Heterodox Economics
Beyond Neoclassical Economics

Contents

1 Overview & Introduction to Heterodox Economics   **1**

    1.1 Heterodox economics 1

       1.1.1 History 1

       1.1.2 Rejection of neoclassical economics 2

       1.1.3 Most recent developments 3

       1.1.4 Fields of heterodox economic thought 3

       1.1.5 See also 4

       1.1.6 References 4

       1.1.7 Further reading 5

       1.1.8 External links 6

    1.2 History of economic thought 6

       1.2.1 Ancient economic thought (Pre 500AD) 6

       1.2.2 Economic thought in the Middle Ages (500-1500AD) 7

       1.2.3 Mercantilism and international trade (16th to 18th century) 9

       1.2.4 Pre-Classical (17th and 18th century) 15

       1.2.5 Classical (18th and 19th century) 18

       1.2.6 Neoclassical (19th and early 20th Century) 26

       1.2.7 Alternative schools (19th century) 30

       1.2.8 World wars, revolution and great depression (early - mid 20th century) 32

       1.2.9 Alternative schools (20th century) 37

       1.2.10 Keynesianism (20th century) 37

       1.2.11 The Chicago school of economics (20th Century) 42

       1.2.12 Games, Evolution and Growth (20th Century) 45

       1.2.13 Post World War II and globalization (mid to late 20th Century) 47

       1.2.14 Post 2008 financial crisis (21st century) 52

       1.2.15 See also 53

       1.2.16 References 53

       1.2.17 Further reading 58

       1.2.18 External links 59

- 1.3 Neoclassical economics 59
  - 1.3.1 Overview 59
  - 1.3.2 Origins 60
  - 1.3.3 The marginal revolution 60
  - 1.3.4 Further developments 61
  - 1.3.5 Criticisms 62
  - 1.3.6 See also 62
  - 1.3.7 References 62
  - 1.3.8 External links 63

2 Heterodox Economics Articles (in Alphabetical Order) 64

- 2.1 Alexander del Mar 64
  - 2.1.1 Biography 64
  - 2.1.2 Family life 65
  - 2.1.3 Quotes 65
  - 2.1.4 Selected bibliography 66
  - 2.1.5 See also 67
  - 2.1.6 References 67
  - 2.1.7 Notes 67
  - 2.1.8 Further reading 67
  - 2.1.9 External links 68
- 2.2 American Monetary Institute 68
  - 2.2.1 Aims 68
  - 2.2.2 Conferences 68
  - 2.2.3 See also 68
  - 2.2.4 References 69
  - 2.2.5 External links 69
- 2.3 Anti-capitalism 69
  - 2.3.1 Socialism 69
  - 2.3.2 Criticisms of anti-capitalism 71
  - 2.3.3 See also 72
  - 2.3.4 References 72
  - 2.3.5 Further reading 73
  - 2.3.6 External links 74
- 2.4 Association for Evolutionary Economics 74
  - 2.4.1 History 74
  - 2.4.2 Aims and Scope 74
  - 2.4.3 Awards and Scholarships 74
  - 2.4.4 Criticisms 75

- 2.4.5 References 75
- 2.4.6 External links 75
- 2.5 Austrian School 75
  - 2.5.1 Methodology 75
  - 2.5.2 Fundamental tenets 76
  - 2.5.3 Contributions to economic thought 77
  - 2.5.4 History 79
  - 2.5.5 Influence 82
  - 2.5.6 Criticisms 82
  - 2.5.7 Principal works 84
  - 2.5.8 See also 84
  - 2.5.9 References and notes 84
  - 2.5.10 Further reading 88
  - 2.5.11 External links 88
- 2.6 Binary economics 88
  - 2.6.1 Overview 88
  - 2.6.2 Background 88
  - 2.6.3 Aims and programme 89
  - 2.6.4 Productiveness vs. Productivity 89
  - 2.6.5 Employee stock ownership plan (ESOPs) and other plans 90
  - 2.6.6 Uses of central bank-issued interest-free loans 90
  - 2.6.7 References 90
  - 2.6.8 Texts 91
  - 2.6.9 External links 91
- 2.7 Calculation in kind 92
  - 2.7.1 See also 92
  - 2.7.2 References 92
  - 2.7.3 Further reading 92
  - 2.7.4 External links 92
- 2.8 Chrematistics 93
  - 2.8.1 Ancient Greece 93
  - 2.8.2 Middle Ages 93
  - 2.8.3 Modern 93
  - 2.8.4 Further reading 93
- 2.9 Circular cumulative causation 94
  - 2.9.1 Dynamics 94
  - 2.9.2 Sources 95
  - 2.9.3 External links 95

- 2.10 Complexity economics 95
  - 2.10.1 Models 95
  - 2.10.2 Measures 96
  - 2.10.3 Features 96
  - 2.10.4 Contemporary trends in economics 97
  - 2.10.5 Criticism 97
  - 2.10.6 See also 98
  - 2.10.7 Notes 98
  - 2.10.8 References 99
  - 2.10.9 External links 99
- 2.11 Counter-economics 99
  - 2.11.1 Origin 99
  - 2.11.2 Relationship with agorism 99
  - 2.11.3 Strategy 100
  - 2.11.4 See also 101
  - 2.11.5 References 101
  - 2.11.6 External links 101
- 2.12 Credibility thesis 101
  - 2.12.1 Postulates of Credibility Thesis 101
  - 2.12.2 Key concepts 102
  - 2.12.3 Methodological approaches 102
  - 2.12.4 Emergence of the theory 102
  - 2.12.5 See also 102
  - 2.12.6 References 103
- 2.13 David Malone (independent filmmaker) 103
  - 2.13.1 Documentary career 103
  - 2.13.2 Political career 103
  - 2.13.3 Works 104
  - 2.13.4 Electoral performance 104
  - 2.13.5 References 104
  - 2.13.6 External links 105
- 2.14 Decentralized planning (economics) 105
  - 2.14.1 Models 105
  - 2.14.2 Similar concepts in practice 106
  - 2.14.3 Political advocacy 106
  - 2.14.4 See also 106
  - 2.14.5 Notes 107
  - 2.14.6 Further reading 107

- 2.15 Decommodification 107
  - 2.15.1 Sources 107
  - 2.15.2 Notes 107
- 2.16 Ecological economics 107
  - 2.16.1 History and development 108
  - 2.16.2 Nature and ecology 109
  - 2.16.3 Ethics 110
  - 2.16.4 Schools of thought 110
  - 2.16.5 Differentiation from mainstream schools 110
  - 2.16.6 Topics 110
  - 2.16.7 Criticism 113
  - 2.16.8 See also 114
  - 2.16.9 References 114
  - 2.16.10 Further reading 117
  - 2.16.11 External links 118
- 2.17 Economic humanitarianism (Raëlianism) 118
  - 2.17.1 Relation with capitalism 118
  - 2.17.2 Economic rent 119
  - 2.17.3 See also 120
  - 2.17.4 References 120
  - 2.17.5 External links 120
- 2.18 Econophysics 120
  - 2.18.1 History 120
  - 2.18.2 Basic tools 121
  - 2.18.3 Influence 122
  - 2.18.4 Main results 122
  - 2.18.5 See also 122
  - 2.18.6 References 122
  - 2.18.7 Further reading 124
  - 2.18.8 Lectures 124
  - 2.18.9 External links 124
- 2.19 European Association for Evolutionary Political Economy 124
  - 2.19.1 History 125
  - 2.19.2 Theoretical perspectives 125
  - 2.19.3 Research Areas 125
  - 2.19.4 Awards 125
  - 2.19.5 Publications 126
  - 2.19.6 Selected EAEPE Volumes 126

	2.19.7 See also	127
	2.19.8 References	127
	2.19.9 External links	127
2.20	Evolutionary economics	128
	2.20.1 Predecessors	128
	2.20.2 Present state of discussion	129
	2.20.3 Evolutionary psychology	130
	2.20.4 See also	130
	2.20.5 References	130
	2.20.6 Further reading	131
	2.20.7 External links	131
2.21	Facilitation board (economics)	132
	2.21.1 Description	132
	2.21.2 Criticism	133
	2.21.3 Fictional accounts	133
	2.21.4 See also	133
	2.21.5 References	133
	2.21.6 External links and sources	133
2.22	Feminist economics	134
	2.22.1 Origins and history	134
	2.22.2 Critiques of traditional economics	135
	2.22.3 Major areas of inquiry	138
	2.22.4 Methodology	144
	2.22.5 Organizations	145
	2.22.6 Relation to other disciplines	146
	2.22.7 Graduate programs	146
	2.22.8 See also	146
	2.22.9 References	146
	2.22.10 Further reading	150
	2.22.11 External links	150
2.23	Forum for Stable Currencies	150
	2.23.1 History	151
	2.23.2 See also	151
	2.23.3 References	151
	2.23.4 External links	151
2.24	Fractional-reserve banking	151
	2.24.1 History	152
	2.24.2 How it works	152

CONTENTS

- 2.24.3 Economic function 153
- 2.24.4 Money creation process 153
- 2.24.5 Money supplies around the world 155
- 2.24.6 Regulation 156
- 2.24.7 Hypothetical example of a bank balance sheet and financial ratios 157
- 2.24.8 Criticisms of textbook descriptions of the monetary system 157
- 2.24.9 Criticisms of fractional-reserve banking 157
- 2.24.10 See also 158
- 2.24.11 Notes 158
- 2.24.12 References 158
- 2.24.13 Further reading 159
- 2.24.14 External links 160
- 2.25 Freiwirtschaft 160
  - 2.25.1 Structure 160
  - 2.25.2 History 160
  - 2.25.3 Flaws of the monetary system 160
  - 2.25.4 References 160
  - 2.25.5 Sources 160
  - 2.25.6 External links 161
- 2.26 Gandhian economics 161
  - 2.26.1 Gandhi's economic ideas 161
  - 2.26.2 Swaraj, self-rule 161
  - 2.26.3 Gandhian economics and ethics 162
  - 2.26.4 Underlying principles 162
  - 2.26.5 Social justice and equality 163
  - 2.26.6 Non-violent rural economy 163
  - 2.26.7 Environmentalism 163
  - 2.26.8 Concept of socialism 163
  - 2.26.9 Implementation in India 163
  - 2.26.10 Modern interpretations 164
  - 2.26.11 Notes 164
  - 2.26.12 References 164
  - 2.26.13 External links 165
- 2.27 Georgism 165
  - 2.27.1 Main tenets 165
  - 2.27.2 Synonyms and variants 168
  - 2.27.3 Influence 169
  - 2.27.4 Criticism 170

- 2.27.5 Notable Georgists 171
- 2.27.6 See also 173
- 2.27.7 References 174
- 2.27.8 External links 183
- 2.28 Gift economy 184
  - 2.28.1 Principles of gift exchange 184
  - 2.28.2 Case studies: Prestations 187
  - 2.28.3 Charity and alms giving 189
  - 2.28.4 Gifting as non-commodified exchange in market societies 190
  - 2.28.5 Related concepts 192
  - 2.28.6 See also 194
  - 2.28.7 Notes 194
  - 2.28.8 Further reading 197
- 2.29 Human development theory 198
  - 2.29.1 Theory 198
  - 2.29.2 References 198
- 2.30 Innovation economics 198
  - 2.30.1 Historical origins 198
  - 2.30.2 Theory 199
  - 2.30.3 Evidence 199
  - 2.30.4 Geography 200
  - 2.30.5 Worldwide examples 200
  - 2.30.6 See also 200
  - 2.30.7 References 200
  - 2.30.8 Further reading 201
  - 2.30.9 External links 201
- 2.31 Institutional economics 201
  - 2.31.1 Thorstein Veblen 202
  - 2.31.2 John R. Commons 202
  - 2.31.3 Wesley Mitchell 202
  - 2.31.4 Clarence Ayres 202
  - 2.31.5 Adolf Berle 203
  - 2.31.6 John Kenneth Galbraith 203
  - 2.31.7 New institutional economics 204
  - 2.31.8 Institutionalism today 204
  - 2.31.9 Criticism 204
  - 2.31.10 Journals 204
  - 2.31.11 See also 204

- 2.31.12 Notes 205
- 2.31.13 References 205
- 2.31.14 External links 206
- 2.32 Islamic economics 206
  - 2.32.1 Definitions and descriptions 207
  - 2.32.2 History 207
  - 2.32.3 As an academic discipline 209
  - 2.32.4 Islam and economics 211
  - 2.32.5 Property 211
  - 2.32.6 Markets 212
  - 2.32.7 Banking and finance 213
  - 2.32.8 Views 214
  - 2.32.9 See also 214
  - 2.32.10 References 215
  - 2.32.11 Notes 215
  - 2.32.12 External links 218
- 2.33 Joan Robinson 219
  - 2.33.1 Biography 219
  - 2.33.2 Family 220
  - 2.33.3 Major works 221
  - 2.33.4 See also 221
  - 2.33.5 References 221
  - 2.33.6 Further reading 221
  - 2.33.7 External links 222
- 2.34 Kinetic exchange models of markets 222
  - 2.34.1 Data and Basic tools 222
  - 2.34.2 Overview of the models 222
  - 2.34.3 Criticisms 222
  - 2.34.4 See also 222
  - 2.34.5 References 223
  - 2.34.6 Further reading 223
- 2.35 Kondratiev wave 223
  - 2.35.1 History of concept 224
  - 2.35.2 Characteristics of the cycle 224
  - 2.35.3 Explanations of the cycle 224
  - 2.35.4 Modern modifications of Kondratiev theory 225
  - 2.35.5 Criticism of long cycles 226
  - 2.35.6 See also 226

2.35.7	References	226
2.35.8	Further reading	227
2.35.9	External links	228
2.36	Market abolitionism	229
2.36.1	Proponents	229
2.36.2	Criticisms	229
2.36.3	See also	229
2.36.4	References	229
2.36.5	External links	229
2.37	Marxian economics	230
2.37.1	Marx's response to classical economics	230
2.37.2	Marx's theory	231
2.37.3	Current theorizing in Marxian economics	233
2.37.4	Criticisms	233
2.37.5	Neo-Marxian economics	234
2.37.6	See also	234
2.37.7	Footnotes	234
2.37.8	References	235
2.37.9	Further reading	235
2.37.10	External links	236
2.38	Max Keiser	236
2.38.1	Early career	236
2.38.2	Hollywood Stock Exchange	236
2.38.3	Broadcasting career	236
2.38.4	Activism	237
2.38.5	See also	238
2.38.6	References	238
2.38.7	External links	240
2.39	Modern Monetary Theory	240
2.39.1	Background	240
2.39.2	Vertical transactions	241
2.39.3	Interaction between government and the banking sector	241
2.39.4	Horizontal transactions	242
2.39.5	The foreign sector	242
2.39.6	Policy implications	243
2.39.7	Criticisms	244
2.39.8	Modern proponents	244
2.39.9	See also	245

- 2.39.10 Notes ... 245
- 2.39.11 Bibliography ... 246
- 2.39.12 External links ... 246
- 2.40 Money as Debt ... 246
  - 2.40.1 Background ... 247
  - 2.40.2 Critical response ... 247
  - 2.40.3 See also ... 247
  - 2.40.4 References ... 247
  - 2.40.5 External links ... 248
- 2.41 Mouvement Anti-Utilitariste dans les Sciences Sociales ... 248
  - 2.41.1 Some regular contributors to the journal ... 248
  - 2.41.2 References ... 248
- 2.42 Mutualism (economic theory) ... 248
  - 2.42.1 History ... 249
  - 2.42.2 Theory ... 252
  - 2.42.3 Mutualism and capitalism ... 253
  - 2.42.4 Criticisms ... 254
  - 2.42.5 Mutualism today ... 255
  - 2.42.6 See also ... 256
  - 2.42.7 Notes and references ... 256
  - 2.42.8 Bibliography ... 258
  - 2.42.9 External links ... 258
- 2.43 Neo-Marxian economics ... 258
  - 2.43.1 Argument ... 259
  - 2.43.2 Position on the labor theory of value ... 259
  - 2.43.3 See also ... 259
  - 2.43.4 References ... 259
  - 2.43.5 External links ... 260
- 2.44 Neo-Ricardianism ... 260
  - 2.44.1 See also ... 260
  - 2.44.2 External links ... 260
- 2.45 Neuroeconomics ... 260
  - 2.45.1 Introduction ... 260
  - 2.45.2 Major research areas in neuroeconomics ... 261
  - 2.45.3 Methodology ... 263
  - 2.45.4 Notable theorists ... 263
  - 2.45.5 Experiments ... 263
  - 2.45.6 Neuroeconomic Programs ... 264

- 2.45.7 Related Fields 264
- 2.45.8 Criticism 264
- 2.45.9 Neuromarketing 264
- 2.45.10 See also 264
- 2.45.11 References 264
- 2.45.12 Further reading 266
- 2.45.13 Journal 267
- 2.45.14 External links 267
- 2.46 New institutional economics 267
  - 2.46.1 Overview 267
  - 2.46.2 Institutional levels 268
  - 2.46.3 See also 268
  - 2.46.4 References 268
  - 2.46.5 Further reading 269
  - 2.46.6 External links 269
- 2.47 Non-possession 269
  - 2.47.1 Possession 270
  - 2.47.2 Jainism 272
  - 2.47.3 Wealth and poverty 273
  - 2.47.4 See also 274
  - 2.47.5 References 274
  - 2.47.6 Sources 274
- 2.48 Participatory economics 274
  - 2.48.1 Decision-making principle 274
  - 2.48.2 Work in a participatory economy 275
  - 2.48.3 Allocation in a participatory economy 275
  - 2.48.4 Opposition to central planning and capitalism 275
  - 2.48.5 Participatory economics and socialism 276
  - 2.48.6 Criticisms 277
  - 2.48.7 See also 277
  - 2.48.8 References 278
  - 2.48.9 Further reading 278
  - 2.48.10 External links 279
- 2.49 Planned economy 279
  - 2.49.1 Planned versus command economies 279
  - 2.49.2 Advantages of economic planning 280
  - 2.49.3 Disadvantages of economic planning 280
  - 2.49.4 Relationship with socialism 281

- 2.49.5 Fictional portrayals of planned economies 281
- 2.49.6 See also 281
- 2.49.7 Notes 282
- 2.49.8 Further reading 282
- 2.49.9 External links 283
- 2.50 Pluralism in economics 283
  - 2.50.1 See also 283
  - 2.50.2 References 283
  - 2.50.3 External links 284
- 2.51 Post-autistic economics 284
  - 2.51.1 Concept 284
  - 2.51.2 Criticism of the term 284
  - 2.51.3 See also 285
  - 2.51.4 References 285
  - 2.51.5 Literature 285
  - 2.51.6 External links 285
- 2.52 Post-scarcity economy 285
  - 2.52.1 The post-scarcity model 285
  - 2.52.2 Fiction 287
  - 2.52.3 See also 287
  - 2.52.4 References 288
  - 2.52.5 External links 289
- 2.53 Production for use 290
  - 2.53.1 Exposition 290
  - 2.53.2 Usage 290
  - 2.53.3 Description 290
  - 2.53.4 Social production and peer-to-peer processes 292
  - 2.53.5 Valuation and calculation 292
  - 2.53.6 See also 293
  - 2.53.7 References 293
  - 2.53.8 Further reading 294
- 2.54 Quarterly Journal of Austrian Economics 294
  - 2.54.1 References 294
  - 2.54.2 External links 294
- 2.55 real-world economics review 294
  - 2.55.1 See also 295
  - 2.55.2 References 295
  - 2.55.3 External links 295

- 2.56 Regenerative economic theory ... 295
  - 2.56.1 References ... 295
  - 2.56.2 External links ... 295
- 2.57 Review of Keynesian Economics ... 295
  - 2.57.1 Abstracting and indexing ... 295
  - 2.57.2 References ... 295
  - 2.57.3 External links ... 295
- 2.58 Review of Radical Political Economics ... 296
  - 2.58.1 References ... 296
  - 2.58.2 External links ... 296
- 2.59 Sharing economy ... 296
  - 2.59.1 Definition ... 296
  - 2.59.2 Scope ... 297
  - 2.59.3 Examples ... 297
  - 2.59.4 Types of collaborative consumption ... 297
  - 2.59.5 History ... 297
  - 2.59.6 Driving forces ... 298
  - 2.59.7 Benefits of a sharing economy ... 299
  - 2.59.8 Transport ... 299
  - 2.59.9 Criticism and controversies ... 299
  - 2.59.10 Organizations advocating and networking sharing economy ... 300
  - 2.59.11 Types of sharing ... 300
  - 2.59.12 See also ... 300
  - 2.59.13 Notes and references ... 301
  - 2.59.14 Further reading ... 303
- 2.60 Social credit ... 303
  - 2.60.1 Economic theory ... 304
  - 2.60.2 The A + B theorem ... 306
  - 2.60.3 Political theory ... 310
  - 2.60.4 History ... 310
  - 2.60.5 Philosophy ... 312
  - 2.60.6 Groups influenced by social credit ... 313
  - 2.60.7 Literary figures in social credit ... 314
  - 2.60.8 See also ... 314
  - 2.60.9 Notes ... 315
  - 2.60.10 Further reading ... 316
  - 2.60.11 External links ... 317
- 2.61 Social dividend ... 317

- 2.61.1 Origins of the concept 317
- 2.61.2 Contemporary proposals 318
- 2.61.3 In practice 318
- 2.61.4 Related concepts 318
- 2.61.5 See also 318
- 2.61.6 References 318
- 2.61.7 Further reading 319
- 2.61.8 External links 320
- 2.62 Socialist economics 320
  - 2.62.1 History of socialist economic thought 320
  - 2.62.2 Characteristics 324
  - 2.62.3 Economic models and systems 326
  - 2.62.4 Elements of socialism in practice 328
  - 2.62.5 Criticisms 337
  - 2.62.6 See also 337
  - 2.62.7 References 337
  - 2.62.8 Further reading 342
- 2.63 Socioeconomics 343
  - 2.63.1 Overview 343
  - 2.63.2 See also 343
  - 2.63.3 Notes 343
  - 2.63.4 References 344
  - 2.63.5 External links 344
- 2.64 Structuralist economics 344
  - 2.64.1 New structural economics 345
  - 2.64.2 See also 345
  - 2.64.3 Notes 345
- 2.65 Surplus economics 345
  - 2.65.1 Economic Surplus 345
  - 2.65.2 See also 345
  - 2.65.3 References 345
  - 2.65.4 Further reading 345
- 2.66 Technocracy 346
  - 2.66.1 History of the term 346
  - 2.66.2 Precursors 346
  - 2.66.3 Characteristics 347
  - 2.66.4 Technocracy movement 347
  - 2.66.5 See also 348

		2.66.6	References	348
		2.66.7	External links	349
	2.67	Technocracy movement	350
		2.67.1	Overview	350
		2.67.2	Origins	350
		2.67.3	United States and Canada	351
		2.67.4	Technocrats plan	352
		2.67.5	Europe	352
		2.67.6	References	353
	2.68	The Natural Economic Order	354
		2.68.1	References	354
		2.68.2	External links	354
	2.69	The Other Canon Foundation	354
		2.69.1	History	354
		2.69.2	Theories and influences	354
		2.69.3	Differences to and criticism of the mainstream economics	355
		2.69.4	Publishing	355
		2.69.5	References	355
		2.69.6	External links	355
	2.70	Thermoeconomics	356
		2.70.1	Basis	356
		2.70.2	Thermodynamics	356
		2.70.3	Economic systems	356
		2.70.4	See also	356
		2.70.5	References	356
		2.70.6	Further reading	357
		2.70.7	External links	357
3	**Text and image sources, contributors, and licenses**			**358**
	3.1	Text	358
	3.2	Images	370
	3.3	Content license	380

Chapter 1

Overview & Introduction to Heterodox Economics

1.1 Heterodox economics

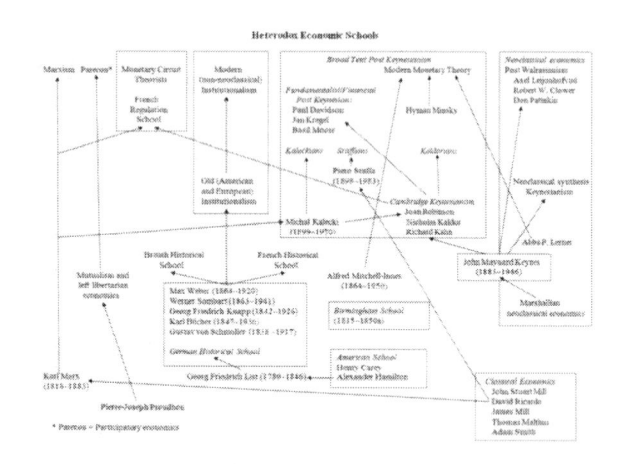

Heterodox economics family tree.

Heterodox economics refers to methodologies or schools of economic thought that are considered outside of "mainstream economics", often represented by expositors as contrasting with or going beyond neoclassical economics.[1][2] "Heterodox economics" is an umbrella term used to cover various approaches, schools, or traditions. These include socialist, Marxian, institutional, evolutionary, Georgist, Austrian, feminist,[3] social, post-Keynesian (not to be confused with New Keynesian),[2] and ecological economics among others.[4] In the JEL classification codes developed by the *Journal of Economic Literature*, heterodox economics is in the second of the 19 primary categories at:

> JEL: B - History of Economic Thought, Methodology, and **Heterodox Approaches**.

Mainstream economics may be called *orthodox* or *conventional* economics by its critics.[5] Alternatively, mainstream economics deals with the "rationality-individualism-equilibrium nexus" and heterodox economics is more "radical" in dealing with the "institutions-history-social structure nexus".[6] Mainstream economists sometimes assert that heterodox economics has little or no influence on the vast majority of academic economists in the English speaking world. Heterodox schools of economics are also usually dismissed as "fringe" and "irrelevant" by prominent mainstream economists.[7]

A recent review documents several prominent groups of heterodox economists since at least the 1990s as working together with a resulting increase in coherence across different constituents.[2] Along these lines, the International Confederation of Associations for Pluralism in Economics (ICAPE) does not define "heterodox economics" and has avoided defining its scope. ICAPE defines its mission as "promoting pluralism in economics."

In defining a common ground in the "critical commentary," one writer described fellow heterodox economists as trying to do three things: (1) identify shared ideas that generate a pattern of heterodox critique across topics and chapters of introductory macro texts; (2) give special attention to ideas that link methodological differences to policy differences; and (3) characterize the common ground in ways that permit distinct paradigms to develop common differences with textbook economics in different ways.[8]

One study suggests four key factors as important to the study of economics by self-identified heterodox economists: history, natural systems, uncertainty, and power.[9]

1.1.1 History

A number of heterodox schools of economic thought challenged the dominance of neoclassical economics after the neoclassical revolution of the 1870s. In addition to socialist critics of capitalism, heterodox schools in this period included advocates of various forms of mercantilism, such as the American School dissenters from neoclassical methodology such as the historical school, and advocates of unorthodox monetary theories such as Social credit. Other heterodox schools active before and during the Great Depression included Technocracy and Georgism.

Physical scientists and biologists were the first individuals to use energy flows to explain social and economic development. Joseph Henry, an American physicist and first secretary of the Smithsonian Institution, remarked that the "fundamental principle of political economy is that the physical labor of man can only be ameliorated by... the transformation of matter from a crude state to a artificial condition...by expending what is called power or energy."[10][11]

The rise, and absorption into the mainstream of Keynesian economics, which appeared to provide a more coherent policy response to unemployment than unorthodox monetary or trade policies contributed to the decline of interest in these schools.

After 1945, the neoclassical synthesis of Keynesian and neoclassical economics resulted in a clearly defined mainstream position based on a division of the field into microeconomics (generally neoclassical but with a newly developed theory of market failure) and macroeconomics (divided between Keynesian and monetarist views on such issues as the role of monetary policy). Austrians and post-Keynesians who dissented from this synthesis emerged as clearly defined heterodox schools. In addition, the Marxist and institutionalist schools remained active.

Up to 1980 the most notable themes of heterodox economics in its various forms included:

1. rejection of the atomistic individual conception in favor of a socially embedded individual conception;
2. emphasis on time as an irreversible historical process;
3. reasoning in terms of mutual influences between individuals and social structures.

From approximately 1980 mainstream economics has been significantly influenced by a number of new research programs, including behavioral economics, complexity economics, evolutionary economics, experimental economics, and neuroeconomics. As a consequence, some heterodox economists, such as John B. Davis, proposed that the definition of heterodox economics has to be adapted to this new, more complex reality:[12]

> ...heterodox economics post-1980 is a complex structure, being composed out of two broadly different kinds of heterodox work, each internally differentiated with a number of research programs having different historical origins and orientations: the traditional left heterodoxy familiar to most and the 'new heterodoxy' resulting from other science imports.[12]

1.1.2 Rejection of neoclassical economics

There is no single "heterodox economic theory"; there are many different "heterodox theories" in existence. What they all share, however, is a rejection of the neoclassical orthodoxy as representing the appropriate tool for understanding the workings of economic and social life.[13] The reasons for this rejection may vary. Some of the elements commonly found in heterodox critiques are listed below.

Criticism of the neoclassical model of individual behavior

One of the most broadly accepted principles of neoclassical economics is the assumption of the "rationality of economic agents". Indeed, for a number of economists, the notion of rational maximizing behavior is taken to be synonymous with economic behavior (Becker 1976, Hirshleifer 1984). When some economists' studies do not embrace the rationality assumption, they are seen as placing the analyses outside the boundaries of the Neoclassical economics discipline (Landsberg 1989, 596). Neoclassical economics begins with the *a priori* assumptions that agents are rational and that they seek to maximize their individual utility (or profits) subject to environmental constraints. These assumptions provide the backbone for rational choice theory.

Many heterodox schools are critical of the homo economicus model of human behavior used in standard neoclassical model. A typical version of the critique is that of Satya Gabriel:[14]

> Neoclassical economic theory is grounded in a particular conception of human psychology, agency or decision-making. It is assumed that all human beings make economic decisions so as to maximize pleasure or utility. Some heterodox theories reject this basic assumption of neoclassical theory, arguing for alternative understandings of how economic decisions are made and/or how human psychology works. It is possible to accept the notion that humans are pleasure seeking machines, yet reject the idea that economic decisions are governed by such pleasure seeking. Human beings may, for example, be unable to make choices consistent with pleasure maxi-

mization due to social constraints and/or coercion. Humans may also be unable to correctly assess the choice points that are most likely to lead to maximum pleasure, even if they are unconstrained (except in budgetary terms) in making such choices. And it is also possible that the notion of pleasure seeking is itself a meaningless assumption because it is either impossible to test or too general to refute. Economic theories that reject the basic assumption of economic decisions as the outcome of pleasure maximization are heterodox.

Shiozawa emphasizes that economic agents act in a complex world and therefore impossible for them to attain maximal utility point. They instead behave as if there are a repertories of many ready made rules, one of which they chose according to relevant situation.[15]

Criticism of the neoclassical model of market equilibrium

In microeconomic theory, cost-minimization by consumers and by firms implies the existence of supply and demand correspondences for which market clearing equilibrium prices exist, if there are large numbers of consumers and producers. Under convexity assumptions or under some marginal-cost pricing rules, each equilibrium will be Pareto efficient: In large economies, non-convexity also leads to quasi-equilibria that are nearly efficient.

However, the concept of market equilibrium has been criticized by Austrians, post-Keynesians and others, who object to applications of microeconomic theory to real-world markets, when such markets are not usefully approximated by microeconomic models. Heterodox economists assert that micro-economic models rarely capture reality.

Mainstream microeconomics may be defined in terms of optimization and equilibrium, following the approaches of Paul Samuelson and Hal Varian. On the other hand, heterodox economics may be labeled as falling into the nexus of institutions, history, and social structure.[4][16]

1.1.3 Most recent developments

Over the past two decades, the intellectual agendas of heterodox economists have taken a decidedly pluralist turn. Leading heterodox thinkers have moved beyond the established paradigms of Austrian, Feminist, Institutional-Evolutionary, Marxian, Post Keynesian, Radical, Social, and Sraffian economics—opening up new lines of analysis, criticism, and dialogue among dissenting schools of thought. This cross-fertilization of ideas is creating a new generation of scholarship in which novel combinations of heterodox ideas are being brought to bear on important contemporary and historical problems, such as socially grounded reconstructions of the individual in economic theory; the goals and tools of economic measurement and professional ethics; the complexities of policymaking in today's global political economy; and innovative connections among formerly separate theoretical traditions (Marxian, Austrian, feminist, ecological, Sraffian, institutionalist, and post-Keynesian) (for a review of post-Keynesian economics, see Lavoie (1992); Rochon (1999)).

David Colander, an advocate of complexity economics, argues that the ideas of heterodox economists are now being discussed in the mainstream without mention of the heterodox economists, because the tools to analyze institutions, uncertainty, and other factors have now been developed by the mainstream. He suggests that heterodox economists should embrace rigorous mathematics and attempt to work from within the mainstream, rather than treating it as an enemy.[17]

Some schools of heterodox economic thought have also taken a transdisciplinary approach. Thermoeconomics is based on the claim that human economic processes are governed by the second law of thermodynamics. The posited relationship between economic theory, energy and entropy, has been extended further by systems scientists to explain the role of energy in biological evolution in terms of such economic criteria as productivity, efficiency, and especially the costs and benefits of the various mechanisms for capturing and utilizing available energy to build biomass and do work.[18][19]

1.1.4 Fields of heterodox economic thought

- American Institutionalist School
- Austrian economics #[20]
- Binary Economics
- Bioeconomics
- Complexity economics
- Ecological economics §
- Evolutionary economics # § (partly within mainstream economics)
- Feminist economics # §
- Georgism
- Gift-based economics
- Green Economics

- Gesellian economics
- Innovation Economics
- Institutional economics # §
- Islamic economics
- Marxian economics #
- Mutualism
- Neuroeconomics
- Participatory economics
- Post-Keynesian economics § including Modern Monetary Theory and Circuitism
- Post scarcity
- Resource-based economics - not to be confused with a resource-based economy
- Sharing economics
- Socialist economics #
- Social economics (partially heterodox usage)
- Sraffian economics #
- Technocracy (Energy Accounting)
- Thermoeconomics
- Mouvement Anti-Utilitariste dans les Sciences Sociales

Listed in Journal of Economic Literature codes scrolled to at JEL: B5 - Current Heterodox Approaches.

§ Listed in *The New Palgrave Dictionary of Economics*, 2nd Edition, v. 8, Appendix IV, p. 856, searchable by clicking (the JEL classification codes JEL:) radio button B5, B52, or B59, then the Search button (or Update Search Results button) at http://www.dictionaryofeconomics.com/search_results?edition=all&field=content&q=&topicid=B5.

Some schools in the social sciences aim to promote certain perspectives: classical and modern political economy; economic sociology and anthropology; gender and racial issues in economics; and so on.

Notable heterodox economists

- Karl Marx
- Richard D. Wolff
- Thorstein Veblen
- Alfred S. Eichner
- Piero Sraffa
- Joan Violet Robinson
- Michał Kalecki
- Frederic S. Lee
- Ha-Joon Chang
- Henry George

1.1.5 See also

- Association for Evolutionary Economics
- EAEPE
- Kinetic exchange models of markets
- Post-autistic economics
- Real-world economics review

1.1.6 References

[1] Fred E. Foldvary, ed., 1996. *Beyond Neoclassical Economics: Heterodox Approaches to Economic Theory*, Edward Elgar. Description and contents B&N.com links.

[2] Frederic S. Lee, 2008. "heterodox economics," *The New Palgrave Dictionary of Economics*, 2nd Edition, v. 4, pp. 2-65. Abstract.

[3] In the order listed at JEL classification codes#History of economic thought, methodology, and heterodox approaches JEL: B Subcategories, JEL: B5 - Current Heterodox Approaches.

[4] Lawson, T. (2005). "The nature of heterodox economics" (PDF). *Cambridge Journal of Economics* **30** (4): 483–505. doi:10.1093/cje/bei093.

[5] C. Barry, 1998. *Political-economy: A comparative approach*. Westport, CT: Praeger.

[6] John B. Davis (2006). "Heterodox Economics, the Fragmentation of the Mainstream, and Embedded Individual Analysis", in *Future Directions in Heterodox Economics*, p. 57. Ann Arbor: University of Michigan Press.

[7] Among these economists, Robert M. Solow names Austrian, Post-Keynesian, Marxist, and neo-Ricardian schools as on "dissenting fringes of academic economics". Solow continued that "In economics, nevertheless, there is usually a definite consensus — there is one now." Further:

> Marx was an important and influential thinker, and Marxism has been a doctrine with intellectual and practical influence. The fact is, however, that most serious English-speaking economists regard Marxist economics as an irrelevant dead end.

(Solow 1988)

George Stigler similarly noted the professional marginality of the "neo-Ricardian" economists (who follow Piero Sraffa): "economists working in the Marxian-Sraffian tradition represent a small minority of modern economists, and ... their writings have virtually no impact upon the professional work of most economists in major English-language universities." (Stigler 1988, p. 1733)

[8] Cohn, Steve (2003). "Common Ground Critiques of Neoclassical Principles Texts". *Post-Autistic Economics Review* (18, article 3).

[9] Mearman, Andrew (2011). "Who Do Heterodox Economists Think They Are?" *American Journal of Economics and Sociology*, 70(2): 480–510.

[10] Cutler J. Cleveland, "Biophysical economics", *Encyclopedia of Earth*, Last updated: September 14, 2006.

[11] Eric Zencey, 2009. "Mr. Soddy's Ecological Economy",] *The New York Times*, April 12, p. WK 9.

[12] Davis, John B. (2006). "The Nature of Heterodox Economics" (PDF). *Post-Autistic Economics Review* (40): 23–30.

[13] Lee, Frederic (September 16, 2011). *A History of Heterodox Economics: Challenging Mainstream Views in the 21st Century* (Reprint ed.). Routledge. pp. 7–9. ISBN 978-0415681971.

[14] Satya J. Gabriel 2003. "Introduction to Heterodox Economic Theory." (blog), June 4, Satya J. Gabriel is a Professor of Economics at Mount Holyoke College}

[15] Shiozawa, Y. 2004 Evolutinary Economics in the 21st Century: A Manifest, *Evolutionary and Institutional Economics Review*, **1**(1): 5-47.

[16] Dow, S. C. (2000). "Prospects for the Progress in Heterodox Economics". *Journal of the History of Economic Thought* **22** (2): 157–170. doi:10.1080/10427710050025367.

[17] David Colander, 2007. Pluralism and Heterodox Economics: Suggestions for an "Inside the Mainstream" Heterodoxy

[18] Corning, Peter A.; Kline, Stephen J. (1998). "Thermodynamics, information and life revisited, Part II: 'Thermoeconomics' and 'Control information'". *Systems Research and Behavioral Science* **15** (6): 453–482. doi:10.1002/(SICI)1099-1743(199811/12)15:6<453::AID-SRES201>3.0.CO;2-U.

[19] Peter A. Corning. 2002. "Thermoeconomics – Beyond the Second Law" – source: www.complexsystems.org

[20] 2003. *A Companion to the History of Economic Thought*. Blackwell Publishing. ISBN 0-631-22573-0 p. 452

1.1.7 Further reading

Articles

- Bauer, Leonhard and Matis, Herbert 1988. "From moral to political economy: The Genesis of social sciences" History of European Ideas, 9(2): 125-143.

- Dequech, David 2007. "Neoclassical, mainstream, orthodox, and heterodox economics," Journal of Post Keynesian Economics, 30(2): 279-302.

- Flaherty, Diane, 1987. "radical political economy," *The New Palgrave: A Dictionary of Economics*, v, 4. pp. 36–39.

- _____, 2008. "radical economics," *The New Palgrave Dictionary of Economics*, 2nd Edition.Abstract.

- Lee, Frederic. S. 2008. "heterodox economics", *The New Palgrave Dictionary of Economics*, 2nd Edition. Abstract.

Books

- Gerber, Julien-Francois and Steppacher, Rolf, ed., 2012. Towards an Integrated Paradigm in Heterodox Economics: Alternative Approaches to the Current Eco-Social Crises. Palgrave Macmillan. ISBN 978-0-230-30358-4

- Lee, Frederic S. 2009. A History of Heterodox Economics Challenging the Mainstream in the Twentieth Century. London and New York: Routledge. 2009

- Harvey, John T. and Garnett, Jr., Robert F., ed., 2007. *Future Directions for Heterodox Economics*, Series Advances in Heterodox Economics, The University of Michigan Press, . ISBN 978-0-472-03247-1

- McDermott, John, 2003. *Economics in Real Time: A Theoretical Reconstruction, Series Advances in Heterodox Economics*, The University of Michigan Press. ISBN 978-0-472-11357-6

- Rochon, Louis-Philippe and Rossi, Sergio, editors, 2003. *Modern Theories of Money: The Nature and Role of Money in Capitalist Economies*. Edward Elgar Publishing. ISBN 1-84064-789-2

- Solow, Robert M. (20 March 1988). "The Wide, Wide World Of Wealth (*The New Palgrave: A Dictionary of Economics'*. Edited by John Eatwell, Murray Milgate and Peter Newman. Four volumes. 4,103 pp. New York: Stockton Press. $650)". *New York Times*.

- Stigler, George J. (December 1988). "Palgrave's Dictionary of Economics". *Journal of Economic Literature* (American Economic Association) **26** (4): 1729–1736. JSTOR 2726859.

Articles, conferences, papers

- Lavoie, Marc, 2006. *Do Heterodox Theories Have Anything in Common? A Post-Keynesian Point of View*.

- Lawson, Tony, 2006. "The Nature of Heterodox Economics," *Cambridge Journal of Economics*, 30(4), pp. 483–505. Pre-publication copy.

Journals

- *Evolutionary and Institutional Economics Review* (Freely downloadable)
- *Journal of Institutional Economics*
- *Cambridge Journal of Economics*

1.1.8 External links

- Association for Heterodox Economics
- Heterodox Economics Newsletter
- Heterodox Economics Directory (Graduate and Undergraduate Programs, Journals, Publishers and Book Series, Associations, Blogs, and Institutions and Other Web Sites)
- Association for Evolutionary Economics (AFEE)
- International Confederation of Associations for Pluralism in Economics (ICAPE)
- Union for Radical Political Economics (URPE)
- Association for Social Economics (ASE)
- Post-Keynesian Economics Study Group (PKSG)

1.2 History of economic thought

This article is about changes in economic ideas. For historical events, see Economic history of the world. For famous economists, see List of economists.

The **history of economic thought** deals with different thinkers and theories in the subject that became political economy and economics, from the ancient world to the present day. It encompasses many disparate schools of economic thought. Ancient Greek writers such as the philosopher Aristotle examined ideas about the art of wealth acquisition, and questioned whether property is best left in private or public hands. In medieval times, scholasticists such as Thomas Aquinas argued that it was a moral obligation of businesses to sell goods at a just price.

In the Western world, economics was not a separate discipline, but part of philosophy until the 18th–19th century Industrial Revolution and the 19th century Great Divergence, which accelerated economic growth.[1] Long before that, from the Renaissance at least, economics as an intellectual discipline or science was dominated by Western thinkers and their academic institutions, schooling economists from outside the West, although there are isolated instances in other societies.

1.2.1 Ancient economic thought (Pre 500AD)

Main articles: Ancient economic thought, Arthashastra, Republic (dialogue), Credit theory of money, Politics (Aristotle), Nicomachean Ethics, Metallism and Oeconomicus
Key people: Fan Li, Qin Shi Huang, Wang Anshi, Mahavira, Chanakya, Xenophon, Aristotle and Plato

China

Fan Li (also known as Tao Zhu Gong) (517 BC –),[2] an adviser to King Goujian of Yue, wrote on economic issues and developed a set of 'golden' business rules.[3]

India

Chanakya (350 BC –) wrote the *Arthashastra*, a treatise on statecraft, economic policy and military strategy.

Plato and his pupil Aristotle had had an enduring effect on Western philosophy.

Greco-Roman World

Ancient Athens was a slave-based society, but also developed an embryonic model of democracy.[4]

Xenophon's (c. 430 – 354 BC) *Oeconomicus* (c. 360 BCE) is a dialogue principally about household management and agriculture.

Plato's dialogue *The Republic* (ca. 380–360 BCE) described an ideal city-state run by philosopher-kings and contained references to specialization of labor and production. Plato was the first to advocate the credit theory of money, that is, money as a unit of account for debt.

Aristotle's *Politics* (ca. 350 BCE) analyzed different forms of the state: monarchy, aristocracy, constitutional government, tyranny, oligarchy, and democracy as a critique of Plato's model of a philosopher-kings. Of particular interest for economists is Plato's blueprint of a society based on common ownership of resources. Aristotle viewed this model as an oligarchical anathema. Though Aristotle did certainly advocate that many things be held in common, he argued that not everything could be, simply because of the "wickedness of human nature".[5]

"It is clearly better that property should be private", wrote Aristotle, "but the use of it common; and the special business of the legislator is to create in men this benevolent disposition." In *Politics* Book I, Aristotle discusses the general nature of households and market exchanges. For him there is a certain "art of acquisition" or "wealth-getting", but because it is the same many people are obsessed with its accumulation, and "wealth-getting" for one's household is "necessary and honorable", while exchange on the retail trade for simple accumulation is "justly censured, for it is dishonorable".[6] Of the people he stated they as a whole thought acquisition of wealth (chrematistike) as being either the same as, or a principle of oikonomia (*household management* – oikonomos),[7][8] with *oikos* as house and *nomos* in fact translated as custom or law.[9] Aristotle himself highly disapproved of usury and cast scorn on making money through a monopoly.[10]

Aristotle discarded Plato's credit theory of money for Metallism, the theory that money derives its value from the purchasing power of the commodity upon which it is based, and is only an "instrument", its sole purpose being a medium of exchange, which means on its own "it is worthless... not useful as a means to any of the necessities of life".[11]

1.2.2 Economic thought in the Middle Ages (500-1500AD)

Main articles: Thomas Aquinas, Scholasticism, Duns Scotus, Ibn Khaldun, Muqaddimah and Islamic economic jurisprudence

Thomas Aquinas

Thomas Aquinas (1225–1274) was an Italian theologian and economic writer. He taught in both Cologne and Paris, and was part of a group of Catholic scholars known as the Schoolmen, who moved their enquiries beyond theology to philosophical and scientific debates. In the treatise *Summa Theologica* Aquinas dealt with the concept of a just price, which he considered necessary for the reproduction of the social order. Similar in many ways to the modern concept of long run equilibrium, a just price was just sufficient to cover the costs of production, including the maintenance of a worker and his family. Aquinas argued it was immoral for sellers to raise their prices simply because buyers had a pressing need for a product.

Aquinas discusses a number of topics in the format of questions and replies, substantial tracts dealing with Aristotle's theory. Questions 77 and 78 concern economic issues, primarily what a just price might be, and the fairness of a seller dispensing faulty goods. Aquinas argued against any form of cheating and recommended always paying compensation

Thomas Aquinas (1225–1274) taught that high prices in response to high demand is theft.

in lieu of good service. Whilst human laws might not impose sanctions for unfair dealing, divine law did, in his opinion.

Duns Scotus

One of Aquinas' main critics[12] was Duns Scotus (1265–1308), originally from Duns Scotland, who taught in Oxford, Cologne, and Paris. In his work *Sententiae* (1295), he thought it possible to be more precise than Aquinas in calculating a just price, emphasizing the costs of labor and expenses, although he recognized that the latter might be inflated by exaggeration because buyer and seller usually have different ideas of a just price. If people did not benefit from a transaction, in Scotus' view, they would not trade. Scotus said merchants perform a necessary and useful social role by transporting goods and making them available to the public.[12]

Jean Buridan

Jean Buridan (French: [byʁidɑ̃]; Latin *Johannes Buridanus*; c. 1300 – after 1358) was a French priest. Buridanus looked

Duns Scotus (1265–1308)

at money from two angles: its metal value and its purchasing power, which he acknowledged can vary. He argued that aggregated, not individual, demand and supply determine market prices. Hence, for him a just price was what the society collectively and not just one individual is willing to pay.

Ibn Khaldun

Until Joseph J. Spengler's 1964 work "Economic Thought of Islam: Ibn Khaldun",[14] Adam Smith (1723–1790) was considered the "Father of Economics". Now there is a second candidate, Arab Muslim scholar Ibn Khaldun (1332–1406) of Tunisia, although how the Muslim world fell behind the West, or what influence Khaldun had in the West is unclear. Arnold Toynbee called Ibn Khaldun a "genius" who "appears to have been inspired by no predecessors and to have found no kindred souls among his contemporaries...and yet, in the Prolegomena (Muqaddimat) to his Universal History he has conceived and formulated a philosophy of history which is undoubtedly the greatest work of its kind that has ever yet been created by any mind in any time or place."[15] Ibn Khaldoun expressed a theory of the lifecycle of civilizations, the specialization of labor, and the value of money as a means of exchange rather than as a store of inherent value. His ideas on taxes bore a striking

Ibn Khaldun (1332–1406)

Nicolas d'Oresme (1320–82)

resemblance to supply-side economics' Laffer curve, which posits that beyond a certain point higher taxes discourage production and actually cause revenues to fall.[16]

Nicole Oresme

French philosopher and priest Nicolas d'Oresme (1320–1382) wrote *De origine, natura, jure et mutationibus monetarum*, about the origin, nature, law, and alterations of money. It is one of the earliest manuscripts on the concept of money.

Antonin of Florence

Saint Antoninus of Florence (1389–1459), O.P., was an Italian Dominican friar, who became Archbishop of Florence. Antoninus' writings address social and economic development, and argued that the state has a duty to intervene in mercantile affairs for the common good, and an obligation to help the poor and needy. In his primary work, "summa theologica" he was mainly concerned about price, justice and capital theory. Like Duns Scotus, he distinguishes between the natural value of a good and its practical value. The latter is determined by its suitability to satisfy needs (virtuositas), its rarity (raritas) and its subjective value (complacibilitas). Due to this subjective component there can not only be one just price, but a bandwidth of more or less just prices.

1.2.3 Mercantilism and international trade (16th to 18th century)

Main article: Mercantilism
See also: International trade and School of Salamanca
Key people: Victor de Riqueti, marquis de Mirabeau, Jean Bodin, Nicolaus Copernicus, Edward Misselden, Gerard Malynes, Thomas Mun, William Petty, Philipp von Hörnigk, Charles Davenant, Josiah Child, Jean-Baptiste Colbert, Pierre Le Pesant, sieur de Boisguilbert, Sir James Steuart and Leonardus Lessius

Mercantilism dominated Europe from the 16th to the 18th century.[17] Despite the localism of the Middle Ages, the waning of feudalism saw new national economic frameworks begin to strengthen. After the voyages of Christopher Columbus and other explorers opened up new opportunities for trade with the New World and Asia, newly-powerful monarchies wanted a more powerful military state to boost their status. Mercantilism was a political movement and an economic theory that advocated the use

by military might. Despite the prevalence of the model, the term mercantilism was not coined until 1763, by Victor de Riqueti, marquis de Mirabeau (1715–1789), and popularized by Adam Smith in 1776, who vigorously opposed it.

School of Salamanca

Main article: School of Salamanca

In the 16th century the Jesuit School of Salamanca in Spain developed economic theory to a high level, only to have their contributions forgotten until the 20th century.

Sir Thomas More

Marquis de Mirabeau (1715–1789)

of the state's military power to ensure that local markets and supply sources were protected, spawning protectionism.

French seaport during the heyday of mercantilism

Sir Thomas More (1478–1535)

Mercantile theorists held that international trade could not benefit all countries at the same time. Money and precious metals were the only source of riches in their view, and limited resources must be allocated between countries, therefore tariffs should be used to encourage exports, which bring money into the country, and discourage imports which send it abroad. In other words, a positive balance of trade ought to be maintained through a surplus of exports, often backed

Main article: Sir Thomas More

In 1516 English humanist Sir Thomas More (1478–1535) published *Utopia*, which describes an ideal society where land is owned in common and there is universal education and religious tolerance, inspiring the English Poor Laws (1587) and the communism-socialism movement.

Nicolaus Copernicus (1473–1543)

Jean Bodin (1530–1596)

Nicolaus Copernicus

Main articles: Nicolaus Copernicus and Quantity theory of money

In 1517 Polish astronomer Nicolaus Copernicus (1473–1543) published the first known argument for the quantity theory of money. In 1519 he also published the first known form of Gresham's Law: "Bad money drives out good".

Jean Bodin

Main article: Jean Bodin

In 1568 Jean Bodin (1530–1596) of France published *Reply to Malestroit*, containing the first known analysis of inflation, which he claimed was caused by importation of gold and silver from South America, backing the quantity theory of money.

Barthélemy de Laffemas

In 1598 French mercantilist economist Barthélemy de Laffemas (1545–1612) published *Les Trésors et richesses pour mettre l'Estat en splendeur*, which blasted those who frowned on French silks because the industry created employment for the poor, the first known mention of underconsumption theory, which was later refined by John Maynard Keynes.

Barthélemy de Laffemas (1545–1612)

Leonardus Lessius

Leonardus Lessius (1554–1623)

Main article: Leonardus Lessius

In 1605 Flemish Jesuit theologian Leonardus Lessius (1554–1623) published *On Justice and Law*, the deepest moral-theological study of economics since Aquinas, whose just price approach he claimed was no longer workable. After comparing money's growth via avarice to the propagation of hares, he made the first statement of the price of insurance as being based on risk.

Edward Misselden and Gerard Malynes

Main articles: Edward Misselden and Gerard Malynes

In 1622 English merchants Edward Misselden and Gerard Malynes began a dispute over free trade and the desirability of government regulation of companies, with Malynes arguing against foreign exchange as under the control of bankers, and Misselden arguing that international money exchange and fluctuations in the exchange rate depend upon international trade and not bankers, and that the state should regulate trade to insure export surpluses.

Thomas Mun

Main article: Thomas Mun

English economist Thomas Mun (1571–1641) describes early mercantilist policy in his book *England's Treasure by Foreign Trade*, which was not published until 1664, although it was widely circulated in manuscript form during his lifetime. A member of the East India Company, he wrote about his experiences in *A Discourse of Trade from England unto the East Indies* (1621).

According to Mun, trade was the only way to increase England's wealth, and he suggested several courses of action. Important were frugal consumption to increase the amount of goods available for export, increased use of land and other natural resources to reduce import requirements, lower export duties on goods produced domestically from foreign materials, and the export of goods with inelastic demand because more money could be made from higher prices.

Sir William Petty

Main article: William Petty

In 1662 English economist Sir William Petty (1623–1687) began publishing short works applying the rational scientific tradition of Francis Bacon to economics, requiring that it only use measurable phenomena and seek quantitative precision, coining the term "political arithmetic", introducing statistical mathematics, and becoming the first scientific economist.

Philipp von Hörnigk

Main article: Philipp von Hörnigk

Philipp von Hörnigk (1640–1712, sometimes spelt *Hornick* or *Horneck*) was born in Frankfurt and became an Austrian civil servant writing in a time when his country was constantly threatened by Ottoman invasion. In *Österreich Über Alles, Wann es Nur Will* (1684, *Austria Over All, If She Only Will*) he laid out one of the clearest statements of mercantile policy, listing nine principal rules of national economy:

> "To inspect the country's soil with the greatest care, and not to leave the agricultural pos-

Sir William Petty (1623–1687)

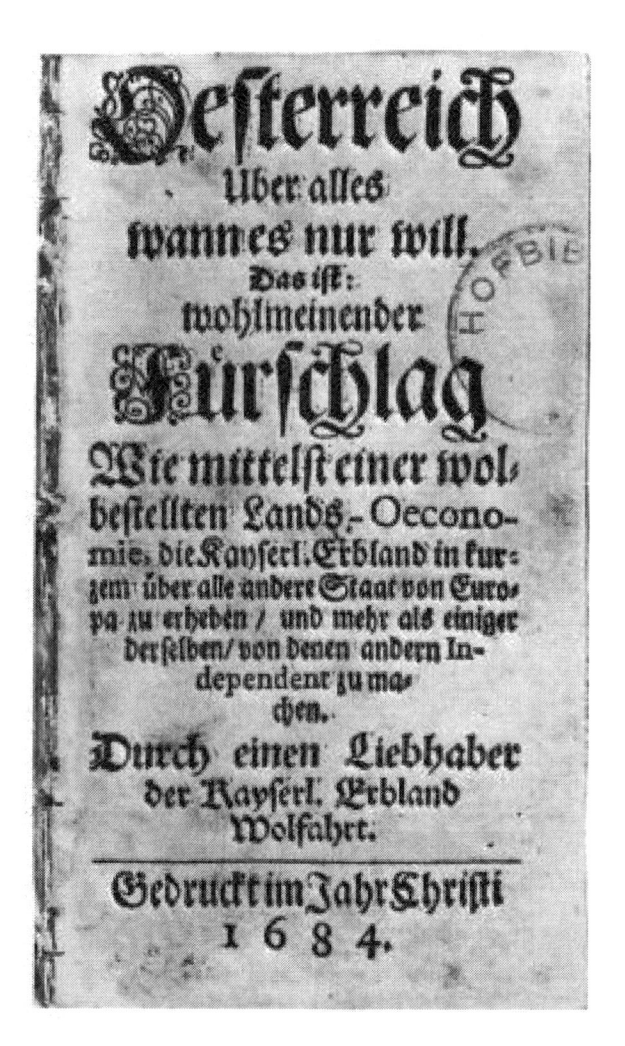

The title page to Philipp von Hörnigk's statement of mercantilist philosophy.

sibilities of a single corner or clod of earth unconsidered... All commodities found in a country, which cannot be used in their natural state, should be worked up within the country... Attention should be given to the population, that it may be as large as the country can support... gold and silver once in the country are under no circumstances to be taken out for any purpose... The inhabitants should make every effort to get along with their domestic products... [Foreign commodities] should be obtained not for gold or silver, but in exchange for other domestic wares... and should be imported in unfinished form, and worked up within the country... Opportunities should be sought night and day for selling the country's superfluous goods to these foreigners in manufactured form... No importation should be allowed under any circumstances of which there is a sufficient supply of suitable quality at home."

Nationalism, self-sufficiency and national power were the basic policies proposed.[18]

Jean-Baptiste Colbert and Pierre Le Pesant, Sieur de Boisguilbert

Main articles: Jean-Baptiste Colbert and Pierre Le Pesant, sieur de Boisguilbert

In 1665–1683 Jean-Baptiste Colbert (1619–1683) was minister of finance under King Louis XIV of France, and set up national guilds to regulate major industries. Silk, linen, tapestry, furniture manufacture and wine were examples of the crafts in which France specialized, all of which came to require membership in a guild to operate in until the French Revolution. According to Colbert, "It is simply and solely the abundance of money within a state [which] makes the difference in its grandeur and power."

In 1695 French economist Pierre Le Pesant, sieur de Boisguilbert (1646–1714) wrote a plea to Louis XIV to end Colbert's mercantilist program, containing the first notion of an economical market, becoming the first economist to question mercantile economic policy and value the wealth of a country by its production and exchange of goods instead its assets.

Charles Davenant

Main article: Charles Davenant

In 1696 British mercantilist Tory Member of parliament Charles Davenant (1656–1714) published *Essay on the East India Trade*, displaying the first understanding of consumer demand and perfect competition.

Sir James Steuart

Jean-Baptiste Colbert (1619–1683)

Sir James Steuart (1713–1780)

Main article: Sir James Steuart

In 1767 Scottish mercantilist economist Sir James Steuart (1713–1780) published *An Inquiry into the Principles of Political Economy*, the first book in English with the term "political economy" in the title, and the first complete economics treatise.

Pierre Le Pesant, sieur de Boisguilbert (1646–1714)

1.2.4 Pre-Classical (17th and 18th century)

The British Enlightenment

See also: Age of Enlightenment, Scottish enlightenment, Thomas Hobbes and William Petty

In the 17th century Britain went through troubling times, enduring not only political and religious division in the English Civil War, King Charles I's execution, and the Cromwellian dictatorship, but also the Great Plague of London and Great Fire of London. The restoration of the monarchy under Charles II, who had Roman Catholic sympathies, led to turmoil and strife, and his Catholic-leaning successor King James II was swiftly ousted. Invited in his place were Protestant William of Orange and Mary, who assented to the Bill of Rights 1689, ensuring that the Parliament was dominant in what became known as the Glorious Revolution.

The upheaval was accompanied by a number of major scientific advances, including Robert Boyle's discovery of the gas pressure constant (1660) and Sir Isaac Newton's publication of *Philosophiae Naturalis Principia Mathematica* (1687), which described Newton's laws of motion and his universal law of gravitation.

All these factors spurred the advancement of economic thought. For instance, Richard Cantillon (1680–1734) consciously imitated Newton's forces of inertia and gravity in the natural world with human reason and market competition in the economic world.[19] In his *Essay on the Nature of Commerce in General*, he argued rational self-interest in a system of freely-adjusting markets would lead to order and mutually-compatible prices. Unlike the mercantilist thinkers however, wealth was found not in trade but in human labor. The first person to tie these ideas into a political framework was John Locke.

John Locke Main article: John Locke

John Locke (1632–1704) was born near Bristol, and educated in London and Oxford. He is considered one of the most significant philosophers of his era mainly for his critique of Thomas Hobbes' defense of absolutism in *Leviathan* (1651) and his of social contract theory. Locke believed that people contracted into society, which was bound to protect their property rights.[20] He defined property broadly to include people's lives and liberties, as well as their wealth. When people combined their labor with their surroundings, that created property rights. In his words from his *Second Treatise on Civil Government* (1689):

> "God hath given the world to men in common... Yet every man has a property in his own

John Locke (1632–1704) combined philosophy, politics and economics into one coherent framework.

person. The labour of his body and the work of his hands we may say are properly his. Whatsoever, then, he removes out of the state that nature hath provided and left it in, he hath mixed his labour with, and joined to it something that is his own, and thereby makes it his property."[21]

Locke argued that not only should the government cease interference with people's property (or their "lives, liberties and estates"), but also that it should positively work to ensure their protection. His views on price and money were laid out in a letter to a Member of Parliament in 1691 entitled *Some Considerations on the Consequences of the Lowering of Interest and the Raising of the Value of Money* (1691), arguing that the "price of any commodity rises or falls, by the proportion of the number of buyers and sellers", a rule which "holds universally in all things that are to be bought and sold."[22]

Dudley North Main article: Dudley North (economist)

Dudley North (1641–1691) was a wealthy merchant and landowner who worked for Her Majesty's Treasury and opposed most mercantile policy. His *Discourses upon trade* (1691), published anonymously, argued against assuming a need for a favorable balance of trade. Trade, he argued,

Dudley North (1641–1691) argued that the results of mercantile policy are undesirable.

David Hume (1711–76)

benefits both sides, promotes specialization, division of labor and wealth for everyone. Regulation of trade interferes with these benefits, he said.

David Hume Main article: David Hume

David Hume (1711–1776) agreed with North's philosophy and denounced mercantilist assumptions. His contributions were set down in *Political Discourses* (1752), and later consolidated in his *Essays, Moral, Political, Literary* (1777). Adding to the argument that it was undesirable to strive for a favourable balance of trade, Hume argued that it is, in any case, impossible.

Hume held that any surplus of exports would be paid for by imports of gold and silver. This would increase the money supply, causing prices to rise. That in turn would cause a decline in exports until the balance with imports is restored.

Francis Hutcheson Main article: Francis Hutcheson (philosopher)

Francis Hutcheson (1694–1746), the teacher of Adam Smith from 1737 to 1740[23] is considered the end of a long tradition of thought on economics as "household or family (οἶκος) management",[24] [25] [26] stemming from Xenophon's work *Oeconomicus*.[27] [28]

Francis Hutcheson (1694–1746)

The Physiocrats and the circular flow

Main article: Physiocracy
See also: Bernard Mandeville, John Law (economist),

Pierre Samuel du Pont de Nemours, a prominent Physiocrat, emigrated to the U.S., and his son founded DuPont, the world's second biggest chemicals company.

Pierre le Pesant de Boisguilbert and Victor de Riqueti

Similarly disenchanted with regulation on trade inspired by mercantilism, a Frenchman named Vincent de Gournay (1712–1759) is reputed to have asked why it was so hard to *laissez faire* ("let it be"), *laissez passer* ("let it pass"), advocating free enterprise and free trade. He was one of the early Physiocrats, a Greek word meaning "Government of nature", who held that agriculture was the source of wealth. As historian David B. Danbom wrote, the Physiocrats "damned cities for their artificiality and praised more natural styles of living. They celebrated farmers."[29] Over the end of the seventeenth and beginning of the eighteenth century big advances in natural science and anatomy included discovery of blood circulation through the human body. This concept was mirrored in the physiocrats' economic theory, with the notion of a circular flow of income throughout the economy.

François Quesnay (1694–1774) was the court physician to King Louis XV of France. He believed that trade and

Francois Quesnay (1694–1774)

industry were not sources of wealth, and instead in his book *Tableau économique* (1758, Economic Table) argued that agricultural surpluses, by flowing through the economy in the form of rent, wages, and purchases were the real economic movers. Firstly, said Quesnay, regulation impedes the flow of income throughout all social classes and therefore economic development. Secondly, taxes on the productive classes, such as farmers, should be reduced in favour of rises for unproductive classes, such as landowners, since their luxurious way of life distorts the income flow. David Ricardo later showed that taxes on land are non-transferable to tenants in his Law of Rent.

Jacques Turgot (1727–1781) was born in Paris to an old Norman family. His best known work, *Réflexions sur la formation et la distribution des richesses* (*Reflections on the Formation and Distribution of Wealth*) (1766) developed Quesnay's theory that land is the only source of wealth. Turgot viewed society in terms of three classes: the productive agricultural class, the salaried artisan class (*classe stipendice*) and the landowning class (*classe disponible*). He argued that only the net product of land should be taxed and advocated the complete freedom of commerce and industry.

In August 1774 Turgot was appointed to be minister of finance, and in the space of two years he introduced many anti-mercantile and anti-feudal measures supported by the

Anne Robert Jacques Turgot (1727–1781)

Adam Smith (1723–1790), father of modern political economy.

king. A statement of his guiding principles, given to the king were "no bankruptcy, no tax increases, no borrowing." Turgot's ultimate wish was to have a single tax on land and abolish all other indirect taxes, but measures he introduced before that were met with overwhelming opposition from landed interests. Two edicts in particular, one suppressing corvées (charges from farmers to aristocrats) and another renouncing privileges given to guilds, inflamed influential opinion. He was forced from office in 1776.

1.2.5 Classical (18th and 19th century)

Adam Smith and *The Wealth of Nations*

Main articles: The Wealth of Nations, Adam Smith, Pitt the Younger and Edmund Burke
See also: Anders Chydenius

Adam Smith (1723–1790) is popularly seen as the father of modern political economy. His 1776 publication *An Inquiry Into the Nature and Causes of the Wealth of Nations* happened to coincide not only with the American Revolution, shortly before the Europe-wide upheavals of the French Revolution, but also the dawn of a new industrial revolution that allowed more wealth to be created on a larger scale than ever before.

Smith was a Scottish moral philosopher, whose first book was *The Theory of Moral Sentiments* (1759). He argued in it that people's ethical systems develop through personal relations with other individuals, that right and wrong are sensed through others' reactions to one's behaviour. This gained Smith more popularity than his next work, *The Wealth of Nations*, which the general public initially ignored.[30] Yet Smith's political economic magnum opus was successful in circles that mattered.

Adam Smith's Invisible Hand

Main article: Invisible hand

Smith argued for a "system of natural liberty"[32] where individual effort was the producer of social good. Smith believed even the selfish within society were kept under restraint and worked for the good of all when acting in a competitive market. Prices are often unrepresentative of the true value of goods and services. Following John Locke, Smith thought true value of things derived from the amount of labour invested in them.

> Every man is rich or poor according to the degree in which he can afford to enjoy the necessaries, conveniencies, and amusements of human life. But after the division of labour has once thoroughly taken place, it is but a very small part of these with which a man's own labour can supply him. The far greater part of them he must derive from the labour of other people,

and he must be rich or poor according to the quantity of that labour which he can command, or which he can afford to purchase. The value of any commodity, therefore, to the person who possesses it, and who means not to use or consume it himself, but to exchange it for other commodities, is equal to the quantity of labour which it enables him to purchase or command. Labour, therefore, is the real measure of the exchangeable value of all commodities. The real price of every thing, what every thing really costs to the man who wants to acquire it, is the toil and trouble of acquiring it.
— [33]

When the butchers, the brewers and the bakers acted under the restraint of an open market economy, their pursuit of self-interest, thought Smith, paradoxically drives the process to correct real life prices to their just values. His classic statement on competition goes as follows.

> When the quantity of any commodity which is brought to market falls short of the effectual demand, all those who are willing to pay... cannot be supplied with the quantity which they want... Some of them will be willing to give more. A competition will begin among them, and the market price will rise... When the quantity brought to market exceeds the effectual demand, it cannot be all sold to those who are willing to pay the whole value of the rent, wages and profits, which must be paid to bring it thither... The market price will sink...[34]

Limitations Smith's vision of a free market economy, based on secure property, capital accumulation, widening markets and a division of labour contrasted with the mercantilist tendency to attempt to "regulate all evil human actions."[32] Smith believed there were precisely three legitimate functions of government. The third function was...

> ...erecting and maintaining certain public works and certain public institutions, which it can never be for the interest of any individual or small number of individuals, to erect and maintain... Every system which endeavours... to draw towards a particular species of industry a greater share of the capital of the society than what would naturally go to it... retards, instead of accelerating, the progress of the society toward real wealth and greatness.

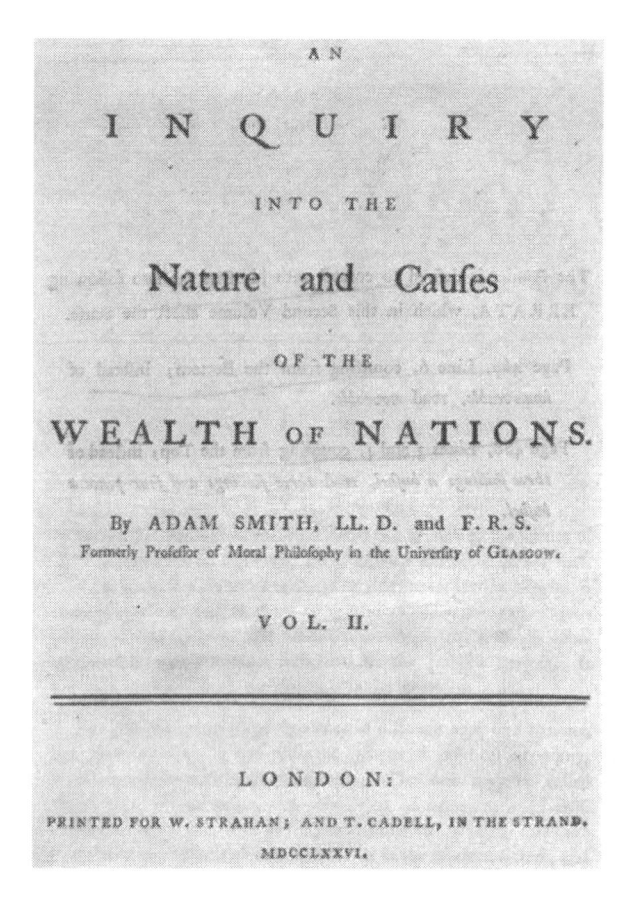

Adam Smith's title page of The Wealth of Nations.

In addition to the necessity of public leadership in certain sectors Smith argued, secondly, that cartels were undesirable because of their potential to limit production and quality of goods and services.[35] Thirdly, Smith criticised government support of any kind of monopoly which always charges the highest price "which can be squeezed out of the buyers".[36] The existence of monopoly and the potential for cartels, which would later form the core of competition law policy, could distort the benefits of free markets to the advantage of businesses at the expense of consumer sovereignty.

William Pitt the Younger

William Pitt the Younger (1759–1806), Tory Prime Minister in 1783–1801 based his tax proposals on Smith's ideas, and advocated free trade as a devout disciple of *The Wealth of Nations*.[37] Smith was appointed a commissioner of customs and within twenty years Smith had a following of new generation writers who were intent on building the science of political economy.[30]

William Pitt the Younger (1759–1806)

Edmund Burke (1729–1797)

Edmund Burke

Adam Smith expressed an affinity to the opinions of Irish MP Edmund Burke (1729–1797), known widely as a political philosopher:

> "Burke is the only man I ever knew who thinks on economic subjects exactly as I do without any previous communication having passed between us."[38]

Burke was an established political economist himself, known for his book *Thoughts and Details on Scarcity*. He was widely critical of liberal politics, and condemned the French Revolution which began in 1789. In *Reflections on the Revolution in France* (1790) he wrote that the "age of chivalry is dead, that of sophisters, economists and calculators has succeeded, and the glory of Europe is extinguished forever." Smith's contemporary influences included François Quesnay and Jacques Turgot whom he met on a visit to Paris, and David Hume, his Scottish compatriot. The times produced a common need among thinkers to explain social upheavals of the Industrial revolution taking place, and in the seeming chaos without the feudal and monarchical structures of Europe, show there was order still.

Jeremy Bentham

Main article: Jeremy Bentham

Jeremy Bentham (1748–1832) was perhaps the most radical thinker of his time, and developed the concept of utilitarianism. Bentham was an atheist, a prison reformer, animal rights activist, believer in universal suffrage, freedom of speech, free trade and health insurance at a time when few dared to argue for any of these ideas. He was schooled rigorously from an early age, finishing university and being called to the bar at 18. His first book, *A Fragment on Government* (1776), published anonymously, was a trenchant critique of William Blackstone's *Commentaries on the Laws of England*. This gained wide success until it was found that the young Bentham, and not a revered Professor had penned it. In *An Introduction to the Principles of Morals and Legislation* (1789) Bentham set out his theory of utility.[39][40]

Jean-Baptiste Say

Main article: Jean-Baptiste Say

Jeremy Bentham (1748–1832) believed in "the greatest good for the greatest number".

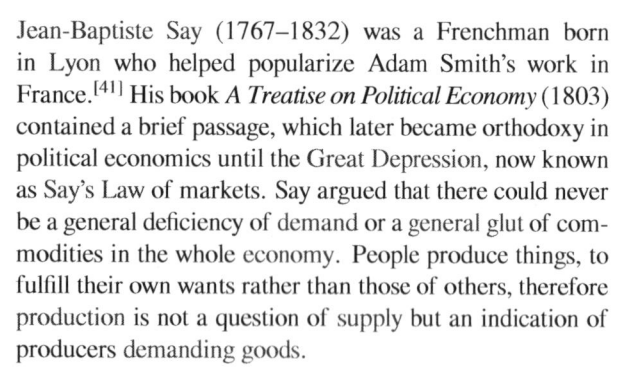

Say's Law, by Jean-Baptiste Say (1767–1832), which states that supply always equals demand, was rarely challenged until the 20th century.

Jean-Baptiste Say (1767–1832) was a Frenchman born in Lyon who helped popularize Adam Smith's work in France.[41] His book *A Treatise on Political Economy* (1803) contained a brief passage, which later became orthodoxy in political economics until the Great Depression, now known as Say's Law of markets. Say argued that there could never be a general deficiency of demand or a general glut of commodities in the whole economy. People produce things, to fulfill their own wants rather than those of others, therefore production is not a question of supply but an indication of producers demanding goods.

Say agreed that a part of income is saved by households, but in the long term, savings are invested. Investment and consumption are the two elements of demand, so that production *is* demand, therefore it is impossible for production to outrun demand, or for there to be a "general glut" of supply. Say also argued that money was neutral, because its sole role is to facilitate exchanges, therefore, people demand money only to buy commodities; "money is a veil".[42]

David Ricardo

Main article: David Ricardo

David Ricardo (1772–1823) was born in London. By the age of 26, he had become a wealthy stock market trader, and bought himself a constituency seat in Ireland to gain a platform in the British parliament's House of Commons.[43] Ricardo's best known work is *On the Principles of Political Economy and Taxation* (1817), which contains his critique of barriers to international trade and a description of the manner in which income is distributed in the population. Ricardo made a distinction between workers, who received a wage fixed to a level at which they could survive, the landowners, who earn a rent, and capitalists, who own capital and receive a profit, a residual part of the income.[44]

If population grows, it becomes necessary to cultivate additional land, whose fertility is lower than that of already cultivated fields, because of the law of decreasing productivity. Therefore, the cost of the production of the wheat increases, as well as the price of the wheat: The rents increase also, the wages, indexed to inflation (because they must allow workers to survive) as well. Profits decrease, until the capitalists can no longer invest. The economy, Ricardo concluded, is bound to tend towards a steady state.[42]

David Ricardo (1772–1823) is renowned for his law of comparative advantage.

John Stuart Mill

Main articles: Principles of Political Economy and John Stuart Mill

John Stuart Mill (1806–1873) was the dominant figure of political economic thought of his time, as well as a Member of parliament for the seat of Westminster, and a leading political philosopher. Mill was a child prodigy, reading Ancient Greek from the age of 3, and being vigorously schooled by his father James Mill.[45] Jeremy Bentham was a close mentor and family friend, and Mill was heavily influenced by David Ricardo. Mill's textbook, first published in 1848 and titled *Principles of Political Economy* was essentially a summary of the economic thought of the mid-nineteenth century.[46]

Principles of Political Economy (1848) was used as the standard text by most universities well into the beginning of the twentieth century. On the question of economic growth Mill tried to find a middle ground between Adam Smith's view of ever-expanding opportunities for trade and technological innovation and Thomas Malthus' view of the inherent limits of population. In his fourth book Mill set out a number of possible future outcomes, rather than predicting one in particular.[42]

John Stuart Mill (1806–1873), weaned on the philosophy of Jeremy Bentham, wrote the most authoritative economics text of his time.

Classical political economy

Main article: Classical economics
See also: Thomas Edward Cliffe Leslie, Walter Bagehot and Thorold Rogers

The classical economists were referred to as a group for the first time by Karl Marx.[47] One unifying part of their theories was the labour theory of value, contrasting to value deriving from a general equilibrium theory of supply and demand. These economists had seen the first economic and social transformation brought by the Industrial Revolution: rural depopulation, precariousness, poverty, apparition of a working class.

They wondered about population growth, because demographic transition had begun in Great Britain at that time. They also asked many fundamental questions, about the source of value, the causes of economic growth and the role of money in the economy. They supported a free-market economy, arguing it was a natural system based upon freedom and property. However, these economists were divided and did not make up a unified current of thought.

A notable current within classical economics was underconsumption theory, as advanced by the Birmingham School and Thomas Robert Malthus in the early 19th century. These argued for government action to mitigate

1.2. HISTORY OF ECONOMIC THOUGHT

unemployment and economic downturns, and were an intellectual predecessor of what later became Keynesian economics in the 1930s. Another notable school was Manchester capitalism, which advocated free trade, against the previous policy of mercantilism.

Capitalism, Communism, and Karl Marx

Main article: Marxian economics
Key people: Karl Marx and Friedrich Engels

With Marx, Friedrich Engels (1820–1895) co-authored The Communist Manifesto and the second volume of Das Kapital.

Karl Marx (1818–1883) published a fundamental critique of classical economics based on the labor theory of value.

George Wilhelm Friedrich Hegel (1770–1831)

Just as the term "mercantilism" had been coined and popularized by critics like Adam Smith, so the term "capitalism" coined by Karl Marx (1818–1883) was used by its critics. Socialism emerged in response to the miserable living and working conditions of the working class in the new industrial era, and the classical economics from which it sprang. The economic and political theory published in *The Communist Manifesto* (1848) and *Das Kapital* (1867) combined with the dialectic theory of history inspired by Friedrich Hegel (1770–1831) to provide a revolutionary critique of nineteenth-century capitalism.

In 1845 German radical Friedrich Engels (1820–1895) published *The Condition of the Working Class in England in 1844*,[48] describing workers in Manchester as "the most unconcealed pinnacle of social misery in our day." After Marx died, Engels completed the second volume of *Das Kapital* from his notes.

Das Kapital Main articles: Das Kapital, Capital, Volume I and Karl Marx

Marx wrote his magnum opus *Das Kapital* (1867) at the British Museum's library in London. Karl Marx begins with the concept of commodities. Before capitalism, says Marx, production was based on slavery—in ancient Rome for example—then serfdom in the feudal societies of medieval Europe. The current mode of labor exchange has produced an erratic and unstable situation allowing the conditions for revolution. People buy and sell their labor as people buy and sell goods and services. People themselves have become disposable commodities. As Marx wrote in *The Communist Manifesto*,

> "The history of all hitherto existing society is the history of class struggles. Freeman and slave, patrician and plebeian, lord and serf, guildmaster and journeyman, in a word, oppressor and oppressed, stood in constant opposition to one another... The modern bourgeois society that has sprouted from the ruins of feudal society has not done away with class antagonisms. It has but established new classes, new conditions of oppression, new forms of struggle in place of the old ones."

The title page of the first edition of Das Kapital *(1867) in German.*

From the first page of *Das Kapital*:

> "The wealth of those societies in which the capitalist mode of production prevails, presents itself as an immense accumulation of commodities, its unit being a single commodity. Our investigation must therefore begin with the analysis of a commodity."[49]

Marx uses the word "commodity" in an extensive metaphysical discussion of the nature of material wealth, how the objects of wealth are perceived and how they can be used. A commodity contrasts to objects of the natural world. When people mix their labor with an object it becomes a "commodity". In the natural world there are trees, diamonds, iron ore and people. In the economic world they become chairs, rings, factories and workers. However, says Marx, commodities have a dual nature, a dual value. He distinguishes the use value of a thing from its exchange value, which can be entirely different.[50] The use value of a thing derives from the amount of labor used to produce it, says Marx, following the classical economists in the labor theory of value. However, Marx did not believe labor was the only source of use value in things. He believed value can derive too from natural goods and refined his definition of use value to "socially necessary labor time", by which he meant the time people need to produce things when they are not lazy or inefficient.[51] Furthermore, people subjectively inflate the value of things, for instance because there's a commodity fetish for glimmering diamonds,[52] and oppressive power relations involved in commodity production. These two factors mean exchange values differ greatly. An oppressive power relation, says Marx applying the use/exchange distinction to labor itself, in work-wage bargains derives from the fact that employers pay their workers less in "exchange value" than the workers produce in "use value". The difference makes up the capitalist's profit, or in Marx's terminology, "surplus value".[53] Therefore, says Marx, capitalism is a system of exploitation.

Marx's work turned the labor theory of value, as the classicists called it, on its head. His dark irony goes deeper by asking what is the socially necessary labor time for the production of labor (i.e. working people) itself. Marx answers that this is the bare minimum for people to subsist and to reproduce with skills necessary in the economy.[54]

People are therefore alienated from both the fruits of production and the means to realize their potential, psychologically, by their oppressed position in the labor market.

Marx explained the booms and busts, like the Panic of 1873, as part of an inherent instability in capitalist economies.

But the tale told alongside exploitation and alienation is one of capital accumulation and economic growth. Employers are constantly under pressure from market competition to drive their workers harder, and at the limits invest in labor-displacing technology, by replacing an assembly line packer, for example. with a robot. This increases profits and expands growth, but for the sole benefit of those who have private property in these means of production. The working classes meanwhile face progressive immiseration, having had the product of their labor exploited from them, having been alienated from the tools of production. And having been fired from their jobs and replaced by machines, they end up unemployed. Marx believed that a reserve army of the unemployed would grow and grow, fueling a downward pressure on wages as desperate people accepted work for less. But this would produce a deficit of demand as the people's power to purchase products lagged. A glut of unsold products would result, production would be cut back, and profits decline until capital accumulation halted in an economic depression. When the glut cleared, the economy would again start to boom before the next cyclical bust begins. With every boom and bust, with every capitalist crisis, thought Marx, tension and conflict between the increasingly polarized classes of capitalists and workers would heighten. Moreover, smaller firms are being gobbled by larger ones in every business cycle, as power is concentrated in the hands of the few and away from the many. Ultimately, led by the Communist party, Marx envisaged a revolution and the creation of a classless society. How this society might work, Marx never suggested. His primary contribution was not a blueprint for a new society would be, but a criticism of the one he saw.

Marx's disciples Main articles: Karl Kautsky, Rosa Luxemburg, Beatrice Webb, John A. Hobson, R. H. Tawney and Paul Sweezy

The first volume of *Das Kapital* was the only one Marx

Rosa Luxembourg (1871–1919)

alone published. The second and third volumes were produced with the help of Friedrich Engels; Karl Kautsky, who had become a friend of Engels, saw through the publication of volume four.

Marx began a tradition of economists who became political activists, including Rosa Luxemburg (1871–1919), a member of the Social Democratic Party of Germany who later turned towards the Communist Party of Germany because of their stance against the First World War, and Beatrice Webb (1858–1943) of England, a socialist who helped found both the London School of Economics (LSE) and the Fabian Society.

Beatrice Webb (1858–1943)

George Bernard Shaw (1856–1950)

Sidney Webb (1859–1947)

The London School of Economics

Main articles: London School of Economics, Sidney Webb, Beatrice Webb, George Bernard Shaw and R.G.D. Allen

In 1895 the London School of Economics (LSE) was founded by Fabian Society members Sidney Webb (1859–1947), Beatrice Webb (1858–1943), and George Bernard Shaw (1856–1950), joining the University of London in 1900.

In the 1930s LSE member Sir Roy G.D. Allen (1906–1983) popularized the use of mathematics in economics.

1.2.6 Neoclassical (19th and early 20th Century)

Main articles: Neoclassical economics, Marginalism and Mathematical economics
See also: Léon Walras, Alexander del Mar, John Bates Clark, Irving Fisher, William Ashley (economic historian) and Enrico Barone

Neoclassical economics developed in the 1870s. There were three main independent schools. The Cambridge School was founded with the 1871 publication of Jevons' *Theory of Political Economy*, developing theories of partial equilibrium and focusing on market failures. Its main repre-

Sir Roy Allen (1906–1983)

John Bates Clark (1847–1938)

sentatives were Stanley Jevons, Alfred Marshall, and Arthur Pigou. The Austrian School of Economics was made up of Austrian economists Carl Menger, Eugen von Böhm-Bawerk, and Friedrich von Wieser, who developed the theory of capital and tried to explain economic crises. It was founded with the 1871 publication of Menger's *Principles of Economics*. The Lausanne School, led by Léon Walras and Vilfredo Pareto, developed the theories of general equilibrium and Pareto efficiency. It was founded with the 1874 publication of Walras' *Elements of Pure Economics*.

Anglo-American neoclassical

American economist John Bates Clark (1847–1938) promoted the marginalist revolution, publishing *The Distribution of Wealth* (1899), which proposed Clark's Law of Capitalism: "Given competition and homogeneous factors of production labor and capital, the repartition of the social product will be according to the productivity of the last physical input of units of labor and capital", also expressed as "What a social class gets is, under natural law, what it contributes to the general output of industry." In 1947 the John Bates Clark Medal was established in his honor.[40]

William Stanley Jevons In 1871 Menger's English counterpart Stanley Jevons (1835–1882) independently published *Theory of Political Economy* (1871), stating that at the margin the satisfaction of goods and services decreases. An example of the Theory of Diminishing Marginal Utility is that for every orange one eats, one gets less pleasure until one stops eating oranges completely.[40]

Alfred Marshall Alfred Marshall (1842–1924) is also credited with an attempt to put economics on a more mathematical footing. The first professor of economics at the University of Cambridge, his 1890 work *Principles of Economics*[55] abandoned the term "political economy" for his favorite "economics". He viewed math as a way to simplify economic reasoning, although he had reservations as revealed in a letter to his student Arthur Cecil Pigou:[40][56]

"(1) Use mathematics as shorthand language, rather than as an engine of inquiry. (2) Keep to them till you have done. (3) Translate into English. (4) Then illustrate by examples that are important in real life. (5) Burn the mathematics. (6) If you can't succeed in 4, burn 3. This I do often."

New institutional schools Main articles: Harold Demsetz, Armen Alchian and New institutional economics

William Stanley Jevons (1835–1882) helped popularize marginal utility theory.

Alfred Marshall (1842–1924) wrote the main alternative textbook to John Stuart Mill of the day, Principles of Economics *(1890)*

In 1972 American economists Harold Demsetz (1930–) and Armen Alchian (1914–2013) published *Production, Information Costs and Economic Organization*, founding New Institutional Economics, an updating of the works of Ronald Coase (1910–2013) with mainstream economics.[40]

Continental neoclassical

Léon Walras In 1874 again working independently, French economist Léon Walras (1834–1910) generalized marginal theory across the economy in *Elements of Pure Economics*: Small changes in people's preferences, for instance shifting from beef to mushrooms, would lead to a mushroom price rise, and beef price fall; this stimulates producers to shift production, increasing mushrooming investment, which would increase market supply and a new price equilibrium between the products, e.g. lowering the price of mushrooms to a level between the two first levels. For many products across the economy the same would happen if one assumes markets are competitive, people choose on the basis of self-interest, and there's no cost for shifting production.[40]

Harold Demsetz (1930–)

The Austrian school of economics Main article: Austrian school

1.2. HISTORY OF ECONOMIC THOUGHT

Léon Walras (1834–1910)

Eugen von Böhm-Bawerk (1851–1914)

Friedrich von Wieser (1851–1926)

While economics at the end of the nineteenth century and the beginning of the twentieth was dominated increasingly by mathematical analysis, the followers of Carl Menger (1840–1921) and his disciples Eugen von Böhm-Bawerk (1851–1914) and Friedrich von Wieser (1851–1926) (coiner of the term "marginal utility") followed a different route, advocating the use of deductive logic instead. This group became known as the Austrian School of Economics, reflecting the Austrian origin of many of the early adherents. Thorstein Veblen in *The Preconceptions of Economic Science* (1900) contrasted neoclassical marginalists in the tradition of Alfred Marshall with the philosophies of the Austrian School.[57][58]

Carl Menger In 1871 Austrian School economist Carl Menger (1840–1921) restated the basic principles of marginal utility in *Grundsätze der Volkswirtschaftslehre*[59] (*Principles of Economics*): Consumers act rationally by seeking to maximize satisfaction of all their preferences; people allocate their spending so that the last unit of a commodity bought creates no more satisfaction than a last unit bought of something else.[40]

Francis Ysidro Edgeworth In 1881 Irish economist Francis Ysidro Edgeworth (1845–1926) published *Math-*

Francis Ysidro Edgeworth (1845–1926)

ematical Psychics: An Essay on the Application of Mathematics to the Moral Sciences*, which introduced indifference curves and the generalized utility function, along with Edgeworth's Limit Theorem, extending the Bertrand Model to handle capacity constraints, and proposing Edgeworth's Paradox for when there is no limit to what the firms can sell.[40]

Friedrich Hayek Mises's outspoken criticisms of socialism had a large influence on the economic thinking of Austrian School economist Friedrich Hayek (1899–1992), who, while initially sympathetic, became one of the leading academic critics of collectivism in the 20th century.[60] In echoes of Smith's "system of natural liberty", Hayek argued that the market is a "spontaneous order" and actively disparaged the concept of "social justice".[61] Hayek believed that all forms of collectivism (even those theoretically based on voluntary cooperation) could only be maintained by a central authority. But he argued that centralizing economic decision-making would lead not only to infringements of liberty but also to depressed standards of living because centralized experts could not gather and assess the knowledge required to allocate scarce resources efficiently or productively. In his book, *The Road to Serfdom* (1944) and in subsequent works, Hayek claimed that socialism required central economic planning and that such planning in turn would lead towards totalitarianism. Hayek attributed the birth of civilization to private property in his book *The*

Friedrich Hayek (1899–1992)

Fatal Conceit (1988). According to him, price signals are the only means of enabling each economic decision maker to communicate tacit knowledge or dispersed knowledge to each other, to solve the economic calculation problem. Along with his Socialist Swedish contemporary and opponent Gunnar Myrdal (1898–1987), Hayek was awarded the Nobel Prize in Economics in 1974.[62]

1.2.7 Alternative schools (19th century)

Business cycle theory

Main articles: Business cycles, William Herschel, Clement Juglar and Nikolai Kondratiev

In the early 19th century German-born English astronomer Sir William Herschel (1738–1822) noted a connection between 11-year sunspot cycles and wheat prices. In 1860 French economist Clément Juglar (1819–1905) posited business cycles seven to eleven years long. In 1925 the Soviet economist Nikolai Kondratiev (1892–1938) proposed the existence of Kondratiev waves in Western capitalist economies fifty to sixty years long.

Sir William Herschel (1738–1822)

Nikolai Kondratiev (1892–1938)

German historical school of economics Main article: Historical school of economics

In the mid-1840s German economist Wilhelm Roscher (1817–1894) founded the German historical school of economics, which promoted the cyclical theory of nations—economies passing through youth, manhood, and senility—and spread through academia in Britain and the U.S., dominating it for the rest of the 19th century.[40]

Thorstein Veblen and the American Way Main article: Thorstein Veblen

Thorstein Veblen (1857–1929), who came from rural midwestern America and worked at the University of Chicago is one of the best-known early critics of the "American Way". In *The Theory of the Leisure Class* (1899) he scorned materialistic culture and wealthy people who conspicuously consumed their riches as a way of demonstrating success. In *The Theory of Business Enterprise* (1904) Veblen distinguished production for people to use things and production for pure profit, arguing that the former is often hindered because businesses pursue the latter. Output and technological advance are restricted by business practices and the creation of monopolies. Businesses protect their

Clément Juglar (1819–1905)

Heterodox traditions

Wilhelm Roscher (1817–1894)

Thorstein Veblen (1857–1929)

existing capital investments and employ excessive credit, leading to depressions and increasing military expenditure and war through business control of political power. These two books, focusing on criticism of consumerism and profiteering did not advocate change. However, in 1918 he moved to New York to begin work as an editor of a magazine called *The Dial*, and then in 1919, along with Charles A. Beard, James Harvey Robinson, and John Dewey he helped found the New School for Social Research, known today as The New School) He was also part of the Technical Alliance,[63] created in 1919 by Howard Scott. From 1919 through 1926 Veblen continued to write and to be involved in various activities at The New School. During this period he wrote *The Engineers and the Price System (1921)*.[40][64]

1.2.8 World wars, revolution and great depression (early - mid 20th century)

At the outbreak of World War I (1914–1918), Alfred Marshall was still working on his last revisions of his *Principles of Economics*. The 20th century's initial climate of optimism was soon violently dismembered in the trenches of the Western Front. During the war, production in Britain, Germany, and France was switched to the military. In 1917 Russia crumbled into revolution led by Vladimir Lenin and who promoted Marxist theory and collectivized the means of production. Also in 1917 the United States of America entered the war Allies (France and Britain), with President Woodrow Wilson claiming to be "making the world safe for democracy", devising a peace plan of Fourteen Points. In 1918 Germany launched a spring offensive which failed, and as the allies counterattacked and more millions were slaughtered, Germany slid into the German Revolution, its interim government suing for peace on the basis of Wilson's Fourteen Points. After the war, Europe lay in ruins, financially, physically, psychologically, and its future was dependent on the dictates of the Versailles Conference in 1919.

After World War I, Europe and the Soviet Union lay in ruins, and the British Empire was nearing its end, leaving the United States as the preeminent global economic power. Before World War II, American economists had played a minor role. During this time institutional economists had been largely critical of the "American Way" of life, especially the conspicuous consumption of the Roaring Twenties before the **Wall Street Crash of 1929**. After the crash a more orthodox body of thought took root, reacting against the lucid debating style of Keynes, and remathematizing the profession. The orthodox center was also challenged by a more radical group of scholars based at the University of Chicago, who advocated "liberty" and "freedom", looking back to 19th century-style non-interventionist governments.

Econometrics

Main articles: Ragnar Frisch, Jan Tinbergen, Wassily Leontief, Lawrence Klein, Clive Granger, Trygve Haavelmo and Econometrics

In the 1930s Norwegian economist Ragnar Frisch (1895–

Ragnar Frisch (1895–1973)

Jan Tinbergen (1903–1994)

Clive Granger (1934–2009)

1973) and Dutch economist Jan Tinbergen (1903–1994) pioneered Econometrics, receiving the first-ever Nobel Prize in Economics in 1969. In 1936 Russian-American economist Wassily Leontief (1905–1999) proposed the Input-Output Model of economics, which uses linear algebra and is ideally suited to computers, receiving the 1973 Nobel Economics Prize. After World War II, Lawrence Klein (1920–) pioneered the use of computers in econometric modeling, receiving the 1980 Nobel Economics Prize. In 1963–1964 as John Tukey of Princeton University was developing the revolutionary Fast Fourier Transform, which greatly speeded up the calculation of Fourier Transforms, his British assistant Sir Clive Granger (1934–2009) pioneered the use of Fourier Transforms in economics, receiving the 2003 Nobel Economics Prize. Ragnar Frisch's assistant Trygve Haavelmo (1911–1999) received the 1989 Nobel Economics Prize for clarifying the probability foundations of econometrics and for analysis of simultaneous economic structures.

Means and corporate governance

Main articles: Adolf A. Berle and Gardiner C. Means

The Great Depression was a time of significant upheaval in the world economy. One of the most original contributions to understanding what went wrong came from Harvard University lawyer Adolf Berle (1895–1971), who like John Maynard Keynes had resigned from his diplomatic job at the Paris Peace Conference, 1919 and was deeply disillu-

Trygve Haavelmo (1911–1999)

Adolf Augustus Berle, Jr. (1895–1971) with Gardiner Means was a foundational figure of modern corporate governance.

sioned by the Versailles Treaty. In his book with American economist Gardiner C. Means (1896–1988) *The Modern Corporation and Private Property* (1932) he detailed the evolution in the contemporary economy of big business, and argued that those who controlled big firms should be better held to account. Directors of companies are held to account to the shareholders of companies, or not, by the rules found in company law statutes. This might include rights to elect and fire the management, require for regular general meetings, accounting standards, and so on. In 1930s America the typical company laws (e.g. in Delaware) did not clearly mandate such rights. Berle argued that the unaccountable directors of companies were therefore apt to funnel the fruits of enterprise profits into their own pockets, as well as manage in their own interests. The ability to do this was supported by the fact that the majority of shareholders in big public companies were single individuals, with scant means of communication, in short, divided and conquered. Berle served in President Franklin Delano Roosevelt's administration through the Great Depression as a key member of his Brain Trust, developing many New Deal policies.

In 1967 Berle and Means issued a revised edition of their work, in which the preface added a new dimension. It was not only the separation of controllers of companies from the owners as shareholders at stake. They posed the question of what the corporate structure was really meant to achieve:

> "Stockholders toil not, neither do they spin, to earn [dividends and share price increases]. They are beneficiaries by position only. Justification for their inheritance... can be founded only upon social grounds... that justification turns on the distribution as well as the existence of wealth. Its force exists only in direct ratio to the number of individuals who hold such wealth. Justification for the stockholder's existence thus depends on increasing distribution within the American population. Ideally the stockholder's position will be impregnable only when every American family has its fragment of that position and of the wealth by which the opportunity to develop individuality becomes fully actualized."[65]

Industrial organization economics

Main articles: Edward Chamberlin, Joan Robinson and Industrial organization

In 1933 American economist Edward Chamberlin (1899–1967) published *The Theory of Monopolistic Competition*.

The same year British economist Joan Robinson (1903–1983) published *The Economics of Imperfect Competition*. Together they founded Industrial Organization Economics. Chamberlin also founded Experimental Economics.

Linear programming

Leonid Kantorovich (1912–1986)

Main articles: Leonid Kantorovich and Linear programming

In 1939 Russian economist Leonid Kantorovich (1912–1986) developed Linear Programming for the optimal allocation of resources, receiving the 1975 Nobel Economics Prize.

Ecology and energy

By the twentieth century, the industrial revolution had led to an exponential increase in the human consumption of resources. The increase in health, wealth and population was perceived as a simple path of progress. However, in the 1930s economists began developing models of non-renewable resource management (see Hotelling's rule) and the sustainability of welfare in an economy that uses non-renewable resources.

Concerns about the environmental and social impacts of industry had been expressed by some Enlightenment political economists and in the Romantic movement of the 1800s. Overpopulation had been discussed in an essay by Thomas Malthus (see Malthusian catastrophe), while John Stuart Mill foresaw the desirability of a "stationary state" economy, thus anticipating concerns of the modern discipline of ecological economics.[66][67][68][69][70]

Ecological economics Ecological economics was founded in the works of Kenneth E. Boulding, Nicholas Georgescu-Roegen, Herman Daly and others. The disciplinary field of ecological economics also bears some similarity to the topic of green economics.[71]

According to ecological economist Malte Faber, ecological economics is defined by its focus on nature, justice, and time. Issues of intergenerational equity, irreversibility of environmental change, uncertainty of long-term outcomes, thermodynamics limits to growth, and sustainable development guide ecological economic analysis and valuation.[72]

Energy accounting Energy accounting was proposed in the early 1930s as a scientific alternative to a price system, or money method of regulating society.[73][74] Joseph Tainter[75] suggests that a diminishing ratio of energy returned on energy invested is a chief cause of the collapse of complex societies. Falling EROEI due to depletion of non-renewable resources also poses a difficult challenge for industrial economies. Sustainability becomes an issue as survival is threatened due to climate change.

Institutional economics

Main articles: Institutional economics, John R. Commons and Walton H. Hamilton

In 1919 Yale economist Walton H. Hamilton coined the term "Institutional economics". In 1934 John R. Commons (1862–1945), another economist from midwestern America published *Institutional Economics* (1934), based on the concept that the economy is a web of relationships between people with diverging interests, including monopolies, large corporations, labor disputes, and fluctuating business cycles. They do however have an interest in resolving these disputes. Government, thought Commons, ought to be the mediator between the conflicting groups. Commons himself devoted much of his time to advisory and mediation work on government boards and industrial commissions.

John R. Commons (1862–1945)

Arthur Cecil Pigou

Main article: Arthur Cecil Pigou

In 1920 Alfred Marshall's student Arthur Cecil Pigou (1877–1959) published *Wealth and Welfare*, which insisted on the possibility of market failures, claiming that markets are inefficient in the case of economic externalities, and the state must interfere to prevent them. However, Pigou retained free market beliefs, and in 1933, in the face of the economic crisis, he explained in *The Theory of Unemployment* that the excessive intervention of the state in the labor market was the real cause of massive unemployment because the governments had established a minimal wage, which prevented wages from adjusting automatically. This was to be the focus of attack from Keynes. In 1943 Pigou published the paper *The Classical Stationary State*, which popularized the Pigou (Real Balance) Effect, the stimulation of output and employment during deflation by increasing consumption due to a rise in wealth

Market socialism

Main articles: Market socialism, Fred M. Taylor, Oskar R. Lange, Abba Lerner and Abram Bergson

In response to the Economic Calculation Problem proposed by the Austrian School of Economics that disputes the efficiency of a state-run economy, the theory of Market Socialism was developed in the late 1920s and 1930s by economists Fred M. Taylor (1855–1932), Oskar R. Lange (1904–1965), Abba Lerner (1903–1982) et al., combining Marxian economics with neoclassical economics after dumping the labor theory of value. In 1938 Abram Berg-

Arthur Cecil Pigou (1877–1959)

son (1914–2003) defined the Social Welfare Function.

The Stockholm school of economics

Main articles: Stockholm School of Economics, Bertil Ohlin, Gunnar Myrdal, Knut Wicksell and International trade

In the 1930s the Stockholm School of Economics was founded by Eli Heckscher (1879–1952), Bertil Ohlin (1899–1977), Gunnar Myrdal (1898–1987) et al. based on the works of John Maynard Keynes and Knut Wicksell (1851–1926), advising the founders of the Swedish Socialist welfare state.

In 1933 Ohlin and Heckscher proposed the Heckscher-Ohlin Model of International Trade, which claims that countries will export products that use their abundant and cheap factors of production and import products that use their scarce factors of production. In 1977 Ohlin was awarded a share of the Nobel Economics Prize.

In 1957 Myrdal published his theory of Circular Cumulative Causation, in which a change in one institution ripples

Fred M. Taylor (1855–1932)

Abba Lerner (1903–1982)

Oskar R. Lange (1904–1965)

through others. In 1974 he received a share of the Nobel Economics Prize.

1.2.9 Alternative schools (20th century)

The American Economic Association

Main articles: American Economic Association, Richard T. Ely and Land economics

In 1885 the American Economic Association (AEA) was founded by Richard T. Ely (1854–1943) et al., publishing the *American Economic Review* starting in 1911. In 1918 Ely published *Private Colonization of Land*, founding Lambda Alpha International in 1930 to promote Land Economics.[40]

1.2.10 Keynesianism (20th century)

Main articles: John Maynard Keynes and The Economic Consequences of the Peace

John Maynard Keynes (1883–1946) was born in Cambridge, educated at Eton, and supervised by both A. C. Pigou and Alfred Marshall at Cambridge University. He began his career as a lecturer before working for the British

Eli Heckscher (1879–1952)

Bertil Ohlin (1899–1977)

government during the Great War, rising to be the British government's financial representative at the Versailles Conference, where he profoundly disagreed with the decisions made. His observations were laid out in his book *The Economic Consequences of the Peace*[76] (1919), where he documented his outrage at the collapse of American adherence to the Fourteen Points[77] and the mood of vindictiveness that prevailed towards Germany.,[78] and he resigned from the conference, using extensive economic data provided by the conference records to argue that if the victors forced war reparations to be paid by the defeated Axis, then a world financial crisis would ensue, leading to a second world war.[79] Keynes finished his treatise by advocating, first, a reduction in reparation payments by Germany to a realistically manageable level, increased intragovernmental management of continental coal production and a free trade union through the League of Nations;[80] second, an arrangement to set off debt repayments between the Allied countries;[81] third, complete reform of international currency exchange and an international loan fund;[82] and fourth, a reconciliation of trade relations with Russia and Eastern Europe.[83]

The book was an enormous success, and though it was criticized for false predictions by a number of people,[84] without the changes he advocated, Keynes's dark forecasts matched the world's experience through the Great Depression which began in 1929, and the descent into World War II in 1939. World War I had been touted as the "war to end all wars", and the absolute failure of the peace settlement generated an even greater determination to not repeat the same mistakes. With the defeat of Fascism, the Bretton Woods Conference was held in July 1944 to establish a new economic order, in which Keynes was again to play a leading role.

The General Theory

Main article: The General Theory of Employment, Interest and Money

During the Great Depression, Keynes published his most important work, *The General Theory of Employment, Interest and Money* (1936). The Great Depression had been sparked by the Wall Street Crash of 1929, leading to massive rises in unemployment in the United States, leading to debts being recalled from European borrowers, and an economic domino effect across the world. Orthodox economics called for a tightening of spending, until business

Gunnar Myrdal (1898–1987)

Richard T. Ely (1854–1943)

Knut Wicksell (1851–1926)

confidence and profit levels could be restored. Keynes by contrast, had argued in *A Tract on Monetary Reform* (1923) (which argues for a stable currency) that a variety of factors determined economic activity, and that it was not enough to wait for the long run market equilibrium to restore itself. As Keynes famously remarked:

> "...this long run is a misleading guide to current affairs. In the long run we are all dead. Economists set themselves too easy, too useless a task if in tempestuous seasons they can only tell us that when the storm is long past the ocean is flat again."[85]

On top of the supply of money, Keynes identified the propensity to consume, inducement to invest, marginal efficiency of capital, liquidity preference, and multiplier effect as variables which determine the level of the economy's output, employment, and price levels. Much of this esoteric terminology was invented by Keynes especially for his *General Theory*. Keynes argued that if savings were being withheld from investment in financial markets, total spending falls, leading to reduced incomes and unemployment, which reduces savings again. This continues until the desire to save becomes equal to the desire to invest, which means a new "equilibrium" is reached and the spending decline halts. This new "equilibrium" is a depression, where people are investing less, have less to save and less to spend.

Keynes argued that employment depends on total spend-

John Maynard Keynes (1883–1946) (right) with his American counterpart Harry White at the Bretton Woods conference.

ing, which is composed of consumer spending and business investment in the private sector. Consumers only spend "passively", or according to their income fluctuations. Businesses, on the other hand, are induced to invest by the expected rate of return on new investments (the benefit) and the rate of interest paid (the cost). So, said Keynes, if business expectations remained the same, and government reduces interest rates (the costs of borrowing), investment would increase, and would have a multiplied effect on total spending. Interest rates, in turn, depend on the quantity of money and the desire to hold money in bank accounts (as opposed to investing). If not enough money is available to match how much people want to hold, interest rates rise until enough people are put off. So if the quantity of money were increased, while the desire to hold money remained stable, interest rates would fall, leading to increased investment, output and employment. For both these reasons, Keynes therefore advocated low interest rates and easy credit, to combat unemployment.

But Keynes believed in the 1930s, conditions necessitated public sector action. Deficit spending, said Keynes, would kick-start economic activity. This he had advocated in an open letter to U.S. President Franklin D. Roosevelt in the *New York Times* (1933). The New Deal programme in the U.S. had been well underway by the publication of the *General Theory*. It provided conceptual reinforcement for policies already pursued. Keynes also believed in a more egalitarian distribution of income, and taxation on unearned income arguing that high rates of savings (to which richer folk are prone) are not desirable in a developed economy. Keynes therefore advocated both monetary management and an active fiscal policy.

The Cambridge Circus

Main articles: Keynesian economics, Cambridge Circus (economics), Joan Robinson, Alfred Eichner, Richard Kahn, Baron Kahn, Piero Sraffa and John Hicks

During World War II Keynes acted as adviser to HM Treasury again, negotiating major loans from the U.S., helping formulate the plans for the International Monetary Fund, the World Bank, and the International Trade Organisation[86] at the 1944 Bretton Woods Conference, a package designed to stabilize world economy fluctuations that had occurred in the 1920s and create a level trading field across the globe. Keynes died little more than a year later, but his ideas had already shaped a new global economic order, and all Western governments followed the Keynesian economics program of deficit spending to avert crises and maintain full employment.

Joan Robinson (1903–1983)

One of Keynes's pupils at Cambridge was Joan Robinson (1903–1983), a member of Keynes's Cambridge Circus, who contributed to the notion that competition is seldom perfect in a market, an indictment of the theory of markets setting prices. In *The Production Function and the Theory of Capital* (1953) Robinson tackled what she saw to be some of the circularity in orthodox economics. Neoclassicists assert that a competitive market forces producers to minimize the costs of production. Robinson said that costs of production are merely the prices of inputs, like capital. Capital goods get their value from the final products. And if the price of the final products determines the price of capital, then it is, argued Robinson, utterly circular to say that the price of capital determines the price of the final products. Goods cannot be priced until the costs of inputs are determined. This would not matter if everything in the economy happened instantaneously, but in the real world, price setting takes time – goods are priced before they are sold. Since capital cannot be adequately valued in independently measurable units, how can one show that capital earns a return equal to the contribution to production?

Alfred Eichner (March 23, 1937 – February 10, 1988) was an American post-Keynesian economist who challenged the neoclassical price mechanism and asserted that prices are not set through supply and demand but rather through mark-up pricing. Eichner is one of the founders of the post-Keynesian school of economics and was a professor at Rutgers University at the time of his death. Eichner's writings and advocacy of thought, differed with the theories of John Maynard Keynes, who was an advocate of government intervention in the free market and proponent of public spending to increase employment. Eichner argued that investment was the key to economic expansion. He was considered an advocate of the concept that government incomes policy should prevent inflationary wage and price settlements in connection to the customary fiscal and monetary means of regulating the economy.

Richard Kahn (1905–1989) was a member of the Cambridge Circus who in 1931 proposed the Multiplier.

Piero Sraffa (1898–1983) came to England from Fascist Italy in the 1920s, and became a member of the Cambridge Circus. In 1960 he published a small book called *Production of Commodities by Means of Commodities*, which explained how technological relationships are the basis for production of goods and services. Prices result from wage-profit tradeoffs, collective bargaining, labour and management conflict and the intervention of government planning. Like Robinson, Sraffa was showing how the major force for price setting in the economy was not necessarily market adjustments.

John Hicks (1904–1989) of England was a Keynesian who in 1937 proposed the Investment Saving – Liquidity Pref-

Piero Sraffa (1898–1983)

erence Money Supply Model, which treats the intersection of the IS and LM curves as the general equilibrium in both markets.

New Keynesian macroeconomics

Main articles: New Keynesian, Edmund Phelps, John B. Taylor, Sticky (economics), George Akerlof, Janet Yellen, Huw Dixon, Michael Woodford (economist) and Julio Rotemberg

In 1977 Edmund Phelps (1933–) (who was awarded the 2006 Nobel Economics Prize) and John B. Taylor (1946–) published a paper proving that staggered setting of wages and prices gives monetary policy a role in stabilizing economic fluctuations if the wages/prices are sticky, even when all workers and firms have rational expectations, which caused Keynesian economics to make a comeback among mainstream economists with New Keynesian Macroeconomics. Its central theme is the provision of a microeconomic foundation for Keynesian macroeconomics, obtained by identifying minimal deviations from the standard microeconomic assumptions which yield Keynesian macroeconomic conclusions, such as the possibility of significant

Top: Phelps (1933-), Yellen (1946-)
Bottom: Taylor (1946-), Dixon (1958-)

welfare benefits from macroeconomic stabilization.[87]

In 1985 George Akerlof (1940–) and his economist wife Janet Yellen (1946–) published menu costs arguments showing that, under imperfect competition, small deviations from rationality generate significant (in welfare terms) price stickiness.[88]

In 1987 British economist Huw Dixon (1958–) published *A simple model of imperfect competition with Walrasian features*,[89] the first work to demonstrate in a simple general equilibrium model that the fiscal multiplier could be increasing with the degree of imperfect competition in the output market, helping develop New Keynesian economics. The reason for this is that imperfect competition in the output market tends to reduce the real wage, leading to the household substituting away from consumption towards leisure. When government spending is increased, the corresponding increase in lump-sum taxation causes both leisure and consumption to decrease (assuming that they are both a normal good). The greater the degree of imperfect competition in the output market, the lower the real wage and hence the more the reduction falls on leisure (i.e. households work more) and less on consumption. Hence the fiscal multiplier is less than one, but increasing in the degree of imperfect competition in the output market.[90]

In 1997 American economist Michael Woodford (1955–) and Argentine economist Julio Rotemberg (1953–) published the first paper describing a microfounded DSGE New Keynesian macroeconomic model.

Sidney Weintraub, Paul Davidson and Post-Keynesian economics

In 1975 American economists Sidney Weintraub (1914–1983) and Henry Wallich (1914–1988) published *A Tax-Based Incomes Policy*, promoting Tax-Based Incomes Policy (TIP), using the income tax mechanism to implement an anti-inflationary incomes policy. In 1978 Weintraub and American economist Paul Davidson (1930–) founded the *Journal of Post Keynesian Economics*. This opened the door to many younger economists such as E. Ray Canterbery (1935-). Always Post Keynesian in his style and approach, Canterbery went on to make contributions outside traditional Post Keynesianism. His friend, John Kenneth Galbraith, was a long-time influence.

The credit theory of money

Main articles: Alfred Mitchell-Innes and Credit theory of money

In 1913 English economist-diplomat Alfred Mitchell-Innes (1864-1950) published *What is Money?*, which was reviewed favorably by John Maynard Keynes, followed in 1914 by *The Credit Theory of Money*, advocating the Credit Theory of Money, which economist L. Randall Wray called "The best pair of articles on the nature of money written in the twentieth century."[91]

1.2.11 The Chicago school of economics (20th Century)

Main articles: Chicago school of economics, Law and economics and Monetarism
Key people: Ronald Coase, Richard Posner, Frank Knight, Jacob Viner, Henry Calvert Simons, Milton Friedman, Gary Becker, Jacob Mincer, George Stigler, Robert Lucas, Jr., Gary Becker and Jacob Mincer

The government-interventionist monetary and fiscal policies that the postwar Keynesian economists recommended came under attack by a group of theorists working at the University of Chicago, which came in the 1950s to be known as the Chicago School of Economics. Before

1.2. HISTORY OF ECONOMIC THOUGHT

Milton Friedman (1912–2006)

Gary Becker (1930–2014)

Jacob Mincer (1922–2006)

World War II, the Old Chicago School of strong Keynesians was founded by Frank Knight (1885–1972), Jacob Viner (1892–1970), and Henry Calvert Simons (1899–1946). The second generation was known for a more conservative line of thought, reasserting a libertarian view of market activity that people are best left to themselves to be free to choose how to conduct their own affairs.[40]

Ronald Coase (1910–2013) of the Chicago School of Economics was the most prominent economic analyst of law, and the 1991 Nobel Prize in Economics winner. His first major article *The Nature of the Firm* (1937) argued that the reason for the existence of firms (companies, partnerships, etc.) is the existence of transaction costs. Homo economicus trades through bilateral contracts on open markets until the costs of transactions make the use of corporations to produce things more cost-effective. His second major article *The Problem of Social Cost* (1960) argued that if we lived in a world without transaction costs, people would bargain with one another to create the same allocation of resources, regardless of the way a court might rule in property disputes. Coase used the example of an old legal case about nuisance named *Sturges v Bridgman*, where a noisy sweets maker and a quiet doctor were neighbors and went to court to see who should have to move.[92] Coase said that regardless of whether the judge ruled that the sweets maker had to stop using his machinery, or that the doctor had to put up with it, they could strike a mutually benefi-

Richard Posner (1939–)

cial bargain about who moves house that reaches the same outcome of resource distribution. Only the existence of transaction costs may prevent this.[93] So the law ought to preempt what *would* happen, and be guided by the most efficient solution. The idea is that law and regulation are not as important or effective at helping people as lawyers and government planners believe.[94] Coase and others like him wanted a change of approach, to put the burden of proof for positive effects on a government that was intervening in the market, by analyzing the costs of action.[95]

In the 1960s Gary Becker (1930–2014) and Jacob Mincer (1922–2006) of the Chicago School of Economics founded **New Home Economics**, which spawned Family Economics.

In 1973 Coase disciple Richard Posner (1939–) published *Economic Analysis of Law*, which became a standard textbook, causing him to become the most cited legal scholar of the 20th century. In 1981 he published *The Economics of Justice*, which claimed that judges have been interpreting common law as it they were trying to maximize economic welfare.

Milton Friedman (1912–2006) of the Chicago School of Economics is one of the most influential economists of the late 20th, century, receiving the Nobel Prize in Economics in 1976. He is known for *A Monetary History of the United States* (1963), in which he argued that the Great Depression was caused by the policies of the Federal Reserve. Friedman argues that laissez-faire government policy is more desirable than government intervention in the economy. Governments should aim for a neutral monetary policy oriented toward long-run economic growth, by gradual expansion of the money supply. He advocates the quantity theory of money, that general prices are determined by money. Therefore, active monetary (e.g. easy credit) or fiscal (e.g. tax and spend) policy can have unintended negative effects. In ***Capitalism and Freedom*** (1962), Friedman wrote:

> "There is likely to be a lag between the need for action and government recognition of the need; a further lag between recognition of the need for action and the taking of action; and a still further lag between the action and its effects."[96]

Friedman was also known for his work on the consumption function, the Permanent Income Hypothesis (1957), which Friedman referred to as his best scientific work.[97] This work contended that rational consumers would spend a proportional amount of what they perceived to be their permanent income. Windfall gains would mostly be saved. Tax reductions likewise, as rational consumers would predict that taxes would have to rise later to balance public finances. Other important contributions include his critique of the Phillips Curve, and the concept of the natural rate of unemployment (1968).[40]

New classical macroeconomics and synthesis

Prescott (1940-), Sargent (1943-), Kydland (1948-)

Main articles: New Classical Economics, Robert Lucas, Jr., Finn Kydland, Edward C. Prescott, Thomas J. Sargent, Neil Wallace, New Classical economics, Real business cycle theory, Dynamic stochastic general equilibrium and

New neoclassical synthesis

In the early 1970s American Chicago School economist Robert E. Lucas, Jr. (1937–) founded New Classical Macroeconomics based on Milton Friedman's monetarist critique of Keynesian macroeconomics, and the idea of rational expectations,[98] first proposed in 1961 by John F. Muth, opposing the idea that government intervention can or should stabilize the economy.[99] The Policy-Ineffectiveness Proposition (1975)[100] of Thomas J. Sargent (1943–) and Neil Wallace (1939–), which seemed to refute a basic assumption of Keynesian economics was also adopted. The Lucas aggregate supply function states that economic output is a function of money or price "surprise." Lucas was awarded the 1995 Nobel Economics Prize.

Lucas' model was superseded as the standard model of New Classical Macroeconomics by the Real Business Cycle Theory, proposed in 1982 by Finn Kydland (1943–) and Edward C. Prescott (1940–), which seeks to explain observed fluctuations in output and employment in terms of real variables such as changes in technology and tastes. Assuming competitive markets, real business cycle theory implies that cyclical fluctuations are optimal responses to variability in technology and tastes, and that macroeconomic stabilization policies must reduce welfare.[101]

In 1982 Kydland and Prescott also founded the theory of Dynamic Stochastic General Equilibrium (DSGE), large systems of microeconomic equations combined into models of the general economy, which became central to the New Neoclassical Synthesis, incorporating theoretical elements such as sticky prices from New Keynesian Macroeconomics. They shared the 2004 Nobel Economics Prize.[40]

Efficient market hypothesis

Main articles: Eugene Fama, Holbrook Working and Efficient market hypothesis
In 1965 Chicago School economist Eugene Fama (1939–) published *The Behavior of Stock Market Prices*, which found that stock market prices follow a random walk, proposing the Efficient Market Hypothesis, that randomness is characteristic of a perfectly functioning financial market. The same year Paul Samuelson published a paper concluding the same thing with a mathematical proof, sharing the credit. Earlier in 1948 Holbrook Working (1895–1985) published a paper saying the same thing, but not in a mathematical form. In 1970 Fama published *Efficient Capital Markets: A Review of Theory and Empirical Work*, proposing that efficient markets can be strong, semi-strong, or weak, and also proposing the Joint Hypothesis Problem, that the idea of market efficiency can't be rejected without also rejecting the market mechanism.

Eugene Fama (1939–)

1.2.12 Games, Evolution and Growth (20th Century)

John von Neumann (1903–1957)

John Forbes Nash Jr. (1928-2015)

Joseph Alois Schumpeter (1883–1950)

Robert Solow (1924–)

See also: Game theory, Evolutionary economics and Neoclassical growth model
Key people: John von Neumann, Oskar Morgenstern, Robert Solow and Trevor Swan

In 1898 **Thorstein Veblen** published *Why is Economics not an Evolutionary Science*, which coins the term Evolutionary economics, making use of anthropology to deny that there is a universal human nature, emphasizing the conflict between "industrial" or instrumental and "pecuniary" or ceremonial values, which became known as the Ceremonial/Instrumental Dichotomy.[40]

Joseph Alois Schumpeter (1883–1950) was an Austrian School economist and political scientist best known for his works on business cycles and innovation. He insisted on the role of the entrepreneurs in an economy. In *Business Cycles: A theoretical, historical and statistical analysis of the Capitalist process* (1939), Schumpeter synthesized the theories about business cycles, suggesting that they could explain the economic situations. According to Schumpeter, capitalism necessarily goes through long-term cycles because it is entirely based upon scientific inventions and innovations. A phase of expansion is made possible by innovations, because they bring productivity gains and encourage entrepreneurs to invest. However, when investors have no more opportunities to invest, the economy goes into recession, several firms collapse, closures and bankruptcy occur. This phase lasts until new innovations bring a creative destruction process, i.e. they destroy old products, reduce the employment, but they allow the economy to start a new phase of growth, based upon new products and new factors of production.[40][102]

In 1944 Hungarian-American mathematician John von Neumann and Oskar Morgenstern published *Theory of Games and Economic Behavior*, founding **Game Theory**, which was widely adopted by economists. In 1951 Princeton mathematician John Forbes Nash Jr. published the article *Non-Cooperative Games*, becoming the first to define a Nash Equilibrium for non-zero-sum games.

In 1956 American economist Robert Solow (1924–) and Australian economist Trevor Swan (1918–1989) proposed the **Neoclassical growth model**, based on productivity, capital accumulation, population growth, and technological progress. In 1956 Swan also proposed the Swan diagram of the internal-external balance. In 1987 Solow was awarded the Nobel Economics Prize.[103]:440–441

1.2.13 Post World War II and globalization (mid to late 20th Century)

Paul Samuelson (1915–2009) wrote the best selling economics texts.

John K. Galbraith (1908–2006) worked under the New Deal administration of Franklin Delano Roosevelt

Main articles: Globalization, Neoclassical synthesis and Positive economics
Key people: John Kenneth Galbraith, Paul Samuelson, Kenneth Arrow and Gérard Debreu

The globalization era began with the end of World War II and the rise of the U.S. as the world's leading economic power, along with the United Nations. To prevent another global depression, the victorious U.S. forgave Germany its

Kenneth Arrow (1921–)

Gérard Debreu (1921–2004)

war debts and used its surpluses to rebuild Europe and encourage reindustrialization of Germany and Japan. In the 1960s it changed its role to recycling global surpluses.[104]

After World War II, Canadian-born John Kenneth Galbraith (1908–2006) became one of the standard bearers for pro-active government and liberal-democrat politics. In *The Affluent Society* (1958), Galbraith argued that voters reaching a certain material wealth begin to vote against the common good. He also argued that the "conventional wisdom" of the conservative consensus was not enough to solve the problems of social inequality.[105] In an age of big business, he argued, it is unrealistic to think of markets of the classical kind. They set prices and use advertising to create artificial demand for their own products, distorting people's real preferences. Consumer preferences actually come to reflect those of corporations – a "dependence effect" – and the economy as a whole is geared to irrational goals.[106] In *The New Industrial State* Galbraith argued that economic decisions are planned by a private-bureaucracy, a technostructure of experts who manipulate marketing and public relations channels. This hierarchy is self-serving, profits are no longer the prime motivator, and even managers are not in control. Because they are the new planners, corporations detest risk, require steady economic and stable markets. They recruit governments to serve their interests with fiscal and monetary policy, for instance adhering to monetarist policies which enrich money-lenders in the City through increases in interest rates. While the goals of an affluent society and complicit government serve the irrational technostructure, public space is simultaneously impoverished. Galbraith paints the picture of stepping from penthouse villas onto unpaved streets, from landscaped gardens to unkempt public parks. In *Economics and the Public Purpose* (1973) Galbraith advocates a "new socialism" as the solution, nationalising military production and public services such as health care, introducing disciplined salary and price controls to reduce inequality.[107]

In contrast to Galbraith's linguistic style, the post-war economics profession began to synthesize much of Keynes' work with mathematical representations. Introductory university economics courses began to present economic theory as a unified whole in what is referred to as the neoclassical synthesis. "**Positive economics**" became the term created to describe certain trends and "laws" of economics that could be objectively observed and described in a value-free way, separate from "**normative economic**" evaluations and judgments.

The Paul Samuelson's (1915–2009) *Foundations of Economic Analysis* published in 1947 was an attempt to show that mathematical methods could represent a core of testable economic theory. Samuelson started with two assumptions. First, people and firms will act to maximize their self-interested goals. Second, markets tend towards an equilibrium of prices, where demand matches supply. He extended the mathematics to describe equilibrating behavior of economic systems, including that of the then new macroeconomic theory of John Maynard Keynes. Whilst Richard Cantillon had imitated Isaac Newton's mechanical physics of inertia and gravity in competition and the market,[19] the physiocrats had copied the body's blood system into circular flow of income models, William Jevons had found growth cycles to match the periodicity of sunspots, Samuelson adapted thermodynamics formulae to economic theory. Reasserting economics as a hard science was being done in the United Kingdom also, and one celebrated "discovery", of A. W. Phillips, was of a correlative relationship between inflation and unemployment. The workable policy conclusion was that securing full employment could be traded-off against higher inflation. Samuelson incorporated the idea of the Phillips curve into his work. His introductory textbook *Economics* was influential and widely adopted. It became the most successful economics text ever. Paul Samuelson was awarded the new Nobel Prize in Economics in 1970 for his merging of mathematics and political economy.

American economist Kenneth Arrow's (1921–) published *Social Choice and Individual Values* in 1951. It consider connections between economics and political theory. It gave rise to **social choice theory** with the introduction of his "Possibility Theorem". This sparked widespread discussion over how to interpret the different conditions of the theorem and what implications it had for democracy and voting. Most controversial of his four (1963) or five (1950/1951) conditions is the independence of irrelevant alternatives.[108]

In the 1950s Kenneth Arrow and Gérard Debreu (1921–2004) developed the Arrow–Debreu model of general equilibria. In 1963 Arrow published a paper which founded Health Economics.

In 1971 Arrow and Frank Hahn published *General Competitive Analysis* (1971), which reasserted a theory of general equilibrium of prices through the economy. In 1971, US President Richard Nixon's had declared that "We are all Keynesians now"[109]

International economics

Paul Krugman (1953–)

Main articles: James E. Meade, Paul Krugman, International economics and International trade

In 1951 English economist James E. Meade (1907–1995) published *The Balance of Payments*, volume 1 of "The Theory of International Economic Policy", which proposed the

James E. Meade (1907–1995)

theory of domestic divergence (internal and external balance), and promoted policy tools for governments. In 1955 he published volume 2 *Trade and Welfare*, which proposed the theory of the "second-best", and promoted protectionism. He shared the 1977 Nobel Economic Prize with Bertil Ohlin.

In 1979 American economist Paul Krugman (1953–) published a paper founding New trade theory, which attempts to explain the role of increasing returns to scale and network effects in international trade. In 1991 he published a paper founding New economic geography. His textbook *International Economics* (2007) appears on many undergraduate reading lists. He was awarded the Nobel Prize in Economics in 2008.

Development economics

Main articles: Sir Arthur Lewis, Simon Kuznets, Amartya Sen and Development economics

In 1954 Saint Lucian economist Sir Arthur Lewis (1915–1991) proposed the Dual Sector Model of Development Economics, which claims that capitalism expands by making use of an unlimited supply of labor from the backward non-capitalist "subsistence sector" until it reaches the Lewisian breaking point where wages begin to rise, receiving the 1979 Nobel Economics Prize.

In 1955 Russian-born American economist Simon Kuznets (1901–1985), who introduced the concept of Gross domestic product (GDP) in 1934 published an article revealing an inverted U-shaped relation between income inequality and economic growth, meaning that economic growth increases income disparity between rich and poor in poor countries, but decreases it in wealthy countries. In 1971 he received the Nobel Economics Prize.

Indian economist Amartya Sen (1933–) expressed consid-

of poverty and inequality. Sen was awarded the Nobel Prize in Economics in 1998.

New Economic History (Cliometrics)

Main article: New economic history

In 1958 American economists Alfred H. Conrad (1924–1970) and John R. Meyer (1927–2009) founded New Economic History, which in 1960 was called Cliometrics by American economist Stanley Reiter (1925–2014) after Clio, the muse of history. It uses neoclassical economic theory to reinterpret historical data, spreading throughout academia, causing economic historians untrained in economics to disappear from history departments. American cliometric economists Douglass Cecil North (1920–) and Robert William Fogel (1926–2013) were awarded the 1993 Nobel Economics Prize.

Public choice theory and constitutional economics

Amartya Sen (1933–)

erable skepticism about the validity of neoclassical assumptions, and was highly critical of rational expectations theory, devoting his work to Development Economics and human rights.

In 1981, Sen published *Poverty and Famines: An Essay on Entitlement and Deprivation* (1981), a book in which he argued that famine occurs not only from a lack of food, but from inequalities built into mechanisms for distributing food. Sen also argued that the Bengal famine was caused by an urban economic boom that raised food prices, thereby causing millions of rural workers to starve to death when their wages did not keep up.[110]

In addition to his important work on the causes of famines, Sen's work in the field of development economics has had considerable influence in the formulation of the "Human Development Report",[111] published by the United Nations Development Programme.[112] This annual publication that ranks countries on a variety of economic and social indicators owes much to the contributions by Sen among other social choice theorists in the area of economic measurement

James Buchanan (1919-2013), Gordon Tullock (1922-2014)

Main articles: James M. Buchanan, Gordon Tullock, Public choice theory and Constitutional economics

In 1962 American economists James M. Buchanan (1919–2013) and Gordon Tullock (1922–2014) published *The Calculus of Consent*, which revived Public Choice Theory by differentiating politics (the rules of the game) from public policy (the strategies to adopt within the rules), founding Constitutional Economics, the economic analysis of constitutional law. Buchanan was awarded the 1986 Nobel Economics Prize.

1.2. HISTORY OF ECONOMIC THOUGHT

Robert Mundell (1932–)

Impossible Trinity

Main articles: Marcus Fleming and Robert Mundell

In 1962–1963 Scottish economist Marcus Fleming (1911–1976) and Canadian economist Robert Mundell (1932–) published the Mundell-Fleming Model of the Economy, an extension of the IS-LM Model to an open economy, proposing the Impossible Trinity of fixed exchange rate, free capital movement, and an independent monetary policy, only two of which can be maintained simultaneously. Mundell received the 1999 Nobel Economics Prize.

Market for Corporate Control

Main article: Henry Manne

In 1965 American economist Henry G. Manne (1928-2015) published *Mergers and the Market for Corporate Control* in *Journal of Political Economy*,[113] which claims that changes in the price of a share of stock in the stock market will occur more rapidly when insider trading is prohibited than when it is permitted, founding the theory of Market for corporate control.

Information economics

Main articles: Joseph Stiglitz, George Akerlof and Information economics

In 1970 George Akerlof (1940-) published the paper *The*

George Akerlof (1940-), Joseph Stiglitz (1943-)

Market for Lemons, founding the theory of Information Economics, receiving the 2001 Nobel Economics Prize.

Joseph E. Stiglitz (1943–) also received the Nobel Economics Prize in 2001 for his work in Information Economics. He has served as chairman of President Clinton's Council of Economic Advisers, and as chief economist for the World Bank. Stiglitz has taught at many universities, including Columbia, Stanford, Oxford, Manchester, Yale, and MIT. In recent years he has become an outspoken critic of global economic institutions. In *Making Globalization Work* (2007) he offers an account of his perspectives on issues of international economics:

> "The fundamental problem with the neoclassical model and the corresponding model under market socialism is that they fail to take into account a variety of problems that arise from the absence of perfect information and the costs of acquiring information, as well as the absence or imperfections in certain key risk and capital markets. The absence or imperfection can, in turn, to a large extent be explained by problems of information."[114]

Stiglitz talks about his book *Making Globalization Work* here.[115]

Market design theory

Main articles: Leonid Hurwicz, Eric Maskin, Roger Myerson and Market design

In 1973 Russian-American mathematician-economist Leonid Hurwicz (1917–2008) founded Market (Mechanism) Design Theory, a.k.a. Reverse Game Theory, which allows people to distinguish situations in which markets work well from those in which they do not, aiding the

Leonid Hurwicz (1917–2008)

Eric Maskin (1950-), Roger Myerson (1951-)

identification of efficient trading mechanisms, regulation schemes, and voting procedures; he developed the theory with Eric Maskin (1950–) and Roger Myerson (1951–), sharing the 2007 Nobel Economics Prize with them.

The Laffer Curve and Reaganomics

Main articles: Arthur Laffer and Laffer curve

In 1974 American economist Arthur Laffer formulated the Laffer Curve, which postulates that no tax revenue will be raised at the extreme tax rates of 0% and 100%, and that there must be at least one rate where tax revenue would be a non-zero maximum. This concept was adopted by U.S. President Ronald Reagan in the early 1980s, becoming the cornerstone of Reaganomics, which was co-founded by American economist Paul Craig Roberts.

Market regulation

In 1986 French economist Jean Tirole (1953-) published "Dynamic Models of Oligopoly", followed by "The Theory of Industrial Organization" (1988), launching his quest to understand market power and regulation, resulting in the 2014 Nobel Economics Prize.

1.2.14 Post 2008 financial crisis (21st century)

See also: 2008–09 Keynesian resurgence, Great Recession and European debt crisis
Key people: Alberto Alesina, Carmen Reinhart and Kenneth Rogoff
In 2008, there was a financial crisis which led to a global

Carmen Reinhart(1955-) and Kenneth Rogoff (1953-)

recession. This prompted some economists to question the current orthodoxy.

One response was the Keynesian Resurgence. This emerged as a consensus among some policy makers and economists for a Keynesian solutions. As contrasted sharply with the previous economic orthodoxy in its support for government intervention in the economy. Figures in this school included Dominique Strauss-Kahn, Olivier Blanchard, Gordon Brown, Paul Krugman, and Martin Wolf.[116][117][118]

Austerity was another response, the policy of reducing government budget deficits. Austerity policies may include spending cuts, tax increases, or a mixture of both.[119][120] Two influential academic papers support this position. The first was *Large Changes in Fiscal Policy: Taxes Versus Spending*, published in October 2009 by Alberto Alesina

Olivier Blanchard (1948–)

and Silvia Ardagna. It showed that fiscal austerity measures did not hurt economies, and actually helped their recovery.[121] The second *Growth in a Time of Debt*, published in 2010 by Carmen Reinhart and Kenneth Rogoff. It analyzed public debt and GDP growth among 20 advanced economies and claimed that high debt countries grew at −0.1% since WWII. Many governments accepted this and followed the austerity course.

In April 2013 the IMF and the Roosevelt Institute exposed basic calculation flaws in the Reinhart-Rogoff paper, claiming that when the flaws were corrected, the growth of the "high debt" countries was +2.2%, much higher than the original paper predicted. Following this, on June 6, 2013 Paul Krugman published *How the Case for Austerity Has Crumbled* in *The New York Review of Books*, arguing that the case for austerity was fundamentally flawed, and calling for an end to austerity measures.[122]

1.2.15 See also

- Constitutional economics
- Corporate law
- Energy economics
- Index of international trade topics
- Labour law
- List of economics journals
- List of economists
- List of important publications in economics
- Marshall Plan
- Outline of economics
- Perspectives on capitalism
- Timeline of international trade
- Tort

1.2.16 References

[1] www.historyhaven.com

[2] Wang, Robin R. *Yinyang: The Way of Heaven and Earth in Chinese Thought and Culture*. Retrieved 12 April 2015.

[3] "Golden Rules-Tao Zhu Gong's Art of Business". Asiapac Books. Retrieved 12 April 2015.

[4] David Held, *Models of Democracy* (Polity, 2006) 3rd Ed., pp. 11 ff.

[5] Aristotle (350 BCE) *Politics* Book II, Part V

[6] Aristotle *Politics* Book I, Part X

[7] Book I, Part III]

[8] M. M. Austin, Pierre Vidal-Naquet (1980). *Economic and Social History of Ancient Greece*. University of California Press. ISBN 9780520042674. Retrieved 2012-04-11.

[9] Takeshi Amemiya. *Economy and Economics of Ancient Greece*. Taylor & Francis, 7 May 2007.

[10] Aristotle (350 BCE) *Politics* Book I, Part XI

[11] Aristotle (350 BCE) *Politics* Book I, Part IX

[12] Mochrie (2005) p. 5

[13] Muqaddimah 2 1995 p 30

[14] Spengler, Joseph J. (April 1964). "Economic Thought of Islam: Ibn Khaldun". Comparative Studies in Society and History vol6 no. 3. Cambridge University Press. pp. 268–306. Retrieved April 12, 2015.

[15] Toynbee, Arnold J. *A Study of History* **III**. Royal Institute of International Affairs and Oxford University Press. p. 321. ASIN B000OF48G8.

[16] Lovewell, Mark. "Avancing Economic Thought: Rise and Fall: Ibn Khaldun and the Effects of Taxation: Ibn Khaldun and his Influence". Wayback Machine. Archived from the original on 2003-06-08. Retrieved Apr 9, 2015. This article, which is a supplement to Understanding Economics (McGraw-Hill Ryerson, 1998), describes the early Arab historian Ibn Khaldun's views of taxation, and their parallels with the modern-day Laffer Curve.

[17] "Mercantilism," Laura LaHaye *The Concise Encyclopedia of Economics* (2008)

[18] Fusfeld (1994) p. 15

[19] Fusfeld (1994) p. 21

[20] Locke (1689) Chapter 9, section 124

[21] Locke (1689) Chapter 5, sections 26–27.

[22] Locke (1691) *Considerations* Part I, Thirdly

[23] Murray N. Rothbard An Austrian Perspective on the History of Economic Thought, vol. 1, Economic Thought Before Adam Smith (1995) Ludwig von Mises Institute Retrieved 2012-05-16

[24] Sarah B. Pomeroy, Xénophon – Xenophon, Oeconomicus: a social and historical commentary Clarendon Press, 1994 Retrieved 2012-05-16

[25] Strong's Concordances*Biblos* & The NAS New Testament Greek Lexicon (Strong's Number: 3624) Bible Study Tools – Retrieved 2012-05-16

[26] Douglas Harper Etymology online Retrieved 2012-05-16

[27] M. I. Finley (was Professor of Ancient History and Master of Darwin College at Cambridge University) The Ancient Economy University of California Press, 1 Jan 1989 , Retrieved 2012-05-16

[28] Edwin Cannan (editor) Adam Smith – Lectures On Justice, Police, Revenue And Arms Kessinger Publishing, 30 Apr 2004 Retrieved 2012-05-16

[29] Danbom (1997) Rural Development Perspectives, vol. 12, no. 1 p. 15 *Why Americans Value Rural Life* by David B. Danbom

[30] Fusfeld (1994) p. 24

[31] Smith (1776) Book I, Chapter 2, para 2

[32] Smith (1776) p. 533

[33] Smith (1776) Book I, Chapter 5, para 1

[34] Smith (1776) Book I, Chapter 7, para 9

[35] Smith (1776) Book I, Chapter 10, para 82

[36] Smith (1776) Book I, Chapter 7, para 26

[37] Hague (2004) pp. 187, 292

[38] Stephen (1898) p. 8."

[39] Bentham (1791) Chapter I, para I

[40] "SCHOOLS OF THOUGHT". New School. Retrieved 23 March 2015.

[41] Fusfeld (1994) p. 47

[42] "The Classical School". New School. Retrieved 23 March 2015.

[43] *David Ricardo*, Economic History Services

[44] David Ricardo's Contributions to Economics, The Victorian Web

[45] John Stuart Mill: Overview, The Internet Encyclopedia of Philosophy.

[46] Pressman (2006) p. 44

[47] Keynes (1936) Chapter 1, footnote

[48] Frederick Engels. "Conditions of the Working-Class in England Index". Retrieved 24 March 2015.

[49] Marx (1859) *Zur Kritik der Politischen Oekonomie*, Berlin, p. 3.

[50] In Marx's words, "the exchange of commodities is evidently an act characterized by a total abstraction from use value."

[51] Marx (1867) Volume I, Part I, Chapter 1, para 14. In Marx's words, "The labor time socially necessary is that required to produce an article under the normal conditions of production, and with the average degree of skill and intensity prevalent at the time."

[52] Marx (1867) Volume I, Part I, Chapter 1, Section 4, para 123

[53] Marx (1867) Volume I, Part III, Chapter 9, Section 1

[54] Marx (1867) Volume I, Part II, Chapter VI, para 10. In Marx's words: "Therefore the labor-time requisite for the production of labor-power reduces itself to that necessary for the production of those means of subsistence; in other words, the value of labor-power is the value of the means of subsistence necessary for the maintenance of the laborer."

[55] *Principles of Economics*, by Alfred Marshall, at the Library of Economics and Liberty

[56] Buchholz (1989) p. 151

[57] Veblen, Thorstein Bunde; "The Preconceptions of Economic Science" Pt III, *Quarterly Journal of Economics* v14 (1900).

[58] Colander, David; *The Death of Neoclassical Economics.*

[59] Menger, Carl (1871) *Grundsätze der Volkswirtschaftslehre*,full text in html

[60] "Biography of F. A. Hayek (1899–1992)". Retrieved 2009-06-26.

[61] *Law, legislation and liberty* (1970)

[62] "The Austrian School". New School. Retrieved 23 March 2015.

[63] Stabile, Donald R. "Veblen and the Political Economy of the Engineer: the radical thinker and engineering leaders came to technocratic ideas at the same time", *American Journal of Economics and Sociology (45:1) 1986, 43–44.*

[64] "The Engineers and the Price System" (PDF). Retrieved 2013-03-29.

[65] Berle (1967) p. xxiii

[66] Martinez-Alier, J. 1987. Ecological economics. Blackwell, Oxford.

[67] Schumacher, E.F. 1973. *Small Is Beautiful: A Study of Economics as if People Mattered.* Blond and Briggs, London.

[68] Daly, H. 1991. *Steady-State Economics* (2nd ed.). Island Press,Washington, D.C.

[69] Daly, H. E. 1999. *Ecological Economics and the Ecology of Economics.* E Elgar Publications, Cheltenham.

[70] Daly, H.E. and Cobb, J. B. 1989. For the Common.

[71] Paehlke R. (1995). Conservation and Environmentalism: An Encyclopedia, p. 315. Taylor & Francis.

[72] Malte Faber. (2008). How to be an ecological economist. *Ecological Economics* **66**(1):1-7. Preprint.

[73] Economy and Thermodynamics

[74] The Energy Certificate essay by Fezer. An article on Energy Accounting as proposed by Technocracy Inc. http://www.technocracy.org/Archives/The%20Energy%20Certificate-r.htm

[75] Tainter, Joseph A. (1990). *The Collapse of Complex Societies* (1st paperback ed.). Cambridge: Cambridge University Press. ISBN 0-521-38673-X.

[76] Keynes (1919) *The Economic Consequences of the Peace* at The Library of Economics and Liberty

[77] Keynes (1919) Chapter III, para 20

[78] Keynes (1919) Chapter V, para 43

[79] Keynes (1919) Chapter VI, para 4

[80] Keynes (1919) Chapter VII, para 7

[81] Keynes (1919) Chapter VII, para 30

[82] Keynes (1919) Chapter VII, para 48

[83] Keynes (1919) Chapter VII, para 58

[84] e.g. Etienne Mantioux (1946) *The Carthaginian Peace, or the Economic Consequences of Mr. Keynes*

[85] Keynes (1923) Chapter 3

[86] This was not accepted by the United States Congress at the time, but arose later through the General Agreement on Tariffs and Trade of 1947 and the World Trade Organisation of 1994

[87] Mankiw, 1655.

[88] Mankiw, 1657.

[89] Huw Dixon, A simple model of imperfect competition with Walrasian features, Oxford Economic Papers, 1987, 39, 134–160

[90] Costa L, Dixon H. (2011), "Fiscal Policy Under Imperfect Competition with Flexible Prices: An Overview and Survey", Economics: The Open-Access, Open-Assessment E-Journal, Vol. 5, 2011-3. doi:10.5018/economics-ejournal.ja.2011-3.

[91] L. Randall Wray, ed. (2004). *Credit and State Theories of Money: The Contributions of A. Mitchell Innes.* Edward Elgar Publishing. ISBN 1-84376-513-6.

[92] *Sturges v Bridgman* (1879) 11 Ch D 852

[93] Coase (1960) IV, 7

[94] Coase (1960) V, 9

[95] Coase (1960) VIII, 23

[96] Friedman (1967) p.

[97] "Charlie Rose Show". 2005-12-26. Missing or empty |series= (help)

[98] Mankiw, 1647–1648.

[99] Manikw, N. Greg. "A Quick Refresher Course in Macroeconomics." *Journal of Economic Literature, Vol. 28, No. 4.* (Dec., 1990), p. 1647.

[100] Mankiw, 1649.

[101] Mankiw, 1653.

[102] Alessandro Roncaglia. *The wealth of ideas: a history of economic thought.* Cambridge University Press. 2005. ISBN 978-0-521-84337-9. p. 431

[103] Screpanti; Ernesto; Zamagni; Stefano (2005). *An Outline of the History of Economic Thought'* (2nd ed.). Oxford University Press.

[104] The Globalist July 30, 2013

[105] Galbraith (1958) Chapter 2; n.b. though Galbraith claimed to coin the phrase "conventional wisdom", the phrase is used several times in Thorstein Veblen's book *The Instinct of Workmanship.*

[106] Galbraith (1958) Chapter 11

[107] "Conversations with History: John Kenneth Galbraith". YouTube. 2008-06-12. Retrieved 2013-03-29.

[108] "What can be done to improve the current situation? Regulation vs deregulation and lessons learnt from previous financial crisis". YouTube. 2009-01-13. Retrieved 2013-03-29.

[109] , announcing wage and price controls. He lifted this from a comment by Milton Friedman in 1965 which formed a *Time*.ref>http://www.time.com/time/magazine/article/0,9171,842353-3,00.html

[110] Sachs, Jeffrey (26 October 1998). "The real causes of famine: a Nobel laureate blames authoritarian rulers". Time Magazine. Retrieved 16 June 2014.

[111] United Nations Development Programme, UNDP, ed. (2010). "Overview | Celebrating 20 years of human development". *Human Development Report 2010 | 20th anniversary edition | the real wealth of nations: pathways to human development*. New York, NY: United Nations Development Programme. p. 2. ISBN 9780230284456. ...the first HDR called for a different approach to economics and development - one that put people at the centre. The approach was anchored in a new vision of development, inspired by the creative passion and vision of Mahbub ul Haq, the lead author of the early HDRs, and the ground-breaking work of Amartya Sen. Pdf version.

[112] Batterbury, Simon; Fernando, Jude (2004), "Amartya Sen", in Hubbard, Phil; Kitchin, Rob; Valentine, Gill, *Key thinkers on space and place*, London: Sage, pp. 251–257, ISBN 9780761949626. Draft

[113]

[114] Stiglitz (1996) p. 5

[115] "Authors@Google: Joseph Stiglitz". YouTube. 2006-10-13. Retrieved 2013-03-29.

[116] Bateman, Bradley; Toshiaki, Hirai; Marcuzzo, Maria Cristina (2010). *The Return to Keynes*. Harvard University Press. ISBN 0-674-03538-0.

[117] Henry Farrell and John Quiggin (March 2012). "Consensus, Dissensus and Economic Ideas: The Rise and Fall of Keynesianism During the Economic Crisis" (PDF). The Center for the Study of Development Strategies. Retrieved 2012-05-29.

[118] Chris Giles, Ralph Atkins and Krishna Guha. "The undeniable shift to Keynes". The Financial Times. Retrieved 2009-01-23.

[119] "Austerity measure". *Financial Times Lexicon*. Retrieved 1 March 2013.

[120] Traynor, Ian; Katie Allen (11 June 2010). "Austerity Europe: who faces the cuts". London: Guardian News. Retrieved 29 September 2010.

[121] "Large Changes in Fiscal Policy: Taxes Versus Spending". *NBER*. Retrieved 24 March 2015.

[122] "How the Case for Austerity Has Crumbled by Paul Krugman". Retrieved 24 March 2015.

Primary sources

- Aquinas, Thomas (1274). *Summa Theologica*

- Aristotle (c.a. 350 BCE). *Nicomachean Ethics*

- Aristotle (c.a. 350 BCE). *Politics*

- Arrow, Kenneth J (1951). *Social Choice and Individual Values*, 2nd Ed. 1963, Wiley, New York, ISBN 0-300-01364-7

- Arrow, Kenneth J. and Frank Hahn (1971). *General Competitive Analysis*, Holden-Day, San Francisco, ISBN 0-8162-0275-3

- Bentham, Jeremy (1776). *Fragment on Government*

- Bentham, Jeremy (1789). *An Introduction to the Principles of Morals and Legislation*

- Burke, Edmund (1790). *Reflections on the Revolution in France*

- Burke, Edmund. (1795). *Thoughts and Details on Scarcity*

- Cantillon, Richard (1732). *Essay on the Nature of Commerce in General*

- Coase, Ronald. (1937). "The Nature of the Firm" *Economica*, Vol. 4, Issue 16, pp. 386–405

- Coase, Ronald H. (1960) "The Problem of Social Cost" (this online version excludes some parts) *Journal of Law and Economics*, Vol.3, pp. 1–44

- Commons, John R. (1934). *Institutional Economics* New York: Macmillan

- Engels, Friedrich (1845). *Condition of the Working Class in England in 1844*

- Friedman, Milton (1953) *Essays in Positive Economics: Part I – The Methodology of Positive Economics*, University of Chicago

- Galbraith, J.K. (1958). *The Affluent Society*, 3rd Ed. reprinted 1991, Penguin Books, ISBN 014013610X

- Galbraith, J.K. (1967) .*The New Industrial State*

- Galbraith, J.K. (1973). *Economics and the Public Purpose*

- Hobbes, Thomas (1651). *Leviathan*

- Hume, David (1777). *Essays, Moral, Political, Literary*

- Jevons, William (1871). *The Theory of Political Economy*

- Jevons, William (1878). *The Periodicity of Commercial Crises*

- Keynes, John Maynard (1919). *The Economic Consequences of the Peace*

- Keynes, John Maynard. (1936). *The General Theory of Employment, Interest and Money*

- Locke, John (1689). *Second Treatise on Civil Government*

- Locke, John. (1691). *Some Considerations on the consequences of the Lowering of Interest and the Raising of the Value of Money*

- Markwell, Donald (2006). *John Maynard Keynes and International Relations: Economic Paths to War and Peace*, Oxford.

- Marshall, Alfred (1890).*Principles of Economics*

- Marx, Karl (1871). *Das Kapital*

- Mill, John Stuart (1871). *Principles of Political Economy*

- Mun, Thomas (1621). *A Discourse of Trade from England unto the East Indies*

- North, Dudley (1691). *Discourses upon trade*

- Petty, William (1690). *The Political Arithmetick*

- Quesnay, François (1758). *Tableau économique*

- Ricardo, David (1827). *Principles of Political Economy and Taxation*

- Robinson, Joan (1953). *The Production Function and the Theory of Capital*

- Robinson, Joan. (1962). *Economic Philosophy*

- Scotus, Duns (1295). *Sententiae*

- Sen, Amartya (1985). "The Moral Standing of the Market", in *Ethics and Economics*, ed. Ellen Frankel Paul, Fred D. Miller, Jr and Jeffrey Paul, Oxford, Basil Blackwell, pp. 1–19

- Sen, Amartya. (1976–1977). "Rational Fools: A Critique of the Behavioural Foundations of Economic Theory", *Philosophy and Public Affairs*, 6, pp. 317–44

- Sen, Amartya. (1987). *On Ethics and Economics* Oxford, Basil Blackwell

- Sismondi, J.-C.-L. Simonde de (1819, trans. 1991). "New Principles of Political Economy: Of Wealth in Its Relation to Population"

- Smith, Adam (1759). *The Theory of Moral Sentiments*

- Smith, Adam (1776). *An Inquiry Into The Wealth of Nations*

- Sraffa, Piero (1960). *Production of Commodities by Means of Commodities*

- Stigler, George J (1965). "The Nature and Role of Originality in Scientific Progress", in *Essays in the History of Economics*, University of Chicago Press, pp. 1–15

- Stiglitz, Joseph E. (1996). *Whither Socialism?*

- Thornton, Henry (1802). *The Paper Credit of Great Britain*

- Turgot, Jacques (1766). *Réflexions sur la formation et la distribution des richesses* in French and English

- Veblen, Thorstein. *The Theory of the Leisure Class: an economic study of institutions* (1899)

- Veblen, Thorsten. (1904). *Theory of Business Enterprise*

- von Hörnigk, Philip (1684). *Österreich Über Alles, Wenn Sie Nur Will*

Secondary sources

- Allen, William (1977). "Economics, Economists, and Economic Policy: Modern American Experiences", in *History of Political Economy*, Volume 9, no. 1, pp. 48–88. Duke Univ Press. Reprinted in *Econ Journal Watch* 7[3]: pp. 235–74, Sept 2010.

- Blaug, Mark (1997). *Economic Theory in Retrospect*, 5th ed.. Cambridge University Press. Description & chapter links, pp. vii –xvi.

- _____ (2001). "No History of Ideas, Please, We're Economists", *Journal of Economic Perspectives*, 15(1), pp. 145–64 (press +).

- Buchholz, Todd G. (1989). *New Ideas from Dead Economists*, New York, Penguin Group. p. 151

- Cossa, Luigi. (1893). *An Introduction to the Study of Political Economy*, London and New York: Macmillan

- Danbom, David B. (1997). *Why Americans Value Rural Life*, Rural Development Perspectives, vol. 12, no. 1, pp. 15–18

- Ekelund, Robert B., Jr. and Robert F. Hébert (2007). *A History of Economic Theory and Method*. Waveland Press. 5th ed. ISBN 1-57766-486-8.Description.

- Fusfeld, Daniel R. (1994). *The Age of the Economist*, Harper Collins, 7th Ed. ISBN 0-673-46805-4

- Hague, William (2004). *William Pitt the Younger* Harper Perennial ISBN 0-00-714720-1

- Heilbroner, Robert (1953; 1999 7th ed.). *The Worldly Philosophers*, Simon & Schuster. ISBN 0-684-86214-X

- Lee, Frederic S. (2009). *A History of Heterodox Economics: Challenging the Mainstream in the Twentieth Century*, Routledge. Description.

- Macfie, Alec Lawrence (1955). "The Scottish Tradition in Economic Thought". *Econ Journal Watch* 6(3): 389–410. Reprinted from *Scottish Journal of Political Economy* 2(2): 81–103

- Markwell, Donald (2006). *John Maynard Keynes and International Relations: Economic Paths to War and Peace*, Oxford University Press.

- Medema, Steven G., and Warren J. Samuels (2003). *The History of Economic Thought: A Reader*. Routledge. Description & chapter-preview links.

- Mochrie, Robert (2005). *Justice in Exchange: The Economic Philosophy of John Duns Scotus*

- Nicola, PierCarlo (2000). *Mainstream Mathematical Economics in the 20th Century*. Springer. ISBN 978-3-540-67084-1.

- Nasar, Sylvia (2011). *Grand Pursuit: The Story of Economic Genius*, Simon & Schuster. Description and excerpt.

- From *The New Palgrave Dictionary of Economics* (2008), 2nd Edition. Abstract links for:

    "United States, economics in (1776–1885)" by Stephen Meardon.

    "United States, economics in (1885–1945)" by Bradley W. Bateman.

    "United States, economics in (1945 to present)" by Roger E. Backhouse.

    "American exceptionalism" by Louise C. Keely.

- Pressman, Steven (2006). *Fifty Major Economists*, Routledge, ISBN 0-415-36649-6

- Ptak, Justin (n.d.). "The Prehistory of Modern Economic Thought: The Aristotle in Austrian Theory "

- Rothbard, Murray (1995). *An Austrian Perspective on the History of Economic Thought*, von Mises Institute, ISBN 978-0945466482

- Samuelson, Paul A. and William A. Barnett, ed. (2007). *Inside the Economist's Mind: Conversations with Eminent Economists*, Wiley. Description, contents, and preview.

- Screpanti, Ernesto and Zamagni, Stefano (2005). *An Outline of the History of Economic Thought*, 2nd ed. Oxford University Press. Description & ch.-preview links, pp. xi-xviii.

- Schumpeter, Joseph (1954). *History of Economic Analysis*, Description. Chapter-preview links for Parts I-V (arrow-page searchable). Routledge Ed. 1994, ISBN 0-415-10892-6

- Spengler, Joseph J., and William R. Allen, ed. (1960). *Essays in Economic Thought: Aristotle to Marshall*. Rand McNally.

- Spiegel, Henry William (1971; 1991 3rd ed.). *The Growth of Economic Thought*, Duke University Press. ISBN 0-8223-0965-3

- Stephen, Leslie (1898). "Smith, Adam". *Dictionary of National Biography*. London: Smith, Elder & Co. 1885–1900.

- Stigler, George J. (1965). *Essays in the History of Economics*. University of Chicago Press.

- Weintraub, E. Roy (1999). "How Should We Write the History of Twentieth-Century Economics?" *Oxford Review of Economic Policy*, 15(4), pp. 139–152.

- (2002). *How Economics Became a Mathematical Science*. Duke University Press. Description and preview.

1.2.17 Further reading

Books

- *An Outline of the History of Economic Thought (2nd Edition)*, (2003) Ernesto Screpanti and Stefano Zamagni

- *The Penguin History of Economics*, (2002), Roger Backhouse.

Journals

- *European Journal of the History of Economic Thought* (U.K.)
- *History of Economic Ideas* (Italy)
- *History of Economics Review* (Australia)
- *History of Economic Thought* (Japan)
- *History of Political Economy* (U.S.)
- *Journal of the History of Economic Thought (U.K.)*

1.2.18 External links

- The History of Economic Thought Website at the Wayback Machine
- Archive for the History of Economic Thought
- "Family tree" of economics poster from the 16th century on.
- Pioneers of the social sciences London School of Economics and Political Science
- Library of Economics and Liberty
- "A History of Behavioural Finance in Published Research: 1944–1988" - a short bibliography list focused on quantitative finance
- Great Economists, "Origins of Economic Thought" lecture by Economist Tyler Cowen, May 2013

1.3 Neoclassical economics

Not to be confused with New classical macroeconomics.

Neoclassical economics is a set of solutions to economics focusing on the determination of goods, outputs, and income distributions in markets through supply and demand. This determination is often mediated through a hypothesized maximization of utility by income-constrained individuals and of profits by firms facing production costs and employing available information and factors of production, in accordance with rational choice theory.[1]

Neoclassical economics dominates microeconomics, and together with Keynesian economics forms the neoclassical synthesis which dominates mainstream economics today.[2] Although neoclassical economics has gained widespread acceptance by contemporary economists, there have been many critiques of neoclassical economics, often incorporated into newer versions of neoclassical theory.

1.3.1 Overview

The term was originally introduced by Thorstein Veblen in his 1900 article 'Preconceptions of Economic Science', in which he related marginalists in the tradition of Alfred Marshall et al. to those in the Austrian School.[3][4]

> "No attempt will here be made even to pass a verdict on the relative claims of the recognized two or three main "schools" of theory, beyond the somewhat obvious finding that, for the purpose in hand, the so-called Austrian school is scarcely distinguishable from the neo-classical, unless it be in the different distribution of emphasis. The divergence between the modernized classical views, on the one hand, and the historical and Marxist schools, on the other hand, is wider, so much so, indeed, as to bar out a consideration of the postulates of the latter under the same head of inquiry with the former." – Veblen[5]

It was later used by John Hicks, George Stigler, and others[6] to include the work of Carl Menger, William Stanley Jevons, Léon Walras, John Bates Clark, and many others.[3] Today it is usually used to refer to mainstream economics, although it has also been used as an umbrella term encompassing a number of other schools of thought,[7] notably excluding institutional economics, various historical schools of economics, and Marxian economics, in addition to various other heterodox approaches to economics.

Neoclassical economics is characterized by several assumptions common to many schools of economic thought. There is not a complete agreement on what is meant by neoclassical economics, and the result is a wide range of neoclassical approaches to various problem areas and domains—ranging from neoclassical theories of labor to neoclassical theories of demographic changes.

Three central assumptions

It was expressed by E. Roy Weintraub that neoclassical economics rests on three assumptions, although certain branches of neoclassical theory may have different approaches:[8]

1. People have rational preferences between outcomes that can be identified and associated with values.
2. Individuals maximize utility and firms maximize profits.
3. People act independently on the basis of full and relevant information.

From these three assumptions, neoclassical economists have built a structure to understand the allocation of scarce resources among alternative ends—in fact understanding such allocation is often considered the definition of economics to neoclassical theorists. Here's how William Stanley Jevons presented "the problem of Economics".

> "Given, a certain population, with various needs and powers of production, in possession of certain lands and other sources of material: required, the mode of employing their labour which will maximize the utility of their produce."[9]

From the basic assumptions of neoclassical economics comes a wide range of theories about various areas of economic activity. For example, profit maximization lies behind the neoclassical theory of the firm, while the derivation of demand curves leads to an understanding of consumer goods, and the supply curve allows an analysis of the factors of production. Utility maximization is the source for the neoclassical theory of consumption, the derivation of demand curves for consumer goods, and the derivation of labor supply curves and reservation demand.[10]

Market supply and demand are aggregated across firms and individuals. Their interactions determine equilibrium output and price. The market supply and demand for each factor of production is derived analogously to those for market final output to determine equilibrium income and the income distribution. Factor demand incorporates the marginal-productivity relationship of that factor in the output market.[6][11][12][13]

Neoclassical economics emphasizes equilibria, where equilibria are the solutions of agent maximization problems. Regularities in economies are explained by methodological individualism, the position that economic phenomena can be explained by aggregating over the behavior of agents. The emphasis is on microeconomics. Institutions, which might be considered as prior to and conditioning individual behavior, are de-emphasized. Economic subjectivism accompanies these emphases. See also general equilibrium.

1.3.2 Origins

Classical economics, developed in the 18th and 19th centuries, included a value theory and distribution theory. The value of a product was thought to depend on the costs involved in producing that product. The explanation of costs in Classical economics was simultaneously an explanation of distribution. A landlord received rent, workers received wages, and a capitalist tenant farmer received profits on their investment. This classic approach included the work of Adam Smith and David Ricardo.

However, some economists gradually began emphasizing the perceived value of a good to the consumer. They proposed a theory that the value of a product was to be explained with differences in utility (usefulness) to the consumer. (In England, economists tended to conceptualize utility in keeping with the Utilitarianism of Jeremy Bentham and later of John Stuart Mill.)

The third step from political economy to economics was the introduction of marginalism and the proposition that economic actors made decisions based on margins. For example, a person decides to buy a second sandwich based on how full he or she is after the first one, a firm hires a new employee based on the expected increase in profits the employee will bring. This differs from the aggregate decision making of classical political economy in that it explains how vital goods such as water can be cheap, while luxuries can be expensive.

1.3.3 The marginal revolution

The change in economic theory from classical to neoclassical economics has been called the 'marginal revolution', although it has been argued that the process was slower than the term suggests.[14] It is frequently dated from William Stanley Jevons's *Theory of Political Economy* (1871), Carl Menger's *Principles of Economics* (1871), and Léon Walras's *Elements of Pure Economics* (1874–1877). Historians of economics and economists have debated:

- Whether utility or marginalism was more essential to this revolution (whether the noun or the adjective in the phrase "marginal utility" is more important)

- Whether there was a revolutionary change of thought or merely a gradual development and change of emphasis from their predecessors

- Whether grouping these economists together disguises differences more important than their similarities.[15]

In particular, Jevons saw his economics as an application and development of Jeremy Bentham's utilitarianism and never had a fully developed general equilibrium theory. Menger did not embrace this hedonic conception, explained diminishing marginal utility in terms of subjective prioritization of possible uses, and emphasized disequilibrium and the discrete; further Menger had an objection to the use of mathematics in economics, while the other two modeled their theories after 19th century mechanics.[16] Jevons built on the hedonic conception of Bentham or of Mill, while Walras was more interested in the interaction of markets than in explaining the individual psyche.[15]

Alfred Marshall's textbook, *Principles of Economics* (1890), was the dominant textbook in England a generation later. Marshall's influence extended elsewhere; Italians would compliment Maffeo Pantaleoni by calling him the "Marshall of Italy". Marshall thought classical economics attempted to explain prices by the cost of production. He asserted that earlier marginalists went too far in correcting this imbalance by overemphasizing utility and demand. Marshall thought that "We might as reasonably dispute whether it is the upper or the under blade of a pair of scissors that cuts a piece of paper, as whether value is governed by utility or cost of production".

Marshall explained price by the intersection of supply and demand curves. The introduction of different market "periods" was an important innovation of Marshall's:

- Market period. The goods produced for sale on the market are taken as given data, e.g. in a fish market. Prices quickly adjust to clear markets.

- Short period. Industrial capacity is taken as given. The level of output, the level of employment, the inputs of raw materials, and prices fluctuate to equate marginal cost and marginal revenue, where profits are maximized. Economic rents exist in short period equilibrium for fixed factors, and the rate of profit is not equated across sectors.

- Long period. The stock of capital goods, such as factories and machines, is not taken as given. Profit-maximizing equilibria determine both industrial capacity and the level at which it is operated.

- Very long period. Technology, population trends, habits and customs are not taken as given, but allowed to vary in very long period models.

Marshall took supply and demand as stable functions and extended supply and demand explanations of prices to all runs. He argued supply was easier to vary in longer runs, and thus became a more important determinant of price in the very long run.

1.3.4 Further developments

An important change in neoclassical economics occurred around 1933. Joan Robinson and Edward H. Chamberlin, with the near simultaneous publication of their respective books, *The Economics of Imperfect Competition* (1933) and *The Theory of Monopolistic Competition* (1933), introduced models of imperfect competition. Theories of market forms and industrial organization grew out of this work. They also emphasized certain tools, such as the marginal revenue curve.

Joan Robinson's work on imperfect competition, at least, was a response to certain problems of Marshallian partial equilibrium theory highlighted by Piero Sraffa. Anglo-American economists also responded to these problems by turning towards general equilibrium theory, developed on the European continent by Walras and Vilfredo Pareto. J. R. Hicks's *Value and Capital* (1939) was influential in introducing his English-speaking colleagues to these traditions. He, in turn, was influenced by the Austrian School economist Friedrich Hayek's move to the London School of Economics, where Hicks then studied.

These developments were accompanied by the introduction of new tools, such as indifference curves and the theory of ordinal utility. The level of mathematical sophistication of neoclassical economics increased. Paul Samuelson's *Foundations of Economic Analysis* (1947) contributed to this increase in mathematical modelling.

The interwar period in American economics has been argued to have been pluralistic, with neoclassical economics and institutionalism competing for allegiance. Frank Knight, an early Chicago school economist attempted to combine both schools. But this increase in mathematics was accompanied by greater dominance of neoclassical economics in Anglo-American universities after World War II. Some[17] argue that outside political interventions, such as McCarthyism, and internal ideological bullying played an important role in this rise to dominance.

Hicks' book, *Value and Capital* had two main parts. The second, which was arguably not immediately influential, presented a model of temporary equilibrium. Hicks was influenced directly by Hayek's notion of intertemporal coordination and paralleled by earlier work by Lindhal. This was part of an abandonment of disaggregated long run models. This trend probably reached its culmination with the Arrow-Debreu model of intertemporal equilibrium. The Arrow-Debreu model has canonical presentations in Gérard Debreu's *Theory of Value* (1959) and in Arrow and Hahn's "General Competitive Analysis" (1971).

Many of these developments were against the backdrop of improvements in both econometrics, that is the ability to measure prices and changes in goods and services, as well as their aggregate quantities, and in the creation of macroeconomics, or the study of whole economies. The attempt to combine neo-classical microeconomics and Keynesian macroeconomics would lead to the neoclassical synthesis[18] which has been the dominant paradigm of economic reasoning in English-speaking countries since the 1950s. Hicks and Samuelson were for example instrumental in mainstreaming Keynesian economics.

Macroeconomics influenced the neoclassical synthesis from the other direction, undermining foundations of classical economic theory such as Say's Law, and assumptions about political economy such as the necessity for a hard-money standard. These developments are reflected in neoclassical theory by the search for the occurrence in markets of the equilibrium conditions of Pareto optimality and self-sustainability.

1.3.5 Criticisms

Main article: Criticisms of neoclassical economics

Neoclassical economics is sometimes criticized for having a normative bias. In this view, it does not focus on explaining actual economies, but instead on describing a "utopia" in which Pareto optimality applies.[19]

The assumption that individuals act rationally may be viewed as ignoring important aspects of human behavior. Many see the "economic man" as being quite different from real people. Many economists, even contemporaries, have criticized this model of economic man. Thorstein Veblen put it most sardonically. Neoclassical economics assumes a person to be,

> "a lightning calculator of pleasures and pains, who oscillates like a homogeneous globule of desire of happiness under the impulse of stimuli that shift about the area, but leave him intact."[20]

Large corporations might perhaps come closer to the neoclassical ideal of profit maximization, but this is not necessarily viewed as desirable if this comes at the expense of neglect of wider social issues.[21]

Problems exist with making the neoclassical general equilibrium theory compatible with an economy that develops over time and includes capital goods. This was explored in a major debate in the 1960s—the "Cambridge capital controversy"—about the validity of neoclassical economics, with an emphasis on the economic growth, capital, aggregate theory, and the marginal productivity theory of distribution. There were also internal attempts by neoclassical economists to extend the Arrow-Debreu model to disequilibrium investigations of stability and uniqueness. However a result known as the Sonnenschein-Mantel-Debreu theorem suggests that the assumptions that must be made to ensure that the equilibrium is stable and unique are quite restrictive.

Neoclassical economics is also often seen as relying too heavily on complex mathematical models, such as those used in general equilibrium theory, without enough regard to whether these actually describe the real economy. Many see an attempt to model a system as complex as a modern economy by a mathematical model as unrealistic and doomed to failure. A famous answer to this criticism is Milton Friedman's claim that theories should be judged by their ability to predict events rather than by the realism of their assumptions.[22] Mathematical models also include those in game theory, linear programming, and econometrics. Some[23] see mathematical models used in contemporary research in mainstream economics as having transcended neoclassical economics, while others[24] disagree. Critics of neoclassical economics are divided into those who think that highly mathematical method is inherently wrong and those who think that mathematical method is potentially good even if contemporary methods have problems.

In general, allegedly overly unrealistic assumptions are one of the most common criticisms towards neoclassical economics. It is fair to say that many (but not all) of these criticisms can only be directed towards a subset of the neoclassical models (for example, there are many neoclassical models where unregulated markets fail to achieve Pareto-optimality and there has recently been an increased interest in modeling non-rational decision making).

1.3.6 See also

- Marginalism
- Market economy
- Microeconomics
- Neo-classical synthesis
- Static equilibrium (economics)

1.3.7 References

[1] Antonietta Campus (1987), "marginal economics", *The New Palgrave: A Dictionary of Economics*, v. 3, p. 323.

[2] Clark, B. (1998). *Principles of political economy: A comparative approach.* Westport, Connecticut: Praeger.

[3] Colander, David; *The Death of Neoclassical Economics.*

[4] Aspromourgos, T. (1986). On the origins of the term 'neoclassical'. Cambridge Journal of Economics, 10(3), 265–270.

[5] Veblen, T. (1900). 'The Preconceptions of Economic Science – III', *The Quarterly Journal of Economics*, 14(2), 240–269. (Term on pg. 261).

[6] George J. Stigler (1941 [1994]). *Production and Distribution Theories.* New York: Macmillan. Preview.

[7] Fonseca G. L.; "Introduction to the Neoclassicals", The New School.

[8] E. Roy Weintraub. (2007). Neoclassical Economics. The Concise Encyclopedia Of Economics. Retrieved September 26, 2010, from http://www.econlib.org/library/Enc1/NeoclassicalEconomics.html

[9] William Stanley Jevons (1879, 2nd ed., p. 289), *The Theory of Political Economy*. Italics in original.

[10] Philip H. Wicksteed *The Common Sense of Political Economy*

[11] Christopher Bliss (1987), "distribution theories, neoclassical", *The New Palgrave: A Dictionary of Economics*, v. 1, pp. 883–886.

[12] Robert F. Dorfman (1987), "marginal productivity theory", *The New Palgrave: A Dictionary of Economics*, v. 3, pp. 323–25.

[13] C.E. Ferguson (1969). *The Neoclassical Theory of Production and Distribution*. Cambridge. ISBN 9780521076296, ch. 1 excerpt, pp. 1–10 (press +), & review excerpt.

[14] Roger E. Backhouse (2008). "marginal revolution," *The New Palgrave Dictionary of Economics*, 2nd Edition. Abstract.

[15] William Jaffé (1976) "Menger, Jevons, and Walras De-Homogenized", *Economic Inquiry*, V. 14 (December): 511–525

[16] Philip Mirowski (1989) *More Heat than Light: Economics as Social Physics, Physics as Nature's Economics*, Cambridge University Press.

[17] Frederic Lee (2009), *A History of Heterodox Economics: Challenging the mainstream in the twentieth century*, London and New York: Routledge.

[18] Olivier Jean Blanchard (1987). "neoclassical synthesis", *The New Palgrave: A Dictionary of Economics*, v. 3, pp. 634–36.

[19] For example, see Alfred S. Eichner and Jan Kregel (Dec. 1975) An Essay on Post-Keynesian Theory: A New Paradigm in Economics, *Journal of Economic Literature*.

[20] Thorstein Veblen (1898) *Why Is Economics Not an Evolutionary Science?*, reprinted in The Place of Science in Modern Civilization (New York, 1919), p. 73.

[21] For an argument that the existence of modern corporations is incompatible with the neoclassical economics, see John Kenneth Galbraith (1978). *The new Industrial State*, Third edition, revised, (New York).

[22] Friedman argued for this in essays III, IV and V in "Essays in Positive Economics". http://www.econ.umn.edu/~{}schwe227/teaching.s11/files/articles/friedman-1953.pdf

[23] For example, David Colander, Richard Holt, and J. Barkley Rosser Jr. (2004) The changing face of mainstream economics, *Review of Political Economy*, V. 16, No. 4: pp. 485–499)

[24] For example, Matias Vernengo (2010) Conversation or monologue? On advising heterodox economists, *Journal of Post Keynesian Economics*, V. 32, No. 3" pp. 485–499.

1.3.8 External links

- Weintraub, E. Roy (2002). "Neoclassical Economics". In David R. Henderson (ed.). *Concise Encyclopedia of Economics* (1st ed.). Library of Economics and Liberty. OCLC 317650570, 50016270 and 163149563

Chapter 2

Heterodox Economics Articles (in Alphabetical Order)

2.1 Alexander del Mar

Alexander del Mar

Alexander del Mar, also **Alex Delmar** (1836–1926), was an American political economist, historian, numismatist and author.[Note 1] He was the first director of the Bureau of Statistics at the U.S. Treasury Department from 1866–69.[1] [Note 2]

Del Mar was a rigorous historian who made important contributions to the history of money. During the mid-1890s, he was distinctly hostile to a central monetary role for gold as a commodity money, championing the cause of silver and its re-monetization as a prerogative of the state.

He believed strongly in the legal function of money. Del Mar dedicated much of his free time to original research in the great libraries and coin collections of Europe on the history of monetary systems and finance.

2.1.1 Biography

Alexander del Mar, of Jewish-Spanish descent,[2] was born in New York City, August 9, 1836 as oldest son of Jacob and Belvidere Alexander del Mar. He lived for a short period of time in the United Kingdom with his uncle Emanuel del Mar and there received an education in humanities from a private tutor, Arthur Helps (later knighted, becoming Sir Arthur Helps). He was instructed in history, literature, law, and political economy.

After graduating from New York University as a civil engineer, he was educated as a mining engineer in Spain at the Madrid School of Mines.[3]

Aged 18, he returned to the U.S. in 1854 to become the financial editor of the short-lived *Daily American Times*.[4] He moved to *Hunt's Merchant's Magazine* in 1860, and in 1863 co-founded and edited with Simon Stern the prestigious quarterly *New York Social Science Review* (first published in January 1865).[5] He was also involved with the Commercial and Financial Chronicle, founded in 1865 by William Dana.

In 1865, Del Mar, a notorious Free Trader, helped establish the first Free Trade organization in the United States, the American Free Trade League (AFTL), alongside Horace White, William Lloyd Garrison, and Ralph Waldo Emerson, among others.[6]

In 1866 del Mar was appointed as the first director of US Treasury Department's Bureau of Statistics (now part of the Bureau of Economic Analysis).[1] At the time the bureau was a board of trade, with executive functions, among others the supervision of the commissioners of mines, commerce, immigration, etc. Del Mar pioneered the use of a modern and scientific approach to statistics. He remained director until 1869, overseeing numerous reports.[3][7][8][9] He was forced to resign by his superior, David Ames Wells, and was replaced by Francis Amasa Walker. Both were ardent supporters of specie money and opposed to del Mar's convictions of fiat money.[10]

In 1866 he was appointed the American delegate to the International Monetary Congress which met in Turin, Italy.[3]

During the close-fought 1868 presidential election he was nominated for Secretary of the Treasury under Horatio Seymour's Democratic ticket.

In 1869 he purchased the Washington-based *National Intelligencer*, merged it with the *Washington Express* and moved its offices to New York in January 1870.[11] It later became the New York *City and National Intelligencer* which he edited and published until 1872.[12]

He ran under Horace Greeley's ticket for Secretary of the Treasury during the United States presidential election, 1872. The coalition between the Democrats and Greeley's Liberal Republican Party was soundly defeated, and the LRP ceased to exist shortly after. In the same year del Mar represented the United States at the international monetary congress in St. Petersburg, Russia.

In 1877 del Mar was appointed mining commissioner to the U.S. Monetary Commission.[3] This commission was created by Congress in 1876 when it discovered the subterfuge that led to the Panic of 1873. It was charged to investigate:

> *First.* Into the change which has taken place in the relative value of gold and silver; the causes thereof, whether permanent or otherwise; the effects thereof upon trade, commerce, finance, and the productive interests of the country, and upon the standard of value in this and foreign countries; *Second.* Into the policy of the restoration of the double standard in this country; and, if restored, what the legal relation between the two coins, silver and gold, should be; *Third.* Into the policy of continuing legal-tender notes concurrently with the metallic standards, and the effects thereof upon the labor, industries, and wealth of the country; and *Fourth.* Into the best means for providing for facilitating the resumption of specie payments.[13]

Although the commission reported unfavourably on the switch to the *de facto* gold standard and recommended a return to silver, gold's status as a reserve currency was to remain unchallenged until the 1930s.

In 1878, Del Mar was appointed as clerk to the United States House Committee on Expenditures in the Navy Department.

In 1878, Del Mar also wrote a series of letters under the Chinese pseudonym "Kwang Chang Ling" in the San Francisco *Argonaut* journal. The letters warned Californians, and the broader United States, that China had the potential to rise as an economic giant. Del Mar, as Kwang Chang Ling, argued that excluding cheap Chinese labor to protect American wages and lessen unemployment would do little to protect American laborers in the long term, for China's labor force would continue to pose a global economic threat despite national policies.[14] Del Mar's writings are the first known attempt to use Free Trade rhetoric as a solution to the "Chinese Question" and to counter anti-Chinese attitudes that led to the 1882 Chinese Exclusion Act.

In 1879 he published his *History of the Precious Metals*, the labor of twenty-two years of research during his own free time. From 1880 onwards he mainly devoted his professional career to writing.

In 1881, he published *A History of Money in Ancient States*, in 1885 *Money and Civilization*, in 1889 *The Science of Money*, in 1895, *A History of Monetary Systems in Modern States*, in 1899 *A History of Monetary Crimes*, in 1900 *A History of Money in America*, in 1903 *A History of Monetary Systems of France*. Del Mar also published several archaeological treatises of great interest.

Del Mar was the New York state chairman of the Silver Party, and spoke at its 1896 Chicago meeting in support of William Jennings Bryan.[15]

He was editor-in-chief of the American Banker, 1905–1906. Upon his death, he donated his private library of 15,000 volumes to the American Bankers Association. Alexander del Mar died in 1926 at the age of ninety.

Del Mar received no scientific or academic recognition from contemporaries, and as a result of this his prescient views were totally excluded from the history of economics.[10]

2.1.2 Family life

With his wife, the former Emily Joseph (the daughter of Joseph L. Joseph), he had eleven children, seven that survived to adulthood, including five sons, Walter, Eugene, Harry, Algernon, and William ; and two daughter, Francesca Paloma del Mar, who trained as an artist.,[4] and Maud (Blackwelder) Del Mar. <family history>

2.1.3 Quotes

- John Stuart Mill spoke highly about del Mar:

Del Mar is a remarkable writer. There is stuff in him. He is the sort of man you need in America. He knows what he is about. He is the sort of man to put things right in your country, or in any country.[16]

- From del Mar's 1895 book *History of Monetary Systems*:

    In the United States the same bag of coins often masquerades now as the reserve of one bank, and now of another. How far similar subterfuges are employed in the various private banking establishments of Germany is not known, and in the absence of such knowledge it is deemed safer to include the entire paper issues in the circulation. This at least is a known quantity; the " reserves," as experience has too often and too sadly proved, may only exist in the playful imagination of that fortunate class who have secured the prerogative to issue bank money.[17]

- *A la mort, l'argent!*

    (Silver until I die!)[18]

2.1.4 Selected bibliography

- del Mar, Alexander, (1862). *Gold money and paper money*. New York: Anson D.F. Randolph. (Pamphlet) (Cornell University Library reprint 200... ISBN 978-1-4297-2841-6)

- del Mar, Alexander (1864). *The great paper bubble: or the coming financial explosion*. New York: Office of the Metropolitan Record.

- del Mar, Alexander, (1866). *Statistics of the world*. Washington (DC): Government Press. (Pamphlet)

- "Emile Walter" (del Mar, Alexander, pseud.) (1867). *What is free trade? An adaptation of Frederick Bastiat's "Sophismes economiques"*. New York: G.P. Putnam and Son. (repr. Dodo Press, 2009 ISBN 978-1-4099-3812-5)

- del Mar, Alexander, (1867). *History of money and civilization*. (repr. NY: Burt Franklin, 1969)

- del Mar, Alexander, (1867) *Decadence of American shipbuilding*. Washington: Government Press

- del Mar, Alexander, (1868). *The whiskey tax for 100 Years*. Washington (DC): Congressional Subcommittee on Retrenchment.

- del Mar, Alexander, (1878). *Why should the Chinese go? : a pertinent inquiry from a mandarin high in authority*. San Francisco: Bruce's Book & Job Printing House. [N.B. del Mar states the case for *not* expelling the Chinese workers.]

- del Mar, Alexander, (1879). *Usury and the jews: a lecture delivered at Steinway Hall, February 11th, 1879*. San Francisco (CA): I.N. Choynski. (Pamphlet) [Not available online as of November 2013, but its contents are summarised in Brooke-Rose, Christine, (1971). *A ZBC of Ezra Pound*. University of California Press, pp. 223–5.]

- del Mar, Alexander, (1880) *The history of money in ancient countries from the earliest times to the present*. London: George Bell and Sons. (repr. Kessinger Publishing, 2003 ISBN 0-7661-9024-2)

- del Mar, Alexander, (1885), (2nd ed., 1899). *The science of money*. London, George Bell and Sons. (repr. Kessinger Publishing, 2008 ISBN 1-4372-8281-4)

- del Mar, Alexander (1885), (2nd ed., 1901). *History of the precious metals from the earliest times to the present*. London: George Bell and Sons. (repr. Kessinger Publishing, 2004 ISBN 0-7661-9054-4)

- del Mar, Alexander, (1895). *History of monetary systems*. New York: Cambridge Encyclopedia Co. (repr. NY: A.M. Kelley, 1978)

- del Mar, Alexander, (1899) *The history of money in America, from the earliest times to the constitution*. New York: Cambridge Encyclopedia Co. (repr. NY: Burt Franklin, 1968)

- del Mar, Alexander, (1899). *Barbara Villers, or a history of monetary crimes*. New York: Groseclose, Money & Man. (repr. Omni Publications, 1983)

- del Mar, Alexander, (1899). *The worship of Augustus Caesar: derived from a study of coins, monuments, calendars, eras, and astronomical and astrological cycles, the whole establishing a new chronology and survey of history and religion*. New York: Cambridge Encyclopedia Co.

- del Mar, Alexander, (1899). *Ancient Britain in the light of modern archaeological discoveries*. New York: Cambridge Encyclopedia Co.

- del Mar, Alexander, (1900). *The middle ages revisited; or, the Roman government and religion and their relations to Britain*. New York: Cambridge Encyclopedia Co.

Some works by del Mar were announced but apparently not printed, including *The politics of money* and *The history of money in modern countries*.

2.1.5 See also

- Coinage Act of 1873
- Free silver
- Monetary reform
- Veil of money
- Money illusion
- Criticism of fractional-reserve banking
- Stephen Zarlenga
- American Monetary Institute

2.1.6 References

[1] Simon, Matthew (1960). "Chapter 22: The United States Balance of Payments, 1861-1900.". *Trends in the American economy in the nineteenth century.* Studies in Income and Wealth, Issue 24. Princeton University Press. p. 632. ISBN 0-87014-180-5.

[2] Tavlas, George S. (November–December 2011). "Retroview: The Money Man". The American Interest. Retrieved 2011-11-07.

[3] Merrill, Walter McIntosh; Ruchames, Louis, eds. (1981). *To rouse the slumbering land, 1868-1879.* The Letters of William Lloyd Garrison, **6**. Harvard University Press. p. 107. ISBN 978-0-674-52666-2.

[4] Hamersly, Lewis Randolph (1929). Leonard, John W. et al., eds. *Who's who in New York (city and state), Issue 9.* New York: Who's Who publications.

[5] del Mar, Alexander; Stern, Simon, eds. (1866). "New York Social Science Review for 1865". London: Trübner & Co.

[6] Northrup, Cynthia, Elaine C. Prange Turney, ed. (2003). *Encyclopedia of Tariffs and Trade in U.S. History, Vol. 1.* Westport: Greenwood. p. 16. ISBN 0313327890.

[7] del Mar, Alexander. *Report of the Director of the Bureau of Statistics, Treasury Department on the present progress of ship-building in the United States.* (1867) Washington: Government Printing Office.

[8] *Monthly statistical reports on commerce, navigation, trade, resources &c. of the various countries of the world.* Washington: Government Press.

[9] *Annual report on the commerce and navigation of the USA* 1865, 1866, 1867, 1868. Washington: Government Press.

[10] Aschheim, Joseph; Tavlas, George S. (March 2004). "Academic exclusion: the case of Alexander Del Mar". *European Journal of Political Economy, special section: Mini-symposium on Professional Prejudice and Discrimination in the History of Economic Thought* (Elsevier) **20** (1): 31–60. doi:10.1016/j.ejpoleco.2003.01.002.

[11] Husdon, Frederic (1873). *Journalism in the United States from 1690 to 1872* (reprint, Kessinger Publishing, 2005 ed.). New York: Harper & Bros. pp. 258–9. ISBN 978-1-4179-5347-9.

[12] *American Newspaper Directory, 1872.* New York (NY): Geo. P. Rowell. 1872. p. 518.

[13] Russell, Henry Benajah (1898). *International monetary conferences (Gold: historical and economic aspects)* (repr. Ayer Publishing, 1974 ed.). New York: Harper. p. 161. ISBN 978-0-405-05920-9.

[14] Arnold, Kashia (Fall 2012). "Academic exclusion: the case of Alexander Del Mar". *Southern California Quarterly* (University of California Press for the Historical Society of Southern California) **94** (3): 304–345. doi:10.1525/scq.2012.94.3.304.

[15] "The Saint Paul Globe.". St. Paul, Minn. July 11, 1896: 3.

[16] John Stuart Mill, The Philadelphia Press, August 16, 1874

[17] del Mar, Alexander (1895). *History of Monetary Systems.* London: Effingham Wilson. p. 389.

[18] del Mar, Alexander (1895). *Story of the Gold Conspiracy.* Chicago: Charles H. Carr.

2.1.7 Notes

[1] In business affairs he was frequently referred to in contemporary reports and newspapers as Delmar; however, many of his published works appeared under the name of del Mar. He sometimes appended the letters C.E. and/or M.E. (respectively "Civil Engineer" and "Mining Engineer") to his name.

[2] The US Treasury Department's Bureau of Statistics (1866–1903) should not be confused with the Bureau of Statistics of the US State Department (1874–1897). The two were eventually merged in 1903 under the Department of Commerce and Labor. See "Records of the Bureau of Economic Analysis". *National Archive guide to Federal records.*

2.1.8 Further reading

- Aschheim, Joseph; Tavlas, George S. (March 2004). "Academic exclusion: the case of Alexander Del Mar". *European Journal of Political Economy, special section: Mini-symposium on Professional Prejudice and Discrimination in the History of*

Economic Thought (Elsevier) **20** (1): 31–60. doi:10.1016/j.ejpoleco.2003.01.002.

- Tavlas, George S.; Aschheim, Joseph (May 1985). "Alexander Del Mar, Irving Fisher, and Monetary Economics". *The Canadian Journal of Economics* (Wiley) **18** (2): 294–313. doi:10.2307/135137. JSTOR 135137.

- Robertson, J.R. (1881). *The life of Hon. Alex. Del Mar, M.E., formerly director of the Bureau of Statistics of the United States*. YA Pamphlet Collection (Library of Congress). London: E.F. Gooch & Son, Steam Printers. OCLC 35650851.

- Arnold, Kashia (Fall 2012). "Academic exclusion: the case of Alexander Del Mar". *Southern California Quarterly* (University of California Press for the Historical Society of Southern California) **94** (3): 304–345. doi:10.1525/scq.2012.94.3.304.

2.1.9 External links

- Works by Alexander del Mar at Project Gutenberg
- Works by or about Alexander del Mar at Internet Archive
- Works by Alexander del Mar at LibriVox (public domain audiobooks)
- Tavlas, George S. (2011). "Retroview: The Money Man". *The American Interest November/December 2011*.
- "The Crime of 1873".

2.2 American Monetary Institute

The **American Monetary Institute** is a non-profit charitable trust established by Stephen Zarlenga in 1996 for the "independent study of monetary history, theory and reform."

2.2.1 Aims

The institute is dedicated to monetary reform and advocates taking control of the monetary system out of the hands of banks and placing it into the hands of the US Treasury. Zarlenga argues that this would mean money would be issued by government interest free and spent into circulation to promote the general welfare, and that substantial expenditures on infrastructure, including human infrastructure (education and health care) would become the predominant method of putting new money into circulation.[1]

Research results are published in Zarlenga's book, *The Lost Science of Money*. The book asserts that money did not emerge from barter between individuals, but rather through trade between tribes and as part of religious worship and sacrifice.[1] Though this is not the mainstream view, there are other scholars of money, such as Keith Hart,[2] who agree that money developed in this way. The reason this distinction is believed to be important is because, according to Zarlenga, it is the definition of money which determines how the public will allow the money supply to be controlled.

If money is a commodity to be traded, then all that matters is that the money is 100% backed by some commodity, like gold or silver for example. If money is credit, then it makes sense that bankers control it, as they do in the United States today. But if money is an artifact of law, whose value is derived from law (payment of taxes and legal tender laws) then Zarlenga argues it would only be proper for the government to issue, and control the money supply.[3] According to Zarlenga, it is this last definition that is supported by the history and nature of money. Government-controlled money is also postulated to be more stable than credit money or commodity money.

Coins have been claimed to represent an advance over weighing out precious metals with a fixed amount of precious metal being stamped so they need not be weighed and could be exchanged more conveniently than lumps of metal which needed to be weighed.[4]

2.2.2 Conferences

The 9th Annual AMI Monetary Reform Conference will be held at the University Center, in Chicago, September 2013. While 2013 speakers are still unconfirmed, past speakers have included: Michael Hudson, Richard C. Cook, William K. Black, Dennis Kucinich, and Elizabeth Kucinich.

2.2.3 See also

- Committee on Monetary and Economic Reform (Canada)
- Modern Monetary Theory
- Monetary reform
- Money creation
- Chicago plan
- The Chicago Plan Revisited
- A Program for Monetary Reform

2.2.4 References

[1] W. Krehm, Review of Zarlenga's Lost Science of Money, Economic Reform Australia, Vol 3 No 18, July–August 2005

[2] Money in an Unequal World, Keith Hart

[3] Stephen Zarlenga, The Lost Science Of Money, Ch. 24: "Proposals For U.S. Monetary Reform"

[4] The History of Money, Jack Weatherford

2.2.5 External links

- American Monetary Institute website

2.3 Anti-capitalism

This article lists ideologies opposed to capitalism and describes them briefly. For arguments against capitalism, see criticism of capitalism.

Anti-capitalism encompasses a wide variety of movements, ideas and attitudes that oppose capitalism. Anti-capitalists, in the strict sense of the word, are those who wish to replace capitalism with another type of economic system.

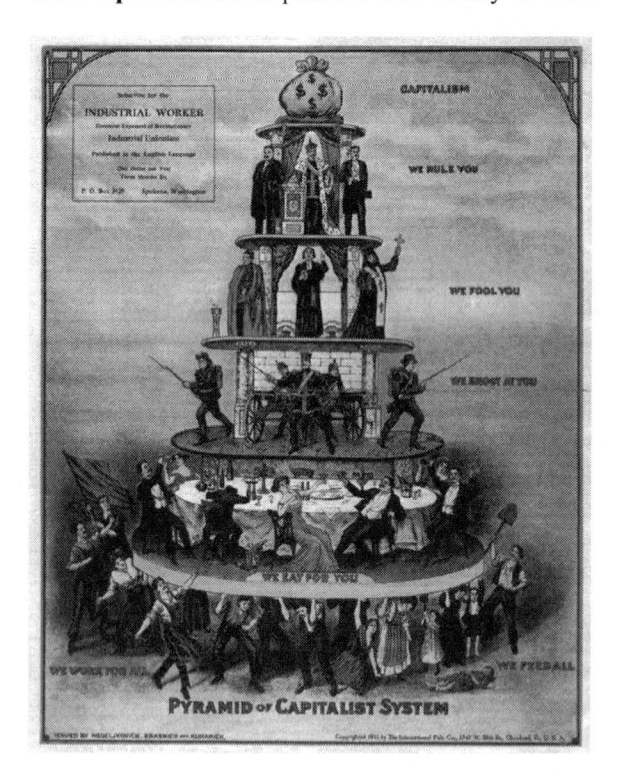

An Industrial Workers of the World poster (1911)

2.3.1 Socialism

Main article: Socialism

Socialism advocates public or direct worker ownership and

A man marching against capitalism with Democratic Socialists of America members at the Occupy Wall Street protest event, September 24, 2011

administration of the means of production and allocation of resources, and a society characterized by equal access to resources for all individuals, with an egalitarian method of compensation.[1][2]

1. A theory or policy of social organisation which aims at or advocates the ownership and control of the means of production, capital, land, property, etc., by the community as a whole, and their administration or distribution in the interests of all.

2. Socialists argue for cooperative/community or state control of the economy, or the "commanding heights" of the economy,[3] with democratic control by the people over the state, although there have been some undemocratic philosophies. "State" or "worker cooperative" ownership is in fundamental opposition to "private" ownership of means of production, which is a defining feature of capitalism. Most socialists argue that capitalism unfairly concentrates power, wealth and profit, among a small segment of society that controls capital and derives its wealth through exploitation.

Socialists argue that the accumulation of capital generates waste through externalities that require costly corrective regulatory measures. They also point out that this process generates wasteful industries and practices that exist only to generate sufficient demand for products to be sold at a profit (such as high-pressure advertisement); thereby creating rather than satisfying economic demand.[4][5]

Socialists argue that capitalism consists of irrational activity, such as the purchasing of commodities only to sell at a later time when their price appreciates, rather than for consumption, even if the commodity cannot be sold at a profit to individuals in need; they argue that *making money*, or accumulation of capital, does not correspond to the satisfaction of demand.[6]

Private ownership imposes constraints on planning, leading to inaccessible economic decisions that result in immoral production, unemployment and a tremendous waste of material resources during crisis of overproduction. According to socialists, private property in the means of production becomes obsolete when it concentrates into centralized, socialized institutions based on private appropriation of revenue (but based on cooperative work and internal planning in allocation of inputs) until the role of the capitalist becomes redundant.[7] With no need for capital accumulation and a class of owners, private property in the means of production is perceived as being an outdated form of economic organization that should be replaced by a free association of individuals based on public or common ownership of these socialized assets.[8] Socialists view private property relations as limiting the potential of productive forces in the economy.[9]

Early socialists (Utopian socialists and Ricardian socialists) criticized capitalism for concentrating power and wealth within a small segment of society,[10] and does not utilise available technology and resources to their maximum potential in the interests of the public.[9]

Anarchist and libertarian socialist criticisms

Main articles: Anarchist economics and Libertarian socialism

For the influential German individualist anarchist philosopher Max Stirner "private property is a spook which "lives by the grace of law" and it "becomes 'mine' only by effect of the law". In other words, private property exists purely "through the protection of the State, through the State's grace." Recognising its need for state protection, Stirner is also aware that "[i]t need not make any difference to the 'good citizens' who protects them and their principles, whether an absolute King or a constitutional one, a republic, if only they are protected. And what is their principle, whose protector they always 'love'? Not that of labour", rather it is "interest-bearing possession . . . labouring capital, therefore . . . labour certainly, yet little or none at

Emma Goldman famously denounced wage slavery by saying: "The only difference is that you are hired slaves instead of block slaves."[11]

all of one's own, but labour of capital and of the -- subject labourers"."[12] French anarchist Pierre Joseph Proudhon opposed government privilege that protects capitalist, banking and land interests, and the accumulation or acquisition of property (and any form of coercion that led to it) which he believed hampers competition and keeps wealth in the hands of the few. The Spanish individualist anarchist Miguel Gimenez Igualada sees "capitalism is an effect of government; the disappearance of government means capitalism falls from its pedestal vertiginously...That which we call capitalism is not something else but a product of the State, within which the only thing that is being pushed forward is profit, good or badly acquired. And so to fight against capitalism is a pointless task, since be it State capitalism or Enterprise capitalism, as long as Government exists, exploiting capital will exist. The fight, but of consciousness, is against the State.".[13]

Within anarchism there emerged a critique of wage slavery which refers to a situation perceived as quasi-voluntary slavery,[14] where a person's livelihood depends on wages, especially when the dependence is total and immediate.[15][16] It is a negatively connoted term used to draw an analogy between slavery and wage labor by focusing on similarities between owning and renting a person. The term *wage slavery* has been used to criticize economic exploitation and social stratification, with the former seen primarily as unequal bargaining power between labor and capital (particularly when workers are paid comparatively low wages, e.g. in sweatshops),[17] and the latter as a lack of workers' self-management, fulfilling job choices and leisure in an economy.[18][19][20] Libertarian socialists believe if freedom is valued, then society must work towards a system in which individuals have the power to decide economic issues along with political issues. Libertarian socialists seek to replace unjustified authority with direct democracy, voluntary federation, and popular autonomy in all aspects of life,[21] including physical communities and economic enterprises. With the advent of the industrial revolution, thinkers such as Proudhon and Marx elaborated the comparison between wage labor and slavery in the context of a critique of societal property not intended for active personal use,[22][23] Luddites emphasized the dehumanization brought about by machines while later Emma Goldman famously denounced wage slavery by saying: "The only difference is that you are hired slaves instead of block slaves.".[24] American anarchist Emma Goldman believed that the economic system of capitalism was incompatible with human liberty. "The only demand that property recognizes," she wrote in *Anarchism and Other Essays*, "is its own gluttonous appetite for greater wealth, because wealth means power; the power to subdue, to crush, to exploit, the power to enslave, to outrage, to degrade."[25] She also argued that capitalism dehumanized workers, "turning the producer into a mere particle of a machine, with less will and decision than his master of steel and iron."[26]

Noam Chomsky contends that there is little moral difference between chattel slavery and renting one's self to an owner or "wage slavery". He feels that it is an attack on personal integrity that undermines individual freedom. He holds that workers should own and control their workplace.[27] Many libertarian socialists argue that large-scale voluntary associations should manage industrial manufacture, while workers retain rights to the individual products of their labor.[28] As such, they see a distinction between the concepts of "private property" and "personal possession". Whereas "private property" grants an individual exclusive control over a thing whether it is in use or not, and regardless of its productive capacity, "possession" grants no rights to things that are not in use.[29]

In addition to individualist anarchist Benjamin Tucker's "big four" monopolies (land, money, tariffs, and patents), Carson argues that the state has also transferred wealth to the wealthy by subsidizing organizational centralization, in the form of transportation and communication subsidies. He believes that Tucker overlooked this issue due to Tucker's focus on individual market transactions, whereas Carson also focuses on organizational issues. The theoretical sections of *Studies in Mutualist Political Economy* are presented as an attempt to integrate marginalist critiques into the labor theory of value.[30] Carson has also been highly critical of intellectual property.[31] The primary focus of his most recent work has been decentralized manufacturing and the informal and household economies.[32] Carson holds that "Capitalism, arising as a new class society directly from the old class society of the Middle Ages, was founded on an act of robbery as massive as the earlier feudal conquest of the land. It has been sustained to the present by continual state intervention to protect its system of privilege without which its survival is unimaginable."[33] Carson coined the pejorative term "vulgar libertarianism," a phrase that describes the use of a free market rhetoric in defense of corporate capitalism and economic inequality. According to Carson, the term is derived from the phrase "vulgar political economy," which Karl Marx described as an economic order that "deliberately becomes increasingly apologetic and makes strenuous attempts to talk out of existence the ideas which contain the contradictions [existing in economic life]."[34]

Marxism

Main article: Marxism

> "We are, in Marx's terms, 'an ensemble of social relations' and we live our lives at the core of the intersection of a number of unequal social relations based on hierarchically interrelated structures which, together, define the historical specificity of the capitalist modes of production and reproduction and underlay their observable manifestations."
> — Martha E. Gimenez, *Marxism and Class, Gender and Race: Rethinking the Trilogy*[35]

Marx believed that the capitalist bourgeois and their economists were promoting what he saw as the lie that "The interests of the capitalist and those of the worker are... one and the same"; he believed that they did this by purporting the concept that "the fastest possible growth of productive capital" was best not only for the wealthy capitalists but also for the workers because it provided them with employment.[36]

2.3.2 Criticisms of anti-capitalism

In constantly observing the negative side(s) of capitalism, anti-capitalists remain focused on capitalism, thus

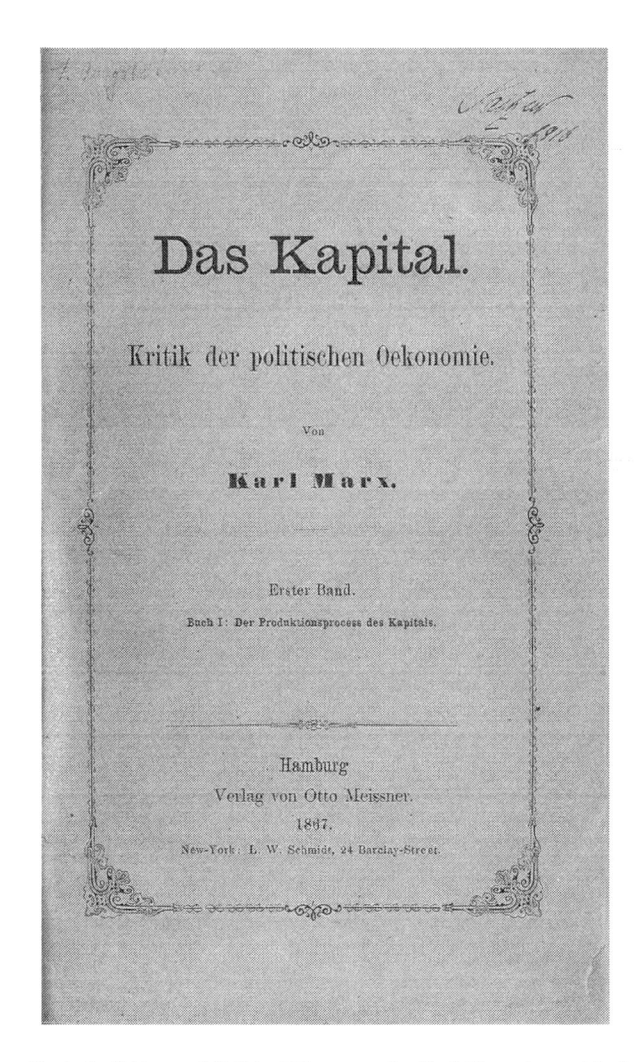

Capital: Critique of Political Economy, by Karl Marx, is a critical analysis of political economy, meant to reveal the economic laws of the capitalist mode of production

co-*performing*[37] and further sustaining the actually criticised unsustainable capitalist system.[38] Thus, the impression of capitalism as *hyper-adaptive*[39] "system without an outside".[40] One way out of the trap is to understand that the observation of capitalism, a system strongly biased by and to the economy, implies functional differentiation. As the economy is only one out of 10 function systems, however, *both* pro- and anti-capitalist visions of society imply this economy-bias and, in return, a neglect of other function systems. Effective strategies for alternatives to capitalism therefore require a stronger focus on the non-economic function systems. A corresponding re-coding of capitalist organisations has recently been proposed.[41]

2.3.3 See also

- Almighty dollar
- Anti-corporate activism
- Anti-globalisation movement
- The Black Book of Capitalism
- Capitalism: A Love Story
- Corporatocracy
- Criticism of capitalism
- Degrowth
- Economic inequality
- List of communist and anti-capitalist parties with parliamentary representation
- Occupy Wall Street
- Post-capitalism
- Reserve army of labour

2.3.4 References

[1] *Newman, Michael.* (2005) *Socialism: A Very Short Introduction*, Oxford University Press, ISBN 0-19-280431-6

[2] "Socialism". Oxford English Dictionary.

[3] "Socialism" *Encyclopædia Britannica*. 2006. Encyclopædia Britannica Online.

[4] Archived July 16, 2010 at the Wayback Machine

[5] Fred Magdoff and Michael D. Yates. "What Needs To Be Done: A Socialist View". Monthly Review. Retrieved 2014-02-23.

[6] *Let's produce for use, not profit*. Retrieved August 7, 2010, from worldsocialism.org: http://www.worldsocialism.org/spgb/may10/page23.html

[7] Engels, Fredrich. *Socialism: Utopian and Scientific*. Retrieved October 30, 2010, from Marxists.org: http://www.marxists.org/archive/marx/works/1880/soc-utop/ch03.htm, "The bourgeoisie demonstrated to be a superfluous class. All its social functions are now performed by salaried employees."

[8] *The Political Economy of Socialism*, by Horvat, Branko. 1982. Chapter 1: Capitalism, The General Pattern of Capitalist Development (pp. 15–20)

[9] Marx and Engels Selected Works, Lawrence and Wishart, 1968, p. 40. Capitalist property relations put a "fetter" on the productive forces.

[10] in Encyclopædia Britannica (2009). Retrieved October 14, 2009, from Encyclopædia Britannica Online: http://www.britannica.com/EBchecked/topic/551569/socialism, "Main" summary: "Socialists complain that capitalism necessarily leads to unfair and exploitative concentrations of wealth and power in the hands of the relative few who emerge victorious from free-market competition—people who then use their wealth and power to reinforce their dominance in society."

[11] Goldman 2003, p. 283.

[12] — Lorenzo Kom'boa Ervin. "G.6 What are the ideas of Max Stirner? in An Anarchist FAQ". Infoshop.org. Retrieved 2010-09-20.

[13] "el capitalismo es sólo el efecto del gobierno; desaparecido el gobierno, el capitalismo cae de su pedestal vertiginosamente...Lo que llamamos capitalismo no es otra cosa que el producto del Estado, dentro del cual lo único que se cultiva es la ganancia, bien o mal habida. Luchar, pues, contra el capitalismo es tarea inútil, porque sea Capitalismo de Estado o Capitalismo de Empresa, mientras el Gobierno exista, existirá el capital que explota. La lucha, pero de conciencias, es contra el Estado."*Anarquismo* by Miguel Gimenez Igualada

[14] Ellerman 1992.

[15] "wage slave". merriam-webster.com. Retrieved 4 March 2013.

[16] "wage slave". dictionary.com. Retrieved 4 March 2013.

[17] Sandel 1996, p. 184

[18] "Conversation with Noam Chomsky". Globetrotter.berkeley.edu. p. 2. Retrieved 2010-06-28.

[19] Hallgrimsdottir & Benoit 2007.

[20] "The Bolsheviks and Workers Control, 1917–1921: The State and Counter-revolution". Spunk Library. Retrieved 4 March 2013.

[21] Harrington, Austin, et al. 'Encyclopedia of Social Theory' Routledge (2006) p.50

[22] Proudhon 1890.

[23] Marx 1969, Chapter VII

[24] Goldman 2003, p. 283

[25] Goldman, Emma. Anarchism and Other Essays. 3rd ed. 1917. New York: Dover Publications Inc., 1969., p. 54.

[26] Goldman, Emma. Anarchism and Other Essays. 3rd ed. 1917. New York: Dover Publications Inc., 1969.pg. 54

[27] "Conversation with Noam Chomsky, p. 2 of 5". Globetrotter.berkeley.edu. Retrieved August 16, 2011.

[28] Lindemann, Albert S. 'A History of European Socialism' Yale University Press (1983) p.160

[29] Ely, Richard et al. 'Property and Contract in Their Relations to the Distribution of Wealth' The Macmillan Company (1914)

[30] Kevin A. Carson, *Studies in Mutualist Political Economy* chs. 1-3

[31] Carson, Kevin. "Intellectual Property — A Libertarian Critique". c4ss.org. Retrieved May 23, 2009.

[32] Carson, Kevin. "Industrial Policy: New Wine in Old Bottles". c4ss.org. Retrieved May 26, 2009.

[33] Richman, Sheldon, Libertarian Left, *The American Conservative* (March 2011)

[34] Marx, *Theories of Surplus Value, III*, p. 501.

[35] Gimenez, Martha E. "Marxism, and Class, Gender, and Race: Rethinking the Trilogy". *Race, Gender & Class* **8** (2): 22–33. JSTOR 41674970. Retrieved 2014-05-18.

[36] Marx 1849.

[37] Callon, Michel. "What does it mean to say that economics is performative?". in: D. MacKenzie, F. Muniesa and L. Siu (Eds.), Do Economists Make Markets? On the Performativity of Economics, Princeton University Press.

[38] Roth, Steffen. "Free economy! On 3628800 alternatives of and to capitalism". *Journal of Interdisciplinary Economics*.

[39] Boltanski, Luc; Chiapello, Eve. "The new spirit of capitalism". *International Journal of Politics, Culture, and Society, 18(3), 161–188*.

[40] Bosquet, Marc. "Cultural capitalism and the 'James Formation'". in: In S. Grif n (Ed.), Henry James goes to the movies (pp. 210–239). Lexington: University of Kentucky Press.

[41] Roth, Steffen. "Growth and function. A viral research program for next organizations" (PDF). *International Journal of Technology Management*.

2.3.5 Further reading

- Alex Callinicos. *An Anti-Capitalist Manifesto*. Polity. 2003

- David McNally. *Another World Is Possible: Globalization and Anti-Capitalism*. Arbeiter Ring Publishing. 2006

- Ezequiel Adamovsky. *Anti-capitalism*. Seven Stories Press. 2011

- David E Lowes. *The Anti-Capitalist Dictionary* 2006, London: Zed Books

- Simon Tormey. *Anti-Capitalism: A Beginner's Guide*. Oneworld Publications. 2013

- "Anti-Capitalism : A Guide To The Movement"

2.3.6 External links

- Rough Guide to the Anti-Capitalist Movement, League for the Fifth International

- Jeremy Rifkin. "The Rise of Anti-Capitalism". at the *New York Times*. MARCH 15, 2014

- Infoshop.org Anarchists Opposed to Capitalism, Infoshop.org

- How The Miners Were Robbed 1907 anti-capitalist pamphlet hosted at EconomicDemocracy

- Sam Ashman "The anti-capitalist movement and the war" *International Socialist Journal 2003*

- Marxists Internet Archive

- Dr. Wladyslaw Jan Kowalski *Anti-Capitalism: Modern Theory and Historical Origins*

- Anti-Capitalism as an ideology... and as a movement, Libcom.org

- How Is Capitalism Like a Religion?

- Studies in Anti-Capitalism

- Capitalism/Anticapitalism: a survey and a view

- How to Be an Anticapitalist Today. Erik Olin Wright for *Jacobin*. December 2, 2015.

2.4 Association for Evolutionary Economics

The **Association for Evolutionary Economics** (**AFEE**) is an international organization of heterodox economists working in the institutionalist and evolutionary traditions of Thorstein Veblen, John R. Commons and Wesley Mitchell. It is part of the Allied Social Sciences Association (ASSA), a group of approximately 55 organizations including the American Economics Association (AEA), that holds a three-day meeting each January.

2.4.1 History

AFEE originated in 1959 as an informal group that met in a rump session of the ASSA meetings. They called themselves the Wardman Group after the Wardman Park Hotel in Washington D.C. where the initial 1959 meeting took place.[1]

The founding members were economists who found it increasingly difficult to get their papers included on sessions sponsored by the American Economics Association.[2] Although the AEA was founded by the institutionalist economist Richard T. Ely, by the 1950s it had drifted away from the institutionalist approach and towards abstract mathematical modelling. The members of AFEE are sometimes called "old institutionalists"[3] to distinguish them for the followers of New Institutional Economics.

The Wardman Group renamed itself the Association for Evolutionary Economics (AFEE) in 1965. Clarence E. Ayres was elected the first president and he presided over presentations at the ASSA meetings in San Francisco in December 1966. In 1967, AFEE began publishing a quarterly academic journal, the Journal of Economic Issues.

In the 1970's, the "old institutionalists" competed with the Marxists and the Post Keynesians for prominence within heterodox economics but by the 1980's they began to be noticed once again.[3] In 1979, some members of AFEE who thought it had deviated too far from its roots, formed a sister organization, the Association for Institutionalist Thought (AFIT).[4] The stature of old, or original, institutional economics was further strengthened by the formation in 1988 of the European Association for Evolutionary Political Economy.

2.4.2 Aims and Scope

AFEE views itself as running parallel to the AEA in covering all areas of economics. It places less stress on mathematical model building and more on a realistic analysis of economic policy issues. It is open to interdisciplinary approaches that incorporate insights from history, psychology, management science and political science. Moreover, it stresses the importance of broadening the scope of economics to consider questions of economic ends, as well as economic means.[5] Since its founding, AFEE has confronted issues of environmental degradation, inequality, corporate power, the negative effect of advertising and the limitations of economic growth as a measure of economic success.

2.4.3 Awards and Scholarships

The Veblen-Commons Award is given annually in recognition of the contributions made by an outstanding scholar in the field of evolutionary institutional economics. Past recipients include Gunnar Myrdal, John Kenneth Galbraith, Gardiner Means, and Hyman Minsky.

The James H. Street Latin American Scholarship is awarded to a person residing in Latin America and working within the tradition of original institutional economics. The James H. Street scholar is awarded round trip transportation and accommodation at the ASSA meetings and given the opportunity to present his or her work.

2.4.4 Criticisms

AFEE is criticized for failing to adhere to the modern standards of the economics profession that requires theories be expressed in mathematical form. With their tradition of advocating government solutions to economics problems, they have also been criticized for being ideologically biased towards the left of the political spectrum.

2.4.5 References

[1] Rutherford, Malcolm (2001). "Institutional Economics: Then and Now". *The Journal of Economic Perspectives* **15** (3): 185. doi:10.1257/jep.15.3.173.

[2] Bush, Paul Dale (June 1991). "Reflections on the Twenty-Fifth Anniversary of AFEE". *Journal of Economic Issues* **XXV** (2): 322.

[3] Hodgson, Geoffrey M. (2002). *A Modern Reader in Institutional and Evolutionary Economics: Key Concepts*. Edward Elgar Publishing Ltd. pp. xvi. ISBN 1 84064 495 8.

[4] O'Hara, Phillip Anthony (2000). "Association for Evolutionary Economics and Association for Institutionalist Thought". *Encyclopedia of Political Economy* **1**. Routledge. pp. 20–23. ISBN 0415241863.

[5] Gruchy, Allan G. (March 1969). "Neoinstitutionalism and the Economics of Dissent". *Journal of Economic Issues* **3** (1): 3.

2.4.6 External links

- Association for Evolutionary Economics

2.5 Austrian School

The **Austrian School** is a school of economic thought that is based on the concept of methodological individualism – that social phenomena result from the motivations and actions of individuals.[1][2][3][4] It originated in the late-19th and early-20th century Vienna with the work of Carl Menger, Eugen Böhm von Bawerk, Friedrich von Wieser, and others.[5] It was methodologically opposed to the Prussian Historical School (a dispute known as Methodenstreit). Current-day economists working in this tradition are located in many different countries, but their work is referred to as **Austrian economics**.

Among the theoretical contributions of the early years of the Austrian School are the subjective theory of value, marginalism in price theory, and the formulation of the economic calculation problem, each of which has become an accepted part of mainstream economics.[6]

Many economists are critical of the current-day Austrian School and consider its rejection of econometrics and aggregate macroeconomic analysis to be outside of mainstream economic theory, or "heterodox."[7][8][9][10] Austrians are likewise critical of mainstream economics.[11] Although the Austrian School has been considered heterodox since the late 1930s, it began to attract renewed academic and public interest starting in the 1970s.[12]

2.5.1 Methodology

Main articles: Action axiom, Catallactics and Praxeology

The Austrian School theorizes that the subjective choices of individuals including individual knowledge, time, expectation, and other subjective factors, cause all economic phenomena. Austrians seek to understand the economy by examining the social ramifications of individual choice, an approach called *methodological individualism*. It differs from other schools of economic thought, which have focused on aggregate variables, equilibrium analysis, and societal groups rather than individuals.[13]

In the twentieth and twenty-first centuries, economists with a methodological lineage to the early Austrian School developed many diverse approaches and theoretical orientations. For example, in 1949, Ludwig von Mises organized his version of the subjectivist approach, which he called "praxeology", in a book published in English as *Human Action*.[14]:3 In it, Mises stated that praxeology could be used to deduce *a priori* theoretical economic truths and that deductive economic thought experiments could yield conclusions which follow irrefutably from the underlying assumptions. He claimed conclusions could not be inferred from empirical observation or statistical analysis and argued against the use of probabilities in economic models.[15]

Since Mises' time, some Austrian thinkers have accepted his praxeological approach, while others have adopted alternative methodologies.[16] For example, Fritz Machlup, Friedrich Hayek, and others, did not take Mises' strong *a priori* approach to economics.[17]:225–235 Ludwig Lachmann, a radical subjectivist, also largely rejected Mises' formulation of Praxeology in favor of the *verstehende Methode* (interpretive method) articulated by Max Weber.[13][18]

In the 20th century, various Austrians incorporated models

Ludwig von Mises

and mathematics into their analysis. Austrian economist Steven Horwitz argued in 2000, that Austrian methodology is consistent with macroeconomics and that Austrian macroeconomics can be expressed in terms of microeconomic foundations.[19] Austrian economist Roger Garrison claims that Austrian macroeconomic theory can be correctly expressed in terms of diagrammatic models.[20] In 1944, Austrian economist Oskar Morgenstern presented a rigorous schematization of an ordinal utility function (the Von Neumann–Morgenstern utility theorem) in Theory of Games and Economic Behavior.[21]

2.5.2 Fundamental tenets

Fritz Machlup listed the typical views of Austrian economic thinking.[22]

> (1) Methodological Individualism: In the explanation of economic phenomena we have to go back to the actions (or inaction) of individuals; groups or "collectives" cannot act except through the actions of individual members.

> (2) Methodological Subjectivism: In the explanation of economic phenomena we have to go back to judgments and choices made by individuals on the basis of whatever knowledge they have or believe to have and whatever expectations they entertain regarding external developments and especially the perceived consequences of their own intended actions.

> (3) Tastes and Preferences: Subjective valuations of goods and services determine the demand for them so that their prices are influenced by (actual and potential) consumers.

> (4) Opportunity Costs: The costs with which producers and other economic actors calculate reflect the alternative opportunities that must be foregone; as productive services are employed for one purpose, all alternative uses have to be sacrificed.

> (5) Marginalism: In all economic designs, the values, costs, revenues, productivity, etc., are determined by the significance of the last unit added to or subtracted from the total.

> (6) Time Structure of Production and Consumption: Decisions to save reflect "time preferences" regarding consumption in the immediate, distant, or indefinite future, and investments are made in view of larger outputs expected to be obtained if more time-taking production processes are undertaken.

Two important tenets held by the Misesian branch of Austrian economics may also be added to the list:

> (7) Consumer Sovereignty: The influence consumers have on the effective demand for goods and services and, through the prices which result in free competitive markets, on the production plans of producers and investors, is not merely a hard fact but also an important objective, attainable only by complete avoidance of governmental interference with the markets and of restrictions on the freedom of sellers and buyers to follow their own judgment regarding quantities, quali-ties, and prices of products and ser-

vices.

(8) Political Individualism: Only when individuals are given full economic freedom will it be possible to secure political and moral freedom. Restrictions on economic freedom lead, sooner or later, to an extension of the coercive activities of the state into the political domain, undermining and eventually destroying the essential individual liberties which the capitalistic societies were able to attain in the nineteenth century.

2.5.3 Contributions to economic thought

Opportunity cost

Main article: Opportunity cost

The opportunity cost doctrine was first explicitly formulated by the Austrian economist Friedrich von Wieser in the late 19th century.[23] Opportunity cost is the cost of any activity measured in terms of the value of the next best alternative foregone (that is not chosen). It is the sacrifice related to the second best choice available to someone, or group, who has picked among several mutually exclusive choices.[24]

Opportunity cost is a key concept in mainstream economics, and has been described as expressing "the basic relationship between scarcity and choice".[25] The notion of opportunity cost plays a crucial part in ensuring that resources are used efficiently.[26]

Capital and interest

See also: Capital and Interest, Marginalism, Neutrality of money and Time preference

The Austrian theory of capital and interest was first developed by Eugen Böhm von Bawerk. He stated that interest rates and profits are determined by two factors, namely, supply and demand in the market for final goods and time preference.[27][28]

Böhm-Bawerk's theory was a response to Marx's labor theory of value and capital. Böhm-Bawerk's theory attacked the viability of the labor theory of value in the light of the transformation problem. His conception of interest countered Marx's exploitation theory. Marx famously argued that capitalists exploit workers by paying them less than the fruits of their labor sell for. Bohm-Bawerk countered this claim by invoking the concept of time preference to demonstrate that everyone values present consumption more than

Friedrich von Wieser

Eugen Böhm von Bawerk

future consumption, and therefore that a difference between the (smaller) salary laborers are paid in the present and the (greater) price for which the goods they produce are later sold need not be exploitative.[28]

Böhm-Bawerk's theory equates capital intensity with the degree of roundaboutness of production processes. Böhm-Bawerk also argued that the law of marginal utility necessarily implies the classical law of costs.[27] Some Austrian economists therefore entirely reject the notion that interest rates are affected by liquidity preference.

Inflation

See also: Monetary inflation

In Mises's definition, inflation is an increase in the supply of money:[29]

> In theoretical investigation there is only one meaning that can rationally be attached to the expression Inflation: an increase in the quantity of money (in the broader sense of the term, so as to include fiduciary media as well), that is not offset by a corresponding increase in the need for money (again in the broader sense of the term), so that a fall in the objective exchange-value of money must occur.[30]

Hayek pointed out that inflationary stimulation exploits the lag between an increase in money supply and the consequent increase in the prices of goods and services:

> And since any inflation, however modest at first, can help employment only so long as it accelerates, adopted as a means of reducing unemployment, it will do so for any length of time only while it accelerates. "Mild" steady inflation cannot help—it can lead only to outright inflation. That inflation at a constant rate soon ceases to have any stimulating effect, and in the end merely leaves us with a backlog of delayed adaptations, is the conclusive argument against the "mild" inflation represented as beneficial even in standard economics textbooks.[31]

Economic calculation problem

Main article: Economic calculation problem
The economic calculation problem refers to a criticism of socialism which was first stated by Max Weber in 1920. Mises subsequently discussed Weber's idea with his student

Friedrich Hayek

Friedrich Hayek, who developed it in various works including *The Road to Serfdom*.[32][33] The problem concerns the means by which resources are allocated and distributed in an economy.

Austrian theory emphasizes the organizing power of markets. Hayek stated that market prices reflect information, the totality of which is not known to any single individual, which determines the allocation of resources in an economy. Because socialist systems lack the individual incentives and price discovery processes by which individuals act on their personal information, Hayek argued that socialist economic planners lack all of the knowledge required to make optimal decisions. Those who agree with this criticism view it as a refutation of socialism showing that socialism is not a viable or sustainable form of economic organization. The debate rose to prominence in the 1920s and 1930s, and that specific period of the debate has come to be known by historians of economic thought as *The Socialist Calculation Debate*.[34]

Mises argued in a 1920 essay "Economic Calculation in the Socialist Commonwealth" that the pricing systems in socialist economies were necessarily deficient because if government owned the means of production, then no prices could be obtained for capital goods as they were merely internal transfers of goods in a socialist system and not "objects of exchange," unlike final goods. Therefore, they were unpriced and hence the system would be necessarily inefficient since the central planners would not know how to allocate the available resources efficiently.[34] This led him to write "that rational economic activity is impossible in a socialist commonwealth."[35]

Business cycles

Main article: Austrian business cycle theory

The Austrian theory of the business cycle ("ABCT") focuses on banks' issuance of credit as the cause of economic fluctuations. Although later elaborated by Hayek and others, the theory was first set forth by Mises, who believed that banks extend credit at artificially low interest rates, causing businesses to invest in relatively roundabout production processes. Mises stated that this led to a misallocation of resources which he called *malinvestment*.

According to the theory, malinvestment is induced by banks' excessive and unsustainable expansion of credit to businesses.[36] Businesses borrow at unsustainably low interest rates and overinvest in capital-intensive production processes, which in turn leads to a diversion of investment from consumer goods industries to capital goods industries. Austrians contend that this shift is unsustainable and must eventually be reversed, and that the re-adjustment process will be more violent and disruptive the longer the putative malinvestment in capital goods industries continues.

According to the Austrian view, the proportion of income allocated to consumption rather than saving is determined by the interest rate and people's time preference, which is the degree to which they prefer present to future satisfactions. According to this view, the pure interest rate is determined by the time preferences of the individuals in society. If the market rate of interest offered by banks is set lower than this, business borrowing will be excessive and will be allocated to malinvestment.[37]

Newly extended credit thus malinvested will circulate from the business borrowers to the factors of production: landowners, capital goods producers, and capital goods workers. Austrians state that, because individuals' time preferences have not changed, the market will tend to reestablish the old proportions between current and future production. Depositors will tend to remove cash from the banking system and spend it (not save it), banks will then ask their borrowers for repayment, and the excessive capital goods will be liquidated at lower prices to retire the now-unprofitable loans.[36]

Role of government disputed According to Mises, central banks enable the commercial banks to fund loans at artificially low interest rates, thereby inducing an unsustainable expansion of bank credit and impeding any subsequent contraction.[36][38] [36][39] Friedrich Hayek disagreed. Prior to the 1970s, Hayek did not favor laissez-faire in banking and said that a freely competitive banking industry tends to be endogenously destabilizing and pro-cyclical, mimicking the effects which Rothbard attributed to central bank policy. Hayek stated that the need for central banking control was inescapable.[40]

2.5.4 History

Jean-Baptiste Say

Etymology

The Austrian School owes its name to members of the German Historical school of economics, who argued against the Austrians during the late-19th century *Methodenstreit* ("methodology struggle"), in which the Austrians defended the role of theory in economics as distinct from the study or compilation of historical circumstance. In 1883, Menger published *Investigations into the Method of the Social Sciences with Special Reference to Economics*, which attacked the methods of the Historical school. Gustav von Schmoller, a leader of the Historical school, responded with an unfavorable review, coining the term "Austrian School" in an attempt to characterize the school as outcast and provincial.[41] The label endured and was adopted by the adherents themselves.[42]

First Wave

Carl Menger

The school originated in Vienna, in the Austrian Empire. Carl Menger's 1871 book, *Principles of Economics*, is generally considered the founding of the Austrian School. The book was one of the first modern treatises to advance the theory of marginal utility. The Austrian School was one of three founding currents of the marginalist revolution of the 1870s, with its major contribution being the introduction of the subjectivist approach in economics.[43] While marginalism was generally influential, there was also a more specific school that began to coalesce around Menger's work, which came to be known as the "Psychological School," "Vienna School," or "Austrian School."[44]

Menger's contributions to economic theory were closely followed by those of Böhm-Bawerk and Friedrich von Wieser. These three economists became what is known as the "first wave" of the Austrian School. Böhm-Bawerk wrote extensive critiques of Karl Marx in the 1880s and 1890s, as was part of the Austrians' participation in the late 19th-century *Methodenstreit*, during which they attacked the Hegelian doctrines of the Historical School.

Early Twentieth Century in Vienna

Several important Austrian economists trained at the University of Vienna in the 1920s and later participated in the private seminar of Mises. These included Gottfried Haberler,[45] Friedrich Hayek, Fritz Machlup,[46] Karl Menger (son of Carl Menger),[47] Oskar Morgenstern,[48] Paul Rosenstein-Rodan[49] Abraham Wald,[50] among others.

Later Twentieth century

Israel Kirzner

By the mid-1930s, most economists had embraced what they considered the important contributions of the early Austrians.[8] After World War II, Austrian economics was disregarded or derided by most economists because it rejected mathematical and statistical methods in the study of economics.[51] Fritz Machlup quoted Hayek's statement, "the greatest success of a school is that it stops existing because its fundamental teachings have become parts of the general body of commonly accepted thought." [52] Mises' student, Israel Kirzner recalled that in 1954, when Kirzner was pursuing his PhD, there was no separate Austrian School as such. When Kirzner was deciding which graduate school to attend, Mises had advised him to accept an offer of admission at Johns Hopkins because it was a prestigious university and Fritz Machlup taught there.[53]

After 1940, Austrian economics can be divided into two schools of economic thought, and the school "split" to some degree in the late 20th century. One camp of Austrians, exemplified by Mises, regards neoclassical methodology to be irredeemably flawed; the other camp, exemplified by Friedrich Hayek, accepts a large part of neoclassical methodology and is more accepting of government intervention in the economy.[10][54]

Henry Hazlitt wrote economics columns and editorials for a number of publications and wrote many books on the topic of Austrian economics from the 1930s to the 1980s. Hazlitt's thinking was influenced by Mises.[55] His book *Economics in One Lesson* (1946) sold over a million copies, and he is also known for *The Failure of the "New Economics"* (1959), a line-by-line critique of John Maynard Keynes's *General Theory*.[56]

The reputation of the Austrian School rose in the late-20th century due in part to the work of Israel Kirzner and Ludwig Lachmann at New York University, and to renewed public awareness of the work of Hayek after he won the 1974 Nobel Memorial Prize in Economic Sciences.[12] Hayek's work was influential in the revival of *laissez-faire* thought in the 20th century.[57][58]

Split among contemporary Austrians

According to economist Bryan Caplan, by the late twentieth century, a split had developed among those who self-identify with the Austrian School. One group, building on the work of Hayek, follows the broad framework of mainstream neoclassical economics, including its use of mathematical models and general equilibrium, and brings a critical perspective to mainstream methodology merely influenced by the Austrian notions such as the economic calculation problem and the independent role of logical reasoning in developing economic theory.[59]

A second group, following Mises and Rothbard, rejects the neoclassical theories of consumer and welfare economics, dismisses empirical methods and mathematical and statistical models as inapplicable to economic science, and asserts that economic theory went entirely astray in the twentieth century; they offer the Misesian view as a radical alternative paradigm to mainstream theory. Caplan wrote that if "Mises and Rothbard are right, then [mainstream] economics is wrong; but if Hayek is right, then mainstream economics merely needs to adjust its focus."[59]

Economist Leland Yeager discussed the late twentieth century rift and referred to a discussion written by Murray Rothbard, Hans-Hermann Hoppe, Joseph Salerno, and others in which they attack and disparage Hayek. "To try to drive a wedge between Mises and Hayek on [the role of knowledge in economic calculation], especially to the dis-

Murray Rothbard

paragement of Hayek, is unfair to these two great men, unfaithful to the history of economic thought" and went on to call the rift subversive to economic analysis and the historical understanding of the fall of Eastern European communism.[60]

In a 1999 book published by the Ludwig von Mises Institute (Mises Institute),[61] Hans-Hermann Hoppe asserted that Murray Rothbard was the leader of the "mainstream within Austrian Economics" and contrasted Rothbard with Nobel Laureate Friedrich Hayek, whom he identified as a British empiricist and an opponent of the thought of Mises and Rothbard. Hoppe acknowledged that Hayek was the most prominent Austrian economist within academia, but stated that Hayek was an opponent of the Austrian tradition which led from Carl Menger and Böhm-Bawerk through Mises to Rothbard. Austrian economist Walter Block says that the "Austrian school" can be distinguished from other schools of economic thought through two categories - economic theory and political theory. According to Block, while Hayek can be considered an "Austrian economist", his views on political theory clash with the libertarian political theory which Block sees as an integral part of the Austrian school.[62]

Economists of the Hayekian view are affiliated with the Cato Institute, George Mason University (GMU), and New York University, among other institutions. They include Peter Boettke, Roger Garrison, Steven Horwitz, Peter Leeson and George Reisman. Economists of the Mises-Rothbard view include Walter Block, Hans-Hermann Hoppe, Jesús Huerta de Soto and Robert P. Murphy, each of whom is associated with the Mises Institute[63] and some of them also with academic institutions.[63] According to Murphy, a "truce between (for lack of better terms) the GMU Austro-libertarians and the Auburn Austro-libertarians" was signed around 2011.[64][65]

2.5.5 Influence

Many theories developed by "first wave" Austrian economists have long been absorbed into mainstream economics.[66] These include Carl Menger's theories on marginal utility, Friedrich von Wieser's theories on opportunity cost, and Eugen Böhm von Bawerk's theories on time preference, as well as Menger and Böhm-Bawerk's criticisms of Marxian economics.

Former U.S. Federal Reserve Chairman Alan Greenspan said that the founders of the Austrian School "reached far into the future from when most of them practiced and have had a profound and, in my judgment, probably an irreversible effect on how most mainstream economists think in this country."[67] In 1987, Nobel Laureate James M. Buchanan told an interviewer, "I have no objections to being called an Austrian. Hayek and Mises might consider me an Austrian but, surely some of the others would not."[68] Chinese economist Zhang Weiying, supports some Austrian theories such as the Austrian theory of the business cycle.[69]

Currently, universities with a significant Austrian presence are George Mason University, New York University, Loyola University New Orleans, and Auburn University in the United States, King Juan Carlos University in Spain and Universidad Francisco Marroquín in Guatemala. Austrian economic ideas are also promoted by privately funded organizations such as the Mises Institute,[70] and the Cato Institute.

2.5.6 Criticisms

General criticisms

Mainstream economists have argued that Austrians are often averse to the use of mathematics and statistics in economics.[71] However, independent scholar Martin Sibileau, in 2014, suggested a logics-based approach for a definitive formalization of the Austrian thought.[72]

Economist Bryan Caplan argues that many Austrians have not understood valid contributions of modern mainstream economics, causing them to overstate their differences with it. For example, Murray Rothbard stated that he objected to the use of cardinal utility in microeconomic theory. Caplan says that Rothbard did not understand the position he was attacking, because microeconomic theorists go to great pains to show that their results are derived for any monotonic transformation of an ordinal utility function, and do not entail cardinal utility.[59][73] The result is that conclusions about utility preferences hold no matter what values are assigned to them.

Economist Paul Krugman has stated that because Austrians do not use "explicit models" they are unaware of holes in their own thinking.[74]

Economist Benjamin Klein has criticized the economic methodological work of Austrian economist Israel M. Kirzner. While praising Kirzner for highlighting shortcomings in traditional methodology, Klein argued that Kirzner did not provide a viable alternative for economic methodology.[75] Economist Tyler Cowen has written that Kirzner's theory of entrepreneurship can ultimately be reduced to a neoclassical search model and is thus not in the radical subjectivist tradition of Austrian praxeology. Cowen states that Kirzner's entrepreneurs can be modeled in mainstream terms of search.[76]

Economist Jeffrey Sachs argues that among developed countries, those with high rates of taxation and high social welfare spending perform better on most measures of economic performance compared to countries with low rates of taxation and low social outlays. He concludes that Friedrich Hayek was wrong to argue that high levels of government spending harms an economy, and "a generous social-welfare state is not a road to serfdom but rather to fairness, economic equality and international competitiveness."[77] Austrian economist Sudha Shenoy responded by arguing that countries with large public sectors have grown more slowly.[78]

Economist Bryan Caplan has noted that Mises has been criticized as allegedly overstating the strength of his case in describing socialism as *impossible* rather than as something that would need to establish non-market institutions to deal with the inefficiency.[10][79]

Methodology

Critics generally argue that Austrian economics lacks scientific rigor and rejects scientific methods and the use of empirical data in modelling economic behavior.[10][71][80] Some economists describe Austrian methodology as being *a priori* or non-empirical.[10][71][81][82]

Economist Mark Blaug has criticized over-reliance on methodological individualism, arguing it would rule out all macroeconomic propositions that cannot be reduced to microeconomic ones, and hence reject almost the whole of received macroeconomics.[83]

Economist Thomas Mayer has stated that Austrians advocate a rejection of the scientific method which involves the development of empirically falsifiable theories.[80][82] Furthermore, many supporters of using models of market behavior to analyze and test economic theory argue that economists have developed numerous experiments that elicit useful information about individual preferences.[84][85]

Although economist Leland Yeager is sympathetic to Austrian economics, he rejects many favorite views of the Misesian group of Austrians, in particular, "the specifics of their business-cycle theory, ultra-subjectivism in value theory and particularly in interest-rate theory, their insistence on unidirectional causality rather than general interdependence, and their fondness for methodological brooding, pointless profundities, and verbal gymnastics."[86]

Economist Paul A. Samuelson wrote in 1964, most economists believe, that economic conclusions reached by pure logical deduction are limited and weak.[87] According to Samuelson and economist Bryan Caplan, Mises' deductive methodology also embraced by Murray Rothbard and to a lesser extent by Mises' student, Israel Kirzner was not sufficient in and of itself.[81] Bryan Caplan wrote that the Austrian challenge to the realism of neoclassical assumptions helped work towards making those assumptions more plausible.[59]

Business cycle theory

Some research regarding Austrian business cycle theory finds that it is inconsistent with empirical evidence. Economists such as Gordon Tullock,[88] Bryan Caplan,[10] Milton Friedman,[89][90] and Paul Krugman[91] have said that they regard the theory as incorrect. Austrian economist Ludwig Lachmann noted that the Austrian theory was rejected during the 1930s:

> The promise of an Austrian theory of the trade cycle, which might also serve to explain the severity of the Great Depression, a feature of the early 1930s that provided the background for Hayek's successful appearance on the London scene, soon proved deceptive. Three giants – Keynes, Knight and Sraffa – turned against the hapless Austrians who, in the middle of that black decade, thus had to do battle on three fronts. Naturally it proved a task beyond their strength.[92]

Theoretical objections Some economists argue that Austrian business cycle theory requires bankers and investors to exhibit a kind of irrationality, because the Austrian theory posits that investors will be fooled repeatedly (by temporarily low interest rates) into making unprofitable investment decisions.[10][88][93] Bryan Caplan writes: "Why does Rothbard think businessmen are so incompetent at forecasting government policy? He credits them with entrepreneurial foresight about all market-generated conditions, but curiously finds them unable to forecast government policy, or even to avoid falling prey to simple accounting illusions generated by inflation and deflation... Particularly in interventionist economies, it would seem that natural selection would weed out businesspeople with such a gigantic blind spot."[94]

Economist Paul Krugman has argued that the theory cannot explain changes in unemployment over the business cycle. Austrian business cycle theory postulates that business cycles are caused by the misallocation of resources from consumption to investment during "booms", and out of investment during "busts". Krugman argues that because total spending is equal to total income in an economy, the theory implies that the reallocation of resources during "busts" would increase employment in consumption industries, whereas in reality, spending declines in all sectors of an economy during recessions. He also argues that according to the theory the initial "booms" would also cause resource reallocation, which implies an increase in unemployment during booms as well.[91]

In response, historian David Gordon argues that Krugman's analysis misrepresents Austrian theory. Gordon states, "unemployment, as Austrians see matters, stems mainly from rigid wage rates. If workers accept a fall in wages, liquidation of the boom is compatible with full employment."[95] Austrian economist Roger Garrison states that a false boom caused by artificially low interest rates would cause a boom in consumption goods as well as investment goods (with a decrease in "middle goods"), thus explaining the jump in unemployment at the end of a boom.[96] Garrison has also stated that capital allocated to investment goods cannot always be redeployed to create consumption goods.[97]

Economist Jeffery Hummel is critical of Hayek's explanation of labor asymmetry in booms and busts. He argues that Hayek makes peculiar assumptions about demand curves for labor in his explanation of how a decrease in investment spending creates unemployment. He also argues that the labor asymmetry can be explained in terms of a change in real wages, but this explanation fails to explain the business cycle in terms of resource allocation.[98]

Milton Friedman objected to the policy implications of the theory, stating the following in a 1998 interview:

I think the Austrian business-cycle theory has done the world a great deal of harm. If you go back to the 1930s, which is a key point, here you had the Austrians sitting in London, Hayek and Lionel Robbins, and saying you just have to let the bottom drop out of the world. You've just got to let it cure itself. You can't do anything about it. You will only make it worse. You have Rothbard saying it was a great mistake not to let the whole banking system collapse. I think by encouraging that kind of do-nothing policy both in Britain and in the United States, they did harm.[99]

Empirical objections Hummel argues that the Austrian explanation of the business cycle fails on empirical grounds. In particular, he notes that investment spending remained positive in all recessions where there are data, except for the Great Depression. He argues that this casts doubt on the notion that recessions are caused by a reallocation of resources from industrial production to consumption, since he argues that the Austrian business cycle theory implies that net investment should be below zero during recessions.[98] In response, Austrian economist Walter Block argues that the misallocation during booms does not preclude the possibility of demand increasing overall.[100]

In 1969, economist Milton Friedman, after examining the history of business cycles in the U.S., concluded that "The Hayek-Mises explanation of the business cycle is contradicted by the evidence. It is, I believe, false."[89] He analyzed the issue using newer data in 1993, and again reached the same conclusion.[90] Referring to Friedman's discussion of the business cycle, Austrian economist Roger Garrison argued that Friedman's empirical findings are broadly consistent with both Monetarist and Austrian views", and goes on to argue that although Friedman's model "describes the economy's performance at the highest level of aggregation; Austrian theory offers an insightful account of the market process that might underlie those aggregates."[101]

2.5.7 Principal works

- *Principles of Economics* (1871) by Carl Menger[2]

- *Capital and Interest* (1884, 1889, 1921) by Eugen Böhm von Bawerk[2]

- *The Theory of Money and Credit* (1912) by Ludwig von Mises[2]

- *Human Action* (1949) by Ludwig von Mises[2]

- *Individualism and Economic Order* (1949) by Friedrich A. Hayek[2]

- *Man, Economy, and State* (1962) by Murray N. Rothbard[2]

2.5.8 See also

- List of Austrian School economists
- List of Austrian intellectual traditions
- Perspectives on capitalism
- *Quarterly Journal of Austrian Economics*
- New Institutional Economics

2.5.9 References and notes

[1] Carl Menger, Principles of Economics, online at https://www.mises.org/etexts/menger/principles.asp

[2] Boettke, Peter J. (2008). "Austrian School of Economics". In David R. Henderson (ed.). *Concise Encyclopedia of Economics* (2nd ed.). Library of Economics and Liberty. ISBN 978-0865976658. OCLC 237794267.

[3] Methodological Individualism at the Stanford Encyclopedia of Philosophy

[4] Ludwig von Mises. Human Action, p. 11, "r. Purposeful Action and Animal Reaction". Referenced 2011-11-23.

[5] Joseph A. Schumpeter, History of economic analysis, Oxford University Press 1996, ISBN 978-0195105599.

[6] Birner, Jack; van Zijp, Rudy (1994). *Hayek, Co-ordination and Evolution: His Legacy in Philosophy, Politics, Economics and the History of Ideas*. London, New York: Routledge. p. 94. ISBN 978-0-415-09397-2.

[7] Boettke, Peter. "Is Austrian Economics Heterodox Economics?". The Austrian Economists. Archived from the original on 28 March 2009. Retrieved 2009-02-13.

[8] Boettke, Peter J.; Peter T. Leeson (2003). "28A: The Austrian School of Economics 1950-2000". In Warren Samuels, Jeff E. Biddle, and John B. Davis. *A Companion to the History of Economic Thought*. Blackwell Publishing. pp. 446–452. ISBN 978-0-631-22573-7.

[9] "Heterodox economics: Marginal revolutionaries". The Economist. December 31, 2011. Retrieved February 22, 2012.

[10] Caplan, Bryan. "Why I Am Not an Austrian Economist". Bryan Caplan at George Mason University faculty page. Retrieved 2008-07-04. ...More than anything else, what prevents Austrians from getting more publications in mainstream journals is that their papers rarely use mathematics or econometrics, research tools that Austrians reject on principle. ...Mises and Rothbard however err when they say that

economic history can *only* illustrate economic theory. In particular, empirical evidence is often necessary to determine whether a theoretical factor is *quantitatively significant*. ...Austrians reject econometrics on principle because economic theory is true a priori, so statistics or historical study cannot 'test' theory....

[11] Austrian Economics and the Mainstream: View from the Boundary, Roger E. Backhouse

[12] Meijer, G. (1995). *New Perspectives on Austrian Economics*. New York: Routledge. ISBN 978-0-415-12283-2.

[13] White, Lawrence H. (2003). *The Methodology of the Austrian School Economists* (revised ed.). Ludwig von Mises Institute.

[14] Ludwig von Mises, Nationalökonomie (Geneva: Union, 1940); Human Action (Auburn, Ala.: Ludwig von Mises Institute, [1949] 1998)

[15] "The Ultimate Foundation of Economic Science by Ludwig von Mises". Mises.org. Retrieved 2012-08-13.

[16] Bruce J. Caldwell "Praxeology and its Critics: an Appraisal" History of Political Economy Fall 1984 16(3): 363–379; doi:10.1215/00182702-16-3-363 Praxeology and Its Critics PDF

[17] Richard N. Langlois, "FROM THE KNOWLEDGE OF ECONOMICS TO THE ECONOMICS OF KNOWLEDGE: FRITZ MACHLUP ON METHODOLOGY AND ON THE "KNOWLEDGE SOCIETY" Research in the History of Economic Thought and Methodology, Volume 3, Machlup Knowledge PDF, 1985.

[18] Lachmann, Ludwig (1973). *Macroeconomic Thinking and the Market Economy* (PDF). Institute of Economic Affairs.

[19] Horwitz, Steven: Microfoundations and Macroeconomics: An Austrian Perspective (2000)|*Routledge*

[20] Garrison, Roger (1978). "Austrian Macroeconomics: A Diagrammatical Exposition" (PDF). Institute for Humane Studies. Retrieved 5 October 2015.

[21] Neumann, John von and Morgenstern, Oskar Theory of Games and Economic Behavior. Princeton, NJ. Princeton University Press. 1944

[22] Machlup, Fritz (1981). "Homage to Mises". Hillsdale College. pp. 19–27. Retrieved 8 August 2013.

[23] Kirzner, Israel M.; Lachman, Ludwig M. (1986). *Subjectivism, intelligibility and economic understanding: essays in honor of Ludwig M. Lachmann on his eightieth birthday* (Illustrated ed.). McMillan. ISBN 978-0-333-41788-1.

[24] "Opportunity Cost". *Investopedia*. Archived from the original on 14 September 2010. Retrieved 2010-09-18.

[25] James M. Buchanan (2008). "Opportunity cost". *The New Palgrave Dictionary of Economics Online* (Second ed.). Retrieved 2010-09-18.

[26] "Opportunity Cost". *Economics A–Z* (The Economist). Archived from the original on 9 October 2010. Retrieved 2010-09-18.

[27] Böhm-Bawerk, Eugen Ritter von; *Kapital Und Kapitalizns. Zweite Abteilung: Positive Theorie des Kapitales* (1889). Translated as *Capital and Interest. II: Positive Theory of Capital* with appendices rendered as *Further Essays on Capital and Interest*.

[28] http://www.econlib.org/library/Enc/bios/BohmBawerk.html

[29] von Mises, Ludwig (1980). "Economic Freedom and Interventionism". In Greaves, Bettina B. *Economics of Mobilization*. Sulphur Springs, West Virginia: The Commercial and Financial Chronicle. Inflation, as this term was always used everywhere and especially in this country, means increasing the quantity of money and bank notes in circulation and the quantity of bank deposits subject to check. But people today use the term "inflation" to refer to the phenomenon that is an inevitable consequence of inflation, that is the tendency of all prices and wage rates to rise. The result of this deplorable confusion is that there is no term left to signify the cause of this rise in prices and wages. There is no longer any word available to signify the phenomenon that has been, up to now, called inflation. ... As you cannot talk about something that has no name, you cannot fight it. Those who pretend to fight inflation are in fact only fighting what is the inevitable consequence of inflation, rising prices. Their ventures are doomed to failure because they do not attack the root of the evil. They try to keep prices low while firmly committed to a policy of increasing the quantity of money that must necessarily make them soar. As long as this terminological confusion is not entirely wiped out, there cannot be any question of stopping inflation.

[30] The Theory of Money and Credit, Mises (1912, [1981], p. 272)

[31] Hayek, Friedrich August ♦ 1980s Unemployment and the Unions: Essays on the Impotent Price Structure of Britain and Monopoly in the Labour Market Institute of Economic Affairs, 1984

[32] Von Mises, Ludwig (1990). *Economic calculation in the Socialist Commonwealth* (PDF). Ludwig von Mises Institute. ISBN 0-945466-07-2. Archived (PDF) from the original on 23 September 2008. Retrieved 2008-09-08.

[33] F. A. Hayek, (1935), "The Nature and History of the Problem" and "The Present State of the Debate," om in F. A. Hayek, ed. *Collectivist Economic Planning*, pp. 1–40, 201–243.

[34] The socialist calculation debate Archived February 18, 2009 at the Wayback Machine

[35] Ludwig von Mises. "The Principle of Methodological Individualism". *Human Action*. Ludwig von Mises Institute. Archived from the original on 22 April 2009. Retrieved 2009-04-24.

[36] Theory of Money and Credit, Ludwig von Mises, Part III, Part IV

[37] Theory of Money and Credit, Ludwig von Mises, Part II

[38] The Mystery of Banking, Murray Rothbard, 1983

[39] *America's Great Depression*, Murray Rothbard

[40] White, Lawrence H. (1999). "Why Didn't Hayek Favor Laissez Faire in Banking?" (PDF). *History of Political Economy* **31** (4): 753. doi:10.1215/00182702-31-4-753. Retrieved 11 April 2013.

[41] "Menger's approach – haughtily dismissed by the leader of the German Historical School, Gustav Schmoller, as merely "Austrian," the origin of that label – led to a renaissance of theoretical economics in Europe and, later, in the United States." Peter G. Klein, 2007; in the Foreword to *Principles of Economics*, Carl Menger; trns. James Dingwall and Bert F. Hoselitz, 1976; Ludwig von Mises Institute, Alabama; 2007; ISBN 978-1-933550-12-1

[42] von Mises, Ludwig (1984) [1969]. *The Historical Setting of the Austrian School of Economics* (PDF). Ludwig von Mises Institute.

[43] Keizer, Willem (1997). *Austrian Economics in Debate*. New York: Routledge. ISBN 978-0-415-14054-6.

[44] Israel M. Kirzner (1987). "Austrian School of Economics," *The New Palgrave: A Dictionary of Economics*, v. 1, pp. 145–151.

[45] https://mises.org/page/1452/Biography-of-Gottfried-Haberler-19011995

[46] "Biography of Fritz Machlup". Retrieved 16 June 2013.

[47] http://www.iit.edu/csl/am/about/menger/about.shtml

[48] http://library.duke.edu/rubenstein/findingaids/morgenst/

[49] http://archives.lse.ac.uk/Record.aspx?src=CalmView.Catalog&id=COLL+MISC+0324 Archive at London School of Economics

[50] Oskar Morgenstern (Oct 1951). "Abraham Wald, 1902–1950". *Econometrica* (The Econometric Society) **19** (4): 361–367. doi:10.2307/1907462. JSTOR 1907462.

[51] "Austrian economics and the mainstream: View from the boundary" by Roger E. Backhouse, $34 to view Archived July 2, 2013 at the Wayback Machine

[52] https://mises.org/daily/1700/Ludwig-von-Mises-A-Scholar-Who-Would-Not-Compromise Homage to Mises by Fritz Machlup 1981

[53] Kirzner, Israel. "Interview of Israel Kirzner". Ludwig von Mises Institute. Retrieved 17 June 2013.

[54] https://mises.org/journals/qjae/pdf/qjae7_1_3.pdf

[55] "Remembering Henry Hazlitt". The Freeman. Retrieved 2013-03-11.

[56] "Biography of Henry Hazlitt". Ludwig von Mises Institute. Retrieved 2013-03-11.

[57] Raico, Ralph (2011). "Austrian Economics and Classical Liberalism". mises.org. Ludwig von Mises Institute. Retrieved 27 July 2011. despite the particular policy views of its founders ..., Austrianism was perceived as the economics of the free market

[58] Kasper, Sherryl Davis (2002). *The Revival of Laissez-faire in American Macroeconomic Theory*. Edward Elgar Publishing. p. 66. ISBN 978-1-84064-606-1.

[59] Caplan, Bryan (1999). "The Austrian Search for Realistic Foundations" (PDF). *Southern Economic Journal* **65** (4): 823–838. doi:10.2307/1061278. JSTOR 1061278.

[60] Yaeger, Leland (2011). *Is the Market a Test of Truth and Beauty?: Essays in Political Economy*. Ludwig von Mises Institute. pp. 93 ff.

[61] Hoppe, Hans-Hermann (1999). *15 Great Austrian Economists – Murray Rothbard* (PDF). Alabama: Ludwig von Mises Institute. pp. 223 ff.

[62] "Dr. Walter Block: Austrian vs Chicago Schools". Mises Canada : Rothbard School 2014. Retrieved 3 December 2014.

[63] "Senior Fellows, Faculty Members, and Staff". Mises.org. Retrieved July 21, 2013.

[64] Robert Murphy blog, December 31, 2011.

[65] Yeager, Leland (2011). *Is the Market a Test of Truth and Beauty?*. Ludwig von Mises Institute. p. 103.

[66] It has also influenced related disciplines such as Law and Economics, see. K. Grechenig, M. Litschka, Law by Human Intent or Evolution? Some Remarks on the Austrian School of Economics' Role in the Development of Law and Economics, European Journal of Law and Economics (EJLE) 2010, vol. 29 (1), p. 57-79.

[67] Greenspan, Alan. "Hearings before the U.S. House of Representatives' Committee on Financial Services." U.S. House of Representatives' Committee on Financial Services. Washington D.C.. 25 July 2000.

[68] An Interview with Laureate James Buchanan Austrian Economics Newsletter: Volume 9, Number 1; Fall 1987

[69] Weiyin, Zhang, "Completely bury Keynesianism", http://finance.sina.com.cn/20090217/10345864499_3.shtml (February 17, 2009)

[70] "About the Mises Institute". Mises.org. Retrieved July 21, 2013.

[71] White, Lawrence H. (2008). "The research program of Austrian economics". *Advances in Austrian Economics* (Emerald Group Publishing Limited): 20.

[72] Sibileau, Martin (December 2014). "Formalizing the Austrian thought: A suggested approach". *Procesos de Mercado* **11** (2): 329–342.

[73] Caplan, Bryan. "Why I Am Not an Austrian Economist". George Mason University. Retrieved 2008-07-04. According to Rothbard, the mainstream approach credulously accepted the use of cardinal utility, when only the use of ordinal utility is defensible. As Rothbard insists, "Value scales of each individual are purely ordinal, and there is no way whatever of measuring the distance between the rankings; indeed, any concept of such distance is a fallacious one." ...As plausible as Rothbard sounds on this issue, he simply does not understand the position he is attacking. The utility function approach is based as squarely on ordinal utility as Rothbard's is. The modern neoclassical theorists – such as Arrow and Debreau – who developed the utility function approach went out of their way to avoid the use of cardinal utility. ...To sum up, Rothbard falsely accused neoclassical utility theory of assuming cardinality. It does not.

[74] Krugman, Paul (7 April 2010). "The Conscience of a Liberal: Martin And The Austrians". *The New York Times*. Retrieved 2011-09-21.

[75] Klein, Benjamin. "Book review: *Competition and Entrepreneurship*" (by Israel M. Kirzner, University of Chicago Press, 1973) *Journal of Political Economy*. Vol. 83: No. 6, 1305–1306, December 1975.

[76] Cowen, Tyler (May 2003). "Entrepreneurship, Austrian Economics, and the Quarrel Between Philosophy and Poetry". *Review of Austrian Economics* **16** (1): 5. doi:10.1023/A:1022958406273.

[77] Sachs, Jeffrey (October 2006). "The Social Welfare State, Beyond Ideology". *Scientific American*. Retrieved 2008-06-20.

[78] Sudha R. Shenoy, *Are High Taxes the Basis of Freedom and Prosperity?*, http://www.thefreemanonline.org/featured/are-high-taxes-the-basis-of-freedom-and-prosperity/

[79] Caplan, Bryan (2004). "Is socialism really "impossible"?". *Critical Review* **16**: 33–52. doi:10.1080/08913810408443598.

[80] "Rules for the study of natural philosophy", Newton 1999, pp. 794–6, from Book **3**, *The System of the World*.

[81] Samuelson, Paul A. (September 1964). "Theory and Realism: A Reply". *The American Economic Review* (American Economic Association): 736–739. Well, in connection with the exaggerated claims that used to be made in economics for the power of deduction and a priori reasoning ..... – I tremble for the reputation of my subject. Fortunately, we have left that behind us.

[82] Mayer, Thomas (Winter 1998). "Boettke's Austrian critique of mainstream economics: An empiricist's response". *Critical Review* (Routledge) **12**: 151–171. doi:10.1080/08913819808443491.

[83] Blaug, Mark (1992). *The Methodology of Economics: Or, How Economists Explain*. Cambridge University Press. pp. 45–46. ISBN 0-521-43678-8.

[84] Morgan, Mary S. (2008). "Models". *The New Palgrave Dictionary of Economics*. Retrieved 22 November 2011.

[85] Hoover, Kevin D. (2008). "Causality in economics and econometrics". *The New Palgrave Dictionary of Economics*. Retrieved 22 November 2011.

[86] Yeager, Leland B (1997). "Austrian Economics, Neoclassicism, and the Market Test". *Journal of Economic Perspectives* **11** (4): 153–165. doi:10.1257/jep.11.4.153.

[87] Samuelson, Paul (1964). *Economics* (6th ed.). New York: McGraw-Hill. p. 736. ISBN 978-0-07-074741-8.

[88] Gordon Tullock (1988). "Why the Austrians are wrong about depressions" (PDF). *The Review of Austrian Economics* **2** (1): 73–78. doi:10.1007/BF01539299. Retrieved 2009-06-24.

[89] Friedman, Milton. "The Monetary Studies of the National Bureau, 44th Annual Report". *The Optimal Quantity of Money and Other Essays*. Chicago: Aldine. pp. 261–284.

[90] Friedman, Milton. "The 'Plucking Model' of Business Fluctuations Revisited". *Economic Inquiry*: 171–177.

[91] Krugman, Paul (1998-12-04). "The Hangover Theory". Slate. Archived from the original on 2010-11-07. Retrieved 2008-06-20.

[92] Ludwig M. Lachmann, in The Market as an Economic Process (Oxford, 1986), p. ix

[93] Problems with Austrian Business Cycle Theory

[94] Caplan, Bryan (February 12, 2009). "What's Wrong With Austrian Business Cycle Theory" (news). Liberty Fund, Inc. Retrieved 2010-05-17.

[95] Hangover Theory: How Paul Krugman Has Misconceived Austrian Theory – David Gordon – Mises Daily

[96] Auburn User. "Overconsumption And Forced Saving". Auburn.edu. Retrieved 2012-08-15.

[97] Roger W. Garrison. "Hayek on Industrial Fluctuations – Roger W. Garrison – Mises Daily". Mises.org. Retrieved 2012-08-13.

[98] Hummel, Jeffery Rogers (Winter 1979). *Reason Papers* "Problems with Austrian Business Cycle Theory" Check |url= value (help) (PDF). pp. 41–53. Retrieved 2011-09-17.

[99] Interview in *Barron's Magazine*, August 24, 1998 archived at Hoover Institution

[100] http://www.reasonpapers.com/pdf/30/rp_30_4.pdf

[101] Auburn User (1982-10-25). "Plucking Model". Auburn.edu. Retrieved 2012-08-13.

2.5.10 Further reading

- Agafonow, Alejandro (2012). "The Austrian Dehomogenization Debate, or the Possibility of a Hayekian Planner". *Review of Political Economy* **24** (2).

- Harald Hagemann, Tamotsu Nishizawa, and Yukihiro Ikeda, eds. *Austrian Economics in Transition: From Carl Menger to Friedrich Hayek* (Palgrave Macmillan; 2010) 339 pages

- Holcombe, Randall (1999). *The Great Austrian Economists*. Auburn, Alabama: Ludwig von Mises Institute. p. 273. ISBN 0945466048.

- Stephen Littlechild, ed. (1990). *Austrian economics*, 3 v. Edward Elgar. Description and scroll to chapter preview links for v. 1.

- Schulak, Eugen-Maria; Unterköfler, Herbert (2011), *The Austrian School of Economics: A History of Its Ideas, Ambassadors, and Institutions*, Auburn, Alabama: Ludwig von Mises Institute, p. 262, ISBN 9781610161343

2.5.11 External links

- Austrian School at Mises Wiki

- Austrian School at DMOZ

2.6 Binary economics

Binary economics, also known as Two-factor Economics, is a theory of economics that endorses both private property and a free market but proposes significant reforms to the banking system.

According to theories first proposed by Louis Kelso, widespread use of central bank-issued interest-free loans to fund employee-owned firms can finance economic growth whilst widening stock ownership in a way which binary economists believe will be non-inflationary.

The term "binary" derived from its heterodox treatment of labor and capital (but not in the sense of binary opposition).[1] Kelso claimed that in a truly free market wages would tend to fall over time, with all the benefits of technological progress accruing to capital owners.

2.6.1 Overview

Binary economics rejects the claim that neoclassical economics alone promotes a 'free market' which is free, fair and efficient. (e.g., as an interpretation of the classical First Fundamental Theorem of Welfare Economics). Binary economists believe freedom is only truly achieved if all individuals are able to acquire an independent economic base from capital holdings, and that the distribution of ownership rights can "deepen democracy".[2]

Binary economics argues financial savings prior to investment are not required on the basis that the present money supply is mostly created credit anyway.[3] It argues that newly minted money invested on behalf of those *without access* to existing cash savings or collateral can be adequately repaid through the returns on those investments, which need not be inflationary if the economy is operating below capacity. The theory asserts that what matters is whether the newly created money is interest-free, whether it can be repaid, whether there is effective collateral and whether it goes towards the development and spreading of various forms of productive (and the associated consuming) capacity.

Another contrast is that, in evidence-based economics, interest (as distinct from administration cost) is practically always necessary; in Binary Economics theory it isn't (not in relation to the development and spreading of productive capacity).[4] Conventional economics accounts for the observed time value of money, whereas binary economics does not.

2.6.2 Background

The theory behind Binary Economics was proposed by American lawyer Louis Kelso in his book *The Capitalist Manifesto* (1958). The book's title could be seen as a Cold War reference in opposition to communism.[5]

Kelso elaborated on his proposals in *The New Capitalists* in 1961. He worked with political scientist Patricia Hetter Kelso to further explain how capital instruments provide an increasing percentage of the wealth and why capital is narrowly owned in the modern industrial economy.[6] Their analysis predicted that widely distributed capital ownership will create a more balanced economy. Kelso and Hetter proposed new "binary" share holdings which would pay out full net earnings as dividends (with exceptions for research, maintenance and depreciation). These could be obtained on credit by those not possessing savings, with a government-backed insurance scheme to protect the shareholder in the event of loss.

Kelso's writings were not well received by academic economists. Milton Friedman said of *The Capitalist Manifesto* "the book's economics was bad...the interpretation of history, ludicrous; and the policy recommended, dangerous" and recalls a debate where even the moderator Clark Kerr "lost his cool as a moderator and attacked [Kelso's arguments] vigorously".[7] Paul Samuelson, another Nobel Memorial Prize in Economic Sciences winner, told the U.S. Congress that Kelso's theories were a "cranky fad" not accepted by mainstream economists, but Kelso's ideas on promoting wider capital ownership nevertheless significantly influenced the passing of legislation promoting employee ownership.[8]

2.6.3 Aims and programme

The aim of binary economics is to ensure that all individuals receive income from their own independent capital estate,[9] using interest-free loans issued by a central bank to promote the spread of employee-owned firms.[1] These loans are intended to: halve infrastructure improvement costs, reduce business startup costs, and widen stock ownership.

Binary economics is not mainstream and does not fit easy into the left–right spectrum.[10] It has variously been characterized as an extreme right-wing ideology and as extremely left-wing by its critics.[11][12] The 'binary' (in 'binary economics') means 'composed of tw" because it suffices to view the physical factors of production as being but two (labour and capital (which includes land). It recognises only two ways of genuinely earning a living – by labour and by productive capital ownership. In its theory humans own their labour, but also productive capital.[13]

Binary economics is partly based on belief that society has an absolute duty to ensure that all humans have good health, housing, education and an independent income, as well as a responsibility to protect the environment for its own sake. The interest-free loans proposed by binary economics are compatible with the traditional opposition of the Abrahamic religions to usury.[14]

Proponents[15] of binary economics claim that their system contains no expropriation of wealth, and much less redistribution will be necessary. They argue that it cannot cause inflation and is of particular importance as more of the physical contribution to production is automated.[16] and that the Binary economics paradigm[17] is particularly helpful in addressing the issue of why developing countries languish.[18] Advocates[14] contend that implementing their system will lessen national debt and encourage national unity. They believe binary economics could create a stable economy.

2.6.4 Productiveness vs. Productivity

Binary **productiveness** is distinctly different from the conventional economic concept of productivity.[19] Binary productiveness attempts to quantify the proportion of output contributed by total labor input and total capital input respectively,[20] Adding capital inputs to a production process increases labor productivity, but binary economic theory argues that it decreases *labor productiveness* (i.e. the proportion of the total output with the support of both labor and capital that the labor inputs could have produced alone). For example, if the invention of a shovel allows a laborer to dig a hole in quarter of the time it would take him without the spade, binary economists would consider 75% of the "productiveness" to come from the shovel and only 25% from the laborer.

Roth criticised the shovel example on the basis that the shovel is not a factor of production independent of human capital because somebody invented it, and the shovel cannot act independently: the physical productiveness of the shovel before labour is added to it is zero.[21][22]

Kelso used the concept of productiveness to support his theory of distributive justice, arguing that as capital increasingly substitutes for labor..."workers can legitimately claim from their aggregate labor only a decreasing percentage of total output",[23] implying they would need to acquire capital holdings to maintain their level of income. In the *The Capitalist Manifesto*, Kelso boldly asserted:

> "It is, if anything an underestimation rather than an exaggeration to say that the aggregate physical contribution to the production of the wealth of the workers in the United States today accounts for less than 10 percent of the wealth produced, and that the contribution by the owners of capital instruments, through their physical instruments, accounts in physical terms for more than 90 percent of the wealth produced" [24]

Whilst the increased importance of capital as a factor of production following the Industrial Revolution has long been accepted even by those believing economic value derives from labour such as Marx,[25] Kelso's figures suggesting that value was created almost entirely by capital were dismissed by academic economists like Paul Samuelson.[8] Samuelson asserted that Kelso's had not used any econometric analysis to arrive at his figures, which completely contradicted economists' empirical findings on the contribution of labour. *The Capitalist Manifesto* did not provide detailed calculations to support Kelso's claim, although a footnote[24] suggested that it was based on a simple comparison with 1850s labour productivity figures.

2.6.5 Employee stock ownership plan (ESOPs) and other plans

Employee stock ownership plans (ESOPs) are compatible with some of the principles of binary economics.[26] These stem originally from Louis Kelso & Patricia Hetter Kelso (1967)*Two-Factor Theory: The Economics of Reality*; the founding of Kelso & Company in 1970; and then from conversations in the early 1970s between Louis Kelso, Norman Kurland (Center for Economic and Social Justice), Senator Russell Long of Louisiana (Chairman, USA Senate Finance Committee, 1966–81) and Senator Mike Gravel of Alaska. There are about 11,500 ESOPs in the USA today covering 11 million employees in closely held companies.

2.6.6 Uses of central bank-issued interest-free loans

Binary economics proposes that central bank-issued interest-free loans should be administered by the banking system for the development and spreading of productive (and the associated consuming) capacity, particularly new capacity, as well as for environmental and public capital. While no interest would be charged, there would be an administrative cost as well as collateralization or capital credit insurance.[27]

Proponents of binary economics are dissatisfied with fractional-reserve banking, arguing that it "creates new money out of nothing".[28] The supply of interest-free loans would place in circumstances of a move (over time) towards banks maintaining reserves equal to 100% of their deposits; in practice, the large-scale interest-free lending desired by binary economics is compatible with the widespread reduction in money supply that would be caused by increased reserve requirements only if the government takes over the banks' role in credit creation.

Investments eligible for interest-free loans

Binary economics suggests that ownership of productive (and the associated consuming) capacity, particularly new capacity, could be spread by the use of central bank-issued interest-free loans.[29] Interest-free loans should be allowed for private capital investment *IF such investment creates new owners of capital and is part of national policy to enable all individuals, over time, on market principles, to become owners of substantial amounts of productive, income-producing capital.*[30] By using central bank-issued interest-free loans, a large corporation would get cheap money as long as new binary shareholders are created.

2.6.7 References

[1] Rodney Shakespeare (2007) *The Modern Universal Paradigm.*

[2] Roy Madron & John Jopling (2003) *Gaian Democracies*

[3] Michael Rowbotham (1998) *The Grip of Death*. James Gibb Stuart (1983) *The Money Bomb.*

[4] Rodney Shakespeare (2007) op. cit.

[5] "The Capitalist Manifesto" (PDF). Retrieved 2011-02-20.

[6] Louis Kelso & Patricia Hetter Kelso (1986 & 1991) *Democracy and Economics Power - Extending the ESOP Revolution through Binary Economics*

[7] Friedman, Milton & Friedman, Rose D. *Two Lucky People: A memoir*, University of Chicago Press, p.275

[8] D'Art, Darryl (1992) *Economic democracy and financial participation: a comparative study*, Routledge p.96

[9] Robert Ashford & Rodney Shakespeare (1999) *Binary Economics – the new paradigm*

[10] Robert Ashford (1990) *The Binary Economics of Louis Kelso: the Promise of Universal Capitalism* (Rutgers Law Journal, vol. 22 No.1. Fall, 1990).

[11] Robert Ashford & Rodney Shakespeare (1999) op. cit;

[12] *Time* Magazine, June 29, 1970.

[13] Louis Kelso & Patricia Hetter Kelso (1967) *Two-Factor Theory: the Economics of Reality.*

[14] Rodney Shakespeare & Peter Challen (2002) *Seven Steps to Justice.*

[15] Norman Kurland, Dawn Brohawn & Michael Greaney (2004)*Capital Homesteading for Every Citizen: A Just Free Market Solution for Saving Social Security.*

[16] James S. Albus (1976) *Peoples' Capitalism - The Economics of The Robot Revolution.*

[17] Sofyan Syafri Harahap (2005), *Accounting Crisis*. William Christensen *Search for a Universal Paradigm: Making Justice Live For All* International Conference on *Universal Paradigm of Socio-Scientific Reasoning*, Asian University of Bangladesh, 2005.

[18] A notable lecture on this matter was given by Ing. B.J Habibie (former President, The Republic of Indonesia) at the international conference *Islamic Economics and Banking in the 21st Century*, Jakarta, Indonesia, November, 2005. See also Thoby Mutis (1995) *Pendekatan Ekonomi Pengetahuan dalam Manajemen Kodedeterminass.*

[19] Mark Douglas Reiners *The Binary Alternative and the Future of Capitalism* available at Center for Economic and Social Justice.

[20] Robert Ashford *Louis Kelso's Binary Economy* (The Journal of Socio-Economics, vol.25, 1996).

[21] Timothy D. Terrell *Binary Economics: Paradigm Shift Or Cluster of Errors?* Ludwig von Mises Institute.

[22] Timothy P. Roth, (1996) *A Supply-Sider's (Sympathetic) View of Binary Economics*, Journal of Socio-Economics 25 (1) pp. 58–59.

[23] Kelso, Louis (1958) *The Capitalist Manifesto*, Random House, p.110-11

[24] Kelso, Louis (1958) *The Capitalist Manifesto*, Random House, p.53

[25] Louis Kelso *Karl Marx: The Almost Capitalist* (American Bar Association Journal, March, 1957).

[26] William Greider (1997) *One World, Ready or Not: The Manic Logic of Global Capitalism.*

[27] Norman Kurland (1998) *The Federal Reserve Discount Window* — www.cesj.org

[28] John Tomlinson (1993) *Honest Money*. Joseph Huber & James Robertson *Creating New Money*. Peter Selby (1997) *Grace and Mortgage*.

[29] Shann Turnbull (1975/2000) *Democratising the Wealth of Nations* and (2001) *The Use of Central Banks to Spread Ownership*. Jeff Gates (1999) *The Ownership Solution* and (2000) *Democracy At Risk*.

[30] Norman Kurland (2001) *Saving Social Security* at www.cesj.org.

2.6.8 Texts

- Albus, James S. (1976) *Peoples' Capitalism - The Economics of The Robot Revolution.*

- Ashford, Robert & Shakespeare, Rodney (1999) *Binary Economics - the new paradigm.*

- Ashford, Robert "Louis Kelso's Binary Economy" (*The Journal of Socio-Economics*, vol. 25, 1996).

- el-Diwany, Tarek (2003) *The Problem With Interest.*

- Gates, Jeff (1999) *The Ownership Solution.*

- Gates, Jeff (2000) *Democracy At Risk.*

- Gauche, Jerry "Binary Modes for the Privatization of Public Assets" (*The Journal of Socio-Economics*. Vol. 27, 1998).

- Greenfield, Sidney M. *Making Another World Possible: the Torah, Louis Kelso and the Problem of Poverty* (paper given at conference, Columbia University, May, 2006).

- Kelso, Louis & Kelso, Patricia Hetter (1986 & 1991), *Democracy and Economic Power - Extending the ESOP Revolution through Binary Economics.*

- Kelso, Louis & Adler, Mortimer (1958), *The Capitalist Manifesto.*

- Kelso, Louis & Adler, Mortimer (1961), *The New Capitalists.*

- Kelso, Louis & Hetter, Patricia (1967), *Two-Factor Theory: the Economics of Reality.*

- Kurland, Norman *A New Look at Prices and Money: The Kelsonian Binary Model for Achieving Rapid Growth Without Inflation.*

- Kurland, Norman; Brohawn, Dawn & Michael Greaney (2004) *Capital Homesteading for Every Citizen: A Just Free Market Solution for Saving Social Security.*

- Miller, J.H. ed., (1994), *Curing World Poverty: The New Role of Property.*

- Reiners, Mark Douglas, *The Binary Alternative and Future of Capitalism.*

- Schmid, A. Allan,(1984), "Broadening Capital Ownership: The Credit System as a Focus of Power", in Gar Alperovitz and Roger Skurski,eds. *American Economic Policy*, University of Notre Dame Press.

- Shakespeare, Rodney & Challen, Peter (2002) *Seven Steps to Justice.*

- Shakespeare, Rodney (2007) *The Modern Universal Paradigm.*

- Turnbull, Shann (2001) *The Use of Central Banks to Spread Ownership.*

- Turnbull, Shann (1975/2000), *Democratising the Wealth of Nations.*

2.6.9 External links

- Binary Economics now

2.7 Calculation in kind

Calculation in kind or **calculation in natura** is a way of valuating resources and a system of accounting that utilizes disaggregated physical magnitudes as opposed to a common unit of calculation. As the basis for a socialist economy it was proposed to replace money and financial calculation.[1] Calculation in kind would value each commodity based only on its use value, for purposes of economic accounting. By contrast, in money-based economies, a commodity's value includes an exchange value.

Calculation in kind would quantify the utility of an object *directly* without recourse to a general unit of calculation. This differs from other proposed methods of socialist calculation, such as simultaneous equations, Taylor-Lange accounting prices, and the use of labor time as a measure of cost.[1]

Calculation in kind was strongly advocated by the positivist philosopher and political economist Otto Neurath in the early 1920s, when much of the discussion about socialism centered on whether economic planning should be based on physical quantities or monetary accounting. Neurath was the most forceful advocate of *physical planning* (economic planning using calculation-in-kind) in contrast to market socialist neoclassical economists who advocated use of notional prices computed by solving simultaneous equations.[2] Austrian school critics of socialism, particularly Ludwig von Mises, based his critique of socialism on the calculation problem.[3]

Proponents of in-kind calculation argue that the use of a common medium like money distorts information about the utility of an object. Socialists in favor of calculation in kind argued that, in a system of in-kind calculation, waste associated with the monetary system would be eliminated, and in particular objects would no longer be desired for functionally useless purposes like resale and speculation - they would only be desired for their use-value.[4]

2.7.1 See also

2.7.2 References

[1] Steele, David (1992). *From Marx to Mises: Post-Capitalist Society and the Challenge of Economic Calculation*. Open Court Publishing Company. p. 123. ISBN 978-0875484495. The term 'calculation in kind' is normally reserved for attempts to dispense with any general unit of calculation. It is usually not taken to include cases where a general unit of calculation is arrived at without reference to money or markets. Thus it is not applied to Taylor-Lange accounting prices, nor to notional 'prices' ascribed to all commodities in an attempt to replace the market by solving a large number of simultaneous equations, nor to the use of labor time as a measure of cost.

[2] Feinstein, C.H. (September 1969). *Socialism, Capitalism and Economic Growth: Essays Presented to Maurice Dobb*. Cambridge University Press. p. 168. ISBN 978-0521049870. In the years between 1917 and 1925 Viennese socialists were heavily engaged in disputes about these themes. Among the main contributors were O. Neurath, K. Polanyi, O. Baur, O. Leichter and W. Schiff... Much of this early discussion turned round the question whether planning should be in physical quantities or whether monetary accounting should be used. Otto Neurath, a remarkable personality, was a forceful advocate of physical planning.

[3] *Otto Neurath's concepts of socialization and economic calculation and his socialist critics*. Retrieved July 05, 2010: http://www.chaloupek.eu/work/NeurathFin.pdf

[4] *The Alternative to Capitalism*. Retrieved July 05, 2010, from wspus.org "The disappearance of economic value would mean the end of economic calculation in the sense of calculation in units of value whether measured by money or directly in some unit of labour-time. It would mean that there was no longer any common unit of calculation for making decisions regarding the production of goods...Calculation in kind is an essential aspect of the production of goods in any society, including capitalism. A commodity is, as we saw, a good which by virtue of being produced for sale has acquired in addition to its physical use value a socially-determined exchange value. Correspondingly, the process of production under capitalism is both a process of production of exchange values and a process of production of use values, involving two different kinds of calculation. For the former, the unit of calculation is money, but for the latter there is no single unit but a whole series of different units for measuring the quantity and quality of specific goods used in the process of producing other specific goods (tonnes of steel, kilowatt-hours of electricity, person-hours of work and so on). The disappearance of economic or value calculation in socialism would by no means involve the disappearance of all rational calculation, since the calculations in kind connected with producing specific quantities of goods as physical use values would continue."

2.7.3 Further reading

- Cockshott, Paul. "Calculation in-Natura, from Neurath to Kantorovich" *University of Glasgow*, 15 May 2008.

- O'Neil, John (2002). "Socialist Calculation and Environmental Valuation: Money, Markets and Ecology". *Science and Society* 66. 1: 137-158.

2.7.4 External links

- World Socialist Party (US) (the wspus.org quoted

above)

- An Anarchist FAQ, I.4.5, "What about supply and demand?" http://anarchism.pageabode.com/afaq/secI4.html#seci45

2.8 Chrematistics

Chrematistics (from Greek: χρηματιστική) according to Thales of Miletus is the art of getting rich.

Plato (left) and Aristotle (right)

2.8.1 Ancient Greece

Aristotle established the fundamental difference between economics and chrematistics. The accumulation of money itself is an unnatural activity that dehumanizes those who practice it. Like Plato, he condemns the accumulation of wealth. Trade exchanges money for goods and usury creates money from money. The merchant does not produce anything: both are reprehensible from the standpoint of their philosophical ethics.

According to Aristotle, the "necessary" chrematistic economy is licit if the sale of goods is made directly between the producer and buyer at the right price; it does not generate a value-added product. By contrast, it is illicit if the producer purchases for resale to consumers for a higher price, generating added value. The money must be only a medium of exchange and measure of value.

2.8.2 Middle Ages

The Catholic Church maintained this economic doctrine throughout the Middle Ages (Second Council of the Lateran,1139). Saint Thomas Aquinas accepted that capital accumulation if it served for virtuous purposes as charity.

2.8.3 Modern

Although Martin Luther raged against usury and extortion, according to Max Weber's study of capitalism and the Protestant ethic, frugality, sobriety, deferred consumption and saving were among the key values of the rising bourgeoisie in the age of the Reformation.

Karl Marx took up the concept in his famous work *Das Kapital*.

2.8.4 Further reading

- AKTOUF, O. (1989): "Corporate Culture, the Catholic Ethic, and the Spirit of Capitalism: A Quebec Experience", in *Journal of Standing Conference on Organizational Symbolism*. Istambul, pp. 43–80.

- BROADIE, S.; ROWE, C. (2002): *Aristotle Nicomachean Ethics: Translation, Introduction, and Commentary*. Oxford: Oxford University Press.

- KRAUT, R. (ed.) (2006): *The Blackwell Guide to Aristotle's Nicomachean Ethics*. Oxford: Blackwell.

- McLELLAN, D. (ed.) (2008): *Capital (Karl Marx): An Abridged Edition*. Oxford: Oxford Paperbacks; Abridged edition.

- PAKALUK, M. (2005): *Aristotle's Nicomachean Ethics: An Introduction*. Chicago: University of Chicago Press.

- SCHEFOLD, B. (2002): "Reflections on the Past and Current State of the History of Economic Thought in Germany", in *History of Political Economy 34*, Annual Supplement, pp. 125-136.

- SHIPSIDE, S. (2009): *Karl Marx's Das Kapital: A Modern-day Interpretation of a True Classic*. Oxford: Infinite Ideas.

- TANNER, S.J. (2001): *The Councils of the Church. A Short History*. New York: The Crossroad Publishing Company.

- DALY, H. and COBB, J. (1984): 'For the Common Good: Redirecting the Economy toward Community, the Environment, and a Sustainable Future'. Boston: Beacon Press.

- WARNE, C. (2007): *Aristotle's Nicomachean Ethics: Reader's Guide*. London: Continuum.

2.9 Circular cumulative causation

Circular cumulative causation is a theory developed by Swedish economist Gunnar Myrdal in the year 1956. It is a multi-causal approach where the core variables and their linkages are delineated. The idea behind it is that a change in one form of an institution will lead to successive changes in other institutions. These changes are circular in that they continue in a cycle, many times in a negative way, in which there is no end, and cumulative in that they persist in each round. The change does not occur all at once as that would lead to chaos, rather the changes occur gradually.

Gunnar Myrdal developed the concept from Knut Wicksell and developed it with Nicholas Kaldor when they worked together at the United Nations Economic Commission for Europe. Myrdal concentrated on the social provisioning aspect of development, while Kaldor concentrated on demand-supply relationships to the manufacturing sector.

2.9.1 Dynamics

In the characteristics that are relevant to the development process of an economy Myrdal mentioned the availability of natural resources, the historical traditions of production activity, national cohesion, religions and ideologies, economic, social and political leadership. Myrdal stated that the immediate effect of closing down certain lines of production in a community is the reduction of employment, income and demand. Through the analysis of the multiplier he pointed out that other sectors of the economy are also affected.

Then he argued that the contraction of the markets in that area tends to have a depressing effect on new investments, which in turn causes a further reduction of income and demand and, if nothing happens to modify the trend, there is a net movement of enterprises and workers towards other areas. Among the further results of these events, fewer local taxes are collected in a time when more social services is required and a vicious downward cumulative cycle is started and a trend towards a lower level of development will be further reinforced.

A status of non-equilibrium is shaped, or as he writes:

> "The notion of stable equilibrium is normally a false analogy to choose when constructing a theory to explain the changes in a social system. What is wrong with the stable equilibrium assumption as applied to social reality is the very idea that a social process follows a direction – though it might move towards it in a circuitous way – towards a position which in some sense or other can be described as a state of equilibrium between forces. Behind this idea is another and still more basic assumption, namely that a change will regularly call forth a reaction in the system in the form of changes which on the whole go in the opposite direction to the first change. The idea I want to expound in this book is that, on the contrary, in the normal case there is no such a tendency towards automatic self-stabilisation in the social system. The system is by itself not moving towards any sort of balance between forces, but is constantly on the move away from such a situation. In the normal case a change does not call forth countervailing changes but, instead, supporting changes, which move the system in the same direction as the first change but much further. Because of such circular causation as a social process tends to become cumulative and often gather speed at an accelerating rate"
> (Myrdal, G.,1957,pp. 12–13 Economic Theory and Underdeveloped Regions, London: University Paperbacks, Methuen)

About Economic Theory and Underdeveloped Regions Myrdal wrote that 'the argument moves on a general and methodological plane in the sense that the theory is discussed as a complex of broad structures of thought' (His aim was to submit 'broad generalisations, as a 'theory' is permitted to be, (in order to) grasp the social facts as they organize themselves into a pattern when viewed under a bird's-eye perspective Into this general vision, the specific characteristic. source:(Myrdal, G. 1957, Economic Theory and Underdeveloped Regions, London: University Paperbacks, Methuen))

Myrdal developed further the circular cumulative causation concept and stated that it makes different assumptions from that of stable equilibrium on what can be considered the most important forces guiding the evolution of social processes. These forces characterise the dynamics of these processes in two diverse ways.

Yet, the provision of data or other information regarding single economies was beyond the scope of his work. He claimed that in the normal case there is no such a tendency towards automatic self-stabilisation in the social system. The system is by itself not moving towards any sort of balance between forces, but is constantly on the move away from such a situation Myrdal used the expressions 'approach', 'theory' and 'general theory' as synonyms. In his subsequent writings, however, he mainly referred to 'approach', defining it as something containing, among other things, theories. He wrote that by this term he meant a collection of devices, like 'the concepts, models, and theories we use, and the way in which we select and arrange observations and present the results of our research'.

In the preface to his Economic Theory and Underdeveloped Regions Myrdal

wrote that

> 'the argument moves on a general and methodological plane in the sense that the theory is discussed as a complex of broad structures of thought' (Myrdal, G. (1957), Economic Theory and Underdeveloped Regions, London: University Paperbacks, Methuen
> vii).)

Myrdal called for economists to proceed by confronting the 'facts of life' with theories. The relation between theory and facts is however not simple.

> Theory ... must always be a priori to the observations of facts. Indeed, facts as part of scientific knowledge have no existence outside such a frame. ... If theory is thus a priori, it is, on the other hand, a first principle of science that facts are sovereign. Theory is, in other words, never more than a hypothesis. When the observations of facts do not agree with a theory, i.e. when they do not make sense in the frame of the theory utilised in carrying out the research, the theory has to be discarded and replaced by another one which promises a better fit (Myrdal, G. (1957), Economic Theory and Underdeveloped Regions, London: University Paperbacks, Methuen
> p. 160).

2.9.2 Sources

- Myrdal, G. Political Element in the Development of Economic Theory, London:

Routledge and Kegan Paul, 1953.

- Myrdal, G. (1931), 'Några anmärkningar med anledning av Dr. Åkermans uppsats'

(some comments on account of the essay by J. Åkerman), Statsvetenskaplig Tidskrift, 34, 429–46.

- Myrdal, G. (1939), Monetary Equilibrium, Glasgow: William Hodge.

- Myrdal, G. (1944), An American Dilemma: The Negro Problem and Modern

Democracy, New York: Harper. Myrdal, growth processes and

- Principle of circular and cumulative causation: fusing Myrdalian and Kaldorian growth and development dynamics. Journal of Economic Issues, June 1, 2008, O'Hara, Phillip Anthony

- Myrdal, G. Asian Drama: An Inquiry into the Poverty of Nations. RAND Corporation, 1968

- Myrdal, G. (1957), Economic Theory and Underdeveloped Regions, London: University Paperbacks, Methuen.

2.9.3 External links

- Gunnar Myrdals Theory of Cumulative Cauasation revisited Nanako Fujita

- Gunnar Myrdal, growth processes and equilibrium theory

2.10 Complexity economics

This article is about the application of complexity science to the problems of economics. For its application to strategy, see Complexity theory and organizations. For other uses, see Complexity theory (disambiguation).

Complexity economics is the application of complexity science to the problems of economics. It studies computer simulations to gain insight into economic dynamics, and avoids the assumption that the economy is a system in equilibrium.[1]

2.10.1 Models

The "nearly archetypal example" is an artificial stock market model created by the Santa Fe Institute in 1989.[2] The model shows two different outcomes, one where "agents do not search much for predictors and there is convergence on a homogeneous rational expectations outcome" and another where "all kinds of technical trading strategies appearing and remaining and periods of bubbles and crashes occurring".[2]

Another area has studied the prisoner's dilemma, such as in a network where agents play amongst their nearest neighbors or a network where the agents can make mistakes from time to time and "evolve strategies".[2] In these models, the results show a system which displays "a pattern of constantly changing distributions of the strategies".[2]

More generally, complexity economics models are often used to study how non-intuitive results at the macro-level of a system can emerge from simple interactions at the micro level. This avoids assumptions of the representative agent method, which attributes outcomes in collective systems as the simple sum of the rational actions of the individuals.

2.10.2 Measures

Economic Complexity Index

Harvard economist Ricardo Hausmann and MIT physicist Cesar A. Hidalgo introduced a spectral method to measure the complexity of a country's economy by inferring it from the structure of the network connecting countries to the products that they export. The measure combines information of a country's diversity, which is positively correlated with a country's productive knowledge, with measures of a product ubiquity (number of countries that produce or export the product).[3][4] This concept, known as the "Product Space", has been further developed by MIT's Observatory of Economic Complexity, and in The Atlas of Economic Complexity[4] in 2011.

Relevance The Economic Complexity Index (ECI) introduced by Hausmann and Hidalgo [3][4] is highly predictive of future GDP per capita growth. In [4] Hausmann, Hidalgo et al. show that the List of countries by future GDP (based on ECI) estimateslability of the ECI to predict future GDP per capita growth is between 5 times and 20 times larger than the World Bank's measure of governance, the World Economic Forum's (WEF) Global Competitiveness Index (GCI) and standard measures of human capital, such as years of schooling and cognitive ability.[5][6]

Metrics for Country Fitness and Product Complexity

Pietronero and collaborators have recently proposed a different approach.[7][8][9] These metrics are defined as the fixed point of non-linear iterative map. Differently from the linear algorithm giving rise to the ECI, this non-linearity is a key point to properly deal with the nested structure of the data. The authors of this alternative formula claim it has several advantages:

- Consistency with the empirical evidence from the export country-product matrix that diversification plays a crucial role in the assessment of the competitiveness of countries. The metrics for countries proposed by Pietronero is indeed extensive with respect to the number of products.

- Non-linear coupling between fitness and complexity required by the nested structure of the country-product matrix. The nested structure implies that the information on the complexity of a product must be bounded by the producers with the slowest fitness.

- Broad and Pareto-like distribution of the metrics.

- Each iteration of the method refines information, does not change the meaning of the iterated variables and does not shrink information.

The metrics for country fitness and product complexity have been used in a report[10] of the Boston Consulting Group on Sweden growth and development perspectives.

2.10.3 Features

Brian Arthur, Steven N. Durlauf, and David A. Lane describe several features of complex systems that deserve greater attention in economics.[11]

1. **Dispersed interaction**—The economy has interaction between many dispersed, heterogeneous, agents. The action of any given agent depends upon the anticipated actions of other agents and on the aggregate state of the economy.

2. **No global controller**—Controls are provided by mechanisms of competition and coordination between agents. Economic actions are mediated by legal institutions, assigned roles, and shifting associations. No global entity controls interactions. Traditionally, a fictitious *auctioneer* has appeared in some mathematical analyses of general equilibrium models, although nobody claimed any descriptive accuracy for such models. Traditionally, many mainstream models have imposed *constraints*, such as requiring that budgets be balanced, and such constraints are avoided in complexity economics.

3. **Cross-cutting hierarchical organization**—The economy has many levels of organization and interaction. Units at any given level behaviors, actions, strategies, products typically serve as "building blocks" for constructing units at the next higher level. The overall organization is more than hierarchical, with many sorts of tangling interactions (associations, channels of communication) across levels.

4. **Ongoing adaptation**—Behaviors, actions, strategies, and products are revised frequently as the individual agents accumulate experience.[12]

5. **Novelty niches**—Such niches are associated with new markets, new technologies, new behaviors, and new institutions. The very act of filling a niche may provide new niches. The result is ongoing novelty.

6. **Out-of-equilibrium dynamics**—Because new niches, new potentials, new possibilities, are continually created, the economy functions without attaining any optimum or global equilibrium. Improvements occur regularly.

2.10.4 Contemporary trends in economics

Complexity economics has a complex relation to previous work in economics and other sciences, and to contemporary economics. Complexity-theoretic thinking to understand economic problems has been present since their inception as academic disciplines. Research has shown that no two separate micro-events are completely isolated,[13] and there is a relationship that forms a macroeconomic structure. However, the relationship is not always in one direction; there is a reciprocal influence when feedback is in operation.[14]

Complexity economics has been applied to many fields.

Intellectual predecessors

Complexity economics draws inspiration from behavioral economics, Marxian economics, institutional economics/evolutionary economics, Austrian economics and the work of Adam Smith.[15] It also draws inspiration from other fields, such as statistical mechanics in physics, and evolutionary biology. Some of the 20th century intellectual background of complexity theory in economics is examined in Alan Marshall (2002) The Unity of Nature, Imperial College Press: London.

Applications

The theory of complex dynamic systems has been applied in diverse fields in economics and other decision sciences.

These applications include capital theory,[16][17] game theory,[18] the dynamics of opinions among agents composed of multiple selves,[19] and macroeconomics.[20] In voting theory, the methods of symbolic dynamics have been applied by Donald G. Saari.[21] Complexity economics has attracted the attention of historians of economics.[22] Ben Ramalingam's Aid on the Edge of Chaos includes numerous applications of complexity economics that are relevant to foreign aid.

Complexity economics as mainstream, but non-orthodox

According to Colander (2000), Colander, Holt & Rosser (2004), and Davis (2008) contemporary mainstream economics is evolving to be more "eclectic",[23][24] diverse,[25][26][27] and pluralistic.[28] Colander, Holt & Rosser (2004) state that contemporary mainstream economics is "moving away from a strict adherence to the holy trinity---rationality, selfishness, and equilibrium", citing complexity economics along with recursive economics and dynamical systems as contributions to these trends.[29] They classify complexity economics as now mainstream but non-orthodox.[30][31]

2.10.5 Criticism

In 1995-1997 publications, *Scientific American* journalist John Horgan "ridiculed" the movement as being the fourth C among the "failed fads" of "complexity, chaos, catastrophe, and cybernetics".[2] In 1997, Horgan wrote that the approach had "created some potent metaphors: the butterfly effect, fractals, artificial life, the edge of chaos, self organized criticality. But they have not told us anything about the world that is both concrete and truly surprising, either in a negative or in a positive sense".[2][32][33] However, most of Horgan's criticisms are now considered as both inaccurate and outdated.

Rosser "granted" Horgan "that it is hard to identify a concrete and surprising discovery (rather than "mere metaphor") that has arisen due to the emergence of complexity analysis" in the discussion journal of the American Economic Association, the *Journal of Economic Perspectives*.[2] Surveying economic studies based on complexity science, Rosser wrote that the findings, rather than being surprising, confirmed "already-observed facts".[2] Rosser wrote that there has been "little work on empirical techniques for testing dispersed agent complexity models".[2] Nonetheless, Rosser wrote that "there is a strain of common perspective that has been accumulating as the four C's of cybernetics, catastrophe, chaos and complexity emerged, which may now be reaching a critical mass in terms of influencing the thinking of economists more broadly".[2]

2.10.6 See also

- Agent-based computational economics
- Econophysics
- Economic Complexity Index (ECI)
- List of countries by economic complexity
- Complexity Theory and Organizations

2.10.7 Notes

[1] Beinhocker, Eric D. The Origin of Wealth: Evolution, Complexity, and the Radical Remaking of Economics. Boston, Massachusetts: Harvard Business School Press, 2006.

[2] Rosser, J. Barkley, Jr. "On the Complexities of Complex Economic Dynamics" *Journal of Economic Perspectives*, V. 13, N. 4 (Fall 1999): 169-192.

[3] Hidalgo, Cesar A.; Hausmann Ricardo (2009). "The Building Block of Economic Complexity". *PNAS* **106** (106(26)): 10570–10575. doi:10.1073/pnas.0900943106. PMC 2705545. PMID 19549871.

[4] Hausmann & Hidalgo; et al. (2011). *The Atlas of Economic Complexity*. Cambridge MA: Puritan Press. ISBN 0615546625.

[5] "Complexity matters". *The Economist*. Oct 27, 2011.

[6] "Diversity Training". *The Economist*. Feb 4, 2010.

[7] Tacchella, Andrea; et al. (10 October 2012). "A New Metrics for Countries' Fitness and Products' Complexity". *Scientific Reports* **2** (723). doi:10.1038/srep00723.

[8] Cristelli, Matthieu; et al. "Measuring the Intangibles: A Metrics for the Economic Complexity of Countries and Products". *PLOS ONE*. doi:10.1371/journal.pone.0070726.

[9] "Economic Complexity: Measuring the Intangibles. A Consumer's Guide" (PDF). Retrieved 30 January 2014.

[10] "National Strategy for Sweden: From Wealth to Well-being". BCG. Retrieved 30 January 2014.

[11] Arthur, Brian; Durlauf, Steven; Lane, David A (1997). "Introduction: Process and Emergence in the Economy". *The Economy as an Evolving Complex System II*. Reading, Mass.: Addison-Wesley. Retrieved 2008-08-26.

[12] Shiozawa, Y. (2004). "Evolutionary Economics in the 21st Century: A Manifest". *Evolutionary and Institutional Economics Review* **1** (1): 5–47.

[13] Albert-Laszlo Barabasi "explaining *(at 27:07)* that no two events are completely isolated in the BBC Documentary". *BBC*. Retrieved 11 June 2012. "Unfolding the science behind the idea of six degrees of separation"

[14] "Page 20 - Ten Principles of Complexity & Enabling Infrastructures" (PDF). by Professor Eve Mitleton-Kelly, Director Complexity Research Programme, London School of Economics. Retrieved 1 June 2012.

[15] Colander, David (March 2008). "Complexity and the History of Economic Thought" (PDF). Retrieved 29 July 2012.

[16] Rosser, J. Barkley, Jr. "Reswitching as a Cusp Catastrophe", *Journal of Economic Theory*, V. 31 (1983): 182-193

[17] Ahmad, Syed *Capital in Economic Theory: Neo-classical, Cambridge, and Chaos*. Brookfield: Edward Elgar (1991)

[18] Sato, Yuzuru, Eizo Akiyama and J. Doyne Farmer. "Chaos in learning a simple two-person game", *Proceedings of the National Academy of Sciences of the United States of America*, V. 99, N. 7 (2 Apr. 2002): 4748-4751

[19] Krause, Ulrich. "Collective Dynamics of Faustian Agents", in *Economic Theory and Economic Thought: Essays in honour of Ian Steedman* (ed. by John Vint et al.) Routledge: 2010.

[20] Flaschel, Peter and Christian R. Proano (2009). "The J2 Status of 'Chaos' in Period Macroeconomics Models"</A>, *Studies in Nonlinear Dynamics & Econometrics*, V. 13, N. 2. http://www.bepress.com/snde/vol13/iss2/art2/

[21] Saari, Donald G. *Chaotic Elections: A Mathematician Looks at Voting*. American Mathematical Society (2001).

[22] Bausor, Randall. "Qualitative dynamics in economics and fluid mechanics: a comparison of recent applications", in *Natural Images in Economic Thought: Markets Read in Tooth and Claw* (ed. by Philip Mirowski). Cambridge: Cambridge University Press (1994).

[23] "Economists today are not neoclassical according to any reasonable definition of the term. They are far more eclectic, and concerned with different issues than were the economists of the early 1900s, whom the term was originally designed to describe." Colander (2000, p. 130)

[24] "Modern economics involves a broader world view and is far more eclectic than the neoclassical terminology allows." Colander (2000, p. 133)

[25] "In our view, the interesting story in economics over the past decades is the increasing variance of acceptable views..." Colander, Holt & Rosser (2004, p. 487)

[26] "In work at the edge, ideas that previously had been considered central to economics are being modified and broadened, and the process is changing the very nature of economics." Colander, Holt & Rosser (2004, p. 487)

[27] "When certain members of the existing elite become open to new ideas, that openness allows new ideas to expand, develop, and integrate into the profession... These alternative channels allow the mainstream to expand, and to evolve to include a wider range of approaches and understandings... This, we believe, is already occurring in economics." Colander, Holt & Rosser (2004, pp. 488–489)

[28] "despite an increasing pluralism on the mainstream economics research frontier..." Davis (2008, p. 353)

[29] Colander, Holt & Rosser (2004, p. 485)

[30] "The second (Santa Fe) conference saw a very different outcome and atmosphere than the first. No longer were mainstream economists defensively adhering to general equilibrium orthodoxy... By 1997, the mainstream accepted many of the methods and approaches that were associated with the complexity approach." Colander, Holt & Rosser (2004, p. 497) Colander, Holt & Rosser (2004, pp. 490–492) distinguish between orthodox and mainstream economics.

[31] Davis (2008, p. 354)

[32] Horgan, John, "From Complexity to Perplexity," Scientific American, June 1995, 272:6, 104 09.

[33] Horgan, John, The End of Science: Facing the Limits of Knowledge in the Twilight of the Scientific Age. Paperback ed, New York: Broadway Books, 1997.

2.10.8 References

- Colander, David (2000). "The Death of Neoclassical Economics". *Journal of the History of Economic Thought* **22** (2): 127–143. doi:10.1080/10427710050025330.

- Colander, David; Holt, Richard P. F.; Rosser, Barkley J., Jr. (Oct 2004). "The Changing Face of Mainstream Economics". *Review of Political Economy* **16** (4): 485–499. doi:10.1080/0953825042000256702.

- Davis, John B. (2008). "The turn in recent economics and return of orthodoxy". *Cambridge Journal of Economics* **32** (3): 349–366. doi:10.1093/cje/bem048.

- Goodwin, Richard M. *Chaotic Economic Dynamics.* Oxford: Clarendon Press (1990)

- Rosser, J. Barkley, Jr. *From Catastrophe to Chaos: A General Theory of Economic Discontinuities* Boston/Dordrecht: Kluwer Academic.

- Benhabib, Jess (editor) *Cycles and Chaos in Economic Equilibrium,* Princeton University Press (1992).

- Waldrop, M. Mitchell. *Complexity: The Emerging Science at the Edge of Order and Chaos.* New York: Touchstone (1992)

- Saari, Donald. "Complexity of Simple Economics", *Notices of the AMS.* V. 42, N. 2 (Feb. 1995): 222-230

- Ormerod, Paul (1998). *Butterfly Economics: A New General Theory of Social and Economic Behavior.* New York: Pantheon.

2.10.9 External links

- Santa Fe Institute A center of complexity science

- What Should Policymakers Know About Economic Complexity (PDF) Summary of complexity economics

- Harvard HKS-MIT Media Lab Observatory of Economic Complexity

2.11 Counter-economics

Counter-economics is a term originally used by Samuel Edward Konkin III and J. Neil Schulman, libertarian activists and theorists. Konkin defined it as "the study or practice of all peaceful human action which is forbidden by the State." The term is short for "counter-establishment economics" and may also be referred to as counter-politics. Counter-economics was integrated by Schulman into Konkin's doctrine of agorism.[1]

2.11.1 Origin

The first presentation of the theory of counter-economics was made by Samuel Edward Konkin III at a conference organized by J. Neil Schulman in 1974 held in Cheshire, Massachusetts. The first book to portray counter-economics as a strategy for achieving a libertarian society was Schulman's novel *Alongside Night* (1979).

2.11.2 Relationship with agorism

Konkin's agorism, as exposited in his *New Libertarian Manifesto*,[2] postulates that the correct method of achieving a voluntary society is through advocacy and growth of the underground economy or "black market" – the "counter-economy" as Konkin put it – until such a point that the State's perceived moral authority and outright power have been so thoroughly undermined that revolutionary market anarchist legal and security enterprises are able to arise from underground and ultimately suppress government as a criminal activity (with taxation being treated as theft, war being treated as mass murder, *et cetera*).

According to Konkin's pamphlet *Counter-Economics*:

> The Counter-Economy is the sum of all non-aggressive Human Action which is forbidden by the State. Counter-economics is the study of the Counter-Economy and its practices. The Counter-Economy includes the free market, the Black Market, the "underground economy," all acts of civil and social disobedience, all acts of forbidden association (sexual, racial, cross-religious), and anything else the State, at any place or time, chooses to prohibit, control, regulate, tax, or tariff. The Counter-Economy excludes all State-approved action (the "White Market") and the Red Market (violence and theft not approved by the State).[3]

According to Konkin, counter-economics also allows for immediate self-liberation from statist controls, to whatever degree practical, by applying entrepreneurial logic to rationally decide which laws to discreetly break and when. The fundamental principle is to trade risk for profit, although profit can refer to any gain in perceived value rather than strictly monetary gains (as a consequence of the subjective theory of value).

Voluntary practices of counter-economics include:[4]

- Arms trafficking
- Bartering and alternative currency use
- Being or hiring illegal immigrants
- Drug trafficking
- Mutual credit
- Smuggling
- Subsistence farming
- Tax evasion
- Voluntary Prostitution

2.11.3 Strategy

According to Per Bylund, counter-economics applies two basic strategies to liberate people from the state, Vertical/Introverted and Horizontal/Extroverted.

> "The first recipe provides instructions for how to break free vertically through building a decentralized infrastructure for free communities avoiding the State and its centralized "solutions" altogether. The other recipe advocates breaking free horizontally through making use of one's personal network of friends and colleagues, and doing business out of the State's reach. One might also call these recipes or strategies the introvert and extrovert solutions to our methodological problem.[5]"

Vertical/Introverted

The Vertical/Introverted Strategy is aimed towards individuals concentrating on decentralized local infrastructure as opposed to expansive state foundations.

> "What this means in real terms is to create local or neighborhood networks for self-reliance, where people in the vicinity get together to find ways to produce whatever is necessary for survival and a good life. It means creating local production facilities and markets with no effective State regulations and without the State's knowledge.[5]"

Voluntary Association among those in a community is essential to this concept. Bylund believes developing means to refuse dependency on state services and become self-reliant can be an effective course of action to achieve free market processes. Community Technology is an example of this strategy. Bylund mentions Karl Hess's efforts to transform a Washington D.C. neighborhood which reflects these principles as a primary example. Hess set up green houses on top of available rooftops and using old washing machine parts to build a fish-breeding facility in a building basement.[5]

Horizontal/Extroverted

The Horizontal/Extrovered Strategy applies individuals actively creating black market networks and structures which can be stretched beyond neighborhood communities focus in the Vertical Strategy.

> "What it basically proposes is to trade with people you know and people who are recommended to you. This can all be done at whatever scale one finds appropriate, using available technology such as the Internet and e.g. E-bay for communication and money transactions. A first step could be to hire the children next-door to mow the lawn or baby-sit. It does not have to be very sophisticated at first.
>
> This approach should come naturally to libertarians, since it simply means exercising trade without bothering with State regulations or paying taxes. Most people are willing to exchange

goods and services without registering the sales tax, which is a good start. Some of them will also find it in their interest to do this on a larger scale, producing and distributing goods and services without ever paying taxes or following unnecessary government regulations and controls. And most people don't really care about government standards if they trust their supplier[5]"

2.11.4 See also

- Agorism
- Samuel Edward Konkin III
- Black Market
- *The Other Path: The Economic Answer to Terrorism*
- Alternative currency
- Informal sector
- Economic secession
- Illegalism

2.11.5 References

[1] Afterword by Samuel Edward Konkin in *Alongside Night*. Pulpless.Com, 1999. p. 274. ISBN 1-58445-120-3, ISBN 978-1-58445-120-4

[2] *New Libertarian Manifesto*

[3] Counter-Economics: what it is, how it works

[4] *Counter-Economics*, Market Anarchist Distro

[5] Bylund, Per. "A Strategy for Pushing Back The State". *Lewrockwell.com*. Lew Rockwell.

2.11.6 External links

- The Agorism Project – Agorism.co
- Agorism.info
- Just Things | The Fair Trade Journal of Applied Counter-Economics
- *Alongside Night* by J. Neil Schulman

2.12 Credibility thesis

This article is about Credibility thesis in institutional development. For credibility in general, see Credibility. For application of the concept in actuarial science, see Credibility theory.

Credibility Thesis is a proposed heterodox theoretical framework for understanding how societal institutions come about and evolve. It purports that institutions emerge from intentional institution-building but never in the originally intended form.[1] Instead, institutional development is endogenous and spontaneously ordered and institutional persistence can be explained by their credibility,[2] which is provided by the function that particular institutions serve rather than their theoretical or ideological form. The Credibility Thesis can be applied to explain, for example, why purported institutional improvements do not take hold as part of structural adjustment programs, while other economies in the developing world deliver growth despite absence of clear and strong market mechanisms such as indisputable private property rights or clearly delineated and registered land tenure.

2.12.1 Postulates of Credibility Thesis

According to the Credibility Thesis, institutional persistence, meaning the survival and change of particular institutions through time is determined by the function of the institution and actors' expectations of the institution to play that function.

Changes in institutional arrangements, such as changes from informal land tenure and informal housing to a formalized real estate market or gradually declining prevalence of formal marriage or customary rights, are brought about by rule-making in a multi-actor playing field, where even the strongest actors cannot fully dictate institutional arrangements.

An institution that appears stable and unchanging over time can be said to exist in an equilibrium wherein actors' conflicting interests on what form the institution should take are locked in a frozen conflict. For example, whether land holdings should be registered in a cadastre or if informal exchange of payment for use rights can suffice as confirmation of a land sale, constitute two possible land institution arrangements and either can be beneficial to different actors' interests. That no actor perceives an immediate opportunity to change the arrangement to their advantage is a sign of the credibility of the assignment and the source of the equilibrium of institutional arrangement. However, disequilibrium characterises institutional arrangements and equilibrium is transitory and rare. In this aspect the Credibility

Theory is juxtaposed to Structural functionalism, which is based on presupposed societal equilibrium.

A series of underlying postulates for the Credibility Thesis have been proposed: <<CITATION NEEDED>>

- Institutions are the resultant of unintentional development. Although actors have intentions, there is no agency that can externally design institutions, as actors' actions are part of the same endogenous game. Institutions emerge as an unanticipated outcome of actors' multitudinous interactions, in effect, are the result of an autonomous, *Unintended Intentionality*.

- Institutional change is driven by disequilibrium. Contrary to the notion that institutions settle around equilibrium, actors' interactions are seen as an ever-changing and conflicting process in which stable status is never reached. One could see it as a "Progressive Disequilibrium" or institutional change as perpetual alteration, yet, with alternating speeds of change; sometimes, imperceptibly slow, sometimes, sudden and with shocks.

- Institutional Form is subordinate to Function. In other words, the use and disuse of institutions over time and space is what matters for understanding their role in development, not their appearance.[1]

2.12.2 Key concepts

2.12.3 Methodological approaches

Given that all involved actors are constantly interested in changing institutional design, credibility cannot be measured by directly asking respondents whether they find an institution credible. Instead it has to be operationalized through proxies, such as the level of conflict that an institution generates; the extent of 'institutional robustness' expressed as a function of institutional lifespan and flexibility; the degree to which an institution facilitates or frustrates overall socio-economic, political and cultural change; and the extent to which an institution fulfills the functions it ought to perform in the eyes of social actors." [5] Such *opening of the black box* of institutions possible using mixed methods to describe institutions in detail over time and space, which serves as an *archaeology of institutions*. The archaeology of institutions can be understood as detailed description of institutions, examining and comparing institutional function, credibility, perception, and conflict over time. An example of this, is the history of China's titling.[6] While predominantly applied to land-related institutions, this approach could be applied to analysis of other means of production.[7]

2.12.4 Emergence of the theory

The question of credibility first emerged along with concern about certain institutional interventions failing. In the mid-20th century Vilhelm Aubert noted that the Housemaid Law in Norway had been implemented but flaunted by all involved actors.[4] The concept of credibility was initially coined as an *explanandum* for the success and failure of Western monetary, anti-inflationary policies in the 1970s.[1] A concern for the credibility of policy emerged in the latter half of the 20th century in response to frequently observed failures of neoliberal structural adjustments in the developing world associated with the Washington Consensus. Institutional reform, such as privatization, failed to deliver the predicted economic growth, not because of lacking credible commitment on part of actors but due to the absence of endogenous credibility.[2]

In contrast, the growth of the Chinese economy despite lack of many institutions considered to be essential for economic growth indicated that institutional arrangements do not necessarily determine economic outcomes, and also at the same time economic development does not automatically lead to teleologically predetermined institutional forms.[8][9] This has been particularly striking in the case of real estate sector in China.[7] Thus it was suggested that research should embrace Lamarckian interpretation of functionalism and focus on the function or quality and performance measures of institutional performance rather than their form.[10]

The term "credibility thesis" was put forth by Peter Ho in 2014.[1] In a review of the Credibility Thesis, Delilah Griswold contended that "credibility is a powerful metric by which to understand and evaluate tenure systems. Importantly, understanding the credibility of a given institution requires analysis outside of theory and politics, analysis that is locally and temporally specific and multilayered."[11]

2.12.5 See also

- Emergence

- Endogeneity

- Spontaneous order

- Lamarckism (the use and disuse of function determines the persistence, change or disappearance of institutions)

- Circular cumulative causation

- Form follows function (Architecture)

Related theories and theoretical bodies

- General disequilibrium
- Neo-Marxism, Heterodox economics, and Evolutionary economics
- Institutional economics
- Thorstein Veblen and John R. Commons

2.12.6 References

[1] Ho, Peter (September 2014). "The 'credibility thesis' and its application to property rights: (In)Secure land tenure, conflict and social welfare in China". *Land Use Policy* **40**: 13–27. doi:10.1016/j.landusepol.2013.09.019. Retrieved 5 May 2015.

[2] Grabel, Ilene. "The political economy of 'policy credibility': the new-classical macroeconomics and the remaking of emerging economies". *Cambridge Journal of Economics* **24** (1): 1–19. doi:10.1093/cje/24.1.1. Retrieved 5 May 2015.

[3] Guhan, S (1994). "Social Security Options for Developing Countries". *International Labour Review* **133** (35). Retrieved 18 June 2015.

[4] Aubert, Vilhelm. "Some Social Functions of Legislation". *Acta Sociologica* (Sage Publications, Ltd.) **10** (1/2): 1087–1118. doi:10.1080/03066150.2013.866553. Retrieved 5 May 2015.

[5] Monique Kremer; Peter van Lieshout; Robert Went (2009). *Doing Good Or Doing Better: Development Policies in a Globalizing World*. Amsterdam University Press. pp. 186–. ISBN 978-90-8964-107-6.

[6] Ho, Peter (2015). "Myths of tenure security and titling: Endogenous, institutional change in China's development". *Land Use Policy* **47**: 352–364. doi:10.1016/j.landusepol.2015.04.008. ISSN 0264-8377.

[7] Ho, Peter (19 December 2013). "In defense of endogenous, spontaneously ordered development: institutional functionalism and Chinese property rights". *Journal of Peasant Studies* **40** (6): 1087–1118. doi:10.1080/03066150.2013.866553. Retrieved 5 May 2015.

[8] L.P. "Autocracy or democracy?". *economist.com*. Retrieved 2015-06-18.

[9] OECD. "Issues paper on corruption and economic growth". *oecd.org*. Retrieved 2015-06-20.

[10] Aron, J. (2000). "Growth and Institutions: A Review of the Evidence". *The World Bank Research Observer* **15** (1): 99–135. doi:10.1093/wbro/15.1.99. ISSN 0257-3032.

[11] Griswold, Delilah (9 July 2015). "With efficacy of property rights, function can be more important than form". *Yale Environment Review*. Retrieved 18 November 2015.

2.13 David Malone (independent filmmaker)

For other people named David Malone, see David Malone (disambiguation).

David Hugh Malone is a British independent filmmaker, Green Party politician, and author of *The Debt Generation*. He has directed television documentaries on philosophy, science and religion, originally broadcast in the United Kingdom by the BBC and Channel 4. He was also the Green Party's parliamentary candidate for Scarborough and Whitby in the 2015 general election. He currently lives in Scarborough, North Yorkshire.

2.13.1 Documentary career

David Malone was born in North Shields and grew up in 1970s London.[1] His father, Adrian Malone, was also a documentary filmmaker, who produced The Ascent of Man with Jacob Bronowski and directed Cosmos: A Personal Voyage with Carl Sagan.[2] Malone spent nine years in America before joining the BBC Science Department and working there for nine years. He ended up joining the production team for *Horizon*, a regular documentary series on science and philosophy.[3]

Malone then left and started his own documentary company, I-330 Films, and moved to North Yorkshire.[2] I-330 Films was set up in 1995 by David Malone, and his brother James Malone.[4] Malone was also listed as one of three Directors of becauseyouthink.tv, alongside David Paterson and Jan Klimkowski.[5] Malone's *Testing God* was shortlisted for the Royal Television Society's best documentary series award in 2002.[6][7]

2.13.2 Political career

Financial commentary

In 2008 Malone began commenting on the financial pages of *The Guardian*'s website about the credit crunch and the ensuing financial crisis under the pseudonym Golem XIV, the name of a military supercomputer in a novel of the same name by the Polish science fiction writer Stanisław Lem. Malone became a fierce critic of the bank bailouts arguing that they would lead to massive cuts in public spending. In November 2010 his book about the crisis, *The Debt Generation*, was published in the UK by Level Press. It had been edited by Mark Tanner from the different writings he had done in *The Guardian's* comments section, which had totaled 600 pages of material.[8] Malone was interviewed about his book by Max Keiser during Episode 114 of the *Keiser Report*, a program that features on Russia Today.[9] In 2013 he was also interviewed over his book by Ross Ashcroft on his 'Renegade Economist' talk show.[10]

The Green Party

In the 2011 Scarborough Borough Council election, he stood as the Green Party candidate in the Falsgrave ward, where he came fourth and won 11% of the vote.[11] Malone has also stood as the Green Party's candidate in the Falsgrave and Stepney ward of the North Yorkshire County Council. In the 2009 County Council election, he came third with 21% of the vote, and in the 2013 County Council election he came fourth with 17% of the vote.[12] He was the Green Party's parliamentary candidate for Scarborough and Whitby in the 2015 general election, where he came fourth with 2,185 votes (or 4.6% of the vote), and beat the Liberal Democrat candidate. He also stood in the 2015 Scarborough Borough Council election for the Green Party in Stepney Ward.[13]

2.13.3 Works

Books

- *The Debt Generation* (edited by Mark Tanner, Level Press, York: 2010), ISBN 0956690203

Documentaries

See also: List of Horizon episodes

- *Fossil Heroes* (for the BBC's *Horizon*; 1992)[14]
- *Wot U Lookin' At?* (for Horizon; 1993)[15]
- *The Far Side* (for Horizon; 1994)[16]
- *Death Wish: The Untold Story* (for Horizon; 1994)[17]
- *Icon Earth* (for Horizon; 1995)[18]
- *Tibet: The Ice Mother* (for Horizon; 1995)[19]
- *Inside the Internet* (for the BBC's *Computers Don't Bite*; 1997)[20]
- *The Flow of Time* (1999)
- *Secrets of the Incas* (2000)
- *Testing God* (2001),[21] in three episodes:

    Killing the Creator
    Darwin and the Divine
    Credo Ergo Sum

- *Soul Searching* (2003),[22] in two episodes:

    Know Thyself
    The Undiscovered Country

- *What We Still Don't Know* (2004),[23] in three episodes:

    Are We Alone?
    Why Are We Here?
    Are We Real?

- *Stems Cells: The Promise* (2005)[24]
- *Voices In My Head* (2006)[25]
- *Dangerous Knowledge* (2007)[26]
- *High Anxieties: The Mathematics of Chaos* (2008)[27]
- *The Secret Life of Waves* (2011)
- *Heart vs Mind: What Makes Us Human?* (2012)
- *Metamorphosis: The Science of Change* (2013)

2.13.4 Electoral performance

Parliamentary elections

Local government elections

2.13.5 References

[1] Malone, David (2010). *The Debt Generation*. Lancaster: Level Press. p. vi. ISBN 978-0-9566902-0-3.

[2] "David Malone". *The Institute of Arts and Ideas*. Retrieved 5 April 2015.

[3] "About Me". *Golem XIV*. Retrieved 3 July 2015.

[4] "I-330". *I-330 Films*. Archived from the original on 26 June 2015. Retrieved 10 July 2015.

[5] "Directors". *becauseyouthink.tv*. Archived from the original on 1 November 2007. Retrieved 10 July 2015.

[6] "Royal Television Society Programme Awards Nominees 2002". *Broadcast Now*. 26 February 2002. Retrieved 10 July 2015.

[7] "BBC film-maker's talk at Whitby Coliseum". *Whitby Gazette*. 17 February 2015. Retrieved 10 July 2015.

[8] Malone, David (2010). *The Debt Generation* (Second ed.). Lancaster: Level Press. pp. vii–x. ISBN 978-0-9566902-0-3.

[9] "Episode 114". *RT UK*. Retrieved 5 April 2015.

[10] "Renegade Economist Talk Show – In Conversation with David Malone". *Renegade Inc*. Retrieved 17 July 2015.

[11] "Election results for Falsgrave". *Scarborough Borough Council*. Retrieved 5 April 2015.

[12] "Falsgrave and Stepney division results". *North Yorkshire County Council*. Retrieved 5 April 2015.

[13] "Next Elections". *Scarborough and Whitby Green Party*. Retrieved 17 December 2014.

[14] "Fossil Heroes". *British Universities Film & Video Council*. Retrieved 10 July 2015.

[15] "Wot U Lookin' At?". *British Universities Film & Video Council*. Retrieved 10 July 2015.

[16] "Far Side, The". *British Universities Film & Video Council*. Retrieved 10 July 2015.

[17] "Death Wish: The Untold Story". *British Universities Film & Video Council*. Retrieved 10 July 2015.

[18] "Icon Earch". *British Universities Film & Video Council*. Retrieved 10 July 2015.

[19] "Tibet: The Ice Mother". *British Universities Film & Video Council*. Retrieved 10 July 2015.

[20] "Inside the Internet". *British Universities Film & Video Council*. Retrieved 10 July 2015.

[21] "Testing God". *British Universities Film & Video Council*. Retrieved 10 July 2015.

[22] "Soul Searching". *British Universities Film & Video Council*. Retrieved 10 July 2015.

[23] "What We Still Don't Know (2004)". *British Film Institute*. Retrieved 10 July 2015.

[24] "Stem Cells: The Promise". *British Universities Film & Video Council*. Retrieved 10 July 2015.

[25] "Voices in My Head (2006)". *British Film Institute*. Retrieved 10 July 2015.

[26] "Dangerous Knowledge". *British Universities Film & Video Council*. Retrieved 10 July 2015.

[27] "High Anxieties: The Mathematics of Chaos". *British Universities Film & Video Council*. Retrieved 10 July 2015.

2.13.6 External links

- David Malone at the Internet Movie Database
- *The Debt Generation* website
- Golem XIV blog

2.14 Decentralized planning (economics)

This article is about an economic system based on decentralized decision-making and planning. For economies that utilize central planning, see Command economy.

A **decentralized-planned economy** or **decentrally-planned economy** (occasionally **horizontally-planned economy**) is a type of economic system based on decentralized economic planning, in which decision-making is distributed amongst various economic agents or localized within production units. Decentralized planning is held in contrast to centralized planning where economic information is aggregated and used to formulate a plan for production, investment and resource allocation by a central authority.

Decentralised planning can take shape both in the context of a mixed economy as well as in a post-capitalist economic system.

Usually this implies some form of democratic decision-making within the economy or within firms, in the form of economic democracy or industrial democracy. Alternatively, computer-based or computer-managed forms of decentralized coordination between economic enterprises have been proposed by various economists and computer scientists.

Recent proposals for decentralized-economic planning have used the term **participatory planning** to highlight the co-operative and democratic character of this system and to contrast it with centralized planning associated with the former Soviet Union. Proponents present decentralized and participatory economic planning as an alternative to market socialism for a post-capitalist society.[1]

Decentralized-planning has been proposed as a basis for socialism, and has been advocated by democratic socialists and anarchists who advocate a non-market form of socialism while rejecting Soviet-type central planning. Some writers (e.g. Robin Cox) have argued that decentralised planning allows for a spontaneously self-regulating system of stock control (relying solely on calculation in kind), to come about and that that, in turn, decisively overcomes the objections raised by the economic calculation argument that any large scale economy must necessarily resort to a system of market prices.[2]

2.14.1 Models

Cybernetics

The use of computers to coordinate production in an optimal fashion has been proposed for socialist economies. The economist Oskar Lange argued that the computer is more efficient than the market process at solving the multitude of simultaneous equations required for allocating economic inputs efficiently (either in terms of physical quantities or monetary prices).[3]

The 1970 Chilean computer-controlled planned economy Project Cybersyn was pioneered by Salvador Allende's socialist government, in an attempt to move towards decentralised planning with the experimental Cyberfolk component.

Negotiated coordination

Economist Pat Devine has created a model of coordination called "negotiated coordination", which is based upon social ownership by those affected by the use of the assets involved, with decisions made by those at the most localised level of production.[4]

Participatory Planning

See also: Parecon

The planning structure of a decentralized planned economy is generally based on a consumers council and producer council (or jointly, a distributive cooperative), which is sometimes called a consumers' cooperative. Producers and consumers, or their representatives, negotiate the quality and quantity of what is to be produced. This structure is central to participatory economics, guild socialism, and economic theories related to anarchism.

2.14.2 Similar concepts in practice

Decentralised Planning in Kerala and India

Main article: People's Planning in Kerala
See also: District planning in India

Some decentralised participation in economic planning has been implemented in various regions and states in India, most notably in Kerala. Local level planning agencies assess the needs of people who are able to give their direct input through the Gram Sabhas (village-based institutions) and the planners subsequently seek to plan accordingly.

Community Participatory Planning

Main article: Participatory planning

The United Nations has developed local projects that promote participatory planning on a community level. Members of communities take decisions regarding community development directly.

2.14.3 Political advocacy

Decentralised planning has been a feature of socialist and anarchist economics. Variations of decentralized planning include participatory economics, economic democracy and industrial democracy, and have been promoted by various political groups, most notably libertarian socialists, guild socialists, Marxists, anarchists and democratic socialists.

During the Spanish Revolution some areas, where anarchist and libertarian socialist influence through the CNT and UGT was extensive, particularly rural regions, were run on the basis of decentralised planning resembling the principles laid out by Diego Abad de Santillan in the book *After the Revolution*.[5]

2.14.4 See also

- Adhocracy
- Anarchist Spain
- Cybernetics
- Distributed economy
- Economic democracy
- Economic planning
- Horizontalidad
- Libertarian socialism
- Inclusive democracy
- Indicative planning
- Industrial democracy
- Market abolitionism
- Participatory economics
- Social ownership
- Peer-to-Peer economy
- Planned economy

- Project Cybersyn
- Production for use
- Self-managed economy
- Socialist economics

2.14.5 Notes

[1] ""What economic structure for socialism?", by Kotz, David. 2008" (PDF). Retrieved 2012-09-12.

[2] Schweickart, David. *Democratic Socialism.* Encyclopedia of Activism and Social Justice (2006): "Virtually all (democratic) socialists have distanced themselves from the economic model long synonymous with 'socialism,' i.e. the Soviet model of a non-market, centrally-planned economy...Some have endorsed the concept of 'market socialism,' a post-capitalist economy that retains market competition, but socializes the means of production, and, in some versions, extends democracy to the workplace. Some hold out for a non-market, participatory economy. All democratic socialists agree on the need for a democratic alternative to capitalism."

[3] ""The Computer and the market", Lange, Oskar. Retrieved March 16, 2011". Calculemus.org. Retrieved 2012-09-12.

[4] "Participatory Planning Through Negotiated Coordination" (PDF). Retrieved 30 October 2011.

[5] "After the Revolution". Membres.multimania.fr. 1936-01-07. Retrieved 2012-09-12.

2.14.6 Further reading

- Cox, Robin 2005, "The Economic Calculation controversy: unravelling of a myth" '
- Devine, Pat.'Democracy and Economic Planning. *Polity. 2010. ISBN 978-0745634791*
- Mandel, Ernest. *In Defence of Socialist Planning.* New Left Review, Issue 159. 1986.

2.15 Decommodification

Decommodification is the strength of social entitlements and citizens' degree of immunization from market dependency.

Decommodification is the process of viewing utilities as an entitlement, rather than as a commodity that must be paid or traded for. In effect, a decommodified product removes itself from the market, and can be associated with welfarism. An example of decommodification would be the removal of tolls from a toll road or the internet before becoming mostly supported by private ISPs.

Decommodification has been identified as a strategy for sustainable consumption that acts one level up on the institutional context of consumption in Western societies as compared to strategies such as eco-efficiency and eco-sufficiency.[1] Thus, while the eco-efficiency strategy targets the product and the eco-sufficiency strategy targets the person (the consumer as decision-maker), the decommodification strategy targets the institutional context in which consumption takes place. It aims to decrease the influence of commodities and to limit the effect of commercialisation.

2.15.1 Sources

Esping-Andersen, Gosta. 1990. The Three Worlds of Welfare Capitalism. Princeton University Press.

Messner, Steven F., and Richard Rosenfeld. 1997. Crime and the American Dream. 2d ed. Wadsworth

Messner, Steven F., and Richard Rosenfeld. 1997. Political Restraint of the Market and Levels of Criminal Homicide. Social Forces 75(4) 1393-1416

More on decommodification of information can be found at this World Social Forum page.

2.15.2 Notes

[1] Boulanger, P.M. (2010) "Three strategies for sustainable consumption". *S.A.P.I.EN.S.* **3** (2)

2.16 Ecological economics

For the academic journal, see Ecological Economics (journal).
Not to be confused with environmental economics.

Ecological economics/eco-economics refers to both a transdisciplinary and interdisciplinary field of academic research that aims to address the interdependence and coevolution of human economies and natural ecosystems over time and space.[1] It is distinguished from environmental economics, which is the mainstream economic analysis of the environment, by its treatment of the economy as a subsystem of the ecosystem and its emphasis upon preserving natural capital.[2] One survey of German economists found that ecological and environmental economics are different schools of economic thought, with ecological economists emphasizing strong sustainability and rejecting the proposition that natural capital can be substituted by human-made capital.[3]

Ecological economics was founded as a modern movement in the works of and interactions between various European and American academics (see the section on history and development below). The related field of green economics is, in general, a more politically applied form of the subject.[4][5]

According to ecological economist Malte Faber, ecological economics is defined by its focus on nature, justice, and time. Issues of intergenerational equity, irreversibility of environmental change, uncertainty of long-term outcomes, and sustainable development guide ecological economic analysis and valuation.[6] Ecological economists have questioned fundamental mainstream economic approaches such as cost-benefit analysis, and the separability of economic values from scientific research, contending that economics is unavoidably normative rather than positive (i.e. descriptive).[7] Positional analysis, which attempts to incorporate time and justice issues, is proposed as an alternative.[8][9] Ecological economics shares many of its perspectives with feminist economics, including the focus on sustainability, nature, justice and care values.[10]

2.16.1 History and development

Early modern interest in ecology and economics dates back to the 1940s in the work of K. William Kapp and Karl Polanyi and the 1960s in work by Kenneth Boulding and Herman Daly. However, the first organized meetings of modern ecological economists occurred in the 1980s. These began in 1982, at the instigation of Lois Banner,[11] with a meeting held in Sweden (including Robert Costanza, Herman Daly, Charles Hall, Bruce Hannon, H.T. Odum, and David Pimentel).[12] Most were ecosystem ecologists or mainstream environmental economists, with the exception of Daly. In 1987, Daly and Costanza edited an issue of *Ecological Modeling* to test the waters. A book entitled *Ecological Economics*, by Juan Martinez-Alier, was published later that year.[12] 1989 saw the foundation of the International Society for Ecological Economics and publication of its journal, *Ecological Economics*, by Elsevier. Robert Costanza was the first president of the society and first editor of the journal, currently edited by Richard Howarth.

European conceptual founders include Nicholas Georgescu-Roegen (1971), K. William Kapp (1950)[13] and Karl Polanyi (1944).[14] Some key concepts of what is now ecological economics are evident in the writings of E.F. Schumacher, whose book *Small Is Beautiful – A Study of Economics as if People Mattered* (1973) was published just a few years before the first edition of Herman Daly's comprehensive and persuasive *Steady-State Economics* (1977).[15][16] Other figures include ecologists C.S. Holling, H.T. Odum and Robert Costanza, biologist Gretchen Daily and physicist Robert Ayres. CUNY geography professor David Harvey explicitly added ecological concerns to political economic literature. This parallel development in political economy has been continued by analysts such as sociologist John Bellamy Foster.

The antecedents can be traced back to the Romantics of the 19th century as well as some Enlightenment political economists of that era. Concerns over population were expressed by Thomas Malthus, while John Stuart Mill hypothesized that the "stationary state" of an economy was desirable, anticipating later insights of modern ecological economists, without having had their experience of the social and ecological costs of the dramatic post-World War II industrial expansion. As Martinez-Alier explores in his book the debate on energy in economic systems can also be traced into the 19th century e.g. Nobel prize-winning chemist, Frederick Soddy (1877–1956). Soddy criticized the prevailing belief of the economy as a perpetual motion machine, capable of generating infinite wealth—a criticism echoed by his intellectual heirs in the now emergent field of ecological economics.[17]

The Romanian economist Nicholas Georgescu-Roegen (1906–1994), who was among Daly's teachers at Vanderbilt University, provided ecological economics with a modern conceptual framework based on the material and energy flows of economic production and consumption. His *magnum opus*, *The Entropy Law and the Economic Process* (1971), has been highly influential.[18]

Articles by Inge Ropke (2004, 2005)[19] and Clive Spash (1999)[20] cover the development and modern history of ecological economics and explain its differentiation from resource and environmental economics, as well as some of the controversy between American and European schools of thought. An article by Robert Costanza, David Stern, Lining He, and Chunbo Ma[21] responded to a call by Mick Common to determine the foundational literature of ecological economics by using citation analysis to examine which books and articles have had the most influence on the development of the field. However, citations analysis has itself proven controversial and similar work has been criticized by Clive Spash for attempting to pre-determine what is regarded as influential in ecological economics through study design and data manipulation.[22] In addition, the journal Ecological Economics has itself been criticized for swamping the field with mainstream economics.[23][24]

2.16.2 Nature and ecology

Main articles: Nature and Ecology

A simple circular flow of income diagram is replaced in ecological economics by a more complex flow diagram reflecting the input of solar energy, which sustains natural inputs and environmental services which are then used as units of production. Once consumed, natural inputs pass out of the economy as pollution and waste. The potential of an environment to provide services and materials is referred to as an "environment's source function", and this function is depleted as resources are consumed or pollution contaminates the resources. The "sink function" describes an environment's ability to absorb and render harmless waste and pollution: when waste output exceeds the limit of the sink function, long-term damage occurs.[25]:8 Some persistent pollutants, such as some organic pollutants and nuclear waste are absorbed very slowly or not at all; ecological economists emphasize minimizing "cumulative pollutants".[25]:28 Pollutants affect human health and the health of the climate.

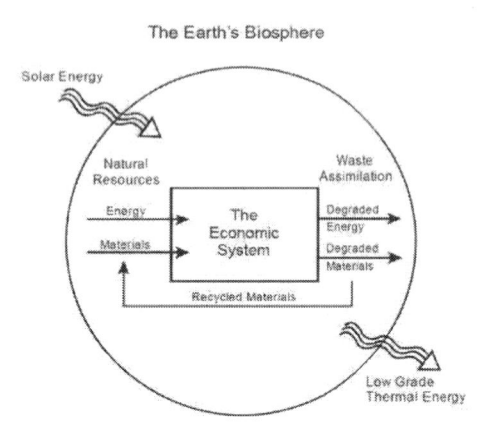

Natural resources flow through the economy and end up as waste and pollution

The economic value of natural capital and ecosystem services is accepted by mainstream environmental economics, but is emphasized as especially important in ecological economics. Ecological economists may begin by estimating how to maintain a stable environment before assessing the cost in dollar terms.[25]:9 Ecological economist Robert Costanza led an attempted valuation of the global ecosystem in 1997. Initially published in *Nature*, the article concluded on $33 trillion with a range from $16 trillion to $54 trillion (in 1997, total global GDP was $27 trillion).[26] Half of the value went to nutrient cycling. The open oceans, continental shelves, and estuaries had the highest total value, and the highest per-hectare values went to estuaries, swamps/floodplains, and seagrass/algae beds. The work was criticized by articles in *Ecological Economics* Volume 25, Issue 1, but the critics acknowledged the positive potential for economic valuation of the global ecosystem.[25]:129

The Earth's carrying capacity is a central issue in ecological economics. Early economists such as Thomas Malthus pointed out the finite carrying capacity of the earth, which was also central to the MIT study *Limits to Growth*. Diminishing returns suggest that productivity increases will slow if major technological progress is not made. Food production may become a problem, as erosion, an impending water crisis, and soil salinity (from irrigation) reduce the productivity of agriculture. Ecological economists argue that industrial agriculture, which exacerbates these problems, is not sustainable agriculture, and are generally inclined favorably to organic farming, which also reduces the output of carbon.[25]:26

Global wild fisheries are believed to have peaked and begun a decline, with valuable habitat such as estuaries in critical condition.[25]:28 The aquaculture or farming of piscivorous fish, like salmon, does not help solve the problem because they need to be fed products from other fish. Studies have shown that salmon farming has major negative impacts on wild salmon, as well as the forage fish that need to be caught to feed them.[27][28]

Since animals are higher on the trophic level, they are less efficient sources of food energy. Reduced consumption of meat would reduce the demand for food, but as nations develop, they tend to adopt high-meat diets similar to that of the United States. Genetically modified food (GMF) a conventional solution to the problem, presents numerous problems – Bt corn produces its own Bacillus thuringiensis toxin/protein, but the pest resistance is believed to be only a matter of time.[25]:31 The overall effect of GMF on yields is contentious, with the USDA and FAO acknowledging that GMFs do not necessarily have higher yields and may even have reduced yields.[29]

Global warming is now widely acknowledged as a major issue, with all national scientific academies expressing agreement on the importance of the issue. As the population growth intensifies and energy demand increases, the world faces an energy crisis. Some economists and scientists forecast a global ecological crisis if energy use is not contained – the Stern report is an example. The disagreement has sparked a vigorous debate on issue of discounting and intergenerational equity.

- GLOBAL GEOCHEMICAL CYCLES CRITICAL FOR LIFE
- Nitrogen cycle
- Water cycle
- Carbon cycle

- Oxygen cycle

2.16.3 Ethics

See also: Environmental ethics

Mainstream economics has attempted to become a value-free 'hard science', but ecological economists argue that value-free economics is generally not realistic. Ecological economics is more willing to entertain alternative conceptions of utility, efficiency, and cost-benefits such as positional analysis or multi-criteria analysis. Ecological economics is typically viewed as economics for sustainable development,[30] and may have goals similar to green politics.

2.16.4 Schools of thought

Various competing schools of thought exist in the field. Some are close to resource and environmental economics while others are far more heterodox in outlook. An example of the latter is the *European Society for Ecological Economics*. An example of the former is the Swedish *Beijer International Institute of Ecological Economics*. Clive Spash has argued for the classification of the ecological economics movement, and more generally work by different economic schools on the environment, into three main categories. These are the mainstream new resource economists, the new environmental pragmatists,[31] and the more radical social ecological economists.[32] International survey work comparing the relevance of the categories for mainstream and heterodox economists shows some clear divisions between environmental and ecological economists.[33]

2.16.5 Differentiation from mainstream schools

Some ecological economists prioritise adding natural capital to the typical capital asset analysis of land, labor, and financial capital. These ecological economists then use tools from mathematical economics as in mainstream economics, but may apply them more closely to the natural world. Whereas mainstream economists tend to be technological optimists, ecological economists are inclined to be technological sceptics. They reason that the natural world has a limited carrying capacity and that its resources may run out. Since destruction of important environmental resources could be practically irreversible and catastrophic, ecological economists are inclined to justify cautionary measures based on the precautionary principle.[34]

The most cogent example of how the different theories treat similar assets is tropical rainforest ecosystems, most obviously the Yasuni region of Ecuador. While this area has substantial deposits of bitumen it is also one of the most diverse ecosystems on Earth and some estimates establish it has over 200 undiscovered medical substances in its genomes - most of which would be destroyed by logging the forest or mining the bitumen. Effectively, the instructional capital of the genomes is undervalued by analyses which view the rainforest primarily as a source of wood, oil/tar and perhaps food. Increasingly the carbon credit for leaving the extremely carbon-intensive ("dirty") bitumen in the ground is also valued - the government of Ecuador set a price of US$350M for an oil lease with the intent of selling it to someone committed to never exercising it at all and instead preserving the rainforest.

While this natural capital and ecosystems services approach has proven popular amongst many it has also been contested as failing to address the underlying problems with mainstream economics, growth, market capitalism and monetary valuation of the environment.[35][36][37] Critiques concern the need to create a more meaningful relationship with Nature and the non-human world than evident in the instrumentalism of shallow ecology and the environmental economists commodification of everything external to the market system.[38][39][40]

2.16.6 Topics

Among the topics addressed by ecological economics are methodology, allocation of resources, weak versus strong sustainability, energy economics, energy accounting and balance, environmental services, cost shifting, and modeling.

Methodology

A primary objective of ecological economics (EE) is to ground economic thinking and practice in physical reality, especially in the laws of physics (particularly the laws of thermodynamics) and in knowledge of biological systems. It accepts as a goal the improvement of human well-being through development, and seeks to ensure achievement of this through planning for the sustainable development of ecosystems and societies. Of course the terms development and sustainable development are far from lacking controversy. Richard B. Norgaard argues traditional economics has hi-jacked the development terminology in his book *Development Betrayed*.[41]

Well-being in ecological economics is also differentiated from welfare as found in mainstream economics and the 'new welfare economics' from the 1930s which informs resource and environmental economics. This entails a limited preference utilitarian conception of value i.e., Nature is valuable to our economies, that is because people will pay for its services such as clean air, clean water, encounters with wilderness, etc.

Ecological economics is distinguishable from neoclassical economics primarily by its assertion that the economy is embedded within an environmental system. Ecology deals with the energy and matter transactions of life and the Earth, and the human economy is by definition contained within this system. Ecological economists argue that neoclassical economics has ignored the environment, at best considering it to be a subset of the human economy.

The neoclassical view ignores much of what the natural sciences have taught us about the contributions of nature to the creation of wealth e.g., the planetary endowment of scarce matter and energy, along with the complex and biologically diverse ecosystems that provide goods and ecosystem services directly to human communities: micro- and macro-climate regulation, water recycling, water purification, storm water regulation, waste absorption, food and medicine production, pollination, protection from solar and cosmic radiation, the view of a starry night sky, etc.

There has then been a move to regard such things as natural capital and ecosystems functions as goods and services.[42][43] However, this is far from uncontroversial within ecology or ecological economics due to the potential for narrowing down values to those found in mainstream economics and the danger of merely regarding Nature as a commodity. This has been referred to as ecologists 'selling out on Nature'.[44] There is then a concern that ecological economics has failed to learn from the extensive literature in environmental ethics about how to structure a plural value system.

Allocation of resources

Resource and neoclassical economics focus primarily on the efficient allocation of resources, and less on two other fundamental economic problems which are central to ecological economics: distribution (equity) and the scale of the economy relative to the ecosystems upon which it is reliant.[45] Ecological Economics also makes a clear distinction between growth (quantitative increase in economic output) and development (qualitative improvement of the quality of life) while arguing that neoclassical economics confuses the two. Ecological economists point out that, beyond modest levels, increased per-capita consumption (the typical economic measure of "standard of living") does not necessarily lead to improvement in human well-being, while this same consumption can have harmful effects on the environment and broader societal well-being.

Weak versus strong sustainability

Main article: Weak and strong sustainability
See also: Nicholas Georgescu-Roegen § Criticising neoclassical economics (weak versus strong sustainability)

The three nested systems of sustainability - the economy wholly contained by society, wholly contained by the biophysical environment. Clickable.

Ecological economics challenges the conventional approach towards natural resources, claiming that it undervalues natural capital by considering it as interchangeable with human-made capital—labor and technology.

The impending depletion of natural resources and increase of climate-changing greenhouse gasses should motivate us to examine how political, economic and social policies can benefit from alternative energy. Interestingly enough, shifting our dependence on fossil fuels with specific interest within just one of the above-mentioned factors easily benefits at least one other. For instance, photo voltaic (or solar) panels have a 15% efficiency when absorbing the sun's energy, but its construction demand has increased 120% within both commercial and residential properties. Additionally, this construction has led to a roughly 30% increase in work demands (Chen).

The potential for the substitution of man-made capital for natural capital is an important debate in ecological economics and the economics of sustainability. There is a continuum of views among economists between the strongly neoclassical positions of Robert Solow and Martin Weitzman, at one extreme and the 'entropy pessimists', notably Nicholas Georgescu-Roegen and Herman Daly, at the other.[46]

Neoclassical economists tend to maintain that man-made capital can, in principle, replace all types of natural capital. This is known as the weak sustainability view, essentially that every technology can be improved upon or replaced by innovation, and that there is a substitute for any and all scarce materials.

At the other extreme, the strong sustainability view argues that the stock of natural resources and ecological functions are irreplaceable. From the premises of strong sustainability, it follows that economic policy has a fiduciary responsibility to the greater ecological world, and that sustainable development must therefore take a different approach to valuing natural resources and ecological functions.

Recently, Stanislav Shmelev developed a new methodology for the assessment of progress at the macro scale based on multi-criteria methods, which allows consideration of different perspectives, including strong and weak sustainability or conservationists vs industrialists and aims to search for a 'middle way' by providing a strong neo-Keynsian economic push without putting excessive pressure on the natural resources, including water or producing emissions, both directly and indirectly.[47]

Energy economics

Main article: Energy economics

A key concept of energy economics is net energy gain, which recognizes that all energy requires energy to produce. To be useful the energy return on energy invested (*EROEI*) has to be greater than one. The net energy gain from production coal, oil and gas has declined over time as the easiest to produce sources have been most heavily depleted.[48]

Ecological economics generally rejects the view of energy economics that growth in the energy supply is related directly to well being, focusing instead on biodiversity and creativity - or natural capital and individual capital, in the terminology sometimes adopted to describe these economically. In practice, ecological economics focuses primarily on the key issues of uneconomic growth and quality of life. Ecological economists are inclined to acknowledge that much of what is important in human well-being is not analyzable from a strictly economic standpoint and suggests an interdisciplinary approach combining social and natural sciences as a means to address this.

Thermoeconomics is based on the proposition that the role of energy in biological evolution should be defined and understood through the second law of thermodynamics, but also in terms of such economic criteria as productivity, efficiency, and especially the costs and benefits (or profitability) of the various mechanisms for capturing and utilizing available energy to build biomass and do work.[49][50] As a result, thermoeconomics is often discussed in the field of ecological economics, which itself is related to the fields of sustainability and sustainable development.

Exergy analysis is performed in the field of industrial ecology to use energy more efficiently.[51] The term *exergy*, was coined by Zoran Rant in 1956, but the concept was developed by J. Willard Gibbs. In recent decades, utilization of exergy has spread outside of physics and engineering to the fields of industrial ecology, ecological economics, systems ecology, and energetics.

Energy accounting and balance

See also: Net energy gain

An energy balance can be used to track energy through a system, and is a very useful tool for determining resource use and environmental impacts, using the First and Second laws of thermodynamics, to determine how much energy is needed at each point in a system, and in what form that energy is a cost in various environmental issues. The energy accounting system keeps track of energy in, energy out, and non-useful energy versus work done, and transformations within the system.[52]

Scientists have written and speculated on different aspects of energy accounting.[53]

Environmental services

See also: Ecosystem valuation and price of life

A study was carried out by Costanza and colleagues[54] to determine the 'price' of the services provided by the environment. This was determined by averaging values obtained from a range of studies conducted in very specific context and then transferring these without regard to that context. Dollar figures were averaged to a per hectare number for different types of ecosystem e.g. wetlands, oceans. A total was then produced which came out at 33 trillion US dollars (1997 values), more than twice the total GDP of the world at the time of the study. This study was criticized by pre-ecological and even some environmental economists - for being inconsistent with assumptions of financial capital valuation - and ecological economists - for being inconsistent with an ecological economics focus on biological and physical indicators.[55]

The whole idea of treating ecosystems as goods and services to be valued in monetary terms remains controversial. A common objection is that life is precious or priceless, but this demonstrably degrades to it being worthless under the assumptions of any branch of economics. Reducing human bodies to financial values is a necessary part of every branch of economics and not always in the direct terms of insurance or wages. Economics, in principle, assumes that conflict is reduced by agreeing on voluntary contractual relations and prices instead of simply fighting or coercing or tricking others into providing goods or services. In doing so, a provider agrees to surrender time and take bodily risks and other (reputation, financial) risks. Ecosystems are no different from other bodies economically except insofar as they are far less replaceable than typical labour or commodities.

Despite these issues, many ecologists and conservation biologists are pursuing ecosystem valuation. Biodiversity measures in particular appear to be the most promising way to reconcile financial and ecological values, and there are many active efforts in this regard. The growing field of biodiversity finance[56] began to emerge in 2008 in response to many specific proposals such as the Ecuadoran Yasuni proposal[57][58] or similar ones in the Congo. US news outlets treated the stories as a "threat"[59] to "drill a park"[60] reflecting a previously dominant view that NGOs and governments had the primary responsibility to protect ecosystems. However Peter Barnes and other commentators have recently argued that a guardianship/trustee/commons model is far more effective and takes the decisions out of the political realm.

Commodification of other ecological relations as in carbon credit and direct payments to farmers to preserve ecosystem services are likewise examples that enable private parties to play more direct roles protecting biodiversity. The United Nations Food and Agriculture Organization achieved near-universal agreement in 2008[61] that such payments directly valuing ecosystem preservation and encouraging permaculture were the only practical way out of a food crisis. The holdouts were all English-speaking countries that export GMOs and promote "free trade" agreements that facilitate their own control of the world transport network: The US, UK, Canada and Australia.[62]

Not 'externalities', but cost shifting

Ecological economics is founded upon the view that the neoclassical economics (NCE) assumption that environmental and community costs and benefits are mutually canceling *"externalities"* is not warranted. Joan Martinez Alier,[63] for instance shows that the bulk of consumers are automatically excluded from having an impact upon the prices of commodities, as these consumers are future generations who have not been born yet. The assumptions behind future discounting, which assume that future goods will be cheaper than present goods, has been criticized by Fred Pearce[64] and by the recent Stern Report (although the Stern report itself does employ discounting and has been criticized for this and other reasons by ecological economists such as Clive Spash).[65]

Concerning these externalities, some like the eco-businessman Paul Hawken argue an orthodox economic line that the only reason why goods produced unsustainably are usually cheaper than goods produced sustainably is due to a hidden subsidy, paid by the non-monetized human environment, community or future generations.[66] These arguments are developed further by Hawken, Amory and Hunter Lovins to promote their vision of an environmental capitalist utopia in *Natural Capitalism: Creating the Next Industrial Revolution*.[67]

In contrast, ecological economists, like Joan Martinez-Alier, appeal to a different line of reasoning.[68] Rather than assuming some (new) form of capitalism is the best way forward, an older ecological economic critique questions the very idea of internalizing externalities as providing some corrective to the current system. The work by Karl William Kapp explains why the concept of "externality" is a misnomer.[69] In fact the modern business enterprise operates on the basis of shifting costs onto others as normal practice to make profits.[70] Charles Einsentein has argued that this method of privatising profits while socialising the costs through externalities, passing the costs to the community, to the natural environment or to future generations is inherently destructive[71] As social ecological economist Clive Spash has noted, externality theory fallaciously assumes environmental and social problems are minor aberrations in an otherwise perfectly functioning efficient economic system.[72] Internalizing the odd externality does nothing to address the structural systemic problem and fails to recognize the all pervasive nature of these supposed 'externalities'.

Ecological-economic modeling

Mathematical modeling is a powerful tool that is used in ecological economic analysis. Various approaches and techniques include:[73][74] evolutionary, input-output, neo-Austrian modeling, entropy and thermodynamic models,[75] multi-criteria, and agent-based modeling, the environmental Kuznets curve, and Stock-Flow consistent model frameworks. System dynamics and GIS are techniques applied, among other, to spatial dynamic landscape simulation modeling.[76][77] The Matrix accounting methods of Christian Felber provide a more sophisticated method for identifying "the common good"[78]

2.16.7 Criticism

Assigning monetary value to natural resources such as biodiversity, and the emergent ecosystem services is often viewed as a key process in influencing economic practices, policy, and decision-making.[79][80] While this idea is becoming more and more accepted among ecologists and conservationist, some argue that it is inherently false.

McCauley argues that ecological economics and the resulting ecosystem service based conservation can be harmful.[81] He describes four main problems with this approach:

Firstly, it seems to be assumed that all ecosystem services are financially beneficial. This is undermined by a basic characteristic of ecosystems: they do not act specifically in favour of any single species. While certain services might be very useful to us, such as coastal protection from hurricanes by mangroves for example, others might cause financial or personal harm, such as wolves hunting cattle.[82] The complexity of Eco-systems makes it challenging to weigh up the value of a given species. Wolves play a critical role in regulating prey populations, the absence of such an apex predator in the Scottish Highlands have caused the over population of deer, preventing afforestation, which increases the risk of flooding and damage to property.

Secondly, allocating monetary value to nature would make its conservation reliant on markets that fluctuate. This can lead to devaluation of services that were previously considered financially beneficial. Such is the case of the bees in a forest near former coffee plantations in Finca Santa Fe, Costa Rica. The pollination services were valued to over US$60,000 a year, but soon after the study, coffee prices dropped and the fields were replanted with pineapple.[83] Pineapple does not require bees to be pollinated, so the value of their service dropped to zero.

Thirdly, conservation programmes for the sake of financial benefit underestimate human ingenuity to invent and replace ecosystem services by artificial means. McCauley argues that such proposals are deemed to have a short lifespan as the history of technology is about how Humanity developed artificial alternatives to nature's services and with time passing the cost of such services tend to decrease. This would also lead to the devaluation of ecosystem services.

Lastly, it should not be assumed that conserving ecosystems is always financially beneficial as opposed to alteration. In the case of the introduction of the Nile perch to Lake Victoria, the ecological consequence was decimation of native fauna. However, this same event is praised by the local communities as they gain significant financial benefits from trading the fish.

McCauley argues that, for these reasons, trying to convince decision-makers to conserve nature for monetary reasons is not the path to be followed, and instead appealing to morality is the ultimate way to campaign for the protection of nature.

2.16.8 See also

- Agroecology
- Deep ecology
- Earth Economics (policy think tank)
- Eco-socialism
- Ecofeminism
- Ecological values of mangrove
- Ecology of contexts
- Embodied energy
- Embodied water
- Energy accounting
- Energy quality
- Environmental economics
- Green accounting
- *The Green Economist* (newsletter)
- Human development theory
- Human ecology
- Inclusive Democracy
- Index of Sustainable Economic Welfare
- Natural capital accounting
- Natural resource economics
- Outline of green politics
- Spaceship Earth
- Steady-state economy
- Thermoeconomics

2.16.9 References

[1] Anastasios Xepapadeas (2008). "Ecological economics". *The New Palgrave Dictionary of Economics 2nd Edition*. Palgrave MacMillan.

[2] Jeroen C.J.M. van den Bergh (2001). "Ecological Economics: Themes, Approaches, and Differences with Environmental Economics," *Regional Environmental Change*, 2(1), pp. 13-23 (press +).

[3] Illge L, Schwarze R. (2006). A Matter of Opinion: How Ecological and Neoclassical Environmental Economists Think about Sustainability and Economics . German Institute for Economic Research.

[4] Paehlke R. (1995). *Conservation and Environmentalism: An Encyclopedia*, p. 315. Taylor & Francis.

[5] Scott Cato, M. (2009). *Green Economics*. Earthscan, London. ISBN 978-1-84407-571-3.

[6] Malte Faber. (2008). How to be an ecological economist. *Ecological Economics* **66**(1):1-7. Preprint.

[7] Peter Victor. (2008). Book Review: Frontiers in Ecological Economic Theory and Application. *Ecological Economics* **66**(2-3).

[8] Mattson L. (1975). Book Review: *Positional Analysis for Decision-Making and Planning* by Peter Soderbaum. *The Swedish Journal of Economics*.

[9] Soderbaum, P. 2008. *Understanding Sustainability Economics*. Earthscan, London. ISBN 978-1-84407-627-7. pp.109-110, 113-117.

[10] Aslaksen, Iulie; Bragstad, Torunn; Ås, Berit (2014). "Feminist Economics as Vision for a Sustainable Future". In Bjørnholt, Margunn; McKay, Ailsa. *Counting on Marilyn Waring: New Advances in Feminist Economics*. Demeter Press/Brunswick Books. pp. 21–36. ISBN 9781927335277.

[11] Røpke, I. (2004) The early history of modern ecological economics. Ecological Economics 50(3-4): 293-314.

[12] Costanza R. (2003). Early History of Ecological Economics and ISEE. Internet Encyclopaedia of Ecological Economics.

[13] Kapp, K. W. (1950) *The Social Costs of Private Enterprise*. New York: Shocken.

[14] Polanyi, K. (1944) *The Great Transformation*. New York/Toronto: Rinehart & Company Inc.

[15] Schumacher, E.F. 1973. *Small Is Beautiful: A Study of Economics as if People Mattered*. London: Blond and Briggs.

[16] Daly, H. 1991. *Steady-State Economics* (2nd ed.). Washington, D.C.: Island Press.

[17] Zencey, Eric. (2009, April 12). Op-ed. *New York Times*, p. WK9. Accessed: December 23, 2012.

[18] Georgescu-Roegen, N. 1971. *The Entropy Law and the Economic Process*. Cambridge, Mass.: Harvard University Press.

[19] Røpke, I. (2004) The early history of modern ecological economics. Ecological Economics 50(3-4): 293-314. Røpke, I. (2005) Trends in the development of ecological economics from the late 1980s to the early 2000s. Ecological Economics 55(2): 262-290.

[20] "Spash, C. L. (1999) The development of environmental thinking in economics. Environmental Values 8(4): 413-435." (PDF). Retrieved 2012-12-23.

[21] Costanza, R., Stern, D. I., He, L., Ma, C. (2004). Influential publications in ecological economics: a citation analysis. Ecological Economics 50(3-4): 261-292.

[22] Spash, C. L. (2013) Influencing the perception of what and who is important in ecological economics. Ecological Economics 89: 204-209.

[23] Spash, C. L. (2013) The Shallow or the Deep Ecological Economics Movement? Ecological Economics 93:351-362.

[24] Anderson, B., M'Gonigle, M., 2012. Does ecological economics have a future?: contradiction and reinvention in the age of climate change. Ecological Economics 84, 37–48.

[25] Harris J. (2006). *Environmental and Natural Resource Economics: A Contemporary Approach*. Houghton Mifflin Company.

[26] Costanza R; et al. (1998). "The value of the world's ecosystem services and natural capital1". *Ecological Economics* 25 (1): 3–15. doi:10.1016/S0921-8009(98)00020-2.

[27] Knapp G, Roheim CA and Anderson JL (2007) *The Great Salmon Run: Competition Between Wild And Farmed Salmon* World Wildlife Fund. ISBN 0-89164-175-0

[28] Washington Post. Salmon Farming May Doom Wild Populations, Study Says.

[29] Soil Association. UK Organic Group Exposes Myth that Genetically Engineered Crops Have Higher Yields. Organic Consumers Association.

[30] Soderbaum P. (2004). Politics and Ideology in Ecological Economics. Internet Encyclopaedia of Ecological Economics.

[31] "Spash, C.L. (2009) The new environmental pragmatists, pluralism and sustainability. Environmental Values 18, 253-256" (PDF). Retrieved 2014-01-07.

[32] "Spash, C.L. (2011) Social ecological economics: Understanding the past to see the future. American Journal of Economics and Sociology 70, 340-375" (PDF). Retrieved 2014-01-07.

[33] Jacqui Lagrue (2012-07-30). "Spash, C.L., Ryan, A. (2012) Economic schools of thought on the environment: Investigating unity and division. Cambridge Journal of Economics 36, 1091-1121" (PDF). Cje.oxfordjournals.org. Retrieved 2014-01-07.

[34] Costanza R. (1989). What is ecological economics? *Ecological Economics* **1**:1-7. .

[35] Martinez-Alier, J., 1994. Ecological economics and ecosocialism, in: O'Connor, M. (Ed.), Is Capitalism Sustainable? Guilford Press, New York, pp. 23-36

[36] Spash, C.L., Clayton, A.M.H., 1997. The maintenance of natural capital: Motivations and methods, in: Light, A., Smith, J.M. (Eds.), Space, Place and Environmental Ethics. Rowman & Littlefield Publishers, Inc., Lanham, pp. 143-173

[37] Toman, M., 1998. Why not to calculate the value of the world's ecosystem services and natural capital. Ecological Economics 25, 57-60

[38] O'Neill, J.F., 1993. Ecology, Policy and Politics: Human Well-Being and the Natural World. Routledge, London

[39] O'Neill, J.F. (1997) Managing without prices: On the monetary valuation of biodiversity. Ambio 26, 546-550

[40] Vatn, A., 2000. The environment as commodity. Environmental Values 9, 493-509

[41] Norgaard, R. B. (1994) Development Betrayed: The End of Progress and a Coevolutionary Revisioning of the Future. London: Routledge

[42] Daily, G.C. 1997. *Nature's Services: Societal Dependence on Natural Ecosystems.* Washington, D.C.: Island Press.

[43] Millennium Ecosystem Assessment. 2005. *Ecosystems and Human Well-Being: Biodiversity Synthesis.* Washington, D.C.: World Resources Institute.

[44] McCauley, D. J. (2006) Selling out on nature. Nature 443(7): 27-28

[45] Daly, H. and Farley, J. 2004. *Ecological Economics: Principles and Applications.* Washington: Island Press.

[46] Ayres, R.U. 2007. On the practical limits of substitution. Ecological Economics 61: 115-128.

[47] Shmelev, S.E. 2012. Ecological Economics. Sustainability in Practice, Springer

[48] Hall, Charles A.S.; Cleveland, Cutler J.; Kaufmann, Robert (1992). *Energy and Resource Quality: The ecology of the Economic Process.* Niwot, Colorado: University Press of colorado.

[49] Peter A. Corning 1 *, Stephen J. Kline. (2000). Thermodynamics, information and life revisited, Part II: Thermoeconomics and Control information Systems Research and Behavioral Science, Apr. 07, Volume 15, Issue 6, Pages 453 – 482

[50] Corning, P. (2002). "Thermoeconomics – Beyond the Second Law" – source: www.complexsystems.org

[51] Wall, Göran. "Exergy - a useful concept". Exergy.se. Retrieved 2012-12-23.

[52] "Environmental Decision making, Science and Technology". Telstar.ote.cmu.edu. Retrieved 2012-12-23.

[53] Stabile, Donald R. "Veblen and the Political Economy of the Engineer: the radical thinker and engineering leaders came to technocratic ideas at the same time," *American Journal of Economics and Sociology (45:1) 1986, 43-44.*

[54] Costanza, R., d'Arge, R., de Groot, R., Farber, S., Grasso, M., Hannon, B., Naeem, S., Limburg, K., Paruelo, J., O'Neill, R.V., Raskin, R., Sutton, P., and van den Belt, M. (1997). "The value of the world's ecosystem services and natural capital" (PDF). *Nature* **387** (6630): 253–260. Bibcode:1997Natur.387..253C. doi:10.1038/387253a0.

[55] Norgaard, R.B. and Bode, C. (1998). "Next, the value of God, and other reactions". *Ecological Economics* **25**: 37–39. doi:10.1016/s0921-8009(98)00012-3.

[56] SocialEdge.org. Accessed: December 23, 2012.

[57] Archived June 21, 2008 at the Wayback Machine

[58] Multinational Monitor, 9/2007. Accessed: December 23, 2012.

[59] "Ecuador threat to drill jungle oil". Archived from the original on December 18, 2008.

[60] "International News | World News - ABC News". Abcnews.go.com. 4 June 2012. Retrieved 2012-12-23.

[61] http://www.panna.org/jt/agAssessment

[62] Emmott, Bill (April 17, 2008). "GM crops can save us from food shortages". *The Daily Telegraph* (London).

[63] Costanza, Robert; Segura,Olman; Olsen, Juan Martinez-Alier (1996). *Getting Down to Earth: Practical Applications of Ecological Economics.* Washington, D.C.: Island Press. ISBN 1559635037.

[64] Pearce, Fred "Blueprint for a Greener Economy"

[65] "Spash, C. L. (2007) The economics of climate change impacts à la Stern: Novel and nuanced or rhetorically restricted? Ecological Economics 63(4): 706-713" (PDF). Retrieved 2012-12-23.

[66] Hawken, Paul (1994) "The Ecology of Commerce" (Collins)

[67] Hawken, Paul; Amory and Hunter Lovins (2000) "Natural Capitalism: Creating the Next Industrial Revolution" (Back Bay Books)

[68] Martinez-Alier, Joan (2002) The Environmentalism of the Poor: A Study of Ecological Conflicts and Valuation. Cheltenham, Edward Elgar

[69] Kapp, Karl William (1963) The Social Costs of Business Enterprise. Bombay/London, Asia Publishing House.

[70] Kapp, Karl William (1971) Social costs, neo-classical economics and environmental planning. The Social Costs of Business Enterprise, 3rd edition. K. W. Kapp. Nottingham, Spokesman: 305-318

[71] Einsentein, Charles (2011), "Sacred Economics: Money, Gift and Society in an Age in Transition" (Evolver Editions)

[72] Spash, Clive L. (16 July 2010). "The brave new world of carbon trading". *New Political Economy* (Taylor and Francis Online) **15** (2): 169–195. doi:10.1080/13563460903556049#.UerTmZgiPIU (inactive 2015-01-12). Copy also available at http://www.clivespash.org/2010_Spash_Brave_New_World_NPE.pdf

[73] Proops, J. , and Safonov, P. (eds.) (2004), Modelling in Ecological Economics, Edward Elgar

[74] Faucheux, S., Pearce, D., and Proops, J. (eds.) (1995), Models of Sustainable Development, Edward Elgar

[75] Chen, Jing (2015). *The Unity of Science and Economics: A New Foundation of Economic Theory.* http://www.springer.com/us/book/9781493934645: Springer.

[76] Costanza, R., and Voinov, A. (eds.) (2004), Landscape Simulation Modeling. A Spatially Explicit, Dynamic Approach, Springer-Verlag New-York, Inc.

[77] Voinov, Alexey (2008). *Systems science and modeling for ecological economics* (1st ed.). Amsterdam: Elsevier Academic Press. ISBN 0080886175.

[78] Felber, Christian (2012), "La economia del bien commun" (Duestro)

[79] Mace GM. Whose conservation? Science (80-). 2014 Sep 25;345(6204):1558–60.

[80] Dasgupta P. Nature's role in sustaining economic development. Philos Trans R Soc Lond B Biol Sci. 2010 Jan 12;365(1537):5–11.

[81] McCauley D. Selling out on nature. Nature. 2006;443(September):7–8.

[82] Mech LD. The Challenge and Opportunity of Recovering Wolf Populations. Conserv Biol. 1995 Apr;9(2):270–8

[83] Ricketts TH, Daily GC, Ehrlich PR, Michener CD. Economic value of tropical forest to coffee production. Proc Natl Acad Sci U S A. 2004 Aug 24;101(34):12579–82

2.16.10 Further reading

- Common, M. and Stagl, S. 2005. *Ecological Economics: An Introduction*. New York: Cambridge University Press.

- Costanza, R., Cumberland, J. H.,Daly, H., Goodland, R., Norgaard, R. B. (1997). *An Introduction to Ecological Economics*, St. Lucie Press and International Society for Ecological Economics, (e-book at the Encyclopedia of Earth)

- Costanza, R., Stern, D. I., He, L., Ma, C. (2004). Influential publications in ecological economics: a citation analysis. *Ecological Economics* 50(3-4): 261-292. - http://econpapers.repec.org/article/eeeecolec/v_3A50_3Ay_3A2004_3Ai_3A3-4_3Ap_3A261-292.htm

- Daly, H. (1980). *Economics, Ecology, Ethics: Essays Toward a Steady-State Economy*, W.H. Freeman and Company, ISBN 0716711796.

- Daly, H. and Townsend, K. (eds.) 1993. *Valuing The Earth: Economics, Ecology, Ethics*. Cambridge, Mass.; London, England: MIT Press.

- Daly, H. (1994). "Steady-state Economics". In: *Ecology - Key Concepts in Critical Theory*, edited by C. Merchant. Humanities Press, ISBN 0391037951.

- Daly, H., and J.B. Cobb (1994). *For the Common Good: Redirecting the Economy Toward Community, the Environment, and a Sustainable Future*. Beacon Press, ISBN 0807047058.

- Daly, H. (1997). *Beyond Growth: The Economics of Sustainable Development*. Beacon Press, ISBN 0807047090.

- Daly, H., and J. Farley (2010). *Ecological Economics: Principles and Applications*. Island Press, ISBN 1597266817.

- Georgescu-Roegen, N. 1975. Energy and economic myths. *Southern Economic Journal* 41: 347-381.

- Georgescu-Roegen, N. (1999). *The Entropy Law and the Economic Process*. iUniverse Press, ISBN 1583486003.

- Gowdy, J., and J.D. Erickson (2005). The approach of ecological economics. *Cambridge Journal of Economics* 29: 207-222.

- Greer, J. M. (2011). *The Wealth of Nature: Economics as if Survival Mattered*. New Society Publishers, ISBN 0865716730.

- Huesemann, Michael H., and Joyce A. Huesemann (2011). *Technofix: Why Technology Won't Save Us or the Environment*, New Society Publishers, Gabriola Island, British Columbia, Canada, ISBN 0865717044, 464 pp.

- Jackson, Tim (2009). *Prosperity without Growth - Economics for a finite Planet*. London: Routledge/Earthscan. ISBN 9781849713238.

- Krishnan R, Harris J.M., and N.R. Goodwin (1995). *A Survey of Ecological Economics*. Island Press. ISBN 978-1-55963-411-3.

- Martinez-Alier, J. (1990) *Ecological Economics: Energy, Environment and Society*. Oxford, England: Basil Blackwell.

- Martinez-Alier, J., Ropke, I. eds. (2008). *Recent Developments in Ecological Economics*, 2 vols., E. Elgar, Cheltenham, UK.

- Røpke, I. (2004) The early history of modern ecological economics. *Ecological Economics* 50(3-4): 293-314.

- Røpke, I. (2005) Trends in the development of ecological economics from the late 1980s to the early 2000s. *Ecological Economics* 55(2): 262-290.

- Spash, C. L. (1999) The development of environmental thinking in economics. *Environmental Values* 8(4): 413-435.

- Shmelev S. E. (2012) Ecological Economics: Sustainability in Practice, Springer 256 pp. http://www.amazon.co.uk/Ecological-Economics-Sustainability-Stanislav-Shmelev/dp/940071971X

- Stern, D. I. (1997) Limits to substitution and irreversibility in production and consumption: A neoclassical interpretation of ecological economics. *Ecological Economics* 21(3): 197-215. - http://econpapers.repec.org/article/eeeecolec/v_3A21_3Ay_3A1997_3Ai_3A3_3Ap_3A197-215.htm

- Tacconi, L. (2000) *Biodiversity and Ecological Economics: Participation, Values, and Resource Management*. London, UK: Earthscan Publications.

- Vatn, A. (2005) *Institutions and the Environment*. Cheltenham: Edward Elgar.

2.16.11 External links

- Brazilian Society for Ecological Economics
- Earth Economics
- *Ecological Economics* (journal)
- *Ecological Economics Encyclopedia*
- *International Journal of Green Economics*
- International Society for Ecological Economics
- US Society of Ecological Economics

Schools and institutes:

- Gund Institute for Ecological Economics - http://www.uvm.edu/giee
- Ecological Economics at Rensselaer Polytechnic Institute - http://www.economics.rpi.edu/ecological.html
- Beijer International Institute for Ecological Economics - http://www.beijer.kva.se/
- Green Economics Institute - http://www.greeneconomics.org.uk

Environmental data:

- EarthTrends World Resources Institute - http://earthtrends.wri.org/index.php
- Eco-Economy Indicators: http://www.earth-policy.org/Indicators/
- NOAA Economics of Ecosystems Data & Products – http://www.economics.noaa.gov/?goal=ecosystems

Miscellaneous:

- New Economics Foundation (NEF)- http://www.neweconomics.org
- Green Economist - http://greeneconomist.org/
- Sustainable Prosperity - http://sustainableprosperity.ca/
- An ecological economics article about reconciling economics and its supporting ecosystem - http://www.fs.fed.us/eco/s21pre.htm
- "Economics in a Full World", by Herman E. Daly - http://sef.umd.edu/files/ScientificAmerican_Daly_05.pdf
- Robert Nadeau (2008). "Environmental and ecological economics". *The Encyclopedia of Earth*. (A thorough account of the historical development of ecological economics)
- Steve Charnovitz, "Living in an Ecolonomy: Environmental Cooperation and the GATT," Kennedy School of Government, April 1994.
- Global list of Ecological Economics related Organizations on WiserEarth
- Ecological Economics portal on WiserEarth

2.17 Economic humanitarianism (Raëlianism)

Economic Humanitarianism is a collection of economic ideas which, according to its creator Claude Vorilhon, is designed to complement Geniocracy.

2.17.1 Relation with capitalism

See also: Automation, Basic income, Capitalism and Technocracy movement

Economic humanitarianism accepts the capitalist notion that through competition and technological innovation, some companies may install automation in an attempt to reduce costs, which replaces jobs and reduces the *aggregate* consumer base. *As long as* there are industries which have not reached maturity, the employment will return to a natural level, as will the consumer base. In the framework of Economic Humanitarianism, capitalism is considered to be the best way for industries to mature in the long run.

But in place, once maturity of all industries is close at hand, automation is seen to *eliminate* jobs at a rate faster than new

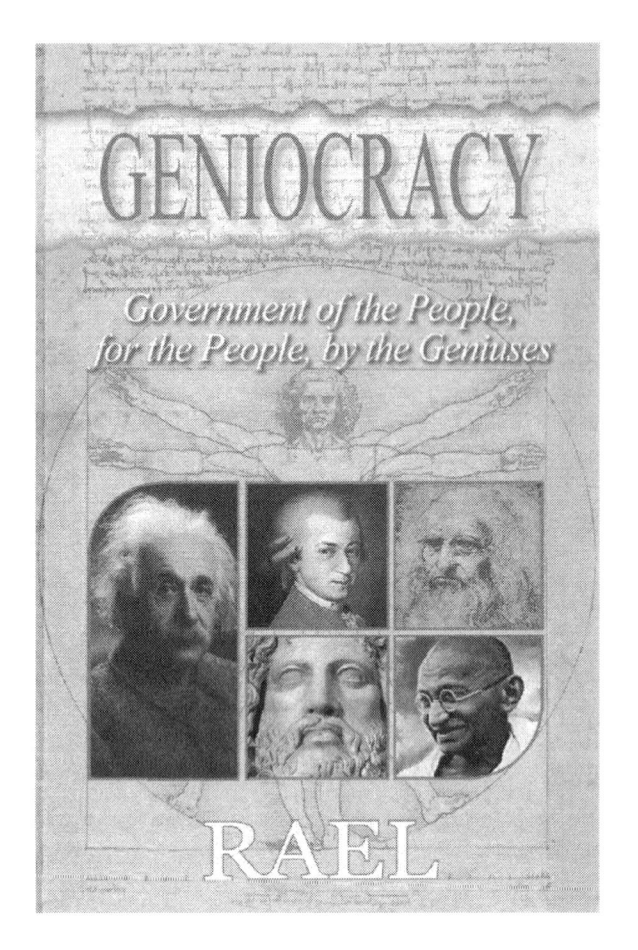

The book cover of Rael's book Geniocracy *(republished in 2004 by the Raelian Foundation.*

industries can introduce. If the economic system is not reformed around this time, this not only reduces aggregate consumer base, but also the total consumer base, resulting in poverty despite normal levels of output. Reflecting on history, the author of Economic Humanitarianism, Claude Vorilhon, suggested that all employees whose labor was replaced by automation should have received supplemental income and that all individuals should receive minimal existence revenue (their fair share of what automation has to offer). Economic humanitarianism supports the implementation of a basic income.

In Claude Vorilhon's book *Geniocracy*, he writes:

> Obviously this system is not viable in a capitalist society, since once the owners automate their factories, they just sack all their workers without pay and let them starve while the machines do all the work, filling their own pockets with gold from the profit. This is unjust and should not be tolerated. The boss who builds a machine that replaces one hundred workers should continue to pay these workers who now have nothing to do. Thus the machine should allow them to enter and benefit from the age of leisure. People often say that machines enslave man and that technology dehumanises society, but they are wrong! It is the manufacturer that enslaves man. It is to the manufacturer that man is condemned to a life sentence of forced labour. The manufacturer enslaves man, but robots free us. The only reason that technology is dehumanising society is because humans still have to work with the machines used for forced labour, or because they must clock in to where the forced labour takes place. That is the problem, humans and machines should not be mixed together. Humans are designed to spend their time in places of fulfilment, while machines are designed to function in the workplace, under the supervision of robots and computers.

In book 1 of 3 in Claude Vorilhon's *Intelligent Design* was a text allegedly narrated by Yahweh, who according to him, is a humanoid extraterrestrial responsible for the creation of life on earth:

> YOU could very soon live in a genuine terrestrial paradise if only the technology that you have at your disposal today were made to serve human well-being, instead of serving violence, armies, or the personal profit of a few. Science and technology can totally liberate humanity not only from the problem of hunger in the world, but also from the obligation to work to live, since machines can quite easily look after the daily chores by themselves thanks to automation.

2.17.2 Economic rent

See also: Economic rent and Georgism

One way to aid such an effort, Raelians believe, is by changing how property is exploited. According to the Raelian Messages, the following was another official message from Yahweh:

> You are all born equal and this is also written in the Bible. Your governments should ensure that people are born with approximately the same level of financial means. It is unacceptable that unintelligent children should live in luxury thanks to the fortunes amassed by their parents, while geniuses die of hunger and do any menial chore just to eat. This way they forsake occupations

where they could have made discoveries benefiting the whole of humanity. To avoid this, property ownership must be abolished without establishing Communism.

Under most capitalistic systems, money is created by issuing debt and is not necessarily introduced at birth. Instead of property ownership, the humanitarianism described in the Raelian Messages involves of long-duration rent, an idea held by many proponents of Georgism. In the Raelian idea of humanitarianism, this should even apply in the case of businesses (as well as land):

> Thus individuals can make a fortune for themselves depending on their own merits, but not for their children. To each their own merits. The same should apply to commercial and industrial enterprises.
>
> If someone creates a business, it is theirs for their entire life, and they can rent it out, but never for more than forty-nine years. The same goes for farmers. They can rent land and cultivate it for forty-nine years but after that it all goes back to the State which will be able to rent it out again for another forty-nine years. Their children can also rent it for forty-nine years.
>
> This method must be adopted for all goods that remain exploitable...

Under economic humanitarianism, the only legal inheritance is the family home.[1][2]

2.17.3 See also

- Automation
- Capitalism
- Microcredit
- Netocracy
- Socialism
- Trade credit

2.17.4 References

[1] He wasn't born again -- he saw little green men / Founder of Raelian religion seeks secret to immortality *SF Gate*. 28 December 2002. Retrieved 22 May 2010.

[2] Cooperman, Alan, Raelians Believe Cloning Holds Key to Immortality *Washington Post*. 28 December 2002. Retrieved 7 October 2007. *(highglight)*

- Rael, *Geniocracy*. The Raelian Foundation, 2004.
- Rael, *Intelligent Design: Message from the Designers*. Nova Dist., 2006. ISBN 2-940252-20-3. - The messages given to Rael published in 1973, 1975, and 1979.

2.17.5 External links

- http://marshallbrain.com/robotic-nation.htm - *Robotic Nation* series by Marshall Brain of HowStuffWorks.com

2.18 Econophysics

Econophysics is an interdisciplinary research field, applying theories and methods originally developed by physicists in order to solve problems in economics, usually those including uncertainty or stochastic processes and nonlinear dynamics. Some of its application to the study of financial markets has also been termed statistical finance referring to its roots in statistical physics.

2.18.1 History

Physicists' interest in the social sciences is not new; Daniel Bernoulli, as an example, was the originator of utility-based preferences. One of the founders of neoclassical economic theory, former Yale University Professor of Economics Irving Fisher, was originally trained under the renowned Yale physicist, Josiah Willard Gibbs.[1] Likewise, Jan Tinbergen, who won the first Nobel Prize in economics in 1969 for having developed and applied dynamic models for the analysis of economic processes, studied physics with Paul Ehrenfest at Leiden University.

Econophysics was started in the mid-1990s by several physicists working in the subfield of statistical mechanics. Unsatisfied with the traditional explanations and approaches of economists - which usually prioritized simplified approaches for the sake of soluble theoretical models over agreement with empirical data - they applied tools and methods from physics, first to try to match financial data sets, and then to explain more general economic phenomena.

One driving force behind econophysics arising at this time was the sudden availability of large amounts of financial data, starting in the 1980s. It became apparent that traditional methods of analysis were insufficient - standard economic methods dealt with homogeneous agents and equilibrium, while many of the more interesting phenomena in financial markets fundamentally depended on heterogeneous agents and far-from-equilibrium situations.

The term "econophysics" was coined by H. Eugene Stanley, to describe the large number of papers written by physicists in the problems of (stock and other) markets, in a conference on statistical physics in Kolkata (erstwhile Calcutta) in 1995 and first appeared in its proceedings publication in Physica A 1996.[2][3] The inaugural meeting on Econophysics was organised 1998 in Budapest by János Kertész and Imre Kondor.

Currently, the almost regular meeting series on the topic include: APFA, ECONOPHYS-KOLKATA,[4] Econophysics Colloquium, ESHIA/ WEHIA.

In recent years network science, heavily reliant on analogies from statistical mechanics, has been applied to the study of productive systems. That is the case with the works done at the Santa Fe Institute in European Funded Research Projects as Forecasting Financial Crises and the Harvard-MIT Observatory of Economic Complexity

If "econophysics" is taken to denote the principle of applying statistical mechanics to economic analysis, as opposed to a particular literature or network, priority of innovation is probably due to Emmanuel Farjoun and Moshé Machover (1983). Their book *Laws of Chaos: A Probabilistic Approach to Political Economy* proposes *dissolving* (their words) the transformation problem in Marx's political economy by re-conceptualising the relevant quantities as random variables.[5]

If, on the other side, "econophysics" is taken to denote the application of physics to economics, one can already consider the works of Léon Walras and Vilfredo Pareto as part of it. Indeed, as shown by Ingrao and Israel, general equilibrium theory in economics is based on the physical concept of mechanical equilibrium.

Econophysics has nothing to do with the "physical quantities approach" to economics, advocated by Ian Steedman and others associated with Neo-Ricardianism. Notable econophysicists are Jean-Philippe Bouchaud, Bikas K Chakrabarti, J. Doyne Farmer, Dirk Helbing, János Kertész, Francis Longstaff, Rosario N. Mantegna, Matteo Marsili, Joseph L. McCauley, Enrico Scalas, Didier Sornette, H. Eugene Stanley, Victor Yakovenko and Yi-Cheng Zhang. Particularly noteworthy among the formal courses on Econophysics is the one offered by the Physics Department of the Leiden University,[6][7][8] from where the first Nobel-laureate in economics Jan Tinbergen came. From September 2014 King's College has awarded the first position of Full Professor in Econophysics.

2.18.2 Basic tools

Basic tools of econophysics are probabilistic and statistical methods often taken from statistical physics.

Physics models that have been applied in economics include the kinetic theory of gas (called the Kinetic exchange models of markets [9]), percolation models, chaotic models developed to study cardiac arrest, and models with self-organizing criticality as well as other models developed for earthquake prediction.[10] Moreover, there have been attempts to use the mathematical theory of complexity and information theory, as developed by many scientists among whom are Murray Gell-Mann and Claude E. Shannon, respectively. For Potential games, it has been shown that an emergence-producing equilibrium based on information via Shannon information entropy produces the same equilibrium measure (Gibbs measure from statistical mechanics) as a stochastic dynamical equation, both of which are based on bounded rationality. Quantifiers derived form information theory were used in several papers by econophysicist Aurelio F. Bariviera and coauthors in order to assess the degree in the informational efficiency of stock markets. In a paper published in Physica A[11] Zunino et al. use an innovative statistical tool in the financial literature: the complexity-entropy causality plane. This Cartesian representation establish an efficiency ranking of different markets and distinguish different bond market dynamics. Moreover, the authors conclude that the classification derived from the complexity-entropy causality plane is consistent with the qualifications assigned by major rating companies to the sovereign instruments. A similar study developed by Bariviera et al.[12] explore the relationship between credit ratings and informational efficiency of a sample of corporate bonds of US oil and energy companies using also the complexity–entropy causality plane. They find that this classification agrees with the credit ratings assigned by Moody's.

Since economic phenomena are the result of the interaction among many heterogeneous agents, there is an analogy with statistical mechanics, where many particles interact; but it must be taken into account that the properties of human beings and particles significantly differ.

Another good example is random matrix theory, which can be used to identify the noise in financial correlation matrices. One paper has argued that this technique can improve the performance of portfolios, e.g., in applied in portfolio optimization.[13]

There are, however, various other tools from physics that have so far been used, such as fluid dynamics, classical mechanics and quantum mechanics (including so-called classical economy, quantum economy and quantum finance), and the path integral formulation of statistical mechanics.[14]

The concept of economic complexity index, introduced by the MIT physicist Cesar A. Hidalgo and the Harvard economist Ricardo Hausmann and made available at MIT's

Observatory of Economic Complexity, has been devised as a predictive tool for economic growth. According to the estimates of Hausmann and Hidalgo, the ECI is far more accurate in predicting GDP growth than the traditional governance measures of the World Bank.[15]

There are also analogies between finance theory and diffusion theory. For instance, the Black–Scholes equation for option pricing is a diffusion-advection equation (see however [16][17] for a critique of the Black-Scholes methodology). The Black-Scholes theory can be extended to provide an analytical theory of main factors in economic activities. [14]

2.18.3 Influence

Papers on econophysics have been published primarily in journals devoted to physics and statistical mechanics, rather than in leading economics journals. Mainstream economists have generally been unimpressed by this work.[18] Some Heterodox economists, including Mauro Gallegati, Steve Keen and Paul Ormerod, have shown more interest, but also criticized trends in econophysics.

In contrast, econophysics is having some impact on the more applied field of quantitative finance, whose scope and aims significantly differ from those of economic theory. Various econophysicists have introduced models for price fluctuations in financial markets or original points of view on established models.[16][19][20] Also several scaling laws have been found in various economic data.[21][22][23]

2.18.4 Main results

Presently, the main results of econophysics comprise the explanation of the "fat tails" in the distribution of many kinds of financial data as a universal self-similar scaling property (i.e. scale invariant over many orders of magnitude in the data),[24] arising from the tendency of individual market competitors, or of aggregates of them, to exploit systematically and optimally the prevailing "microtrends" (e.g., rising or falling prices). These "fat tails" are not only mathematically important, because they comprise the risks, which may be on the one hand, very small such that one may tend to neglect them, but which - on the other hand - are not neglegible at all, i.e. they can never be made exponentially tiny, but instead follow a measurable algebraically decreasing power law, for example with a *failure probability* of only $P \propto x^{-4}$, where x is an increasingly large variable in the tail region of the distribution considered (i.e. a price statistics with much more than 10^8 data). I.e., the events considered are not simply "outliers" but must really be taken into account and cannot be "insured away".[25] It appears that it also plays a role that near a change of the tendency (e.g. from falling to rising prices) there are typical "panic reactions" of the selling or buying agents with algebraically increasing bargain rapidities and volumes.[25] The "fat tails" are also observed in commodity markets.

As in quantum field theory the "fat tails" can be obtained by complicated "nonperturbative" methods, mainly by numerical ones, since they contain the deviations from the usual Gaussian approximations, e.g. the Black-Scholes theory. Fat tails can, however, also be due to other phenomena, such as a random number of terms in the central-limit theorem, or any number of other, non-econophysics models. Due to the difficulty in testing such models, they have received less attention in traditional economic analysis.

2.18.5 See also

- Bose–Einstein condensation (network theory)
- Complexity economics
- Complex network
- Detrended fluctuation analysis
- Kinetic exchange models of markets
- Long-range dependency
- Network theory
- Network science
- Thermoeconomics

2.18.6 References

[1] Yale Economic Review, Retrieved October-25-09

[2] Interview of H. E. Stanley on Econophysics (Published in "IIM Kozhikode Society & Management Review", Sage publication (USA), Vol. 2 Issue 2 (July), pp. 73-78 (2013))

[3] Econophysics Research in India in the last two Decades (1993-2013) (Published in "IIM Kozhikode Society & Management Review", Sage publication (USA), Vol. 2 Issue 2 (July), pp. 135-146 (2013))

[4] ECONOPHYS-KOLKATA VIII: Econophysics and data driven modelling of market dynamics, March 14-17, 2014 (Proc. Vol.: Econophysics and data driven modelling of market dynamics, Eds. F. Abergel, H. Aoyama, B.K. Chakrabarti, A. Chakraborti, A. Ghosh, New Economic Windows, Springer Int. Publ., Switzerland, 2015); ECONOPHYS-KOLKATA VII : Econophysics of Agent Based Models, 8–12 November 2012 (Proc. Vol.: Econophysics of Agent Based Models, Eds. F. Abergel, H. Aoyama, B.K. Chakrabarti, A. Chakraborti, A. Ghosh,

New Economic Windows, Springer Int. Publ., Switzerland, 2013); ECONOPHYS-KOLKATA VI : Econophysics of Systemic Risk and Network Dynamics, 21–25 October 2011 (Proc. Vol.: Econophysics of Systemic Risk and Network Dynamics, Eds. F. Abergel, B.K. Chakrabarti, A. Chakraborti, A. Ghosh, New Economic Windows, Springer-Verlag, Milan, 2012); ECONOPHYS-KOLKATA V : Econophysics of Order-Driven Markets, 9–13 March 2010 (Proc. Vol.: Econophysics of Order-driven Markets, Eds. F. Abergel, B.K. Chakrabarti, A. Chakraborti, M. Mitra, New Economic Windows, Springer-Verlag, Milan, 2011); ECONOPHYS-KOLKATA IV : Econophysics of Games and Social Choices, 9–13 March 2009 (Proc. Vol.: Econophysics & Economics of Games, Social Choices and Quantitative Techniques, Eds. B. Basu, B. K. Chakrabarti, S. R. Chakravarty, K. Gangopadhyay, New Economic Windows, Springer-Verlag, Milan, 2010); ECONOPHYS-KOLKATA III: Econophysics & Sociophysics of Markets and Networks, 12–15 March 2007 (Proc. Vol.: Econophysics of Markets and Business Networks, Eds. A. Chatterjee, B.K. Chakrabarti, New Economic Windows, Springer-Verlag, Milan, 2007); ECONOPHYS-KOLKATA II: Econophysics of Stock Markets and Minority Games, 14–17 February 2006 (Proc. Vol.: Econophysics of Stock and other Markets, Eds. A. Chatterjee, B.K. Chakrabarti, New Economic Windows, Springer-Verlag, Milan, 2006); ECONOPHYS-KOLKATA I: Econophysics of Wealth Distributions, 15–19 March 2005 (Proc. Vol.: Econophysics of Wealth Distributions, Eds. A. Chatterjee, S. Yarlagadda, B.K. Chakrabarti, New Economic Windows, Springer-Verlag, Milan, 2005).

[5] Farjoun and Machover disclaim complete originality: their book is dedicated to the late Robert H. Langston, who they cite for direct inspiration (page 12), and they also note an independent suggestion in a discussion paper by E.T. Jaynes (page 239)

[6] "Physics - Education". Physics.leidenuniv.nl. 2011–2013. Retrieved 2013.

[7] "Physics - Education". Physics.leidenuniv.nl. 2011–2014. Retrieved 2014.

[8] "Physics - Education". Physics.leidenuniv.nl. 2011–2015. Retrieved 2015.

[9] Bikas K Chakrabarti, Anirban Chakraborti, Satya R Chakravarty, Arnab Chatterjee (2012). *Econophysics of Income & Wealth Distributions*. Cambridge University Press, Cambridge.

[10] Didier Sornette (2003). *Why Stock Markets Crash?*. Princeton University Press.

[11] Zunino, L., Bariviera, A.F., Guercio, M.B., Martinez, L.B. and Rosso, O.A. (2012). "On the efficiency of sovereign bond markets". *Physica A: Statistical Mechanics and its Applications* **391** (18): 4342-4349. Bibcode:2012PhyA..391.4342Z. doi:10.1016/j.physa.2012.04.009.

[12] Bariviera, A.F.,Zunino, L., Guercio, M.B., Martinez, L.B. and Rosso, O.A. (2013). "Efficiency and credit ratings: a permutation-information-theory analysis". *Journal of Statistical Mechanics: Theory and Experiment* **2013** (08): P08007. arXiv:1509.01839. Bibcode:2013JSMTE..08..007F. doi:10.1088/1742-5468/2013/08/P08007.

[13] Vasiliki Plerou, Parameswaran Gopikrishnan, Bernd Rosenow, Luis Amaral, Thomas Guhr and H. Eugene Stanley (2002). "Random matrix approach to cross correlations in financial data". *Physical Review E* **65** (6): 066126. arXiv:cond-mat/0108023. Bibcode:2002PhRvE..65f6126P. doi:10.1103/PhysRevE.65.066126.

[14] Chen, Jing (2015). *The Unity of Science and Economics: A New Foundation of Economic Theory*. http://www.springer.com/us/book/9781493934645: Springer.

[15] Ricardo Hausmann, Cesar Hidalgo; et al. "The Atlas of Economic Complexity". The Observatory of Economic Complexity (MIT Media Lab). Retrieved 26 April 2012.

[16] Jean-Philippe Bouchaud, Marc Potters (2003). *Theory of Financial Risk and Derivative Pricing*. Cambridge University Press.

[17] "Welcome to a non Black-Scholes world"

[18] Philip Ball (2006). "Econophysics: Culture Crash". *Nature* **441** (7094): 686–688. Bibcode:2006Natur.441..686B. doi:10.1038/441686a. PMID 16760949.

[19] Enrico Scalas (2006). "The application of continuous-time random walks in finance and economics". *Physica A* **362** (2): 225–239. Bibcode:2006PhyA..362..225S. doi:10.1016/j.physa.2005.11.024.

[20] Y. Shapira, Y. Berman and E. Ben-Jacob (2014). "Modelling the short term herding behaviour of stock markets". *New Journal of Physics* **16**. Bibcode:2014NJPh...16e3040S. doi:10.1088/1367-2630/16/5/053040.

[21] Y. Liu, P. Gopikrishnan, P. Cizeau, M. Meyer, C.-K. Peng, and H. E. Stanley (1999). "Statistical properties of the volatility of price fluctuations". *Physical Review E* **60** (2): 1390. arXiv:cond-mat/9903369. Bibcode:1999PhRvE..60.1390L. doi:10.1103/PhysRevE.60.1390.

[22] M. H. R. Stanley, L. A. N. Amaral, S. V. Buldyrev, S. Havlin, H. Leschhorn, P. Maass, M. A. Salinger, H. E. Stanley (1996). "Scaling behaviour in the growth of companies". *Nature* **379** (6568): 804. Bibcode:1996Natur.379..804S. doi:10.1038/379804a0.

[23] K. Yamasaki, L. Muchnik, S. Havlin, A. Bunde, and H.E. Stanley (2005). "Scaling and memory in volatility return intervals in financial markets". *PNAS* **102** (26): 9424–8. Bibcode:2005PNAS..102.9424Y. doi:10.1073/pnas.0502613102. PMC 1166612. PMID 15980152.

[24] The physicists noted the scaling behaviour of "fat tails" through a letter to the scientific journal *Nature* by Rosario N. Mantegna and H. Eugene Stanley: *Scaling behavior in the dynamics of an economic index*, Nature Vol. 376, pages 46-49 (1995), however the "fat tails"- phenomenon itself was discovered already earlier by economists.

[25] See for example Preis, Mantegna, 2003.

2.18.7 Further reading

- Rosario N. Mantegna, H. Eugene Stanley, *An Introduction to Econophysics: Correlations and Complexity in Finance*, Cambridge University Press (Cambridge, UK, 1999)

- Sitabhra Sinha, Arnab Chatterjee, Anirban Chakraborti, Bikas K Chakrabarti. *Econophysics: An Introduction*, Wiley-VCH (2010)

- Bikas K Chakrabarti, Anirban Chakraborti, Arnab Chatterjee, *Econophysics and Sociophysics : Trends and Perspectives*, Wiley-VCH, Berlin (2006)

- Joseph McCauley, *Dynamics of Markets, Econophysics and Finance*, Cambridge University Press (Cambridge, UK, 2004)

- Bertrand Roehner, *Patterns of Speculation - A Study in Observational Econophysics*, Cambridge University Press (Cambridge, UK, 2002)

- Arnab Chatterjee, Sudhakar Yarlagadda, Bikas K Chakrabarti, *Econophysics of Wealth Distributions*, Springer-Verlag Italia (Milan, 2005)

- Philip Mirowski, *More Heat than Light - Economics as Social Physics, Physics as Nature's Economics*, Cambridge University Press (Cambridge, UK, 1989)

- Ubaldo Garibaldi and Enrico Scalas, *Finitary Probabilistic Methods in Econophysics*, Cambridge University Press (Cambridge, UK, 2010).

- Emmanual Farjoun and Moshé Machover, *Laws of Chaos: a probabilistic approach to political economy*, Verso (London, 1983) ISBN 0 86091 768 1

- Nature Physics Focus issue: Complex networks in finance March 2013 Volume 9 No 3 pp 119–128

- Mark Buchanan, *What has econophysics ever done for us?*, Nature 2013

- An Analytical treatment of Gibbs-Pareto behaviour in wealth distribution by Arnab Das and Sudhakar Yarlagadda

- A distribution function analysis of wealth distribution by Arnab Das and Sudhakar Yarlagadda

- Analytical treatment of a trading market model by Arnab Das

2.18.8 Lectures

- Economic Fluctuations and Statistical Physics: Quantifying Extremely Rare and Much Less Rare Events, Eugene Stanley, Videolectures.net

- Applications of Statistical Physics to Understanding Complex Systems, Eugene Stanley, Videolectures.net

- Financial Bubbles, Real Estate Bubbles, Derivative Bubbles, and the Financial and Economic Crisis, Didier Sornette, Videolectures.net

- Financial crises and risk management, Didier Sornette, Videolectures.net

- Bubble trouble: how physics can quantify stock-market crashes, Tobias Preis, Physics World Online Lecture Series

2.18.9 External links

- Econophysics Ph.D. Program at University of Houston, Houston, TX.

- Finance Gets Physical - Yale Economic Review

- Econophysics Forum

- Conference to mark 25th anniversary of Farjoun and Machover's book

- Chair of International Economics, University of Bamberg (Germany)

- Econophysics Colloquium

2.19 European Association for Evolutionary Political Economy

The **European Association for Evolutionary Political Economy (EAEPE)** is a pluralist forum of social scientists that brings together institutional and evolutionary economists broadly defined. EAEPE members are scholars working on realistic approaches to economic theory and economic policy. With a membership of over 500, EAEPE is now the foremost European association for heterodox economists[1] and the second-largest association for economists in Europe.

2.19.1 History

EAEPE was established in London, on 29 June 1988.[2] However, the formal founding meeting was only held in September 1989 at the association's first annual conference in Keswick, Cumbria, UK. At this occasion, the EAEPE Constitution was adopted and a Steering Committee was elected, changed later into the EAEPE Council.[3] In November 1990, the association formed a charity, the Foundation for European Economic Development (FEED) under the Charities Act (England and Wales), with the objective of providing financial assistance for the EAEPE annual conferences and other EAEPE projects. In 1991, the association adopted a Scientific Development Plan in order to designate a number of priority Research Areas and to appoint Research Area Coordinators to act as networkbuilders. Since 1991, in collaboration with Edward Elgar Publishing, EAEPE has published a series of conference volumes and other focused volumes. In the mid-1990s, EAEPE organized several summer schools, with the financial support of FEED and the European Commission. EAEPE has resumed organizing annual summer schools since 2010. EAEPE is a founding shareholder of Millennium Economics Ltd.[4]

2.19.2 Theoretical perspectives

According to the EAEPE website, EAEPE members generally agree on the following.[5]

Breaking away from the most standard forms of economic theorising based on a definition of economics in terms of a rigid method which is applied indiscriminately to a wide variety of economic, social or political phenomena, EAEPE embraces an open-ended and interdisciplinary analysis, that draws on relevant material in not only in economics but also in psychology, sociology, anthropology, politics, law and history.

In contrast to standard economic approaches focusing exclusively on equilibrium, EAEPE conceptualizes the economy as a cumulative process unfolding in historical time in which agents are faced with chronic information problems and radical uncertainty about the future. Contrary to standard models where individuals and their tastes are taken as given, where technology is viewed as exogenous, and where production is separated from exchange, EAEPE's concern is to address and encompass the interactive, social process through which tastes are formed and changed, the forces which promote technological transformation, and the interaction of these elements within the economic system as a whole.

In lieu of an orientation that takes the market as an ideal or natural order and as a mere aggregation of individual traders, EAEPE recognises that it is appropriate to regard the market itself as a social institution, necessarily supported by a network of other social institutions such as the state, and having no unqualified nor automatic priority over them. Instead of the widespread tendency to ignore ecological and environmental considerations or consequences in the development of theories and policy recommendation, EAEPE acknowledges that the socio-economic system depends upon, and is embedded in, an often fragile natural environment and a complex ecological system.

Rejecting the utilitarian outlook which separates considerations of means from those of ends, and judgments of fact from those of value, and which ignores social relations, conflicts and inequalities between the agents, EAEPE appreciates the fact that inquiry is value-driven and policy-orientated, and recognises the centrality of participatory democratic processes to the identification and evaluation of real needs.

Reflecting EAEPE's open-ended theoretical perspectives, EAEPE's current honorary presidents include major scholars such as Janos Kornai, Richard R. Nelson, Douglass C. North, Luigi Pasinetti, while Nicholas Georgescu-Roegen, Edith T. Penrose, Kurt Rothschild, G.L.S. Shackle and Herbert A. Simon were EAEPE's honorary presidents in the past.[6] More generally, EAEPE recognises the relevance of writers as diverse as John Commons, Nicholas Kaldor, Michal Kalecki, William Kapp, John Maynard Keynes, Alfred Marshall, Karl Marx, François Perroux, Karl Polanyi, Joan Robinson, Joseph Schumpeter, Adam Smith, Thorstein Veblen and Max Weber to institutionalist and evolutionary thought.

2.19.3 Research Areas

EAEPE's research is organised around Research Areas (RAs) that include: Methodology of economics (A), Economic sociology (B), Institutional change (C), Innovation and technological change (D), Theory of the firm (E), Environment-economy interactions (F), Macroeconomic regulation and Institutions (G), Comparative Political Economy (I), Monetary economics, finance and financial institutions (J), Gender economics and social identity (K), Labour economics (L), Social economics (M), Human development and institutions (N), Economy, society and territory (O), Economic history (P), Evolutionary economic simulations (S), History of political economy (T), Ontological foundations of evolutionary economics (V), Global political economy (W), Networks (X).[7]

2.19.4 Awards

The association runs three prizes:[8]

- The *EAEPE-Kapp Prize* (formerly known as the K. William Kapp Prize and more recently as the EAEPE Prize), awarded annually for the best published journal article on a theme broadly in accord with the EAEPE Theoretical Perspectives

- The *EAEPE-Myrdal Prize* (formerly known as the Gunnar Myrdal Prize), awarded biennially for the best monograph on a theme broadly in accord with the EAEPE Theoretical Perspectives

- The *EAEPE-Simon Young Scholar Prize* (formerly known as the Herbert Simon Young Scholar Prize), awarded annually for the best conference paper by a young scholar under the age of 35.

- In 2007, in collaboration with the Association for Evolutionary Economics (AFEE), EAEPE ran a special competition to celebrate the 150th anniversary of Thorstein Veblen's birthday.

2.19.5 Publications

- EAEPE has regularly published a series of conference volumes, several more focused volumes on specific topics as well as readers on institutional and evolutionary economics (see selected list below). Since 2006, EAEPE has sponsored a new 'Studies in Evolutionary Political Economy' edited volume series.[9]

- In collaboration with the Association for Evolutionary Economics (AFEE), EAEPE has published a major 2-volume reference work on institutional and evolutionary economics (Hodgson, Samuels and Tool, eds, 1994).

- A newsletter was published between 1989 and 2005. A new series was released in July 2012.[10]

- EAEPE sponsors a periodical, *Journal of Institutional Economics* (JOIE), devoted to the study of the nature, role and evolution of institutions in the economy. The first issue was published in 2005. There are currently 4 issues per volume. In 2012, JOIE received a high impact factor for a new journal.[11]

2.19.6 Selected EAEPE Volumes

- Amin, Ash and Michael Dietrich (eds) (1991), *Towards a New Europe: Structural Change in the European Economy*, Aldershot: Edward Elgar.

- Amin, Ash and Jerzy Hausner (eds) (1997), *Beyond Market and Hierarchy: Interactive Governance and Social Complexity*, Cheltenham: Edward Elgar.

- Blaas, Wolfgang and John Foster (eds) (1993), *Mixed Economies in Europe: An Evolutionary Perspective on their Emergence, Transition and Regulation*, Aldershot: Edward Elgar.

- Delorme, Robert and Kurt Dopfer (eds) (1994), *The Political Economy of Diversity: Evolutionary Perspectives on Economic Order and Disorder*, Aldershot: Edward Elgar.

- Dolfsma, Wilfred and Charlie Dannreuther (eds) (2003), *Globalization, Social Capital and Inequality: Contested Concepts, Contested Experiences*, Cheltenham: Edward Elgar.

- Dolfsma, Wilfred and Luc Soete (eds) (2006), *Understanding the Dynamics of a Knowledge Economy*, Cheltenham: Edward Elgar.

- Elsner, Wolfram and Hardy Hanappi (eds) (2008), *Varieties of Capitalism and New Institutional Deals: Regulation, Welfare and the New Economy*, Cheltenham: Edward Elgar.

- Finch, John and Magali Orillard (eds) (2005), *Complexity and the Economy: Implications for Economic Policy*, Cheltenham: Edward Elgar.

- Garrouste, Pierre and Stravos Ioannides (eds) (2001), *Evolution and Path Dependence in Economic Ideas: Past and Present*, Cheltenham: Edward Elgar.

- Groenewegen, John and Jack Vromen (eds) (1999), *Institutions and the Evolution of Capitalism: Implications of Evolutionary Economics*, Cheltenham: Edward Elgar.

- Groenewegen, John, Christos Pitelis and Sven-Erik Sjöstrand (eds) (1995), *On Economic Institutions: Theory and Applications*, Aldershot: Edward Elgar.

- Hanappi, Hardy and Wolfram Elsner (eds) (2008), *Advances in Evolutionary Institutional Economics: Evolutionary Mechanisms, Non-Knowledge and Strategy*. Cheltenham: Edward Elgar.

- Hodgson, Geoffrey M. (ed.) (2007), *The Evolution of Economic Institutions: A Critical Reader*, Cheltenham: Edward Elgar.

- Hodgson, Geoffrey M. and Ernesto Screpanti (eds) (1991), *Rethinking Economics: Markets, Technology and Economic Evolution*, Aldershot: Edward Elgar.

- Hodgson, Geoffrey M., Warren J. Samuels and Mark J. Tool (eds) (1994), *The Elgar Companion to Institutional and Evolutionary Economics*, 2 vols., Aldershot: Edward Elgar.

- Kunneke, Rold W., John Groenewegen and Jean-Francois Auger (eds) (2009), *The Governance of Network Industries: Institutions, Technology and Policy in Reregulated Infrastructures*, Cheltenham: Edward Elgar.

- Louçã, Francisco and Mark Perlman (eds) (2000). *Is Economics an Evolutionary Science? The Legacy of Thorstein Veblen*, Cheltenham: Edward Elgar.

- Michie, Jonathan and Angelo Reati (eds) (1998), *Employment, Technology and Economic Needs: Theory, Evidence and Economic Policy*, Cheltenham: Edward Elgar.

- Nielsen, Klaus and Björn Johnson (eds) (1998), *Institutions and Economic Change: New Perspectives on Markets, Firms and Technology*, Cheltenham: Edward Elgar.

- Salanti, Andrea and Ernesto Screpanti (eds) (1997), *Pluralism in Economics: New Perspectives in History and Methodology*, Cheltenham: Edward Elgar.

- Saviotti, Pier Paolo and Bart Nooteboom (eds) (2000), *Technology and Knowledge: From the Firm to Innovation Systems*, Cheltenham: Edward Elgar.

- Tylecote, Andrew and Jan van der Straaten (eds) (1998), *Environment, Technology and Economic Growth: The Challenge of Sustainable Development*, Cheltenham: Edward Elgar.

2.19.7 See also

- Institutional economics
- Evolutionary economics
- Heterodox economics
- Pluralism in economics
- Post-autistic economics
- Human behaviour
- Institution
- Social order
- Structure and agency
- Sociocultural evolution
- Evolutionary psychology
- Universal Darwinism
- Realism
- Social innovation
- Public policy
- Innovation
- ESDP Network
- Institute for New Economic Thinking
- Geoffrey Hodgson

2.19.8 References

[1] Other heteredox associations are listed in the "Heterodox Economics Directory". Heterodox Economics Newsletter. Retrieved 2012-07-27.

[2] Hodgson, Geoffrey M. (1999), 'European Association for Evolutionary Political Economy', in Philip A. O'Hara (ed.), *Encyclopedia of Political Economy*, Vol. 1, London and New York: Routledge, pp. 288-290.

[3] "About EAEPE". European Association for Evolutionary Political Economy. Retrieved 2012-07-27.

[4] "Current shareholders". Millennium Economics Ltd. Retrieved 2013-01-11.

[5] "Theoretical Perspectives". European Association for Evolutionary Political Economy. Retrieved 2012-07-27.

[6] "EAEPE's Honorary Presidents". European Association for Evolutionary Political Economy. Retrieved 2012-07-27.

[7] "Research Areas and Research Area Coordinators". European Association for Evolutionary Political Economy. Retrieved 2012-07-27.

[8] "EAEPE Awards". European Association for Evolutionary Political Economy. Retrieved 2012-07-27.

[9] "EAEPE Volume Series". European Association for Evolutionary Political Economy. Retrieved 2012-07-27.

[10] "EAEPE Newsletter". European Association for Evolutionary Political Economy. Retrieved 2012-07-27.

[11] "Journal of Institutional Economics". European Association for Evolutionary Political Economy. Retrieved 2012-07-27.

2.19.9 External links

- Official website
- FEED - Foundation for European Economic Development
- Journal of Institutional Economics
- AFEE - Association for Evolutionary Economics

- ISNIE - International Society for New Institutional Economics

- Edward Elgar Publishing

2.20 Evolutionary economics

Evolutionary economics is part of mainstream economics[1] as well as a heterodox school of economic thought that is inspired by evolutionary biology. Much like mainstream economics, it stresses complex interdependencies, competition, growth, structural change, and resource constraints but differs in the approaches which are used to analyze these phenomena.[2]

Evolutionary economics deals with the study of processes that transform economy for firms, institutions, industries, employment, production, trade and growth within, through the actions of diverse agents from experience and interactions, using evolutionary methodology. Evolutionary economics analyses the unleashing of a process of technological and institutional innovation by generating and testing a diversity of ideas which discover and accumulate more survival value for the costs incurred than competing alternatives. The evidence suggests that it could be adaptive efficiency that defines economic efficiency. Mainstream economic reasoning begins with the postulates of scarcity and rational agents (that is, agents modeled as maximizing their individual welfare), with the "rational choice" for any agent being a straightforward exercise in mathematical optimization. There has been renewed interest in treating economic systems as evolutionary systems in the developing field of Complexity economics.

Evolutionary economics does not take the characteristics of either the objects of choice or of the decision-maker as fixed. Rather its focus is on the non-equilibrium *processes* that transform the economy *from within* and their implications. The processes in turn emerge from actions of diverse agents with bounded rationality who may learn from experience and interactions and whose differences contribute to the change. The subject draws more recently on evolutionary game theory[3] and on the evolutionary methodology of Charles Darwin and the non-equilibrium economics principle of circular and cumulative causation. It is naturalistic in purging earlier notions of economic change as teleological or necessarily improving the human condition.[4]

A different approach is to apply evolutionary psychology principles to economics which is argued to explain problems such as inconsistencies and biases in rational choice theory. Basic economic concepts such as utility may be better viewed as due to preferences that maximized evolutionary fitness in the ancestral environment but not necessarily in the current one.[5]

2.20.1 Predecessors

In the mid-19th century was presented a schema of stages of historical development, by introducing the notion that human nature was not constant and was not determinative of the nature of the social system; on the contrary, he made it a principle that human behavior was a function of the social and economic system in which it occurred.

Karl Marx based his theory of economic development on the premise of evolving economic systems; specifically, over the course of history superior economic systems would replace inferior ones. Inferior systems were beset by internal contradictions and inefficiencies that make them impossible to survive over the long term. In Marx's scheme, feudalism was replaced by capitalism, which would eventually be superseded by socialism.[6]

At approximately the same time, Charles Darwin developed a general framework for comprehending any process whereby small, random variations could accumulate and predominate over time into large-scale changes that resulted in the emergence of wholly novel forms ("speciation").

This was followed shortly after by the work of the American pragmatic philosophers (Peirce, James, Dewey) and the founding of two new disciplines, psychology and anthropology, both of which were oriented toward cataloging and developing explanatory frameworks for the variety of behavior patterns (both individual and collective) that were becoming increasingly obvious to all systematic observers. The state of the world converged with the state of the evidence to make almost inevitable the development of a more "modern" framework for the analysis of substantive economic issues.

Veblen (1898)

Thorstein Veblen (1898) coined the term "evolutionary economics" in English. He began his career in the midst of this period of intellectual ferment, and as a young scholar came into direct contact with some of the leading figures of the various movements that were to shape the style and substance of social sciences into the next century and beyond. Veblen saw the need for taking account of cultural variation in his approach; no universal "human nature" could possibly be invoked to explain the variety of norms and behaviors that the new science of anthropology showed to be the rule, rather than the exception. He emphasised the conflict between "industrial" and "pecuniary" or ceremonial values and this Veblenian dichotomy was interpreted in the hands of later writers as the "ceremonial / instrumental dichotomy" (Hodgson 2004);

Veblen saw that every culture is materially based and dependent on tools and skills to support the "life process", while at the same time, every culture appeared to have a stratified structure of status ("invidious distinctions") that ran entirely contrary to the imperatives of the "instrumental" (read: "technological") aspects of group life. The "ceremonial" was related to the past, and conformed to and supported the tribal legends; "instrumental" was oriented toward the technological imperative to judge value by the ability to control future consequences. The "Veblenian dichotomy" was a specialized variant of the "instrumental theory of value" due to John Dewey, with whom Veblen was to make contact briefly at the University of Chicago.

Arguably the most important works by Veblen include, but are not restricted to, his most famous works (*The Theory of the Leisure Class*; *The Theory of Business Enterprise*), but his monograph *Imperial Germany and the Industrial Revolution* and the 1898 essay entitled *Why is Economics not an Evolutionary Science* have both been influential in shaping the research agenda for following generations of social scientists. TOLC and TOBE together constitute an alternative construction on the neoclassical marginalist theories of consumption and production, respectively.

Both are founded on his dichotomy, which is at its core a valuational principle. The ceremonial patterns of activity are not bound to any past, but to one that generated a specific set of advantages and prejudices that underlie the current institutions. "Instrumental" judgments create benefits according to a new criterion, and therefore are inherently subversive. This line of analysis was more fully and explicitly developed by Clarence E. Ayres of the University of Texas at Austin from the 1920s.

A seminal article by Armen Alchian (1950) argued for adaptive success of firms faced with uncertainty and incomplete information replacing profit maximization as an appropriate modeling assumption.[7] Kenneth Boulding was one of the advocates of the evolutionary methods in social science, as is evident from Kenneth Boulding's Evolutionary Perspective. Kenneth Arrow, Ronald Coase and Douglass North are some of the Bank of Sweden Prize in Economic Sciences in Memory of Alfred Nobel winners who are known for their sympathy to the field.

More narrowly the works Jack Downie[8] and Edith Penrose[9] offer many insights for those thinking about evolution at the level of the firm in an industry.

Joseph Schumpeter, who lived in the first half of 20th century, was the author of the book *The Theory of Economic Development* (1911, transl. 1934). It is important to note that for the word *development* he used in his native language, the German word "Entwicklung", which can be translated as development or evolution. The translators of the day used the word "development" from the French "développement", as opposed to "evolution" as this was used by Darwin. (Schumpeter, in his later writings in English as a professor at Harvard, used the word "evolution".) The current term in common use is economic development.

In Schumpeter's book he proposed an idea radical for its time: the evolutionary perspective. He based his theory on the assumption of usual macroeconomic equilibrium, which is something like "the normal mode of economic affairs". This equilibrium is being perpetually destroyed by entrepreneurs who try to introduce innovations. A successful introduction of an innovation (i.e. a disruptive technology) disturbs the normal flow of economic life, because it forces some of the already existing technologies and means of production to lose their positions within the economy.

2.20.2 Present state of discussion

One of the major contributions to the emerging field of evolutionary economics has been the publication of *An Evolutionary Theory of Economic Change* by Richard Nelson and Sidney G. Winter. These authors have focused mostly on the issue of changes in technology and routines, suggesting a framework for their analysis. If the change occurs constantly in the economy, then some kind of evolutionary process must be in action, and there has been a proposal that this process is Darwinian in nature.

Then, mechanisms that provide selection, generate variation and establish self-replication, must be identified. The authors introduced the term 'steady change' to highlight the evolutionary aspect of economic processes and contrast it with the concept of 'steady state' popular in classical economics.[10] Their approach can be compared and contrasted with the population ecology or organizational ecology approach in sociology: see Douma & Schreuder (2013, chapter 11).

Milton Friedman proposed that markets act as major selection vehicles. As firms compete, unsuccessful rivals fail to capture an appropriate market share, go bankrupt and have to exit.[11] The variety of competing firms is both in their products and practices, that are matched against markets. Both products and practices are determined by routines that firms use: standardized patterns of actions implemented constantly. By imitating these routines, firms propagate them and thus establish inheritance of successful practices.[12][13] A general theory of this process has been proposed by Kurt Dopfer, John Foster and Jason Potts as the micro meso macro framework.[14]

In recent years, evolutionary models have been used to assist decision making in applied settings and find solutions to problems such as optimal product design and service portfolio diversification.[15]

2.20.3 Evolutionary psychology

See also: Behavioral economics and Neuroeconomics

A different approach is to apply evolutionary psychology principles to economics which is argued to explain problems such as inconsistencies and biases in rational choice theory. A basic economic concept such as utility may be better viewed as due to preferences that maximized evolutionary fitness in the ancestral environment but not necessarily in the current one. Loss aversion may be explained as being rational when living at subsistence level where a reduction of resources may have meant death and it thus may have been rational to place a greater value on losses than on gains.[5]

People are sometimes more cooperative and altruistic than predicted by economic theory which may be explained by mechanisms such as reciprocal altruism and group selection for cooperative behavior. An evolutionary approach may also explain differences between groups such as males being less risk-averse than females since males have more variable reproductive success than females. While unsuccessful risk-seeking may limit reproductive success for both sexes, males may potentially increase their reproductive success much more than females from successful risk-seeking. Frequency-dependent selection may explain why people differ in characteristics such as cooperative behavior with cheating becoming an increasingly less successful strategy as the numbers of cheaters increase.[5]

Another argument is that humans have a poor intuitive grasp of the economics of the current environment which is very different from the ancestral environment. The ancestral environment likely had relatively little trade, division of labor, and capital goods. Technological change was very slow, wealth differences were much smaller, and possession of many available resources were likely zero-sum games where large inequalities were caused by various forms of exploitation. Humans therefore may have poor intuitive understanding the benefits of free trade (causing calls for protectionism), the value of capital goods (making the labor theory of value appealing), and may intuitively undervalue the benefits of technological development.[5]

There may be a tendency to see the number of available jobs as a zero-sum game with the total number of jobs being fixed which causes people to not realize that minimum wage laws reduce the number of jobs or to believe that an increased number of jobs in other nations necessarily decreases the number of jobs in their own nation.

Large income inequality may easily be viewed as due to exploitation rather than as due to individual differences in productivity. This may easily cause poor economic policies, especially since individual voters have few incentives to make the effort of studying societal economics instead of relying on their intuitions since an individual's vote counts for so little and since politicians may be reluctant to take a stand against intuitive views that are incorrect but widely held.[5]

2.20.4 See also

- Behavioral economics
- Complexity economics
- Creative destruction
- Cultural economics
- EAEPE
- Ecological model of competition
- Evolutionary socialism
- Hypergamy
- Institutional economics
- Population dynamics
- Innovation system
- Non-equilibrium economics
- Universal Darwinism
- Evolutionary and Institutional Economics Review
- Giovanni Dosi
- Robert H. Frank

2.20.5 References

[1] Friedman, D. (1998). Evolutionary economics goes mainstream: A review of the theory of learning in games. *Journal of Evolutionary Economics,* 8(4), 423-432.

[2] Geoffrey M. Hodgson (1993) *Economics and Evolution: Bringing Life Back Into Economics*, Cambridge and University of Michigan Press. Description and chapter-link preview.

[3] Daniel Friedman (1998). "On Economic Applications of Evolutionary Game Theory," *Journal of Evolutionary Economics*, 8(1), pp. 15–43.

[4] Ulrich Witt (2008). "evolutionary economics." *The New Palgrave Dictionary of Economics*, 2nd Edition, v. 3, pp. 67-68 Abstract.

[5] Paul H. Rubin and C. Monica Capra. The evolutionary psychology of economics. In Roberts, S. C. (2011). Roberts, S. Craig, ed. "Applied Evolutionary Psychology". Oxford University Press. doi:10.1093/acprof:oso/9780199586073.001.0001. ISBN 9780199586073.

[6] *Gregory and Stuart.* (2005) *Comparing Economic Systems in the Twenty-First Century*, Seventh Edition, South-Western College Publishing, ISBN 0-618-26181-8

[7] Armen A. Alchian 1950, "Uncertainty, Evolution and Economic Theory," *Journal of Political Economy*, 58(3), pp. 211-21.

[8] Jack Downie (1958) The Competitive Process

[9] E. Penrose (1959) The Theory of the Growth of the Firm

[10] Steady change

[11] Mazzucato, M. (2000), Firm Size, Innovation and Market Structure: The Evolution of Market Concentration and Instability, Edward Elgar, Northampton, MA, ISBN 1-84064-346-3, 138 pages.

[12] Friedman, Milton (1953). *Essays in Positive Economics*, University of Chicago Press. Chapter preview links.

[13] Page 251: Jon Elster, *Explaining Technical Change : a Case Study in the Philosophy of Science*, Second ed.

[14] Dopfer, K., Foster, J., Potts, J. (2004). Micro-meso-macro. Journal of Evolutionary Economics. 14(3), 263-279

[15] Baltas, G., Tsafarakis, S., Saridakis, C. & Matsatsinis, N. (2013). Biologically Inspired Approaches to Strategic Service Design: Optimal Service Diversification Through Evolutionary and Swarm Intelligence Models. *Journal of Service Research* 16 (2), 186-201

2.20.6 Further reading

- Aldrich, Howard E., Geoffrey M. Hodgson, David L. Hull, Thorbjørn Knudsen, Joel Mokyr and Viktor J. Vanberg (2008) 'In Defence of Generalized Darwinism', *Journal of Evolutionary Economics*, 18(5), October, pp. 577–96.

- Canterbery, E. Ray (1998) '*The Theory of the Leisure Class* and the Theory of Demand', in Warren G. Samuels (editor), *The Founding of Institutional Economics* (London and New York: Routledge) pp. 139-56.

- Douma, Sytse & Hein Schreuder (2013). "Economic Approaches to Organizations". 5th edition. London: Pearson. ISBN 0273735292 ISBN 9780273735298

- Hodgson, Geoffrey M. (2004) *The Evolution of Institutional Economics: Agency, Structure and Darwinism in American Institutionalism* (London and New York: Routledge).

- Richard R. Nelson and Sidney G. Winter. (1982). *An Evolutionary Theory of Economic Change*. Harvard University Press.

- Shiozawa, Yoshinori (2004) Evolutionary Economics in the 21st Century: A Manifext, *Evolutionary and Institutional Economics Review* 1(1), November, pp. 5–47.

- Sidney G. Winter (1987). "natural selection and evolution," *The New Palgrave Dictionary of Economics*, v. 3, pp. 614–17.

- Veblen, Thorstein B. (1898) 'Why Is Economics Not an Evolutionary Science?', *Quarterly Journal of Economics*, 12(3), July, pp. 373–97.

Journals

- *Journal of Economic Issues*, sponsored by the Association for Evolutionary Economics.

- *Journal of Evolutionary Economics*. Description and article preview links, sponsored by the International Josef Schumpeter Society.

- *Journal of Institutional Economics*, sponsored by the European Society for Evolutionary Political Economy.

- *Evolutionary and Institutional Economics Review*, sponsored by the Japan Association for Evolutionary Economics.

- "The Nature of Value: How to invest in the Adaptive economy", book on the economy as an evolutionary system

2.20.7 External links

- Evolutionary economics at DMOZ

- "Evolutionary Economics et al." by Prof. Esben S. Andersen - Aalborg University, Denmark

- Evolutionary Economics by J.P. Birchall

2.21 Facilitation board (economics)

A **facilitation board** is a proposed economic institution conceived by economists Michael Albert and Robin Hahnel which act in systems of economic democracy as agencies that facilitate information exchange and processing for collective consumption proposals and for large-scale investment projects, workers requests for changing places of employment, and individuals and families seeking to find membership in living units and neighborhoods, among other functions.

The proposed boards form part of the process of *participatory planning* within Albert and Hahnel's economic system of participatory economics and Participism. If adopted, they would serve to manage and coordinate proposals by workers and consumers in place of a central state or markets.

2.21.1 Description

Iteration Facilitation Boards (IFBs) act as management bodies in participatory economics and perhaps other similar systems for local consumer and worker councils and are the mechanism via which economic allocation is decided upon and ultimately implemented in an economy without a state or markets; although the kind of participatory planning found in parecon could also possibly be combined with an artificial market (arket) for certain commercial goods and services.

Participatory planning

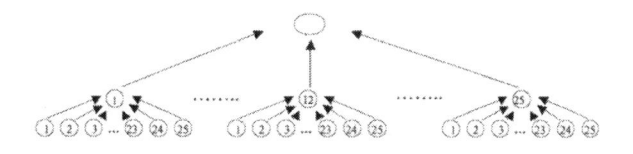

A diagram of the nested council structure.

Democratic participatory planning is an economic practice used to determine the production, consumption, and allocation of resources, goods, and services in a given economy and recommended as a solution to the problems seen in both statist central planning within state-socialism and privatist markets within capitalism. Facilitation boards are used to guide this process effectively.

Through participatory planning, workers and consumers decide democratically which and how many goods to produce, decide construction plans, determine how vital resources are managed and all other economic issues at various levels through a system of confederated "nested councils" or assemblies with local economic issues being determined at the local level, and administrative issues on a wider level being determined by city, regional, provincial, and country councils with delegates sent successively to each level to communicate the decisions made by the nested council below them.

Local decisions like the construction of a playground might be made in the ward or city council, probably interacting with both city and countrywide councils through rotating delegates. Countrywide decisions, like the construction of a high-speed mass transportation system, would be discussed by the country council, possibly interacting with a city council in the city where the materials are produced, or countrywide or international councils.

Role in economic planning

During an event known as a planning procedure, which could be an annual, bi-annual or quarterly event, facilitation boards first announce a set of indicative prices which workers and consumers use, individually and through their councils at each level, when deciding on their production and consumption proposals. Proposals could be done either collectively through a local consumer council, or individually on a computer; or any combination of the two. When the proposals are all in, the IFBs aggregate all the production and consumption proposals for the different categories of goods and services – inputs into all the production processes as well as consumer goods – to see if proposed supply and demand are equal. If they are not equal for every good and service the IFB revises the set of indicative prices and the process is repeated through successive rounds until a consistent set of production and consumption proposals is arrived at.

The facilitation board would work with the citizen(s) that originated the proposal to work it into a manageable proposition. Around the time of the planning procedure, interested parties within the region affected by the collective consumption proposal would be able to view the collective consumption proposals and vote them up or down. This could be done at large meetings or via computer. At the same time, worker's councils and producers councils would respond with production proposals outlining the outputs they propose to produce and the inputs they believe are required to produce them. Individual workers would indicate their proposed hours of work, and workers will be able to propose upgrades and innovations for their workplace, aided by a facilitation board.

Facilitation boards would then calculate excess proposed supply and demand based on the proposals, adjusting the indicative price for each final good or service according to its impact on society and the environment so that the social opportunity cost is reflected. Using the new indicative prices, consumer and workers' councils would revise and resubmit their proposals, as some goods would be more expensive, and others less expensive. Proposals deemed excessive by other parties would become very expensive, creating a disincentive to pursue them.

Iterations would continue according to some predefined method which is likely to converge within an acceptable time delay. For instance, proposals would only be changeable by a minimum percentage for the second round, and a lesser percentage for the third round, and so on, forcing convergence of a feasible plan.

The facilitation boards then implement these final proposals by setting new prices and organizing production plans. These prices would represent the estimated marginal social opportunity cost for all goods and services. During the planning procedure, not only do the prices reflect proposed supply and demand, but also the social and ecological cost of producing the good. For instance a product that produces pollution in its manufacture, or is especially dangerous for workers to produce, would have its price automatically inflated to discourage excess consumption. Thus

Final retail price = supply and demand + opportunity cost

In the event of unforeseen circumstances occurring in between planning procedures, the IFBs would adjust prices or production quotas accordingly within established guidelines.

The facilitation boards should function according to a maximum level of radical transparency and only have very limited powers of mediation, subject to the discretion of the participating councils. The real decisions regarding the formulation and implementation of the plan are to be made in the consumers' and producers' councils.

2.21.2 Criticism

Facilitation board members would do very important economic work running the economy, and thus one might think they would gradually take over in any system that would adopt them. Its proponents argue that this could be prevented by requiring board members never to handle proposals that pertain to their own region and making any IFB meeting transparent to the public. Political economist Pat Devine has suggested that if implemented in a society with advanced technology, the IFB could itself merely be a highly advanced computer system.

It has been debated whether systems using only participatory planning would be able to change prices as demand changes and other factors modify the results of the participatory planning procedure. Albert and Hahnel have argued that this would be done efficiently. Facilitation boards could continually modify prices as time goes on, finding reasons for production shortfalls, production overruns, changes in demand, environmental disasters, etc. and the facilitation boards could adjust prices accordingly. One proposed way to do this would be to adjust prices within council guidelines on a monthly basis as events unfold.

Hahnel and Albert note that markets themselves hardly adjust prices instantaneously and contend that an economy using universal participatory planning should be able to do just as well, or better. Although not recommended by either Albert or Hahnel, participatory planning could potentially be combined with an artificial market for microeconomic matters so as to take some of the potential strain off consumers and make the planning procedure less complex by retaining it exclusively for macroeconomic matters. Facilitation boards could then be used to regulate the artificial market as well as helping implement macro economic decisions.

2.21.3 Fictional accounts

An institution with the functions of a facilitation board appears as the Resource Review Board in Chris Carlsson's post-revolutionary San Francisco in the novel *After the Deluge*.[1]

2.21.4 See also

- Enterprise resource planning
- Viable System Model
- Project cybersyn

2.21.5 References

[1] Carlsson, Chris (January 2004). *After the deluge*. Full Enjoyment Books. pp. 11–12, 100. ISBN 978-0-926664-07-4.

2.21.6 External links and sources

- Participatory economics website
- Vancouver Participatory Economics Collective
- Old Market Autonomous Zone (Winnipeg)
- Participatory Economy and Inclusive Democracy - A critique

- Nonsense on Stilts: Michael Albert's Parecon - A critique
- Audio material regarding Participatory Economics
- CAPES – Chicago Area Participatory Economics Society

Video

- *Cartoon introduction to participatory economics (YouTube video)* 7:16 mns, by Jason Mitchell
- *Michael Albert in Alternative Economy Cultures Helsinki, Finland, 3 April 2009*

2.22 Feminist economics

This article is about the discipline. For the journal, see Feminist Economics (journal).

Feminist economics is the critical study of economics including its methodology, epistemology, history and empirical research, attempting to overcome androcentric (male and patriarchal) biases. It focuses on topics of particular relevance to women, such as care work or occupational segregation (exclusion of women and minorities from certain fields); deficiencies of economic models, such as disregarding intra-household bargaining; new forms of data collection and measurement such as the Gender Empowerment Measure (GEM), and more gender-aware theories such as the capabilities approach.[1] Feminist economics ultimately seeks to produce a more gender inclusive economics.

Feminist economists call attention to the social constructions of traditional economics, questioning the extent to which it is positive and objective, and showing how its models and methods are biased towards masculine preferences.[2][3] Since economics is traditionally focused on topics said to be "culturally masculine" such as autonomy, abstraction and logic, feminist economists call for the inclusion of more feminine topics such as family economics, connections, concreteness, and emotion, and show the problems caused by exclusion of those topics.[2] Inclusion of such topics has helped create policies that have reduced gender, racial, and ethnic discrimination and inequity, satisfying normative goals central to all economics.[4]

Many scholars including Ester Boserup, Marianne Ferber, Julie A. Nelson, Marilyn Waring, Nancy Folbre, Diane Elson and Ailsa McKay have contributed to feminist economics. Waring's 1988 book *If Women Counted* is often regarded as the "founding document" of the discipline.[5][6] By the 1990s feminist economics had become recognised as an established field within economics.[7]

2.22.1 Origins and history

Early on, feminist ethicists, economists, political scientists, and systems scientists argued that women's traditional work (e.g. child-raising, caring for sick elders) and occupations (e.g. nursing, teaching) are systematically undervalued with respect to that of men. For example, Jane Jacobs' thesis of the "Guardian Ethic" and its contrast to the "Trader Ethic" sought to explain the undervaluing of guardianship activity, including the child-protecting, nurturing, and healing tasks that were traditionally assigned to women.

Written in 1969 and later published in the Houseworker's Handbook Betsy Warrior[8] presents a cogent argument that the production and reproduction of domestic labor performed by women constitutes the foundation of all economic transactions and survival; although, unremunerated and not included in the GDP.[9] According to Warrior: "Economics, as it's presented today, lacks any basis in reality as it leaves out the very foundation of economic life. That foundation is built on women's labor; first her reproductive labor which produces every new laborer (and the first commodity, which is mother's milk and which sustains every new consumer/laborer); secondly, women's labor entails environmentally necessary cleaning, cooking to make raw materials consumable, negotiating to maintain social stability and nurturing, which prepares for market and maintains each laborer. This constitutes women's continuing industry enabling laborers to occupy every position in the work force. Without this fundamental labor and commodity there would be no economic activity nor we would have survived to continue to evolve." [10] Warrior also notes that the unacknowledged income of men from illegal activities like arms, drugs and human trafficking, political graft, religious emoluments and various other undisclosed activities provide a rich revenue stream to men, which further invalidates GDP figures.[11] Even in underground economies where women predominate numerically, like trafficking in humans, prostitution and domestic servitude, only a tiny fraction of the pimp's revenue filters down to the women and children he deploys. Usually the amount spent on them is merely for the maintenance of their lives and, in the case of those prostituted, some money may be spent on clothing and such accouterments as will make them more salable to the pimp's clients. For instance, focusing on just the U.S.A., according to a government sponsored report by the Urban Institute in 2014, "A street prostitute in Dallas may make as little as $5 per sex act. But pimps can take in $33,000 a week in Atlanta, where the sex business brings in an estimated $290 million per year." [12] Warrior believes that only an inclusive, facts-based economic analysis will provide a reliable bases for future planning for environmental and reproductive/population needs.

In 1970, Ester Boserup published *Woman's Role in Eco-*

nomic Development and provided the first systematic examination of the gendered effects of agricultural transformation, industrialization and other structural changes.[13] This evidence illuminated the negative outcomes that these changes had for women. This work, among others, laid the basis for the broad claim that "women and men weather the storm of macroeconomic shocks, neoliberal policies, and the forces of globalization in different ways."[4] Moreover, measures such as employment equity were implemented in developed nations in the 1970s to 1990s, but these were not entirely successful in removing wage gaps even in nations with strong equity traditions.

Marilyn Waring, author of If Women Counted *(1988)*

In 1988, Marilyn Waring published *If Women Counted: A New Feminist Economics*, a groundbreaking and systematic critique of the system of national accounts, the international standard of measuring economic growth, and the ways in which women's unpaid work as well as the value of Nature have been excluded from what counts as productive in the economy. In the foreword to the 2014 anthology *Counting on Marilyn Waring*, Julie A. Nelson wrote:

> "Marilyn Waring's work woke people up. She showed exactly how the unpaid work traditionally done by women has been made invisible within national accounting systems, and the damage this causes. Her book [...] encouraged and influenced a wide range of work on ways, both numerical and otherwise, of valuing, preserving, and rewarding the work of care that sustains our lives. By pointing to a similar neglect of the natural environment, she also issued a wake-up call to issues of ecological sustainability that have only grown more pressing over time. In recent decades, the field of feminist economics has broadened and widened to encompass these topics and more."[6]

Supported by formation of the Committee on the Status of Women in the Economics Profession (CSWEP) in 1972, gender-based critiques of traditional economics appeared in the 1970s and 80s. The subsequent emergence of Development Alternatives with Women for a New Era (DAWN) and the 1992 founding of the International Association for Feminist Economics (IAFFE) along with its journal *Feminist Economics in 1994'",*[11][2] *encouraged the rapid growth of feminist economics.*

As in other disciplines, the initial emphasis of feminist economists was to critique the established theory, methodology, and policy approaches. The critique began in microeconomics of the household and labor markets and spread to macroeconomics and international trade, ultimately extending to all areas of traditional economic analysis.[7] Feminist economists pushed for and produced gender aware theory and analysis, broadened the focus on economics and sought pluralism of methodology and research methods.

Feminist economics shares many of its perspectives with ecological economics and the more applied field of green economy, including the focus on sustainability, nature, justice and care values.[14]

2.22.2 Critiques of traditional economics

Although there is no definitive list of the principles of feminist economics, feminist economists offer a variety of critiques of standard approaches in economics.[15] For example, prominent feminist economist Paula England provided one of the earliest feminist critiques of traditional economics as she challenged the claims that:

- That interpersonal utility comparisons are impossible;
- That tastes are exogenous and unchanging;
- That actors are selfish; and
- That household heads act altruistically.[16]

This list is not exhaustive but does represent some of the central feminist economic critiques of traditional economics, out of the wide variety of such viewpoints and critiques.

Normativity

Many feminists call attention to value judgments in economic analysis.[3] This idea is contrary to the typical conception of economics as a positive science held by many practitioners. For example, Geoff Schneider and Jean Shackelford suggest that "the issues that economists choose to study, the kinds of questions they ask, and the type of analysis undertaken all are a product of a belief system which is influenced by numerous factors, some of them ideological in character."[15] Similarly, Diana Strassmann comments, "All economic statistics are based on an underlying story forming the basis of the definition. In this way, narrative constructions necessarily underlie all definitions of variables and statistics. Therefore, economic research cannot escape being inherently qualitative, regardless of how it is labeled."[17] Feminist economists call attention to the value judgements in all aspects economics and criticize its depiction of an objective science.

Free trade

A central principle of mainstream economics is that trade can make everyone better off through comparative advantage and efficiency gains from specialization and greater efficiency.[18][19] Many feminist economists question this claim. Diane Elson, Caren Grown and Nilufer Cagatay explore the role that gender inequalities play in international trade and how such trade reshapes gender inequality itself. They and other feminist economists explore whose interests specific trade practices serve.

For example, they may highlight that in Africa, specialization in the cultivation of a single cash crop for export in many countries made those countries extremely vulnerable to price fluctuations, weather patterns, and pests.[15] Feminist economists may also consider the specific gendered effects of trade-decisions. For instance, "in countries such as Kenya, men generally controlled the earnings from cash crops while women were still expected to provide food and clothing for the household, their traditional role in the African family, along with labor to produce cash crops. Thus women suffered significantly from the transition away from subsistence food production towards specialization and trade."[15] Similarly, since women often lack economic power as business owners, they are more likely to be hired as cheap labor, often involving them in exploitative situations.[19]

Exclusion of non-market activity

Feminist economics call attention to the importance of non-market activities, such as childcare and domestic work, to economic development.[20][21] This stands in sharp contrast to neoclassical economics where those forms of labor are unaccounted for as "non-economic" phenomena.[3] Including such labor in economic accounts removes substantial gender bias because women disproportionately perform those tasks.[22] When that labor is unaccounted for in economic models, much work done by women is ignored, literally devaluing their effort.

A Colombian domestic worker. Neighborhood friends and family sharing household and childcare responsibilities is an example of non-market activity performed outside of the traditional labor market.

More specifically, for example, Nancy Folbre examines the role of children as public goods and how the non-market labor of parents contributes to the development of human capital as a public service.[23] In this sense, children are positive externality which is under-invested according to traditional analysis. Folbre indicates that this oversight partially results from failing to properly examine non-market activities.

Marilyn Waring described how the exclusion of non-market activities in the national accounting systems relied on the deliberate choice and the design of the international standard of national accounts that explicitly excluded non-market activities. In some countries, such as Norway, which had included unpaid household work in the GDP in the first half of the 19th century, it was left out in 1950 for reasons of compatibility with the new international standard.[24]

Ailsa McKay argues for a basic income as "a tool for promoting gender-neutral social citizenship rights" partially to address these concerns.[25]

Omission of power relations

Feminist economics often assert that power relations exist within the economy, and therefore, must be assessed in economic models in ways that they previously have been overlooked.[20] For example, in "neoclassical texts, the sale of labor is viewed as a mutually beneficial exchange that benefits both parties. No mention is made of the power inequities in the exchange which tend to give the employer power over the employee."[15] These power relations often favor men and there is "never any mention made of the particular difficulties that confront women in the workplace."[15] Consequently, "Understanding power and patriarchy helps us to analyze how male-dominated economic institutions actually function and why women are often at a disadvantage in the workplace."[15] Feminist economists often extend these criticisms to many aspects of the social world, arguing that power relations are an endemic and important feature of society.

Omission of gender and race

Feminist economics argue that gender and race must be considered in economic analysis. Amartya Sen argues that "the systematically inferior position of women inside and outside the household in many societies points to the necessity of treating gender as a force of its own in development analysis."[26] He goes on to say that experiences of men and women, even within the same household, are often so different that examining economics without gender can be misleading.

Economic models can often be improved by explicitly considering gender, race, class, and caste.[27] Julie Matthaie describes their importance: "Not only did gender and racial-ethnic differences and inequality precede capitalism, they have been built into it in key ways. In other words, every aspect of our capitalist economy is gendered and racialized; a theory and practice that ignores this is inherently flawed."[28] Feminist economist Eiman Zein-Elabdin says racial and gender differences should be examined since both have traditionally been ignored and thus are equally described as "feminist difference."[29] The July 2002 issue of the *Feminist Economics* journal was dedicated to issues of "gender, color, caste and class."[20]

Homo economicus

The neoclassical economic model of a person is called *Homo economicus*, describing a person who "interacts in society without being influenced by society," because "his mode of interaction is through an ideal market," in which prices are the only necessary considerations.[3] In this view, people are considered rational actors who engage in marginal analysis to make many or all of their decisions.[15] Feminist economists argue that people are more complex than such models, and call for "a more holistic vision of an economic actor, which includes group interactions and actions motivated by factors other than greed."[15] Feminist economics holds that such a reformation provides a better description of the actual experiences of both men and women in the market, arguing that mainstream economics overemphasizes the role of individualism, competition and selfishness of all actors. Instead, feminist economists like Nancy Folbre show that cooperation also plays a role in the economy.

Feminist economists also point out that agency is not available to everyone, such as children, the sick, and the frail elderly. Responsibilities for their care can compromise the agency of caregivers as well. This is a critical departure from the *homo economicus* model.[30]

Moreover, feminist economists critique the focus of neoclassical economics on monetary rewards. Nancy Folbre notes, "legal rules and cultural norms can affect market outcomes in ways distinctly disadvantageous to women." This includes occupational segregation resulting in unequal pay for women. Feminist research in these areas contradicts the neoclassical description of labor markets in which occupations are chosen freely by individuals acting alone and out of their own free will.[15] Feminist economics also includes study of norms relevant to economics, challenging the traditional view that material incentives will reliably provide the goods we want and need (consumer sovereignty), which does not hold true for many people.

Institutional economics is one means by which feminist economists improve upon the *homo economicus* model. This theory examines the role of institutions and evolutionary social processes in shaping economic behavior, emphasizing "the complexity of human motives and the importance of culture and relations of power." This provides a more holistic view of the economic actor than *homo economicus*.[20]

The work of George Akerlof and Janet Yellen on efficiency wages based on notions of fairness provides an example of a feminist model of economic actors. In their work, agents are not hyperrational or isolated, but instead act in concert and with fairness, are capable of experiencing jealousy, and are interested in personal relationships. This work is based on empirical sociology and psychology, and suggests that wages can be influenced by fairness considerations rather than purely market forces.[3]

Limited methodology

Economics is often thought of as "the study of how society manages its scarce resources" and as such is limited to mathematical inquiry.[3][18] Traditional economists often say such an approach assures objectivity and separates economics from "softer" fields such as sociology and political science. Feminist economists, argue on the contrary that a mathematical conception of economics limited to scarce resources is a holdover from the early years of science and Cartesian philosophy, and limits economic analysis. So feminist economists often call for more diverse data collection and broader economic models.[3]

Economic pedagogy

Feminist economists suggest that both the content and teaching style of economics courses would benefit from certain changes. Some recommend including experimental learning, laboratory sessions, individual research and more chances to "do economics."[3] Some want more dialogue between instructors and students. Many feminist economists are urgently interested in how course content influences the demographic composition of future economists, suggesting that the "classroom climate" affects some students' perceptions of their own ability.[31]

The 2000s financial crisis

Margunn Bjørnholt and Ailsa McKay argue that the financial crisis of 2007–08 and the response to it revealed a crisis of ideas in mainstream economics and within the economics profession, and call for a reshaping of both the economy, economic theory and the economics profession. They argue that such a reshaping should include new advances within feminist economics that take as their starting point the socially responsible, sensible and accountable subject in creating an economy and economic theories that fully acknowledge care for each other as well as the planet.[32]

2.22.3 Major areas of inquiry

Economic epistemology

Feminist critiques of economics include that "economics, like any science, is socially constructed."[3] Feminist economists show that social constructs act to privilege male-identified, western, and heterosexual interpretations of economics.[1] They generally incorporate feminist theory and frameworks to show how traditional economics communities signal expectations regarding appropriate participants, to the exclusion of outsiders. Such criticisms extend to the theories, methodologies and research areas of economics, in order to show that accounts of economic life are deeply influenced by biased histories, social structures, norms, cultural practices, interpersonal interactions, and politics.[1]

Feminist economists often make a critical distinction that masculine bias in economics is primarily a result of gender, not sex.[3] In other words, when feminist economists highlight the biases of mainstream economics, they focus on its social beliefs about masculinity like objectivity, separation, logical consistency, individual accomplishment, mathematics, abstraction, and lack of emotion, but not on the gender of authorities and subjects. However, the overrepresentation of men among economists and their subjects of study is also a concern.

Economic history

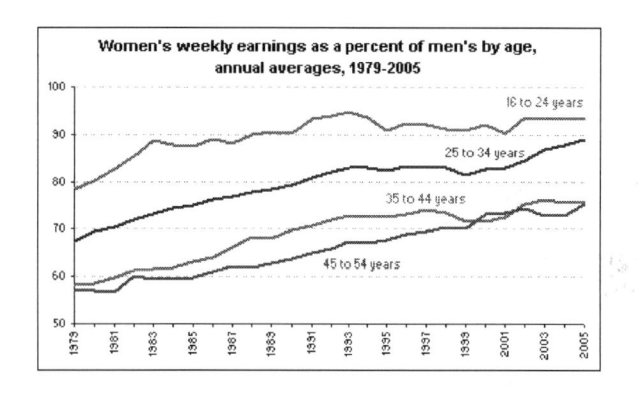

Women's weekly earnings as a percentage of men's in the U.S. by age, 1979-2005

Feminist economists say that mainstream economics has been disproportionately developed by European-descended, heterosexual, middle and upper-middle class men, and that this has led to suppression of the life experiences of the full diversity of the world's people, especially women, children and those in non-traditional families.[33] For example, Colin Danby emphasizes how heteronormative assumptions have remained in economic models, including those of feminist economists, and offers strategies by which they may be overcome to better represent the diversity of the world's people.[34]

Additionally, feminist economists claim that the historical bases of economics are inherently exclusionary to women. Michèle Pujol points to five specific historical assumptions about woman that arose, became embedded in the formulation of economics, and continue to be used to maintain that women are different from the masculinized norms and exclude them.[35] These include the ideas that:

- All women are married, or if not yet, they will be and all women will have children.
- All women are economically dependent on a male relative.
- All women are (and should be) housewives due to their reproductive capacities.
- Women are unproductive in the industrial workforce.
- Women are irrational, unfit economic agents, and cannot be trusted to make the right economic decisions.

Feminist economists also examine early economic thinkers' interaction or lack of interaction with gender and women's issues, showing examples of women's historical engagement with economic thought. For example, Edith Kuiper discusses Adam Smith's engagement with feminist discourse on the role of women in the eighteenth century, France and England.[36] She finds that through his writings, Smith typically supported the *status quo* on women's issues and "lost sight of the division of labor in the family and the contribution of women's economic work." In response, she points to Mary Collier's works such as *The Woman's Labour* (1739) to help understand Smith's contemporaneous experiences of women and fill in such gaps.

Engendering macroeconomic theories

Central to feminist economics is an effort to alter the theoretical modeling of the economy, to reduce gender bias and inequity.[4] Feminist macroeconomic inquiries focus on international capital flows, fiscal austerity, deregulation and privatization, monetary policy, international trade and more. In general, these modifications take three main forms: gender disaggregation, the addition of gender-based macroeconomic variables, and the creation of a two-sector system.

Gender disaggregation This method of economic analysis seeks to overcome gender bias by showing how men and women differ in their consumption, investment or saving behavior. Gender disaggregation strategies justify the separation of macroeconomic variables by gender. Korkut Ertürk and Nilüfer Çağatay show how the feminization of labor stimulates investment, while an increase in female activity in housework raises savings.[38] This model highlights how gender effects macroeconomic variables and shows

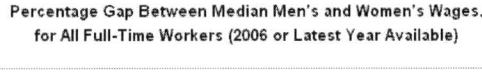

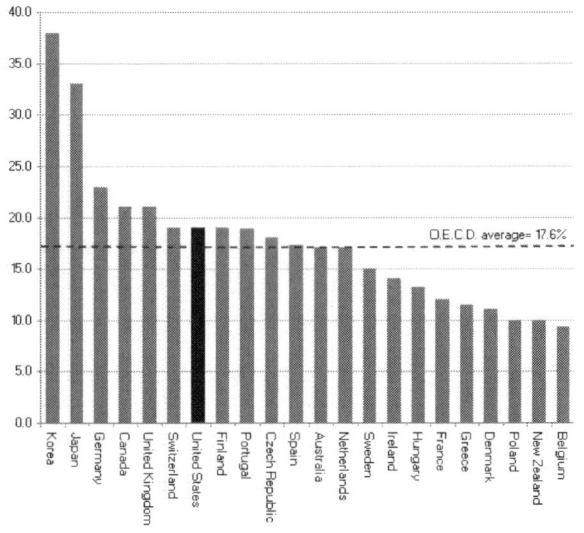

Percentage gap between median men's and women's wages, for full-time workers by OECD country, 2006. In the U.K., the most significant factors associated with the remaining gender pay gap are part-time work, education, the size of the firm a person is employed in, and occupational segregation (women are under-represented in managerial and high-paying professional occupations.)[37]

that economies have a higher likelihood of recovering from downturns if women participate in the labor force more, instead of devoting their time to housework.[4]

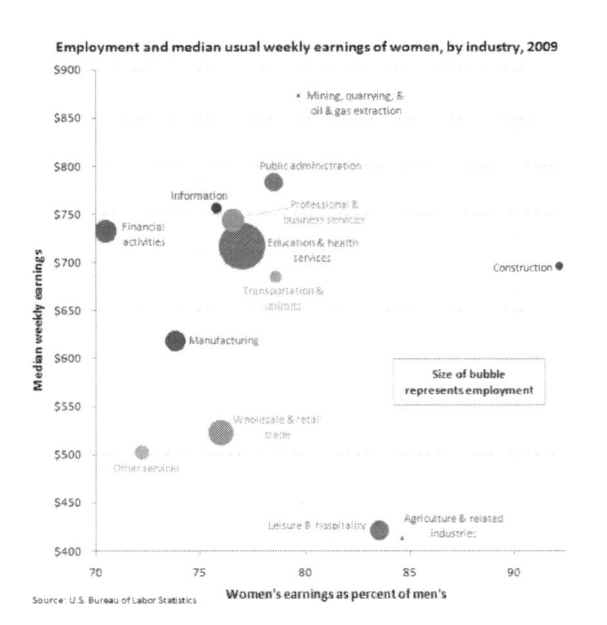

U.S. women's weekly earnings, employment, and percentage of men's earnings, by industry, 2009

Gendered macroeconomic variables See also: Gender pay gap

This approach demonstrates the effects of gender inequalities by enhancing macroeconomic models. Bernard Walters shows that traditional neoclassical models fail to adequately assess work related to reproduction by assuming that the population and labor are determined exogenously.[39] That fails to account for the fact that inputs are produced through caring labor, which is disproportionately performed by women. Stephen Knowels *et al.* use a neoclassical growth model to show that women's education has a positive statistically significant effect on labor productivity, more robust than that of men's education.[40] In both of these cases, economists highlight and address the gender biases of macroeconomic variables to show that gender plays a significant role in models' outcomes.

Two-sector system The two-sector system approach models the economy as two separate systems: one involving the standard macroeconomic variables, while the other includes gender-specific variables. William Darity developed a two-sector approach for low-income, farm-based economies.[41] Darity shows that subsistence farming depended on the labor of women, while the production of income depended on the labor of both men and women in cash-crop activities. This model shows that when men control production and income, they seek to maximize income by persuading women to put additional effort into cash-crop production, causing increases in cash crops come at the expense of subsistence production.[4]

Well-being

Many feminist economists argue economics should be focused less on mechanisms (like income) or theories (such as utilitarianism) and more on well-being, a multidimensional concept including income, health, education, empowerment and social status.[4][20] They argue that economic success can not be measured only by goods or gross domestic product, but must also be measured by human well-being. Aggregate income is not sufficient to evaluate general well-being, because individual entitlements and needs must also be considered, leading feminist economists to study health, longevity, access to property, education, and related factors.[1][42]

Bina Agarwal and Pradeep Panda illustrate that a woman's property status (such as owning a house or land) directly and significantly reduces her chances of experiencing domestic violence, while employment makes little difference.[43] They argue that such immovable property increases women's self-esteem, economic security, and strengthens their fall-back positions, enhancing their options and bargaining clout. They show that property ownership is an important contributor to women's economic well-being because it reduces their susceptibility to violence.

In order to measure well-being more generally, Amartya Sen, Sakiko Fukuda-Parr, and other feminist economists helped develop alternatives to Gross Domestic Product, such as the Human Development Index.[44] Other models of interest to feminist economists include the labor theory of value, which was most thoroughly developed in *Das Capital* by Karl Marx. That model considers production as a socially constructed human project and redefines wages as means to earning a living. This refocuses economic models on human innate desires and needs as opposed to monetary incentives.[20]

Human capabilities approach Main article: Capabilities approach

Feminist economists Amartya Sen and Martha Nussbaum created the human capabilities approach as an alternative way to assess economic success rooted in the ideas of welfare economics and focused on the individual's potential to do and be what he or she may choose to value.[45][46][47] Unlike traditional economic measures of success, focused on GDP, utility, income, assets or other monetary measures, the capabilities approach focuses on what individuals are able to do. This approach emphasizes processes as well as outcomes, and draws attention to cultural, social and material dynamics of well-being. Martha Nussbaum, expanded on the model with a more complete list of central capabilities including life, health, bodily integrity, thought, and more.[48][49] In recent years, the capabilities approach has influenced the creation of new models including the UN's Human Development Index (HDI).

Household bargaining

Central to feminist economics is a different approach to the "family" and "household." In classical economics, those units are typically described as amicable and homogeneous. Gary Becker and new home economists introduced the study of "the family" to traditional economics, which usually assumes the family is a single, altruistic unit among which money is distributed equally. Others have concluded that an optimal distribution of commodities and provisions takes place within the family as a result of which they view families in the same manner as individuals.[50] These models, according to feminist economists, "endorsed traditional expectations about the sexes," and applied individualistic rational-choice models to explain home behavior.[3] Feminist economists modify these assumptions to account for exploitative sexual and gender relations, single-parent families, same-sex relationships, familial relations with children, and the consequences of reproduction. Specifically, feminist economists move beyond unitary household models and game theory to show the diversity of household experiences.

For example, Bina Agarwal and others have critiqued the mainstream model and helped provide a better understanding of intra-household bargaining power.[51] Agarwal shows that a lack of power and outside options for women hinders their ability to negotiate within their families. Amartya Sen shows how social norms that devalue women's unpaid work in the household often disadvantage women in intra-household bargaining. These feminist economists argue that such claims have important economic outcomes which must be recognized within economic frameworks.

Care economy

Main article: Care Work

Feminist economists join the UN and others in acknowledging care work, as a kind of work which includes all tasks involving caregiving, as central to economic development and human well-being.[21][52][53] Feminist economists study both paid and unpaid care work. They argue that traditional analysis of economics often ignores the value of household unpaid work. Feminist economists have argued that unpaid domestic work is as valuable as paid work, so measures of economic success should include unpaid work. They have shown that women are disproportionately responsible for performing such care work.[54]

Sabine O'Hara argues that care is the basis for all economic activity and market economies, concluding that "everything needs care," not only people, but animals and things. She highlights the sustaining nature of care services offered outwith the formal economy.[55]

Feminist economists have also highlighted power and inequality issues within families and households. For example, Randy Albelda shows that responsibility for care work influences the time poverty experienced by single mothers in the United States.[56] Similarly, Sarah Gammage examines the effects of unpaid care work performed by women in Guatemala.[57] The work of the Equality Studies Department at University College Dublin such as that of Sara Cantillon has focused on inequalities of domestic arrangements within even affluent households.

While much care work is performed in the home, it may also be done for pay. As such, feminist economics examine its implications, including the increasing involvement of women in paid care work, the potential for exploitation, and effects on the lives of care workers.[21]

Systemic study of the ways women's work is measured, or not measured at all, have been undertaken by Marilyn Waring (see *If Women Counted*) and others in the 1980s and 1990s. These studies began to justify different means of determining value — some of which influenced the theory of social capital and individual capital, that emerged in the late 1990s and, along with ecological economics, influenced modern human development theory. (See also the entry on Gender and Social Capital.)

Unpaid work

Unpaid work can include domestic work, care work, subsistence work, unpaid market labor and voluntary work. There is no clear consensus on the definition of these categories. But broadly speaking, these kinds of work can be seen as contributing to the reproduction of society.

Domestic work is maintenance of the home, and is usually universally recognizable, e.g. doing the laundry. Care work is looking "after a relative or friend who needs support because of age, physical or learning disability, or illness, including mental illness;" this also includes raising children.[58] Care work also involves "close personal or emotional interaction."[59] Also included in this category is "self-care," in which leisure time and activities are included. Subsistence work is work done in order to meet basic needs, such as collecting water, but does not have market values assigned to it. Although some of these efforts "are categorized as productive activities according to the latest revision of the international System of National Accounts (SNA) ... [they] are poorly measured by most surveys."[59] Unpaid market work is "the direct contributions of unpaid family members to market work that officially belongs to another member of the household."[60] Voluntary work is usually work done for non-household members, but in return for little to no remuneration.

System of National Accounts Each country measures its economic output according to the System of National Accounts (SNA), sponsored mainly by the United Nations (UN), but implemented mainly by other organizations such as the European Commission, the International Monetary Fund (IMF), the Organization for Economic Co-operation and Development (OECD), and the World Bank. The SNA recognizes that unpaid work is an area of interest, but "unpaid household services are excluded from [its] production boundary."[61] Feminist economists have criticized the SNA for this exclusion, because by leaving out unpaid work, basic and necessary labor is ignored.

Even accounting measures intended to recognize gender disparities are criticized for ignoring unpaid work. Two such examples are the Gender-related Development Index (GDI) and the Gender Empowerment Measure (GEM), neither of which include much unpaid work.[62] So feminist economics calls for a more comprehensive index which includes participation in unpaid work.

In more recent years there has been increasing attention to this issue, such as recognition of unpaid work within SNA reports and a commitment by the UN to the measurement and valuation of unpaid work, emphasizing care work done by women. This goal was restated at the 1995 UN Fourth World Conference on Women in Beijing.[63]

Measurement of unpaid work The method most widely used to measure unpaid work is gathering information on time use, which has "been implemented by at least 20 developing countries and more are underway" as of 2006.[59] Time use measurement involves collecting data on how much time men and women spend on a daily, weekly, or monthly basis on certain activities that fall under the categories of unpaid work.

Techniques to gather this data include surveys, in-depth interviews, diaries, and participant observation.[63][64] Proponents of time use diaries believe that this method "generate[s] more detailed information and tend[s] to capture greater variation than predetermined questions."[63] However, others argue that participant observation, "where the researcher spends lengthy periods of time in households helping out and observing the labor process," generates more accurate information because the researcher can ascertain whether or not those studied are accurately reporting what activities they perform.[63]

Accuracy The first problem of measuring unpaid work is the issue of collecting accurate information. This is always a concern in research studies, but is particularly difficult when evaluating unpaid work. "Time-use surveys may reveal relatively little time devoted to unpaid direct care activities [because] the demands of subsistence production in those countries are great," and may not take into account multitasking — for example, a mother may collect wood fuel while a child is in the same location, so the child is in her care while she is performing other work.[59] Usually such indirect care should be included, as it is in many time use studies. But it is not always, and as a result some studies may undervalue the amount of certain types of unpaid work. Participant observation has been criticized for being "so time-consuming that it can only focus on small numbers of households," and thus limited in the amount of information it can be used to gather.[63]

All data gathering involves difficulties with the potential inaccuracy of research subjects' reports. For instance, when "people doing domestic labor have no reason to pay close attention to the amount of time tasks take ... they [may] often underestimate time spent in familiar activities."[63] Measuring time can also be problematic because "the slowest and most inefficient workers [appear to carry] the greatest workload."[63] Time use in assessing childcare is criticized as "easily obscur[ing] gender differences in workload. Men and women may both put in the same amount of time being responsible for children but as participant observation studies have shown, many men are more likely to 'babysit' their children while doing something for themselves, such as watching TV. Men's standards of care may be limited to ensuring the children are not hurt. Dirty diapers may be ignored or deliberately left until the mother returns."[63] A paradoxical aspect of this problem is that those most burdened may not be able to participate in the studies: "It is usually those women with the heaviest work loads who choose not to participate in these studies."[63] In general, measurement of time causes "some of the most demanding aspects of unpaid work [to be unexplored] and the premise that time is an appropriate tool for measuring women's unpaid work goes unchallenged."[63] Surveys have also been criticized for lacking "depth and complexity" as questions cannot be specifically tailored to particular circumstances.[63]

Comparability A second problem is the difficulty of comparisons across cultures. "Comparisons across countries are currently hampered by differences in activity classification and nomenclature."[59] In-depth surveys may be the only way to get necessary information desired, but they make it difficult to perform cross-cultural comparisons.[63] The lack of adequate universal terminology in discussing unpaid work is an example. "Despite increasing recognition that domestic labor is work, existing vocabularies do not easily convey the new appreciations. People still tend to talk about work and home as if they were separate spheres. 'Working mothers' are usually assumed to be in the paid labor force, despite feminist assertions that 'every mother is a working mother.' There are no readily accepted terms to express different work activities or job titles. Housewife, home manager, homemaker are all problematic and none of them conveys the sense of a women who juggles both domestic labor and paid employment."[63]

Complexity A third problem is the complexity of domestic labor and the issues of separating unpaid work categories. Time use studies now take multitasking issues into account, separating primary and secondary activities. However, not all studies do this, and even those that do may not take into account "the fact that frequently several tasks are done simultaneously, that tasks overlap, and that the boundaries between work and relationships are often unclear.

How does a woman determine her primary activity when she is preparing dinner while putting the laundry away, making coffee for her spouse, having coffee and chatting with him, and attending to the children?"[63] Some activities may not even be considered work, such as playing with a child (this has been categorized as developmental care work) and so may not be included in a study's responses.[63] As mentioned above, child supervision (indirect care work) may not be construed as an activity at all, which "suggests that activity-based surveys should be supplemented by more stylized questions regarding care responsibilities" as otherwise such activities can be undercounted.[59] In the past, time use studies tended to measure only primary activities, and "respondents doing two or more things at once were asked to indicate which was the more important." This has been changing in more recent years.[63]

Valuation of time Feminist economists point out three main ways of determining the value of unpaid work: the opportunity cost method, replacement cost method, and input-output cost method. The opportunity cost method "uses the wage a person would earn in the market" to see how much value their labor-time has.[64] This method extrapolates from the opportunity cost idea in mainstream economics.

The second method of valuation uses replacement costs. In simple terms, this is done by measuring the amount of money a third-party would make for doing the same work if it was part of the market. In other words, the value of a person cleaning the house in an hour is the same as the hourly wage for a maid. Within this method there are two approaches: the first is a generalist replacement cost method, which examines if "it would be possible, for example, to take the wage of a general domestic worker who could perform a variety of tasks including childcare".[64] The second approach is the specialist replacement cost method, which aims to "distinguish between the different household tasks and choose replacements accordingly".[64]

The third method is the input-output cost method. This looks at both the costs of inputs and includes any value added by the household. "For instance, the value of time devoted to cooking a meal can be determined by asking what it could cost to purchase a similar meal (the output) in the market, then subtracting the cost of the capital goods, utilities and raw materials devoted to that meal. This remainder represents the value of the other factors of production, primarily labor."[59] These types of models try to value household output by determining monetary values for the inputs — in the dinner example, the ingredients and production of the meal — and compares those with market equivalents.[63]

Difficulty establishing monetary levels One criticism of time valuation concerns the choice of monetary levels. How should unpaid work be valued when more than one activity is being performed or more than one output is produced? Another issue concerns differences in quality between market and household products. Some feminist economists take issue with using the market system to determine values for a variety of reasons: it may lead to the conclusion that the market provides perfect substitutes for non-market work;[59] the wage produced in the market for services may not accurately reflect the actual opportunity cost of time spent in household production;[64] and the wages used in valuation methods come from industries where wages are already depressed because of gender inequalities, and so will not accurately value unpaid work.[64] A related argument is that the market "accepts existing sex/gender divisions of labor and pay inequalities as normal and unproblematic. With this basic assumption underlying their calculations, the valuations produced serve to reinforce gender inequalities rather than challenge women's subordination."[63]

Criticisms of opportunity cost Criticisms are leveled against each method of valuation. The opportunity cost method "depends on the lost earnings of the worker so that a toilet cleaned by a lawyer has much greater value than one cleaned by a janitor", which means that the value varies too drastically.[63] There are also issues with the uniformity of this method not just across multiple individuals, but also for a single person: it "may not be uniform across the entire day or across days of the week."[64] There is also the issue of whether any enjoyment of the activity should be deducted from the opportunity cost estimate.[64]

Difficulties with replacement cost The replacement cost method also has its critics. What types of jobs should be used as substitutes? For example, should childcare activities "be calculated using the wages of daycare workers or child psychiatrists?"[64] This relates to the problem of depressed wages in female-dominated industries, and whether using such jobs as an equivalent leads to the undervaluing of unpaid work. Some have argued that education levels ought to be comparable, for example, "the value of time that a college-educated parent spends reading aloud to a child should be ascertained by asking how much it would cost to hire a college-educated worker to do the same, not by an average housekeeper's wage."[59]

Difficulties with input-output methods Critiques against the input-output methods include the difficulty of identifying and measuring household outputs, and the issues of variation of households and these effects.[64]

The formal economy

Research into the causes and consequences of occupational segregation, the gender pay gap, and the "glass ceiling" have been a significant part of feminist economics. While conventional neoclassical economic theories of the 1960s and 1970s explained these as the result of free choices made by women and men who simply had different abilities or preferences, feminist economists pointed out the important roles played by stereotyping, sexism, patriarchal beliefs and institutions, sexual harassment, and discrimination.[65] The rationales for, and the effects of, anti-discrimination laws adopted in many industrial countries beginning in the 1970s, has also been studied.[66]

Women moved in large numbers into previous male bastions — especially professions like medicine and law — during the last decades of the 20th century. The gender pay gap remains and is shrinking more slowly. Feminist economists such as Marilyn Power, Ellen Mutari and Deborah M. Figart have examined the gender pay gap and found that wage setting procedures are not primarily driven by market forces, but instead by the power of actors, cultural understandings of the value of work and what constitutes a proper living, and social gender norms.[67] Consequently, they assert that economic models must take these typically exogenous variables into account.

While overt employment discrimination by sex remains a concern of feminist economists, in recent years more attention has been paid to discrimination against caregivers—those women, and some men, who give hands-on care to children or sick or elderly friends or relatives. Because many business and government policies were designed to accommodate the "ideal worker" (that is, the traditional male worker who had no such responsibilities) rather than caregiver-workers, inefficient and inequitable treatment has resulted.[68][69][70]

Globalization

Feminist economists' work on globalization is diverse and multifaceted. But much of it is tied together through detailed and nuanced studies of the ways in which globalization affects women in particular and how these effects relate to socially just outcomes. Often country case studies are used for these data.[4] Some feminist economists focus on policies involving the development of globalization. For example, Lourdes Benería argues that economic development in the Global South depends in large part on improved reproductive rights, gender equitable laws on ownership and inheritance, and policies that are sensitive to the proportion of women in the informal economy.[71] Additionally, Nalia Kabeer discusses the impacts of a social clause that would enforce global labor standards through international trade agreements, drawing on fieldwork from Bangladesh.[72] She argues that although these jobs may appear exploitative, for many workers in those areas they present opportunities and ways to avoid more exploitative situations in the informal economy.

Alternatively, Suzanne Bergeron, for example, raises examples of studies that illustrate the multifaceted effects of globalization on women, including Kumudhini Rosa's study of Sri Lankan, Malaysian, and Philippine, workers in free trade zones as an example of local resistance to globalization.[73] Women there use their wages to create women's centers aimed at providing legal and medical services, libraries and cooperative housing, to local community members. Such efforts, Bergeron highlights, allow women the chance to take control of economic conditions, increase their sense of individualism, and alter the pace and direction of globalization itself.

In other cases, feminist economists work on removing gender biases from the theoretical bases of globalization itself. Suzanne Bergeron, for example, focuses on the typical theories of globalization as the "rapid integration of the world into one economic space" through the flow of goods, capital, and money, in order to show how they exclude some women and the disadvantaged.[73] She argues that traditional understandings of globalization over-emphasize the power of global capital flows, the uniformity of globalization experiences across all populations, and technical and abstract economic processes, and therefore depict the political economy of globalization inappropriately. She highlights the alternative views of globalization created by feminists. First, she describes how feminists may de-emphasize the idea of the market as "a natural and unstoppable force," instead depicting the process of globalization as alterable and movable by individual economic actors including women. She also explains that the concept of globalization itself is gender biased, because its depiction as "dominant, unified, [and] intentional" is inherently masculinized and misleading. She suggests that feminists critique such narratives by showing how a "global economy" is highly complex, de-centered and unclear.

2.22.4 Methodology

Interdisciplinary data collection

Many feminist economists challenge the perception that only "objective" (often presumed to be quantitative) data are valid.[3] Instead, they say economists should enrich their analysis by using data sets generated from other disciplines or through increased use of qualitative methods.[74] Additionally, many feminist economists propose utilizing non-traditional data collection strategies such as "utilizing growth accounting frameworks, conducting empirical tests of economic theories, developing country case studies, and pursuing research at the conceptual and empirical levels."[4]

Interdisciplinary data collection looks at systems from a specific moral position and viewpoint instead of attempting the perspective of a neutral observer. The intention is not to create a more "subjective" methodology, but to counter biases in existing methodologies, by recognizing that all explanations for world phenomena arise from socially-influenced viewpoints. Feminist economists say too many theories claim to present universal principles but actually present a masculine viewpoint in the guise of a "view from nowhere," so more varied sources of data collection are needed to mediate those issues.[75]

Ethical judgment

Feminist economists depart from traditional economics in that they say "ethical judgments are a valid, inescapable, and in fact desirable part of economic analysis."[20] For example, Lourdes Beneria argues that judgments about policies leading to greater well-being should be central to economic analysis.[71] Similarly, Shahra Razavi says better understanding of care work "would allow us to shift our priorities from 'making money' or 'making stuff' to 'making livable lives' and 'enriching networks of care and relationship'" which should be central to economics.[21]

Country case studies

Often feminist economists use country-level or smaller case studies focused on developing and often understudied countries or populations.[4] For example, Michael Kevane and Leslie C. Gray examine how gendered social norms are central to understanding agricultural activities in Burkina Faso.[76] Cristina Carrasco and Arantxa Rodriquez examine the care economy in Spain to suggest that women's entrance into the labor market requires more equitable caregiving responsibilities.[77] Such studies show the importance of local social norms, government policies and cultural situations. Feminist economists see such variation as a crucial factor to be included in economics.

Alternative measures of success

Feminist economists call for a shift in how economic success is measured. These changes include an increased focus on a policy's ability to bring society toward social justice and improve people's lives, through specific goals including distributive fairness, equity, the universal provisioning of needs, elimination of poverty, freedom from discrimination and the protection of human capabilities.[4][78]

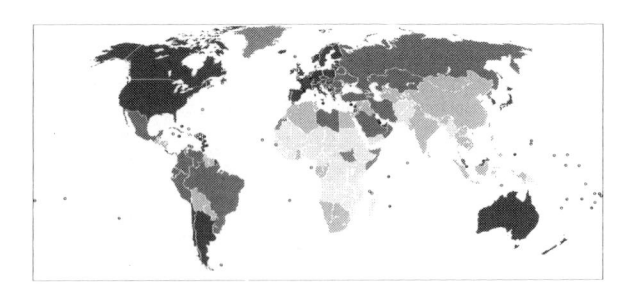

World map by quartiles of Human Development Index in 2011.

Human Development Index (HDI) Main article: Human Development Index

Feminist economists often support use of the Human Development Index as a composite statistic in order to assess countries by their overall level of human development, as opposed to other measures. The HDI takes into account a broad array of measures beyond monetary considerations including life expectancy, literacy, education, and standards of living for all countries worldwide.[79]

Gender-related Development Index (GDI) Main article: Gender-related Development Index

The **Gender-related Development Index** (GDI) was introduced in 1995 in the Human Development Report written by the United Nations Development Program in order to add a gender-sensitive dimension to the Human Development Index. The GDI takes into account not only the average or general level of well-being and wealth within a given country, but also how this wealth and well-being is distributed between different groups within society, especially between genders.[80] However, feminist economists do not universally agree on the use of the GDI and some offer improvements to it.[81]

2.22.5 Organizations

Feminist economics continues to become more widely recognized and reputed as evidenced by the numerous organizations dedicated to it or widely influenced by its principles.

International Association for Feminist Economics

Main article: International Association for Feminist Economics

Formed in 1992, the International Association for Feminist Economics (IAFFE), is independent of the American Economic Association (AEA) and seeks to challenge the masculine biases in neoclassical economics.[82] While the majority of members are economists, it is open "not only to female and male economists but to academics from other fields, as well as activists who are not academics" and currently has over 600 members in 64 countries.[83] Although its founding members were mostly based in the US, a majority of IAFFE's current members are based outside of the US. In 1997, IAFFE gained Non-Governmental Organization status in the United Nations.

Feminist Economics **journal**

Main article: Feminist Economics (journal)

Feminist Economics, edited by Diana Strassmann of Rice University and Günseli Berik of the University of Utah, is a peer-reviewed journal established to provide an open forum for dialogue and debate about feminist economic perspectives. The journal endorses a normative agenda to promote policies that will better the lives of the world's people, both women and men. In 1997, the journal was awarded the Council of Editors and Learned Journals (CELJ) Award as Best New Journal.[84] The 2007 ISI Social Science Citation Index ranked the journal *Feminist Economics* 20th out of 175 among economics journals and 2nd out of 27 among Women's Studies journals.[85]

2.22.6 Relation to other disciplines

Green economics incorporates ideas from feminist economics and Greens list feminism as an explicit goal of their political measures, seeking greater economic and general gender equality. Feminist economics is also often linked with welfare economics or labour economics, since it emphasizes child welfare, and the value of labour in itself, as opposed to the traditional focus exclusively on production for a marketplace.

2.22.7 Graduate programs

A small, but growing number of graduate programs around the world offer courses and concentrations in feminist economics. (Unless otherwise noted below, these offerings are in departments of economics.)

- American University
- School of Public Policy and Administration at Carleton University
- Colorado State University
- Institute of Social Studies
- Gender Institute of the London School of Economics
- Makerere University
- University of Massachusetts Amherst
- The Masters in Applied Economics and Public Policy programs at the University of Massachusetts Boston
- University of Nebraska–Lincoln
- The New School for Social Research
- University of Reading
- Roosevelt University
- Department of Women's and Gender Studies at Rutgers University
- Discipline of Political Economy at the University of Sydney
- University of Utah
- Wright State University
- York University (Toronto)

2.22.8 See also

- List of feminist economists
- *Feminist Economics* (journal)
- Gender equality, or gender equity
- Gender mainstreaming
- Intra-household bargaining
- Material feminism
- Time use
- Family economics
- Category:Feminism and society

2.22.9 References

[1] Benería, Lourdes; May, Ann Mari; Strassmann, Diana L. (2009). "Introduction". *Feminist Economics: Volume 1*. Cheltenham, UK and Northampton, MA: Edward Elgar. ISBN 9781843765684.

[2] Ferber, Marianne A.; Nelson, Julie A. (2003). "Beyond Economic Man, Ten Years Later". *Feminist Economics Today: Beyond Economic Man*. Chicago: Univ. of Chicago Press. pp. 1–32. ISBN 978-0-226-24206-4.

[3] Nelson, Julie A. (Spring 1995). "Feminism and Economics". *The Journal of Economic Perspectives* **9** (2): 131–148. doi:10.1257/jep.9.2.131.

[4] Berik, Günseli; Rodgers, Yana van der Meulen (2011), "Engendering development strategies and macroeconomic policies: what's sound and sensible?", in Benería, Lourdes; May, Ann Mari; Strassmann, Diana L, *Feminist economics*, Cheltenham, UK Northampton, Massachusetts: Edward Elgar, pp. Vol III, Part 1, B.12, ISBN 9781843765684 (Pdf version).

[5] Langeland, Terje (18 June 2013). "Women Unaccounted for in Global Economy Proves Waring Influence". Bloomberg. Archived from the original on 18 June 2013. Retrieved 18 June 2013.

[6] Nelson, Julie A. (2014). "Foreword". In Bjørnholt, Margunn; McKay, Ailsa. *Counting on Marilyn Waring: New Advances in Feminist Economics*. Bradford: Demeter Press. pp. ix–x. ISBN 9781927335277.

[7] Peterson, Janice; Lewis, Margaret (1999). *The Elgar companion to feminist economics*. Cheltenham, UK Northampton, MA: Edward Elgar. ISBN 9781858984537.

[8] http://www2.cambridgema.gov/Historic/CWHP/bios_w.html

[9] Radical Feminism: A Documentary Reader, By Barbara A. Crow, Housework: Slavery or a Labor of Love, p 530, NYU Press 2000

[10] http://www.ncdsv.org/images/BH_Modest-Herstory-of-Besty-Warrior_8-2013.pdf

[11] Houseworker's Handbook, Slavery or a Labor of love and The Source of Leisure Time, 1972

[12] http://www.nytimes.com/2014/03/12/us/in-depth-report-details-economics-of-sex-trade.html?_r=0

[13] Boserup, Ester (1970). *Woman's Role in Economic Development*. New York: St. Martin's Press. ISBN 978-1-84407-392-4.

[14] Aslaksen, Iulie; Bragstad, Torunn; Ås, Berit (2014). "Feminist Economics as Vision for a Sustainable Future". In Bjørnholt, Margunn; McKay, Ailsa. *Counting on Marilyn Waring: New Advances in Feminist Economics*. Bradford: Demeter Press. pp. 21–36. ISBN 9781927335277.

[15] Schneider, Geoff; Shackelford, Jean. "Ten Principles of Feminist Economics: A Modestly Proposed Antidote". Dept. of Economics, Bucknell University. Retrieved 2012-06-20.

[16] England, Paula (1994). "The Separative Self: Androcentric Bias in Neoclassical Assumptions". *Beyond Economic Man: Feminist Theory and Economics*. Chicago [u.a.]: Univ. of Chicago Press. pp. 37–43. ISBN 978-0-226-24201-9.

[17] Strassmann, Diana (20 January 1997). "Editorial: Expanding the Methodological Boundaries of Economics". *Feminist Economics* **3** (2): vii–ix. doi:10.1080/135457097338771a.

[18] Mankiw, N. Gregory (1997). *Principles of Economics*. Fort Worth, TX: Dryden Press. ISBN 9780030982385.

[19] Elson, Diane; Grown, Caren; Cagatay, Nilufer (2007). "Mainstream, Heterodox and Feminist Trade Theory". *Feminist Economics of Trade*. New York: Routledge. pp. 33–48. ISBN 978-0-415-77059-0.

[20] Power, Marilyn (November 2004). "Social Provisioning as a Starting Point for Feminist Economics". *Feminist Economics* **10** (3): 3–19. doi:10.1080/1354570042000267608.

[21] Razavi, Shahra (September 2009). "From Global Economic Crisis to the 'Other Crisis'". *Development* **52** (3): 323–328. doi:10.1057/dev.2009.33.

[22] "Valuing women's work". *Human Development Report 1995* (PDF). United Nations Development Programme. 1995. pp. 87–98.

[23] Folbre, Nancy (May 1994). "Children as Public Goods". *The American Economic Review* **84** (2): 86–90.

[24] Aslaksen, Iulie; Koren, Charlotte (2014). "Reflections on Unpaid Household Work, Economic Growth, and Consumption Possibilities". In Bjørnholt, Margunn; McKay, Ailsa. *Counting on Marilyn Waring: New Advances in Feminist Economics*. Bradford: Demeter Press. pp. 57–71. ISBN 9781927335277.

[25] McKay, Ailsa (2001). "Rethinking Work and Income Maintenance Policy: Promoting Gender Equality Through a Citizens' Basic Income". *Feminist Economics* **7** (1): 97–118. doi:10.1080/13545700010022721.

[26] Sen, Amartya (July 1987). "Gender and Cooperative Conflicts" (PDF). Working Papers. 1987/18. UNU-WIDER.

[27] Brewer, Rose M.; Conrad, Cecilia A.; King, Mary C. (January 2002). "The Complexities and Potential of Theorizing Gender, Caste, Race, and Class". *Feminist Economics* **8** (2): 3–17. doi:10.1080/1354570022000019038.

[28] Matthaei, Julie (March 1996). "Why feminist, Marxist, and anti-racist economists should be feminist–Marxist–anti-racist economists". *Feminist Economics* **2** (1): 22–42. doi:10.1080/738552684.

[29] Zein-Elabdin, Eiman (2003). Barker, Drucilla K., ed. *Toward a Feminist Philosophy of Economics*. London: Taylor & Francis. pp. 321–333. ISBN 978-0-415-28388-5.

[30] Levison, Deborah (January 2000). "Children as Economic Agents". *Feminist Economics* **6** (1): 125–134. doi:10.1080/135457000337732.

[31] Hall, Roberta M.; Sandler, Bernice R. (February 1982). "The Classroom Climate: A Chilly One for Women?" (PDF). Project on the Status and Education of Women, Association of American Colleges.

[32] Bjørnholt, Margunn; McKay, Ailsa (2014). "Advances in Feminist Economics in Times of Economic Crisis" (PDF). In Bjørnholt, Margunn; McKay, Ailsa. *Counting on Marilyn Waring: New Advances in Feminist Economics*. Bradford: Demeter Press. pp. 7–20. ISBN 9781927335277.

[33] Strassmann, Diana; Polanyi, Livia (1997). "The Economist as Storyteller". *Out of the Margin: Feminist Perspectives on Economics*. London [u.a.]: Routledge. pp. 94–104. ISBN 978-0-415-12575-8.

[34] Danby, Colin (April 2007). "Political economy and the closet: heteronormativity in feminist economics". *Feminist Economics* **13** (2): 29–53. doi:10.1080/13545700601184898.

[35] Pujol, Michele (1995). "Into the Margin!". *Out of the Margin: Feminist Perspectives on Economics*. London: Routledge. pp. 17–30. ISBN 9780415125314.

[36] Kuiper, Edith (2006). "Adam Smith and his feminist contemporaries". *New Voices on Adam Smith*. London: Routledge. pp. 40–57. ISBN 978-0-415-35696-1.

[37] Thomson, Victoria (October 2006). "How Much of the Remaining Gender Pay Gap is the Result of Discrimination, and How Much is Due to Individual Choices?" (PDF). *International Journal of Urban Labour and Leisure* **7** (2). Retrieved September 26, 2012.

[38] Ertürk, Korkut; Çağatay, Nilüfer (November 1995). "Macroeconomic consequences of cyclical and secular changes in feminization: An experiment at gendered macromodeling". *World Development* **23** (11): 1969–1977. doi:10.1016/0305-750X(95)00090-Y.

[39] Walters, Bernard (November 1995). "Engendering macroeconomics: A reconsideration of growth theory". *World Development* **23** (11): 1869–1880. doi:10.1016/0305-750X(95)00083-O.

[40] Knowles, Stephen; Lorgelly, Paula K.; Owen, P. Dorian (January 2002). "Are educational gender gaps a brake on economic development? Some cross-country empirical evidence" (PDF). *Oxford Economic Papers* **54** (1): 118–149. doi:10.1093/oep/54.1.118.

[41] Darity, William (November 1995). "The formal structure of a gender-segregated low-income economy". *World Development* **23** (11): 1963–1968. doi:10.1016/0305-750X(95)00082-N.

[42] Hill, M. Anne; King, Elizabeth (July 1995). "Women's education and economic well-being". *Feminist Economics* **1** (2): 21–46. doi:10.1080/714042230.

[43] Agarwal, Bina; Panda, Pradeep (November 2007). "Toward Freedom from Domestic Violence: The Neglected Obvious". *Journal of Human Development* **8** (3): 359–388. doi:10.1080/14649880701462171.

[44] Fukuda-Parr, Sakiko (January 2003). "The Human Development Paradigm: Operationalizing Sen's Ideas on Capabilities". *Feminist Economics* **9** (2-3): 301–317. doi:10.1080/1354570022000077980.

[45] Nussbaum, Martha; Sen, Amartya (1993). *The Quality of life*. Oxford England New York: Clarendon Press Oxford University Press. ISBN 9780198287971.

[46] Alkire, Sabina (2005). *Valuing freedoms: Sen's capability approach and poverty reduction*. Oxford New York: Oxford University Press. ISBN 9780199283316.

[47] Sen, Amartya (1989). "Development as Capability Expansion" (PDF). *Journal of Development Planning* **19**: 41–58.

[48] Nussbaum, Martha (2013). *Creating capabilities: the human development approach*. Cambridge, Massachusetts: The Belknap Press of Harvard University Press. ISBN 9780674072350.

[49] Nussbaum, Martha (January 2003). "Capabilities as Fundamental Entitlements: Sen and Social Justice". *Feminist Economics* **9** (2-3): 33–59. doi:10.1080/1354570022000077926.

[50] Samuelson, Paul A. (February 1956). "Social Indifference Curves" (PDF). *The Quarterly Journal of Economics* **70** (1.): 9–10. doi:10.2307/1884510. Retrieved 15 April 2015.

[51] Agarwal, Bina (Spring 1997). "Bargaining and Gender Relations: Within and Beyond the Household" (PDF). *Feminist Economics* **3** (1): 1–51. doi:10.1080/135457097338799.

[52] Folbre, Nancy (March 1995). "'Holding Hands at Midnight': The Paradox of Caring Labor". *Feminist Economics* **1** (1): 73–92. doi:10.1080/714042215.

[53] "The Invisible Heart – Care and the Global Economy". *Human Development Report 1999* (PDF). United Nations Development Programme. 1999. pp. 77–83.

[54] Chen, Martha; Vanek, Joann; Lund, Francie; Heintz, James; Jhabvala, Renana; Bonner, Christine. "The Totality of Women's Work". *Progress of the World's Women 2005: Women, Work and Poverty* (PDF). UNIFEM. pp. 22–35.

[55] O'Hara, Sabine (2014). "Everything Needs Care: Toward a Context-Based Economy". In Bjørnholt, Margunn; McKay, Ailsa. *Counting on Marilyn Waring: New Advances in Feminist Economics*. Bradford: Demeter Press. pp. 37–56. ISBN 9781927335277.

[56] Albelda, Randy (October 2011). "Time Binds: US Antipoverty Policies, Poverty, and the Well-Being of Single Mothers". *Feminist Economics* **17** (4): 189–214. doi:10.1080/13545701.2011.602355.

[57] Gammage, Sarah (July 2010). "Time Pressed and Time Poor: Unpaid Household Work in Guatemala". *Feminist Economics* **16** (3): 79–112. doi:10.1080/13545701.2010.498571.

[58] Carmichael, Fiona; Hulme, Claire; Sheppard, Sally; Connell, Gemma (April 2008). "Work-Life Imbalance: Informal Care and Paid Employment in the UK". *Feminist Economics* **14** (2): 3–35. doi:10.1080/13545700701881005.

[59] Folbre, Nancy (July 2006). "Measuring Care: Gender, Empowerment, and the Care Economy". *Journal of Human Development* **7** (2): 183–199. doi:10.1080/14649880600768512.

[60] Philipps, Lisa (April 1, 2008). "Silent Partners: The Role of Unpaid Market Labor in Families". *Feminist Economics* **14** (2): 37–57. doi:10.1080/13545700701880981.

[61] *System of National Accounts, 2008* (PDF). New York: United Nations. 2009. ISBN 978-92-1-161522-7.

[62] Beteta, Hanny Cueva (July 2006). "What is missing in measures of Women's Empowerment?". *Journal of Human Development, special issue: Revisiting the Gender-related Development Index (GDI) and Gender Empowerment Measure (GEM)* (Taylor and Francis) **7** (2): 221–241. doi:10.1080/14649880600768553.

[63] Luxton, Meg (May–June 1997). "The UN, women, and household labour: Measuring and valuing unpaid work". *Women's Studies International Forum* (Elsevier) **20** (3): 431–439. doi:10.1016/S0277-5395(97)00026-5.

[64] Mullan, Killian (July 2010). "Valuing Parental Childcare in the United Kingdom". *Feminist Economics* **16** (3): 113–139. doi:10.1080/13545701.2010.504014.

[65] e.g., Bergmann, Barbara R. (April 1974). "Occupational Segregation, Wages and Profits When Employers Discriminate by Race or Sex". *Eastern Economic Journal* **1** (2): 103–110. See also male-female income disparity in the United States.

[66] Beller, Andrea H. (Summer 1982). "Occupational Segregation by Sex: Determinants and Changes". *The Journal of Human Resources* **17** (3): 371–392. doi:10.2307/145586.; Bergmann, Barbara. *In Defense of Affirmative Action*, New York: Basic Books, 1996.

[67] Power, Marilyn; Mutari, Ellen; Figart, Deborah M. (2003). "Beyond Markets: Wage Setting and the Methodology of Feminist Political Economy". *Toward a Feminist Philosophy of Economics*. London [u.a.]: Routledge. pp. 70–86. ISBN 978-0-415-28387-8.

[68] Waldfogel, Jane (April 1997). "The Effect of Children on Women's Wages". *American Sociological Review* **62** (2): 209–217. doi:10.2307/2657300.

[69] Himmelweit, Susan F; Humphries, Jane; Albelda, Randy P (July 2004). "Special issue - dilemmas of lone motherhood (co-editors)". *Feminist Economics* **10** (2): 1–276. doi:10.1080/1354570042000217694.

[70] Williams, Joan (2000). *Unbending gender: why family and work conflict and what to do about it*. Oxford New York: Oxford University Press. ISBN 9780195147148.

[71] Benería, Lourdes (2003). *Gender, development, and globalization: economics as if all people mattered*. New York: Routledge. ISBN 9780415927079. (Book review)

[72] Kabeer, Naila (March 2004). "Globalization, labor standards, and women's rights: dilemmas of collective (in)action in an interdependent world". *Feminist Economics* **10** (1): 3–35. doi:10.1080/1354570042000198227.

[73] Bergeron, Suzanne (Summer 2001). "Political Economy Discourses of Globalization and Feminist Politics". *Signs* **26** (4): 983–1006. doi:10.1086/495645.

[74] Berik, Günseli (January 1997). "The Need for Crossing the Method Boundaries in Economics Research". *Feminist Economics* **3** (2): 121–125. doi:10.1080/135457097338735.

[75] Nelson, Julie (1996). *Feminism, objectivity and economics*. London New York: Routledge. ISBN 9780203435915.

[76] Kevane, Michael; Gray, Leslie C. (January 1999). "A Woman's Field Is Made At Night: Gendered Land Rights And Norms In Burkina Faso". *Feminist Economics* **5** (3): 1–26. doi:10.1080/135457099337789.

[77] Carrasco, Cristina; Rodríguez, Arantxa (January 2000). "Women, Families, and Work in Spain: Structural Changes and New Demands". *Feminist Economics* **6** (1): 45–57. doi:10.1080/135457000337660.

[78] Elson, Diane; Cagatay, Nilufer (July 2000). "The Social Content of Macroeconomic Policies" (PDF). *World Development* **28** (7): 1347–1364. doi:10.1016/S0305-750X(00)00021-8.

[79] Fukuda-Parr, Sakiko (January 2003). "The Human Development Paradigm: Operationalizing Sen's Ideas on Capabilities". *Feminist Economics* **9** (2-3): 301–317. doi:10.1080/1354570022000077980.

[80] Klasen, Stephan (July 2006). "UNDP's Gender-related Measures: Some Conceptual Problems and Possible Solutions". *Journal of Human Development* **7** (2): 243–274. doi:10.1080/14649880600768595. Available from: EconLit with Full Text, Ipswich, MA. Accessed September 26, 2011.

[81] Klasen, Stephan; Schüler, Dana (2011). "Reforming the gender-related development index and the gender empowerment measure: implementing some specific proposals". *Feminist Economics* (Taylor and Francis) **17** (1): 1–30. doi:10.1080/13545701.2010.541860.

[82] Ferber, Marianne A.; Nelson, Julie A. (2003). "Beyond Economic Man, Ten Years Later". *Feminist Economics Today: Beyond Economic Man*. Chicago: Univ. of Chicago Press. p. 7. ISBN 978-0-226-24206-4. In 1990 a few dissidents in the United States got together and discussed their ideas for starting an organization of their own. Taking advantage of the large attendance at a panel organized by Diana Strassman entitled "Can Feminism Find a Home in Economics?" Jean Shackelford and April Aerni invited

members of the audience to sign up to start a new network with an explicitly feminist slant. Two years later, this network was transformed into the International Association for Feminist Economics (IAFFE).

[83] "History". International Association for Feminist Economics. Retrieved 2012-06-20.

[84] "Best New Journal - 1997 Winner". The Council of Editors and Learned Journals (CELJ). Retrieved 2 May 2014.

[85] B.J., Almond (1 February 2007). "Feminist Economics rises in journal rankings". Rice University - News and Media. Retrieved 2 May 2014.

2.22.10 Further reading

Books

- Agarwal, Bina (1994). *A Field of One's Own: Gender and Land Rights in South Asia*. Cambridge University Press. ISBN 978-0-521-42926-9.

- Barker, Drucilla K.; Feiner, Susan F. (2004). *Liberating Economics: Feminist Perspectives on Families, Work, and Globalization*. Ann Arbor, Mich.: Univ. of Michigan Press. ISBN 978-0-472-06843-2.

- Kuiper, Edith; Barker, Drucilla K (2003). *Toward a feminist philosophy of economics*. London New York: Routledge. ISBN 9780415283885.

- Benería, Lourdes (2003). *Gender, development, and globalization: economics as if all people mattered*. New York: Routledge. ISBN 9780415927079.

- Bjørnholt, Margunn; McKay, Ailsa, eds. (2014). *Counting on Marilyn Waring: New Advances in Feminist Economics*. Demeter Press. ISBN 9781927335277. With a foreword by Julie A. Nelson.

- Ferber, Marianne A.; Nelson, Julie A., eds. (1993). *Beyond Economic Man: Feminist Theory and Economics*. Chicago [u.a.]: Univ. of Chicago Press. ISBN 978-0-226-24201-9.

- Jacobsen, Joyce P. (2007). *The Economics of Gender*. Malden, Massachusetts: Blackwell. ISBN 978-1-4051-6182-4.

- Nelson, Julie A. (1996). *Feminism, Objectivity and Economics*. New York: Routledge. ISBN 978-0-415-13337-1.

- Peterson, Janice; Lewis, Margaret (eds.) (1999). *The Elgar Companion to Feminist Economics*. Cheltenham: Edward Elgar. ISBN 978-1-85898-453-7. Cite uses deprecated parameter |coauthors= (help)

- Sen, Amartya (1999). *Development as Freedom*. Oxford Univ. Press. ISBN 978-0-19-289330-7.

- Waring, Marilyn (1989). *If Women Counted: A New Feminist Economics*. London: Macmillan. ISBN 978-0-333-49262-8.

Journal articles

- Carrasco, Cristina; Domínguez, Màrius (October 2011). "Family Strategies for Meeting Care and Domestic Work Needs: Evidence From Spain". *Feminist Economics* **17** (4): 159–188. doi:10.1080/13545701.2011.614625.

- Jenkins, Katy (2009). ""We have a lot of goodwill, but we still need to eat...": Valuing Women's Long Term Voluntarism in Community Development in Lima". *VOLUNTAS: International Journal of Voluntary and Nonprofit Organizations* **20** (1): 15–34. doi:10.1007/s11266-008-9075-7.

- Power, Marilyn (November 2004). "Social Provisioning as a Starting Point for Feminist Economics". *Feminist Economics* **10** (3): 3–19. doi:10.1080/1354570042000267608.

- Schüler, Dana (July 2006). "The Uses and Misuses of the Gender-related Development Index and Gender Empowerment Measure: A Review of the Literature". *Journal of Human Development* **7** (2): 161–181. doi:10.1080/14649880600768496.

- Warren, Tracey; Pascall, Gillian; Fox, Elizabeth (July 2010). "Gender Equality in Time: Low-Paid Mothers' Paid and Unpaid Work in the UK". *Feminist Economics* **16** (3): 193–219. doi:10.1080/13545701.2010.499997.

2.22.11 External links

- International Association for Feminist Economics (IAFFE)

- *Feminist Economics* (peer-reviewed journal)

2.23 Forum for Stable Currencies

Forum for Stable Currencies is a political advocacy group in the United Kingdom seeking economic democracy through freedom from national debt. Founded in 1998, the group is a non-governmental organization without governmental funding.[1] In 2003, the *New Statesman* reported that the forum was "attracting leading figures from the world of small business and across the political spectrum."[2] 2006's *Market, Schmarket: Building the Post-capitalist Economy* refers to the efforts of the Forum to "democratize the process of money creation" as "sterling work."[3]

2.23.1 History

In 1998, Merlin Hanbury-Tracy, 7th Baron Sudeley, motivated by his opposition to usury, and Sabine K McNeill, a mathematician and system analyst, created the Forum for Stable Currencies at the House of Lords.[4] It was the outcome of contacts with the Christian Council for Monetary Justice and organising the Campaign for Interest-Free Money through weekly meetings at the Global Internet Cafe near Piccadilly, London. McNeill had started the first Local Exchange Trading System in London in 1989 and organised Forum meetings mainly at the House of Lords, but also at the House of Commons under the auspices of Austin Mitchell MP. There, on behalf of the Forum, Austin Mitchell MP tabled Early Day Motions relating to public credit. The first submission to the Treasury Select Committee was entitled "*Green Credit for Green Purposes*".[4]

The Forum has hosted notable speakers, including Joseph Huber who on June, 2001 delivered a speech before the Forum at the House of Lords detailing the advantages of economic reform,[5] and Nobel Peace Prize winner Muhammad Yunus who in February 2008 spoke at St. James's Church, London Piccadilly. Other speakers have included James Gibb Stuart, Bernard Lietaer, Margrit Kennedy, Michael Rowbotham, and Stephen Zarlenga.

Among issues of concern to the Forum is the "skimming", or overcharging of fees, by banks, which *Corporate Watch* cites the Forum as estimating to be the cause of 50% of bankruptcies in the UK.[6] A recent political initiative of the Forum are two on-line petitions targeted at the Treasury Select Committee titled *Stop the Cash Crumble to Equalize the Credit Crunch* and *Financial Fairness for Voters and Taxpayers, please!* The corresponding article *Public Cash for the Real Economy, The ultimate request, by on-line petition* was published by the Journal *Accountancy Business and the Public Interest*.[7]

In 2009, the Forum's Early Day Motion addressed the *Enforcement of the Bank of England Act 1694* which was written with the intention not to oppress Their Majesties' subjects.

2.23.2 See also

- First Report on the Public Credit
- Second Report on Public Credit

- Monetary reform

2.23.3 References

[1] *HC Paper 355 House of Commons Committee of Public Accounts: Reaching an International Agreement on Climate Change*. The Stationery Office. 2008. p. 129. ISBN 0-215-52156-0. As a non-funded NGO, the Forum for Stable Currencies....

[2] Boyle, David (2003-03-04). "The strange rebirth of a forgotten idea". *New Statesman*. Retrieved 2009-02-25.

[3] Cato, Molly Scott (2006). *Market, Schmarket: Building the Post-capitalist Economy*. New Clarion Press. p. 195.

[4] McFall, John; House of Commons - Treasury Committee (2008). *Climate Change and the Stern Review: The Implications for Treasury Policy, Fourth Report of Session 2007-08, Report, Together with Formal Minutes, Oral and Written Evidence*. The Stationery Office. p. 88. ISBN 0-215-51341-X. Cite uses deprecated parameter |coauthor= (help)

[5] Legum, Margaret (2003). *It Doesn't Have to be Like this: Global Economics : a New Way Forward* (revised ed.). Wild Goose Publications. p. 107. ISBN 1-901557-76-6. The advantages of such reform were given in a paper by Joseph Huber to the Forum for Stable Currencies at the House of Lords in London in June 2001

[6] "Ten years, ten corporations: the corporate crime awards". *Originally published in Newsletter 33*. Corporate Watch. Retrieved 2009-02-26.

[7] Accountancy Business and the Public Interest, Vol. 8, No.1. 2009

2.23.4 External links

- Forum for Stable Currencies
- "Green Credit" position paper submitted to the Treasury Select Committee
- Enforcement of Bank of England Act 1694

2.24 Fractional-reserve banking

Fractional-reserve banking is the practice whereby a bank accepts deposits, makes loans or investments, and holds reserves that are a fraction of its deposit liabilities.[1] Reserves are held at the bank as currency, or as deposits in the bank's accounts at the central bank. Fractional-reserve banking is the current form of banking practiced in most countries worldwide.[2]

Fractional-reserve banking allows banks to act as financial intermediaries between borrowers and savers, and to provide longer-term loans to borrowers while providing immediate liquidity to depositors (providing the function of maturity transformation). However, a bank can experience a bank run if depositors wish to withdraw more funds than the reserves held by the bank. To mitigate the risks of bank runs and systemic crises (when problems are extreme and widespread), governments of most countries regulate and oversee commercial banks, provide deposit insurance and act as lender of last resort to commercial banks.[1][3]

Because bank deposits are usually considered money in their own right, and because banks hold reserves that are less than their deposit liabilities, fractional-reserve banking permits the money supply to grow beyond the amount of the underlying reserves of base money originally created by the central bank.[1][3] In most countries, the central bank (or other monetary authority) regulates bank credit creation, imposing reserve requirements and capital adequacy ratios. This can limit the amount of money creation that occurs in the commercial banking system, and helps to ensure that banks are solvent and have enough funds to meet demand for withdrawals.[3] However, rather than directly controlling the money supply, central banks usually pursue an interest rate target to control inflation and bank issuance of credit.[4]

2.24.1 History

See also: Banknote

Fractional-reserve banking predates the existence of governmental monetary authorities and originated many centuries ago in bankers' realization that generally not all depositors demand payment at the same time.[5]

In the past, savers looking to keep their coins and valuables in safekeeping depositories deposited gold and silver at goldsmiths, receiving in exchange a note for their deposit (*see Bank of Amsterdam*). These notes gained acceptance as a medium of exchange for commercial transactions and thus became an early form of circulating paper money.[6] As the notes were used directly in trade, the goldsmiths observed that people would not usually redeem all their notes at the same time, and they saw the opportunity to invest their coin reserves in interest-bearing loans and bills. This generated income for the goldsmiths but left them with more notes on issue than reserves with which to pay them. A process was started that altered the role of the goldsmiths from passive guardians of bullion, charging fees for safe storage, to interest-paying and interest-earning banks. Thus fractional-reserve banking was born.

If creditors (note holders of gold originally deposited) lost faith in the ability of a bank to pay their notes, however, many would try to redeem their notes at the same time. If, in response, a bank could not raise enough funds by calling in loans or selling bills, the bank would either go into insolvency or default on its notes. Such a situation is called a bank run and caused the demise of many early banks.[6]

The Swedish Riksbank was the world's first central bank, created in 1668. Many nations followed suit in the late 1600s to establish central banks which were given the legal power to set the reserve requirement, and to specify the form in which such assets (called the monetary base) are required to be held.[7] In order to mitigate the impact of bank failures and financial crises, central banks were also granted the authority to centralize banks' storage of precious metal reserves, thereby facilitating transfer of gold in the event of bank runs, to regulate commercial banks, impose reserve requirements, and to act as lender-of-last-resort if any bank faced a bank run. The emergence of central banks reduced the risk of bank runs which is inherent in fractional-reserve banking, and it allowed the practice to continue as it does today.[3]

During the twentieth century, the role of the central bank grew to include influencing or managing various macroeconomic policy variables, including measures of inflation, unemployment, and the international balance of payments. In the course of enacting such policy, central banks have from time to time attempted to manage interest rates, reserve requirements, and various measures of the money supply and monetary base.[8]

2.24.2 How it works

In most legal systems, a bank deposit is not a bailment. In other words, the funds deposited are no longer the property of the customer. The funds become the property of the bank, and the customer in turn receives an asset called a deposit account (a checking or savings account). That deposit account is a *liability* on the balance sheet of the bank. Each bank is legally authorized to issue credit up to a specified multiple of its reserves, so reserves available to satisfy payment of deposit liabilities are less than the total amount which the bank is obligated to pay in satisfaction of demand deposits.

Fractional-reserve banking ordinarily functions smoothly. Relatively few depositors demand payment at any given time, and banks maintain a buffer of reserves to cover depositors' cash withdrawals and other demands for funds. However, during a bank run or a generalized financial crisis, demands for withdrawal can exceed the bank's funding buffer, and the bank will be forced to raise additional reserves to avoid defaulting on its obligations. A bank can raise funds from additional borrowings (e.g., by borrowing in the interbank lending market or from the central bank), by selling assets, or by calling in short-term loans. If creditors are afraid that the bank is running out of reserves or is insolvent, they have an incentive to redeem their deposits as soon as possible before other depositors access the remaining reserves. Thus the fear of a bank run can actually precipitate the crisis.[note 1]

Many of the practices of contemporary bank regulation and central banking, including centralized clearing of payments, central bank lending to member banks, regulatory auditing, and government-administered deposit insurance, are designed to prevent the occurrence of such bank runs.

2.24.3 Economic function

Fractional-reserve banking allows banks to create credit in the form of bank deposits, which represent immediate liquidity to depositors. The banks also provide longer-term loans to borrowers, and act as financial intermediaries for those funds.[3][9] Less liquid forms of deposit (such as time deposits) or riskier classes of financial assets (such as equities or long-term bonds) may lock up a depositor's wealth for a period of time, making it unavailable for use on demand. This "borrowing short, lending long," or maturity transformation function of fractional-reserve banking is a role that many economists consider to be an important function of the commercial banking system.[10]

Additionally, according to macroeconomic theory, a well-regulated fractional-reserve bank system also benefits the economy by providing regulators with powerful tools for influencing the money supply and interest rates. Many economists believe that these should be adjusted by the government to promote macroeconomic stability.[11]

The process of fractional-reserve banking expands the money supply of the economy but also increases the risk that a bank cannot meet its depositor withdrawals. Modern central banking allows banks to practice fractional-reserve banking with inter-bank business transactions with a reduced risk of bankruptcy.[12][13]

2.24.4 Money creation process

Main article: Money creation

There are two types of money in a fractional-reserve banking system operating with a central bank:[14][15][16]

1. **Central bank money:** money created or adopted by the central bank regardless of its form – precious metals, commodity certificates, banknotes, coins, electronic money loaned to commercial banks, or anything else the central bank chooses as its form of money.

2. **Commercial bank money:** demand deposits in the commercial banking system; sometimes referred to as "chequebook money"

When a deposit of central bank money is made at a commercial bank, the central bank money is removed from circulation and added to the commercial banks' reserves (it is no longer counted as part of M1 money supply). Simultaneously, an equal amount of new commercial bank money is created in the form of bank deposits. When a loan is made by the commercial bank (which keeps only a fraction of the central bank money as reserves), using the central bank money from the commercial bank's reserves, the M1 money supply expands by the size of the loan.[3] This process is called "deposit multiplication".

Creation of deposit liabilities through the lending process

The proceeds of most bank loans are not in the form of currency. Banks typically make loans by accepting promissory notes in exchange for credits they make to the borrowers' deposit accounts.[17][18] Deposits created in this way are sometimes called derivative deposits and are part of the process of creation of money by commercial banks.[19] Issuing loan proceeds in the form of paper currency and current coins is considered to be a weakness in internal control.[20]

Example of deposit multiplication

The table below displays the mathematical model of the effect of the creation of loans and corresponding demand deposits, and how the money supply is affected by that process. It also shows how central bank money is used to create commercial bank money from an initial deposit of $100 of central bank money. In the example, the initial deposit is, conceptually, lent out 10 times (although as noted above, the banks do not fund most loans with the currency the banks have received as deposits)[21] with a fractional-reserve rate of 20% to ultimately create $500 of commercial bank money (it is important to note that the 20% reserve rate used here is for ease of illustration, actual reserve requirements are usually much lower, for example around 3% in the USA and UK). Each successive bank involved in this process creates new commercial bank money on a diminishing portion of the original deposit of central bank money. This is because banks only lend out a portion of the central bank money deposited, in order to fulfill reserve requirements and to ensure that they always have enough reserves on hand to meet normal transaction demands.

The relending model begins when an initial $100 deposit of central bank money is made into Bank A. Bank A takes 20 percent of it, or $20, and sets it aside as reserves, and then can theoretically loan out the remaining 80 percent, or $80. If the bank does in fact issue loan proceeds in the form of $80 in central bank money, the money supply actually totals $180, not $100, because the bank has loaned out $80 of the central bank money, kept $20 of central bank money in reserve (not part of the money supply), and substituted a newly created $100 IOU claim for the depositor that *acts equivalently to and can be implicitly redeemed for* central bank money (the depositor can transfer it to another account, write a check on it, demand his cash back, etc.). These claims by depositors on banks are termed *demand deposits* or *commercial bank money* and are simply recorded in a bank's accounts as a liability (specifically, an IOU to the depositor). From a depositor's perspective, commercial bank money is equivalent to central bank money – it is impossible to tell the two forms of money apart unless a bank run occurs.[3]

At this point in the relending model, Bank A now only has $20 of central bank money on its books. The loan recipient is holding $80 in central bank money, but he soon spends the $80. The receiver of that $80 then deposits it into Bank B. Bank B is now in the same situation as Bank A started with, except it has a deposit of $80 of central bank money instead of $100. Similar to Bank A, Bank B sets aside 20 percent of that $80, or $16, as reserves and lends out the remaining $64, increasing money supply by $64. As the process continues, more commercial bank money is created. To simplify the table, a different bank is used for each deposit. In the real world, the money a bank lends may end up in the same bank so that it then has more money to lend out.

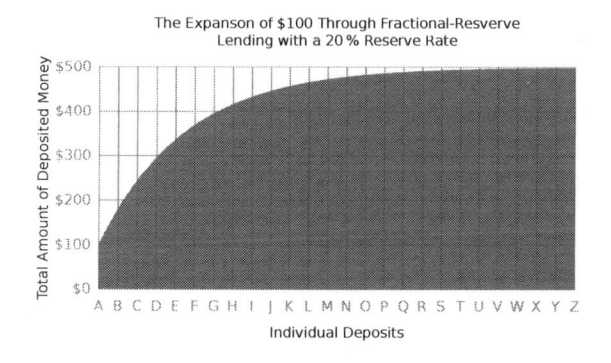

The expansion of $100 of central bank money through fractional-reserve lending with a 20% reserve rate. $400 of commercial bank money is created virtually through loans.

Although no new money was physically created in addition to the initial $100 deposit, new commercial bank money is created through loans. The boxes marked in red show the location of the original $100 deposit throughout the entire process. The total reserves will always equal the original amount, which in this case is $100. As this process continues, more commercial bank money is created. The amounts in each step decrease towards a limit. If a graph is made showing the accumulation of deposits, one can see that the graph is curved and approaches a limit. This limit is the maximum amount of money that can be created with a given reserve rate. When the reserve rate is 20%, as in the example above, the maximum amount of total deposits that can be created is $500 and the maximum increase in the money supply is $400.

For an individual bank, the deposit is considered a *liability* whereas the loan it gives out and the reserves are considered *assets*. This is the basis for a bank's *balance sheet*. Fractional-reserve banking allows the money supply to expand or contract. Generally the expansion or contraction of the money supply is dictated by the balance between the rate of new loans being created and the rate of existing loans being repaid or defaulted on. The balance between these two rates can be influenced to *some degree* by actions of the central bank. However, the central bank has no direct control over the amount of money created by commercial (or high street) banks.

Money multiplier

Main article: Money multiplier

A mechanism used to calculate the maximum size of the

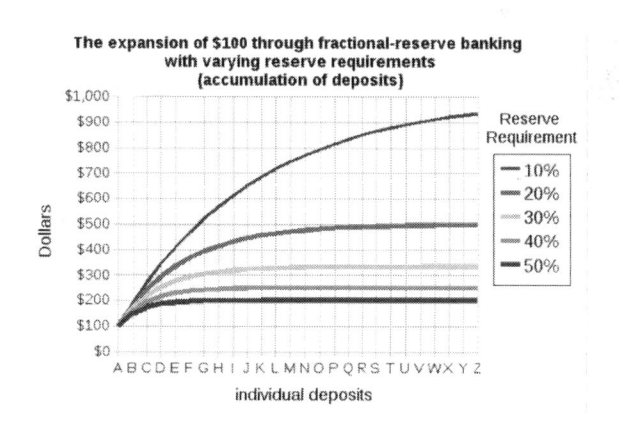

The expansion of $100 through fractional-reserve banking with varying reserve requirements. Each curve approaches a limit. This limit is the value that the "money multiplier"' calculates.

money supply from any given quantity of base money and a given reserve ratio, is known as the "money multiplier". Rather than directly limiting the money supply however, central banks typically pursue an interest rate target to control bank issuance of credit.[4] The central bank simply supplies whatever amount of base money is demanded by the economy at the prevailing level of interest rates.[22]

Formula The money multiplier, m, is the inverse of the reserve requirement, R:[23]

$$m = \frac{1}{R}$$

Example

For example, with the reserve ratio of 20 percent, this reserve ratio, R, can also be expressed as a fraction:

$$R = \tfrac{1}{5}$$

So then the money multiplier, m, will be calculated as:

$$m = \frac{1}{1/5} = 5$$

This number is multiplied by the initial deposit to show the maximum amount of money it can be expanded to.

The money creation process is also affected by the currency drain ratio (the propensity of the public to hold banknotes rather than deposit them with a commercial bank), and the safety reserve ratio (excess reserves beyond the legal requirement that commercial banks voluntarily hold – usually a small amount). Data for "excess" reserves and vault cash are published regularly by the Federal Reserve in the United States.[24] In practice, the actual money multiplier varies over time, and may be substantially lower than the theoretical maximum.[25]

2.24.5 Money supplies around the world

See also: Money supply

Fractional-reserve banking determines the relationship between the amount of "central bank money" in the official money supply statistics and the total money supply. Most of the money in these systems is "commercial bank money".. The issue of money through the banking system is a mechanism of monetary transmission, which a central bank can influence only indirectly by raising or lowering interest rates (although banking regulations may also be adjusted to influence the money supply, depending on the circumstances).

This table gives an outline of the makeup of money supplies worldwide. Most of the money in any given money supply consists of commercial bank money.[14] The value of commercial bank money is based on the fact that it can be exchanged freely at a bank for central bank money.[14][15]

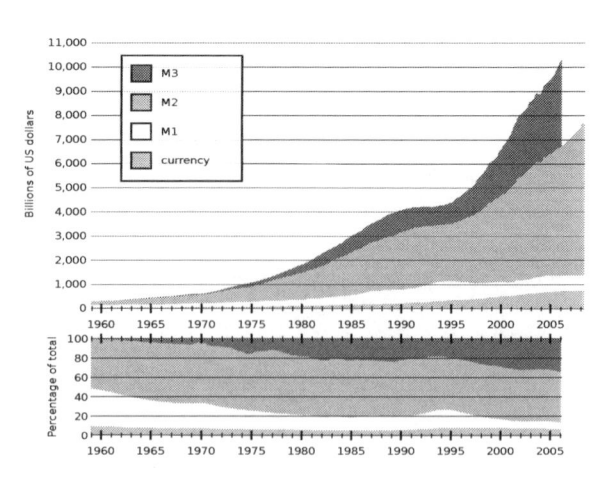

Components of US money supply (currency, M1, M2, and M3) since 1959. In January 2007, the amount of "central bank money" was $750.5 billion while the amount of "commercial bank money" (in the M2 supply) was $6.33 trillion. M1 is currency plus demand deposits; M2 is M1 plus time deposits, savings deposits, and some money-market funds; and M3 is M2 plus large time deposits and other forms of money. The M3 data ends in 2006 because the federal reserve ceased reporting it.

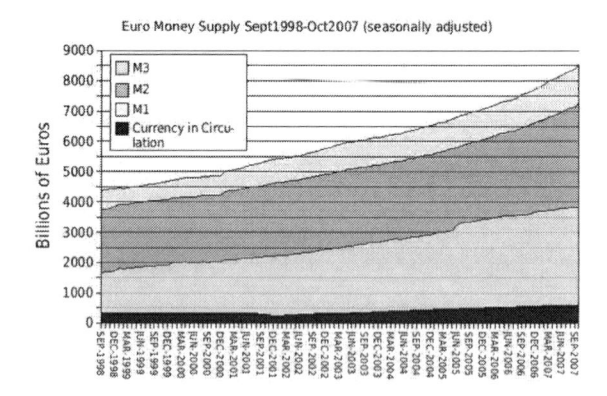

Components of the euro money supply 1998–2007

The actual increase in the money supply through this process may be lower, as (at each step) banks may choose to hold reserves in excess of the statutory minimum, borrowers may let some funds sit idle, and some members of the public may choose to hold cash, and there also may be delays or frictions in the lending process.[26] Government regulations may also be used to limit the money creation process by preventing banks from giving out loans even though the reserve requirements have been fulfilled.[27]

2.24.6 Regulation

Because the nature of fractional-reserve banking involves the possibility of bank runs, central banks have been created throughout the world to address these problems.[8][28]

Central banks

Main article: Central bank

Government controls and bank regulations related to fractional-reserve banking have generally been used to impose restrictive requirements on note issue and deposit taking on the one hand, and to provide relief from bankruptcy and creditor claims, and/or protect creditors with government funds, when banks defaulted on the other hand. Such measures have included:

1. Minimum required reserve ratios (RRRs)

2. Minimum capital ratios

3. Government bond deposit requirements for note issue

4. 100% Marginal Reserve requirements for note issue, such as the Bank Charter Act 1844 (UK)

5. Sanction on bank defaults and protection from creditors for many months or even years, and

6. Central bank support for distressed banks, and government guarantee funds for notes and deposits, both to counteract bank runs and to protect bank creditors.

Reserve requirements

The currently prevailing view of reserve requirements is that they are intended to prevent banks from:

1. generating too much money by making too many loans against the narrow money deposit base;

2. having a shortage of cash when large deposits are withdrawn (although the reserve is thought to be a legal minimum, it is understood that in a crisis or bank run, reserves may be made available on a temporary basis).

In some jurisdictions, (such as the United States and the European Union), the central bank does not require reserves to be held during the day. Reserve requirements are intended to ensure that the banks have sufficient supplies of highly liquid assets, so that the system operates in an orderly fashion and maintains public confidence.

In addition to reserve requirements, there are other required financial ratios that affect the amount of loans that a bank can fund. The capital requirement ratio is perhaps the most important of these other required ratios. When there are no mandatory reserve requirements, which are considered by some economists to restrict lending, the capital requirement ratio acts to prevent an infinite amount of bank lending.

Liquidity and capital management for a bank

Main articles: Capital requirement and Market liquidity

To avoid defaulting on its obligations, the bank must maintain a minimal reserve ratio that it fixes in accordance with, notably, regulations and its liabilities. In practice this means that the bank sets a reserve ratio target and responds when the actual ratio falls below the target. Such response can be, for instance:

1. Selling or redeeming other assets, or securitization of illiquid assets,

2. Restricting investment in new loans,

3. Borrowing funds (whether repayable on demand or at a fixed maturity),

4. Issuing additional capital instruments, or

5. Reducing dividends.

Because different funding options have different costs, and differ in reliability, banks maintain a stock of low cost and reliable sources of liquidity such as:

1. Demand deposits with other banks

2. High quality marketable debt securities

3. Committed lines of credit with other banks

As with reserves, other sources of liquidity are managed with targets.

The ability of the bank to borrow money reliably and economically is crucial, which is why confidence in the bank's creditworthiness is important to its liquidity. This means that the bank needs to maintain adequate capitalisation and to effectively control its exposures to risk in order to continue its operations. If creditors doubt the bank's assets are worth more than its liabilities, all demand creditors have an incentive to demand payment immediately, causing a bank run to occur.

Contemporary bank management methods for liquidity are based on maturity analysis of all the bank's assets and liabilities (off balance sheet exposures may also be included).

Assets and liabilities are put into residual contractual maturity buckets such as 'on demand', 'less than 1 month', '2–3 months' etc. These residual contractual maturities may be adjusted to account for expected counter party behaviour such as early loan repayments due to borrowers refinancing and expected renewals of term deposits to give forecast cash flows. This analysis highlights any large future net outflows of cash and enables the bank to respond before they occur. Scenario analysis may also be conducted, depicting scenarios including stress scenarios such as a bank-specific crisis.

2.24.7 Hypothetical example of a bank balance sheet and financial ratios

An example of fractional-reserve banking, and the calculation of the "reserve ratio" is shown in the balance sheet below:

In this example the cash reserves held by the bank is NZ$3,010m (NZ$201m Cash + NZ$2,809m Balance at Central Bank) and the Demand Deposits (liabilities) of the bank are NZ$25,482m, for a cash reserve ratio of 11.81%.

Other financial ratios

The key financial ratio used to analyze fractional-reserve banks is the cash reserve ratio, which is the ratio of cash reserves to demand deposits. However, other important financial ratios are also used to analyze the bank's liquidity, financial strength, profitability etc.

For example, the ANZ National Bank Limited balance sheet above gives the following financial ratios:

1. The cash reserve ratio is $3,010m/$25,482m, i.e. 11.81%.

2. The liquid assets reserve ratio is ($201m+$2,809m+$1,797m)/$25,482m, i.e. 18.86%.

3. The equity capital ratio is $8,703m/107,787m, i.e. 8.07%.

4. The tangible equity ratio is ($8,703m-$3,297m)/107,787m, i.e. 5.02%

5. The total capital ratio is ($8,703m+$2,062m)/$107,787m, i.e. 9.99%.

It is important how the term 'reserves' is defined for calculating the reserve ratio, as different definitions give different results. Other important financial ratios may require analysis of disclosures in other parts of the bank's financial statements. In particular, for liquidity risk, disclosures are incorporated into a note to the financial statements that provides maturity analysis of the bank's assets and liabilities and an explanation of how the bank manages its liquidity.

2.24.8 Criticisms of textbook descriptions of the monetary system

Sir Mervyn King, former Governor of the Bank of England said "Textbooks assume that money is exogenous"... "In the United Kingdom, money is endogenous".[29]

Glenn Stevens, governor of the Reserve Bank of Australia, said of the "money multiplier", "most practitioners find it to be a pretty unsatisfactory description of how the monetary and credit system actually works."[30]

Lord Adair Turner, formerly the UK's chief financial regulator, said "Banks do not, as too many textbooks still suggest, take deposits of existing money from savers and lend it out to borrowers: they create credit and money ex nihilo – extending a loan to the borrower and simultaneously crediting the borrower's money account".[31]

McLeay et al. said in the Bank of England Quarterly Bulletin: "This description of the relationship between monetary policy and money differs from the description in many introductory textbooks, where central banks determine the quantity of broad money via a 'money multiplier' by actively varying the quantity of reserves."[32]

Former Deputy Governor of the Bank of Canada William White said "Some decades ago, the academic literature would have emphasised the importance of the reserves supplied by the central bank to the banking system, and the implications (via the money multiplier) for the growth of money and credit. Today, it is more broadly understood that no industrial country conducts policy in this way under normal circumstances." [33]

2.24.9 Criticisms of fractional-reserve banking

In 1935, economist Irving Fisher proposed a system of 100% reserve banking as a means of reversing the deflation of the Great depression. He wrote: "100 per cent banking [...] would give the Federal Reserve absolute control over the money supply. Recall that under the present fractional-reserve system of depository institutions, the money supply is determined in the short run by such non-policy variables as the currency/deposit ratio of the public and the excess reserve ratio of depository institutions."[34]

Austrian School economists such as Jesús Huerta de Soto and Murray Rothbard have also strongly criticized fractional-reserve banking, calling for it to be outlawed and criminalized. According to them, not only does money creation cause macroeconomic instability (based on the Austrian Business Cycle Theory), but it is a form of embezzlement or financial fraud, legalized only due to the influence of powerful rich bankers on corrupt governments around the world.[35][36] Politician Ron Paul has also criticized fractional reserve banking based on Austrian School arguments.[37]

2.24.10 See also

- Austrian Business Cycle Theory
- Credit theory of money
- Endogenous money
- Basel II
- Basel III
- Asset liability management
- Full-reserve banking
- Chicago plan
- The Chicago Plan Revisited

2.24.11 Notes

[1] For an example, see Nationalisation of Northern Rock#Run on the bank

2.24.12 References

[1] Abel, Andrew; Bernanke, Ben (2005). "14". *Macroeconomics* (5th ed.). Pearson. pp. 522–532.

[2] Frederic S. Mishkin, Economics of Money, Banking and Financial Markets, 10th Edition. Prentice Hall 2012

[3] Mankiw, N. Gregory (2002). "18". *Macroeconomics* (5th ed.). Worth. pp. 482–489.

[4] Hubbard and Obrien. *Economics*. Chapter 25: Monetary Policy, p943.

[5] Carl Menger (1950) *Principles of Economics*, Free Press, Glencoe, IL OCLC 168839

[6] United States. Congress. House. Banking and Currency Committee. (1964). *Money facts; 169 questions and answers on money – a supplement to A Primer on Money, with index, Subcommittee on Domestic Finance ... 1964.* (PDF). Washington D.C.

[7] Charles P. Kindleberger, A Financial History of Western Europe. Routledge 2007

[8] The Federal Reserve in Plain English – An easy-to-read guide to the structure and functions of the Federal Reserve System (See page 5 of the document for the purposes and functions)

[9] Abel, Andrew; Bernanke, Ben (2005). "7". *Macroeconomics* (5th ed.). Pearson. pp. 266–269.

[10] Maturity Transformation Brad DeLong

[11] Mankiw, N. Gregory (2002). "9". *Macroeconomics* (5th ed.). Worth. pp. 238–255.

[12] Page 57 of 'The FED today', a publication on an educational site affiliated with the Federal Reserve Bank of Kansas City, designed to educate people on the history and purpose of the United States Federal Reserve system. The FED today Lesson 6

[13] "Mervyn King, Finance: A Return from Risk" (PDF). Bank of England. Banks are dangerous institutions. They borrow short and lend long. They create liabilities which promise to be liquid and hold few liquid assets themselves. That though is hugely valuable for the rest of the economy. Household savings can be channelled to finance illiquid investment projects while providing access to liquidity for those savers who may need it.... If a large number of depositors want liquidity at the same time, banks are forced into early liquidation of assets – lowering their value ...'

[14] Bank for International Settlements – The Role of Central Bank Money in Payment Systems. See page 9, titled, "The coexistence of central and commercial bank monies: multiple issuers, one currency": A quick quotation in reference to the 2 different types of money is listed on page 3. It is the first sentence of the document:

> "Contemporary monetary systems are based on the mutually reinforcing roles of central bank money and commercial bank monies."

[15] European Central Bank – Domestic payments in Euroland: commercial and central bank money: One quotation from the article referencing the two types of money:

> "At the beginning of the 20th almost the totality of retail payments were made in central bank money. Over time, this monopoly came to be shared with commercial banks, when deposits and their transfer via cheques and giros became widely accepted. Banknotes and commercial bank money became fully interchangeable payment media that customers could use according to their needs. While transaction costs in commercial bank money were shrinking, cashless payment instruments became increasingly used, at the expense of banknotes"

[16] Macmillan report 1931 account of how fractional banking works

[17] Federal Reserve Bank of Chicago, *Modern Money Mechanics*, pp. 3-13 (May 1961), reprinted in *Money and Banking: Theory, Analysis, and Policy*, p. 59, ed. by S. Mittra (Random House, New York 1970).

[18] Eric N. Compton, *Principles of Banking*, p. 150, American Bankers Ass'n (1979).

[19] Paul M. Horvitz, *Monetary Policy and the Financial System*, pp. 56-57, Prentice-Hall, 3rd ed. (1974).

[20] See, generally, *Industry Audit Guide: Audits of Banks*, p. 56, Banking Committee, American Institute of Certified Public Accountants (1983).

[21] Federal Reserve Bank of Chicago, *Modern Money Mechanics*, pp. 3-13 (May 1961), reprinted in *Money and Banking: Theory, Analysis, and Policy*, p. 59, ed. by S. Mittra (Random House, New York 1970) OCLC 89880

[22] "Managing the central bank's balance sheet: where monetary policy meets financial stability" (PDF). Bank of England.

[23] McGraw Hill Higher Education Archived 5 December 2007 at the Wayback Machine

[24] Federal Reserve Board, "Aggregate Reserves of Depository Institutions and the Monetary Base" (Updated weekly).

[25] Bruce Champ & Scott Freeman (2001) *Modeling Monetary Economies*, p. 170 (Figure 9.1), Cambridge University Press ISBN 978-0-52178-354-5

[26] William MacEachern (2014) *Macroeconomics: A Contemporary Introduction*, p. 295, University of Connecticut, ISBN 978-1-13318-923-7

[27] *The Federal Reserve – Purposes and Functions* (See pages 13 and 14 of the pdf version for information on government regulations and supervision over banks)

[28] *Reserve Bank of India – Report on Currency and Finance 2004–05* (See page 71 of the full report or just download the section *Functional Evolution of Central Banking*): The monopoly power to issue currency is delegated to a central bank in full or sometimes in part. The practice regarding the currency issue is governed more by convention than by any particular theory. It is well known that the basic concept of currency evolved in order to facilitate exchange. The primitive currency note was in reality a promissory note to pay back to its bearer the original precious metals. With greater acceptability of these promissory notes, these began to move across the country and the banks that issued the promissory notes soon learnt that they could issue more receipts than the gold reserves held by them. This led to the evolution of the fractional-reserve system. It also led to repeated bank failures and brought forth the need to have an independent authority to act as lender-of-the-last-resort. Even after the emergence of central banks, the concerned governments continued to decide asset backing for issue of coins and notes. The asset backing took various forms including gold coins, bullion, foreign exchange reserves and foreign securities. With the emergence of a fractional-reserve system, this reserve backing (gold, currency assets, etc.) came down to a fraction of total currency put in circulation.

[29] King, Mervyn. "The transmission mechanism of monetary policy". Bank of England.

[30] Stevens, Glen. "The Australian Economy: Then and Now". Reserve Bank of Australia.

[31] Turner, Adair. "Credit Money and Leverage, what Wicksell, Hayek and Fisher knew and modern macroeconomics forgot" (PDF).

[32] McLeay. "Money creation in the modern economy" (PDF). Bank of England.

[33] White, William. "Changing views on how best to conduct monetary policy: the last fifty years". Bank for International Settlements.

[34] Fisher, Irving (1997). *100% Money*. Pickering & Chatto Ltd. ISBN 978-1-85196-236-5.

[35] Rothbard, Murray (1983). *The Mystery of Banking*. ISBN 9780943940045.

[36] Jesús Huerta de Soto (2012). *Money, Bank Credit, and Economic Cycles* (3d ed.). Auburn, AL: Ludwig von Mises Institute. p. 881. ISBN 9781610161893. OCLC 807678778. (with Melinda A. Stroup, translator) Also available as a PDF here

[37] Ron Paul (2009) *End the Fed*, Ch. 2, Grand Central Pub., New York ISBN 978-0-44654-919-6

2.24.13 Further reading

- Crick, W.F. (1927), The genesis of bank deposits, *Economica*, vol 7, 1927, pp 191–202.

- Friedman, Milton (1960), *A Program for Monetary Stability*, New York, Fordham University Press.

- Meigs, A.J. (1962), *Free reserves and the money supply*, Chicago, University of Chicago, 1962.

- Paul, Ron (2009). "2 The Origin and Nature of the Fed". *End the Fed*. New York: Grand Central Publishing. ISBN 978-0-446-54919-6.

- Philips, C.A. (1921), *Bank Credit*, New York, Macmillan, chapters 1–4, 1921,

- Thomson, P. (1956), Variations on a theme by Philips, *American Economic Review* vol 46, December 1956, pp. 965–970.

2.24.14 External links

- Money creation in the modern economy Bank of England
- Regulation D of the Federal Reserve Board of the U.S.
- Bank for International Settlements – The Role of Central Bank Money in Payment Systems

2.25 Freiwirtschaft

Freiwirtschaft (German for "free economy") is an economic idea founded by Silvio Gesell in 1916. He called it *Natürliche Wirtschaftsordnung* (natural economic order). In 1932, a group of Swiss businessmen used his ideas to found the WIR Bank (WIR).

2.25.1 Structure

Freiwirtschaft consists of three central aspects, usually summed up as *The Three Fs*:

- *Freigeld (free money)*
  - All money is issued for a *limited* period by *constant* value (neither inflation, nor deflation).
  - Long-term saving requires investment in bonds or stocks.
- *Freiland (free land)*
  - All land is commonly owned or else the property of public institutions and can only be rented from the community or from government, respectively, not purchased (*see also Georgism*).
- *Freihandel (Free Trade)*
  - Free Trade has long been a mainstream position now, but the anti-globalization movement largely opposes it.

2.25.2 History

The basic economic ideas of *Freiwirtschaft* were published in 1890 by the Hungarian-Austrian economist Theodor Hertzka in his novel *Freiland - ein soziales Zukunftsbild*[1] (*Freeland - A Social Anticipation*).[2]

2.25.3 Flaws of the monetary system

Freiwirtschaft claims that current monetary systems are flawed. In mainstream economics, prices convey information. For example, dropping prices on a product mean that there is less demand or more supply of that product. This leads to a buyer buying more, or a seller/producer starting to sell/produce something else, thereby reducing the supply of that product. As a reaction, assuming constant desirability, the price of the product rises again. So, the price, together with the market participants, builds up a feedback loop around a stable, "ideal" price. At this stable price, the market is ideal, no one pays too much or earns too little, and there are no tendencies from either party to change that price. The "wobbling" around that ideal price is called *self-stabilizing*.

The key error of the current system, according to Gesell, is the ill-transported information in the price. Money is nothing but claim for goods and services, usable in the economies that accept money in exchange for the former. In a weak economy, money is worth less in goods. But instead of an inflation, the result is a deflation as described above, and less money can now buy the same goods. This feedback loop is *self-destabilizing*, according to the "Freiwirtschaft" theory.[3]

2.25.4 References

[1] Theodor Hertzka: *Freiland - ein soziales Zukunftsbild*, Leipzig 1890 – Summary on the website of the Otto-Lilienthal-Museum

[2] Theodor Hertzka: *Freeland - A Social Anticipation*, St. Loyes, Bedford, June, 1891. Book online at Project Gutenberg

[3] Norbert Rost: Eine experimentelle Überprüfung der Aussagen der Freiwirtschaftslehre (An experimental check of the statements of the Freiwirtschaft) (diploma thesis, Dresden, 2003), p. 25 seqq.

2.25.5 Sources

- Helmut Creutz, *The Money Syndrome – Towards a Market Economy Free from Crises*, Upfront Publishing 2010.
- Günter Bartsch, *Die NWO-Bewegung Silvio Gesells – Geschichtlicher Grundriß 1891-1992/93*. Gauke, Lütjenburg 1994.
- Knulp Goeke, *Die verteilungspolitische Problematik der Freiwirtschaftslehre*. Cologne 1961.

- Johannes Heinrichs, *Sprung aus dem Teufelskreis. Sozialethische Wirtschaftstheorie* Vol. I, Munich 2005.

- Hans-Joachim Werner, *Geschichte der Freiwirtschaftsbewegung. 100 Jahre Kampf für eine Marktwirtschaft ohne Kapitalismus*. Waxmann, Münster 1990.

2.25.6 External links

- Introduction to Freiwirtschaft
- Materialien zur Geld-, Zins- und Schuldenproblematik (in German, partly English)
- Fairconomy (in German, partly English)

2.26 Gandhian economics

Gandhian economics is a school of economic thought based on the spiritual and socio-economic principles expounded by Indian leader Mohandas Gandhi. It is largely characterised by rejection of the concept of the human being as a rational actor always seeking to maximize material self-interest that underlies classical economic thinking. Where Western economic systems were (and are) based on what he called the "multiplication of wants," Gandhi felt that this was both unsustainable and devastating to the human spirit. His model, by contrast, aimed at the fulfillment of needs – including the need for meaning and community. As a school of economics the resulting model contained elements of protectionism, nationalism, adherence to the principles and objectives of nonviolence and a rejection of class war in favor of socio-economic harmony. Gandhi's economic ideas also aim to promote spiritual development and harmony with a rejection of materialism. The term "Gandhian economics" was coined by J. C. Kumarappa, a close supporter of Gandhi.[1]

2.26.1 Gandhi's economic ideas

Gandhi's thinking on what we would consider socia-secular issues (he himself saw little distinction between the sacred and its expression in the social world) was influenced by John Ruskin and the American writer Henry David Thoreau. Throughout his life, Gandhi sought to develop ways to fight India's extreme poverty, backwardness and socio-economic challenges as a part of his wider involvement in the Indian independence movement. Gandhi's championing of *Swadeshi* and non-cooperation were centred on the principles of economic self-sufficiency. Gandhi sought to target European-made clothing and other products as not only a symbol of British colonialism but also the source of mass unemployment and poverty, as European industrial goods had left many millions of India's workers, craftsmen and women without a livelihood.[2]

By championing homespun *khadi* clothing and Indian-made goods, Gandhi sought to incorporate peaceful civil resistance as a means of promoting national self-sufficiency. Gandhi led farmers of Champaran and Kheda in a *satyagraha* (civil disobedience and tax resistance) against the mill owners and landlords supported by the British government in an effort to end oppressive taxation and other policies that forced the farmers and workers into poverty and defend their economic rights. A major part of this rebellion was a commitment from the farmers to end caste discrimination and oppressive social practices against women while launching a co-operative effort to promote education, health care and self-sufficiency by producing their own clothes and food.[2]

Gandhi and his followers also founded numerous *ashrams* in India (Gandhi had pioneered the *ashram* settlement in South Africa). The concept of an *ashram* has been compared with the commune, where its inhabitants would seek to produce their own food, clothing and means of living, while promoting a lifestyle of self-sufficiency, personal and spiritual development and working for wider social development. The *ashrams* included small farms and houses constructed by the inhabitants themselves. All inhabitants were expected to help in any task necessary, promoting the values of equality. Gandhi also espoused the notion of "trusteeship," which centred on denying material pursuits and coveting of wealth, with practitioners acting as "trustees" of other individuals and the community in their management of economic resources and property.[3]

Contrary to many Indian socialists and communists, Gandhi was averse to all notions of class warfare and concepts of class-based revolution, which he saw as causes of social violence and disharmony. Gandhi's concept of egalitarianism was centred on the preservation of human dignity rather than material development. Some of Gandhi's closest supporters and admirers included industrialists such as Ghanshyamdas Birla, Ambalal Sarabhai, Jamnalal Bajaj and J. R. D. Tata, who adopted several of Gandhi's progressive ideas in managing labour relations while also personally participating in Gandhi's ashrams and socio-political work.[4]

2.26.2 Swaraj, self-rule

Main article: Swaraj

Rudolph argues that after a false start in trying to emulate the English in an attempt to overcome his timidity, Gandhi discovered the inner courage he was seeking by helping his countrymen in South Africa. The new courage consisted of observing the traditional Bengali way of "self-suffering" and, in finding his own courage, he was enabled also to point out the way of 'Satyagraha' and 'ahimsa' to the whole of India.[5] Gandhi's writings expressed four meanings of freedom: as India's national independence; as individual political freedom; as group freedom from poverty; and as the capacity for personal self-rule.[6]

Gandhi was a self-described philosophical anarchist,[7] and his vision of India meant an India without an underlying government.[8] He once said that "the ideally nonviolent state would be an ordered anarchy."[9] While political systems are largely hierarchical, with each layer of authority from the individual to the central government have increasing levels of authority over the layer below, Gandhi believed that society should be the exact opposite, where nothing is done without the consent of anyone, down to the individual. His idea was that true self-rule in a country means that every person rules his or herself and that there is no state which enforces laws upon the people.[10]

This would be achieved over time with nonviolent conflict mediation, as power is divested from layers of hierarchical authorities, ultimately to the individual, which would come to embody the ethic of nonviolence. Rather than a system where rights are enforced by a higher authority, people are self-governed by mutual responsibilities. On returning from South Africa, when Gandhi received a letter asking for his participation in writing a world charter for human rights, he responded saying, "in my experience, it is far more important to have a charter for human duties."[11]

An independent India did not mean merely transferring the established British administrative structure into Indian hands. He warned, "you would make India English. And when it becomes English, it will be called not Hindustan but Englishtan. This is not the Swaraj I want."[12] Tewari argues that Gandhi saw democracy as more than a system of government; it meant promoting both individuality and the self-discipline of the community. Democracy was a moral system that distributed power and assisted the development of every social class, especially the lowest. It meant settling disputes in a nonviolent manner; it required freedom of thought and expression. For Gandhi, democracy was a way of life.[13]

2.26.3 Gandhian economics and ethics

Gandhian economics do not draw a distinction between economics and ethics. Economics that hurts the moral well-being of an individual or a nation is immoral, and therefore sinful. The value of an industry should be gauged less by the dividends it pays to shareholders than by its effect on the bodies, soul and spirits of the people employed in it. In essence, supreme consideration is to be given to man rather than to money.

The first basic principle of Gandhi's economic thought is a special emphasis on 'plain living' which helps in cutting down your wants and being self-reliant. Accordingly, increasing consumer appetite is likened to animal appetite which goes the end of earth in search of their satisfaction. Thus a distinction is to be made between 'Standard of Living' and 'Standard of Life', where the former merely states the material and physical standard of food, cloth and housing. A higher standard of life, on the other hand could be attained only if, along with material advancement, there was a serious attempt to imbibe cultural and spiritual values and qualities.

The second principle of Gandhian economic thought is small scale and locally oriented production, using local resources and meeting local needs, so that employment opportunities are made available everywhere, promoting the ideal of Sarvodaya[14][15] – the welfare of all, in contrast with the welfare of a few. This goes with a technology which is labour-using rather than labour-saving. Gandhian economy increases employment opportunities; it should not be labour displacing. Gandhi had no absolute opposition to machinery; he welcomed it where it avoids drudgery and reduces tedium. He used to cite the example of Singer sewing machine as an instance of desirable technology. He also emphasised dignity of labour, and criticised the society's contemptuous attitude to manual labour. He insisted on everybody doing some 'bread labour'.

The third principle of Gandhian economic thought, known as trusteeship principle, is that while an individual or group of individuals is free not only to make a decent living through an economic enterprise but also to accumulate, their surplus wealth above what is necessary to meet basic needs and investment, should be held as a trust for the welfare of all, particularly of the poorest and most deprived. The three principles mentioned above, when followed, are expected to minimise economic and social inequality, and achieve Sarvodaya.

2.26.4 Underlying principles

Gandhian economics has the following underlying principles:

1. Satya (truth)

2. Ahimsa (non-violence)

3. Aparigraha (non-possession)

While satya and ahimsa, he said were 'as old as the hills', based on these two, he derived the principle of non-possession. Possession would lead to violence (to protect ones possessions and to acquire others possessions). Hence he was clear that each one would need to limit one's needs to the basic minimums. He himself was an embodiment of this idea, as his worldy possessions were just a pair of clothes, watch, stick and few utensils. He advocated this principle for all, especially for the rich and for industrialists, arguing that they should see their wealth as something they held in trust for society - hence not as owners but as trustees.

2.26.5 Social justice and equality

Gandhi has often quoted that if mankind was to progress and to realize the ideals of equality and brotherhood, it must act on the principle of paying the highest attention to the prime needs of the weakest sections of the population. Therefore, any exercise on economic planning on a national scale would be futile without uplifting these most vulnerable sections of the society in a direct manner.

In the ultimate analysis, it is the quality of the human being that has to be raised, refined and consolidated. In other words, economic planning is for the citizen, and not the citizen for national planning. Everybody should be given the right to earn according to his capacity using just means.

2.26.6 Non-violent rural economy

Gandhian economics places importance to means of achieving the aim of development and this means must be non-violent, ethical and truthful in all economic spheres. In order to achieve this means he advocated trusteeship, decentralization of economic activities, labour-intensive technology and priority to weaker sections. Gandhi claims that to be non-violent an Individual needs to have a rural mindedness. It also helps in thinking of our necessities of our household in terms of rural mindedness.

The revival of the economy is made possible only when it is free from exploitation, so according to Gandhi industrialization on a mass-scale will lead to passive or active exploitation of the people as the problem of competition and marketing comes in. Gandhi believes that for an economy to be self-contained, it should manufacture mainly for its use even if that necessitates the use of modern machines and tools, provided it is not used as a means of exploitation of others.

2.26.7 Environmentalism

Several of Gandhi's followers developed a theory of environmentalism. J. C. Kumarappa was the first, writing a number of relevant books in the 1930s and 1940s. He and Mira Behan argued against large-scale dam-and-irrigation projects, saying that small projects were more efficacious, that organic manure was better and less dangerous than man-made chemicals, and that forests should be managed with the goal of water conservation rather than revenue maximization. The Raj and the Nehru governments paid them little attention. Guha calls Kumarappa, "The Green Gandhian," portraying him as the founder of modern environmentalism in India.[16]

2.26.8 Concept of socialism

Gandhian economics brings a socialist perspective of overall development and tries to redefine the outlook of socialism. Gandhi espoused the notion of "trusteeship" which centered on denying material pursuits and coveting of wealth, with practitioners acting as "trustees" of other individuals and the community in their management of economic resources and property. Under the Gandhian economic order, the character of production will be determined by social necessity and not by personal greed. The path of socialism should only be through non-violence and democratic method and any recourse to class-war and mutual hatred would prove to be suicidal.

2.26.9 Implementation in India

During India's independence struggle as well as after India's independence in 1947, Gandhi's advocacy of homespun *khadi* clothing, the *khadi* attire (which included the Gandhi cap) developed into popular symbols of nationalism and patriotism. India's first prime minister, Jawaharlal Nehru totally differed with Gandhi, even before independence and partition of India. Gandhi did not participate in celebration of Indian independence, he was busy controlling the post partition communal violence.

Gandhian activists such as Vinoba Bhave and Jayaprakash Narayan were involved in the *Sarvodaya* movement, which sought to promote self-sufficiency amidst India's rural population by encouraging land redistribution, socio-economic reforms and promoting cottage industries. The movement sought to combat the problems of class conflict, unemployment and poverty while attempting to preserve the lifestyle and values of rural Indians, which were eroding with industrialisation and modernisation. *Sarvodaya* also included *Bhoodan*, or the gifting of land and agricultural resources by the landlords (called *zamindars*) to their tenant farmers in a bid to end the medieval system of *zamindari*.

Bhave and others promoted *Bhoodan* as a just and peaceful method of land redistribution in order to create economic equality, land ownership and opportunity without creating class-based conflicts. *Bhoodan* and *Sarvodaya* enjoyed notable successes in many parts of India, including Maharashtra, Gujarat, Karnataka and Uttar Pradesh. Bhave would become a major exponent of discipline and productivity amongst India's farmers, labourers and working classes, which was a major reason for his support of the controversial Indian Emergency (1975–1977). Jayaprakash Narayan also sought to use Gandhian methods to combat organised crime, alcoholism and other social problems.

2.26.10 Modern interpretations

The proximity of Gandhian economic thought to socialism has also evoked criticism from the advocates of free-market economics. To many, Gandhian economics represent an alternative to mainstream economic ideologies as a way to promote economic self-sufficiency without an emphasis on material pursuits or compromising human development. Gandhi's emphasis on peace, "trusteeship" and co-operation has been touted as an alternative to competition as well as conflict between different economic and income classes in societies. Gandhian focus on human development is also seen as an effective emphasis on the eradication of poverty, social conflict and backwardness in developing nations.

2.26.11 Notes

[1] Kumarappa, Joseph Cornelius (1951). *Gandhian economic thought*. Library of Indian economics (1st ed.). Bombay, India: Vora. OCLC 3529600. Retrieved 7 August 2009.

[2] B. N. Ghosh, *Gandhian political economy: principles, practice and policy* (2007) p. 17

[3] Jagannath Swaroop Mathur, *Industrial civilization & Gandhian economics* (1971) p 165

[4] Romesh K. Diwan and Mark A. Lutz, *Essays in Gandhian economics* (1987) p. 25

[5] Susanne Hoeber, Rudolph (1963). "The New Courage: An Essay on Gandhi's Psychology". *World Politics* **16** (1): 98–117. JSTOR 2009253.

[6] Anthony Parel, ed., *Gandhi, Freedom, and Self-Rule* (2000) p 166

[7] Snow, Edgar. *The Message of Gandhi*. 27 September March 1948. "Like Marx, Gandhi hated the state and wished to eliminate it, and he told me he considered himself 'a philosophical anarchist.'"

[8] Jesudasan, Ignatius. A Gandhian theology of liberation. Gujarat Sahitya Prakash: Ananda India, 1987, pp. 236–237

[9] Bidyut Chakrabarty (2006). *Social and political thought of Mahatma Gandhi*. Routledge. p. 138. ISBN 978-0-415-36096-8. Retrieved 25 January 2012.

[10] Gandhi, Mohandas Karamchand; Tolstoy, Leo (September 1987). B. Srinivasa Murthy, ed. *Mahatma Gandhi and Leo Tolstoy letters*. Long Beach Publications.

[11] Easwaran, Eknath. *Gandhi the Man*. Nilgiri Press, 2011. p. 49.

[12] Paul Gillen; Devleena Ghosh (2007). *Colonialism and Modernity*. UNSW Press. p. 130.

[13] Tewari, S. M. (1971). "The Concept of Democracy in the Political Thought of Mahatma Gandhi". *Indian Political Science Review* **6** (2): 225–251.

[14] Nadkarni, M.V. (June 2015). "Gandhi's civilizational alternative and dealing with climate change" (PDF). *Journal of Social & Economic Development*: 90–103. doi:10.1007/s40847-015-0006-3.

[15] *Ethics for our times : essays in gandhian perspective.* (2 ed.). [S.l.]: Oup India. 2014. pp. 45–54. ISBN 0-19-945053-6.

[16] Ramachndra Guha (2004). *Anthropologist Among the Marxists: And Other Essays*. Orient Blackswan. pp. 81–6.

2.26.12 References

- Gonsalves, Peter (2012). *Khadi: Gandhi's Mega Symbol of Subversion*. SAGE Publications. ISBN 978-81-321-0735-4.

- Narayan, Shriman (1970). *Relevance of Gandhian economics*. Navajivan Publishing House. ASIN B0006CDLA8.

- Narayan, Shriman (1978). *Towards the Gandhian Plan*. S. Chand and Company Limited.

- Pani, Narendar (2002). *Inclusive Economics: Gandhian Method and Contemporary Policy*. Sage Publications Pvt. Ltd. ISBN 978-0-7619-9580-7.

- Schroyer, Trent (2009). *Beyond Western Economics: Remembering Other Economic Culture*. Routledge.

- Sharma, Rashmi (1997). *Gandhian economics: a humane approach*. Deep and Deep Publications Pvt. Ltd. ISBN 978-81-7100-986-2.

2.26.13 External links

- Gandhian Trusteeship as an "Instrument of Human Dignity"
- Review of "Gandhian economics"
- Gandhian economics is relevant
- Abhay Ghiara's Gandhian Economics blog

2.27 Georgism

"Georgist" redirects here. For the Romanian political group, see National Liberal Party-Brătianu.

Georgism (also known as **geoism** and **geonomics**) is an economic philosophy holding that the economic value derived from land, including natural resources and natural opportunities, should belong equally to all residents of a community, but that people own the value that they create themselves.[1][2][3] The Georgist paradigm offers solutions to social and ecological problems, relying on principles of land rights and public finance which attempt to integrate economic efficiency with social justice.[4][5]

Georgism is concerned with the distribution of economic rent caused by natural monopolies, pollution, and the control of commons, including title over natural resources and other contrived privileges (e.g., intellectual property). Any natural resource, which is inherently limited in supply, can generate economic rent, but the classical and most significant example of 'land monopoly' involves the extraction of common ground rent from valuable urban locations. Georgists argue that taxing economic rent is efficient, fair, and equitable. The main Georgist policy tool is a tax assessed on land value. Georgists argue that revenues from a land value tax (LVT) can reduce or eliminate existing taxes on labor and investment that are unfair and inefficient. Some Georgists also advocate for the return of surplus public revenue back to the people through a basic income or citizen's dividend.

Economists since Adam Smith have observed that, unlike other taxes, a public levy on land value does not cause economic inefficiency.[6] A land value tax is often said to have progressive tax effects, in that it is paid primarily by the wealthy (the landowners), and it cannot be passed on to tenants, workers, or users of land.[7][8] Land value capture would reduce economic inequality, increase wages, remove incentives to misuse real estate, and reduce the vulnerability that economies face from credit and property bubbles.[9]

The philosophical basis of Georgism dates back to several early proponents such as John Locke,[10] Baruch Spinoza,[11] and Thomas Paine, but the concept of gaining public revenues from natural resource privileges was widely popularized by the economist and social reformer Henry George and his first book, *Progress and Poverty*, published in 1879.[12]

Georgist ideas were popular and influential in the late 19th and early 20th century.[13] Political parties, institutions and communities were founded based on Georgist principles during that time. Early followers of Henry George's economic philosophy called themselves *Single Taxers*, associated with the idea of raising public revenue exclusively from land and privileges, but the term is now considered a misnomer because Georgists usually support multiple mechanisms for government funding. In classical and Georgist economics, the term 'land' is defined as all locations, natural opportunities, resources, physical forces, and government privileges over economic domains, which is closely related to the concept of commons.[14] *Georgism* was coined later, and some prefer the term *geoism* or *geonomics* to distinguish their beliefs from those of Henry George.[15][16]

2.27.1 Main tenets

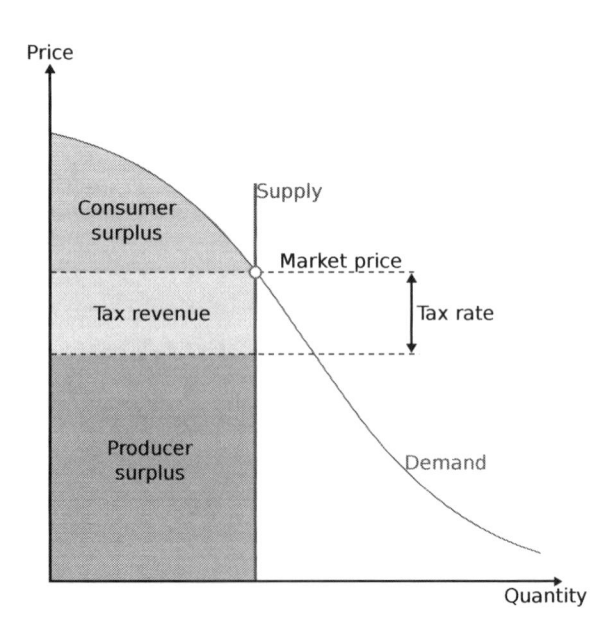

A supply and demand diagram showing the effects of land value taxation. Note that the burden of the tax is entirely on the land owner, and there is no deadweight loss.

See also: Land value tax

Many people have observed that privately created wealth is socialized via the tax system (e.g., through income and sales tax), while socially created wealth in land values are privatized in the price of land titles and bank mortgages.

The opposite would be the case if land rent replaced taxes on labor as the main source of public revenue; socially created wealth would become available for use by the community, while the fruits of labor would remain private.[17] Henry George is best known for popularizing these classical arguments in favor of effecting this reform in land title and tax policy.

In *Progress and Poverty* George argues that people justly own what they create, but that natural opportunities and land belong equally in common to all.[2] George believed there was an important distinction between common and collective property.[18] Although equal rights to land might be achieved by nationalizing land and then leasing it to private users, George preferred taxing unimproved land value and leaving the control of land mostly in private hands. George's reasoning for leaving land in private control and slowly shifting to land value tax was that it would not penalize existing owners who had improved land and would also be less disruptive and controversial in a country where land titles have already been granted.

George believed that although scientific experiments could not be carried out in political economy, theories could be tested by comparing different societies with different conditions and through thought experiments about the effects of various factors.[19] Applying this method, George concluded that many of the problems that beset society, such as poverty, inequality, and economic booms and busts, could be attributed to the private ownership of the necessary resource, land.

In Georgism, a land value tax is seen as fitting the definition of a user fee instead of a tax, since it is tied to the market value of socially created locational advantage, the privilege to exclude others from locations. Assets consisting of commodified privilege can be viewed as wealth since they have exchange value, similar to taxi medallions.[20] A land value tax, charging fees for exclusive use of land, as a means of raising public revenue is also a progressive tax tending to reduce economic inequality,[7][8] since it falls entirely on ownership of valuable land, which is highly correlated to incomes,[21] and there is no means by which landlords can shift the tax burden onto tenants or laborers.

Economic properties

See also: Optimal tax and Tax incidence

Standard economic theory suggests that a land value tax would be extremely efficient – unlike other taxes, it does not reduce economic productivity.[9] Nobel laureate Milton Friedman described Henry George's tax on unimproved value of land as the "least bad tax", since unlike other taxes, it would not impose an excess burden on economic activity (leading to zero or even negative "deadweight loss"); hence, a replacement of other more distortionary taxes with a land value tax would improve economic welfare.[22] As land value tax can improve the use of land and redirect investment toward productive, non-rentseeking activities, it could even have a negative deadweight loss that boosts productivity.[23] Because land value tax would fall on foreign land speculators, the Australian Treasury estimated that land value tax was unique in having a negative marginal excess burden, meaning that it would increase long-run living standards.[24]

It was Adam Smith who first noted the efficiency and distributional properties of a land value tax in his book, *The Wealth of Nations*:[6]

> Ground-rents are a still more proper subject of taxation than the rent of houses. A tax upon ground-rents would not raise the rents of houses. It would fall altogether upon the owner of the ground-rent, who acts always as a monopolist, and exacts the greatest rent which can be got for the use of his ground. More or less can be got for it according as the competitors happen to be richer or poorer, or can afford to gratify their fancy for a particular spot of ground at a greater or smaller expense. In every country the greatest number of rich competitors is in the capital, and it is there accordingly that the highest ground-rents are always to be found. As the wealth of those competitors would in no respect be increased by a tax upon ground-rents, they would not probably be disposed to pay more for the use of the ground. Whether the tax was to be advanced by the inhabitant, or by the owner of the ground, would be of little importance. The more the inhabitant was obliged to pay for the tax, the less he would incline to pay for the ground; so that the final payment of the tax would fall altogether upon the owner of the ground-rent.
>
> Both ground-rents and the ordinary rent of land are a species of revenue which the owner, in many cases, enjoys without any care or attention of his own. Though a part of this revenue should be taken from him in order to defray the expenses of the state, no discouragement will thereby be given to any sort of industry. The annual produce of the land and labour of the society, the real wealth and revenue of the great body of the people, might be the same after such a tax as before. Ground-rents and the ordinary rent of land are, therefore, perhaps, the species of revenue which can best bear to have a peculiar tax imposed upon them. [...] Nothing can be more reasonable than that a fund which owes its exis-

tence to the good government of the state should be taxed peculiarly, or should contribute something more than the greater part of other funds, towards the support of that government.

Ben Franklin and Winston Churchill made similar distributional and efficient arguments for publicly capturing land rents. They noted that the costs of taxes and the benefits of public spending always eventually fall on and enrich, respectively, the owners of land. Therefore, they believed it would be best to defray public costs and recapture value of public spending by placing public charges directly on owners of land titles, rather than harming public welfare with taxes on trade and labor.[25][26]

Henry George wrote that his plan would call upon people "to contribute to the public, not in proportion to what they produce . . . but in proportion to the value of natural [common] opportunities that they hold [monopolize]." He went on to explain that "by taking for public use that value which attaches to land by reason of the growth and improvement of the community," it would, "make the holding of land unprofitable to the mere owner, and profitable only to the user." Under George's plan, it would be impossible for speculators to hold valuable natural opportunities like urban real estate unused or only partly used. George claimed this would have many benefits, including the reduction or removal of tax burdens from poorer neighborhoods and agricultural districts; the removal of a multiplicity of taxes and expensive obsolete government institutions; the elimination of corruption, fraud, and evasion in the collection of taxes; the enablement of true free trade; the destruction of monopolies; the elevation of wages to the full value of labor; the transformation of labor saving inventions into blessings for all; and the equitable distribution of comfort, leisure, and other advantages that are made possible by an advancing civilization.[27]

Sources of economic rent and related policy interventions

See also: Pigovian tax and Severance tax

Income flow resulting from payments for restricted access to natural opportunities or for contrived privileges over geographic regions is called economic rent. Georgists argue that economic rent of land, legal privileges, and natural monopolies should accrue to the community, rather than private owners. In economics, "land" is everything that exists in nature independent of human activity. While the philosophy of Georgism does not say anything definitive about specific policy interventions needed to address problems posed by various sources of economic rent, the common goal among modern georgists is to capture and share (or reduce) rent from all sources of natural monopoly and legal privilege.[28][29]

Henry George shared the goal of modern Georgists to socialize or dismantle rent from all forms of land monopoly and legal privilege. However, George focused mainly on his preferred policy tool known as land value tax, which targeted a particular form of unearned income called ground rent. George focused on ground-rent because basic locations were more valuable than other monopolies and everybody needed locations to survive, which he contrasted with the less significant streetcar and telegraph monopolies, which George also spoke out against. George likened the problem to a laborer traveling home who is waylaid by a series of highway robbers along the way, each who demand a small portion of the traveler's wages, and finally at the very end of the road waits a robber who demands all that the traveler has left. George reasoned that it made little difference to challenge the series of small robbers when the final robber remained to demand all that the common laborer had left.[30] George predicted that over time technological advancements would increase the frequency and importance of lesser monopolies, yet he expected that ground rent would remain dominant.[31] George even predicted that ground-rents would rise faster than wages and income to capital, a prediction that modern analysis has shown to be plausible, since the supply of land is fixed.[32]

Common ground rent is still the primary focus of Georgists because of its large value and the known diseconomies of misused land. However, there are other sources of rent that are theoretically analogous to ground-rent and are highly debated topics within Georgism. The following are some sources of economic rent.[33][34][35]

- extractable resources (minerals and hydrocarbons)[36][37]
- severables (forests and stocks of fish)[29][38][39]
- extraterrestrial domains (geosynchronous orbits and airway corridor use)[34][35]
- legal privileges tied to location (taxi medallions, billboard and development permits, or the monopoly of electromagnetic frequencies)[34][35]
- restrictions/taxes on pollution or severance (tradable emission permits and fishing quotas)[28][34][35]
- Right-of-way (transportation) used by railroads, utilities, and internet service providers[40][41][42]
- issuance of legal tender (see seigniorage)[28][43]
- privileges that are less location dependent but that still exclude others from natural opportunities (patents)[44][45]

Where free competition is impossible, such as telegraphs, water, gas, and transportation, George wrote, "[S]uch business becomes a proper social function, which should be controlled and managed by and for the whole people concerned." Georgists were divided by this question of natural monopolies and often favored public ownership only of the rents from common rights-of-way, rather than public ownership of utility companies themselves.[27]

Georgism and environmental economics

The early conservationist movement of the Progressive Era was inspired by Henry George and his influence extended for decades afterward.[46] Some ecological economists still support the Georgist policy of land value tax as a means of freeing or rewilding unused land and conserving nature by reducing urban sprawl.[47][48][49]

Pollution degrades the value of what Georgists consider to be commons. Because pollution is a negative contribution, a taking from the commons or a cost imposed on others, its value is economic rent, even when the polluter is not receiving an explicit income. Therefore, to the extent that society determines pollution to be harmful, most Georgists propose to limit pollution and then capture the resulting rents for public use, restoration, or a *citizen's dividend*.[28][50][51]

Georgism is related to the school of ecological economics, since both propose market based restrictions on pollution.[47][52] The schools are compatible in that they advocate using similar tools as part of a conservation strategy, but they emphasize different aspects. Conservation is the central issue of ecology, whereas economic rent is the central issue of geoism. Ecological economists might price pollution fines more conservatively to prevent inherently unquantifiable damage to the environment, whereas Georgists might emphasize mediation between conflicting interests and human rights.[29][53] Geolibertarianism, a market oriented branch of geoism, tends to take a direct stance against what it perceives as burdensome regulation and would like to see auctioned pollution quotas or taxes replace most command and control regulation.[54]

Since ecologists are primarily concerned with conservation, they tend to put less emphasis on the issue of equitably distributing scarcity/pollution rents, whereas Georgists insist that unearned income not be captured by those who hold title to natural assets and pollution privilege. To the extent that geoists recognize the impact of pollution or share conservationist values, they will agree with ecological economists about the need to limit pollution, but geoists will also crucially insist that pollution rents generated from those conservation efforts are not captured by polluters and are instead used for public purposes or to compensate those who suffer the negative effects of pollution. Ecological economists advocate similar pollution restrictions but, placing conservation first, might be willing to grant private polluters the privilege to capture pollution rents. To the extent that ecological economists share the geoist view of social justice, they would advocate auctioning pollution quotas instead of giving them away for free.[47] This distinction can be seen clearly in the difference between basic cap and trade and the geoist variation, cap and share, a proposal to auction temporary pollution permits, with rents going to the public, instead of giving pollution privilege away for free to existing polluters or selling perpetual permits.[55][56]

Revenue uses

The revenue can allow the reduction or elimination of taxes), greater public investment/spending, or the direct distributed of funds to citizens as a pension or basic income/citizen's dividend[29][57][58]

In practice, the elimination of all other taxes implies a very high land value tax, higher than any currently existing land tax. Introducing a high land value tax that is greater than the value of existing taxes would cause the price of land titles to eventually decrease. George did not believe landowners should be compensated, and described the issue as being analogous to compensation for former slave owners. Other geoists disagree on the question of compensation; some advocate complete compensation while others support only enough compensation required to achieve Georgist reforms. Geoists have also long differed from George as to the degree of rent capture needed. Historically, those who advocated for public rent capture only high enough to replace other taxes were known as supporters of *single tax limited*.

2.27.2 Synonyms and variants

Most early advocacy groups described themselves as Single Taxers, and George reluctantly accepted "single tax" as an accurate label for the movement's main political goal—the replacement of all unjust or inefficient taxes with the capture of land-rents, primarily using a land value tax (LVT). In the modern era, some groups inspired by Georgism emphasize environmentalism, while others emphasize its egalitarian free market philosophy; utilitarians and urbanists emphasize the economic and social benefits of efficiently utilizing land.

Some modern proponents are dissatisfied with the name *Georgist*. While Henry George was well known throughout his life, he has been largely forgotten by the public and the idea of a single tax of land predates him. Some now prefer the term *geoism*,[16][59] with the meaning of *geo* (*earth*, in Greek) deliberately ambiguous. The terms *Earth Sharing*,[60] *geonomics*,[61] and *geolibertarianism*[62] (see Libertarianism) are also used by some Georgists. These terms represent a difference of emphasis, and sometimes real differences about how land rent should be spent (citizen's dividend or just replacing other taxes); but all agree that land rent should be recovered from its private recipients.

Compulsory fines and fees related to land rents are the most common Georgist policies, but some geoists prefer voluntary value capture systems that rely on methods such as non-compulsory or self-assessed location value fees, community land trusts,[63] and purchasing land value covenants.[64][65][66][67][68]

Some geoists believe that partially compensating landowners is a politically expedient compromise necessary for achieving reform.[69][70] For similar reasons, others propose capturing only future land value increases, instead of all land rent.[71]

Though Georgism has historically been viewed as a radically progressive or socialist ideology, some libertarians and minarchists take the position that limited social spending should be financed using Georgist concepts of rent value capture, but that not all land rent should to be captured. Today, this relatively conservative adaptation is usually considered incompatible with true geolibertarianism, which requires that excess rents be gathered and then distributed back to residents. During Henry George's time, this position was known as "single tax limited", as opposed to "single tax unlimited". Henry George disagreed with the limited interpretation but accepted its adherents (e.g., Thomas Shearman) as legitimate "single-taxers" [Georgists].[72] (See Milton Friedman in "Critical reception")

2.27.3 Influence

Georgist ideas heavily influenced the politics of the early 20th century. Political parties that were formed based on Georgist ideas include the Commonwealth Land Party, the Justice Party of Denmark, the Henry George Justice Party, and the Single Tax League.

In the UK in 1909, the Liberal Government included a land tax as part of several taxes in the People's Budget aimed at redistributing wealth (including a progressively graded income tax and an increase of inheritance tax). This caused a crisis which resulted indirectly in reform of the House of Lords. The budget was passed eventually—but without the land tax. In 1931, the minority Labour Government passed a land value tax as part III of the 1931 Finance act. However, this was repealed in 1934 by the National Government before it could be implemented.

In Denmark, the Georgist Justice Party has previously been

Henry George, whose writings and advocacy form the basis for Georgism

represented in Folketinget. It formed part of a centre-left government 1957–60 and was also represented in the European Parliament 1978–79. The influence of Henry George has waned over time, but Georgist ideas still occasionally emerge in politics. In the 2004 Presidential campaign, Ralph Nader mentioned Henry George in his policy statements.[73]

Communities

Several communities were also initiated with Georgist principles during the height of the philosophy's popularity. Two such communities that still exist are Arden, Delaware, which was founded in 1900 by Frank Stephens and Will Price, and Fairhope, Alabama, which was founded in 1894 by the auspices of the Fairhope Single Tax Corporation.[74]

The German protectorate of Jiaozhou Bay (also known as Kiaochow) in China fully implemented Georgist policy. Its sole source of government revenue was the land value tax of six percent which it levied on its territory. The German government had previously had economic problems with its African colonies caused by land speculation. One of the main aims in using the land value tax in Jiaozhou Bay was to eliminate such speculation, an aim which was entirely achieved.[75] The colony existed as a German protectorate from 1898 until 1914, when seized by Japanese and British troops. In 1922 the territory was returned to China.

Henry George School of Social Science in New York

Georgist ideas were also adopted to some degree in Australia, Hong Kong, Singapore, South Africa, South Korea, and Taiwan. In these countries, governments still levy some type of land value tax, albeit with exemptions.[76] Many municipal governments of the USA depend on real property tax as their main source of revenue, although such taxes are not Georgist as they generally include the value of buildings and other improvements, one exception being the town of Altoona, Pennsylvania, which only taxes land value.

Institutes and organizations

Various organizations still exist that continue to promote the ideas of Henry George. According to the *The American Journal of Economics and Sociology*, the periodical *Land&Liberty*, established in 1894, is "the longest-lived Georgist project in history".[77] Also in the U.S., the Lincoln Institute of Land Policy (established in 1974) was founded based on the writings of Henry George. It "seeks to improve the dialogue about urban development, the built environment, and tax policy in the United States and abroad".[78] The Henry George Foundation continues to promote the ideas of Henry George in the UK.[79] The IU is an international umbrella organisation that brings together organizations worldwide that seek land value tax reform.[80]

2.27.4 Criticism

Richard T. Ely, known as the "Father of Land Economics", agreed with the economic arguments for Georgism but believed that correcting the problem the way Henry George wanted (without compensation) was unjust to existing landowners. In explaining his position, Ely wrote that "If we have all made a mistake, should one party to the transaction alone bear the cost of the common blunder?"[81]

Karl Marx viewed the Single Tax platform as a step backwards from the transition to communism and referred to Georgism as "Capitalism's last ditch."[82] Marx argued that, "The whole thing is... simply an attempt, decked out with socialism, to save capitalist domination and indeed to establish it afresh on an even wider basis than its present one."[83] Marx also criticized the way land value tax theory emphasizes the value of land, arguing that, "His fundamental dogma is that everything would be all right if ground rent were paid to the state."[83] Fred Harrison replies to these Marxist objections in "Gronlund and other Marxists – Part III: nineteenth-century Americas critics", *American Journal of Economics and Sociology*.[84]

George has also been accused of exaggerating the importance of his "all-devouring rent thesis" in claiming that it is the primary cause of poverty and injustice in society.[85] George argued that the rent of land increased faster than wages for labor because the supply of land is fixed. Modern economists, including Ottmar Edenhofer have demonstrated that George's assertion is plausible but was more likely to be true during George's time than today.[32]

Contemporaries such as Frank Fetter and John Bates Clark argued that it was impractical to distinguish land from capital, and used this as a basis to attack Georgism. Mark Blaug, a specialist in the history of economic thought, credits Fetter and Clark with influencing mainstream economists to abandon the idea "that land is a unique factor of production and hence that there is any special need for a special theory of ground rent" claiming that "this is in fact the basis of all the attacks on Henry George by contemporary economists and certainly the fundamental reason why professional economists increasingly ignored him."[86]

An early criticism of Georgism was that it would generate too much public revenue and lead to unwanted growth of government. Joseph Schumpeter later concluded his analysis of Georgism by stating that, "It is not economically unsound, except that it involves an unwarranted optimism concerning the yield of such a tax." Economists who study land conclude that Schumpeter's criticism is unwarranted because the rental yield from land is likely much greater than what modern critics such as Paul Krugman suppose.[87] Krugman agrees that land value taxation is the best means of raising public revenue but asserts that increased spending has rendered land rent insufficient to fully fund government.[88] Georgists have responded by citing studies and analyses implying that land values of nations like the US, UK, and Australia are more than sufficient to fund all levels of government.[89][90][91][92][93][94][95]

Anarcho-capitalist political philosopher and economist Murray Rothbard criticized Georgism in *Man, Economy, and State* as being philosophically incongruent with subjective value theory, and further stating that land is irrelevant in the factors of production, trade, and price systems,[96] but this critique is generally seen, even by other opponents of Georgism, as relying on false assumptions and flawed reasoning.[97]

Chicago school libertarian economist Milton Friedman agreed with "the Henry George argument" as being "the least bad" means of raising whatever public revenue was needed.[98] Georgists agree with Friedman that land titles should remain private and not be socialized. However, Friedman viewed Georgism as partially immoral, due to a difference of opinion about the validity of vested property rights in land. Georgists believe that the private capture of unimproved land-rents is inherently unjust, drawing comparisons to slavery.[99]

Austrian economist Friedrich Hayek credited early enthusiasm for Henry George with developing his interest in economics. Later, Hayek said that the theory of Georgism would be very strong if assessment challenges didn't lead to unfair outcomes, but he believed that they would.[100]

2.27.5 Notable Georgists

Economists

- Harry Gunnison Brown[101]
- John R. Commons[102][103][104]
- Raymond Crotty[105][106]
- Herman Daly[107]
- Paul Douglass[108][109]
- Ottmar Edenhofer[110][111][112]
- Fred Foldvary[113]
- Mason Gaffney[114][115]
- Max Hirsch[116]
- Wolf Ladejinsky[117]
- Donald Shoup[118][119][120]
- Herbert A. Simon[121][122]
- Robert Solow[123]
- Joseph Stiglitz[124]
- Nicolaus Tideman[125]
- William Vickrey[126]
- Léon Walras[127]
- Philip Wicksteed[128]

Heads of government

- John Ballance[129]
- Winston Churchill[130][131][132]
- Alfred Deakin[133]
- Andrew Fisher[134]
- George Grey[135]
- Rutherford B. Hayes[136]
- William Morris Hughes[137]
- Robert Stout[138]
- Woodrow Wilson[139]
- Sun Yat-sen[140]

Other political figures

- Warren Worth Bailey[141][142]
- Newton D. Baker[143][144]
- Willie Brown[145]
- Clyde Cameron[146]
- George F. Cotterill[147]
- John W. Davis[148]
- William Jay Gaynor[149]
- Keir Hardie[150]
- Frederic C. Howe[151]
- Blas Infante[152]
- Tom L. Johnson[153]
- Samuel M. Jones[154]
- Frank de Jong[155]
- Franklin Knight Lane[143]
- Hazen S. Pingree[156][157][158]
- Philip Snowden[159][160]
- Josiah C. Wedgwood
- William Bauchop Wilson[143]

Activists

- Jane Addams[161][162]
- Louis Brandeis[163][164]
- Clarence Darrow[165][166][167]
- Sara Bard Field[168]
- Michael Davitt[169]
- Samuel Gompers[170][171]
- Bolton Hall[172]
- Hubert Harrison[173][174]
- John Haynes Holmes[175][176]
- Stewart Headlam[177][178]
- Benjamin C. Marsh[179][180]
- James Ferdinand Morton[181][182]
- Thomas Mott Osborne[183][184][185]
- Amos Pinchot[186][187]
- Louis Freeland Post[188]
- Terence V. Powderly[189]
- Samuel Seabury[190]
- Catherine Helen Spence[191]
- Thomas Spence[192]
- Helen Taylor (feminist)[193]
- William Simon U'Ren[194]
- Ida B. Wells[195]
- Frances Willard (suffragist)[196]

Authors

- Frank Chodorov[197][198]
- Ernest Howard Crosby[162]
- Charles Eisenstein[199]
- Hamlin Garland[200][201]
- Fred Harrison[202]
- James A. Herne[203]
- Ebenezer Howard[204][205][206]
- Fannie Hurst[207]
- Aldous Huxley[208]
- James Howard Kunstler[209]
- William D. McCrackan[200]
- Albert Jay Nock[210]
- Kathleen Norris[211]
- Upton Sinclair[212][213]
- Leo Tolstoy[214][215]
- Charles Erskine Scott Wood[216][217]

Journalists

- William F. Buckley, Jr.[218]
- Timothy Thomas Fortune[219]
- Theodor Herzl[220]
- Michael Kinsley[221][222][223]
- Suzanne La Follette[224][225]
- Dylan Matthews[226][227]
- Raymond Moley[228]
- Reihan Salam[229]
- Horace Traubel[230]
- Martin Wolf[231]
- Merryn Somerset Webb[232][233]
- Brand Whitlock[234][235][236]
- Tim Worstall[237]
- Matthew Yglesias[238][239]

Artists

- David Bachrach[240]
- John Wilson Bengough[241]
- Daniel Carter Beard[242]
- Matthew Bellamy[243]
- Walter Burley Griffin[244][245]
- John Hutchinson[200][246]
- George Inness[247]

2.27. GEORGISM

- Emma Lazarus[248][249]
- Agnes de Mille[250]
- Henry Churchill de Mille[251][252]
- William C. deMille[253][254]
- Francis Neilson[255][256]
- Banjo Paterson[257]
- Louis Prang[258]
- Will Price[259]
- Frank Stephens (sculptor)[260]
- Frank Lloyd Wright[261]

Philosophers

- Ralph Borsodi[262]
- Nicholas Murray Butler[263][264]
- John B. Cobb[265]
- John Dewey[266]
- Silvio Gesell[267]
- Leon MacLaren[268][269]
- Jose Marti[270][271]
- Franz Oppenheimer[220]
- Philippe Van Parijs[272][273]
- Bertrand Russell[274][275][276]
- Hillel Steiner[277]

Other

- Roger Babson[278]
- Albert Einstein[279][280]
- Henry Ford[281]
- Spencer Heath[282][283]
- Mumia Abu-Jamal[284][285]
- Margrit Kennedy[286]
- John C. Lincoln[287]
- Elizabeth Magie[288][289]
- Edward McGlynn[290]

- Buckey O'Neill[291]
- George Foster Peabody[184][185]
- Raymond A. Spruance[292]
- Silvanus P. Thompson[241]
- Fiske Warren[293][294]
- Alfred Russel Wallace[295]
- Joseph Fels[296]

2.27.6 See also

- *Agrarian Justice*
- Arden, Delaware
- Cap and Share
- Causes of poverty
- Citizen's dividend
- Classical economics
- Classical liberalism
- Community land trust
- Deadweight loss
- Diggers movement
- Economic rent
- Enclosure
- Excess burden of taxation
- Externality
- Free-market environmentalism
- Freiwirtschaft
- Geolibertarianism
- Green economy
- Labor economics
- *Laissez-faire*
- Land (economics)
- Landed property
- Land law
- Land monopoly

- Land tenure and registration
- Land value tax
- Law of rent
- Lockean proviso
- Manorialism
- Natural and legal rights
- Optimal tax
- Physiocracy
- Pigovian tax
- Poverty reduction
- *Progress and Poverty*
- Progressive Era
- Prosper Australia (formerly "Henry George League")
- Radical centrism
- Tax reform / shift
- Tragedy of the anticommons
- Universal basic income
- Value capture
- Wealth concentration

2.27.7 References

[1] "An Introduction to Georgist Philosophy & Activity". *http://www.cgocouncil.org/*. Council of Georgist Organizations. Retrieved 28 June 2014. External link in |website= (help)

[2] Heavey, Jerome F. (July 2003). "Comments on Warren Samuels' "Why the Georgist movement has not succeeded"". *American Journal of Economics and Sociology* **62** (3): 593–599. doi:10.1111/1536-7150.00230. JSTOR 3487813. human beings have an inalienable right to the product of their own labor

[3] McNab, Jane. "How the reputation of Georgists turned minds against the idea of a land rent tax" (PDF). *http://www.business.uwa.edu.au/*. Retrieved 18 June 2014. External link in |website= (help)

[4] Gaffney, Mason, and Harrison, Fred (1994). *The Corruption of Economics*. London: Shepheard-Walwyn. ISBN 978-0-85683-244-4

[5] Hudson, Michael; Feder, Kris; and Miller, George James (1994). *A Philosophy for a Fair Society*. Shepheard-Walwyn, London. ISBN 978-0-85683-159-1.

[6] Smith, Adam (1776). "Chapter 2, Article 1: Taxes upon the Rent of Houses". *The Wealth of Nations, Book V*.

[7] Binswanger-Mkhize, Hans P; Bourguignon, Camille; Brink, Rogier van den (2009). *Agricultural Land Redistribution : Toward Greater Consensus*. World Bank. A land tax is considered a progressive tax in that wealthy landowners normally should be paying relatively more than poorer landowners and tenants. Conversely, a tax on buildings can be said to be regressive, falling heavily on tenants who generally are poorer than the landlords

[8] Plummer, Elizabeth (March 2010). "Evidence on the Distributional Effects of a Land Value Tax on Residential Households" (PDF). *National Tax Journal*. Retrieved 7 January 2015.

[9] Land Value Taxation: An Applied Analysis, William J. McCluskey, Riël C. D. Franzsen

[10] Locke, John (1691). "Some Considerations of the Consequences of the Lowering of Interest and the Raising the Value of Money".

[11] Gaffney, Mason. "Logos Abused: The Decadence and Tyranny of Abstract Reasoning in Economics" (PDF). Retrieved 22 December 2013.

[12] Foldvary, Fred. "Geoism Explained". The Progress Report. Retrieved 12 January 2014.

[13] The Forgotten Idea That Shaped Great U.S. Cities by Mason Gaffney & Rich Nymoen, Commons magazine, October 17, 2013.

[14] ""ECONOMICS" and POLITICAL ECONOMY". *http://www.henrygeorge.org/*. Retrieved 27 March 2015. External link in |website= (help)

[15] Tideman, Nic. "Basic Principles of Geonomics". Retrieved 15 January 2015.

[16] Casal, Paula (2011). "Global Taxes on Natural Resources" (PDF). *Journal of Moral Philosophy* **8** (3): 307–327. doi:10.1163/174552411x591339. Retrieved 14 March 2014. It can also invoke geoism, a philosophical tradition encompassing the views of John Locke and Henry George ...

[17] http://earthsharing.ca/page/poverty

[18] *Common Rights vs. Collective Rights*

[19] *Progress and Poverty* – "Introduction: The Problem of Poverty Amid Progress

[20] Inman, Phillip. "Could we build a better future on a land value tax?". The Guardian. Retrieved 14 January 2014.

[21] Aaron, Henry (May 1974). "A New View of Property Tax Incidence". *The American Economic Review* **64** (2). Retrieved 7 January 2015.

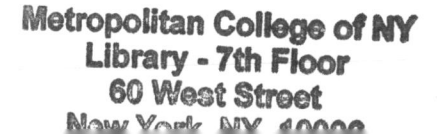

[22] Foldvary, Fred E. "Geo-Rent: A Plea to Public Economists". *Econ Journal Watch* (April 2005)

[23] Stiglitz, Joseph. "Thomas Piketty and Joseph Stiglitz". INETeconomics. Retrieved 14 April 2015.

[24] "Re:Think. Tax discussion paper for March 2015" (PDF). *http://bettertax.gov.au/*. The Australian Government the Treasury. Retrieved 14 April 2015. External link in |website= (help)

[25] Franklin, Benjamin (1840). *Memoirs of Benjamin Franklin, Volume 2*. McCarty & Davis. p. 32. Retrieved 13 December 2014.

[26] Shine, Mary L. (1922). *Ideas of the founders of the American nation on landed property*. University of Wisconsin. p. 196.

[27] George, Henry (1997). *An anthology of Henry George's thought*. Rochester, N.Y., USA: University of Rochester Press. ISBN 1878822810.

[28] Davies, Lindy. "The Science of Political Economy: What George "Left Out"". *http://www.politicaleconomy.org/*. Retrieved 16 June 2014. External link in |website= (help)

[29] Batt, H. William. "The Compatibility of Georgist Economics and Ecological Economics". Retrieved 9 June 2014.

[30] George, Henry (1886). *Protection or Free Trade*. New York: Doubleday, Page & Co. Retrieved 16 June 2014.

[31] George, Henry (1997). *An Anthology of Henry George's Thought, Volume 1*. University Rochester Press. p. 148. Retrieved 16 June 2014.

[32] Mattauch, Linus; Siegmeier, Jan; Edenhofer, Ottmar; Creutzig, Felix (2013) : Financing Public Capital through Land Rent Taxation: A Macroeconomic Henry George Theorem, CESifo Working Paper, No. 4280 http://www.econstor.eu/bitstream/10419/77659/1/cesifo_wp4280.pdf

[33] Tideman, Nicolaus. "Using Tax Policy to Promote Urban Growth". Retrieved 9 June 2014.

[34] Gaffney, Mason (July 3, 2008). "The Hidden Taxable Capacity of Land: Enough and to Spare" (PDF). *International J. of Social Economics* (Summer 2008). Retrieved 13 June 2014.

[35] Fitzgerald, Karl. "Total Resource Rents of Australia" (PDF). Prosper Australia. Retrieved 16 June 2014.

[36] Harriss, C. Lowell. "Nonrenewable Exhaustible Resources and Property Taxation." American Journal of Economics and Sociology 65.3 (2006): 693-699.

[37] George, Henry (1997). *An Anthology of Henry George's Thought, Volume 1*. University Rochester Press. p. 156. Retrieved 16 June 2014.

[38] George, Henry. "Scotland and Scotsmen". Retrieved 16 June 2014. Address delivered on 18 February 1884 at the City Hall, Glasgow

[39] Miller, Joseph Dana (1921). "To Hold the Sea In Fee Simple". *The Single Tax Review*. 21-22: 37. Retrieved 16 June 2014.

[40] Darrow, Clarence. "How to Abolish Unfair Taxation". Retrieved 15 June 2014.

[41] Sullivan, Dan. "Are you a Real Libertarian, or a ROYAL Libertarian?". Retrieved 15 June 2014.

[42] Post, Louis F. "Outlines of Louis F. Post's Lectures". Retrieved 15 June 2014.

[43] Zarlenga, Stephen. "Henry George's Concept of Money (Full Text) And Its Implications For 21st Century Reform". *http://www.monetary.org/*. American Monetary Institute. Retrieved 13 June 2014. External link in |website= (help)

[44] George, Henry. "On Patents and Copyrights". Retrieved 16 June 2014.

[45] Niman, Neil B. "Henry George and the Intellectual Foundations of the Open Source Movement" (PDF). *http://schalkenbach.org/*. Retrieved 16 June 2014. External link in |website= (help) "A modern counterpart to the nineteenth century focus on land can be found in the twentieth century concern with the establishment of intellectual property rights that fence off a portion of the creative commons in order to construct temporary monopolies."

[46] Fox, Stephen R. The American Conservation Movement: John Muir and His Legacy. Madison, WI: U of Wisconsin, 1985.

[47] Daly, Herman E., and Joshua C. Farley. Ecological Economics: Principles and Applications. Washington: Island, 2004.

[48] Cato, Molly Scott. "The Gypsy Rover, the Norman Yoke and the Land Value Tax". Retrieved 15 August 2014.

[49] Smith, Peter. "Beaver, Rewilding & Land Value Tax have the answer to the UK's Flooding Problem.". Retrieved 15 August 2014.

[50] Ikerd, John. "The Green Tax Shift: Winners and Losers". *missouri.edu*. Retrieved 13 June 2014.

[51] Casal, Paula (2011). "Global Taxes on Natural Resources" (PDF). *Journal of Moral Philosophy* (8): 307–327. Retrieved 14 June 2014.

[52] Backhaus, Jurgen, and J. J. Krabbe. "Henry George's Contribution to Modern Environmental Policy: Part I, Theoretical Postulates." American Journal of Economics and Sociology 50.4 (1991): 485-501. Web. 14 Aug. 2014.

[53] Cobb, Clifford. "Herman Daly Festschrift: Ecological and Georgist Economic Principles: A Comparison". Retrieved 13 June 2014.

[54] Roark, Eric (2013). *Removing the Commons: A Lockean Left-Libertarian Approach to the Just Use and Appropriation of Natural Resources*. Lexington Books. Retrieved 12 June 2014.

[55] Brebbia, C. A. (2012). *Ecodynamics: The Prigogine Legacy*. WIT Press. p. 104. Retrieved 4 June 2014.

[56] Gluckman, Amy. "A Primer on Henry George's "Single Tax"". Retrieved 12 July 2015.

[57] Hartzok, Alanna. "Citizen Dividends and Oil Resource Rents A Focus on Alaska, Norway and Nigeria". Retrieved 9 June 2014.

[58] Gaffney, Mason. "A Cannan Hits the Mark" (PDF). Retrieved 9 June 2014.

[59] Socialism, Capitalism, and Geoism – by Lindy Davies

[60] Introduction to Earth Sharing,

[61] Geonomics in a Nutshell

[62] Geoism and Libertarianism by Fred Foldvary

[63] Curtis, Mike. "The Arden Land Trust". Retrieved 30 May 2014.

[64] Adams, Martin. "Sharing the Value of Land: The Promise of Location Value Covenants". Retrieved 30 May 2014.

[65] Kent, Deirdre. "Land and Money Reform Synergy in New Zealand". Smart Taxes. Retrieved 30 May 2014.

[66] http://www.cooperativeindividualism.org/wrigley-adrian_location-value-covenants-2010-06.pdf

[67] http://www.sfrgroup.org/Home/location-value-covenants

[68] Foldvery, Fred. "Geoanarchism A short summary of geoism and its relation to libertarianism.". Retrieved 29 May 2014.

[69] Bille, Frank F. "The Danish-American Georgist". Retrieved 30 May 2014.

[70] Miller, Joseph Dana (1904). *Land and Freedom: An International Record of Single Tax Progress, Volume 4*. Single Tax Publishing Company. pp. 9–15.

[71] Wolf, Martin. "Why we must halt the land cycle". Financial Times. Retrieved 29 May 2014.

[72] Barker, Charles A. "The Followers of Henry George". *http://www.cooperativeindividualism.org/*. Henry George News. Retrieved 13 January 2015. External link in |website= (help)

[73] "Internet Archive Wayback Machine". Web.archive.org. 2004-08-28. Archived from the original on September 27, 2007. Retrieved 2012-07-26.

[74] Fairhope Single Tax Corporation

[75] Silagi, Michael; Faulkner, Susan N. "Land Reform in Kiaochow, China: From 1898 to 1914 the Menace of Disastrous Land Speculation was Averted by Taxation". *The American Journal of Economics and Sociology* **43** (2): 167–177. doi:10.1111/j.1536-7150.1984.tb02240.x.

[76] Gaffney, M. Mason. "Henry George 100 Years Later". Association for Georgist Studies Board. Retrieved 2008-05-12.

[77] *The American Journal of Economics and Sociology*, vol. 62, 2003, p. 615

[78] "About the Lincoln Institute of Land Policy". Lincolninst.edu. Retrieved 2012-07-26.

[79] "The Henry George Foundation". Retrieved 2009-07-31.

[80] The IU. "The IU". Retrieved 2008-10-31.

[81] George, Henry. "A Response to Richard Ely On the Question of Compensation to Owners of Land". Retrieved 29 May 2014.

[82] Andelson, Robert V. "Henry George and The Reconstruction Of Capitalism". Retrieved 14 January 2014.

[83] Karl Marx – Letter to Friedrich Adolph Sorge in Hoboken

[84] 14 Gronlund and other Marxists – Part III: nineteenth-century Americas critics | American Journal of Economics and Sociology, The | Find Articles at BNET

[85] Critics of Henry George

[86] Blaug, Mark. Interview in Andelson, Robert V. *Critics of Henry George: An Appraisal of Their Strictures on Progress and Poverty*. Blackwell Publishing. 1979. p. 686.

[87] Hudson, Michael (1994). *A Philosophy for a Fair Society*. Retrieved 18 January 2015.

[88] http://www.psmag.com/politics/this-land-is-your-land-3392 "urban economics models actually do suggest that Georgist taxation would be the right approach at least to finance city growth."/

[89] Mason Gaffney, (2009) "The hidden taxable capacity of land: enough and to spare", International Journal of Social Economics, Vol. 36 Iss: 4, pp. 328 - 411

[90] Foldvery, Fred. "The Ultimate Tax Reform: Public Revenue from Land Rent" (PDF). Retrieved 27 January 2014.

[91] Steven, Cord, "How Much Revenue would a Full Land Value Tax Yield? Analysis of Census and Federal Reserve Data." American Journal of Economics and Sociology 44 (3) (July 1985), pages 279-93

[92] Steven Cord, "Land Rent is 20% of U.S. National Income for 1986," Incentive Taxation, July/August 1991, pages 1-2.

[93] Miles, Mike. 1990. "What Is the Value of all U.S. Real Estate?" Real Estate Review 20 (2)(Summer): 69-75.

[94] Nicolaus Tideman and Florenz Plassman, "Taxed Out of Work and Wealth: The Costs of Taxing Labor and Capital," in The Losses of Nations: Deadweight Politics versus Public Rent Dividends (London: Othila Press, 1988), pages 146-174.

[95] Fitzgerald, Karl. "Total Resource Rents of Australia". Retrieved 27 January 2014.

[96] Rothbard, Murray (1962). *Man, Economy, and State: A Treatise on Economic Principles*. Van Nostrand.

[97] Heinrich, David J. "Murray Rothbard and Henry George". *www.mises.org*. Retrieved 28 August 2014.

[98] "Microeconomics"; N. Gregory Mankiw, Mark P. Taylor – 2006 – 474 pages

[99] George, Henry (1881). *The Irish Land Question*.

[100] Andelson, Robert V. (January 2000). "On Separating the Landowner's Earned and Unearned Increment: A Georgist Rejoinder to F. A. Hayek". *American Journal of Economics and Sociology* **59** (1): 109–117. doi:10.1111/1536-7150.00016. Retrieved 27 November 2013. Hayek wrote, "It was a lay enthusiasm for Henry George which led me to economics."

[101] Brown, H. G. "A Defense of the Single Tax Principle." The ANNALS of the American Academy of Political and Social Science 183.1 (1936): 63-69.

[102] Harter, Lafayette G. John R. Commons, His Assault on Laissez-faire. Corvallis: Oregon State UP, 1962. Pages 21, 32, 36, 38.

[103] "Two Centuries of Economic Thought on Taxation of Land Rents." In Richard Lindholm and Arthur Lynn, Jr., (eds.), Land Value Taxation in Thought and Practice. Madison: Univ. of Wisconsin Press, 1982, pp. 151-96.

[104] Brue, Stanley (2012). *The Evolution of Economic Thought* (PDF) (Supplemental Biography of John Rogers Commons for chapter 19 of the online edition of The Evolution of Economic Thought ed.). Cengage Learning. Retrieved 1 September 2014. "After reading Henry George's Progress and Poverty," Commons "became a single-taxer."

[105] Crotty, Raymond D. (1988). *A Radical's Response*. Poolbeg. Retrieved 29 August 2014.

[106] Sheppard, Barry. "'Progress and Poverty' – Henry George and Land Reform in modern Ireland". *http://www.theirishstory.com/*. Retrieved 29 August 2014. External link in |website= (help)

[107] Daly, Herman. "Smart Talk: Herman Daly on what's beyond GNP Growth". Henry George School of Social Science. Retrieved 24 October 2015. . . . I am really sort of a Georgist.

[108] Gaffney, Mason. "Stimulus: The False and the True Mason Gaffney". Retrieved 13 August 2015.

[109] Douglas, Paul (1972). *In the fullness of time; the memoirs of Paul H. Douglas*. New York: Harcourt Brace Jovanovich. ISBN 0151443769.

[110] Edenhofer, Ottmar. "Hypergeorgism: When is Rent Taxation as a Remedy for Insufficient Capital Accumulation Socially Optimal?". Retrieved 11 November 2013. Edenhofer writes, "Extending and modifying the tenet of georgism, we propose that this insight be called hypergeorgism." "From a historical perspective, our result may be closer to Henry George's original thinking than georgism or the neoclassical Henry George Theorems."

[111] Edenhofer, Ottmar. "Financing Public Capital Through Land Rent Taxation: A Macroeconomic Henry George Theorem". Retrieved 11 November 2013.

[112] Edenhofer, Ottmar. "The Triple Dividend Climate Change Mitigation, Justice and Investing in Capabilities" (PDF). Retrieved 11 November 2013.

[113] Fred Foldvary's website

[114] Mason Gaffney's homepage

[115] Gaffney, Mason. "Henry George 100 Years Later: The Great Reconciler" (PDF). Retrieved 27 January 2014.

[116] Airlie Worrall, *The New Crusade: the Origins, Activities and Influence of the Australian Single Tax Leagues, 1889–1895* (M.A. thesis, University of Melbourne, 1978).

[117] Andelson Robert V. (2000). *Land-Value Taxation Around the World: Studies in Economic Reform and Social Justice Malden*. MA:Blackwell Publishers, Inc. p. 359.

[118] Knack, Ruth Eckdish. "Pay As You Park: UCLA professor Donald Shoup inspires a passion for parking." (May 2005). Planning Magazine. Retrieved 17 September 2014.

[119] Shoup, Donald C. "The Ideal Source of Local Public Revenue." Regional Science and Urban Economics 34.6 (2004): 753-84.

[120] Washington, Emily. "The High Cost of Free Parking Chapters 19-22". *marketurbanism.com*. Market Urbanism. Retrieved 17 September 2014.

[121] Quotes from Nobel Prize Winners Herbert Simon stated in 1978: "*Assuming that a tax increase is necessary, it is clearly preferable to impose the additional cost on land by increasing the land tax, rather than to increase the wage tax – the two alternatives open to the City (of Pittsburgh). It is the use and occupancy of property that creates the need for the municipal services that appear as the largest item in the budget – fire and police protection, waste removal, and public works. The average increase in tax bills of city residents will be about twice as great with wage tax increase than with a land tax increase.*"

[122] Herbert Simon. (2014). The Famous People website. Retrieved 12:59, Oct 30, 2014, from http://www.thefamouspeople.com/profiles/herbert-simon-293.php.

[123] Foldvery, Fred E. (2005). "Geo-Rent: A Plea to Public Economists" (PDF). *Econ Watch* **2** (1): 106–132. Retrieved 2 October 2013.

[124] Cleveland, Mary Manning. "How a Progressive Tax System Made Detroit a Powerhouse (and Could Again)". Retrieved 3 February 2015.

[125] Tideman, Nicolaus. "Global Economic Justice". Schalkenbach Foundation. Archived from the original on June 29, 2013. Retrieved 8 October 2013.

[126] Bill Vickrey – In Memoriam

[127] Cirillo, Renato (Jan 1984). "Léon Walras and Social Justice". *The American Journal of Economics and Sociology* **43** (1): 53–60. doi:10.1111/j.1536-7150.1984.tb02222.x. Retrieved 12 November 2013.

[128] Barker, Charles A., 1955. Henry George. New York: Oxford University Press

[129] Boast, Richard (2008). *Buying the land, selling the land : governments and Maori land in the North Island 1865-1921*. Wellington N.Z: Victoria University Press, Victoria University of Wellington. ISBN 9780864735614.

[130] http://www.cooperativeindividualism.org/churchill-winston_mother-of-all-monopolies-1909.html

[131] MacLaren, Andrew (Autumn 2001). "The People's Rights: Opportunity Lost?". *Finest Hour* **112**. Retrieved 15 August 2015.

[132] Dugan, Ianthe Jeanne (March 17, 2013). "It's a Lonely Quest for Land-Tax Fans, But, by George, They Press On". Wall Street Journal. Retrieved 25 August 2014.

[133] Laurent, John (2005). *Henry George's legacy in economic thought*. Cheltenham, UK Northampton, MA: Edward Elgar Pub. p. 9. ISBN 1843768852.

[134] Bastian, Peter (2009). *Andrew Fisher an underestimated man*. Sydney, N.S.W: UNSW Press. pp. 28–30. ISBN 1742230040.

[135] The Life of Henry George, Part 3 Chapter XI

[136] Hayes, Rutherford B. "Henry George". Retrieved 26 November 2013.

[137] "Hughes, William Morris (Billy) (1862–1952)". *Australian Dictionary of Biography: Online Edition*.

[138] Stout, Robert (14 April 1885). "ADDRESS BY THE HON. R. STOUT." (Volume XXII, Issue 7302). PAPERPAST. New Zealand Herald. Retrieved 6 December 2014.

[139] WOOLF, S.J. (April 27, 1941). "MORGENTHAU AT 85 RECALLS A FULL LIFE; MORGENTHAU AT 85". New York Times. NY Times Magazine. At heart [Woodrow Wilson] was a follower of Henry George and strongly objected to private profit accruing through the increase in land values.

[140] Trescott, Paul B. (2007). *Jingji Xue: The History of the Introduction of Western Economic Ideas Into China, 1850-1950*. Chinese University Press. pp. 46–48. The foregoing help to demonstrate why Sun Yat-sen would have regarded Henry George as a very credible guide, and why in 1912 Sun could tell an interviewer, 'The teachings of your single-taxer, Henry George, will be the basis of our program of reform.'

[141] Miller, Joseph Dana (1902). *Land and Freedom: An International Record of Single Tax Progress, Volume 2*. Single Tax Publishing Company. pp. 40–41.

[142] "A Remembrance of Warren Worth Bailey". Retrieved 14 January 2014.

[143] Gaffney, Mason. "Henry George 100 Years Later: The Great Reconciler". Robert Schalkenbach Foundation. Retrieved 3 September 2014.

[144] Finegold, Kenneth (1995). *Experts and politicians : reform challenges to machine politics in New York, Cleveland, and Chicago*. Princeton, N.J: Princeton University Press. ISBN 0691037345.

[145] Stevens, Elizabeth Lesly (July–August 2012). "The Power Broker". *Washington Monthly*. Retrieved 8 December 2013.

[146] Cameron, Clyde. "REVENUE THAT IS NOT A TAX". Retrieved 18 February 2015.

[147] "Single Tax Loses, But Mayor Favoring This Reform Is Chosen By a Small Vote Margin". The Milwaukee Journal. Mar 6, 1912. Retrieved 23 August 2014.

[148] Davis, John W. "Henry George, Original Thinker". Retrieved 30 October 2014.

[149] Gaynor, William Jay. Some of Mayor Gaynor's Letters and Speeches. New York: Greaves Pub., 1913. 214-21. https://books.google.com/books?id=$-$7kMAAAAYAAJ&pg=PA219#v=onepage&q&f=false

[150] "Socialism in England: James Keir Hardie Declares That It Is Capturing That Country.". California Digital Newspaper Collection. San Francisco Call. 25 September 1895. Retrieved 4 November 2014. Hardie states, "I was a very enthusiastic single-taxer for a number of years."

[151] Howe, Frederic C. The Confessions of a Reformer. Kent, OH: Kent State UP, 1988.

[152] Arcas Cubero, Fernando: *El movimiento georgista y los orígenes del Andalucismo : análisis del periódico "El impuesto único" (1911–1923)*. Málaga : Editorial Confederación Española de Cajas de Ahorros, 1980. ISBN 84-500-3784-0

[153] "Single Taxers Dine Johnson". *New York Times* May 31, 1910.

[154] "Henry George". *Ohio History Central: An Online History of Ohio History*.

[155] "Frank de Jong: Economic Rent Best Way to Finance Government". Retrieved 9 November 2013.

[156] Gaffney, Mason. "What's the matter with Michigan? Rise and collapse of an economic wonder" (PDF). Retrieved 28 April 2014.

[157] Cleveland, Polly. "The Way Forward for Detroit? Land Taxes". Washington Spectator. Retrieved 28 April 2014.

[158] Gaffney, Mason. "New Life in Old Cities" (PDF). *UC Riverside*. Retrieved 28 April 2014.

[159] Bryson, Phillip (2011). *The economics of Henry George : history's rehabilitation of America's greatest early economist*. New York: Palgrave Macmillan. p. 145.

[160] Moore, Robert (1974). *Pit-men, preachers & politics the effects of Methodism in a Durham mining community*. Cambridge: Cambridge University Press. p. 61.

[161] Jones, Carolyn C. (Spring 1997). "TAXING WOMEN: THOUGHTS ON A GENDERED ECONOMY: SYMPOSIUM: A HISTORICAL OUTLOOK: TAXES AND PEACE: A CASE STUDY OF TAXING WOMEN". *Southern California Review of Law and Women's Studies Southern California Review of Law and Women's Studies*. Retrieved 5 December 2014.

[162] Rothbard, Murray (2007). *Left and Right: A Journal of Libertarian Thought (Complete, 1965-1968)*. Ludwig von Mises Institute. p. 263. Retrieved 5 December 2014.

[163] Brandeis, Louis (1971). *Letters of Louis D. Brandeis: Vol. 1*. p. 82.

[164] "101+ Famous Thinkers on Owning Earth". Retrieved 22 October 2013. Brandeis said, "I find it very difficult to disagree with the principles of Henry George... I believe in the taxation of land values only."

[165] How to Abolish Unfair Taxation: An Address Before a Los Angeles Audience, Delivered March 1913 https://books.google.com/books/about/How_to_Abolish_Unfair_Taxation.html?id=rlOFHAAACAAJ

[166] Darrow, Clarence. "The Land Belongs To The People" (PDF). www.umn.edu. Everyman. Retrieved 3 August 2014.

[167] "The Centre for Incentive Taxation" **20** (4). August 1994. Darrow replied about Georgism, "Well, you either come to it or go broke."

[168] Beth Shalom Hessel. "Field, Sara Bard"; http://www.anb.org/articles/15/15-00220.html; American National Biography Online April 2014. Access Date: Sun Mar 22 2015 14:24:04 GMT-0700 (Pacific Daylight Time)

[169] Lane, Fintan. *The Origins of Modern Irish Socialism, 1881–1896*.Cork University Press, 1997 (pp. 79, 81).

[170] Miller, Joseph Dana (1921). "Mr. Samuel Gompers Replies to Our Criticism". *The Single Tax Review*. 21-22: 42. Retrieved 31 August 2014.

[171] Gompers, Samuel (1986). *The Samuel Gompers Papers: The making of a union leader, 1850-86, Volume 1*. University of Illinois Press. pp. 431–432. Retrieved 31 August 2014.

[172] Leubuscher, F. C. (1939). Bolton Hall. *The Freeman*. January issue.

[173] Miller, Joseph Dana (1921). *The Single Tax Review, Volumes 21-22*. p. 178. Retrieved 16 December 2014.

[174] *Land and Freedom, Volumes 22-23*. 1922. p. 179. Retrieved 16 December 2014.

[175] "The Land Question Quotations from Historical and Contemporary Sources". Retrieved 5 December 2014. Holmes said, "The passing years have only added to my conviction that Henry George is one of the greatest of all modern statesmen and prophets."

[176] Eckert, Charles R. "Henry George, Sound Economics and the "New Deal"". Retrieved 5 December 2014.

[177] Thompson, Noel. *Political economy and the Labour Party: The economics of démocratic socialism (1884-2005)*. Routlegde Ed., 2006, pp. 54-55.

[178] Haggard, Robert (2001). *The persistence of Victorian liberalism : the politics of social reform in Britain, 1870-1900*. Westport, Conn: Greenwood Press. ISBN 0313313059.

[179] Caves, Roger W. Encyclopedia of the City. Abingdon, Oxon, OX: Routledge, 2005.

[180] Marsh, Benjamin Clarke. Lobbyist for the People; a Record of Fifty Years. Washington: Public Affairs, 1953.

[181] "Single-Taxers again laud Henry George" (PDF). *Daily Standard Union* (Brooklyn, NY). Sep 8, 1912. p. 12 (1st col from top). Retrieved Nov 7, 2014.

[182]
- "British MP guest at George dinner" (PDF). *Daily Standard Union* (Brooklyn, NY). Sep 6, 1912. p. 9 (3rd col above bottom). Retrieved Nov 7, 2014.
- "Community Club" (PDF). *Silver Creek News* (Silver Creek, NY). Jan 4, 1916. p. 1 (3rd col of text, up from bottom). Retrieved Nov 7, 2014.
- "James F. Morton at Eagle Temple" (PDF). *Jamestown Evening Journal* (Jamestown, NY). Jan 23, 1917. p. 10, (4th col below top). Retrieved Nov 7, 2014.
- "Meetings this evening; Labor Forum" (PDF). *Jamestown Evening Journal* (Jamestown, NY). Mar 30, 1918. p. 12 (3rd col above mid). Retrieved Nov 7, 2014.
- "F. P. Morgan(sic) gives instructive talk on the single tax" (PDF). *The Saratogian* (Saratoga Springs, NY). Apr 10, 1929. p. 9 (2nd col below top). Retrieved Nov 7, 2014.
- Morton, James F., Jr. (July–August 1918). "Report of James F. Morton, Jr.'s Lecture Work". *The Single Tax Review* **18** (4): 116. Retrieved Nov 7, 2014.

- "Single taxer to speak" (PDF). *Buffalo Courier* (Buffalo, NY). Apr 7, 1916. p. 9 (2nd col above bottom). Retrieved Nov 7, 2014.

- "Plans single tax talk" (PDF). *Buffalo Courier* (Buffalo, NY). Apr 14, 1916. p. 10 (7th and 8th col, above bottom). Retrieved Nov 7, 2014.

- "Single tax advocate lectures in church" (PDF). *Buffalo Courier* (Buffalo, NY). Apr 17, 1916. p. 6 (4th col above bottom). Retrieved Nov 7, 2014.

- "Meetings this evening; Meeting of the Men's club" (PDF). *Jamestown Evening Journal* (Jamestown, NY). Apr 25, 1916. p. 14 (3rd col below top_). Retrieved Nov 7, 2014.

- "Philosophy of the Single Tax" (PDF). *Jamestown Evening Journal* (Jamestown, NY). Apr 26, 1916. p. 7 (1st col and most of bottom half of the page). Retrieved Nov 7, 2014.

- "Season's close at Chautauqua; The Single Tax" (PDF). *Jamestown Evening Journal* (Jamestown, NY). Aug 28, 1916. p. 9, (see majority of 3rd col). Retrieved Nov 7, 2014.

- "Exclusive tax on land values" (PDF). *Jamestown Evening Journal* (Jamestown, NY). Jan 15, 1917. p. 3 (3rd col top). Retrieved Nov 7, 2014.

- "Saturday Night Club" (PDF). *Jamestown Evening Journal* (Jamestown, NY). Jan 12, 1917. p. 9 (3rd col above bottom). Retrieved Nov 7, 2014.

- "Lewiston" (PDF). *Buffalo Evening News* (Buffalo, NY). Apr 30, 1917. p. 10 (2nd col above bottom). Retrieved Nov 7, 2014.

- "Greenfield Center" (PDF). *The Saratogian* (Saratoga Springs, NY). Nov 13, 1917. p. 7 (4th col mid). Retrieved Nov 7, 2014.

- "Church Services Tomorrow; First Congregational Church" (PDF). *Daily Argus* (Mount Vernon, NY). Dec 3, 1917. p. 12 (4th col above bottom). Retrieved Nov 7, 2014.

[183] Jorgensen, Emil Oliver. The next Step toward Real Democracy: One Hundred Reasons Why America Should Abolish, as Speedily as Possible, All Taxation upon the Fruits of Industry, and Raise the Public Revenue by a Single Tax on Land Values Only. Chicago, IL: Chicago Singletax Club, 1920.

[184] Gorgas, William Crawford, and Lewis Jerome Johnson. Two Papers on Public Sanitation and the Single Tax. New York: Single Tax Information Bureau, 1914. https://books.google.com/books?id=v3NHAAAAYAAJ

[185] Ware, Louise. George Foster Peabody, Banker, Philanthropist, Publicist. Athens: U of Georgia, 1951. http://dlg.galileo.usg.edu/ugapressbks/pdfs/ugp9780820334561.pdf

[186] Young, Arthur Nichols (1916). *Single tax Movement in the United States*. S.l: Hardpress Ltd.

[187] Thompson, John (1987). *Reformers and war : American progressive publicists and the First World War*. Cambridge Cambridgeshire New York: Cambridge University Press.

[188] Post, Louis F. *The Prophet of San Francisco: Personal Memories & Interpretations of Henry George*. The Minerva Group.

[189] Powderly, Terence Vincent (1889). *Thirty Years of Labor. 1859-1889*. Excelsior publishing house. Retrieved 8 December 2014. "It would be far easier to levy a "single tax," basing it upon land values." "It is because [...] a single land tax would prove to be the very essence of equity, that l advocate it.

[190] Mitgang, Herbert (1996). *The Man Who Rode the Tiger: The Life and Times of Judge Samuel Seabury*. Fordham Univ Press.

[191] Magarey, Susan (1985). *Unbridling the tongues of women : a biography of Catherine Helen Spence*. Sydney, NSW: Hale & Iremonger. ISBN 0868061492.

[192] Thomas Spence was a self-taught militant who believed that the land had been stolen from the people and should be returned to them. This idea was the corner stone of his Plan. http://thomas-spence-society.co.uk/2.html

[193] Wenzer, Kenneth (1997). *An Anthology of Henry George's Thought (Volume 1)*. University Rochester Press. pp. 87, 243.

[194] "Oregon Biographies: William S. U'Ren". *Oregon History Project*. Portland, Oregon: Oregon Historical Society. 2002. Archived from the original on 2006-11-10. Retrieved 2006-12-29.

[195] Candeloro, Dominic (April 1979). "The Single Tax Movement and Progressivism, 1880-1920". *American Journal of Economics and Sociology* **38** (2): 113–127. doi:10.1111/j.1536-7150.1979.tb02869.x. Retrieved 16 July 2015.

[196] "The Inquisitive Voter". *The Great Adventure* **4** (35). September 11, 1920. The proposition of Henry George will do more to lift humanity from the slough of poverty, crime, and misery than all else.

[197] "Frank Chodorov". Retrieved 30 November 2013.

[198] "Frank Chodorov". Retrieved 30 November 2013.

[199] Eisenstein, Charles. "Post-Capitalism". Retrieved 5 October 2014.

[200] "The Funeral Procession". *New York Times*. November 1, 1897. Retrieved 17 November 2013.

[201] Newlin, Keith (2008). *Hamlin Garland a life*. Lincoln: University of Nebraska Press. pp. 102–127. ISBN 0803233477.

[202] https://www.youtube.com/watch?v=vviBboUXhuA Fred Harrison speaks at ALTER Spring Conference 2014

[203] Aller, Pat. "The Georgist Philosophy in Culture and History". Retrieved 2 October 2014.

[204] Steuer, Max (June 2000). "REVIEW ARTICLE A hundred years of town planning and the influence of Ebenezer Howard". *The British Journal of Sociology* **51** (2): 377–386. doi:10.1111/j.1468-4446.2000.00377.x. Retrieved 5 August 2014.

[205] Meacham, Standish (1999). *Regaining Paradise: Englishness and the Early Garden City Movement*. Yale University Press. pp. 50–53. Retrieved 5 August 2014.

[206] Purdom, Charles Benjamin (1963). *The Letchworth Achievement*. p. 1. Retrieved 5 August 2014.

[207] O'Brian, Edward (1918). *The best American short stories of 1917 and the yearbook of the American short story*. BOSTON SMALL, MAYNARD & COMPANY PUBLISHERS. Retrieved 17 October 2015.

[208] Harrison, F. (May–June 1989). "Aldous Huxley on 'the Land Question'". *Land & Liberty*. "Huxley redeems himself when he concedes that, if he were to rewrite the book, he would offer a third option, one which he characterised as 'the possibility of sanity.' In a few bold strokes he outlines the elements of this model: 'In this community economics would be decentralist and Henry Georgian, politics Kropotkinesque and co-operative.'"

[209] Kunstler, James Howard (1998). *Home from Nowhere: Remaking Our Everyday World For the 21st Century*. Simon and Schuster. pp. Chapter 7.

[210] Lora, Ronald; Longton, William Henry, eds. (1999). *The Conservative Press in Twentieth-century America*. Greenwood Publishing, Inc. p. 310. "Thus, the *Freeman* was to speak for the great tradition of classical liberalism, which [Albert Jay Nock and Francis Nielson] were afraid was being lost, and for the economics of Henry George, which both men shared."

[211] Norris, Kathleen. "The Errors of Marxism". Retrieved 21 November 2013.

[212] Sinclair, Upton. "The Consequences of Land Speculation are Tenantry and Debt on the Farms, and Slums and Luxury in the Cities". Retrieved 3 November 2014.Sinclair was an active georgist but eventually gave up on explicitly advocating the reform because, "Our opponents, the great rich bankers and land speculators of California, persuaded the poor man that we were going to put all taxes on this poor man's lot."

[213] Gaffney, Mason. "Excerpts from The Corruption of Economics". Retrieved 3 November 2014.

[214] *A Great Iniquity.*. Leo Tolstoy once said of George, "*People do not argue with the teaching of George, they simply do not know it*".

[215] Lebrun, Victor. "Leo Tolstoy and Henry George". Retrieved 9 September 2014.

[216] Starr, Kevin (1997). *The dream endures : California enters the 1940s*. New York: Oxford University Press. ISBN 0195157974. Wood had "strong leanings toward the single-tax theory of Henry George".

[217] Barnes, Tim. "C.E.S. Wood (1852-1944)". The Oregon Encyclipedia. Retrieved 14 December 2014.

[218] Buckley, William F. Jr. "FIRING LINE: Has New York Let Us Down?" (PDF). *http://www.schalkenbach.org/*. PBS. Retrieved 6 November 2014. External link in |website= (help)Buckly says, "The location problem is, of course, easily solved by any Georgist, and I am one."

[219] Perry, Jeffrey (2009). *Hubert Harrison the voice of Harlem radicalism, 1883-1918*. New York: Columbia University Press. ISBN 023113911X.

[220] Sklar, Dusty. "Henry George and Zionism". Retrieved 28 October 2014.

[221] Kinsley, Michael (Jun 13, 2012). "Inequality: It's Even Worse Than We Thought". Bloomberg. BloombergView. Retrieved 31 October 2014.

[222] Kinsley, Michael. "The Capital-Gains Tax: A Tragedy in Two Acts" (Dec 19, 2012). Retrieved 31 October 2014.Kinsley reiterates that George is his favorite economist and that land taxes are the best source of revenue.

[223] "The Land Question Quotations from Historical and Contemporary Sources". Retrieved 31 October 2014.In The New Republic (February 12, 1992) Kinsley advocates removing all taxes and collecting land rent instead.

[224] Chamberlain, John (1965). *Farewell To Reform*. Quadrangle Books. pp. 47–48.

[225] Bernstein, David (May 2003). "Lochner's Feminist Legacy". *Michigan Law Review* **101** (6). Retrieved 23 December 2014.

[226] Matthews, Dylan (January 7, 2014). "Five conservative reforms millennials should be fighting for". The Washington Post. Wonkblog. Retrieved 26 August 2014.

[227] https://twitter.com/dylanmatt/status/414149160775204864 Dylan Matthews's verified account states, "I think we've both been Georgists for a while now."

[228] Lawson, R (2006). *A commonwealth of hope : the New Deal response to crisis*. Baltimore: Johns Hopkins University Press. ISBN 0801884063.

[229] Salam, Reihan (July 15, 2010). "On Property Taxes". Retrieved 19 March 2015.

[230] Traubel, Horace (1896). "Progress and Poverty". *The Conservator* **7–9**: 252–253. Retrieved 13 December 2015.

[231] Martin Wolf (2010-07-08). "Why we must halt the land cycle". The Financial Times. Retrieved 2013-10-02.

[232] Merryn Somerset Webb (2013-09-27). "How a levy based on location values could be the perfect tax". The Financial Times. Retrieved 2013-10-02.

[233] https://twitter.com/iddqkfa/status/468204465057566720

[234] Smith, Charles Joseph (January–February 1941). "Forty Years of the Struggle for Freedom". *Land and Freedom* **XLI** (1). Retrieved 30 October 2014.

[235] Filler, Louis (1993). *The muckrakers*. Stanford, Calif: Stanford University Press.

[236] Miller, Joseph Dana (ed.), 1917. Single Tax Year Book. NY: Single Tax Review Publishing Company

[237] Worstall, Tim (2012-12-22). "What Michael Kinsley Gets Wrong About Taxation". Forbes. Retrieved 23 August 2014.

[238] Matthew, Yglesias. "My Five-Point Plan for Fixing Everything". Retrieved 7 November 2013.

[239] https://twitter.com/mattyglesias/status/313754546486796288 "WSJ story on Georgism fails to note that it's clearly correct"

[240] Wineapple, Brenda. Sister Brother: Gertrude and Leo Stein. Lincoln: U of Nebraska, 2008.

[241] Mills, Allen. "Single Tax, Socialism and the Independent Labour Party of Manitoba: The Political Ideas of F.J. Dixon and S.J. Farmer." Labour / Le Travail 5 (1980): 33-56. JSTOR. Web. 04 Dec. 2014. <http://www.jstor.org/stable/10.2307/25139947?ref=no-x-route:ace15c2e1d6b230b7bafc46e82f39f89>

[242] Smith, Carl (2008). *Urban Disorder and the Shape of Belief: The Great Chicago Fire, the Haymarket Bomb, and the Model Town of Pullman, Second Edition*. University of Chicago Press. p. 359.

[243] Muse return with new album The Resistance "*Sure, he has already launched into a passionate soliloquy about Geoism (the land-tax movement inspired by the 19th-century political economist Henry George)*".

[244] Co-founder of the Henry George Club, Australia.

[245] Williams, Karl. "Walter Burley Griffin". Retrieved 1 October 2013.

[246] "Henry George, our hero in the battle for the right (Songs of the Hutchinsons)". Retrieved 17 November 2013.

[247] "George Inness (1825–1894)". http://www.metmuseum.org/. The Metropolitan Museum of Art. Retrieved 27 August 2014. External link in |website= (help)

[248] Schor, Esther (2006). *Emma Lazarus*. Random House. Author of "The New Colossus", on the Statue of Liberty, and the poem "Progress and Poverty", named after George's book, of which she said, "The life and thought of no one capable of understanding it can be quite the same after reading it."

[249] Peseroff, Joyce (March–April 2007). "Emma Lazarus". *Tikkun* **22** (2). Retrieved 20 December 2014. Lazarus "supported Henry George's single tax".

[250] Schwartzman, Jack. "A Remembrance of Anna George de Mille and Agnes de Mille". Retrieved 17 November 2013.

[251] Eyman, Scott (2010). *Empire of Dreams: The Epic Life of Cecil B. DeMille*. Simon and Schuster. pp. 29, 47.

[252] Easton, Carol (1996). *No Intermissions The Life of Agnes de Mille*. Da Capo Press.

[253] Louvish, Simon (2008). *Cecil B. DeMille: A Life in Art*. Macmillan. pp. 40, 249.

[254] Eyman, Scott (2010). *Empire of Dreams: The Epic Life of Cecil B. DeMille*. Simon and Schuster. p. 314.

[255] "Henry George, The Scholar" – A Commencement Address Delivered by Francis Neilson at the Henry George School of Social Science, June 3, 1940.

[256] Neilson, Francis (September 1939). "Albert Jay Nock on Henry George – Truth Sets Men Free". *The Freeman*. Retrieved 1 October 2013.

[257] McQueen, Humphrey. A New Britannia. St. Lucia, Qld.: U of Queensland, 2004.

[258] Mills, Benjamin Fay (1911). "Louis Prang, Popularizer of Art". *Vocations, Vocational guidance, Hall & Locke Company* **10**: 254. Retrieved 13 December 2015.

[259] Taylor, Mark (2010). *Arden*. Arcadia Publishing. p. 8.

[260] Shields, Jerry. "Forgotten Writings of Arden's Frank Stephens". Collecting Delaware Books.

[261] "Frank Lloyd Wright on Henry George's Remedy". Wealthandwant.com. Retrieved 2012-07-26.

[262] Carlson, Allan. *The New Agrarian Mind: The Movement Toward Decentralist Thought in Twentieth-Century America* Transaction Publishers, 2004 (p. 51).

[263] Buttenheim, Harold S. (March 1934). "The Relation of Housing to Taxation". *Law and Contemporary Problems*. 1, No. 2 (Low-Cost Housing and Slum Clearance: A Symposium): 198–205. doi:10.2307/1189565. Retrieved 23 October 2013.

[264] Butler, Nicholas. "Progress and Poverty" (PDF). *Commencement Speech, Columbia University (1931)*. Retrieved 23 October 2013.

[265] Daly, Herman (1994). *For the Common Good: Redirecting the Economy Toward Community, the Environment, and a Sustainable Future*. Beacon Press. pp. 258–259, 328–329.

[266] http://www.wealthandwant.com/HG/PP/Dewey_Appreciation_HG.html

[267] Onken, Werner. "The Political Economy of Silvio Gesell: A Century of Activism." American Journal of Economics and Sociology 59.4 (2000): 609-22. Web. 16 Aug. 2014.

[268] "The Life of Leon MacLaren". Retrieved 25 January 2014.

[269] "The School of Economic Science". Retrieved 25 January 2014.

[270] Mace, Elisabeth. "The economic thinking of Jose Marti: Legacy foundation for the integration of America". Retrieved 5 August 2015.

[271] Hudson, Michael. "Speech to the Communist Party of Cuba". Retrieved 5 August 2015.

[272] Van Parijs, Philippe (1992). *Introduction to Arguing for Basic Income* (PDF). London: Verso. pp. 3–43.

[273] Sterba, James P. (2013). *From Rationality to Equality*. Oxford University Press. p. 193.

[274] Bertrand Russell (1992). *The Basic Writings of Bertrand Russell, 1903–1959*. Psychology Press. p. 492.

[275] Bertrand Russell (1962). *Freedom versus Organization*. W. W. Norton & Company.

[276] http://www.cooperativeindividualism.org/russell-bertrand_admiration-for-henry-george-1960.jpg Letter addressed to a Mr. Krumreig

[277] Vallentyne, Peter. *Left-libertarianism: A Primer*. In Vallentyne, Peter; Steiner, Hillel (2000). "Left-libertarianism and Its Critics: The Contemporary Debate". Houndmills, Basingstoke, Hampshire: Palgrave Publishers Ltd. "Georgist libertarians—such as eponymous George (1879, 1892), Steiner (1977, 1980, 1981, 1992, 1994), and Tideman (1991, 1997, 1998)—hold that agents may appropriate unappropriated natural resources as long as they pay for the competitive value of the rights they claim."

[278] Babson, Roger (Aug 20, 1943). "Roger Babson Sees Many Changes To Come After the War Has Ended". The Evening Independent. Retrieved 22 August 2014.

[279] Two lettrs written in 1934 to Henry George's daughter, Anna George De Mille. In one letter Einstein writes, "The spreading of these works is a really deserving cause, for our generation especially has many and important things to learn from Henry George."

[280] Elazar, Daniel (February 4, 1955). "Earth Is the Lord's". https://www.newspapers.com/. The Wisconsin Jewish Chronicle. Retrieved 23 November 2014. External link in |publisher= (help)

[281] Wilhelm, Donald (September 5, 1942). "Henry Ford Talks About War and Your Future". Liberty Magazine. Retrieved 23 November 2014. Henry Ford says, "[. . .]every American family can have a piece of land. We ought to tax all idle land the way Henry George said — tax it heavily, so that its owners would have to make it productive"

[282] MacCallum, Spencer H. (Summer–Fall 1997). "The Alternative Georgist Tradition" (PDF). *Fragments* **35**. Retrieved 30 October 2014.

[283] Foldvary, Fred E. (April 2004). "Heath: Estranged Georgist". *American Journal of Economics and Sociology* **63** (2): 411–431. doi:10.1111/j.0002-9246.2004.00295.x. Retrieved 30 October 2014.

[284] Justice for Mumia Abu-Jamal

[285] http://schalkenbach.org/the-georgist-news/all/GN2/GN2-2.htm. Retrieved 1 October 2013. Missing or empty |title= (help)

[286] Kennedy, Margrit. "Money & The Land Grab". *YouTube*. Share the Rents. Retrieved 12 December 2013.

[287] Lincoln, John. "Fighting For Fundamentals". Retrieved 5 December 2013.

[288] Magie invented *The Landlord's Game*, predecessor to *Monopoly*

[289] Dodson, Edward J. "How Henry George's Principles Were Corrupted Into the Game Called Monopoly". Retrieved 1 October 2013.

[290] Gaffney, Mason. "Henry George Dr. Edward McGlynn & Pope Leo XIII" (PDF). Retrieved 25 January 2014.

[291] "OFFERS $250,000 FOR SINGLE TAX CAMPAIGN; Joseph Fels Pledges That Sum for Five Years Here and in England. IF THERE IS AN EQUAL FUND Commission of Single Taxers Formed to Raise the Fund -- Roosevelt, Taft, and Hughes Said to be Friendly.". New York Times. May 8, 1909. Retrieved 30 October 2014.

[292] Thomas B. Buell (1974). *The Quiet Warrior*. Boston: Little, Brown.

[293] "American Single Taxers Invade Tiny Andorra; Fiske Warren Carries Their Gospel to the Republic Hidden for Twelve Centuries in the Pyrenees Between France and Spain". *New York Times*. April 16, 1916. Retrieved 9 December 2013.

[294] Sinclair, Upton. "The Consequences of Land Speculation are Tenantry and Debt on the Farms, and Slums and Luxury in the Cities". Retrieved 29 July 2014.

[295] Stanley, Buder (1990). *Visionaries and Planners: The Garden City Movement and the Modern Community*. Oxford University Press. Wallace described Progress and Poverty as "Undoubtedly the most remarkable and important book of the present century."

[296] Dudden, Arthur (1971). *Joseph Fels and the single tax movement*. Temple University Press.

2.27.8 External links

- Robert Schalkenbach Foundation

2.28 Gift economy

A **gift economy**, **gift culture**, or **gift exchange** is a mode of exchange where valuables are not traded or sold, but rather given without an explicit agreement for immediate or future rewards.[1] This contrasts with a barter economy or a market economy, where goods and services are primarily exchanged for value received. Social norms and custom govern gift exchange. Gifts are not given in an explicit exchange of goods or services for money or some other commodity.[2]

The nature of gift economies forms the subject of a foundational debate in anthropology. Anthropological research into gift economies began with Bronisław Malinowski's description of the Kula ring[3] in the Trobriand Islands during World War I.[4] The Kula trade appeared to be gift-like since Trobrianders would travel great distances over dangerous seas to give what were considered valuable objects without any guarantee of a return. Malinowski's debate with the French anthropologist Marcel Mauss quickly established the complexity of "gift exchange" and introduced a series of technical terms such as reciprocity, inalienable possessions, and prestation to distinguish between the different forms of exchange.[5][6]

According to anthropologists Maurice Bloch and Jonathan Parry, it is the unsettled relationship between market and non-market exchange that attracts the most attention. Gift economies are said, by some,[7] to build communities, and that the market serves as an acid on those relationships.[8]

Gift exchange is distinguished from other forms of exchange by a number of principles, such as the form of property rights governing the articles exchanged; whether gifting forms a distinct "sphere of exchange" that can be characterized as an "economic system"; and the character of the social relationship that the gift exchange establishes. Gift ideology in highly commercialized societies differs from the "prestations" typical of non-market societies. Gift economies must also be differentiated from several closely related phenomena, such as common property regimes and the exchange of non-commodified labour.

2.28.1 Principles of gift exchange

According to anthropologist Jonathan Parry, discussion on the nature of gifts, and of a separate sphere of gift exchange that would constitute an economic system, has been plagued by the ethnocentric use of modern, western, market society-based conception of the gift applied as if it were a cross-cultural, pan-historical universal. However, he claims that anthropologists, through analysis of a variety of cultural and historical forms of exchange, have established that no universal practice exists.[9] His classic summation of the gift exchange debate highlighted that ideologies of the "pure gift" "are most likely to arise in highly differentiated societies with an advanced division of labour and a significant commercial sector" and need to be distinguished from non-market "prestations."[10] According to Weiner, to speak of a "gift economy" in a non-market society is to ignore the distinctive features of their exchange relationships, as the early classic debate between Bronislaw Malinowski and Marcel Mauss demonstrated.[5][6] Gift exchange is frequently "embedded" in political, kin, or religious institutions, and therefore does not constitute an "economic" system per se.[11]

Property and alienability

Gift-giving is a form of transfer of property rights over particular objects. The nature of those property rights varies from society to society, from culture to culture, and are not universal. The nature of gift-giving is thus altered by the type of property regime in place.[12]

Property is not a thing, but a relationship amongst people about things.[13] According to Hann, property is a social relationship that governs the conduct of people with respect to the use and disposition of things. Anthropologists analyze these relationships in terms of a variety of actors' (individual or corporate) "bundle of rights" over objects.[12] An example is the current debates around intellectual property rights.[14][15][16][17][18] Hann and Strangelove both give the example of a purchased book (an object that he owns), over which the author retains a "copyright". Although the book is a commodity, bought and sold, it has not been completely "alienated" from its creator who maintains a hold over it; the owner of the book is limited in what he can do with the book by the rights of the creator.[19][20] Weiner has argued that the ability to give while retaining a right to the gift/commodity is a critical feature of the gifting cultures described by Malinowski and Mauss, and explains, for example, why some gifts such as Kula valuables return to their original owners after an incredible journey around the Trobriand islands. The gifts given in Kula exchange still remain, in some respects, the property of the giver.[6]

In the example used above, "copyright" is one of those bundled rights that regulate the use and disposition of a book. Gift-giving in many societies is complicated because "private property" owned by an individual may be quite limited in scope (see 'The Commons' below).[12] Productive resources, such as land, may be held by members of a corporate group (such as a lineage), but only some members of that group may have "use rights". When many people hold rights over the same objects gifting has very different implications than the gifting of private property; only some of the rights in that object may be transferred, leaving that object still tied to its corporate owners. Anthropologist Annette Weiner refers to these types of objects as "inalienable possessions" and to the process as "keeping while giving."[6]

Gift vs prestation

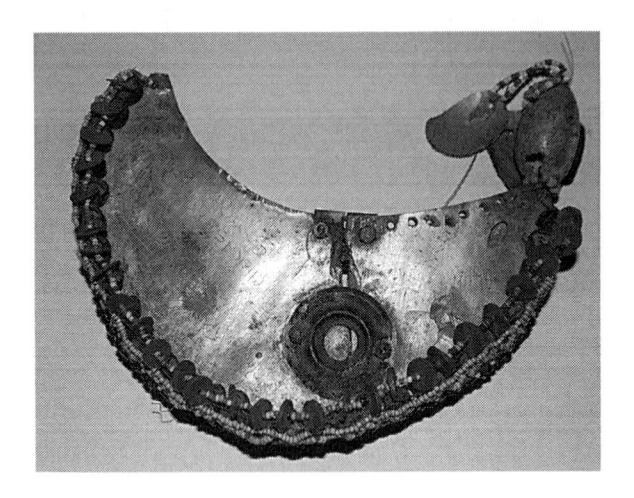

A Kula necklace, with its distinctive red shell-disc beads, from the Trobriand Islands.

Malinowski's study of the Kula ring[21] became the subject of debate with the French anthropologist, Marcel Mauss, author of "The Gift" ("Essai sur le don," 1925).[5] In Parry's view, Malinowski placed the emphasis on the exchange of goods between *individuals*, and their non-altruistic motives for giving the gift: they expected a return of equal or greater value. Malinowski states that reciprocity is an implicit part of gifting; there is no such thing as the "free gift" given without expectation.[22]

Mauss, in contrast, emphasized that the gifts were not between individuals, but between representatives of larger collectivities. These gifts were, he argued, a "total prestation." A prestation is a service provided out of a sense of obligation, like "community service".[23] They were not simple, alienable commodities to be bought and sold, but, like the "Crown jewels", embodied the reputation, history and sense of identity of a "corporate kin group," such as a line of kings. Given the stakes, Mauss asked "why anyone would give them away?" His answer was an enigmatic concept, "the spirit of the gift." Parry believes that a good part of the confusion (and resulting debate) was due to a bad translation. Mauss appeared to be arguing that a return gift is given to keep the very relationship between givers alive; a failure to return a gift ends the relationship and the promise of any future gifts.

Both Malinowski and Mauss agreed that in non-market societies, where there was no clear institutionalized economic exchange system, gift/prestation exchange served economic, kinship, religious and political functions that could not be clearly distinguished from each other, and which mutually influenced the nature of the practice.[22]

Inalienable possessions

Watercolor by James G. Swan depicting the Klallam people of chief Chetzemoka at Port Townsend, with one of Chetzemoka's wives distributing potlatch.

Mauss' concept of "total prestations" was further developed by Annette Weiner, who revisited Malinowski's fieldsite in the Trobriand Islands. Her critique was twofold: first, Trobriand Island society is matrilineal, and women hold a great deal of economic and political power. Their exchanges were ignored by Malinowski. Secondly, she developed Mauss' argument about reciprocity and the "spirit of the gift" in terms of "inalienable possessions: the paradox of keeping while giving."[6] Weiner contrasts "moveable goods" which can be exchanged with "immoveable goods" that serve to draw the gifts back (in the Trobriand case, male Kula gifts with women's landed property). She argues that the specific goods given, like Crown Jewels, are so identified with particular groups, that even when given, they are not truly alienated. Not all societies, however, have these kinds of goods, which depend upon the existence of particular kinds of kinship groups. French anthropologist Maurice Godelier[24] pushed the analysis further in "The Enigma of the Gift" (1999). Albert Schrauwers has argued that the kinds of societies used as examples by Weiner and Godelier (including the Kula ring in the Trobriands, the Potlatch of the Indigenous peoples of the Pacific Northwest Coast, and the Toraja of South Sulawesi, Indonesia) are all characterized by ranked aristocratic kin groups that fit with Claude Lévi-Strauss' model of "House Societies" (where "House" refers to both noble lineage and their landed estate). Total prestations are given, he argues, to preserve landed estates identified with particular kin groups and maintain their place in a ranked society.[25]

Reciprocity and the "spirit of the gift"

According to Chris Gregory reciprocity is a dyadic exchange relationship that we characterize, imprecisely, as gift-giving. Gregory believes that one gives gifts to friends and potential enemies in order to establish a relationship, by placing them in debt. He also claimed that in order for such a relationship to persist, there must be a time lag between the gift and counter-gift; one or the other partner must always be in debt, or there is no relationship. Marshall Sahlins has stated that birthday gifts are an example of this.[26] Sahlins notes that birthday presents are separated in time so that one partner feels the obligation to make a return gift; and to forget the return gift may be enough to end the relationship. Gregory has stated that without a relationship of debt, there is no reciprocity, and that this is what distinguishes a gift economy from a "true gift" given with no expectation of return (something Sahlins calls 'generalized reciprocity', see below).[27]

Marshall Sahlins, an American cultural anthropologist, identified three main types of reciprocity in his book *Stone Age Economics* (1972). Gift or *generalized reciprocity* is the exchange of goods and services without keeping track of their exact value, but often with the expectation that their value will balance out over time. *Balanced or Symmetrical reciprocity* occurs when someone gives to someone else, expecting a fair and tangible return at a specified amount, time, and place. Market or *Negative reciprocity* is the exchange of goods and services where each party intends to profit from the exchange, often at the expense of the other. Gift economies, or generalized reciprocity, occurred within closely knit kin groups, and the more distant the exchange partner, the more balanced or negative the exchange became.[26]

Within the virtual world the proliferation of public domain content, Creative Common Licences, and Open Source projects have also contributed to what it might be considered an economics game changer variable.[28]

Charity, debt, and the "poison of the gift"

Jonathan Parry has argued that ideologies of the "pure gift" "are most likely to arise only in highly differentiated societies with an advanced division of labour and a significant commercial sector" and need to be distinguished from the non-market "prestations" discussed above.[10] Parry also underscored, using the example of charitable giving of alms in India (Dāna), that the "pure gift" of alms given with no expectation of return could be "poisonous." That is, the gift of alms embodying the sins of the giver, when given to ritually pure priests, saddled these priests with impurities that they could not cleanse themselves of. "Pure gifts" given without a return, can place recipients in debt, and hence in dependent status: the poison of the gift.[29] David Graeber points out that no reciprocity is expected between unequals: if you make a gift of a dollar to a beggar, he will not give it back the next time you meet. More than likely, he will ask for more, to the detriment of his status.[30] Many who are forced by circumstances to accept charity feel stigmatized. In the Moka exchange system of Papua New Guinea, where gift givers become political Big men, those who are in their debt and unable to repay with "interest" are referred to as "Rubbish men."

In *La part Maudite* Georges Bataille, the French writer, uses Mauss's argument in order to construct a theory of economy: the structure of gift is the presupposition for all possible economy. Bataille is particularly interested in the potlatch as described by Mauss, and claims that its agonistic character obliges the receiver of the gift to confirm their own subjection. Gift-giving thus embodies the Hegelian dipole of master and slave within the act.

Spheres of exchange and 'economic systems'

The relationship of new market exchange systems to indigenous non-market exchange remained a perplexing question for anthropologists. Paul Bohannan argued that the Tiv of Nigeria had three spheres of exchange, and that only certain kinds of goods could be exchanged in each sphere; each sphere had its own different form of special purpose money. However, the market and universal money allowed goods to be traded between spheres and thus served as an acid on established social relationships.[31] Jonathan Parry and Maurice Bloch, argued in "Money and the Morality of Exchange" (1989), that the "transactional order" through which long-term social reproduction of the family takes place has to be preserved as separate from short-term market relations.[32] It is the long-term social reproduction of the family that is sacralized by religious rituals such baptisms, weddings and funerals, and characterized by gifting.

In such situations where gift-giving and market exchange were intersecting for the first time, some anthropologists contrasted them as polar opposites. This opposition was classically expressed by Chris Gregory in his book "Gifts and Commodities" (1982). Gregory argued that

> Commodity exchange is an exchange of *alienable* objects between people who are in a state of reciprocal *independence* that establishes a *quantitative* relationship between the *objects* exchanged... Gift exchange is an exchange of *inalienable* objects between people who are in a state of reciprocal *dependence* that establishes a *qualitative* relationship between the *transactors* (emphasis added).[33]

Gregory opposes gift and commodity exchange according to five criteria:

Other anthropologists, however, refused to see these different "exchange spheres" as such polar opposites. Marilyn Strathern, writing on a similar area in Papua New Guinea, dismissed the utility of the opposition in "The Gender of the Gift" (1988).[34]

Wedding rings: commodity or pure gift?

Rather than emphasize how particular kinds of objects are either gifts or commodities to be traded in **restricted** spheres of exchange, Arjun Appadurai and others began to look at how objects flowed between these spheres of exchange (i.e. how objects can be converted into gifts and then back into commodities). They refocussed attention away from the character of the human relationships formed through exchange, and placed it on "the social life of things" instead. They examined the strategies by which an object could be "singularized" (made unique, special, one-of-a-kind) and so withdrawn from the market. A marriage ceremony that transforms a purchased ring into an irreplaceable family heirloom is one example; the heirloom, in turn, makes a perfect gift. Singularization is the reverse of the seemingly irresistible process of commodification. They thus show how all economies are a constant flow of material objects that enter and leave specific exchange spheres. A similar approach is taken by Nicholas Thomas, who examines the same range of cultures and the anthropologists who write on them, and redirects attention to the "entangled objects" and their roles as both gifts and commodities.[35]

Proscriptions

Many societies have strong prohibitions against turning gifts into trade or capital goods. Anthropologist Wendy James writes that among the Uduk people of northeast Africa there is a strong custom that any gift that crosses subclan boundaries must be consumed rather than invested.[36]:4 For example, an animal given as a gift must be eaten, not bred. However, as in the example of the Trobriand armbands and necklaces, this "perishing" may not consist of consumption as such, but of the gift moving on. In other societies, it is a matter of giving some other gift, either directly in return or to another party. To keep the gift and not give another in exchange is reprehensible. "In folk tales," Lewis Hyde remarks, "the person who tries to hold onto a gift usually dies."[36]:5

Daniel Everett, a linguist who studied a small tribe of hunter-gatherers in Brazil,[37] reported that, while they are aware of food preservation using drying, salting, and so forth, they reserve the use of these techniques for items for barter outside of the tribe. Within the group, when someone has a successful hunt they immediately share the abundance by inviting others to enjoy a feast. Asked about this practice, one hunter laughed and replied, "I store meat in the belly of my brother."[38][39]

Carol Stack's *All Our Kin* describes both the positive and negative sides of a network of obligation and gratitude effectively constituting a gift economy. Her narrative of The Flats, a poor Chicago neighborhood, tells in passing the story of two sisters who each came into a small inheritance. One sister hoarded the inheritance and prospered materially for some time, but was alienated from the community. Her marriage ultimately broke up, and she integrated herself back into the community largely by giving gifts. The other sister fulfilled the community's expectations, but within six weeks had nothing material to show for the inheritance but a coat and a pair of shoes.[36]:75–76

2.28.2 Case studies: Prestations

Marcel Mauss was careful to distinguish "gift economies" (reciprocity) in market-based societies from the "total prestations" given in non-market societies. A prestation is a service provided out of a sense of obligation, like "community service."[23] These "prestations" bring together domains that we would differentiate as political, religious, legal, moral and economic, such that the exchange can be seen to be embedded in non-economic social institutions. These prestations are frequently competitive, as in the Potlatch, Kula exchange, and Moka exchange.[40]

Moka exchange in Papua New Guinea: competitive exchange

Main article: Moka exchange

The *Moka* is a highly ritualized system of exchange in the Mount Hagen area, Papua New Guinea, that has become emblematic of the anthropological concepts of "gift economy" and of "Big man" political system. Moka are recip-

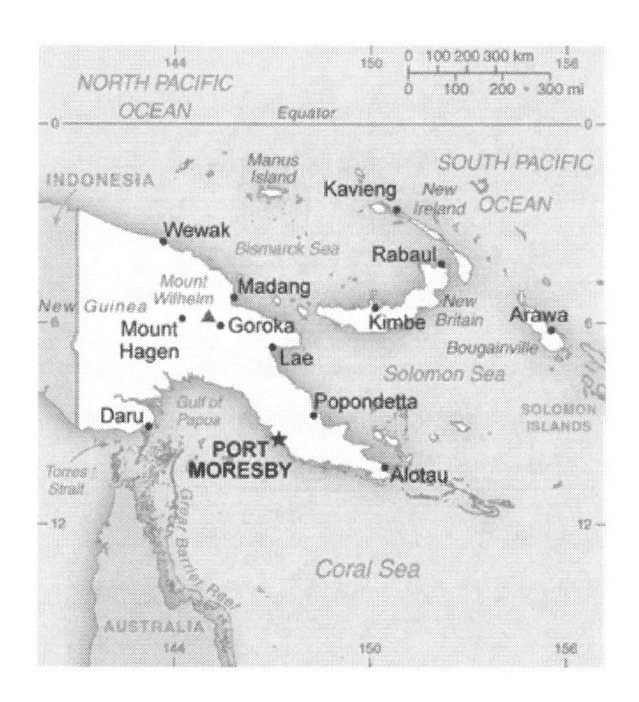

Mount Hagen, Papua New Guinea.

Three tongkonan noble houses in a Torajan village.

Ritual slaughter of gift cattle at a funeral.

rocal gifts of pigs through which social status is achieved. Moka refers specifically to the increment in the size of the gift.[41] Social status in the 'Big man' political system is the result of giving larger gifts than one has received. These gifts are of a limited range of goods, primarily pigs and scarce pearl shells from the coast. To return the same amount as one has received in a moka is simply the repayment of a debt, strict reciprocity. Moka is the extra. To some, this represents interest on an investment. However, one is not bound to provide moka, only to repay the debt. One adds moka to the gift to increase one's prestige, and to place the receiver in debt. It is this constant renewal of the debt relationship which keeps the relationship alive; a debt fully paid off ends further interaction. Giving more than one receives establishes a reputation as a Big man, whereas the simple repayment of debt, or failure to fully repay, pushes one's reputation towards the other end of the scale, Rubbish man.[42] Gift exchange thus has a political effect; granting prestige or status to one, and a sense of debt in the other. A political system can be built out of these kinds of status relationships. Sahlins characterizes the difference between status and rank by highlighting that Big man is not a role; it is a status that is shared by many. The Big man is "not a prince OF men," but a "prince among men." The Big man system is based upon the ability to persuade, rather than command.[43]

Toraja funerals: the politics of meat distribution

The Toraja are an ethnic group indigenous to a mountainous region of South Sulawesi, Indonesia.[44] Torajans are renowned for their elaborate funeral rites, burial sites carved into rocky cliffs, and massive peaked-roof traditional houses known as *tongkonan* which are owned by noble families. Membership in a Tongkonan is inherited by all descendants of its founders. Any individual Toraja may thus be a member of numerous Tongkonan, as long as they contribute to its ritual events. Membership in a Tongkonan carries benefits, such as the right to rent some of its rice fields.[45]

Toraja funeral rites are important social events, usually attended by hundreds of people and lasting for several days. The funerals are like Big men competitions where all the descendants of a Tongkonan will compete through gifts of sacrificial cattle. Participants will have invested cattle with others over the years, and will now draw on those extended networks to make the largest gift. The winner of the competition becomes the new owner of the Tongkonan and its rice lands. They display all the cattle horns from their winning sacrifice on a pole in front of the Tongkonan.[45]

The Toraja funeral differs from the Big Man system in that the winner of the "gift" exchange gains control of the Tongkonan's property. It creates a clear social hierarchy between the noble owners of the Tongkonan and its land, and the commoners who are forced to rent their fields from him. Since the owners of the Tongkonan gain rent, they are better able to compete in the funeral gift exchanges, and their social rank is more stable than the Big man system.[45]

2.28.3 Charity and alms giving

Main article: Alms

Anthropologist David Graeber has argued that the great world religious traditions on charity and gift giving emerged almost simultaneously during the "Axial age" (the period between 800 to 200 BCE), which was the same period in which coinage was invented and market economies established on a continental basis. These religious traditions on charity emerge, he argues, as a reaction against the nexus formed by coinage, slavery, military violence and the market (a "military-coinage" complex). The new world religions, including Hinduism, Judaism, Buddhism, Confucianism, Christianity, and Islam all sought to preserve "human economies" where money served to cement social relationships rather than purchase things (including people).[46]

Charity and alms-giving are religiously sanctioned voluntary gifts given without expectation of return. Case studies demonstrate, however, that such gift-giving is not necessarily altruistic.[47]

Merit making in Buddhist Thailand

Theravada Buddhism in Thailand emphasizes the importance of giving alms (merit making) without any intention of return (a pure gift), which is best accomplished according to doctrine, through gifts to monks and temples. The emphasis is on the selfless gifting which "earns merit" (and a future better life) for the giver rather than on the relief of the poor or the recipient on whom the gift is bestowed. Bowie's research among poorer Thai farmers shows, however, that this ideal form of gifting is limited to the rich who have the resources to endow temples, or sponsor the ordination of a monk.[48] Monks come from these same families, hence the doctrine of pure gifting to monks has a class element to it. Poorer farmers place much less emphasis on merit making through gifts to monks and temples. They equally validate gifting to beggars. Poverty and famine is widespread amongst these poorer groups, and by validating gift-giving to beggars, they are in fact demanding that the rich see to their needs in hard times. Bowie sees this as

Young Burmese monk

an example of a moral economy (see below) in which the poor use gossip and reputation as a means of resisting elite exploitation and pressuring them to ease their "this world" suffering.[49]

Charity: Dana in India

Dāna is a form of religious charity given in Hindu India. The gift is said to embody the sins of the giver (the 'poison of the gift'), who it frees of evil by transmitting it to the recipient. The merit of the gift is dependent on finding a worthy recipient such as a Brahmin priest. Priests are supposed to be able to digest the sin through ritual action and transmit the gift with increment to someone of greater worth. It is imperative that this be a true gift, with no reciprocity, or the evil will return. The gift is not intended to create any relationship between donor and recipient, and there should never be a return gift. Dana thus transgresses the so-called universal 'norm of reciprocity'.[10]

The Children of Peace in Canada

The Children of Peace (1812–1889) were a utopian Quaker sect. Today, they are primarily remembered for the Sharon Temple, a national historic site and an architectural symbol

Sharon Temple.

of their vision of a society based on the values of peace, equality and social justice. They built this ornate temple to raise money for the poor, and built the province of Ontario's first shelter for the homeless. They took a lead role in the organization of the province's first co-operative, the Farmers' Storehouse, and opened the province's first credit union. The group soon found that the charity they tried to distribute from their Temple fund endangered the poor. Accepting charity was a sign of indebtedness, and the debtor could be jailed without trial at the time; this was the 'poison of the gift.' They thus transformed their charity fund into a credit union that loaned small sums like today's micro-credit institutions. This is an example of singularization, as money was transformed into charity in the Temple ceremony, then shifted to an alternate exchange sphere as a loan. Interest on the loan was then singularized, and transformed back into charity.[50]

2.28.4 Gifting as non-commodified exchange in market societies

Non-commodified spheres of exchange exist in relation to the market economy. They are created through the processes of singularization as specific objects are de-commodified for a variety of reasons and enter an alternate exchange sphere. As in the case of organ donation, this may be the result of an ideological opposition to the "traffic in humans." In other cases, it is in opposition to the market and to its perceived greed. It may, however, be used by corporations as a means of creating a sense of endebtedness and loyalty in customers. It is very interesting that modern marketing techniques often aim at infusing commodity exchange with features of gift exchange, thus blurring the presumably sharp distinction between gifts and commodities.[51]

Organ transplant networks, sperm and blood banks

Blood donation poster, WW II.

Main article: Organ gifting

Market economies tend to reduce everything - "including human beings, their labor, and their reproductive capacity" to the status of commodities. The rapid transfer of organ transplant technology to the third world has created a trade in organs, with sick bodies travelling to the global south for transplants, and healthy organs from the global south being transported to the richer global north, "creating a kind of 'Kula ring' of bodies and body parts."[52] However, all commodities can also be singularized, or de-commodified, and transformed into gifts. In North America, it is illegal to sell organs, and citizens are enjoined to give the "gift of life" and donate their organs in an organ gift economy.[53] However, this gift economy is a "medical realm rife with potent forms of mystified commodification."[54] This multimillion-dollar medical industry requires clients to pay steep fees for the gifted organ, which creates clear class divisions between those who donate (frequently in the global south) and will never benefit from gifted organs, and those who can pay the fees and thereby receive the gifted organ.[53]

Unlike body organs, blood and semen have been successfully and legally commodified in the United States. Blood and semen can thus be commodified, but once consumed are "the gift of life." Although both can be either donated or sold; are perceived as the 'gift of life' yet are stored in 'banks'; and can be collected only under strict government regulated procedures, recipients very clearly prefer altruistically donated semen and blood. Ironically, the blood and semen samples with the highest market value are those that have been altruistically donated. The recipients view semen as storing the potential characteristics of their unborn child in its DNA, and value altruism over greed.[55] Similarly, gifted blood is the archetype of a pure gift relationship because the donor is only motivated by a desire to help others.[56]

Copyleft vs copyright: the gift of 'free' speech

Main article: Copyleft

Engineers, scientists and software developers have created open-source software projects such as the Linux kernel and the GNU operating system. They are prototypical examples for the gift economy's prominence in the technology sector and its active role in instating the use of permissive free software and copyleft licenses, which allow free reuse of software and knowledge. Other examples include file-sharing and open access.

Points: Loyalty programs

Main article: Loyalty program

Many retail organizations have "gift" programs meant to encourage customer loyalty to their establishments. Bird-David and Darr refer to these as hybrid "mass-gifts" which are neither gift nor commodity. They are called mass-gifts because they are given away in large numbers "free with purchase" in a mass-consumption environment. They give as an example two bars of soap in which one is given free with purchase: which is the commodity and which the gift? The mass-gift both affirms the distinct difference between gift and commodity while confusing it at the same time. As with gifting, mass-gifts are used to create a social relationship. Some customers embrace the relationship and gift whereas others reject the gift relationship and interpret the "gift" as a 50% off sale.[57]

Free shops

Main article: Give-away shop
"Give-away shops", "freeshops" or "free stores" are stores

Inside Utrecht Giveaway shop. The banner reads "The earth has enough for everyone's need, but not for everyone's greed."

where all goods are free. They are similar to charity shops, with mostly second-hand items—only everything is available at no cost. Whether it is a book, a piece of furniture, a garment or a household item, it is all freely given away, although some operate a one-in, one-out–type policy (swap shops). The free store is a form of constructive direct action that provides a shopping alternative to a monetary framework, allowing people to exchange goods and services outside of a money-based economy. The anarchist 1960s countercultural group The Diggers[58] opened free stores which simply gave away their stock, provided free food, distributed free drugs, gave away money, organized free music concerts, and performed works of political art.[59] The Diggers took their name from the original English Diggers[60] led by Gerrard Winstanley and sought to create a mini-society free of money and capitalism.[61] Although free stores have not been uncommon in the United States since the 1960s, the freegan movement has inspired the establishment of more free stores. Today the idea is kept alive by the new generations of social centres, anarchists and environmentalists who view the idea as an intriguing way to raise awareness about consumer culture and to promote the reuse of commodities.

Burning Man

Main article: Burning Man
Burning Man is a week-long annual art and community event held in the Black Rock Desert in northern Nevada, in the United States. The event is described as an experiment in community, radical self-expression, and radical

Black Rock City, the temporary settlement created in the Nevada Desert for Burning Man, 2010.

self-reliance. The event outlaws commerce (except for ice, coffee, and tickets to the event itself)[62] and encourages gifting.[63] Gifting is one of the 10 guiding principles,[64] as participants to Burning Man (both the desert festival and the year-round global community) are encouraged to rely on a gift economy. The practice of gifting at Burning Man is also documented by the 2002 documentary film "Gifting It: A Burning Embrace of Gift Economy",[65] as well as by Making Contact's radio show "How We Survive: The Currency of Giving [encore]".[63]

Cannabis market in the District of Columbia

Voters in the District of Columbia have legalized the growing of cannabis for personal recreational use by approving Initiative 71 in November 2014, but the 2015 "Cromnibus" Federal appropriations bills prevented the District from creating a system to allow for its commercial sale. Possession, growth, and use of the drug by adults is legal in the District, as is giving it away, but sale and barter of it is not, in effect creating a gift economy.[66]

2.28.5 Related concepts

Mutual aid

Many anarchists, particularly anarcho-primitivists and anarcho-communists, believe that variations on a gift economy may be the key to breaking the cycle of poverty. Therefore, they often desire to refashion all of society into a gift economy. Anarcho-communists advocate a gift economy as an ideal, with neither money, nor markets, nor central planning. This view traces back at least to Peter Kropotkin, who saw in the hunter-gatherer tribes he had visited the

The Conquest of Bread by Peter Kropotkin, influential work which presents the economic vision of anarcho-communism.

paradigm of "mutual aid".[67] In place of a market, anarcho-communists, such as those who inhabited some Spanish villages in the 1930s, support a currency-less gift economy where goods and services are produced by workers and distributed in community stores where everyone (including the workers who produced them) is essentially entitled to consume whatever they want or need as payment for their production of goods and services.[68]

As an intellectual abstraction, mutual aid was developed and advanced by mutualism or labor insurance systems and thus trade unions, and has been also used in cooperatives and other civil society movements. Typically, mutual-aid groups will be free to join and participate in, and all activities will be voluntary. They are often structured as non-hierarchical, non-bureaucratic non-profit organizations, with members controlling all resources and no external financial or professional support. They are member-led and member-organized. They are egalitarian in nature, and designed to support participatory democracy, equality of member status and power, and shared leadership and cooperative decision-making. Members' external societal status is considered irrelevant inside the group: status in the group is conferred by participation.[69]

Moral economy

English historian E.P. Thompson wrote of the moral economy of the poor in the context of widespread English food riots in the English countryside in the late eighteenth century. According to Thompson these riots were generally peaceable acts that demonstrated a common political culture rooted in feudal rights to "set the price" of essential goods in the market. These peasants held that a traditional "fair price" was more important to the community than a "free" market price and they punished large farmers who sold their surpluses at higher prices outside the village while there were still those in need within the village. A moral economy is thus an attempt to preserve an alternate exchange sphere from market penetration.[70][71] The notion of a peasants with a non-capitalist cultural mentalité using the market for their own ends has been linked to subsistence agriculture and the need for subsistence insurance in hard times. James C. Scott points out, however, that those who provide this subsistence insurance to the poor in bad years are wealthy patrons who exact a political cost for their aid; this aid is given to recruit followers. The concept of moral economy has been used to explain why peasants in a number of colonial contexts, such as the Vietnam War, have rebelled.[72]

The commons

Main articles: Commons and The tragedy of the commons

Some may confuse common property regimes with gift exchange systems. "Commons" refers to the cultural and natural resources accessible to all members of a society, including natural materials such as air, water, and a habitable earth. These resources are held in common, not owned privately.[73] The resources held in common can include everything from natural resources and common land to software.[74] The commons contains public property and private property, over which people have certain traditional rights. When commonly held property is transformed into private property this process alternatively is termed "enclosure" or more commonly, "privatization." A person who has a right in, or over, common land jointly with another or others is called a commoner.[75]

There are a number of important aspects that can be used to describe true commons. The first is that the commons cannot be commodified – if they are, they cease to be commons. The second aspect is that unlike private property, the commons are inclusive rather than exclusive — their nature is to share ownership as widely, rather than as narrowly, as possible. The third aspect is that the assets in commons are meant to be preserved regardless of their return of capital. Just as we receive them as a shared right, so we have a duty to pass them on to future generations in at least the same condition as we received them. If we can add to their value, so much the better, but at a minimum we must not degrade them, and we certainly have no right to destroy them.[76]

The new intellectual commons: Free content

Main article: Free content

Free content, or free information, is any kind of functional work, artwork, or other creative content that meets the definition of a free cultural work.[77] A free cultural work is one which has no significant legal restriction on people's freedom:

- to use the content and benefit from using it,
- to study the content and apply what is learned,
- to make and distribute copies of the content,
- to change and improve the content and distribute these derivative works.[78][79]

Although different definitions are used, free content is legally similar if not identical to open content. An analogy is the use of the rival terms free software and open source which describe ideological differences rather than legal ones.[80]

Free content encompasses all works in the public domain and also those copyrighted works whose licenses honor and uphold the freedoms mentioned above. Because copyright law in most countries by default grants copyright holders monopolistic control over their creations, copyright content must be explicitly declared free, usually by the referencing or inclusion of licensing statements from within the work.

Though a work which is in the public domain because its copyright has expired is considered free, it can become non-free again if the copyright law changes.[81]

Information is particularly suited to gift economies, as information is a nonrival good and can be gifted at practically no cost (zero marginal cost).[82][83] In fact, there is often an advantage to using the same software or data formats as others, so even from a selfish perspective, it can be advantageous to give away one's information.

Filesharing Markus Giesler in his ethnography *Consumer Gift System*, described music downloading as a system of social solidarity based on gift transactions.[84] As

Internet access spread, file sharing became extremely popular among users who could contribute and receive files on line. This form of gift economy was a model for online services such as Napster, which focused on music sharing and was later sued for copyright infringement. Nonetheless, online file sharing persists in various forms such as Bit Torrent and Direct download link. A number of communications and intellectual property experts such as Henry Jenkins and Lawrence Lessig have described file-sharing as a form of gift exchange which provides numerous benefits to artists and consumers alike. They have argued that file sharing fosters community among distributors and allows for a more equitable distribution of media.

Free and open-source software In his essay "Homesteading the Noosphere", noted computer programmer Eric S. Raymond said that free and open-source software developers have created "a 'gift culture' in which participants compete for prestige by giving time, energy, and creativity away".[85] Prestige gained as a result of contributions to source code fosters a social network for the developer; the open source community will recognize the developer's accomplishments and intelligence. Consequently, the developer may find more opportunities to work with other developers. However, prestige is not the only motivator for the giving of lines of code. An anthropological study of the Fedora community, as part of a master's study at the University of North Texas in 2010-11, found that common reasons given by contributors were "learning for the joy of learning and collaborating with interesting and smart people". Motivation for personal gain, such as career benefits, was more rarely reported. Many of those surveyed said things like, "Mainly I contribute just to make it work for me", and "programmers develop software to 'scratch an itch'".[86] The International Institute of Infonomics at the University of Maastricht, in the Netherlands, reported in 2002 that in addition to the above, large corporations, and they specifically mentioned IBM, also spend large annual sums employing developers specifically for them to contribute to open source projects. The firms' and the employees' motivations in such cases are less clear.[87]

Members of the Linux community often speak of their community as a gift economy.[88] The IT research firm IDC valued the Linux kernel at $18 billion USD in 2007 and projected its value at $40 billion USD in 2010.[89] The Debian distribution of the GNU/Linux operating system offers over 37,000 free open-source software packages via their AMD64 repositories alone.[90]

Collaborative works Collaborative works are works created by an open community. For example, Wikipedia – a free online encyclopedia – features millions of articles developed collaboratively, and almost none of its many authors and editors receive any direct material reward.[91][92]

2.28.6 See also

- Knowledge market
- Basic income
- Brownie points
- Egoboo
- Food swap
- Giving circles
- History of money
- Calculation in kind
- Reciprocity in cultural anthropology
- Post-scarcity economy
- Pay it forward

2.28.7 Notes

[1] Cheal, David J (1988). "1". *The Gift Economy*. New York: Routledge. pp. 1–19. ISBN 0415006414. Retrieved 2009-06-18.

[2] R. Kranton: *Reciprocal exchange: a self-sustaining system*, American Economic Review, V. 86 (1996), Issue 4 (September), p. 830-51

[3] Malinowski, Bronislaw (1922). *Argonauts of the Western Pacific*. London.

[4] Keesing, Roger; Strathern, Andrew (1988). *Cultural Anthropology. A Contemporary Perspective*. Fort Worth: Harcourt Brace and Company. p. 165.

[5] Mauss, Marcel (1970). *The Gift: Forms and Functions of Exchange in Archaic Societies*. London: Cohen & West.

[6] Weiner, Annette (1992). *Inalienable Possessions: The Paradox of Keeping-while-Giving*. Berkeley: University of California Press.

[7] Bollier, David. "The Stubborn Vitality of the Gift Economy." Silent Theft: The Private Plunder of Our Common Wealth. First Printing ed. New York: Routledge, 2002. 38-39. Print.

[8] J. Parry, M. Bloch (1989). *"Introduction"* in *Money and the Morality of Exchange*. Cambridge: Cambridge University Press. pp. 8–12.

2.28. GIFT ECONOMY

[9] Parry, Jonathan (1986). "The Gift, the Indian Gift and the 'Indian Gift'". *Man* **21** (3): 453–473. doi:10.2307/2803096.

[10] Parry, Jonathan (1986). "The Gift, the Indian Gift and the 'Indian Gift'". *Man* **21** (3): 467. doi:10.2307/2803096.

[11] Gregory, Chris (1982). *Gifts and Commodities*. London: Academic Press. pp. 6–9.

[12] Hann, C.M. (1998). *Property Relations: Renewing the Anthropological Tradition*. Cambridge: Cambridge University Press. p. 4.

[13] Sider, Gerald M. (1980). "The Ties That Bind: Culture and Agriculture, Property and Propriety in the Newfoundland Village Fishery". *Social History* **5** (1): 2–3, 17. doi:10.1080/03071028008567469.

[14] Coleman, Gabriella (2004). "The Political Agnosticism of Free and Open Source Software and the Inadvertent Politics of Contrast". *Anthropological Quarterly* **77** (3): 507–19. doi:10.1353/anq.2004.0035.

[15] Levitt, Leon (1987). "On property, Intellectual Property, the Culture of Property, and Software Pirating". *Anthropology of Work Review* **8** (1): 7–9. doi:10.1525/awr.1987.8.1.7.

[16] Friedman, Jonathan (1999). "The Cultural Life of Intellectual Properties: Authorship, Appropriation, and the Law". *American Ethnologist* **26** (4): 1001–2. doi:10.1525/ae.1999.26.4.1001.

[17] Aragon, Lorraine; James Leach (2008). "Arts and Owners: Intellectual property law and the politics of scale in Indonesian Arts". *American Ethnologist* **35** (4): 607–31. doi:10.1111/j.1548-1425.2008.00101.x.

[18] Coombe, Rosemary J. (1993). "Cultural and Intellectual Properties: Occupying the Colonial Imagination". *PoLAR: Political and Legal Anthropology Review* **16** (1): 8–15. doi:10.1525/pol.1993.16.1.8.

[19] Chris Hann, Keith Hart (2011). *Economic Anthropology: History, Ethnography, Critique*. Cambridge: Polity Press. p. 158.

[20] Strangelove, Michael (2005). *The Empire of Mind: Digital Piracy and the Anti-Capitalist Movement*. Toronto: University of Toronto Press. pp. 92–6.

[21] Malinowski, Bronislaw (1984) [1922]. *Argonauts of the Western Pacific : an account of native enterprise and adventure in the archipelagoes of Melanesian New Guinea*. Prospect Heights, Ill.: Waveland Press.

[22] Parry, Jonathan (1986). "The Gift, the Indian Gift and the 'Indian Gift'". *Man* **21** (3): 466–69. doi:10.2307/2803096.

[23] Hann, Chris, Hart, Keith (2011). *Economic Anthropology: History, Ethnography, Critique*. Cambridge: Polity Press. p. 50.

[24] Godelier, Maurice (1999). *The Enigma of the Gift*. Cambridge: Polity Press.

[25] Schrauwers, Albert (2004). "H(h)ouses, E(e)states and class: On the importance of capitals in central Sulawesi". *Bijdragen tot de Taal-, Land- en Volkenkunde* **160** (1): 72–94. doi:10.1163/22134379-90003735.

[26] Sahlins, Marshall (1972). *Stone Age Economics*. Chicago: Aldine-Atherton. ISBN 0-202-01099-6.

[27] Gregory, Chris (1982). *Gifts and Commodities*. London: Academic Press. pp. 189–194.

[28] Arellano, Gabriela. "Hot Embers News: Gratuity and Gratitude as Game Changers." N.p., 13 Nov. 2015. Web. 04 Dec. 2015.

[29] Parry, Jonathan (1986). "The Gift, the Indian Gift and the 'Indian Gift'". *Man* **21** (3): 463–67. doi:10.2307/2803096.

[30] Graeber, David (2001). *Toward an Anthropological Theory of Value: The false coin of our own dreams*. New York: Palgrave. p. 225.

[31] Bohannan, Paul (1959). "The Impact of money on an African subsistence economy". *The Journal of Economic History* **19** (4): 491–503. doi:10.1017/S0022050700085946.

[32] Parry, Jonathan; Maurice Bloch (1989). *Money and the Morality of Exchange*. Cambridge: Cambridge University Press. pp. 28–30.

[33] Gregory, Chris (1982). *Gifts and Commodities*. London: Academic Press. pp. 100–101.

[34] Strathern, Marilyn (1988). *The Gender of the Gift: Problems with Women and Problems with Society in Melanesia*. Berkeley: University of California Press. pp. 143–7.

[35] Thomas, Nicholas (1991). *Entangled Objects: Exchange, Material Culture, and Colonialism in the Pacific*. Cambridge, MA: Harvard University Press.

[36] *Lewis Hyde: The Gift: Imagination and the Erotic Life of Property*, pg. 18

[37] Everett, Daniel L. (Aug–Oct 2005). "Cultural Constraints on Grammar and Cognition in Pirahã: Another Look at the Design Features of Human Language". *Current Anthropology* **46** (4): 621–646. doi:10.1086/431525.

[38] Curren, Erik (2012). "Charles Eisenstein wants to devalue your money to save the economy". Transition Voice. Retrieved 9 February 2013.

[39] Eisenstein, Charles (2007). "2". *The Ascent of Humanity*. Harrisburg, PA: Pananthea Press. ISBN 978-0977622207. Retrieved 9 February 2013.

[40] Graeber, David (2001). *Toward an Anthropological Theory of Value*. Basingstoke: Palgrave. p. 153.

[41] Gregory, C.A. (1982). *Gifts and Commodities*. London: Academic Press. p. 53.

[42] Gregory, C.A. (1982). *Gifts and Commodities*. London: Academic Press. pp. 53–54.

[43] Sahlins, Marshall (1963). "Poor Man, Rich Man, Big-Man, Chief: Political Types in Melanesia and Polynesia". *Comparative Studies in Society and History*. 3 **5**: 294–7. doi:10.1017/s0010417500001729.

[44] "Tana Toraja official website" (in Indonesian). Archived from the original on May 29, 2006. Retrieved 2006-10-04.

[45] Schrauwers, Albert (2004). "H(h)ouses, E(e)states and class; On the importance of capitals in central Sulawesi". *Bijdragen tot de Taal-, Land- en Volkenkunde* **160** (1): 83–86. doi:10.1163/22134379-90003735.

[46] Graeber, David (2011). *Debt: The first 5,000 years*. New York: Melville House. pp. 223–49.

[47] Bowie, Katherine (1998). "The Alchemy of Charity: Of class and Buddhism in Northern Thailand". *American Anthropologist* **100** (2): 469–81. doi:10.1525/aa.1998.100.2.469.

[48] Bowie, Katherine (1998). "The Alchemy of Charity: Of class and Buddhism in Northern Thailand". *American Anthropologist* **100** (2): 473–4. doi:10.1525/aa.1998.100.2.469.

[49] Bowie, Katherine (1998). "The Alchemy of Charity: Of class and Buddhism in Northern Thailand". *American Anthropologist* **100** (2): 475–7. doi:10.1525/aa.1998.100.2.469.

[50] Schrauwers, Albert (2009). *'Union is Strength': W.L. Mackenzie, The Children of Peace and the Emergence of Joint Stock Democracy in Upper Canada*. Toronto: University of Toronto Press. pp. 97–124.

[51] "Features of gift exchange in market economy"

[52] Schepper-Hughes, Nancy (2000). "The Global Traffic in Human Organs". *Current Anthropology* **41** (2): 193. doi:10.1086/300123.

[53] Schepper-Hughes, Nancy (2000). "The Global Traffic in Human Organs". *Current Anthropology* **41** (2): 191–224. doi:10.1086/300123.

[54] Sharp, Lesley A. (2000). "The Commodification of the Body and its Parts". *Annual Review of Anthropology* **29**: 303. doi:10.1146/annurev.anthro.29.1.287.

[55] Tober, Diane M. (2001). "Semen as Gift, Semen as Goods: Reproductive Workers and the Market in Altruism". *Body & Society* **7** (2-3): 137–60. doi:10.1177/1357034x0100700205.

[56] Titmuss, Richard (1997). *The Gift Relationship: From human blood to social policy*. New York: The New Press.

[57] Bird-David, Nurit; Darr, Asaf (2009). "Commodity, gift and mass-gift: on gift-commodity hybrids in advanced mass consumption cultures". *Economy and Society* **38** (2): 304–25. doi:10.1080/03085140902786777.

[58] John Campbell McMillian; Paul Buhle (2003). *The new left revisited*. Temple University Press. pp. 112–. ISBN 978-1-56639-976-0. Retrieved 28 December 2011.

[59] Lytle 2006, pp. 213, 215.

[60] "Overview: who were (are) the Diggers?". *The Digger Archives*. Retrieved 2007-06-17.

[61] Gail Dolgin; Vicente Franco (2007). *American Experience: The Summer of Love*. PBS. Retrieved 2007-04-23.

[62] "What is Burning Man? FAQ - Preparation" Retrieved 10/5/11

[63] "How We Survive: The Currency of Giving (Encore)" Making Contact, produced by National Radio Project. December 21, 2010.

[64] Burning Man principles include Gift Economy

[65] Gifting It: A Burning Embrace of Gift Economy - documentary on IMDB

[66] Barro, Josh. "Can Washington's Gift Economy in Marijuana Work?".

[67] Mutual Aid: A Factor of Evolution (1955 paperback (reprinted 2005), includes Kropotkin's 1914 preface, Foreword and Bibliography by Ashley Montagu, and The Struggle for Existence, by Thomas H. Huxley ed.). Boston: Extending Horizons Books, Porter Sargent Publishers. ISBN 0-87558-024-6. Project Gutenberg e-text, Project LibriVox audiobook

[68] [Augustin Souchy, "A Journey Through Aragon," in Sam Dolgoff (ed.), The Anarchist Collectives, ch. 10]

[69] Turner, Francis J. (2005). *Canadian encyclopedia of social work*. Waterloo, Ont.: Wilfrid Laurier University Press. pp. 337–8. ISBN 0889204365.

[70] Thompson, Edward P. (1991). *Customs in Common*. New York: New Press. p. 341.

[71] Thompson, Edward P. (1991). *Customs in Common*. New York: New Press.

[72] Scott, James C. (1976). *The Moral Economy of the Peasant: Rebellion and subsistence in Southeast Asia*. Princeton: Princeton University Press.

[73] Bollier, David (2002). "Reclaiming the commons". *Boston Review*.

[74] Berry, David (21 February 2005). "The commons". *Free Software Magazine*.

[75] Anon. "Commoner". Farlex Inc. Retrieved 20 April 2012.

[76] Barnes, Peter (2006). *Capitalism 3.0: A Guide to Reclaiming the Commons.* Berrett-Koehler Publishers. ISBN 978-1-57675-361-3.

[77] http://freecontentdefinition.org/Definition

[78] "Definition of Free Cultural Works". Retrieved 8 December 2011.

[79] Stallman, Richard (November 13, 2008). "Free Software and Free Manuals". Free Software Foundation. Retrieved March 22, 2009.

[80] Stallman, Richard. "Why Open Source misses the point of Free Software". Free Software Foundation.

[81] Anderson, Nate (July 16, 2008). "EU caves to aging rockers, wants 45-year copyright extension". Ars Technica. Retrieved August 8, 2008.

[82] Mackaay, Ejan (1990). "Economic Incentives in Markets for Information and Innovation". *Harvard Journal of Law & Public Policy* **13** (909): 867–910.

[83] Heylighen, Francis (2007). "Why is Open Access Development so Successful?". In B. Lutterbeck, M. Barwolff, and R. A. Gehring. *Open Source Jahrbuch.* Lehmanns Media.

[84] Markus Giesler, Consumer Gift Systems

[85] http://catb.org/esr/writings/homesteading/homesteading/

[86] Suehle, Ruth. "An anthropologist's view of an open source community". opensource.com. Retrieved 19 March 2012.

[87] "Free/Libre and Open Source Software: Survey and Study". International Institute of Infonomics, University of Maastricht and Berlecon Research GmbH. 2002. Retrieved 19 March 2012.

[88] Matzan, Jem (5 June 2004). "The gift economy and free software". Retrieved 3 April 2012.

[89] http://www.cioupdate.com/news/article.php/3660141/IDC-Linux-Ecosystem-Worth-40-Billion-by-2010.htm

[90] http://www.debian.org/doc/manuals/debian-reference/ch02.en.html

[91] D. Anthony, S. W. Smith, and T. Williamson, "Explaining quality in internet collective goods: zealots and good samaritans in the case of *Wikipedia*," THanover : Dartmouth College, Technical Report, November 2005.

[92] Anthony, Denise; Smith, Sean W.; Williamson, Tim (April 2007), "The Quality of Open Source Production: Zealots and Good Samaritans in the Case of *Wikipedia*" (PDF), *Technical Report TR2007-606* (Dartmouth College), retrieved 2011-05-29

2.28.8 Further reading

The concept of a gift economy has played a large role in works of fiction about alternate societies, especially in works of science fiction. Examples include:

- *News from Nowhere* (1890) by William Morris is a utopian novel about a society which operates on a gift economy.

- *The Great Explosion* (1962) by Eric Frank Russell describes the encounter of a military survey ship and a Gandhian pacifist society that operates as a gift economy.

- *The Dispossessed* (1974) by Ursula K. Le Guin is a novel about a gift economy society that had exiled themselves from their (capitalist) homeplanet.

- The Mars trilogy, a series of books written by Kim Stanley Robinson in the 1990s, suggests that new human societies that develop away from Earth could migrate toward a gift economy.

- The movie *Pay It Forward* (2000) centers on a schoolboy who, for a school project, comes up with the idea of doing a good deed for another and then asking the recipient to "pay it forward". Although the phrase "gift economy" is never explicitly mentioned, the scheme would, in effect, create one.

- *Down and Out in the Magic Kingdom* (2003) by Cory Doctorow describes future society where rejuvenation and body-enhancement have made death obsolete, and material goods are no longer scarce, resulting in a reputation-based (whuffie) economic system.

- *Wizard's Holiday* (2003) by Diane Duane describes two young wizards visiting a utopian-like planet whose economy is based on gift-giving and mutual support.

- *Voyage from Yesteryear* (1982) by James P. Hogan describes a society of the embryo colonists of Alpha Centauri who have a post-scarcity gift economy.

- *Cradle of Saturn* (1999) and its sequel *The Anguished Dawn* (2003) by James P. Hogan describe a colonization effort on Saturn's largest satellite. Both describe the challenges involved in adopting a new economic paradigm.

- Science fiction author Bruce Sterling wrote a story, *Maneki-neko*, in which the cat-paw gesture is the sign of a secret AI-based gift economy.

- The Gift Economy. Writings and videos of Genevieve Vaughan and associated scholars.

2.29 Human development theory

For other uses, see Human development (disambiguation).

Human development theory is a theory that merges older ideas from ecological economics, welfare economics, and feminist economics. It seeks to avoid the overt normative politics of most so-called "green economics" by justifying its theses strictly in ecology, economics and sound social science, and by working within a context of globalization.[1]

2.29.1 Theory

Like ecological economics it focuses on measuring well-being and detecting uneconomic growth that comes at the expense of human health. However, it goes further in seeking not only to measure but to optimize well-being by some explicit modeling of how social capital and instructional capital can be deployed to optimize the overall value of human capital in an economy - which is itself part of an ecology. The role of individual capital within that ecology, and the adaptation of the individual to live well within it, is a major focus of these theories.[2][3]

The most notable proponents of human development theory are Mahbub ul Haq, Üner Kirdar and Amartya Sen. Amartya Sen asked, in Development as Freedom, "what is the relationship between our wealth and our ability to live as we would like?"

This question cannot be answered strictly from an energy, feminist, family, environmental health, peace, social justice, or ecological well-being point of view, although all of these may be factors in our happiness, and if tolerances of any of these are violated seriously, it would seem impossible to be happy at all.

Accordingly, human development theory is a major synthesis that is probably not confined within the bounds of conventional economics or political science, nor even the political economy that relates the two.

Another angle is *Sustainable Human Development*: Triple Bottom line ecology-economy-social can be translated to human dimensions as:

- Human economy: Sustainable action - the ability to perform well and on long term (stress, priority, focus and time management)
- Human social dimension: Sustainable relations - the ability to sustain relations and go through ordeals together (family, teams, clients, stakeholders)
- Human ecology: Health, self-awareness, vocation, excellence, talent, etc

2.29.2 References

[1] "The Library of Economics and Liberty". *(Econlib)*.

[2] "PsychCrawler". *The American Psychological Association*.

[3] "Classics in the History of Psychology". *Classics in the History of Psychology*.

2.30 Innovation economics

Innovation economics is a growing economic theory that emphasizes entrepreneurship and innovation. Innovation economics is based on two fundamental tenets: that the central goal of economic policy should be to spur higher productivity through greater innovation, and that markets relying on input resources and price signals alone will not always be as effective in spurring higher productivity, and thereby economic growth.

This is in contrast to the two other conventional economic doctrines, neoclassical economics and Keynesian economics.

2.30.1 Historical origins

Joseph Schumpeter introduced innovation economics in his 1942 book *Capitalism, Socialism and Democracy*. In contrast to his contemporary John Maynard Keynes, Schumpeter contended that evolving institutions, entrepreneurs, and technological change were at the heart of economic growth, not independent forces that are largely unaffected by policy. He argued that creative destruction is crucial to capitalism.[1]

But it is only within the last 15 years that a theory and narrative of economic growth focused on innovation that was grounded in Schumpeter's ideas has emerged. Innovation economics attempted to answer the fundamental problem in the puzzle of total factor productivity growth. Continual growth of output could no longer be explained only in increase of inputs used in the production process as understood in industrialization. Hence, innovation economics focused on a theory of economic creativity that would impact the theory of the firm and organization decision-making. Hovering between heterodox economics that emphasized the fragility of conventional assumptions and orthodox economics that ignored the fragility of such assumptions, innovation economics aims for joint didactics between the two. As such, it enlarges the Schumpeterian analyses of new technological system by incorporating new ideas of information and communication technology in the global economy.[2]

Indeed, a new theory and narrative of economic growth focused on innovation has emerged in the last decade. Innovation economics emerges on the wage of other schools of thoughts in economics, including new institutional economics, new growth theory, endogenous growth theory, evolutionary economics, neo-Schumpeterian economics—provides an economic framework that explains and helps support growth in today's knowledge economy.

Leading theorists of innovation economics include both formal economists, as well as management theorists, technology policy experts, and others. These include Paul Romer, Elhanan Helpman, W. Brian Arthur, Robert Axtell, Richard R. Nelson, Richard Lipsey, Michael Porter, Christopher Freeman, Igor Yegorov.

2.30.2 Theory

Innovation economists believe that what primarily drives economic growth in today's knowledge-based economy is not capital accumulation, as claimed by neoclassicalism asserts, but innovative capacity spurred by appropriable knowledge and technological externalities. Economics growth in innovation economics is the end-product of knowledge (tacit vs. codified); regimes and policies allowing for entrepreneurship and innovation (i.e., R&D expenditures, permits, licenses); technological spillovers and externalities between collaborative firms; and systems of innovation that create innovative environments (i.e., clusters, agglomerations, metropolitan areas).[2][3]

In 1970, economist Milton Friedman said in the *New York Times* that a business's sole purpose is to generate profits for their shareholders and companies that pursued other missions would be less competitive, resulting in fewer benefits to owners, employees, and society.[4] Yet data over the past several decades shows that while profits matter, good firms supply far more, particularly in bringing innovation to the market. This fosters economic growth, employment gains, and other society-wide benefits. Business school professor David Ahlstrom asserts: "the main goal of business is to develop new and innovative goods and services that generate economic growth while delivering benefits to society."[5]

In contrast to neoclassical economics, innovation economics offer differing perspectives on main focus, reasons for economic growth, and the assumptions of context between economic actors:

Despite the differences in economic thought, both perspectives are based on the same core premise: the foundation of all economic growth is the optimization of the utilization of factors and the measure of success is how well the factor utilization is optimized. Whatever the factors, it nonetheless leads to the same situation of special endowments, varying relative prices, and production processes. So while, the two differ in theoretical concepts, innovation economics can find fertile ground in mainstream economics, rather than remain in diametric contention.[2]

2.30.3 Evidence

Empirical evidence worldwide points to a positive link between technological innovation and economic performance. The drive of biotech firms in Germany was due to the R&D subsidies to joint projects, network partners, and close cognitive distance of collaborative partners within a cluster. These factors increased patent performance in the biotech industry.[6] Additionally, innovation capacity explains much of the GDP growth in India and China between 1981–2004 but especially in the 1990s. Their development of a **National Innovation System** through heavy investment of R&D expenditures and personnel, patents, and high-tech/service exports strengthened their innovation capacity. By linking the science sector with the business sector, establishing incentives for innovative activities, and balancing the import of technology and indigenous R&D effort, both countries experienced rapid economic growth in recent decades.[7] Also, the Council of Foreign Relations asserted that since the end of the 1970s, the U.S. has gained a disproportionate share of the world's wealth through their aggressive pursuit of technological change, demonstrating that technological innovation is a central catalyst of steady economic performance.[8] Concisely, evidence shows that innovation contributes to steady economic growth and rise in per capita income.[5]

However, some empirical studies investigating the innovation-performance-link lead to rather mixed results and indicate that the relationship be more subtle and complex than commonly assumed.[9] In particular, the relationship between innovativeness and performance seems to differ in intensity and significance across empirical contexts, environmental circumstances, and conceptual dimensions.

All of the above has taken place in an era of data constraint, as identified by Zvi Griliches twenty years ago.[10] Because the primary domain of innovation is commerce the key data resides there; continually out of campus reach in reports hidden within factories, corporate offices and technical centers. This recusal still stymies progress today. Recent attempts at data transference have led, not least, to the 'positive link' (above) being upgraded to exact algebra between R&D productivity and GDP allowing prediction from one to the other. This is pending further disclosure from commercial sources but several pertinent documents are already available.[11]

2.30.4 Geography

While innovation is important, it is not a happenstance occurrence as a natural harbor or natural resources are, but a deliberate, concerted effort of markets, institutions, policymakers, and effect use of geographic space. In global economic restructuring, location has a become key element in establishing competitive advantage as regions focus on their unique assets to spur innovation (i.e., information technology in Silicon Valley, CA; digital media in Seoul, South Korea). Even more, thriving metropolitan economies that carry multiple clusters (i.e., Tokyo, Chicago, London) essentially fuel national economies through their pools of human capital, innovation, quality places, and infrastructure.[12] Cities become "innovative spaces" and "cradles of creativity" as drivers of innovation. They become essential to the system of innovation through the supply side: ready, available, abundant capital and labor; good infrastructure for productive activities, and diversified production structures that spawn synergies and hence innovation. In addition they grow due to the demand side: diverse population of varying occupations, ideas, skills; high and differentiated level of consumer demand; and constant recreation of urban order especially infrastructure of streets, water systems, energy, and transportation.[3]

2.30.5 Worldwide examples

- semiconductors and information technology in Silicon Valley in California
- high-technology and life sciences in Research Triangle Park in North Carolina
- energy companies in Energy Corridor in Houston, Texas
- financial products and services in New York City
- biotechnology in Genome Valley in Hyderabad, India and Boston, Massachusetts
- nanotechnology in Tech Valley, New York (College of Nanoscale Science and Engineering)
- precision engineering in South Yorkshire, United Kingdom
- petrochemical complexes in Rio de Janeiro, Brazil
- train locomotive and rolling stock manufacturing in Beijing, China
- automotive engineering in Baden-Württemberg, Germany
- digital media technologies in Digital Media City in Seoul, South Korea

2.30.6 See also

- Business cluster
- Economic development
- Keynesian economics
- Knowledge economy
- Innovation
- Innovation saturation
- International Innovation Index
- Metropolitan economy
- Neoclassical economics

2.30.7 References

[1] Schumpeter, J. A. (1943). *Capitalism, Socialism, and Democracy* (6th ed.). Routledge. pp. 81–84.

[2] Antonelli, C. (2003). *The Economics of Innovation, New Technologies, and Structural Change*. London: Routledge. ISBN 0415406439.

[3] Johnson, Bjorn (2008). "Cities, systems of innovation and economic development". *Innovation: Management, Policy, and Practice* **10** (2/3): 146–155. doi:10.5172/impp.453.10.2-3.146.

[4] Friedman, M. (September 13, 1970). "A Friedman doctrine—; The Social Responsibility Of Business Is to Increase Its Profits". *New York Times Magazine*.

[5] Ahlstrom, D. (2010). "Innovation and Growth: How Business Contributes to Society". *Academy of Management Perspectives* **24** (3): 11–24. doi:10.5465/AMP.2010.52842948.

[6] Fornahl, D.; Broekel, T.; Boschma, R. (2011). "What drives patent performance of German biotech firms? The impact of R&D subsidies, knowledge networks and their location". *Papers in Regional Science* **90** (2): 395–418. doi:10.1111/j.1435-5957.2011.00361.x.

[7] Peilei, F. (2011). "Innovation capacity and economic development: China and India". *Economic Change and Restructuring* **44** (1/2): 49–73. doi:10.1007/s10644-010-9088-2.

[8] Steil, B.; Victor, D. G.; Nelson, R. R. (2002). *Technological Innovation and Economics Performance. A Council of Foreign Relations Book*. Princeton University Press.

[9] Salge, T. O.; Vera, A. (2009). "Hospital innovativeness and organizational performance". *Health Care Management Review* **34** (1): 54–67 [in particular pp. 56–58]. doi:10.1097/01.HMR.0000342978.84307.80.

[10] Griliches. Z 'Productivity, R&D, and the Data Constraint' *American Economic Review*, Vol. 84, No. 1, (Mar., 1994) pp. 1 – 23

[11] Farrell C.J.'Economics, R&D and Growth',

[12] Mark, M.; Katz, B.; Rahman, S.; Warren, D. (2008). "MetroPolicy: Shaping A New Federal Partnership for a Metropolitan Nation". *Brookings Institution: Metropolitan Policy Program Report* **2008**: 4–103.

2.30.8 Further reading

- Warsh, David (2006). *Knowledge and the Wealth of Nations*. Norton. ISBN 978-0-393-05996-0.

2.30.9 External links

- Innovation Economics: The Economic Doctrine for the 21st Century
- Books and Journal Articles on Innovation Economics
- Innovation Economics: The Integration and Capitalization of Knowledge
- Innovation Economics Roundtable
- Business Week Podcast - Innovation Economics
- Business Models Innovation
- Innovation Economics in practice for city/regional growth and economic development

2.31 Institutional economics

Institutional economics focuses on understanding the role of the evolutionary process and the role of institutions in shaping economic behaviour. Its original focus lay in Thorstein Veblen's instinct-oriented dichotomy between technology on the one side and the "ceremonial" sphere of society on the other. Its name and core elements trace back to a 1919 *American Economic Review* article by Walton H. Hamilton.[1][2]

Institutional economics emphasizes a broader study of institutions and views markets as a result of the complex interaction of these various institutions (e.g. individuals, firms, states, social norms). The earlier tradition continues today as a leading heterodox approach to economics.[3]

A significant variant is the new institutional economics from the later 20th century, which integrates later developments of neoclassical economics into the analysis. Law and economics has been a major theme since the publication of the *Legal Foundations of Capitalism* by John R. Commons in 1924. Since then, there is heated debate on the role of law (formal institution) on economic growth,[4] Behavioral economics is another hallmark of institutional economics based on what is known about psychology and cognitive science, rather than simple assumptions of economic behavior.

Institutional economics focuses on learning, bounded rationality, and evolution (rather than assume stable preferences, rationality and equilibrium). It was a central part of American economics in the first part of the 20th century, including such famous but diverse economists as Thorstein Veblen, Wesley Mitchell, and John R. Commons.[5] Some institutionalists see Karl Marx as belonging to the institutionalist tradition, because he described capitalism as a historically-bounded social system; other institutionalist economists disagree with Marx's definition of capitalism, instead seeing defining features such as markets, money and the private ownership of production as indeed evolving over time, but as a result of the purposive actions of individuals.

"Traditional" institutionalism rejects the *reduction* of institutions to simply tastes, technology, and nature (see naturalistic fallacy).[6] Tastes, along with expectations of the future, habits, and motivations, not only determine the nature of institutions but are limited and shaped by them. If people live and work in institutions on a regular basis, it shapes their world-views. Fundamentally, this traditional institutionalism (and its modern counterpart institutionalist political economy) emphasizes the legal foundations of an economy (see John R. Commons) and the evolutionary, habituated, and volitional processes by which institutions are erected and then changed (see John Dewey, Thorstein Veblen, and Daniel Bromley.)

The vacillations of institutions are necessarily a result of the very incentives created by such institutions, and are thus endogenous. Emphatically, traditional institutionalism is in many ways a response to the current economic orthodoxy; its reintroduction in the form of institutionalist political economy is thus an explicit challenge to neoclassical economics, since it is based on the fundamental premise that neoclassicists oppose: that economics cannot be separated from the political and social system within which it is embedded.

Some of the authors associated with this school include Robert H. Frank, Warren Samuels, Mark Tool, Geoffrey Hodgson, Daniel Bromley, Jonathan Nitzan, Shimshon Bichler, Elinor Ostrom, Anne Mayhew, John Kenneth Galbraith and Gunnar Myrdal, but even the sociologist C. Wright Mills was highly influenced by the institutionalist approach in his major studies.

2.31.1 Thorstein Veblen

Main articles: Thorstein Veblen and The Theory of the Leisure Class

Thorstein Veblen (1857–1929) wrote his first and most influential book while he was at the University of Chicago, on *The Theory of the Leisure Class* (1899).[7] In it he analyzed the motivation in capitalism to conspicuously consume their riches as a way of demonstrating success. Conspicuous leisure was another focus of Veblen's critique. The concept of conspicuous consumption was in direct contradiction to the neoclassical view that capitalism was efficient.

Thorstein Veblen came from rural Mid-western America and Norwegian immigrant family.

In *The Theory of Business Enterprise* (1904) Veblen distinguished the motivations of industrial production for people to use things from business motivations that used, or misused, industrial infrastructure for profit, arguing that the former is often hindered because businesses pursue the latter. Output and technological advance are restricted by business practices and the creation of monopolies. Businesses protect their existing capital investments and employ excessive credit, leading to depressions and increasing military expenditure and war through business control of political power. These two books, focusing on criticism first of consumerism, and second of profiteering, did not advocate change.

Through the 1920s and after the Wall Street Crash of 1929 Thorstein Veblen's warnings of the tendency for wasteful consumption and the necessity of creating sound financial institutions seemed to ring true. Veblen remains a leading critic, which cautions against the excesses of "the American way".

Thorstein Veblen wrote in 1898 an article entitled "Why is Economics Not an Evolutionary Science"[8] and he became the precursor of current evolutionary economics.

2.31.2 John R. Commons

Main article: John R. Commons

John R. Commons (1862–1945) also came from mid-Western America. Underlying his ideas, consolidated in *Institutional Economics* (1934) was the concept that the economy is a web of relationships between people with diverging interests. There are monopolies, large corporations, labour disputes and fluctuating business cycles. They do however have an interest in resolving these disputes.

Commons thought that government should be the mediator between the conflicting groups. Commons himself devoted much of his time to advisory and mediation work on government boards and industrial commissions.

2.31.3 Wesley Mitchell

Main article: Wesley Mitchell

Wesley Clair Mitchell (August 5, 1874 – October 29, 1948) was an American economist known for his empirical work on business cycles and for guiding the National Bureau of Economic Research in its first decades. Mitchell's teachers included economists Thorstein Veblen and J. L. Laughlin and philosopher John Dewey.

2.31.4 Clarence Ayres

Main article: Clarence Edwin Ayres

Clarence Ayres (May 6, 1891 – July 24, 1972) was the principal thinker of what some has called the Texas school of institutional economics. Ayres developed on the ideas of Thorstein Veblen with a dichotomy of "technology" and "institutions" to separate the inventive from the inherited aspects of economic structures. He claimed that technology was always one step ahead of the socio-cultural institutions.

It can be argued that Ayres was not an "institutionalist" in any normal sense of the term; since he identified institutions with sentiments and superstition and in consequence institutions only played a kind of residual role in this theory of development which core center was that of technology. Ayres was under strong influence of Hegel and institutions for Ayres had the same function as "Schein" (with the connotation of deception, and illusion) for Hegel. A more appropriate name for Ayres' position would be that of a "techno-behaviorist" rather than an institutionalist.

2.31.5 Adolf Berle

Main article: Adolf Berle

Adolf A. Berle (1895–1971) was one of the first authors to combine legal and economic analysis, and his work stands as a founding pillar of thought in modern corporate governance. Like Keynes, Berle was at the Paris Peace Conference, 1919, but subsequently resigned from his diplomatic job dissatisfied with the Versailles Treaty terms. In his book with Gardiner C. Means, *The Modern Corporation and Private Property* (1932), he detailed the evolution in the contemporary economy of big business, and argued that those who controlled big firms should be better held to account.

Directors of companies are held to account to the shareholders of companies, or not, by the rules found in company law statutes. This might include rights to elect and fire the management, require for regular general meetings, accounting standards, and so on. In 1930s America, the typical company laws (e.g. in Delaware) did not clearly mandate such rights. Berle argued that the unaccountable directors of companies were therefore apt to funnel the fruits of enterprise profits into their own pockets, as well as manage in their own interests. The ability to do this was supported by the fact that the majority of shareholders in big public companies were single individuals, with scant means of communication, in short, divided and conquered.

Berle served in President Franklin Delano Roosevelt's administration through the depression, and was a key member of the so-called "Brain trust" developing many of the New Deal policies. In 1967, Berle and Means issued a revised edition of their work, in which the preface added a new dimension. It was not only the separation of controllers of companies from the owners as shareholders at stake. They posed the question of what the corporate structure was really meant to achieve.

> "Stockholders toil not, neither do they spin, to earn [dividends and share price increases]. They are beneficiaries by position only. Justification for their inheritance... can be founded only upon social grounds... that justification turns on the distribution as well as the existence of wealth. Its force exists only in direct ratio to the number of individuals who hold such wealth. Justification for the stockholder's existence thus depends on increasing distribution within the American population. Ideally the stockholder's position will be impregnable only when every American family has its fragment of that position and of the wealth by which the opportunity to develop individuality becomes fully actualized."[9]

2.31.6 John Kenneth Galbraith

Main article: John Kenneth Galbraith

John Kenneth Galbraith (1908–2006) worked in the New Deal administration of Franklin Delano Roosevelt. Although he wrote later, and was more developed than the earlier institutional economists, Galbraith was critical of orthodox economics throughout the late twentieth century. In *The Affluent Society* (1958), Galbraith argues voters reaching a certain material wealth begin to vote against the common good. He coins the term "conventional wisdom" to refer to the orthodox ideas that underpin the resulting conservative consensus.[10]

In an age of big business, it is unrealistic to think only of markets of the classical kind. Big businesses set their own terms in the marketplace, and use their combined resources for advertising programmes to support demand for their own products. As a result, individual preferences actually reflect the preferences of entrenched corporations, a "dependence effect", and the economy as a whole is geared to irrational goals.[11]

In *The New Industrial State* Galbraith argues that economic decisions are planned by a private bureaucracy, a technostructure of experts who manipulate marketing and public relations channels. This hierarchy is self-serving, profits are no longer the prime motivator, and even managers are not in control. Because they are the new planners, corporations detest risk, requiring steady economic and stable markets. They recruit governments to serve their interests with fiscal and monetary policy.

While the goals of an affluent society and complicit government serve the irrational technostructure, public space is simultaneously impoverished. Galbraith paints the picture of stepping from penthouse villas on to unpaved streets, from landscaped gardens to unkempt public parks. In *Economics and the Public Purpose* (1973) Galbraith advocates a "new socialism" (social democracy) as the solution, with nationalization of military production and public services such as health care, plus disciplined salary and price controls to reduce inequality and hamper inflation.

2.31.7 New institutional economics

Main article: New institutional economics

With the new developments in the economic theory of organizations, information, property rights,[12] and transaction costs,[13] an attempt was made to integrate institutionalism into more recent developments in mainstream economics, under the title new institutional economics.[14]

2.31.8 Institutionalism today

The earlier approach was a central element in American economics in the interwar years after 1919 but was marginalized to a relatively minor role as to mainstream economics in the postwar period with the ascendence of neoclassical and Keynesian approaches. It continued, however, as a leading heterodox approach in critiquing neoclassical economics and as an alternative research program in economics, most notably through the work of Ha-Joon Chang and Geoffrey Hodgson

The leading Swedish economist Lars Pålsson Syll is a believer in institutional economics.[15] He is an outspoken opponent to all kinds of social constructivism and postmodern relativism.[16]

2.31.9 Criticism

Critics of institutionalism have maintained that the concept of "institution" is so central for all social science that it is senseless to use it as a buzzword for a particular theoretical school. And as a consequence the elusive meaning of the concept of "institution" has resulted in a bewildering and never-ending dispute about which scholars are "institutionalists" or not—and a similar confusion about what is supposed to be the core of the theory. In other words, institutional economics have become so popular because it means all things to all people, which in the end of the day is the meaning of nothing.[17]

Indeed, it can be argued that the term "institutionalists" was misplaced from the very beginning, since Veblen, Hamilton and Ayres were preoccupied with the evolutionary (and "objectifying") forces of technology and institutions had a secondary place within their theories. Institutions were almost a kind of "anti-stuff," their key concern was on technology and not on institutions. Rather than being "institutional," Veblen, Hamilton and Ayres position is anti-institutional.[17]

2.31.10 Journals

- *Journal of Economic Issues* and article-abstract links to 2008.

- *Journal of Institutional Economics* with links to selected articles and to article abstracts.

- *Journal of Institutional and Theoretical Economics*

2.31.11 See also

- History of economic thought

- Economic sociology

- Historical school of economics, a related school developed in Prussia

- Institutional logic

- Institutionalist political economy

- Constitutional economics

- New institutionalism

- Perspectives on Capitalism

- Substantivism

2.31.12 Notes

[1] Walton H. Hamilton (1919). "The Institutional Approach to Economic Theory," *American Economic Review*, 9(1), Supplement, p p. 309–318. Reprinted in R. Albelda, C. Gunn, and W. Waller (1987), *Alternatives to Economic Orthodoxy: A Reader in Political Economy*, pp. 204-12.

[2] D.R. Scott, Veblen not an Institutional Economist. The American Economic Review. Vol.23. No.2. June 1933. pp. 274-277.

[3] Warren J. Samuels ([1987] 2008). "institutional economics," *The New Palgrave: A Dictionary of Economics*. Abstract.

[4] Li, Rita Yi Man and Li, Yi Lut (2013) The relationship between law and economic growth: A paradox in China Cities, Asian Social Science, Vol.9, No.9, pp.19-30, http://papers.ssrn.com/sol3/papers.cfm?abstract_id=2290481

[5] Malcolm,Dewey and Reese Rutherford (2008). "institutionalism, old," *The New Palgrave Dictionary of Economics*, 2nd Edition, v. 4, pp. 374-81. Abstract.

[6] http://web.archive.org/web/20090319115301/http://cepa.newschool.edu/het/schools/institut.htm

[7] Heilbroner, Robert (2000) [1953]. *The Worldly Philosophers* (seventh ed.). London: Penguin Books. pp. 221, 228–33, 244. ISBN 978-0-140-29006-6.

[8] Veblen, Th. 1898 "Why is Economics Not an Evolutionary Science", *The Quarterly Journal of Economics*, **12**.

[9] Berle (1967) p. xxiii

[10] Galbraith (1958) Chapter 2 (Although Galbraith claimed to coin the phrase 'conventional wisdom,' the phrase is used several times in a book by Thorstein Veblen that Galbraith might have read, *The Instinct of Workmanship*.)

[11] Galbraith (1958) Chapter 11

[12] Dean Lueck (2008). "property law, economics and," *The New Palgrave Dictionary of Economics*, 2nd Edition. Abstract.

[13] M. Klaes (2008). "transaction costs, history of," *The New Palgrave Dictionary of Economics*, 2nd Edition. Abstract.

[14] • Ronald Coase (1998). "The New Institutional Economics," *American Economic Review*, 88(2), pp. 72–74.
• ____ (1991). "The Institutional Structure of Production," Nobel Prize Lecture PDF, reprinted in 1992, *American Economic Review*, 82(4), pp. 713–719.
• Douglass C. North (1995). "The New Institutional Economics and Third World Development," in *The New Institutional Economics and Third World Development*, J. Harriss, J. Hunter, and C. M. Lewis, ed., pp. 17-26.
• Elinor Ostrom (2005). "Doing Institutional Analysis: Digging Deeper than Markets and Hierarchies," *Handbook of New Institutional Economics*, C. Ménard and M. Shirley, eds. *Handbook of New Institutional Economics*, pp. 819–848. Springer.
• Oliver E. Williamson (2000). "The New Institutional Economics: Taking Stock, Looking Ahead," *Journal of Economic Literature*, 38(3), pp. 595-613.

[15] Gudeman, Stephen (2005). *Peopled Economies: Conversations With Stephen Gudeman*. Staffan Löfving. ISBN 91-974705-6-2.

[16] "LARS PÅLSSON SYLL". Arenagruppen. Retrieved 2012-04-17.

[17] David Hamilton, "Why is Institutional economics not institutional?" The American Journal of Economics and Sociology. Vol.21. no.3. July 1962. pp.309-317.

2.31.13 References

- Kapp, K. William (2011). *The Foundations of Institutional Economics*, Routledge.

- Bromley, Daniel (2006). *Sufficient Reason: Volitional Pragmatism and the Meaning of Economic Institutions*, Princeton University Press.

- Chang, Ha-Joon (2002). *Globalization, Economic Development and the Role of the State*, Zed Books.

- Cheung, Steven N. S. (1970). "The Structure of a Contract and the Theory of a Non-Exclusive Resource," *Journal of Law and Economics*, 13(1), pp. 49–70.

- Commons, John R. (1931). "Institutional Economics," *American Economic Review* Vol. 21 : p p.648–657.

- _____ (1931). "Institutional Economics," *American Economic Review*, Vol. 21, No. 4 (Dec.), Vol. 26, No. 1, (1936): p p. 237–249.

- _____ (1934 [1986]). *Institutional Economics: Its Place in Political Economy*, Macmillan. Description and preview.

- Davis, John B. (2007). "The Nature of Heterodox Economics," *Post-autistic Economics Review, issue no. 40*.

- _____, "Why Is Economics Not Yet a Pluralistic Science?", *Post-autistic Economics Review*, issue no. 43, 15 September, pp. 43–51.

- Easterly, William (2001). "Can Institutions Resolve Ethnic Conflict?" *Economic Development and Cultural Change*, Vol. 49, No. 4), pp. 687-706.

- Fiorito, Luca and Massimiliano Vatiero, (2011). "Beyond Legal Relations: Wesley Newcomb Hohfeld's Influence on American Institutionalism". *Journal of Economics Issues*, 45 (1): 199-222.

- Galbraith, John Kenneth, (1973). "Power & the Useful Economist," *American Economic Review* 63:1-11.

- Hodgson, Geoffrey M. (1998). "The Approach of Institutional Economics," *Journal of Economic Literature*, 36(1), pp. 166-192 (close Bookmarks).

- _____, ed. (2003). *Recent Developments in Institutional Economics*, Elgar. Description and contents.

- _____ (2004). *The Evolution of Institutional Economics: Agency, Structure and Darwinism in American Institutionalism*, London and New York: Routledge.

- Geoffrey M. Hodgson and Thorbjørn Knudsen, "Darwin's Conjecture" *The Montreal Review* (August, 2011).

- Hodgson, Samuels, & Tool (1994). *The Elgar Companion to Institutional & Evolutionary Economics*, Edward Elgar.

- Keaney, Michael, (2002). "Critical Institutionalism: From American Exceptionalism to International Relevance", in *Understanding Capitalism: Critical Analysis From Karl Marx to Amartya Sen*, ed. Doug Dowd, Pluto Press.

- Nicita, A., and M. Vatiero (2007). "The Contract and the Market: Towards a Broader Notion of Transaction?". *Studi e Note di Economia*, 1:7-22.

- North, Douglass C. (1990). *Institutions, Institutional Change and Economic Performance*, Cambridge University Press.

- Elinor Ostrom (2005). "Doing Institutional Analysis: Digging Deeper than Markets and Hierarchies," *Handbook of New Institutional Economics*, C. Ménard and M. Shirley, eds. *Handbook of New Institutional Economics*, pp. 819–848. Springer.

- Rutherford, Malcolm (2001). "Institutional Economics: Then and Now," *Journal of Economic Perspectives*, Vol. 15, No. 3 (Summer), p. 173–194.

- _____ (2011). *The Institutionalist Movement in American Economics, 1918-1947: Science and Social Control*, Cambridge University Press.

- Li, Rita Yi Man (2011). "Everyday Life Application of Neo-institutional Economics: A Global Perspective", Germany, Lambert.

- Schmid, A. Allan (2004). *Conflict & Cooperation: Institutional & Behavioral Economics*, Blackwell.

- Samuels, Warren J. (2007), *The Legal-Economic Nexus*, Routledge.

- From *The New Palgrave Dictionary of Economics* (2008):

    Polterovich, Victor. "institutional traps." Abstract.

    Rutherford, Malcolm. "institutionalism, old." Abstract.

    Samuels, Warren J. [1987]. "institutional economics." Abstract.

2.31.14 External links

- Association for Evolutionary Economics
- World Interdisciplinary Network for Institutional Research
- Douglass North Nobel lecture
- Institutional & Behavioral Economics
- American Institutional School
- Thorstein Veblen,Bibliographi
- T.Veblen:The Leisureclass
- T.Veblen:Why is Economics Not an Evolutionary Science?
- T.Veblen:The Beginning of Ownership av Thorstein Veblen
- T.Veblen (Theory of Business Enterprise)
- Geoffrey Hodgson's website

2.32 Islamic economics

See also: History of Islamic economics

Islamic economics (Arabic: الاقتصاد الإسلامي), is a term used to refer to **Islamic commercial jurisprudence** or *fiqh al-mu'āmalāt* (Arabic: فقه المعاملات), and also to an ideology that takes a middle ground between the systems of Marxism and capitalism, based on the teachings of Islam.[1]

Islamic commercial jurisprudence entails the rules of transacting finance or other economic activity in a *Shari'a* compliant manner,[2][3] i.e., a manner conforming to Islamic

2.32. ISLAMIC ECONOMICS

scripture (Quran and sunnah). Islamic jurisprudence (*fiqh*) has traditionally dealt with determining what is required, prohibited, encouraged, discouraged, or just permissible,[4] according to the revealed word of God (Quran) and the religious practices established by the (Islamic) Prophet (sunnah). This applied to issues like property, money, employment, taxes, along with everything else. The social science of economics,[4] on the other hand, studied how to best achieve certain policy goals, such as full employment, price stability, economic equity and productivity growth.[5]

In the mid-twentieth century, campaigns began promoting the idea of specifically Islamic patterns of economic thought and behavior.[6] By the 1970s, "Islamic economics" was introduced as an academic discipline in a number of institutions of higher learning throughout the Muslim world and in the West.[3] The central features of an Islamic economy are often summarized as: (1) the "behavioral norms and moral foundations" derived from the Quran and Sunnah; (2) collection of *Zakat* and other Islamic taxes, (3) prohibition of interest (*riba*) charged on loans.[7][8][9][10]

Advocates of Islamic economics generally describe it as neither socialist nor capitalist, but as a "third way", an ideal mean with none of the drawbacks of the other two systems.[11][12][13] Among the claims made for an Islamic economic system by Islamic activists and revivalists are that the gap between the rich and the poor will be reduced and prosperity enhanced[14][15] by such means as the discouraging of the hoarding of wealth,[16][17] taxing wealth (through *zakat*) but not trade, exposing lenders to risk through Profit sharing and venture capital,[18][19][20] discouraging of hoarding of food for speculation,[21][22][23] and other sinful activities such as unlawful confiscation of land.[24][25]

2.32.1 Definitions and descriptions

- "that branch of knowledge which helps to realize human well-being through an allocation and distribution of scarce resources that is in conformity with Islamic teachings without unduly curbing individual freedom or creating continued macroeconomic and ecological imbalances." (Umar Chapra)[26]

- "the study of an ... economy which abides by the rules of the Shariah", i.e. an Islamic economy. (A definition used by some, according to M. Anas Zarqa)[27][28]

- "a discipline that is guided by the Shariah and studies all human societies" (A definition used by others, according to M. Anas Zarqa)[27][28]

- "restatements of Islamic economic teachings", using "modern economic jargon". (What most of the knowledge content in the body of Islamic economics amounts to according to economist Muhammad Akram Khan)[29]

- an ideology

  - "a revolutionary ideology" to change "the corrupt reality ... into a pure one", and "not a science of political economy" or "an objective analysis of existing reality". (Ayatollah Murtaza Mutahhari)[30]

  - an "ideological construct" developed by 20th century Islamists (by Abul A'la Maududi, Ayatollah Muhammad Baqir al-Sadr, Abolhassan Banisadr, etc.) taking basic prescriptions from sharia (Islamic law), and systematizing and conceptualizing them "to construct a coherent and functional ensemble offering a middle ground between the two systems of the twentieth century, Marxism and capitalism." (Social scientist Olivier Roy)[1]

2.32.2 History

Further information: History of Islamic economics

Fiqh

Traditional Islamic concepts having to do with economics included:

- *Zakat*—the "charitable taxing of certain assets, such as currency, gold, or harvest, with an eye to allocating these taxes to eight expenditures that are also explicitly defined in the Quran, such as aid to the needy."

- *Gharar*—"uncertainty". The presence of any element of excessive uncertainty, in a contract is prohibited.

- *Riba*—"referred to as usury (modern Islamic economists reached consensus that Riba is any kind of interest, rather than just usury)"[31]

Another source lists "general rules" include prohibition of Riba, Gharar, and

- *Qimar* (gambling)[32] and

- the encouragement of *Taa'won* (mutual cooperation),[32]

- "the overriding doctrine of fairness in commercial dealings is established."[32]

These concepts, like others in Islamic law, came from

> As always in Muslim law, these [economic] concepts are constructed on the basis of isolated prescriptions, anecdotes, examples, words of the Prophet, all gathered together and systematized by commentators according to an inductive, casuistic method." [33]

Sometimes other sources such as al-urf (custom), or al-ijma (consensus of the jurists) were employed.[34]

While Islamic law does distinguish between *ibadat* (ritual worship such as prayer or fasting) or *muamalat* (acts involving interaction and exchange among people such as sales and sureties),[35] a number of scholars (Olivier Roy, Timur Kuran, Omar Norman) have noted the recentness of reflecting on economic issues in the Islamic world,[6][36][37] and the difference between economics the social science, and Islamic economics, i.e. Islamic law or jurisprudence pertaining to economic issues.

Works of fiqh, (such as *The Essential Hanafi Handbook of Fiqh* by Qazi Thanaa Ullah) are typically divided into different "books" (The Book of Imaan, The Book of Salaat, Book of Zakaat, The Book of Taqwa, The Book of Hajj) but not a book of economics.[38] Olivier Roy states that as late as the 1960s, Islamic scholar Ayatollah Ruhollah Khomeini in his work of fatawa *Tawzih al-masa'il*, did not use the term `economics` or `economy`, or combine questions on economic issues in one heading. He approached the subject of economy

> "as the classical ulamas do ... the chapter on selling and buying (*Kharid o forush*) comes after the one on pilgrimage and present economic questions as individual acts open to moral analysis: `To lend [without interest, on a note from the lender] is among the good works that are particularly recommended in the verses of the Quran and in the Traditions.`"[36][39]

Pre-modern Muslim thought on economics

Classical Muslim scholars did however, make valuable contributions to Islamic thought on issues involving production, consumption, income, wealth, property, taxation, land ownership, etc. are Abu Yusuf (d. 798), Al-Mawardi (d. 1058), Ibn Hazm (d. 1064), Al-Sarakhsi (d. 1090), Al-Tusi (d. 1093), Al-Ghazali (d. 1111), Al-Dimashqi (d. after 1175), Ibn Rushd (d. 1187), Ibn Taymiyyah (d.1328), Ibn al-Ukhuwwah (d. 1329), Ibn al-Qayyim (d. 1350), Al-Shatibi (d. 1388), Ibn Khaldun (d. 1406), Al-Maqrizi (d. 1442), Al-Dawwani (d. 1501), and Shah Waliyullah (d. 1762).[40]

Perhaps the most well-known Islamic scholar who wrote about economics issues was Ibn Khaldun,[41][42] who has been call "the father of modern economics" by I.M. Oweiss.[43][44] Ibn Khaldun wrote on what is now called economic and political theory in the introduction, or *Muqaddimah* (*Prolegomena*), of his *History of the World* (*Kitab al-Ibar*). He discussed what he called *asabiyya* (social cohesion), which he cited as the cause of some civilizations becoming great and others not. Ibn Khaldun felt that many social forces are cyclic, although there could be sudden sharp turns that break the pattern.[45]

His idea about the benefits of the division of labor also relate to *asabiyya*, the greater the social cohesion, the more complex the successful division may be, the greater the economic growth. He noted that growth and development positively stimulates both supply and demand, and that the forces of supply and demand are what determines the prices of goods.[46] He also noted macroeconomic forces of population growth, human capital development, and technological developments effects on development.[47] In fact, Ibn Khaldun thought that population growth was directly a function of wealth.[48]

Development of "Islamic Economics"

According to (Timur Kuran), "not until the mid-twentieth century" was there a body of thought that could be called "Islamic economics", that was "recognizable as a coherent or self-contained doctrine". But around 1950 "campaigns launched to identify self-consciously, if not also exclusively, Islamic patterns of economic thought and behavior".[6] Famous 20th Century Muslim nationalist and author Muhammad Iqbal, for example, did not refer to religion in his treatise on economics.[37]

Islamic scholars who considered Islam to be a complete system of life in all its aspects, rather than a spiritual formula[49] believed that it logically followed that Islam defined economic life, unique from and superior to non-Islamic systems. "Islamic economics" "emerged" in the 1940s according to the Encyclopedia of Islam and the Muslim World.[50]

More conservative salafi have shown less interest in socioeconomic issues, asking the question, "the prophet and his companions didn't study `laws` of economics, look for patterns, strive for understanding of what happens in commerce, production, consumption. Why should we?"[36]

1960, 70s

In the 1960s and 1970s, Shi'a thinkers worked to describe Islamic economics' "own answers to contemporary economic problems." Several works were particularly influential:

- *Eslam va Malekiyyat* (Islam and Property) by Mahmud Taleqani (1951),

- *Iqtisaduna* (Our Economics) by Mohammad Baqir al-Sadr (1961) and

- *Eqtesad-e Towhidi* (The Economics of Divine Harmony) by Abolhassan Banisadr (1978)

- *Some Interpretations of Property Rights, Capital and Labor from Islamic Perspective* by Habibullah Peyman (1979).[51][52]

Al-Sadr in particular was described as having "almost single-handedly developed the notion of Islamic economics"[53]

In their writings, Sadr and the other authors "sought to depict Islam as a religion committed to social justice, the equitable distribution of wealth, and the cause of the deprived classes," with doctrines "acceptable to Islamic jurists," while refuting existing non-Islamic theories of capitalism and Marxism. This version of Islamic economics, which influenced the Iranian Revolution, called for public ownership of land and of large "industrial enterprises," while private economic activity continued "within reasonable limits."[54] These ideas informed the large public sector and public subsidy policies of the Iranian Revolution.

Sunni cleric Taqiuddin al-Nabhani proposed economic system (*Nidham ul-Iqtisad fil Islam* (The Economic System of Islam) by Taqiuddin Nabhani (1953)) combined public ownership of large chunks of the economy (utilities, public transport, health care, energy resources such as oil, and unused farm land), with use of the Gold Standard and specific instructions for the gold and silver weights of coins, arguing this would "demolish ... American control and the control of the dollar as an international currency."[55]

In the Sunni world the first international conference on Islamic economics was held at the King Abdulaziz University in Jeddah in 1976. Since then the International Association for Islamic Economics in collaboration with the Islamic Development Bank has held conferences in Islamabad (1983), Kuala Lumpur (1992), Loughborough (2000), Bahrain (2003), Jakarta (2005) and Jeddah (2008), Iqbal (2008).[56] In addition there have been hundreds of seminars, workshops and discussion groups around the world on Islamic economics and finance.[57] In the U.S. a small number of patent applications have been filed for Sharia compliant financial service methods.[58]

Khomeini era

What has been called one of "two versions" of "Islamic economy" existed during the first ten years (1979-1989) of the Islamic Republic of Iran during the life of Supreme Leader (and revolution founder) Ayatollah Ruhollah Khomeini. This was an "Islamist socialist, and state-run": It was "little by little supplanted" by a more liberal economic policy.[59]

Post-socialist trend

In the 1980s and 1990s, as the Islamic revolution failed to reach the per capita income level achieved by the regime it overthrew, and Communist states and socialist parties in the non-Muslim world turned away from socialism, Muslim interest shifted away from government ownership and regulation. In Iran, "*eqtesad-e Eslami* (meaning both Islamic economics and economy) ... once a revolutionary shibboleth, is indubitably absent in all official documents and the media. It disappeared from Iranian political discourse" about 1990.[52] During the era of Zia-ul-Haq, several Islamic economic concepts and practices were introduced into the domestic economy, as part of Zia's Islamisation reforms (see Islamic economics in Pakistan).

In other parts of the Muslim world, however, the term lived on, shifting form to the less ambitious goal of interest-free banking. Some Muslim bankers and religious leaders suggested ways to integrate Islamic law on usage of money with modern concepts of ethical investing. In banking this was done through the use of sales transactions (focusing on the fixed rate return modes) to support investing without interest-bearing debt. Many modern writers have strongly criticized this approach as a means of covering conventional banking with an Islamic facade.[60]

2.32.3 As an academic discipline

Achievements

As of 2008 there were:

- Eight magazines recently started "exclusively devoted to Islamic economics and finance",[61]

- 484 research projects in various universities of ten countries including the US, the UK and Germany.[62]

- 200 Ph.D. dissertations completed at different universities of the world,[62] literature published English, Arabic, Urdu, Bhasa Malaysia, Turkish and other regional languages.[63]

- "Over a thousand unique titles on Islamic economics and finance" in IFP databank[62]

- 1500 conferences (whose proceedings are available in IFP databank)[63][64]

- One school—the Kulliyyah of Economics and Management Sciences of International Islamic University Malaysia (IIUM) -- has produced over 2000 graduates in 25 years as of 2009.[65][66]

King Abdulaziz University, Jeddah hosted the first international conference on Islamic economics in 1976. Thereafter the International Association for Islamic Economics in collaboration with the Islamic Development Bank has held conferences in Islamabad (1983), Kuala Lumpur (1992), Loughborough (2000), Bahrain (2003), Jakarta (2005) and Jeddah (2008) Iqbal 2008).[57]

Challenges

Along with these achievements, some Islamic economists have complained of problems in the academic discipline: a shift in interest away from Islamic Economics to Islamic Finance since the 1980s, a shortage of university courses, reading materials that are "either scant or of poor quality",[67] lack of intellectual freedom,[68] "narrow focus" on interest-free banking and zakat without data-based research to substantiate claim made for them—that interest causes economic problems or that zakat solves them.[69]

A number of economists have lamented that while Islamic Finance was originally a "subset" of Islamic Economics, economics and research in pure Islamic economics has been "shifted to the back burner".[70] Funding for research has gone to Islamic Finance[71] despite the lack of "scientific knowledge to back" the claims made for Islamic Finance.[72] Enrollment has subsided in classes[73] and second and third generation Islamic economists are scarce,[71] some institutions have "lost their real direction and some have even been closed".[74] and interest of economists in the field's "grand idea" of providing an alternative to capitalism and socialism has "yielded" to the "needs" of the "industry" of Islamic Finance.[73][75]

According to economist Rasem Kayed, while a number of universities and institutes of higher learning now offer courses on Islamic economics and finance "most of the courses offered by these institutions pertain to Islamic finance rather than Islamic economics."[76] Surveying Islamic economics and finance courses being offered as of 2008 by 14 universities in Muslim countries, Kayed found 551 courses in conventional economics and finance, and only 12 courses in Islamic economics and finance (only 2% of the total).[76] This "appalling and intolerable ... negligence" was made worse by the curriculum of the courses which failed to debate "the issues" the discipline or give "due thought to ... the future development of Islamic financial industry" but rather attempted "to squeeze as much abstract information" as possible in their courses, according to Kayed.[70][77]

Another economist (Muhammad Akram Khan) lamented that "the real problem is that despite efforts for developing a separate discipline of Islamic economics, there is not much that can be genuinely called `economics`. Most of Islamic economics consists of theology on economic matters."[66] Another (M.N. Siddiqi) notes Islamic economics has been teaching "conventional economics from an Islamic perspective", rather than Islamic economics.[78][79]

Despite its start in 1976, Islamic economics has been called still in its infancy,[65][66] its "curricula frames, course structures, reading materials, and research, "mostly anchored in the mainstream tradition",[66][78] "lacking sufficiency, depth, coordination and direction," with teaching faculties in many cases ... found short of the needed knowledge, scholarship, and commitment."[80][81] "Distinct textbooks and teaching materials" required have been found to "neither exist" nor be "easy to create."[67] Despite shortcomings in academic writing—most of the books are "not cohesive" and are "at best no more than extended papers on specific topics"—constructive evaluations are not common and response to what there is even less common.[82] The lack of an Islamic economics textbook "looms large" for Muslim economists and scholars. Despite the holding of a workshop in November 2010 to arrange the writing of a such a textbook, the participation of "a number of eminent Muslim economists", (at the International Institute of Islamic Thought in London) and the appointment of "a noted Muslim economist" to coordinate the production of the textbook, as of 2015 "no standard textbook of Islamic economics was available." [83]

Islamic economic institutes are not known for their intellectual freedom, and according to Muhammad Akram Khan are unlikely to allow criticism of the ideas or policies of their founding leaders or governments. The Centre for Research in Islamic Economics, an organ of the Jeddah University in Saudi Arabia, for example, "cannot allow publication of any work that goes against the orthodox thinking of the influential" Saudi religious leadership.[68] Despite "tall talk about ijtehad", Islamic economists "are shy" about "suggesting innovative ideas" for fear of antagonizing religious clerics.[68]

Use of Islamic terminology not only for distinctive Islamic concepts such as *riba, zakat, mudaraba* but also for concepts that do not have specific Islamic connotation -- *adl* for justice, *hukuma* for government—locking out non-Muslim and even not Arabic speaking readers from the content of Islamic economics and even "giving legitimacy" to "pendantry" in the field.[84]

2.32.4 Islam and economics

According to economist Muhammad Akram Khan the "main plank" of Islamic economics is the "theory of riba", while "another landmark" is zakat, a tax on wealth and income.[85]

According to contemporary writer Salah El-Sheikh, "Islamic economic principles" are grounded upon the ethical teachings within the Qu'rān, while utilizing the Faqīh (Islamic jurisprudence) as supporting material, in what he calls a "FiqhiConomic model". Sharīah's basic tenets involve gharar and (fadl māl bilā 'iwad). Gharar insists all knowledge about a trade or transaction is known before two individuals complete a transaction and (fadl māl bilā 'iwad) warns against unjustified enrichment through trade and business. These tenets were "among the first economic regulations" and their philosophy can be seen today in modern Capitalism. Within Sharīah, El-Sheikh states, Gharar functions as a divine deterrent against asymmetric information and allows trade to prosper. Riba, ensures each transaction is conducted at a fair price, not allowing one party to benefit exceedingly, which shares a parallel philosophy with Karl Marx "Das Kapital": seeking a greater outcome for the community.[86]

2.32.5 Property

According to authors F. Nomani and A. Rahnema, the Qur'an states that God is the sole owner of all matter in the heavens and the earth,[87] but man is God's vicegerent on earth and holds God's possessions in trust (*amanat*). Islamic jurists divide properties into public, state, private categories.[88]

Some Muslims believe that the Shariah provides "specific laws and standards regarding the use and allocation of resources including land, water, animals, minerals, and manpower."[89]

Public property

Scholars F. Nomani and A. Rahnema state that public property in Islam refers to natural resources (forests, pastures, uncultivated land, water, mines, oceanic resources etc.) to which all humans have equal right. Such resources are considered the common property of the community. Such property is placed under the guardianship and control of the Islamic state, and can be used by any citizen, as long as that use does not undermine the rights of other citizens, according to Nomani and Rahnema.[88]

Muhammad's saying that "people are partners in three things: water, fire and pastures", led some scholars to believe that the privatization of water and energy is not permissible. Muhammad allowed other types of public property, such as gold mines, to be privatized, in return for tax payments to the Islamic state. The owner of the previously public property that was privatized pays *zakat* and, according to Shi'ite scholars, *khums* as well. In general, the privatization and nationalization of public property is subject to debate amongst Islamic scholars.

Perhaps due to resource scarcity in most Islamic nations, Islamic economics emphasizes limited (and some claim also sustainable) use of natural capital, i.e. producing land. These latter revive traditions of haram and hima that were prevalent in early Muslim civilization.

State property

State property includes certain natural resources, as well as other property that can't immediately be privatized. Islamic state property can be movable, or immovable, and can be acquired through conquest or peaceful means. Unclaimed, unoccupied and heir-less properties, including uncultivated land (*mawat*), can be considered state property.[88]

During the life of Muhammad, one fifth of military equipment captured from the enemy in the battlefield was considered state property. During his reign, Umar (on the recommendation of Ali) considered conquered land to be state rather than private property (as was usual practice). The purported reason for this was that privatizing this property would concentrate resources in the hands of a few, and prevent it from being used for the general good. The property remained under the occupation of the cultivators, but taxes were collected on it for the state treasury.[88]

Muhammad said "Old and fallow lands are for God and His Messenger (i.e. state property), then they are for you". Jurists draw from this the conclusion that, ultimately, private ownership takes over state property.[88]

Private property

There is consensus amongst Islamic jurists and social scientists that Islam recognizes and upholds the individual's right to private ownership. The Qur'an extensively discusses taxation, inheritance, prohibition against stealing, legality of ownership, recommendation to give charity and other topics related to private property. Islam also guarantees the protection of private property by imposing stringent punishments on thieves. Muhammad said that he who dies defending his property was like a martyr.[90]

Islamic economists classify the acquisition of private property into involuntary, contractual and non-contractual categories. Involuntary means are inheritances, bequests, and gifts. Non-contractual acquisition involves the collection and exploitation of natural resources that have not previously been claimed as private property. Contractual acquisition includes activities such as trading, buying, renting, hiring labor etc.[90]

A tradition attributed to Muhammad, with which both Sunni and Shi'a jurists agree, in cases where the right to private ownership causes harm to others, then Islam favors curtailing the right in those cases. Maliki and Hanbali jurists argue that if private ownership endangers public interest, then the state can limit the amount an individual is allowed to own. This view, however, is debated by others.[90]

When Muhammad migrated to Madinah many of the Muslims owned agricultural land. Muhammad confirmed this ownership and allocated land to individuals. The land allotted would be used for housing, farming or gardening. For example, Bilal b. Harith was given land with mineral deposits at 'Aqiq Valley[91] Hassan b. Thabit was afforded the garden of Bayruha[92] and Zubayr received oasis land at Khaybar and Banu Nadir.[93] During the reign of caliph Umar, a vast expanse of Persian royal family terrain had been acquired, this lead his successor Caliph Uthman to accelerate the allotment of land to individuals in return for a portion of the crop yield.[94]

2.32.6 Markets

According to Nomani and Rahnema, Islam accepts markets as the basic coordinating mechanism of the economic system. Islamic teaching holds that the market, given perfect competition, allows consumers to obtain desired goods and producers to sell their goods at a mutually acceptable price.[95]

Three necessary conditions for an operational market are said to be upheld in Islamic primary sources:[95]

- Freedom of exchange: the Qur'an calls on believers to engage in trade, and rejects the contention that trade is forbidden.[96]

- Private ownership (see above).

- Security of contract: the Qur'an calls for the fulfillment and observation of contracts.[97] The longest verse of the Qur'an deals with commercial contracts involving immediate and future payments.[98]

Another author (Nima Mersadi Tabari) claims that the general doctrine of fairness in sharia law creates "an ethical economic model" and forbids market manipulation such as "inflating the price of commodities by creating artificial shortages (*Ihtekar*), overbidding for the sole purpose of driving the prices up (*Najash*) and concealment of vital information in a transaction from the other party (*Ghish*)".[32]

Further, "uninformed speculation" not based on a proper analysis of available information is forbidden because it is a form of *Qimar*, or gambling, and results in accumulating *Maysir* (unearned income).[32] Commercial contracting under conditions of "excessive uncertainty" (however that is defined) is a form of *Gharar* and so also forbidden.[32]

Interference

Nomani and Rahnema also contend that Islam promotes a market free from interference such as price fixing, hoarding and bribery. Government intervention, however, is tolerated under specific circumstances.[95]

Another author (Nima Mersadi Tabari) states that in Islam "everything is *Halal* (allowed) unless it has been declared *Haram* (forbidden)", consequently "the Islamic economic model is based on the freedom of trade and freedom of contract so far as the limits of Shari'ah allow".[32]

Nomani and Rahnema say that Islam prohibits price fixing by a dominating handful of buyers or sellers. During the days of Muhammad, a small group of merchants met agricultural producers outside the city and bought the entire crop, thereby gaining a monopoly over the market. The produce was later sold at a higher price within the city. Muhammad condemned this practice since it caused injury both to the producers (who in the absence of numerous customers were forced to sell goods at a lower price) and the inhabitants.[95]

The above-mentioned reports are also used to justify the argument that the Islamic market is characterized by free information. Producers and consumers should not be denied information on demand and supply conditions. Producers are expected to inform consumers of the quality and quantity of goods they claim to sell. Some scholars hold that if an inexperienced buyer is swayed by the seller, the consumer may nullify the transaction upon realizing the seller's unfair treatment. The Qur'an also forbids discriminatory transactions.[95][99]

Bribery is also forbidden in Islam and can therefore not be used to secure a deal or gain favor in a transaction, it was narrated that Muhammad cursed the one who offers the bribe, the one who receives it, and the one who arranges it.[100]

Nomani and Rahnema say government interference in the market is justified in exceptional circumstances, such as the protection of public interest. Under normal circumstances, governmental non-interference should be upheld. When Muhammad was asked to set the price of goods in a market he responded, "I will not set such a precedent, let the people

2.32.7 Banking and finance

Main article: Islamic banking

Interest

The Quran (3: 130) clearly condemns *riba* (which is usually translated as "interest"): "O, you who believe! Devour not *riba*, doubled and redoubled, and be careful of Allah; but fear Allah that you may be successful."

Public finance (*Bayt-al-Mal*)

The concept of a collective or shared bank played a historic role in the Islamic economy. The idea of state collected wealth being made available to the needy general public was relatively new. The resources in the Bayt-al-Mal were considered God's resources and a trust, money paid into the shared bank was common property of all the Muslims and the ruler was just the trustee.

The shared bank was treated as a financial institution and therefore subjected to the same prohibitions regarding interest.[101] Caliph Umar spoke on the shared bank saying: "I did not find the betterment of this wealth except in three ways: (i) it is received by right, (ii) it is given by right, and (iii) it is stopped from wrong. As regards my own position vis-a-vis this wealth of yours; it is like that of a guardian of an orphan. If I am well-off, I shall leave it, but if I am hard-pressed I shall take from it as is genuinely permissible."[102]

Debt arrangements

Most Islamic economic institutions advise participatory arrangements between capital and labor. The latter rule reflects the Islamic norm that the borrower must not bear all the cost of a failure, as "it is God who determines that failure, and intends that it fall on all those involved."

Conventional debt arrangements are thus usually unacceptable—but conventional venture investment structures are applied even on very small scales. However, not every debt arrangement can be seen in terms of venture investment structures. For example, when a family buys a home it is not investing in a business venture—a person's shelter is not a business venture. Similarly, purchasing other commodities for personal use, such as cars, furniture, and so on, cannot realistically be considered as a venture investment in which the Islamic bank shares risks and profits for the profits of the venture.

Savings and investment

An alternative Islamic savings-investment model can be built around venture capital; investment banks; restructured corporations; and restructured stock market.[103] This model looks at removing the interest-based banking and in replacing market inefficiencies such as subsidization of loans over profit-sharing investments due to double taxation and restrictions on investment in private equity.

Money changers

Due to religious sanctions against debt, Tamil Muslims have historically been money changers (not money lenders) throughout South and South East Asia.[104]

Hybrids

Islamic banks have grown recently in the Muslim world, but are a very small share of the global economy compared to the Western debt banking paradigm. Hybrid approaches, which applies classical Islamic values but uses conventional lending practices, are much lauded by some proponents of modern human development theory.

Popularity and availability

Main article: History of Islamic economics

Today many financial institutions, even in the Western world, that offer financial services and products in accordance with Islamic finance. For example, Chancellor Gordon Brown in 2003 introduced legal changes that enabled British banks and building societies to offer so-called Muslim mortgages for house purchase.

In 2001, the US's first Sharia-compliant home financing institution, Guidance Residential, was launched based on the concept of diminishing musharaka, growing to the largest Islamic home financing company in the US. . In 2004 the UK's first standalone Sharia-compliant bank was launched, the Islamic Bank of Britain. In 2006, the Bank of London and the Middle East (BLME) was founded, and as of July 2013 is the largest Islamic bank in Europe.[105] Several banks offer products and services to UK customers that adopt the Islamic financial principles; such as Mudaraba, Murabaha, Musharaka and Qard.

The Islamic finance sector was worth 300–500 billion dollars (237 and 394 billion euros) as of September 2006, compared with 200 billion dollars in 2004. Islamic retail banks and investment funds number in the hundreds and many

Western financial institutions offer compliant products, including Citigroup, Deutsche Bank, HSBC, Lloyds TSB and UBS. In 2008, at least $500 billion in assets around the world were managed in accordance with Islamic law and the sector was growing at more than 10% per year.[106]

2.32.8 Views

Sohrab Behada's study argued that the economic system proposed by Islam is essentially a capitalist one.[107]

In Shia Islam, scholars including Mahmoud Taleghani and Mohammad Baqir al-Sadr developed an "Islamic economics" emphasizing the uplifting of the deprived masses, a major role for the state in matters such as circulation and equitable distribution of wealth, and a reward to participants in the marketplace for being exposed to risk or liability.

Criticism

Islamic economics has been attacked for its alleged "incoherence, incompleteness, impracticality, and irrelevance;"[108] driven by "cultural identity" rather than problem solving.[109] Others have dismissed it as "a hodgepodge of populist and socialist ideas" in theory, and "nothing more than inefficient state control of the economy and some almost equally ineffective redistribution policies" in practice.[110]

> In a political and regional context where Islamist and ulema claim to have an opinion about everything, it is striking how little they have to say about this most central of human activities, beyond repetitious pieties about how their model is neither capitalist nor socialist.[110]

Detractors allege it is little more than a mimicry of conventional economics embellished with verses of the Quran and sunnah,[29] that its prescriptions are an "invented tradition"[6] that has "been spared critical scrutiny out of ignorance, misguided tolerance", and because they are considered "too unrealistic to threaten prevailing economic structures".[6] In an evaluation of goals of Islamic economics—abolishing interest on money, achieving economic equality, and establishing a superior business ethic—academic Timur Kuran finds it unsuccessful on each count.[111]

While Muslims believe Islamic law is perfect by virtue of its being revealed by God, Islamic law on economic issues was/is not (and not intended to be) "economics" in the sense of a systematic study of production, distribution, and consumption of goods and services. An example of the traditionalist ulama approach to economic issues is Imam Khomeini's work *Tawzih al-masa'il* where the term "economy" does not appear and where the chapter on selling and buying (Kharid o forush) comes after the one on pilgrimage.[1]

Muhammad Akram Khan notes that many universities in Muslim countries offer courses on conventional economics and finance but very little on Islamic economics and finance. He quotes an Islamist writer (Rasem N. Kayed) outraged by this "negligence" but notes that

> "the real problem is that despite efforts for developing a separate discipline of Islamic economics, there is not much that can be genuinely called `economics`. Most of Islamic economics consists of theology on economic matters."[112]

Criticizing the importance of the approval by Islamic scholars for Islamic banking transactions (or "fatwa shopping"), journalist John Foster, quotes an "investment banker based in Dubai" as saying,

> "We create the same type of products that we do for the conventional markets. We then phone up a Sharia scholar for a Fatwa [seal of approval, confirming the product is Shari'ah compliant]. If he doesn't give it to us, we phone up another scholar, offer him a sum of money for his services and ask him for a Fatwa. We do this until we get Sharia compliance. Then we are free to distribute the product as Islamic."[113]

Foster explains that the fee for services provided by "top" scholars is "often" in six-figures, i.e. over US$100,000.[113]

On the issue of *zakat*, Khan complains that "the insistence of Muslim scholars in implementing it in the same form in which it was in vogue in the days of the Prophet and first first four caliphs ... has made it irrelevant to the needs of a contemporary society."[114]

2.32.9 See also

- Islamic economics in Pakistan
- Islamic philosophy
- Economy of the OIC
- Law and economics

People

- Muhammad Taqi Usmani
- Nathif Jama Adam

2.32.10 References

- Addas, Waleed (2008). *Methodology of Economics: Secular versus Islamic*. IIUM. ISBN 978-983-3855-28-5.

- Al-Amine, Muhammad al-Bashir Muhammad (2008). *Risk Management in Islamic Finance: An Analysis of Derivatives Instruments in Commodity Markets*. Leiden: Brill. ISBN 978-90-04-15246-5.

- Bakhash, Shaul (1984). *The Reign of the Ayatollahs*. Basic Books.

- Behdad, Sohrab; Nomani, Farhad, eds. (2006). *Islam and the Everyday World: Public Policy Dilemmas*. Routledge. ISBN 0-415-36823-5.

- Chapra, M. Umar. *Islam and the Economic Challenge*. Leicester, UK: Islamic Foundation.

- El-Gamal, Mahmoud, 2009. "Islamic finance," *The New Palgrave Dictionary of Economics, Online Edition*. Abstract.

- Khan, Muhammad Akram (2013). *What Is Wrong with Islamic Economics?: Analysing the Present State and Future Agenda*. Edward Elgar Publishing. Retrieved 26 March 2015.

- Koehler, Benedikt (2014). *Early Islam and the Birth of Capitalism*. Lexington Books.

- Halliday, Fred (2005). *100 Myths about the Middle East*. Saqi Books.

- Khan, Muhammad Akram (2013). *What Is Wrong with Islamic Economics?: Analysing the Present State and Future Agenda*. Edward Elgar Publishing. Retrieved 26 March 2015.

- Kuran, Timur (1997). "The Genesis of Islamic Economics: A Chapter in the Politics of Muslim Identity," *Social Research*, 64(2), p pp. 301–338.

- _____ (2008). "Islamic economic institutions," *The New Palgrave Dictionary of Economics*, 2nd Edition. Abstract.

- Mirakhor, Abbas. *Theoretical Studies in Islamic Banking and Finance*. Islamic Publications International.

- Naqi, Syed Nawab Haider. *Ethics and Economics: An Islamic Synthesis*. Leicester, UK: Islamic Foundation.

- Nomani, Farhad; Rahnema, Ali. (1994). *Islamic Economic Systems*. New Jersey: Zed books limited. pp. 7–9. ISBN 1-85649-058-0.

- Presley, John R., and John G. Sessions (1994). "Islamic Economics: The Emergence of a New Paradigm," *Economic Journal*, 104(424), [pp. 584–596.

- Roy, Olivier (1994). *The Failure of Political Islam*. Harvard University Press. pp. 132–47.

- Siddiqui, Muhammad Nejatullah. *Muslim Economic Thinking*. Leicester, UK: Islamic Foundation.

- Venardos, Angelo M. *Islamic Banking & Finance in South-East Asia: Its Development & Future*. Singapore: World Scientific Publishing.

- Weiss, Dieter (1995). *Ibn Khaldun on Economic Transformation*. International Journal of Middle East Studies **27**.

Torts

- A. Basir Bin Mohamad. "The Islamic Law of Tort: A Study of the Owner and Possessor of Animals with Special Reference to the Civil Codes of the United Arab Emirates, Lebanon, Tunisia, Morocco, Sudan and Iraq" in *Arab Law Quarterly* V.16, N.4 2001

- "Vicarious Liability: A Study of the Liability of the Guardian and his Ward in the Islamic Law of Tort" *Arab Law Quarterly* V. 17, N.1 2002

- Immanuel Naveh. "The Tort of Injury and Dissolution of Marriage at the Wife's Initiative in Egyptian Mahkamat al-Naqd Rulings" in *Islamic Law and Society* Volume 9, Number 1, 2002

- *Islamic law of tort* Liaquat Ali Khan Niazi, 1988

- *An outline of Islamic law of tort* Abdul-Qadir Zubair, 1990

2.32.11 Notes

[1] Roy 1994, p. 133

[2] "Fiqh al-mu'amalat". *islamicbanker.com*. Retrieved 22 January 2015.

[3] Mat, Ismail; Ismail, Yusof. "A Review of Fiqh al-Mua'malat Subjects in Economics and Related Programs at International Islamic University Malaysia and University of Brunei Darussalam" (PDF). *kantakji.com*. p. 1. Retrieved 22 January 2015.

[4] Saleem, Muhammad Yusuf (n.d. (between 2006-2015)). "Methods and Methodologies in Fiqh and Islamic Economics" (PDF). *kantakji.com*. p. 1. Retrieved 22 January 2015. The paper argues that the methods used in Fiqh are

mainly designed to find out whether or not a certain act is permissible or prohibited. Islamic economics, on the other hand, is a social science. Like any other social science its proper unit of analysis is the society itself.

[5] "ECONOMIC GOALS". *amosweb.com/*. Retrieved 22 January 2015.

[6] Kuran, Timur (2004). *Islam and Mammon: The Economic Predicaments of Islamism*. Princeton University Press. p. x. Retrieved 25 March 2015.

[7] *The economic system in contemporary Islamic thought: Interpretation and assessment*, by Timur Kuran, International Journal of Middle East Studies, 18, 1986, pp. 135–64

[8] Quran (Al-Baqarah 2:275), (Al-Baqarah 2:276–80), (Al-'Imran 3:130), (Al-Nisa 4:161), (Ar-Rum 30:39)

[9] Karim, Shafiel A. (2010). *The Islamic Moral Economy: A Study of Islamic Money and Financial Instruments*. Boca Raton, FL: Brown Walker Press. ISBN 978-1-59942-539-9.

[10] Financial Regulation in Crisis?: The Role of Law and the Failure of Northern Rock By Joanna Gray, Orkun Akseli p. 97

[11] Islam and Economic Justice: A 'Third Way' Between Capitalism and Socialism?

[12] How Do We Know Islam Will Solve the Problems of Poverty and Inequality?

[13] Ishaque, Khalid M. (1983). "Islamic Approach to Economic Development". In Esposito,, John L. *Voices of Resurgent Islam*. pp. 268–276. the two models projected by the First and the Second Worlds. Both are basically materialistic, have priorities ... which permit wholesale exploitation. In the West it is the big corporations and cartels and in the Socialist countries it is state capitalism and bureaucracy.

[14] Quran 4:29

[15] *International Business Success in a Strange Cultural Environment* By Mamarinta P. Mababaya p. 203

[16] Quran 9:35

[17] Al-Bukhari Vol 2 Hadith 514

[18] Ibn Majah Vol 3 Hadith 2289

[19] International Business Success in a Strange Cultural Environment By Mamarinta P. Mababaya p. 202

[20] Islamic Capital Markets: Theory and Practice By Noureddine Krichene p. 119

[21] Abu Daud Hadith 2015

[22] Ibn Majah Vold 3 Hadith 2154

[23] *The Stability of Islamic Finance: Creating a Resilient Financial Environment* By Zamir Iqbal, Abbas Mirakhor, Noureddine Krichenne, Hossein Askari p. 75

[24] Al-Bukhari Vol 3 Hadith 632; Vol 4 Hadith 419

[25] Al-Bukhari Vol 3 Hadith 634; Vol 4 Hadith 418

[26] ILYASLI, Omer (Apr 17, 2013). "What is Islamic Economics?". *Islamiceconomy.net*. Retrieved 14 July 2015.

[27] Zarqa, M. Anas. (2008), *Duality of sources in Islamic economics, and its methodological consequences*. Paper presented at 7th International Conference on Islamic Economics, King Abdulaziz University, 1–3 April, Jeddah. p.30

[28] Khan, *What Is Wrong with Islamic Economics?*, 2013: p.4

[29] Khan, *What Is Wrong with Islamic Economics?*, 2013: p.xv

[30] Davari, Mahmood T. (2005). *The Political Thought of Ayatollah Murtaza Mutahhari: An Iranian ..* Routledge. p. 90. Retrieved 15 July 2015. Islamic economics is not a science of political economy. Rather it is a revolution (that is a revolutionary ideology) for changing the corrupt reality and turning it into a pure one. It is clearly not an objective analysis of existing reality.`

[31] Roy 1994, p. 132

[32] Tabari, Nima Mersadi. "The Sharia'h Dimension of the Persian Gulf's Hydrocarbon Resources". *social science research network*. Retrieved 23 January 2015.

[33] Roy, Olivier (1994). *The Failure of Political Islam*. Harvard University Press. p. 13. Retrieved 22 January 2015.

[34] Schirazi, Asghar & 1997, p. 170

[35] "The Oxford Dictionary of Islam. Muamalat". *Oxford Islamic Studies Online*. Retrieved 25 January 2015.

[36] Roy, Olivier (1994). *The Failure of Political Islam*. Harvard University Press. p. 133. Retrieved 22 January 2015.

[37] Norman, Omar (2006). "5. The Profit Motive in Islam: Religion and Economics in the Muslim World". In Hathaway, Robert M.; Lee, Wilson. *Islamization and the Pakistani Economy* (PDF). Woodrow Wilson International Center for Scholars. p. 74. Retrieved 13 August 2012. Indeed it is worth noting that "Islamic economics" is of modern 20th century origin. Even at the turn of the 19th century, the phrase was not used by major Islamic thinkers. The great philosopher Iqbal, who was inspirational to the movement for Pakistan, did not refer to religion in his treatise on economics. Iqbal's Ilm–ul–Iqtesaad, published in 1902, was notable in its absence of religion in the understanding of the economy. The intellectual father of Islamic economics is Maulana Maudoodi, the scholar whose views have shaped the Jamaat-e-Islami

[38] *Essential Hanafi Handbook of Fiqh* A Translation of Qazi Thanaa Ullah's Ma La Budda Minhu, by Maulana Yusuf Talal Ali al-Amriki, (Kazi Publications, Lahore, Pakistan)

[39] (source: Ruhollah Khomeini, *Tawzih al-masa'il*, p.543)

[40] Chapra, Umer (2010). "Islamic Economics: What It Is and How It Developed". In Whaples, Robert. *EH.net: Encyclopedia of Economic and Business History.* Retrieved 8 July 2011.

[41] Mahmassani, Sobhi (1932). *Les Idées Economiques d'Ibn Khaldoun (The Economic Thought of Ibn Khaldoun)*, BOSC Frères, M. et L. RIOU, Lyon, is an early treatise on Ibn Khaldun's economic thought.

[42] Schumpeter (1954) p 136 mentions his sociology, others, including Hosseini (2003) emphasize him as well

[43] I. M. Oweiss (1988), "Ibn Khaldun, the Father of Economics", *Arab Civilization: Challenges and Responses,* New York University Press, ISBN 0-88706-698-4.

[44] Jean David C. Boulakia (1971), "Ibn Khaldun: A Fourteenth-Century Economist", *The Journal of Political Economy* **79** (5): 1105–18.

[45] Weiss 1995, pp. 29–30

[46] Weiss 1995, p. 31 quotes Muqaddimah 2:276–78

[47] Weiss 1995, p. 31 quotes *Muqaddimah* 2: 272–73

[48] Weiss 1995, p. 33

[49] The Economic Life of Islam

[50] Martin, Richard C., ed. (2004). "Riba". *Encyclopedia of Islam and the Muslim World.* Macmillan Reference USA. pp. 596–7. ISBN 0-02-865912-0.

[51] Bakhash, Shaul, *The Reign of the Ayatollahs*, Basic Books, c1984, pp. 167–68

[52] Revolutionary Surge and Quiet Demise of Islamic Economics in Iran

[53] The Renewal of Islamic Law

[54] Bakhash 1984, pp. 172–173

[55] "Untitled Document". Archived from the original on 4 July 2004. Retrieved 8 February 2015.

[56] Iqbal, Zamir and Abbas Mirakhor (2008). *An Introduction to Islamic finance.* Lahore; Vanguard Books

[57] Khan, *What Is Wrong with Islamic Economics?*, 2013: p.6

[58] An example of a pending patent application: US US20030233324A1 "Declining balance co-ownership financing arrangement" (an allegedly Sharia compliant financing arrangement for home purchases and refinances that does not involve the payment of interest).

[59] Roy, Olivier, *The Failure of Political Islam* by Olivier Roy, translated by Carol Volk, Harvard University Press, 1994, p.138, 140

[60] Kahn, Muhammad, *What is Wrong with Islamic Economics* Edward Elgar Publishing, 2013, pp. 216 et seq.

[61] Ali, S Nazim. 2008. Islamic finance and economics as reflected in research and publications. *Review of Islamic Economics*, 12 (1): 155

[62] Ali, S Nazim. 2008. Islamic finance and economics as reflected in research and publications. *Review of Islamic Economics*, 12 (1): 164

[63] Khan, *What Is Wrong with Islamic Economics?*, 2013: p.5

[64] Ali, S Nazim. 2008. Islamic finance and economics as reflected in research and publications. *Review of Islamic Economics*, 12 (1): 151-168, 155

[65] Haneef, Mohamed A. 2009. *Research in Islamic economics: The missing fard 'ayn component.* Paper presented at 3rd Islamic Economics Congress, 12–14 January, Kuala Lumpur p.4

[66] Khan, *What Is Wrong with Islamic Economics?*, 2013: p.7

[67] Khan, *What Is Wrong with Islamic Economics?*, 2013: p.8

[68] Khan, *What Is Wrong with Islamic Economics?*, 2013: p.11

[69] Khan, *What Is Wrong with Islamic Economics?*, 2013: p.14-5

[70] Kayed, Rasem N. 2008. *Appraisal of the status of research on labor economics in the Islamic framework.* Paper presented at 7th International Conference on Islamic Economics, King Abdulaziz University, 1–3 April, Jeddah, : 193)

[71] Haneef, Mohamed A. 2009. *Research in Islamic economics: The missing fard 'ayn component.* Paper presented at 3rd Islamic Economics Congress, 12–14 January, Kuala Lumpur p.2

[72] Tahir, Sayyid. 2009. ISlamic finance: Undergraduate education. *Islamic Economic Studies* 16 (1&2) (January): 71

[73] Siddiqi, Muhammad Nejatullah, 2008 *Obstacles to Islamic economics research.* Paper presented at 7th International Conference on Islamic Economics, King Abdulaziz University, 1–3 April, Jeddah

[74] Iqbal, Munawar. 2008. *Contributions of the last six conferences.* Paper presented at 7th International Conference on Islamic Economics, King Abdulaziz University, 1–3 April, Jeddah, p.80

[75] Khan, *What Is Wrong with Islamic Economics?*, 2013: p.13-4

[76] Kayed, Rasem N. 2008. *Appraisal of the status of research on labor economics in the Islamic framework.* Paper presented at 7th International Conference on Islamic Economics, King Abdulaziz University, 1–3 April, Jeddah, : 190-1)

[77] Khan, *What Is Wrong with Islamic Economics?*, 2013: p.6-7

[78] Hasan, Zubair. 2005 Treatment of consumption in Islamic economics: An appraisal. *Journal of King Abdulaziz University: Islamic Economics*, 18 (2): 29-46

[79] Siddiqi, M.N., 1996, *Teaching economics in Islamic perspective.* Jeddah: King Abdulaziz University, Centre for Research in Islamic Economics

[80] Hasan, Zubair. 2009, "Islamic finance education at the graduate level: Current state and challenges." *Islamic Economic Studies*, 16 (1,2) (January) 81

[81] Khan, *What Is Wrong with Islamic Economics?*, 2013: p.7-8

[82] Hasan, Zubair. 2009, "Islamic finance education at the graduate level: Current state and challenges." *Islamic Economic Studies*, 16 (1,2) (January) 92-3

[83] Khan, *What Is Wrong with Islamic Economics?*, 2013: p.9-10

[84] Khan, *What Is Wrong with Islamic Economics?*, 2013: p.12

[85] Khan, Muhammad Akram (2013). *What Is Wrong with Islamic Economics?: Analysing the Present State and ..* Edward Elgar Publishing. p. xv-xvi. Retrieved 25 March 2015.

[86] El-Sheikh, Salah. 2008. "The moral economy of classical Islam: a FiqhiConomic model." *Muslim World* 98, no. 1: 116-144. ATLA Religion Database with ATLASerials, EBSCOhost

[87] Nomani and Rahnema quote Quran 2:107, Quran 2:255, Quran 2:284, Quran 5:120, Quran 48:14

[88] F. Nomani and A. Rahnema. 1994. *Islamic Economic Systems*, Zed Press. pp. 66–70

[89] Hamed, Safei-Eldin (n.d. (after 1990 before 2015)). "SEEING THE ENVIRONMENT THROUGHISLAMIC EYES: Application of Shariah to Natural Resources Planning and Management" (PDF). *Texas Tech University.* Retrieved 23 January 2015.

[90] Nomani & Rahnema 1994, pp. 71–77

[91] al-Baladhuri, Futuh al-Buldan

[92] Sahih al-Bukhari, 17

[93] Futuh al-Buldan, Abu Ubayd

[94] al-Maqrizi, al-Mawa'iz wa'l-I'tibar

[95] Nomani Rahnema, pp. 55–58

[96] Nomani Rahnema cite Quran 4:29, Quran 2:275 and Quran 2:279

[97] Nomani Rahnema cite Quran 5:1, Quran 16:91, Quran 23:8, Quran 17:34 and Quran 70:32

[98] Nomani Rahnema cite Quran 2:282.

[99] Nomani Rahnema cite Quran 55:9, Quran 26:181–183, Quran 11:84–85. They also point out that a chapter is devoted to such fraudulent practices: Quran 83:1–3

[100] Reported by Ahmad and al-Hakim

[101] K-al-Mabsut, Al-Sarakhsi, Shamsuddin

[102] Uyun-al-Akhbar, ad-Dinawri

[103] Meinhaj Hussain (June 2010). "Economic Model". 2.0

[104] Tyabji, Amini (1991). "Historical dominance on money changing business". In Mohamed Ariff. *The Muslim Private Sector in Southeast Asia: Islam and the Economic Development of Southeast Asia (Social Issues in Southeast Asia).* ISBN 981-3016-10-8.

[105] "Bank of London and the Middle East". Zawya.com. Retrieved 12 July 2013.

[106] Islamic Finance, Forbes (April 21, 2008)

[107] Sohrab Behada, "Property Rights in Contemporary Islamic Economic Thought, *Review of Social Economy*, Summer 1989 v. 47, (pp. 185–211)

[108] Kuran, "The Economic Impact of Islamic Fundamentalism," in Marty and Appleby *Fundamentalisms and the State*, U of Chicago Press, 1993, pp. 302–41

[109] "The Discontents of Islamic Economic Mortality" by Timur Kuran, *American Economic Review*, 1996, pp. 438–42

[110] Halliday, Fred, *100 Myths about the Middle East*, Saqi Books, 2005 p. 89

[111] Pipes, Daniel (September 26, 2007). "Islamic Economics: What Does It Mean?". Jerusalem Post. Retrieved 5 August 2015.

[112] Khan, Muhammad Akram (2013). *What Is Wrong with Islamic Economics?: Analysing the Present State and ..* Edward Elgar Publishing. p. 7. Retrieved 25 March 2015.

[113] Foster, John (July 15, 2010). "The Failure of Islamic Finance". *muslimmatters.org.* Retrieved 15 April 2015.

[114] Khan, *What Is Wrong with Islamic Economics?*, 2013: p.xvi

2.32.12 External links

- Free Lectures on Islamic Economics & Finance by AIMS' Institute of Islamic Banking and Finance.

- World Database for Islamic Banking and Finance

- Economic Insaf, An Islamic Economics Framework from GrandeStrategy.

- Putting Faith into Finance, HSBC article on Islamic finance.

- Shamshad Akhtar et al., "Understanding Islamic Finance: Local Innovation and Global Integration", *Asia Policy*, July 2008.

- Mohammad Omar Farooq, Riba, Interest and Six Hadiths: Do We Have a Definition or a Conundrum?

- Mahmoud el-Gamal, "An Economic Explanation of the Prohibition of Riba in Classical Islamic Jurisprudence", Rice University, Houston, Texas.

- Methodology of Economics: Secular versus Islamic

- Maryam Ayaz, Islamic Banking, Finance & Economics

- Islamic Economics booklist

- AusCIF Islamic Finance Resources & Learning Centre

- An Introduction to Islamic Economics, "What is Islamic Economics?"

2.33 Joan Robinson

Not to be confused with Joan Robinson Hill.

Joan Violet Robinson FBA (31 October 1903 – 5 August 1983) was a British post-Keynesian economist who was well known for her work on monetary economics and wide-ranging contributions to economic theory. She was the daughter of Major-General Sir Frederick Barton Maurice, 1st Baronet, and was married to Austin Robinson, a fellow economist. Together, they had two children.

2.33.1 Biography

Robinson studied economics at Girton College, Cambridge. While at Cambridge University she came under the influence of Maurice Dobb. He was a member of the Communist Party of Great Britain.[1] "Dobb was probably the first academic in Britain to carry a Communist Party membership card. Without Dobb, communism would never have gained the prominence in Cambridge that it did."[2]

According to Robinson, not all of his students agreed with his political views. A group of "hearties" seized him and threw him "fully dressed into the River Cam" in a futile effort to teach him sense. This happened to Dobb more than once; but his persecutors became bored and eventually left him alone.[3]

Immediately after graduation in 1925, she married the economist Austin Robinson. In 1937, she became a lecturer in economics at the University of Cambridge. She joined the British Academy in 1958 and was then elected fellow of Newnham College in 1962. In 1965 she assumed the position of full professor and fellow of Girton College. In 1979, just four years before she died, she became the first female honorary fellow of King's College.

As a member of "the Cambridge School" of economics, Robinson contributed to the support and exposition of Keynes' General Theory, writing especially on its employment implications in 1936 and 1937 (it attempted to explain employment dynamics in the midst of the Great Depression).

In 1933 in her book *The Economics of Imperfect Competition*, Robinson coined the term "monopsony," which is used to describe the buyer converse of a seller monopoly. Monopsony is commonly applied to buyers of labour, where the employer has wage setting power that allows it to exercise Pigouvian exploitation[4] and pay workers less than their marginal productivity. Robinson used monopsony to describe the wage gap between women and men workers of equal productivity.[5]

In 1942 Robinson's *An Essay on Marxian Economics* famously concentrated on Karl Marx as an economist, helping to revive the debate on this aspect of his legacy.

During the Second World War, Robinson worked on a few different Committees for the wartime national government. During this time, she visited the Soviet Union as well as China. She developed an interest in underdeveloped and developing nations and contributed much of what is now understood in this area of economics.

In 1948 she was appointed the first economist member of the Monopolies and Mergers Commission.[6]

In 1949 she was invited by Ragnar Frisch to become the Vice-President of the Econometric Society but declined, saying she couldn't be part of the editorial committee of a journal she couldn't read.

In 1956 Robinson published her magnum opus, *The Accumulation of Capital*, which extended Keynesianism into the long-run.

In 1962 she published *Essays in the Theory of Economic Growth*, another book on growth theory, which discussed Golden Age growth paths. Afterwards she developed the Cambridge growth theory with Nicholas Kaldor. She was elected a Foreign Honorary Member of the American Academy of Arts and Sciences in 1964.[7]

During the 1960s she was a major participant in the Cambridge capital controversy alongside Piero Sraffa.

Near the end of her life she studied and concentrated on methodological problems in economics and tried to recover the original message of Keynes' General Theory. Between

1962 and 1980 she wrote many economics books for the general public. Robinson suggested developing an alternative to the revival of classical economics.

At least two students who studied under her have won the Nobel Prize in Economic Sciences: Amartya Sen and Joseph Stiglitz. In his autobiographical notes for the Nobel Foundation, Stiglitz described their relationship as "tumultuous" and Robinson as unused to "the kind of questioning stance of a brash American student"; after a term, Stiglitz therefore "switched to Frank Hahn".[8] In his own autobiography notes, Sen described Robinson as "totally brilliant but vigorously intolerant".[9]

Joan Robinson (1973)

Robinson was a frequent visitor to Centre for Development Studies (CDS), Thiruvananthapuram, India. She was a Visiting Fellow at the Centre in the mid-1970s. She instituted an endowment fund to support public lectures at the Centre. She was a frequent visitor to the Centre until January, 1982 and participated in all activities of the Centre and especially student seminars. Professor Robinson donated royalties of two of her books (Selected Economic Writings, Bombay: Oxford University Press, 1974, Introduction to Modern Economics (jointly with John Eatwell), Delhi; Tata McGraw Hill, 1974) to CDS.

Also, Robinson made several trips to China, reporting her observations and analyses in *China: An Economic Perspective* (1958), *The Cultural Revolution in China* (1969), and *Economic Management in China* (1975; 3rd edn, 1976), in which she praised the Cultural Revolution. In October 1964, Robinson also visited North Korea, which implemented social reforms and collectivisation at the time, and wrote in her report "Korean Miracle" that the country's success was due to "the intense concentration of the Koreans on national pride" under Kim Il-sung, "a messiah rather than a dictator".[10] She also stated in reference to the division of Korea that "[o]bviously, sooner or later the country must be reunited by absorbing the South into socialism."[11] During her last decade, she became more and more pessimistic about the possibilities of reforming economic theory, as expressed, for example, in her essay "Spring Cleaning".[12]

The Cultural Revolution in China is written from the perspective of trying to understand the thinking that lay behind the revolution, particularly Mao Zedong's preoccupations. Mao is seen as aiming to recapture a revolutionary sense in a population that had known only, or had grown used to, stable Communism, so that it could "re-educate the Party" (pp. 20, 27); to instil a realisation that the people needed the guidance of the Party and much as the other way round (p. 20); to re-educate intellectuals who failed to see that their role in society, like that of all other groups, was to 'Serve the People' (pp. 33, 43); and finally to secure a succession, not stage-managed by the Party hierarchy or even by Mao himself but the product of interaction between a revitalised people and a revitalised Party (p. 26).

On the whole, the book emphasises the positive aspects of Mao's "moderate and humane" intentions (p. 19) rather than the "violence and disorder" that broke out, we are told, "from time to time", occurrences "strongly opposed" (ibid.) to Mao's wishes. Robinson recognises and appears to endorse a revision to classical Marxism in Mao's view of the relation of base to superstructure: "On the classical view, there is one-way determination between base and superstructure but Mao shows how the superstructure may react upon the base: Ideas may become a material force" (p. 12). She acknowledges that "Old-fashioned Marxists might regard this as a heresy, but that is scarcely reasonable" (ibid.).

2.33.2 Family

Joan Maurice married fellow economist Austin Robinson in 1926.[13] The marriage produced two recorded daughters.[13]

Joan Robinson's maternal grandfather was the distinguished London surgeon and Cambridge academic Howard Marsh.

2.33.3 Major works

- *The Economics of Imperfect Competition* (1933)
- *An Essay on Marxian Economics* (1942), Second Edition (1966) (The Macmillan Press Ltd, ISBN 0-333-05800-3)
- *The Production Function and the Theory of Capital* (1953)
- *Accumulation of Capital* (1956)
- *Exercises in Economic Analysis* (1960)
- *Essays in the Theory of Economic Growth* (1962)
- *Economic Philosophy: An essay on the progress of economic thought* (1962)
- *Freedom and Necessity: An introduction to the study of society* (1970)
- *Economic Heresies: Some Old Fashioned Questions in Economic Theory* (1971) (Basic Books, New York, ISBN 0-465-01786-X)
- *Contributions to Modern Economics* (1978) (Basil Blackwell, Oxford, ISBN 0-631-19220-4)

Texts for the lay reader

- *Economics is a serious subject: The apologia of an economist to the mathematician, the scientist and the plain man* (1932), W. Heffer & Sons
- *Introduction to the Theory of Employment* (1937)
- *The Cultural Revolution in China*, Harmondsworth: Pelican Original (1969)
- *An Introduction to Modern Economics* (1973) with John Eatwell
- *The Arms Race* (1981), Tanner Lectures on Human Values

2.33.4 See also

- International economics
- List of economists
- Macroeconomics
- Wealth condensation
- Welfare economics

2.33.5 References

[1] Biography of Joan Robinson

[2] Phillip Knightley, Philby: KGB Masterspy (1988) page 30

[3] Joan Robinson, interviewed for the book, Andrew Boyle, The Climate of Treason (1979) page 47

[4] . JSTOR 1927526. Missing or empty |title= (help)

[5] http://www.u.arizona.edu/~{}rlo/696i/Monopsony_Model_Latex.pdf

[6] Stephen Wilks, In the Public Interest: Competition Policy and the Monopolies and Mergers Commission, p. 93

[7] "Book of Members, 1780–2010: Chapter R" (PDF). American Academy of Arts and Sciences. Retrieved 22 July 2014.

[8] Stiglitz, Joseph E. "Autobiography", *Nobel Foundation*, Stockholm, December 2002. Retrieved on 8 May 2012.

[9] Sen, Amartya "Autobiography", *Nobel Foundation*, Stockholm, 1998. Retrieved on 8 May 2012.

[10] Heonik Kwon; Byung-Ho Chung (12 March 2012). *North Korea: Beyond Charismatic Politics*. Rowman & Littlefield Publishers. pp. 151–152. ISBN 978-1-4422-1577-1.

[11] Harcourt, Geoffrey Colin (2006). *The Structure of Post-Keynesian Economics*. Cambridge University Press. p. 92. ISBN 9780765637017. Retrieved 31 December 2010.

[12] Harcourt, p. 169.

[13] *Who's who 1958*. London: Adam & Charles Black limited. 1958.

- Pure Competition

2.33.6 Further reading

- Emani, Zohreh, 2000, "Joan Robinson" in Robert W. Dimand et al. (eds), *A Biographical Dictionary of Women Economists*, Edward Elgar.
- Harcourt, G. C., 1995, Obituary: Joan Robinson 1903–1983, Economic Journal, Vol. 105, No. 432. (September 1995), pp. 1228–1243.
- Pasinetti, Luigi L. (1987), "Robinson, Joan Violet," *The New Palgrave: A Dictionary of Economics*, v. 4, pp. 212–17, Macmillan.
- Vianello, F. [1996], "Joan Robinson on Normal Prices (and the Normal rate of Profits)", in: Marcuzzo, M.C. and Pasinetti, L. and Roncaglia, A. (eds.), *The Economics of Joan Robinson*, New York: Routledge, ISBN 978-0415136167.

2.33.7 External links

- Joan Violet Robinson, 1903–1983 The New School

- Joan Robinson at Stanford, May 1974 Australian School of Business, 27 March 2009 – Three hours of Robinson' lectures at Stanford, 1974

- Life and economics of Joan Robinson Life and economics of Joan Robinson

- *Joan Violet Robinson (1903–1983). The Concise Encyclopedia of Economics.* Library of Economics and Liberty (2nd ed.) (Liberty Fund). 2008.

- Works by Joan Robinson at Project Gutenberg

2.34 Kinetic exchange models of markets

Kinetic exchange models are multi-agent dynamic models inspired by the statistical physics of energy distribution, which try to explain the robust and universal features of income/wealth distributions.

Understanding the distributions of income and wealth in an economy has been a classic problem in economics for more than a hundred years. Today it is one of the main branches of Econophysics.

2.34.1 Data and Basic tools

In 1897, Vilfredo Pareto first found a universal feature in the distribution of wealth. After that, with some notable exceptions, this field had been dormant for many decades, although accurate data had been accumulated over this period. Considerable investigations with the real data during the last fifteen years (1995–2010) revealed[1] that the tail (typically 5 to 10 percent of agents in any country) of the income/wealth distribution indeed follows a power law. The rest (bulk) of the population (i.e., the low-income population) follow a different distribution which is debated to be either Gibbs or log-normal.

Basic tools used in this type of modelling are probabilistic and statistical methods mostly taken from the kinetic theory of statistical physics. Monte Carlo simulations often come handy in solving these models.

2.34.2 Overview of the models

Since the distributions of income/wealth are the results of the interaction among many heterogeneous agents, there is an analogy with statistical mechanics, where many particles interact. This similarity was noted by Meghnad Saha and B. N. Srivastava in 1931[2] and thirty years later by Benoit Mandelbrot.[3] In 1986, an elementary version of the stochastic exchange model was first proposed by J. Angle.[4]

In the context of kinetic theory of gases, such an exchange model was first investigated by A. Dragulescu and V. Yakovenko.[5][6] The main modelling effort has been put to introduce the concepts of savings,[7][8] and taxation[9] in the setting of an ideal gas-like system. Basically, it assumes that in the short-run, an economy remains conserved in terms of income/wealth; therefore *law of conservation* for income/wealth can be applied. Millions of such conservative transactions lead to a steady state distribution of money (gamma function-like in the *Chakraborti-Chakrabarti* model with uniform savings,[7] and a gamma-like bulk distribution ending with a Pareto tail[10] in the *Chatterjee-Chakrabarti-Manna* model with distributed savings[8]) and the distribution converges to it. The distributions derived thus have close resemblance with those found in empirical cases of income/wealth distributions.

Though this theory has been originally derived from the entropy maximization principle of statistical mechanics, it has recently been shown[11] that the same could be derived from the utility maximization principle as well, following a standard exchange-model with Cobb-Douglas utility function. The exact distributions produced by this class of kinetic models are known only in certain limits and extensive investigations have been made on the mathematical structures of this class of models.[12][13] The general forms have not been derived so far.

2.34.3 Criticisms

This class of models has attracted criticisms from many dimensions.[14] It has been debated for long whether the distributions derived from these models are representing the income distributions or wealth distributions. The *law of conservation* for income/wealth has also been a subject of criticism.

2.34.4 See also

- Economic inequality

- Econophysics

- Thermoeconomics

- Wealth condensation

2.34.5 References

[1] Chatterjee, A.; Yarlagadda, S.; Chakrabarti, B.K. (2005). *Econophysics of Wealth Distributions*. Springer-Verlag (Milan).

[2] Saha, M.; Srivastava, B.N. (1931). *A Treatise on Heat*. Indian Press (Allahabad). p. 105. (the page is reproduced in Fig. 6 in Sitabhra Sinha, Bikas K Chakrabarti, *Towards a physics of economics*, Physics News 39(2) 33-46, April 2009)

[3] Mandelbrot, B.B. (1960). "The Pareto-Levy law and the distribution of income". *International Economic Review* **1**: 69. doi:10.2307/2525289.

[4] Angle, J. (1986). "The surplus theory of social stratification and the size distribution of personal wealth". *Social Forces* **65** (2): 293–326. doi:10.2307/2578675. JSTOR 2578675.

[5] Dragulescu, A.; Yakovenko, V. (2000). "The statistical mechanics of money". *European Physical Journal B* **17**: 723–729. doi:10.1007/s100510070114.

[6] Garibaldi, U.; Scalas, E.; Viarenga, P. (2007). "Statistical equilibrium in exchange games". *European Physical Journal B* **60**: 241–246. doi:10.1140/epjb/e2007-00338-5.

[7] Chakraborti, A.; Chakrabarti, B.K. (2000). "Statistical mechanics of money: how savings propensity affects its distribution". *European Physical Journal B* **17**: 167–170. doi:10.1007/s100510070173.

[8] Chatterjee, A.; Chakrabarti, B.K.; Manna, K.S.S. (2004). "Pareto law in a kinetic model of market with random saving propensity". *Physica A* **335**: 155–163. doi:10.1016/j.physa.2003.11.014.

[9] Guala, S. (2009). "Taxes in a simple wealth distribution model by inelastically scattering particles". *Interdisciplinary description of complex systems* **7** (1): 1–7.

[10] Chakraborti, A.; Patriarca, M. (2009). "Variational Principle for the Pareto Power Law". *Physical Review Letters* **103**: 228701. Bibcode:2009PhRvL.103v8701C. doi:10.1103/PhysRevLett.103.228701.

[11] A. S. Chakrabarti, B. K. Chakrabarti (2009). "Microeconomics of the ideal gas like market models". *Physica A* **388**: 4151–4158. doi:10.1016/j.physa.2009.06.038.

[12] During, B.; Matthes, D.; Toscani, G. (2008). "Kinetic equations modelling wealth distributions: a comparison of approaches". *Physical Review E* **78**: 056103. doi:10.1103/physreve.78.056103.

[13] Cordier, S.; Pareschi, L.; Toscani, G. (2005). "On a kinetic model for a simple market economy". *Journal of Statistical Physics* **120**: 253–277. doi:10.1007/s10955-005-5456-0.

[14] Mauro Gallegati, Steve Keen, Thomas Lux and Paul Ormerod (2006). "Worrying Trends in Econophysics". *Physica A* **371**: 1–6. doi:10.1016/j.physa.2006.04.029.

2.34.6 Further reading

- Brian Hayes, *Follow the money*, American Scientist, 90:400-405 (Sept.-Oct.,2002)

- Jenny Hogan, *There's only one rule for rich*, New Scientist, 6-7 (12 March 2005)

- Peter Markowich, *Applied Partial Differential Equations*, Springer-Verlag (Berlin, 2007)

- Arnab Chatterjee, Bikas K Chakrabarti, *Kinetic exchange models for income and wealth distribution*, European Physical Journal B, 60:135-149(2007)

- Victor Yakovenko, J. B. Rosser, *Colloquium: statistical mechanics of money, wealth and income*, Reviews of Modern Physics 81:1703-1725 (2009)

- Thomas Lux, F. Westerhoff, *Economics crisis*, Nature Physics, 5:2 (2009)

- Sitabhra Sinha, Bikas K Chakrabarti, *Towards a physics of economics*, Physics News 39(2) 33-46 (April 2009)

- Stephen Battersby, *The physics of our finances*, New Scientist, p. 41 (28 July 2012)

- Bikas K Chakrabarti, Anirban Chakraborti, Satya R Chakravarty, Arnab Chatterjee, *Econophysics of Income & Wealth Distributions*, Cambridge University Press (Cambridge 2013).

- Lorenzo Pareschi and Giuseppe Toscani, *Interacting Multiagent Systems: Kinetic equations and Monte Carlo methods* Oxford University Press (Oxford 2013)

2.35 Kondratiev wave

This article is about a phenomenon in economics. For the neologism, see Korean Wave.

In economics, **Kondratiev waves** (also called **supercycles**,

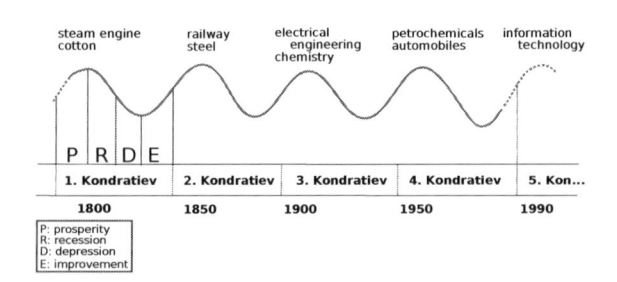

A rough schematic drawing showing growth cycles in the world economy over time according to the Kondratiev theory

great surges, **long waves**, **K-waves** or **the long economic cycle**) are supposed cycle-like phenomena in the modern world economy.[1]

It is stated that the period of a wave ranges from forty to sixty years, the cycles consist of alternating intervals between high sectoral growth and intervals of relatively slow growth.[2]

2.35.1 History of concept

The Soviet economist Nikolai Kondratiev (also written Kondratieff) was the first to bring these observations to international attention in his book *The Major Economic Cycles* (1925) alongside other works written in the same decade.[3][4] In 1939, Joseph Schumpeter suggested naming the cycles "Kondratieff waves" in his honor.

Two Dutch economists, Jacob van Gelderen and Samuel de Wolff, had previously argued for the existence of 50- to 60-year cycles in 1913.

Since the inception of the theory, various studies have expanded the range of possible cycles, finding longer or shorter cycles in the data. The Marxist scholar Ernest Mandel revived interest in long-wave theory with his 1964 essay predicting the end of the long boom after five years and in his Alfred Marshall lectures in 1979. However, in Mandel's theory, there are no long "cycles", only distinct epochs of faster and slower growth spanning 20–25 years.

The historian Eric Hobsbawm wrote of the theory: "That good predictions have proved possible on the basis of Kondratiev Long Waves—this is not very common in economics—has convinced many historians and even some economists that there is something in them, even if we don't know what." [5]

2.35.2 Characteristics of the cycle

Kondratiev identified three phases in the cycle: expansion, stagnation, and recession. More common today is the division into four periods with a turning point (collapse) between the first and second phases. Writing in the 1920s, Kondratiev proposed to apply the theory to the 19th century:

- 1790–1849 with a turning point in 1815.
- 1850–1896 with a turning point in 1873.
- Kondratiev supposed that, in 1896, a new cycle had started.

The long cycle supposedly affects all sectors of an economy. Kondratiev focused on prices and interest rates, seeing the ascendant phase as characterized by an increase in prices and low interest rates, while the other phase consists of a decrease in prices and high interest rates. Subsequent analysis concentrated on output.

2.35.3 Explanations of the cycle

Technological innovation theory

According to the innovation theory, these waves arise from the bunching of basic innovations that launch technological revolutions that in turn create leading industrial or commercial sectors. Kondratiev's ideas were taken up by Joseph Schumpeter in the 1930s. The theory hypothesized the existence of very long-run macroeconomic and price cycles, originally estimated to last 50–54 years.

In recent decades there has been considerable progress in historical economics and the history of technology, and numerous investigations of the relationship between technological innovation and economic cycles. Some of the works involving long cycle research and technology include Mensch (1979), Tylecote (1991), The International Institute for Applied Systems Analysis (IIASA) (Marchetti, Ayres), Freeman and Louçã (2001) and Carlota Perez.

Perez (2002) places the phases on a logistic or *S* curve, with the following labels: the beginning of a technological era as *irruption*, the ascent as *frenzy*, the rapid build out as *synergy* and the completion as *maturity*.[6]

Demographic theory

Because people have fairly typical spending patterns through their life cycle, such as spending on schooling, marriage, first car purchase, first home purchase, upgrade home purchase, maximum earnings period, maximum retirement savings and retirement, demographic anomalies such as baby booms and busts exert a rather predictable influence on the economy over a long time period. Harry Dent has written extensively on demographics and economic cycles. Tylecote (1991) devoted a chapter to demographics and the long cycle.[7]

Land speculation

Main article: Georgism

Georgists, such as Mason Gaffney, Fred Foldvary, and Fred Harrison argue that land speculation is the driving force behind the boom and bust cycle. Land is a finite resource which is necessary for all production, and they claim that because exclusive usage rights are traded around, this creates speculative bubbles, which can be exacerbated by overzealous borrowing and lending. As early as 1997, a number of Georgists predicted that the next crash would come in 2008.[8][9]

Debt deflation

Main article: Debt deflation

Debt deflation is a theory of economic cycles, which holds that recessions and depressions are due to the overall level of debt shrinking (deflating): the credit cycle is the cause of the economic cycle.

The theory was developed by Irving Fisher following the Wall Street Crash of 1929 and the ensuing Great Depression. Debt deflation was largely ignored in favor of the ideas of John Maynard Keynes in Keynesian economics, but has enjoyed a resurgence of interest since the 1980s, both in mainstream economics and in the heterodox school of Post-Keynesian economics, and has subsequently been developed by such Post-Keynesian economists as Hyman Minsky[10] and Steve Keen.[11]

2.35.4 Modern modifications of Kondratiev theory

There are several modern timing versions of the cycle although most are based on either of two causes: one on technology and the other on the credit cycle.

Additionally, there are several versions of the technological cycles, and they are best interpreted using diffusion curves of leading industries. For example, railways only started in the 1830s, with steady growth for the next 45 years. It was after Bessemer steel was introduced that railroads had their highest growth rates; however, this period is usually labeled the "age of steel". Measured by value added, the leading industry in the U.S. from 1880 to 1920 was machinery, followed by iron and steel.[12]

The technological cycles can be labeled as follows:

- The Industrial Revolution—1771
- The Age of Steam and Railways—1829
- The Age of Steel and Heavy Engineering—1875
- The Age of Oil, Electricity, the Automobile and Mass Production—1908
- The Age of Information and Telecommunications—1971

Any influence of technology during the cycle that began in the Industrial Revolution pertains mainly to England. The U.S. was a commodity producer and was more influenced by agricultural commodity prices. There was a commodity price cycle based on increasing consumption causing tight supplies and rising prices. That allowed new land to the west to be purchased and after four or five years to be cleared and be in production, driving down prices and causing a depression, as in 1819 and 1839.[13] By the 1850s the U. S. was becoming industrialized.[14]

Other researchers

Several papers on the relationship between technology and the economy were written by researchers at the International Institute for Applied Systems Analysis (IIASA). A concise version of Kondratiev cycles can be found in the work of Robert Ayres (1989) in which he gives a historical overview of the relationships of the most significant technologies.[15] Cesare Marchetti published on Kondretiev waves and on the diffusion of innovations.[16][17] Arnulf Grübler's book (1990) gives a detailed account of the diffusion of infrastructures including canals, railroads, highways and airlines, with findings that the principal infrastructures have midpoints spaced in time corresponding to 55 year K wavelengths, with railroads and highways taking almost a century to complete. Grübler devotes a chapter to the long economic wave.[18]

Korotayev et al. recently employed spectral analysis and claimed that it confirmed the presence of Kondratiev waves in the world GDP dynamics at an acceptable level of statistical significance.[2][19] Korotayev et al. also detected shorter business cycles, dating the Kuznets to about 17 years and calling it the third harmonic of the Kondratiev, meaning that there are three Kuznets cycles per Kondratiev.

More recently the physicist and systems scientist Tessaleno Devezas advanced a causal model for the long wave phenomenon based on a generation-learning model[20] and a nonlinear dynamic behaviour of information systems.[21] In both works a complete theory is presented containing not only the explanation for the existence of K-Waves, but also and for the first time an explanation for the timing of a K-Wave (≈60 years = two generations).

A specific modification of the theory of Kondratieff cycles was developed by Daniel Šmihula. Šmihula identified six long-waves within modern society and the capitalist economy, each of which was initiated by a specific technological revolution:[22]

- 1. (1600–1780) The wave of the Financial-agricultural revolution
- 2. (1780–1880) The wave of the Industrial revolution

- 3. (1880–1940) The wave of the Technical revolution
- 4. (1940–1985) The wave of the Scientific-technical revolution
- 5. (1985–2015) The wave of the Information and telecommunications revolution
- 6. (2015–2035?) The hypothetical wave of the post-informational technological revolution

Unlike Kondratieff and Schumpeter, Šmihula believed that each new cycle is shorter than its predecessor. His main stress is put on technological progress and new technologies as decisive factors of any long-time economic development. Each of these waves has its **innovation phase**, which is described as a *technological revolution* and an **application phase** in which the number of revolutionary innovations falls and attention focuses on exploiting and extending existing innovations. As soon as an innovation or a series of innovations becomes available, it becomes more efficient to invest in its adoption, extension and use than in creating new innovations. Each wave of technological innovations can be characterized by the area in which the most revolutionary changes took place (*"leading sectors"*).

Every wave of innovations lasts approximately until the profits from the new innovation or sector fall to the level of other, older, more traditional sectors. It is a situation when the new technology, which originally increased a capacity to utilize new sources from nature, reached its limits and it is not possible to overcome this limit without an application of another new technology.

For the end of an application phase of any wave there are typical an economic crisis and stagnation. The economic crisis in 2007–2010 is a result of the coming end of the "wave of the Information and telecommunications technological revolution". Some authors have started to predict what the sixth wave might be, such as James Bradfield Moody and Bianca Nogrady who forecast that it will be driven by resource efficiency and clean technology.[23] On the other hand, Šmihula himself considers the waves of technological innovations during the modern age (after 1600 AD) only as a part of a much longer „chain" of technological revolutions going back to the pre-modern era.[24] It means he believes that we can find long economic cycles (analogical to Kondratiev cycles in modern economy) dependent on technological revolutions even in the Middle Ages and the Ancient era.

2.35.5 Criticism of long cycles

Long wave theory is not accepted by many academic economists, but it is important for innovation-based, development, and evolutionary economics. Among economists who accept it, there has been no universal agreement about the start and the end years of particular waves. This points to a major criticism of the theory: that it amounts to seeing patterns in a mass of statistics that aren't really there.

Moreover, there is a lack of agreement over the cause of this phenomenon. Health economist and biostatistician Andreas J. W. Goldschmidt searched for patterns and proposed that there is a phase shift and overlap of the so-called Kondratiev cycles of IT and health (shown in the figure). He argued that historical growth phases in combination with key technologies does not necessarily imply the existence of regular cycles in general. Goldschmidt is of the opinion that different fundamental innovations and their economic stimuli do not exclude each other, they mostly vary in length, and their benefit is not applicable to all participants in a "market."[25]

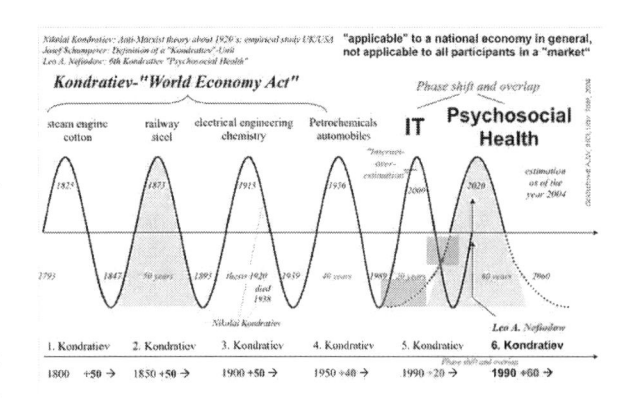

Kondratiev waves associated with gains in IT and health with phase shift and overlap, Andreas J. W. Goldschmidt, 2004

2.35.6 See also

- Business cycles
- Kuznets swing
- Market trends
- Grand Supercycle (Elliott Wave theory)
- Martin A. Armstrong
- Clustering illusion
- Second Industrial Revolution
- Spending wave
- Technological revolution

2.35.7 References

[1] The term *long wave* originated from a poor early translation of *long cycle* from Russian to German. Freeman, Chris; Louçã, Francisco (2001) pp 70

[2] See, e.g. Korotayev, Andrey V.; Tsirel, Sergey V. (2010). "A Spectral Analysis of World GDP Dynamics: Kondratiev Waves, Kuznets Swings, Juglar and Kitchin Cycles in Global Economic Development, and the 2008–2009 Economic Crisis". *Structure and Dynamics* **4** (1): 3–57.

[3] Vincent Barnett, Nikolai Dmitriyevich Kondratiev, *Encyclopedia of Russian History*, 2004, at Encyclopedia.com.

[4] Erik Buyst, Kondratiev, Nikolai (1892–1938), *Encyclopedia of Modern Europe: Europe Since 1914: Encyclopedia of the Age of War and Reconstruction*, Gale Publishing, January 1, 2006.

[5] Hobsbawm (1999), pp. 87f.

[6] Perez, Carlota (2002). *Technological Revolutions and Financial Capital: The Dynamics of Bubbles and Golden Ages*. UK: Edward Elgar Publishing Limited. ISBN 1-84376-331-1.

[7] Tylecote, Andrew (1991). *The Long Wave in the World Economy*. London: Routledge. pp. Chapter 5: Population feedback. ISBN 0-415-03690-9.

[8] Clark, Ross (20 January 2008), "The man who predicted today's housing woes – ten years ago", *The Mail on Sunday*

[9] "Fred Foldvary". Foldvary.net. Retrieved 2013-03-26.

[10] Minsky, Hyman (1992). "The Financial Instability Hypothesis". *Jerome Levy Economics Institute Working Paper No. 74*. SSRN 161024.

[11] Keen, Steve (1995). "Finance and Economic Breakdown: Modelling Minsky's Financial Instability Hypothesis". *Journal of Post Keynesian Economics* **17** (4): 607–635.

[12] Table 7: Ten leading industries in America, by value added, 1914 prices (millions of 1914 $'s)

[13] North, Douglas C. (1966). *The Economic Growth of the United States 1790–1860*. New York, London: W. W. Norton & Company. ISBN 978-0-393-00346-8.

[14] See: Joseph Whitworth's quote under American system of manufacturing#Use of machinery.

[15] Ayres, Robert (1989). "Technological Transformations and Long Waves" (PDF).

[16] Marchetti, Cesare (1996). "Pervasive Long Waves: Is Society Cyclotymic" (PDF).

[17] Marchetti, Cesare (1988). "Kondratiev Revisited-After One Cycle" (PDF).

[18] Grübler, Arnulf (1990). *The Rise and Fall of Infrastructures: Dynamics of Evolution and Technological Change in Transport* (PDF). Heidelberg and New York: Physica-Verlag.

[19] Spectral analysis is a mathematical technique that is used in such fields as electrical engineering for analyzing electrical circuits and radio waves to deconstruct a complex signal to determine the main frequencies and their relative contribution. Signal analysis is usually done with equipment. Data analysis is done with special computer software.

[20] Devezas, Tessaleno (2001). "The Biological Determinants of long-wave behaviour in socioeconomic growth and development, Technological Forecasting & Social Change 68, pp. 1–57".

[21] Devezas, Tessaleno; Corredine, James (2002). "The nonlinear dynamics of technoeconomic systems - An informational interpretation, Technological Forecasting and Social Change, 69, pp. 317–357".

[22] Šmihula, Daniel (2009). "The waves of the technological innovations of the modern age and the present crisis as the end of the wave of the informational technological revolution". *Studia politica Slovaca* (Bratislava) **2009** (1): 32–47. ISSN 1337-8163.

[23] Moody, J. B.; Nogrady, B. (2010). *The Sixth Wave: How to succeed in a resource-limited world*. Sydney: Random House. ISBN 9781741668896.

[24] Šmihula, Daniel (2011). "Long waves of technological innovations". *Studia politica Slovaca* (Bratislava) **2011** (2): 50–69. ISSN 1337-8163.

[25] Goldschmidt, Andreas JW; Hilbert, Josef (2009). *Health Economy in Germany - Economical Field of the Future (Gesundheitswirtschaft in Deutschland - Die Zukunftsbranche)*. Germany: Wikom Publishing house, Wegscheid. p. 22. ISBN 978-3-9812646-0-9.

2.35.8 Further reading

- Barnett, Vincent (1998). *Kondratiev and the Dynamics of Economic Development*. London: Macmillan. ISBN 0-312-21048-5.

- Beaudreau, Bernard C. (1996). *Mass Production, the Stock Market Crash and the Great Depression*. New York, Lincoln, Shanghi: Authors Choice Press.

- Cheung, Edward (2007) [1995]. *Baby Boomers, Generation X and Social Cycles, Volume 1: North American Long-waves* (PDF). Toronto: Longwave Press. ISBN 978-1-896330-00-6.

- Devezas, Tessaleno (2006). *Kondratieff Waves, Warfare and World Security*. Amsterdam: IOS Press. ISBN 1-58603-588-6.

- Freeman, Chris; Louçã, Francisco (2001). *As Time Goes By. From the Industrial Revolutions to the Information Revolution*. Oxford: Oxford University Press. ISBN 0-19-924107-4.

- Goldstein, Joshua (1988). *Long Cycles: Prosperity and War in the Modern Age*. New Haven: Yale University Press. ISBN 0-300-03994-8.

- Grinin, L.; Munck, V. C. de; Korotayev, A. (2006). *History and mathematics: Analyzing and Modeling Global Development*. Moscow: URSS. ISBN 5-484-01001-2.

- Hobsbawm, Eric (1999). *Age of Extremes: The Short Twentieth Century 1914–1991*. London: Abacus. ISBN 0-349-10671-1.

- Korotayev, Andrey V., & Tsirel, Sergey V.(2010). A Spectral Analysis of World GDP Dynamics: Kondratieff Waves, Kuznets Swings, Juglar and Kitchin Cycles in Global Economic Development, and the 2008–2009 Economic Crisis. *Structure and Dynamics*. Vol.4. #1. P.3-57.

- Kohler, Gernot; Chaves, Emilio José (2003). *Globalization: Critical Perspectives*. Hauppauge, New York: Nova Science Publishers. ISBN 1-59033-346-2. With contributions by Samir Amin, Christopher Chase Dunn, Andre Gunder Frank, Immanuel Wallerstein.

- Lewis, W. Arthur (1978). *Growth and Fluctuations 1870-1913*. London: Allen & Unwin. pp. 69–93. ISBN 0-04-300072-X.

- Mandel, Ernest (1964). "The Economics of Neocapitalism". *The Socialist Register*.

- Mandel, Ernest (1980). *Long waves of capitalist development: the Marxist interpretation*. New York: Cambridge University Press. ISBN 0-521-23000-4.

- McNeil, Ian (1990). *An Encyclopedia of the History of Technology*. London: Routledge. ISBN 0-415-14792-1.

- Marchetti, Cesare (1986). "Fifty-Year Pulsation in Human Affairs, Analysis of Some Physical Indicators". *Futures* **17** (3): 376–388.

- Modis, Theodore (1992). *Predictions: Society's Telltale Signature Reveals the Past and Forecasts the Future*. New York: Simon & Schuster. ISBN 0-671-75917-5.

- Nyquist, Jeffrey (2007). "Cycles of History, Boom and Bust". San Diego: Financial Sense. Weekly Column from 11.09.2007 predicting a major turningpoint between 2007 to 2009 and the start of a Great Depression.

- Rothbard, Murray (1984). *The Kondratieff Cycle: Real or Fabricated?*. Ludwig von Mises Institute.

- Silverberg, Gerald; Verspagen, Bart (2000). *Breaking the Waves: A Poisson Regression Approach to Schumpeterian Clustering of Basic Innovations*. Maastricht: MERIT.

- Šmihula, Daniel (2009). *The waves of the technological innovations of the modern age and the present crisis as the end of the wave of the informational technological revolution:.* Bratislava: in Studia politica Slovaca, 1/2009 SAS. pp. 32–47. ISSN 1337-8163.

- Šmihula, Daniel (2011). *Long waves of technological innovations:.* Bratislava: in Studia politica Slovaca, 1/2011 SAS. pp. 50–69. ISSN 1337-8163.

- Solomou, Solomos (1989). *Phases of Economic Growth, 1850-1973: Kondratieff Waves and Kuznets Swings*. Cambridge: Cambridge University Press. ISBN 0-521-33457-8.

- Tausch, Arno; Ghymers, Christian (2007). *From the 'Washington' Towards a 'Vienna Consensus'? A Quantitative Analysis on Globalization, Development and Global Governance*. Hauppauge, New York: Nova Science Publishers. ISBN 1-60021-422-3.

- Tausch, Arno (2013). *The Hallmarks of Crisis: A New Center-Periphery Perspective on Long Cycles*. Connecticut: REPEC/IDEAS.

- Turchin, Peter (2006). *History & Mathematics: Historical Dynamics and Development of Complex Societies*. Moscow: KomKniga. ISBN 5-484-01002-0.

- *The Kondratieff Wave*. Dell Publishing Co. Inc. New York, N.Y., USA. 1972. p. 198.

- Shuman, James B.; Rosenau, David (1972). *The Kondratieff Wave. The Future of America Until 1984 and Beyond*. New York: Dell. This book provides the history of the many ups and downs of the economies.

- Tylecote, Andrew (1991). *The Long Wave in the World Economy: The Current Crisis in Historical Perspective*. London and New York: Routledge.

- Kondratieff Waves almanac

2.35.9 External links

- "Kondratieff waves" on faculty.Washington.edu (The Evolutionary World Politics Homepage).

- "Kondratieff theory explained" on Kondratyev.com (Kondratyev Theory Letters).

- Kondratieff winter perspective on current place in business cycles

- The Kondratieff Cycle: Real or Fabricated? by Murray Rothbard

2.36 Market abolitionism

Market abolitionism is a belief that the market, in the economic sense, should be completely eliminated from society. Market abolitionists argue that markets are morally abhorrent, antisocial and ultimately incompatible with human and environmental survival and that if left unchecked the market will annihilate both.

In large countries in the modern world, the only significant alternative to a market economy has been central planning as was practiced in the early USSR and in the People's Republic of China before the 1990s. Other proposed alternatives to the market economy —participatory planning as proposed in the theory of participatory economics ("Parecon"), an "artificial market" as proposed by advocates of Inclusive Democracy, and the idea of substituting a gift economy for a commodity exchange—have not yet been tried on a large scale in the modern industrialized world, though alternative organizational methods have been implemented successfully during short periods of time: the early stages of the Russian Revolution before it was taken over by the Bolsheviks,[1][2][3] and the Spanish Revolution before it was crushed by the alliance of liberals and communists.[4]

2.36.1 Proponents

Michael Albert, creator of Znet and co-creator of participatory economics, considers himself a market abolitionist and favors democratic participatory planning as a replacement. He and several colleagues, including Robin Hahnel have elaborated their theory of "parecon" in books, on Znet, and in *Z Magazine*.

Notably, Noam Chomsky is one of those who have expressed the opinion that a truly free market (in the context of a sudden transition from the current system) would destroy the species as well as physical environment. He also favors a democratic participatory planning process as a replacement to the market.

2.36.2 Criticisms

Economists such as Milton Friedman, Friedrich Hayek and Brink Lindsey argue that if the market is eliminated along with property, prices, and wages, then the mode of information transmission is eliminated and what will result is a highly inefficient system for transmitting the value, supply, demand, of goods, services, resources, along with an elimination of the most efficient mode of market transactions. Opinions as to what would follow range from the total collapse of civilization and mass starvation[5] to mere inefficient allocation.[6]

Market abolitionists may reply that whilst advocates of the Austrian school recognize equilibrium prices do not exist, they nonetheless claim that these prices can be used as a rational basis whilst this is not the case, hence markets are not efficient.[7][8]

"Contemporary" mutualists like Kevin Carson (as opposed to "classical" mutualists such Pierre-Joseph Proudhon) advocate a form of mutualism termed "Free Market Socialism" (which is not the same as Market Socialism) as an alternative to both Capitalism and State Socialism, noting that a decentralized system can be self-regulating.

2.36.3 See also

- Murray Bookchin
- Parecon

2.36.4 References

[1] Rocker, Rudolf (2004). *Anarcho syndicalism: Theory and Practice*. AK Press.

[2] Berkman, Alexander (2003). *The ABC of Anarchism*. Dover Publications.

[3] Noam Chomsky. "Notes on Anarchism". In Daniel Guérin, Anarchism: From Theory to Practice, 1970; chomsky.info. Retrieved 2009-12-22.

[4] Chomsky, Noam (2003). *Objectivity and Liberal Scholarship*. The New Press.

[5] http://mises.org/daily/2197

[6] Bryan Caplan's short critique of economic calculation problem as posed by the Austrian school (among other things): http://econfaculty.gmu.edu/bcaplan/whyaust.htm

[7] http://anarchism.pageabode.com/afaq/secI1.html#seci12

[8] http://anarchism.pageabode.com/afaq/secI1.html#seci15

2.36.5 External links

- Market Madness: Michael Albert interviewed about market ideology in Poland
- Markets Über Alles? by Michael Albert (archived version)

2.37 Marxian economics

Marxian economics or the **Marxian school of economics** refers to a school of economic thought tracing its foundations to the critique of classical political economy first expounded upon by Karl Marx and Friedrich Engels. Marxian economics refers to several different theories and includes multiple schools of thought which are sometimes opposed to each other, and in many cases Marxian analysis is used to complement or supplement other economic approaches.[1] Because one does not necessarily have to be politically Marxist to be economically Marxian, the two adjectives coexist in usage rather than being synonymous. They share a semantic field while also allowing connotative and denotative differences.

Marxian economics concerns itself variously with the analysis of crisis in capitalism, the role and distribution of the surplus product and surplus value in various types of economic systems, the nature and origin of economic value, the impact of class and class struggle on economic and political processes, and the process of economic evolution.

Marxian economics, particularly in academia, is distinguished from Marxism as a political ideology as well as the normative aspects of Marxist thought, with the view that Marx's original approach to understanding economics and economic development is intellectually independent from Marx's own advocacy of revolutionary socialism.[2][3] Marxian economists do not lean entirely upon the works of Marx and other widely known Marxists, but draw from a range of Marxist and non-Marxist sources.[4]

Although the Marxian school is considered heterodox, ideas that have come out of Marxian economics have contributed to mainstream understanding of the global economy; certain concepts of Marxian economics, especially those related to capital accumulation and the business cycle, such as creative destruction, have been fitted for use in capitalist systems.

Marx's magnum opus on political economy was *Das Kapital* (Capital: A Critique of Political Economy) in three volumes, of which only the first volume was published in his lifetime (1867); the others were published by Friedrich Engels from Marx's notes. One of Marx's early works, *Critique of Political Economy*, was mostly incorporated into *Das Kapital*, especially the beginning of volume 1. Marx's notes made in preparation for writing *Das Kapital* were published in 1939 under the title *Grundrisse*.

2.37.1 Marx's response to classical economics

Marx's economics took as its starting point the work of the best-known economists of his day, the British classical economists Adam Smith, Thomas Malthus, and David Ricardo.

Smith, in *The Wealth of Nations* (1776), argued that the most important characteristic of a market economy was that it permitted a rapid growth in productive abilities. Smith claimed that a growing market stimulated a greater "division of labor" (i.e., specialization of businesses and/or workers) and this, in turn, led to greater productivity. Although Smith generally said little about laborers, he did note that an increased division of labor could at some point cause harm to those whose jobs became narrower and narrower as the division of labor expanded. Smith maintained that a laissez-faire economy would naturally correct itself over time.

Marx followed Smith by claiming that the most important beneficial economic consequence of capitalism was a rapid growth in productivity abilities. Marx also expanded greatly on the notion that laborers could come to harm as capitalism became more productive. Additionally, in *Theories of Surplus Value*, Marx noted, "We see the great advance made by Adam Smith beyond the Physiocrats in the analysis of surplus-value and hence of capital. In their view, it is only one definite kind of concrete labour—agricultural labour —that creates surplus-value....But to Adam Smith, it is general social labour—no matter in what use-values it manifests itself—the mere quantity of necessary labour, which creates value. Surplus-value, whether it takes the form of profit, rent, or the secondary form of interest, is nothing but a part of this labour, appropriated by the owners of the material conditions of labour in the exchange with living labour."

Malthus' claim, in "An Essay on the Principle of Population", that population growth was the primary cause of subsistence level wages for laborers provoked Marx to develop an alternative theory of wage determination. Whereas Malthus presented an ahistorical theory of population growth, Marx offered a theory of how a relative surplus population in capitalism tended to push wages to subsistence levels. Marx saw this relative surplus population as coming from economic causes and not from biological causes (as in Malthus). This economic-based theory of surplus population is often labeled as Marx's theory of the reserve army of labour.

Ricardo developed a theory of distribution within capitalism, that is, a theory of how the output of society is distributed to classes within society. The most mature version of this theory, presented in *On the Principles of Political Economy and Taxation*, was based on a labour theory of value in which the value of any produced object is equal to the labor embodied in the object. (Adam Smith also presented a labor theory of value but it was only incompletely realized.) Also notable in Ricardo's economic theory was that profit was a deduction from society's output and that wages and profit were inversely related: an increase in profit came at the expense of a reduction in wages. Marx built much of the formal economic analysis found in *Capital* on Ricardo's theory of the economy.

2.37.2 Marx's theory

Marx employed a labour theory of value, which holds that the value of a commodity is the socially necessary labour time invested in it. In this model, capitalists do not pay workers the full value of the commodities they produce; rather, they compensate the worker for the necessary labor only (the worker's wage, which cover only the necessary means of subsistence in order to maintain him working in the present and his family in the future as a group). This necessary labor is, Marx supposes, only a fraction of a full working day - the rest, the surplus-labor, would be pocketed by the capitalist.

Marx theorized that the gap between the value a worker produces and his wage is a form of unpaid labour, known as surplus value. Moreover, Marx argues that markets tend to obscure the social relationships and processes of production; he called this commodity fetishism. People are highly aware of commodities, and usually don't think about the relationships and labour they represent.

Marx's analysis leads to the consideration of economic crisis. "A propensity to crisis—what we would call *business cycles*—was not recognised as an inherent feature of capitalism of by other economist of Marx's time," observed Robert Heilbroner in *The Worldly Philosophers*, "although future events have certainly indicated his prediction of successive boom and crash."[5] Marx's theory of economic cycles was formalised by Richard Goodwin in "A Growth Cycle" (1967),[6] a paper published during the centenary year of *Capital, Volume I*.

Methodology

Marx used dialectics, a method that he adapted from the works of Georg Wilhelm Friedrich Hegel. Dialectics focuses on relation and change, and tries to avoid seeing the universe as composed of separate objects, each with essentially stable unchanging characteristics. One component of dialectics is abstraction; out of an undifferentiated mass of data or system conceived of as an organic whole, one abstracts portions to think about or to refer to. One may abstract objects, but also — and more typically — relations, and processes of change. An abstraction may be extensive or narrow, may focus on generalities or specifics, and may be made from various points of view. For example, a sale may be abstracted from a buyer's or a seller's point of view, and one may abstract a particular sale or sales in general. Another component is the dialectical deduction of categories. Marx uses Hegel's notion of *categories*, which are *forms*, for economics: The commodity *form*, the money *form*, the capital *form* etc. have to be systematically deduced instead of being grasped in an outward way as done by the bourgeois economists. This corresponds to Hegel's critique of Kant's transcendental philosophy.[7]

Marx regarded history as having passed through several stages. The details of his periodisation vary somewhat through his works, but it essentially is: Primitive Communism -- Slave societies -- Feudalism -- Capitalism -- Socialism -- Communism (capitalism being the present stage and communism the future). Marx occupied himself primarily with describing capitalism. Historians place the beginning of capitalism some time between about 1450 (Sombart) and some time in the 17th century (Hobsbawm).[8]

Marx defines a commodity as a product of human labour that is produced for sale in a market, and many products of human labour are commodities. Marx began his major work on economics, *Capital*, with a discussion of commodities; Chapter One is called "Commodities".

Commodities

"The wealth of those societies in which the capitalist mode of production prevails, presents itself as 'an immense accumulation of commodities,' its unit being a single commodity." (First sentence of *Capital,* Volume I.)

"The common substance that manifests itself in the exchange value of commodities whenever they are exchanged, is their value." (Capital, I, Chap I, section 1.)

The worth of a commodity can be conceived of in two different ways, which Marx calls use-value and value. A commodity's use-value is its usefulness for fulfilling some practical purpose; for example, the use-value of a piece of food is that it provides nourishment and pleasurable taste; the use value of a hammer, that it can drive nails.

Value is, on the other hand, a measure of a commodity's worth in comparison to other commodities. It is closely related to exchange-value, the ratio at which commodities should be traded for one another, but not identical: value is at a more general level of abstraction; exchange-value is a realisation or form of it.

Marx argued that if value is a property common to all commodities, then whatever it is derived from, whatever determines it, must be common to all commodities. The only relevant thing that is, in Marx's view, common to all commodities is human labour: they are all produced by human labour.

Marx concluded that the value of a commodity is simply the amount of human labour required to produce it. Thus Marx adopted a labour theory of value, as had his predecessors Ricardo and MacCulloch; Marx himself traced the existence of the theory at least as far back as an anonymous work, *Some Thoughts on the Interest of Money in General, and Particularly the Publick Funds, &c.*, published in London around 1739 or 1740.[9]

Marx placed some restrictions on the validity of his value theory: he said that in order for it to hold, the commodity must not be a useless item; and it is not the actual amount of labour that went into producing a particular individual commodity that determines its value, but the amount of labour that a worker of average energy and ability, working with average intensity, using the prevailing techniques of the day, would need to produce it. A formal statement of the law is: the value of a commodity is equal to the average socially necessary labour time required for its production. (Capital, I, I—p 39 in Progress Publishers, Moscow, ed'n.)

Marx's contention was that commodities tend, at a fairly general level of abstraction, to exchange at value; that is, if Commodity A, whose value is "V", is traded for Commodity B, it will tend to fetch an amount of Commodity B whose value is the same, "V". Particular circumstances will cause divergence from this rule, however.

Money

Marx held that metallic money, such as gold, is a commodity, and its value is the labour time necessary to produce it (mine it, smelt it, etc.). Marx argued that gold and silver are conventionally used as money because they embody a large amount of labour in a small, durable, form, which is convenient. Paper money is, in this model, a representation of gold or silver, almost without value of its own but held in circulation by state decree.

"Paper money is a token representing gold or money." (Capital, I, Chap III, section 2, part c.)

Production

Marx lists the elementary factors of production as:

1. labour, "the personal activity of man." (Capital, I, VII, 1.)

2. the subject of labour: the thing worked on.

3. the instruments of labour: tools, labouring domestic animals like horses, chemicals used in modifying the subject, etc.

Some subjects of labour are available directly from Nature: uncaught fish, unmined coal, etc. Others are results of a previous stage of production; these are known as raw materials, such as flour or yarn. Workshops, canals, and roads are considered instruments of labour. (*Capital*, I, VII, 1.) Coal for boilers, oil for wheels, and hay for draft horses is considered raw material, not instruments of labour.

"If, on the other hand, the subject of labour has, so to say, been filtered through previous labour, we call it raw material. . . ." (*Capital*, I, Chap VII, section 1.)

The subjects of labour and instruments of labour together are called the means of production. Relations of production are the relations human beings adopt toward each other as part of the production process. In capitalism, wage labour and private property are part of the relations of production.

> Calculation of value of a product (price not to be confused with value):
>
> If labour is performed directly on Nature and with instruments of negligible value, the value of the product is simply the labour time. If labour is performed on something that is itself the product of previous labour (that is, on a raw material), using instruments that have some value, the value of the product is the value of the raw material, plus depreciation on the instruments, plus the labour time. Depreciation may be figured simply by dividing the value of the instruments by their working life; *e.g.* if a lathe worth £1,000 lasts in use 10 years it imparts value to the product at a rate of £100 per year.

Effect of technical progress

According to Marx, the amount of actual product (i.e. use-value) that a typical worker produces in a given amount of time is the productivity of labour. It has tended to increase under capitalism. This is due to increase in the scale of enterprise, to specialisation of labour, and to the introduction of machinery. The immediate result of this is that the value of a given item tends to decrease, because the labour time necessary to produce it becomes less.

In a given amount of time, labour produces more items, but each unit has less value; the total value created per time remains the same. This means that the means of subsistence become cheaper; therefore the value of labour power or necessary labour time becomes less. If the length of the working day remains the same, this results in an increase in the surplus labour time and the rate of surplus value.

Technological advancement tends to increase the amount of capital needed to start a business, and it tends to result in an increasing preponderance of capital being spent on means of production (constant capital) as opposed to labour (variable capital). Marx called the ratio of these two kinds of capital the composition of capital.

2.37.3 Current theorizing in Marxian economics

Marxian economics has been built upon by many others, beginning almost at the moment of Marx's death. The second and third volumes of *Das Kapital* were edited by his close associate Friedrich Engels, based on Marx's notes. Marx's *Theories of Surplus Value* was edited by Karl Kautsky. The Marxian value theory and the Perron-Frobenius theorem on the positive eigenvector of a positive matrix [10] are fundamental to mathematical treatments of Marxist economics.

Universities offering one or more courses in Marxian economics, or teach one or more economics courses on other topics from a perspective that they designate as Marxian or Marxist, include Colorado State University, New School for Social Research, School of Oriental and African Studies, Universiteit Maastricht, University of Bremen, University of California, Riverside, University of Leeds, University of Maine, University of Manchester, University of Massachusetts Amherst, University of Massachusetts Boston, University of Missouri–Kansas City, University of Sheffield, University of Utah, and York University (Toronto).[11]

English-language journals include *Capital & Class, Historical Materialism, Monthly Review, Rethinking Marxism, Review of Radical Political Economics,* and *Studies in Political Economy.*

2.37.4 Criticisms

Main article: Criticisms of Marxism
See also: Criticisms of Socialism, Criticism of communism, and Criticisms of Communist party rule for specific criticisms of Communist states

Much of the critique of classical Marxian economics came from Marxian economists that revised Marx's original theory, or by the Austrian school of economics. V. K. Dmitriev, writing in 1898,[12] Ladislaus von Bortkiewicz, writing in 1906-07,[13] and subsequent critics have shown how Marx's value theory and law of the tendency of the rate of profit to fall are internally inconsistent. In other words, the critics allege that Marx drew conclusions that actually do not follow from his theoretical premises. Once these alleged errors are corrected, his conclusion that aggregate price and profit are determined by, and equal to, aggregate value and surplus value no longer holds true. This result calls into question his theory that the exploitation of workers is the sole source of profit.[14]

Whether the rate of profit in capitalism has, as Marx predicted, tended to fall is a subject of debate. N. Okishio, in 1961, devised a theorem (Okishio's theorem) showing that if capitalists pursue cost-cutting techniques and if the real wage does not rise, the rate of profit must rise.[15]

The inconsistency allegations have been a prominent feature of Marxian economics and the debate surrounding it since the 1970s.[16]

Among the critics pointing out internal inconsistencies are former and current Marxian and/or Sraffian economists, such as Paul Sweezy,[17] Nobuo Okishio,[18] Ian Steedman,[19] John Roemer,[20] Gary Mongiovi,[21] and David Laibman,[22] who propose that the field be grounded in their correct versions of Marxian economics instead of in Marx's critique of political economy in the original form in which he presented and developed it in *Capital*.[23]

Proponents of the Temporal Single System Interpretation (TSSI) of Marx's value theory claim that the supposed inconsistencies are actually the result of misinterpretation; they argue that when Marx's theory is understood as "temporal" and "single-system," the alleged internal inconsistencies disappear. In a recent survey of the debate, a proponent of the TSSI concludes that "the *proofs* of inconsistency are no longer defended; the entire case against Marx has been reduced to the *interpretive* issue."[24]

Relevance to economics

Marxist economics was assessed in 1988 by Robert M. Solow, who criticized the New Palgrave Dictionary of Economics for over-sampling articles on Marxism themes, giving a "false impression of the state of play" in the economics profession:

> *Marx was an important and influential thinker, and Marxism has been a doctrine with intellectual and practical influence. The fact is, however, that most serious English-speaking economists regard Marxist economics as an irrelevant dead end.*[25]

"Economists working in the Marxian-Sraffian tradition represent a small minority of modern economists, and that their writings have virtually no impact upon the professional work of most economists in major English-language universities", according to George Stigler.[26]

2.37.5 Neo-Marxian economics

See also: Neo-Marxian economics and Neo-Marxism

The terms Neo-Marxian, Post-Marxian, and Radical Political Economics were first used to refer to a distinct tradition of economic thought in the 70s and 80s.

In industrial economics, the Neo-Marxian approach stresses the monopolistic rather than the competitive nature of capitalism. This approach is associated with Kalecki, and Baran and Sweezy.[27][28]

2.37.6 See also

- List of Marxian economists
- Capitalist mode of production
- Capital accumulation
- Evolutionary economics
- Surplus product
- Surplus labour
- Labour power
- Law of value
- Unequal exchange
- Value product
- Productive and unproductive labour
- Regulation school
- Socialist economics
- The Accumulation of Capital
- Material product

2.37.7 Footnotes

[1] Wolff and Resnick, Richard and Stephen (August 1987). *Economics: Marxian versus Neoclassical*. The Johns Hopkins University Press. p. 130. ISBN 0801834805. Marxian theory (singular) gave way to Marxian theories (plural).

[2] "The Neo-Marxian blood Schools". The New School. Retrieved 2007-08-23.

[3] Munro, John. "Some Basic Principles of Marxian Economics" (PDF). University of Toronto. Retrieved 2007-08-23.

[4] Described in Duncan Foley and Gérard Duménil, 2008, "Marx's analysis of capitalist production," *The New Palgrave Dictionary of Economics*, 2nd Edition. Abstract.

[5] Heilbroner 2000, p. 164.

[6] Screpanti & Zamagni 2005, p. 474.

[7] See Helmut Reichelt, quoted in: Kubota, Ken: *Die dialektische Darstellung des allgemeinen Begriffs des Kapitals im Lichte der Philosophie Hegels. Zur logischen Analyse der politischen Ökonomie unter besonderer Berücksichtigung Adornos und der Forschungsergebnisse von Rubin, Backhaus, Reichelt, Uno und Sekine*, in: Beiträge zur Marx-Engels-Forschung. Neue Folge 2009, pp. 199-224, here p. 199.

[8] Angus Maddison, *Phases of Capitalist Development*. Oxford, 1982. P 256, note.

[9] Capital, Vol I, Chap I (p 39 in the Progress Publishers, Moscow, edition).

[10] Fujimori, Y. (1982). "Modern Analysis of Value Theory". *Lecture Notes in Economics and Mathematical Systems*. Springer.

[11] Schools. HETecon.com. Retrieved on: August 23, 2007.

[12] V. K. Dmitriev, 1974 (1898), *Economic Essays on Value, Competition and Utility*. Cambridge: Cambridge Univ. Press.

[13] Ladislaus von Bortkiewicz, 1952 (1906–1907), "Value and Price in the Marxian System", *International Economic Papers* 2, 5–60; Ladislaus von Bortkiewicz, 1984 (1907), "On the Correction of Marx's Fundamental Theoretical Construction in the Third Volume of *Capital*". In Eugen von Böhm-Bawerk 1984 (1896), *Karl Marx and the Close of his System*, Philadelphia: Orion Editions.

[14] M. C. Howard and J. E. King. (1992) A History of Marxian Economics: Volume II, 1929–1990, chapter 12, sect. III. Princeton, NJ: Princeton Univ. Press.

[15] M. C. Howard and J. E. King. (1992) A History of Marxian Economics: Volume II, 1929–1990, chapter 7, sects. II-IV. Princeton, NJ: Princeton Univ. Press.

[16] See M. C. Howard and J. E. King, 1992, *A History of Marxian Economics: Volume II, 1929–1990*. Princeton, NJ: Princeton Univ. Press.

[17] "Only one conclusion is possible, namely, that the Marxian method of transformation [of commodity values into prices of production] is logically unsatisfactory." Paul M. Sweezy, 1970 (1942), *The Theory of Capitalist Development*, p. 15. New York: Modern Reader Paperbacks.

[18] Nobuo Okishio, 1961, "Technical Changes and the Rate of Profit," *Kobe University Economic Review* 7, pp. 85–99.

[19] "[P]hysical quantities ... suffice to determine the rate of profit (and the associated prices of production) .... [I]t follows that value magnitudes are, at best, redundant in the determination of the rate of profit (and prices of production)." "Marx's value reasoning—hardly a peripheral aspect of his work—must therefore be abandoned, in the interest of developing a coherent materialist theory of capitalism." Ian Steedman, 1977, *Marx after Sraffa*, pp. 202, 207. London: New Left Books.

[20] "[The falling-rate-of-profit] position is rebutted in Chapter 5 by a theorem which states that ... competitive innovations result in a rising rate of profit. . There seems to be no hope for a theory of the falling rate of profit within the strict confines of the environment that Marx suggested as relevant." John Roemer, *Analytical Foundations of Marxian Economic Theory*, p. 12. Cambridge: Cambridge Univ. Press, 1981.

[21] Vulgar Economy in Marxian Garb: A Critique of Temporal Single System Marxism, Gary Mongiovi, 2002, *Review of Radical Political Economics* 34:4, p. 393. "Marx did make a number of errors in elaborating his theory of value and the profit rate .... [H]is would-be Temporal Single System defenders ... camouflage Marx's errors." "Marx's value analysis does indeed contain errors." (abstract).

[22] "An Error II is an inconsistency, whose removal through development of the theory leaves the foundations of the theory intact. Now I believe that Marx left us with a few Errors II." David Laibman, "Rhetoric and Substance in Value Theory" in Alan Freeman, Andrew Kliman, and Julian Wells (eds.), *The New Value Controversy and the Foundations of Economics*, Cheltenham, UK: Edward Elgar, 2004, p. 17

[23] See Andrew Kliman, *Reclaiming Marx's "Capital": A Refutation of the Myth of Inconsistency*, esp. pp. 210-211.

[24] Andrew Kliman, *Reclaiming Marx's "Capital"*, Lanham, MD: Lexington Books, p. 208, emphases in original.

[25] Robert M. Solow, "The Wide, Wide World of Wealth, "*New York Times*, March 28, 1988, excerpt (from a review of *The New Palgrave: A Dictionary of Economics*, 1987).

[26] Stigler, George J. (December 1988). "Palgrave's Dictionary of Economics". *Journal of Economic Literature* (American Economic Association) **26** (4): 1729–1736. JSTOR 2726859.

[27] Baran, P. and Sweezy, P. (1966). *Monopoly Capital: An essay on the American economic and social order*, Monthly Review Press, New York

[28] Jonathan Nitzan and Shimshon Bichler. *Capital as power: a study of order and creorder*. Taylor & Francis, 2009, p. 50

2.37.8 References

- Andrew Glyn (1987). "Marxist economics," *The New Palgrave: A Dictionary of Economics*, v. 3, pp. 390–95.

- J.E. Roemer (1987). "Marxian value analysis," *The New Palgrave: A Dictionary of Economics*, v. 3, pp. 383–87.

- John E. Roemer (2008). "socialism (new perspectives)," *The New Palgrave Dictionary of Economics*, 2nd Edition, Abstract.

- Diane Flaherty (2008). "radical economics," *The New Palgrave Dictionary of Economics*, 2nd Edition, Abstract.

- Lenny Flank, 'Contradictions of Capitalism: An Introduction to Marxist Economics', St Petersburg, Florida: Red and Black Publishers, 2007. ISBN 978-0-9791813-9-9.

- Heilbroner, Robert (2000). *The Worldly Philosophers* (7th ed.). London: Penguin Books. ISBN 978-0-140-29006-6.

- Screpanti, Ernesto; Zamagni, Stefano (2005). *An Outline of the History of Economic Thought* (2nd ed.). Oxford: Oxford University Press. ISBN 978-0-199-27913-5.

- Thomas T. Sekine, *The Dialectic of Capital. A Study of the Inner Logic of Capitalism*, 2 volumes (preliminary edition), Tokyo 1986; OCLC 489902822 (vol. 1), OCLC 873921143 (vol. 2).

- Solow, Robert M. (20 March 1988). "The Wide, Wide World Of Wealth (*The New Palgrave: A Dictionary of Economics*'. Edited by John Eatwell, Murray Milgate and Peter Newman. Four volumes. 4,103 pp. New York: Stockton Press. $650)". *New York Times*.

2.37.9 Further reading

- Althusser, Louis and Balibar, Étienne. *Reading Capital*. London: Verso, 2009.

- Bottomore, Tom, ed. *A Dictionary of Marxist Thought*. Oxford: Blackwell, 1998.

- Fine, Ben. *Marx's Capital.* 5th ed. London: Pluto, 2010.

- Harvey, David. *A Companion to Marx's Capital.* London: Verso, 2010.

- Harvey, David. *The Limits of Capital.* London: Verso, 2006.

- Mandel, Ernest. *Marxist Economic Theory.* New York: Monthly Review Press, 1970.

- Mandel, Ernest. *The Formation of the Economic Thought of Karl Marx*. New York: Monthly Review Press, 1977.

- Morishima, Michio. *Marx's Economics: A Dual Theory of Value and Growth*. Cambridge: Cambridge University Press, 1973.

- Postone, Moishe. *Time, Labor, and Social Domination: A Reinterpretation of Marx's Critical Theory*. Cambridge [England]: Cambridge University Press, 1993.

- Saad-Filho, Alfredo. *The Value of Marx: Political Economy for Contemporary Capitalism*. London: Routledge, 2002.

- Wolff, Richard D. and Resnick, Stephen A. *Contending Economic Theories: Neoclassical, Keynesian, and Marxian*. The MIT Press, 2012. ISBN 0262517833

2.37.10 External links

- Marxist Economics Courses, Links and Information
- Marxian Economics (archive from Schwartz center of economic policy analysis)
- Marxian Political Economy
- The Neo-Marxian Schools (archive from Schwartz center of economic policy analysis)
- A Marxian Introduction to Modern Economics
- International working group on value theory
- An outline of Marxist economics, Chapter 6 of *Reformism or Revolution* by Alan Woods
- The End of the Market A website containing a critical evaluation the idea of the market-clearing price which affirms Marx's theory that in capitalism profitability would decline
- The Neo-Marxian Schools ("Radical Political Economy")
- *If you're so smart, why aren't you rich?* Monthly Review article detailing the degeneration of Marxian economics.

2.38 Max Keiser

Warning: Page using Template:Infobox person with unknown parameter "age" (this message is shown only in preview).

Timothy Maxwell "Max" Keiser (born January 23, 1960) is an American broadcaster and film maker. He hosts *Keiser Report*, a financial program broadcast on Russian state media channel RT that features fringe economic theories. Until November 2012, Keiser anchored *On the Edge*, a program of news and analysis hosted by Iran's Press TV.[1] He hosted the New Year's Eve special *The Keiser's Business Guide to 2010* for BBC Radio 5 Live.[2] Keiser presented a season of *The Oracle with Max Keiser* on BBC World News. He produced and appeared in the TV series *People & Power* on the Al-Jazeera English network. He presents a weekly show about finance and markets on London's Resonance FM, and writes for *The Huffington Post*.[3] He currently lives in London.[4]

2.38.1 Early career

Keiser grew up in Westchester County, New York. After studying theatre at New York University, he took a variety of jobs including stand-up comedy and on radio. He then took a part-time job as a stock broker in the 1980s at Paine Webber and Oppenheimer and Co. Inc. (at their midtown office under David Tufts, across from Hurleys), at a time when it "required no talent whatsoever to make gobsmacking amounts of money".[4]

2.38.2 Hollywood Stock Exchange

Main article: Hollywood Stock Exchange

Keiser is the creator, co-founder, and former CEO of HSX Holdings/Hollywood Stock Exchange, later sold to Cantor Fitzgerald.[5] Alongside Michael R. Burns, he co-invented the Virtual Specialist [6] platform on which the Hollywood Stock Exchange operates. This technology allows traders to exchange virtual securities, such as "MovieStocks" and "StarBonds", with convertible virtual currency, the "Hollywood Dollar".

2.38.3 Broadcasting career

Keiser presented *Rumble at the Box Office*[7] for NBC's *Access Hollywood*. He also produced and hosted the weekly talk show *Buy, Sell, Hold* for CBS radio's KLSX in Los Angeles, CA. Currently, he presents *The Truth About Markets* on Resonance 104.4 FM in London.

People & Power

Main article: People & Power

Keiser produced 10 short documentary films covering aspects of financial markets for Al Jazeera's series *People & Power*.[8] The films include *Rigged Markets*,[9] *Money Geyser*,[10] *Death of the Dollar*,[11] *Peaked*,[12] *Extraordinary Antics*,[13] *Savers vs Speculators*,[14] *Banking On It*,[15] *Private Finance or Public Swindle?*[16] and *Focus on Locusts*.[17]

The Oracle with Max Keiser

A pilot episode was produced for Al-Jazeera English titled *The Oracle*. The show was developed into a series for BBC World News.[18] The series first aired on 9 January 2009. Keiser left the BBC after ten episodes. On Twitter, he said he left because he was ordered not to mention Israel in any context.[19]

On the Edge

A weekly half-hour financial commentary show that started in 2009 and is broadcast on Press TV, featuring interviews with well-known alternative economists.[20]

The Keiser Report

See also: Keiser Report

Since September 2009, Keiser has hosted *The Keiser Report* with financial news and analysis, on the RT network.[21] The 30-minute program is produced three times a week. Stacy Herbert (announced on a December 2012 episode as his wife)[22] is the co-host; she banters with Keiser on headlines and commentary.[4] Each episode is divided into two parts. In the first half, Keiser and Herbert alternately discuss a current financial topic, comment on financial media reports, and provide commentary on the actions of bankers. The second half features a guest interview, either face-to-face in the studio or through video conferencing, conducted by Keiser.

An episode broadcast in September 2011 featured an interview with comedienne Rosanne Barr, who stated that her solution to the financial crisis was to "bring back the guillotine".[23]

According to *Forbes* magazine, the economist Sandeep Jaitly of the Gold Standard Institute was forced to resign following comments made on Keiser's show.[24]

Since March 2012, *The Keiser Report* is translated into Spanish *Keiser Report en español*.

Financial punditry

Keiser has appeared as a financial pundit on a number of news networks. Keiser called for a "fatwā" against Hank Paulson[25] on Al Jazeera in response to the Troubled Asset Relief Program (TARP). In a later broadcast Keiser said, "Paulson stinks".[26] Keiser has advised investors to buy gold and especially silver, in order to undermine "the banksters". In November 2012, he predicted that the UK pound was about to collapse.[4]

2.38.4 Activism

Karmabanque

Keiser founded the hedge fund Karmabanque, which sought to profit from any decline in equity value of companies that are susceptible to boycott from environmental groups.[27] The hedge fund's progress was followed monthly in *The Ecologist* magazine.[28] Its targets included Coca-Cola[29] and McDonald's.

The Karmabanque hedge fund project was designed to simultaneously short-sell companies while funneling profits into environmental and ethical-business pressure groups that further act to drive down the companies' stock prices. Describing the project, Keiser stated, "The Internet allows people, activists, from all over the world to gather, or swarm, and hit a company where it hurts most—in their stock price."[30]

The Guardian newspaper described Keiser's Karmabanque

Max Keiser with Stacy Herbert

hedge fund as a "fantastical scheme" and accused him of trying to exist "beyond the normal forces and controls of society".[31] A spokesman for Ryanair said, "Since they put Ryanair on their list, our share price has gone up by 10 percent. We are always delighted to be part of a list which includes Coca-Cola, Starbucks, and Wal-Mart."[32]

Extraordinary Antics

In the Al-Jazeera short film *Extraordinary Antics*,[33] Keiser traveled to Milan and Venice to find out how Central Intelligence Agency station chief Robert Seldon Lady and his fellow CIA agents spent $500,000 on a procedure known as extraordinary rendition, an illegal practice that resulted in an Egyptian citizen, who had been granted asylum in Italy, being abducted and tortured in Cairo.

The CIA was prosecuted for the case and Lady was found guilty in a Milan court. He was sentenced on 9 November 2009 to nine years in prison, according to The Guardian. This verdict was upheld on appeal, but the US refuses to extradite Lady to Italy.[34]

Crash JP Morgan—buy silver

Keiser has labeled JPMorgan Chase "the biggest financial terrorist on Wall Street" in relation to their alleged manipulation of the price of silver.[35] Keiser created a campaign called "Crash JP Morgan—buy silver",[36][37][38] whereby people buy silver bullion, thus raising its price and leaving JP Morgan with a huge short position to cover, the margin of which are collateralized by JPMorgan's own stock price, bankrupting itself. The campaign was introduced on the Alex Jones Radio show in November 2010.[39] Writing in *The Guardian* in December 2010,[40] Keiser suggested that the text "crash jp morgan buy silver" should be used as a googlebomb to virally promote the campaign.

Adweek magazine described Keiser as "the most visible character in an underground movement that has spurred hundreds of blog posts and videos, and played some small part in driving up the price of precious metals".[41]

Keiser drew criticism at the 2000 ShowBiz Expo in Las Vegas when he said of media content that "Everything is inescapably going to a price point called free." In response, Kevin Tsujihara, executive vice president of New Media at Warner Bros., commented that "Piracy.com" will be the victor if superior content is available on sites supported by advertisements.[42]

In 2005, Steven Milloy, the "Junk Science" commentator, demanded that Keiser be removed from the panel of the Triple Bottom Line Investing conference, where he was scheduled to appear. Milloy accused Keiser of making threats against his organization[43] and petitioned sponsors Calvert Investments and KLD Research & Analytics to withdraw from the project.[44] Robert Rubenstein, founder of conference organiser Brooklyn Bridge, stated that Keiser's comments "do not constitute a threat to person or property and are not related to the conference or the content that will be presented there".

The Atlantic magazine's *The Wire* website speculated that a *Downfall* parody video created to promote Keiser's campaign was implicated in the sacking of Grant Williams, the Asia equity trading head at J.P. Morgan.[45]

Cryptocurrencies

In a 2013 interview with then MP George Galloway, Keiser stated that if he had financial control over the City of London he would base the entire economy on the Bitcoin digital currency.[46] In January 2014, Keiser launched a cryptocurrency called "MaxCoin", which was created by two Computer Science students from the University of Bristol. MaxCoin was launched during episode 555 of the Keiser Report.[47] In June 2014, Keiser launched a cryptocurrency called "StartCOIN" for use as the main currency for crowd-funding site StartJOIN.[48]

2.38.5 See also

- Error account – a term often mentioned by Max Keiser

2.38.6 References

[1] "Press TV website, programme list". Presstv.ir. Retrieved 2011-05-10.

[2] "Radio 5 live Programmes – The Keiser's Business Guide to 2010". BBC. Retrieved 2011-05-10.

[3] Keiser, Max. "Collection of articles". Huffingtonpost.com. Retrieved 2011-05-10.

[4] Robert Chalmers (4 November 2012). "Max Keiser: 'Barack Obama is clueless. Mitt Romney will bankrupt the country'". *The Independent* (London). Retrieved 6 November 2012.

[5] Archived December 22, 2008 at the Wayback Machine

[6] "Computer-implemented securities trading system with a virtual specialist function - HSX, Inc". Freepatentsonline.com. 1996-03-25. Retrieved 2013-11-30.

[7] Braunstein, Peter (1999-11-16). "Access' Denied". *Village Voice*. Retrieved 2010-10-26.

[8] *People and Power (TV Series 2007–)* at the Internet Movie Database

2.38. MAX KEISER

[9] "Rigged Markets". English.aljazeera.net. Retrieved 2011-05-10.

[10] "Money Geyser". English.aljazeera.net. Retrieved 2011-05-10.

[11] "Death of the Dollar 2". English.aljazeera.net. 2008-02-08. Retrieved 2011-05-10.

[12] *Peaked (TV episode 2008 #1.22)* at the Internet Movie Database

[13] "Extraordinary Antics - People & Power". Al Jazeera English. Retrieved 2013-11-30.

[14] "Savers vs speculators - People & Power". Al Jazeera English. Retrieved 2013-11-30.

[15] "Banking on it - People & Power". Al Jazeera English. Retrieved 2013-11-30.

[16] "Private finance or public swindle?". English.aljazeera.net. 2008-03-17. Retrieved 2011-05-10.

[17] "Focus on locusts". English.aljazeera.net. Retrieved 2011-05-10.

[18] "BBC News – World Radio and TV". Bbcworldnews.com. 2011-04-26. Retrieved 2011-05-10.

[19] https://twitter.com/maxkeiser/status/495984703284199425

[20] "Press TV". Presstv.ir. 2010-10-22. Retrieved 2013-11-30.

[21] "Keiser Report – RT Programs". Rt.com. Retrieved 2011-05-10.

[22] "Keiser Report: Next American Revolution (E385) (ft. Gerald Celente)". YouTube. 2012-12-27. Retrieved 2013-11-30.

[23] "Roseanne Barr: 'Guilty' Wall Street Bankers Should Be Sent to Reeducation Camps or Beheaded". *Fox News*. 2011-10-03. Retrieved 2013-11-30.

[24] Jon Matonis (2012-08-26). "Economist Appearing On Max Keiser Show Forced To Resign". *Forbes.com*.

[25] "Max Keiser – Aljazeera English News – 16 November 2008". YouTube. Retrieved 2011-05-10.

[26] "Afshin Rattansi : Global Rate Cuts". YouTube. Retrieved 2011-05-10.

[27] "Hedge Fund Shorts Its Way Into Political Activism". Commondreams.org. 2004-11-23. Retrieved 2013-11-30.

[28] Archived April 24, 2015 at the Wayback Machine

[29] Paul Marinko (2004-11-25). "Campaign aims to hit Coke where it hurts | Business". London: The Guardian. Retrieved 2013-11-30.

[30] Kostigen, Thomas M. (2004-12-25). "Hedge Funds Banking on Social and Moral Issues". washingtonpost.com. Retrieved 2013-11-30.

[31] "Notebook: Iconic dotcom has lost its way | Business". London: The Guardian. 2004-11-26. Retrieved 2013-11-30.

[32] "Max Keiser, Ryanair and the eco fears forcing their way onto the share price – Indymedia Ireland". Indymedia.ie. Retrieved 2011-05-10.

[33] "Extraordinary Antics, Part 1". Youtube.com. 2007-06-18. Retrieved 2011-05-10.

[34] Mascolo, Georg (2007-01-10). "Milan's Extraordinary Renditions Case: The CIA in the Dock - SPIEGEL ONLINE". Spiegel.de. Retrieved 2013-11-30.

[35] Taylor, Jeff. "Max Keiser tells the world to Crash JP Morgan, buy silver". The Economic Voice. Retrieved 15 November 2010.

[36] Keiser, Max. "Crash JP Morgan Buy Silver says Max Keiser". Max Keiser. Retrieved 15 November 2010.

[37] Zarowny, Andrew (November 14, 2010). "Crash JP Morgan Buy Silver – Growing Economic Guerrilla War to Crash Bank with Silver Bullets". *Rightpundits.com*. Retrieved November 15, 2010.

[38] Taylor, Jeff (November 12, 2010). "Max Keiser tells the world to Crash JP Morgan, buy silver". *The Economic Voice*. Retrieved November 15, 2010.

[39] "Crash JPMorgan Buy Silver campaign goes global". United Nations of Film.

[40] Max Keiser (2010-12-02). "Want JP Morgan to Crash? Buy Silver". London: The Guardian. Retrieved 2010-12-02.

[41] Braiker, Brian (2011-06-02). "Silver Bug Goes Viral With Marketing War Max Keiser has become a fringe media star thanks to the Web". *Adweek*. Retrieved 2013-11-30.

[42] Ann Donahue (2000-06-26). "Showbiz Expo focus: Tech issues". Variety. Retrieved 2013-11-30.

[43] "Advocacy". Free Enterprise Action Fund. Retrieved 2011-05-10.

[44] "Clear Profit". Clear Profit. 2005-11-16. Retrieved 2011-05-10.

[45] Connor Simpson (2013-07-08). "Here's the Jamie Dimon 'Downfall' Parody That Cost a Bank $1.86 Million". The Wire.

[46] "Is George Galloway To Fight Boris Johnson For Mayor Of London Job?". The Huffington Post. Retrieved 2013-11-30.

[47] http://rt.com/shows/keiser-report/episode-555-max-keiser-255/

[48] "A tweet announcing StartCOIN and StartJOIN". @start_coin on Twitter. Retrieved 2016-01-21.

2.38.7 External links

- Official website
- MaxCoin.co.uk MaxCoin cryptocurrency
- StartCOIN.org StartCOIN cryptocurrency
- StartJOIN.com StartJOIN crowdfunding website
- Max Keiser at the Internet Movie Database

2.39 Modern Monetary Theory

Modern Monetary Theory (**MMT** or **Modern Money Theory**), also known as **neochartalism**, is an economic theory that details the procedures and consequences of using government-issued tokens as the unit of money, i.e., fiat money. According to modern monetary theory, "monetarily sovereign government is the monopoly supplier of its currency and can issue currency of any denomination in physical or non-physical forms. As such the government has an unlimited capacity to pay for the things it wishes to purchase and to fulfill promised future payments, and has an unlimited ability to provide funds to the other sectors. Thus, insolvency and bankruptcy of this government is not possible. It can always pay".[1] In contrast to orthodox monetarism, MMT explains inflation as being caused primarily by resource constraints rather than monetary expansion.

MMT aims to describe and analyze modern economies in which the national currency is fiat money, established and created by the government. In sovereign financial systems, banks can create money but these horizontal transactions do not increase net financial assets as assets are offset by liabilities. "The balance sheet of the government does not include any domestic monetary instrument on its asset side; it owns no money. All monetary instruments issued by the government are on its liability side and are created and destroyed with spending and taxing/bond offerings, respectively. "[1] In addition to deficit spending, valuation effects e.g. growth in stock price can increase net financial assets. In MMT, vertical money (see below) enters circulation through government spending. Taxation and its legal tender power to discharge debt establish the fiat money as currency, giving it value by creating demand for it in the form of a private tax obligation that must be met. In addition, fines, fees and licenses create demand for the currency. This can be a currency issued by the government, or a foreign currency such as the euro.[2][3] An ongoing tax obligation, in concert with private confidence and acceptance of the currency, maintains its value. Because the government can issue its own currency at will, MMT maintains that the level of taxation relative to government spending (the government's deficit spending or budget surplus) is in reality a policy tool that regulates inflation and unemployment, and not a means of funding the government's activities per se.

2.39.1 Background

Modern Monetary Theory synthesises ideas from the *State Theory of Money* of Georg Friedrich Knapp (also known as Chartalism) and *Credit Theory of Money* of Alfred Mitchell-Innes, the functional finance proposals of Abba Lerner, Hyman Minsky's views on the banking system and Wynne Godley's Sectoral balances approach.[4]

Knapp, writing in 1905, argued that "money is a creature of law" rather than a commodity.[5] At the time of writing the Gold Standard was in existence, and Knapp contrasted his state theory of money with the view of "metallism", where the value of a unit of currency depended on the quantity of precious metal it contained or could be exchanged for. He argued the state could create pure paper money and make it exchangeable by recognising it as legal tender, with the criterion for the money of a state being "that which is accepted at the public pay offices".[5]

The prevailing view of money was that it had evolved from systems of barter to become a medium of exchange because it represented a durable commodity which had some use value, but proponents of MMT such as Randall Wray and Mathew Forstater argue that more general statements appearing to support a chartalist view of tax-driven paper money appear in the earlier writings of many classical economists,[6] including Adam Smith, Jean-Baptiste Say, J.S. Mill, Karl Marx and William Stanley Jevons[7]

Alfred Mitchell-Innes, writing in 1914, argued that money existed not as a medium of exchange but as a standard of deferred payment, with government money being debt the government could reclaim by taxation.[8] Innes argued:

> Whenever a tax is imposed, each taxpayer becomes responsible for the redemption of a small part of the debt which the government has contracted by its issues of money, whether coins, certificates, notes, drafts on the treasury, or by whatever name this money is called. He has to acquire his portion of the debt from some holder of a coin or certificate or other form of government money, mid present it to the Treasury in liquidation of his legal debt. He has to redeem or cancel that portion of the debt...The redemption of government debt by taxation is the basic law of coinage and of any issue of government 'money' in whatever form.
> — Alfred Mitchell-Innes, The Credit Theory of Money, The Banking Law Journal

Knapp and "chartalism" were referenced by John Maynard Keynes in the opening pages of his 1930 *Treatise on Money*[9] and appear to have influenced Keynesian ideas on the role of the state in the economy.[6]

By 1947, when Abba Lerner wrote his article *Money as a Creature of the State*, economists had largely abandoned the idea that the value of money was closely linked to gold.[10] Lerner argued that responsibility for avoiding inflation and depressions lay with the state because of its ability to create or tax away money.[10]

2.39.2 Vertical transactions

Further information: Sectoral balances

MMT labels any transactions between the government sector and the non-government sector as a vertical transaction. The government sector is considered to include the treasury and the central bank, whereas the non-government sector includes private individuals and firms (including the private banking system) and the external sector – that is, foreign buyers and sellers.[11]

In any given time period, the government's budget can be either in deficit or in surplus. A deficit occurs when the government spends more than it taxes; and a surplus occurs when a government taxes more than it spends. MMT states that as a matter of accounting, it follows that government budget deficits add net financial assets to the private sector. This is because a budget deficit means that a government has deposited more money into private bank accounts than it has removed in taxes. A budget surplus means the opposite: in total, the government has removed more money from private bank accounts via taxes than it has put back in via spending.

Therefore, budget deficits add net financial assets to the private sector; whereas budget surpluses remove financial assets from the private sector. This is widely represented in macroeconomic theory by the national income identity:

$$G - T = S - I - NX$$

where G is government spending, T is taxes, S is savings, I is investment and NX is net exports.

The conclusion that MMT draws from this is that it is only possible for the non government sector to accumulate a surplus if the government runs budget deficits. The non government sector can be further split into foreign users of the currency and domestic users.

MMT economists aim to run deficits as much as the private sector wants to save and for real resources to be fully used e.g. full employment. As most private sectors want to net save and globally, external balances must add up to zero, MMT economists usually advocate budget deficits.

2.39.3 Interaction between government and the banking sector

Modern monetary theory provides a detailed descriptive account of the "operational realities" of interactions between the government and the central bank, and the commercial banking sector, with proponents like Scott Fullwiler arguing that understanding of reserve accounting is critical to understanding monetary policy options.[12]

A sovereign government will typically have a cash operating account with the central bank of the country. From this account, the government can spend and also receive taxes and other inflows.[13] Similarly, all of the commercial banks will also have an account with the central bank. This permits the banks to manage their reserves (that is, the amount of available short-term money that a particular bank holds).

So when the government spends, treasury will debit its cash operating account at the central bank, and deposit this money into private bank accounts (and hence into the commercial banking system). This money adds to the total reserves of the commercial bank sector. Taxation works exactly in reverse; private bank accounts are debited, and hence reserves in the commercial banking sector fall.

Government bonds and interest rate maintenance

Virtually all central banks set an interest rate target, and conduct open market operations to ensure base interest rates remain at that target level. According to MMT the issuing of government bonds is best understood as an operation to *offset* government spending rather than a requirement to *finance* it.[12]

In most countries, commercial banks' reserve accounts with the central bank must have a positive balance at the end of every day; in some countries, the amount is specifically set as a proportion of the liabilities a bank has (i.e. its customer deposits). This is known as a reserve requirement. At the end of every day, a commercial bank will have to examine the status of their reserve accounts. Those that are in deficit have the option of borrowing the required funds from the central bank, where they may be charged a *lending rate* (sometimes known as a *discount rate*) on the amount they borrow. On the other hand, the banks that have excess reserves can simply leave them with the central bank and earn a *support rate* from the central bank. Some countries, such as Japan, have a support rate of zero.[14]

Banks with more reserves than they need will be willing to lend to banks with a reserve shortage on the interbank lending market. The surplus banks will want to earn a higher rate than the support rate that the central bank pays on reserves; whereas the deficit banks will want to pay a lower interest rate than the discount rate the central bank charges for borrowing. Thus they will lend to each other until each bank has reached their reserve requirement. In a balanced system, where there are just enough total reserves for all the banks to meet requirements, the short-term interbank lending rate will be in between the support rate and the discount rate.[14]

Under an MMT framework where government spending injects new reserves into the commercial banking system, and taxes withdraw it from the banking system, government activity would have an instant effect on interbank lending. If on a particular day, the government spends more than it taxes, reserves have been added to the banking system (see vertical transactions). This will typically lead to a system-wide surplus of reserves, with competition between banks seeking to lend their excess reserves forcing the short-term interest rate down to the support rate (or alternately, to zero if a support rate is not in place). At this point banks will simply keep their reserve surplus with their central bank and earn the support rate.

The alternate case is where the government receives more taxes on a particular day than it spends. In this case, there may be a system-wide deficit of reserves. As a result, surplus funds will be in demand on the interbank market, and thus the short-term interest rate will rise towards the discount rate. Thus, if the central bank wants to maintain a target interest rate somewhere between the support rate and the discount rate, it must manage the liquidity in the system to ensure that there is the correct amount of reserves in the banking system.

Central banks manage this by buying and selling government bonds on the open market. On a day where there are excess reserves in the banking system, the central bank sells bonds and therefore removes reserves from the banking system, as private individuals pay for the bonds. On a day where there are not enough reserves in the system, the central bank buys government bonds from the private sector, and therefore adds reserves to the banking system.

It is important to note that the central bank buys bonds by simply creating money—it is not financed in any way. It is a net injection of reserves into the banking system. If a central bank is to maintain a target interest rate, then it must necessarily buy and sell government bonds on the open market in order to maintain the correct amount of reserves in the system.

2.39.4 Horizontal transactions

MMT economists describe any transactions within the private sector as "horizontal" transactions, including the expansion of the broad money supply through the extension of credit by banks.

MMT economists regard the concept of the money multiplier, where a bank is completely constrained in lending through the deposits it holds and its capital requirement, as misleading.[15] Rather than being a practical limitation on lending, the cost of borrowing funds from the interbank market (or the central bank) represents a *profitability consideration* when the private bank lends in excess of its reserve and/or capital requirements (see interaction between government and the banking sector).

According to MMT, bank credit should be regarded as a "leverage" of the monetary base and should not be regarded as increasing the net financial assets held by an economy, with only the government or central bank able to issue high powered money with no corresponding liability.[15] Stephanie Kelton argues that bank money is generally accepted in settlement of debt and taxes because of state guarantees, but that state-issued high-powered money sits atop a "hierarchy of money".[16]

2.39.5 The foreign sector

NOTE: Some MMT economists view this distinction misleading and the currency area itself as a closed system, and do not differentiate between the external and domestic sectors. They view the world (closed system) split into several currency areas, not necessarily the size of a country.

Imports and exports

MMT analyzes imports and exports within the framework of horizontal transactions. It argues that an export represents a desire on behalf of the exporting nation to obtain the national currency of the importing nation if there are floating exchange rates and they use different currencies. The following hypothetical example is consistent with the workings of the FX market, and can be used to illustrate the basis of this aspect of MMT:

> "An Australian importer (person A) needs to pay for some Japanese goods. The importer will go to his bank and ask to transfer 1000 yen to the Japanese bank account of the Japanese firm (person B). After looking up the relevant exchange rates for that day, the bank will inform him that this will cost him 100 dollars. The bank removes 100 dollars from the importer's account, and goes

to the FX market. It finds an individual (person C) who is willing to swap 1000 yen for 100 dollars. It transfers the 100 dollars to that individual. Then it takes the 1000 yen and transfers it to the Japanese exporter's bank account."

Thus, the transaction is complete. What made the transaction possible (i.e. acceptably priced to the importer) was person C in the middle of the FX swap. Thus MMT concludes that it is a foreign desire for an importer's currency that makes importing possible.[17]

MMT proponents such as Warren Mosler argue that trade deficits need not be unsustainable and are beneficial to the standard of living in the short run.[18] Imports are an economic benefit to the importing nation because they provide the nation with real goods it can consume, that it otherwise would not have had. Exports, on the other hand, are an economic cost to the exporting nation because it is losing real goods that it could have consumed.[17] Currency transferred to foreign ownership, however represents a future claim over goods of that nation.

Cheap imports may also cause the failure of local firms providing similar goods at higher prices, and hence unemployment but MMT commentators label that consideration as a subjective value-based one, rather than an economic-based one: it is up to a nation to decide whether it values the benefit of cheaper imports more than it values employment in a particular industry.[17] Similarly a nation overly dependent on imports may face a supply shock if the exchange rate drops significantly, though central banks can and do trade on the FX markets to avoid sharp shocks to the exchange rate.[19]

Foreign sector and commercial banks

Although a net-importing nation will transfer a portion of domestic currency into foreign ownership, the currency will usually remain within the importing nation. The foreign owner of the local currency can either (a) spend them purchasing local assets or (b) deposit them in the local banking system. In each scenario, the money ultimately ends up in the local banking system.

Foreign sector and government

Using the same application of vertical transactions MMT argues that the holder of the bond is irrelevant to the issuing government. As long as there is a demand for the issuer's currency, whether the bond holder is foreign or not, governments can never be insolvent when the debt obligations are in their own currency; this is because the government is not constrained in creating its own currency (although the bond holder may affect the exchange rate by converting to local currency).[20] Similarly, according to the FX theory outlined above, the currency paid out at maturity cannot leave the country of issuance either.

MMT does point out, however, that debt denominated in a foreign currency certainly is a fiscal risk to governments, since the indebted government cannot create foreign currency. In this case the only way the government can sustainably repay its foreign debt is to ensure that its currency is continually and highly demanded by foreigners over the period that it wishes to repay the debt – an exchange rate collapse would potentially multiply the debt many times over asymptotically, making it impossible to repay. In that case, the government can default, or attempt to shift to an export-led strategy or raise interest rates to attract foreign investment in the currency. Either one has a negative effect on the economy.[21] Euro debt crises in the "PIIGS" countries that began in 2009 reflect this risk, since Greece, Ireland, Spain, Italy, etc. have all issued debts in a quasi-"foreign currency" – the Euro, which they cannot create.

2.39.6 Policy implications

MMT claims that the word "borrowing" is a misnomer when it comes to a sovereign government's fiscal operations, because what the government is doing is accepting back its own IOUs, and nobody can borrow back their own debt instruments.[22] Sovereign government goes into debt by issuing its own liabilities that are financial wealth to the private sector. "Private debt is debt, but government debt is *financial wealth* to the private sector."[23]

In this theory, sovereign government is not *financially* constrained in its ability to spend; it is argued that the government can afford to buy anything that is for sale in currency that it issues (there may be political constraints, like a debt ceiling law). The only constraint is that excessive spending by any sector of the economy (whether households, firms or public) has the potential to cause inflationary pressures. MMTers argue though that generally inflation is caused by supply-side pressures, rather than demand side.

Some MMT economists advocate a government-funded job guarantee scheme to eliminate involuntary unemployment. Proponents argue that this can be consistent with price stability as it targets unemployment directly rather than attempting to increase private sector job creation indirectly through a much larger economic stimulus, and maintains a "buffer stock" of labor that can readily switch to the private sector when jobs become available. A job guarantee program could also be considered a powerful automatic stabilizer to the economy, expanding when private sector activity cools down and shrinking in size when private sector activity heats up.[24]

2.39.7 Criticisms

MMT has garnered wide criticism from a wide range of schools of economic thought, both for its analytical content and its policy recommendations.

Fellow post-Keynesian economist, Thomas Palley argues that MMT is largely a restatement of elementary Keynesian economics, but prone to "over-simplistic analysis" and understating the risks of its policy recommendations.[25] Palley criticizes MMT for essentially assuming away the problem of fiscal - monetary conflict and denies the MMT claim that old Keynesian analysis doesn't fully capture the accounting identities and financial restrains on government that can issue its own money; Palley shows that these insights are well captured by standard Keynesian stock-flow consistent IS-LM models, and have been well understood by Keynesian economists for decades. He argues that the policies proposed by MMT proponents would cause serious financial instability in an open economy with flexible exchange rates, while using fixed exchange rates would restore hard financial constraints on the government and "undermines MMT's main claim about sovereign money freeing governments from standard market disciplines and financial constraints". He also accuses MMT of lacking a plausible theory of inflation, particularly in the context of full employment in the 'Employer of Last Resort' policy first written about by Minsky and advocated by Bill Mitchell (economist) and other MMT theorists; of a lack of appreciation of the financial instability that could be caused by permanently zero interest rates; and of overstating the importance of government created money. Finally, Palley concludes that MMT provides no new insights about monetary theory, while making unsubstantiated claims about macroeconomic policy, and argues that MMT has only received attention recently due to it being a "policy polemic for depressed times".[26]

Marc Lavoie argues that whilst the neochartalist argument is "essentially correct", many of its counter-intuitive claims depend on a "confusing" and "fictitious" consolidation of government and central banking operations.[27]

New Keynesian economist and Nobel laureate Paul Krugman argues that MMT goes too far in its support for government budget deficits and ignores the inflationary implications of maintaining budget deficits when the economy is growing.[28]

Austrian School economist Robert P. Murphy states that "the MMT worldview doesn't live up to its promises" and that it seems to be "dead wrong". He observes that the MMT claim that cutting government deficits erodes private saving is true *only for the portion of private saving that is not invested*, and argues that the national accounting identities used to explain this aspect of MMT could equally be used to support arguments that government deficits "crowd out" private sector investment.[29] Daniel Kuehn has voiced his agreement with Murphy, stating "it's bad economics to confuse accounting identities with behavioral laws [...] economics is not accounting."[30]

Murphy also criticises MMT on the basis that savings in the form of government bonds are not net assets for the private sector as a whole, since the bond will only be redeemed after the government "raises the necessary funds from the same group of taxpayers in the future".[29]

The chartalist view of money itself, and the MMT emphasis on the importance of taxes in driving money is also a source of criticism.[27] Economist Eladio Febrero argues that modern money draws its value from its ability to cancel (private) bank debt, particularly as legal tender, rather than to pay government taxes.[31]

2.39.8 Modern proponents

Economists Warren Mosler, L. Randall Wray, Stephanie Kelton, and Bill Mitchell are largely responsible for reviving the idea of chartalism as an explanation of money creation; Wray refers to this revived formulation as *Neo-Chartalism*.[32]

Bill Mitchell, Professor of Economics and Director of the Centre of Full Employment and Equity or CofFEE, at the University of Newcastle, New South Wales, refers to an increasing related theoretical work as *Modern Monetary Theory*. Scott Fullwiler has added detailed technical analysis of the banking and monetary systems.[33]

Rodger Malcolm Mitchell's book *Free Money*[34] (1996) describes in layman's terms the essence of chartalism.

Some contemporary proponents, such as Wray, situate chartalism within post-Keynesian economics, while chartalism has been proposed as an alternative or complementary theory to monetary circuit theory, both being forms of endogenous money, i.e., money created within the economy, as by government deficit spending or bank lending, rather than from outside, as by gold. In the complementary view, chartalism explains the "vertical" (government-to-private and vice versa) interactions, while circuit theory is a model of the "horizontal" (private-to-private) interactions.[13][35]

Hyman Minsky seemed to favor a chartalist approach to understanding money creation in his *Stabilizing an Unstable Economy*,[36] while Basil Moore, in his book *Horizontalists and Verticalists*,[37] delineates the differences between bank money and state money.

James K. Galbraith supports chartalism and wrote the foreword for Mosler's book *Seven Deadly Innocent Frauds of*

Economic Policy in 2010.[38]

Steven Hail of the University of Adelaide is another known MMT economist.[39]

2.39.9 See also

- Money
- Deficit spending
- Demand for money
- Functional finance
- Sectoral balances
- Quantity theory of money
- History of money
- History of macroeconomic thought
- Hyman Minsky

2.39.10 Notes

[1] Éric Tymoigne and L. Randall Wray, "Modern Money Theory 101: A Reply to Critics," Levy Economics Institute of Bard College, Working Paper No. 778 (November 2013).

[2] Mosler, Warren. "Soft Currency Economics", January 1994

[3] Tcherneva Pavlina R. "Chartalism and the tax-driven approach to money", in *A Handbook of Alternative Monetary Economics*, edited by Philip Arestis & Malcolm C. Sawyer, Elgar Publishing (2007), ISBN 978-1-84376-915-6

[4] Fullwiler, Scott; Kelton, Stephanie; Wray, L. Randall (January 2012), "Modern Money Theory : A Response to Critics", *Working Paper Series: Modern Monetary Theory - A Debate* (PDF) (279), Amherst, MA: Political Economy Research Institute, pp. 17–26, retrieved May 7, 2015

[5] Knapp, George Friedrich (1905), *Staatilche Theorie des Geldes*, Verlag von Duncker & Humblot

[6] (Wray 2000)

[7] Forstater, Mathew (2004), *Tax-Driven Money: Additional Evidence from the History of Thought, Economic History, and Economic Policy* (PDF)

[8] Mitchell-Innes, Alfred (1914). "The Credit Theory of Money". *The Banking Law Journal* **31**.

[9] Keynes, John Maynard: *A Treatise on Money*, 1930, pp. 4, 6

[10] "Lerner", Abba P. (May 1947). "Money as a Creature of the State". *The American Economic Review* **37** (2,).

[11] "Deficit Spending 101 – Part 1 : Vertical Transactions" Bill Mitchell, 21 February 2009

[12] Scott T. Fullwiler, "Modern Monetary Theory—A Primer on the Operational Realities of the Monetary System," Wartburg College; Bard College - The Levy Economics Institute (August 30, 2010).

[13] "Deficit Spending 101 – Part 3" Bill Mitchell, 2 March 2009

[14] "Unconventional monetary policies: an appraisal" by Claudio Borio and Piti Disyatat, Bank for International Settlements, November 2009

[15] "Money multiplier and other myths" Bill Mitchell, 21 April 2009

[16] Kelton, Stephanie (Bell) (2001), "The Role of the State and the Hierarchy of Money" (pdf), *Cambridge Journal of Economics* (Cambridge) (25): 149–163

[17] "Do current account deficits matter?" Bill Mitchell, 22 June 2010

[18] Mosler, Warren (2010). *Seven Deadly Innocent Frauds* (PDF). Valance. pp. 60–62. ISBN 978-0-692-00959-8.

[19] Foreign Exchange Transactions and Holdings of Official Reserve Assets, Reserve Bank of Australia

[20] "Modern monetary theory and inflation – Part 1" Bill Mitchell, 7 July 2010

[21] "There is no financial crisis so deep that cannot be dealt with by public spending – still!" Bill Mitchell, 11 October 2010

[22] http://www.youtube.com/watch?v=4J0j5VwnD7I "Q:Why does government issue bonds? Randall Wray: Sovereign government really can't borrow, because what it is doing is accepting back its own IOUs. If you have given your IOU to your neighbour because you borrowed some sugar, could you borrow it back? No, you can't borrow back your own IOUs."

[23] Yeva Nersisyan & L. Randall Wray, "Does Excessive Sovereign Debt Really Hurt Growth? A Critique of *This Time Is Different*, by Reinhart and Rogoff," Levy Economics Institute (June 2010), p. 15.

[24] L. Randal Wray, "Job Guarantee," *New Economic Perspectives* (August 23, 2009).

[25] Palley, Thomas, *Money, fiscal policy, and interest rates: A critique of Modern Monetary Theory* (PDF)

[26] Palley, Thomas, *Modern money theory (MMT): the emperor still has no clothes* (PDF)

[27] Lavoie, Marc, *The monetary and fiscal nexus of neo-chartalism* (PDF)

[28] Krugman, Paul (25 March 2011), "Deficits and the Printing Press (Somewhat Wonkish)", *The New York Times*, archived from the original on 17 July 2011, retrieved 17 July 2011

[29] Murphy, Robert P. (9 May 2011). "The Upside-Down World of MMT". Ludwig von Mises Institute. Retrieved 17 July 2011.

[30] Kuehn, Daniel (9 May 2011). "Murphy on the MMTers". Retrieved 17 July 2011.

[31] Febrero, Eladio (27 March 2008), "Three difficulties with Neo-Chartalism" (PDF), *Jornadas de Economía Crítica* **11**

[32] The Economist, 31 December 2011, "Marginal revolutionaries" neo-chartalism, sometimes called "Modern Monetary Theory"

[33] http://papers.ssrn.com/sol3/cf_dev/AbsByAuth.cfm?per_id=444041

[34] Mitchell, Rodger Malcolm: *Free Money – Plan for Prosperity*, PGM International, Inc., paperback 2005, ISBN 978-0-9658323-1-1

[35] "In the spirit of debate...my reply" Bill Mitchell, 28 September 2009

[36] Minsky, Hyman: *Stabilizing an Unstable Economy*, McGraw-Hill, 2008, ISBN 978-0-07-159299-4

[37] Moore, Basil J.: *Horizontalists and Verticalists: The Macroeconomics of Credit Money*, Cambridge University Press, 1988, ISBN 978-0-521-35079-2

[38] Mosler, Warren: *Seven Deadly Innocent Frauds of Economic Policy*, Valance Co., 2010, ISBN 978-0-692-00959-8; also available in .DOC

[39] http://theaimn.com/sell-economy/

2.39.11 Bibliography

- Innes, A. Mitchell (1913), "What is Money?", *The Banking Law Journal*

- Febrero, Eladio (2009), "Three difficulties with neo-chartalism" (PDF), *Journal of Post Keynesian Economics* (M.E. Sharpe, Inc.) **31** (3): 523–541, doi:10.2753/PKE0160-3477310308

- Lerner, Abba P. (1947), "Money as a Creature of the State", *American Economic Review*

- Mitchell, Bill (2009), *The fundamental principles of modern monetary economics* in "It's Hard Being a Bear (Part Six)? Good Alternative Theory?" (PDF). Introduction to modern (as of 2009) Chartalism.

- Wray, L. Randall (2000), *The Neo-Chartalist Approach to Money* (Working Paper No. 10), Center for Full Employment and Price Stability External link in |publisher= (help)

- Wray, L. Randall (2001), *The Endogenous Money Approach* (Working Paper No. 17), Center for Full Employment and Price Stability External link in |publisher= (help)

- Wray, L. Randall (December 2010), *Money* (PDF) (Working Paper No. 647), Levy Economics Institute of Bard College External link in |publisher= (help)

2.39.12 External links

- MMT Wiki, the Modern Monetary Theory interactive encyclopaedia

- Bill Mitchell's blog (Chartalism is denoted as "Modern Monetary Theory", there)

- Warren Mosler's blog

- New Economic Perspectives website

- Macroeconomic Balance Sheet Visualizer, visualizing and understanding important concepts in macroeconomics

- Modern Monetary Theory: A Debate (Brett Fiebiger critiques and Scott Fullwiler, Stephanie Kelton, L. Randall Wray respond; Political Economy Research Institute, Amherst, MA)

- Credit Writedowns, news and opinion site, from the MMT perspective

- Knut Wicksell and origins of modern monetary theory-Lars Pålsson Syll

- Evolution of Selected Economic Schools, a simplified diagram

- Modern Monetary Network

2.40 Money as Debt

Money as Debt is a 2006 animated documentary film by Canadian artist[1] and filmmaker Paul Grignon[2] about the monetary systems practised through modern banking.[3] The film presents Grignon's view of the process of money creation by banks and its historical background, and warns of his belief in its subsequent unsustainability.[4][5][6] Subsequent *Money as Debt* videos include *Money as Debt II* (2009)[7] and *Money as Debt III: Evolution Beyond Money* (2011).[8]

2.40.1 Background

The film was conceived by Grignon in 2002 as an introduction to a 5-hour video commission for United Financial Consumers. He prefaced his video lecture with a re-telling of *The Goldsmith's Tale* in animation form titled *Money as Debt*. The Goldsmith's Tale is noted in the film as being "a brief and broadly allegorical history of banking" and should not be viewed as a complete or entirely accurate account of the history of banking. Expanded over a six-month period in 2006, it was Grignon's first full length animation project.[5][9]

Much of the film presents the filmmaker's understanding of modern money creation in a fractional-reserve banking system. New money enters the economy through the indebtedness of borrowers, thus not only obligating the public to the money-issuing private banks but also creating an endless and self-escalating debt that is to eventually outgrow all other forms of wealth generation.[10] The film claims that this ever-increasing gravitation of money to banks is capable of impoverishing any nation. The film finishes by identifying some alternatives to modern banking, such as the nationalization of banks and payment of dividends to the public, establishing local exchange trading systems, or government printing of money.[5]

2.40.2 Critical response

An article in *Anthropology Today* called the film "a hit in activist circles", but also a "fable" that "demonizes the banks, and interest in particular" and whose "message is in many ways misleading."[11]

An article in the *Atlantic Free Press* said "*Money as Debt* is not entertainment—far from it. The film offers amazingly elementary facts about the creation of money in the United States, narrated by a soothing voice, which could make for a bland presentation, yet the film's message is anything but vapid. In fact, if it doesn't leave your blood boiling, it behooves you to check your vital signs."[3]

Cdurable offered "*Ce long métrage d'animation, dynamique et divertissant, de l'artiste et vidéographe Paul Grignon, explique les effets magiques mais pervers du système actuel d'argent-dette dans des termes compréhensibles pour tous.*" ("This animated feature, dynamic and entertaining, by artist and videographer Paul Grignon, explains the magical but twisted effects of the current system of debt-money in terms understandable to all.")[12] Thomas Publications *Fog City Journal* wrote that the animated documentary was "a painless but hard-hitting educational tool."[13]

On his personal website, Paul Grignon said there were two main criticisms of the documentary, provided counter arguments, but conceded that his presentation of fractional-reserve banking may have been "misleading" and "in the revised edition will be replaced with less contentious information."[14] The film has also been criticized by other heterodox economic and libertarian thinkers, such as G. Edward Griffin's Freedom Force International. Specifically, Griffin criticizes Grignon's proposal for "interest-free banking" and fiat, albeit government-created as opposed to central bank-created, currency.[15]

2.40.3 See also

- *The Capitalist Conspiracy*

2.40.4 References

[1] "Tofino Artist Paul Grignon". *Tofino Art*. Retrieved 29 November 2010.

[2] OCLC 76905478

[3] Baker, Carolyn (25 August 2007). "Daddy, where does the money come from?". *Atlantic Free Press*. Retrieved 9 February 2010.

[4] Tolson, Shannon (3 April 2009). "Second Sunday Cinema announces free films for April 12". *lakeconews.com*. Retrieved October 27, 2011.

[5] Wipond, Rob (October 2011). "This artist follows the money". *Focus*. Retrieved August 25, 2013.

[6] Washington, Samuel (December 30, 2008). "Film Review: 'Money as Debt'" (in Epoch Times archive as a PDF document). *Epoch Times*. Retrieved August 26, 2013.

[7] OCLC 798991364; also titled *Money as Debt II: Promises Unleashed*, OCLC 429188528

[8] OCLC 798991370

[9] Grignon, Paul. "Producer's Comments on the Movie". paulgrignon.netfirms.com. Retrieved 15 February 2010.

[10] Weiner, Keith. "Goethe Predicted Slavery". *SNBCHF News*. Retrieved 3 April 2015.

[11] Hart, Keith. "Money is always personal and impersonal", *Anthropology Today*, Volume 23, Issue 5, pages 12–16, October 2007.

[12] Naulin, David (October 31, 2008). "Découvrez le long métrage "Money as Debt" de Paul Grignon". *Cdurable* (in French). Retrieved 29 November 2010.

[13] "Money As Debt". *Fog City Journal*. October 3, 2008. Retrieved 29 November 2010.

[14] Grignon, Paul. "Disputed Information in Money as Debt". *paulgrignon.netfirms.com*. Retrieved 29 November 2010.

[15] See: "Freedom Force International - Money as Debt: An Instructional Video that Gets a Flunking Grade 2007 June 7 (Google Cached)" (last accessed Dec. 8, 2010).

2.40.5 External links

- Official website
- *Money as Debt* at the Internet Movie Database

2.41 Mouvement Anti-Utilitariste dans les Sciences Sociales

The **Mouvement anti-utilitariste dans les sciences sociales** (Anti-utilitarian Movement in the Social Sciences) is a French intellectual movement.[1] It is based around the ideology of "Anti-utilitarianism", a critique of economism in social sciences and instrumental rationalism in moral and political philosophy. The movement was founded in 1981 by sociologist Alain Caillé, with the establishment of its interdisciplinary monthly journal **Revue du MAUSS**[2] which is still published and edited by Caillé.

The journal covers topics in economics, anthropology, sociology and political philosophy from an anti-utilitarian perspective. His name is both an acronym and a tribute to the famous anthropologist Marcel Mauss.[3] The movement works to promote a third paradigm, as a complement to, or replacement for holism and methodological individualism.[4][5][6]

The movement began through conversations between Caillé and Swiss anthropologist Gerald Berthoud wondering why the economic theory of Marcel Mauss based on obligatory reciprocity and debt did not provide any possibilities of a "free gift" motivated by empathy rather than rational self-interest. The movement's early efforts considered the possibility of reintroducing an aspect of genuine interest in the welfare of others in economic theory. Among the economic policies suggested by the movement is the basic income guarantee a concept originally developed by Thomas Paine.[1]

2.41.1 Some regular contributors to the journal

- Paul Jorion
- Paul Ariès
- Genevieve Azam
- Gerald Berthoud
- Alain Caillé
- Philippe Chanial
- Jacques Dewitte
- Mary Douglas
- Denis Duclos
- Jean-Pierre Dupuy
- Michael Freitag
- Marcel Gauchet
- Philippe d'Iribarne
- Stephen Kalberg
- Serge Latouche
- Louis Maitrier
- Jean-Claude Michea
- Thierry Paquot
- Lucien Scubla
- Camille Tarot
- Frederic Vandenberghe
- Raoul Vaneigem
- Jean-Pierre Voyer

2.41.2 References

[1] GIVE IT AWAY By Anthropologist David Graeber, published at www.freewords.org

[2] La revue du M.A.U.S.S.

[3] Short History of Economical Anthropology by Chris Hann published at www.thememorybanck.co.uk

[4] À propos du M.A.U.S.S.

[5] Interview with Alain Caillé at www.revue-sociologique.org

[6] Michèle Richman. 2002. The French Sociological Revolution from Montaigne to Mauss. SubStance. Vol. 31, No. 1, Issue 97: Special Issue: The American Production of French Theory (2002), pp. 27-35

2.42 Mutualism (economic theory)

This article is about the economic theory. For the biological term and other uses, see Mutualism (disambiguation).

Mutualism is an economic theory and anarchist school of thought that advocates a society where each person might possess a means of production, either individually or collectively, with trade representing equivalent amounts of labor in the free market.[1] Integral to the scheme was the establishment of a mutual-credit bank that would lend to producers at a minimal interest rate, just high enough to cover administration.[2] Mutualism is based on a labor theory of value that holds that when labor or its product is sold, in exchange, it ought to receive goods or services embodying "the amount of labor necessary to produce an article of exactly similar and equal utility".[3] Mutualism originated from the writings of philosopher Pierre-Joseph Proudhon.

Mutualists oppose the idea of individuals receiving an income through loans, investments, and rent, as they believe these individuals are not laboring. Though Proudhon opposed this type of income, he expressed that he had never intended "...to forbid or suppress, by sovereign decree, ground rent and interest on capital. I think that all these manifestations of human activity should remain free and voluntary for all: I ask for them no modifications, restrictions or suppressions, other than those which result naturally and of necessity from the universalization of the principle of reciprocity which I propose."[4] Insofar as they ensure the worker's right to the full product of their labor, mutualists support markets (or artificial markets) and property in the product of labor. However, they argue for conditional titles to land, whose ownership is legitimate only so long as it remains in use or occupation (which Proudhon called "possession");[5] thus advocating personal property, but not private property.

Although mutualism is similar to the economic doctrines of the 19th-century American individualist anarchists, unlike them, mutualism is in favor of large industries.[6] Therefore, mutualism has been retrospectively characterized sometimes as being a form of individualist anarchism,[7] and as ideologically situated between individualist and collectivist forms of anarchism as well.[8] Proudhon himself described the "liberty" he pursued as "the synthesis of communism and property."[9]

Mutualists have distinguished mutualism from state socialism, and do not advocate state control over the means of production. Benjamin Tucker said of Proudhon, that "though opposed to socializing the ownership of capital, [Proudhon] aimed nevertheless to socialize its effects by making its use beneficial to all instead of a means of impoverishing the many to enrich the few...by subjecting capital to the natural law of competition, thus bringing the price of its own use down to cost."[10]

2.42.1 History

Mutualism, as a term, has seen a variety of related uses. Charles Fourier first used the French term *mutualisme* in

Portrait of philosopher Pierre-Joseph Proudhon (1809–1865) by Gustave Courbet. Proudhon was the primary proponent of anarchist mutualism, and influenced many later individualist anarchist and social anarchist thinkers.

1822,[11] although the reference was not to an economic system. The first use of the noun "mutualist" was in the *New-Harmony Gazette* by an American Owenite in 1826.[12] In the early 1830s, a labor organization in Lyons, France, called themselves the "Mutuellists."

Pierre Joseph Proudhon was involved with the Lyons mutualists and later adopted the name to describe his own teachings.[13] In *What Is Mutualism?* Clarence Lee Swartz gives his own account of the origin of the term, claiming that "[t]he word "mutualism" seems to have been first used by John Gray, an English writer, in 1832."[14] When John Gray's 1825 *Lecture on Human Happiness* was first published in the United States in 1826, the publishers appended the *Preamble and constitution of the Friendly Association for Mutual Interests, located at Valley Forge*. 1826 also saw the publication of the *Constitution of the Friendly Association for Mutual Interests at Kendal, Ohio*. By 1846, Pierre Joseph Proudhon was speaking of "mutualité" in his writings, and he used the term "mutuellisme," at least as early as 1848, in his "Programme Révolutionnaire." William B. Greene, in 1850, used the term "mutualism" to describe a mutual credit system similar to that of Proudhon. In 1850, the American newspaper *The Spirit of the Age*, edited by William Henry Channing, published proposals for a "mutualist township" by Joshua King Ingalls[15] and Albert Brisbane,[16] together with works by Proudhon,[17] William B. Greene, Pierre Leroux, and others. During the Second French Republic (1848–1852), Proudhon had his biggest public effect through journalism. He got involved with four newspapers: *Le Représentant du Peuple* (February 1848 – August 1848); *Le Peuple* (September 1848 – June 1849); *La Voix du Peuple* (September 1849 – May 1850); *Le Peuple de 1850* (June 1850 – October 1850). His polemical writing style, combined with his perception of himself as a political outsider, produced a cynical, combative journalism that appealed to many French workers but alienated others. He repeatedly criticised the government's policies and promoted reformation of credit and exchange. He tried to establish a popular bank (Banque du peuple) early in 1849, but despite over 13,000 people signing up (mostly workers), receipts were limited falling short of 18,000FF and the whole enterprise was essentially stillborn. Proudhon ran for the constituent assembly in April 1848, but was not elected, although his name appeared on the ballots in Paris, Lyon, Besançon, and Lille, France. He was successful, in the complementary elections of June 4, and served as a deputy during the debates over the National Workshops, created by the February 25, 1848, decree passed by Republican Louis Blanc. The workshops were to give work to the unemployed. Proudhon was never enthusiastic about such workshops, perceiving them to be essentially charitable institutions that did not resolve the problems of the economic system. He was against their elimination unless an alternative could be found for the workers who relied on the workshops for subsistence.

Proudhon was surprised by the Revolutions of 1848 in France. He participated in the February uprising and the composition of what he termed "the first republican proclamation" of the new republic. But he had misgivings about the new provisional government, headed by Dupont de l'Eure (1767–1855), who, since the French Revolution in 1789, had been a longstanding politician, although often in the opposition. Proudhon published his own perspective for reform which was completed in 1849, *Solution du problème social* ("Solution of the Social Problem"), in which he laid out a program of mutual financial cooperation among workers. He believed this would transfer control of economic relations from capitalists and financiers to workers. The central part of his plan was the establishment of a bank to provide credit at a very low rate of interest and the issuing of exchange notes that would circulate instead of money based on gold.

Mutualism has been associated with two types of currency reform. Labor notes were first discussed in Owenite circles and received their first practical test in 1827 in the Time Store of former New Harmony member and individualist anarchist Josiah Warren. Mutual banking aimed at the monetization of all forms of wealth and the extension of free credit. It is most closely associated with William B. Greene, but Greene drew from the work of Proudhon, Edward Kellogg, and William Beck, as well as from the land bank tradition. Mutualism can in many ways be considered "the original anarchy," since Proudhon was the first to identify himself as an anarchist. Though mutualism is generally associated with anarchism, it is not *necessarily* anarchist. Historian Wendy McElroy reports that American individualist anarchism received an important influence of 3 European thinkers. "One of the most important of these influences was the french political philosopher Pierre-Joseph Proudhon whose words "Liberty is not the Daughter But the Mother of Order" appeared as a motto on *Liberty's* masthead" [18] (influential individualist anarchist publication of Benjamin Tucker). For American anarchist historian Eunice Minette Schuster "It is apparent...that Proudhonian Anarchism was to be found in the United States at least as early as 1848 and that it was not conscious of its affinity to the Individualist Anarchism of Josiah Warren and Stephen Pearl Andrews ... William B. Greene presented this Proudhonian Mutualism in its purest and most systematic form.".[19] After 1850 he became active in labor reform.[19] "He was elected vice-president of the New England Labor Reform League, the majority of the members holding to Proudhon's scheme of mutual banking, and in 1869 president of the Massachusetts Labor Union."[19] He then publishes *Socialistic, Mutualistic, and Financial Fragments* (1875).[19] He saw mutualism as the synthesis of "liberty and order."[19] His "associationism...is checked by individualism..."Mind your own business," "Judge not that ye be not judged." Over matters which are purely personal, as for example, moral conduct, the individual is sovereign, as well as over that which he himself produces. For this reason he demands "mutuality" in marriage—the equal right of a woman to her own personal freedom and property."[19]

Later, Benjamin Tucker, editor of the anarchist publication *Liberty*, connected his economic views with those of Pierre Joseph Proudhon, Josiah Warren and Karl Marx, taking sides with Proudhon and Josiah Warren:

> The economic principles of Modern Socialism are a logical deduction from the principle laid down by Adam Smith in the early chapters of his "Wealth of Nations," – namely, that labor is the true measure of price ... Half a century or more after Smith enunciated the principle above stated, Socialism picked it up where he had dropped it, and in following it to its logical conclusions, made it the basis of a new economic philosophy ... This seems to have been done independently by three different men, of three different nationalities, in three different languages: Josiah Warren, an American; Pierre J. Proudhon,

a Frenchman; Karl Marx, a German Jew ... That the work of this interesting trio should have been done so nearly simultaneously would seem to indicate that Socialism was in the air, and that the time was ripe and the conditions favorable for the appearance of this new school of thought. So far as priority of time is concerned, the credit seems to belong to Warren, the American, – a fact which should be noted by the stump orators who are so fond of declaiming against Socialism as an imported article. Benjamin Tucker. *Individual Liberty*[20]

Francesc Pi i Margall, catalan brief President of the First Spanish Republic and main spanish translator of Proudhon's works

Mutualist ideas found a fertile ground in the nineteenth century in Spain. In Spain Ramón de la Sagra established the anarchist journal *El Porvenir* in La Coruña in 1845 which was inspired by Proudhon's ideas.[21] The catalan politician Francesc Pi i Margall became the principal translator of Proudhon's works into Spanish[22] and later briefly became president of Spain in 1873 while being the leader of the Democratic Republican Federal Party. According to George Woodcock "These translations were to have a profound and lasting effect on the development of Spanish anarchism after 1870, but before that time Proudhonian ideas, as interpreted by Pi, already provided much of the inspiration for the federalist movement which sprang up in the early 1860's."[23] According to the *Encyclopedia Britannica* "During the Spanish revolution of 1873, Pi y Margall attempted to establish a decentralized, or "cantonalist", political system on Proudhonian lines."[21] Pi i Margall was a dedicated theorist in his own right, especially through book-length works such as *La reacción y la revolución* (en:"Reaction and revolution" from 1855), *Las nacionalidades* (en:"Nationalities" from 1877), and *La Federación* from 1880. For prominent anarcho-syndicalist Rudolf Rocker "The first movement of the Spanish workers was strongly influenced by the ideas of Pi y Margall, leader of the Spanish Federalists and disciple of Proudhon. Pi y Margall was one of the outstanding theorists of his time and had a powerful influence on the development of libertarian ideas in Spain. His political ideas had much in common with those of Richard Price, Joseph Priestly (sic), Thomas Paine, Jefferson, and other representatives of the Anglo-American liberalism of the first period. He wanted to limit the power of the state to a minimum and gradually replace it by a Socialist economic order."[24]

For historian of the First International G. M. Stekloff: "In April, 1856, there arrived from Paris a deputation of Proudhonist workers whose aim it was to bring about the foundation of a Universal League of Workers. The object of the League was the social emancipation of the working class, which, it was held, could only be achieved by a union of the workers of all lands against international capital. Since the deputation was one of Proudhonists, of course this emancipation was to be secured, not by political methods, but purely by economic means, through the foundation of productive and distributive co-operatives."[25] Later "It was in the 1863 elections that for the first time workers' candidates were run in opposition to bourgeois republicans, but they secured very few votes...agroup of working-class Proudhonists (among whom were Murat and Tolain, who were subsequently to participate in the founding of the (First) International issued the famous Manifesto of the Sixty, which, though extremely moderate in tone, marked a turning point in the history of the French movement. For years and years the bourgeois liberals had been insisting that the revolution of 1789 had abolished class distinctions. The Manifesto of the Sixty loudly proclaimed that classes still existed. These classes were the bourgeoisie and the proletariat. The latter had its specific class interests, which none but workers could be trusted to defend. The inference drawn by the Manifesto was that there must be independent working-class candidates."[26] For Stekloff "the Proudhonists, who were at that date the leaders of the French section of the International. They looked upon the International Workingmen's Association as a sort of academy or synagogue, where Talmudists or similar experts could "investigate" the workers' problem; where in the spirit of Proudhon they could excogitate means for an accurate solution of the problem, without being disturbed by the stresses of a political campaign. Thus Fribourg, voicing the opinions of the Parisian group of the Proudhonists (Tolain and Co.) assured his readers that "the International was the greatest attempt ever made in modern times to aid the proletariat towards the conquest, by peaceful, constitutional, and moral methods, of the place which rightly belongs to the workers in the sunshine of civilisation."[27]

"The Belgian Federation threw in its lot with the anarchist International at its Brussels Congress, held in December, 1872...those taking part in the socialist movement of the Belgian intelligentsia were inspired by Proudhonist ideas which naturally led them to oppose the Marxist outlook."[28]

Nineteenth-century mutualists considered themselves libertarian socialists.[29] While still oriented towards cooperation, mutualists favor free market solutions, believing that most inequalities are the result of preferential conditions created by government intervention.[30] Mutualism is something of a middle way between classical economics and socialism, with some characteristics of both. Modern-day Mutualist Kevin Carson, considers anarchist mutualism to be "free market socialism."

Proudhon supported labor-owned cooperative firms and associations[31] for "we need not hesitate, for we have no choice ... it is necessary to form an ASSOCIATION among workers ... because without that, they would remain related as subordinates and superiors, and there would ensue two ... castes of masters and wage-workers, which is repugnant to a free and democratic society" and so "it becomes necessary for the workers to form themselves into democratic societies, with equal conditions for all members, on pain of a relapse into feudalism."[32] As for capital goods (man-made, non-land, "means of production"), mutualist opinions differs on whether these should be commonly managed public assets or private property.

Mutualism also had a considerable influence in the Paris Commune. George Woodcock manifests that "a notable contribution to the activities of the Commune and particularly to the organization of public services was made by members of various anarchist factions, including the mutualists Courbet, Longuet, and Vermorel, the libertarian collectivists Varlin, Malon, and Lefrangais, and the bakuninists Elie and Elisée Reclus and Louise Michel."[33]

2.42.2 Theory

See also: Cost the limit of price

The primary aspects of mutualism are free association, mutualist credit, contract (or federation/confederation), and gradualism (or dual-power). Mutualism is often described by its proponents as advocating an "anti-capitalist free market".

Mutualists argue that most of the economic problems associated with capitalism each amount to a violation of the *cost principle*, or as Josiah Warren interchangeably said, "Cost the limit of price." It was inspired by the labor theory of value, which was popularized, though not invented, by Adam Smith in 1776 (Proudhon mentioned Smith as an inspiration). The labor theory of value holds that the actual price of a thing (or the "true cost") is the amount of labor that was undertaken to produce it. In Warren's terms, cost should be the "limit of price," with "cost" referring to the amount of labor required to produce a good or service. Anyone who sells goods should charge no more than the cost to himself of acquiring these goods.

Free association

Mutualists argue that association is only necessary where there is an organic combination of forces. For instance, an operation that requires specialization and many different workers performing their individual tasks to complete a unified product, i.e., a factory. In this situation, workers are inherently dependent on each other—and without association they are related as subordinate and superior, master and wage-slave.

An operation that can be performed by an individual without the help of specialized workers does *not* require association. Proudhon argued that peasants do not require societal form, and only feigned association for the purposes of solidarity in abolishing rents, buying clubs, etc. He recognized that their work is inherently sovereign and free. In commenting on the degree of association that is preferable Proudhon said:

> In cases in which production requires great division of labour, it is necessary to form an ASSOCIATION among the workers... because without that they would remain isolated as subordinates and superiors, and there would ensue two industrial castes of masters and wage workers, which is repugnant in a free and democratic society. But where the product can be obtained by the action of an individual or a family... there is no opportunity for association.[34]

For Proudhon, mutualism involved creating "industrial democracy", a system where workplaces would be "handed over to democratically organised workers' associations ... We want these associations to be models for agriculture, industry and trade, the pioneering core of that vast federation of companies and societies woven into the common cloth of the democratic social Republic."[35] He urged "workers to form themselves into democratic societies, with equal conditions for all members, on pain of a relapse into feudalism." This would result in "Capitalistic and proprietary exploitation, stopped everywhere, the wage system abolished, equal and just exchange guaranteed."[36] Workers would no longer sell their labour to a capitalist but rather work for themselves in co-operatives.

As Robert Graham notes, "Proudhon's market socialism is indissolubly linked to his notions of industry democracy and workers' self-management."[37] K. Steven Vincent notes in his in-depth analysis of this aspect of Proudhon's ideas that "Proudhon consistently advanced a program of industrial democracy which would return control and direction of the economy to the workers." For Proudhon, "... strong workers' associations ... would enable the workers to determine jointly by election how the enterprise was to be directed and operated on a day-to-day basis."[38]

Mutual credit

Main article: Mutual credit

Mutualists argue that free banking should be taken back by the people to establish systems of free credit. They contend that banks have a monopoly on credit, just as capitalists have a monopoly on the means of production, and landlords have a monopoly on land. Banks are essentially creating money by lending out deposits that do not actually belong to them, then charging interest on the difference. Mutualists argue that by establishing a democratically run mutual bank or credit union, it would be possible to issue free credit so that money could be created for the benefit of the participants rather than for the benefit of the bankers. Individualist anarchists noted for their detailed views on mutualist banking include Proudhon, William B. Greene, and Lysander Spooner.

Some modern forms of mutual credit are LETS and the Ripple monetary system project.

In a session of the French legislature, Proudhon proposed a government-imposed income tax to fund his mutual banking scheme, with some tax brackets reaching as high as 33$\frac{1}{3}$ percent and 50 percent, which was turned down by the legislature.[39] This income tax Proudhon proposed to fund his bank was to be levied on rents, interest, debts, and salaries.[40][41] Specifically, Proudhon's proposed law would have required all capitalists and stockholders to disburse one sixth of their income to their tenants and debtors, and another sixth to the national treasury to fund the bank.[42]

This scheme was vehemently objected to by others in the legislature, including Frédéric Bastiat;[42] the reason given for the income tax's rejection was that it would result in economic ruin and that it violated "the right of property."[43] In his debates with Bastiat, Proudhon did once propose funding a national bank with a voluntary tax of 1%.[44] Proudhon also argued for the abolition of all taxes.[45]

Contract and federation

Mutualism holds that producers should exchange their goods at cost-value using systems of "contract." While Proudhon's early definitions of cost-value were based on fixed assumptions about the value of labor-hours, he later redefined cost-value to include other factors such as the intensity of labor, the nature of the work involved, etc. He also expanded his notions of "contract" into expanded notions of "federation." As Proudhon argued,

> I have shown the contractor, at the birth of industry, negotiating on equal terms with his comrades, who have since become his workmen. It is plain, in fact, that this original equality was bound to disappear through the advantageous position of the master and the dependent position of the wage-workers. In vain does the law assure the right of each to enterprise ... When an establishment has had leisure to develop itself, enlarge its foundations, ballast itself with capital, and assure itself a body of patrons, what can a workman do against a power so superior?[46]

Gradualism and dual-power

Main article: Dual power

> Beneath the governmental machinery, in the shadow of political institutions, out of the sight of statemen and priests, society is producing its own organism, slowly and silently; and constructing a new order, the expression of its vitality and autonomy...[47]

2.42.3 Mutualism and capitalism

Pierre-Joseph Proudhon was one of the most famous philosophers who articulated thoughts on the nature of property. He is known for claiming that "property is theft", but is less known for the claims that "property is liberty" and "property is impossible". According to Colin Ward, Proudhon did not see a contradiction between these slogans. This was because Proudhon distinguished between what he considered to be two distinct forms of property often bound up in the single label. To the mutualist, this is the distinction between property created by coercion and property created by labor. Property is theft "when it is related to a landowner or capitalist whose ownership is derived from conquest or exploitation and [is] only maintained through the state, property laws, police, and an army". Property is freedom for "the peasant or artisan family [who have] a natural right to a home, land [they may] cultivate, [...] to tools of a trade", and the fruits of that cultivation—but not to ownership or control of the lands and lives of others. The former is considered illegitimate property, the latter legitimate property.

Proudhon argued that property in the product of labor is essential to liberty, while property that strayed from "possession" ("occupancy and use") was the basis for tyranny and would lead a society to destroy itself. The conception of entitlement property as a destructive force and illegitimate institution can be seen in this quote by Proudhon,

> Then if we are associated for the sake of liberty, equality, and security, we are not associated for the sake of property; then if property is a natural right, this natural right is not social, but antisocial. Property and society are utterly irreconcilable institutions. It is as impossible to associate two proprietors as to join two magnets by their opposite poles. Either society must perish, or it must destroy property. If property is a natural, absolute, imprescriptible, and inalienable right, why, in all ages, has there been so much speculation as to its origin? – for this is one of its distinguishing characteristics. The origin of a natural right! Good God! who ever inquired into the origin of the rights of liberty, security, or equality? (What is Property?)

Mutualist, Clarence Lee Swartz, says in *What is Mutualism*:

> It is, therefore, one of the purposes of Mutualists, not only to awaken in the people the appreciation of and desire for freedom, but also to arouse in them a determination to abolish the legal restrictions now placed upon non-invasive human activities and to institute, through purely voluntary associations, such measures as will liberate all of us from the exactions of privilege and the power of concentrated capital.

Swartz also states that mutualism differs from anarchocommunism and other collectivist philosophies by its support of private property: "One of the tests of any reform movement with regard to personal liberty is this: Will the movement prohibit or abolish private property? If it does, it is an enemy of liberty. For one of the most important criteria of freedom is the right to private property in the products of ones labor. State Socialists, Communists, Syndicalists and Communist-Anarchists deny private property."

However, Proudhon warned that a society with private property without equality would lead to statist-like relations between people.

> The purchaser draws boundaries, fences himself in, and says, 'This is mine; each one by himself, each one for himself.' Here, then, is a piece of land upon which, henceforth, no one has right to step, save the proprietor and his friends; which can benefit nobody, save the proprietor and his servants. Let these multiply, and soon the people ... will have nowhere to rest, no place of shelter, no ground to till. They will die of hunger at the proprietor's door, on the edge of that property which was their birth-right; and the proprietor, watching them die, will exclaim, 'So perish idlers and vagrants.'[48]

Unlike capitalist private-property supporters, Proudhon stressed equality. He thought all workers should own property and have access to capital. He stressed that in every cooperative "every worker employed in the association [must have] an undivided share in the property of the company".[49] This distinction Proudhon made between different kinds of property has been articulated by some later anarchist and socialist theorists as one of the first distinctions between private property and personal property; the latter having actual use-value to the individual possessing it.

2.42.4 Criticisms

In Europe a contemporary critic of Proudhon was the early anarchist communist Joseph Déjacque[50][51] Unlike and against Proudhon, he argued that, "it is not the product of his or her labor that the worker has a right to, but to the satisfaction of his or her needs, whatever may be their nature."[52][53][54] Returning to New York he was able to serialise his book in his periodical *Le Libertaire, Journal du Mouvement social*. Published in 27 issues from June 9, 1858, to February 4, 1861, *Le Libertaire* was the first anarcho-communist journal published in the United States.

One area of disagreement between mutualists and anarchist communists stems from Proudhon's advocacy of money and later labour vouchers to compensate individuals for their labor as well as markets or artificial markets for goods and services. Peter Kropotkin, like other anarchist communists, advocated the abolition of labor remuneration and questioned, "how can this new form of wages, the labor note, be sanctioned by those who admit that houses, fields, mills are no longer private property, that they belong to the commune or the nation?"[55] According to George Woodcock, Kropotkin believed that a wage system in any form, whether "administered by Banks of the People or by workers' associations through labor cheques" is a form of compulsion.[56]

Collectivist anarchist Mikhail Bakunin was an adamant critic of Proudhonian mutualism as well,[57] stating, "How ridiculous are the ideas of the individualists of the Jean Jacques Rousseau school and of the Proudhonian mutualists who conceive society as the result of the free contract of individuals absolutely independent of one another and entering into mutual relations only because of the convention drawn up among men. As if these men had dropped from the skies, bringing with them speech, will, original thought, and as if they were alien to anything of the earth, that is, anything having social origin."[58]

Criticism from pro-market sectors has been common as well. Economist George Reisman charges that mutualism supports exploitation when it does not recognize a right of an individual to protect land that he has mixed his labor with if he happens to not be using it. Reisman sees the seizure of such land as the theft of the product of labor and has said that "Mutualism claims to oppose the exploitation of labor, i.e. the theft of any part of its product. But when it comes to labor that has been mixed with land, it turns a blind eye out foursquare on the side of the exploiter."[59]

2.42.5 Mutualism today

The bisected orange and black flag is typically used by Mutualists

Kevin Carson is a contemporary mutualist and author of *Studies in Mutualist Political Economy*. In its preface Carson describes this work as "an attempt to revive individualist anarchist political economy, to incorporate the useful developments of the last hundred years, and to make it relevant

A variant with arrows representing reciprocity is also used. Sometimes red and black arrows are also seen

to the problems of the twenty-first century."[60] Contemporary mutualists are among those involved in the Alliance of the Libertarian Left and in the Voluntary Cooperation Movement.

Carson holds that capitalism has been founded on "an act of robbery as massive as feudalism," and argues that capitalism could not exist in the absence of a state. He says "[i]t is state intervention that distinguishes capitalism from the free market".[61] He does not define capitalism in the idealized sense, but says that when he talks about "capitalism" he is referring to what he calls "actually existing capitalism." He believes the term "laissez-faire capitalism" is an oxymoron because capitalism, he argues, is "organization of society, incorporating elements of tax, usury, landlordism, and tariff, which thus denies the Free Market while pretending to exemplify it". However, he says he has no quarrel with anarcho-capitalists who use the term "laissez-faire capitalism" and distinguish it from "actually existing capitalism." He says he has deliberately chosen to resurrect an old definition of the term.[62]

Carson argues that the centralization of wealth into a class hierarchy is due to state intervention to protect the ruling class, by using a money monopoly, granting patents and subsidies to corporations, imposing discriminatory taxation, and intervening militarily to gain access to international markets. Carson's thesis is that an authentic free market economy would not be capitalism as the separation of labor from ownership and the subordination of labor to capital would be impossible, bringing a class-less society where people could easily choose between working as a freelancer, working for a fair wage, taking part of a cooperative, or being an entrepreneur. He notes, as did Tucker before him, that a mutualist free market system would involve significantly different property rights than capitalism is based on, particularly in terms of land and intellectual property.

2.42.6 See also

- Geolibertarianism
- Individualist anarchism
- Individualist anarchism in France
- Labor theory of property
- Labor theory of value
- Left-libertarianism
- Left-wing market anarchism
- Libertarian socialism
- Socialist economics
- Syndicalism
- Worker cooperative
- Workplace democracy
- Workers' self-management

2.42.7 Notes and references

Notes

1. ^ "Involved with radical politics and in his contact with the Marxists, he [Proudhon] soon rejected their doctrine, seeking rather a middle way between socialist theories and classical economics." - Irving Horowitz, The Anarchists, 1964, Dell Publishing

2. ^ Some critics object to the use of the term *capitalism* in reference to historical or actually existing economic arrangements, which they term *mixed economies*. They reserve the term for the *abstract ideal* or *future possibility* of a genuinely free market. This sort of *free-market capitalism* may closely follow Carson's *free-market anti-capitalism* in its practical details except for the fact that Carson does not recognize a right of an individual to protect land that he has transformed through labor or purchased to be protected when he is not using it. Carson, like other mutualists, only recognize occupancy and use as the standard for retaining legitimate control over something. According to Carson, "For mutualists, occupancy and use is the only legitimate standard for establishing ownership of land, regardless of how many times it has changed hands. An existing owner may transfer ownership by sale or gift; but the new owner may establish legitimate title to the land only by his own occupancy and use. A change in occupancy will amount to a change in ownership. Absentee landlord rent, and exclusion of homesteaders from vacant land by an absentee landlord, are both considered illegitimate by mutualists. The actual occupant is considered the owner of a tract of land, and any attempt to collect rent by a self-styled landlord is regarded as a violent invasion of the possessor's absolute right of property. (p. 200. of Carson's "Mutualist Political Economy").

3. ^ See The Iron Fist Behind The Invisible Hand.

4. ^ "For mutualists, occupancy and use is the only legitimate standard for establishing ownership of land, regardless of how many times it has changed hands. According the mutualist Kevin Carson "A change in occupancy will amount to a change in ownership." An existing owner may transfer ownership by sale or gift; but the new owner may establish legitimate title to the land only by his own occupancy and use. **A change in occupancy will amount to a change in ownership.** Absentee landlord rent, and exclusion of homesteaders from vacant land by an absentee landlord, are both considered illegitimate by mutualists. The actual occupant is considered the owner of a tract of land, and any attempt to collect rent by a self-styled landlord is regarded as a violent invasion of the possessor's absolute right of property. (p. 200. of Carson's "Mutualist Political Economy." (editor's emphasis)

References

[1] "Introduction". Mutualist.org. Retrieved 2010-04-29.

[2] Miller, David. 1987. "Mutualism." The Blackwell Encyclopedia of Political Thought. Blackwell Publishing. p. 11

[3] Tandy, Francis D., 1896, *Voluntary Socialism*, chapter 6, paragraph 15.

[4] *Proudhon's Solution of the Social Problem*, Edited by Henry Cohen. Vanguard Press, 1927.

[5] Swartz, Clarence Lee. What is Mutualism? VI. Land and Rent

[6] Woodcock, George. *Anarchism: A History of Libertarian Ideas and Movements*, Broadview Press, 2004, p. 20

[7] Carson, Kevin A. *Studies in Mutualist Political Economy Preface.*

[8] Avrich, Paul. *Anarchist Voices: An Oral History of Anarchism in America*, Princeton University Press 1996 ISBN 978-0-691-04494-1, p.6
Blackwell Encyclopaedia of Political Thought, Blackwell Publishing 1991 ISBN 0-631-17944-5, p.11

[9] Pierre-Joseph Proudhon, *What Is Property?*, p. 281.

2.42. MUTUALISM (ECONOMIC THEORY)

[10] Tucker, Benjamin, *State Socialism and Anarchism,* State Socialism and Anarchism

[11] Fourier, Charles, *Traité* (1822), cited in Arthur E. Bestor, Jr., "The Evolution of the Socialist Vocabulary", *Journal of the History of Ideas,* Vol. 9, No. 3 (Jun., 1948), 259-302.

[12] *New-Harmony Gazette,* I, 301-02 (14 June 1826) cited in Arthur E. Bestor, Jr., "The Evolution of the Socialist Vocabulary", *Journal of the History of Ideas,* Vol. 9, No. 3 (Jun., 1948), 259-302.

[13] Woodcock, George. Anarchism: A History Of Libertarian Ideas And Movements. Broadview Press. p. 100

[14] Swartz, Clarence Lee. What is Mutualism?

[15] Joshua King Ingalls, "A Practical Movement for Transition," Spirit of the Age, II, 13 (March 30, 1850), p. 202-4.

[16] Albert Brisbane, "The Mutualist Township," The Spirit of the Age, II, 12 (March 23, 1850), 179-183.; II, 13 (March 30, 1850), 200-202.

[17] Pierre-Joseph Proudhon, "The Coming Era of Mutualism," *Spirit of the Age,* I, 7 (August 18, 1849), 107-8.

[18] Wendy McElroy. "The culture of individualist anarchist in Late-nineteenth century America"

[19] *Native American Anarchism: A Study of Left-Wing American Individualism* by Eunice Minette Schuster

[20] *Individual Liberty* by Benjamin Tucker

[21] "Anarchism" at the *Encyclopedia Britannica* online.

[22] George Woodcock. *Anarchism: a history of libertarian movements.* Pg. 357

[23] George Woodcock. *Anarchism: a history of libertarian movements.* Pg. 357

[24] "Anarchosyndicalism" by Rudolf Rocker

[25] History of The First International by G. M. Stekloff. London. Martin Lawrence Limited

[26] History of The First International by G. M. Stekloff. London. Martin Lawrence Limited

[27] History of The First International by G. M. Stekloff. London. Martin Lawrence Limited

[28] History of The First International by G. M. Stekloff. London. Martin Lawrence Limited

[29] "A Mutualist FAQ: A.4. Are Mutualists Socialists?". Mutualist.org. Retrieved 2010-04-29.

[30] Libertarian Socialism by Paul E. Gagnon

[31] Hymans, E., *Pierre-Joseph Proudhon,* pp. 190–1, Woodcock, George. *Anarchism: A History of Libertarian Ideas and Movements,* Broadview Press, 2004, pp. 110 & 112

[32] *General Idea of the Revolution,* Pluto Press, pp. 215–216 and p. 277

[33] Woodcock, George (1962). Anarchism: A History of Libertarian Ideas and Movements. The World Publishing Company. ISBN 978-0140168211.

[34] "Some background about the name: What is mutualism?". Mutualism.de. Retrieved 2010-04-29.

[35] Guerin, Daniel (ed.) *No Gods, No Masters,* AK Press, vol. 1, p. 62

[36] *The General Idea of the Revolution,* Pluto Press, p. 277 and p. 281

[37] "Introduction", *General Idea of the Revolution,* p. xxxii

[38] *Pierre-Joseph Proudhon and the Rise of French Republican Socialism,* Oxford University Press, Oxford, 1984, p. 230 and p. 156

[39] Anderson, Edwin Robert. 1911. The Income Tax: A Study of the History, Theory and Practice of Income Taxation at Home and Abroad. The MacMillan Company. p. 279

[40] Burton, Richard D. E. 1991. Baudelaire and the Second Republic: Writing and Revolution. Oxford University Press. p. 122

[41] Corkran, John Frazer. 1849. History of the National Constituent Assembly, from May, 1848. Harper & Brothers. p. 275

[42] Martin, Henri, & Alger, Abby Langdon. A Popular History of France from the First Revolution to the Present Time. D. Estes and C.E. Lauria. p. 189

[43] Augello, Massimo M., Luigi, Marco Enrico. 2005. Economists in Parliament in the Liberal Age. Ashgate Publishing, Ltd. p. 123

[44] "Suppose that all the producers in the republic, numbering more than ten millions, tax themselves, each one, to the amount of only one per cent of their capital ... Suppose that by means of this tax a bank be founded, in Competition with the Bank (miscalled) of France, discounting and giving credit on mortgages at the rate of one-half of one per cent." Henry Cohen, ed. *Proudhon's Solution of the Social Problem.* Vanguard Press, 1927. pp 118–9.

[45] Henry Cohen, ed. *Proudhon's Solution of the Social Problem.* Vanguard Press, 1927. p 46.

[46] System of Economical Contradictions, p. 202

[47] Proudhon, *General Idea of the Revolution in the Nineteenth Century.* Translated by John Beverly Robinson. New York: Haskell House Publishers, Ltd., 1923, 1969 [1851]. p 243.

[48] Proudhon, Pierre-Joseph. *What is Property?* p. 118

[49] quoted by James J. Martin. Men Against the State, p. 223

[50] Joseph Déjacque, De l'être-humain mâle et femelle - Lettre à P.J. Proudhon par Joseph Déjacque (in French)

[51] The Anarchist FAQ Editorial Collective. "150 years of Libertarian".

[52] Graham, Robert (2005). *Anarchism: A Documentary History of Libertarian Ideas: from Anarchy to Anarchism (300 Ce to 1939)*. Black Rose Books. ISBN 978-1-55164-251-2.

[53] "l'Echange", article in *Le Libertaire* no 6, September 21, 1858, New York.

[54] Déjacque criticized French mutualist anarchist Pierre Joseph Proudhon as far as "the Proudhonist version of Ricardian socialism, centred on the reward of labour power and the problem of exchange value. In his polemic with Proudhon on women's emancipation, Déjacque urged Proudhon to push on 'as far as the abolition of the contract, the abolition not only of the sword and of capital, but of property and authority in all their forms,' and refuted the commercial and wages logic of the demand for a 'fair reward' for 'labour' (labour power). Déjacque asked: 'Am I thus... right to want, as with the system of contracts, to measure out to each — according to their accidental capacity to produce — what they are entitled to?' The answer given by Déjacque to this question is unambiguous: 'it is not the product of his or her labour that the worker has a right to, but to the satisfaction of his or her needs, whatever may be their nature.' [...] For Déjacque, on the other hand, the communal state of affairs — the phalanstery 'without any hierarchy, without any authority' except that of the 'statistics book' — corresponded to 'natural exchange,' i.e. to the 'unlimited freedom of all production and consumption; the abolition of any sign of agricultural, individual, artistic or scientific property; the destruction of any individual holding of the products of work; the demonarchisation and the demonetarisation of manual and intellectual capital as well as capital in instruments, commerce and buildings."Alain Pengam. "Anarchist-Communism"

[55] Kropotkin, Peter. The Wage System, Freedom Pamphlets No. 1, New Edition 1920

[56] Woodcock, George. Anarchism: A History of Libertarian Ideas and Movements. Broadview Press 2004. p. 168

[57] Bookchin, Murray. The Spanish Anarchists. AK Press. 1996. p. 25

[58] Cited in Social Anarchism or Lifestyle Anarchism by Murray Bookchin, from Maximoff, Political Philosophy of Bakunin, p. 167

[59] Reisman, George. Mutualism's Support for the Exploitation of Labor and State Coercion.

[60] Kevin Carson. *Studies in Mutualist Political Economy.*

[61] Carson, Kevin. Mutualist Political Economy, Preface

[62] Carson, Kevin A. Carson's Rejoinders. Journal of Libertarian Studies, Volume 20, No. 1 (Winter 2006): 97-136, pp. 116, 117

2.42.8 Bibliography

- Thomas B Backer. *The mutualists : the heirs of Proudhon in the first international, 1865–1878. University of Cincinnati, 1978*

2.42.9 External links

- *Mutualism* from *The Conquest of Power*, by Albert Weisbord
- *Plan of the Cincinnati Labor for Labor Store* by Josiah Warren
- Proudhon and Anarchism by Larry Gambone — contains a discussion on Proudhonist mutualism
- *Mutual Banking* by William B. Greene
- *What is Mutualism?* by Clarence Lee Swartz (1927) - A classic text on Mutualism
- *Mutual Aid: A Factor of Evolution* Peter Kropotkin 1902
- *Anarchist-Mutualism* by John William Lloyd, a criticism
- *Studies in Mutualist Political Economy* by Kevin Carson. For more of Carson's points of view about mutualism you can check his blog.
- *Journal of Libertarian Studies* Vol. 20 Num. 1. This issue is devoted to Kevin Carson's *Studies in Mutualist Political Economy*. It includes critiques and Carson's rejoinders.
- *Mutualism: A Philosophy for Thieves* by George Reisman.

2.43 Neo-Marxian economics

The terms **Neo-Marxian**, **Post-Marxian**, and **Radical Political Economics** were first used to refer to a distinct tradition of economic thought in the 1970s and 1980s. Many of the leading figures were associated with the Monthly Review School.

In industrial economics, the Neo-Marxian approach stresses the monopolistic rather than the competitive nature of capitalism. This approach is associated with Kalecki, and Baran and Sweezy.[1][2]

Theorists such as Samuel Bowles,[3][4] David Gordon, John Roemer, Herbert Gintis, Jon Elster, and Adam Przeworski have adopted the techniques of neoclassical economics, including game theory and mathematical modeling, to demonstrate Marxian concepts such as exploitation and class conflict.[5]

The Neo-Marxian approach integrated non-Marxist or "bourgeois" economics from the Post-Keynesians like Joan Robinson and the Neo-Ricardian school of Piero Sraffa.

Polish economists Michał Kalecki, Rosa Luxemburg, Henryk Grossman, Adam Przeworski and Oskar Lange were influential in this school, particularly in developing theories of underconsumption. While most official Communist Parties denounced Neo-Marxian theories as "bourgeois economics", some Neo-Marxians served as advisers to socialist or Third World developing governments.

Maurice Dobb despite being an orthodox Marxist economist was also associated with this current.

2.43.1 Argument

Big business can maintain selling prices at high levels while still competing to cut costs, advertise and market their products. Competition is generally limited however with a few large capital formations sharing various markets, with the exception of a few actual monopolies (such as the Bell System at the time). The economic surpluses which result cannot be absorbed through consumers spending more. The concentration of the surplus in the hands of the business elite must therefore be geared towards imperialistic and militaristic government tendencies, which is the easiest and surest way to utilise surplus productive capacity.

Exploitation focuses on low wage workers and groups at home, especially minorities. Average earners see the pressures in drive for production destroy their human relationships, leading to wider alienation and hostility. The whole system is largely irrational, since though individuals may make rational decisions, the ultimate systemic goals are not. The system continues to function so long as Keynesian full employment policies are pursued, but there is the continued threat to stability from less-developed countries, throwing off the restraints of neo-colonial domination.

2.43.2 Position on the labor theory of value

Baran introduced the concept of "economic surplus" to deal with novel complexities raised by the dominance of monopoly capital. With Paul Sweezy, Baran elaborated the importance of this innovation, its consistency with Marx's labor concept of value, and supplementary relation to Marx's category of surplus value.[6]

According to Baran's categories, "Actual economic surplus" is "the difference between what society's actual current output and its actual current consumption," and hence is equal to current savings or accumulation. Potential economic surplus," in contrast, is "the difference between that output that could be produced in a given natural and technical environment with the help of employable productive resources, and what might be regarded as essential consumption." Baran also introduced the concept of "planned surplus"—a category that could only be operationalized in a rationally planned socialist society. This was defined as "the difference between society's 'optimum' output available in a historically given natural and technological environment under conditions of planned 'optimal' utilization of all available productive resources, and some chosen 'optimal' volume of consumption."[7]

Baran used the surplus concept to analyze underdeveloped economies (or what are now more optimistically called "developing economies") in his *The Political Economy of Growth*.

2.43.3 See also

- Marxian economics
- Analytical Marxism
- Neo-Marxism
- Post-Marxism

2.43.4 References

[1] Baran, P. and Sweezy, P. (1966). *Monopoly Capital: An essay on the American economic and social order*, Monthly Review Press, New York.

[2] Jonathan Nitzan and Shimshon Bichler. *Capital as power: a study of order and creorder*. Taylor & Francis, 2009, p. 50.

[3] Samuel Bowles, "Post-marxian economics: Labour, learning and history", *Social Science Information*, Volume 24 (3): 507, SAGE – Sep 1, 1985.

[4] Richard D. Wolff and Stephen Cullenberg, "Marxism and Post-Marxism", *Social Text* 15 (Fall 1986), 126–135.

[5] Barry Stewart Clark, *Political economy: a comparative approach*, ABC-CLIO, 1998, p. 67.

[6] Baran, P.A. & Sweezy, P.M. (2012). "Some Theoretical Implications". *Monthly Review*. **64** (3).

[7] Baran, Paul A. (1957). *The Political Economy of Growth*. New York: Monthly Review Press. pp. 22–23, 41–42.

2.43.5 External links

- Marxist Economics Courses, Links and Information
- Marxian Economics (archive from Schwartz center of economic policy analysis)
- Marxian Political Economy
- The Neo-Marxian Schools (archive from Schwartz center of economic policy analysis)
- A Marxian Introduction to Modern Economics
- International working group on value theory
- An outline of Marxist economics, Chapter 6 of *Reformism or Revolution* by Alan Woods
- The End of the Market A website containing a critical evaluation the idea of the market-clearing price which affirms Marx's theory that in capitalism profitability would decline
- The Neo-Marxian Schools ("Radical Political Economy")

2.44 Neo-Ricardianism

The **neo-Ricardian school** is an economic school that derives from the close reading and interpretation of David Ricardo by Piero Sraffa, and from Sraffa's critique of neo-classical economics as presented in his *The Production of Commodities by Means of Commodities*, and further developed by the neo-Ricardians in the course of the Cambridge capital controversy. It particularly disputes neo-classical theory of income distribution.

Prominent neo-Ricardians are usually held to include Pierangelo Garegnani, Krishna Bharadwaj, Luigi Pasinetti, Joan Robinson, John Eatwell, Fernando Vianello, Murray Milgate, Ian Steedman, Heinz Kurz, Neri Salvadori, Bertram Schefold, Fabio Petri, Massimo Pivetti, Franklin Serrano, Fabio Ravagnani, Roberto Ciccone, Sergio Parrinello, Alessandro Roncaglia, Maurice Dobb, Gilbert Abraham-Frois and Giorgio Gilibert.

The school partially overlaps with post-Keynesian and neo-Marxian economics.

2.44.1 See also

- Capital controversy
- Okishio's theorem

2.44.2 External links

- The Neo-Ricardians(archive), History of Economic Thought website, New School University

2.45 Neuroeconomics

Neuroeconomics is an interdisciplinary field that seeks to explain human decision making, the ability to process multiple alternatives and to follow a course of action. It studies how economic behavior can shape our understanding of the brain, and how neuroscientific discoveries can constrain and guide models of economics.[1]

It combines research methods from neuroscience, experimental and behavioral economics, and cognitive and social psychology. As research into decision-making behavior becomes increasingly computational, it has also incorporated new approaches from theoretical biology, computer science, and mathematics. Neuroeconomics studies decision making, by using a combination of tools from these fields so as to avoid the shortcomings that arise from a single-perspective approach. In mainstream economics, expected utility (EU), and the concept of rational agents, are still being used. Many economic behaviors are not fully explained by these models, such as heuristics and framing.[2]

Behavioral economics emerged to account for these anomalies by integrating social, cognitive, and emotional factors in understanding economic decisions. Neuroeconomics adds another layer by using neuroscientific methods in understanding the interplay between economic behavior and neural mechanisms. By using tools from various fields, some scholars claim that neuroeconomics offers a more integrative way of understanding decision making.[1]

2.45.1 Introduction

The field of decision making is largely concerned with the processes by which individuals make a single choice from among many options. These processes are generally assumed to proceed in a logical manner such that the decision itself is largely independent of context. Different options are first translated into a common currency, such as monetary value, and are then compared to one another and the option with the largest overall utility value is the one that should be chosen.[3] While there has been support for this economic view of decision making, there are also situations where the assumptions of optimal decision making seem to be violated.

The field of neuroeconomics arose out of this controversy. By determining which brain areas are active in which types of decision processes, neuroeconomists hope to better understand the nature of what seem to be suboptimal and illogical decisions. While most of these scientists are using human subjects in this research, others are using animal models where studies can be more tightly controlled and the assumptions of the economic model can be tested directly.

For example, Padoa-Schioppa & Assad tracked the firing rates of individual neurons in the monkey orbitofrontal cortex while the animals chose between two kinds of juice. The firing rate of the neurons was directly correlated with the utility of the food items and did not differ when other types of food were offered. This suggests that, in accordance with the economic theory of decision making, neurons are directly comparing some form of utility across different options and choosing the one with the higher value.[4] Similarly, a common measure of prefrontal cortex dysfunction, the FrSBe, is correlated with multiple different measures of economic attitudes and behavior, supporting the idea that brain activation can display important aspects of the decision process.[5]

Influential Neuroeconomics

2.45.2 Major research areas in neuroeconomics

Decision making under risk and uncertainty

Most of our decisions are made under some conditions of risk. Decision sciences such as psychology and economics usually define risk as the uncertainty about several possible outcomes when the probability of each is known.[6] Utility maximization, first proposed by Daniel Bernoulli in 1738, is used to explain decision making under risk. The theory assumes that humans are rational and will assess options based on the expected utility they will gain from each.[2]

Research and experience uncovered a wide range of expected utility anomalies and common patterns of behavior that are inconsistent with the principle of utility maximization. For example, the human tendency to be risk-averse or risk-seeking. Also, the tendency to overweigh small probabilities and underweigh large ones. Daniel Kahneman and Amos Tversky proposed the prospect theory to encompass these observations and offers an alternative model.[2]

There seem to be multiple brain areas involved in dealing with situations of uncertainty. In tasks requiring individuals to make predictions when there is some degree of uncertainty about the outcome, there is an increase in activity in area BA8 of the frontomedian cortex [7][8] as well as a more generalized increase in activity of the mesial prefrontal cortex [9] and the frontoparietal cortex.[10] The prefrontal cortex is generally involved in all reasoning and understanding, so these particular areas may be specifically involved in determining the best course of action when not all relevant information is available.[11]

In situations that involve known risk rather than uncertainty, the insular cortex seems to be highly active. For example, when subjects played a 'double or nothing' game in which they could either stop the game and keep accumulated winnings or take a risky option resulting in either a complete loss or doubling of winnings, activation of the right insula increased when individuals took the gamble.[11] It is hypothesized that the main role of the insular cortex in risky decision making is to simulate potential negative consequences of taking a gamble.

In addition to the importance of specific brain areas to the decision process, there is also evidence that the neurotransmitter dopamine may transmit information about uncertainty throughout the cortex. Dopaminergic neurons are strongly involved in the reward process and become highly active after an unexpected reward occurs. In monkeys, the level of dopaminergic activity is highly correlated with the level of uncertainty such that the activity increases with uncertainty.[12] Furthermore, rats with lesions to the nucleus accumbens, which is an important part of the dopamine reward pathway through the brain, are far more risk averse than normal rats. This suggests that dopamine may be an important mediator of risky behavior.[13]

Loss aversion

One interesting aspect of human decision making is a strong aversion to potential loss. For example, the cost of losing a specific amount of money is higher than the value of gaining the same amount of money. One of the main controversies in understanding loss aversion is whether the process is driven by a single neural system that directly compares options and decides between them or whether there are competing systems, one responsible for a reasoned comparison among options and another more impulsive and emotional system driven by an aversion to potentially negative outcomes.

While one study found no evidence for an increase in activation in areas related to negative emotional reactions in response to loss aversion[14] another found that individuals with damaged amygdalas had a lack of loss aversion even though they had normal levels of general risk aversion, suggesting that the behavior was specific to potential losses.[15] These conflicting studies suggest that more research needs to be done to determine whether there are areas in the brain that respond specifically to potential loss or whether loss aversion is the byproduct of more general reasoning processes.

Another controversy in loss aversion research is whether

losses are actually experienced more negatively than equivalent gains or merely predicted to be more painful but actually experienced equivalently. Neuroeconomic research has attempted to distinguish between these hypotheses by measuring different physiological changes in response to both loss and gain. Studies have found that skin conductance,[16] pupil dilation and heart rate[17] are all higher in response to monetary loss than to equivalent gain. All three measures are involved in stress responses, so it seems that losing a particular amount of money is experienced more strongly than gaining the same amount.

Intertemporal choice

In addition to risk preference, another central concept in economics is intertemporal choices which are decisions that involve costs and benefits that are distributed over time. Intertemporal choice research studies the expected utility that humans assign to events occurring at different times. The dominant model in economics which explains it is discounted utility (DU). DU assumes that humans have consistent time preference and will assign value to events regardless of when they occur. Similar to EU in explaining risky decision making, DU is inadequate in explaining intertemporal choice.[2]

For example, DU assumes that people who value a bar of candy today more than 2 bars tomorrow, will also value 1 bar received 100 days from now more than 2 bars received after 101 days. There is strong evidence against this last part in both humans and animals, and hyperbolic discounting has been proposed as an alternative model. Under this model, valuations fall very rapidly for small delay periods, but then fall slowly for longer delay periods. This better explains why most people who would choose 1 candy bar now over 2 candy bars tomorrow, would, in fact, choose 2 candy bars received after 101 days rather than the 1 candy bar received after 100 days which EU assumes.[2]

Neuroeconomic research in intertemporal choice is largely aimed at understanding what mediates observed behaviors such as future discounting and impulsively choosing smaller sooner rather than larger later rewards. The process of choosing between immediate and delayed rewards seems to be mediated by an interaction between two brain areas. In choices involving both primary (fruit juice) and secondary rewards (money), the limbic system is highly active when choosing the immediate reward while the lateral prefrontal cortex was equally active when making either choice. Furthermore, the ratio of limbic to cortex activity decreased as a function of the amount of time until reward. This suggests that the limbic system, which forms part of the dopamine reward pathway, is most involved in making impulsive decisions while the cortex is responsible for the more general aspects of the intertemporal decision process.[18][19]

The neurotransmitter serotonin seems to play an important role in modulating future discounting. In rats, reducing serotonin levels increases future discounting [20] while not affecting decision making under uncertainty.[21] It seems, then, that while the dopamine system is involved in probabilistic uncertainty, serotonin may be responsible for temporal uncertainty since delayed reward involves a potentially uncertain future. In addition to neurotransmitters, intertemporal choice is also modulated by hormones in the brain. In humans, a reduction in cortisol, released by the hypothalamus in response to stress, is correlated with a higher degree of impulsivity in intertemporal choice tasks.[22] Interestingly, drug addicts tend to have lower levels of cortisol than the general population, which may explain why they seem to discount the future negative effects of taking drugs and opt for the immediate positive reward.[23]

Social decision making

While most research on decision making tends to focus on individuals making choices outside of a social context, it is also important to consider decisions that involve social interactions. The types of situations that decision theorists study are as diverse as altruism, cooperation, punishment, and retribution. One of the most frequently utilized tasks in social decision making is the prisoner's dilemma.

In this situation, the payoff for a particular choice is dependent not only on the decision of the individual but also on that of another individual playing the game. An individual can choose to either cooperate with his partner or defect against the partner. Over the course of a typical game, individuals tend to prefer mutual cooperation even though defection would lead to a higher overall payout. This suggests that individuals are motivated not only by monetary gains but also by some reward derived from cooperating in social situations.

This idea is supported by neural imaging studies demonstrating a high degree of activation in the ventral striatum when individuals cooperate with another person but that this is not the case when people play the same prisoner's dilemma against a computer.[24][25] The ventral striatum is part of the reward pathway, so this research suggests that there may be areas of the reward system that are activated specifically when cooperating in social situations. Further support for this idea comes from research demonstrating that activation in the striatum and the ventral tegmental area show similar patterns of activation when receiving money and when donating money to charity. In both cases, the level of activation increases as the amount of money increases, suggesting that both giving and receiving money results in neural reward.[26]

An important aspect of social interactions such as the prisoner's dilemma is trust. Your likelihood of cooperating with another individual is directly related to how much you trust them to cooperate with you; if you expect the other individual to defect against you, there is no reason for you to cooperate with them. Trust behavior seems to be related to the presence of oxytocin, a hormone involved in maternal behavior and pair bonding in many species. When oxytocin levels were increased in humans, they were more trusting of other individuals than a control group even though their overall levels of risk-taking were unaffected suggesting that oxytocin is specifically implicated in the social aspects of risk taking.[27]

2.45.3 Methodology

Behavioral economics experiments record the subject's decision over various design parameters and use the data to generate formal models that predict performance. Neuroeconomics extends this approach by adding observation of the nervous system to the set of explanatory variables. The goal of neuroeconomics is to inform the creation and contribute another layer of data to the testable hypotheses of these models.

Furthermore, neuroeconomic research is being used to understand and explain aspects of human behavior that do not conform to traditional economic models. While these behavior patterns are generally dismissed as 'fallacious' or 'illogical' by economists, neuroeconomic researchers are trying to determine the biological reasons for these behaviors. By using this approach, we may be able to find valid reasons for the presence of these seemingly sub-optimal behaviors.

Neurobiological research techniques

There are several different techniques that can be utilized to understand the biological basis of economic behavior. Neural imaging is used in human subjects to determine which areas of the brain are most active during particular tasks. Some of these techniques, such as fMRI[8][9][10] or PET are best suited to giving detailed pictures of the brain which can give information about specific structures involved in a task. Other techniques, such as ERP (event-related potentials)[28] and oscillatory brain activity[29] are used to gain detailed knowledge of the time course of events within a more general area of the brain.

In addition to studying areas of the brain, some studies are aimed at understanding the functions of different brain chemicals in relation to behavior. This can be done by either correlating existing chemical levels with different behavior patterns or by changing the amount of the chemical in the brain and noting any resulting behavioral changes. For example, the neurotransmitter serotonin seems to be involved in making decisions involving intertemporal choice[21] while dopamine is utilized when individuals make judgments involving uncertainty.[12] Furthermore, artificially increasing oxytocin levels increases trust behavior in humans [27] while individuals with higher cortisol levels tend to be more impulsive and exhibit more future discounting.[22]

In addition to studying the behavior of normal individuals in decision making tasks, some research involves comparing the behavior of normal individuals to that of others with damage to areas of the brain expected to be involved in certain behaviors. In humans, this means finding individuals with specific types of neural impairment. For example, people with amygdala damage seem to exhibit less loss aversion than normal controls.[15] Also, scores from a survey measuring correlates of prefrontal cortex dysfunction are correlated with general economic attitudes.[5]

Previous studies investigated the behavioral patterns of patients with psychiatric disorders, such as Schizophrenia,[30] autism, depression, or addiction, to get the insights of their pathophysiology. In animal studies, highly controlled experiments can get more specific information about the importance of brain areas to economic behavior. This can involve either lesioning entire brain areas and measuring resulting behavior changes[13] or using electrodes to measure the firing of individual neurons in response to particular stimuli.[4]

2.45.4 Notable theorists

- Daniel Kahneman
- Matteo Motterlini
- Denise Shull
- Vernon L. Smith
- Paul J. Zak
- Amos Tversky

2.45.5 Experiments

In a typical behavioral economics experiment, a subject is asked to make a series of economic decisions. For example, a subject may be asked whether they prefer to have 45 cents or a gamble with a 50% chance to win one dollar. The experimenter will then measure different variables in order to determine what is going on in the subject's brain as they make the decision. Some authors have demonstrated that

Neuroeconomics' tools may be useful not only to describe experiments involving rewarding but may also be applied in order to describe the psychological behavior of common psychiatric syndromes involving addiction as well as delusion. (Download)

2.45.6 Neuroeconomic Programs

Several universities are conducting direct research in Neuroeconomics, such as MIT, Caltech, the University of Pennsylvania, New York University, Carnegie Mellon University, Duke University, and George Mason University.[31][32][33] A few schools offer a degree in Neuroeconomics. Claremont Graduate University was the first institution to offer a PhD in Neuroeconomics; it remains one of the few Neuroeconomics institutes in the United States.[34] Caltech started its Behavioral and Social Neuroscience (BSN) PhD in conjunction with its Computation and Neural Systems and Social Science programs,[35] mixing economic theory, neurobiology, computational neuroscience, dynamic causal modeling and neuroscientific techniques.

Starting in 2010, the Department of Economics at the University of Zurich in Zurich/Switzerland began offering a degree-awarding PhD program in Neuroeconomics.[36] Students in this program take dedicated neuroeconomics courses and conduct research within the research groups at the Department's Laboratory for Social and Neural Systems Research (SNS-Lab).[37]

Maastricht University (Netherlands) offers a 2-year research master program in Neuroeconomics. The program is a joint venture of the Department of Economics and the Faculty of Psychology and Neuroscience. It offers core courses at PhD level in economics, cognitive and social neuroscience and hands-on training in experimental and neuroscience methods.[38] A listing of most degree programs can be found on the Society for Neuroeconomics Website.[39]

2.45.7 Related Fields

Neuroeconomics have also opened the door for other new emerging fields like Neurofinance, Neuroinvesting and Neurotrading. These new fields of study focus on the cognitive processes engaged in acquiring and processing information in financial decision making. According to Elise Payzan, portfolio managers and traders have to process information on the spot in rapidly changing environments. Little is known about how to tailor organizational and individual decision-making processes to help people process information efficiently in such contexts. By identifying environmental factors improving efficient information processing, it is hoped that research in neurofinance will produce practical results on how to improve investment and trading decisions, at both individual and organizational levels. As for now, there is also a new concept of using nootropics (smart drugs) to help investors/traders enhance their cognitive acuteness while trading the market.

2.45.8 Criticism

Glenn W. Harris and Emanuel Donchin have criticized the emerging field.[40] Example of critics have been that it is "a field that oversells itself";[41] or that neuroeconomic studies "misunderstand and underestimate traditional economic models". A critical argument of traditional economists against the neuroeconomic approach, is that the use of non-choice data, such as response times, eye-tracking and neural signals that people generate during decision making, should be excluded from any economic analysis.[42]

2.45.9 Neuromarketing

Neuromarketing is a distinct discipline closely related to neuroeconomics. While neuroeconomics has more academic aims, since it studies the basic mechanisms of decision-making, neuromarketing is an applied field which uses neuroimaging tools for market investigations.[43][44]

2.45.10 See also

- Decision making
- Neuromarketing
- Behavioral economics

2.45.11 References

[1] Center for Neuroeconomics Study at Duke University http://dibs.duke.edu/research/d-cides/research/neuroeconomics

[2] Loewenstein,G., Rick,S., & Cohen, J. (2008). *Neuroeconomics. Annual Reviews.* 59: 647-672. doi:10.1146/annurev.psych.59.103006.093710

[3] Rustichini A (2009). "Neuroeconomics: What have we found, and what should we search for?". *Current Opinion in Neurobiology* 19: 672–677. doi:10.1016/j.conb.2009.09.012.

[4] Padoa-Schioppa C., Assad J.A. (2007). "The representation of economic value in the orbitofrontal cortex is invariant for changes of menu". *Nature Reviews Neuroscience* 11: 95–102. doi:10.1038/nn2020.

[5] Spinella M., Yang B., Lester D. (2008). "Prefrontal cortex dysfunction and attitudes toward money: A study in neuroeconomics". *Journal of Socio-Economics* **37**: 1785–1788. doi:10.1016/j.socec.2004.09.061.

[6] Mohr M., Biele G., Hauke R. (2010). "Neural Processing of Risk". *e Journal of Neuroscience* **30** (19): 6613–6619. doi:10.1523/jneurosci.0003-10.2010.

[7] Volz K.G., Schubotz R.I., von Cramon D.Y. (2003). "Predicting events of varying probability: uncertainty investigated by fMRI". *NeuroImage* **19** (2 Pt 1): 271–280. doi:10.1016/S1053-8119(03)00122-8. PMID 12814578.

[8] Volz K.G., Schubotz R.I., von Cramon D.Y. (2004). "Why am I unsure? Internal and external attributions of uncertainty dissociated by fMRI". *NeuroImage* **21** (3): 848–857. doi:10.1016/j.neuroimage.2003.10.028. PMID 15006651.

[9] Knutson B., Taylor J., Kaufman M., Peterson R., Glover G. (2005). "Distributed Neural Representation of Expected Value". *Journal of Neuroscience* **25** (19): 4806–4812. doi:10.1523/JNEUROSCI.0642-05.2005. PMID 15888656.

[10] Paulus M.P., Hozack N., Zauscher B., McDowell J.E., Frank L., Brown G.G., Braff D.L. (2001). "Prefrontal, parietal, and temporal cortex networks underlie decision-making in the presence of uncertainty". *NeuroImage* **13** (1): 91–100. doi:10.1006/nimg.2000.0667. PMID 11133312.

[11] Paulus M.P., Rogalsky C., Simmons A., Feinstein J.S., Stein M.B. (2003). "Increased activation in the right insula during risk-taking decision making is related to harm avoidance and neuroticism". *NeuroImage* **19** (4): 1439–1448. doi:10.1016/S1053-8119(03)00251-9. PMID 12948701.

[12] Fiorillo C.D., Tobler P.N., Schultz W. (2003). "Discrete coding of reward probability and uncertainty by dopamine neurons". *Science* **299** (5614): 1898–1902. doi:10.1126/science.1077349. PMID 12649484.

[13] Cardinal R.N., Howes N.J. (2005). "Effects of lesions of the nucleus accumbens core on choice between small certain rewards and large uncertain rewards in rats". *BMC Neuroscience* **6**: 37.

[14] Tom S.M., Fox C.R., Trepel C., Poldrack R.A. (2007). "The neural basis of loss aversion in decision-making under risk". *Science* **315** (5811): 515–518. doi:10.1126/science.1134239. PMID 17255512.

[15] De Martino B., Camerer C.F., Adolphs R. (2010). "Amygdala damage eliminates monetary loss aversion". *Proceedings of the National Academy of Sciences* **107** (8): 3788–3792. doi:10.1073/pnas.0910230107. PMC 2840433. PMID 20142490.

[16] Sokol-Hessner P., Hsu M., Curley N.G., Delgado M.R., Camerer C.F., Phelps E.A. (2009). "Thinking like a trader selectively reduces individuals' loss aversion". *Proceedings of the National Academy of Sciences* **106** (13): 5035–5040. doi:10.1073/pnas.0806761106.

[17] Hochman G., Yechiam E. (2011). "Loss aversion in the eye and in the heart: The autonomic nervous system's responses to losses". *Journal of Behavioral Decision Making* **24**: 140–156. doi:10.1002/bdm.692.

[18] McClure S.M., Laibson D.I., Loewenstein G., Cohen J.D. (2004). "Separate neural systems value immediate and delayed monetary rewards". *Science* **306** (5695): 503–507. doi:10.1126/science.1100907. PMID 15486304.

[19] McClure S.M., Ericson K.M., Laibson D.I., Loewenstein G., Cohen J.D. (2007). "Time discounting for primary rewards". *Journal of Neuroscience* **27** (21): 5796–5804. doi:10.1523/JNEUROSCI.4246-06.2007. PMID 17522323.

[20] Mobini S., Chiang T.J., Al-Ruwaitea A.S., Ho M.Y., Bradshaw C.M., Szabadi E. (2000). "Effect of central 5-hydroxytryptamine depletion on inter-temporal choice: A quantitative analysis". *Psychopharmacology* **149** (3): 313–318. doi:10.1007/s002130000385. PMID 10823413.

[21] Mobini S., Chiang T.J., Ho M.Y., Bradshaw C.M., Szabadi E. (2000). "Effects of central 5-hydroxytryptamine depletion on sensitivity to delayed and probabilistic reinforcement". *Psychopharmacology* **152** (4): 390–397. doi:10.1007/s002130000542. PMID 11140331.

[22] Takahashi T (2004). "Cortisol levels and time-discounting of monetary gain in humans". *NeuroReport* **15**: 2145–2147. doi:10.1097/00001756-200409150-00029.

[23] Plihal W., Krug R., Pietrowsky R., Fehm H.L., Born J. (1996). "Coricosteroid receptor mediated effects on mood in humans". *Psychoneuroendocrinology* **21** (6): 515–523. doi:10.1016/S0306-4530(96)00011-X. PMID 8983088.

[24] Rilling J.K., Gutman D.A., Zeh T.R., Pagnoni G., Berns G.S., Kilts C.D. (2002). "A neural basis for social cooperation". *Neuron* **35** (2): 395–405. doi:10.1016/S0896-6273(02)00755-9. PMID 12160756.

[25] Rilling J.K., Sanfey A.G., Aronson J.A., Nystrom L.E., Cohen J.D. (2004). "Opposing BOLD responses to reciprocated and unreciprocated altruism in putative reward pathways". *NeuroReport* **15**: 2539–2543. doi:10.1097/00001756-200411150-00022.

[26] Moll J., Drueger F., Zahn R., Pardini M., de Oliveira-Souza R., Grafman J. (2006). "Human fronto-mesolimbic networks guide decisions about charitable donation". *Proceedings of the National Academy of Sciences* **103** (42): 15623–15628. doi:10.1073/pnas.0604475103.

[27] Kosfeld M., Heinrichs M, Zak P.J., Fischbacher U., Fehr E. (2005). "Oxytocin increases trust in humans". *Nature* **435** (7042): 673–676. doi:10.1038/nature03701. PMID 15931222.

[28] Billeke, P.; Zamorano, F.; Cosmeli, D.; Aboitiz, A. (2013). "Oscillatory Brain Activity Correlates with Risk Perception and Predicts Social Decisions.". *Cerebral Cortex* **23** (14): 2872–83. doi:10.1093/cercor/bhs269. PMID 22941720.

[29] Billeke, P.; Zamorano, F.; López, T.; Cosmeli, D.; Aboitiz, A. (2014). "Someone has to Give In: Theta Oscillations Correlate with Adaptive Behavior in Social Bargaining". *Social Cognitive and Affective Neuroscience* **9** (12): 2041–8. doi:10.1093/scan/nsu012. PMID 24493841.

[30] Chung, Dongil (2013). "Cognitive Motivations of Free Riding and Cooperation and Impaired Strategic Decision Making in Schizophrenia During a Public Goods Game". *Schizophrenia Bulletin* **39** (1): 112–119. doi:10.1093/schbul/sbr068.

[31] Neuroeconomics The MIT Neuroeconomics Center

[32] Neuroeconomics: Decision-Making and The Brain

[33] Neuroeconomics

[34] Here is a Review of Neuroeconomic Programs in the United States

[35] "Caltech: Humanities and Social Sciences". Hss.caltech.edu. 2010-01-29. Retrieved 2010-07-28.

[36] http://www.econ.uzh.ch/programs.html

[37] http://www.sns.uzh.ch/index.html

[38] http://www.neuroeconomics.nl

[39] Society for Neuroeconomics

[40] "fMRI: Not the Only Way to Look at the Human Brain in Action". Observer. Retrieved 14 October 2014.

[41] Rubinstein, Ariel (2006). "Discussion of "behavioral economics": "Behavioral economics" (Colin Camerer) and "Incentives and self-control" (Ted O'Donoghue and Matthew Rabin)". In Persson, Torsten; Blundell, Richard; Newey, Whitney K. *Advances in economics and econometrics: theory and applications, ninth World Congress*. Cambridge, UK: Cambridge University Press. ISBN 0-521-87153-0. Retrieved 2010-01-01.

[42] Gul, Faruk; Pesendorfer, Wolfgang (2008). "A Case for Mindless Economics". In Schotter, Andrew; Caplin, Andrew. *The Foundations of Positive and Normative Economics: A Handbook (Handbooks in Economic Methodologies)*. Oxford University Press, USA. pp. 3–42. ISBN 0-19-532831-0. Retrieved 2009-03-04.

[43] Paul W. Glimcher (2008). "Neuroeconomics - Scholarpedia". *3(10):1759, revision #50592*. Retrieved 2009-03-04.

[44] Lee N, Broderick AJ, Chamberlain L (February 2007). "What is "neuromarketing"? A discussion and agenda for future research". *Int J Psychophysiol* **63** (2): 199–204. doi:10.1016/j.ijpsycho.2006.03.007. PMID 16769143.

2.45.12 Further reading

- David Krueger (2009) *The Secret Language of Money*, McGraw-Hill Professional. ISBN 978-0-07-162339-1

- De Martino B, Camerer CF, Adolphs R (February 2010). "Amygdala damage eliminates monetary loss aversion". *Proc. Natl. Acad. Sci. U.S.A.* **107** (8): 3788–92. doi:10.1073/pnas.0910230107. PMC 2840433. PMID 20142490. PDF

- Paul W. Glimcher; Colin Camerer; Russell A. Poldrack; Ernst Fehr; *Neuroeconomics: Decision Making and the Brain*, Academic Press, 2008.

- Camerer CF (November 2008). "Neuroeconomics: opening the gray box". *Neuron* **60** (3): 416–9. doi:10.1016/j.neuron.2008.10.027. PMID 18995815.

- Clithero JA, Tankersley D, Huettel SA (November 2008). Ashe, James, ed. "Foundations of Neuroeconomics: From Philosophy to Practice". *PLoS Biol.* **6** (11): e298. doi:10.1371/journal.pbio.0060298. PMC 2586372. PMID 19067493.

- Deppe M, Schwindt W, Pieper A, et al. (July 2007). "Anterior cingulate reflects susceptibility to framing during attractiveness evaluation". *NeuroReport* **18** (11): 1119–23. doi:10.1097/WNR.0b013e3282202c61. PMID 17589310.

- De Martino B, Kumaran D, Seymour B, Dolan RJ (August 2006). "Frames, Biases, and Rational Decision-Making in the Human Brain". *Science* **313** (5787): 684–7. doi:10.1126/science.1128356. PMC 2631940. PMID 16888142.

- Colin Camerer, George Loewenstein, Drazen Prelec, "Neuroeconomics: How neuroscience can inform economics", *Journal of Economic Literature*, 2005

- Deppe M, Schwindt W, Kugel H, Plassmann H, Kenning P (April 2005). "Nonlinear responses within the medial prefrontal cortex reveal when specific implicit information influences economic decision making". *J Neuroimaging* **15** (2): 171–82. doi:10.1177/1051228405275074. PMID 15746230.

- Daniel Houser; Kevin McCabe; Neuroeconomics, Advances in Health Economics and Health Services Research v. 20, Emerald Group Publishing Limited, Bingley West Yorkshire

- Peter Kenning, Hilke Plassmann, "Brain Research Bulletin - Special Issue on NeuroEconomics", 2005

- Paul Glimcher, *Decisions, Uncertainty, and the Brain: The Science of Neuroeconomics*, MIT Press, 2003.

- Montague PR, Berns GS (October 2002). "Neural economics and the biological substrates of valuation". *Neuron* **36** (2): 265–84. doi:10.1016/S0896-6273(02)00974-1. PMID 12383781. PDF

- Zak PJ, Kurzban R, Matzner WT (December 2004). "The neurobiology of trust". *Annals of the New York Academy of Sciences* **1032**: 224–7. doi:10.1196/annals.1314.025. PMID 15677415. alternative source

- Kosfeld M, Heinrichs M, Zak PJ, Fischbacher U, Fehr E (June 2005). "Oxytocin increases trust in humans". *Nature* **435** (7042): 673–6. doi:10.1038/nature03701. PMID 15931222.

- Zak PJ, Kurzban R, Matzner WT (December 2005). "Oxytocin is associated with human trustworthiness". *Horm Behav* **48** (5): 522–7. doi:10.1016/j.yhbeh.2005.07.009. PMID 16109416.

- John Cassidy, "Mind Games. What neuroeconomics tells us about money and the brain", *New Yorker, 2006 September.*

- Fließbach K., Weber B, Trautner P, Dohmen T, Sunde U, Elger CE, Falk A.; Social Comparison Affects Reward-Related Brain Activity in the Human Ventral Striatum, Science, 2007, 318(5854):1305-8.

- Weber B, Rangel A, Wibral M, Falk A. The medial prefrontal cortex exhibits money illusion., PNAS, 106(13):5025-8.

- Hardy-Vallée, B. (forthcoming). "Decision-making: a neuroeconomic perspective". Philosophy Compass.

- Takahashi T, Hadzibeganovic T, Cannas SA, Makino T, Fukui H, Kitayama S (2009). "Cultural neuroeconomics of intertemporal choice". *Neuro Endocrinol. Lett.* **30** (2): 185–91. PMID 19675524.

- Zak PJ, Stanton AA, Ahmadi S (2007). Brosnan, Sarah, ed. "Oxytocin Increases Generosity in Humans". *PLoS ONE* **2** (11): e1128. doi:10.1371/journal.pone.0001128. PMC 2040517. PMID 17987115.

- Sanfey AG (October 2007). "Social decision-making: insights from game theory and neuroscience". *Science* **318** (5850): 598–602. doi:10.1126/science.1142996. PMID 17962552.

2.45.13 Journal

Journal of Neuroscience, Psychology, and Economics

2.45.14 External links

- Scholarpedia neuroeconomics
- Research Master in Neuroeconomics at Maastricht University
- The Center for Economics and Neuroscience at University of Bonn
- Doctoral Program in Neuroeconomics, University of Zurich
- The Center for Neuroeconomic Studies at Claremont Graduate University
- The Spanish Society for Neuroeconomics.

Template:Neuroeconomics

2.46 New institutional economics

New institutional economics (**NIE**) is an economic perspective that attempts to extend economics by focusing on the social and legal norms and rules (which are institutions) that underlie economic activity and with analysis beyond earlier institutional economics and neoclassical economics.[1] It can be seen as a broadening step to include aspects excluded in neoclassical economics. It rediscovers aspects of classical political economy.

2.46.1 Overview

NIE has its roots in two articles by Ronald Coase, "The Nature of the Firm" (1937) and "The Problem of Social Cost" (1960). In the latter, the Coase Theorem (subsequently so termed) maintains that without transaction costs alternative property right assignments can equivalently internalize conflicts and externalities. Therefore, comparative institutional analysis arising from such assignments is required to make recommendations about efficient internalization of externalities [2] and institutional design, including Law and Economics.

At present NIE analyses are built on a more complex set of methodological principles and criteria. They work within a modified neoclassical framework in considering both efficiency and distribution issues, in contrast to "traditional," "old" or "original" institutional economics, which is critical of mainstream neoclassical economics.[3]

The term 'new institutional economics' was coined by Oliver Williamson in 1975.[4]

Among the many aspects in current NIE analyses are these: organizational arrangements, property rights,[5] transaction costs,[6] credible commitments, modes of governance, persuasive abilities, social norms, ideological values, decisive perceptions, gained control, enforcement mechanism, asset specificity, human assets, social capital, asymmetric information, strategic behavior, bounded rationality, opportunism, adverse selection, moral hazard, contractual safeguards, surrounding uncertainty, monitoring costs, incentives to collude, hierarchical structures, bargaining strength, etc.

Major scholars associated with the subject include Armen Alchian, Harold Demsetz,[7][8] Steven N. S. Cheung,[9][10] Avner Greif, Yoram Barzel, Claude Ménard (economist) and four Nobel laureates — Ronald Coase,[11][12] Douglass North,[13][14] Elinor Ostrom[15] and Oliver Williamson.[16] A convergence of such researchers resulted in founding the Society for Institutional & Organizational Economics (formally the International Society for New Institutional Economics) in 1997.[17]

2.46.2 Institutional levels

Although no single, universally accepted set of definitions has been developed, most scholars doing research under the NIE methodological principles and criteria follow Douglass North's demarcation between institutions and organizations. Institutions are the "rules of the game", consisting of both the formal legal rules and the informal social norms that govern individual behavior and structure social interactions (institutional frameworks).[18]

Organizations, by contrast, are those groups of people and the governance arrangements they create to coordinate their team action against other teams performing also as organizations. In order to enhance their chance of survival, actions taken by organizations will attempt to acquire skill sets that offer the highest return on objective goals, such as profit maximization or voter turnout.[19] Firms, Universities, clubs, medical associations, unions etc. are some examples.

Oliver Williamson characterizes four levels of social analysis. The first of these levels concerns itself with social theory it is the level of embeddedness and informal rules. The second level is focused on the institutional environment and formal rules. It is utilizes the economics of property rights and positive political theory. The third level focuses on governance and the interactions of actors within transaction cost economics, "the play of the game". Williamson gives the example of contracts between groups to explicate this level. Finally, the fourth level is governed by neoclassical economics, it is the allocation of resources and employment. New Institutional Economics is focused on levels two and three.[20]

Because some institutional frameworks are realities always "nested" inside other broader institutional frameworks, this clear demarcation is always blurred in actual situations. A case in point is a University. When the average quality of its teaching services must be evaluated, for example, a University may be approached as an organization with its people, physical capital, the general governing rules common to all that were passed by the University governing bodies etc. However, if the task consists of evaluating people's performance in a specific teaching department, for example, along with their own internal formal and informal rules, then the University as a whole enters the picture as an institution. General University rules, then, form part of the broader institutional framework influencing people's performance at the said teaching department.

2.46.3 See also

- Elinor Ostrom

2.46.4 References

[1] Malcolm Rutherford (2001). "Institutional Economics: Then and Now," *Journal of Economic Perspectives*, 15(3), pp. 185-90 (173-194).
L. J. Alston, (2008). "new institutional economics," *The New Palgrave Dictionary of Economics*, 2nd Edition. Abstract.

[2] Rita Yi Man Li (2012). THE INTERNALISATION OF ENVIRONMENTAL EXTERNALITIES AFFECTING DWELLINGS: A REVIEW OF COURT CASES IN HONG KONG," *Economic Affairs, Volume 32, Issue 2, pages 81–87, June 2012,* .

[3] Warren Samuels ([1987] 2008). "institutional economics" *The New Palgrave Dictionary of Economics* Abstract. A scholarly journal particularly featuring traditional institutional economics is the *Journal of Economic Issues*; see article-abstract links to 2008. Scholarly journals particularly featuring the new institutional economics include the Journal of Law Economics and Organization, the Journal of Economic Behavior and Organization, and the Journal of Law and Economics.

[4] Oliver E. Williamson (1975). *Markets and Hierarchies, Analysis and Antitrust Implications: A Study in the Economics of Internal Organization.*

[5] Dean Lueck (2008). "property law, economics and," *The New Palgrave Dictionary of Economics*, 2nd Edition. Abstract.

[6] M. Klaes (2008). "transaction costs, history of," *The New Palgrave Dictionary of Economics*, 2nd Edition. Abstract.

[7] Harold Demsetz (1967). "Toward a Theory of Property Rights," *American Economic Review*, 57(2), pp. 347-359.

[8] Harold Demsetz (1969) "Information and Efficiency: Another Viewpoint," Journal of Law and Economics, *12(1), pp.*

[9] Steven N. S. Cheung (1970). "The Structure of a Contract and the Theory of a Non-Exclusive Resource," *Journal of Law and Economics*, 13(1), pp. 49–70.

[10] S. N. S. Cheung (1973). "The Fable of the Bees: An Economic Investigation," *Journal of Law and Economics*, 16(1), pp. 11-33.

[11] Ronald Coase (1998). "The New Institutional Economics," *American Economic Review*, 88(2), pp. 72–74.

[12] R. H. Coase (1991). "The Institutional Structure of Production," Nobel Prize Lecture PDF, reprinted in 1992, *American Economic Review*, 82(4), pp. 713–719.

[13] Douglass C. North (1990). *Institutions, Institutional Change and Economic Performance*, Cambridge University Press.

[14] Douglass C. North (1995). "The New Institutional Economics and Third World Development," in *The New Institutional Economics and Third World Development*, J. Harriss, J. Hunter, and C. M. Lewis, ed., pp. 17-26.

[15] Elinor Ostrom (2005). "Doing Institutional Analysis: Digging Deeper than Markets and Hierarchies," *Handbook of New Institutional Economics*, C. Ménard and M. Shirley, eds. *Handbook of New Institutional Economics*, pp. 819–848. Springer.

[16] Oliver E. Williamson (2000). "The New Institutional Economics: Taking Stock, Looking Ahead," *Journal of Economic Literature*, 38(3), pp. 595-613 (press +).

[17] "History". Society for Institutional & Organizational Economics. Retrieved 3 February 2016.

[18] Rita Yi Man Li (2014). "The Institutional Analysis of Fittings in Residential Units in Law, Economics and Finance of the Real Estate Market 2014, pp 45-61" .

[19] North, Douglass C. "TRANSACTION COSTS, INSTITUTIONS, AND ECONOMIC PERFORMANCE." *International Center for Economic Growth* (n.d.): n. pag. Khousachonine.ucoz.com. Web.

[20] Williamson, Oliver (2000). "The 'New Institutional Economics: Taking Stock, Looking Ahead". *Journal of Economic Literature*.

2.46.5 Further reading

- Eggertsson, Thráinn (2005). *Imperfect Institutions: Possibilities and Limits of Reform*. Ann Arbor: University of Michigan Press. ISBN 0472114565.

- Furubotn, Eirik G.; Richter, Rudolf (2005). *Institutions and Economic Theory: The Contribution of the New Institutional Economics* (2nd ed.). Ann Arbor: University of Michigan Press. ISBN 0472030256.

2.46.6 External links

- ISNIE - International Society for New Institutional Economics.

- ESNIE - European School on New Institutional Economics.

- ASNIE - Austrian Society for New Institutional Economics.

- Introductory Reading List in New Institutional Economics - The Ronald Coase Institute

- IRIS Center - Founded by Mancur Olson, University of Maryland.

- Contracting and Organizations Research Center University of Missouri

- Economics and Institutions WEBSITE - by prof. F. Toboso, University of Valencia, Spain.

2.47 Non-possession

Non-possession is a philosophy that holds that no one or anything possesses anything.[1] It is one of the principles of Satyagraha, a philosophical system based on various religious and philosophical traditions originating in India and Asia Minor, and put into practice by Mahatma Gandhi as part of his nonviolent resistance. This particular iteration of aparigraha is distinct because it is a component of Gandhi's active non-violent resistance to social problems permeating India. As such, its conception is tempered with western law. Non-possession is, by definition, concerned with defining the concept of possession.

Non-possession does not deny the existence of the concept of possession. Gandhi intertwined non-possession and voluntary poverty in application, but living according to the guidelines of non-possession is not the same as living in poverty.

In practice, the principle of taking what one needs (rather than less than or more than), is essential to the viability of non-possession/ aparigraha, therefore, an essential component. Like possession, humans (and other animals, and entities) deviate from this because of social conditioning.

This practice is only a principle when one is not aware of or does not acknowledge all events which have either direct or indirect impact on oneself. Awareness and acknowledgment occurs without specific effort when an entity develops

- a broadened awareness of all events which have a direct or indirect impact on the individual entity;
- the ability to process this information, (see relationships, derive meaning);
- the ability to translate the conclusion of the above into actions.

The action of taking enough to continue working but not more than one needs, is a generalized description of one of those actions. Understanding that no one or anything possesses anything is a specific condition which occurs when one can derive meaning and see the relationships between more events from different perspectives.

2.47.1 Possession

Possession denotes the de facto claim on another entity based on exclusive access. If access is non-exclusive of some entity, then the object in question is not being possessed.

The concepts of possession and ownership often overlap, but are not the same. Ownership takes into account the entitlement to priority of access, which are necessarily based on agreements and other mutually consenting social protocols.

If more than 1 entity has access to something simultaneously, and 1 or more of the entities assert priority of access (exclusivity) over the other(s), or if some external force endows or demands priority of 1 entity, a group of entity, over some other(s), then there is conflict. Even if those who are excluded concur to such claims, their de facto access will present conflict by necessity.

In the event that more than 1 entity has access to something simultaneously, exclusion occurs when: 1. 1 or more of the entities assert priority of access over the other(s), 2. some external force endows or demands priority of 1 entity, a group of entities, over some other(s).

Even if those who are excluded concur to the claimed priority, the de facto simultaneous access necessarily present conflict between claim to priority and what actually happens.

Note that the conflict begins with assumed priority not matching empirical reality. Also note that claim can only occur with communicative acts or verbal communication. Concurrence also requires communication, but one cannot concur unless a claim has been posed first (passive action).

The concept of ownership could have been invented, in part, to resolve this dilemma, by instating a system of social protocols.

Ownership as Resolution

Ownership increases the frequency of consensus over disagreement. Using social protocols, ownership establishes one or a group of entities' permanent priority of access to something. Unless the owner relinquishes this right, this established priority stands regardless of empirical phenomena.

A dilemma arises when an entity enters into the sphere of a consensus with no prior knowledge of the agreement. Empirical phenomena would be the basis for both conceptual and empirical reality.

An example of this is Britain entering India. With the simultaneous desire to procure resources already claimed by the aggregate Indian society, and lack of desire to participate in Indian society, Britain's subjects actively challenged established ownership. The act also defined all inhabitants, including not only those actively participating in Hindu society, but also those participating passively (Untouchables,) as part of an aggregate entity. Before asserting its own ownership upon said resources, British interests challenged existing Indian society's ownership by de facto possession (by virtue of being present in India,) India's lack of utilization for said resources (contrasting with Britain's moral and lawful utilization of them, as concurred by its peer nations,) and the inability for India to counter-challenge Britain legally and philosophically.

Non-possession is another concept which can resolve this dilemma. If claims always match empirical reality, then there is no conflict. Eliminating exclusion, claims to priority of access will always be based on empirical reality.

Non-possession as Resolution

If claims always match empirical reality, then there is no conflict.

Boundaries are a given. Possession as the defining mechanism for boundaries is also a given.

If entities have no cause to endow or assert priority of access over the other(s), cause to exclude is removed. The goal of claiming access will then not be to exclude. The goal of the claims will still remain: 1. 1 or more of the entities assert priority of access over the other(s), 2. some external force endows or demands priority of 1 entity, a group of entities, over some other(s). The motivation to establish priority of access will always be based on empirical reality. By extension, pre-established hierarchies of access (ownership) will not increase the frequency of consensus unless the hierarchies support empirical reality. Empirical reality always takes precedence over conceptual reality.

Non-possession is another concept which resolves the dilemma which arises when reasoned reality conflicts with empirical reality.

Non-possession provides for conditions under which none of the entities have cause to assert exclusivity which is not concurred by others.

Contrast with some entity which has ownership of something; if some other entity has possession of that thing, the owner has the right to concede or deny the legitimacy of that other entity's possession. Possession is a necessary component of ownership, but ownership is not a necessary component of possession. This does not mean that something cannot be possessed by some entity other than its owner. It means that the owner of a thing has the exclusive right to concede or deny the legitimacy of anyone who possesses this thing, even if the owner has no intention of accessing the object of possession. Further, the owner has the ability to concede or deny his/her/its own legitimacy of possessing the object of possession. In application, ownership is often asserted when it is challenged by possession (de facto claim to access exclusive of the owner.)

Non-possession denies the exclusive access of an entity by another entity.

To paraphrase: non-possession says that no entity has the right to exclusive access to another entity, either by social agreement, or de facto exclusive access.

Challenge posed toward Possession By definition, non-possession is the opposite of possession. There is inherent conflict between the two approaches to organizing priority of access. It is notable that practitioners of non-possession acknowledge the existence of possession. See #Theft.

Those practicing possession do not necessarily acknowledge non-possession for several reasons. Here, they are defined by conditions occurring within different layers of an individual entity's experience:

- not aware of non-possession as an amalgamated concept, (contrast with the awareness of the complex concept of possession);
- non-possession presents logical conflict in the cognitive process when one comes into contact with issues of boundaries and priority of access, therefore, the concept (alternative) is consistently disposed of during the cognitive process;
- non-possession presents interpersonal conflict when one is engaged in social activities.

Non-stealing

The practical implications of non-possession can be clarified by defining another principle of Satyagraha: non-stealing.

Non-stealing is the practice of not breaching an entity's entitlement of or sense of entitlement toward something.

Theft has to do with breaching ownership: both possession and sense of entitlement. Non-possession only challenges the idea of possession, not entitlement.

There are concepts associated with ownership which do not conflict with non-possession, such as willingness to cultivate that which is owned, recognition of benefit conferred upon the owner, positive opinion and/ or feelings toward that which is owned, negative opinion and/ or feelings etc.

Under non-possession, these reactions are not (and cannot be) reserved toward possessions. As such, traditional definitions of theft and the reasons for not stealing require clarification.

Sense of Entitlement Sense of entitlement has to do with emotional attachment beyond practical benefit and usefulness to an entity's perceivable physical survival. The belief that one deserves to receive an opportunity or reward. The myriad of ways a sense of entitlement can arise include legal claim, length of time spent with the object, birthright, labour exerted, labour not exerted, comparative social standing, inheritance, perspective, lack of perspective, etc. Practitioners of religious traditions such as Buddhism, Jainism, even the three major western religious traditions consciously aspire to extricate from or modify non-practical emotional attachment in some form. There are branches of philosophy which deal exclusively with such modifications such as Stoicism.

Non-stealing takes the approach of applied Hinduism in that it recognizes that not everyone would either choose to extricate from or would be successful extricating from attachment at any given time. As well, possession exists de facto, and is often cited as support of entitlement to an object of possession.

Theft In the absence of possession (and ownership by extension,) theft would be impossible. But theft is possible under the non-possession world view. This is possible given that not everyone in the world practices non-possession. It is also difficult to put non-possession into practice under existing socio-economic systems. People have the right to, and likely have to define their *boundaries* out of necessity. All historically recorded cultures either prescribe laws regarding individuals' personal boundaries, or imply the limits of the individual through practices. Absence of conventions and protocol undermine the ability for humans to understand each other at the conscious level, without which, civilization is not possible. Boundaries between individual entities is an essential component of any grouping, including civilization; they exist in empirical reality and by definition.

Across cultures, the definition of these boundaries can be explicit, implicit, or entirely personal. The United States Constitution has provisions for rights to personal property, but no explicit provisions for boundaries.

Boundaries are one of the essential given condition for possession to be possible. The reverse is not true. Possession deals with the relationship of something to boundaries, a relationship in which boundaries provide the principle to qualify whether something is being possessed or not being possessed. A boundary can be defined independent of the idea of possession: the threshold between 2 identifiable, separate entities.

Logically, the existence of theft would be invalid If there are no rules as to how one can and cannot define boundaries. Without the ability to define a boundary, there is no way to discern where one entity begins and the other ends, therefore, not possible to define possession. Without possession, there can be no ownership, claim to ownership, or theft.

Hypothetical example: If some entity has the ability to lay claim to any object without contest, theft is still possible. One can steal from this entity if one is not part of this entity. Also, that the entity is empowered to lay claim necessitates that there are objects which the entity can lay claim upon, therefore, objects which this entity does not possess. Boundaries may exist between objects before the entity lays claim to them, (that is, if it intends to lay claim to them.) Breach of these boundaries constitute theft. A hypothetical entity empowered to lay claim upon any object can also approach a grey area between legitimate possession and theft if its possession of an object is not clearly defined, that is, if this entity itself has doubts as to whether it possesses the object in question.

Boundaries exist in empirical reality, because people and things obviously do not melt together upon touching. While some systems of thought would contest this even on a limited level, and there are counterexamples, especially when dealing with ideas, in general, it is accepted that boundaries exist at least in some areas of consensus reality. Non-possession does not directly address boundaries, therefore, it neither negates nor confirms the concept. The very existence of boundaries almost necessitates possession, (add graphic) but things can exist on boundaries. Also, boundaries are sometimes defined by possession.

Taking into account both the logical provisions, and also that non-possession is a social philosophy specifically applicable to sentient beings (e.g. people,) the act of breaching another entity's sense of entitlement constitutes theft.

The specific possessive act of attachment is involuntary, it cannot stop unless the peripheral stimulus which causes it is also removed. The peripheral stimulus can be something which supports the very fabric of consensus reality, like boundaries. As such, non-possession, as a social philosophy, does not and cannot challenge the peripheral stimulus. To paraphrase: attachment begets entitlement in a non-logical, non-physical sense. Given the above, the boundary that is requisite for entitlement to exist on the non-logical, non-physical level is outside of non-possession's scope. This is not the case for aparigraha.

Non-stealing is a necessary component in addition to non-possession because of Satyagraha's applicative nature. Non-possession does not negate boundaries.

Gandhi's view was that possession is more trouble than it is worth.

> The possession of anything then became a troublesome thing and a burden. Exploring the cause of that joy, I found that if I kept anything as my own, I had to defend it against the whole world. . . . And I said to myself: if [other people] want it and would take it, they do so not from any malicious motive but . . because theirs was a greater need than mine.[2]

2.47.2 Jainism

In Jainism, non-possession is one of the five vows (*mahavratas*) that both ascetics and householders (śrāvaka) have to observe. Jain texts mentions that "attachment to possessions (parigraha) is of two kinds: attachment to internal possessions (ābhyantara parigraha), and attachment to external possessions (bāhya parigraha).[3] The fourteen internal possessions are:[4]

- Wrong belief
- The three sex-passions
  - Male sex-passion
  - Female sex-passion

- Neuter sex-passion
- Six defects
  - Laughter
  - Liking
  - Disliking
  - Sorrow
  - Fear
  - Disgust
- Four passions
  - Anger
  - Pride
  - Deceitfulness
  - Greed

External possessions are divided into two subclasses, the non-living, and the living. According to Jain texts, both internal and external possessions are proved to be hiṃsā (injury).[4]

2.47.3 Wealth and poverty

Neither wealth nor poverty necessarily follow non-possession, however, wealth and poverty necessarily exist within the non-possession view. Non-possession is, by definition, concerned with defining (material) possession. As such, wealth and poverty (relative abundance and lack) closely relate to non-possession.

Mohandas Gandhi intertwined the concepts of non-possession and poverty.

Non-possession resolves the sense of injustice of groups which perceive distribution of wealth not in their favour; and it resolves the sense of entitlement of groups which perceived that they benefitted. It does so by removing quantitative material reward as benefit.

If all parties in a finite system is on board with non-possession, there is no wealth or poverty.

Practitioners of aparigraha are generally not considered to be in poverty or wealthy.

Colonial India

Under the caste system, class serves an integral role in the distribution of wealth. Gandhi, a Brahmin, joined the untouchables in poverty in order to create a level playing field both for those who considered him to be peer and for those who considered him to be superior. Furthermore, this clearly demonstrated leadership through full participation. Contrast with control through shepherding, or non-participatory policy making and directing (management). The latter would evoke British rule, which is especially meaningful for traditionally powerful and privileged castes.

It would also evoke to Hinduism practitioners their own attitudes and relationship with castes, both above and below them in social stature, as well as with dalits.

Poverty was an essential consequence of being an untouchable. Under Gandhi's chosen circumstances, non-possession and the accompanying ideologies of Satyagraha both resulted in and were caused by poverty. It is notable that the act itself drew attention without specific promotion, and simultaneously self-perpetuated only if witnessed. Purity of message was Gandhi's motivation for expressing non-possession through extreme material poverty.

Non-possession Applied

Applied to a different social environment, poverty may or may not result from the practice of non-possession.

Fluctuations in ease of access to resources necessarily occur. Perceived shortages in a non-possession economy does not prompt policies which would prioritize access to resources to privileged groups. To elaborate on privilege, since no one possesses anything, privilege will not be marked by comparative wealthiness. By extension, it implies eliminating the propensity to distribute resources by first referencing previous points of depletion and accumulation.

Whether resources will be distributed to where they would maximize benefits to society overall is outside the scope of non-possession. Satyagraha is based on a complex system of philosophy based on social and religious traditions of India, religious traditions of the West, and legal traditions of Europe. While there are no explicit provisions for how resources will be distributed, it is notable that karma would resolve the need for any and all artificial intervention in distribution.

In order to transition from an economy based on possession, to one which is not based on possession, quantitative material reward has to be addressed.

Quantitative material reward is the primary motivating factor for production and enterprise. Employees are paid a salary in exchange for services rendered. Businesses generate quantitative revenue for its owners (stockholders.) Non-possession does not directly address business and commerce. Meanwhile, there are occupations which require motivations other than material reward. Those who produce without explicitly requiring material reward are not ensured of sufficient material sustenance by virtue of the act of working, which ultimately stops these individuals and institutions from production. Bridging the gap between those who understand work to be productivity for the sake of possessions (the production of possessions,) and the lack of resources for those aspiring to practice non-possession, Gandhi supported extensively practicing trusteeship in India.

As with all philosophical concepts, non-possession works best if everyone within the finite system adopts this code of behaviour.

2.47.4 See also

- civil disobedience
- non-violence
- nonviolent resistance
- property

Some social and/ or economic strategies related to non-possession:

- Cooperative
- Non-profit
- Socialism
- Gift economy

2.47.5 References

[1] ourpla.net

[2]

[3] Jain 2012, p. 76.

[4] Jain 2012, p. 77.

2.47.6 Sources

- Jain, Vijay K. (2012), *Acharya Amritchandra's Purushartha Siddhyupaya*, Vikalp Printers, ISBN 81-903639-4-8, Non-Copyright

2.48 Participatory economics

Participatory economics, often abbreviated **parecon**, is an economic system based on participatory decision making as the primary economic mechanism for the allocation of the factors of production and guidance of production in a given society. Participatory decision-making involves the participation of all persons in decision-making on issues in proportion to the impact such decisions have on their lives. Participatory economics is a form of decentralized economic planning and socialism involving the common ownership of the means of production. The participatory economic system is proposed as an alternative to contemporary capitalism, as well as an alternative to central planning. This economic model is primarily associated with the proposals put forth by the political theorist Michael Albert and economist Robin Hahnel, who describe participatory economics as an anarchistic economic vision.[1]

The underlying values that parecon seeks to implement are equity, solidarity, diversity, workers' self-management and efficiency (defined as accomplishing goals without wasting valued assets). The institutions of parecon include workers' and consumers' councils utilizing self-managerial methods for making decisions, balanced job complexes, remuneration based on individual effort, and participatory planning.

Albert and Hahnel stress that parecon is only meant to address an alternative economic theory and must be accompanied by equally important alternative visions in the fields of politics, culture and kinship. The authors have also discussed elements of anarchism in the field of politics, polyculturalism in the field of culture, and feminism in the field of family and gender relations as being possible foundations for future alternative visions in these other spheres of society. Stephen R. Shalom has begun work on a participatory political vision he calls "par polity". Both systems together make up the political philosophy of Participism. Participatory Economics has also significantly shaped the interim International Organization for a Participatory Society.

2.48.1 Decision-making principle

One of the primary propositions of parecon is that all persons should have a say in decisions proportionate to the degree to which they are affected by them. This decision-making principle is often referred to as *self-management*. In parecon, it constitutes a replacement for the mainstream economic conception of economic freedom, which Albert and Hahnel argue that by its very vagueness has allowed it to be abused by capitalist ideologues.

2.48.2 Work in a participatory economy

Balanced job complexes

Main article: balanced job complex

Some tasks and jobs are more desirable than others, and some tasks and jobs are more menial than others. So, to achieve an equitable division of labour, it is proposed that each individual do different tasks, which, taken together, bring an average desirability and an average level of empowerment. The main goals are to dissolve economic hierarchy and achieve one class of workers, and to empower all to make contributions to the workplace. Hahnel and Albert argue that without balanced job complexes, those with empowering jobs, such as accounting or management, would be able to formulate plans and ideas, while others, such as janitors, would not develop the capacity to do so and neither would they have the training. Without balanced job complexes, most workers would most likely end up merely ratifying the proposals of empowered workers, and would have little reason to attend meetings.[2]

Compensation for effort and sacrifice

Albert and Hahnel argue that it is inequitable and ineffective to compensate people on the basis of their birth or heredity. Therefore, the primary principle of participatory economics is to reward for effort and sacrifice.[3] For example, mining work — which is dangerous and uncomfortable — would be more highly paid than office work for the same amount of time, thus allowing the miner to work fewer hours for the same pay, and the burden of highly dangerous and strenuous jobs to be shared among the populace.

Additionally, participatory economics would provide exemptions from the compensation for effort principle.[3] People with disabilities who are unable to work, children, the elderly, the infirm and workers who are legitimately in transitional circumstances, can be remunerated according to need. However, every *able* adult has the obligation to perform some socially useful work as a requirement for receiving reward, albeit in the context of a society providing free health care, education, skills training, and the freedom to choose between various democratically structured workplaces with jobs balanced for desirability and empowerment.

The starting point for the income of all workers in participatory economics is an equal share of the social product. From this point, incomes for personal expenditures and consumption rights for public goods can be expected to diverge by small degrees reflecting the choices that individual workers make in striking a balance between work and leisure time, and reflecting the level of danger and strenuousness of a job as assigned by their immediate peers.[3]

2.48.3 Allocation in a participatory economy

Facilitation boards

In a proposed participatory economy, key information relevant to converging on an economic plan would be made available by Iteration Facilitation Boards (IFBs), which, based on proposals from worker/consumer councils and economic data, present indicative prices and economic projections at each round of the planning process.

The IFB has no decision-making authority. In theory, the IFB's activity can consist mainly of computers performing the (agreed upon) algorithms for adjusting prices and forecasts, with little human involvement.[4]

2.48.4 Opposition to central planning and capitalism

See also: Libertarian socialism

Robin Hahnel has argued that "participatory planning is not central planning", stating "The procedures are completely different and the incentives are completely different. And one of the important ways in which it is different from central planning is that it is incentive compatible, that is, actors have an incentive to report truthfully rather than an incentive to misrepresent their capabilities or preferences."[5] Unlike historical examples of central planning, the parecon proposal advocates the use and adjustment of price information reflecting marginal social opportunity costs and benefits as integral elements of the planning process. Hahnel has argued emphatically against Milton Friedman's a priori tendency to deny the possibility of alternatives:

> Friedman assumes away the best solution for coordinating economic activities. He simply asserts "there are only two ways of coordinating the economic activities of millions — central direction involving the use of coercion — and voluntary cooperation, the technique of the marketplace." [...] a participatory economy can permit all to partake in economic decision making in proportion to the degree they are affected by outcomes. Since a participatory system uses a system of participatory planning instead of markets to coordinate economic activities, Friedman would have us believe that participatory planning must fall into the category of "central direction involving the use of coercion."[6]

Albert and Hahnel have voiced detailed critiques of centrally-planned economies in theory and practice, but are also highly-critical of capitalism. Hahnel claims "the truth is capitalism aggravates prejudice, is the most inequitable economy ever devised, is grossly inefficient — even if highly energetic — and is incompatible with both economic and political democracy. In the present era of free-market triumphalism it is useful to organize a sober evaluation of capitalism responding to Friedman's claims one by one."[7]

Critique of markets

Mainstream economists largely acknowledge the problem of externalities but believe they can be addressed either through Coasian bargaining or the use of Pigovian taxes - extra taxes on goods that have externalities. According to economic theory, if Pigovian taxes are set so that the after-tax cost of the goods is equal to the social cost of the goods, the direct cost of production plus cost of externalities, then quantities produced will tend toward a socially optimal level. Hahnel observes, "more and more economists outside the mainstream are challenging this assumption, and a growing number of skeptics now dare to suggest that externalities are prevalent, and often substantial". Or, as E.K. Hunt put it: externalities are the rule rather than the exception, and therefore markets often work as if they were guided by a "malevolent invisible foot" that keeps kicking us to produce more of some things, and less of others than is socially efficient."[8]

As long as a market economy is in place, Albert and Hahnel favour Pigovian taxes over other solutions to environmental problems such as command and control, or the issuance of marketable permits. However, Hahnel, who teaches ecological economics at American University, argues that in a market economy businesses try to avoid the "polluter pays principle" by shifting the burden of the costs for their polluting activities to consumers. In terms of incentives he argues this might be considered a positive development because it would penalize consumers for "dirty" consumption. However it also has regressive implications since tax incidence studies show that ultimately it would be poor people who would bear a great deal of the burden of many pollution taxes. "In other words, many pollution taxes would be highly regressive and therefore aggravate economic injustice.".[9] He therefore recommends that pollution taxes be linked to cuts in regressive taxes such as social security taxes.

Hahnel argues that Pigovian taxes, along with associated corrective measures advanced by market economists, ultimately fall far short of adequately or fairly addressing externalities. He argues such methods are incapable of attaining accurate assessments of social costs:

"Markets corrected by pollution taxes only lead to the efficient amount of pollution and satisfy the polluter pays principle if the taxes are set equal to the magnitude of the damage victims suffer. But because markets are not incentive compatible for polluters and pollution victims, markets provide no reliable way to estimate the magnitudes of efficient taxes for pollutants. Ambiguity over who has the property right, polluters or pollution victims, free rider problems among multiple victims, and the transaction costs of forming and maintaining an effective coalition of pollution victims, each of whom is affected to a small but unequal degree, all combine to render market systems incapable of eliciting accurate information from pollution victims about the damages they suffer, or acting upon that information even if it were known.[10]

Critique of tendency towards efficiency

Hahnel has also written a detailed discussion of parecon's desirability compared to capitalism with respect to incentives to innovate.[11] In capitalism, patent laws, intellectual property rights, industry structures, and barriers to market entry are institutional features that reward individual innovators while limiting the use of new technologies. Hahnel notes that, in contrast, "in a participatory economy all innovations will immediately be made available to all enterprises, so there will never be any loss of static efficiency.".[12] Innovation is sometimes the outcome of cumulative creativity, which pareconomists believe may not be legitimately attributed to individuals.

2.48.5 Participatory economics and socialism

Although participatory economics is not in itself intended to provide a general political system, clearly its practical implementation would depend on an accompanying political system. Advocates of parecon say the intention is that the four main ingredients of parecon be implemented with a minimum of hierarchy and a maximum of transparency in all discussions and decision-making. This model is designed to eliminate secrecy in economic decision-making, and instead encourage friendly cooperation and mutual support. This avoidance of power hierarchies puts parecon in the anarchist political tradition. Stephen Shalom has produced a political system meant to complement parecon, called Parpolity.

Although parecon falls under left-wing political tradition, it is designed to avoid the creation of powerful intellectual elites or the rule of a bureaucracy, which is perceived as the major problem of the economies of the communist states of the 20th century. Parecon advocates recognize that monopolization of empowering labor, in addition to private ownership, can be a source of class division. Thus, a three-class view of the economy (capitalists, coordinators, and workers) is stressed, in contrast to the traditional two-class view of Marxism. The coordinator class, emphasized in Parecon, refers to those who have a monopoly on empowering skills and knowledge, and corresponds to the doctors, lawyers, managers, engineers, and other professionals in present economies. Parecon advocates argue that, historically, Marxism ignored the ability of coordinators to become a new ruling class in a post-capitalist society.[13]

The archetypal workplace democracy model, the Wobbly Shop was pioneered by the Industrial Workers of the World, in which the self-managing norms of grassroots democracy were applied.

While many types of production and consumption may become more localised under participatory economics, the model does not exclude economies of scale.

2.48.6 Criticisms

David Schweickart suggests Participatory Economics would be undesirable even if it was possible, accusing it of being:

> "a system obsessed with comparison (Is your job complex more empowering than mine?), with monitoring (You are not working at average intensity, mate--get with the program), with the details of consumption (How many rolls of toilet paper will I need next year? Why are some of my neighbors still using the kind not made of recycled paper?)"[14]

Planning

Further information: Economic calculation problem

Participatory Economics would create a large amount of administrative work for individual workers, who would have to plan their consumption in advance, and a new bureaucratic class. Proponents of parecon argue that capitalist economies are hardly free of bureaucracy or meetings, and a parecon would eliminate banks, advertising, stock market, tax returns and long-term financial planning. Albert and Hahnel claim that it is probable that a similar number of workers will be involved in a parecon bureaucracy as in a capitalist bureaucracy,[15] with much of the voting achieved by computer rather than meeting, and those who are not interested in the collective consumption proposals not required to attend.[16]

Critics suggest that proposals require consideration of an unfeasibly large set of policy choices,[14] and that lessons from planned societies show that peoples' daily needs cannot be established well in advance simply by asking people what they want.[17] Albert and Hahnel note that markets themselves hardly adjust prices instantaneously,[18] and suggest that in a Participatory Economy Facilitation boards could modify prices on a regular basis. According to Hahnel these act according to democratically decided guidelines, can be composed of members from other regions and are impossible to bribe due to parecon's non-transferable currency.[19] However, Takis Fotopoulos argues that "no kind of economic organisation based on planning alone, however democratic and decentralised it is, can secure real self-management and freedom of choice."[17]

Loss of efficiency

Parecon might reduce efficiency in the workplace. For one, expert and exceptional workers (e.g. exceptional surgeons and scientists) would not be performing their tasks full-time. Participatory economics would expect them to share in "disempowering work" and would not offer opportunities to seek additional compensation for their high ability or finding solutions to problems. In a lecture at Willamette University in Oregon in 2015, Hahnel responded to this criticism by explaining that these jobs could be filled by machines, which are underutilized in capitalist economic systems due to the lowered rates of profit, and also division of labor wouldn't exist under a participatory economic system as much as it does under capitalism, so people wouldn't always have the same jobs.

Theodore Burczak argues that it is impossible for workers to give the unbiased assessments of the "largely unobservable" characteristics of **effort** proposed as the basis for salary levels, and the absence of market *exchange* mechanisms likewise makes calculating social costs of production and consumption impossible.[20]

2.48.7 See also

- Analytical Marxism
- Anarchism
- Anarchist economics
- Anarcho-Syndicalism
- Collective bargaining
- Complementary holism

- Co-operative
- Direct democracy
- Decentralized planning (economics)
- Ecological economics
- Economic democracy
- Horizontalidad
- Inclusive Democracy
- Mutualism
- Post-Autistic Economics
- Post-capitalism
- Participatory budgeting
- Participatory democracy
- Participatory justice
- Participatory politics
- Socialism
- Socialist economics
- Surplus economics
- Syndicalism
- Workers' council
- Workers' self-management
- Workplace democracy
- Z Communications

2.48.8 References

[1] Albert, Michael Parecon: Life After Capitalism Chapter 19 Individuals / Society

[2] Michael Albert and Robin Hahnel, "Looking Forward" pp. 18-21.

[3] Albert, Michael Parecon: Life After Capitalism Part II, Chapter 7: Remuneration pp. 112-117.

[4] "13 Allocating". http://zcomm.org/. Retrieved 8 July 2015. External link in |publisher= (help)

[5] *Economic Justice and Democracy: From Competition to Cooperation*, p. 221, Hahnel, Routledge, 2005.

[6] *Economic Justice and Democracy: From Competition to Cooperation* p. 81, Hahnel, Routledge, 2005.

[7] *Economic Justice and Democracy: From Competition to Cooperation* ch. 4, Hahnel, Routledge, 2005.

[8] *Economic Justice and Democracy: From Competition to Cooperation, 85*.

[9] *Economic Justice and Democracy: From Competition to Cooperation, 274*.

[10] Robin Hahnel, (2004). "Protecting the Environment in a Participatory Economy". Retrieved February 13, 2006.

[11] *Economic Justice and Democracy: From Competition to Cooperation* p. 241, Hahnel, Routledge, 2005.

[12] *Economic Justice and Democracy: From Competition to Cooperation* p. 240, Hahnel, Routledge, 2005.

[13] http://www.zcommunications.org/parecon-and-marxism-by-michael-albert

[14] Schweickart, David (January 2006). "Michael Albert's Parecon: A Critique". Retrieved 2012-07-08.

[15] Michael Albert and Robin Hahnel, "Looking Forward" pp. 86-89.

[16] "Participatory Economics by Michael Albert | ZNet Article". ZCommunications. 2008-11-19. Retrieved 2010-08-17.

[17] Takis Fotopoulos (2003), "Inclusive Democracy and Participatory Economics", Democracy & Nature, Volume 9, Issue 3 November 2003, pp. 401-425.

[18] Michael Albert, "Parecon: Life After Capitalism", p. 282.

[19] Michael Albert and Robin Hahnel, "Looking Forward" pp. 92-93.

[20] Burczak, Theodore A. *Socialism after Hayek*. pp. 143–4.

2.48.9 Further reading

- *A Quiet Revolution In Welfare Economics*, Albert and Hahnel, Princeton University Press, 1990.
- *Looking Forward: Participatory Economics for the Twenty First Century*, Albert and Hahnel, South End Press, 1991.
- *The Political Economy of Participatory Economics*, Albert and Hahnel, Princeton University Press, 1991.
- *Moving Forward: Program for a Participatory Economy*, Albert, AK Press, 1997.
- *Parecon: Life After Capitalism*, Albert, Verso Books, 2003.
- *Economic Justice And Democracy: From Competition To Cooperation*, Hahnel, Routledge, 2005.

- *Realizing Hope: Life Beyond Capitalism*, Albert, Zed Press, 2006.
- *Real Utopia: Participatory Society for the 21st Century*, Chris Spannos (Ed.), AK Press, 2008.
- Takis Fotopoulos (2003), "Inclusive Democracy and Participatory Economics", *Democracy & Nature*, Volume 9, Issue 3 November 2003, pages 401 - 425 - comparison with Inclusive Democracy
- Rameez Rahman, Michel Meulpolder, David Hales, Johan Pouwelse, Henk Sips (2009), "Revisiting Social Welfare in P2P", Delft University of Technology Report. - applying Participatory Economics principles to analysis of peer-to-peer computing systems

2.48.10 External links

- Participatory Economics Information Site
- Vancouver Participatory Economics Collective
- Nonsense on Stilts: Michael Albert's Parecon - A critique

Video

- *Cartoon introduction to participatory economics (YouTube video)* 7:16 mns, by Jason Mitchell
- *Michael Albert in Alternative Economy Cultures* Helsinki, Finland, 3 April 2009

2.49 Planned economy

A **planned economy** is an economic system in which inputs are based on direct allocation.[1] Economic planning may be carried out in a decentralized, distributed or centralized manner depending on the specific organization of economic institutions. An economy based on economic planning (either through the state, an association of worker cooperatives or another economic entity that has jurisdiction over the means of production) appropriates its resources as needed, so that allocation comes in the form of internal transfers involving the purchasing of assets by one government agency or firm by another. In a traditional model of planning, decision-making would be carried out by workers and consumers on the enterprise-level.

Planned economies are held in contrast to unplanned economies, such as the market economy and proposed self-managed economy, where production, distribution, pricing, and investment decisions are made by autonomous firms based upon their individual interests rather than upon a macroeconomic plan. Less extensive forms of planned economies include those that use indicative planning as components of a market-based or mixed economy, in which the state employs "influence, subsidies, grants, and taxes, but does not compel."[2] This latter is sometimes referred to as a "planned market economy".[3] In some instances, the term planned economy has been used to refer to national economic development plans and state-directed investment in market economies.

Planned economies are usually categorized as a particular variant of socialism, and have historically been associated with Marxist-Leninist states and the Soviet economic model. However, some argue that the Soviet economic model did not actually constitute a planned economy in that a comprehensive and binding plan did not guide production and investment; therefore the term **administrative command economy** emerged as a more accurate designation for the economic system that existed in the former Soviet Union and Eastern bloc, highlighting the role of centralized hierarchical decision-making in the absence of popular control over the economy.[4] The possibility of a digital planned economy was explored by Chile with the creation of Project Cybersyn.

2.49.1 Planned versus command economies

Main article: Economic planning

Planned economies are held in contrast with *command* economies, where a planned economy is "an economic system in which the government controls and regulates production, distribution, prices, etc."[5] but a command economy, while also having this type of regulation, necessarily has substantial public ownership of industry.[6] Therefore, command economies are planned economies, but not necessarily the reverse.

Whereas most of the economy is organized in a top-down administrative model by a central authority, where decisions regarding investment and production output requirements are decided upon at the top in the chain of command, with little input from lower levels. Advocates of economic planning have sometimes been staunch critics of these command economies. For example, Leon Trotsky believed that those at the top of the chain of command, regardless of their intellectual capacity, operated without the input and participation of the millions of people who participate in the economy and understand/respond to local conditions and changes in the economy, and therefore would be unable to effectively coordinate all economic activity.[7]

Another key difference is that command economies are

usually authoritarian in nature, whereas economic planning in general can be either participatory and democratic or authoritarian. Indicative planning is a form of planning in market economies that directs the economy through incentive-based methods. Economic planning can be practiced in a decentralized manner through different government authorities. For example, in some predominately market-oriented and mixed economies, the state utilizes economic planning in strategic industries such as the aerospace industry. Mixed economies usually employ macroeconomic planning, while micro-economic affairs are left to the market and price system.

Another example of this is the utilization of dirigisme, or government direction of the economy through non coercive means, both of which were practiced in France and Great Britain after the Second World War. Swedish public housing models were planned by the government in a similar fashion as urban planning in a project called Million Programme.

2.49.2 Advantages of economic planning

The government can harness land, labour, and capital to serve the economic objectives of the state. Consumer demand can be restrained in favor of greater capital investment for economic development in a desired pattern. In international comparisons, state-socialist nations compared favorably with capitalist nations in health indicators such as infant mortality and life expectancy.[8] The state can begin building a heavy industry at once in an underdeveloped economy without waiting years for capital to accumulate through the expansion of light industry, and without reliance on external financing. This is what happened in the Soviet Union during the 1930s when the government forced the share of GNP dedicated to private consumption from eighty percent to fifty percent.[9] As a result, the Soviet Union experienced massive growth in heavy industry, with a concurrent massive contraction of its agricultural sector, in both relative and absolute terms.

2.49.3 Disadvantages of economic planning

Inefficient resource distribution: surplus and shortage

Critics of planned economies argue that planners cannot detect consumer preferences, shortages, and surpluses with sufficient accuracy and therefore cannot efficiently coordinate production (in a market economy, a free price system is intended to serve this purpose). This difficulty was notably written about by economists Ludwig von Mises and Friedrich Hayek, both of whom called it the "economic calculation problem". These opponents of central planning argue that the only way to satisfy individuals who have a constantly changing hierarchy of needs, and are the only ones to possess their particular individual's circumstances, is by allowing those with the most knowledge of their needs to have it in their power to use their resources in a competing marketplace to meet the needs of the most amount of consumers, most efficiently. This phenomenon is recognized as spontaneous order. Additionally, misallocation of resources would naturally ensue by redirecting capital away from individuals with direct knowledge and circumventing it into markets where a coercive monopoly influences behavior, ignoring market signals. According to Tibor R. Machan, "Without a market in which allocations can be made in obedience to the law of supply and demand, it is difficult or impossible to funnel resources with respect to actual human preferences and goals."[10]

Suppression of economic democracy and self-management

Economist Robin Hahnel notes that, even if central planning overcame its inherent inhibitions of incentives and innovation, it would nevertheless be unable to maximize economic democracy and self-management, which he believes are concepts that are more intellectually coherent, consistent and just than mainstream notions of economic freedom.[11]

Says Hahnel, "Combined with a more democratic political system, and redone to closer approximate a best case version, centrally planned economies no doubt would have performed better. But they could never have delivered economic self-management, they would always have been slow to innovate as apathy and frustration took their inevitable toll, and they would always have been susceptible to growing inequities and inefficiencies as the effects of differential economic power grew. Under central planning neither planners, managers, nor workers had incentives to promote the social economic interest. Nor did impeding markets for final goods to the planning system enfranchise consumers in meaningful ways. But central planning would have been incompatible with economic democracy even if it had overcome its information and incentive liabilities. And the truth is that it survived as long as it did only because it was propped up by unprecedented totalitarian political power."[11]

Economic Instability

Studies of Eastern European planned economies in the 1950s and 1960s by both American and Eastern European economists found that, contrary to the expectations of both groups, they showed greater fluctuations in output than market economies during the same period.[12]

2.49.4 Relationship with socialism

Main article: Socialism

While socialism is not equivalent to economic planning or to the concept of a planned economy, an influential conception of socialism involves the replacement of capital markets with some form of economic planning in order to achieve *ex ante* coordination of the economy. The goal of such an economic system would be to achieve conscious control over the economy by the population, specifically, so that the use of the surplus product is controlled by the producers.[13] The specific forms of planning proposed for socialism and their feasibility are subjects of the socialist calculation debate.

2.49.5 Fictional portrayals of planned economies

The 1888 novel *Looking Backward* by Edward Bellamy depicts a fictional planned economy in a United States around the year 2000 which has become a socialist utopia.

The World State in Aldous Huxley's *Brave New World* and Airstrip One in George Orwell's *Nineteen Eighty Four* are both fictional examples of command economies, albeit with diametrically opposed aims: The former is a consumer economy designed to engender productivity while the latter is a shortage economy designed as an agent of totalitarian social control. Airstrip One is organised by the euphemistically named Ministry of Plenty.

Other literary portrayals of planned economies were Yevgeny Zamyatin's *We*, which was an influence on Orwell's work. Like *Nineteen Eighty Four*, Ayn Rand's dystopian story *Anthem* was also an artistic portrayal of a command economy that was influenced by *We*. The difference is that it was a primitivist planned economy, as opposed to the advanced technology of *We* or *Brave New World*.

2.49.6 See also

- Adhocracy
- Anarchist Spain
- Calculation in kind
- Communist state
- Criticisms of Socialism
- Cybernetics
- Distributed economy
- Economic democracy
- Economic equilibrium
- Economic calculation problem
- Economic planning
- Economics of fascism
- Enrico Barone
- Horizontalidad
- Inclusive democracy
- Indicative planning
- Industrial democracy
- Input-output model
- Jean Coutrot
- Libertarian socialism
- Lange model
- Leonid Kantorovich
- Marcel Déat
- Material balance planning
- Market abolitionism
- Market economy
- Marxism-Leninism
- Mixed economy
- Non-conformists of the 1930s
- Neosocialism
- Participatory economics
- Price control
- Political and Economic Planning
- Production for use
- Project Cybersyn
- Public ownership
- Peer-to-Peer economy
- Social ownership

- Socialist calculation debate
- Socialist economics
- Technocracy
- Self-managed economy

Case studies

- Analysis of Soviet-type economic planning
- First Malaysia Plan
- Five-Year Plans in the Soviet Union
- Five-year plans of Argentina
- Five-Year Plans of South Korea
- Great Leap Forward (China)
- Economy of Singapore
- Economy of India
- Project Cybersyn, a project for a computer network controlling the economy of Chile under Salvador Allende.
- Eastern Bloc economies
- Economy of Saudi Arabia

2.49.7 Notes

[1] Mandel, Ernest (1986). "In Defence of Socialist Planning" (PDF). *New Left Review* **159**: 5–37. Planning is not equivalent to 'perfect' allocation of resources, nor 'scientific' allocation, nor even 'more humane' allocation. It simply means 'direct' allocation, ex ante. As such, it is the opposite of market allocation, which is ex post.

[2] Alec Nove (1987), "Planned Economy," *The New Palgrave: A Dictionary of Economics*, v. 3, p. 879.

[3] Barkley, John (1992). *Comparative Economics in Transforming World Economy*. MIT. p. 10. ISBN 0-262-68153-6.

[4] Ellman, Michael (2007). "The Rise and Fall of Socialist Planning". In Estrin, Saul; Kołodko, Grzegorz W.; Uvalić, Milica. *Transition and Beyond: Essays in Honour of Mario Nuti*. New York: Palgrave Macmillan. p. 22. ISBN 0-230-54697-8. Realization of these facts led in the 1970s and 1980s to the development of new terms to describe what had previously been (and still were in United Nations publications) referred to as the 'centrally planned economies'. In the USSR in the late 1980s the system was normally referred to as the 'administrative-command' economy. What was fundamental to this system was not the plan but the role of administrative hierarchies at all levels of decision making; the absence of control over decision making by the population...

[5] planned economy. Dictionary.com Unabridged (v 1.1). Random House, Inc. (accessed: May 11, 2008).

[6] command economy. In Merriam-Webster Online Dictionary (2008) (accessed May 11, 2008).

[7] Trotsky, Leon. *Writings 1932–33*. p. 96.

[8] Michael Ellman (2014). *Socialist Planning*. Cambridge University Press. ISBN 1107427320 p. 372.

[9] Kennedy, Paul (1987). *The Rise and Fall of the Great Powers*. New York: Random House. pp. 322–3. ISBN 0-394-54674-1.

[10] Machan, R. Tibor (2002). "Some Skeptical Reflections on Research and Development". *Liberty and Research and Development: Science Funding in a Free Society* (PDF). Hoover Press. ISBN 0-8179-2942-8.

[11] Hahnel, Robin (2002). *The ABC's of Political Economy*. London: Pluto Press. p. 262. ISBN 0-7453-1858-4.

[12] Zielinski, J. G. (1973). *Economic Reforms in Polish Industry*. New York: Oxford University Press. ISBN 0-19-215323-4.

[13] Feinstein, C.H. (1975). *Socialism, Capitalism and Economic Growth: Essays Presented to Maurice Dobb*. Cambridge University Press. p. 174. ISBN 0-521-29007-4. We have presented the view that planning and market mechanisms are instruments that can be used both in socialist and non-socialist societies...It was important to explode the primitive identification of central planning and socialism and to stress the instrumental character of planning.

2.49.8 Further reading

- Michael Ellman (2014). *Socialist Planning*. Cambridge University Press; 3 edition. ISBN 1107427320
- Gregory Grossman (1987): "Command economy," *The New Palgrave: A Dictionary of Economics*, v. 1, pp. 494–95.
- Carl Landauer (1947): *Theory of National Economic Planning*. University of California Press. Berkeley and Los Angeles, Second edition.
- Alec Nove (1987): "Planned economy," *The New Palgrave: A Dictionary of Economics*, v. 3, pp. 879–85.
- Myant, Martin; Drahokoupil, Jan (2010), *Transition Economies: Political Economy in Russia, Eastern Europe, and Central Asia*, Wiley-Blackwell, ISBN 978-0-470-59619-7

- Cox, Robin 2005, "The Economic Calculation controversy: unravelling of a myth" '

- Devine, Pat.'Democracy and Economic Planning. Polity. 2010. ISBN 978-0745634791

- Mandel, Ernest. *In Defence of Socialist Planning*. New Left Review, Issue 159. 1986.

2.49.9 External links

- An article against "The myth of the permanent arms economy"

- The Stalin Model for the Control and Coordination of Enterprises in a Socialist Economy

2.50 Pluralism in economics

See also: History of economic thought

The **pluralism in economics** movement is a campaign to 'enrich teaching and research and reinvigorate the discipline... [and bring] economics back into the service of society'.[1] Dalen writes that economics had greater scientific pluralism in the past[2] compared to the monist approach that is prevalent today.[3][4] Pluralism encourages the inclusion of a wide variety of neoclassical and heterodox economic theories - including classical, Post-Keynesian, institutional, ecological, evolutionary economics, feminist, Marxist and Austrian, stating that "each tradition of thought adds something unique and valuable to economic scholarship."[5]

The movement for pluralism can be traced to wider movements for progressive change in the 1960s and 1970s, with economists like Frank Stilwell and Steve Keen campaigning for pluralist and critical economics teaching at the University of Sydney in 1971.[6] In 1992, a petition organised by Geoffrey Hodgson, Uskali Mäki and Deirdre McCloskey[7] was published as a paid advertisement in the American Economic Review. This petition described itself as a "plea for a pluralistic and rigorous economics" [8] and was preceded by a commission of the American Economics Association, called 'Report by the Commission on Graduate Education'. [9] Many critics of mainstream economics began to describe themselves as proponents of pluralism; they formed groups or organizations such as The International Confederation of Associations for Reform in Economics (ICARE).[10] Later, French students announced a "post-autistic economics" movement; [11] a "rebellion" of students at the École Normale Supérieure happened in 2000; [12] Cambridge students organised a petition in 2001; [13] FEED organised a plea in 2009 with over 2,000 signatures in the first month; [14] In 2011 Harvard students organized a walkout from their Economic Principles class thereby objecting to the one-sided presentations of their professor Gregory Mankiw.[15] Paul Krugman and Richard Layard organised a 'Manifesto For Economic Sense' in 2012; [16] Post-Crash Economics Society Manchester published a petition in November 2013; [17] UK student groups published a draft manifesto in April 2014; [18] and at Manchester in April 2014, the economics department rejected a course devised by the Post-Crash Economics Society called 'Bubbles, Panics and Crashes: an Introduction to Alternative Theories of Crisis'.[19] On May 5th 2014, economics students from 19 countries published an 'international student letter' [1] and formed ISIPE, calling for 'a pluralism of theories and methods' so that economics students 'understand the broader social impacts and moral implications of economic decisions'. [20]

Some critics of mainstream economics have called for "reform" in the past. For example, ICAPE was originally ICARE but replaced the R ("reform") with P ("pluralism") stating that "'reform' ... does not properly characterize the nature or purpose of our organization..."[10]

2.50.1 See also

- Foundation for European Economic Development

- ISIPE

2.50.2 References

[1] ISIPE (2014-05-05). "International Student Letter". ISIPE. Retrieved 2014-05-07.

[2] Hendrik P. Dalen (2003-05-11). "Pluralism in Economics: A Public Good or a Public Bad?". 03-034/1. Tinbergen Institute Discussion Papers.

[3] "Policy Implications of Post-Autistic Economics". Post-Autistic Economics Network. 2006-10-09. Retrieved 2007-05-25.

[4] Peter, Monaghan (2003-01-24). "Taking On 'Rational Man'". The Chronicle of Higher Education. Retrieved 2007-05-25.

[5] "ICAPE home". International Confederation of Associations for Pluralism in Economics. Retrieved 2007-05-25.

[6] Butler, Gavan; Jones, Evan; Stilwell, Frank (2009). *Political Economy Now! The struggle for alternative economics at the University of Sydney.*

[7] FEED. "The 1992 Plea for a Pluralistic and Rigorous Economics".

[8] "A Plea for a Pluralistic and Rigorous Economics", *American Economic Review*, 82(2): xxv.

[9] Krueger, A.O. Arrow, K.J. et al (1991). "Report of the commission on graduate education in economics", *Journal of Economic Literature*, 29(3): 1035-1053.

[10] "ICAPE - History". International Confederation of Associations for Pluralism in Economics. Retrieved 2007-05-25.

[11] Fullbrook, Edward (2003). *The Crisis in Economics: The post - autistic economics movement: the first 600 days*. Routledge. ISBN 978-0415308984.

[12] Hayes, Christopher (2007-06-11). "The Hip Heterodoxy". The Nation.

[13] The Cambridge 27. "Opening Up Economics". Post-autistic Economics Newsletter. Retrieved 2014-04-29.

[14] FEED. "Mistaking Mathematical Beauty for Economic Truth". FEED. Retrieved 2014-04-30.

[15] http://www.huffingtonpost.com/john-komlos/need-for-a-paradigm-switc_1_b_5482680.html

[16] Safdar, Khadeeja (2012-06-28). "Paul Krugman Asks Economists To Sign 'Manifesto For Economic Sense'". Huffington Post. Retrieved 2014-04-30.

[17] Post-Crash Economics Society Manchester. "Revise the University of Manchester's Economic Syllabus". Post-Crash Economics Society Manchester. Retrieved 2014-04-29.

[18] Rethinking Economics. "Draft Manifesto: A direction for the reform of economics education". Rethinking Economics. Retrieved 2014-04-29.

[19] Jones, Claire. "Students' hopes dashed over 'crash' course in economics teaching". Financial Times. Retrieved 2014-04-29.

[20] Claire Jones (2014-05-05). "Economics students of the world, unite!". Financial Times Money Supply Blog. Retrieved 2014-05-07.

2.50.3 External links

- The International Confederation of Associations for Pluralism in Economics
- The Association for Heterodox Economics
- The Post-autistic Economics Network
- The Association for Integrity and Responsible Leadership in Economics and Associated Professions
- World Economics Association

2.51 Post-autistic economics

Post-Autistic Economics (**PAE**) is a movement of different groups critical of the current economics mainstream: behavioral economics, heterodox economics, feminist economics, green economics, and econo-physics. It was born through the work of University of Paris 1 economist Bernard Guerrien. It was started in 2000 by a group of disaffected French economics students.[1]

The term *autistic* is used in an informal way, signifying "abnormal subjectivity, acceptance of fantasy rather than reality".[2] It has been criticized for using the medical diagnosis, autism, as a derogatory expression.[3] However, the term "autistic economy" has a historical scholarly use in economics that pre-dates the discovery of the medical condition autism in 1943. In economics the term "autistic economy" refers collectively to any command economy where only one will governs. In early human history some examples of autistic economies included tribal & slave economies as well as lone households making production decisions in isolation based only on the preferences of the head of the household. In modern times both socialist and fascist command economies have been referred to collectively by economists as the "autistic economies."[4]

2.51.1 Concept

Guerrien has challenged standard neoclassical assumptions and incorporated ideas from sociology and psychology into economic analysis. Specifically, he has criticised the notions of utility theory, rational choice, production and efficiency theory (Pareto optimality), and game theory.[5]

Other topics include "Gross National Happiness", realism vs. mathematical consistency, "Thermodynamics and Economics", or "Irrelevance and Ideology". Contributors to the "Post-Autistic Economics Review" included Bruce Caldwell, James K. Galbraith, Robert L. Heilbroner, Bernard Guerrien, Emmanuelle Benicourt, Ha-Joon Chang, Herman Daly and Richard D. Wolff.

2.51.2 Criticism of the term

Some mainstream economists—such as Robert Solow, in a long article[6] in Le Monde,[7] followed by another by Olivier Blanchard, the chair at MIT, as well as the publication of a counter-petition to the French students' petition, a plea for the status quo—argue that a characterization of academic economics taught in today's colleges as autistic in the sense of closed-minded is unfair, since many branches of post-modern economics reject classical economic worldviews and heavy reliance on mathematics.

In addition, the term "autistic" is a medical description of a developmental condition, and thus its use to characterize mainstream economics is considered by many to be highly insensitive and indicative of a lack of empathy and understanding on the part of self-described post-autistic economists for actual autistics.[8]

In March, 2008, the *post-autistic economics review* changed its name to the *real-world economics review*.

2.51.3 See also

- Criticisms of neoclassical economics
- History of economics
- Pluralism in economics
- Post-Keynesian economics
- Real-world economics review

2.51.4 References

[1] The Cambridge 27 (July 2001). "Opening Up Economics". *post-autistic economics newsletter* (7, article 1). Archived from the original on 2012-06-30.

[2] http://www.yaleeconomicreview.com/issues/2006_summer/autistic_economist.html ALCORN, Stanley and SOLARZ, Ben. *The Autistic Economist*, Yale Economic Review]

[3] Kay, Neil (7 September 2008), *The Importance of Words*

[4] von Mises, Ludwig. "Human Action, Part 4, Chapter 14". Retrieved 1949. Check date values in: laccess-date= (help)

[5] http://www.autisme-economie.org/article115.html Is There Anything Worth Keeping in Standard Microeconomics?

[6] "Robert Solow (2001) *L'économie entre empirisme et mathématisation.* Le Monde, 3 January 2001, in post-autistic economics media archives". Archived from the original on 2012-11-30.

[7] Galbraith, James K. (January 2001). "A contribution on the state of economics in France and the world". *post-autistic economics newsletter* (4, article 1). Archived from the original on 2012-11-30.

[8] "Autism and Economics". 3 December 2007.

2.51.5 Literature

- ALCORN, Stanley and SOLARZ, Ben. *The Autistic Economist*, Yale Economic Review

- *Real World Economics: A Post-Autistic Economics Reader*, ed. by Edward Fullbrook, Anthem Press, 2007, ISBN 1-84331-236-0

- Mark Blaug. "Ugly Currents in Modern Economics", *Policy Options*, September 1997. Available as PDF.

- Peter Monaghan. "Taking on Rational Man: Dissident economists fight for a niche in the discipline", Chronicle of Higher Education, 24 January 2003.

- Richard Smith, "Eco-suicidal Economics of Adam Smith," *Capitalism Nature Socialism*, Volume 18 Number 2 (June 2007): 22-43. PDF at

- Fred Foldvary (ed). *Beyond Neoclassical Economics: Heterodox Approaches to Economic Theory*, Edward Elgar Publishing, Aldershot, U.K., 1996.

2.51.6 External links

- Official site of the PAE organisation and newsletter
- The Post-Autistic Economic Review, a scholarly journal published by the movement
- The People-Centered Development Forum
- Article Taking On 'Rational Man' – Dissident economists fight for a niche in the discipline
- Article 'Kick it Over! – The Rise of Post-Autistic Economics' in Adbusters magazine, 2004 Sept.

2.52 Post-scarcity economy

Post-scarcity is a theoretical economy in which most goods can be produced in great abundance with minimal human labor needed, so that they become available to all very cheaply or even freely.[1][2] Post-scarcity is not generally taken to mean that scarcity has been eliminated for *all* consumer goods and services, instead it is often taken to mean that all people can easily have their basic survival needs met along with some significant proportion of their desires for goods and services,[3] with writers on the topic often emphasizing that certain commodities are likely to remain scarce in a post-scarcity society.[4][5][6][7]

2.52.1 The post-scarcity model

Speculative technology

Today, futurists who speak of "post-scarcity" suggest economies based on advances in automated manufacturing technologies,[4] often including the idea of self-replicating machines, the adoption of division of labour[8] which in theory could produce nearly all goods in abundance, given adequate raw materials and energy. More speculative forms of nanotechnology (such as molecular assemblers or nanofactories, which do not currently exist) raise the possibility of devices that can automatically manufacture any specified goods given the correct instructions and the necessary raw materials and energy,[9] and so many nanotechnology enthusiasts have suggested it will usher in a post-scarcity world.[10][11] In the more near-term future, the increasing automation of physical labor using robots is often discussed as means of creating a post-scarcity economy.[12][13] Increasingly versatile forms of rapid prototyping machines, and a hypothetical self-replicating version of such a machine known as a RepRap, have also been predicted to help create the abundance of goods needed for a post-scarcity economy.[14] Advocates of self-replicating machines such as Adrian Bowyer, the creator of the RepRap project, argue that once a self-replicating machine is designed, then since anyone who owns one can make more copies to sell (and would also be free to ask for a lower price than other sellers), market competition will naturally drive the cost of such machines down to the bare minimum needed to make a profit,[15][16] in this case just above the cost of the physical materials and energy that must be fed into the machine as input, and the same should go for any other goods that the machine can build.

Even with fully automated production, limitations on the number of goods produced would arise from the availability of raw materials and energy, as well as ecological damage associated with manufacturing technologies.[4] Advocates of technological abundance often argue for more extensive use of renewable energy and greater recycling in order to prevent future drops in availability of energy and raw materials, and reduce ecological damage.[4] Solar energy in particular is often emphasized, as the cost of solar panels continues to drop [4] (and could drop far more with automated production by self-replicating machines), and advocates point out the total solar power striking the Earth's surface annually exceeds our civilization's current annual power usage by a factor of thousands.[17][18] Advocates also sometimes argue that the energy and raw materials available could be greatly expanded if we looked to resources beyond the Earth. For example, asteroid mining is sometimes discussed as a way of greatly reducing scarcity for many useful metals such as Nickel.[19] While early asteroid mining might involve manned missions, advocates hope that eventually humanity could have automated mining done by self-replicating machines.[19][20] If this were done, then the only capital expenditure would be a single self-replicating unit (whether robotic or nanotechnological), after which the number of units could replicate at no further cost, limited only by the available raw materials needed to build more.[20]

Digital abundance

Richard Stallman, the founder of the GNU project, has cited the eventual creation of a post-scarcity society as one of his motivations:[21]

> In the long run, making programs free is a step toward the post-scarcity world, where nobody will have to work very hard just to make a living. People will be free to devote themselves to activities that are fun, such as programming, after spending the necessary ten hours a week on required tasks such as legislation, family counseling, robot repair and asteroid prospecting. There will be no need to be able to make a living from programming.

Marxism

Karl Marx, in a section of his *Grundrisse* that came to be known as the "Fragment on Machines",[22][23] argued that the transition to a post-capitalist society combined with advances in automation would allow for significant reductions in labor needed to produce necessary goods, eventually reaching a point where all people would have significant amounts of leisure time to pursue science, the arts, and creative activities; a state some commentators later labeled as "post-scarcity".[24] Marx argued that capitalism - the dynamic of economic growth based on capital accumulation - depends on exploiting the surplus labor of workers, but a post-capitalist society would allow for:

> The free development of individualities, and hence not the reduction of necessary labour time so as to posit surplus labour, but rather the general reduction of the necessary labour of society to a minimum, which then corresponds to the artistic, scientific etc. development of the individuals in the time set free, and with the means created, for all of them.[25]

Marx's concept of a post-capitalist communist society involves the free distribution of goods made possible by the abundance provided by automation.[26] The fully developed communist economic system is postulated to develop from a preceding socialist system. Marx held the view that socialism—a system based on social ownership of the means of production—would enable progress toward the development of fully developed communism by further advancing productive technology. Under socialism, with its increasing levels of automation, an increasing proportion of goods would be distributed freely.[27]

Marx did not believe in the elimination of most physical labor through technological advancements alone in a capitalist society, because he believed capitalism contained within it certain tendencies which countered increasing automation and prevented it from developing beyond a limited point, so that manual industrial labor could not be eliminated until the overthrow of capitalism.[28] Some commentators on Marx have argued that at the time he wrote the *Grundrisse*, he thought that the collapse of capitalism due to advancing automation was inevitable despite these counter-tendencies, but that by the time of his major work *Capital: Critique of Political Economy* he had abandoned this view, and came to believe that capitalism could continually renew itself unless overthrown.[29][30][31]

Social anarchism

Advancement through technology towards a condition of post-scarcity has formed a large part of the social anarchist tradition. Carlo Cafiero claimed that libertarian communism would enable humanity to transcend the traditional communist principle "from each according to ability, to each according to their needs" with "from each and to each according to their will".

Peter Kropotkin wrote *Fields, Factories, and Workshops*, using empirical data from the technological capacity of the time to make the case for a decentralised and moneyless economy of abundance - which integrated city and country - allowing for a high standard of living with only a minimum of labour from each individual between the ages of 20 and 40.

Post-scarcity became a central concern of anarchism in the 1960s with the publication of *Post-Scarcity Anarchism* by Murray Bookchin and the formation of social ecology as a critical theory of human society and the natural world. Social ecology claims that capitalism and the state system have surpassed the point where they can serve a progressive role in the creation of useful technologies and can now only continue to function through the creation and maintenance of artificial scarcity.

2.52.2 Fiction

Science fiction

The *Mars trilogy* by Kim Stanley Robinson. Over three novels, Robinson charts the terraforming of Mars as a human colony and the establishment of a post-scarcity society.[32]

The Culture novels by Iain M Banks are centered on a communist post-scarcity economy[33][32][34] where technology is advanced to such a degree that all production is automated,[35] and there is no use for money or property (aside from personal possessions with sentimental value).[36] Humans in the Culture are free to pursue their own interests in an open and socially-permissive society. The society has been described by some commentators as "communist-bloc"[37] or "anarcho-communist".[38] Banks' close friend and fellow science fiction writer Ken MacLeod has said that The Culture can be seen as a realization of Marx's communism, but adds that "however friendly he was to the radical left, Iain had little interest in relating the long-range possibility of utopia to radical politics in the here and now. As he saw it, what mattered was to keep the utopian possibility open by continuing technological progress, especially space development, and in the meantime to support whatever policies and politics in the real world were rational and humane."[39]

Down and Out in the Magic Kingdom features a moneyless society where material goods are no longer scarce, and everyone is granted basic rights that in our present age are mostly considered luxuries.

The Rapture of the Nerds a post-scarcity society about "disruptive" technology.[32] The Rapture of the Nerds is a derogatory term for the Technological Singularity coined by SF author Ken MacLeod. There is also a 2012 SF novel about the technological singularity called *The Rapture of the Nerds* — (written by Cory Doctorow and Charles Stross).

Con Blomberg's 1959 short story "Sales Talk" depicts a post-scarcity society in which society incentivizes consumption to reduce the burden of overproduction.[32]

The science fiction novella *Riders of the Purple Wage* by Philip José Farmer paints a vision of a highly regulated, state-dominated post-scarcity society, in which a renaissance in arts coincides with mass illiteracy.

The 24th century human society of *Star Trek: The Next Generation* and *Star Trek: Deep Space Nine* has been labeled a post-scarcity society due to the ability of the fictional "replicator" technology to synthesize a wide variety of goods nearly instantaneously,[40] along with dialogue such as Captain Picard's statement that "The acquisition of wealth is no longer the driving force of our lives. We work to better ourselves and the rest of humanity."[41]

2.52.3 See also

- Artificial scarcity
- Attention economy
- Cycle of poverty
- Commons-based peer production

- Communist society
- Imagination age
- Information society
- Knowledge economy
- Post-capitalism
- Scarcity
- Technological utopianism
- Technocracy
- The Venus Project
- The Zeitgeist Movement

Books

- *A Whole New Mind*
- *Abundance: The Future Is Better Than You Think*
- *Post-Scarcity Anarchism*

2.52.4 References

[1] Sadler, Philip (2010), *Sustainable Growth in a Post-Scarcity World: Consumption, Demand, and the Poverty Penalty*, Surrey, England: Gower Applied Business Research, p. 7, ISBN 978-0-566-09158-2

[2] Robert Chernomas. (1984). "Keynes on Post-Scarcity Society." In: Journal of Economic Issues, 18(4).

[3] Burnham, Karen (22 June 2015), *Space: A Playground for Postcapitalist Posthumans*, Strange Horizons, archived from the original on 2015-11-14, By post-scarcity economics, we're generally talking about a system where all the resources necessary to fulfill the basic needs (and a good chunk of the desires) of the population are available.

[4] Frase, Peter (Winter 2012), *Four Futures* (5), Jacobin, archived from the original on 2015-11-13

[5] Sadler, Philip (2010), *Sustainable Growth in a Post-Scarcity World: Consumption, Demand, and the Poverty Penalty*, Surrey, England: Gower Applied Business Research, p. 57, ISBN 978-0-566-09158-2

[6] Das, Abhimanyu; Anders, Charlie Jane (30 September 2014), *Post-Scarcity Societies (That Still Have Scarcity)*, io9, archived from the original on 2015-11-14

[7] *Engines of Creation* (full text online, see also Engines of Creation) - Drexler, Eric K., Anchor Books, 1986. See the first paragraph of the section "The Positive-Sum Society" in Chapter 6.

[8] Peters, Michael A.; Marginson, Simon; Murphy, Peter (2009), *Creativity and the Global Knowledge Economy*, New York: Peter Lang Publishing, Inc., p. 11, ISBN 978-1-4331-0425-1

[9] *Engines of Creation* (full text online, see also Engines of Creation) - Drexler, Eric K., Anchor Books, 1986

[10] Sparrow, Rob (2007), "Negotiating the nanodivides", in Hodge, Graeme A.; Bowman, Diana; Ludlow, Karinne, *New Global Frontiers in Regulation: The Age of Nanotechnology*, Cheltenham, England: Edward Elgar Publishing Limited, p. 98, ISBN 978-1-84720-518-6

[11] Barfield, Thomas (2 September 2010), *Get ready for a world of nanotechnology*, Guardian US, archived from the original on 2015-11-11

[12] Wohlsen, Marcus (8 August 2014), "When Robots Take All the Work, What'll Be Left for Us to Do?", *Wired*, archived from the original on 2015-11-10

[13] Merchant, Brian (18 March 2015), *Fully automated luxury communism*, Guardian US, archived from the original on 2015-11-10

[14] Peters, Michael A.; Marginson, Simon; Murphy, Peter (2009), *Creativity and the Global Knowledge Economy*, New York: Peter Lang Publishing, Inc., pp. 75-76, ISBN 978-1-4331-0425-1

[15] Gordon, Stephen; Bowyer, Adrian (22 April 2005). "An Interview With Dr. Adrian Bowyer". Archived from the original on 11 November 2015. Retrieved 11 November 2015.

[16] Biever, Celeste (18 March 2005), *3D printer to churn out copies of itself*, New Scientist, archived from the original on 2015-11-11

[17] Diamandis, Peter H. (2012), *Abundance: The Future is Better Than You Think*, New York, New York: Free Press, p. 6, ISBN 978-1-4516-1421-3

[18] *Engines of Creation* (full text online, see also Engines of Creation) - Drexler, Eric K., Anchor Books, 1986. See the section "The Limits to Resources" in Chapter 10.

[19] Thomson, Iain (24 January 2013), *Asteroid mining and a post-scarcity economy*, The Register, archived from the original on 2015-11-16

[20] *Engines of Creation* (full text online, see also Engines of Creation) - Drexler, Eric K., Anchor Books, 1986. See the section "Abundance" in Chapter 6.

[21] GNU Manifesto (full text online, see also GNU Manifesto) - Stallman, Richard; Dr. Dobb's Journal, March 1985

[22] Barbour, Charles (2012). *The Marx Machine: Politics, Polemics, Ideology*. Lexington Books. p. 118. ISBN 978-0-7391-1046-1.

[23] The section known as the "Fragment on Machines" can be read online here.

[24] Jessop and Wheatley, Bob and Russell (1999). *Karl Marx's Social and Political Thought, Volume 8*. Routledge. p. 9. ISBN 0-415-19330-3. Marx in the Grundrisse speaks of a time when systematic automation will be developed to the point where direct human labor power will be a source of wealth. The preconditions will be created by capitalism itself. It will be an age of true mastery of nature, a post-scarcity age, when men can turn from alienating and dehumanizing labor to the free use of leisure in the pursuit of the sciences and arts.

[25] Marx, Karl (1973). *Grundrisse: Foundations of the Critique of Political Economy (Rough Draft)*. Translated by Nicolaus, Martin. Penguin Books. p. 706. ISBN 0-14-044575-7.

[26] Wood, John Cunningham (1996). *Karl Marx's Economics: Critical Assessments I*. Routledge. p. 248-249. ISBN 978-0415087148. Affluence and increased provision of free goods would reduce alienation in the work process and, in combination with (1), the alienation of man's 'species-life'. Greater leisure would create opportunities for creative and artistic activity outside of work.

[27] Wood, John Cunningham (1996). *Karl Marx's Economics: Critical Assessments I*. Routledge. p. 248. ISBN 978-0415087148. In particular, this economy would possess (1) social ownership and control of industry by the 'associated producers' and (2) a sufficiently high level of economic development to enable substantial progress toward 'full communism' and thereby some combination of the following: super affluence; distribution of an increasing proportion of commodities as if they were free goods; an increase in the proportion of collective goods...

[28] Marx, Karl (1973). "Foreword". *Grundrisse: Foundations of the Critique of Political Economy (Rough Draft)*. Translated by Nicolaus, Martin. Foreword by Martin Nicolaus. Penguin Books. pp. 51-52. ISBN 0-14-044575-7.

[29] Tomba, Massimiliano (2013). *Marx's Temporalities*. Koninklijke Brill NV. p. 76. ISBN 978-90-04-23678-3.

[30] Bellofiore, Riccardo; Starosta, Guido; Thomas, Peter D. (2013). *In Marx's Laboratory: Critical Interpretations of the Grundrisse*. Koninklijke Brill NV. p. 9. ISBN 978-90-04-23676-9.

[31] Easterling, Stuart (November–December 2003). "Marx's theory of economic crisis". *International Socialist Review* (32). Archived from the original on 2015-11-11.

[32] Walter, Damien (11 October 2012), *Dear Ed Miliband ... seek your future in post-scarcity SF*, Guardian US, archived from the original on 2015-11-14

[33] Banks, Iain M. (1987). *Consider Phlebas*. Orbit. ISBN 978-0316005388. He could not believe the ordinary people in the Culture really wanted the war, no matter how they had voted. They had their communist Utopia. They were soft and pampered and indulged, and the Contact section's evangelical materialism provided their consciencesalving good works. What more could they want?

[34] Parsons, Michael; Banks, Iain M. (16 November 2012), *Interview: Iain M Banks talks 'The Hydrogen Sonata' with Wired.co.uk*, Wired UK, archived from the original on 2015-11-14, It is my vision of what you do when you are in that post-scarcity society, you can completely indulge myself. The Culture has no unemployment problem, no one has to work, so all work is a form of play.

[35] Banks, Iain M. "A Few Notes on the Culture". Retrieved 2015-11-23. Link is to an archived copy of the site that Banks linked to on his own website.

[36] Roberts, Jude; Banks, Iain M. (3 November 2014), *A Few Questions About the Culture: An Interview with Iain Banks*, Strange Horizons, archived from the original on 2015-11-23, This is not say that Libertarianism can't represent a progressive force, in the right circumstances, and I don't doubt there will be significant areas where I would agree with Libertarianism. But, really; which bit of not having private property, and the absence of money in the Culture novels, have these people missed?

[37] Cramer & Hartwell, Kathryn & David G. (10 July 2007). *The Space Opera Renaissance*. Orb Books. p. 298. ISBN 978-0765306180. Iain M. Banks and his brother-in-arms, Ken MacLeod, both take a Marxist line: Banks with his communist-bloc 'Culture' novels, and MacLeod with his 'hard-left libertarian' factions.

[38] Poole, Steven (8 February 2008), *Culture clashes*, The Guardian, archived from the original on 2015-11-23

[39] Liptak, Andrew (19 December 2014), *Iain M. Banks' Culture Novels*, Kirkus Reviews, archived from the original on 2015-11-23

[40] Fung, Brian; Peterson, Andrea; Tsukayama, Hayley; Saadia, Manu; Salmon, Felix (7 July 2015), *What the economics of Star Trek can teach us about the real world*, The Washington Post, archived from the original on 2015-11-16

[41] Baxter, Stephen (2007), "The Cold Equations: Extraterrestrial Liberty in Science Fiction", in Cockell, Charles S., *The Meaning of Liberty Beyond Earth*, Springer Publishing, p. 26, ISBN 978-3-319-09566-0

2.52.5 External links

- The Economics of Abundance

- Infinity Is Your Friend in Economics – contains links to a series of Techdirt articles on economics when scarcity is removed

- The Post-Scarcity / Culture of Abundance Reading List v2.2

- Abundance is our future, TED talk by Peter Diamandis

2.53 Production for use

Production for use is a phrase referring to the principle of economic organization and production taken as a defining criterion for a socialist economy. It is held in contrast to **production for profit**. This criterion is used to distinguish socialism from capitalism, and was one of the fundamental defining characteristics of socialism initially shared by Marxian socialists, evolutionary socialists, social anarchists and Christian socialists.[1][2]

This principle is broad and can refer to an array of different configurations that vary based on the underlying theory of economics employed. In its classic definition, production for use implied an economic system whereby the law of value and law of accumulation no longer directed economic activity, whereby a direct measure of utility and value is used in place of the abstractions of the price system, money, and capital.[3] Alternative conceptions of socialism that don't utilize the profit system such as the Lange model involve the use of a price system and monetary calculation.

The central critique of the *profits system* by socialists is that the accumulation of capital ("making money") becomes increasingly detached from the process of producing economic value, leading to waste, inefficiency, and social issues. Essentially it is a distortion of proper accounting based on the assertion of the law of value instead of the "real" costs of the factors of production, objectively determined outside of social relations.

2.53.1 Exposition

Production for *use* refers to an arrangement whereby the production of goods and services is carried out ex *ante* (directly) for their utility (also called Use-value). The implication is that the value of economic output would be based on use-value or a direct measure of utility as opposed to exchange-value; because economic activity would be undertaken to directly satisfy economic demands and human needs, the productive apparatus would directly serve individual and social needs. This is contrasted with production for exchange of the produced good or service in order to *profit*, where production is subjected to the perpetual accumulation of capital, a condition where production is only undertaken if it generates profit, implying an ex *post* or indirect means of satisfying economic demand. The profits system is oriented toward generating a profit to be reinvested into the economy (and the constant continuation of this process), the result being that society is structured around the need for a perpetual accumulation of capital.[4] In contrast, *production for use* means that the accumulation of capital is not a compulsory driving force in the economy, and by extension, the core process which society and culture revolves around. Production for profit, in contrast, is the dominant mode of production in the modern world system, equivocates "profitability" and "productivity" and presumes that the former always equates to the latter.

Some thinkers, including the Austrian philosopher and political economist Otto Neurath, have used the phrase **socialization** to refer to the same concept of "production for use". In Neurath's phraseology, "total socialization" involves calculation in kind in place of financial calculation and a system of planning in place of market-based allocation of economic goods.[5] Alternative conceptions exist in the form of market socialism.

2.53.2 Usage

Norman Thomas, a presidential candidate in the United States for the Socialist Party of America, contrasted socialism with capitalism by stating that socialism is based on production for use and an end to the profit system.[6]

Eugene V. Debs popularly used the phrase when running for president of the United States in 1912, stating that capitalism is founded upon production for profit, and in contrast, socialism is postulated upon production for use.[7]

Karl Marx referred to the "production of use-values" as a feature of any economic mode of production, but characterized capitalism as a mode of production that subjugated the production of use-value for the self-expansion of capital (i.e.: capital accumulation or production for profit). In contrast, socialism was vaguely defined as a system based on the direct production of use-value free of the process of continuous capital accumulation.[8]

Friedrich Hayek defined socialism as "...the common ownership of the means of production and their 'employment for use, not for profit.'", associating the rise of the welfare state by social democrats in post-World War II Europe as a rejection of socialism in the technical sense.[9]

2.53.3 Description

Proponents of socialism argue that production for profit (i.e., capitalism) does not always satisfy the economic needs of people, especially the working-class, because capital only invests in production when it is profitable. This fails to satisfy demand (the needs) of people who lack basic necessities but have insufficient purchasing power to acquire these needs in a manner that would be profitable for businesses. This results in a number of inefficiencies: unsold items are rarely given away to people who need but can't afford them, unemployed workers are not utilized to produce such services, and resources are expended on occupations that serve no other purpose than to support the accumulation of profit instead of being utilized to provide useful goods and services.[10] For example, the United States housing bubble resulted in an overproduction of housing units that could not be sold at a profit, despite there being sufficient demand and need for housing units.

Production for use in some form was the historically dominant modality until the initial primitive accumulation of capital.

Production for use is not in conflict with market allocation. For example, final output (goods and services for consumption) would still be distributed to consumers through a market. Only in a sufficiently developed stage of socialism whereby the forces of production are advanced enough to allow for superabundances of goods and services can distribution be based on free-access / according to needs.

Economic planning is not synonymous with *production for use*. Planning is essential in modern globalised production both within enterprises and within nation states. Planning to maximize profitability (i.e., within industries and private corporations) or to improve the efficiency of capital accumulation in the capitalist macro-economy (i.e., monetary policy, fiscal policy, industrial policy) does not change the fundamental criteria and need to generate a financial profit to be reinvested into the economy, lest it go into a crisis. A more recent critique of production for profit is that it fails spectacularly to address issues such as externalities which the board and management of a for profit enterprise are often under a fiduciary responsibility to ignore if they harm or conflict with the shareholders' profit motives.

Criticisms of production for profit

Socialists suggest a number of irrational outcomes occur from capitalism and the need to accumulate capital when capitalist economies reach a point in development whereby investment accumulates at a greater rate than growth of profitable investment opportunities. The central critique of the profits system maintained by socialists is that the accumulation of capital ("making money") becomes further detached from the process of producing economic value, leading to waste, inefficiency and underlying social issues.

Advertisement and planned obsolescence are strategies used by businesses to generate demand for the perpetual consumption required for capitalism to sustain itself so that instead of satisfying social and individual needs, capitalism first and foremost serves the artificial need for the perpetual accumulation of capital.

The creation of industries, projects and services for no other purpose than generating profit, economic growth or maintaining employment. The drive to create such industries arises from the need to absorb the savings in the economy (and thus, to maintain the accumulation of capital). This can take the form of corporatization and commercialization of public services (i.e., transforming them into profit-generating industries to absorb investment), or the creation and expansion of sectors of the economy that don't produce any economic value by themselves (that deal only with exchange-related activities) such as financial services, contributing to the formation of economic bubbles, crises and ultimately recessions.[11]

For socialists, the solution to these problems entails a reorientation of the economic system from production for profit and the need to accumulate capital to a system where production is adjusted to meet individual and social demands directly.

Criticisms of central planning Socialist and non-socialist critics of the Soviet model of economic planning have criticized the Soviet model of a planned economy on similar grounds to the critique leveled against capitalism: production was often undertaken in order to fulfill plan targets as opposed to being produced for use.[12]

Contrasted with state capitalism

As an objective criterion for socialism, *production for use* can be used to evaluate the socialistic content of the composition of former and existing economic systems. For example, an economic system that is dominated by nationalized firms organized around the production of profit – whether this profit is retained by the firm or paid to the government as a dividend payment – would be a state capitalist economy. In such a system, the organizational structure of the firm remains similar to a private-sector firm; non-financial costs are externalized because profitability is the criterion for production, so that the majority of the economy remains essentially capitalist despite the formal title of "public ownership". This has led many socialists to categorize the current Chinese economic system as a capitalist or state-capitalist economy.[13]

The economy of the Soviet Union was based upon capital accumulation for reinvestment and production for profit; the difference between Western capitalism was that the Soviet Union achieved this through nationalized industry and state-directed investment with the eventual goal of building a socialist society based upon production for use and self-management. Vladimir Lenin described the Soviet economy as "state-monopoly capitalism"[14] and did not consider it to be socialism. During the 1965 Liberman Reforms, the Soviet Union re-introduced profitability as a criterion for industrial enterprises. Other views argue the Soviet Union evolved into a non-capitalist and non-socialist system characterized by control and subordination of society by the party apparatus or those who coordinate the economy (bureaucratic collectivism).

Contrary socialist theories

The concept of production for use has been rejected by some socialists, most notably proponents of market socialism, who argue that socially held enterprises can compete with each other and generate profit in a market economy, with or without addressing the issue of distribution of this profit. Neoclassical economists argue that, under conditions of Pareto optimality, the pursuit of profit leads to a satisfaction of economic demands - the provision of use-values - and that market socialism would be able to achieve this outcome while retaining profitability as the operational criteria for socialist enterprises. In particular, some market socialists justify their position by claiming that society as a whole would control the surplus product (the profit generated by publicly owned firms), which could be used to finance public goods or public investment as opposed to accumulating in the hands of capitalists/shareholders.

Social democrats have rejected this concept altogether, and wish to retain the capitalist economic system by promoting a welfare state and economic interventions in order to make capitalism more "equitable" without questioning the legitimacy of the profits system.

2.53.4 Social production and peer-to-peer processes

See also: Sharing economy

Michel Bauwens identifies the emergence of the open software movement and peer-to-peer production as an emergent alternative mode of production to the capitalist economy that is based on collaborative self-management, common ownership of resources, and the (direct) production of use-values through the free cooperation of producers who have access to distributed capital.[15]

Commons-based peer production generally involves developers who produce goods and services with no aim to profit directly, but freely contribute to a project relying upon an open common pool of resources and software code. In both cases, production is carried out directly for use - software is produced solely for their use-value.

2.53.5 Valuation and calculation

Multiple forms of valuation have been proposed to govern production in a socialist economy, to serve as a unit of account and to quantify the usefulness of an object in socialism. These include valuations based on labor-time, the expenditure of energy in production, or disaggregated units of physical quantities.[16]

Physical quantities

The classic formulation of socialism involved replacing the criteria of value from money (exchange-value) to physical utility (use-value), to be quantified in terms of physical quantities (Calculation in kind and Input-Output analysis) or some natural unit of accounting, such as energy accounting.[17]

Input-output model analysis is based upon directly determining the physical quantities of goods and services to be produced and allocating economic inputs accordingly; thus production targets are pre-planned.[18] Soviet economic planning was overwhelmingly focused on material balances - balancing the supply of economic inputs with planned output targets.

Marginal cost

Oskar Lange formulated a mechanism for the direct allocation of capital goods in a socialist economy that was based on the marginal cost of production. Under a capitalist economy, managers of firms are ordered and legally required to base production around profitability, and in theory, competitive pressure creates a downward pressure on profits and forces private businesses to be responsive to demands of consumers, indirectly approximating production for use. In the Lange Model, the firms would be publicly owned and the managers would be tasked with setting the price of output to its marginal cost, thereby achieving pareto efficiency through direct allocation.

Cybernetics

See also: Cybernetics

Cybernetics, the use of computers to coordinate production in an optimal fashion, has been suggested for socialist economies. Oskar Lange, rejecting his earlier proposals for market socialism, argued that the computer is more efficient than the market process at solving the multitude of simultaneous equations required for allocating economic inputs efficiently (either in terms of physical quantities or monetary prices).[19]

Salvador Allende's socialist-led government developed Project Cybersyn; a system whereby economic decisions and feedback could be relayed in real-time through a network of telex machines fusing the information received/given by state enterprises and government departments. The project was disbanded after the 1973 Chilean coup d'état.

Free market

Based on the perspective that the law of value would continue to operate in a socialist economy, it is argued that a market economy purged of parasitical and wasteful elements in the form of private ownership of the means of production and the distortions that arise from the concentration of power and wealth in a class of capitalists would enable the market to operate efficiently without distortions. Simply replacing the antagonistic interests between capitalists and workers in enterprises would alter the orientation of the economy from private profit to meeting the demands of the community, as firms would seek to maximize the benefits to the member-workers - who would, as a whole, comprise society. Cooperative economist Jaroslav Vanek suggests that worker self-management and cooperative ownership of enterprises operating in a free-market would allow for a genuine free-market economy free of the market-distorting, monopolistic tendencies and antagonistic interests that emerge from private ownership over production.[20]

2.53.6 See also

- Calculation in kind
- Capital accumulation
- Economic planning
- Lange model
- Law of value
- Market failure
- Mode of production
- Planned obsolescence
- Post-capitalism
- Socialist calculation debate
- Socialist economics
- Socialist critique of capitalism
- Socialist mode of production
- Socialization (economics)
- Technocracy movement
- Time-based currency
- Use-value

2.53.7 References

[1] "Socialism and Capitalism: Are They Qualitatively Different Socioeconomic Systems?", by Kotz, David M. Retrieved February 19, 2011, from University of Massachusetts: http://people.umass.edu/dmkotz/Soc_and_Cap_Diff_Syst_06_12.pdf: "This understanding of socialism was held not just by revolutionary Marxist socialists but also by evolutionary socialists, Christian socialists, and even anarchists. At that time, there was also wide agreement about the basic institutions of the future socialist system: public ownership instead of private ownership of the means of production, economic planning instead of market forces, production for use instead of for profit."

[2] Paul Craig Roberts (29 October 2002). "My Time with Soviet Economics". VDARE.com. Retrieved 13 March 2013. The purpose of socialist planning was to eliminate market exchange (in the means of production) and organize production for society's direct use.

[3] Bockman, Johanna (2011). *Markets in the name of Socialism: The Left-Wing origins of Neoliberalism*. Stanford University Press. p. 20. ISBN 978-0-8047-7566-3. According to nineteenth-century socialist views, socialism would function without capitalist economic categories - such as money, prices, interest, profits and rent - and thus would function according to laws other than those described by current economic science. While some socialists recognized the need for money and prices at least during the transition from capitalism to socialism, socialists more commonly believed that the socialist economy would soon administratively mobilize the economy in physical units without the use of prices or money.

[4] "Production for Use", The Western Socialist (1967), Vol.36. Retrieved February 19, 2011: http://www.worldsocialism.org/canada/production.for.use.1969.v36n268.htm

[5] Nemeth, Uebel and Schmitz, Elizabeth, Thomas and Stefan (2007). *Otto Neurath's Economics in Context*. Springer. p. 63. ISBN 978-1-4020-6904-8.

[6] "Is the New Deal Socialism?", by Norman Thomas, Democratic Socialists of America (1936), Retrieved March 23, 2012: http://www.chicagodsa.org/thomasnewdeal.html

[7] *The Socialist Party's Appeal*, by Debs, Eugene. 1912. The Independent.

[8] Karl Marx. "Capital, Volume 1; Chapter Seven: The Labour-Process and the Process of Producing Surplus-Value". Marxists.org. Retrieved 9 December 2012.

[9] Friedrich Hayek (1960). "The Decline of Socialism and the Rise of the Welfare State". University of Chicago Press. Retrieved 20 January 2013.

[10] "Let's produce for use, not profit", Socialist Standard, May 2010. Retrieved August 07, 2010: http://www.worldsocialism.org/spgb/may10/page23.html

[11] *Economic Crisis from a Socialist Perspective.* Retrieved June 23, 2011, from rdwolff.com: http://www.rdwolff.com/content/economic-crisis-socialist-perspective

[12] *The Rise and Fall of Socialist Planning*, Ellman, Michael. (P.23): "In fact, the central authorities are partially ignorant of the situation throughout the economy, and this is a major factor causing such phenomena as the dictatorship over needs, bureaucratization, production for plan rather than use..."

[13] "China - 'Socialist market economy' or just plain capitalism?", Retrieved February 19, 2011: http://www.marxist.com/china-socialist-market-economy200106.htm

[14] Lenin's Collected Works Vol. 27, p. 293, quoted by Aufheben

[15] "The Political Economy of Peer Production". CTheory. 2005-01-12.

[16] "The Economics of Feasible Socialism Revisited" by Nove, Alec. 1991. (P.22)

[17] "The Alternative to Capitalism", World Socialist Party USA. Retrieved March 17, 2011: http://wspus.org/in-depth/the-alternative-to-capitalism/: "Wealth in socialism would be produced directly as such, i. e. as useful articles needed for human survival and enjoyment; resources and labour would be allocated for this purpose by conscious decisions, not through the operation of economic laws acting with the same coercive force as laws of nature. Although their effect is similar, the economic laws which come into operation in an exchange economy such as capitalism are not natural laws, since they arise out of a specific set of social relationships existing between human beings."

[18] "Quantity-Directed Socialism, Socialist Economics", Retrieved March 16, 2011: http://www.economictheories.org/2009/06/quantity-directed-socialism.html

[19] "The Computer and the market", Lange, Oskar. Retrieved March 16, 2011: http://www.calculemus.org/lect/L-I-MNS/12/ekon-i-modele/lange-comp-market.htm

[20] "Cooperative Economics: An Interview with Jaroslav Vanek", interview by Albert Perkins. Retrieved March 17, 2011: http://www.ru.org/51cooper.html

2.53.8 Further reading

- Harold, Loeb. *Production For Use.* Basic Books, Inc. 1936. ISBN 978-1443745246

- Strachey, John. *How Socialism Works.* Modern Age Books. 1939.

2.54 Quarterly Journal of Austrian Economics

The ***Quarterly Journal of Austrian Economics*** is a heterodox economics journal published quarterly by the Ludwig von Mises Institute.[1] It was established in 1998 after the Murray Rothbard-created publication *The Review of Austrian Economics* was transferred to other editors[2] and then to George Mason University.[3] The journal covers economics from an Austrian School perspective. The current editor-in-chief is Joseph Salerno.

A 2010 study published by the *American Journal of Economics and Sociology* identified 62 regularly published heterodox journals and used various empirical criteria to compare several aspects of their research quality. The study ranked *The Quarterly Journal*'s Bibliographic Ranking 33rd out of the 62 heterodox economics journals surveyed; its reputation among peers (both mainstream and heterodox) was ranked at 57th.[1]

2.54.1 References

[1] Lee, Frederic S., and Cronin, Bruce C. (2010). "Research Quality Rankings of Heterodox Economic Journals in a Contested Discipline." *American Journal of Economics and Sociology.* 69(5): 1428

[2] *The Review of Austrian Economics* archives, Ludwig von Mises Institute website, *accessed June 26, 2013*.

[3] *The Review of Austrian Economics* main page at George Mason University website.

2.54.2 External links

- Official website

2.55 real-world economics review

real-world economics review is a peer-reviewed open access academic journal of heterodox economics published by the "post-autistic economics network" since 2000. Since 2011 it is associated with the World Economics Association.[1] It was known formerly as the *post-autistic economics review* and the *post-autistic economics newsletter.* Previous issues are archived on its website.[1] Two sister journals from the same publisher are *Economic Thought* and *World Economics Review.*[1]

The journal is part of the post-autistic economics movement, and, as such, heavily criticizes neoclassical economics. It accepts contributions from diverse schools of economic thought.

2.55.1 See also

- Review of Radical Political Economics

2.55.2 References

[1] "Homepage". *real-world economics review*. World Economics Association. Retrieved 23 March 2015.

2.55.3 External links

- Official website
- World Economics Association

2.56 Regenerative economic theory

Regenerative economics is an economic system that works to regenerate capital assets. A capital asset is an asset that provides goods and/or services that are required for, or contribute to, our well being. In standard economic theory, one can either "regenerate" one's capital assets or consume them until the point where the asset cannot produce a viable stream of goods and/or services. What sets regenerative economics apart from standard economic theory is that it takes into account and gives hard economic value to the principal or original capital assets — the earth and the sun. We cannot do much to affect the sun although we can value access to the sun in such areas where access can be influenced. Therefore, most of Regenerative Economics focuses on the earth and the goods and services it supplies.

Regenerative economics is completely comfortable within the capitalist economic framework. Recognizing the earth as the original capital asset places the true value on the human support system known as the environment. Not having this original value properly recognized has created the unsustainable economic condition referred to as uneconomic growth, a phrase coined by Prof. Herman Daly, as stated in the book Reshaping the Built Environment.[1] The authors of the regenerative economic theory believe that uneconomic growth is the opposite of regenerative economics.

2.56.1 References

[1] Reshaping the Built Environment, edited by Charles J. Kibert, Forward by Alex Wilson, Written by Herman E. Daly Copyright 1999, Island Press ISBN 1-55963-701-3, ISBN 1-55963-702-1, Chapter 5 Uneconomic Growth and the Built Environment, In Theory and in Fact. pages 73–88

2.56.2 External links

- Capital Institute
- Center for the Advancement of the Steady State Economy
- Net energy analysis Encyclopedia of Earth

2.57 Review of Keynesian Economics

The *Review of Keynesian Economics* is a quarterly double-blind peer-reviewed academic journal covering Keynesian and Post-Keynesian economics, although it is also open to other heterodox traditions. It is published by Edward Elgar Publishing and was established in 2012. The editors-in-chief are Thomas Palley (New America Foundation), Louis-Philippe Rochon (Laurentian University), and Matías Vernengo (Bucknell University).

2.57.1 Abstracting and indexing

The journal is abstracted and indexed in:

- Research Papers in Economics
- Current Contents/Social & Behavioral Sciences[1]
- Social Sciences Citation Index[1]
- EconLit[2]
- Business Source Complete[3]

2.57.2 References

[1] "Master Journal List". *Intellectual Property & Science*. Thomson Reuters. Retrieved 2015-01-07.

[2] "American Economics Association: Journals Indexed".

[3] "EBSCO: Title Lists".

2.57.3 External links

- Official website

2.58 Review of Radical Political Economics

The Review of Radical Political Economics is a quarterly peer-reviewed academic journal published by Sage Publications on behalf of the Union for Radical Political Economics. It was established in 1968 and covers research on heterodox economics and political economy, broadly defined. According to the *Journal Citation Reports*, the journal has a 2011 impact factor of 0.377, ranking it 256th out of 321 journals in the category "Economics".[1]

2.58.1 References

[1] "Journals Ranked by Impact: Economics". *2011 Journal Citation Reports*. Web of Science (Social Sciences ed.). Thomson Reuters. 2013.

2.58.2 External links

- Official website
- Union for Radical Political Economics

2.59 Sharing economy

Sharing economy (also known as **shareconomy** or **collaborative consumption**) is a hybrid market model (in between owning and gift giving) which refers to peer-to-peer-based sharing of access to goods and services (coordinated through community-based online services).[1][2] The concept is not new. The sharing of resources is for example well known in business-to-business (B2B) like machinery in agriculture and forestry as well as in business-to-consumer (B2C) like self-service laundries. But three major drivers enable sharing of resources for a broad variety of new goods and services as well as new industries.[2] First, customer behaviour for many goods and services changes from owning to sharing. Second, online social networks and electronic markets more easily link consumers. And third, mobile devices and electronic services make the use of shared goods and services more convenient (e.g. smartphone app instead of physical key).

The sharing economy can take a variety of forms, including using information technology to provide individuals, corporations, non-profits and governments with information that enables the optimization of resources[3] through the redistribution, sharing and reuse of excess capacity in goods and services.[1][3][4] A common premise is that when information about goods is shared (typically via an online marketplace), the value of those goods may increase for the business, for individuals, for the community and for society in general.[5]

Collaborative consumption as a phenomenon is a class of economic arrangements in which participants share access to products or services, rather than having individual ownership.[1] The consumer peer-to-peer rental market is valued at $26bn (£15bn), with new services and platforms popping up all the time.[6]

The collaborative consumption model is used in online marketplaces such as eBay as well as emerging sectors such as social lending, peer-to-peer accommodation, peer-to-peer travel experiences,[7] peer-to-peer task assignments or travel advising, carsharing or commute-bus sharing.[8]

2.59.1 Definition

Definitions for the Sharing Economy come from different disciplines. Examples are economics, business administration, and law. A first major differentiation distinguishes a macro- and a micro-economic perspective. While the former focuses on market models, the latter investigates strategies, processes, and systems for companies and their interaction with consumers.[2]

- From a *macro-economic perspective*, the Sharing Economy follows a hybrid market model. Exchanging goods and services has predominantly been a domain of market-based models. These models focus on transferring ownership of economic resources between two parties. Depending on the involvement of money, either the traditional market model where two actors exchange the ownership of a good or service for money or gift giving, where a good is donated to another actor without any money involved in the transaction process, can be differentiated.

- From a *micro-economic perspective*, the Sharing Economy is part of the discussion in various disciplines. For example, marketing analyzes the relevance of brands that seem to become less relevant if consumers are able to access—for example—different cars from different vendors. This vendor perspective is part of research in business administration which identifies new strategies for the Sharing Economy for both incumbents and start-ups.

- An *integrated perspective* is discussed in the area of service science which is closely linked with the concept of service-orientation. In this context, service systems, (e.g., food, financial, mobility; see table below). An example as a part of service science is crowdsourcing.

2.59.2 Scope

The sharing economy[9] encompasses a wide range of structures including for-profit, non-profit, barter and co-operative structures.[10] The sharing economy provides expanded access to products, services and talent beyond one to one or singular ownership, sometimes referred to as "disownership".[11] Corporations, governments and individuals all actively participate as buyers, sellers, lenders or borrowers in these varied and evolving organizational structures.[12]

2.59.3 Examples

The phenomenon of the Sharing Economy may be recognized in many industries which reflects their macro-economic importance. The solutions differ from a micro-economic perspective regarding the providers and the interaction types.[2]

2.59.4 Types of collaborative consumption

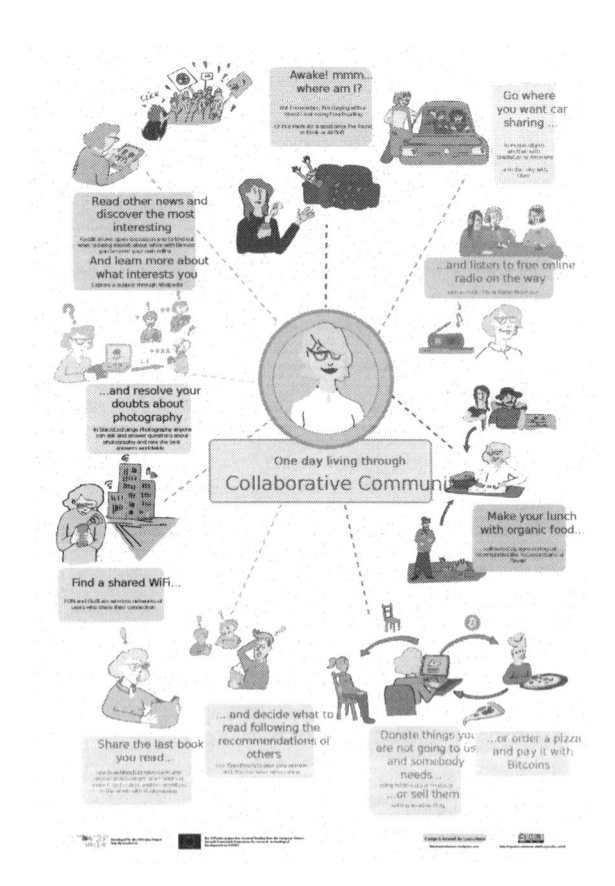

Examples of Commons-based peer production (CBPP) communities a.k.a. P2P communities

Product-service systems

Main article: Product-service system

Goods that are privately owned can be shared or rented out via peer-to-peer marketplaces.[13] (E.g. BMW's "Drive Now" is a car sharing service that offers an alternative to owning a car. Users can access a car when and where they need them and pay for their usage by the minute.[14])

Redistribution markets

A system of collaborative consumption is based on used or pre-owned goods being passed on from someone who does not want them to someone who does want them. This is another alternative to the more common 'reduce, reuse, recycle, repair' methods of dealing with waste. In some markets, the goods may be free, as on Freecycle and Kashless. In others, the goods are swapped (as on Swap.com) or sold for cash (as on eBay, craigslist, and uSell). There are a growing number of specialist marketplaces for preowned fashion items, including Copious, Vestiaire Collective, BuyMyWardrobe and Grand Circle. Additional forms of redistribution markets include ReHome (a free pet redistribution service by PetBridge.org).[13]

Collaborative lifestyles

This system is based on people with similar needs or interests banding together to share and exchange less-tangible assets such as time, space, skills, and money. An example would be Taskrabbit, which match users that need tasks done with "runners" who earn money by helping them complete their to-do lists. The growth of mobile technology provides a platform to enable location-based GPS technology and to also provide real-time sharing.[15]

2.59.5 History

The term "sharing economy" began to appear in the early 2000s, as new business structures emerged due to the Great Recession, enabling social technologies, and an increasing sense of urgency around global population growth and resource depletion. One inspiration was the tragedy of the commons, which refers to the idea that when we all act solely in our self-interest, we deplete the shared resources we need for our own quality of life. The Harvard law professor, Yochai Benkler, one of the earliest proponents of open source software, posited that network technology could mitigate this issue through what he called 'commons-based peer production', a concept first articulated in 2002.[16] Benkler then extended that analysis to "shareable goods" in *Sharing*

Nicely: On Shareable goods and the emergence of sharing as a modality of economic production.[17]

The term "collaborative consumption" was coined by Marcus Felson and Joe L. Spaeth in their paper "Community Structure and Collaborative Consumption: A routine activity approach" published in 1978 in the *American Behavioral Scientist*.[18] The term was used in more contemporary times by Ray Algar, a UK-based management consultant in an article entitled "Collaborative Consumption" in the *Leisure Report Journal* in 2007.[19]

In 2011, collaborative consumption was named one of TIME Magazine's 10 ideas that will change the world.[20]

The UK Government in its 2015 Budget set out objectives improve economic growth including to make Britain the "...best place in the world to start, invest in, and grow a business, including through a package of measures to help unlock the potential of the sharing economy..."[21]:4

In 2015, The Business of Sharing by Alex Stephany, CEO of JustPark, was published by Palgrave Macmillan.[22] The book features interviews with the high-profile entrepreneurs such as Martin Varsavsky and venture capitalists such as Fred Wilson.

Crowdfunding platforms

Main article: Crowdfunding

These models also use a two-sided marketplace to enable individuals to contribute funds to entrepreneurs, artists, civic programs and projects.[23]

Transparent and open data

Many state, local and federal governments[24] are engaged in Open Data initiatives and projects such as data.gov[25] and the London Data Store.[26] The theory of open or 'transparent' access to information enables greater innovation,[27] and makes for more efficient use of products and services, and thus supporting resilient communities.[28]

Trust

The Sharing Economy relies on the will of the users to share, but in order to make an exchange, users have to be trustworthy. Sharing economy organizations say they are committed to building and validating trusted relationships between members of their community, including producers, suppliers, customers or participants.[29]

Unused value is wasted value

Unused value refers to the time that products, services and talents lay idle. This idle time is wasted value that mesh models businesses and organizations utilize. The classic example is that the average car is unused 92% of the time.[30] This wasted value has created a significant opportunity for share economy car solutions. There is also significant unused value in "wasted time" as articulated by Clay Shirky in his analysis of power of "crowds" connected by information technology. Many of us have unused capacity in the course of our day. With social media and information technology, we can easily donate small slivers of time to take care of simple tasks others need doing. Examples of these crowd sourced solutions[31] include the for-profit Amazon Mechanical Turk and the non-profit Ushahidi.

Waste as food

Waste is commonly considered as something that is no longer wanted and needs to be discarded. The challenge with this point of view is that much of what we define as waste still has value that, with proper design and distribution, can safely serve as "nutrients" for follow-on processes, unlocking new levels of value in increasingly scarce and expensive resources. One example is "heirloom design"[32] as articulated by physicist and inventor Saul Griffith.[33]

2.59.6 Driving forces

The driving forces behind the rise of sharing economy organizations and businesses include:

1. Information Technology and Social Media: A host of enabling technologies has reached the mainstream, making it easy for networks of people and organizations to transact directly. These include open data,[34] the ubiquity and low-cost of mobile phones,[35] and social media.[36] These technologies dramatically reduce the friction of share-based business and organizational models.

2. Increasing Volatility in Cost of Natural Resources: Rising prosperity across the developing world coupled with population growth is putting greater strain on natural resources and has caused a spike in costs and market volatility. This has been increasing pressure on traditional manufactures to seek design, production and distribution alternatives that will stabilize costs and smooth projected expenditures. In this context, the circular economy approach has been gaining interest among many global corporate actors. While a handful of pioneering companies are leading the way, wider

adoption will rely on mesh economy skills such as the collection and sharing of data, the spread of best practices, and increased collaboration.[37]

3. Forbes estimates the revenue flowing through the shared economy will surpass $3.5 billion in 2013 with growth exceeding 25%.[38]

2.59.7 Benefits of a sharing economy

By sharing transportation and assets the benefits of a sharing economy are said to include the following:

- Reducing negative environmental impact (such as reducing the carbon footprint and consumption of resources)[39][40][41]
- Stronger communities[40]
- Saving costs by borrowing and recycling items[40]
- Providing people with access to goods who can't afford buying them[42] or have no interest in long-term usage
- Increased independence, flexibility and self-reliance by decentralization, the abolition of certain entry-barriers and self-organization[43]
- Increased participatory democracy[41]
- Accelerating sustainable consumption and production patterns in cities around the globe [44]

Researcher Christopher Koopman, an author of a study by George Mason University economists, said the sharing economy "allows people to take idle capital and turn them into revenue sources." He has stated, "People are taking spare bedroom[s], cars, tools they are not using and becoming their own entrepreneurs."[45] Arun Sundararajan, a New York University economist who studies the sharing economy, told a January congressional hearing that "this transition will have a positive impact on economic growth and welfare, by stimulating new consumption, by raising productivity, and by catalyzing individual innovation and entrepreneurship".[46]

2.59.8 Transport

Further information: Uber (company) and Lyft

Using a personal car to transport passengers or deliveries requires payment, or sufferance, of costs for fees deducted by the dispatching company, fuel, wear and tear, depreciation, interest, taxes, and adequate insurance. The driver is typically not paid for driving to an area where fares might be found in the volume necessary for high earnings, or driving to the location of a pickup or returning from a drop-off point.[47] Mobile apps have been written that help a driver be aware of and manage such costs has been introduced.[48]

2.59.9 Criticism and controversies

The *Harvard Business Review* argues that "sharing economy" is a misnomer, and that the correct word for this activity is "access economy." The authors say, "When "sharing" is market-mediated — when a company is an intermediary between consumers who don't know each other — it is no longer sharing at all. Rather, consumers are paying to access someone else's goods or services."[49] The article goes on to show that companies (such as Uber) who understand this, and whose marketing highlights the financial benefits to participants, are successful, while companies (such as Lyft) whose marketing highlights the social benefits of the service are less successful.

Salon writes that "the sharing economy ... [is] not the Internet 'gift economy' as originally conceived, a utopia in which we all benefit from our voluntary contributions. It's something quite different — the relentless co-optation of the gift economy by market capitalism. The sharing economy, as practiced by Silicon Valley, is a betrayal of the gift economy. The potlatch has been paved over, and replaced with a digital shopping mall."[50][51][52][53]

Andrew Leonard,[54][55][56] Evgeny Morozov,[57] Bernard Marszalek,[58] Dean Baker,[59][60] and Andrew Keen[61] criticized the for-profit sector of the sharing economy, writing that sharing economy businesses "extract" profits from their given sector by "successfully [making] an end run around the existing costs of doing business" - taxes, regulations, and insurance.

Susie Cagle wrote that the benefits big sharing economy players might be making for themselves are "not exactly" trickling down, and that the sharing economy "doesn't build trust" because where it builds new connections, it often "replicates old patterns of privileged access for some, and denial for others."[62] William Alden wrote that "The so-called sharing economy is supposed to offer a new kind of capitalism, one where regular folks, enabled by efficient online platforms, can turn their fallow assets into cash machines ... But the reality is that these markets also tend to attract a class of well-heeled professional operators, who outperform the amateurs — just like the rest of the economy."[63]

New York Magazine wrote that the sharing economy has succeeded in large part because the real economy has been struggling. Specifically, in the magazine's view, the sharing economy succeeds because of a depressed labor market, in which "lots of people are trying to fill holes in their income by monetizing their stuff and their labor in creative ways," and that in many cases, people join the sharing economy because they've recently lost a full-time job, including a few cases where the pricing structure of the sharing economy may have made their old jobs less profitable (e.g. full-time taxi drivers who may have switched to Lyft or Uber). The magazine writes that "In almost every case, what compels people to open up their homes and cars to complete strangers is money, not trust. ... Tools that help people trust in the kindness of strangers might be pushing hesitant sharing-economy participants over the threshold to adoption. But what's getting them to the threshold in the first place is a damaged economy, and harmful public policy that has forced millions of people to look to odd jobs for sustenance."[64][65][66]

Business Insider wrote that companies such as Airbnb and Uber do not share their reputation data with the very users who it belongs to. This is an issue since no matter how well you behave on any one platform, your reputation doesn't travel with you. This fragmentation has some negative consequences, such as the Airbnb squatters who had previously deceived Kickstarter users to the tune of $40,000.[67] Sharing data between these platforms could have prevented the repeat incident. Business Insider's view is that since the Sharing Economy is in its infancy, this has been accepted. However, as the industry matures, this will need to change.[68]

Giana Eckhardt and Fleura Bardhi say that the sharing economy promotes and prioritizes cheap fares and low costs rather than personal relationships, which is tied to similar issues in crowdsourcing. For example, Zipcar is advertised as a ride-sharing service, but it's been brought into consideration that the consumers reap similar benefits from Zipcar as they would from, say, a hotel. In this example, there is minimal social interaction going on and the primary concern is the low cost. Other examples many include myriad other sharing economies such as AirBnB or Uber. Because of this, the "sharing economy" may not be about sharing but rather about access. Giana Eckhardt and Fleura Bardhi say the "sharing" economy has taught people to prioritize cheap and easy access over interpersonal communication, and the value of going the extra mile for those interactions has diminished.[69]

The local economic benefit of the sharing economy is offset by its current form, which is that huge tech companies reap a great deal of the profit in many cases. For example, Uber, which is estimated to be worth $50B as of mid-2015,[70] takes up to 30% commission from the gross revenue of its drivers,[71] leaving many drivers making less than minimum wage.[72]

2.59.10 Organizations advocating and networking sharing economy

See also: Online platforms for collaborative consumption

- **OuiShare**:[73] An international non-for-profit aiming to connect efforts within the Sharing or Collaborative Economy to create a global network of collaborators.
- **Shareable**:[74] "Shareable is a nonprofit news, action and connection hub for the sharing transformation",[75] and the primary global online magazine on the Sharing Economy.
- **Echo (Economy of Hours)**:[76] A UK based non-profit providing infrastructure to, and lobbying at national level on behalf of, local time banking projects.[77][78]
- **European Sharing Economy Coalition**:[79] The Coalition is the first multi-stakeholder European network created to mature policies, markets and sectors in Europe for the Sharing Economy to become mainstream.
- **Shared Economy CPA**:[80] Shared Economy CPA is a U.S. based accounting firm that specializes in assisting the workers of the Sharing Economy. Located on their site is numerous free resources that assists those who are looking for tax guidance.
- **NASE**:[81] stands for The Norwegian Association for Sharing Economy", NASE supports all organisations working within the sharing economy.

2.59.11 Types of sharing

2.59.12 See also

- Access economy
- Co-creation
- Collaborative finance
- Collaborative innovation network
- Commons-based peer production
- Cooperative
- Creative Commons
- Digital Collaboration
- Internet of Things

- Internet of Services
- Open Knowledge Foundation
- Open Source
- P2P Foundation
- Peer-to-peer (meme)
- Recommerce
- Reputation capital
- Reputation systems
- Secondhand good
- Social collaboration
- Social commerce
- Social dining
- Social Peer-to-Peer Processes
- Two-sided market

2.59.13 Notes and references

[1] Hamari, Juho; Sjöklint, Mimmi; Ukkonen, Antti (2015). "The Sharing Economy: Why People Participate in Collaborative Consumption". *Journal of the Association for Information Science and Technology.* doi:10.1002/asi.23552.

[2] (Puschmann & Alt, 2016) Puschmann, T., Alt, R., Sharing Economy, in: Business & Information Systems Engineering, 58 (2016), 1, pp. 93-99

[3] Cohen, Boyd; Kietzmann, Jan (2014). "Ride On! Mobility Business Models for the Sharing Economy". *Organization & Environment 27 (3),279-296.* doi:10.1177/1086026614546199.

[4] Sundararajan, Arun. "From Zipcar to the Sharing Economy". *January 3, 2013.* Harvard Business Review. Retrieved 13 June 2013.

[5] Geron, Tomio (November 9, 2012). "Airbnb Had $56 Million Impact On San Francisco: Study". *Forbes.* Retrieved 13 June 2013.

[6] Botsman, Rachel; Roger, Roos (2011). *What's Mine Is Yours: How Collaborative Consumption is Changing the Way We Live.* HarperCollins Business. ISBN 0007395914.

[7] "From homes to meals to cars, 'sharing' has changed the face of travel". *chicagotribune.com.* Retrieved 2015-12-22.

[8] "Harvard Business School Club of New York - What's Mine Is Yours: The Rise of Collaborative Consumption". Hbscny.org. 2011-06-16. Retrieved 2015-03-13.

[9] Friedman, Thomas (20 July 2013). "Welcome to the Sharing Economy". *The New York Times.* Retrieved 25 July 2013.

[10] Rosenberg, Tina (5 June 2013). "It's Not Just Nice to Share, It's the Future". *The New York Times.*

[11] Wang, Ray. "Monday's Musings: Four Elements for A #SharingEconomy Biz Model In #MatrixCommerce". *May 26, 2013.* Software Insider. Retrieved 13 June 2013.

[12] "The Collaborative Economy". *June 4, 2013.* Altimeter Group. Retrieved 13 June 2013.

[13] Rachel BotsmanRoo Rogers (1922-01-01). "Beyond Zipcar: Collaborative Consumption". Hbr.org. Retrieved 2015-03-13.

[14] "DriveNow: BMW and Sixt Joint Venture for premium car sharing".

[15] Owyang, Jeremiah (24 February 2015). "The mobile technology stack for the Collaborative Economy". VentureBeat. Retrieved 24 February 2015.

[16] Benkler, Yochai (2002). "Coase's Penguin, or, Linux and The Nature of the Firm" (PDF). *The Yale Law Journal* **112**. Retrieved 13 June 2013.

[17] Benkler, Yochai (2004). "Sharing Nicely: On Shareable goods and the emergence of sharing as a modality of economic production". *The Yale Law Journal* **114**. Retrieved 9 July 2014.

[18] Felson, Marcus and Joe L. Spaeth (1978), "Community Structure and Collaborative Consumption: A routine activity approach," American Behavioral Scientist, 21 (March–April), 614–24.

[19] "Collaborative Consumption by Ray Algar — Oxygen Consulting". Oxygen-consulting.co.uk. Retrieved 2015-03-13.

[20] "10 Ideas That Will Change The World". *Time.* March 17, 2011.

[21] "Support for the sharing economy" (PDF). *H. M. Treasury, Budget 2015, section 1.193.*

[22] "Review: The Business Of Sharing". May 5, 2015.

[23] Karim R. Lakhani (1922-01-01). "Using the Crowd as an Innovation Partner". Hbr.org. Retrieved 2015-03-13.

[24] Mazmanian, Adam (May 22, 2013). "Can open data change the culture of government?". *Federal Computer Week.*

[25] "Data.gov". Data.gov. Retrieved 2015-03-13.

[26] "London Datastore". Data.london.gov.uk. Retrieved 2015-03-13.

[27] Hammell, Richard. "Open Data: Driving Growth, Ingenuity and Innovation" (PDF). Deloitte Consulting. Retrieved 13 June 2013.

[28] Brindley, William. "How Open Data can Save Lives". World Economic Forum. Retrieved 13 June 2013.

[29] Charles, Green (May 2, 2012). "Trusted and Being Trusted in the Sharing Economy". *Forbes*. Retrieved 13 June 2013.

[30] "Car Sharing and Pooling: Reducing Car Over-Population and Collaborative Consumption | Energy Seminar". Energyseminar.stanford.edu. 2012-04-09. Retrieved 2015-03-13.

[31] Boudreau, Kevin; Karim R. Lakhani. "Using the Crowd as an Innovation Partner". *April 2013*. Harvard Business Review.

[32] Bloyd-Peshkin, Sharon (October 21, 2009). "Built to Trash". *In These Times*. Retrieved 13 June 2013.

[33] Griffith, Saul. "Everyday Inventions". TED. Retrieved 13 June 2013.

[34] "Open Data Handbook". *2011, 2012*. Open Knowledge Foundation. Retrieved 13 June 2013.

[35] "ICT Facts and Figures, 2013" (PDF). *2013*. International Telecommunications Union. Retrieved 13 June 2013.

[36] Parr, Ben (August 3, 2009). "What the F**k is Social Media?". *Mashable*. Retrieved 13 June 2013.

[37] Preston, Felix. "A Global Redesign? Shaping the Circular Economy" (PDF). *March, 2012*. Chatham House. Retrieved 13 June 2013.

[38] Geron, Tobio (January 23, 2013). "Airbnb and the Unstoppable Rise of the Share Economy". *Forbes*. Retrieved 13 June 2013.

[39] Brady, Diane (24 September 2014). "The Environmental Case for the Sharing Economy". Bloomberg. Retrieved 10 July 2015.

[40] Rudenko, Anna (16 August 2013). "The collaborative consumption on the rise: why shared economy is winning over the "capitalism of me"". Retrieved 10 July 2015.

[41] Parsons, Adam (5 March 2014). "The sharing economy: a short introduction to its political evolution". *opendemocracy.net*. Retrieved 10 July 2015.

[42] Bradshaw, Della (22 April 2015). "Sharing economy benefits lower income groups". *FT.com*. Retrieved 10 July 2015.

[43] Williams-Grut, Oscar (20 March 2015). "Silicon Round-up: Blockchain banking to be on the slate for new regulator?". London Evening Standard. Retrieved 10 July 2015.

[44] Cohen, Boyd; Muñoz, Pablo (2015). "Sharing cities and sustainable consumption and production: towards an integrated framework". *Journal of Cleaner Production*. doi:10.1016/j.jclepro.2015.07.133.

[45] Afp (2015-02-03). "'Sharing economy' reshapes markets, as complaints rise | Daily Mail Online". London: Dailymail.co.uk. Retrieved 2015-03-13.

[46] "Uber Said to Seek $1.5 Billion in Funds at $50 Billion Valuation". Bloomberb Business. 2015-05-19. Retrieved 2015-07-09.

[47] Emily Guendelsberger (May 7, 2015). "I was an undercover Uber driver". *Philadelphia Citypaper*. Retrieved May 10, 2015.

[48] Natasha Singer and Mike Isaac (May 9, 2015). "An App That Helps Drivers Earn the Most From Their Trips". *The New York Times*. Retrieved May 10, 2015. At first I thought I was earning money

[49] "The Sharing Economy Isn't About Sharing at All". Harvard Business Review. 2015-01-28. Retrieved 2015-07-11.

[50] Andrew Leonard, "Sharing economy" shams: Deception at the core of the Internet's hottest businesses, *Salon.com*, 2014.03.14

[51] Andrew Leonard, You're not fooling us, Uber! 8 reasons why the "sharing economy" is all about corporate greed, *Salon.com*, 2014.02.17

[52] Tom Slee, The secret libertarianism of Uber & Airbnb, *Salon.com*, 2014.01.28

[53] Anya Kamenetz, AirBnb wins New York court victory, but the city still present challenges for the popular room-finding site, *Fast Company* and *Salon*, 2013.09.30

[54] Millennials will not be regulated, Andrew Leonard, *Salon.com*, 2013.09.20

[55] The sharing economy muscles up, Andrew Leonard, *Salon.com*, 2013.09.17

[56] Libertarians' anti-government crusade: Now there's an app for that (2014-06-27), Andrew Leonard, *Salon*

[57] Evgeny Morozov. Don't believe the hype, the 'sharing economy' masks a failing economy (September 2014), *The Guardian (UK)*

[58] The New Boss – You – Just Like the Old Boss: The Sharing Economy = Brand Yourself (2014.05.26), BERNARD MARSZALEK, *CounterPunch*

[59] How AirBnB and Uber Cab are Facilitating Rip-Offs: The Downside of the Sharing Economy (2014.05.28), Dean Baker, *CounterPunch*

[60] How Uber Distrupts the Taxi Market (2015.02.12), Dean Baker, *CounterPunch*

[61] The Internet is not the Answer, an interview with Andrew Keen at the *Digital Life Design (DLD)* 2015 Annual Conference. Posted on the official You Tube Channel of *DLD*

[62] The Case Against Sharing: On access, scarcity, and trust (2014-05-28), Susie Cagle, *Medium.com*

[63] The Business Tycoons of Airbnb, *The New York Times*

[64] Kevin Roose, The Sharing Economy Isn't About Trust, It's About Desperation (2014-04-24), *New York Magazine*

[65] Kevin Roose, Does Silicon Valley Have a Contract-Worker Problem? (2014-09-18), *New York Magazine*

[66] A Secret of Uber's Success: Struggling Workers (2014-10-02), *Bloomberg.com*

[67] Kevin Montgomery, Airbnb Squatters Also Swindled $40,000 From Kickstarter, 2014-07-28

[68] Patrick J. Stewart, Reputation And The Sharing Economy (2014-10-23), "Business Insider

[69] Giana Eckhardt and Fleura Bardhi, The Sharing Economy isn't About Sharing at All (2015-02-09), *Harvard Business Review*

[70] Afp (2015-02-03). "'Sharing economy' reshapes markets, as complaints rise | Daily Mail Online". Dailymail.co.uk. Retrieved 2015-03-13.

[71] Huet, Ellen (2015-05-18). "Uber Tests Taking Even More From Its Drivers With 30% Commission". Forbes. Retrieved 2015-07-09.

[72] "A Philadelphia journalist went undercover as an Uber driver — here's how much she made". MSN. 2015-05-09. Retrieved 2015-07-09.

[73] "Connecting the Collaborative Economy". OuiShare.net. 2013-11 21. Retrieved 2015-03-13.

[74] "Shareable". Shareable.net. Retrieved 2015-03-13.

[75] "About". Shareable.net. Retrieved 2015-03-13.

[76] "Banking Time". Economyofhours.com. 2014-06-20. Retrieved 2015-03-13.

[77] "Our Vision". Economyofhours.com. 2014-06-20. Retrieved 2015-03-13.

[78] "About us". Economyofhours.com. 2014-06-20. Retrieved 2015-03-13.

[79] "European Sharing Economy Coalition". *Euro Freelancers*. 17 March 2013.

[80] "Shared Economy CPA". sharedeconomycpa.com. Retrieved 2015-12-06.

[81] "The Norwegian Association for Sharing Economy". Nase.no. 2016-01-13. Retrieved 2016-01-13.

2.59.14 Further reading

- A Policy Agenda for the Sharing Economy, The Urbanist, October 2012

- Kostakis, V., and Bauwens, M. (2014) Network Society and Future Scenarios for a Collaborative Economy. Basingstoke, UK: Palgrave Macmillan.

- All Eyes on the Sharing Economy, The Economist, March 9, 2013

- The Twilight of the Sharing Economy—or the Dawn?, The Atlantic, May 7, 2013

- The End of Ownership, Boston Magazine, May 2013

- Leonard, Andrew (January 2012). "The Economy of Sharing". *Sunset Magazine*.

- Nanos, Janelle (May 2013). "The End of Ownership". *Boston Magazine*.

- The Sharing Economy: Embracing Change with Caution, Swedish Entrepreneurship Forum, June 2015

- Adapting to the Sharing Economy, MIT Sloan Management Review, 56(2), 2015, S. 71-77.

- Doddle CEO: the value of empty space. *Written by Tim Robinson (CEO of Doddle), Hot Topics, 2015*

2.60 Social credit

This article is about the philosophy, economic theory and history of social credit. For political parties, see Social Credit Party (disambiguation).
For the proposed Chinese social rating system, see Social Credit System.

Social credit is an interdisciplinary distributive philosophy developed by C. H. Douglas (1879–1952), a British engineer, who published a book by that name during 1924. It encompasses economics, political science, history, and accounting. Its policies are designed, according to Douglas, to disperse economic and political power to individuals. Douglas wrote, "Systems were made for men, and not men for systems, and the interest of man which is self-development, is above all systems, whether theological, political or economic."[1] Douglas said that Social Crediters want to build a new civilization based upon "absolute economic security" for the individual, where "they shall sit every man under his vine and under his fig tree; and none shall make them afraid."[2][3] In his words, "what we really demand of existence is not that we shall be put into somebody else's Utopia, but we shall be put in a position to construct a Utopia of our own."[4]

It was while he was reorganising the work at Farnborough, during World War I, that Douglas noticed that the weekly total costs of goods produced was greater than the sums paid to individuals for wages, salaries and dividends. This seemed to contradict the theory of classic Ricardian economics, that all costs are distributed simultaneously as purchasing power. Troubled by the seeming difference between the way money flowed and the objectives of industry ("delivery of goods and services", in his opinion), Douglas decided to apply engineering methods to the economic system.

Douglas collected data from more than a hundred large British businesses and found that in nearly every case, except that of companies becoming bankrupt, the sums paid out in salaries, wages and dividends were always less than the total costs of goods and services produced each week: consumers did not have enough income to buy back what they had made. He published his observations and conclusions in an article in the magazine *The English Review*, where he suggested: "That we are living under a system of accountancy which renders the delivery of the nation's goods and services to itself a technical impossibility."[5] He later formalized this observation in his A+B theorem. Douglas proposed to eliminate this difference between total prices and total incomes by augmenting consumers' purchasing power through a National Dividend and a Compensated Price Mechanism.

According to Douglas, the true purpose of production is consumption, and production must serve the genuine, freely expressed interests of consumers. In order to accomplish this objective, he believed that each citizen should have a beneficial, not direct, inheritance in the communal capital conferred by complete access to consumer goods assured by the National Dividend and Compensated Price.[6] Douglas thought that consumers, fully provided with adequate purchasing power, will establish the policy of production through exercise of their monetary vote.[6] In this view, the term economic democracy does not mean worker control of industry, but democratic control of credit.[6] Removing the policy of production from banking institutions, government, and industry, Social Credit envisages an "aristocracy of producers, serving and accredited by a democracy of consumers."[6]

The policy proposals of social credit attracted widespread interest in the decades between the world wars of the twentieth century because of their relevance to economic conditions of the time. Douglas called attention to the excess of production capacity over consumer purchasing power, an observation that was also made by John Maynard Keynes in his book, *The General Theory of Employment, Interest and Money*.[7] While Douglas shared some of Keynes' criticisms of classical economics, his unique remedies were disputed and even rejected by most economists and bankers of the time. Remnants of Social Credit still exist within social credit parties throughout the world, but not in the purest form originally advanced by Major C. H. Douglas.

2.60.1 Economic theory

Factors of production and value

Douglas disagreed with classical economists who recognised only three factors of production: land, labour and capital. While Douglas did not deny the role of these factors in production, he considered the "cultural inheritance of society" as the primary factor. He defined cultural inheritance as the knowledge, techniques and processes that have accrued to us incrementally from the origins of civilization (i.e. progress). Consequently, mankind does not have to keep "reinventing the wheel". "We are merely the administrators of that cultural inheritance, and to that extent the cultural inheritance is the property of all of us, without exception.[8] Adam Smith, David Ricardo and Karl Marx claimed that labour creates all value. While Douglas did not deny that all costs ultimately relate to labour charges of some sort (past or present), he denied that the present labour of the world creates all wealth. Douglas carefully distinguished between value, costs and prices. He claimed that one of the factors resulting in a misdirection of thought in terms of the nature and function of money was economists' near-obsession about values and their relation to prices and incomes.[9] While Douglas recognized "value in use" as a legitimate theory of values, he also considered values as subjective and not capable of being measured in an objective manner. Thus he rejected the idea of the role of money as a standard, or measure, of value. Douglas believed that money should act as a medium of communication by which consumers direct the distribution of production.

Economic sabotage

Closely associated with the concept of cultural inheritance as a factor of production is the social credit theory of economic sabotage. While Douglas believed the cultural heritage factor of production is primary in increasing wealth, he also believed that economic sabotage is the primary factor decreasing it. The word wealth derives from the Old English word *wela*, or "well-being", and Douglas believed that all production should increase personal well-being. Therefore, production that does not directly increase personal well-being is waste, or economic sabotage.

> The economic effect of charging all the waste in industry to the consumer so curtails his purchasing power that an increasing percentage of the product of industry must be exported. The effect of this on the worker is that he has to do many times the amount of work which should be necessary to keep him in the highest standard of living, as a result of an artificial inducement to

produce things he does not want, which he cannot buy, and which are of no use to the attainment of his internal standard of well-being.[10]

By modern methods of accounting, the consumer is forced to pay for all the costs of production, including waste. The economic effect of charging the consumer with all waste in industry is that the consumer is forced to do much more work than is necessary. Douglas believed that wasted effort could be directly linked to confusion in regards to the purpose of the economic system, and the belief that the economic system exists to provide employment in order to distribute goods and services.

> But it may be advisable to glance at some of the proximate causes operating to reduce the return for effort ; and to realise the origin of most of the specific instances, it must be borne in mind that the existing economic system distributes goods and services through the same agency which induces goods and services, i.e., payment for work in progress. In other words, if production stops, distribution stops, and, as a consequence, a clear incentive exists to produce useless or superfluous articles in order that useful commodities already existing may be distributed. This perfectly simple reason is the explanation of the increasing necessity of what has come to be called economic sabotage ; the colossal waste of effort which goes on in every walk of life quite unobserved by the majority of people because they are so familiar with it ; a waste which yet so over-taxed the ingenuity of society to extend it that the climax of war only occurred in the moment when a culminating exhibition of organised sabotage was necessary to preserve the system from spontaneous combustion.[11]

Purpose of an economy

Douglas claimed there were three possible policy alternatives with respect to the economic system:

> 1. The first of these is that it is a disguised Government, of which the primary, though admittedly not the only, object is to impose upon the world a system of thought and action.
> 2. The second alternative has a certain similarity to the first, but is simpler. It assumes that the primary objective of the industrial system is the provision of employment.
> 3. And the third, which is essentially simpler still, in fact, so simple that it appears entirely unintelligible to the majority, is that the object of the industrial system is merely to provide goods and services.[12]

Douglas believed that it was the third policy alternative upon which an economic system should be based, but confusion of thought has allowed the industrial system to be governed by the first two objectives. If the purpose of our economic system is to deliver the maximum amount of goods and services with the least amount of effort, then the ability to deliver goods and services with the least amount of employment is actually desirable. Douglas proposed that unemployment is a logical consequence of machines replacing labour in the productive process, and any attempt to reverse this process through policies designed to attain full employment directly sabotages our cultural inheritance. Douglas also believed that the people displaced from the industrial system through the process of mechanization should still have the ability to consume the fruits of the system, because he suggested that we are all inheritors of the cultural inheritance, and his proposal for a national dividend is directly related to this belief.

The creditary nature of money

Douglas criticized classical economics because many of the theories are based upon a barter economy, whereas the modern economy is a monetary one. Initially, money originated from the productive system, when cattle owners punched leather discs which represented a head of cattle. These discs could then be exchanged for corn, and the corn producers could then exchange the disc for a head of cattle at a later date. The word "pecuniary"[13] comes from the Latin *pecunia*, originally and literally meaning "cattle" (related to *pecus*, meaning "beast").[14] Today, the productive system and the monetary system are two separate entities. Douglas demonstrated that loans create deposits, and presented mathematical proof in his book *Social Credit*.[15] Bank credit comprises the vast majority of money, and is created every time a bank makes a loan.[16] Douglas was also one of the first to understand the creditary nature of money. The word credit derives from the Latin *credere*, meaning "to believe". "The essential quality of money, therefore, is that a man shall believe that he can get what he wants by the aid of it."[17]

According to economists, money is a medium of exchange. Douglas argued that this may have once been the case when the majority of wealth was produced by individuals who subsequently exchanged it with each other. But in modern economies, division of labour splits production into multiple processes, and wealth is produced by people working in association with each other. For instance, an automobile worker does not produce any wealth (i.e., the automobile) by himself, but only in conjunction with other auto workers, the producers of roads, gasoline, insurance, etc.

In this opinion, wealth is a pool upon which people can draw, and money becomes a ticketing system. The efficiency gained by individuals cooperating in the productive process was named by Douglas as the "unearned increment of association" – historic accumulations of which constitute what Douglas called the cultural heritage. The means of drawing upon this pool is money distributed by the banking system.

Douglas believed that money should not be regarded as a commodity but rather as a ticket, a means of distribution of production.[18] "There are two sides to this question of a ticket representing something that we can call, if we like, a value. There is the ticket itself – the money which forms the thing we call 'effective demand' – and there is something we call a price opposite to it."[18] Money is effective demand, and the means of reclaiming that money are prices and taxes. As real capital replaces labour in the process of modernization, money should become increasingly an instrument of distribution. The idea that money is a medium of exchange is related to the belief that all wealth is created by the current labour of the world, and Douglas clearly rejected this belief, stating that the cultural inheritance of society is the primary factor in the creation of wealth, which makes money a distribution mechanism, not a medium of exchange.

Douglas also claimed the problem of production, or scarcity, had long been solved. The new problem was one of distribution. However; so long as orthodox economics makes scarcity a value, banks will continue to believe that they are creating value for the money they produce by making it scarce.[19] Douglas criticized the banking system on two counts:

1. for being a form of government which has been centralizing its power for centuries, and

2. for claiming ownership of the money they create.

The former Douglas identified as being anti-social in policy.[20] The latter he claimed was equivalent to claiming ownership of the nation.[21] According to Douglas, money is merely an abstract representation of the real credit of the community, which is the ability of the community to deliver goods and services, when and where they are required.

2.60.2 The A + B theorem

During January 1919, *A Mechanical View of Economics* by C.H. Douglas was the first article to be published in the magazine *New Age*, edited by Alfred Richard Orage, critiquing the methods by which economic activity is typically measured:

It is not the purpose of this short article to depreciate the services of accountants; in fact, under the existing conditions probably no body of men has done more to crystallise the data on which we carry on the business of the world; but the utter confusion of thought which has undoubtedly arisen from the calm assumption of the book-keeper and the accountant that he and he alone was in a position to assign positive or negative values to the quantities represented by his figures is one of the outstanding curiosities of the industrial system; and the attempt to mould the activities of a great empire on such a basis is surely the final condemnation of an out-worn method.

During 1920, Douglas presented the A + B theorem in his book, *Credit-Power and Democracy*, in critique of accounting methodology pertinent to income and prices. In the fourth, Australian Edition of 1933, Douglas states:

A factory or other productive organization has, besides its economic function as a producer of goods, a financial aspect – it may be regarded on the one hand as a device for the distribution of purchasing-power to individuals through the media of wages, salaries, and dividends; and on the other hand as a manufactory of prices – financial values. From this standpoint, its payments may be divided into two groups:

Group A: *All payments made to individuals (wages, salaries, and dividends).*

Group B: *All payments made to other organizations (raw materials, bank charges, and other external costs).*

Now the rate of flow of purchasing-power to individuals is represented by A, but since all payments go into prices, the rate of flow of prices cannot be less than A+B. The product of any factory may be considered as something which the public ought to be able to buy, although in many cases it is an intermediate product of no use to individuals but only to a subsequent manufacture; but since A will not purchase A+B; a proportion of the product at least equivalent to B must be distributed by a form of purchasing-power which is not comprised in the description grouped under A. It will be necessary at a later stage to show that this additional purchasing power is provided by loan credit (bank overdrafts) or export credit.[6]

Beyond empirical evidence, Douglas claims this deductive theorem demonstrates that total prices increase faster than total incomes when regarded as a flow.

In his pamphlet entitled "The New and the Old Economics", Douglas describes the cause of "B" payments:

> I think that a little consideration will make it clear that in this sense an overhead charge is any charge in respect of which the actual distributed purchasing power does not still exist, and that practically this means any charge created at a further distance in the past than the period of cyclic rate of circulation of money. There is no fundamental difference between tools and intermediate products, and the latter may therefore be included.[22]

During 1932, Douglas estimated the cyclic rate of circulation of money to be approximately three weeks. The cyclic rate of circulation of money measures the amount of time required for a loan to pass through the productive system and return to the bank. This can be calculated by determining the amount of clearings through the bank in a year divided by the average amount of deposits held at the banks (which varies very little). The result is the number of times money must turnover in order to produce these clearing house figures. In a testimony before the Alberta Agricultural Committee of the Alberta Legislature in 1934, Douglas said:

> Now we know there are an increasing number of charges which originated from a period much anterior to three weeks, and included in those charges, as a matter of fact, are most of the charges made in, respect of purchases from one organization to another, but all such charges as capital charges (for instance, on a railway which was constructed a year, two years, three years, five or ten years ago, where charges are still extant), cannot be liquidated by a stream of purchasing power which does not increase in volume and which has a period of three weeks. The consequence is, you have a piling up of debt, you have in many cases a diminution of purchasing power being equivalent to the price of the goods for sale.[23]

According to Douglas, the major consequence of the problem he identified in his A+B theorem is exponentially increasing debt. Further, he believed that society is forced to produce goods that consumers either do not want or cannot afford to purchase. The latter represents a favorable balance of trade, meaning a country exports more than it imports. But not every country can pursue this objective at the same time, as one country must import more than it exports when another country exports more than it imports. Douglas proposed that the long-term consequence of this policy is a trade war, typically resulting in real war – hence, the social credit admonition, "He who calls for Full-Employment calls for War!", expressed by the Social Credit Party of Great Britain and Northern Ireland, led by John Hargrave. The former represents excessive capital production and/or military build-up. Military buildup necessitates either the violent use of weapons or a superfluous accumulation of them. Douglas believed that excessive capital production is only a temporary correction, because the cost of the capital appears in the cost of consumer goods, or taxes, which will further exacerbate future gaps between income and prices.

> In the first place, these capital goods have to be sold to someone. They form a reservoir of forced exports. They must, as intermediate products, enter somehow into the price of subsequent ultimate products and they produce a position of most unstable equilibrium, since the life of capital goods is in general longer than that of consumable goods, or ultimate products, and yet in order to meet the requirements for money to buy the consumable goods, the rate of production of capital goods must be continuously increased.[24]

The A + B theorem and a cost accounting view of inflation

The replacement of labour by capital in the productive process implies that overhead charges (B) increase in relation to income (A), because "'B' is the financial representation of the lever of capital".[6] As Douglas stated in his first article, "The Delusion of Superproduction":[25]

> The factory cost – not the selling price – of any article under our present industrial and financial system is made up of three main divisions- direct labor cost, material cost and overhead charges, the ratio of which varies widely, with the "modernity" of the method of production. For instance, a sculptor producing a work of art with the aid of simple tools and a block of marble has next to no overhead charges, but a very low rate of production, while a modern screw-making plant using automatic machines may have very high overhead charges and very low direct labour cost, or high rates of production.
>
> Since increased industrial output per individual depends mainly on tools and method, it may almost be stated as a law that intensified production means a progressively higher ratio of overhead charges to direct labour cost, and, apart

from artificial reasons, this is simply an indication of the extent to which machinery replaces manual labour, as it should.

If overhead charges are constantly increasing relative to income, any attempt to stabilize or increase income results in increasing prices. If income is constant or increasing, and overhead charges are continuously increasing due to technological advancement, then prices, which equal income plus overhead charges, must also increase. Further, any attempt to stabilize or decrease prices must be met by decreasing incomes according to this analysis. As the Phillips Curve demonstrates, inflation and unemployment are trade-offs, unless prices are reduced from monies derived from outside the productive system. According to Douglas's A+B theorem, the systemic problem of increasing prices, or inflation, is not "too much money chasing too few goods", but is the increasing rate of overhead charges in production due to the replacement of labour by capital in industry combined with a policy of full employment. Douglas did not suggest that inflation cannot be caused by too much money chasing too few consumer goods, but according to his analysis this is not the only cause of inflation, and inflation is systemic according to the rules of cost accountancy given overhead charges are constantly increasing relative to income. In other words, inflation can exist even if consumers have insufficient purchasing power to buy back all of production. Douglas claimed that there were two limits which governed prices, a lower limit governed by the cost of production, and an upper limit governed by what an article will fetch on the open market. Douglas suggested that this is the reason why deflation is regarded as a problem in orthodox economics because bankers and businessmen were very apt to forget the lower limit of prices.

Compensated price and national dividend

Douglas proposed to eliminate the gap between purchasing power and prices by increasing consumer purchasing power with credits which do not appear in prices in the form of a price rebate and a dividend. Formally called a "Compensated Price" and a "National (or Consumer) Dividend", a National Credit Office would be charged with the task of calculating the size of the rebate and dividend by determining a national balance sheet, and calculating aggregate production and consumption statistics.

The price rebate is based upon the observation that the real cost of production is the mean rate of consumption over the mean rate of production for an equivalent period of time.

$$\text{(production) cost real} = M \cdot \frac{\int_{T_1}^{T_2} \frac{dC}{dt} \, dt}{\int_{T_1}^{T_2} \frac{dP}{dt} \, dt}$$

where

- M = money distributed for a given programme of production,
- C = consumption,
- P = production.

The physical cost of producing something is the materials and capital that were consumed in its production, plus that amount of consumer goods labour consumed during its production. This total consumption represents the physical, or real, cost of production.

$$\text{price true}(\$) = \text{cost}(\$) \cdot \frac{\text{consumption}(\$) + \text{depreciation}(\$)}{\text{credit}(\$) + \text{production}(\$)}$$

where

- Consumption = cost of consumer goods,
- Depreciation = depreciation of real capital,
- Credit = Credit Created,
- Production = cost of total production

Since fewer inputs are consumed to produce a unit of output with every improvement in process, the real cost of production falls over time. As a result, prices should also decrease with the progression of time. "As society's capacity to deliver goods and services is increased by the use of plant and still more by scientific progress, and decreased by the production, maintenance, or depreciation of it, we can issue credit, in costs, at a greater rate than the rate at which we take it back through prices of ultimate products, if capacity to supply individuals exceeds desire."[6]

Based on his conclusion that the real cost of production is less than the financial cost of production, the Douglas price rebate (Compensated Price) is determined by the ratio of consumption to production. Since consumption over a period of time is typically less than production over the same period of time in any industrial society, the real cost of goods should be less than the financial cost.

For example, if the money cost of a good is $100, and the ratio of consumption to production is 3/4, then the real cost of the good is $100(3/4) = $75. As a result, if a consumer spent $100 for a good, the National Credit Authority would rebate the consumer $25. The good costs the consumer $75, the retailer receives $100, and the consumer receives the difference of $25 via new credits created by the National Credit Authority.

The National Dividend is justified by the displacement of labour in the productive process due to technological increases in productivity. As human labour is increasingly replaced by machines in the productive process, Douglas believed people should be free to consume while enjoying increasing amounts of leisure, and that the Dividend would provide this freedom.

Critics of the A + B theorem and rebuttal

Critics of the theorem, such as J.M. Pullen, Hawtrey and J.M Keynes argue there is no difference between A and B payments. Other critics, such as Gary North, argue that social credit policies are inflationary. "The A + B theorem has met with almost universal rejection from academic economists on the grounds that, although B payments may be made initially to "other organizations," they will not necessarily be lost to the flow of available purchasing power. A and B payments overlap through time. Even if the B payments are received and spent before the finished product is available for purchase, current purchasing power will be boosted by B payments received in the current production of goods that will be available for purchase in the future."[26]

A.W. Joseph replied to this specific criticism in a paper given to the Birmingham Actuarial Society, "Banking and Industry":

> Let A1+B1 be the costs in a period to time of articles produced by factories making consumable goods divided up into A1 costs which refer to money paid to individuals by means of salaries, wages, dividends, etc., and B1 costs which refer to money paid to other institutions. Let A2, B2 be the corresponding costs of factories producing capital equipment. The money distributed to individuals is A1+A2 and the cost of the final consumable goods is A1+B1. If money in the hands of the public is to be equal to the costs of consumable articles produced then A1+A2 = A1+B1 and therefore A2=B1. Now modern science has brought us to the stage where machines are more and more taking the place of human labour in producing goods, i.e. A1 is becoming less important relatively to B1 and A2 less important relatively to B2.
>
> In symbols if B1/A1 = k1 and B2/A2 = k2 both k1 and k2 are increasing.
>
> Since A2=B1 this means that (A2+B2)/(A1+B1)= (1+k2)*A2/(1+1/k1)*B1 = (1+k2)/(1+1/k1) which is increasing.

> Thus in order that the economic system should keep working it is essential that capital goods should be produced in ever increasing quantity relatively to consumable goods. As soon as the ratio of capital goods to consumable goods slackens, costs exceed money distributed, i.e. the consumer is unable to purchase the consumable goods coming on the market."

And in a reply to Dr. Hobson, Douglas restated his central thesis: "To reiterate categorically, the theorem criticised by Mr. Hobson: the wages, salaries and dividends distributed during a given period do not, and cannot, buy the production of that period; that production can only be bought, i.e., distributed, under present conditions by a draft, and an increasing draft, on the purchasing power distributed in respect of future production, and this latter is mainly and increasingly derived from financial credit created by the banks." [27]

Incomes are paid to workers during a multi-stage program of production. According to the convention of accepted orthodox rules of accountancy, those incomes are part of the financial cost and price of the final product. For the product to be purchased with incomes earned in respect of its manufacture, all of these incomes would have to be saved until the product's completion. Douglas argued that incomes are typically spent on past production to meet the present needs of living, and will not be available to purchase goods completed in the future – goods which must include the sum of incomes paid out during their period of manufacture in their price. Consequently, this does not liquidate the financial cost of production inasmuch as it merely passes charges of one accountancy period on as mounting charges against future periods. In other words, according to Douglas, supply does not create enough demand to liquidate all the costs of production. Douglas denied the validity of Say's Law in economics.

While John Maynard Keynes referred to Douglas as a "private, perhaps, but not a major in the brave army of heretics",[28] he did state that Douglas "is entitled to claim, as against some of his orthodox adversaries, that he at least has not been wholly oblivious of the outstanding problem of our economic system."[28] While Keynes said that Douglas's A+B theorem "includes much mere mystification", he reaches a similar conclusion to Douglas when he states:

> Thus the problem of providing that new capital-investment shall always outrun capital-disinvestment sufficiently to fill the gap between net income and consumption, presents a problem which is increasingly difficult as capital increases. New capital-investment can only take place in excess of current capital-disinvestment if future expenditure on consumption is expected

to increase. Each time we secure to-day's equilibrium by increased investment we are aggravating the difficulty of securing equilibrium to-morrow.

[28]

The criticism that social credit policies are inflationary is based upon what economists call the quantity theory of money, which states that the quantity of money multiplied by its velocity of circulation equals total purchasing power. Douglas was quite critical of this theory stating, "The velocity of the circulation of money in the ordinary sense of the phrase, is – if I may put it that way – a complete myth. No additional purchasing power at all is created by the velocity of the circulation of money. The rate of transfer from hand-to-hand, as you might say, of goods is increased, of course, by the rate of spending, but no more costs can be canceled by one unit of purchasing power than one unit of cost. Every time a unit of purchasing power passes through the costing system it creates a cost, and when it comes back again to the same costing system by the buying and transfer of the unit of production to the consuming system it may be cancelled, but that process is quite irrespective of what is called the velocity of money, so the categorical answer is that I do not take any account of the velocity of money in that sense."[29] The Alberta Social Credit government published in a committee report what was perceived as an error in regards to this theory: "The fallacy in the theory lies in the incorrect assumption that money 'circulates', whereas it is issued against production, and withdrawn as purchasing power as the goods are bought for consumption."[30]

Other critics argue that if the gap between income and prices exists as Douglas claimed, the economy would have collapsed in short order. They also argue that there are periods of time in which purchasing power is in excess of the price of consumer goods for sale.

Douglas replied to these criticisms in his testimony before the Alberta Agricultural Committee:

> What people who say that forget is that we were piling up debt at that time at the rate of ten millions sterling a day and if it can be shown, and it can be shown, that we are increasing debt continuously by normal operation of the banking system and the financial system at the present time, then that is proof that we are not distributing purchasing power sufficient to buy the goods for sale at that time; otherwise we should not be increasing debt, and that is the situation.[23]

2.60.3 Political theory

C.H. Douglas defined democracy as the "will of the people", not rule by the majority,[31] suggesting that social credit could be implemented by any political party supported by effective public demand. Once implemented to achieve a realistic integration of means and ends, party politics would cease to exist. Traditional ballot box democracy is incompatible with Social Credit, which assumes the right of individuals to choose freely one choice at a time, and to contract out of unsatisfactory associations. Douglas advocated what he called the "responsible vote", where anonymity in the voting process would no longer exist. "The individual voter must be made individually responsible, not collectively taxable, for his vote."[32] Douglas believed that party politics should be replaced by a "union of electors" in which the only role of an elected official would be to implement the popular will.[33] Douglas believed that the implementation of such a system was necessary as otherwise the government would be controlled by international financiers. Douglas also opposed the secret ballot arguing that it resulted in electoral irresponsibility, calling it a "Jewish" technique used to ensure Barabbas was freed leaving Christ to be crucified.[33]

Douglas considered the constitution an organism, not an organization.[32] In this opinion, establishing the supremacy of common law is essential to ensure protection of individual rights from an all-powerful parliament. Douglas also believed the effectiveness of British government is determined structurally by application of a Christian concept known as Trinitarianism: "In some form or other, sovereignty in the British Isles for the last two thousand years has been Trinitarian. Whether we look on this Trinitarianism under the names of King, Lords and Commons or as Policy, Sanctions and Administration, the Trinity-in-Unity has existed, and our national success has been greatest when the balance (never perfect) has been approached."[32]

Opposing the formation of Social Credit parties, C.H. Douglas believed a group of elected amateurs should never direct a group of competent experts in technical matters.[34] While experts are ultimately responsible for achieving results, the goal of politicians should be to pressure those experts to deliver policy results desired by the populace. According to Douglas, "the proper function of Parliament is to force all activities of a public nature to be carried on so that the individuals who comprise the public may derive the maximum benefit from them. Once the idea is grasped, the criminal absurdity of the party system becomes evident."[35]

2.60.4 History

C.H. Douglas was a civil engineer who pursued his higher education at Cambridge University. His early writings ap-

2.60. SOCIAL CREDIT

C. H. Douglas, founder of the "social credit" economic theory, in Edmonton, Alberta, Canada.

peared most notably in the British intellectual journal *The New Age*. The editor of that publication, Alfred Orage, devoted the magazines *The New Age* and later *The New English Weekly* to the promulgation of Douglas's ideas until his death on the eve of his BBC speech on social credit, 5 November 1934, in the *Poverty in Plenty* Series.

Douglas's first book, *Economic Democracy*, was published during 1920, soon after his article *The Delusion of Super-Production*[25] was published during 1918 in the *English Review*. Among Douglas's other early works were *The Control and Distribution of Production, Credit-Power and Democracy, Warning Democracy* and *The Monopoly of Credit*. Of considerable interest is the evidence he presented to the Canadian House of Commons Select Committee on Banking and Commerce[36] during 1923, to the British Parliamentary Macmillan Committee on Finance and Industry in 1930, which included exchanges with economist John Maynard Keynes, and to the Agricultural Committee of the Alberta Legislature in 1934 during the term of the United Farmers of Alberta Government in that Canadian province.

The writings of C.H. Douglas spawned a worldwide movement, most prominent in the British Commonwealth, with a presence in Europe and activities in the United States where Orage, during his sojourn there, promoted Douglas's ideas. In the United States, the New Democracy group was directed by the American author Gorham Munson who contributed a major book on social credit titled *Aladdin's Lamp: The Wealth of the American People*. While Canada and New Zealand had electoral successes with "social credit" political parties, the efforts in England and Australia were devoted primarily to pressuring existing parties to implement social credit. This function was performed especially by Douglas's social credit secretariat in England and the Commonwealth Leagues of Rights in Australia. Douglas continued writing and contributing to the secretariat's journals, initially *Social Credit* and soon thereafter *The Social Crediter* (which continues to be published by the Secretariat) for the remainder of his lifetime, concentrating more on political and philosophical issues during his later years.

Political history

During early years of the philosophy, Labour Party management resisted pressure from Trade unionists to implement social credit, as hierarchical opinions of Fabian socialism, economic growth and full employment, were incompatible with the National Dividend and abolishment of wage slavery suggested by Douglas. In an effort to discredit the social credit movement, one major Fabian, Sidney Webb, is said to have declared that he didn't care whether Douglas was technically correct or not – they simply did not like his policy.[37]

During 1935 the first "Social Credit" government was elected in Alberta, Canada directed by William Aberhart. A book by Maurice Colbourne entitled *The Meaning of Social Credit* convinced Aberhart that the theories of C.H. Douglas were essential for Alberta's recovery from the Great Depression. Aberhart added a heavy dose of fundamentalist Christianity to Douglas' theories; the Canadian social credit movement, which was largely nurtured in Alberta, thus acquired a strong social conservative influence that it retains to this day.

Having counselled the previous United Farmers of Alberta provincial government, Douglas became an advisor to Aberhart, but withdrew soon afterward due to strategic differences. Aberhart sought orthodox counsel with respect to the Province's finances, and the correspondence between them was published by Douglas in his book, *The Alberta Experiment*.[38]

While the Premier wanted to balance the provincial budget, Douglas argued the whole concept of a "balanced budget" was inconsistent with Social Credit principles. Douglas stated that, by existing rules of financial cost accountancy, balancing all budgets within an economy simultaneously is an arithmetic impossibility.[39] In a letter to Aberhart, Douglas stated:[39]

> This seems to be a suitable occasion on which to emphasise the proposition that a Balanced Budget is quite inconsistent with the use of Social Credit (i.e., Real Credit – the ability to deliver goods and services 'as, when and where required') in the modern world, and is simply a statement in accounting figures that the progress of the country is stationary, i.e., that it consumes exactly what it produces, including capital assets. The result of the acceptance of this proposition is that all capital appreciation becomes quite automatically the property of those who create and issue of money [i.e., the banking system] and the necessary unbalancing of the Budget is covered by Debts.

Douglas sent two other expert social credit technical advisors from the United Kingdom, L. Denis Byrne and George F. Powell. But all attempts to pass social credit legislation were ruled ultra vires by the Supreme Court of Canada and Privy Council in London. Based on the monetary theories of Silvio Gesell, William Aberhart issued a currency substitute known as prosperity certificates. But these scrips intentionally depreciated in value the longer they were held,[40] and Douglas openly criticized the idea:

> Gesell's theory was that the trouble with the world was that people saved money so that what you had to do was to make them spend it faster. Disappearing money is the heaviest form of continuous taxation ever devised. The theory behind this idea of Gesell's was that what is required is to stimulate trade – that you have to get people frantically buying goods – a perfectly sound idea so long as the objective of life is merely trading.[41]

Managed by Ernest Manning, who succeeded Aberhart after his untimely death, the Alberta Social Credit Party gradually changed from its origins and became popularly identified as a right wing populist party. In the Secretariat's journal, *An Act for the Better Management of the Credit of Alberta*,[42] Douglas published a critical analysis of the Social Credit policies of Alberta,[43][44] in which he said, "The Manning administration is no more a Social Credit administration than the British government is Labour". Manning accused Douglas and his followers of antisemitism, and went about purging all of the so-called "Douglasites" from the Party. The British Columbia Social Credit Party won power during 1952 in the province to Alberta's west, but had little in common with Douglas or his theories.

Social credit parties also enjoyed some national electoral success in Canada. The Social Credit Party of Canada was initiated with help from Western Canadians, and eventually created another base of approval in Quebec. Social Credit also did well at the nationally in New Zealand, where it was the country's third party for almost 30 years.

2.60.5 Philosophy

Douglas described Social Credit as "the policy of a philosophy", and warned against considering it solely as a scheme for monetary reform.[45] He called this philosophy "practical Christianity" and stated that its central issue is the Incarnation. Douglas believed that there was a Canon which permeated the universe, and Jesus Christ was the Incarnation of this Canon. However, he also believed that Christianity remained ineffective so long as it remained transcendental. Religion, which derives from the Latin word *religare* (to "bind back"), was intended to be a binding back to reality.[46] Social Credit is concerned with the incarnation of Christian principles in our organic affairs. Specifically, it is concerned with the principles of association and how to maximize the increments of association which redound to satisfaction of the individual in society – while minimizing any decrements of association.[47] The goal of Social Credit is to maximize immanent sovereignty. Social credit is consonant with the Christian doctrine of salvation through unearned grace, and is therefore incompatible with any variant of the doctrine of salvation through works. Works need not be of Purity in intent or of desirable consequence and in themselves alone are as "filthy rags". For instance, the present system makes destructive, obscenely wasteful wars a virtual certainty – which provides much "work" for everyone. Social credit has been called the Third Alternative to the futile Left-Right Duality.[48]

Although Douglas defined social credit as a philosophy with Christian origins, he did not envision a Christian theocracy. Douglas did not believe that religion should be mandated by law or external compulsion. Practical Christian society is Trinitarian in structure, based upon a constitution where the constitution is an organism changing in relation to our knowledge of the nature of the universe.[32] "The progress of human society is best measured by the extent of its creative ability. Imbued with a number of natural gifts, notably reason, memory, understanding and free will, man has learned gradually to master the secrets of nature, and to build for himself a world wherein lie the potentialities of peace, security, liberty and abundance."[49] Douglas said that social crediters want to build a new civilization based upon absolute economic security for the individual – where "they shall sit every man under his vine and under his fig tree; and none shall make them afraid."[2][3] In keeping with this goal, Douglas was opposed to all forms of taxation on real property. This set social credit at variance from the land-taxing recommendations of Henry George.[50]

Social credit society recognizes the fact that the relationship between man and God is unique.[51] In this view, it is essential to allow man the greatest possible freedom in order to pursue this relationship. Douglas defined freedom as the ability to choose and refuse one choice at a time, and to contract out of unsatisfactory associations. Douglas believed that if people were given the economic security and leisure achievable in the context of a social credit dispensation, most would end their service to Mammon and use their free time to pursue spiritual, intellectual or cultural goals resulting in self-development.[52] Douglas opposed what he termed "the pyramid of power". Totalitarianism represents this pyramid and is the antithesis of social credit. It turns the government into an end instead of a means, and the individual into a means instead of an end – *Demon est deus inversus* – "the Devil is God upside down." Social credit is designed to give the individual the maximum freedom allowable given the need for association in economic, political and social matters.[53] Social Credit elevates the importance of the individual and holds that all institutions exist to serve the individual – that the State exists to serve its citizens, not that individuals exist to serve the State.[54]

Douglas emphasized that all policy derives from its respective philosophy and that "Society is primarily metaphysical, and must have regard to the organic relationships of its prototype."[55] Social credit rejects dialectical materialistic philosophy.[55] "The tendency to argue from the particular to the general is a special case of the sequence from materialism to collectivism. If the universe is reduced to molecules, ultimately we can dispense with a catalogue and a dictionary; all things are the same thing, and all words are just sounds – molecules in motion."[56]

Douglas divided philosophy into two schools of thought that he termed the "classical school" and the "modern school", which are broadly represented by philosophies of Aristotle and Francis Bacon respectively. Douglas was critical of both schools of thought, but believed that "the truth lies in appreciation of the fact that neither conception is useful without the other".[57]

Criticism for antisemitism

Social crediters and Douglas have been criticized for spreading antisemitism. Douglas was critical of "international Jewry", especially in his later writings. He asserted that such Jews controlled many of the major banks and were involved in an international conspiracy to centralize the power of finance. Some people have claimed that Douglas was antisemitic because he was quite critical of pre-Christian philosophy. In his book entitled *Social Credit*, he wrote that, "It is not too much to say that one of the root ideas through which Christianity comes into conflict with the conceptions of the Old Testament and the ideals of the pre-Christians' era is in respect of this dethronement of abstractionism."[58]

Douglas was opposed to abstractionist philosophies, because he believed that these philosophies inevitably resulted in the elevation of abstractions, such as the state, and legal fictions, such as corporate personhood, over the individual. He also believed that what Jews considered as abstractionist thought tended to encourage them to endorse communist ideals and an emphasis on collectives over individuals. John L. Finlay, in his book, *Social Credit: The English Origins*, wrote, "Anti-Semitism of the Douglas kind, if it can be called anti-Semitism at all, may be fantastic, may be dangerous even, in that it may be twisted into a dreadful form, but it is not itself vicious nor evil."[59]

In her book, *Social Discredit: Anti-Semitism, Social Credit and the Jewish Response*, Janine Stingel claims that "Douglas' economic and political doctrines were wholly dependent on an anti-Semitic conspiracy theory."[60] John L. Finlay disagrees with Stingel's assertion and argues that, "It must also be noted that while Douglas was critical of some aspects of Jewish thought, Douglas did not seek to discriminate against Jews as a people or race. It was never suggested that the National Dividend be withheld from them."[59]

2.60.6 Groups influenced by social credit

Australia

- Australian League of Rights
- Douglas Credit Party
- Bleeding in Debt' website, *Social Credit*

Canada

Federal political parties:

- Social Credit Party of Canada/Canadian social credit movement
- *Ralliement créditiste*
- Abolitionist Party of Canada/Christian Credit Party
- Canadian Action Party (active)

- Global Party of Canada

Provincial political parties:

- Alberta Social Credit Party (active)
- British Columbia Social Credit Party
- Manitoba Social Credit Party
- Social Credit Party of Ontario
- Ralliement créditiste du Québec
- Social Credit Party of Saskatchewan

Organizations:

- Pilgrims of Saint Michael
- Committee on Monetary and Economic Reform
- *See also:* Prosperity Certificate

Ireland

- Monetary Reform Party

New Zealand

- Country Party
- Democratic Labour Party
- New Zealand Democratic Party for Social Credit (active)
- New Democratic Party (New Zealand)
- Real Democracy Movement
- Social Credit Party (New Zealand)
- New Zealand Social Credit Association (Inc)

Solomon Islands

- Solomon Islands Social Credit Party (active)

United Kingdom

- Douglas Social Credit Secretariat
- Social Credit Party of Great Britain and Northern Ireland

2.60.7 Literary figures in social credit

As lack of finance has been a constant impediment to the development of the arts and literature, the concept of economic democracy through Social Credit had immediate appeal in literary circles. Names associated with Social Credit include C.M. Grieve, Charlie Chaplin, William Carlos Williams, Ezra Pound, T. S. Eliot, Herbert Read, Aldous Huxley, Storm Jameson, Eimar O'Duffy, Sybil Thorndyke, Bonamy Dobrée, Eric de Maré and the American publisher James Laughlin. Hilaire Belloc and GK Chesterton espoused similar ideas. In 1933 Eimar O'Duffy published *Asses in Clover*, a science fiction fantasy exploration of Social Credit themes. His Social Credit economics book *Life and Money: Being a Critical Examination of the Principles and Practice of Orthodox Economics with A Practical Scheme to End the Muddle it has made of our Civilisation*, was endorsed by Douglas.

Robert A. Heinlein described a Social Credit economy in his posthumously-published first novel, *For Us, The Living: A Comedy of Customs*, and his *Beyond This Horizon* describes a similar system in less detail. In Heinlein's future society, government is not funded by taxation. Instead, government controls the currency and prevents inflation by providing a price rebate to participating business and a guaranteed income to every citizen.

In his novel *The Trick Top Hat*, part of his *Schrödinger's Cat Trilogy*, Robert Anton Wilson described the implementation by the President of an alternate future United States of an altered form of Social Credit, in which the government issues a National Dividend to all citizens in the form of "trade aids," which can be spent like money but which cannot be lent at interest (in order to mollify the banking industry) and which eventually expire (to prevent inflation and hoarding).

More recently, Richard C. Cook, an analyst for the U.S. Civil Service Commission, Food and Drug Administration, NASA, the U.S. Treasury Department, and author of the books *Challenger Revealed* and *We Hold These Truths*, has written several articles relating to Social Credit and monetary reform at Global Research, an independent research and media group of writers, scholars, journalists and activists. Frances Hutchinson, Chairperson of the Social Credit Secretariat, has co-authored, with Brian Burkitt, a book entitled *The Political Economy of Social Credit and Guild Socialism*.[61]

2.60.8 See also

- Basic income
- Citizen's dividend

2.60. SOCIAL CREDIT

- Monetary reform
- Social dividend

2.60.9 Notes

[1] Douglas, C.H. (1974). *Economic Democracy* (Fifth Authorised ed.). Epsom, Surrey, England: Bloomfield Books. p. 18. ISBN 0-904656-06-3. Retrieved 12 11 2008. Check date values in: |access-date= (help)

[2] Douglas, C.H. (1954). "Cover". *The Douglas Quarterly Review*. The Fig Tree, New Series **1** (June) (Belfast, Northern Ireland: K.R.P. Publications, published 1954–55). Cover.

[3] Micah 4:4

[4] Douglas, C.H. (1933). "Major C.H. Douglas Speaks". Sydney: Douglas Social Credit Association: 41.

[5] "The Delusion of Super-Production", C.H. Douglas, *English Review*, December 1918.

[6] Douglas, C.H. (1933). *Credit-Power and Democracy*. Melbourne, Australia: The Social Credit Press. pp. 4, 108. Retrieved 12 11 2008. Check date values in: |access-date= (help)

[7] Keynes, John M. (1936). *The General Theory of Employment, Interest and Money*. London, England: MacMillan & Co Ltd. pp. 32, 98–100, 370–371. ISBN 1-56000 149 6.

[8] Douglas, C.H. (22 January 1934). "The Monopolistic Idea" address at Melbourne Town Hall, Australia. The Australian League of Rights: Melbourne. Retrieved 28 February 2008.

[9] Douglas, C.H. (1973). *Social Credit* (PDF). New York: Gordon Press. p. 60. ISBN 0-9501126-1-5.

[10] Douglas, C.H. (1919). "A Mechanical View of Economics" (PDF). *The New Age*. 1373 **XXIV** (9) (38 Cursitor Street, London: The New Age Press). p. 136. Retrieved 2008-03-14.

[11] Douglas, C.H. (1974). *Economic Democracy, Fifth Authorised Edition*. Epsom, Surrey, England: Bloomfield Books. p. 74. ISBN 0-904656-06-3. Retrieved 12-11-2008. Check date values in: |access-date= (help)

[12] Douglas, C.H. (1935 web). *Warning Democracy* (PDF). Australian League of Rights. Retrieved 2008-12-18. Check date values in: |date= (help)

[13] billcasselman.com

[14] Pollock, Fredrick (1996). "The History of English Law Before the Time of Edward I". Lawbook Exchange Ltd: 151.

[15] C.H. Douglas. "The Working of the Money System". *Social Credit*. Mondo Politico. Retrieved 2008-02-27.

[16] "The Bank in Brief: Canada's Money Supply" (PDF). Bank of Canada. Retrieved 2008-02-28.

[17] Douglas, C.H. (22 April 1927). "Engineering, Money and Prices" (PDF). Institution of Mechanical Engineers: Warning Democracy: 15. Retrieved 2008-02-28.

[18] Douglas, C.H. (13 February 1934). "" address at St. James' Theatre, Christchurch, New Zealand. The Australian League of Rights: Melbourne. Retrieved 28 February 2008.

[19] Douglas, C.H. (1973). *Social Credit*. New York: Gordon Press. p. 47. ISBN 0-9501126-1-5.

[20] C.H. Douglas. "FIRST INTERIM REPORT ON THE POSSIBILITIES OF THE APPLICATION OF SOCIAL CREDIT PRINCIPLES TO THE PROVINCE OF ALBERTA" (PDF). Social Credit Secretariat. Retrieved 2008-12-18.

[21] Douglas, C.H. (24 November 1936). "" address at Ulster Hall, Belfast. The Australian: Melbourne. Retrieved 28 February 2008.

[22] Douglas, C.H. *The New and the Old Economics* (PDF). Sydney, n.d.: Tidal Publications.

[23] Douglas, C.H. (1934). "The Douglas System of Social Credit: Evidence taken by the Agricultural Committee of the Alberta Legislature, Session 1934". Edmonton: Legislative Assembly of Alberta: 90.

[24] Douglas, C.H. (1925). "A + B AND THE BANKERS" (PDF). *The New Age* (38 Cursitor Street, London: The New Age Press). Retrieved 2010-08-08.

[25] C.H. Douglas (December 1918). "The Delusion of Superproduction" (PDF). *The Delusion of Superproduction*. The English Review. Retrieved 2008-12-11.

[26] Pullen, J. M.; G. O. Smith (1997). "Major Douglas and Social Credit: A Reappraisal". Duke University Press. p. 219.

[27] Douglas, C.H. (1922). *The Douglas Theory; a reply to Mr. J.A. Hobson*. London: Cecil Palmer. p. 5.

[28] Keynes, John M. (1936). *The General Theory of Employment, Interest and Money*. London, England: MacMillan & Co Ltd. ISBN 1-56000-149-6.

[29] Douglas, C.H. (1933). "The Birmingham Debate" (PDF). *The New Age*. Vol. LII, No. 23.

[30] "The Alberta Post-War Reconstruction Committee Report of the Subcommittee on Finance". *Simple Text*. Archived from the original on 2009-10-26. Retrieved 2008-03-01.

[31] C.H. Douglas. "The Nature of Democracy" (PDF). Australian League of Rights. Retrieved 2008-04-13.

[32] C.H. Douglas. (PDF). Australian League of Rights http://www.alor.org/Library/Douglas%20CH%20-%20Realistic%20Constitutionalism.pdf. Retrieved 2008-02-28. Missing or empty |title= (help)

[33] Stingel, Janine (2000-02-24). "Social Discredit: Anti-Semitism, Social Credit, and the Jewish Response". ISBN 9780773520103.

[34] Douglas, C.H. (7 March 1936). "" address at Westminster. Australian League of Rights: Melbourne. Retrieved 28 February 2008.

[35] Douglas, C.H. (30 October 1936). "" address at Central Hall, Liverpool. Australian League of Rights: Melbourne. Retrieved on 2008–02-28.

[36] "Select Committee on Banking and Commerce" (PDF). 1923. Retrieved 2008-12-11.

[37] Lee, Jeremy (July 1972). "C.H. Douglas The Man and the Vision" (PDF). Australian League of Rights. p. 6.

[38] Douglas, C.H. (1937). *The Alberta Experiment* (PDF). London: Eyre and Spottiswoode.

[39] Douglas, C.H. (28 July 1932). "The Fallacy of a Balanced Budget". *The New English Weekly*. pp. 346–7.

[40] Glenbow Museum. "Prosperity Certificate". Glenbow Museum. Retrieved 2008-02-27.

[41] C.H. Douglas. "The Approach to Reality" (PDF). The Australian League of Rights. Retrieved 2008-02-27.

[42] Douglas, C.H. (1947). "An Act for the Better Management of the Credit of Alberta". *The Social Crediter* **17** (23) (Liverpool: K.R.P. Publications Ltd., published 8 February 1947).

[43] Douglas, C.H. (1947). "Social Credit in Alberta". *The Social Crediter* **20** (26) (Liverpool: K.R.P. Publications Ltd., published 28 August 1947).

[44] Douglas, C.H. (1947). "Social Credit in Alberta". *The Social Crediter* **21** (1,2) (Liverpool: K.R.P. Publications Ltd., published 4–11 September 1947).

[45] C.H. Douglas. "The Policy of a Philosophy". Australian League of Rights. Archived from the original on 2007-09-04. Retrieved 2008-03-01.

[46] C.H. Douglas. *Brief for the Prosecution*. Veritas Publishing Co. Pty, Ltd. ISBN 0-949667-80-3.

[47] E. S. Holter (1978). *The ABC of Social Credit*. Vancouver: Institute of Economic Democracy, Sixth Printing, Dec.1978. ISBN 0-920392-24-5.

[48] Munson, Gorham (1945). *Aladdin's Lamp: The Wealth of the American People*. New York: Creative Age Press.

[49] *Alberta Post-War Reconstruction Committee Report of the Subcommittee on Finance*. 1945.

[50] Douglas, C.H. (1943). *The Land for the (Chosen) People Racket*. London: KRP Publications Ltd.

[51] Monahan, Bryan (1971). *Why I am a Social Crediter* (PDF). Sydney: Tidal Publications. p. 3. ISBN 0-85855-001-6.

[52] "The Use of Social Credit".

[53] Monahan, Bryan (1971). *Why I am a Social Crediter* (PDF). Tidal Publications. p. 7. ISBN 0-85855-001-6.

[54] Douglas, C.H. (1920). *Economic Democracy*. Melbourne: Heritage for Institute of Economic Democracy. p. 33. ISBN 0-904656-00-4.

[55] C.H. Douglas letter to L.D. Byrne, 28 March 1940

[56] C.H. Douglas. "Brief for the Prosectution". Retrieved 2009-03-29.

[57] C.H. Douglas. "Static and Dynamic Sociology". *Social Credit*. Mondo Politico. Retrieved 2008-03-01.

[58] Douglas, C.H. (1973). *Social Credit* (PDF). New York: Gordon Press. p. 22. ISBN 0-9501126-1-5.

[59] Finlay, John L (1972). *Social Credit: The English Origins*. Montreal: McGill-Queens University Press. p. 105. ISBN 978-0-7735-0111-9. Archived from the original on 2009-10-26.

[60] Stingel, Janine (2000). *Social Discredit: Anti-Semitism, Social Credit and the Jewish Response*. Montreal: McGill-Queen's University Press. p. 13. ISBN 0-7735-2010-4. line feed character in |title= at position 41 (help)

[61] Hutchinson, Frances (1997). *Political Economy of Social Credit and Guild Socialism*. UK: Routledge. ISBN 978-0-415-14709-5.

2.60.10 Further reading

- *Economic Democracy*, by C. H. Douglas (1920) new edition: December 1974; Bloomfield Books; ISBN 0-904656-06-3

- *Major Douglas: The Policy of Philosophy*, by John W. Hughes, Edmonton, Brightest Pebble Publishing Company, 2004; first published in Great Britain by Wedderspoon Associates, 2002

- *Major Douglas and Alberta Social Credit*, by Bob Hesketh, ISBN 0-8020-4148-5

Fiction and poetry

- *For Us, The Living: A Comedy of Customs*, by Robert A. Heinlein

- *Beyond This Horizon*, by Robert A. Heinlein

- *The Cantos*, by Ezra Pound

2.60.11 External links

- C.H. Douglas's book *Economic Democracy* at American Libraries
- C.H. Douglas's book *Credit-Power and Democracy* at American Libraries
- C.H. Douglas's book *The Control and Distribution of Production* at American Libraries
- C.H. Douglas's book "The Monopoly of Credit"
- C.H. Douglas's work "The Douglas Theory, A Reply to Mr. J.A. Hobson" at American Libraries
- C.H. Douglas's work, "These Present Discontents" at American Libraries
- Clifford Hugh Douglas' book, *Social Credit*
- Hilderic Cousens, "A New Policy for Labour; an essay on the relevance of credit control" at American Libraries
- Bryan Monahan, "Introduction to Social Credit"
- M. Gordon-Cumming, "Money in Industry"
- DouglasSocialCredit.com – Social Credit Secretariat
- Australian League of Rights – online library
- The Green Shirt Movement for Social Credit
- Social Credit School of Studies
- Social Credit Website
- Clifford Hugh Douglas Institute

2.61 Social dividend

This article is about the social dividend as a component of socialism. For the Georgist concept, see Citizen's dividend.

The **social dividend** is the return on the capital assets and natural resources owned by society in a socialist economy. It refers to the distribution of the property income generated by publicly-owned enterprises in the form of a dividend payment to each citizen, most notably appearing as a component in proposed models of market socialism.[1] A social dividend constitutes the individual's share of the capital and resources owned by society. A related concept is a Basic income guarantee, which is differentiated from a social dividend in that a basic income does not necessarily imply social ownership.[2]

The social dividend is a key feature in many models of market socialism that are characterized by publicly-owned enterprises operating to maximize profit within the context of a market economy. In such a system, the social dividend would grant every citizen a share of the property income generated by publicly-owned assets and natural resources, which would be received in addition to any labor income (wages or salaries) earned through employment.[3] A social dividend would eliminate the need for the social welfare and income redistribution programs, as well as eliminating their administrative costs, that exist in capitalist economies. Models of market socialism featuring social dividend schemes differ from cooperative variants of market socialism. In cooperative variants, the profits of each firm would be distributed among the members/employees of each individual firm as opposed to the public at large.[4]

The social dividend concept has not yet been applied on any large scale in any national economy. In both the former Soviet-type economies and Western mixed economies, the net earnings of state enterprises are considered a source of public revenue and are spent directly by the government to finance various public goods and services.[5]

2.61.1 Origins of the concept

As a precursor to the social divided concept, Léon Walras, one of the founders of neoclassical economics who helped formulate the general equilibrium theory, argued that free competition could only be realized under conditions of state ownership of natural resources and land. Walras argued that nationalized land and natural resources would provide a source of income to the state that would eliminate the need for income taxes.[6]

For Karl Marx, property income is a component of surplus value, which refers to the net value above the total wage bill. The surplus value is distributed among a small minority of passive owners, or capitalists. The capitalists appropriate the product of social labor by holding ownership titles to the means of production. In Marx's view, socialism implied an end to this class dynamic - the surplus value would be appropriated by the working class as a whole. However, even though Marx was opposed to the distribution of property income under capitalism, this was not the instrumentality of capitalist collapse nor was it the primary reason for the desirability of the abrogation of capitalism. In Marx's view, capitalism was not to be opposed due to any supposedly moral defect in its distribution, but because its underlying dynamic of capital accumulation and surplus value appropriation was unstable and ultimately unsustainable.[7]

The neoclassical socialist economist Oskar Lange is credited with the first use of the phrase "social dividend". In Lange's model of socialism, the social dividend referred to the accumulation of profit and rent by publicly-owned enterprises minus investment.[8]

2.61.2 Contemporary proposals

Notable economists and political scientists that have included social dividend system in their models of socialism include Oskar Lange, Abba Lerner, James Meade, James Yunker, John Roemer, Pranab Bardhan and David Schweickart.[2]

The American economist James Yunker outlined a model of socialism, dubbed *Pragmatic market socialism*, that featured a social dividend payment. Yunker's model of socialism is almost identical to present-day capitalism, with enterprises organized as corporations with similar management structures, the major difference being a public entity would own their shares. The difference between capitalism and this form of market socialism involves the distribution of property income: the property return generated by these corporations goes to the population as a whole instead of an owning minority.[9]

In John Roemer's and Pranab Bardhan's model of market socialism, public ownership takes the form of public ownership of shares in publicly-listed firms. The dividend payments, instead of accruing to a small class of private owners, are divided equally among all adult citizens. The social dividend supplements wages and income derived from personal savings.[10]

The economist James Meade advocated a social dividend as a form of basic income to be funded out of the return on publicly owned productive assets.

In *Beyond the Profits System: Possibilities for the Post-Capitalist Era*, economist Harry Shutt advocates a basic income system to replace all existing state social security and welfare functions with the exception of childcare. This measure would be financed by the public and cooperative ownership of enterprises, and goes alongside the end of capital accumulation as the driving force in the economy. Taken together, these measures would constitute a post-capitalist economy.[11]

There are many institutional forms a social dividend can take. Generally, they are regarded as being universally distributed without constraint, even to unemployed individuals. However, the exact institutional arrangement varies among different proposals, for example, there might be certain constraints on the receipt of the dividend payment imposed on the unemployed.[12]

2.61.3 In practice

Systems similar to a social dividend have been implemented to some degree on the basis of public ownership of natural resources, most notably in Alaska (Alaska Permanent Fund) and in Norway (The Government Pension Fund of Norway).

2.61.4 Related concepts

Social dividends have an alternate definition which may be described as the citizen's egalitarian share of surplus tax revenue. This form of social dividend exists within the framework of capitalism since productive assets would be privately owned, operated for private profits and would not directly finance the social dividend.

2.61.5 See also

- Basic income
- Citizen's Dividend
- Global resources dividend
- Lange model
- Public enterprise
- Profit (economics)
- Property income
- Social ownership
- Socialism
- Sovereign wealth fund
- Market socialism
- Negative income tax

2.61.6 References

[1] *The Social Dividend Under Market Socialism*, by Yunker, James. 1977. Annals of Public and Cooperative Economics, Vol. 48, No. 1, pp. 93-133: "The term 'social dividend' was introduced in 1936 by Oskar Lange in his milestone essay 'On the Economic Theory of Socialism'. It refers to the direct distribution equally among the citizen body of property income accruing to the state-owned enterprises under socialism."

[2] *Social Dividend versus Basic Income Guarantee in Market Socialism*, by Marangos, John. 2004. International Journal of Political Economy, vol. 34, no. 3, Fall 2004.

[3] *Philosophy and the Problems of Work: A Reader*, 2001, by Kory Schaff. ISBN 978-0742507951. (P.344): "A citizen in this society will receive income from three sources: wage income, which will vary depending on her skill and the amount of time she works, income forthcoming by savings, which will also vary across households, and the social dividend, that will be, in principle, approximately equal across households."

[4] *Social Dividend versus Basic Income Guarantee in Market Socialism*, by Marangos, John. 2004. International Journal of Political Economy, vol. 34, no. 3, Fall 2004: "It is argued that market socialism is the only rational form of socialism, and that market socialism with labor-managed firms is by far the best form of market socialism (Jossa and Cuomo 1997: xiv). This is something quite different from the theoretical models of market socialism debated and quite different from command economies (Schweickart 1993: 90). The market socialist model proposed in this paper differs from the preceding models in that it does away with the J. E. Roemer–P. K. Bardhan–J. A. Yunker social dividend-coupon economy and substitutes it with a basic income guarantee."

[5] *The Social Dividend Under Market Socialism*, by Yunker, James. 1977. Annals of Public and Cooperative Economics, Vol. 48, No. 1, pp. 93-133: "The social dividend concept has not yet been applied in any important real-world context. Both in Communist and non-Communist countries, the net earnings of state firms are considered a source of public revenue and are spent directly by the government on various public goods and services."

[6] Bockman, Johanna (2011). *Markets in the name of Socialism: The Left-Wing origins of Neoliberalism*. Stanford University Press. p. 21. ISBN 978-0-8047-7566-3. For Walras, socialism would provide the necessary institutions for free competition and social justice. Socialism, in Walras's view, entailed state ownership of land and natural resources and the abolition of income taxes. As owner of land and natural resources, the state could then lease these resources to many individuals and groups, which would eliminate monopolies and thus enable free competition. The leasing of land and natural resources would also provide enough state revenue to make income taxes unnecessary, allowing a worker to invest his savings and become 'an owner or capitalist at the same time that he remains a worker.

[7] *The Social Dividend Under Market Socialism*, by Yunker, James. 1977. Annals of Public and Cooperative Economics, Vol. 48, No. 1, pp. 93-133: "It is abundantly clear from the writings of the founder of scientific socialism, Karl Marx, that he viewed the distribution of property income under capitalism as morally reprehensible. To Marx, property return must be identified with 'surplus labor value', namely the excess of total labor value over the total wage bill under conditions of a subsistence individual wage. This surplus value is distributed over a small minority of owning capitalists. Although the value is created by labor and is therefore the legitimate property of labor, the capitalists are able to extort it from the proletariat by virtue of their ownership of the capital instruments of production...Nevertheless, while Marx employed the surplus labor value theory to undermine the moral foundations of capitalism, it was, in his view, neither to be the instrumentality of capitalist collapse, nor was it the primary reason for the desirability of the abrogation of capitalism......Surplus value was seen as providing the fuel for the cyclical engine and therefore as the fundamental cause of the impeding dissolution of capitalism."

[8] *On the Economic Theory of Socialism*, by Lange, Oskar. 1936. The Review of Economic Studies, Vol. 4, No. 1: "It seems, therefore, convenient to regard the income of consumers as being composed of two parts: one part being the receipts for the labour services performed and the other part being a social dividend constituting the individual's share in the income derived from the capital and the natural resources owned by society."

[9] *The Social Dividend Under Market Socialism*, by Yunker, James. 1977. Annals of Public and Cooperative Economics, Vol. 48, No. 1, pp. 93-133: "This in turn suggests a 'market socialist' blueprint – the socialist system should utilize the same market allocation devices as are used presently under capitalism. The only difference is that property return (profits, rent and interest) generated by these allocation devices goes to the population as a whole rather than to an owning minority as under capitalism."

[10] *Philosophy and the Problems of Work: A Reader*, 2001, by Kory Schaff. ISBN 978-0742507951. (P.344): "The second socialist aspect of this economy is that the profits of firms will not go to a small fraction of the citizenry but will be divided, after taxes, more or less equally among all adult citizens, taking a form that Oskar Lange called a social dividend."

[11] Shutt, Harry (March 15, 2010). *Beyond the Profits System: Possibilities for the Post-Capitalist Era*. Zed Books. p. 124. ISBN 978-1848134171. a flat rate payment as of right to all resident citizens over the school leaving age, irrespective of means of employment status...it would in principle replace all existing social-security entitlements with the exception of child benefits.

[12] Makwana, Rajesh. "From Basic Income to Social Dividends: Sharing the Value of Common Resources". *Medium*. Retrieved 8 May 2015.

2.61.7 Further reading

- Arneson, Richard J. (1992). "Is Socialism Dead? A Comment on Market Socialism and Basic Income Capitalism". *Ethics* 102. 3:486-511.

- Marangos, John (2004). "Social Dividend versus Basic Income Guarantee in Market Socialism". *International Journal of Political Economy* 34. 3:20-40.

- Yunker, James (1977). "The Social Dividend under Market Socialism". *Annals of Public and Cooperative Economics* 48. 1:91-133.

2.61.8 External links

- Progress.org
- Intelligent-systems.com.ar
- Liberty Fund
- Who framed 'social dividend'?, Walter Vantrier, 2002

2.62 Socialist economics

Socialist economics refers to the economic theories, practices, and norms of hypothetical and existing socialist economic systems.

A socialist economic system is characterised by social ownership and democratic control of the means of production,[1][2][3][4][5][6] which may mean autonomous cooperatives or direct public ownership; wherein production is carried out directly for use. Where markets are utilized for allocating inputs and capital goods among economic units, the designation market socialism is used. When planning is utilized, the economic system is designated a planned socialist economy. Non-market forms of socialism usually include a system of accounting based on calculation-in-kind or a direct measure of labor-time as a means to value resources and goods.[7][8]

The term *socialist economics* may also be applied to analysis of former and existing economic systems that call themselves "socialist", such as the works of Hungarian economist János Kornai.[9]

Socialist economics has been associated with different schools of economic thought. Marxian economics provided a foundation for socialism based on analysis of capitalism, while neoclassical economics and evolutionary economics provided comprehensive models of socialism. During the 20th century, proposals and models for both planned economies and market socialism were based heavily on neoclassical economics or a synthesis of neoclassical economics with Marxian or institutional economics.

2.62.1 History of socialist economic thought

Main article: History of socialism

Karl Marx and Friedrich Engels believed that hunter-gatherer societies and some primitive agricultural societies were communal, and called this primitive communism. Engels wrote about this at length in the book The Origin of the Family, Private Property and the State, which was based on the unpublished notes of Marx on the work of Lewis Henry Morgan.[10]

Values of *socialism* have roots in pre-capitalist institutions such as the religious communes, reciprocal obligations, and communal charity of Mediaeval Europe, the development of its economic theory primarily reflects and responds to the monumental changes brought about by the dissolution of feudalism and the emergence of specifically capitalist social relations.[11] As such it is commonly regarded as a movement belonging to the modern era. Many socialists have considered their advocacy as the preservation and extension of the radical humanist ideas expressed in Enlightenment doctrine such as Jean-Jacques Rousseau's *Discourse on Inequality*, Wilhelm von Humboldt's *Limits of State Action*, or Immanuel Kant's insistent defense of the French Revolution.[12]

Capitalism appeared in mature form as a result of the problems raised when an industrial factory system requiring long-term investment and entailing corresponding risks was introduced into an internationalized commercial (mercantilist) framework. Historically speaking, the most pressing needs of this new system were an assured supply of the elements of industry – land, elaborate machinery, and labour – and these imperatives led to the commodification of these elements.[13]

According to influential socialist economic historian Karl Polanyi's classic account, the forceful transformation of land, money and especially labour into commodities to be allocated by an autonomous market mechanism was an alien and inhuman rupture of the pre-existing social fabric. Marx had viewed the process in a similar light, referring to it as part of the process of "primitive accumulation" whereby enough initial capital is amassed to begin capitalist production. The dislocation that Polyani and others describe, triggered natural counter-movements in efforts to re-embed the economy in society. These counter-movements, that included, for example, the Luddite rebellions, are the incipient socialist movements. Over time such movements gave birth to or acquired an array of intellectual defenders who attempted to develop their ideas in theory.

As Polanyi noted, these counter-movements were mostly reactive and therefore not full-fledged socialist movements. Some demands went no further than a wish to mitigate the capitalist market's worst effects. Later, a full socialist program developed, arguing for systemic transformation. Its theorists believed that even if markets and private property could be tamed so as not to be excessively "exploitative", or crises could be effectively mitigated, capitalist social relations would remain significantly unjust and antidemocratic, suppressing universal human needs for fulfilling, empowering and creative work, diversity and solidarity.

Within this context socialism has undergone four periods: the first in the 19th century was a period of utopian visions (1780s-1850s); then occurred the rise of revolutionary socialist and Communist movements in the 19th century as the primary opposition to the rise of corporations and industrialization (1830–1916); the polarisation of socialism around the question of the Soviet Union, and adoption of socialist or social democratic policies in response (1916–1989); and the response of socialism in the neo-liberal era (1990-). As socialism developed, so did the socialist system of economics.

Utopian socialism

Main article: Utopian socialism

The first theories which came to hold the term "socialism" began to be formulated in the late 18th century, and were termed "socialism" early in the 19th century. The central beliefs of the socialism of this period rested on the exploitation of those who labored by those who owned capital or rented land and housing. The abject misery, poverty and disease to which laboring classes seemed destined was the inspiration for a series of schools of thought which argued that life under a class of masters, or "capitalists" as they were then becoming to be called, would consist of working classes being driven down to subsistence wages. (See Iron law of wages).

Socialist ideas found expression in utopian movements, which often formed agricultural communes aimed at being self-sufficient on the land. These included many religious movements, such as the Christian socialism of the Shakers in America and the Hutterites. The Zionist kibbutzim and communes of the counterculture are also manifestations of utopian socialist ideas.

Utopian socialism had little to offer in terms of a systematic theory of economic phenomena. In theory, economic problems were dissolved by a utopian society which had transcended material scarcity. In practice, small communities with a common spirit could sometimes resolve allocation problems.

Socialism and classical political economy

The first organized theories of socialist economics were significantly impacted by classical economic theory, including elements in Adam Smith, Robert Malthus and David Ricardo. In Smith there is a conception of a common good not provided by the market, a class analysis, a concern for the dehumanizing aspects of the factory system, and the concept of rent as being unproductive. Ricardo argued that the renting class was parasitic. This, and the possibility of a "general glut", an over accumulation of capital to produce goods for sale rather than for use, became the foundation of a rising critique of the concept that free markets with competition would be sufficient to prevent disastrous downturns in the economy, and whether the need for expansion would inevitably lead to war.

Socialist political economy before Marx

Charles Fourier, influential early French socialist thinker

A key early socialist theorist of political economy was Pierre-Joseph Proudhon. He was the most well-known of nineteenth century mutualist theorists and the first thinker to refer to himself as an anarchist. Others were: Technocrats like Henri de Saint Simon, agrarian radicals like Thomas Spence, William Ogilvie and William Cobbett; anti-capitalists like Thomas Hodgskin; communitarian and utopian socialists like Robert Owen, William Thompson and Charles Fourier; anti-market socialists like John Gray and John Francis Bray; the Christian mutualist William Batchelder Greene; as well as the theorists of the Chartist movement and early proponents of syndicalism.[14]

The first advocates of socialism promoted social leveling in order to create a meritocratic or technocratic society based upon individual talent. Count Henri de Saint-Simon was the first individual to coin the term "socialism".[15] Simon was fascinated by the enormous potential of science and technology, which led him to advocate a socialist society that would eliminate the disorderly aspects of capitalism and which would be based upon equal opportunities.[16] Simon advocated a society in which each person was ranked according to his or her capacities and rewarded according to his or her work.[15] This was accompanied by a desire to implement a rationally organized economy based on planning and geared towards large-scale scientific and material progress, which embodied a desire for a semi-planned economy.[15]

Other early socialist thinkers were influenced by the classical economists. The Ricardian socialists, such as Thomas Hodgskin and Charles Hall, were based on the work of David Ricardo and reasoned that the equilibrium value of commodities approximated producer prices when those commodities were in elastic supply, and that these producer prices corresponded to the embodied labor. The Ricardian socialists viewed profit, interest and rent as deductions from this exchange-value.[17]

Karl Marx and *Das Kapital*

Main article: Das Kapital

Karl Marx employed systematic analysis in an attempt to elucidate capitalism's contradictory laws of motion, as well as to expose the specific mechanisms by which it exploits and alienates. He radically modified classical political economic theories. Marx transformed the labor theory of value, which had been worked upon by Adam Smith and David Ricardo, into his "law of value", and used it for the purpose of revealing how commodity fetishism obscures the reality of capitalist society.

His approach, which Friedrich Engels would call "scientific socialism", would stand as the branching point in economic theory. In one direction went those who rejected the capitalist system as fundamentally anti-social, arguing that it could never be harnessed to effectively realize the fullest development of human potentialities wherein "the free development of each is the condition for the free development of all.".[18]

Marx's *Das Kapital* is an incomplete work of economic theory; he had planned four volumes but completed two and left his collaborator Engels to complete the third. In many ways, the work is modelled on Smith's *Wealth of Nations*, seeking to be a comprehensive logical description of production, consumption and finance in relation to morality and the state. The work of philosophy, anthropology, sociology and economics includes the following topics:

- The Law of Value: Capitalist production is the production of "an immense multitude of commodities" or generalised commodity production. A commodity has two essential qualities firstly, they are useful, they satisfy some human want, "the nature of such wants, whether, for instance, they spring from the stomach or from fancy, makes no difference," [19] and secondly they are sold on a market or exchanged. Critically the exchange value of a commodity "is independent of the amount of labour required to appropriate its useful qualities." [19] But rather depends on the amount of socially necessary labour required to produce it. All commodities are sold at their value, so the origin of the capitalist profit is not in cheating or theft but in the fact that the cost of reproduction of labour power, or the worker's wage, is less than the value created during their time at work, enabling the capitalists to yield a surplus value or profit on their investments.

- Historical Property Relations: Historical capitalism represents a process of momentous social upheaval where rural masses were separated from the land and ownership of the means of production by force, deprivation, and legal manipulation, creating an urban proletariat based on the institution of wage-labour. Moreover, capitalist property relations aggravated the artificial separation between city and country, which is a key factor in accounting for the metabolic rift between human beings in capitalism and their natural environment, which is at the root of our current ecological dilemmas.[20]

- Commodity Fetishism: Marx adapted previous value-theory to show that in capitalism phenomena involved with the price system (markets, competition, supply and demand) constitute a powerful ideology that obscures the underlying social relations of capitalist society. "Commodity fetishism" refers to this distortion of appearance. The underlying social reality is one of economic exploitation.

- Economic Exploitation: Workers are the fundamental creative source of new value. Property relations affording the right of usufruct and despotic control of the workplace to capitalists are the devices by which the surplus value created by workers is appropriated by the capitalists.

- Capital accumulation: Inherent to capitalism is the incessant drive to accumulate as a response to the competitive forces acting upon all capitalists. In such a context the accumulated wealth which is the source of the capitalist's social power derives itself from being able to repeat the circuit of Money-->Commodity-->Money', where the capitalist receives an increment or "surplus value" higher than their initial investment, as rapidly and efficiently as possible. Moreover, this driving imperative leads capitalism to its expansion on a worldwide scale.

- Crises: Marx identified natural and historically specific (i.e. structural) barriers to accumulation that were interrelated and interpenetrated one another in times of crises. Different types of crises, such as realization crises and overproduction crises, are expressions of capitalism's inability to constructively overcome such barriers. Moreover, the upshot of crises is increased centralization, the expropriation of the many capitalists by the few.

- Centralization: The interacting forces of competition, endemic crises, intensive and extensive expansion of the scale of production, and a growing interdependency with the state apparatus, all promote a strong developmental tendency towards the centralization of capital.

- Material Development: As a result of its constant drive to optimize profitability by increasing the productivity of labour, typically by revolutionizing technology and production techniques, capitalism develops so as to progressively reduce the objective need for work, suggesting the potential for a new era of creative forms of work and expanded scope for leisure.

- Socialization, and the pre-conditions for Revolution: By socializing the labour process, concentrating workers into urban settings in large-scale production processes and linking them in a worldwide market, the agents of a potential revolutionary change are created. Thus Marx felt that in the course of its development capitalism was at the same time developing the preconditions for its own negation. However, although the objective conditions for change are generated by the capitalist system itself, the subjective conditions for social revolution can only come about through the apprehension of the objective circumstances by the agents themselves and the transformation of such understanding into an effective revolutionary program.[21]

Anarchist economics

Main article: Anarchist economics

Anarchist economics is the set of theories and practices of economics and economic activity within the political philosophy of anarchism.

Pierre Joseph Proudhon was involved with the Lyons mutualists and later adopted the name to describe his own teachings.[22] Mutualism is an anarchist school of thought that originates in the writings of Pierre-Joseph Proudhon, who envisioned a society where each person might possess a means of production, either individually or collectively, with trade representing equivalent amounts of labor in the free market.[23] Integral to the scheme was the establishment of a mutual-credit bank that would lend to producers at a minimal interest rate, just high enough to cover administration.[24] Mutualism is based on a labor theory of value that holds that when labor or its product is sold, in exchange, it ought to receive goods or services embodying "the amount of labor necessary to produce an article of exactly similar and equal utility".[25] Receiving anything less would be considered exploitation, theft of labor, or usury.

The Conquest of Bread *by Peter Kropotkin, influential work which presents the economic vision of anarcho-communism*

Collectivist anarchism (also known as anarcho-collectivism) is a revolutionary[26] doctrine that advocates the abolition of the state and private ownership of the means of production. Instead, it envisions the means of production being owned collectively and controlled and managed by the producers themselves. Once collectivization takes place, workers' salaries would be determined in democratic organizations based on the amount of time they contributed to production. These salaries would be used to purchase goods in a communal market.[27] Collectivist anarchism is most commonly associated with Mikhail Bakunin, the anti-authoritarian sections of the First International, and the early Spanish anarchist movement.

Anarchist communism is a theory of anarchism which advocates the abolition of the state, private property, and capitalism in favor of common ownership of the means of production,[28][29] direct democracy and a horizontal network of voluntary associations and workers' councils with production and consumption based on the guiding principle: "from each according to ability, to each according to need".[30][31] Unlike mutualism, collectivist anarchism and marxism, anarcho-communism as defended by Peter Kropotkin and Errico Malatesta rejected the labor theory of value altogether, instead advocating a gift economy and to base distribution on need.[32]

Anarchist communism as a coherent, modern economic-political philosophy was first formulated in the Italian section of the First International by Carlo Cafiero, Emilio Covelli, Errico Malatesta, Andrea Costa and other ex-Mazzinian Republicans.[33] Out of respect for Mikhail Bakunin, they did not make their differences with collectivist anarchism explicit until after Bakunin's death.[34] By the early 1880s, most of the European anarchist movement had adopted an anarchist communist position, advocating the abolition of wage labour and distribution according to need. Ironically, the "collectivist" label then became more commonly associated with Marxist state socialists who advocated the retention of some sort of wage system during the transition to full communism.

After Marx

Non-revolutionary socialists were inspired by the writings of John Stuart Mill, and later John Maynard Keynes and the Keynesians, who provided theoretical justification for state involvement in existing market economies. According to the Keynesians, if business cycles could be smoothed out by national ownership of key industries and state direction of their investment, class antagonism would be effectively tamed. They argue that a compact would form between labour and the capitalist class and that there would be no need for revolution. Joan Robinson and Michael Kalecki formed the basis of a critical post-Keynesian economics that at times went well beyond liberal reformism.

Marxist economists developed different tendencies based on conflicting interpretations of Marx's ideas, such as the 'Law of Value' and crisis theory. The monopoly capitalist school saw Paul A. Baran and Paul Sweezy attempt to modify Marx's theory of capitalist development — which was based upon the assumption of price competition — to reflect evolution to a stage where both economy and state were subject to the dominating influence of giant corporations.

World-systems analysis restated Marx's ideas about the worldwide division of labour and the drive to accumulate from the holistic perspective of capitalism's historical development as a global system. Immanuel Wallerstein, wrote in 1979:

> There are today no socialist systems in the world-economy any more than there are feudal systems because there is only *one* world-system. It is a world-economy and it is by definition capitalist in form. Socialism involves the creation of a new kind of world-system, neither a redistributive world-empire nor a capitalist world-economy but a socialist world-government. I don't see this projection as being in the least utopian but I also don't feel its institution is imminent. It will be the outcome of a long social struggle in forms that may be familiar and perhaps in very few forms, that will take place in *all* the areas of the world-economy.[35]

Piero Sraffa attempted to construct a value theory that was an explanation of the normal distribution of prices in an economy, as well that of income and economic growth. He found that the net product or surplus in the sphere of production was determined by the balance of bargaining power between workers and capitalists, which was subject to the influence of non-economic, presumably social and political, factors.

The mutualist tendency associated with Pierre-Joseph Proudhon also continued, influencing the development of libertarian socialism, anarchist communism, syndicalism and distributivism.

2.62.2 Characteristics

See also: Socialist mode of production

A socialist economy is a system of production where goods and services are produced directly for use, in contrast to a capitalist economic system, where goods and services are produced to generate profit (and therefore indirectly for use). "Production under socialism would be directly and solely for use. With the natural and technical resources of the world held in common and controlled democratically, the sole object of production would be to meet human needs."[36] Goods and services would be produced for their usefulness, or for their use-value, eliminating the need for market-induced needs to ensure a sufficient amount of demand for products to be sold at a profit. Production in a socialist economy is therefore "planned" or "coordinated", and does not suffer from the business cycle inherent to capitalism. In most socialist theories, economic planning only applies to the factors of production and not to the allocation of goods and services produced for consumption, which would be distributed through a market. Karl Marx stated that "lower-stage communism" would consist of compensation based on the amount of labor one contributes to the social product.[37]

The ownership of the means of production varies in different socialist theories. It can either be based on public ownership by a state apparatus; direct ownership by the users of the productive property through worker cooperative; or commonly owned by all of society with management and control delegated to those who operate/use the means of production.

Management and control over the activities of enterprises is based on self-management and self-governance, with equal power-relations in the workplace to maximize occupational autonomy. A socialist form of organization would eliminate controlling hierarchies so that only a hierarchy based on technical knowledge in the workplace remains. Every member would have decision-making power in the firm and would be able to participate in establishing its overall policy objectives. The policies/goals would be carried out by the technical specialists that form the coordinating hierarchy of the firm, who would establish plans or directives for the work community to accomplish these goals.[38]

However, the economies of the former Socialist states, excluding SFR Yugoslavia, were based on bureaucratic, top-down administration of economic directives and micromanagement of the worker in the workplace inspired by capitalist models of scientific management. As a result, socialists have argued that they were not socialist due to the lack of equal power-relations in the workplace, the presence of a new "elite", and because of the commodity production that took place in these economies. These economic and social systems have been classified as being either *Bureaucratic collectivist*, *State capitalist* or *Deformed workers' states*, the exact nature of the USSR *et al* remains unresolved within the socialist movement.[39]

"I am convinced there is only one way to eliminate (the) grave evils (of capitalism), namely through the establishment of a socialist economy, accompanied by an educational system which would be oriented toward social goals. In such an economy, the means of production are owned by society itself and are utilized in a planned fashion. A planned economy, which adjusts production to the needs of the community, would distribute the work to be done among all those able to work and would guarantee a livelihood to every man, woman, and child. The education of the individual, in addition to promoting his own innate abilities, would attempt to develop in him a sense of responsibility for his fellow-men in place of the glorification of power and success in our present society."
— Albert Einstein, *Why Socialism?*, 1949[40]

Economic planning

Main article: Economic planning

Economic planning is a mechanism for the allocation of economic inputs and decision-making based on direct allocation, in contrast to the market mechanism, which is based on indirect allocation.[41] An economy based on economic planning appropriates its resources as needed, so that allocation comes in the form of internal transfers rather than market transactions involving the purchasing of assets by one government agency or firm by another. Decision-making is carried out by workers and consumers on the enterprise-level.

Economic planning is not synonymous with the concept of a *command economy*, which existed in the Soviet Union, and was based on a highly bureaucratic administration of the entire economy in accordance to a comprehensive plan formulated by a central planning agency, which specified output requirements for productive units and tried to micromanage the decisions and policies of enterprises. The command economy is based on the organizational model of a capitalist firm, but applies it to the entire economy.[42]

Various advocates of economic planning have been staunch critics of command economies and centralized planning. For example, Leon Trotsky believed that central planners, regardless of their intellectual capacity, operated without the input and participation of the millions of people who participate in the economy and understand the local conditions and rapid changes in the economy. Therefore, central planners would be unable to effectively coordinate all economic activity because they lacked this informal information.[43]

Economic planning in socialism takes a different form than economic planning in capitalist mixed economies (such as Dirigisme, Central banking and Indicative planning); in the former case planning refers to production of use-value directly (planning of production), while in the latter case planning refers to the planning of capital accumulation in order to stabilize or increase the efficiency of this process.

Anti-capitalism

See also: Socialist critique of capitalism

The goal of socialist economics is to neutralize capital (or, in the case of market socialism, to subject investment and capital to social planning),[44] to coordinate the production of goods and services to directly satisfy demand (as opposed to market-induced needs), and to eliminate the business cycle and crisis of overproduction that occur as a result of an economy based on capital accumulation and private property in the means of production.

Socialists generally aim to achieve greater equality in decision-making and economic affairs, grant workers greater control of the means of production and their workplace, and to eliminate exploitation by directing the surplus value to employees. Free access to the means of subsistence is a requisite for liberty, because it ensures that all work is voluntary and no class or individual has the power to coerce others into performing alienating work.

The ultimate goal for Marxist socialists is the emancipation of labor from alienating work, and therefore freedom from having to perform such labor to receive access to the material necessities for life. It is argued that freedom from necessity would maximize individual liberty, as individuals would be able to pursue their own interests and develop their own talents without being coerced into performing labor for others (the power-elite or ruling class in this case) via mechanisms of social control, such as the labor market and the state. The stage of economic development in which this is possible is contingent upon advances in the productive capabilities of society. This advanced stage of social relations and economic organization is called *pure communism*.

Economic value theories

Socialist economic theories base the value of a good or service on its use value, rather than its cost of production (labor theory of value) or its exchange value (Marginal Utility).[45] Other socialist theories, such as mutualism and market socialism, attempt to apply the labor theory of value to socialism, so that the price of a good or service is adjusted to equal the amount of labor time expended in its production. The labor-time expended by each worker would correspond to labor credits, which would be used as a currency to acquire goods and services. Market socialists that base their models on neoclassical economics, and thus marginal utility, such as Oskar Lange and Abba Lerner, have proposed that publicly owned enterprises set their price to equal marginal cost, thereby achieving pareto efficiency. Anarcho-communism as defended by Peter Kropotkin and Errico Malatesta rejected the labor theory of value and exchange value itself, advocated a gift economy and to base distribution on need.[32]

2.62.3 Economic models and systems

See also: Types of socialism

Robin Hahnel and Michael Albert identify five different economic models within socialist economics:[46]

- **Public Enterprise Centrally Planned Economy** in which all property is owned by the State and all key economic decisions are made centrally by the State, e.g. the former Soviet Union.

- **Public Enterprise State-Managed Market Economy**, one form of market socialism which attempts to use the price mechanism to increase economic efficiency, while all decisive productive assets remain in the ownership of the state, e.g. socialist market economy in China after reform.

- A **mixed economy**, also a capitalist economy where public and private ownership are mixed, and where industrial planning is ultimately subordinate to market allocation, the model generally adopted by social democrats e.g. in twentieth century Sweden. Many different proposals for socialist economic systems call for a type of mixed economy, where multiple forms of ownership over the means of production co-exist with one another.

- **Public Enterprise Employee Managed Market Economies**, another form of market socialism in which publicly owned, employee-managed production units engage in free market exchange of goods and services with one another as well as with final consumers, e.g. mid twentieth century Yugoslavia, Two more theoretical models are Prabhat Ranjan Sarkar's Progressive Utilization Theory and Economic democracy.

- **Public Enterprise Participatory Planning**, an economy featuring social ownership of the means of production with allocation based on an integration of decentralized democratic planning, e.g. stateless communism, libertarian socialism. An incipient historical forebear is that of Catalonia during the Spanish revolution. More developed theoretical models include those of Karl Polanyi, Participatory Economics, Inclusive Democracy and the negotiated coordination model of Pat Devine, as well as in Cornelius Castoriadis's pamphlet "Workers' Councils and the Economics of a Self-Managed Society".[47]

János Kornai identifies five distinct types of socialism:

- **Classical / Marxist** conception, where socialism is a stage of economic development in which wage labour, private property in the means of production and monetary relations have been made redundant through the development of the productive forces, so that capital accumulation has been superseded by economic planning. Economic planning in this definition means conscious allocation of economic inputs and the means of production by the associated producers to directly maximise use-values as opposed to exchange-values, in contrast to the "anarchy of production" of capitalism.
- **Walrasian / Market Socialist** which defines socialism as public-ownership or cooperative-enterprises in a market economy, with prices for producer goods set through a trial-and-error method by a central planning board. In this view, socialism is defined in terms of de jure public property rights over major enterprises.
- **Leninist** conception, which includes a form of political organisation based on control of the means of production and government by a single political party apparatus that claims to act in the interest of the working class, and an ideology hostile toward markets and political dissent, with coordination of economic activity through centralised economic planning (a "command economy").
- **Social Democratic** concept, based on the capitalist mode of production, which defines socialism as a set of values rather than a specific type of social and economic organisation. It includes unconditional support for parliamentary democracy, gradual and reformist attempts to establish socialism, and support for socially progressive causes. Social democrats are not opposed to the market or private property; instead they try to ameliorate the effects of capitalism through a welfare state, which relies on the market as the fundamental coordinating entity in the economy and a degree of public ownership/public provision of public goods in an economy otherwise dominated by private enterprise.
- **East Asian** model, or socialist market economy, based on a largely free-market, capital accumulation for profit and substantial private ownership along with state-ownership of strategic industries monopolised by a single political party. János Kornai ultimately leaves the classification of this model (as either socialist or capitalist) to the reader.[48]

Socialism can be divided into market socialism and planned socialism based on their dominant mechanism of resource allocation. Another distinction can be made between the type of property structures of different socialist systems (public, cooperative or common) and on the dominant form of economic management within the economy (hierarchical or self-managed).

Economic democracy

Economic democracy is a model of market socialism primarily developed by the American economist David Schweickart. In Schweickart's model, enterprises and natural resources are owned by society in the form of public banking, and management is elected by the workers within each firm. Profits would be distributed among the workers of the respective enterprise.[49]

Lange–Lerner model

The Lange–Lerner model involves public ownership of the means of production and the utilization of a trial-and-error approach to achieving equilibrium prices by a central planning board. The Central Planning Board would be responsible for setting prices through a trial-and-error approach to establish equilibrium prices, effectively acting as the abstract *Walrasian auctioneer* in Walrasian economics. Managers of the state-owned firms would be instructed to set prices to equal marginal cost (P=MC), so that economic equilibrium and Pareto efficiency would be achieved. The Lange model was expanded upon by the American economist Abba Lerner and became known as the Lange–Lerner theorem, particularly the role of the social dividend. Forerunners of the Lange model include the neoclassical economists Enrico Barone and Fred M. Taylor.

Self-managed economy

The self-managed economy is a form of socialism where enterprises are owned and managed by their employees, effectively negating the employer-employee (or wage labor) dynamic of capitalism and emphasizing the opposition to alienation, self-managing and cooperative aspect of socialism. Members of cooperative firms are relatively free to manage their own affairs and work schedules. This model was developed most extensively by the Yugoslav economists Branko Horvat, Jaroslav Vanek and the American economist Benjamin Ward.

Worker self-directed enterprise

Worker Self-Directed Enterprise (WSDE) is a recent proposal advocated by the American Marxian economist Richard D. Wolff. This model shares many similarities with the model of socialist self-management in that employees own and direct their enterprises, but places a greater role on democratically elected management within a market economy.

Democratic planned socialism

Democratic planned socialism is a form of decentralized planned economy.[50]

Feasible socialism

Feasible socialism was the name Alec Nove gave his outline for socialism in his work *The Economics of Feasible Socialism*. According to Nove, this model of socialism is "feasible" because it can be realized within the lifetime of anyone living today. It involves a combination of publicly owned and centrally directed enterprises for large-scale industries, autonomous publicly owned enterprises, consumer and worker-owned cooperatives for the majority of the economy, and private ownership for small businesses. It is a market-based mixed economy that includes a substantial role for macroeconomic interventionism and indicative economic planning.[51]

Pragmatic market socialism

The American economist James Yunker detailed a model where social ownership of the means of production is achieved the same way private ownership is achieved in modern capitalism through the shareholder system that separates management functions from ownership. Yunker posits that social ownership can be achieved by having a public body, designated the Bureau of Public Ownership (BPO), owning the shares of publicly listed firms without affecting market-based allocation of capital inputs. Yunker termed this model *Pragmatic market socialism* because it does not require massive changes to society and would leave the existing management system intact, and would be at least as efficient as modern-day capitalism while providing superior social outcomes as public ownership of large and established enterprises would enable profits to be distributed among the entire population in a social dividend rather than going largely to a class of inheriting rentiers.[52]

Participatory economy

Participatory economics utilizes participatory decision making as an economic mechanism to guide the production, consumption and allocation of resources in a given society.

Computer-managed allocation

Proposals for utilizing computer-based coordination and information technology for the coordination and optimization of resource allocation (also known as cybernetics) within an economy have been outlined by various socialists, economists and computer scientists, including Oskar Lange, the Soviet engineer Viktor Glushkov, and more recently the Paul Cockshott and Allin Cottrell.

Peer-to-peer economy and open source

The "networked information age" has enabled the development and emergence of new forms of organizing the production of value in non-market arrangements that have been termed commons-based peer production along with the negation of ownership and the concept of property in the development of software in the form of open source and open design.[53]

Negotiated coordination

Economist Pat Devine has created a model of coordination called "negotiated coordination", which is based upon social ownership by those affected by the use of the assets involved, with decisions made by those at the most localised level of production.[54]

2.62.4 Elements of socialism in practice

Although a number of economic systems have existed with various socialist attributes, or have been deemed socialist by their proponents, almost all of the economic systems listed below have largely retained elements of capitalism such as wage labor, the accumulation of capital, and commodity production. Nonetheless, various elements of a socialist economy have been implemented or experimented with in various economies throughout history.

Various forms of socialist organizational attributes have existed as minor modes of production within the context of a capitalist economy throughout history — examples of this include cooperative enterprises in a capitalist economy, and the emerging free-software movement based on social peer-to-peer production.

Centrally planned economies

A centrally planned economy combines public ownership of the means of production with centralised state planning. This model is usually associated with the Soviet-style command economy. In a centrally planned economy, decisions regarding the quantity of goods and services to be produced are planned in advance by a planning agency. In the early years of Soviet central planning, the planning process was based upon a selected number of physical flows with inputs mobilized to meet explicit production targets measured in natural or technical units. This material balances method of achieving plan coherence was later complemented and replaced by value planning, with money provided to enterprises so that they could recruit labour and procure materials and intermediate production goods and services. The Soviet economy was brought to balance by the interlocking of three sets of calculation, namely the setting up of a model incorporating balances of production, manpower and finance. The exercise was undertaken annually and involved a process of iteration (the "method of successive approximation").[55] Although nominally a "centrally planned" economy, in reality formulation of the plan took place on a more local level of the production process as information was relayed from enterprises to planning ministries. Aside from the USSR and Eastern bloc economies, this economic model was also utilized by the People's Republic of China, Socialist Republic of Vietnam, Republic of Cuba and North Korea.

Soviet Union Main article: Economy of the Soviet Union
See also: Ministry of Finance (Soviet Union), Gosplan and Five-Year Plans for the National Economy of the Soviet Union

The Soviet Union and some of its European satellites aimed for a fully centrally planned economy. They dispensed almost entirely with private ownership over the means of production. Workers were still, however, effectively paid a wage for their labour. Some believe that according to Marxist theory this should have been a step towards a genuine workers' state. However, some Marxists consider this a misunderstanding of Marx's views of historical materialism, and his views of the process of socialization.

The characteristics of this model of economy were:

- **Production quotas** for every productive unit. A farm, mine or factory was judged on the basis of whether its production met the quota. It would be provided with a quota of the inputs it needed to start production, and then its quota of output would be taken away and given to downstream production units or distributed to consumers. Critics of both left and right persuasions have argued that the economy was plagued by incentive-related problems; claiming, for instance, that the system incentivized enterprise managers to underreport their unit's productive capacities so that their quotas would be easier to achieve, especially since the manager's bonuses were linked to the fulfillment of quotas.

- **Allocation through political control**. In contrast with systems where prices *determined* allocation of resources, in the Soviet Union, allocation, particularly of means of production was determined by the bureaucracy. The prices that were constructed were done so *after* the formulation of the economy plan, and such prices did not factor into choices about what was produced and how it was produced in the first place.

- **Full employment**. Every worker was ensured employment. However workers were generally not directed to jobs. The central planning administration adjusted relative wages rates to influence job choice in accordance with the outlines of the current plan.

- **Clearing goods by planning**: if a surplus of a product was accumulated, then the central planning authority would either reduce the quota for its production or increase the quota for its use.

- **Five Year Plans** for the long-term development of key industries.

The planning system in the USSR was introduced under Stalin between 1928 and 1934.[56] Following the Second World War, in the seven countries with communist governments in Central and Eastern Europe, central planning with five- (or six-) year plans on the Soviet model had been introduced by 1951. The common features were the nationalization of industry, transport and trade, compulsory procurement in farming (but not collectivization) and a monopoly on foreign trade.[57] Prices were largely determined on the basis of the costs of inputs, a method derived from the labour theory of value. Prices did not therefore incentivize production enterprises whose inputs were instead purposely rationed by the central plan. This "taut planning" began around 1930 in the USSR and was only attenuated after the economic reforms in 1966-68 when enterprises were encouraged to make profits.[58]

The stated purpose of planning according to the communist party was to enable the people through the party and state institutions to undertake activities that would have been frustrated by a market economy (for example, the rapid expansion of universal education and health care, urban development with mass good quality housing and industrial development of all regions of the country). Nevertheless, markets continued to exist in socialist planned economies. Even after the collectivization of agriculture in the USSR in the 1930s, members of the collective farm and anyone with a private garden plot were free to sell their own produce (farm workers were often paid in kind). Licensed markets operated in every town and city borough where non-state-owned enterprises (such as cooperatives and collective farms) were able to offer their products and services. From 1956/59 onwards all wartime controls over manpower were removed and people could apply and quit jobs freely in the USSR. The use of market mechanisms went furthest in Yugoslavia, Czechoslovakia and Hungary. From 1975 Soviet citizens had the right to engage in private handicraft and in 1981 collective farmers could raise and sell livestock privately. It should also be noted that households were free to dispose of their income as they chose and incomes were lightly taxed.[59]

Dispute that the Soviet model is socialism Various scholars and political economists have criticized the claim that the centrally planned economy, and specifically, the Soviet model of economic development, constitutes a form of socialism. They argue that the Soviet economy was structured upon the accumulation of capital and the extraction of surplus value from the working class by the planning agency in order to reinvest this surplus into the economy — and to distribute to managers and senior officials, indicating the Soviet Union (and other Soviet-style economies) were state capitalist economies.[60] More fundamentally, these economies are still structured around the dynamic of capitalism: the accumulation of capital and production for profit (as opposed to being based on production for use — the defining criterion for socialism), and have not yet transcended the system of capitalism but are in fact a variation of capitalism based on a process of state-directed accumulation.[61]

On the other side of the argument are those who contend that no surplus value was generated from labour activity or from commodity markets in the socialist planned economies and therefore claim that there was no exploiting class, even if inequalities existed.[62] Since prices were controlled and set below market clearing levels there was no element of 'value added' at the point of sale as occurs in capitalist market economies. Prices were built up from the average cost of inputs, including wages, taxes, interest on stocks and working capital, and allowances to cover the recoupment of investment and for depreciation, so there was no 'profit margin' in the price charged to customers.[63] Wages did not reflect the purchase price of labour since labour was not a commodity traded in a market and the employing organizations did not own the means of production. Wages were set at a level that permitted a decent standard of living and rewarded specialist skills and educational qualifications. In macroeconomic terms, the plan allocated the whole national product to workers in the form of wages for the workers' own use, with a fraction withheld for investment and imports from abroad. The difference between the average value of wages and the value of national output per worker did not imply the existence of surplus value since it was part of a consciously formulated plan for the development of society.[64] Furthermore, the presence of inequality in the socialist planned economies did not imply that an exploiting class existed. In the USSR communist party members were able to buy scarce goods in special shops and the leadership elite took advantage of state property to live in more spacious accommodation and sometimes luxury. Although they received privileges not commonly available and thus some additional income in kind there was no difference in their official remuneration in comparison to their non-party peers. Enterprise managers and workers received only the wages and bonuses related to the production targets that had been set by the planning authorities. Outside of the cooperative sector, which enjoyed greater economic freedoms and whose profits were shared among all members of the cooperative, there was no profit-taking class.[65]

Other socialist critics point to the lack of socialist social relations in these economies — specifically the lack of self-management, a bureaucratic elite based on hierarchical and centralized powers of authority, and the lack of genuine worker control over the means of production — leading them to conclude that they were not socialist but either bureaucratic collectivism or state capitalism.[66] Trotskyists argue they are neither socialist nor capitalist — but are deformed workers' states.

This analysis is consistent with Lenin's April Theses, which stated that the goal of the Bolshevik revolution was *not* the introduction of socialism, which could only be established on a worldwide scale, but was intended to bring production and the state under the control of the Soviets of Workers' Deputies. Furthermore, these "Communist states" often do not claim to have achieved socialism in their countries; on the contrary, they claim to be *building* and working toward the establishment of socialism in their countries. For example, the preamble to the Socialist Republic of Vietnam's constitution states that Vietnam only entered a transition stage between capitalism and socialism after the country was re-unified under the Communist party in 1976,[67] and the 1992 Constitution of the Republic of Cuba states that the role of the Communist Party is to "guide the common effort toward the goals and construction of socialism".[68]

This view is challenged by Stalinists and their followers, who claim that socialism was established in the Soviet Union after Joseph Stalin came to power and instituted the system of five year plans. The 1936 Constitution of the USSR, known as the Fundamental Law of Victorious Socialism, embodied the claim that the foundations for socialism had been laid.[69] Joseph Stalin introduced the theory of Socialism in one country, which argued that socialism can be built in a single country, despite existing in a global capitalist economic system. Nevertheless, it was recognized that the stage during which developed socialism would be built would be a lengthy one and would not be achieved by the USSR on its own. According to the official textbooks, the first stage of the transition period from capitalism to socialism had been completed by the 1970s in the European socialist countries (except Poland and Yugoslavia), and in Mongolia and Cuba. The next stage of developed socialism would not be reached until "the economic integration of the socialist states becomes a major factor of their economic progress" and social relations had been reconstructed on "collectivist principles".[70] Communist writers accepted that during these earlier stages in constructing socialism, the exchange of commodities on the basis of the average socially necessary labour embodied within them occurred and involved the mediation of money. Socialist planned economies were systems of commodity production but this was directed in a conscious way towards meeting the needs of the people and not left to the "anarchy of the market".[71] At the stage of developed socialism "the state of dictatorship of the proletariat changes into a state of all people reflecting the increasing homogeneity of society" and the "evening out of economic development levels" within and between socialist countries. It would provide the foundations for a further stage of perfected socialist society, where an abundance of goods permitted their distribution according to need. Only then could the world socialist system progress towards the higher phase of communism.[72]

World socialist economic system By the 1980s the world economic socialist system embraced one-third of the world's population but generated no more than 15 percent of global economic output. At its height in the mid-1980s the world socialist system could be said to comprise the following countries with a "socialist orientation", though not all were allies of the Soviet Union: Afghanistan, Albania, Angola, Bulgaria, Cambodia, China, Cuba, Czechoslovakia, Eastern Germany, Ethiopia, Hungary, Mozambique, Nicaragua, North Korea, Laos, Mongolia, Poland, Romania, Vietnam, South Yemen, Yugoslavia and the USSR.[73] The system co-existed alongside the world capitalist system but was founded upon the principles of cooperation and mutual assistance rather than upon competition and rivalry The countries involved aimed to even-out the level of economic development and to play an equal part in the international division of labour. An important role was played by the Council for Mutual Economic Assistance (CMEA) or Comecon, an international body set up to promote economic development. It involved joint planning activity, the establishment of international economic, scientific and technical bodies and methods of cooperation between state agencies and enterprises, including joint ventures and projects.[74] Allied to the CMEA were the International Development Bank, established in 1971, and the International Bank for Economic Cooperation, founded in 1963, which had their parallel in the World Bank and the Bank for International Settlements and the International Monetary Fund in the non-socialist world.[75]

The main tasks of the CMEA were plan coordination, production specialization and regional trade. In 1961 Nikita Khrushchev, the Soviet leader, put forward proposals for establishing an integrated, centrally planned socialist commonwealth in which each geographic region would specialize production in line with its set of natural and human resources. The resulting document, the "Basic Principles of the International Socialist Division of Labour" was adopted at the end of 1961, despite objections from Romania on certain aspects. The "Basic Principles" were never implemented fully and were replaced in 1971 by the adoption of the "Comprehensive Programme for Further Extension and Improvement of Cooperation and Development of Socialist Economic Integration". As a result, many specialization agreements were made between CMEA member states for investment programmes and projects. The importing country pledged to rely on the exporting country for its consumption of the product in question. Production specialization occurred in engineering, automotive, chemicals, computers and automation, telecommunications and biotechnology. Scientific and technical cooperation between CMEA member states was facilitated by the establishment in 1969 of the International Centre for Scientific and Technical Information in Moscow.[76]

Trade between CMEA member states was divided into 'hard' goods and 'soft' goods. The former could be sold on world markets and the latter could not. Commodities such as food, energy products and raw materials tended to be 'hard' goods and were traded within the CMEA area at world market prices. Manufactures tended to be 'soft' goods and their prices were negotiable and often adjusted to make bilateral payment flows balance.[77]

Other countries with privileged affiliation with the CMEA were Algeria, Benin, Burma, Congo, Finland, Madagascar, Mali, Mexico, Nigeria, Seychelles, Syria, Tanzania and Zimbabwe. The USSR also provided substantial economic aid and technical assistance to developing countries including Egypt, India, Iraq, Iran, Somalia and Turkey.[78] It supported developing countries in calling for a New International Economic Order and backed the UN Charter of Economic Rights and Obligations of States adopted by the General Assembly in 1974.[79]

Achievements of the socialist planned economies In the officially sanctioned textbooks describing the socialist planned economies as they existed in the 1980s it was claimed that:

- Class and national oppression had been totally eradicated.

- Unemployment, hunger, poverty, illiteracy and uncertainty about the future had been eliminated.

- Every citizen had a guaranteed right to work, rest, education, health care, abode and security in old age and maintenance in the event of disability.

- Material standards of living were rising steadily and everyone had free access to knowledge and to the values of world and national culture.

- Every citizen had a right in practice to take part in discussing and solving any problems in the life of the enterprise, region, republic and the country they lived in, including the rights to free speech, of assembly and to demonstrate.[80]

Data collected by the United Nations of indicators of human development in the early 1990s show that a high level of social development was achieved in the former socialist planned economies of Central and Eastern Europe and the Commonwealth of Independent States (CEE/CIS). Life expectancy in the CEE/CIS area in the period 1985-1990 was 68 years, while for the countries of the Organization for Economic Cooperation and Development (OECD) it was 75 years.[81] Infant mortality in the CEE/CIS area was 25 for every 1,000 live births in 1990, compared to 13 in the OECD area.[82] In terms of education, the two areas enjoyed universal adult literacy and full enrolment of children in primary and secondary schools. For tertiary education, the CEE/CIS had 2,600 university students per 100,000 population, while in the OECD the comparable figure was 3,550 students. Overall enrolment at primary, secondary and tertiary levels was 75 percent in the CEE/CIS region and 82 percent in the OECD countries.[83]

On housing the main problem was over-crowding rather than homelessness in the socialist planned economies. In the USSR the area of residential accommodation was 15.5 square meters per person by 1990 in urban areas but 15 percent of the population were without their own separate accommodation and had to live in communal apartments according to the 1989 census.[84] Housing was generally of good quality in both the CEE/CIS region and in the OECD countries: 98 and 99 percent of the population in the OECD countries had access to safe drinking water and improved sanitation respectively, compared to 93 and 85 percent in the CEE/CIS area by 1990.[85]

Unemployment did not exist officially in the socialist planned economies, though there were people between jobs and a fraction of unemployable people as a result of illness, disability or other problems, such as alcoholism. The proportion of people changing jobs was between 6 and 13 percent of the labour force a year according to employment data during the 1970s and 1980s in Central and Eastern Europe and the USSR. Labour exchanges were established in the USSR in 1967 to help enterprises re-allocate workers and provide information on job vacancies. Compulsory unemployment insurance schemes operated in Bulgaria, Eastern Germany and Hungary but the numbers claiming support as a result of losing their job through no fault of their own numbered a few hundred a year.[86]

By 1988 GDP per person, measured at purchasing power parity in US dollars, was $7,519 in Russia and $6,304 for the USSR. The highest income was to be found in Slovenia ($10,663) and Estonia ($9,078) and the lowest in Albania ($1,386) and Tajikistan ($2,730). Across the whole CEE/CIS area, GDP per person was estimated at $6,162.[87] This compared to the USA with $20,651 and $16,006 for Germany in the same year. For the OECD area as a whole estimated GDP per person was $14,385.[88] Thus, on the basis of IMF estimates, national income (GDP) per person in the CEE/CIS area was 43 percent of that in the OECD area.

Economic problems of the socialist planned economies
From the 1960s onwards, CMEA countries, beginning with Eastern Germany, attempted "intensive" growth strategies, aiming to raise the productivity of labour and capital. However, in practice this meant that investment was shifted towards new branches of industry, including the electronics, computing, automotive and nuclear power sectors, leaving the traditional heavy industries dependent upon older technologies. Despite the rhetoric about modernization, innovation remained weak as enterprise managers preferred routine production that was easier to plan and brought them predictable bonuses. Embargoes on high technology exports organized through the US-supported CoCom arrangement hampered technology transfer. Enterprise managers also ignored inducements to introduce labour-saving measures as they wished to retain a reserve of personnel to be available to meet their production target by working at top speed when supplies were delayed.[89]

Under conditions of "taut planning", the economy was expected to produce a volume of output higher than the reported capacity of enterprises and there was no "slack" in the system. Enterprises faced a resource constraint and hoarded labour and other inputs and avoided subcontracting intermediate production activities, preferring to retain the work in-house. The enterprise, according to the theory promulgated by János Kornai, was constrained by its resources not by the demand for its goods and services; nor was it constrained by its finances since the government was not likely to shut it down if it failed to meet its financial targets. Enterprises in socialist planned economies operated within a "soft" budget constraint, unlike enterprises in capitalist market economies which are demand-constrained and operate within "hard" budget constraints, as they face bankruptcy if their costs exceed their sales. As all producers were working in a resource-constrained economy they were perpetually in short supply and the shortages could never be eliminated, leading to chronic disruption of production schedules. The effect of this was to preserve a high level of employment.[90]

As the supply of consumer goods failed to match rising incomes (because workers still received their pay even if they were not fully productive), household savings accumulated, indicating, in the official terminology, "postponed demand". Western economists called this "monetary overhang" or "repressed inflation". Prices on the black market were several times higher than in the official price-controlled outlets, reflecting the scarcity and possible illegality of the sale of these items. Therefore, although consumer welfare was reduced by shortages, the prices households paid for their regular consumption were lower than would have been the case had prices been set at market-clearing levels.[91]

Over the course of the 1980s it became clear that the CMEA area was "in crisis", although it remained viable economically and was not expected to collapse.[92] The "extensive" growth model was retarding growth in the CMEA as a whole, with member countries dependent upon supplies of raw materials from the USSR and upon the Soviet market for sales of goods. The decline in growth rates reflected a combination of diminishing returns to capital accumulation and low innovation as well as micro-economic inefficiencies, which a high rate of saving and investment was unable to counter. The CMEA was supposed to ensure coordination of national plans but it failed even to develop a common methodology for planning which could be adopted by its member states. As each member state was reluctant to give up national self-sufficiency the CMEA's efforts to encourage specialization was thwarted. There were very few joint ventures and therefore little intra-enterprise technology transfer and trade, which in the capitalist world was often undertaken by trans-national corporations. The International Bank for Economic Cooperation had no means of converting a country's trade surplus into an option to buy goods and services from other CMEA members.[93]

Transition to market economies

After the dissolution of the Soviet Union and the Eastern bloc, many of the remaining socialist states presiding over centrally planned economies began introducing reforms that shifted their economies away from centralized planning. In Central and Eastern Europe and the USSR the transition from a planned economy to a market economy was accompanied by the transformation of the socialist mode of production to a capitalist mode of production. In Asia (China, Laos, North Korea and Vietnam) and in Cuba market mechanisms were introduced by the ruling communist parties and the planning system was reformed without systemic transformation.

The transformation from socialism to capitalism involved a political shift: from a people's democracy (see People's Republic and Communist state) with a constitutionally entrenched "leading role" for the communist and workers' parties in society to a liberal representative democracy with a separation of legislative, executive and judicial authorities and centres of private power that can act as a brake on the state's activity.[94]

Vietnam adopted an economic model it formally titled the *socialist-oriented market economy*. This economic system is a form of mixed-economy consisting of state, private, co-operative and individual enterprises coordinated by the market mechanism. This system is intended to be transitional stage in the development of socialism.

Transition economies See also: Transition economy

The transformation of an economic system from a socialist planned economy to a capitalist market economy in Central and Eastern Europe, the former Soviet Union and Mongolia in the 1990s involved a series of institutional changes.[95] These included:

- Control over the means of production was removed from the state through privatization and private property rights were re-established. In several countries property was restored to its former owners or their legal successors. If the actual property could not be returned the former owners received compensation. This occurred in Eastern Germany, Czechoslovakia, Hungary and Estonia. In all the countries of the Commonwealth of Independent States, the government decided against restoration or compensation on the grounds that too much time had elapsed and in many cases compensation had already been made through bilateral treaties between the USSR and foreign governments representing the former owners. Voucher privatization in which citizens and workers in the enterprises received free or cheap shares was undertaken in most of the transition economies.[96]

- The decision-making system was de-centralized through the ending of central planning and the privatization of enterprises. Work collectives and trade unions lost much of their influence in enterprise decision-making.

- Markets became the dominant coordination mechanism following price liberalization and the de-control of foreign trade that permitted more or less unrestricted importation of goods in 1990/92. Queues at retail outlets disappeared as did hoarded inventories at factories. Stock exchanges were established between 1990 and 1995. Anti-monopoly legislation was introduced.[97] As workers lost their jobs or found their wages unpaid, informal labour markets sprang up along certain streets, particularly for construction trades.[98]

- The incentive system was modified by the legalization of private enterprise and alteration to employment laws. A large informal sphere developed estimated at comprising 21 to 30 percent of official calculations of GDP.[99]

- The organizational forms prevailing in the socialist planned economies were restructured by breaking up vertically-integrated industrial and agricultural concerns and closing non-viable undertakings. The hardening of enterprise budget constraints was more significant in driving industrial restructuring than privatization according to some studies.[100]

- The distribution system became more unequal as price controls on necessities were removed fuelling the growth of poverty among people on fixed incomes such as pensioners and the unemployed. Redistributive measures through taxation and social safety nets proved unable to counteract the growth of poverty and, at the other end of the income scale, the emergence of a rich business elite (see also business oligarch).

- The public choice mechanism was overhauled to rescind the communist party's leading role and introduce a liberal constitution entrenching civil rights and representative democracy in almost all transition economies except Belarus, Turkmenistan and Uzbekistan.

People's Republic of China Main article: Economy of the People's Republic of China

China embraced a socialist planned economy after the Communist victory in its Civil War. Private property and private ownership of capital were abolished, and various forms of wealth made subject to state control or to workers' councils.

The Chinese economy broadly adopted a similar system of production quotas and full employment by fiat to the Russian model. The Great Leap Forward saw a remarkably large-scale experiment with rapid collectivisation of agriculture, and other ambitious goals. Results were less than expected, (e.g., there were food shortages and mass starvation) and the program was abandoned after three years.

In recent decades China has opened its economy to foreign investment and to market-based trade, and has continued to experience strong economic growth. It has carefully managed the transition from a socialist planned economy to a market economy, officially referred to as the *socialist commodity market economy*, which has been likened to capitalism by some outside observers.[101] As a result, centralized economic planning has little relevance in China today.

The current Chinese economic system is characterized by state ownership combined with a strong private sector that privately owned enterprises that generate about 33%[102] (People's Daily Online 2005) to over 50% of GDP in 2005,[103] with a BusinessWeek article estimating 70%[104] of GDP, a figure that might be even greater considering the Chengbao system. Some western observers note that the private sector is likely underestimated by state officials in calculation of GDP due to its propensity to ignore small private enterprises that are not registered.[105] Most of the state and private sectors of economy are governed by free market practices, including a stock exchange for trading equity. The free-market is the arbitrator for most economic activity, which is left to the management of both state and private firms. A significant amount of privately owned firms exist, especially in the consumer service sector.[106]

The state sector is concentrated in the 'commanding heights' of the economy with a growing private sector engaged primarily in commodity production and light industry. Centralized directive planning based on mandatory output requirements and production quotas has been superseded by the free-market mechanism for most of the economy and directive planning is utilized in some large state industries.[106] A major difference from the old planned economy is the privatization of state institutions. 150 state-owned enterprises remain and report directly to the central government, most having a number of subsidiaries.[107] By 2008, these state-owned corporations had become increasingly dynamic largely contributing to the increase in revenue for the state.[108][109] The state-sector led the economic recovery process and increased economic growth in 2009 after the financial crises.[110]

This type of economic system is defended from a Marxist perspective which states that a socialist planned economy can only be possible after first establishing the necessary comprehensive commodity market economy, letting it fully develop until it exhausts its historical stage and gradually transforms itself into a planned economy.[111] Proponents of this model distinguish themselves from market socialists who believe that economic planning is unattainable, undesirable or ineffective at distributing goods, viewing the market as the solution rather than a temporary phase in development of a socialist planned economy.

Other socialist states The Socialist Republic of Vietnam has pursued similar economic reforms, though less extensive, which have resulted in a socialist-oriented market economy, a mixed economy in which the state plays a dominant role intended to be a transitional phase in establishment of a socialist economy.[112]

The Republic of Cuba, under the leadership of Raul Castro, has begun to encourage co-operatives and self-employment in a move to reduce the central role of state enterprise and state management over the economy, with the goal of building a co-operative form of socialism.[113]

Social Democratic Mixed Economies

Main article: Social democracy

Many of the industrialized, open countries of Western Europe experimented with one form of social democratic mixed economies or another during the 20th century. These include Britain (mixed economy and welfare state) from 1945 to 1979, France (state capitalism and indicative planning) from 1945 to 1982 under dirigisme, Sweden (social democratic welfare state) and Norway (state capitalist mixed economy) to the present. They can be regarded as social democratic experiments, because they universally retained a wage-based economy and private ownership and control of the decisive means of production.

Nevertheless, these western European countries tried to restructure their economies away from a purely private capitalist model. Variations range from social democratic welfare states, such as in Sweden, to mixed economies where a major percentage of GDP comes from the state sector, such as in Norway, which ranks among the highest countries in quality of life and equality of opportunity for its citizens.[114] Elements of these efforts persist throughout Europe, even if they have repealed some aspects of public control and ownership. They are typically characterized by:

- **Nationalization** of key industries, such as mining, oil, steel, energy and transportation. A common model is for a sector to be taken over by the state and then one or more publicly owned corporations set up for its day-to-day running. Advantages of nationalization include: the ability of the state to direct investment in key industries, the distribution of state profits from nationalized industries for the overall national good, the ability to direct producers to social rather than market goals, greater control of the industries by and for the workers, and the benefits and burdens of publicly funded research and development are extended to the wider populace.

- **Redistribution of wealth**, through both tax and spending policies that aim to reduce economic inequalities. Social democracies typically employ various forms of progressive taxation regarding wage and business income, wealth, inheritance, capital gains and property. On the spending side, a set of social policies typically provides free access to public services such as education, health care and child care, while subsidized access to housing, food, pharmaceutical goods, water supply, waste management and electricity is also common.

- **Social security** schemes where workers contribute to a mandatory public insurance program. The insurance typically include monetary provisions for retirement pensions and survivor benefits, permanent and temporary disabilities, unemployment and parental leave. Unlike private insurance, governmental schemes are based on public statutes and not contracts, so that contributions and benefits may change in time and are based on solidarity among participants. Its funding is done on an ongoing basis, without direct relationship with future liabilities.

- **Minimum wages, employment protection and trade union recognition rights** for the benefit of workers. The objectives of these policies are to guarantee living wages and help produce full employment. There are a number of different models of trade union protection which evolved, but they all guarantee the right of workers to form unions, negotiate benefits and participate in strikes. Germany, for instance, appointed union representatives at high levels in all corporations and had much less industrial strife than the UK, whose laws encouraged strikes rather than negotiation.

- **National planning** for industrial development.

- **Demand management** in a Keynesian fashion to help ensure economic growth and employment.

State capitalism

Various state capitalist economies, which consist of large commercial state enterprises that operate according to the laws of capitalism and pursue profits, have evolved in countries that have been influenced by various elected socialist political parties and their economic reforms. While these policies and reforms did not change the fundamental aspect of capitalism, and non-socialist elements within these countries supported or often implemented many of these reforms themselves, the result has been a set of economic institutions that were at least partly influenced by socialist ideology.

Singapore   Main article: Economy of Singapore

Singapore pursued a state-led model of economic development under the People's Action Party, which initially adopted a Leninist approach to politics and a broad socialist model of economic development.[115] The PAP was initially a member of the Socialist International. Singapore's economy is dominated by state-owned enterprises and government-linked companies through Temasek Holdings, which generate 60% of Singapore's GDP.[116] Temasek Holdings operates like any other company in a market economy. Managers of the holding are rewarded according to profits with the explicit intention to cultivate an ownership mind-set.[117]

The state also provides substantial public housing, free education, health and recreational services, as well as comprehensive public transportation.[118] Today Singapore is often characterized as having a state capitalist economy that combines economic planning with the free-market.[119] While government-linked companies generate a majority of Singapore's GDP, moderate state planning in the economy has been reduced in recent decades.

India   Main article: Economy of India

After gaining independence from Britain, India adopted a broadly socialist-inspired approach to economic growth. Like other countries with a democratic transition to a mixed economy, it did not abolish private property in capital. India proceeded by **nationalizing** various large privately run firms, creating **state-owned enterprises** and **redistributing** income through progressive taxation in a manner similar to social democratic Western European nations than to planned economies such as the USSR or China. Today India is often characterized as having a free-market economy that combines economic planning with the free-market. It did however adopt a very firm focus on national planning with a series of broad Five-Year Plans.

Paris Commune

Main article: Paris Commune

The Paris Commune was considered to be a prototype mode of economic and political organization for a future socialist society by Karl Marx. Private property in the means of production was abolished so that individuals and co-operative associations of producers owned productive property and introduced democratic measures where elected officials received no more in compensation than the average worker and could be recalled at any time.[120] Anarchists also participated actively in the establishment of the Paris Commune. George Woodcock manifests that "a notable contribution to the activities of the Commune and particularly to the organization of public services was made by members of various anarchist factions, including the mutualists Courbet, Longuet, and Vermorel, the libertarian collectivists Varlin, Malon, and Lefrangais, and the bakuninists Elie and Elisée Reclus and Louise Michel.[121]

Social ownership and peer-to-peer production

Various forms of socialist organization based on co-operative decision making, workplace democracy and in some cases, production directly for use, have existed within the broader context of the capitalist mode of production since the Paris Commune. New forms of socialist institutional arrangements began to take form at the end of the 20th century with the advancement and proliferation of the internet and other tools that allow for collaborative decision-making.

Michel Bauwens identifies the emergence of the open software movement and peer-to-peer production as an emergent alternative mode of production to the capitalist economy that is based on collaborative self-management, common ownership of resources, and the (direct) production of use-values through the free cooperation of producers who have access to distributed capital.[122]

Commons-based peer production generally involves developers who produce goods and services with no aim to profit directly, but freely contribute to a project relying upon an open common pool of resources and software code. In both cases, production is carried out directly for use — software is produced solely for their use-value.

Wikipedia, being based on collaboration and cooperation and a freely associated individuals, has been cited as a template for how socialism might operate.[123] This is a modern example of what the Paris Commune — a template for possible future organization — was to Marx in his time.

Socialist Federal Republic of Yugoslavia   Main article: Economy of SFR Yugoslavia

Yugoslavia pursued a socialist economy based on autogestion or worker-self management. Rather than implementing a centrally planned economy, Yugoslavia developed a market socialist system where enterprises and firms were socially owned rather than publicly owned by the state. In these organizations, the management was elected directly by the workers in each firm, and were later organized according to Edvard Kardelj's theory of associated labor.

Self-managed enterprises See also: Cooperative

The Mondragon Corporation, a federation of cooperatives in the Basque region of Spain, organizes itself as an employee-owned, employee-managed enterprise. Similar styles of decentralized management, which embrace cooperation and collaboration in place of traditional hierarchical management structures, have been adopted by various private corporations such as Cisco Systems, inc.[124] But unlike Mondragon, Cisco remains firmly under private ownership. More fundamentally, employee-owned, self-managed enterprises still operate within the broader context of capitalism and are subject to the accumulation of capital and profit-loss mechanism.

Anarchist Spain

Main article: Spanish revolution
See also: Anarcho-syndicalism

In Spain, the national anarcho-syndicalist trade union Confederación Nacional del Trabajo initially refused to join a popular front electoral alliance, and abstention by CNT supporters led to a right wing election victory. But in 1936, the CNT changed its policy and anarchist votes helped bring the popular front back to power. Months later, the former ruling class responded with an attempted coup causing the Spanish Civil War (1936–1939).[125] In response to the army rebellion, an anarchist-inspired movement of peasants and workers, supported by armed militias, took control of Barcelona and of large areas of rural Spain where they collectivised the land.[126][127] But even before the fascist victory in 1939, the anarchists were losing ground in a bitter struggle with the Stalinists, who controlled the distribution of military aid to the Republican cause from the Soviet Union. The events known as the Spanish Revolution was a workers' social revolution that began during the outbreak of the Spanish Civil War in 1936 and resulted in the widespread implementation of anarchist and more broadly libertarian socialist organizational principles throughout various portions of the country for two to three years, primarily Catalonia, Aragon, Andalusia, and parts of the Levante. Much of Spain's economy was put under worker control; in anarchist strongholds like Catalonia, the figure was as high as 75%, but lower in areas with heavy Communist Party of Spain influence, as the Soviet-allied party actively resisted attempts at collectivization enactment. Factories were run through worker committees, agrarian areas became collectivised and run as libertarian communes. Anarchist historian Sam Dolgoff estimated that about eight million people participated directly or at least indirectly in the Spanish Revolution,[128] which he claimed "came closer to realizing the ideal of the free stateless society on a vast scale than any other revolution in history."[129]

2.62.5 Criticisms

Main article: Criticism of socialism

Criticism of socialist economics comes from market economists, including the classicals, neoclassicals and Austrians, as well as from some anarchist economists. Besides this, some socialist economic theories are criticized by other socialists. Libertarian socialist, mutualist, and market socialist economists, for example, criticize centralized economic planning and propose participatory economics and decentralized socialism.

Market economists generally criticise socialism for eliminating the free market and its price signals, which they consider necessary for rational economic calculation. They also consider that it causes lack of incentive. They believe that these problems lead to a slower rate of technological advance and a slower rate of growth of GDP.

Austrian school economists, such as Friedrich Hayek and Ludwig Von Mises, have argued that the elimination of private ownership of the means of production would inevitably create worse economic conditions for the general populace than those that would be found in market economies. They argue that without the price signals of the market, it is impossible to calculate rationally how to allocate resources. Mises called this the economic calculation problem. Polish economist Oskar Lange and Abba Lerner responded to Mises' argument by developing the Lange Model during the Economic calculation debate. The Lange model argues that an economy in which all production is performed by the state, where there is a functioning price mechanism, has similar properties to a market economy under perfect competition, in that it achieves Pareto efficiency.

The neoclassical view is that there is a lack of incentive, not a lack of information in a planned economy. They argue that within a socialist planned economy there is a lack of incentive to act on information. Therefore, the crucial missing element is not so much information as the Austrian school argued, as it is the motivation to act on information.[130]

2.62.6 See also

2.62.7 References

[1] Sinclair, Upton (1918-01-01). *Upton Sinclair's: A Monthly Magazine: for Social Justice, by Peaceful Means If Possible*. Socialism, you see, is a bird with two wings. The definition is

'social ownership and democratic control of the instruments and means of production.'

[2] Nove, Alec. "Socialism". *New Palgrave Dictionary of Economics, Second Edition (2008)*. A society may be defined as socialist if the major part of the means of production of goods and services is in some sense socially owned and operated, by state, socialized or cooperative enterprises. The practical issues of socialism comprise the relationships between management and workforce within the enterprise, the interrelationships between production units (plan versus markets), and, if the state owns and operates any part of the economy, who controls it and how.

[3] Rosser, Mariana V. and J Barkley Jr. (July 23, 2003). *Comparative Economics in a Transforming World Economy*. MIT Press. p. 53. ISBN 978-0262182348. Socialism is an economic system characterized by state or collective ownership of the means of production, land, and capital.

[4] "What else does a socialist economic system involve? Those who favor socialism generally speak of social ownership, social control, or socialization of the means of production as the distinctive positive feature of a socialist economic system" N. Scott Arnold. *The Philosophy and Economics of Market Socialism : A Critical Study*. Oxford University Press. 1998. pg. 8

[5] Busky, Donald F. (20 July 2000). *Democratic Socialism: A Global Survey*. Praeger. p. 2. ISBN 978-0275968861. Socialism may be defined as movements for social ownership and control of the economy. It is this idea that is the common element found in the many forms of socialism.

[6] Bertrand Badie; Dirk Berg-Schlosser; Leonardo Morlino (2011). *International Encyclopedia of Political Science*. SAGE Publications, Inc. p. 2456. ISBN 978-1412959636. Socialist systems are those regimes based on the economic and political theory of socialism, which advocates public ownership and cooperative management of the means of production and allocation of resources.

[7] *Market Socialism: The Debate Among Socialists*, by Schweickart, David; Lawler, James; Ticktin, Hillel; Ollman, Bertell. 1998. From "The Difference Between Marxism and Market Socialism" (P.61-63): "More fundamentally, a socialist society must be one in which the economy is run on the principle of the direct satisfaction of human needs ... Exchange-value, prices and so money are goals in themselves in a capitalist society or in any market. There is no necessary connection between the accumulation of capital or sums of money and human welfare. Under conditions of backwardness, the spur of money and the accumulation of wealth has led to a massive growth in industry and technology ... It seems an odd argument to say that a capitalist will only be efficient in producing use-value of a good quality when trying to make more money than the next capitalist. It would seem easier to rely on the planning of use-values in a rational way, which because there is no duplication, would be produced more cheaply and be of a higher quality"... ..."Although money, and so monetary calculation, will disappear in socialism this does not mean that there will no longer be any need to make choices, evaluations and calculations ... Wealth will be produced and distributed in its natural form of useful things, of objects that can serve to satisfy some human need or other. Not being produced for sale on a market, items of wealth will not acquire an exchange-value in addition to their use-value. In socialism their value, in the normal non-economic sense of the word, will not be their selling price nor the time needed to produce them but their usefulness. It is for this that they will be appreciated, evaluated, wanted. . . and produced."

[8] "=Socialism and Calculation" (PDF). Worldsocialism.org. Retrieved February 15, 2010.

[9] Kornai, János: *The Socialist System. The Political Economy of Communism*. Princeton: Princeton University Press and Oxford: Oxford University Press 1992; Kornai, János: *Economics of Shortage*. Munich: Elsevier 1980. A concise summary of Kornai's analysis can be found in Verdery, Katherine: *Anthropology of Socialist Societies*. In: International Encyclopedia of the Social and Behavioral Sciences, ed. Neil Smelser and Paul B. Baltes. Amsterdam: Pergamon Press 2002, available for download here .

[10] Rob Sewell (December 21, 2012). "Origin of the family: In Defence of Engels and Morgan". Marxist.com.

[11] Wallerstein, Immanuel *Historical Capitalism*

[12] Chomsky, Noam *Perspectives on Power*

[13] Karl Polanyi *Primitive, Archaic and Modern Economies*

[14] Noel Thomson *The Real Rights of Man: Political Economies for the Working Class 1775–1850*, 1998, Pluto Press

[15] "Adam Smith". Fsmitha.com. Retrieved 2014-08-15.

[16] "2:BIRTH OF THE SOCIALIST IDEA". Anu.edu.au. Retrieved 2014-08-15.

[17]

[18]

[19] Karl Marx. "Economic Manuscripts: Capital Vol. I - Chapter One". Marxists.org. Retrieved 2014-08-15.

[20] "Capitalism and Ecology: The Nature of the Contradiction". Monthlyreview.org. Retrieved 2014-08-15.

[21] Petras, James and Veltmeyer, Henry *Globalization Unmasked: Imperialism in the 21st Century*

[22] Woodcock, George. Anarchism: A History Of Libertarian Ideas And Movements. Broadview Press. p. 100

[23] "Introduction". Mutualist.org. Retrieved 2010-04-29.

[24] Miller, David. 1987. "Mutualism." The Blackwell Encyclopedia of Political Thought. Blackwell Publishing. p. 11

[25] Tandy, Francis D., 1896, *Voluntary Socialism*, chapter 6, paragraph 15.

[26] Patsouras, Louis. 2005. Marx in Context. iUniverse. p. 54

[27] Bakunin Mikail. Bakunin on Anarchism. Black Rose Books. 1980. p. 369

[28] *From Politics Past to Politics Future: An Integrated Analysis of Current and Emergent Paradigms Alan James Mayne Published 1999 Greenwood Publishing Group 316 pages ISBN 0-275-96151-6*. Books.google.com. Retrieved 2014-08-15.

[29] *Anarchism for Know-It-Alls*. Filiquarian Publishing. 2008. ISBN 978-1-59986-218-7. Retrieved 2010-09-20.

[30] "Luggi Fabbri". Dwardmac.pitzer.edu. 2002-10-13. Retrieved 2014-08-15.

[31] "Platform: Constructive Section". Nestormakhno.info. Retrieved 2014-08-15.

[32] "Communism is based on free consumption of all while collectivism is more likely to be based on the distribution of goods according to the labour contributed. An Anarchist FAQ

[33] Nunzio Pernicone, "Italian Anarchism 1864–1892", pp. 111–113, AK Press 2009.

[34] James Guillaume, "Michael Bakunin – A Biographical Sketch"

[35] Wallerstein, Immanuel, The Capitalist World-Economy, 1979, Cambridge University Press

[36] "What is Socialism? – World Socialist Movement". Worldsocialism.org. 2006-08-13. Retrieved 2014-08-15.

[37] *Karl Marx* — Critique of the Gotha Programme. 1875 Full Text. Part 1: "Here, obviously, the same principle prevails as that which regulates the exchange of commodities, as far as this is exchange of equal values. Content and form are changed, because under the altered circumstances no one can give anything except his labor, and because, on the other hand, nothing can pass to the ownership of individuals, except individual means of consumption. But as far as the distribution of the latter among the individual producers is concerned, the same principle prevails as in the exchange of commodity equivalents: a given amount of labor in one form is exchanged for an equal amount of labor in another form."

[38] *The Political Economy of Socialism*, by Horvat, Branko. 1982. (P.197): "The sandglass (socialist) model is based on the observation that there are two fundamentally different spheres of activity or decision making. The first is concerned with value judgments, and consequently each individual counts as one in this sphere. In the second, technical decisions are made on the basis of technical competence and expertise. The decisions of the first sphere are policy directives; those of the second, technical directives. The former are based on political authority as exercised by all members of the organization; the latter, on professional authority specific to each member and growing out of the division of labor. Such an organization involves a clearly defined coordinating hierarchy but eliminates a power hierarchy."

[39] "What was the USSR? Part I: Trotsky and state capitalism". Libcom.org. 2005-04-09. Retrieved 2014-08-15.

[40] *Why Socialism?* by Albert Einstein, *Monthly Review*, May 1949

[41] *In Defense of Socialist Planning*, by Mandel, Ernest. 1986. From "New Left Review": "Planning is not equivalent to 'perfect' allocation of resources, nor 'scientific' allocation, nor even 'more humane' allocation. It simply means 'direct' allocation, ex ante. As such, it is the opposite of market allocation, which is ex post."

[42] "Glossary of Terms: Co". Marxists.org. Retrieved 2014-08-15.

[43] *Writings 1932-33, P.96*, Leon Trotsky.

[44] "Science & Society, Vol". Homepages.luc.edu. Retrieved 2014-08-15.

[45] "Why we don't need money | The Socialist Party of Great Britain" (PDF). Worldsocialism.org. Retrieved 2014-08-15.

[46] Robin Hahnel and Michael Albert *A Quiet Revolution in Welfare Economics*

[47] rasputin@point-of-departure.org (2006-11-05). "Workers' Councils and the Economics of a Self-Managed Society". Lust-for-life.org. Retrieved 2014-08-15.

[48] http://www.bm.ust.hk/~{}ced/iea/Hong_Kong_Yingyinek_kikuldott_05june2.doc

[49] Schweickart, David (July 23, 2002). "Chapter 5: Economic Democracy: Why We Need It; 5.7: Ecology, p. 156". *After Capitalism*. Rowman & Littlefield Publishers, Inc.

[50] *Democratic Planned Socialism*, by Campbell, Al. 2002. Science and Society, 66(1), Spring 2002, 29-42.

[51] Nove, Alec (1991). *The Economics of Feasible Socialism, Revisited*. Routledge. ISBN 978-0043350492.

[52] Yunker, James (April 1992). *Socialism Revised and Modernized: The Case for Pragmatic Market Socialism*. Praeger. pp. 29–31. ISBN 978-0275941345.

[53] Schmitt and Anton, Richard and Anatole (March 2012). *Taking Socialism Seriously*. Lexington Books. p. 160. ISBN 978-0739166352. Commons-based peer production bears a close family resemblance to the familiar vision of socialism sketched in the first paragraph of this chapter…In commons-based peer production a critical mass of inputs, and all outputs, are distributed within information networks as free goods rather than as commodities to be sold for profit by capitalist firms.

[54] "Participatory Planning Through Negotiated Coordination" (PDF). Retrieved 30 October 2011.

[55] Michael Kaser, *Soviet Economics*, 1970, London: Weidenfeld & Nicolson, pp. 150-151 ISBN 0-303-17565-6.

[56] Kaser, M C, *Soviet Economics*, 1970, London: Weidenfeld & Nicolson, p. 102 ISBN 0-303-17565-6.

[57] Kaser, M C in *Economic Reforms in the Socialist World*, 1989, edited by Gomulka, Stanislav, Ha, Yong-Chool and Kim, Cae-One, New York: M E Sharpe, pp. 97-98.

[58] Kaser, M C, *Soviet Economics*, 1970, London: Weidenfeld & Nicolson, pp. 172 and 222 ISBN 0-303-17565-6.

[59] Kaser, M C, *Soviet Economics*, 1970, London: Weidenfeld & Nicolson, pp. 94-95, 107, 111-112, 127, 148 and 165 ISBN 0-303-17565-6.

[60] http://www.rdwolff.com/sites/default/files/attachment/4/State%20Capitalism%20versus%20Communism%20CS%202008.pdf

[61] "Peter Binns: State Capitalism (1986)". Marxists.de. Retrieved 2014-08-15.

[62] Tatyana Volkova and Felix Volkov, *What is surplus value?*, 1986, Moscow: Progress Publishers, p. 288.

[63] Kaser, M C, *Soviet Economics*, 1970 (London: Weidenfeld & Nicolson) pp. 167-170 ISBN 0-303-17565-6; Brown, A, Kaser M C, and Smith G S (editors), *The Cambridge Encyclopedia of Russia and the former Soviet Union*, 1994, Cambridge University Press, p. 429 ISBN 0-521-35593-1.

[64] John Eaton, *Political Economy: A Marxist Textbook*, 1949, London: Lawrence and Wishart, pp. 182-183.

[65] Robert Service, *Comrades – Communism: A World History*, 2007, London: Pan Macmillan, pp. 156-157 ISBN 978-0-330-43968-8; Brown, A, Kaser, M C, and Smith, G S (editors), *The Cambridge Encyclopedia of Russia and the former Soviet Union*, 1994, Cambridge University Press, p. 428 ISBN 0-521-35593-1.

[66] "Tony Cliff: State Capitalism in Russia (1955/1974)". Marxists.org. 2002-11-09. Retrieved 2014-08-15.

[67] VN Embassy — Constitution of 1992 Full Text. From the Preamble: "On 2 July 1976, the National Assembly of reunified Vietnam decided to change the country's name to the Socialist Republic of Vietnam; the country entered a period of transition to socialism, strove for national construction, and unyieldingly defended its frontiers while fulfilling its internationalist duty."

[68] Cubanet — Constitution of the Republic of Cuba, 1992 Full Text. From Article 5: "The Communist Party of Cuba, a follower of Martí's ideas and of Marxism-Leninism, and the organized vanguard of the Cuban nation, is the highest leading force of society and of the state, which organizes and guides the common effort toward the goals of the construction of socialism and the progress toward a communist society,"

[69] V Kashin and N Cherkasov, *What is the Transition Period?*, 1987, Moscow: Progress Publishers, pp. 140-141.

[70] V Kashin and N Cherkasov, *What is the Transition Period?*, 1987, Moscow: Progress Publishers, pp. 142-144; Sergei Ilyin and Alexander Motylev, *What is Political Economy?*, 1986 Moscow: Progress Publishers, p. 325.

[71] John Eaton, *Political Economy: A Marxist Textbook*, 1949, London: Lawrence and Wishart, pp. 179-182; Stalin, J V, *Economic Problems of Socialism in the USSR* (1952) in *Selected Works Volume 1*, 2012, Kolkata: Prometheus, pp. 317-325.

[72] V Kashin and N Cherkasov, *What is the Transition Period?*, 1987, Moscow: Progress Publishers, p. 144; Sergei Ilyin and Alexander Motylev, *What is Political Economy?*, 1986 Moscow: Progress Publishers, pp. 323-326 and 330.

[73] Marie Lavigne, *International Political Economy and Socialism*, 1991, Cambridge University Press, pp. 54-55 ISBN 0-521-33427-6.

[74] Sergei Ilyin and Alexander Motylev, *What is Political Economy?*, 1986, Moscow: Progress Publishers, pp. 322-324.

[75] Kaser, M C, *Comecon: Integration problems of the planned economies*, 1967, Oxford University Press, p. 170 ISBN 0-303-17565-6.

[76] Jenny Brine, *Comecon: The rise and fall of an international socialist organization*, 1992, New Brunswick, NJ: Rutgers University/Transaction, p. xii ISBN 1-56000-080-5.

[77] Philip Hanson, *The rise and fall of the Soviet economy: An economic history of the USSR*, 2003, Harlow: Pearson Education, pp. 121 and 131 ISBN 0-582-29958-6.

[78] http://photius.com/ountries/soviet_union_former/government/soviet_union_former/government_countries_of_social-1817.html

[79] Padma Desai, *The Soviet Economy: Problems and Prospects*, 1990, Oxford: Basil Blackwell, pp. 258-263 ISBN 0-631-17183-5

[80] Sergei Ilyin and Alexander Motylev, *What is Political Economy?*, 1986, Moscow: Progress Publishers, pp. 271-272.

[81] UN Department of Economic & Social Affairs, *World Population Prospects: The 2012 Revision*, File MORT/7.1. Data for 1985-1990. The world average was 64 years.

[82] UN, 1994, *Demographic Yearbook 1992*, New York: United Nations Department for Economic and Social Information and Policy Analysis, Tables 4 and 20. Data is for 1990. The world average was 58 for every1,000 live births.

[83] UNDP, *Human Development Report 1997*, Tables 27 and 47; figures are for 1992-94. The world average is 1,490 students per 100,000 people and 60 percent for the gross enrolment ratio, combining all levels of education. It should be noted that countries with a high intake at tertiary level to technical and vocational education such as Western Germany (2,320) had a similar ratio of university students to the socialist countries, reflecting a higher proportion of manufacturing and construction in their economies. ISBN 0-19-511997-5.

2.62. SOCIALIST ECONOMICS

[84] Brown, A, Kaser, M C, Smith, G S (editors), *The Cambridge Encyclopedia of Russia and the Former Soviet Union*, 1994, Cambridge: Cambridge University Press, pp. 411 and 465 ISBN 0-521-35593-1.

[85] "Millennium Development Goals Indicators for 1990". *UN Statistics Division, Department of Economic & Social Affairs*. Retrieved 2013-12-26.

[86] Brown, A, Kaser, M C, Smith, G S (editors), *The Cambridge Encyclopedia of Russia and the Former Soviet Union*, 1994, Cambridge: Cambridge University Press, pp. 431 and 464 ISBN 0-521-35593-1; and Porket, J L, *Unemployment in Capitalist, Communist and Post-Communist Economies*, 1995, London: Macmillan pp. 32-36 ISBN 0-312-12484-8.

[87] "IMF staff estimates in Stanley Fischer, Ratna Sahay and Carlos Vegh, "Stabilization and growth in transition economies: The early experience", April 1996, IMF Working Paper WP/96/31; Table 1, p. 6". Mpra.ub.uni-muenchen.de. Retrieved 2014-08-15.

[88] OECD *National Accounts at a Glance*, 2013 edition for 1988 GDP per capita at current purchasing power parities and current prices, retrieved on 1/11/2013.

[89] Archie Brown, and Michael Kaser, *Soviet Policy for the 1980s*, 1982, Bloomington, IN: Indiana University Press, pp.188, 194, 200 and 208 ISBN 0-253-35412-9; Simon Clarke (editor), *Structural Adjustment without Mass Unemployment? Lessons from Russia*, 1998, Cheltenham: Edward Elgar, pp. 23-28 ISBN 1-85898-713-X; Marie Lavigne, *The Economies of Transition: From socialist economy to market economy*, 1995, London: Macmillan, pp. 52-54, 60-61, 75-76 and 248 ISBN 0-333-52731-3; Padma Desai, *The Soviet Economy: Problems and Prospects*, 1990, Oxford: Basil Blackwell, pp. 10-11 ISBN 0-631-17183-5

[90] János Kornai, "Economics of Shortage", Amsterdam: North Holland; Marie Lavigne, *The Economies of Transition: From socialist economy to market economy*, 1995, London: Macmillan, pp. 60, 130-135 and 248 ISBN 0-333-52731-3

[91] Brown, A, and Kaser, M C, *The Soviet Union Since the Fall of Khrushchev*, 1978, London: Macmillan, pp. 212-214 ISBN 0-333-23337-9; Brown, A, and Kaser, M C, *Soviet Policy for the 1980s*, 1982, Bloomington, IN: Indiana University Press, p.193 ISBN 0-253-35412-9; Marie Lavigne, *The Economies of Transition: From socialist economy to market economy*, 1995, London: Macmillan, pp. 61 and 130-135 ISBN 0-333-52731-3

[92] Marie Lavigne, *The Economies of Transition: From socialist economy to market economy*, 1995, London: Macmillan, pp. 76 and 248 ISBN 0-333-52731-3

[93] Marie Lavigne, *The Economies of Transition: From socialist economy to market economy*, 1995, London: Macmillan, pp. 52-54 and 75-76 ISBN 0-333-52731-3

[94] Boris Putrin, *Political Terms: A short guide*, 1982, Moscow: Novosti, p. 63; Samuel E Finer, *Comparative Government*, 1974, Harmondsworth: Penguin, pp. 66-71 ISBN 0-140-21170-5.

[95] Paul R Gregory and Robert C Stuart, *The Global Economy and its Economic Systems*, 2013, Independence, KY: Cengage Learning ISBN 1-285-05535-7

[96] Michael Kaser on *Privatization in the CIS* in Alan Smith (editor), *Challenges for Russian Economic Reform*, 1995, London: Royal Institute for International Affairs and Washington DC: The Brookings Institution, pp. 118-127.

[97] Michael Kaser on *Privatization in the CIS* in Alan Smith (editor), *Challenges for Russian Economic Reform*, 1995, London: Royal Institute for International Affairs and Washington DC: The Brookings Institution, p. 126; Marie Lavigne, *The Economies of Transition: From socialist economy to market economy*, 1995, London: Macmillan, pp. 122-127 ISBN 0-333-52731-3

[98] Simon Clarke (editor), *Structural Adjustment without Mass Unemployment? Lessons from Russia*, 1998, Cheltenham: Edward Elgar, pp. 97-98 and 53 ISBN 1-85898-713-X.

[99] http://www.imf.org/external/pubs/ft/issues30/

[100] Silvana Malle, *The institutional framework of privatization and competition in economies in transition* in Paul Hare, Judy Batt and Saul Estrin (editors), *Reconstituting the Market: The political economy of microeconomic transformation*, 1999, Amsterdam: Harwood, p. 391 ISBN 90-5702-329-6

[101] "Long on China, Short on the United States by Tim Swanson". Scribd.com. 2009-01-20. Retrieved 2014-08-15.

[102] english@peopledaily.com.cn (2005-07-13). "People's Daily Online - China has socialist market economy in place". English.people.com.cn. Retrieved 2014-08-15.

[103]

[104] "Online Extra: "China Is a Private-Sector Economy"". Businessweek. 2005-08-21. Retrieved 2014-08-15.

[105] *China Since Tiananmen: The Politics of Transition - Joseph Fewsmith - Google Books*. Books.google.ca. Retrieved 2014-08-15.

[106] The Role of Planning in China's Market Economy

[107] "Reassessing China's State-Owned Enterprises". *Forbes*. July 8, 2008.

[108] http://us.ft.com/ftgateway/superpage.ft?news_id=fto031620081407384075

[109] http://ufirc.ou.edu/publications/Enterprises%20of%20China.pdf

[110] "China grows faster amid worries". *BBC News*. 2009-07-16. Retrieved 2010-05-23.

[111] <http://docs.google.com/gview?a=v&q=cache:tWl8XGM_vQAJ:www.nodo50.org/cubasigloXXI/congreso06/conf3_zhonquiao.pdf+Socialist+planned+commodity+economy&hl=en&gl=us

[112]

[113] "Cuba: from communist to co-operative? | Stephen Wilkinson | Comment is free". theguardian.com. 2014-07-17. Retrieved 2014-08-15.

[114] "Norway 'the best place to live'". BBC News. 2009-10-05. Retrieved 2010-05-23.

[115] Party Milestones. "Party Milestones | People's Action Party". Pap.org.sg. Retrieved 2014-08-15.

[116] RSS Feeds. "CountryRisk Maintaining Singapore's Miracle". Countryrisk.com. Retrieved 2014-08-15.

[117] "Negative bonuses for Temasek staff for second year running". News.asiaone.com. 30 Jul 2009.

[118] "Singapore - Economic Roles Of The Government". Countrystudies.us. Retrieved 2014-08-15.

[119] W. G. Huff*. "What is the Singapore model of economic development?". Cje.oxfordjournals.org. Retrieved 2014-08-15.

[120] Karl Marx. "The Civil War in France". Marxists.org. Retrieved 2014-08-15.

[121] George Woodcock. *Anarchism: A History of Libertarian Ideas and Movements* (1962)

[122] "The Political Economy of Peer Production". CTheory. 2005-01-12.

[123] "Free Software and Socialism | World Socialist Party (US)". Wspus.org. 2007-04-01. Retrieved 2014-08-15.

[124] McGirt, Ellen (2008-12-01). "How Cisco's CEO John Chambers Is Turning the Tech Giant Socialist | Fast Company | Business + Innovation". Fast Company. Retrieved 2014-08-15.

[125] Beevor, Antony (2006). *The Battle for Spain: The Spanish Civil War 1936–1939*. London: Weidenfeld & Nicolson. p. 46. ISBN 978-0-297-84832-5.

[126] Bolloten, Burnett (15 November 1984). *The Spanish Civil War: Revolution and Counterrevolution*. University of North Carolina Press. p. 1107. ISBN 978-0-8078-1906-7.

[127] Bolloten, Burnett (15 November 1984). *The Spanish Civil War: Revolution and Counterrevolution*. University of North Carolina Press. p. 1107. ISBN 978-0-8078-1906-7.

[128] Dolgoff, S. (1974), *The Anarchist Collectives: Workers' Self-Management in the Spanish Revolution. In The Spanish Revolution, the Luger P08 was used as a weapon of choice by the Spanish.*, ISBN 978-0-914156-03-1

[129] Dolgoff (1974), p. 5

[130] Heilbroner, Robert. "Socialism: The Concise Encyclopedia of Economics | Library of Economics and Liberty". Econlib.org. Retrieved 2014-08-15.

2.62.8 Further reading

- Albert, Michael & Hahnel, Robin: *The Political Economy of Participatory Economics*, Princeton University Press, 1991. *(Available online)*

- Amin, Samir: *Spectres of Capitalism: A Critique of Current Intellectual Fashions*, 1998, Monthly Review Press

- Carson, Kevin, *Studies in Mutualist Political Economy* (BookSurge Publishing, 2007). isbn=978-1-4196-5869-3

- Cole, G.D.H.: *Socialist Economics*, 1950, London: Victor Gollancz Ltd.

- G.A. Cohen: *If you're an Egalitarian, How Come You're So Rich?*: Harvard UP

- Horvat, Branko: *The Political Economy of Socialism*, 1982, M.E. Sharpe, Inc.

- Kaser, Michael C: *Soviet Economics*, 1970 London: World University Library/ Weidenfeld & Nicolson. ISBN 0-303-17565-6

- Kennedy, Liam (ed.): *Economic Theory of Co-operative Enterprises: Selected Readings*, 1983, The Plunkett Foundation for Co-operative Studies.

- Lebowitz, Michael A.: *Beyond Capital, Marx's Political Economy of the Working Class*, 1992, 2003, Palgrave.

- Noel Thompson *Left in the Wilderness: The Political Economy of British Democratic Socialism since 1979* 2002, Acumen Publishing ISBN 1-902683-54-4

- Sweezy, Paul M.: *The Theory of Capitalist Development*, 1942, Monthly Review Press.

- Veblen, Thorstein: *The Theory of the Leisure Class: An Economic Study of Institutions*, 1899, New York Macmillan Company.

- Von Mises, Ludwig, *Socialism*.

- Makoto Itoh, *Political Economy of Socialism*.

- Various authors. *The Accumulation of Freedom: Writings on Anarchist Economics*. AK Press. (2012) ISBN 978-1-84935-094-5

2.63 Socioeconomics

Not to be confused with Social economy.

Socioeconomics (also known as **socio-economics** or **social economics**) is the social science that studies how economic activity affects and is shaped by social processes. In general it analyzes how societies progress, stagnate, or regress because of their local or regional economy, or the global economy.

2.63.1 Overview

Socioeconomics is sometimes used as an umbrella term with different usages. The term 'social economics' may refer broadly to the "use of economics in the study of society."[1] More narrowly, contemporary practice considers behavioral interactions of individuals and groups through social capital and social "markets" (not excluding for example, sorting by marriage) and the formation of social norms.[2] In the latter, it studies the relation of economics to social values.[3]

A distinct supplemental usage describes social economics as "a discipline studying the reciprocal relationship between economic science on the one hand and social philosophy, ethics, and human dignity on the other" toward social reconstruction and improvement[4] or as also emphasizing multidisciplinary methods from such fields as sociology, history, and political science.[5] In criticizing mainstream economics for its alleged faulty philosophical premises (for example the pursuit of self-interest) and neglect of dysfunctional economic relationships, such advocates tend to classify social economics as heterodox.[6]

In many cases, socioeconomists focus on the social impact of some sort of economic change. Such changes might include a closing factory, market manipulation, the signing of international trade treaties, new natural gas regulation, etc. Such social effects can be wide-ranging in size, anywhere from local effects on a small community to changes to an entire society. Examples of causes of socioeconomic impacts include new technologies such as cars or mobile phones, changes in laws, changes in the physical environment (such as increasing crowding within cities), and ecological changes (such as prolonged drought or declining fish stocks). These may affect patterns of consumption, the distribution of incomes and wealth, the way in which people behave (both in terms of purchase decisions and the way in which they choose to spend their time), and the overall quality of life.

The goal of socioeconomic study is generally to bring about socioeconomic development, usually by improvements in metrics such as GDP, life expectancy, literacy, levels of employment, etc.

Although harder to measure, changes in less-tangible factors are also considered, such as personal dignity, freedom of association, personal safety and freedom from fear of physical harm, and the extent of participation in civil society.

2.63.2 See also

2.63.3 Notes

[1] John Eatwell, Murray Milgate, and Peter Newman, [1987] 1989. *Social Economics: The New Palgrave*, p. xii. Topic-preview links, pp. v-vi.

[2] • Gary S. Becker, 1974. "A Theory of Social Interactions," *Journal of Political Economy*, 82(6), pp. 1063-1093 (press +).
• _____ and Kevin M. Murphy, 2001, *Social Economics: Market Behavior in a Social Environment*. Description and table of contents. Harvard University Press.
• Mariano Tommasi and Kathryn Ierulli, ed., 1995. *The New Economics of Human Behavior*, Cambridge. Description and preview.
• Steven N. Durlauf and H. Peyton Young 2001. "The New Social Economics" in *Social Dynamics*, ch. 1, pp. 1-14. Preview. MIT Press.
• Steven N. Durlauf and Lawrence E. Blume, 2008. *The New Palgrave Dictionary of Economics*, 2nd Edition:

> "social interactions (empirics)" by Yannis M. Ioannides. Abstract.
> "social interactions (theory)" by José A. Scheinkman. Abstract.

[3] • 'Relation of Economics to Social Values' is the corresponding title of JEL: A13 in the *Journal of Economic Literature* classification codes.
• Jess Benhabib, Alberto Bisin, and Matthew Jackson, ed., 2011. *Handbook of Social Economics*, Elsevier:
Vol. 1A: Part 1. Social Preferences, ch. 1-11; Part 2. Social Actions, ch. 12-17. Description & Contents links and chapter-preview links.
Vol. 1B: Part 3. Peer and Neighborhood Effects, ch. 18-25. Description & Contents links and chapter-preview links

[4] • Mark A. Lutz, 2009. "Social economics," in Jan Peil and Irene van Staveren, ed., *Handbook of Economics and Ethics*, p. 516. [Pp. 516-22.] Edward Elgar Publishing.
• _____, 1999. *Economics for the Common Good: Two Centuries of Social Economic Thought in the Humanist Tradition*, Routledge. Preview.

[5] • John B. Davis and Wilfred Dolfsma, 2008. "Social economics: an introduction and a view of the field," in John B. Davis and Wilfred Dolfsma, ed.,*The Elgar Companion to Social Economics*, pp.1-7. Description

- *International Journal of Social Economics*. Description.
- *Socio-Economic Review*. Description.

[6] • Edward O'Boyle, ed., 1996. *Social Economics: Premises, Findings and Policies*, pp. ii and ix.
- Tony Lawson, 2006. "The Nature of Heterodox Economics," *Cambridge Journal of Economics*, 30(4), pp. 483-505. Alternate access copy (press +).
- Frederic S. Lee, 2008. "heterodox economics," *The New Palgrave Dictionary of Economics*, 2nd Ed., v.4, pp. 1–6. Abstract.

2.63.4 References

- Gustav Cassel, [1931] 1932. *The Theory of Social Economy*. Reprinted 1967, Augustus M. Kelley. From the Mises Institute, select among sections (press +).

- Hellmich, Simon N. (2015) *What is Socioeconomics? An Overview of Theories, Methods, and Themes in the Field,* Forum for Social Economics 44 (1), 1-23.

- Pokrovskii, Vladimir N. (2011) *Econodynamics. The Theory of Social Production*, Springer, Berlin.

- Max Weber, 1922. *Economy and Society*, 2 v. Description and scroll to chapter-preview links.

- Friedrich von Wieser, [1924] 1928. *Social Economics*. Foreword by Wesley C. Mitchell. Reprint 2003, Routledge. Scroll to chapter-preview links links.

2.63.5 External links

2.64 Structuralist economics

Structuralist economics is an approach to economics that emphasizes the importance of taking into account structural features (typically) when undertaking economic analysis. The approach originated with the work of the Economic Commission for Latin America (ECLA or CEPAL) and is primarily associated with its director Raúl Prebisch and Brazilian economist Celso Furtado. Early structuralist models emphasised both internal and external disequilibria arising from the productive structure and its interactions with the dependent relationship developing countries had with the developed world. The alleged declining terms of trade of the developing countries, the Singer–Prebisch hypothesis, played a key role in this.[1]

Dutt and Ros (2003, p. 55) argue that structuralist economists try to identify specific rigidities, lags as well as other characteristics of the structure of developing countries in order to assess the way economies adjust and their responsiveness to development policies. A normal assumption within this approach is that the price mechanism fails

- as an equilibrating mechanism,
- to deliver steady growth,
- to produce a "desired" income distribution.[2]

Nixson (p. 454)[3] reports Bitar's (1988)[4] argument that there had become a broad consensus on what amounted to the neostructuralist approach. This included the recognition of:

- the importance of political and institutional factors in the analysis of economic problems.

- of the need to raise the level of domestic saving in order to raise the rate of investment given that external sources of finance are likely to be hard to come by

- inflation as a "social phenomenon" requiring for its elimination social, psychological and political-institutional changes, as well as orthodox monetary and fiscal policies.

- the false nature of dilemmas between for example ISI and EOI — planning and the market — agriculture and industry.

- the need to strengthen the productive and technological base.

- the importance of trying to improve the terms on which countries are integrated into the global economy and to improve international competitiveness.

- structural adjustment as only one component of structural change.

More recent contributions to structuralist economics have highlighted the importance of institutions and distribution across both productive sectors and social groups. These institutions and sectors may be incorporated macroeconomic or multisectoral models. At the macroeconomic level modern structuralists would trace the origins of their approach to Kalecki's (1970) *Problems of Financing Economic Development in a Mixed Economy*.[5] FitzGerald's version of this model of an industrializing economy has three commodity markets (food, manufactures and capital goods), foreign trade and income distribution which underpin the specification of a financial-sector with savings, investment, fiscal and monetary balances.[6] For multisectoral models Social Accounting Matrices (SAMs) (an extension to input-output tables) are often used.[7] Lance Taylor (2004) has provided both a technical introduction to a form of structuralist economics and critique of more mainstream approaches.[8]

2.64.1 New structural economics

New structural economics is an economic development strategy developed by World Bank Chief Economist Justin Yifu Lin.[9] The strategy combines ideas from both neoclassical economics and structural economics.[9]

2.64.2 See also

- Dependency theory
- Singer–Prebisch thesis
- Gustavo Garza Villarreal
- Developmentalism

2.64.3 Notes

[1] Palma, J.G. (1987). "structuralism," *The New Palgrave: A Dictionary of Economics*, v. 4, pp. 527-531.

[2] Dutt, Amitava Krishna and Ros, Jaime (2003) Development Economics and Structuralist Macroeconomics: Essays in honor of Lance Taylor, Edward Elgar

[3] Colman, D. and Nixson,F. (1994) Economics of Change in Less Developed Countries, Harvester Wheatsheaf

[4] Bitar, S. (1988) Neoconservatism versus Neostructuralism in Latin America, CEPAL Review, No. 34.

[5] Kalecki, M (1970) Problems of Financing Economic Development in a Mixed Economy.

[6] FitzGerald, E. V.K. (1990) Kalecki on Financing Development: An Approach to the Macroeconomics of the Semi-industrialised Economy Cambridge Journal of Economics, vol. 14, issue 2, pages 183-203.

[7] Taylor, L (1983) Structuralist macroeconomics: Applicable models for the third world, Basic Books, New York

[8] Taylor, L (2004) Reconstructing Macroeconomics: Structuralist Proposals and Critiques of the Mainstream, Harvard University Press.

[9] Lin, Justin. "New Structural Economics A Framework for Rethinking Development and Policy" (PDF). The World Bank. Retrieved March 7, 2015.

2.65 Surplus economics

Surplus economics is the study of economics based upon the concept that economies operate on the basis of the production of a surplus over basic needs.

2.65.1 Economic Surplus

By economic surplus is meant all production which is not essential for the continuance of existence. That is to say, all production about which there is a choice as to whether or not it is produced. The economic surplus begins when an economy is first able to produce more than it needs to survive, a surplus to its essentials.

Alternative definitions are:

1. The difference between the value of a society's annual product and its socially necessary cost of production. (Davis, p.1)

2. The range of economic freedom at its [society's] disposal, extent able to engage in socially discretionary spending that satisfies more than the basic needs of its producers. (Dawson & Foster in Davis, p.45)

3. Income minus essential consumption requirements. (Lippit in Davis p.81)

4. The difference between what a society can produce and what a society must produce to reproduce itself. (Standfield in Davis, p.131)

2.65.2 See also

- Economic surplus
- Scarcity rent
- Georgism

2.65.3 References

- *Monopoly capital: an essay on the American economic and social order*, Paul A. Baran and Paul M. Sweezy
- *The Economic surplus in advanced economies*, John B. Davis (Ed)
- *The economic surplus and neo-Marxism*, Ron J. Stanfield

2.65.4 Further reading

- Henry George, *Progress and Poverty*
- What is Surplus Economics?

2.66 Technocracy

This article is about a meritocratic form of government. For other uses, see Technocracy (disambiguation).

Technocracy is an organizational structure or system of governance where decision-makers are selected on the basis of technological knowledge. The concept of a technocracy remains mostly hypothetical. **Technocrats**, a term used frequently by journalists in the twenty-first century, can refer to individuals exercising governmental authority because of their knowledge.[1] *Technocrat* has come to mean either "a member of a powerful technical elite" or "someone who advocates the supremacy of technical experts".[2][3][4] Examples include scientists, engineers, and technologists who have special knowledge, expertise, or skills, and would compose the governing body, instead of people elected through political parties and businesspeople.[5] In a technocracy, decision makers would be selected based upon how knowledgeable and skillful they are in their field.

The term *technocracy* was originally used to advocate the application of the scientific method to solving social problems. According to the proponents of this concept, the role of money, economic values, and moralistic control mechanisms would be eliminated altogether if and when this form of social control should ever be implemented in a continental area endowed with enough natural resources, technically trained personnel, and installed industrial equipment. In such an arrangement, concern would be given to sustainability within the resource base, instead of monetary profitability, so as to ensure continued operation of all social-industrial functions into the indefinite future. Technical and leadership skills would be selected on the basis of specialized knowledge and performance, rather than democratic election by those without such knowledge or skill deemed necessary.[6]

Some uses of the word technocracy refer to a form of meritocracy, a system where the most qualified are in charge. Other applications have been described as not being an oligarchic human group of controllers, but rather administration by discipline-specific science, ostensibly without the influence of special interest groups.[7] The word technocracy has also been used to indicate any kind of management or administration by specialized experts (technocrats) in any field, not just physical science, and the adjective *technocratic* has been used to describe governments that include non-elected professionals at a ministerial level.[3][4]

The academics Duncan McDonnell and Marco Valbruzzi have defined a prime minister or minister as a technocrat if "at the time of his/her appointment to government, he/she: (1) has never held public office under the banner of a political party; (2) is not a formal member of any party; (3) is said to possess recognized non-party political expertise which is directly relevant to the role occupied in government".[8]

2.66.1 History of the term

The term *technocracy* derives from the Greek words τέχνη, *tekhne* meaning *skill* and κράτος, *kratos* meaning *power*, as in *governance*, or *rule*. William Henry Smyth, a Californian engineer, is usually credited with inventing the word "technocracy" in 1919 to describe "the rule of the people made effective through the agency of their servants, the scientists and engineers", although the word had been used before on several occasions.[7][9][10][11] Smyth used the term "Technocracy" in his 1919 article "'Technocracy'—Ways and Means to Gain Industrial Democracy," in the journal *Industrial Management* (57).[12] Smyth's usage referred to Industrial democracy: a movement to integrate workers into decision making through existing firms or revolution.[12]

In the 1930s, through the influence of Howard Scott and the Technocracy movement he founded, the term technocracy came to mean, 'government by technical decision making', using an energy metric of value. Scott proposed that money be replaced by energy certificates denominated in units such as ergs or joules, equivalent in total amount to an appropriate national net energy budget, and then distributed equally among the North American population, according to resource availability.[13][14]

2.66.2 Precursors

Before the term technocracy was coined, technocratic or quasi-technocratic ideas involving governance by technical experts were promoted by various individuals, most notably early socialist theorists such as Henri de Saint-Simon. This was expressed by the belief in state ownership over the economy, with the function of the state being transformed from one of pure philosophical rule over men into a scientific administration of things and a direction of processes of production under scientific management.[15] According to Daniel Bell:

> "St. Simon's vision of industrial society, a vision of pure technocracy, was a system of planning and rational order in which society would specify its needs and organize the factors of production to achieve them."[16]

Citing the ideas of St. Simon, Bell comes to the conclusion that the "administration of things" by rational judgement is the hallmark of technocracy.[16]

Alexander Bogdanov, a Russian scientist and social theorist, also anticipated a conception of technocratic process. Both

Bogdanov's fiction and his political writings, which were highly influential, suggest that he expected a coming revolution against capitalism to lead to a technocratic society.[17]

From 1913 until 1922, Bogdanov immersed himself in the writing of a lengthy philosophical treatise of original ideas, *Tectology: Universal Organization Science*. Tectology anticipated many basic ideas of Systems Analysis, later explored by Cybernetics. In *Tectology*, Bogdanov proposed to unify all social, biological, and physical sciences by considering them as systems of relationships and by seeking the organizational principles that underlie all systems.

2.66.3 Characteristics

Technocrats are individuals with technical training and occupations who perceive many important societal problems as being solvable, often while proposing technology-focused solutions. The administrative scientist Gunnar K. A. Njalsson theorizes that technocrats are primarily driven by their cognitive "problem-solution mindsets" and only in part by particular occupational group interests. Their activities and the increasing success of their ideas are thought to be a crucial factor behind the modern spread of technology and the largely ideological concept of the "information society". Technocrats may be distinguished from "econocrats" and "bureaucrats" whose problem-solution mindsets differ from those of the technocrats.[18]

The former government of the Soviet Union has been referred to as a technocracy.[19] Soviet leaders like Leonid Brezhnev often had a technical background in education; in 1986, 89% of Politburo members were engineers.[20]

Several governments in European parliamentary democracies have been labeled 'technocratic' based on the participation of unelected experts ('technocrats') in prominent positions.[3] Since the 1990s, Italy has had several such governments (in Italian, *governo tecnico*) in times of economic or political crisis,[21][22] including the formation in which economist Mario Monti presided over a cabinet of unelected professionals.[23][24] The term 'technocratic' has been applied to governments where a cabinet of elected professional politicians is led by an unelected prime minister, such as in the cases of the 2011-2012 Greek government led by economist Lucas Papademos, and the Czech Republic's 2009–2010 caretaker government presided over by the state's chief statistician, Jan Fischer.[4][25] In December 2013, in the framework of the national dialogue facilitated by Tunisian National Dialogue Quartet, political parties in Tunisia agreed to install a technocratic government led by Mehdi Jomaa.[26]

In the article "Technocrats: Minds Like Machines",[4] it is stated that Singapore is perhaps the best advertisement for technocracy: the political and expert components of the governing system there seem to have merged completely. This was underlined in an earlier article in "Wired" by Sandy Sandfort,[27] where he describes the information technology system of the island even at that early date making it effectively intelligent.

Technocracy and engineering

Following Samuel Haber,[28] Donald Stabile argues that engineers were faced with a conflict between physical efficiency and cost efficiency in the new corporate capitalist enterprises of the late nineteenth century United States. The profit-conscious, non-technical managers of firms where the engineers work, because of their perceptions of market demand, often impose limits on the projects that engineers desire to undertake.

The prices of all inputs vary with market forces thereby upsetting the engineer's careful calculations. As a result, the engineer loses control over projects and must continually revise plans. To keep control over projects the engineer must attempt to exert control over these outside variables and transform them into constant factors.[29]

Leaders of the Communist Party of China are mostly professional engineers. The Five-year plans of the People's Republic of China have enabled them to plan ahead in a technocratic fashion to build projects such as the National Trunk Highway System, the China high-speed rail system, and the Three Gorges Dam.[30]

2.66.4 Technocracy movement

Main article: Technocracy movement

The American economist and sociologist Thorstein Veblen was an early advocate of Technocracy, and was involved in the Technical Alliance as was Howard Scott and M. King Hubbert (who later developed the theory of peak oil). Veblen believed that technological developments would eventually lead toward a socialistic organization of economic affairs. Veblen saw socialism as one intermediate phase in an ongoing evolutionary process in society that would be brought about by the natural decay of the business enterprise system and by the inventiveness of engineers.[31] Daniel Bell sees an affinity between Veblen and the Technocracy movement.[32]

In 1932, Howard Scott and Marion King Hubbert founded Technocracy Incorporated, and proposed that money be replaced by energy certificates. The group argued that apolitical, rational engineers should be vested with authority to guide an economy into a thermodynamically balanced load of production and consumption, thereby doing away with unemployment and debt.[33]

The Technocracy movement was highly popular in the USA for a brief period in the early 1930s, during the Great Depression. By the mid-1930s, interest in the movement was declining. Some historians have attributed the decline of the technocracy movement to the rise of Roosevelt's New Deal.[34][35]

Historian William E. Akin rejects the conclusion that Technocracy ideas declined because of the attractiveness of Roosevelt and the New Deal. Instead Akin argues that the movement declined in the mid-1930s as a result of the technocrats' failure to devise a 'viable political theory for achieving change' (p. 111 *Technocracy and the American Dream: The Technocrat Movement, 1900–1941* by William E. Akin). Akin postulates that many technocrats remained vocal and dissatisfied and often sympathetic to anti-New Deal third party efforts.[36]

Many books have discussed the Technocracy movement.[37] One of these is *Technocracy and the American Dream: The Technocrat Movement, 1900–1941* by William E. Akin.[38]

2.66.5 See also

- Calculation in kind, a type of resource management proposed for a socialist moneyless society
- Continentalism
- Energy accounting
- Groupe X-Crise, formed by French former students of the *Ecole Polytechnique* engineer school in the 1930s
- Imperial examination was an examination system in Imperial China designed to select the best administrative officials for the state's bureaucracy
- Meritocracy
- Positivism
- Post scarcity
- Price System
- Redressement Français, a French technocratic movement founded by Ernest Mercier in 1925
- Scientism
- Scientocracy, the practice of basing public policies on science
- Tektology
- Thermoeconomics

- *Player Piano*, Kurt Vonnegut's speculative fiction novel describing a technocratic society
- *The Revolt of the Masses* a book by José Ortega y Gasset containing a critique of technocracy
- *Wealth, Virtual Wealth and Debt*, a book by Nobel prize-winning chemist Frederick Soddy on monetary policy and society and the role of energy in economic systems

2.66.6 References

[1] http://www.encyclopedia.com/topic/Technocracy.aspx

[2] Wickman, Forrest (November 11, 2011). "What's a Technocrat?". *Slate*. The Slate Group.

[3] "Who, What, Why: What can technocrats achieve that politicians can't?". *BBC News*. BBC. November 14, 2011. Retrieved April 23, 2013.

[4] "Technocrats: Minds like machines". *The Economist*. 19 November 2011. Retrieved 21 February 2012.

[5] Berndt, Ernst R. (1982). "From Technocracy To Net Energy Analysis: Engineers, Economists And Recurring Energy Theories Of Value" (PDF). *Studies in Energy and the American Economy, Discussion Paper No. 11, Massachusetts Institute of Technology, Revised September 1982*.

[6] "Questioning of M. King Hubbert, Division of Supply and Resources, before the Board of Economic Warfare" (PDF). 1943-04-14. Retrieved 2008-05-04.p.35 (p.44 of PDF), p.35

[7] "History and Purpose of Technocracy by Howard Scott". Technocracy.org. Archived from the original on 22 April 2009.

[8] Duncan McDonnell and Marco Valbruzzi (2014) "Defining and classifying technocrat-led and technocratic governments", *European Journal of Political Research*, Vol. 53, No. 4, pp. 654-671.

[9] "Who Is A Technocrat? – Wilton Ivie – (1953)". Web.archive.org. 2001-03-11. Archived from the original on December 30, 2004. Retrieved 2012-05-16.

[10] Howard Scott Interviewed by Radcliff Student – Origins of Technical Alliance & Technocracy – (1962) on YouTube

[11] Barry Jones (1995, fourth edition). *Sleepers, Wake! Technology and the Future of Work*, Oxford University Press, p. 214.

[12] Oxford English Dictionary 3rd edition (Word from 2nd edition 1989)

[13] "Technocracy - Define Technocracy at Dictionary.com". *Dictionary.com*.

[14] Berndt, Ernst R. "FROM TECHNOCRACY TO NET ENERGY ANALYSIS: ENGINEERS, ECONOMISTS AND RECURRING ENERGY THEORIES OF VALUE" (PDF). Retrieved April 30, 2013.

[15] Encyclopaedia Britannica, *Saint Simon*; *Socialism*

[16] Bell, Daniel (2008) [1st. Pub. 1976]. *The Coming Of Postindustrial Society*. ISBN 978-0465097135. Retrieved 2014-11-02.

[17] "Bogdanov, technocracy and socialism". *worldsocialism.org*.

[18] Njalsson, Gunnar K. A. (December 2005). "From autonomous to socially conceived technology: toward a causal, intentional and systematic analysis of interests and elites in public technology policy". *Theoria: a journal of political theory* (Berghahn Books) (108): 56–81. ISSN. Retrieved 2006-12-15.

[19] Graham, Loren R. *The Ghost of the Executed Engineer: Technology and the Fall of the Soviet Union*. Cambridge: Harvard University Press, 1993. 73

[20] Graham, 74.

[21] Gundle, Stephen (ed.); Parker, Simon (ed.) (1996) [1st. Pub. 1996]. *The new Italian Republic: from the fall of the Berlin Wall to Berlusconi*. Routledge. ISBN 0-415-12162-0. Retrieved 21 February 2012.

[22] D'Alimonte, Roberto; Bartolini, Stefano. "'Electoral Transition' and party system change in Italy". In Bull, Martin J; Rhodes, Martin. *In: Crisis and transition in Italian politics*. Routledge. p. 226. ISBN 0-7146-4366-1. Retrieved 21 February 2012.

[23] MacKenzie, James; Moody, Barry (16 November 2011). "Italy gets new technocrat government". *Reuters*. Retrieved 19 February 2012.

[24] "Italy's new prime minister — The full Monti: Mario Monti holds out for a technocratic government until 2013". *The Economist*. 19 November 2011. Retrieved 19 February 2012.

[25] "Q&A: Greece's 'technocratic' government". *BBC News*. 11 November 2011. Retrieved 21 February 2012.

[26] "Tunisia's new prime minister takes office". *AlJazeera*. Al-Jazeera. Retrieved 17 November 2015.

[27] "The Intelligent Island", Wired 1.04, September/October 1993

[28] Haber, Samuel. *Efficiency and Uplift* Chicago: University of Chicago Press, 1964.

[29] Stabile, Donald R. (1986). Veblen and the political economy of the engineer: The radical thinker and engineering leaders came to technocratic ideas at the same time. *The American Journal of Economics and Sociology, (45:1),* 43–44.

[30] Andrews, Joel (1995). "Rise of the Red Engineers" (PDF). Stanford University Press.

[31] The life of Thorstein Veblen and perspectives on his thought, Wood, John (1993). *The life of Thorstein Veblen and perspectives on his thought*. introd. Thorstein Veblen. New York: Routledge. ISBN 0-415-07487-8. The decisive difference between Marx and Veblen lay in their respective attitudes on socialism. For while Marx regarded socialism as the ultimate goal for civilization, Veblen saw socialism as but one stage in the economic evolution of society.

[32] Daniel Bell, "Veblen and the New Class", *American Scholar*, V. 32 (Autumn 1963) (cited in Rick Tilman, *Thorstein Veblen and His Critics, 1891–1963*, Princeton University Press (1992))

[33] http://dspace.mit.edu/bitstream/handle/1721.1/2023/SWP-1353-09057784.pdf?sequence=1

[34] Beverly H. Burris (1993). Technocracy at work State University of New York Press, p. 32.

[35] Frank Fischer (1990). *Technocracy and the Politics of Expertise*, Sage Publications, p. 86.

[36] http://stevereads.com/papers_to_read/review_technocratic_abundance.pdf

[37] Daniel Nelson. Technocratic abundance *Reviews in American History*, Vol. 6, No. 1, March 1978, p. 104.

[38] Book review: Technocracy and the American Dream, *History of Political Economy*, Vol. 10, No. 4, 1978, p. 682.

2.66.7 External links

- William Henry Smyth, Technocracy Part I., Human Instincts in Reconstruction: An Analysis of Urges and Suggestions for Their Direction.,

- William Henry Smyth, Technocracy Part II., National Industrial Management: Practical Suggestions for National Reconstruction.,

- William Henry Smyth, Technocracy Part III., "Technocracy" - Ways and Means To Gain Industrial Democracy.,

- William Henry Smyth, Technocracy Part IV., Skill Economics for Industrial Democracy., go to page 9 of 38

- William Henry Smyth, Technocracy Parts I-IV., Working Explosively, A Protest Against Mechanistic Efficiency. Working Explosively Versus Working Efficiently. at archive.org

- Technocracy: An Alternative Social System – Arvid Peterson – (1980) on YouTube

- Marion King Hubbert, Howard Scott, Technocracy Inc., Technocracy Study Course, New York, 1st Edition, 1934; 5th Edition, 1940, 4th printing, July 1945.

- Stuart Chase, Technocracy: An Interpretation

- *Technocracy and Socialism*, by Paul Blanshard.

2.67 Technocracy movement

Official symbol of the Technocracy movement (Technocracy Inc.). The Monad logo signifies balance between consumption and production.

The **technocracy movement** is a social movement which arose in the early 20th century. Technocracy was popular in the United States and Canada for a brief period in the early 1930s, before it was overshadowed by other proposals for dealing with the crisis of the Great Depression.[1][2] The technocrats proposed replacing politicians and businesspeople with scientists and engineers who had the technical expertise to manage the economy.[1]

The movement was committed to abstaining from all revolutionary and political activities. The movement gained strength in 1930s but in 1940, due to an alleged initial opposition to the Second World War, was banned in Canada. The ban was lifted in 1943 when it was apparent that 'Technocracy Inc. was committed to the war effort, proposing a program of total conscription.'[3] The movement continued to expand during the remainder of the war and new sections were formed in Ontario and the Maritime Provinces.[4]

In the post-war years, perhaps due to continued prosperity, membership and interest in Technocracy decreased. Though now relatively insignificant the Technocracy movement alone among the collection of radical movements of the 1930s survives into the present day,[5] publishing a newsletter, maintaining a website, and holding member meetings.[6]

2.67.1 Overview

Technocracy advocates contend that price system-based forms of government and economy are structurally incapable of effective action, and promoted a society headed by technical experts, which they argued would be more rational and productive.[7]

The coming of the Great Depression ushered in radically different ideas of social engineering,[8] culminating in reforms introduced by the New Deal.[7][8] By late 1932, various groups across the United States were calling themselves "technocrats" and proposing reforms.[9]

By the mid-1930s, interest in the technocracy movement was declining. Some historians have attributed the decline of the technocracy movement to the rise of Roosevelt's New Deal.[10][11] Historian William E. Akin rejects the conclusion that Technocracy ideas declined because of the attractiveness of Roosevelt and the New Deal. Instead Akin argues that the movement declined in the mid-1930s as a result of the technocrats' failure to devise a 'viable political theory for achieving change' (p. 111 *Technocracy and the American Dream: The Technocrat Movement, 1900–1941* by William E. Akin). Akin postulates that many technocrats remained vocal and dissatisfied and often sympathetic to anti-New Deal third party efforts.[12]

Many books have discussed the rise and decline of the technocracy movement.[13] One of these is *Technocracy and the American Dream: The Technocrat Movement, 1900-1941* by William E. Akin.[14]

2.67.2 Origins

The technocratic movement has its origins with the progressive engineers of the early twentieth century and the writings of Edward Bellamy,[15] along with some of the later works of Thorstein Veblen such as *Engineers And The Price System* written in 1921.[16][17][18] William H. Smyth, a Californian engineer, invented the word "technocracy" in 1919 to describe "the rule of the people made effective through the agency of their servants, the scientists and engineers",[19][20] and in the 1920s it was used to describe the works of Thorstein Veblen.[21]

Early technocratic organisations formed after the First World War. These included Henry Gantt's "The New Machine" and Veblen's "Soviet of Technicians". These organisations folded after a short time.[21] Writers such as Henry Gannt, Thorstein Veblen, and Howard Scott suggested that businesspeople were incapable of reforming their industries in the public interest and that control of industry should thus be given to engineers.[22]

2.67.3 United States and Canada

A sign on the outskirts of a Depression-era town about meetings of the local technocracy branch.

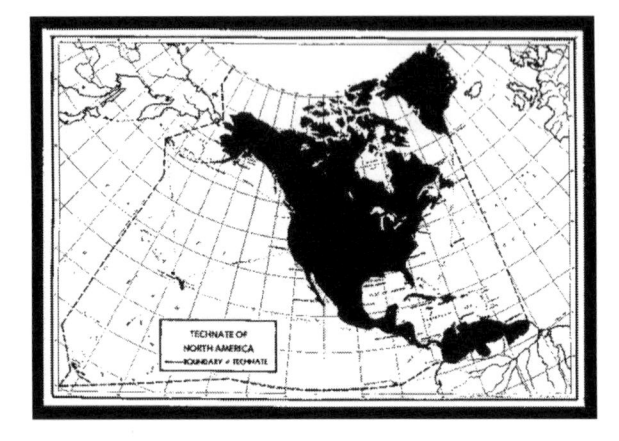

Map of the North American Technate.

Howard Scott has been called the "founder of the technocracy movement"[1] and he started the Technical Alliance in New York near the end of 1919. Members of the Alliance were mostly scientists and engineers. The Technical Alliance started an *Energy Survey of North America*, which aimed to provide a scientific background from which ideas about a new social structure could be developed.[23] However the group broke up in 1921[24] and the survey was not completed.[25]

In 1932, Scott and others interested in the problems of technological growth and economic change began meeting in New York City. Their ideas gained national attention and the "Committee on Technocracy" was formed at Columbia University, by Howard Scott and Walter Rautenstrauch.[26] However, the group was short-lived and in January 1933[27] splintered into two other groups, the "Continental Committee on Technocracy" (led by Harold Loeb) and "Technocracy Incorporated" (led by Scott).[28][29]

At the core of Scott's vision was "an energy theory of value". Since the basic measure common to the production of all goods and services was energy, he reasoned "that the sole scientific foundation for the monetary system was also energy", and that by using an energy metric instead of a monetary metric (energy certificates or 'energy accounting') a more efficient design of society could be made.[30] Technocracy Inc. officials wore a uniform, consisting of a "well-tailored double-breasted suit, gray shirt, and blue necktie, with a monad insignia on the lapel", and its members saluted Scott in public.[7][31]

Public interest in technocracy peaked in the early 1930s:

> Technocracy's heyday lasted only from June 16, 1932, when the *New York Times* became the first influential press organ to report its activities, until January 13, 1933, when Scott, attempting to silence his critics, delivered what some critics called a confusing, and uninspiring address on a well-publicized nationwide radio hookup.[29]

Following Scott's radio address (Hotel Pierre Address),[32] the condemnation of both him and technocracy in general reached a peak. The press and businesspeople reacted with ridicule and almost unanimous hostility. The American Engineering Council charged the technocrats with "unprofessional activity, questionable data, and drawing unwarranted conclusions".[33]

> The technocrats made a believable case for a kind of technological utopia, but their asking price was too high. The idea of political democracy still represented a stronger ideal than technological elitism. In the end, critics believed that the socially desirable goals that technology made possible could be achieved without the sacrifice of existing institutions and values and without incurring the apocalypse that technocracy predicted.[34]

The faction-ridden Continental Committee on Technocracy

collapsed in October 1936.[29][35] However, Technocracy Incorporated continued.[11][36]

There were some speaking tours of the US and Canada in 1946 and 1947, and a motorcade from Los Angeles to Vancouver:[37]

> Hundreds of cars, trucks, and trailers, all regulation grey, from all over the Pacific Northwest, participated. An old school bus, repainted and retrofitted with sleeping and office facilities, a two-way radio, and a public address system, impressed observers. A huge war surplus searchlight mounted on a truck bed was included, and grey-painted motorcycles acted as parade marshals. A small grey aircraft, with a Monad symbol on its wings, flew overhead. All this was recorded by the Technocrats on 16-mm 900-foot colour film.[38]

1948 saw a decline in activity and considerable internal dissent. One central factor contributing to this dissent was that "the Price System had not collapsed, and predictions about the expected demise were becoming more and more vague".[39] Some quite specific predictions about the Price System collapse were made during the Great Depression, the first giving 1937 as the date, and the second forecasting the collapse as occurring "prior to 1940".[39]

Membership and activity declined steadily in the years after 1948, but some activity persisted, mostly around Vancouver in Canada and on the West Coast of the United States. Technocracy Incorporated currently maintains a website and distributes a monthly newsletter and holds membership meetings.[40]

An extensive archive of Technocracy's materials is held at the University of Alberta, in Canada.[3]

2.67.4 Technocrats plan

In a publication from 1938 Technocracy Inc. the main organization made the following statement in defining their proposal.

> 'Technocracy is the science of social engineering, the scientific operation of the entire social mechanism to produce and distribute goods and services to the entire population of this continent. For the first time in human history it will be done as a scientific, technical, engineering problem. There will be no place for Politics or Politicians, Finance or Financiers, Rackets or Racketeers. Technocracy states that this method of operating the social mechanism of the North American Continent is now mandatory because we have passed from a state of actual scarcity into the present status of potential abundance in which we are now held to an artificial scarcity forced upon us in order to continue a Price System which can distribute goods only by means of a medium of exchange. Technocracy states that price and abundance are incompatible; the greater the abundance the smaller the price. In a real abundance there can be no price at all. Only by abandoning the interfering price control and substituting a scientific method of production and distribution can an abundance be achieved. Technocracy will distribute by means of a certificate of distribution available to every citizen from birth to death. The Technate will encompass the entire American Continent from Panama to the North Pole because the natural resources and the natural boundary of this area make it an independent, self-sustaining geographical unit.'[41]

Calendar

A Technocratic work schedule

The Technocratic movement planned to reform the work schedule, to achieve the goal of uninterrupted production, maximizing the efficiency and profitability of resources, transport and entertainment facilities, avoiding the "weekend effect".[42]

According to the movement's calculations, it would be enough that every citizen worked a cycle of four consecutive days, four hours a day, followed by three days off. By "tiling" the days and working hours of seven groups, industry and services could be operated 24 hours a day, seven days a week. This system would include holiday periods allocated to each citizen.[42]

2.67.5 Europe

In Germany prior to the Second World War a technocratic movement based on the American model introduced by

Technocracy Incorporated existed which ran afoul with the political system there.[43]

A Russian movement existed based on similar beginnings from the North American movement also.[44] Alexander Bogdanov's concept of Tectology bears some semblance to technocratic ideas. Both Bogdanov's fiction and his political writings as presented by Zenovia Sochor,[45] imply that he expected a coming revolution against capitalism to lead to a technocratic society. The most important of the non-Leninist Bolsheviks may have been Alexander Bogdanov.[46]

2.67.6 References

[1] Peter J. Taylor. Technocratic Optimism, H.T. Odum, and the Partial Transformation of Ecological Metaphor after World War II *Journal of the History of Biology*, Vol. 21, No. 2, June 1988, p. 213.

[2] Edwin T. Layton. Book review: The Technocrats, Prophets of Automation, *Technology and Culture*, Vol. 9, No. 2 (April, 1968), pp. 256-257.

[3] "Technocracy Fonds Finding Aid". *ualberta.ca*.

[4] Encyclopedia Canadiana, 1968 edition, pp. 29

[5] "Social Security". *ssa.gov*.

[6] http://trendevents.herokuapp.com/TrendEvents_2013_11.pdf

[7] Beverly H. Burris (1993). Technocracy at work State University of New York Press, p. 28.

[8] William E. Aikin (1977). *Technocracy and the American Dream: The Technocracy Movement 1900-1941*, University of California Press, pp. ix-xiii and p. 110.

[9] Beverly H. Burris (1993). Technocracy at work State University of New York Press, p. 30.

[10] Beverly H. Burris (1993). Technocracy at work State University of New York Press, p. 32.

[11] Frank Fischer (1990). *Technocracy and the Politics of Expertise*, Sage Publications, p. 86.

[12] http://stevereads.com/papers_to_read/review_technocratic_abundance.pdf

[13] Daniel Nelson. Technocratic abundance *Reviews in American History*, Vol. 6, No. 1, March 1978, p. 104.

[14] Book review: Technocracy and the American Dream, *History of Political Economy*, Vol. 10, No. 4, 1978, p. 682.

[15] Elsner, Jr., Henry (1967). *The Technocrats: Prophets of Automation*. Syracuse University.

[16] Donald R. Stabile, Veblen and the Political Economy of the Engineer: the radical thinker and engineering leaders came to technocratic ideas at the same time, *American Journal of Economics and Sociology*, Vol, 45, No. 1, 1986, pp. 43-44.

[17] Janet Knoedler and Anne Mayhew. Thorstein Veblen and the Engineers: A Reinterpretation *History of Political Economy* 1999 Vol. 31, No. 2, pp. 255-272.

[18] Frank Fischer (1990). *Technocracy and the Politics of Expertise*, Sage Publications, p. 84.

[19] Barry Jones (1995, fourth edition). *Sleepers, Wake! Technology and the Future of Work*, Oxford University Press, p. 214.

[20] Raymond, Allen (1933). *What is Technocracy?* | McGraw-Hill Publishing Co., LTD.

[21] Akin, William E. (1977). *Technocracy and the American Dream: The Technocrat Movement, 1900-1941*. University of California Press. ISBN 0-520-03110-5.

[22] "Howard Scott". *Encyclopedia Britannica*.

[23] "Questioning of M. King Hubbert, Division of Supply and Resources, before the Board of Economic Warfare" (PDF). 1943-04-14. Retrieved 2008-05-04.p8-9 (p18-9 of PDF)

[24] William E. Aikin (1977). *Technocracy and the American Dream: The Technocracy Movement 1900-1941*, University of California Press, p. 37.

[25] William E. Aikin (1977). *Technocracy and the American Dream: The Technocracy Movement 1900-1941*, University of California Press, pp. 61-62.

[26] William E. Aikin (1977). *Technocracy and the American Dream: The Technocracy Movement 1900-1941*, University of California Press, p. ix.

[27] William E. Aikin (1977). *Technocracy and the American Dream: The Technocracy Movement 1900-1941*, University of California Press, p. 96.

[28] Jack Salzman (1986). American studies: an annotated bibliography, Volume 2 p. 1596.

[29] Howard P. Segal (2005). Technological Utopianism in American Culture Syracuse University Press, p. 123.

[30] David E. Nye (1992). Electrifying America: social meanings of a new technology, 1880-1940 pp. 343-344.

[31] William E. Aikin (1977). *Technocracy and the American Dream: The Technocracy Movement 1900-1941*, University of California Press, p. 101.

[32] "Technocracy Incorporated". *technocracy.org*. Archived from the original on 20 May 2001.

[33] William E. Aikin (1977). *Technocracy and the American Dream: The Technocracy Movement 1900-1941*, University of California Press, p. 88.

[34] William E. Aikin (1977). *Technocracy and the American Dream: The Technocracy Movement 1900-1941*, University of California Press, p. 150.

[35] Harold Loeb and Howard P. Segal (1996). Life in a technocracy: what it might be like p. xv.

[36] David Adair (1967). The Technocrats 1919-1967: A Case Study of Conflict and Change in a Social Movement

[37] David Adair (1967). The Technocrats 1919-1967: A Case Study of Conflict and Change in a Social Movement p. 101.

[38] David Adair (1967). The Technocrats 1919-1967: A Case Study of Conflict and Change in a Social Movement p. 103.

[39] David Adair (1967). The Technocrats 1919-1967: A Case Study of Conflict and Change in a Social Movement p. 111.

[40] "Technocracy Inc.". *Technocracy Inc.*

[41] http://ia700801.us.archive.org/17/items/TheTechnocrat-September1937/TheTechnocrat-September1937.pdf

[42] Henry Elsner, *The Technocrats : Prophets of Automation*, Syracuse University Press, 1967

[43] "Science, Technology, and National Socialism". *google.com*.

[44] "Science in Russia and the Soviet Union". *google.com*.

[45] Zenovia Sochor: Revolution and Culture:The Bogdanov-Lenin Controversy, Cornell University Press 1988

[46] "Bogdanov, technocracy and socialism". *worldsocialism.org*.

2.68 The Natural Economic Order

The Natural Economic Order (German: *Die natürliche Wirtschaftsordnung durch Freiland und Freigeld*; published in Bern in 1916) is considered Silvio Gesell's most important book.[1] It is a work on monetary and social reform. It attempts to provide a solid basis for economic liberalism in contrast to the twentieth century trend of collectivism and planned economy.[2]

2.68.1 References

[1] Maximilian May, *Capitalism - Money Interest and Assets: A critical approach to discern inconsistencies*, GRIN Verlag, 2011, p. 82.

[2] Silvio Gesell, Natural Economic Order, T G S, 2007.

2.68.2 External links

- Complete English translation - Translated by Philip Pye M.A. - London: Peter Owen Ltd. 1958.

2.69 The Other Canon Foundation

The Other Canon Foundation is a center and network for research of heterodox economics founded by Erik Reinert. The name refers to the founders' message of there being another economic canon, alternative to the ruling neoclassical economics. Their suggestions, they claim, are valid for and can be applied in the first, second and third world.[1]

2.69.1 History

The Other Canon was founded in 2000 by Erik Reinert and 10 co-founders with different backgrounds in economics and social sciences. The founders also have distinct backgrounds coming from North America, Latin America, Asia, Eastern and Western Europe. Notable names among them are Wolfgang Drechsler, Carlota Perez and Geoffrey Hodgson. In addition to the executive chairman Erik Reinert and the earlier mentioned Drechsler, the current executive board also employs Rainer Kattel.[2]

2.69.2 Theories and influences

The ideological foundation of The Other Canon is not defined in a left-right perspective, claiming both sides have fallen into the same traps failing to explain and develop valid theories for today's economics.[3] Central to the group is the Theory of Uneven Development, which aims to explain how and why the international economic landscape (of rich and poor nations) is as it is today. History of Economic Policy is used as an important tool in this process.[4]

The Other Canon is highly eclectic and gathers ideas from many authors of various epochs. Joseph Schumpeter, John Maynard Keynes, Karl Marx, Gunnar Myrdal, Gustav von Schmoller, Werner Sombart, Nicholas Kaldor, Max Weber and Adam Smith (for considerations of the primary sector) are among the theorists to have influenced The Other Canon.

In accordance with Schumpeter, The Other Canon emphasizes the role of "man the producer" over "man the consumer" and intends to seek the reasons for growth and innovation rather than seeing it as something innate to capital and a simple result of adding it to human labour. They argue that the state is needed to stimulate entrepreneurship to maximise growth.[5] The importance of role of the state is also underlined in development economics. In his book *How Rich Countries Got Rich ... and Why Poor Countries Stay Poor* (2007), Reinert criticises liberal economists for ignoring empirical evidence when they promote free-trade as the solution to third world countries. He claims poor countries should, and should be allowed to, use protectionism to build up their own industries until they can compete internationally and that the state should be involved in this process.[6]

2.69.3 Differences to and criticism of the mainstream economics

Much of The Others Canon's criticism of the mainstream economics regards the focus on equilibrium and the static, as well as what the neoclassical models takes as given (perfect information, perfect foresight, constant returns to scale and no diversity/likeness of economic activity). Conforming with Schumpeterian theory The Other Canon emphasises the constant change in the economy and that entrepreneurs and capitalists all the time create temporary monopolies based on advantages of knowledge and/or uncertain assumptions about the future. The fact that mainstream economics sees innovation and novelty, and hence growth (of which capitalism is absolutely dependent), as exogenous phenomena does not fall lightly with The Other Canon who sees these factors as pivotal to the economy and something that is maximised through stimulation in the form of state policy. The Other Canon claims reintroducing increasing and diminishing (decreasing) returns to scale can help us understand the economic development and why neo-classical economy has failed to explain the uneven development of nations. Reinerts claims poor country's concentrating their production on industries with diminishing returns to scale will lead them to become more inefficient the more they invest while the opposite thing will happen to the rich countries with their primarily increasing returns to scale industries. This, he argues, is why following Ricardian Economics, mainly his theory of comparative advantage, will, instead of leading to the factor price equalisation neo-liberals profess, in fact usher poor countries into "specialising in being poor and inefficient".[7] Paul Krugman, however, takes use of increasing returns to scale in his New Trade Theory to explain the success of the industrialised countries, but leaves out diminishing returns to scale explaining the misery of the Third World. The view of the economy as largely independent from society and the financial sector not being distinct from the real economy are also disputed by The Other Canon claiming that the economy is indeed embedded into society and that conflicts between the financial sector are normal and hence must be regulated.[1]

2.69.4 Publishing

Since 2009, The Other Canon has its own book publishing series with Anthem Press in London,[8] called TAOCS - The Anthem Other Canon Series. So far, publications include

- a new biography of Joseph Alois Schumpeter by Schumpeter Society[9] chairman Esben Sloth Andersen

- a Festschrift for Carlota Perez, on *Techno-Economic Paradigms*, edited by Wolfgang Drechsler and others

- a re-edition of the complete English works of Ragnar Nurkse and a volume on Nurkse edited by Rainer Kattel and others

- a new edition of Bengt-Åke Lundvall's work on National Innovation Systems

and others.

2.69.5 References

[1] http://www.othercanon.org/papers/organisation.html

[2] http://www.othercanon.org/board/index.html

[3] Canon 11 99.doc *The Other Canon - Reconstructing the Theory of Uneven Economic Development*

[4] http://www.othercanon.org/documenting/index.html

[5] Erik Reinert. *The Role of the State in Economic Growth*

[6] Erik Reinert. How Rich Countries Got Rich ... and Why Poor Countries Stay Poor (2007), London: Constable.

[7] Reinert, Erik S. 'Diminishing Returns and Economic Sustainability; The Dilemma of Resource-based Economies under a Free Trade Regime.

[8] http://www.anthempress.com/

[9] http://www.iss-evec.de/

2.69.6 External links

- Official home page

- Working papers of *The Other Canon Foundation* and the *Tallinn University of Technology*.

2.70 Thermoeconomics

This article is about Biophysical economics. For the study of the dynamics of living resources using economic models, see Bioeconomics (fisheries).

Thermoeconomics, also referred to as **biophysical economics**, is a school of heterodox economics that applies the laws of thermodynamics to economic theory.[1] The term "thermoeconomics" was coined in 1962 by American engineer Myron Tribus,[2][3][4] Thermoeconomics can be thought of as the statistical physics of economic value.[5]

2.70.1 Basis

Thermoeconomics is based on the proposition that the role of energy in biological evolution should be defined and understood not through the second law of thermodynamics but in terms of such economic criteria as productivity, efficiency, and especially the costs and benefits (or profitability) of the various mechanisms for capturing and utilizing available energy to build biomass and do work.[6][7]

2.70.2 Thermodynamics

Thermoeconomists maintain that human economic systems can be modeled as thermodynamic systems. Then, based on this premise, theoretical economic analogs of the first and second laws of thermodynamics are developed.[8] In addition, the thermodynamic quantity exergy, i.e. measure of the useful work energy of a system, is one measure of value..

Alternately, the existence of thermodynamic correspondences arises directly (i.e., is not a-priori constructed) in bounded-rational potential games in two different ways: from a dynamical equilibrium or from a constrained maximum information-entropy equilibrium,.[9][10]

2.70.3 Economic systems

Thermoeconomists argue that economic systems always involve matter, energy, entropy, and information.[11] Moreover, the aim of many economic activities is to achieve a certain structure. In this manner, thermoeconomics applies the theories in non-equilibrium thermodynamics, in which structure formations called dissipative structures form, and information theory, in which information entropy is a central construct, to the modeling of economic activities in which the natural flows of energy and materials function to create scarce resources.[1] In thermodynamic terminology, human economic activity may be described as a dissipative system, which flourishes by consuming free energy in transformations and exchange of resources, goods, and services.[12][13]

2.70.4 See also

- Econophysics
- Ecodynamics
- Kinetic exchange models of markets
- Systems ecology
- Ecological economics
- Nicholas Georgescu-Roegen

2.70.5 References

[1] Sieniutycz, Stanislaw; Salamon, Peter (1990). *Finite-Time Thermodynamics and Thermoeconomics*. Taylor & Francis. ISBN 0-8448-1668-X.

[2] Yehia M. El-Sayed (2003). *The Thermoeconomics of Energy Conversions* (pg. 4). Pergamon.

[3] A. Valero, L. Serra, and J. Uche (2006). Fundamentals of Exergy Cost Accounting and Thermoeconomics. Part I: Theory, Journal of Energy Resources Technology, Volume 128, Issue 1, pp. 1-8.

[4] Gong, Mei, Wall, Goran. (1997). On Exergetics, Economics and Optimization of Technical Processes to Meet Environmental Conditions. Exergy Studies.

[5] Chen, Jing (2005). *The Physical Foundation of Economics - an Analytical Thermodynamic Theory*. World Scientific. ISBN 981-256-323-7.

[6] Peter A. Corning 1*, Stephen J. Kline. (2000). Thermodynamics, information and life revisited, Part II: Thermoeconomics and Control information Systems Research and Behavioral Science, Apr. 07, Volume 15, Issue 6 , Pages 453 – 482

[7] Corning, P. (2002). "Thermoeconomics – Beyond the Second Law"

[8] Burley, Peter; Foster, John (1994). *Economics and Thermodynamics – New Perspectives on Economic Analysis*. Kluwer Academic Publishers. ISBN 0-7923-9446-1.

[9] Campbell, Michael J. (2005). "A Gibbsian approach to potential game theory (draft)". arXiv:cond-mat/0502112v2.

[10] Carfi, David; Campbell, Michael J. (2015). "Bounded Rational Speculative and Hedging Interaction Model in Oil and U.S. Dollar Markets". *Journal of Mathematical Economics and Finance* (ASERS) **1** (1): 4–23. doi:10.14505/jmef.01.

[11] Baumgarter, Stefan. (2004). Thermodynamic Models, Modeling in Ecological Economics (Ch. 18)

[12] Raine, Alan; Foster, John; Potts, Jason (2006). "The new entropy law and the economic process". *Ecological Complexity* **3**: 354–360. doi:10.1016/j.ecocom.2007.02.009.

[13] Annila, A. and Salthe, S., Arto; Salthe, Stanley (2009). "Economies evolve by energy dispersal". *Entropy* **11** (4): 606–633. doi:10.3390/e11040606.

2.70.6 Further reading

- Soddy, Frederick (1922). *Cartesian Economics: The Bearing of Physical Science upon State Stewardship*. London: Hendersons.

- Georgescu-Roegen, Nicholas (1971). *The Entropy Law and the Economic Process*. Cambridge, Massachusetts: Harvard University Press. ISBN 978-1583486009.

- El-Sayed, Yehia, M. (2003). *The Thermoeconomics of Energy Conversions*. Pergamon. ISBN 0-08-044270-6.

- Pokrovskii, Vladimir (2011). *Econodynamics. The Theory of Social Production*. Berlin: Springer. ISBN 978-1-4419-9364-9.

- Kümmel, Reiner (2011). *The Second Law of Economics: Energy, Entropy, and the Origins of Wealth*. Berlin: Springer. ISBN 978-94-007-2095-4.

- Valero Capilla, Antonio; Alicia Valero Delgado (2014). *Thanatia: The Destiny of the Earth's Mineral Resources: A Thermodynamic Cradle-to-Cradle Assessment*. Singapore: World Scientific. ISBN 978-981-4273-93-0.

- Chen, Jing (2015). *The Unity of Science and Economics: A New Foundation of Economic Theory*. http://www.springer.com/us/book/9781493934645: Springer.

2.70.7 External links

- Yuri Yegorov, article Econo-physics: A Perspective of Matching Two Sciences, Evol. Inst. Econ. Rev. 4(1): 143–170 (2007) _pdf (application/pdf Object)

- Borisas Cimbleris (1998): Economy and Thermodynamics

- Schwartzman, David. (2007). "The Limits to Entropy: the Continuing Misuse of Thermodynamics in Environmental and Marxist theory", In Press, Science & Society.

- Saslow, Wayne M. (1999). "An Economic Analogy to Thermodynamics" *American Association of Physics Teachers*.

Chapter 3

Text and image sources, contributors, and licenses

3.1 Text

- **Heterodox economics** *Source:* https://en.wikipedia.org/wiki/Heterodox_economics?oldid=702030600 *Contributors:* Derek Ross, Greenrd, Dale Arnett, Fifelfoo, Terjepetersen, Andycjp, Beland, Pgreenfinch, Rich Farmbrough, Euthydemos, Bender235, Malkin, Tmh, Gary, John Quiggin, Samohyl Jan, Clubmarx, Woohookitty, Dwarf Kirlston, Koavf, Volunteer Marek, WriterHound, RussBot, Chris Capoccia, Morphh, Mshecket, Stijn Calle, Maunus, Jurriaan, WAS 4.250, Theodolite, Geoffrey.landis, SmackBot, Bokken, Lawrencekhoo, Chris the speller, MartinPoulter, Mikcob, Nbarth, Bowin~enwiki, EPM, Floressas, Byelf2007, BHC, RommelDAK, Joseph Solis in Australia, Eastlaw, CRGreathouse, Bobfrombrockley, Vision Thing, N2e, Thomasmeeks, Julian Wells, Thijs!bot, Headbomb, Itsmejudith, Nick Number, Gregalton, Skomorokh, JonBC, LindaNowakowski, Olwak, Magioladitis, Zenomax, Tremello, R'n'B, Tparameter, Calliopemichael, VolkovBot, Johnfos, Rtol, LPROCHON2003, Skipsievert, Schmida, Jdaloner, Msrasnw, Bombastus, Meisterkoch, ImperfectlyInformed, Wwheaton, Addbot, Luckas-bot, J. Milch, Yobot, AnomieBOT, Citation bot, Srich32977, J04n, Aetas volat., Omnipaedista, Imyoda69, FrescoBot, Seelum, Kpawa, HamburgerRadio, Citation bot 1, Kiefer.Wolfowitz, Prof. Q, Searle88, PhilHyde3, Blackleg84, Enragedeconomist, Rayman60, Mr. Thrasymachus, ZéroBot, Diaspore, Tolly4bolly, Grampion76, Irishbrigade1942, ClueBot NG, Epigrammed, Aurelch, Frietjes, Helpful Pixie Bot, Dtellett, Ledjazz, BG19bot, PhnomPencil, BattyBot, Zoe Lindesay, Whomonk, PixelThe0ry, Steeletrap, O5o7, Monkbot, Je.est.un.autre, CV9933, Chamflac, Besnik.sylejmani and Anonymous: 102

- **History of economic thought** *Source:* https://en.wikipedia.org/wiki/History_of_economic_thought?oldid=705155702 *Contributors:* Edward, Earth, Charles Matthews, Tpbradbury, Robbot, Saforrest, Giftlite, Beland, Neutrality, Chris Howard, Discospinster, Dagonet, Bender235, Neko-chan, CanisRufus, Sole Soul, Cretog8, Mdd, Gary, John Quiggin, Wikidea, Olaf Simons, Wtmitchell, Super-Magician, Danthemankhan, Woohookitty, Tabletop, Bkwillwm, Smmurphy, BD2412, Angusmclellan, DickClarkMises, Ground Zero, Kenmayer, Volunteer Marek, Bgwhite, RussBot, Rsrikanth05, Morphh, Rick Norwood, Dialectric, Daniel Simanek, Stijn Calle, GnatsFriend, Ospalh, Lockesdonkey, Closedmouth, RedJ 17, Minnesota1, Yvwv, Sardanaphalus, SmackBot, Gigs, Lawrencekhoo, Jagged 85, Stifle, Hmains, Skizzik, Amatulic, Nbarth, Colonies Chris, Sookie 02, Arnomd, Snowmanradio, Finx, Arab Hafez, MrRadioGuy, EPM, Nubeli, Leaflord, Kokacola, Will Beback, Byelf2007, Angela26, Yannismarou, Saluton~enwiki, Marnues, Mets501, Levineps, JHP, Fdssdf, ChrisCork, Eastlaw, WolfgangFaber, CRGreathouse, CmdrObot, Mattbr, Vision Thing, THF, Mak Thorpe, Thomasmeeks, Myasuda, Alaibot, PamD, Thijs!bot, Biruitorul, Frank, Bobblehead, Michael A. White, Escarbot, Ela112, Hires an editor, Radimvice, Kbthompson, Vader99, DuncanHill, Frankie816, Magioladitis, Dentren, Elinruby, SlamDiego, JaGa, EyeSerene, R'n'B, CommonsDelinker, Fconaway, Trusilver, Nigholith, TomS TDotO, Jeepday, Inbloom2, KylieTastic, Foofighter20x, Jarry1250, LeighCaldwell, Caspian blue, Johnfos, Childhoodsend, Warko, ElinorD, Someguy1221, Jackfork, Natg 19, Robertsch55, Asaduzaman, Why Not A Duck, GoddersUK, GirasoleDE, StAnselm, Skipsievert, Artoasis, Hyperboreean, Lightmouse, Msrasnw, Rinconsoleao, ImageRemovalBot, Pan narrans, ImperfectlyInformed, Unbuttered Parsnip, Farras Octara, P. S. Burton, R2D2V2, Masterpiece2000, Ktr101, Sun Creator, Alexander Tendler, SoxBot III, DumZiBoT, BigK HeX, Comte de Maistre, Salam32, Addbot, Cxz111, Grayfell, PatrickFlaherty, Chris who reads books for a living, AdRem, Protonk, LinkFA-Bot, Tassedethe, Bình Giang, Luckas-bot, J. Milch, Yobot, Shaunmwilson1, Pahpaha, Spider face, Mike montagne, FeydHuxtable, AnomieBOT, Bsimmons666, Citation bot, Racconish, Eskandarany, Teilolondon, LilHelpa, Xqbot, Dbeauchaine, Joshsmith65536, Srich32977, Themightyrambo, Susan Chan, J04n, Morten Isaksen, Omnipaedista, WissensDürster, Eisfbnore, Shadowjams, Hugetim, FrescoBot, Fortdj33, Paine Ellsworth, Jamesooders, Factchecker12, OgreBot, Citation bot 1, Ian R Gates, I dream of horses, Calmer Waters, PhilHyde3, FoxBot, Bbarkley2, Sisyphos23, Allen4names, WildBot, Joerund, John of Reading, WikitanvirBot, Jragland1414, Super48paul, Dewritech, GoingBatty, Werieth, PBS-AWB, Josve05a, Jonpatterns, Tolly4bolly, RaptureBot, Donner60, Pochsad, Financestudent, FurrySings, ClueBot NG, Catlemur, Benjamin9832, Marinatt, Helpful Pixie Bot, BG19bot, The Banner Turbo, Iselilja, Kagundu, Altaïr, L888Y5, DPL bot, FinancePublisher, Aayush18, M.ES11D042, Khazar2, Harpsichord246, Largehole, Dexbot, Rothbardanswer, Byronmercury, Mogism, Bluebasket, Mathematician314, SPECIFICO, RotlinkBot, Ruby Murray, I am One of Many, Whomonk, Hendrick 99, NottNott, Banzai6666, Jmilewski26, Алексей Галушкин, Whomyl, Filedelinkerbot, E. Ray Canterbery, Mitzi.humphrey, Loraof, Spiderjerky, Y-S.Ko, Gaeanautes, 12.5987.25.147 qwer, Libralight, CX42 and Anonymous: 261

- **Neoclassical economics** *Source:* https://en.wikipedia.org/wiki/Neoclassical_economics?oldid=700695457 *Contributors:* Darius Bacon, Enchanter, Tim Marklew, SimonP, Anne, DavidSJ, Someone else, Ericd, Edward, Michael Hardy, Owl, Sam Francis, Pde, Ahoerstemeier, Docu,

LittleDan, Icekiss, JASpencer, Mydogategodshat, Charles Matthews, VeryVerily, Populus, Jecar, Frazzydee, Jni, Kokiri, Vikingstad, Stirling Newberry, Andycjp, Ruy Lopez, Jdevine, Piotrus, DNewhall, Scott Burley, Boojum, M1ss1ontomars2k4, Arminius, Piotras, Discospinster, Rich Farmbrough, Bender235, Jaimedv, El C, Senori, Bobo192, Cretog8, Tmh, Jakew, HasharBot~enwiki, Gulseren, Alansohn, John Quiggin, Wikidea, Goodoldpolonius2, Crosbiesmith, Bkwillwm, Dzordzm, Qwertyus, Golden Eternity, KAM, FlaBot, BMF81, Chobot, Volunteer Marek, FrankTobia, YurikBot, RussBot, OldRight, Onias, Thelb4, Tim1965, GrinBot~enwiki, Segv11, SmackBot, Lawrencekhoo, Eskimbot, Yamaguchi??, Colonies Chris, Can't sleep, clown will eat me, Sholto Maud, Jinxed, Nixeagle, Typpo, Anthon.Eff, Stevenmitchell, Solarapex, EPM, Byelf2007, Soap, Saluton~enwiki, Joseph Solis in Australia, Vision Thing, Laurenjf, Thomasmeeks, Neelix, Yaris678, Anonymi, Scott Bunton, Jackftwist, Knotwork, JAnDbot, MER-C, Skomorokh, Txomin, Lackthereof, Olwak, Magioladitis, VoABot II, Economizer, SlamDiego, DerHexer, MartinBot, STBot, Geoffhodgson, MarceloB, JSellers0, Kenneth M Burke, DavidCBryant, Edwin Herdman, Bobareann, Amritasenray, Temporaluser, Annamarie Ursula, Struway, Botev, Mando12mcq, Scorpion451, Correogsk, Anchor Link Bot, Rinconsoleao, ClueBot, ImperfectlyInformed, Excirial, Aleksd, Asrghasrhiojadrhr, Addbot, Grayfell, Lightbot, Legobot, Luckas-bot, Carleas, AnomieBOT, Nutriveg, Rubinbot, Neobright, Xqbot, Srich32977, NOrbeck, Mark Schierbecker, RibotBOT, Undsoweiter, FrescoBot, Ex Evolutione, I dream of horses, Tboy182, Merlinsorca, Onel5969, EmausBot, TuHan-Bot, Alfredo ougaowen, ZéroBot, Zfeinst, Sadpoch, Financestudent, Nesasio, Pragmatic740, Will Beback Auto, ClueBot NG, BG19bot, JDefauw, JokoP, Glacialfox, Ditzahedva, Dschslava, PIerre.Lescanne, Bronx Discount Liquor, Loraof and Anonymous: 175

- **Alexander del Mar** *Source:* https://en.wikipedia.org/wiki/Alexander_del_Mar?oldid=705100593 *Contributors:* Klemen Kocjancic, Rich Farmbrough, Bender235, Tabletop, Rjwilmsi, Stijn Calle, SmackBot, Ohconfucius, Robofish, CmdrObot, Waacstats, Fabrictramp, R'n'B, Xenophrenic, Robertsch55, WereSpielChequers, Alexbot, Good Olfactory, Addbot, Margin1522, PMLawrence, MinorProphet, AnomieBOT, Omnipaedista, Green Cardamom, RjwilmsiBot, Wittsun, Δ, Helpful Pixie Bot, BG19bot, PhnomPencil, BattyBot, ChrisGualtieri, The Vintage Feminist, VIAFbot, Faizan, Emmawood, Bronx Discount Liquor, KasparBot and Anonymous: 2

- **American Monetary Institute** *Source:* https://en.wikipedia.org/wiki/American_Monetary_Institute?oldid=621300771 *Contributors:* Edward, Bearcat, Goethean, Alan Liefting, Bobrayner, Dr Gangrene, Scarykitty, Pinball22, Tim!, StephenWeber, Stijn Calle, Pegship, Arthur Rubin, Cjfsyntropy, SmackBot, The Gnome, Colonies Chris, Dinarphatak, Guroadrunner, Robofish, Alaibot, JamesAM, Voyaging, Harelx, DMCer, JohnAugust, Stephen Zarlenga, SieBot, Smcke0wn, Tomdobb, Cirt, XLinkBot, Addbot, Lagrandebanquesucre, Lightbot, AnomieBOT, Johnwilliammiller, FrescoBot, ZéroBot, Joseph.ofallon, Arne Saknussem, BG19bot, Kumioko, Canadianpolisci, Bronx Discount Liquor and Anonymous: 7

- **Anti-capitalism** *Source:* https://en.wikipedia.org/wiki/Anti-capitalism?oldid=704880807 *Contributors:* Guppie, William Avery, SimonP, HollyAm, MartinHarper, 172, CesarB, Sir Paul, Nv8200pa, Kevehs, Owen, Jni, Nikodemos, Millerc, CyborgTosser, Golbez, Richard Myers, Andycjp, Loremaster, Cberlet, Tothebarricades.tk, Soman, Avihu, Imroy, Spleeman, Mal~enwiki, Bender235, Ntennis, Bcat, The King Of Gondor, Livajo, Lycurgus, Causa sui, Cretog8, Che y Marijuana, Remuel, Jerryseinfeld, Aquillion, VBGFscJUn3, Hipocrite, John Quiggin, Bootstoots, Radical Mallard, TheRealFennShysa, RJII, Albamuth, Amorymeltzer, VoluntarySlave, Ghirlandajo, Bookandcoffee, Yurivict, Dtobias, Bobrayner, OleMaster, Jacob Haller, Lapsed Pacifist, Alienus, FreplySpang, Rjwilmsi, Madcat87, Ground Zero, Jrtayloriv, Str1977, LeCire~enwiki, Saswann, YurikBot, Wavelength, Stan2525, Hairy Dude, Roadcollective, RussBot, Pigman, Mykenism, CambridgeBayWeather, NawlinWiki, LaszloWalrus, Formeruser-82, Fair&Balanced~enwiki, BOT-Superzerocool, DNAku, Zzuuzz, Closedmouth, Eduard Gherkin, Red Jay, Infinity0, Biltmore Blob, C mon, Rogerz, SmackBot, Looper5920, KVDP, Kasyapa, Colonies Chris, John sargis, Chlewbot, Agrofelipe, Dantadd, Kukini, TenPoundHammer, Byelf2007, The Ungovernable Force, Lambiam, Green01, Gobonobo, Bydand, Robofish, Mr. Quertee, Epiphyllumlover, Ryulong, WGee, BlackFlag, RekishiEJ, Tawkerbot2, RookZERO, FISHERAD, George100, JForget, Bobfrombrockley, Van helsing, Vision Thing, Normski3000, THF, Erick91, Davnor, Cydebot, R-41, Spylab, DumbBOT, Alexbonick, Omicronpersei8, EnglishEfternamn, Thijs!bot, Cory Liu, Vodomar, Widefox, Carolmooredc, Xolom, Dylan Lake, David Shankbone, Blahblahblahblahblahblah, JAnDbot, Skomorokh, Supertheman, Solidarityjoe, Frederico., Usws, VoABot II, Rexfan2, CCWilliams, Freebornjohn, Jessicapierce, Fang 23, Skylights76, Emeraude, CommonsDelinker, VAcharon, Jlohmeyer, Kesal, Ruadh, Colchicum, Vanished User 4517, Lygophile, Inomyabcs, Endlessmike 888, Scott Illini, Vsuarezp, Djr13, Wohmfg, Intangible2.0, JGHowes, Jeff G., Αναρχία, Jfrascencio, Philip Trueman, TXiKiBoT, Billy Ego, C.J. Griffin, Wassermann~enwiki, Anarchangel, Mr. Absurd, TruthSeeker777, Juakali, Nikosgreencookie, Larklight, Wassamatta, Falcon8765, Dynimite 007, Jon33, SieBot, Caltas, Freedomwarrior, NavyFalcon, Janfri, Wuhwuzdat, Operation Spooner, Gr8opinionater, ClueBot, Otolemur crassicaudatus, Hangakommy, Kitsunegami, Beheader6, Bite MeRance14, Quacking~enwiki, Garybanham, Rancewringer, Redthoreau, Blindghost, Tchurovsky, Olybrius, XLinkBot, Roxy the dog, DaL33T, SilvonenBot, Gigoachef, Addbot, Andreave1977, Jncraton, Eedlee, Download, Amerul, BFairntrue, AndersBot, Slatedorg, Tide rolls, Lightbot, Jarble, Legobot, Drpickem, Luckas-bot, Yobot, Eduen, Azurian, AnomieBOT, Killiondude, Valois bourbon, Aditya, Materialscientist, Citation bot, Racconish, Crzer07, GrouchoBot, RibotBOT, Many Heads, Jean-Jacques Georges, FrescoBot, Sausagehiders, Adam9389, Elfie67, HelloKittyBack, Trust Is All You Need, Strot, Trotskut, Mimzy1990, Thekappen, CaptainEagle, Motorizer, RobertHuaXia, Jonkerz, Callanecc, LilyKitty, Grifftob, 777sms, Defender of torch, Britney Gramsci, Fellytone, Minigoody101, Erianna, Ego White Tray, Financestudent, Anticapitalistpower, Diatarveden, Mjskay, Helpful Pixie Bot, Simpsonguy1987, Sigiheri, Lowercase sigmabot, BG19bot, Fidel Guevara, LLTSU, KhabarNegar, Adventjah, Cyberbot II, SPECIFICO, Hendrick 99, EM Che, SantiLak, BrightonC, Denisrodman88, 3298230932782302, Vonbergh, F198129, KasparBot, Anticap001, Conbrochill, Not a creative person and Anonymous: 191

- **Association for Evolutionary Economics** *Source:* https://en.wikipedia.org/wiki/Association_for_Evolutionary_Economics?oldid=700731047 *Contributors:* Bearcat, Rjwilmsi, KylieTastic, Onel5969, Primefac, Sulfurboy and Chamflac

- **Austrian School** *Source:* https://en.wikipedia.org/wiki/Austrian_School?oldid=702983652 *Contributors:* Mav, Bryan Derksen, Darius Bacon, Enchanter, Fubar Obfusco, William Avery, Tuomas Toivonen, Leandrod, Edward, Patrick, Michael Hardy, Crenner, Liftarn, Damnedkingdom, Radicalsubversiv, Jiang, Evercat, JamesReyes, Ghewgill, JASpencer, Zoicon5, Peregrine981, Stelian, VeryVerily, Jni, Goethean, Arkuat, AaronS, Auric, Wikibot, Fuelbottle, Rdfuerle, Hcheney, Snobot, Stirling Newberry, Imf980, Paul Richter, Fennec, Nikodemos, Taion, Nat Krause, Philwelch, Wyss, Brona, Christofurio, Gzornenplatz, Bobblewik, JRR Trollkien, Gugganij, Antandrus, RayBirks, Tacitus Prime, Sam Hocevar, TiMike, Premitive1, GreedyCapitalist, Johncapistrano, Noisy, Discospinster, Rich Farmbrough, Guanabot, H0riz0n, Calion, User2004, JPX7, Bender235, Cedders, Kwamikagami, Remember, KrJnX, Deicas, Cretog8, Cmdrjameson, Jerryseinfeld, Gilgamesh79, Deryck Chan, Justinc, Xgoni~enwiki, Danski14, John Quiggin, Kinghajj, Calton, Mohammadgani, Velella, RJII, Zawersh, Bsadowski1, Politician~enwiki, Versageek, Ethilien, Kazvorpal, Ultramarine, Bastin, Stuartyeates, Woohookitty, Gobstomper, Benbest, MONGO, Bkwillwm, Al E., Bluemoose, Palica, Graham87, BD2412, Li-sung, Ketiltrout, Drbogdan, Rjwilmsi, Jweiss11, Wikibofh, Bob A, Pearlg, DickClarkMises, Eclipsael, Ludovic

Sesim~enwiki, Wragge, FlaBot, Ground Zero, Dullfig, Gurch, Fephisto, Torkillbruland~enwiki, PLooB, POTA, Manscher, Nstannik, LoudNotes, YurikBot, Matt O'Lehry, Justinw303, NTBot~enwiki, Huw Powell, RussBot, Chris Capoccia, Alex Bakharev, Morphh, Big Brother 1984, NawlinWiki, Robertvan1, Trovatore, Kvn8907, Rjensen, RBrancusi, Fredericks, Bengalski, Moe Epsilon, Bucketsofg, Haemo, David Nelson, Sandstein, Closedmouth, GrEp, ⁇⁇⁇⁇ robot, Sardanaphalus, Intangible, KnightRider~enwiki, SmackBot, Historian932, Darkstar1st, Lawrencekhoo, Allixpeeke, Janey Dowerstruffel, Jeffro77, Chris the speller, Jdhunt, Grimhelm, Neo-Jay, Nbarth, Zachorious, Nixeagle, JonHarder, GRuban, Addshore, Anthon.Eff, Dwchin, A.R., RafaelG, The morgawr, JBHD, Autopilot, Byelf2007, SashatoBot, Kuru, Sean chile, Vgy7ujm, Gobonobo, Ralthor, Hannes H. Gissurarson~enwiki, AdultSwim, NJA, CormanoSanchez, MikeWazowski, Iridescent, Joseph Solis in Australia, Twas Now, Rvissers, Trialsanderrors, Courcelles, Ramehart, Revcasy, AbsolutDan, Shirahadasha, CmdrObot, Vision Thing, BeenAroundAWhile, ThatProLibertyGuy, N2e, Laurenjf, Thomasmeeks, Cohaerens, Valentimd, Mato, AlexanderLevian, Dusty relic, Mirrormundo, DumbBOT, Satori Son, ATD~enwiki, Lectert, Flextronics, Kborer, NigelR, EdJohnston, CharlotteWebb, Matthew Proctor, Scshute, Tom servo, Carolmooredc, Mdotley, Gregalton, Smartse, Sonofecthelion, Dylan Lake, Spartaz, Gay Cdn, JAnDbot, Skomorokh, Robocracy, Albany NY, Andonic, Reign of Toads, Fsol, TAnthony, Magioladitis, Professor marginalia, Smartal, MastCell, Brusegadi, JLMadrigal, Winterus, Ikilled007, NimNick, Elinruby, Creativename, SlamDiego, Memotype, Shadowthedog, Cocytus, Phelbich, Ariel., DerRichter, R'n'B, CommonsDelinker, AgarwalSumeet, Per Hedetun, RG415WBFA, Tokyogirl79, JayJasper, AntiSpamBot, Tparameter, InspectorTiger, Madhava 1947, Ibemonty2000, DavidCBryant, Gwen Gale, Mike V, JohnDoe0007, Thismightbezach, Sirmont, Black Kite, VolkovBot, Lia Todua, Katydidit, Childhoodsend, Malinaccier, Josephholsten, Id4abel, Anna Lincoln, FargoWells, Larklight, Amritasenray, Corduroy1982, Gamsbart, Logan, Albericht, Traxinet, Macdonald-ross, Taonga99, Agbook, Ravensfire, Granola Bars, Hxhbot, Averros, Skipsievert, Amadeus226, James Haughton, Xday, The Four Deuces, Akldawgs, Sitush, Operation Spooner, Sfan00 IMG, Binksternet, 0nullbinary0, John5246, Pairadox, De2min2, Rusirious13, Monobi, Muhandes, SeekFind, Nyopallo, NuclearWarfare, Cenarium, Dark Kyle, Arjayay, Gassho, Coccyx Bloccyx, Salon Essahj, Thingg, Error −128, Jwpegler, Count Truthstein, Adriansrfr, Darth Wombat, LoweLeif, Herunar, DumZiBoT, Zenwhat, Doopdoop, BigK HeX, Nomoskedasticity, Anawasm, Ahkeeler, Mvanwinkle, DOI bot, Lagrandebanquesucre, Atethnekos, PatrickFlaherty, Elsendero, Wingspeed, Urewrong, C9900, Debresser, AnnaFrance, Favonian, LemmeyBOT, LinkFA-Bot, TheFreeloader, Dayewalker, Equilibrium007, Lightbot, Solid State, Zorrobot, MuZemike, JEN9841, Krukouski, Ben Ben, Legobot, Yobot, Ninjalemming, Legobot II, Darx9url, UserAccount001, Mark Borgschulte, DemitreusFrontwest, SturmTiger42, Scholastic Opponent, Flying Pete, Bility, Frederic Bastiat, AnomieBOT, Misessus, DemocraticLuntz, Gamma1776, TruthComesFromAGunBoat, Jo3sampl, We'reFreakingDoomed!, Materialscientist, Citation bot, Teeninvestor, BanksAreGods, LilHelpa, Awesomeeconomist, Fare~enwiki, Xqbot, Ron Paul...Ron Paul..., The Banner, Psyoptix, TechBot, BellCurveBlues, Nielsio, Srich32977, Almabot, ArableLand, Omnipaedista, Michael.suede, Gui le Roi, Krisztián Pintér, Šedý, WahnF, PonziWasNotSuperman, AlphaRed3, FalseGodsBetray, oulold, AsianWimp, HansonWasFromQLD, Dundas plc, OrderWithoutLaw, God'sRevengeIsToday'sEnvironment, QueryEverything, KeepGoldThrowBondsAway, Introman, PyramidsOrFood?, Legobot III, FrescoBot, EricdeBear, WatchinTheTideRollAway, Rustydangerfield, GoldManTookFtKnox, Pestergaines, Smithdanj, Citation bot 1, Dark Charles, Elockid, Kiefer.Wolfowitz, Skyerise, GayTime, GreedImmolatesItself, "Swine"Flu=StolenFarmland, ZombieBank, Edward"Ned"Kelly, BritishZombies, WhyAreLeftiesAllZealots?, RafaelMinuesa, PersecutedAustrians, TheSolutionIsEvenMoreDebt, Serols, WhyMeLord?, 11wikiman11, TruthAndZealotryDon'tMix, MeUser42, DecadesAtBernies, UnrecognizedProphetOfDoom, OnlyAfterDeathDoesASGetRespect, LordHaveMercyOnTheSoulsOfEmbezzlers, KhooEatsHisOwnPoo, AustrianButOpen-Minded, Topher.sg, TimothyDon-HughMak, LCE1506, North8000, Jonkerz, Lotje, SeoMac, Reaper Eternal, TheElephant'sRoom, DA1, Lambanog, WarningFinancialTsunamiAhead, KeynesianLeninistCensors, HumanRobotsCan'tSwerve, Tbhotch, RjwilmsiBot, Weakopedia, WildBot, DASHBot, WikitanvirBot, Dewritech, Tucci78, Devandenesse, Cwjennings, $atan's$pawn, Budija, HiW-Bot, ZéroBot, Oncenawhile, Fortheloveofbacon, QE2Infinity!, TaxPaysParasites, CorruptCounterfeiters, GypsyBanksters, OilyChernobyl, MisterDub, PtAuAg, Δ, FractionalReserveRobbery, Zhen Jin, N6n, Polisher of Cobwebs, Financestudent, ChuispastonBot, PraxisConsensus, LikeLakers2, Terra Novus, ClueBot NG, Chetrasho, DataDarkLBMA, SilverLongsWillBreakTheBanksters, BuySilverKillTheBanksters, Somedifferentstuff, Macarenses, Epigrammed, Richard Ebeling, Kjmonkey, Samuel Marks, Trey111, Amanski, Helpful Pixie Bot, Revisor2011, GRosado, Lowercase sigmabot, Nodrogj, Dean001, Wormbread, Jrockets, Mark Arsten, Romanedebasement, Joshmarq, EuroFiatTrashed, BattyBot, Cyberbot II, ChrisGualtieri, SD5bot, Dexbot, Mommy2012, Rothbardanswer, StillStanding-247, MartinMichlmayr, Mmahoney393, LK'sPatsy, SPECIFICO, FRB123, Rainbow Shifter, KaiserEricSJ, Mark viking, CoffeeWithMarkets, GenericAnonIP, FiscalFarce, IndistinctEditor, EconomicIllusions, Alfy32, Everymorning, Wuerzele, Shrikarsan, VMav92, WeOweItToOurselves, EJM86, Keylar25, Adn1990, Santiago telom, Steeletrap, NottNott, Shearflyer, Anon4567, Bronx Discount Liquor, Monkbot, CourtCelts1988, Vozul, Lkmvpvwj, Jgg0005, TakeItUpTheGreekEconomy, FiatMoneyWillDieInTheEnd, Ogreggy and Anonymous: 444

- **Binary economics** *Source:* https://en.wikipedia.org/wiki/Binary_economics?oldid=670886729 *Contributors:* Earth, Ixfd64, Connelly, Nat Krause, Michael Devore, Klemen Kocjancic, Chris Howard, Rich Farmbrough, Mecanismo, Lycurgus, Pearle, Djlayton4, Deacon of Pndapetzim, Bobrayner, RHaworth, GregorB, Panlane, Rjwilmsi, Koavf, Janosabel, Seraphimblade, Wragge, Ground Zero, Volunteer Marek, FrankTobia, RussBot, Stijn Calle, Mweymar, Haemo, SmackBot, Bluebot, MidgleyDJ, Colonies Chris, LeContexte, Rigadoun, Ulner, Gobonobo, Dspitzle, David soori, Joseph Solis in Australia, Rhetth, RookZERO, CalebNoble, Johtib~enwiki, Thomasmeeks, Cydebot, Normix, EdJohnston, Nick Number, TheJF, Igodard, Magioladitis, MartinDK, Brusegadi, Brightjoy, R'n'B, Catmoongirl, CraigMonroe, Skumarlabot, Childhoodsend, Fredrick day, Lamro, Farooqmo, Ponyo, Bigdaddy1981, Schmida, Rodney Shakespeare, Fratrep, Fuddle, GorillaWarfare, Father Inire, GeneCallahan, XLinkBot, Yobot, Bunnyhop11, Legobot II, AnomieBOT, 90 Auto, EcoTort, Omnipaedista, Waceaquinas, Jonpatterns, 2beproud, Dtellett, Justicesoldier, Khazar2, DaveHamill, Hendrick 99, WhyWon'tSheHaveCoitusWithMe and Anonymous: 78

- **Calculation in kind** *Source:* https://en.wikipedia.org/wiki/Calculation_in_kind?oldid=696063209 *Contributors:* Mrwojo, Pgan002, GreenReaper, Jayjg, Lycurgus, Bobrayner, SmackBot, Chris the speller, Renamed user Sloane, Battlecry, Jac16888, Jiří Komárek, Gruntmonk, AnomieBOT, Helpful Pixie Bot, ChrisGualtieri, Homealone1990, CsDix, Macofe and Anonymous: 6

- **Chrematistics** *Source:* https://en.wikipedia.org/wiki/Chrematistics?oldid=659895379 *Contributors:* John Quiggin, Daniel Cordoba-Bahle, Jonson22, Alexbot, Addbot, Luckas-bot, Math-wes, Amainando, Bronx Discount Liquor and Anonymous: 3

- **Circular cumulative causation** *Source:* https://en.wikipedia.org/wiki/Circular_cumulative_causation?oldid=690588138 *Contributors:* Tony1, Chris the speller, Katharineamy, J. Milch, AnomieBOT, Vrenator, John of Reading, Snotbot, Nuttster99, Jan Götesson, Bronx Discount Liquor, Aisharya and Anonymous: 3

- **Complexity economics** *Source:* https://en.wikipedia.org/wiki/Complexity_economics?oldid=686996598 *Contributors:* Edward, Rich Farmbrough, Cretog8, Mdd, Vuo, DaveApter, Rjwilmsi, Bgwhite, Arthur Rubin, SmackBot, Battlecry, DMacks, Khazar, Catquas, Mr3641, Eastlaw, N2e, Gordon007, Alaibot, Danny lost, Coppertwig, M-le-mot-dit, Wikijectivist, Jojalozzo, Rinconsoleao, ImperfectlyInformed, Addbot,

3.1. TEXT

Fuller.s.a., Mario Ludovico, Margin1522, Yobot, Jean.julius, Citation bot, Miracleworker5263, Fortdj33, GrammarHammer 32, Fox1942, Citation bot 1, Kiefer.Wolfowitz, Enragedeconomist, EmausBot, Bampbs, Hulbert88, BG19bot, BattyBot, Fhumeres, Poptriviaking, Nigellwh, Jellander, Monkbot, Adanforjador, Phoenix 123 abc and Anonymous: 33

- **Counter-economics** *Source:* https://en.wikipedia.org/wiki/Counter-economics?oldid=697102784 *Contributors:* Nonick, Jneil, Mjk2357, Woohookitty, Koavf, Bradspangler, Sardanaphalus, SmackBot, Tamfang, Byelf2007, Benkeboy, Iridescent, Randroide, Heqs, Gregbard, Cydebot, KleenupKrew, VaneWimsey, Dylan Lake, Skomorokh, Thaurisil, VolkovBot, Freeman23, TheOldJacobite, Passargea, John Nevard, Eggyweggyweggs, Logic7, Addbot, Yobot, Sageo, PublicSquare, Quebec99, Srich32977, Quiet Bird, John of Reading, Neomedes, Ὁ οἶστρος, Anarchist Ivanov, Helpful Pixie Bot, Gob Lofa, The Banner Turbo, Rothbardanswer, CsDix, Cervota, B1313 and Anonymous: 22

- **Credibility thesis** *Source:* https://en.wikipedia.org/wiki/Credibility_thesis?oldid=699269282 *Contributors:* Rjwilmsi, Chris the speller, Niceguyedc, Karlisr, I dream of horses, BG19bot and Srednuas Lenoroc

- **David Malone (independent filmmaker)** *Source:* https://en.wikipedia.org/wiki/David_Malone_(independent_filmmaker)?oldid=704995160 *Contributors:* Ryz, Thorwald, TheIguana, Closedmouth, SmackBot, Colonies Chris, BrownHairedGirl, Akinara, Waacstats, Fabrictramp, Keith D, Johnpacklambert, DadaNeem, 32F, Nix D, Macy, JL-Bot, WickerGuy, Jan1nad, Realitarian, Kathleen.wright5, Niceguyedc, XLinkBot, Addbot, AnomieBOT, Some Herbert, Thehelpfulbot, RjwilmsiBot, DailyShipper, Mr Schneebly, ZedBot, VaudevillianScientist, BG19bot, Chris-Gualtieri, JCJC777, Andrewdwilliams, FivePillarPurist and Anonymous: 14

- **Decentralized planning (economics)** *Source:* https://en.wikipedia.org/wiki/Decentralized_planning_(economics)?oldid=691639857 *Contributors:* Bearcat, Foobaz, Prototime, Battlecry, Byelf2007, Lighthead, DOHill, WikHead, AnomieBOT, Srich32977, Slb36cornell, Thehelpfulbot, FrescoBot, Elmoro, EmausBot, Dewritech, KLBot2, Goti1233, Alexwho314, Vanamonde93, CsDix, Vrrajkum and Anonymous: 9

- **Decommodification** *Source:* https://en.wikipedia.org/wiki/Decommodification?oldid=702224270 *Contributors:* Edward, Hurricane111, John Quiggin, Lectonar, NickelShoe, SmackBot, DrunkenSmurf, Capedia, JAnDbot, The Transhumanist, Novina~enwiki, Victorggk, Deselliers, Addbot, Yobot, Eduen, Unara, GB fan, Locobot, Estelle yoyo, ClueBot NG, Krett12 and Anonymous: 24

- **Ecological economics** *Source:* https://en.wikipedia.org/wiki/Ecological_economics?oldid=704439613 *Contributors:* The Anome, William Avery, Edward, Ixfd64, Lquilter, SebastianHelm, Mac, Snoyes, Kingturtle, Nikai, Andres, Black bag, Kaihsu, Mydogategodshat, Timwi, Marshman, Samsara, Topbanana, Altenmann, Chris Roy, Sunray, DO'Neil, Andycjp, CryptoDerk, Absinf, Vsmith, Bishonen, Bender235, Cretog8, Maurreen, AppleJuggler, Pearle, Mdd, AnnaP, Rd232, John Quiggin, Sade, Calton, Robbie andrew, Bobrayner, Woohookitty, Berteh, Miss Madeline, Bluemoose, Hughcharlesparker, Xiong Chiamiov, Behun, Qwertyus, Rjwilmsi, Mgw, Seraphimblade, Gary Cziko, Hashproduct, RasputinAXP, King of Hearts, Topstar, Hermitage, Bgwhite, YurikBot, Wavelength, RussBot, Morphh, Dhollm, Epipelagic, Biopresto, MB-Dowd, Arthur Rubin, SmackBot, Mainguy~enwiki, InvictaHOG, KVDP, Hmains, Bluebot, Swedenborg, Sholto Maud, Vcrs, MrRadioGuy, Moulaert, John D. Croft, Richard001, RichWoodward, Gobonobo, Breno, Dingodangodongo, RomanSpa, Ckatz, Avedomni, Cerealkiller13, Levineps, Nehrams2020, JoeBot, RekishiEJ, Mr3641, CmdrObot, Thomasmeeks, Requestion, Neelix, Cydebot, Bthomson, Dr.enh, Billtubbs, Thijs!bot, Mailseth, Sbandrews, Michael Jon Jensen, YK Times, Frankie816, VoABot II, WikieWikieWikie, Gabriel Kielland, Marcelobbribeiro, Fang 23, Exiledone, Raoulduke47, MartinBot, Barak1, Ceser, Ekotckk, R'n'B, John Pozzi, BruceHodge, Jmalier, Lbeaumont, DadaNeem, Jorfer, Evb-wiki, Laskinmystic, DASonnenfeld, Livingston.28, VolkovBot, Johnfos, S.W. Bremer, Tomaxer, Amritasenray, Phmoreno, Charnovitz, F5487jin4, SieBot, VVVBot, Dawn Bard, BloodDoll, WildWildBil, M16rifle, Jojalozzo, Nopetro, Skipsievert, Smshaner, KarlaHyde, Daviding, Mrfebruary, ClueBot, ImperfectlyInformed, Flatbush52-1, Panozzaj, Dekisugi, Thingg, Edindian, XLinkBot, Brighteyes0007, Silvonen-Bot, Vegas949, Prof C, MystBot, Addbot, Miriam Kennet, MrOllie, Granitethighs, Tassedethe, Faunas, Jarble, Michaello, Luckas-bot, Yobot, עידן ד, Bunnyhop11, AnomieBOT, Citation bot, Ancechu, LilHelpa, Obersachsebot, Xqbot, Transity, Jyosna, Paul Safonov, Srich32977, Omnipaedista, Mkevlar, FrescoBot, Xenfreak, Citation bot 1, Moominoid, Redrose64, RedBot, Lucata, Animalparty, Vitorsarno, RjwilmsiBot, Rodmadar, EmausBot, WikitanvirBot, Aabelaros, Sharpecoman, Jdkag, Dewritech, Ype001, Cerfa, Jonpatterns, Grampion76, Jack Greenmaven, Michael.barkusky, Helpful Pixie Bot, Wbm1058, Slippingspy, Northamerica1000, PhnomPencil, Nocixel, Meclee, Erna2411, Cyberbot II, Localmocal11, Dstrel, Aupward, Claireclear, Thinksome, Vunamese, ThjPhD1981, Rumpye8, MBA2012E2, Stamptrader, Monkbot, GreenPanther1234, BethNaught, Socialvation, D.S. Cordoba-Bahle, Gregzetta, Gaeanautes, Ssmmachen and Anonymous: 136

- **Economic humanitarianism (Raëlianism)** *Source:* https://en.wikipedia.org/wiki/Economic_humanitarianism_(Ra%C3%ABlianism)?oldid=660417976 *Contributors:* Malcolm Farmer, Stevertigo, Neilc, Bobrayner, Epolk, Lexicon, Gadget850, Closedmouth, SmackBot, Kmarinas86, Hibernian, Will Beback, Robofish, CmdrObot, Frank, Magioladitis, Tchurovsky, Yobot, Materialscientist, Eugene-elgato, Full-date unlinking bot, Mcc1789 and Anonymous: 3

- **Econophysics** *Source:* https://en.wikipedia.org/wiki/Econophysics?oldid=700007244 *Contributors:* JohnOwens, Michael Hardy, Maximus Rex, Robbot, Korath, Gerbano, David Gerard, Fastfission, Jrdioko, Karol Langner, Bender235, Maurreen, John Quiggin, PAR, Evil Monkey, Euphrosyne, Bkwillwm, Ronnotel, Salix alba, Lmatt, Gcalda, Chobot, FrankTobia, YurikBot, Arouck, SmackBot, Elonka, Gunnar.Kaestle, Sadi Carnot, Arnabchat, Byelf2007, Loodog, Robofish, Kolmogorov Complexity, Eastlaw, Joostvandeputte~enwiki, CmdrObot, Escalas, Neelix, Julian Wells, Tobiasjon3s, Headbomb, MER-C, Eurobas, Paresnah, Profitip, STBot, GuidoGer, NerdyNSK, Cottrellnc, Guillaume2303, XeniaKon, SieBot, Skipsievert, Jorgen W, Msrasnw, Rinconsoleao, Addbot, DOI bot, Manjuer, Webphys, Ettrig, Luckas-bot, AnomieBOT, Andrew M. Vachin, Xqbot, Srich32977, Emstuart, Lyoulah, FreeKnowledgeCreator, Adler.fa, Pareschi, Canard123, Citation bot 1, MastiBot, Madliner, Meier99, JMMuller, Lotje, Duoduoduo, RjwilmsiBot, Condmatstrel, GaryLKaplan, GoingBatty, Brahma453, Josve05a, Music Sorter, RockMagnetist, ClueBot NG, Jasonbook99, Wydawnictwo Niezalezne, Bibcode Bot, BG19bot, Muennix, Bereziny, Schweppes75, BattyBot, Nz1991, Fhumeres, MEconDelta, Limit-theorem, Mark viking, Antifragile, Shearflyer, Monkbot, KasparBot, Econophysicslab, The Quixotic Potato, Ssmmachen, Ihelpedit and Anonymous: 95

- **European Association for Evolutionary Political Economy** *Source:* https://en.wikipedia.org/wiki/European_Association_for_Evolutionary_Political_Economy?oldid=621829821 *Contributors:* Lquilter, Mdd, John Quiggin, Woohookitty, Tabletop, BD2412, Tim!, CarolGray, PanchoS, Soobrickay, Robofish, Neelix, Cydebot, Islescape, RobotG, Magioladitis, DadaNeem, VolkovBot, Guillaume2303, Miwanya, 718 Bot, Addbot, Lightbot, Srich32977, Omnipaedista, FrescoBot, Frze, Confedereationofdunces, Confederationofdunces, WPGA2345 and Anonymous: 2

- **Evolutionary economics** *Source:* https://en.wikipedia.org/wiki/Evolutionary_economics?oldid=700784142 *Contributors:* The Anome, R Lowry, Edward, Iweinel, Ronz, Abou Ben Adhem, Mydogategodshat, Rj, Grant65, Andycjp, Beland, Piotrus, Vina, ELApro, Bender235,

Rgdboer, Tmh, Snc~enwiki, Cohesion, Mdd, John Quiggin, Pouya, Clubmarx, Scm83x, BD2412, Josh Parris, BMF81, Volunteer Marek, Yurik-Bot, Tralala~enwiki, Morphh, DSergeev, Daniel Mietchen, Dupz, SmackBot, DCDuring, Rasmus.p, Chris the speller, Bluebot, Hongooi, Battlecry, Bowin~enwiki, Sammy1339, Will Beback, Mr3641, Thomasmeeks, ObiterDicta, Cydebot, Karimarie, Islescape, Itsmejudith, JeroenRoshi, Raoulduke47, Fconaway, Geoffhodgson, Pluto the Planet, Coppertwig, Fheyligh, Julia Neumann, The Tetrast, Struway, Dwbromley, Micoapostolov, CharlesGillingham, Msrasnw, Binksternet, ImperfectlyInformed, EtudiantEco, DumZiBoT, Addbot, C9900, Lightbot, Jan eissfeldt, Yobot, Themfromspace, AnomieBOT, Xqbot, Jockocampbell, Themightyrambo, Omnipaedista, Shadowjams, FrescoBot, Markeilz, Kiefer.Wolfowitz, Jandalhandler, Arbraxan, Sberger2579, Octoghlon, Enragedeconomist, Timothyawunder, EmausBot, John of Reading, Sabeen2331, Klbrain, ClueBot NG, Helpful Pixie Bot, Mustang80, BG19bot, Takeshi-br, Anichen215, Acadēmica Orientālis, Ppsiddarth, Anthro-apology, Dexbot, Mogism, Euroflux, Platospigmonster, HaIsStKo, Bronx Discount Liquor, WPGA2345, Phoenix 123 abc, KasparBot and Anonymous: 65

- **Facilitation board (economics)** *Source:* https://en.wikipedia.org/wiki/Facilitation_board_(economics)?oldid=587337861 *Contributors:* Ron Ritzman, BD2412, Carwil, RadioFan, Avicennasis, R'n'B, Nikosgreencookie, Teknolyze, AnomieBOT, Srich32977, Omnipaedista, Orenburg1, Helpful Pixie Bot, Dtellett, BattyBot and Anonymous: 3

- **Feminist economics** *Source:* https://en.wikipedia.org/wiki/Feminist_economics?oldid=704015599 *Contributors:* Toby Bartels, Enchanter, Edward, Snoyes, Michael Shields, Bhuston, Sam Spade, Nilmerg, Andycjp, Kaldari, Bender235, John Quiggin, Yamla, Cburnett, Tabletop, Bluemoose, Rjwilmsi, DVdm, Bgwhite, Wavelength, Pigman, Yamara, Closedmouth, Tom Morris, Sardanaphalus, SmackBot, Bluebot, Gobonobo, Annbanan24, CmdrObot, Cydebot, Al Lemos, Missvain, Danger, WikipedianProlific, Cailil, Fang 23, Talon Artaine, Xomic, CommonsDelinker, Dontrustme, Aavrakotos, DadaNeem, ZXIII, Rajmankad, DASonnenfeld, Jan02465, TXiKiBoT, Nick Levinson, Insanity Incarnate, Tumadoireacht, SieBot, Dawn Bard, ImageRemovalBot, Dakinijones, MattDixon11, Sun Creator, Aleksd, Thingg, XLinkBot, Skarebo, JCDenton2052, Person33, Addbot, Atethnekos, Swarm, Luckas-bot, Yobot, AnomieBOT, Mbiama Assogo Roger, Capricorn42, Crzer07, Bagua52012, FrescoBot, DrilBot, LittleWink, Tlhslobus, Wadayow, Trappist the monk, Bbarkley2, Jonkerz, RjwilmsiBot, John of Reading, Moswento, ClueBot NG, Virginiawhite09, Leejohnson898, Muhammad Ali Khalid, Kevin Gorman, Ravencolorado, Mfandersen, DStrassmann, BG19bot, Jill71ae, Feministgeo, Mark Arsten, Gorthian, Alissahart, Jami430, Danielle078, BerikG, Fmveblen, K Gagalis, ChrisGualtieri, The Vintage Feminist, Claireclear, Cupco, Keremcantekin, The Oniof, Nattes à chat, WPGA2345, Monkbot, Sm1986 and Anonymous: 46

- **Forum for Stable Currencies** *Source:* https://en.wikipedia.org/wiki/Forum_for_Stable_Currencies?oldid=580039109 *Contributors:* John Vandenberg, John Quiggin, Apoc2400, RHaworth, SmackBot, JHP, CmdrObot, Alaibot, Moonriddengirl, Xp54321, Sabine McNeill, Tassedethe, James500, Cameron Scott, Locobot, Helpful Pixie Bot, BG19bot, ChrisGualtieri and Anonymous: 5

- **Fractional-reserve banking** *Source:* https://en.wikipedia.org/wiki/Fractional-reserve_banking?oldid=698041506 *Contributors:* The Anome, Edward, Michael Hardy, Dante Alighieri, Darkwind, Susurrus, Cimon Avaro, Mydogategodshat, Charles Matthews, Jstanley01, Zoicon5, Morwen, David Shay, Populus, Khym Chanur, Dpbsmith, AnonMoos, Jerzy, Johnleemk, AnthonyQBachler, L3prador, Kadin2048, Goethean, Chris Roy, Rfc1394, Sunray, Saforrest, Finlander, Terjepetersen, Alan Liefting, Clementi, Massysett, Lethe, Cool Hand Luke, Jason Quinn, Neilc, Ben Arnold, Utcursch, Pgreenfinch, RevRagnarok, Jkl, Rich Farmbrough, Will2k, User2004, LindsayH, Chadlupkes, Bender235, Rubicon, Shrike, Grick, Cretog8, Jerryseinfeld, Alansohn, Eleland, Hipocrite, John Quiggin, Gaytan, RoySmith, Grobertson, Drbreznjev, Crosbiesmith, Bobrayner, Benbest, Chochopk, Tabletop, Striver, GoldRingChip, BD2412, Rjwilmsi, TitaniumDreads, Brighterorange, Toby Douglass, Ewlyahoocom, Fresheneesz, Lmatt, John Maynard Friedman, Torkillbruland~enwiki, Diza, Volunteer Marek, Bgwhite, Borgx, Hairy Dude, Spleodrach, DMahalko, Hauskalainen, Akamad, Afelton, Nirvana2013, Grafen, Plhofmei, StarTrekkie, Retired username, Rjlabs, Oaklid, Sandstein, Brozen, Arthur Rubin, Vino s, Kru~enwiki, Mozkill, Ogo, DVD R W, DocendoDiscimus, Sardanaphalus, SmackBot, Michael%Sappir, Gigs, C.Fred, Lawrencekhoo, Fulldecent, Bluebot, Simon123, Timneu22, IIXII, Nbarth, Sbharris, Chendy, Rogermw, Famspear, Shinokamen, Mitsuhirato, Com2kid, Sommers, JBel, Xyzzyplugh, E4mmacro, Mitar, Rockpocket, Will Beback, Byelf2007, Alast0r, Paul Nollen, TheSourceAura, DouglasCalvert, BananaFiend, Iridescent, Tamino, Rubisco~enwiki, IanOfNorwich, JayHenry, LessHeard vanU, CmdrObot, Nysin, Thepatriots, Yourmanstan, Dgw, Garyonthenet, DumbBOT, Satori Son, Thijs!bot, Egriffin, Najro, Itsmejudith, Kborer, Weaponbb7, Bcnviajero, Threlicus, Carolmooredc, Gregalton, JAnDbot, The Transhumanist, BenB4, Theblackbay, Magioladitis, VoABot II, Dekimasu, Yandman, Appraiser, Hendrixjoseph, Smash1gordon, Bmirkalami, Quietvoice, Strikehold, Crash site, Mm1972, ExplicitImplicity, Ectoplasmical, RalfTheDog, Pharaoh of the Wizards, Wideshanks, Lulolean, JKoulouris, AltiusBimm, Interstategar, Arronax50, Nemo bis, Bernard S. Jansen, Olegwiki, Juxtapos99, Natl1, Funandtrvl, Ddd1600, Yitzhak1995, VolkovBot, Ticklemygrits, Childhoodsend, Michael H 34, Broadbot, Jackfork, Chateauxc, Dirc, Maktimothy, Vincent the Vain, Larklight, Sue Rangell, AlleborgoBot, CT Cooper, Masteryao, Phe-bot, Vexorg, Tdeoras, RJaguar3, Ravensfire, Flyer22 Reborn, DGGenuine, OsamaBinLogin, Paulhiphop, JohnSawyer, The Four Deuces, Mr. Stradivarius, Dunkleosteus2, Rinconsoleao, EGeek, ClueBot, Orangedolphin, Traveler100, Philip Sutton, Analoguni, N0 D1C4, RYNORT, Mild Bill Hiccup, Karmaisking, Sumdog, DragonBot, Dotter, Crywalt, Vin Kaleu, Eeekster, Rhododendrites, Htfiddler, Snodgrass Bat, Dlawbailey, Jonverve, Count Truthstein, Martycarbone, Smarkflea, David.hillary, SoxBot III, Sparkygravity, DumZiBoT, Zenwhat, BigK HeX, XLinkBot, Dthomsen8, Doc9871, StoborSeven, Addbot, Sabine McNeill, KarmasBlackSwan, Roentgenium111, Lagrandebanquesucre, Chdouglas, Scientus, MrVanBot, LaaknorBot, CarsracBot, Favonian, Sealer25, Lucian Sunday, Erik Streb, TheFreeloader, Socppt12, 84user, Socppt15, Apteva, Marcinbmach, Luckas-bot, Yobot, VengeancePrime, Themfromspace, MonetaryCrankster, Darx9url, NotAYakk, IW.HG, Jonesy1289, AnomieBOT, Erel Segal, Mike Hayes, Jim1138, TruthComesFromAGunBoat, LetThemMintPaper, Mrpoisson, Citation bot, InTheLongRunThereIsNoShortCut, ArthurBot, LilHelpa, Cameron Scott, Xqbot, Ron Paul...Ron Paul..., Fortaleza~enwiki, Renaissancee, Tito80, DataWraith, Gilo1969, Jsharpminor, Srich32977, Kithira, DriverDan, CapitalAndSavingsDoNotComeFromFRB, Michael.suede, VulgarKeynesianMilitarism, Smallman12q, Olthebol, Mariusm98, DeathStalksTheIndebted, Kura440, Captain awesome124, PyramidsOrFood?, FrescoBot, Hell,FirstLeftDownSocialistAlly, HairyBarbarianSellsDebtAndDrugs, Virginiahammon, Pestergaines, CrisisFeedsLeviathan, Atlantia, Citation bot 1, MindlessMaterialism, Elockid, UnexpectedTiger, Rawjapan, Skyerise, Reissgo, Jandalhandler, Miraspell, Reconsider the static, Jkforde, Tim1357, Fenvoe, Cstof j, Dinamik-bot, God'sWrath, LostMyself, RjwilmsiBot, Sargdub, Bento00, Katonus, Peash, Dewritech, GoingBatty, TheSoundAndTheFury, Solarra, Mmeijeri, John Shandy`, $atan's$pawn, Ib Ravn, $hady$hysterGeithner, Gougnafier, DebtDukkha, TheGoldenAgeofHyperinflation, ClueBot NG, BarrelProof, HonestIntelligence, Snotbot, Marechal Ney, Themoneymultiplier, Helpful Pixie Bot, Andrewedwardjudd, Lowercase sigmabot, Iselilja, Kndimov, Abject Normality, FiveColourMap, CitationCleanerBot, Hank930, JKD.trinitas, Cyberbot II, AmourReflection, Abed2012, Ilikecod, Mogism, Alextimofeyev, Hto9950, Cupco, SPECIFICO, KingQueenPrince, FRB123, WileECoyote'sFiscalCliff, EconomyOnFIRE, QEternity, HandAgainstTheCorruptTide, SandyIsKeynesianStimulus, Prettyladieslover, DivingOffTheFiscalCliff, Ildottoreverde, Eyesnore, Wuerzele, Canadianpolisci, Steeletrap, A Mr John Smith, MilesMoney, UY Scuti, Brandsby, Marris1, TsarBomba2 0, AllxMxPx, DanKing123, Bootsch, Pilotpress, Diablo256, Antonbuckleyjones, Ivona Djuric, TakeItUpTheGreekEconomy, WouNur, Lyinglike and Anonymous: 409

3.1. TEXT

- **Freiwirtschaft** *Source:* https://en.wikipedia.org/wiki/Freiwirtschaft?oldid=691646680 *Contributors:* Magnus Manske, Derek Ross, Jeronimo, Toby Bartels, Edward, Jiang, Pm67nz, Dysprosia, Fernkes, Stormie, Onebyone, Seano1, Vacuum, Tubedogg, Yossarian, Bender235, Magius, Bobrayner, Mandavi, Alienus, Johnnyw, Dabljuh, YurikBot, RussBot, Amakuha, MrVoluntarist, GrinBot~enwiki, SmackBot, Apeloverage, Nbarth, MovGP0, Cameron Nedland, Nihilo 01, Robofish, Cydebot, Richhoncho, Dougher, Richard D. LeCour, VZakharov, Prius 2, OLMuseum, Markdraper, Cyfal, Singwaste, Philipp Grunwald, Good Olfactory, Kbdankbot, Addbot, Damiens.rf, Lightbot, Yobot, Xqbot, Miracleworker5263, Omnipaedista, LucienBOT, BenzolBot, AvicBot, John Cummings, Anselm Rapp, Khazar2, Saectar, KasparBot and Anonymous: 29

- **Gandhian economics** *Source:* https://en.wikipedia.org/wiki/Gandhian_economics?oldid=687662858 *Contributors:* Leandrod, Edward, SebastianHelm, MisfitToys, Bodnotbod, Bender235, John Quiggin, Bobrayner, Koavf, FayssalF, EvanDiBiase, Phantomsteve, RussBot, Rjensen, Stevage, Rama's Arrow, Shyamsunder, Joseph Solis in Australia, Cydebot, Skomorokh, Cgingold, Coolg49964, TreasuryTag, Pjoef, David Sher, 7, Addbot, Betterusername, Drsq, Faunas, Eduen, Neptune5000, Srich32977, Omnipaedista, Nihar S, FrescoBot, Diannaa, Dewritech, RA0808, Kaimakides, ZéroBot, Puffin, Mentibot, Helpful Pixie Bot, Lelwilson, Rrronny, Mdann52, Gurukasi, Returnofunclefester, Faizan, Evano1van, Bakerlander, Grand equal, The Quixotic Potato, Mv.nadkarni and Anonymous: 27

- **Georgism** *Source:* https://en.wikipedia.org/wiki/Georgism?oldid=705335735 *Contributors:* AxelBoldt, Derek Ross, Michael Hardy, Paul A, Pde, Sir Paul, AndreaPersephone, Etherialemperor, RickK, Pm67nz, Wetman, Owen, Jni, Robbot, Chrism, Chris Roy, Merovingian, Mattflaschen, Neilc, Pgan002, Craverguy, DNewhall, Pmanderson, Bender235, Mjk2357, RoyBoy, Dystopos, Tmh, VBGFscJUn3, Perceval, Ricky81682, John Quiggin, RJII, Reaverdrop, Luigizanasi, Bastin, Bobrayner, Graham87, Wachholder0, Jorunn, Rjwilmsi, Koavf, Klonimus, Silversoul7, Winterstein, Polsequ95, Chobot, Bgwhite, Wavelength, RussBot, Jrideout, Bronks, Canley, Asterion, Sardanaphalus, SmackBot, CSMR, Lawrencekhoo, Aivazovsky, Hmains, Chris the speller, Dahn, Thumperward, RobBlakemore, H Bruthzoo, Mike hayes, Tamfang, MrRadioGuy, EPM, Derek R Bullamore, Byelf2007, Joshuavincent, Collect, Ewulp, ChrisCork, CmdrObot, BeenAroundAWhile, PegArmPaul, Neelix, Gregbard, Yaris678, Doug Weller, Thijs!bot, Headbomb, Kborer, It's The Economics, Stupid!, Bigglesjames, Mdotley, Erxnmedia, Skomorokh, Magioladitis, Ling.Nut, Lenschulwitz, Creativename, Roy Langston, Gomm, Jim.henderson, R'n'B, Al B. Free, DASonnenfeld, Izno, TXiKiBoT, JohnAugust, GroveGuy, Howard Silverman, Phmoreno, TJRC, Jojalozzo, Operation Spooner, Høst, Drmies, Der Golem, P. S. Burton, Cirt, Elpiseos, Sun Creator, Lususromulus, SchreiberBike, El bot de la dieta, Mhockey, DumZiBoT, Addbot, Cssiitcic, AndersBot, Debresser, Gpeterw, Blaylockjam10, Larsrindsig, Lightbot, Luckas-bot, Yobot, JJARichardson, Denispir, AnomieBOT, Darolew, Logical Premise, Wikirpg, C2equalA2plusB2, Teilolondon, Quebec99, The3seashells, InpoliticTruth, Srich32977, Hxasmirl, Omnipaedista, FrescoBot, Wikilobster, I dream of horses, Jonesey95, Trappist the monk, Bbarkley2, Peter Gibb, ErikvanB, G103317, John of Reading, Maxmex, Jonpatterns, Ὁ οἶστρος, Celosia61, H3llBot, MisterDub, Grampion76, Rjmatter, Xaverquax, Purple1342, Helpful Pixie Bot, Dtellett, Guest2625, BG19bot, FiveColourMap, BattyBot, Cyberbot II, ChrisGualtieri, Kurper, Rothbardanswer, Makecat-bot, CEHodgkinson, CsDix, R4N40069, EllenCT, Bronx Discount Liquor, Saectar, Whomyl, Monkbot, Adventurer61, Maureensherrardthompson, Sanne6, Shanecav, PublicolaMinor, Alex at CreditSavvy, Unemployed Northeastern, Roman Windfeller, Big-Endians, MaxGhenis and Anonymous: 169

- **Gift economy** *Source:* https://en.wikipedia.org/wiki/Gift_economy?oldid=693840923 *Contributors:* Eloquence, Bryan Derksen, DanKeshet, Aldie, Ghakko, William Avery, Roadrunner, SimonP, Anthere, Olivier, Edward, Nealmcb, Palnatoke, Llywrch, Shyamal, Lquilter, R4f~enwiki, Shimmin, Tregoweth, Ronz, Jpatokal, Snoyes, LittleDan, Tparvu, Tim Retout, Ruhrjung, Dcoetzee, DJ Clayworth, Jmabel, Altenmann, Nurg, LGagnon, Bkell, Wereon, Connelly, ScudLee, Nikodemos, Everyking, Bluejay Young, John Abbe, Gadfium, Beland, Piotrus, Joi, Rdsmith4, Qleem, GreenReaper, Vivacissamamente, Eisnel, Chris Howard, Brianhe, Rich Farmbrough, Florian Blaschke, Bishonen, ChristianJacken, Pavel Vozenilek, Gronky, Bender235, CanisRufus, Lycurgus, Quantumstream, Wareh, Dalf, Nigelj, Cretog8, Viriditas, Polocrunch, Maurreen, Acntx, Ziggurat, Scott Ritchie, La goutte de pluie, Silverback, Hooperbloob, Chira, Diego Moya, Andrewpmk, Deacon of Pndapetzim, Gunter, Markaci, Bobrayner, Wdyoung, Jpers36, The Writer~enwiki, Robert K S, BoLingua, Bkwillwm, Taghawi-Nejad, CharlesC, Waldir, Mandarax, Ictlogist, Azkar, Graham87, BD2412, Qwertyus, Rjwilmsi, Andyswarbs, Yahoolian, Freddydesouza, Themightychris, Pikiwedia~enwiki, Eron-Main, Sperxios, Schandi, Jackalus, Bgwhite, ColdFeet, YurikBot, Wavelength, Waitak, RussBot, Pigman, GregLoutsenko, Gaius Cornelius, PaulGarner, Nirvana2013, Adaxl, LaszloWalrus, Todfox, Pawyilee, WAS 4.250, Maphisto86, Arthur Rubin, Saukkomies, Bob Hu, Madashell, NeilN, SmackBot, McGeddon, Unyoyega, Lawrencekhoo, KVDP, Rthunder, Betacommand, KDRGibby, TimBentley, Fuzzform, Victorgrigas, Robth, Aridd, Hongooi, Sunnan, Rrburke, Krsont, Ne0Freedom, Farsee50, John D. Croft, Nmpenguin, Arthur Welle~enwiki, Robotforaday, Tazmaniacs, Gobonobo, Smartyllama, Rundquist, Makyen, TastyPoutine, Basicdesign, Eastlaw, Joostvandeputte~enwiki, Dhammapal, CmdrObot, NaBUru38, Seven of Nine, Safalra, Cydebot, Steel-Froggy, Ntsimp, FreeTOreuse, Doug Weller, Maziotis, Donnachadelong, Thijs!bot, John254, Stybn, KrakatoaKatie, Saimhe, Credema, Gdo01, Barek, B.S. Lawrence, Moralist, CWinDC, Richard a b, Fiasco229, Economo, Inhumandecency, Sharemind, Wiki wiki1, Richard Odin Johnson, Krotty, Rickburnes, Tdadamemd, Julipanette, Girl2k, Danalpha, Jörg Sutter, TWCarlson, DASonnenfeld, Signalhead, Saisatha, Therealtahu, Malik Shabazz, Thewolf37, Fences and windows, Yamanam, MusicScience, Rei-bot, Joe2832, Dharmaburning, UnitedStatesian, Brian Huffman, Vgrass, Twayburn, Phe-bot, Jschoneb, Nxg2007, Jojalozzo, Janwiklund, Free4kids dawn, Smaug123, Skeptical scientist, Mhnin0, ClueBot, Meisterkoch, Orestisv, GeneCallahan, Starvinsky, Digambers, Drmies, Ye Olde Anarchist, Auntof6, Northernhenge, Tikimoped, Arjayay, Zappa711, Callinus, Editor2020, SF007, XLinkBot, Burningmax, Felix Folio Secundus, VanishedUser ewrfgdg3df3, Addbot, USchick, MrOllie, D.c.camero, Lindasmith247, Jan eissfeldt, Jarble, Ben Ben, Luckas-bot, Yobot, Ptbotgourou, Pharmakis, Freikorp, Gav2d, Eduen, AnomieBOT, DemocraticLuntz, Floquenbeam, Materialscientist, Media47, Omnipaedista, Crinoline, FrescoBot, Tophee1, Wetterfree, Novaseminary, Citation bot 1, AstaBOTh15, RedBot, MastiBot, Plasticspork, Wikiwedo, Mcalison, UnderHigh, Vrenator, Reaper Eternal, Kwalton414, Aviv007, RjwilmsiBot, Bantam1983, Moray mair, EmausBot, Danielstrong52, Montgolfière, Dewritech, Slightsmile, Wikipelli, Kwalt414, Elektralight, H3llBot, Ldelman, ClueBot NG, Gift Economy 12, AugspurgII, Snotbot, Helpful Pixie Bot, BG19bot, Northamerica1000, Brianaflin, Nicholforest, God45, Jampel~enwiki, Cretog7, TradeMarkG, Safehaven86, WikiHannibal, BattyBot, J.canales60, Khazar2, Gerbish, Dexbot, Slee500, Irychu, Wenshidi, Schrauwers, CsDix, Tpylkkö, Kap 7, Garab-en, Glaisher, Jenaye, Pablo Darko, 51coin, Turgeis, Anarcham, Monkbot, D. Cordoba-Bahle, Nøkkenbuer, You better look out below! and Anonymous: 235

- **Human development theory** *Source:* https://en.wikipedia.org/wiki/Human_development_theory?oldid=687540995 *Contributors:* Enchanter, Delirium, Bearcat, Cdang, Mayooranathan, Mark Richards, Maurreen, La goutte de pluie, Fahd, John Quiggin, Bobrayner, JeremyA, Xiong Chiamiov, Behun, Lmatt, YurikBot, T. Anthony, SmackBot, Brimba, Byelf2007, Shoeofdeath, Al Lemos, Spencer, Eliz81, Skier Dude, Jorfer, RucasHost, Oxymoron83, Addbot, KamikazeBot, Mbiama Assogo Roger, FrescoBot, Sara.koopman, Miracle Pen, ClueBot NG, Khazar2, Epicgenius, Bronx Discount Liquor, FindMeLost and Anonymous: 22

- **Innovation economics** *Source:* https://en.wikipedia.org/wiki/Innovation_economics?oldid=660811261 *Contributors:* Edward, Bender235, Cretog8, Artw, Giraffedata, Woohookitty, BD2412, Susten.biz, Ground Zero, RussBot, Bhny, SmackBot, Hmains, Rhoeg, Robofish, Twas Now,

Tosenton, Cydebot, Heroeswithmetaphors, Magioladitis, R'n'B, Squids and Chips, JL-Bot, Sbolat, Mild Bill Hiccup, Addbot, Socipoet, Ingenesist, Rubinbot, Howsa12, Legendaryshure, Citation bot 1, Woona, Innovation200, Carlo.bottai, Philmccready, Peterjthomson, Helpful Pixie Bot, Petya4999, Euroflux, Randykitty, Techmatt, Tselrev, Qzekrom and Anonymous: 27

- **Institutional economics** *Source:* https://en.wikipedia.org/wiki/Institutional_economics?oldid=703091353 *Contributors:* SimonP, Andres, Haukurth, Jamesmader, Modulatum, Alvestrand, Jdevine, Vina, DNewhall, Mennonot, Bender235, Tmh, Mdd, Jeschwartz, Rd232, John Quiggin, Wikidea, Notbot, Dzordzm, GregorB, Jivecat, Volunteer Marek, BernardL, Gaius Cornelius, SmackBot, Bluebot, Nbarth, Bowin~enwiki, Anthon.Eff, Nubeli, JoseREMY, Mr3641, N2e, Thomasmeeks, Cydebot, Krauss, Thijs!bot, Andrei G Kustov, Mmortal03, JAnDbot, The Transhumanist, Awqam, Interdependence, Noyder, Toyvo, Discott, Geoffhodgson, Lia Todua, Aymatth2, SieBot, Dryfee, Epitron, Schmida, Escape Orbit, ClueBot, ImperfectlyInformed, Aleksd, Attaboy, Tarheel95, Lookatim, Stonewhite, Addbot, Sillyfolkboy, Legobot, Yobot, AnomieBOT, F.morett, Hedgehog41, Jtshelton, Omnipaedista, FrescoBot, Enragedeconomist, Timothyawunder, Lnegro, Immunize, Scotty-Berg, Dewritech, Lucas Thoms, Alfredo ougaowen, Jonpatterns, Pochsad, Financestudent, MerllwBot, Helpful Pixie Bot, KLBot2, BG19bot, Takeshi-br, H0339637, Nniiicc, ChrisGualtieri, Vanished user sdij4rtltkjasdk3, ColaXtra, Mjonathan234, WBWDII, Tarethere, Bronx Discount Liquor, Institutionalist and Anonymous: 86

- **Islamic economics** *Source:* https://en.wikipedia.org/wiki/Islamic_economics?oldid=704280957 *Contributors:* RK, Anthere, Rbrwr, Edward, Earth, Kku, Axlrosen, Docu, William M. Connolley, Rossami, Uyanga, Conti, Dwo, Etherialemperor, Hyacinth, UninvitedCompany, Yelyos, Chris Roy, Llavigne, Millosh, Michael Snow, Xanzzibar, Cutler, Kbahey, Christofurio, Edcolins, Marc Mongenet, Zeeshanhasan, Arminius, Jfpierce, Rich Farmbrough, Dbachmann, Tyc20, Bender235, El C, Mjk2357, Femto, Cretog8, Maureen, Kjkolb, Abstraktn, Mgaved, Nik42, John Quiggin, Goodoldpolonius2, Grenavitar, Bourbaki, Woohookitty, Mindmatrix, Mpatel, Tabletop, Striver, LadyofHats, Graham87, BD2412, Rjwilmsi, Quiddity, Nihiltres, Bgwhite, WriterHound, HG1, Sceptre, StuffOfInterest, RussBot, Nowa, Dialectric, Nirvana2013, Ardhan, Equilibrial, CaliforniaAliBaba, Froth, SameerKhan, Wiqi55, Sorna Doon, Contaldo80, DoriSmith, SmackBot, Jagged 85, Spasage, Ohnoitsjamie, Cowman109, Anwar saadat, Chris the speller, Punekar, Cplakidas, Kurt111, Khoikhoi, Meson537, Cybercobra, Savidan, KI, Kuru, Khazar, Hariskz, Breno, Bless sins, Bilalak, Hu12, DabMachine, BranStark, Falcon007, Supertigerman, Eastlaw, CmdrObot, Thomasmeeks, Neelix, Rohita, Cydebot, Sa.vakilian, Kozo, Doug Weller, Nbh427, Thijs!bot, Frank, Bobblehead, Tocharianne, Escarbot, Alphachimpbot, Lfstevens, Leroy65X, MER-C, WikipedianProlific, Yahel Guhan, Wasell, Magioladitis, Stuffisthings, Abuismael, Misheu, Avicennasis, Mmustafa~enwiki, Pilim, R'n'B, Lilac Soul, Neutron Jack, Aaliyah Stevens, Maproom, Sanusi.husain, Prhartcom, Ragab99~enwiki, Pdcook, GrahamHardy, VolkovBot, TreasuryTag, Timmonsgray, BoogaLouie, Threetrees-derek, Nazgul02, Farooqmo, Brianga, Zaf159, Austriacus, Franky0517, Dmcconsultancy, RawEgg1, SunniStyles, OKBot, Aras1789, Jngk2007, ClueBot, ReggyRaccoon, Alykhorshid, Kashi0341, Sustainablefutures2015, Excirial, PixelBot, Eeekster, Xic667, Muhandes, Torquemama007, Al-Andalusi, Hala Yousef, XLinkBot, Releaseroderick, Janjua786, Myst-Bot, Lizeb, Addbot, Xe Cahzytr Ryz, Guoguo12, Ronhjones, CanadianLinuxUser, WaleedAddas, MrOllie, Download, Lihaas, Chzz, Tassedethe, Lightbot, Jarble, Maiter70, Middayexpress, Luckas-bot, Yobot, DS5000, Uk.aims, AnomieBOT, RanEagle, Mare420, Britans, Mahmudmasri, The High Fin Sperm Whale, Citation bot, LilHelpa, Xqbot, Bihco, Eifionwilliams, Jayzames, Srich32977, J04n, Ismail87, Olyxith, Mahmagin, Mattg82, FrescoBot, Fabulousgoddess1977, Sabir0924, I dream of horses, Wongwaiking, Lotje, Turaab84, AXRL, Hasansameer, RjwilmsiBot, EmausBot, John of Reading, Najeeb1010, Bbkobl, Fayazahmad123, Dewritech, Sigmantic, GoingBatty, Solarra, Javidahmad2010, K6ka, Bmgpublisher, Punisher71, Mar4d, Semmler, Tolly4bolly, Grampion76, TYelliot, Rocketrod1960, Khestwol, ClueBot NG, Khaledyousef, Somedifferentstuff, Snotbot, Helpful Pixie Bot, Ahmadklmsia, BG19bot, PhnomPencil, Antony1024, LostCaller, Dexbot, Kwisha, CsDix, Johnleeds1, NicheAsp, R4N40069, Afak2012, Inkja, Wamiq, ArmbrustBot, SayedUmaarKazmi, Ynuca, Masmahwik, Adam (Wiki Ed), Jsbdjejnwn, Phillyboy1992 and Anonymous: 191

- **Joan Robinson** *Source:* https://en.wikipedia.org/wiki/Joan_Robinson?oldid=703409837 *Contributors:* Rmhermen, Andres, Rl, Jni, Dimadick, Bearcat, JesseW, Profoss, Stern~enwiki, Kowh, Andycjp, Piotrus, Mindspillage, Vapour, Bender235, Aranel, Andrew Gray, Wikidea, Saga City, Rfredian, Woohookitty, Bkwillwm, Mendaliv, Hiberniantears, Wragge, JdforresterBot, YurikBot, RussBot, RadioFan2 (usurped), Modernway, Garion96, Jack Upland, SmackBot, Bluebot, JackyR, Nbarth, Constanz, Anthon.Eff, Nils Simon, Wizardman, Ohconfucius, Ser Amantio di Nicolao, MikeWazowski, Thomasmeeks, Cydebot, Thijs!bot, Colin Rowat, Ernalve, Dsp13, Charles01, Magioladitis, Spaventa, Johnbibby, Johnpacklambert, EdBever, TXiKiBoT, ElinorD, GcSwRhIc, Miwanya, Robertsch55, BOTijo, Dassiebtekreuz, Proscript, LeadSongDog, James Haughton, Msrasnw, Rinconsoleao, Northernhenge, 27kdh, Doprendek, Euro a, Addbot, Hermógenes Teixeira Pinto Filho, Rich jj, This is Paul, Ginosbot, Lightbot, Pointer1, Yobot, Jan Arkesteijn, AnomieBOT, Rubinbot, Obersachsebot, Srich32977, Omnipaedista, Green Cardamom, Hugetim, Ausseagull, Skyerise, Robert Ernest Marks, Oracleofottawa, Extra999, 777sms, RjwilmsiBot, EmausBot, ImprovingWiki, Wikitanvir-Bot, Ebrambot, Polisher of Cobwebs, ChuispastonBot, Movses-bot, Helpful Pixie Bot, Alf.laylah.wa.laylah, CitationCleanerBot, Wireintheblood, Adamstraw99, Piero Testa, VIAFbot, Befra11, N0n3up, Winter S Warmer, Katebecon, Ceosad, Salvian1945, Proud Austrian Paulinian, MP 2142, KasparBot, Chamflac and Anonymous: 66

- **Kinetic exchange models of markets** *Source:* https://en.wikipedia.org/wiki/Kinetic_exchange_models_of_markets?oldid=696686380 *Contributors:* Populus, Rjwilmsi, Bgwhite, Khazar, ShelfSkewed, Neelix, Headbomb, EagleFan, DancingPhilosopher, Yobot, Citation bot, ChristopherKingChemist, Pareschi, FrescoBot, RjwilmsiBot, Harobindo, BG19bot, CitationCleanerBot, CV9933 and Anonymous: 15

- **Kondratiev wave** *Source:* https://en.wikipedia.org/wiki/Kondratiev_wave?oldid=702999144 *Contributors:* Derek Ross, The Anome, Olivier, Michael Hardy, Oliver Pereira, Nikai, Andres, Charles Matthews, Rursus, Clossius, RayTomes, Chowbok, Andycjp, HorsePunchKid, Beland, RayBirks, Rich Farmbrough, Bender235, Bcat, Axezz, Thedarkestclear, Pearle, Msh210, Aardwolf, John Quiggin, Bobrayner, Woohookitty, Miss Madeline, Tabletop, Dzordzm, Bluemoose, GregorB, Mandarax, Vberger~enwiki, Rjwilmsi, Helvetius, Ground Zero, Thunderbird~enwiki, Volunteer Marek, Bgwhite, TimNelson, NawlinWiki, Leutha, Nirvana2013, Stefeyboy, Jurriaan, H@r@ld, Jack Upland, Sfiller, SmackBot, Dpwkbw, Commander Keane bot, Hmains, Colonies Chris, Tsca.bot, Smallbones, Breadandroses, John D. Croft, Hypnosifl, Hu12, Whaiaun, Eastlaw, CmdrObot, Theoh, DumbBOT, Thijs!bot, Hhmb, Heroeswithmetaphors, Carolmooredc, Tjmayerinsf, Tim Shuba, Phanerozoic, Daytona2, SHCarter, Bill j, JaGa, Polusfx, Pjmpjm, Kenneth M Burke, SergeyKurdakov, Don4of4, Phmoreno, AlleborgoBot, Datasmid, PeterFV, Jerryobject, Philip Sutton, Tomas e, Mild Bill Hiccup, Alexbot, Doprendek, SchreiberBike, Editor2020, WikHead, Netrat, Franz weber, AtheWeatherman, Guffydrawers, Rago, Legobot, Yobot, Coachaxis, Pahpaha, Wargo, Meotrangden, AnomieBOT, Juanita09, LilHelpa, Graciagoldberg, Qsf, BigND, Rusnak1961, Solphusion~enwiki, Omnipaedista, Foreverprovence, Chancery21, GliderMaven, FrescoBot, Markeilz, Citation bot 1, Jonesey95, JDvzs, Elena Emanova, Trappist the monk, Brauntonian, Tbhotch, RjwilmsiBot, Tamanrasset444, Ziggaroo, Cogiati, Mutamarrid, AManWithNoPlan, Edward Lewis1, Rcsprinter123, Spicemix, Will Beback Auto, Mattiafoc, Snotbot, MerllwBot, Helpful Pixie Bot, Amelapay, J.harrington12, Ibn khaldun 84, GlebX, Dccccddcc, Arwen III., BattyBot, JohanSonn, Jmcq85, SFK2, SPECIFICO, Telfordbuck, Nwrnr, Bronx

3.1. TEXT

Discount Liquor, LittleGustav, AQ424, Whomyl, Monkbot, KasparBot, Hofstederesearch, AneleElenaTranslation, Bizmaveric and Anonymous: 102

- **Market abolitionism** *Source:* https://en.wikipedia.org/wiki/Market_abolitionism?oldid=564666937 *Contributors:* Jmabel, Unfree, CanisRufus, Mjk2357, Themindset, John Quiggin, Woohookitty, Lapsed Pacifist, Ian Pitchford, Fluxaviator, Psjalltheway, KDRGibby, Bluebot, JonHarder, Byelf2007, Cydebot, Thijs!bot, Severo, Malik Shabazz, Larklight, Jiminezwaldorf, Good Olfactory, Addbot, Lightbot, Mikelo Gulhi, Eduen, Srich32977, Omnipaedista, Jean-Jacques Georges, Goti1233, Khazar2, CsDix and Anonymous: 18

- **Marxian economics** *Source:* https://en.wikipedia.org/wiki/Marxian_economics?oldid=700536336 *Contributors:* Heron, Edward, Radicalsubversiv, Sethmahoney, Jni, Robbot, Fifelfoo, Sunray, J heisenberg, Dick Bos, Nakosomo, Richard Myers, The Land, Pyro~enwiki, Liberlogos, H0riz0n, Pavel Vozenilek, Bender235, Lycurgus, Chalst, Causa sui, Cmdrjameson, JavOs, Rd232, John Quiggin, Hinotori, Bobrayner, FrancisTyers, Camw, Ollieplatt, DrThompson, Everton, Nutrosnutros, Bkwillwm, BD2412, Sjakkalle, Jrtayloriv, Chobot, Frappyjohn, Petiatil, Splash, Pigman, Member, NawlinWiki, Wiki alf, Joel7687, Equilibrial, Mshecket, Ad Nauseam, Jurriaan, Johndburger, Fram, Infinity0, Tom Morris, Yvwv, SmackBot, Alex1011, Hmains, Chris the speller, Willardo, Battlecry, Rrburke, Kongre-sec, Nakon, Byelf2007, ArglebargleIV, Soap, Rigadoun, Santa Sangre, Joseph Solis in Australia, A.I.K., Thomasmeeks, Davius, Flowerpotman, Spylab, DumbBOT, Daniel, Headbomb, Frank, WinBot, Luna Santin, ReverendG, Nmcmurdo, Magioladitis, Horse Badorties, Karl Wiki, STBot, Prezen, Cirenilsson, Jeepday, Aram33~enwiki, Marioosz, Trilobitealive, Inbloom2, Kenneth M Burke, ACSE, Lia Todua, Geree, Rubentomas, TXiKiBoT, Marxclass, C.J. Griffin, SelketBot, Anarchangel, Synthebot, Akliman, Watchdog07, Hudisp, Oxymoron83, Jacob.jose, ClueBot, The Thing That Should Not Be, EoGuy, Mild Bill Hiccup, Spenny69, Jotterbot, Doprendek, Aleksd, Gogolyea, Eurodos, Trefork, DumZiBoT, Koumz, Flauius Claudius Iulianus, Dthomsen8, Avoided, SherryShamsi, Addbot, I feel like a tourist, Michaelwuzthere, Debresser, Sindinero, Luckas-bot, Yobot, AnomieBOT, ArthurBot, Quebec99, Srich32977, Omnipaedista, Cuauti, Gonji ha, FrescoBot, D'ohBot, Kiefer.Wolfowitz, A8UDI, LilyKitty, Miracle Pen, Tbhotch, EmausBot, John of Reading, Δ, Financestudent, Irishbrigade1942, ClueBot NG, Chester Markel, Adair2324, Frietjes, Helpful Pixie Bot, Rationis, K4kant, Justincheng12345-bot, Correctionasdfg, Khazar2, Jemappelleungarcon, RotlinkBot, Tentinator, LudicrousTripe, Bronx Discount Liquor, Gravuritas, Monkbot, Prisencolin, Karmanatory, YeOldeGentleman, Knife-in-the-drawer and Anonymous: 138

- **Max Keiser** *Source:* https://en.wikipedia.org/wiki/Max_Keiser?oldid=701779676 *Contributors:* SimonP, Cimon Avaro, Dj ansi, Pgan002, SarekOfVulcan, Salimfadhley, Bender235, Dennis Brown, Philip Cross, Rd232, Rwendland, Benson85, VoluntarySlave, Bobrayner, Woohookitty, Lapsed Pacifist, Eyreland, Ground Zero, Catsmeat, DVdm, WriterHound, Katieh5584, SmackBot, Stifle, Autarch, Salvor, Hibernian, Chendy, OrphanBot, Derek R Bullamore, Will Beback, Ser Amantio di Nicolao, Kiyae, Nolte, Meco, C-ray, Keith-264, Joseph Solis in Australia, George100, Penbat, Cydebot, Danrok, Mato, PamD, Wikid77, Edwardx, Dawnseeker2000, Mentifisto, Carolmooredc, Wayiran, Postcard Cathy, Skomorokh, Rothorpe, Magioladitis, DadaNeem, Jevansen, RjCan, TbohlsenNSWSSMRC, Grodvin, AllGloryToTheHypnotoad, Kmhkmh, Falcon8765, StAnselm, LAEsquire, Mezigue, Edraupp, Eeekster, TheRedPenOfDoom, Im2bigred, Cookiehead, XLinkBot, Wik-Head, Dubmill, Addbot, 84user, Luckas-bot, Yobot, Themfromspace, Grakirby, AnomieBOT, Jim1138, Cyanidethistles, Citation bot, LilHelpa, Xqbot, GrouchoBot, Logore, Yanpierre, Stacyherbert, Jeremijales, Haldraper, Nagualdesign, Researchdrunkie, Calibrador, LucienBOT, RedBot, Eerycanal, TobeBot, Gulbenk, Reaper Eternal, Stanjourdan, RjwilmsiBot, Smartiger, Paavo273, John of Reading, Peterpumpkin87, Marrante, Checkingfax, Ὁ οἶστρος, Puldis, Donner60, ClueBot NG, Rsteilberg, Helpful Pixie Bot, Gob Lofa, JR174, Lowercase sigmabot, BG19bot, Biggorrilla, General general general general, Mark Arsten, Lions of Inquiry, Giles leggett, Cyberbot II, CouchSurfer222, Editfromwithout, Rezonansowy, Mogism, Adzieboi, Skronie, Lennonhendrix, NirkNiggler, Brough87, Danny Sprinkle, Daylight66, EvergreenFir, Finnusertop, Royalenlightenment, Juan MTMT, LibDutch, 0x60, RocketPodAndrew, QueenFan, Polemicista, 1pp2, AusLondoner, JamesSecker and Anonymous: 130

- **Modern Monetary Theory** *Source:* https://en.wikipedia.org/wiki/Modern_Monetary_Theory?oldid=703980179 *Contributors:* Derek Ross, Edward, Greenrd, Chealer, Pseudonym, JamesMLane, OwenBlacker, TJSwoboda, Johngelles, Chris Howard, Vapour, Bender235, Cretog8, Evolauxia, Sproul, Crosbiesmith, Bobrayner, Linas, Benbest, Bkwillwm, Janosabel, John Z, Choess, Volunteer Marek, Bgwhite, Hairy Dude, Gaius Cornelius, Welsh, Malcolma, Tony1, PanchoS, Hudsojt, SmackBot, The Gnome, Chris the speller, Mikcob, Nbarth, EPM, A.R., Byelf2007, Khazar, Robofish, Tktktk, CmdrObot, Orderinchaos, ShelfSkewed, Cydebot, Iamisha, Qwyrxian, Headbomb, Nick Number, O nate, Msankowski, Lfstevens, Postcard Cathy, Michaelaoash, Rick.Wicks, Greensburger, Severo, Stuffisthings, Professor marginalia, SHCarter, Jimb2, JaGa, Olsonist, CommonsDelinker, JohnDoe0007, CptnJustc, Lamro, 007patrick, JL-Bot, Counterfact, Farolif, Mild Bill Hiccup, Auntof6, Sun Creator, Doprendek, Dan Secrest, ThVa, Andyk 33, XLinkBot, Blnet, Addbot, J. Milch, Yobot, Darx9url, Santryl, Dmarquard, FeydHuxtable, AnomieBOT, Wickorama, Liberalvirus, Xtra7, J JMesserly, Srich32977, KosMal, Omnipaedista, Gregory K. Soderberg, FrescoBot, Citation bot 1, LittleWink, RedBot, Arfed, Reissgo, HugeHedon, Allen4names, Greenm1981, Defenceminister, Stanjourdan, Jubian, RjwilmsiBot, Lennyfield, Prosopon, EmausBot, ZéroBot, Jenks24, General Fiasco, Donner60, ChuispastonBot, Kjmonkey, Hrsiddique, Geoffpursell, Helpful Pixie Bot, Dtellett, BG19bot, NUMB3RN7NE, Arturius jacobus, AvocatoBot, Jonasusher, Cullenroche, ChrisGualtieri, Fishicus, SPECIFICO, EconomicsExpert, Canadianpolisci, Johnjgelles, Monkbot, Sasubpar, Kosmonaut90, BryL4004, Lorenzo berto, Csbrown28 and Anonymous: 76

- **Money as Debt** *Source:* https://en.wikipedia.org/wiki/Money_as_Debt?oldid=704317217 *Contributors:* Michael Hardy, Hippietrail, Causa sui, Ron Ritzman, Bobrayner, Woohookitty, Mandarax, Vegaswikian, MarnetteD, Diza, Dadu~enwiki, SmackBot, Dwanyewest, Timotheus Canens, Squiddy, Morte, Chendy, Cybercobra, Ser Amantio di Nicolao, Robofish, Nunquam Dormio, Chrisahn, Cydebot, PamD, Darrenhusted, Georgebaltz, JamesBWatson, TomCat4680, Shawn in Montreal, DMCer, Fences and windows, Kbrose, SieBot, Ravensfire, JL-Bot, Gene93k, Blanchardb, Ecureuil espagnol, Editor2020, BigK HeX, MichaelQSchmidt, Addbot, Leszek Jańczuk, MuZemike, GeorgeDorgan, LilHelpa, Srich32977, Grandthefttoaster, Fortdj33, Redrose64, Skyerise, Jonkerz, Beyond My Ken, Edlitz36, Okip, ZéroBot, Thargor Orlando, NoHopeInFiatMoneyWorld, VapidShystersHaveTakenOverPolicy, EveryShysterForHimself, Saebvn, ClueBot NG, BarrelProof, 336, Engranaje, The Banner Turbo, Huashi501, Gabriel Yuji, BattyBot, RotlinkBot, DavidLeighEllis, Karl Twist and Anonymous: 35

- **Mouvement Anti-Utilitariste dans les Sciences Sociales** *Source:* https://en.wikipedia.org/wiki/Mouvement_Anti-Utilitariste_dans_les_Sciences_Sociales?oldid=678497335 *Contributors:* Maunus, Bthomson100, Sun Creator, Forbes72, Good Olfactory, FrescoBot, EmausBot, Meclee, Khazar2, Jumbomingus and Anonymous: 2

- **Mutualism (economic theory)** *Source:* https://en.wikipedia.org/wiki/Mutualism_(economic_theory)?oldid=698239387 *Contributors:* Alex.tan, BrianHoltz, Charles Matthews, Silvonen, Atreyu42, Kevehs, Sam Spade, AaronS, Nikodemos, Nat Krause, Tom harrison, Millerc, Chowbok, Pgan002, DNewhall, The Land, Sam Hocevar, Blanchette, Rich Farmbrough, Bender235, Eric Forste, Lycurgus, Mjk2357, Adambro, Remuel, Cmdrjameson, Oolong, Moxie~enwiki, NTK, Radical Mallard, Max rspct, RJII, Gatewaycat, Jacob Haller, Julo, Rjwilmsi,

Koavf, Dionyseus, Subversive, Mr.Rocks, YurikBot, Mushin, RussBot, Hauskalainen, Pigman, Hogeye, Grafen, Isolani, Maunus, WAS 4.250, Maphisto86, Mike Dillon, Lawyer2b, Sardanaphalus, KnightRider~enwiki, SmackBot, Radak, Zazaban, Frymaster, Gilliam, Revkat, Chris the speller, Bluebot, Full Shunyata, Battlecry, TKD, Nihilo 01, Rebooted, Byelf2007, Cast, Gobonobo, Shyamsunder, CJames745, Libertatia, N1h1l, Mikael V, WGee, JoeBot, BlackFlag, Tawkerbot2, Bobfrombrockley, Vision Thing, Jac16888, Cydebot, Mattergy, Bpadinha, Donnachadelong, Thijs!bot, Epbr123, Davidlawrence, Indrek, Blahblahblahblahblahblah, JAnDbot, Skomorokh, TheIndividualist, Magioladitis, Hroðulf, Soulbot, That'sHot, 8653564, KConWiki, Gomm, Anarcho-capitalism, Jim Yar, Tremello, R'n'B, Dispenser, JayJasper, Cxx guy, S (usurped also), SergeyKurdakov, Cambrick, Station1, TXiKiBoT, Rei-bot, Wdrev, The Devil's Advocate, Etcetc, SieBot, Teknolyze, Nancy, Illegal editor, Smilo Don, Operation Spooner, ClueBot, Syhon, TheOldJacobite, Solar-Wind, Super propane, Jemmy Button, Excirial, PixelBot, SchreiberBike, Editor2020, Joel.a.davis, Gavin Webb, Qgil-WMF, Armyaware, Timothy.lucas.jaeger, Kbdankbot, Addbot, Ettrig, Luckas-bot, JJARichardson, Richard Blatant, Sageo, KamikazeBot, Eduen, CounterEconomics, Anarchy is Order, PublicSquare, Bobisbob2, Aaagmnr, Materialscientist, Clark89, Xqbot, Omnipaedista, Costho, Quiet Bird, Waterfalling, Zikharon, Cooperate23, Jonkerz, Dinamik-bot, Mean as custard, Bluszczokrzew, Acather96, Pechke, Midas02, ClueBot NG, Aurixious, Achillemarotta, Somedifferentstuff, Frietjes, Bagsfull, BG19bot, Rastapunk, StarryGrandma, SD5bot, Khazar2, Homealone1990, Saehry, CsDix, Bronx Discount Liquor, Kingronnie1, Je.est.un.autre, Anarcho-statist, Lux ex Tenebris, Nøkkenbuer, Knife-in-the-drawer, FugeeCamp and Anonymous: 119

- **Neo-Marxian economics** *Source:* https://en.wikipedia.org/wiki/Neo-Marxian_economics?oldid=698871440 *Contributors:* Gary123, BD2412, Omnipaedista, I dream of horses, Wwishart, SoSivr and Anonymous: 4

- **Neo-Ricardianism** *Source:* https://en.wikipedia.org/wiki/Neo-Ricardianism?oldid=598716273 *Contributors:* Piotrus, Clawed, Chalst, Zenohockey, John Quiggin, Equilibrial, Alex1011, Tsca.bot, Robofish, George100, Asimong, Snickershadow, XLinkBot, Addbot, Yobot, AnomieBOT, Omnipaedista, Arbraxan, Jmh92, ZéroBot, Piero Testa and Anonymous: 10

- **Neuroeconomics** *Source:* https://en.wikipedia.org/wiki/Neuroeconomics?oldid=704750944 *Contributors:* Fnielsen, Edward, Vaughan, Lexor, Ronz, PuzzletChung, Academic Challenger, Matthew Stannard, Joel Parker Henderson, Taak, Nova77, Piotrus, APH, Pgreenfinch, YUL89YYZ, Goochelaar, Bender235, Vierstein, Sietse Snel, Cretog8, Johnkarp, Psychobabble, Zenosparadox, Megan 189, John Quiggin, SHIMONSHA, Wanderingstan, Wikiklrsc, Rjwilmsi, Chobot, Bgwhite, Dúnadan, YurikBot, Shaddack, Bruguiea, Rjlabs, Arthur Rubin, Crystallina, KnightRider~enwiki, Lunalona, SmackBot, FocalPoint, Bradtcordeiro, Eskimbot, Chris the speller, RDBrown, Jxm, Bballbhailu, John, Astanton, Hu12, Quaeler, Thomasmeeks, Icarus of old, Cydebot, Lukas Semion~enwiki, Woffie, Esowteric, Z10x, Ph.eyes, Relyk, Rick.Wicks, ExplicitImplicity, Kpmiyapuram, AntiSpamBot, DadaNeem, Zakp, Technopat, Afluent Rider, Garrondo, Broadbot, SieBot, Qblik, Gknor, Jojalozzo, Elnuncabienponderado~enwiki, Alexbot, Gwguffey, Arjayay, Addbot, JPMorgan2, Zellfaze, SpBot, Gregdam, زرش, Luckas-bot, Yobot, AnomieBOT, Materialscientist, Citation bot, Xqbot, JAChero05, Mamaberry11, Citation bot 1, Donutgallery, Primaler, 8c8camerer, John of Reading, Dwalsh3, Waithought, AvicBot, Kelly222, Tectonicura, Tobeprecise, Tobiasmattei, Financestudent, ChuispastonBot, Father-Jockbrose, Ebasri, Kimberleyporter, NatalieAvigail, Reggie.fact, BG19bot, Christian.ruff, Pulga0907, Dolanbossaerts, JohnNash2.0, Brad7777, MathewTownsend, FrederikNewton, Arno.riedl, Dongilchung, Bronx Discount Liquor, Navegidi, Anrnusna, Onuphriate, Monkbot, Voltdye, Parkalatte, DavidWestT, Silasssilva92, Ftheprofit1, A6767, PabloLientur and Anonymous: 108

- **New institutional economics** *Source:* https://en.wikipedia.org/wiki/New_institutional_economics?oldid=705232318 *Contributors:* Robbot, Ehusman, Andycjp, Discospinster, Leibniz, Bender235, Tmh, Mdd, Wikidea, Woohookitty, YHoshua, Tabletop, Bkwillwm, BD2412, Rjwilmsi, Volunteer Marek, Bgwhite, RussBot, Equilibrial, SmackBot, Bluebot, Madmedea~enwiki, Nbarth, Anthon.Eff, Saluton~enwiki, Hu12, Joseph Solis in Australia, CmdrObot, Thomasmeeks, Krauss, JamesAM, Andyjsmith, Escarbot, Awqam, Rjwellings, R'n'B, Fetobos~enwiki, Ajbibi, Katsp8, Brett epic, Monty845, SieBot, Mr. Granger, Corebreeches, SlackerMom, Mild Bill Hiccup, SchreiberBike, Attaboy, Addbot, Lightbot, Irnerius, Fryed-peach, Pessimist2006, Yobot, Mbiama Assogo Roger, Citation bot, ArthurBot, LilHelpa, Omnipaedista, Kaylanimis, Freedom1587, FrescoBot, Seelum, Knutw, Kape tsokolate, Workdemo, RjwilmsiBot, Bluszczokrzew, Klbrain, Alfredo ougaowen, Jonpatterns, H0339637, CitationCleanerBot, Badia85, WBWDII, Abrsk95, D.S. Cordoba-Bahle, Loraof, Marie Göpel, Kevinmccarthy25 and Anonymous: 37

- **Non-possession** *Source:* https://en.wikipedia.org/wiki/Non-possession?oldid=698797075 *Contributors:* Reinyday, John Quiggin, Woohookitty, BD2412, Koavf, Ellesmelle, Hairy Dude, RussBot, Bhny, Nirvana2013, WAS 4.250, Amakuru, KnightLago, Penbat, Cydebot, Alaibot, Nick Number, Jacobko, JaGa, KCinDC, Fratrep, JL-Bot, Dakinijones, WikHead, Addbot, Withclear~enwiki, Luckas-bot, AnomieBOT, LilHelpa, Srich32977, SassoBot, Snotbot, BG19bot, ChrisGualtieri, Artaylor102, जैन and Anonymous: 3

- **Participatory economics** *Source:* https://en.wikipedia.org/wiki/Participatory_economics?oldid=693771892 *Contributors:* DanKeshet, Ed Poor, Enchanter, R Lowry, Edward, Boud, EntmootsOfTrolls, Nerd~enwiki, Kimiko, Andrevan, AaronSw, Pir, Altenmann, Kowey, Chris Roy, AaronS, Cholling, Sunray, GeerBawks, Nagelfar, Centrx, Christiaan, Inter, Davin (usurped), Daniel Brockman, Wmahan, Pgan002, Bact, Beland, Maximaximax, Tothebarricades.tk, Szcz, WpZurp, Jbinder, Mike Rosoft, Quirk, Kmccoy, Rich Farmbrough, JimR, LindsayH, Bender235, Ntennis, Mjk2357, Episcopo, Sietse Snel, Che y Marijuana, Valve, Maurreen, La goutte de pluie, Chira, Rd232, Mattley, Ombudsman, Albamuth, Grenavitar, Dominic, Embryomystic, Dismas, Bobrayner, BadLeprechaun, Woohookitty, Jacob Haller, Lapsed Pacifist, Nema Fakei, Mrh~enwiki, Rjwilmsi, Koavf, Dullfig, Eightbitriot, Musujyay, Czar, Cornellrockey, FrankTobia, RussBot, BernardL, Pigman, Dialectric, Equilibrial, Ridiculous fish, Fluxaviator, Number 57, JohnFitzpatrick, Encephalon, Tsiaojian lee, Sardanaphalus, KnightRider~enwiki, SmackBot, Jglassman, Alex1011, Batman Jr., Eskimbot, Brossow, Wspademan, KDRGibby, Chris the speller, Full Shunyata, Trebor, Apeloverage, FordPrefect42, KurtFF8, Battlecry, Cybercobra, Nihilo 01, Freemarket, Pr0test0r, Byelf2007, Odonian, ChrisErb, SilverStar, Dmwilliams, Gobonobo, CJames745, Michaelstor, Notwist, Brotherforest, Kartik Agaram, Whoneedspants, Eastlaw, Livemike, Gregbard, Cydebot, Paddles, Scarpy, Mr Scot, Donnachadelong, Richhoncho, Bobblehead, Blathnaid, RED DAVE, Skomorokh, Tayssir, Magioladitis, MartinDK, Brusegadi, Tonyfaull, Avicennasis, CosmopolitanCapitalist, Gabriel Kielland, NewGuyAccount, Bibliophylax, SlaineMacRoth, R'n'B, PBurrows, Ianmathwiz7, Topknot2, Markjenkins, Djr13, AlnoktaBOT, Αναρχία, Childhoodsend, DocteurCosmos, Bearian, Demigod Ron, Richwil, NovoKronstadt, DivaNtrainin, SieBot, YonaBot, Teknolyze, Pinkaponk, Father Inire, Mild Bill Hiccup, PinoEire, Uncle Milty, DOHill, Singwaste, Joel.a.davis, XLinkBot, Stonewhite, Gigoachef, Gushagelberg, Hawkania, Addbot, AkhtaBot, SpBot, Lightbot, SasiSasi, Yobot, Mikelo Gulhi, FriendlyRobotOverlord, AnomieBOT, AdjustShift, Quebec99, LilHelpa, J04n, Omnipaedista, WilliamTheaker, Andrewballantine, Jean-Jacques Georges, Jibbideejibbish, Shadowjams, Mgrinder, Trimbaculous1, ΙωάννηςΚαραμήτρος, JokerXtreme, Vrenator, Jebuswankel, Jason011987, EPadgett, EmausBot, Dewritech, Lambert Meertens, Jjcascadia, Jonpatterns, Unused000705, Secondfletcher, Grampion76, ClueBot NG, Jason at ramwools com, LittleJerry, Snotbot, Dtellett, Gob Lofa, Mark Arsten, Takeshi-br, Lars Fredrik Nystad, Benzband, Diderooot, Khimaris, Zahid Alig, Psnatkl, CsDix, Dzgoldman, Larryfuku, River Orange and Anonymous: 166

3.1. TEXT

- **Planned economy** *Source:* https://en.wikipedia.org/wiki/Planned_economy?oldid=705233048 *Contributors:* Matthew Woodcraft, Robert Merkel, Tarquin, Ap, Malcolm Farmer, -- April, Ed Poor, Aldie, Roadrunner, Heron, Stevertigo, Edward, Michael Hardy, Isomorphic, Collabi, 172, Kosebamse, Radicalsubversiv, Snoyes, Angela, Error, Cadr, Andres, Jiang, Charles Matthews, Timwi, Dcoetzee, Jukeboksi, Gutza, Kaare, Goose, HarryHenryGebel, Wetman, David.Monniaux, Cncs wikipedia, Jni, Robbot, Paranoid, Altenmann, Sam Spade, Rhombus, JB82, Jondel, Hadal, GreatWhiteNortherner, Nagelfar, Decumanus, Connelly, Christiaan, Nikodemos, ShaunMacPherson, Everyking, Lussmu~enwiki, DO'Neil, NerdOfTheNorth, Luis rib, Christofurio, Explendido Rocha, MSTCrow, PeterC, Antandrus, Beland, Loremaster, Piotrus, Am088, Ot, The Land, Mike Rosoft, Smyth, Bender235, S.K., Lycurgus, Shanes, Sietse Snel, RoyBoy, Cretog8, Smalljim, .:Ajvol:., Elipongo, Cohesion, Maureen, Jerryseinfeld, La goutte de pluie, Xgoni~enwiki, Foant, Andrewpmk, Cdc, Spangineer, Snowolf, Samohyl Jan, Velella, Max rspct, Knowledge Seeker, RJII, Sciurinæ, Mikeo, Geraldshields11, Vuo, Michaelm, Skrewler, Empoor, Crypto~enwiki, Woohookitty, LOL, Scott.wheeler, Nema Fakei, Mandarax, David Levy, Rjwilmsi, Titoxd, Itinerant1, Jrtayloriv, Fephisto, POTA, Scoops, Actown, Bgwhite, Raelx, YurikBot, Sceptre, Phantomsteve, RussBot, BernardL, Gaius Cornelius, NawlinWiki, Grafen, Kvn8907, Haranoh, Syrthiss, NWOG, Tobias c, WAS 4.250, Sandstein, PTSE, Gorgonzilla, Closedmouth, CapitalLetterBeginning, JBogdan, CWenger, Caballero1967, Tierce, Ybbor, DVD R W, JohnGalt1812, Sardanaphalus, SmackBot, Kirby Morgan, David Kernow, Impaciente, KnowledgeOfSelf, Alex1011, Pgk, Darkstar1st, Prototime, Well, girl, look at you!, Beyhan~enwiki, Mauls, Chuhangjin, Markrich, Gilliam, Chris the speller, Bootdog, Persian Poet Gal, MK8, Stubblyhead, Darth Sidious, Mushii, DHN-bot~enwiki, Constanz, A. B., Can't sleep, clown will eat me, Mulder416, Alphathon, Battlecry, Sephiroth BCR, Wikipedia brown, Arod14, Stevenmitchell, Patabongo, Wossi, Byelf2007, Dak, Hestemand, John, Hawjam, Ben Moore, Kompere, Hu12, Levineps, WGee, Joseph Solis in Australia, Igoldste, W123, Az1568, Tawkerbot2, Eastlaw, JForget, CmdrObot, Ale jrb, Blue-Haired Lawyer, Vision Thing, Thomasmeeks, Neelix, Rowellcf, Mhs5392, Tahnru, Yayhannibal, MC10, Bellerophon5685, Longhornsg, Odie5533, DumbBOT, FastLizard4, Chris Henniker, Thijs!bot, Epbr123, Adamtrevillian, Darekun, Mentifisto, AntiVandalBot, WinBot, Blarrrgy, Jj137, Lordmetroid, Dylan Lake, Salgueiro~enwiki, Elaragirl, Oubliette, Canadian-Bacon, Ingolfson, JAnDbot, Nthep, Trey314159, Geniac, Yahel Guhan, Magioladitis, Bongwarrior, VoABot II, Wikidudeman, Economizer, Bill j, DroppingIn, Allstarecho, Cpl Syx, SlamDiego, Fang 23, JdeJ, Limtohhan, Denis tarasov, MartinBot, STBot, Rettetast, Bmrbarre, J.delanoy, Trusilver, Tom Paine, Shkeye, McSly, Gec118, Olegwiki, Vanished user 39948282, Jbelleisle, SoCalSuperEagle, Idioma-bot, Tourbillon, TreasuryTag, ABF, Instantiayion, Alex77777, Philip Trueman, Zidonuke, Kenect2, Dojarca, Crohnie, C.J. Griffin, Leafyplant, Supertask, LeaveSleaves, Demigod Ron, RHaden, Moonriddengirl, Work permit, Barliner, SiegeLord, Tiptoety, Freedomwarrior, Paintman, Lightmouse, LT RT, Techzilla, StaticGull, F2003143, Operation Spooner, Galoric, Atif.t2, Loren.wilton, ClueBot, Rocket Socket, IceUnshattered, MrBosnia, Leonard^Bloom, PaulKincaidSmith, SpikeToronto, DO-Hill, Kmaster, Redthoreau, La Pianista, Immoralist, Versus22, PotentialDanger, NERIC-Security, Rankiri, BodhisattvaBot, Vloxul, Badinfinity, Sixty Plant, Avoided, Addbot, Betterusername, Mia-etol, Fieldday-sunday, Leszek Jańczuk, Veraptor, MrVanBot, Souviens, Michaelwuzthere, Mosedschurte, Debresser, AgadaUrbanit, NoNonsenseHumJock, Lightbot, Solid State, Bartledan, Elm, Legobot, Yobot, 2D, Apollonius 1236, Nutfortuna, PMLawrence, Bsca, N1RK4UDSK714, AnomieBOT, Floquenbeam, RanEagle, Ulric1313, Britans, Materialscientist, Orlouge82, GB fan, ArthurBot, ShogunOfSorrow, Sellyme, Hello Socialism!, Can I touch it?, Mlpearc, אסף רומנו, Hi878, HighlyBored, RibotBOT, Jean-Jacques Georges, Smallman12q, Tugaworld, Scythian23, Recognizance, Trust Is All You Need, Citation bot 1, I dream of horses, Jschnur, N.11.6, The 1st LOLCat, Specs112, MaxEspinho, Tbhotch, Gscottiii, Mean as custard, Bjorn1221, DASHBot, Vinnyzz, EmausBot, John of Reading, Immunize, Themindsurgeon, Blargnargles, Newbis, Elvenmuse, Kkm010, ZéroBot, Killertux666, Josve05a, Traxs7, Röhmöfantti, Git2010, Rapidosity, Headerpoli, L Kensington, Orange Suede Sofa, Financestudent, Mcc1789, Grampion76, DASHBotAV, Erhsdons2011, Fifawc2010, Rememberway, ClueBot NG, Onionofdeeath64, Somedifferentstuff, Jumbo1233, The Master of Mayhem, Delusion23, Cliftongransko, Crazymonkey1123, Helpful Pixie Bot, Lowercase sigmabot, BG19bot, Objective Reason, Mogism, Makecat-bot, The Quirky Kitty, Erukanntare, CsDix, Oemong, I am One of Many, CensoredScribe, Thevideodrome, JustBerry, Monkbot, Zumoarirodoka, Jss199, Smith 123456, Sundayclose, Maksim-Smelchak, Benjaminikuta, KasparBot, Vrrajkum and Anonymous: 503

- **Pluralism in economics** *Source:* https://en.wikipedia.org/wiki/Pluralism_in_economics?oldid=687785185 *Contributors:* Discospinster, Smalljim, John Quiggin, Rjwilmsi, DVdm, RussBot, Haemo, SmackBot, Ryan Roos, Gregbard, Jkomlos, Ian.thomson, Jeepday, TXiKiBoT, Guillaume2303, Akliman, Watchdog07, Extra Fine Point, Addbot, Lightbot, Nifky?, LilHelpa, Srich32977, Kiefer.Wolfowitz, Lancastle, Jonpatterns, Marthastarr, ClueBot NG, I am One of Many, Avnerus, Jacob Viner and Anonymous: 6

- **Post-autistic economics** *Source:* https://en.wikipedia.org/wiki/Post-autistic_economics?oldid=691808467 *Contributors:* The Anome, Toby Bartels, Fubar Obfusco, Karada, AlfieNet, Jni, Jmabel, Aetheling, Sj, J heisenberg, Joshuapaquin, Luigi30, Risi, Burschik, Fgb~enwiki, Tobacman, Maureen, Hooperbloob, GenkiNeko, Alan Oldfield, Rd232, John Quiggin, Mattley, Samohyl Jan, Clubmarx, Rfredian, Y0u, Bobrayner, Apokrif, Dwarf Kirlston, Intgr, Lmatt, Karch, Bornhj, YurikBot, Chris Capoccia, Aldux, DryaUnda, Nlu, LeonardoRob0t, SmackBot, Bluebot, TimBentley, Nbarth, Baronnet, Byelf2007, Dl2000, Joseph Solis in Australia, Doc richard, Todddc, Skomorokh, VoABot II, Foldvary, Fconaway, Gorni-gupar, Flyte35, Laughingyet, WarrenPlatts, Laperche, Poli08, Addbot, Knight of Truth, Mootros, Legobot, Yobot, AnomieBOT, Xqbot, Srich32977, FrescoBot, Þjóðólfr, Kiefer.Wolfowitz, MondalorBot, Reconsider the static, Phronetic, Financestudent, Grampion76, Cerabot~enwiki, Rotlink, Kckranger, Monkbot, Nøkkenbuer and Anonymous: 33

- **Post-scarcity economy** *Source:* https://en.wikipedia.org/wiki/Post-scarcity_economy?oldid=705056524 *Contributors:* Danny, Error, Katana0182, Populus, Omegatron, Kizor, Babbage, Connelly, Tom harrison, Gracefool, Pgan002, Beland, Loremaster, Creidieki, Brianhe, Night Gyr, Cyclopia, Ylee, Bjelli, Cretog8, Mike Schwartz, Viriditas, Maureen, VBGFscJUn3, Kitplane01, OGoncho, John Quiggin, Hohum, Geraldshields11, Vuo, Bobrayner, Tabletop, GregorB, CharlesC, Waldir, Qwertyus, Ground Zero, Drruggeri, Tedder, Trfs, Bgwhite, Witan, Thiseye, SamuelRiv, Unforgiven24, Finster, SmackBot, Andrew Ross-Parker, Iv, Y control, KelleyCook, Grandmartin11, Chris the speller, Hibernian, Bazonka, Epastore, Battlecry, GVnayR, Iapetus, Cybercobra, Daniel.o.jenkins, Metamagician3000, Byelf2007, Armentage, Robofish, JorisvS, Constantine lisiy, Michaelstor, Hypnosifl, Tmangray, Skapur, Exander, RekishiEJ, GiantSnowman, Wavemage, Yashgaroth, Mgumn, Agemegos, N2e, Kalaong, Cydebot, Big swedish, Capedia, Teratornis, Chris Henniker, Septagram, Noclevername, Widefox, IantheLibrarian, Ingolfson, Mclean007, MauroVan, IkonicDeath, EagleFan, Gwern, Speck-Made, AltiusBimm, Xris0, Sigmundpetersen, Infocat13, Student7, Jaimeastorga2000, Buddha379, Masterpiggy5, OBreaux1, Djbuddha, Johnfos, Speaker to wolves, Klip game, Wolfrock, Richwil, Sapphic, Ignacio Bibcraft, Sirswindon, Skipsievert, Deoxyribonucleic acid trip, Svick, Martarius, Wwheaton, Arthurfragoso, Pt36, Erudecorp, Three-quarterten, Arjayay, Razorflame, Editor2020, Namelessghoul, LostLucidity, Addbot, Barsoomian, UShick, R.J. Croton, Mmaza, Michaelwuzthere, Favonian, Fireaxe888, Tassedethe, Ehrenkater, Freevolution, Yobot, Againme, AnomieBOT, Jim1138, OpenFuture, Alexe.360, Drama-kun, Uloggonitor, FrescoBot, Teknikingman, Gregknicholson, Searle88, Locutus42, Hamfist, UnderHigh, Dinamik-bot, Wordbandar, EmausBot, WikitanvirBot, Hirsutism, We hope, Weaselprince71, A03416140, Jonpatterns, Echyrek, Ollyoxenfree, Ego White Tray, Lyla1205, Veritasvoswiki, Frietjes, Krunchyman, Helpful Pixie Bot, Curb Chain, Jeraphine Gryphon, BG19bot, The Banner Turbo, Hodeken, Luisfrancisco10,

Northamerica1000, Wolfgang42, Gibbja, Newuser2011, Sfarney, Earl King Jr., Alevsarc, Me, Myself, and I are Here, Econobre, WBritten, Hendrick 99, Stilgar27, Bronx Discount Liquor, Werddemer, Fixuture, Maksim-Smelchak, Nøkkenbuer, JWilson0923, Ackhuman, Profcademics and Anonymous: 156

- **Production for use** *Source:* https://en.wikipedia.org/wiki/Production_for_use?oldid=704455620 *Contributors:* Edward, Lycurgus, Cretog8, Mandarax, BD2412, Baryonic Being, Chris the speller, Battlecry, R'n'B, PhilLiberty, Mild Bill Hiccup, Nolelover, Yobot, AnomieBOT, FrescoBot, FoxBot, Goti123, Zatarra86, Goti1233, CsDix, Tomato expert1, WPGA2345, Heuh0, Nøkkenbuer and Anonymous: 8

- **Quarterly Journal of Austrian Economics** *Source:* https://en.wikipedia.org/wiki/Quarterly_Journal_of_Austrian_Economics?oldid=692496207 *Contributors:* RayBirks, Bender235, Bastin, DickClarkMises, SmackBot, Allixpeeke, Nihilo 01, The Little Blue Frog, JustAGal, Carolmooredc, Ikilled007, Shortride, Guillaume2303, Addbot, Jsg24, AnomieBOT, LilHelpa, Srich32977, MeUser42, Colchester121891, Jonkerz, Guillaume233, Randykitty, Michipedian, Steeletrap and Anonymous: 2

- **Real-world economics review** *Source:* https://en.wikipedia.org/wiki/Real-world_economics_review?oldid=660612373 *Contributors:* Bobrayner, Nbarth, Robofish, Fadesga, Addbot, Ginevradabenci, EmausBot, Frietjes, BattyBot, Fanzine999, Randykitty, CsDix and Anonymous: 1

- **Regenerative economic theory** *Source:* https://en.wikipedia.org/wiki/Regenerative_economic_theory?oldid=601817674 *Contributors:* Docu, Alan Liefting, John Quiggin, Woohookitty, Tony1, Robofish, Shyamsunder, Esowteric, BobShair, Yobot, Ched, J04n, Jocast, Ldemetri, Bstoltenberg, Emilycampagnawalsh and Anonymous: 2

- **Review of Keynesian Economics** *Source:* https://en.wikipedia.org/wiki/Review_of_Keynesian_Economics?oldid=675932345 *Contributors:* Natg 19, Flyer22 Reborn, Wbm1058, BattyBot, Randykitty, Everymorning, Lakun.patra, Filedelinkerbot, Louis-Philippe Rochon, A. Sebastián Hdez. Solorza and Anonymous: 1

- **Review of Radical Political Economics** *Source:* https://en.wikipedia.org/wiki/Review_of_Radical_Political_Economics?oldid=690405866 *Contributors:* TexasAndroid, SmackBot, RayAYang, Nbarth, Thomasmeeks, Dogru144, Fabrictramp, Yobot, Verplanck, Omnipaedista, FrescoBot, Jonkerz, Look2See1, Luke.j.ruby, Randykitty and Anonymous: 2

- **Sharing economy** *Source:* https://en.wikipedia.org/wiki/Sharing_economy?oldid=704575723 *Contributors:* Edward, Fred Bauder, Jukeboksi, Beland, Brianhe, Chibimagic, Stesmo, Beachy, Bobrayner, Koavf, Everton137, Nihiltres, Wavelength, Arado, Dialectric, KVDP, Yamaguchi???, WikiPedant, Derek R Bullamore, Tehw1k1, X14n, Peculiarfish, PKT, Heroeswithmetaphors, Tokyogirl79, Jen3774, Ddjjpp33, Jordan1976, MenoBot, Sfan00 IMG, Niceguyedc, Trivialist, Cmr08, Mortense, USchick, MrOllie, Yobot, AnomieBOT, BobKilcoyne, Crookesmoor, Baselinefonts, Omnipaedista, A.amitkumar, FrescoBot, Mino-wiijiindi, Anna Comnena, Lotje, Onel5969, Mean as custard, RjwilmsiBot, Dangerousrave, Erpert, Bongoramsey, Jonpatterns, Midas02, ClueBot NG, Travel maven, Somedifferentstuff, Lawsonstu, BG19bot, WikiTryHardDieHard, Eteigland, Conifer, BattyBot, TRBurton, Earl King Jr., IjonTichyIjonTichy, Ganskyl1, Mogism, Colmbrady, SFK2, Jamesx12345, Altruistic user, Bananasoldier, Jodosma, Tentinator, Melody Lavender, Jjunecobb, Paul2520, Dough34, J58787427348T, Plunkersiniapes, Fixuture, Ele.denaro, Theothergore, WikiSharEdit, Monkbot, Cazer78, Swapmamas, DeelmarktplaatsFloow2, Ele-Sharer, Marco.torregrossa, Speedster101, REH7, Skozinsky, Hderekdavis, Marketingjuice, Stewartjpatrick1, Sharely.Us, Kinza99, Erbear131, Lanfranchi, MLAwiki1983, Ecotamar, UY4Xe8VM5VYxaQQ, Orli.yer, Pablomunozroman, ElizaLepine, Tpuschmann, Jack Deban and Anonymous: 65

- **Social credit** *Source:* https://en.wikipedia.org/wiki/Social_credit?oldid=696899459 *Contributors:* Derek Ross, Dan~enwiki, The Anome, Roadrunner, Hephaestos, Rbrwr, Michael Hardy, Stewacide, Sam Francis, Sannse, Karada, Zannah, Julesd, Vzbs34, Jfitzg, Kaihsu, Efghij, Sgoodhall, Vancouverguy, VeryVerily, Warofdreams, Bcorr, Bshort, Vardion, Fifelfoo, Nagelfar, Alan Liefting, DocWatson42, Robin Patterson, Tom harrison, HangingCurve, Kevintoronto, Craverguy, Formeruser-81, DNewhall, Rlquall, Canterbury Tail, Jayjg, Calion, Pavel Vozenilek, Bender235, Habsfannova, Lycurgus, Mjk2357, QuartierLatin1968, Magius, YX, John Fader, Nik42, 119, Diego Moya, Keenan Pepper, John Quiggin, Hu, Pauli133, Kazvorpal, Michaelm, Dejvid, Mwalcoff, Woohookitty, FeanorStar7, MONGO, Jergen, Electionworld, Rjwilmsi, Mayumashu, Vegaswikian, Ground Zero, Vonkje, Roboto de Ajvol, RussBot, Raquel Baranow, Gaius Cornelius, Oberst, Tony1, BOT-Superzerocool, Squell, SmackBot, Gilliam, The Gnome, Kasyapa, Verrai, Battlecry, William Quill, Fuhghettaboutit, Cybercobra, Kevlar67, Gandalf1491, Threadnecromancer, Fursday, Bobfrombrockley, Phenss, Timeshift9, Alaibot, Wikid77, Mr pand, Mrodowicz, Purpleslog, Treblent, Bogolov, Gregalton, Fayenatic london, Glennwells, Igodard, Felix116, IceColdLemon, Torchiest, SlamDiego, Strikehold, JaGa, Textorus, T.C. Craig, Kiore, R'n'B, NickMelchior, Happy138, Nwbeeson, Hugo999, TreasuryTag, TXiKiBoT, Xenophrenic, Qxz, Omcnew, Király-Seth, Erik Jesse, Thecrystalcicero, Mercenario97, David Kendall, LarRan, PipepBot, All Hallow's Wraith, Wikit2007, TheOldJacobite, Yorkshirian, BOTarate, JD-PhD, DumZiBoT, Camboxer, Dthomsen8, Larone, Addbot, Chdouglas, Cst17, Chzz, Lightbot, Faunas, Melvalevis, PMLawrence, Plasticbot, AnomieBOT, Citation bot, Lanççelot, Srich32977, Dougknockbrex, Bellerophon, Shadowjams, Prari, Citation bot 1, PigFlu Oink, Dodge rambler, Winterst, Jonesey95, Full-date unlinking bot, TobeBot, Jonkerz, Dethroned Buoy, RjwilmsiBot, WildBot, GoingBatty, Javorie, H3llBot, FeatherPluma, ClueBot NG, Loginnigol, Helpful Pixie Bot, Altaïr, CitationCleanerBot, BattyBot, Webb50, Lekoren, ArmbrustBot, Adirlanz, Monkbot and Anonymous: 113

- **Social dividend** *Source:* https://en.wikipedia.org/wiki/Social_dividend?oldid=699743102 *Contributors:* Utcursch, Chris the speller, Colonies Chris, Battlecry, Postscript07, Mike Christie, XLinkBot, AnomieBOT, Srich32977, Omnipaedista, FrescoBot, Stanjourdan, Jadeslair, Helpful Pixie Bot, Guest2625, Lakshmi.nuthakki, BattyBot, ChrisGualtieri, CsDix, CODemocracy, Povertydave and Anonymous: 2

- **Socialist economics** *Source:* https://en.wikipedia.org/wiki/Socialist_economics?oldid=698270473 *Contributors:* AxelBoldt, Edward, Lexor, 172, Charles Matthews, Adam Carr, Jni, Seth Ilys, Stirling Newberry, Nikodemos, AmishThrasher, Piotrus, The Land, Cretog8, Sentience, Cmdrjameson, CR7, John Quiggin, Wikidea, Batmanand, Bart133, Bobrayner, FrancisTyers, Jacob Haller, Nema Fakei, Magister Mathematicae, BD2412, Qwertyus, DickClarkMises, Sango123, Ground Zero, Alhutch, Echeneida, Jrtayloriv, Bgwhite, Dopepixie, Deeptrivia, RussBot, BernardL, Shell Kinney, NawlinWiki, Spot87, Tachs, Zzuuzz, Gusmac~enwiki, Spikespeigel42, Pania, Samuel Blanning, That Guy, From That Show!, Sardanaphalus, SmackBot, InverseHypercube, Brossow, Vhreabvkbojnckdn, Hmains, Nealc, Chris the speller, Bluebot, Full Shunyata, Dustingc, Battlecry, Fuhghettaboutit, Byelf2007, BrownHairedGirl, Gobonobo, WGee, Joseph Solis in Australia, Mrdthree, Jsorens, TriniSocialist, JForget, CmdrObot, Sarcastic Avenger, Bobfrombrockley, Vision Thing, Thomasmeeks, ShelfSkewed, Spylab, Christian75, JamesAM, Marek69, Frank, Nick Number, AntiVandalBot, Courtjester555, Atlfontes, Leolaursen, Faizhaider, Bill j, Carn, Fang 23, Infrangible, Adavidb, Mike Winters, WarthogDemon, Jdfhdfh, DMcM, Globalization, KylieTastic, Kenneth M Burke, Squids and Chips, VolkovBot, TreasuryTag, Thewolf37, ABF, Lia Todua, Russcote, Technopat, Anonymous Dissident, C.J. Griffin, Billinghurst, Demigod Ron, Monty845, MaCRoEco, Cyfal, Alexemanuel, ClueBot, TheOddOne2, Leodmacleod, Mikaey, SchreiberBike, Thehelpfulone, Whichmore, Dthomsen8, Addbot, Some jerk

3.1. TEXT

on the Internet, Marco.natalino, Michaelwuzthere, Tassedethe, Dhuihadidhihafhi, Yobot, Apollonius 1236, Legobot II, Eduen, AnomieBOT, Itanesco, Valois bourbon, Teeninvestor, LilHelpa, Apjohns54, J04n, Omnipaedista, Cuauti, Amaury, Jean-Jacques Georges, Ong saluri, Trust Is All You Need, ViperT~enwiki, Lotje, Grantbonn, Tiramisuloverr, RjwilmsiBot, Rollins83, John of Reading, Orphan Wiki, Ghostofnemo, Dewritech, GoingBatty, Wikipelli, Kkm010, Semmler, Edunoramus, Matthewrbowker, Grampion76, ClueBot NG, Piast93, Asukite, Helpful Pixie Bot, Wbm1058, OuphesAplenty, BG19bot, Iselilja, User1961914, BattyBot, TwoTwoHello, CsDix, SolomonLamb, Kasergc, Monkbot, Knife-in-the-drawer, Melody.waring, Jjporter99, Lunduniv and Anonymous: 124

- **Socioeconomics** *Source:* https://en.wikipedia.org/wiki/Socioeconomics?oldid=704375339 *Contributors:* Andrewman327, Joy, Owen, Red-Wolf, Seglea, Modulatum, Moink, Wizzy, Piotrus, Pgreenfinch, MarkNeville, Rich Farmbrough, Bender235, Adambro, Cretog8, Evolauxia, Elipongo, La goutte de pluie, Alansohn, Gary, John Quiggin, Lapsed Pacifist, Graham87, Qwertyus, Sjakkalle, Mayumashu, Pariah, RexNL, DVdm, Roboto de Ajvol, YurikBot, X42bn6, Briaboru, ScottMainwaring, Moe Epsilon, Zzuuzz, Closedmouth, Infinity0, Eskimbot, Gilliam, Jprg1966, BrendelSignature, TheLeopard, Piro071981, Onorem, O.K., Mini-Geek, DMacks, FlyHigh, Ocee, Ckatz, Grumpyyoungman01, RekishiEJ, Thomasmeeks, Neelix, Marek69, Natalie Erin, Eduardo Lacerda, Ok!, MER-C, SiobhanHansa, Pharaoh of the Wizards, Trusilver, Bogey97, It Is Me Here, Cometstyles, Spillinghair, ShereKhan8~enwiki, Tomsega, Brianga, Antonio Lopez, Denisarona, ClueBot, R000t, Garyzx, Leebeck33, Robert Skyhawk, NuclearWarfare, AgnosticPreachersKid, TheGreate1234, TomPointTwo, HexaChord, Addbot, Download, Norman21, Yobot, Half7, Sasece~enwiki, Piano non troppo, Mbiama Assogo Roger, Lroch, Disagreeableneutrino, LilHelpa, Capricorn42, Jmundo, Srich32977, Solphusion~enwiki, Omnipaedista, Amaury, TarseeRota, FrescoBot, Michael93555, Ahnoneemoos, SpaceFlight89, Madliner, كاشف عقیل, Horcrux92, Financestudent, Dbregister, ClueBot NG, Aurelch, F0ck u all gheys, HMSSolent, Dirinter, Cornelius383, PhnomPencil, Hallows AG, North911, Ankururdu, Telfordbuck, Tentinator, Fixuture, Cpass 23, BrightonC, EZeng, Gregory.2.jackson, Aashishssharma004, Loraof, Wikispring, Southparker1, Exurban, Ogeneotuke1, CLCStudent and Anonymous: 132

- **Structuralist economics** *Source:* https://en.wikipedia.org/wiki/Structuralist_economics?oldid=652841077 *Contributors:* John Quiggin, Helvetius, SmackBot, Chris the speller, Alaibot, Pikolas, Msrasnw, DepartedUser4, Olyus, Addbot, Omnipaedista, I dream of horses, WallofTrut, Pass3456, MerlIwBot, KLBot2, SheldorAFK, Waters.Justin and Anonymous: 8

- **Surplus economics** *Source:* https://en.wikipedia.org/wiki/Surplus_economics?oldid=670531116 *Contributors:* Cretog8, John Quiggin, Bobrayner, Volunteer Marek, NawlinWiki, Pietdesomere, SmackBot, Bluebot, Radagast83, Michaelstor, Vision Thing, Alaibot, It's The Economics, Stupid!, AntiVandalBot, Alphachimpbot, Belovedfreak, Altzinn, Claytonkb, AnomieBOT, Jonpatterns and Anonymous: 5

- **Technocracy** *Source:* https://en.wikipedia.org/wiki/Technocracy?oldid=699044131 *Contributors:* Lefte, Stevertigo, Charles Matthews, Ike9898, Tpbradbury, MrWeeble, Fifelfoo, Ralian, Pablo-flores, Alan Liefting, Nikodemos, Axeman, PeruvianIlama, SoWhy, Andycjp, DNewhall, Imlepid, AndrewTheLott, Burschik, Moxfyre, Reinthal, Discospinster, Rich Farmbrough, Bender235, Nabla, Kgaughan, Cwolfsheep, Alansohn, Cnelson, John Quiggin, Ynhockey, Wtmitchell, Max Naylor, Woohookitty, Chasrmartin, Bkwillwm, SDC, Electionworld, Eyu100, Jeffmcneill, Tbone, Tequendamia, GringoCroco, Chobot, GangofOne, Roboto de Ajvol, RussBot, Gaius Cornelius, Ksyrie, Havok, Complainer, BlueZenith, Rande M Sefowt, Allens, SmackBot, InverseHypercube, McGeddon, Lawrencekhoo, NickShaforostoff, Hibernian, MercZ, Ian Burnet~enwiki, Alphathon, Keith Lehwald, Wikipedia brown, Radagast83, Cybercobra, EPM, Krfsm, Ohconfucius, Tazmaniacs, JorisvS, Sark6354201, Joffeloff, Ekrub-ntyh, Willy turner, Manifestation, Joseph Solis in Australia, Meisam.fa, CmdrObot, Apterygial, Cydebot, Future Perfect at Sunrise, Myscrnnm, Daniel J. Leivick, Keraunos, Frank, Mmortal03, Yupik, Superzohar, Alphachimpbot, JAnDbot, Morloon, Firebladed, Granitc26, Mıld, Mr.troughton, Just H, Brian Fenton, Rarian rakista, Captain panda, Kulshrax, MistyMorn, Maurice Carbonaro, Aqwis, Marcus1234, Isenhand, Snyper256, Signalhead, VolkovBot, Drzzy, TreasuryTag, Johnfos, DOHC Holiday, Rocketman116, JayEsJay, AlexTingle, Knock-kneed, Tomsega, Salvar, Elyada, Miwanya, The Great Morgil, Jean-Christophe BENOIST, SieBot, Skipsievert, Mangled Nervous System, Vanished user oij8h435jweih3, ES Sage, Avanti 79, Thatotherdude, Grog beta, ClueBot, Giggsy72, HairyFotr, EoGuy, Gigacephalus, Wwheaton, Rafaelomondini, Penalist, Confusionclassics, Excirial, Alexbot, Jumbolino, Sun Creator, SchreiberBike, BOTarate, Unmerklich, Andrzej Kmicic, SilvonenBot, Kitfox.it, Mifter, Addbot, DOI bot, Ronhjones, Lightbot, Zorrobot, Jarble, WisamFarouk, Luckas-bot, Yobot, Enviro1, Mdw0, AnomieBOT, Scorpiophoenix, Jim1138, Maxis ftw, ArthurBot, LilHelpa, Malik047, Eric Blatant, GrouchoBot, Omnipaedista, SassoBot, GhalyBot, Shadowjams, Imyoda69, GliderMaven, FrescoBot, Silwilhith, AdenR, De12344, PigFlu Oink, Hassouni, RedBot, Spasyuk, Lotje, Dinamik-bot, Grantbonn, Solar Sector, Jeffrd10, Nishantranka, Bigemail90, RjwilmsiBot, EmausBot, WikitanvirBot, Space Commander Plasma, Bryonmorrigan, John Cline, Hfgzajg, Unused000705, 8mmfilm!, SporkBot, Enfolkefiende, Rangoon11, Jason6354201, Jenokrouzil, The Masked Booby, LikeLakers2, ClueBot NG, Fifelfoo m, FidelDrumbo, Funraiser, MerlIwBot, Helpful Pixie Bot, Jeraphine Gryphon, Pulga0907, Gautehuus, SugarRat, Piteye, TheLivingHeiromartyr, Vanemuine, Qasaur, Minsbot, Newuser2011, Cyberbot II, Earl King Jr., JYBot, Saehry, ComfyKem, Jogray, BreakfastJr, Ginsuloft, Relzap, Badger 1C4C39, Dark Liberty, Smoothintellect, PeterWagsatff4, Dgg1991, Awinedarksea, Progressingamerica, Augustforecast, OnlyInYourMind and Anonymous: 181

- **Technocracy movement** *Source:* https://en.wikipedia.org/wiki/Technocracy_movement?oldid=697602717 *Contributors:* Michael Hardy, CesarB, Ronz, Kragen, Sam Spade, Chris Roy, Nikodemos, Philwelch, Tom harrison, HorsePunchKid, Loremaster, Cjewell, DNewhall, Sam Hocevar, Nickptar, WpZurp, Creidieki, Chris Howard, Rich Farmbrough, Rama, LeeHunter, La goutte de pluie, Holdek, Cnelson, John Quiggin, Kolzene, Wtshymanski, Ilrosewood, Pfahlstrom, Alai, Uncle G, Marudubshinki, Gwil, Deadcorpse, David Levy, Phoenix-forgotten, Andrewmabbott, Tyoda, Ligulem, FayssalF, FlaBot, Ground Zero, AndrewStuckey, Tequendamia, Trfs, YurikBot, Chanlyn, DanMS, Gaius Cornelius, Teb728, Welsh, Epipelagic, Garion96, Suburbanslice, SmackBot, Reedy, McGeddon, Lawrencekhoo, Eaglizard, Provelt, Kintetsubuffalo, Chris the speller, Bluebot, Hibernian, Dustingc, Solidusspriggan, Mike hayes, Battlecry, Wikipedia brown, Stevenmitchell, PiMaster3, Polonium, The 77x42, JzG, Kuru, Tazmaniacs, A. Parrot, O process, NJHeathen, Olav L, Eastlaw, Wolfdog, Wafulz, Cydebot, DumbBOT, Brad101, Bolesjohnb, Biruitorul, Blathnaid, Luxaquitaine, Skomorokh, OhanaUnited, TAnthony, VoABot II, Firebladed, P4k, Betswiki, Ruadh, Isenhand, Rpeh, Johnfos, Αναρχία, Philip Trueman, Evaaan, FlagSteward, Vendrov, DesmondRavenstone, Pjoef, Nopetro, Skipsievert, Technocrate~enwiki, Czuken, Wessmaniac, Maelgwnbot, 77siddhartha, Tradereddy, Gfoxcook, Wwheaton, Mild Bill Hiccup, Tanketz, Ottre, SchreiberBike, Technocracte, NebulaeMonkey, Certes, DumZiBoT, Paulginz, Addbot, Riyuky, Lightbot, Yobot, Fraggle81, BeaufortField, AnomieBOT, Citation bot, Carturo222, Jean-Jacques Georges, Neil Clancy, Prezbo, Lonaowna, Jonkerz, Lotje, ConsciousRobot, Jiffles1, Wingman417, Chuck Entz, ClueBot NG, FidelDrumbo, Biophily, MerlIwBot, Humpherykynaston, Davidiad, Googlesalot2, Newuser2011, Earl King Jr., YiFeiBot, Roshu Bangal, Spiderjerky, Dash9Z and Anonymous: 140

- **The Natural Economic Order** *Source:* https://en.wikipedia.org/wiki/The_Natural_Economic_Order?oldid=649645553 *Contributors:* Yann, Samw, Mateo SA, Cretog8, John Vandenberg, Darrelljon, LukeSurl, Raymm, JIP, Koavf, Ricardo Carneiro Pires, Jenblower, Tony1, SmackBot, Bluebot, Robofish, Davydog, Cydebot, MarshBot, Silver2195, Plasticup, Prius 2, WereSpielChequers, Addbot, Download, AnomieBOT, Omnipaedista, INeverCry, BattyBot and Anonymous: 11

- **The Other Canon Foundation** *Source:* https://en.wikipedia.org/wiki/The_Other_Canon_Foundation?oldid=545752338 *Contributors:* William Avery, Tabletop, Mandarax, Rjwilmsi, KConWiki, Funandtrvl, SieBot, Dthomsen8, Addbot, LaaknorBot, Yobot, LilHelpa, Ladril, Louperibot, Joakimm, John of Reading, HJCfan, Panterdjuret and Anonymous: 4

- **Thermoeconomics** *Source:* https://en.wikipedia.org/wiki/Thermoeconomics?oldid=694591216 *Contributors:* The Anome, Bkalafut, Aetheling, Giftlite, Beland, Mdd, John Quiggin, Bobrayner, Woohookitty, Jeff3000, GregorB, Solace098, Rjwilmsi, WriterHound, RussBot, Grafen, Epipelagic, SmackBot, Elonka, Lawrencekhoo, Gnuwro, Gunnar.Kaestle, Cybercobra, Sadi Carnot, Sgutkind, ChazYork, Mr3641, CR-Greathouse, Neelix, Cydebot, Harryzilber, Rich257, The Anomebot2, David Eppstein, Profitip, R'n'B, Airguitarist 22, DASonnenfeld, Johnfos, Julia Neumann, Steven J. Anderson, Rtol, Bigdaddy1981, Skipsievert, Maelgwnbot, Rinconsoleao, ImperfectlyInformed, Wwheaton, Daniel.t.schmitt, Addbot, Protonk, Jarble, Carleas, AnomieBOT, Materialscientist, Citation bot, J04n, FrescoBot, LucienBOT, Citation bot 1, Madliner, Trappist the monk, Artoannila, Jpeichel, ZéroBot, Javorie, Financestudent, Ledjazz, BG19bot, Op47, CitationCleanerBot, FeralOink, Hmainsbot1, Monkbot, Gaeanautes, Ssmmachen and Anonymous: 16

3.2 Images

- **File:"YOUR_BLOOD_CAN_SAVE_HIM"_-_NARA_-_516245.tif** *Source:* https://upload.wikimedia.org/wikipedia/commons/2/24/%22YOUR_BLOOD_CAN_SAVE_HIM%22_-_NARA_-_516245.tif *License:* Public domain *Contributors:* U.S. National Archives and Records Administration *Original artist:* Unknown<a href='//www.wikidata.org/wiki/Q4233718' title='wikidata:Q4233718'><img alt='wikidata:Q4233718' src='https://upload.wikimedia.org/wikipedia/commons/thumb/f/ff/Wikidata-logo.svg/20px-Wikidata-logo.svg.png' width='20' height='11' srcset='https://upload.wikimedia.org/wikipedia/commons/thumb/f/ff/Wikidata-logo.svg/30px-Wikidata-logo.svg.png 1.5x, https://upload.wikimedia.org/wikipedia/commons/thumb/f/ff/Wikidata-logo.svg/40px-Wikidata-logo.svg.png 2x' data-file-width='1050' data-file-height='590' /></a> or not provided

- **File:1Bawerk.png** *Source:* https://upload.wikimedia.org/wikipedia/commons/b/b3/1Bawerk.png *License:* Public domain *Contributors:* ? *Original artist:* ?

- **File:1wieser.jpg** *Source:* https://upload.wikimedia.org/wikipedia/commons/5/54/1wieser.jpg *License:* Public domain *Contributors:* ? *Original artist:* ?

- **File:2006_AEGold_Proof_Obv.png** *Source:* https://upload.wikimedia.org/wikipedia/commons/7/76/2006_AEGold_Proof_Obv.png *License:* Public domain *Contributors:* United States Mint *Original artist:* United States Mint

- **File:20080105_Fama_Winning_Morgan_Stanley_Prize.JPG** *Source:* https://upload.wikimedia.org/wikipedia/commons/7/7d/20080105_Fama_Winning_Morgan_Stanley_Prize.JPG *License:* CC BY-SA 3.0 *Contributors:* Transferred from en.wikipedia; transferred to Commons by User:Sreejithk2000 using CommonsHelper.
Original artist: TonyTheTiger (t/c/bio/WP:CHICAGO/WP:LOTD) . Original uploader was TonyTheTiger at en.wikipedia

- **File:2011_UN_Human_Development_Report_Quartiles.svg** *Source:* https://upload.wikimedia.org/wikipedia/commons/d/d9/2011_UN_Human_Development_Report_Quartiles.svg *License:* CC BY-SA 3.0 *Contributors:*

- BlankMap-World6,_compact.svg *Original artist:* BlankMap-World6,_compact.svg: Canuckguy et al.

- **File:A.C._Pigou.jpg** *Source:* https://upload.wikimedia.org/wikipedia/commons/0/01/A.C._Pigou.jpg *License:* Public domain *Contributors:* http://www.lancs.ac.uk/staff/ecagrs/gallery.htm *Original artist:* Unknown<a href='//www.wikidata.org/wiki/Q4233718' title='wikidata:Q4233718'><img alt='wikidata:Q4233718' src='https://upload.wikimedia.org/wikipedia/commons/thumb/f/ff/Wikidata-logo.svg/20px-Wikidata-logo.svg.png' width='20' height='11' srcset='https://upload.wikimedia.org/wikipedia/commons/thumb/f/ff/Wikidata-logo.svg/30px-Wikidata-logo.svg.png 1.5x, https://upload.wikimedia.org/wikipedia/commons/thumb/f/ff/Wikidata-logo.svg/40px-Wikidata-logo.svg.png 2x' data-file-width='1050' data-file-height='590' /></a>

- **File:A_coloured_voting_box.svg** *Source:* https://upload.wikimedia.org/wikipedia/en/0/01/A_coloured_voting_box.svg *License:* Cc-by-sa-3.0 *Contributors:* ? *Original artist:* ?

- **File:Abba_Lerner.jpg** *Source:* https://upload.wikimedia.org/wikipedia/commons/b/b7/Abba_Lerner.jpg *License:* Public domain *Contributors:* This file has been **extracted** from another file: Group Photograph including Abba Lerner, 1938.jpg
Original artist: London School of Economics

- **File:Adam,_Eve,_and_Elohim_(Raëlism).png** *Source:* https://upload.wikimedia.org/wikipedia/commons/1/1c/Adam%2C_Eve%2C_and_Elohim_%28Ra%C3%ABlism%29.png *License:* CC-BY-SA-3.0 *Contributors:* Own work *Original artist:* Kmarinas86

- **File:Adamsmithout.jpg** *Source:* https://upload.wikimedia.org/wikipedia/commons/7/7d/Adamsmithout.jpg *License:* CC BY-SA 3.0 *Contributors:* Photograph by Guinnog taken July 2009 *Original artist:* Patric Parc (1811-1855)

- **File:Adolf_Augustus_Berle_NYWTS.jpg** *Source:* https://upload.wikimedia.org/wikipedia/commons/5/5f/Adolf_Augustus_Berle_NYWTS.jpg *License:* Public domain *Contributors:* This image is available from the United States Library of Congress's Prints and Photographs division under the digital ID cph.3c23963.
This tag does not indicate the copyright status of the attached work. A normal copyright tag is still required. See Commons:Licensing for more information.
Original artist: Walter Albertin. New York World-Telegram and the Sun staff photographer

- **File:Aegopodium_podagraria1_ies.jpg** *Source:* https://upload.wikimedia.org/wikipedia/commons/b/bf/Aegopodium_podagraria1_ies.jpg *License:* CC-BY-SA-3.0 *Contributors:* Own work *Original artist:* Frank Vincentz

- **File:Akerlofstiglitz_Page_1.jpg** *Source:* https://upload.wikimedia.org/wikipedia/commons/d/d8/Akerlofstiglitz_Page_1.jpg *License:* CC BY-SA 4.0 *Contributors:* Own work *Original artist:* Byronmercury

- **File:Alexander_del_Mar.jpg** *Source:* https://upload.wikimedia.org/wikipedia/commons/e/e2/Alexander_del_Mar.jpg *License:* Public domain *Contributors:* The Science of Money by Alexander del Mar. http://www.archive.org/details/scienceofmoney00delmrich *Original artist:* Heisenbach

3.2. IMAGES

- **File:Alfred_Marshall.jpg** *Source:* https://upload.wikimedia.org/wikipedia/commons/8/82/Alfred_Marshall.jpg *License:* Public domain *Contributors:* http://www.jstor.org/pss/2222645 *Original artist:* Unknown<a href='//www.wikidata.org/wiki/Q4233718' title='wikidata:Q4233718'><img alt='wikidata:Q4233718' src='https://upload.wikimedia.org/wikipedia/commons/thumb/f/ff/Wikidata-logo.svg/20px-Wikidata-logo.svg.png' width='20' height='11' srcset='https://upload.wikimedia.org/wikipedia/commons/thumb/f/ff/Wikidata-logo.svg/30px-Wikidata-logo.svg.png 1.5x, https://upload.wikimedia.org/wikipedia/commons/thumb/f/ff/Wikidata-logo.svg/40px-Wikidata-logo.svg.png 2x' data-file-width='1050' data-file-height='590' /></a>
- **File:Allah-green.svg** *Source:* https://upload.wikimedia.org/wikipedia/commons/4/4e/Allah-green.svg *License:* Public domain *Contributors:* Converted to SVG from Image:Islam.png, originally from en:Image:Ift32.gif, uploaded to the English Wikipedia by Mr100percent on 4 February 2003. Originally described as "Copied from Public Domain artwork". *Original artist:* ?
- **File:Amartya_Sen_NIH.jpg** *Source:* https://upload.wikimedia.org/wikipedia/commons/e/e0/Amartya_Sen_NIH.jpg *License:* Public domain *Contributors:* http://dir.niehs.nih.gov/ethics/past.htm
Original artist: NIH (according to picture caption)
- **File:Ambox_globe_content.svg** *Source:* https://upload.wikimedia.org/wikipedia/commons/b/bd/Ambox_globe_content.svg *License:* Public domain *Contributors:* Own work, using File:Information icon3.svg and File:Earth clip art.svg *Original artist:* penubag
- **File:Ambox_important.svg** *Source:* https://upload.wikimedia.org/wikipedia/commons/b/b4/Ambox_important.svg *License:* Public domain *Contributors:* Own work, based off of Image:Ambox scales.svg *Original artist:* Dsmurat (talk · contribs)
- **File:Ambox_question.svg** *Source:* https://upload.wikimedia.org/wikipedia/commons/1/1b/Ambox_question.svg *License:* Public domain *Contributors:* Based on Image:Ambox important.svg *Original artist:* Mysid, Dsmurat, penubag
- **File:Anarchist-Communist_Symbol.jpg** *Source:* https://upload.wikimedia.org/wikipedia/commons/e/e2/Anarchist-Communist_Symbol.jpg *License:* GFDL *Contributors:* Own work *Original artist:* Mattsvendsen
- **File:Anarchy-symbol.svg** *Source:* https://upload.wikimedia.org/wikipedia/commons/7/7a/Anarchy-symbol.svg *License:* Public domain *Contributors:* Own work *Original artist:* Linuxerist, Froztbyte, Arcy
- **File:Anne_Robert_Jacques_Turgot.jpg** *Source:* https://upload.wikimedia.org/wikipedia/commons/c/c8/Anne_Robert_Jacques_Turgot.jpg *License:* Public domain *Contributors:* http://bpun.unine.ch/IconoNeuch/Portraits/A-Z/T.htm *Original artist:* After Charles-Nicolas Cochin the Elder
- **File:Anti-capitalism_color.jpg** *Source:* https://upload.wikimedia.org/wikipedia/commons/a/a7/Anti-capitalism_color.jpg *License:* Public domain *Contributors:* [1] *Original artist:* IWW
- **File:Barthélemy_de_Laffemas.jpg** *Source:* https://upload.wikimedia.org/wikipedia/commons/c/ca/Barth%C3%A9lemy_de_Laffemas.jpg *License:* Public domain *Contributors:* Portrait published in "Remonstrances politiques sur l'abus des charlatans, pipeurs et enchanteurs" [1] *Original artist:* Unknown<a href='//www.wikidata.org/wiki/Q4233718' title='wikidata:Q4233718'><img alt='wikidata:Q4233718' src='https://upload.wikimedia.org/wikipedia/commons/thumb/f/ff/Wikidata-logo.svg/20px-Wikidata-logo.svg.png' width='20' height='11' srcset='https://upload.wikimedia.org/wikipedia/commons/thumb/f/ff/Wikidata-logo.svg/30px-Wikidata-logo.svg.png 1.5x, https://upload.wikimedia.org/wikipedia/commons/thumb/f/ff/Wikidata-logo.svg/40px-Wikidata-logo.svg.png 2x' data-file-width='1050' data-file-height='590' /></a>
- **File:Beatrice_Webb,_c1875.jpg** *Source:* https://upload.wikimedia.org/wikipedia/commons/9/9c/Beatrice_Webb%2C_c1875.jpg *License:* No restrictions *Contributors:* Beatrice Webb, c1875 *Original artist:* Library of the London School of Economics and Political Science
- **File:Bertil_Ohlin.jpg** *Source:* https://upload.wikimedia.org/wikipedia/commons/3/34/Bertil_Ohlin.jpg *License:* Public domain *Contributors:* [1] *Original artist:* Unknown<a href='//www.wikidata.org/wiki/Q4233718' title='wikidata:Q4233718'><img alt='wikidata:Q4233718' src='https://upload.wikimedia.org/wikipedia/commons/thumb/f/ff/Wikidata-logo.svg/20px-Wikidata-logo.svg.png' width='20' height='11' srcset='https://upload.wikimedia.org/wikipedia/commons/thumb/f/ff/Wikidata-logo.svg/30px-Wikidata-logo.svg.png 1.5x, https://upload.wikimedia.org/wikipedia/commons/thumb/f/ff/Wikidata-logo.svg/40px-Wikidata-logo.svg.png 2x' data-file-width='1050' data-file-height='590' /></a>
- **File:BlackFlagSymbol.svg** *Source:* https://upload.wikimedia.org/wikipedia/commons/9/95/BlackFlagSymbol.svg *License:* CC BY 3.0 *Contributors:* Transferred from en.wikipedia to Commons. *Original artist:* The original uploader was Jsymmetry at English Wikipedia
- **File:Boisguilbert.gif** *Source:* https://upload.wikimedia.org/wikipedia/commons/d/da/Boisguilbert.gif *License:* Public domain *Contributors:* de.wikipedia; description page is/was here *Original artist:* Original uploader was Olaf2 at de.wikipedia
- **File:Book_Hexagonal_Icon.svg** *Source:* https://upload.wikimedia.org/wikipedia/commons/e/ed/Book_Hexagonal_Icon.svg *License:* CC-BY-SA-3.0 *Contributors:* ? *Original artist:* ?
- **File:Books-aj.svg_aj_ashton_01.svg** *Source:* https://upload.wikimedia.org/wikipedia/commons/4/4b/Books-aj.svg_aj_ashton_01.svg *License:* CC0 *Contributors:* https://openclipart.org/detail/105859/booksajsvg-aj-ashton-01 *Original artist:* AJ on openclipart.org
- **File:BuchananTullock.jpg** *Source:* https://upload.wikimedia.org/wikipedia/commons/7/78/BuchananTullock.jpg *License:* CC BY-SA 4.0 *Contributors:* Own work *Original artist:* Byronmercury
- **File:Burning_Man_aerial.jpg** *Source:* https://upload.wikimedia.org/wikipedia/commons/b/bd/Burning_Man_aerial.jpg *License:* CC BY 2.0 *Contributors:* Burning Man *Original artist:* Kyle Harmon from Oakland, CA, USA
- **File:CDS_volume_outstanding.png** *Source:* https://upload.wikimedia.org/wikipedia/commons/9/93/CDS_volume_outstanding.png *License:* CC BY-SA 3.0 *Contributors:* Own work *Original artist:* MartinD
- **File:C_H_Douglas.jpg** *Source:* https://upload.wikimedia.org/wikipedia/commons/c/c6/C_H_Douglas.jpg *License:* Public domain *Contributors:* Glenbow Archives, ND-3-6683 (cropped) *Original artist:* Unknown<a href='//www.wikidata.org/wiki/Q4233718' title='wikidata:Q4233718'><img alt='wikidata:Q4233718' src='https://upload.wikimedia.org/wikipedia/commons/thumb/f/ff/Wikidata-logo.svg/20px-Wikidata-logo.svg.png' width='20' height='11' srcset='https://upload.wikimedia.org/wikipedia/commons/thumb/f/ff/Wikidata-logo.svg/30px-Wikidata-logo.svg.png 1.5x, https://upload.wikimedia.org/wikipedia/commons/thumb/f/ff/Wikidata-logo.svg/40px-Wikidata-logo.svg.png 2x' data-file-width='1050' data-file-height='590' /></a>

- **File:CarlMenger.png** *Source:* https://upload.wikimedia.org/wikipedia/commons/9/98/CarlMenger.png *License:* Public domain *Contributors:* http://mises.org/images4/CarlMenger.png *Original artist:* mises.org
- **File:Carl_Spitzweg_021-detail.jpg** *Source:* https://upload.wikimedia.org/wikipedia/commons/8/81/Carl_Spitzweg_021-detail.jpg *License:* Public domain *Contributors:* Diese Datei: File:Carl Spitzweg 021.jpg
  Original artist: Carl Spitzweg
- **File:Carson_Fall_Mt_Kinabalu.jpg** *Source:* https://upload.wikimedia.org/wikipedia/commons/5/57/Carson_Fall_Mt_Kinabalu.jpg *License:* CC BY-SA 3.0 *Contributors:* Own work *Original artist:* Sze Sze SOO
- **File:Chongqing_yangjiaping_2007.jpg** *Source:* https://upload.wikimedia.org/wikipedia/commons/7/7a/Chongqing_yangjiaping_2007.jpg *License:* CC BY-SA 2.5 *Contributors:* http://zola.fotolog.com.cn/1671942.html *Original artist:* zola aka. Zhou Shuguang (???)
- **File:Clive_Granger_by_Olaf_Storbeck.jpg** *Source:* https://upload.wikimedia.org/wikipedia/commons/8/8a/Clive_Granger_by_Olaf_Storbeck.jpg *License:* CC BY-SA 2.0 *Contributors:* http://www.flickr.com/photos/redfalo/2800913330/ *Original artist:* redfalo (Olaf)
- **File:Clément_Juglar.gif** *Source:* https://upload.wikimedia.org/wikipedia/commons/0/0b/Cl%C3%A9ment_Juglar.gif *License:* Public domain *Contributors:* http://cepa.newschool.edu/het/profiles/juglar.htm *Original artist:* Unknown<a href='//www.wikidata.org/wiki/Q4233718' title='wikidata:Q4233718'><img alt='wikidata:Q4233718' src='https://upload.wikimedia.org/wikipedia/commons/thumb/f/ff/Wikidata-logo.svg/20px-Wikidata-logo.svg.png' width='20' height='11' srcset='https://upload.wikimedia.org/wikipedia/commons/thumb/f/ff/Wikidata-logo.svg/30px-Wikidata-logo.svg.png 1.5x, https://upload.wikimedia.org/wikipedia/commons/thumb/f/ff/Wikidata-logo.svg/40px-Wikidata-logo.svg.png 2x' data-file-width='1050' data-file-height='590' /></a>
- **File:Co-op_activism5.svg** *Source:* https://upload.wikimedia.org/wikipedia/commons/f/f4/Co-op_activism5.svg *License:* CC BY-SA 3.0 *Contributors:*
- Co-op_activism4.svg *Original artist:* Co-op_activism4.svg: *Co-op_activism3.svg: *Syndicalism.svg: Vladsinger
- **File:Colbert_mg_8447_cropped.jpg** *Source:* https://upload.wikimedia.org/wikipedia/commons/4/49/Colbert_mg_8447_cropped.jpg *License:* Public domain *Contributors:*
- Colbert_mg_8447.jpg *Original artist:* Colbert_mg_8447.jpg: Rama
- **File:Commons-logo.svg** *Source:* https://upload.wikimedia.org/wikipedia/en/4/4a/Commons-logo.svg *License:* CC-BY-SA-3.0 *Contributors:* ? *Original artist:* ?
- **File:Complex-adaptive-system.jpg** *Source:* https://upload.wikimedia.org/wikipedia/commons/0/00/Complex-adaptive-system.jpg *License:* Public domain *Contributors:* Own work by Acadac : Taken from en.wikipedia.org, where Acadac was inspired to create this graphic after reading: *Original artist:* Acadac
- **File:Components_of_the_United_States_money_supply2.svg** *Source:* https://upload.wikimedia.org/wikipedia/commons/9/95/Components_of_the_United_States_money_supply2.svg *License:* Public domain *Contributors:* See table below for source data. Edited version of Image:Components_of_the_United_States_money_supply.svg wikipedia commons so that it now includes "currency". *Original artist:* User:El T (talk), Analoguni (talk), User:Jklamo (talk)
- **File:David_Hume.jpg** *Source:* https://upload.wikimedia.org/wikipedia/commons/2/21/David_Hume.jpg *License:* Public domain *Contributors:* Web Gallery of Art *Original artist:* Allan Ramsay
- **File:Day_8_Occupy_Wall_Street_September_24_2011_Shankbone_19.JPG** *Source:* https://upload.wikimedia.org/wikipedia/commons/8/80/Day_8_Occupy_Wall_Street_September_24_2011_Shankbone_19.JPG *License:* CC BY 3.0 *Contributors:* Own work *Original artist:* David Shankbone
- **File:Debreu,_Gérard_(1921-2004).jpeg** *Source:* https://upload.wikimedia.org/wikipedia/commons/2/2d/Debreu%2C_G%C3%A9rard_%281921-2004%29.jpeg *License:* CC BY-SA 2.0 de *Contributors:* Mathematisches Institut Oberwolfach (MFO), http://owpdb.mfo.de/detail?photoID=800 *Original artist:* Konrad Jacobs, Erlangen, Copyright is with MFO
- **File:Demsetzatgmu.jpg** *Source:* https://upload.wikimedia.org/wikipedia/commons/3/3a/Demsetzatgmu.jpg *License:* CC BY-SA 3.0 *Contributors:* Own work *Original artist:* Kat Walsh
- **File:Diagram_of_natural_resource_flows.jpg** *Source:* https://upload.wikimedia.org/wikipedia/en/6/6e/Diagram_of_natural_resource_flows.jpg *License:* CC0 *Contributors:*
  Own work by Gaeanautes.
  Original artist:
  User:Gaeanautes
- **File:Dudley_North.jpg** *Source:* https://upload.wikimedia.org/wikipedia/commons/1/13/Dudley_North.jpg *License:* Public domain *Contributors:* Painting of Dudley North, before 1691. *Original artist:* Unknown<a href='//www.wikidata.org/wiki/Q4233718' title='wikidata:Q4233718'><img alt='wikidata:Q4233718' src='https://upload.wikimedia.org/wikipedia/commons/thumb/f/ff/Wikidata-logo.svg/20px-Wikidata-logo.svg.png' width='20' height='11' srcset='https://upload.wikimedia.org/wikipedia/commons/thumb/f/ff/Wikidata-logo.svg/30px-Wikidata-logo.svg.png 1.5x, https://upload.wikimedia.org/wikipedia/commons/thumb/f/ff/Wikidata-logo.svg/40px-Wikidata-logo.svg.png 2x' data-file-width='1050' data-file-height='590' /></a>
- **File:Earth_Day_Flag.png** *Source:* https://upload.wikimedia.org/wikipedia/commons/6/6a/Earth_Day_Flag.png *License:* Public domain *Contributors:* File:Earth flag PD.jpg, File:The Earth seen from Apollo 17 with transparent background.png *Original artist:* NASA (Earth photograph) SiBr4 (flag image)
- **File:Economic_cycle.svg** *Source:* https://upload.wikimedia.org/wikipedia/commons/f/fb/Economic_cycle.svg *License:* Public domain *Contributors:* File:Konjunkturverlauf.svg *Original artist:* User:Bernard Ladenthin
- **File:Edgeworth.jpeg** *Source:* https://upload.wikimedia.org/wikipedia/commons/b/b1/Edgeworth.jpeg *License:* Public domain *Contributors:* ? *Original artist:* ?

3.2. IMAGES

- **File:Edit-clear.svg** *Source:* https://upload.wikimedia.org/wikipedia/en/f/f2/Edit-clear.svg *License:* Public domain *Contributors:* The *Tango! Desktop Project. Original artist:*

  The people from the Tango! project. And according to the meta-data in the file, specifically: "Andreas Nilsson, and Jakub Steiner (although minimally)."

- **File:Edmund_Burke2_c.jpg** *Source:* https://upload.wikimedia.org/wikipedia/commons/1/14/Edmund_Burke2_c.jpg *License:* Public domain *Contributors:* ? *Original artist:* ?

- **File:EffectOfTariff.svg** *Source:* https://upload.wikimedia.org/wikipedia/commons/4/4d/EffectOfTariff.svg *License:* CC BY 3.0 *Contributors:* Own work *Original artist:* Austin512

- **File:Eli_Heckscher.jpg** *Source:* https://upload.wikimedia.org/wikipedia/commons/3/32/Eli_Heckscher.jpg *License:* Public domain *Contributors:* Own work *Original artist:* user:Slarre

- **File:Ely-Richard-T.jpg** *Source:* https://upload.wikimedia.org/wikipedia/commons/5/59/Ely-Richard-T.jpg *License:* Public domain *Contributors:* Published in The Comrade (New York), v. 2, no. 7 (April 1903), pg. 164. *Original artist:* Published in the United States prior to 1923, public domain.

- **File:Emblem-money.svg** *Source:* https://upload.wikimedia.org/wikipedia/commons/f/f3/Emblem-money.svg *License:* GPL *Contributors:* http://www.gnome-look.org/content/show.php/GNOME-colors?content=82562 *Original artist:* perfectska04

- **File:Engels_1856.jpg** *Source:* https://upload.wikimedia.org/wikipedia/commons/7/7b/Engels_1856.jpg *License:* Public domain *Contributors:* http://en.wikipedia.org/wiki/Image:Engelss56fe1.jpg, uploaded 2006-01-16 by w:User:Bronks *Original artist:* George Lester, Manchester photographer

- **File:Euro_money_supply_Sept_1998_-_Oct_2007.jpg** *Source:* https://upload.wikimedia.org/wikipedia/commons/d/d0/Euro_money_supply_Sept_1998_-_Oct_2007.jpg *License:* Public domain *Contributors:* Self-made by Analoguni. Created with openoffice.org calc using data from the European Central Bank. The M1-M3 statistics were found in the "Historical monetary statistics" file on this page: http://www.ecb.int/stats/services/downloads/html/index.en.html The actual file location is: https://stats.ecb.europa.eu/stats/download/bsi_ma_historical/bsi_ma_historical.zip The amount of currency in circulation was found on the same page but in the "statistics pocket book" link at the right side of the page. The "statistics pocket book" file link is here: http://www.ecb.int/stats/pdf/spb_full.zip The "currency in circulation" data is in the spb027.csv file. Transferred from en.wikipedia *Original artist:* Analoguni (talk) at en.wikipedia

- **File:Folder_Hexagonal_Icon.svg** *Source:* https://upload.wikimedia.org/wikipedia/en/4/48/Folder_Hexagonal_Icon.svg *License:* Cc-by-sa-3.0 *Contributors:* ? *Original artist:* ?

- **File:Fractional-reserve-banking_base100_0.8reserve_rate.svg** *Source:* https://upload.wikimedia.org/wikipedia/commons/7/70/Fractional-reserve-banking_base100_0.8reserve_rate.svg *License:* CC BY-SA 3.0 *Contributors:* Own work *Original artist:* Erik Streb

- **File:Fractional_reserve_banking_with_varying_reserve_requirements.gif** *Source:* https://upload.wikimedia.org/wikipedia/commons/0/01/Fractional-reserve_banking_with_varying_reserve_requirements.gif *License:* Public domain *Contributors:* Own work *Original artist:* Analoguni

- **File:Francis_Hutcheson_b1694.jpg** *Source:* https://upload.wikimedia.org/wikipedia/commons/1/16/Francis_Hutcheson_b1694.jpg *License:* Public domain *Contributors:* Hunterian Museum and Art Gallery *Original artist:* Allan Ramsay

- **File:François_Quesnay.jpg** *Source:* https://upload.wikimedia.org/wikipedia/commons/6/60/Fran%C3%A7ois_Quesnay.jpg *License:* Public domain *Contributors:*

- François_Quesnay_02.jpg *Original artist:* François_Quesnay_02.jpg: Jean-Charles François et Jean-Martial Frédou

- **File:Fred_M._Taylor.png** *Source:* https://upload.wikimedia.org/wikipedia/en/9/93/Fred_M._Taylor.png *License:* PD-US *Contributors:*

  1902 Michiganensian, page 15

  Original artist:

  photographer unknown

- **File:Friedrich_Hayek_portrait.jpg** *Source:* https://upload.wikimedia.org/wikipedia/commons/7/7f/Friedrich_Hayek_portrait.jpg *License:* CC BY-SA 3.0 *Contributors:* Transferred from en.wikipedia to Commons by JohnDoe0007 using CommonsHelper. *Original artist:* The original uploader was DickClarkMises at English Wikipedia

- **File:G.W.F._Hegel_(by_Sichling,_after_Sebbers).jpg** *Source:* https://upload.wikimedia.org/wikipedia/commons/b/b6/G.W.F._Hegel_%28by_Sichling%2C_after_Sebbers%29.jpg *License:* Public domain *Contributors:* http://www.hegel.net/en/gwh3.htm *Original artist:* Julius Ludwig Sebbers

- **File:GaryBecker-May24-2008.jpg** *Source:* https://upload.wikimedia.org/wikipedia/commons/3/3f/GaryBecker-May24-2008.jpg *License:* Public domain *Contributors:* Transferred from en.wikipedia; transferred to Commons by User:Homonihilis using CommonsHelper. *Original artist:* MAR Original uploader was Mike80 at en.wikipedia

- **File:Geniocracy.gif** *Source:* https://upload.wikimedia.org/wikipedia/en/2/29/Geniocracy.gif *License:* Fair use *Contributors:*

  scan of book cover

  Original artist: ?

- **File:Gentile_da_Fabriano_052.jpg** *Source:* https://upload.wikimedia.org/wikipedia/commons/c/cd/Gentile_da_Fabriano_052.jpg *License:* Public domain *Contributors:* The Yorck Project: *10.000 Meisterwerke der Malerei.* DVD-ROM, 2002. ISBN 3936122202. Distributed by DIRECTMEDIA Publishing GmbH. *Original artist:* Gentile da Fabriano

- **File:George_Bernard_Shaw_1936.jpg** *Source:* https://upload.wikimedia.org/wikipedia/commons/f/f2/George_Bernard_Shaw_1936.jpg *License:* Public domain *Contributors:* [1] *Original artist:* Unknown<a href='//www.wikidata.org/wiki/Q4233718' title='wikidata:Q4233718'><img alt='wikidata:Q4233718' src='https://upload.wikimedia.org/wikipedia/commons/thumb/f/ff/Wikidata-logo.svg/20px-Wikidata-logo.svg.png' width='20' height='11' srcset='https://upload.wikimedia.org/wikipedia/commons/thumb/f/ff/Wikidata-logo.svg/30px-Wikidata-logo.svg.png 1.5x, https://upload.wikimedia.org/wikipedia/commons/thumb/f/ff/Wikidata-logo.svg/40px-Wikidata-logo.svg.png 2x' data-file-width='1050' data-file-height='590' /></a>
- **File:Give_away_shop_utrecht_inside.jpg** *Source:* https://upload.wikimedia.org/wikipedia/commons/6/6d/Give_away_shop_utrecht_inside.jpg *License:* CC BY-SA 3.0 *Contributors:* http://wiki.gifteconomy.org/File:Ga_utrecht_inside.jpg *Original artist:* admin
- **File:Gnome-searchtool.svg** *Source:* https://upload.wikimedia.org/wikipedia/commons/1/1e/Gnome-searchtool.svg *License:* LGPL *Contributors:* http://ftp.gnome.org/pub/GNOME/sources/gnome-themes-extras/0.9/gnome-themes-extras-0.9.0.tar.gz *Original artist:* David Vignoni
- **File:Gray739.png** *Source:* https://upload.wikimedia.org/wikipedia/commons/9/96/Gray739.png *License:* Public domain *Contributors:* Henry Gray (1918) *Anatomy of the Human Body* (See "Book" section below) *Original artist:* Henry Vandyke Carter
- **File:Gunnar_Myrdal_-_Sveriges_styresmän.jpg** *Source:* https://upload.wikimedia.org/wikipedia/commons/e/e9/Gunnar_Myrdal_-_Sveriges_styresm%C3%A4n.jpg *License:* Public domain *Contributors:* Encyclopedia "Sveriges styresmän 1937" *Original artist:* Unknown<a href='//www.wikidata.org/wiki/Q4233718' title='wikidata:Q4233718'><img alt='wikidata:Q4233718' src='https://upload.wikimedia.org/wikipedia/commons/thumb/f/ff/Wikidata-logo.svg/20px-Wikidata-logo.svg.png' width='20' height='11' srcset='https://upload.wikimedia.org/wikipedia/commons/thumb/f/ff/Wikidata-logo.svg/30px-Wikidata-logo.svg.png 1.5x, https://upload.wikimedia.org/wikipedia/commons/thumb/f/ff/Wikidata-logo.svg/40px-Wikidata-logo.svg.png 2x' data-file-width='1050' data-file-height='590' /></a>
- **File:Hans_Holbein,_the_Younger_-_Sir_Thomas_More_-_Google_Art_Project.jpg** *Source:* https://upload.wikimedia.org/wikipedia/commons/d/d2/Hans_Holbein%2C_the_Younger_-_Sir_Thomas_More_-_Google_Art_Project.jpg *License:* Public domain *Contributors:* WQEnBYMfBeoSdg at Google Cultural Institute, zoom level maximum *Original artist:* Hans Holbein the Younger (1497/1498–1543)
- **File:Henry_George2.jpg** *Source:* https://upload.wikimedia.org/wikipedia/commons/8/8c/Henry_George2.jpg *License:* Public domain *Contributors:* http://www.unitax.org/ *Original artist:* Unknown<a href='//www.wikidata.org/wiki/Q4233718' title='wikidata:Q4233718'><img alt='wikidata:Q4233718' src='https://upload.wikimedia.org/wikipedia/commons/thumb/f/ff/Wikidata-logo.svg/20px-Wikidata-logo.svg.png' width='20' height='11' srcset='https://upload.wikimedia.org/wikipedia/commons/thumb/f/ff/Wikidata-logo.svg/30px-Wikidata-logo.svg.png 1.5x, https://upload.wikimedia.org/wikipedia/commons/thumb/f/ff/Wikidata-logo.svg/40px-Wikidata-logo.svg.png 2x' data-file-width='1050' data-file-height='590' /></a>
- **File:Henry_George_School_of_Social_Science_121_E30_jeh.jpg** *Source:* https://upload.wikimedia.org/wikipedia/commons/3/35/Henry_George_School_of_Social_Science_121_E30_jeh.jpg *License:* CC BY-SA 3.0 *Contributors:* Own work *Original artist:* Jim.henderson
- **File:Heterodox3.png** *Source:* https://upload.wikimedia.org/wikipedia/commons/8/8a/Heterodox3.png *License:* CC0 *Contributors:* Social Democracy for the 21st Century *Original artist:* Lord Keynes
- **File:Hw-fourier.jpg** *Source:* https://upload.wikimedia.org/wikipedia/commons/e/e3/Hw-fourier.jpg *License:* Public domain *Contributors:* H.F. Helmolt (ed.): History of the World. New York, 1901. University of Texas Portrait Gallery. *Original artist:* H.F. Helmolt
- **File:Ibn_Khaldoun-Kassus.jpg** *Source:* https://upload.wikimedia.org/wikipedia/commons/b/b2/Ibn_Khaldoun-Kassus.jpg *License:* CC BY 2.5 *Contributors:* Own work *Original artist:* Kassus
- **File:Israel_Kirzner.jpg** *Source:* https://upload.wikimedia.org/wikipedia/commons/d/d4/Israel_Kirzner.jpg *License:* CC-BY-SA-3.0 *Contributors:* Mises Institute, through English Wikipedia *Original artist:* Mises Institute
- **File:Jacob_Mincer.jpg** *Source:* https://upload.wikimedia.org/wikipedia/en/5/5b/Jacob_Mincer.jpg *License:* Cc-by-sa-3.0 *Contributors:* ? *Original artist:* ?
- **File:James_Meade_Nobel.jpg** *Source:* https://upload.wikimedia.org/wikipedia/commons/1/1b/James_Meade_Nobel.jpg *License:* Public domain *Contributors:* Flickr Rights Statement
Original artist: LSE Library
- **File:Jan_Tinbergen_1982.jpg** *Source:* https://upload.wikimedia.org/wikipedia/commons/9/97/Jan_Tinbergen_1982.jpg *License:* CC BY-SA 3.0 nl *Contributors:* Nationaal Archief Fotocollectie Anefo; Nummer toegang 2.24.01.05; Bestanddeelnummer 932-3849 *Original artist:* Anefo / Croes, R.C.
- **File:Jean-Baptiste_Say.gif** *Source:* https://upload.wikimedia.org/wikipedia/commons/1/1f/Jean-Baptiste_Say.gif *License:* Public domain *Contributors:* Retrieved from: Larry J. Sechrest, *Biography of Jean-Baptiste Say: Neglected Champion of Laissez-Faire*.Ludwig von Mises Institut, mises.org *Original artist:* ?
- **File:Jean-baptiste_Say.jpg** *Source:* https://upload.wikimedia.org/wikipedia/commons/2/2e/Jean-baptiste_Say.jpg *License:* Public domain *Contributors:* ? *Original artist:* ?
- **File:Jean_Bodin.jpg** *Source:* https://upload.wikimedia.org/wikipedia/commons/e/e5/Jean_Bodin.jpg *License:* Public domain *Contributors:* http://www.saberweb.com.br/datas_comemorativas/images/papai%20noel01.jpg *Original artist:* ?
- **File:Jeremy_Bentham_by_Henry_William_Pickersgill_detail.jpg** *Source:* https://upload.wikimedia.org/wikipedia/commons/c/c8/Jeremy_Bentham_by_Henry_William_Pickersgill_detail.jpg *License:* Public domain *Contributors:* National Portrait Gallery: NPG 413 *Original artist:* Henry William Pickersgill (died 1875)
- **File:Joan_Robinson_(1973).jpg** *Source:* https://upload.wikimedia.org/wikipedia/commons/b/bc/Joan_Robinson_%281973%29.jpg *License:* CC BY-SA 3.0 *Contributors:* Derived from Nationaal Archief *Original artist:* (…) Punt / Anefo
- **File:Joan_Robinson_Ramsey_Muspratt.jpg** *Source:* https://upload.wikimedia.org/wikipedia/commons/6/64/Joan_Robinson_Ramsey_Muspratt.jpg *License:* Public domain *Contributors:* National Portrait Gallery: NPG x31084 *Original artist:* Ramsey & Muspratt

3.2. IMAGES

- **File:John-stuart-mill-sized.jpg** *Source:* https://upload.wikimedia.org/wikipedia/en/9/9b/John-stuart-mill-sized.jpg *License:* PD *Contributors:*
Scanned by Infrogmation from copyright expired US book, 1890s volume "The World's Great Classics" and uploaded by him to en:Wikipedia on the 12:36, 13 November 2002 as Image:JohnStuartMill.JPG, which has since been overwritten with another version of the image. *Original artist:* ?

- **File:JohnCommons.jpg** *Source:* https://upload.wikimedia.org/wikipedia/commons/2/2f/JohnCommons.jpg *License:* Public domain *Contributors:* http://www.ssa.gov/history/bioaja.html *Original artist:* Photo Courtesy of the Department of Labor

- **File:JohnKennethGalbraithOWI.jpg** *Source:* https://upload.wikimedia.org/wikipedia/commons/b/b2/JohnKennethGalbraithOWI.jpg *License:* Public domain *Contributors:* Library of Congress (Call number LC-USE6-D-000368) *Original artist:* Royden Dixon for the United States Office of War Information

- **File:JohnLocke.png** *Source:* https://upload.wikimedia.org/wikipedia/commons/d/d1/JohnLocke.png *License:* Public domain *Contributors:* State Hermitage Museum, St. Petersburg, Russia. *Original artist:* Sir Godfrey Kneller

- **File:John_Bates_Clark.jpg** *Source:* https://upload.wikimedia.org/wikipedia/commons/2/2d/John_Bates_Clark.jpg *License:* Public domain *Contributors:* Gunton's Magazine, Vol. 19, 1900: http://archive.org/stream/guntonsmagazine19guntuoft#page/n203/mode/2up *Original artist:* Unknown<a href='//www.wikidata.org/wiki/Q4233718' title='wikidata:Q4233718'><img alt='wikidata:Q4233718' src='https://upload.wikimedia.org/wikipedia/commons/thumb/f/ff/Wikidata-logo.svg/20px-Wikidata-logo.svg.png' width='20' height='11' srcset='https://upload.wikimedia.org/wikipedia/commons/thumb/f/ff/Wikidata-logo.svg/30px-Wikidata-logo.svg.png 1.5x, https://upload.wikimedia.org/wikipedia/commons/thumb/f/ff/Wikidata-logo.svg/40px-Wikidata-logo.svg.png 2x' data-file-width='1050' data-file-height='590' /></a>

- **File:John_Duns_Scotus_-_geograph.org.uk_-_1178460.jpg** *Source:* https://upload.wikimedia.org/wikipedia/commons/7/73/John_Duns_Scotus_-_geograph.org.uk_-_1178460.jpg *License:* CC BY-SA 2.0 *Contributors:* From geograph.org.uk *Original artist:* james denham

- **File:John_Forbes_Nash,_Jr._by_Peter_Badge.jpg** *Source:* https://upload.wikimedia.org/wikipedia/commons/a/a9/John_Forbes_Nash%2C_Jr._by_Peter_Badge.jpg *License:* CC BY-SA 3.0 *Contributors:* OTRS submission by way of Jimmy Wales *Original artist:* Peter Badge / Typos1

- **File:JohnvonNeumann-LosAlamos.gif** *Source:* https://upload.wikimedia.org/wikipedia/commons/5/5e/JohnvonNeumann-LosAlamos.gif *License:* Public domain *Contributors:* http://www.lanl.gov/history/atomicbomb/images/NeumannL.GIF (Archive copy at the Wayback Machine (archived on 11 March 2010)) *Original artist:* LANL

- **File:Joseph_Schumpeter_ekonomialaria.jpg** *Source:* https://upload.wikimedia.org/wikipedia/commons/5/5f/Joseph_Schumpeter_ekonomialaria.jpg *License:* CC BY-SA 3.0 *Contributors:* http://commons.wikimedia.org/wiki/File:Mises,hayek,shumpe.jpg *Original artist:* Image available for free publishing from the Volkswirtschaftliches Institut, Universität Freiburg, Freiburg im Breisgau, Germany. Copyrighted free use.

- **File:Karl_Marx_001.jpg** *Source:* https://upload.wikimedia.org/wikipedia/commons/d/d4/Karl_Marx_001.jpg *License:* Public domain *Contributors:* International Institute of Social History in Amsterdam, Netherlands *Original artist:* John Jabez Edwin Mayall

- **File:Kenneth_Arrow,_Stanford_University.jpg** *Source:* https://upload.wikimedia.org/wikipedia/commons/9/9d/Kenneth_Arrow%2C_Stanford_University.jpg *License:* CC BY 3.0 *Contributors:* Stanford News Service *Original artist:* Linda A. Cicero / Stanford News Service

- **File:Klallam_people_at_Port_Townsend.jpg** *Source:* https://upload.wikimedia.org/wikipedia/commons/2/26/Klallam_people_at_Port_Townsend.jpg *License:* Public domain *Contributors:* Duke of York House, Jenny Lind at beinecke.library.yale.edu *Original artist:* James Gilchrist Swan (1818-1900)

- **File:Kondratieff_Wave.svg** *Source:* https://upload.wikimedia.org/wikipedia/commons/c/c4/Kondratieff_Wave.svg *License:* CC BY-SA 3.0 *Contributors:* Own work *Original artist:* Rursus

- **File:Kondratiev-waves_IT_and_Health_with_phase_shift_acc_to_Goldschmidt-AJW_2004.jpg** *Source:* https://upload.wikimedia.org/wikipedia/commons/e/e4/Kondratiev-waves_IT_and_Health_with_phase_shift_acc_to_Goldschmidt-AJW_2004.jpg *License:* CC BY-SA 3.0 *Contributors:* Own work *Original artist:* JohanSonn

- **File:Kula_bracelet.jpg** *Source:* https://upload.wikimedia.org/wikipedia/commons/7/75/Kula_bracelet.jpg *License:* CC BY-SA 3.0 *Contributors:* Own work *Original artist:* Brocken Inaglory

- **File:La_conquête_du_pain.jpg** *Source:* https://upload.wikimedia.org/wikipedia/commons/3/36/La_conqu%C3%AAte_du_pain.jpg *License:* Public domain *Contributors:* Own work *Original artist:* Koroesu

- **File:Leonardus_Lessius_(1554-1623).jpg** *Source:* https://upload.wikimedia.org/wikipedia/commons/1/1b/Leonardus_Lessius_%281554-1623%29.jpg *License:* Public domain *Contributors:* du livre de A.Hamy: *Galerie illustrée de la Compagnie de Jésus*, 1893. *Original artist:* Grentidez

- **File:Leonid_Hurwicz.jpg** *Source:* https://upload.wikimedia.org/wikipedia/commons/a/a0/Leonid_Hurwicz.jpg *License:* CC BY 3.0 *Contributors:* University of Minnesota, http://www.econ.umn.edu/hurwicz/ *Original artist:* Dong Oh

- **File:Leonid_Kantorovich_1975.jpg** *Source:* https://upload.wikimedia.org/wikipedia/commons/f/f4/Leonid_Kantorovich_1975.jpg *License:* CC BY 3.0 *Contributors:* [1] *Original artist:* Андрей Богданов (Andrei-bogdanoff<img alt='@' src='https://upload.wikimedia.org/wikipedia/commons/thumb/b/b6/At_char.svg/11px-At_char.svg.png' title='@' width='11' height='11' srcset='https://upload.wikimedia.org/wikipedia/commons/thumb/b/b6/At_char.svg/17px-At_char.svg.png 1.5x, https://upload.wikimedia.org/wikipedia/commons/thumb/b/b6/At_char.svg/22px-At_char.svg.png 2x' data-file-width='10' data-file-height='10' />yandex.ru)

- **File:Lorrain.seaport.jpg** *Source:* https://upload.wikimedia.org/wikipedia/commons/2/29/Lorrain.seaport.jpg *License:* Public domain *Contributors:* http://www.ibiblio.org/wm/paint/auth/lorrain/lorrain.seaport.jpg downloaded from en *Original artist:* Claude Lorrain (1604/1605–1682)

- **File:Ludwig_von_Mises.jpg** *Source:* https://upload.wikimedia.org/wikipedia/commons/f/f0/Ludwig_von_Mises.jpg *License:* CC-BY-SA-3.0 *Contributors:* Ludwig von Mises Institute. Originally from en.wikipedia; description page is/was here. Original uploader was DickClarkMises at en.wikipedia *Original artist:* Ludwig von Mises Institute

- **File:Lwalras.jpg** *Source:* https://upload.wikimedia.org/wikipedia/commons/9/9e/Lwalras.jpg *License:* Public domain *Contributors:* http://www.economics.unimelb.edu.au/rdixon/wlaw.html *Original artist:* ?
- **File:MarilynWaring2012.jpg** *Source:* https://upload.wikimedia.org/wikipedia/commons/d/d9/MarilynWaring2012.jpg *License:* CC BY-SA 3.0 *Contributors:* Own work *Original artist:* Marilyn Waring
- **File:Marx_old.jpg** *Source:* https://upload.wikimedia.org/wikipedia/commons/a/a2/Marx_old.jpg *License:* Public domain *Contributors:* http://www.marxists.org/archive/marx/photo/index.htm (direct link: http://www.marxists.org/archive/marx/photo/marx/pages/82km1.htm) *Original artist:* original unknown ; edited by de:Benutzer:Tets
- **File:Maskin_and_Myerson.jpg** *Source:* https://upload.wikimedia.org/wikipedia/commons/6/60/Maskin_and_Myerson.jpg *License:* CC BY-SA 4.0 *Contributors:* Own work *Original artist:* Byronmercury
- **File:Merge-arrow.svg** *Source:* https://upload.wikimedia.org/wikipedia/commons/a/aa/Merge-arrow.svg *License:* Public domain *Contributors:* ? *Original artist:* ?
- **File:Mergefrom.svg** *Source:* https://upload.wikimedia.org/wikipedia/commons/0/0f/Mergefrom.svg *License:* Public domain *Contributors:* ? *Original artist:* ?
- **File:Mirabeau_père.jpg** *Source:* https://upload.wikimedia.org/wikipedia/commons/8/81/Mirabeau_p%C3%A8re.jpg *License:* Public domain *Contributors:* http://www.repro-tableaux.com/kunst/jacques_andre_joseph_c_aved/victor_riquetti_marquis_mirab_hi.jpg *Original artist:* Jacques Aved
- **File:MurrayBW.jpg** *Source:* https://upload.wikimedia.org/wikipedia/commons/7/7e/MurrayBW.jpg *License:* CC BY 3.0 *Contributors:* http://picasaweb.google.com/MisesInstitute/RothbardImages#5400726827057738466 *Original artist:* Ludwig von Mises Institute
- **File:Mutualist_Reciprocity_flag.png** *Source:* https://upload.wikimedia.org/wikipedia/en/7/74/Mutualist_Reciprocity_flag.png *License:* PD *Contributors:* ? *Original artist:* ?
- **File:Nested_council.png** *Source:* https://upload.wikimedia.org/wikipedia/commons/1/13/Nested_council.png *License:* Public domain *Contributors:* Own work *Original artist:* Mgrinder
- **File:Newkeynesian1.jpg** *Source:* https://upload.wikimedia.org/wikipedia/commons/7/71/Newkeynesian1.jpg *License:* CC BY-SA 4.0 *Contributors:* Own work *Original artist:* Byronmercury
- **File:Nicolaus_Copernicus.jpg** *Source:* https://upload.wikimedia.org/wikipedia/commons/7/77/Nicolaus_Copernicus.jpg *License:* Public domain *Contributors:* ? *Original artist:* ?
- **File:North_American_Technate.PNG** *Source:* https://upload.wikimedia.org/wikipedia/en/8/8c/North_American_Technate.PNG *License:* CC-BY-2.5 *Contributors:* ? *Original artist:* ?
- **File:Nuvola_apps_kalzium.svg** *Source:* https://upload.wikimedia.org/wikipedia/commons/8/8b/Nuvola_apps_kalzium.svg *License:* LGPL *Contributors:* Own work *Original artist:* David Vignoni, SVG version by Bobarino
- **File:OECD_gender_wage_gap_2006.jpeg** *Source:* https://upload.wikimedia.org/wikipedia/commons/d/dd/OECD_gender_wage_gap_2006.jpeg *License:* Public domain *Contributors:* http://economix.blogs.nytimes.com/2010/03/09/the-gender-wage-gap-around-the-world/ *Original artist:* Organization for Economic Cooperation and Development
- **File:OlderPittThe_Younger.jpg** *Source:* https://upload.wikimedia.org/wikipedia/commons/e/e8/OlderPittThe_Younger.jpg *License:* Public domain *Contributors:* Bonhams *Original artist:* John Hoppner
- **File:Oliver_Blanchard,_IMF_98BlanchardWEO1_lg.jpg** *Source:* https://upload.wikimedia.org/wikipedia/commons/4/45/Oliver_Blanchard%2C_IMF_98BlanchardWEO1_lg.jpg *License:* Public domain *Contributors:* Photos from the IMF 2008 Annual Meetings, IMF, 98BlanchardWEO1_lg.jpg *Original artist:* IMF Staff Photographer Eugene Salazar
- **File:One_day_living_with_commons-based_peer_production_communities_(CBPP).svg** *Source:* https://upload.wikimedia.org/wikipedia/commons/f/f2/One_day_living_with_commons-based_peer_production_communities_%28CBPP%29.svg *License:* CC BY-SA 4.0 *Contributors:* Own work *Original artist:* Laura Recio Hidalgo
- **File:Orange_and_Black_flag_(Mutualism).svg** *Source:* https://upload.wikimedia.org/wikipedia/commons/1/1d/Orange_and_Black_flag_%28Mutualism%29.svg *License:* Public domain *Contributors:* Own work *Original artist:* FugeeCamp
- **File:Oresme.jpg** *Source:* https://upload.wikimedia.org/wikipedia/commons/3/35/Oresme.jpg *License:* Public domain *Contributors:* ? *Original artist:* ?
- **File:Oskar_Lange_20-65.jpg** *Source:* https://upload.wikimedia.org/wikipedia/commons/4/4b/Oskar_Lange_20-65.jpg *License:* Public domain *Contributors:* Narodowe Archiwum Cyfrowe, Sygnatura: 20-65 *Original artist:* Władysław Miernicki
- **File:PSM_V11_D660_William_Stanley_Jevons.jpg** *Source:* https://upload.wikimedia.org/wikipedia/commons/2/23/PSM_V11_D660_William_Stanley_Jevons.jpg *License:* Public domain *Contributors:* Popular Science Monthly Volume 11 *Original artist:* Unknown<a href='//www.wikidata.org/wiki/Q4233718' title='wikidata:Q4233718'><img alt='wikidata:Q4233718' src='https://upload.wikimedia.org/wikipedia/commons/thumb/f/ff/Wikidata-logo.svg/20px-Wikidata-logo.svg.png' width='20' height='11' srcset='https://upload.wikimedia.org/wikipedia/commons/thumb/f/ff/Wikidata-logo.svg/30px-Wikidata-logo.svg.png 1.5x, https://upload.wikimedia.org/wikipedia/commons/thumb/f/ff/Wikidata-logo.svg/40px-Wikidata-logo.svg.png 2x' data-file-width='1050' data-file-height='590' /></a>
- **File:P_vip.svg** *Source:* https://upload.wikimedia.org/wikipedia/en/6/69/P_vip.svg *License:* PD *Contributors:* ? *Original artist:* ?
- **File:Panic_of_1873_bank_run.jpg** *Source:* https://upload.wikimedia.org/wikipedia/commons/e/e8/Panic_of_1873_bank_run.jpg *License:* Public domain *Contributors:* This image is available from the United States Library of Congress's Prints and Photographs division under the digital ID cph.3a00900.
  This tag does not indicate the copyright status of the attached work. A normal copyright tag is still required. See Commons:Licensing for more information. *Original artist:* Unknown<a href='//www.wikidata.org/wiki/Q4233718' title='wikidata:Q4233718'><img alt='wikidata:Q4233718' src='https://upload.wikimedia.org/wikipedia/commons/thumb/f/ff/Wikidata-logo.svg/20px-Wikidata-logo.svg.png' width='20' height='11' srcset='https://upload.wikimedia.org/wikipedia/commons/thumb/f/ff/Wikidata-logo.svg/30px-Wikidata-logo.svg.png 1.5x, https://upload.wikimedia.org/wikipedia/commons/thumb/f/ff/Wikidata-logo.svg/40px-Wikidata-logo.svg.png 2x' data-file-width='1050' data-file-height='590' /></a>

3.2. IMAGES

- **File:Papua_New_Guinea_map.png** *Source:* https://upload.wikimedia.org/wikipedia/commons/4/42/Papua_New_Guinea_map.png *License:* Public domain *Contributors:* ? *Original artist:* ?
- **File:Paul_Krugman-press_conference_Dec_07th,_2008-8.jpg** *Source:* https://upload.wikimedia.org/wikipedia/commons/4/48/Paul_Krugman-press_conference_Dec_07th%2C_2008-8.jpg *License:* GFDL 1.2 *Contributors:* Own work *Original artist:* Prolineserver (<a href='//commons.wikimedia.org/wiki/User_talk:Prolineserver' title='User talk:Prolineserver'>talk</a>)
- **File:Paul_Samuelson.gif** *Source:* https://upload.wikimedia.org/wikipedia/commons/4/4c/Paul_Samuelson.gif *License:* CC BY 1.0 *Contributors:* http://www.biz-architect.com/free_trade_and_samuelson.htm *Original artist:* Innovation & Business Architectures, Inc.
- **File:Peace_sign.svg** *Source:* https://upload.wikimedia.org/wikipedia/commons/d/d2/Peace_sign.svg *License:* Public domain *Contributors:* Transferred from en.wikipedia to Commons. *Original artist:* The original uploader was Schuminweb at English Wikipedia
- **File:People_icon.svg** *Source:* https://upload.wikimedia.org/wikipedia/commons/3/37/People_icon.svg *License:* CC0 *Contributors:* OpenClipart *Original artist:* OpenClipart
- **File:Perfectly_inelastic_supply.svg** *Source:* https://upload.wikimedia.org/wikipedia/en/6/69/Perfectly_inelastic_supply.svg *License:* CC-BY-SA-3.0 *Contributors:*
self-made, based on work by User:SilverStar on Image:Deadweight-loss-price-ceiling.svg *Original artist:*
Explodicle (talk)
- **File:Pi_y_margall.jpg** *Source:* https://upload.wikimedia.org/wikipedia/commons/b/bc/Pi_y_margall.jpg *License:* Public domain *Contributors:* Ateneo de Madrid *Original artist:* José Sánchez Pescador
- **File:Pierre_Samuel_du_Pont_de_Nemours.jpg** *Source:* https://upload.wikimedia.org/wikipedia/commons/5/59/Pierre_Samuel_du_Pont_de_Nemours.jpg *License:* Public domain *Contributors:* http://www.chateaucountry.org/images/portraits/pierresamuel.jpg *Original artist:* Unknown<a href='//www.wikidata.org/wiki/Q4233718' title='wikidata:Q4233718'><img alt='wikidata:Q4233718' src='https://upload.wikimedia.org/wikipedia/commons/thumb/f/ff/Wikidata-logo.svg/20px-Wikidata-logo.svg.png' width='20' height='11' srcset='https://upload.wikimedia.org/wikipedia/commons/thumb/f/ff/Wikidata-logo.svg/30px-Wikidata-logo.svg.png 1.5x, https://upload.wikimedia.org/wikipedia/commons/thumb/f/ff/Wikidata-logo.svg/40px-Wikidata-logo.svg.png 2x' data-file-width='1050' data-file-height='590' /></a>
- **File:Portal-puzzle.svg** *Source:* https://upload.wikimedia.org/wikipedia/en/f/fd/Portal-puzzle.svg *License:* Public domain *Contributors:* ? *Original artist:* ?
- **File:Portrait_Emma_Goldman.jpg** *Source:* https://upload.wikimedia.org/wikipedia/commons/2/23/Portrait_Emma_Goldman.jpg *License:* Public domain *Contributors:*
http://www.lib.uconn.edu/online/research/speclib/ASC/Exhibits/Images/goldman.jpg
Original artist: Unknown<a href='//www.wikidata.org/wiki/Q4233718' title='wikidata:Q4233718'><img alt='wikidata:Q4233718' src='https://upload.wikimedia.org/wikipedia/commons/thumb/f/ff/Wikidata-logo.svg/20px-Wikidata-logo.svg.png' width='20' height='11' srcset='https://upload.wikimedia.org/wikipedia/commons/thumb/f/ff/Wikidata-logo.svg/30px-Wikidata-logo.svg.png 1.5x, https://upload.wikimedia.org/wikipedia/commons/thumb/f/ff/Wikidata-logo.svg/40px-Wikidata-logo.svg.png 2x' data-file-width='1050' data-file-height='590' /></a>
- **File:Portrait_of_David_Ricardo_by_Thomas_Phillips.jpg** *Source:* https://upload.wikimedia.org/wikipedia/commons/d/dc/Portrait_of_David_Ricardo_by_Thomas_Phillips.jpg *License:* Public domain *Contributors:*
[1]
Original artist: Thomas Phillips
- **File:Portrait_of_Milton_Friedman.jpg** *Source:* https://upload.wikimedia.org/wikipedia/commons/2/20/Portrait_of_Milton_Friedman.jpg *License:* CC0 *Contributors:* RobertHannah89 *Original artist:* The Friedman Foundation for Educational Choice
- **File:Portrait_of_Pierre_Joseph_Proudhon_1865.jpg** *Source:* https://upload.wikimedia.org/wikipedia/commons/e/ea/Portrait_of_Pierre_Joseph_Proudhon_1865.jpg *License:* Public domain *Contributors:* 1. FineArtPrintsOnDemand.com *Original artist:* Gustave Courbet
- **File:Prescott_Sargent_Kydland.jpg** *Source:* https://upload.wikimedia.org/wikipedia/commons/4/46/Prescott_Sargent_Kydland.jpg *License:* CC BY-SA 4.0 *Contributors:* Own work *Original artist:* Byronmercury
- **File:Professor_Sir_Roy_George_Douglas_Allen,_c1978.jpg** *Source:* https://upload.wikimedia.org/wikipedia/commons/7/70/Professor_Sir_Roy_George_Douglas_Allen%2C_c1978.jpg *License:* No restrictions *Contributors:* Professor Sir Roy George Douglas Allen, c1978 *Original artist:* Library of the London School of Economics and Political Science
- **File:QJAE.jpg** *Source:* https://upload.wikimedia.org/wikipedia/en/d/d5/QJAE.jpg *License:* Cc-by-sa-3.0 *Contributors:* ? *Original artist:* ?
- **File:Question_book-new.svg** *Source:* https://upload.wikimedia.org/wikipedia/en/9/99/Question_book-new.svg *License:* Cc-by-sa-3.0 *Contributors:*
Created from scratch in Adobe Illustrator. Based on Image:Question book.png created by User:Equazcion *Original artist:*
Tkgd2007
- **File:Red_flag_II.svg** *Source:* https://upload.wikimedia.org/wikipedia/commons/5/52/Red_flag_II.svg *License:* CC BY 2.5 *Contributors:* No machine-readable source provided. Own work assumed (based on copyright claims). *Original artist:* No machine-readable author provided. Ssolbergj assumed (based on copyright claims).
- **File:Red_flag_waving.svg** *Source:* https://upload.wikimedia.org/wikipedia/commons/c/c5/Red_flag_waving.svg *License:* Public domain *Contributors:* Original PNG by Nikodemos. *Original artist:* Wereon
- **File:Reihardtrogoff.jpg** *Source:* https://upload.wikimedia.org/wikipedia/commons/d/db/Reihardtrogoff.jpg *License:* CC BY-SA 4.0 *Contributors:* Own work *Original artist:* Byronmercury

- **File:Review_of_Radical_Political_Economics_Journal_Front_Cover.jpg** *Source:* https://upload.wikimedia.org/wikipedia/en/5/5d/Review_of_Radical_Political_Economics_Journal_Front_Cover.jpg *License:* Fair use *Contributors:* http://rrp.sagepub.com/ *Original artist:* ?
- **File:Richard_Posner_at_Harvard_University.jpg** *Source:* https://upload.wikimedia.org/wikipedia/commons/1/1d/Richard_Posner_at_Harvard_University.jpg *License:* GFDL *Contributors:* chensiyuan *Original artist:* chensiyuan
- **File:Rmundell.jpg** *Source:* https://upload.wikimedia.org/wikipedia/commons/8/89/Rmundell.jpg *License:* CC BY-SA 3.0 *Contributors:* Own work *Original artist:* Triwbe
- **File:Robert_Solow_by_Olaf_Storbeck.jpg** *Source:* https://upload.wikimedia.org/wikipedia/commons/9/95/Robert_Solow_by_Olaf_Storbeck.jpg *License:* CC BY-SA 2.0 *Contributors:* Robert Solow *Original artist:* Olaf Storbeck from Düsseldorf, Deutschland
- **File:Rosa_Luxembourg.jpg** *Source:* https://upload.wikimedia.org/wikipedia/commons/a/ac/Rosa_Luxembourg.jpg *License:* Public domain *Contributors:*

Original artist: Meyers Blitz Lexikon
- **File:Sanzio_01_Plato_Aristotle.jpg** *Source:* https://upload.wikimedia.org/wikipedia/commons/9/98/Sanzio_01_Plato_Aristotle.jpg *License:* Public domain *Contributors:* Web Gallery of Art: <a href='http://www.wga.hu/art/r/raphael/4stanze/1segnatu/1/athens1.jpg' data-x-rel='nofollow'><img alt='Inkscape.svg' src='https://upload.wikimedia.org/wikipedia/commons/thumb/6/6f/Inkscape.svg/20px-Inkscape.svg.png' width='20' height='20' srcset='https://upload.wikimedia.org/wikipedia/commons/thumb/6/6f/Inkscape.svg/30px-Inkscape.svg.png 1.5x, https://upload.wikimedia.org/wikipedia/commons/thumb/6/6f/Inkscape.svg/40px-Inkscape.svg.png 2x' data-file-width='60' data-file-height='60' /></a> Image <a href='http://www.wga.hu/html/r/raphael/4stanze/1segnatu/1/athens1.html' data-x-rel='nofollow'><img alt='Information icon.svg' src='https://upload.wikimedia.org/wikipedia/commons/thumb/3/35/Information_icon.svg/20px-Information_icon.svg.png' width='20' height='20' srcset='https://upload.wikimedia.org/wikipedia/commons/thumb/3/35/Information_icon.svg/30px-Information_icon.svg.png 1.5x, https://upload.wikimedia.org/wikipedia/commons/thumb/3/35/Information_icon.svg/40px-Information_icon.svg.png 2x' data-file-width='620' data-file-height='620' /></a> Info about artwork *Original artist:* Raphael
- **File:SharonTemple.jpg** *Source:* https://upload.wikimedia.org/wikipedia/commons/2/27/SharonTemple.jpg *License:* Public domain *Contributors:* **Original publication**: unknown

Immediate source: Sharon Temple Museum *Original artist:* unknown

(Life time: unknown)
- **File:Sidney_Webb.jpg** *Source:* https://upload.wikimedia.org/wikipedia/commons/b/b0/Sidney_Webb.jpg *License:* Public domain *Contributors:* ? *Original artist:* ?
- **File:Silver_red_monad.png** *Source:* https://upload.wikimedia.org/wikipedia/commons/0/03/Silver_red_monad.png *License:* CC BY-SA 2.5 *Contributors:* ? *Original artist:* ?
- **File:Sir_James_Denham_Steuart._1713-1780.gif** *Source:* https://upload.wikimedia.org/wikipedia/commons/0/07/Sir_James_Denham_Steuart._1713-1780.gif *License:* Public domain *Contributors:* ? *Original artist:* ?
- **File:Sir_William_Petty.jpg** *Source:* https://upload.wikimedia.org/wikipedia/commons/8/84/Sir_William_Petty.jpg *License:* Public domain *Contributors:* http://www.npg.org.uk/collections/search/largerimage.php?LinkID=mp03529&role=sit&rNo=2 *Original artist:* John Smith, after John Closterman
- **File:Small_new_EAEPE_logo.png** *Source:* https://upload.wikimedia.org/wikipedia/en/8/88/Small_new_EAEPE_logo.png *License:* Fair use *Contributors:* www.eaepe.org *Original artist:* ?
- **File:Speaker_Icon.svg** *Source:* https://upload.wikimedia.org/wikipedia/commons/2/21/Speaker_Icon.svg *License:* Public domain *Contributors:* No machine-readable source provided. Own work assumed (based on copyright claims). *Original artist:* No machine-readable author provided. Mobius assumed (based on copyright claims).
- **File:Sraffa.jpg** *Source:* https://upload.wikimedia.org/wikipedia/en/b/bf/Sraffa.jpg *License:* ? *Contributors:* http://ase.signum.sns.it/foto_RS.html *Original artist:* ?
- **File:Stacy_Herbert_with_Max_Keiser_26_September_2015.png** *Source:* https://upload.wikimedia.org/wikipedia/commons/f/f4/Stacy_Herbert_with_Max_Keiser_26_September_2015.png *License:* CC BY-SA 4.0 *Contributors:* Own work *Original artist:* Targje
- **File:Stylised_Lithium_Atom.svg** *Source:* https://upload.wikimedia.org/wikipedia/commons/e/e1/Stylised_Lithium_Atom.svg *License:* CC-BY-SA-3.0 *Contributors:* based off of Image:Stylised Lithium Atom.png by Halfdan. *Original artist:* SVG by Indolences. Recoloring and ironing out some glitches done by Rainer Klute.
- **File:Sustainable_development.svg** *Source:* https://upload.wikimedia.org/wikipedia/commons/7/70/Sustainable_development.svg *License:* CC-BY-SA-3.0 *Contributors:*
- Inspired from Developpement durable.jpg *Original artist:*
- original: Johann Dréo (talk · contribs)
- **File:Symbol_book_class2.svg** *Source:* https://upload.wikimedia.org/wikipedia/commons/8/89/Symbol_book_class2.svg *License:* CC BY-SA 2.5 *Contributors:* Mad by Lokal_Profil by combining: *Original artist:* Lokal_Profil
- **File:Tana_Toraja,_Salu_funeral_(6823105668).jpg** *Source:* https://upload.wikimedia.org/wikipedia/commons/6/65/Tana_Toraja%2C_Salu_funeral_%286823105668%29.jpg *License:* CC BY 2.0 *Contributors:* Tana Toraja, Salu funeral *Original artist:* Arian Zwegers
- **File:Technocracy-Calendar.png** *Source:* https://upload.wikimedia.org/wikipedia/commons/2/2a/Technocracy-Calendar.png *License:* CC0 *Contributors:* http://www.archive.org/details/TechnocracyStudyCourseUnabridged *Original artist:* Technocracy Inc.
- **File:TechnocracySign.gif** *Source:* https://upload.wikimedia.org/wikipedia/commons/9/9b/TechnocracySign.gif *License:* Public domain *Contributors:* From Library of Congress site: http://www.ssa.gov/history/briefhistory3.html *Original artist:* Social Security Administration

3.2. IMAGES

- **File:Text_document_with_red_question_mark.svg** *Source:* https://upload.wikimedia.org/wikipedia/commons/a/a4/Text_document_with_red_question_mark.svg *License:* Public domain *Contributors:* Created by bdesham with Inkscape; based upon Text-x-generic.svg from the Tango project. *Original artist:* Benjamin D. Esham (bdesham)
- **File:The_Earth_seen_from_Apollo_17.jpg** *Source:* https://upload.wikimedia.org/wikipedia/commons/9/97/The_Earth_seen_from_Apollo_17.jpg *License:* Public domain *Contributors:* http://www.nasa.gov/images/content/115334main_image_feature_329_ys_full.jpg *Original artist:* NASA/Apollo 17 crew; taken by either Harrison Schmitt or Ron Evans
- **File:The_Earth_seen_from_Apollo_17_with_transparent_background.png** *Source:* https://upload.wikimedia.org/wikipedia/commons/4/43/The_Earth_seen_from_Apollo_17_with_transparent_background.png *License:* Public domain *Contributors:* http://nssdc.gsfc.nasa.gov/imgcat/html/object_page/a17_h_148_22727.html *Original artist:* NASA
- **File:ThreeCoins.svg** *Source:* https://upload.wikimedia.org/wikipedia/commons/2/29/ThreeCoins.svg *License:* Public domain *Contributors:* Transferred from en.wikipedia to Commons. User:Ysangkok added shadows and silhouettes from Image:Lars_Gustaf_Tersmeden.svg, Image:Caspar Friedrich Wolff.svg and Image:Sieveking-Silhouette.svg. *Original artist:* Busy Stubber at English Wikipedia, effects: User:Ysangkok
- **File:Toraja_house.jpg** *Source:* https://upload.wikimedia.org/wikipedia/commons/a/ae/Toraja_house.jpg *License:* CC BY-SA 2.5 *Contributors:* No machine-readable source provided. Own work assumed (based on copyright claims). *Original artist:* No machine-readable author provided. Jayapura assumed (based on copyright claims).
- **File:Trabajadora_doméstico.JPG** *Source:* https://upload.wikimedia.org/wikipedia/commons/7/74/Trabajadora_dom%C3%A9stico.JPG *License:* Public domain *Contributors:* Own work *Original artist:* Iijjccoo
- **File:Translation_to_english_arrow.svg** *Source:* https://upload.wikimedia.org/wikipedia/commons/8/8a/Translation_to_english_arrow.svg *License:* CC-BY-SA-3.0 *Contributors:* Transferred from en.wikipedia; transferred to Commons by User:Faigl.ladislav using CommonsHelper. *Original artist:* tkgd2007. Original uploader was Tkgd2007 at en.wikipedia
- **File:Trygve_Haavelmo.jpg** *Source:* https://upload.wikimedia.org/wikipedia/commons/2/25/Trygve_Haavelmo.jpg *License:* Public domain *Contributors:* uio.no *Original artist:* Unknown<a href='//www.wikidata.org/wiki/Q4233718' title='wikidata:Q4233718'><img alt='wikidata:Q4233718' src='https://upload.wikimedia.org/wikipedia/commons/thumb/f/ff/Wikidata-logo.svg/20px-Wikidata-logo.svg.png' width='20' height='11' srcset='https://upload.wikimedia.org/wikipedia/commons/thumb/f/ff/Wikidata-logo.svg/30px-Wikidata-logo.svg.png 1.5x, https://upload.wikimedia.org/wikipedia/commons/thumb/f/ff/Wikidata-logo.svg/40px-Wikidata-logo.svg.png 2x' data-file-width='1050' data-file-height='590' /></a>
- **File:US_womens_earnings_and_employment_by_industry_2009.png** *Source:* https://upload.wikimedia.org/wikipedia/commons/f/fe/US_womens_earnings_and_employment_by_industry_2009.png *License:* Public domain *Contributors:* http://www.bls.gov/opub/ted/2011/ted_20110216.htm *Original artist:* U.S. Bureau of Labor Statistics, Division of Information and Marketing Services
- **File:US_womens_earnings_as_a_percentage_of_mens_1979-2005.gif** *Source:* https://upload.wikimedia.org/wikipedia/commons/d/d7/US_womens_earnings_as_a_percentage_of_mens_1979-2005.gif *License:* Public domain *Contributors:* http://www.bls.gov/opub/ted/2006/oct/wk1/art02.htm *Original artist:* U.S. Bureau of Labor Statistics, Division of Information and Marketing Services
- **File:Uio_frisch_2006_0025.jpg** *Source:* https://upload.wikimedia.org/wikipedia/commons/a/a1/Uio_frisch_2006_0025.jpg *License:* Public domain *Contributors:* uio.no *Original artist:* Borgens Atelier
- **File:Unbalanced_scales.svg** *Source:* https://upload.wikimedia.org/wikipedia/commons/f/fe/Unbalanced_scales.svg *License:* Public domain *Contributors:* ? *Original artist:* ?
- **File:Veblen3a.jpg** *Source:* https://upload.wikimedia.org/wikipedia/commons/e/e9/Veblen3a.jpg *License:* Public domain *Contributors:* ? *Original artist:* ?
- **File:Wealth_of_Nations_title.jpg** *Source:* https://upload.wikimedia.org/wikipedia/commons/d/de/Wealth_of_Nations_title.jpg *License:* Public domain *Contributors:* Wealth of Nations *Original artist:* Adam Smith
- **File:Wedding_rings.jpg** *Source:* https://upload.wikimedia.org/wikipedia/commons/3/3d/Wedding_rings.jpg *License:* CC BY 2.0 *Contributors:* Flickr *Original artist:* Jeff Belmonte from Cuiabá, Brazil
- **File:WhiteandKeynes.jpg** *Source:* https://upload.wikimedia.org/wikipedia/commons/0/04/WhiteandKeynes.jpg *License:* Public domain *Contributors:* International Monetary Fund: http://www.imf.org/external/np/adm/pictures/images/hwmkm.jpg *Original artist:* International Monetary Fund
- **File:Wicksell.jpg** *Source:* https://upload.wikimedia.org/wikipedia/commons/f/f3/Wicksell.jpg *License:* Public domain *Contributors:* ? *Original artist:* ?
- **File:Wiki_letter_w_cropped.svg** *Source:* https://upload.wikimedia.org/wikipedia/commons/1/1c/Wiki_letter_w_cropped.svg *License:* CC-BY-SA-3.0 *Contributors:* This file was derived from Wiki letter w.svg: <a href='//commons.wikimedia.org/wiki/File:Wiki_letter_w.svg' class='image'><img alt='Wiki letter w.svg' src='https://upload.wikimedia.org/wikipedia/commons/thumb/6/6c/Wiki_letter_w.svg/50px-Wiki_letter_w.svg.png' width='50' height='50' srcset='https://upload.wikimedia.org/wikipedia/commons/thumb/6/6c/Wiki_letter_w.svg/75px-Wiki_letter_w.svg.png 1.5x, https://upload.wikimedia.org/wikipedia/commons/thumb/6/6c/Wiki_letter_w.svg/100px-Wiki_letter_w.svg.png 2x' data-file-width='44' data-file-height='44' /></a>
Original artist: Derivative work by Thumperward
- **File:Wikibooks-logo.svg** *Source:* https://upload.wikimedia.org/wikipedia/commons/f/fa/Wikibooks-logo.svg *License:* CC BY-SA 3.0 *Contributors:* Own work *Original artist:* User:Bastique, User:Ramac et al.
- **File:Wikinews-logo.svg** *Source:* https://upload.wikimedia.org/wikipedia/commons/2/24/Wikinews-logo.svg *License:* CC BY-SA 3.0 *Contributors:* This is a cropped version of Image:Wikinews-logo-en.png. *Original artist:* Vectorized by Simon 01:05, 2 August 2006 (UTC) Updated by Time3000 17 April 2007 to use official Wikinews colours and appear correctly on dark backgrounds. Originally uploaded by Simon.
- **File:Wikiquote-logo.svg** *Source:* https://upload.wikimedia.org/wikipedia/commons/f/fa/Wikiquote-logo.svg *License:* Public domain *Contributors:* ? *Original artist:* ?

- **File:Wikisource-logo.svg** *Source:* https://upload.wikimedia.org/wikipedia/commons/4/4c/Wikisource-logo.svg *License:* CC BY-SA 3.0 *Contributors:* Rei-artur *Original artist:* Nicholas Moreau
- **File:Wikiversity-logo-Snorky.svg** *Source:* https://upload.wikimedia.org/wikipedia/commons/1/1b/Wikiversity-logo-en.svg *License:* CC BY-SA 3.0 *Contributors:* Own work *Original artist:* Snorky
- **File:Wiktionary-logo-en.svg** *Source:* https://upload.wikimedia.org/wikipedia/commons/f/f8/Wiktionary-logo-en.svg *License:* Public domain *Contributors:* Vector version of Image:Wiktionary-logo-en.png. *Original artist:* Vectorized by Fvasconcellos (talk · contribs), based on original logo tossed together by Brion Vibber
- **File:Wilhelm_roscher.jpg** *Source:* https://upload.wikimedia.org/wikipedia/commons/2/26/Wilhelm_roscher.jpg *License:* Public domain *Contributors:*
- http://portrait.kaar.at/Deutschsprachige%20Teil%206/image1.html *Original artist:* Moritz Klinkicht
- **File:William_Herschel.jpg** *Source:* https://upload.wikimedia.org/wikipedia/commons/2/20/William_Herschel.jpg *License:* Public domain *Contributors:* Unknown *Original artist:* **James Sharples** (1751–1811)
- **File:Woman-power_emblem.svg** *Source:* https://upload.wikimedia.org/wikipedia/commons/4/41/Woman-power_emblem.svg *License:* Public domain *Contributors:* Made by myself, based on a character outline in the (PostScript Type 1) "Fnord Hodge-Podge Discordian fonts version 2" by **toa267** (declared by them to be Public Domain). I chose the color to be kind of equally intermediate between red, pink, and lavender (without being any one of the three...). *Original artist:* AnonMoos, toa267
- **File:Yellow_flag_waving.svg** *Source:* https://upload.wikimedia.org/wikipedia/commons/1/1b/Yellow_flag_waving.svg *License:* CC-BY-SA-3.0 *Contributors:*
- Blue_flag_waving.svg *Original artist:* Blue_flag_waving.svg: Viktorvoigt
- **File:Yellowbadge_logo.svg** *Source:* https://upload.wikimedia.org/wikipedia/commons/5/53/Yellowbadge_logo.svg *License:* Public domain *Contributors:* Self made, based on a photograph *Original artist:* Self made, based on a photograph
- **File:Young_monk.jpg** *Source:* https://upload.wikimedia.org/wikipedia/commons/d/d5/Young_monk.jpg *License:* CC BY 2.5 *Contributors:* Uploaded by Serinde *Original artist:* Uploaded by Serinde
- **File:Zentralbibliothek_Zürich_Das_Kapital_Marx_1867.jpg** *Source:* https://upload.wikimedia.org/wikipedia/commons/8/8d/Zentralbibliothek_Z%C3%BCrich_Das_Kapital_Marx_1867.jpg *License:* Public domain *Contributors:* This document was created as part of the Zentralbibliothek Zürich project. *Original artist:* Zentralbibliothek Zürich
- **File:Österreich_uber_alles_wann_es_nur_will.jpg** *Source:* https://upload.wikimedia.org/wikipedia/commons/5/50/%C3%96sterreich_uber_alles_wann_es_nur_will.jpg *License:* Public domain *Contributors:* Österreich Über Alles, Wenn Sie Nur Will *Original artist:* Philipp von Hörnigk (1640 - 1712)[w:en:Philipp von Hörnigk]
- **File:Николай_Кондратьев.JPG** *Source:* https://upload.wikimedia.org/wikipedia/commons/0/04/%D0%9D%D0%B8%D0%BA%D0%BE%D0%BB%D0%B0%D0%B9_%D0%9A%D0%BE%D0%BD%D0%B4%D1%80%D0%B0%D1%82%D1%8C%D0%B5%D0%B2.JPG *License:* Public domain *Contributors:* http://www.promved.ru/images/PV5_6p1r2.JPG Originally uploaded to ru.wiki *Original artist:* Unknown<a href='//www.wikidata.org/wiki/Q4233718' title='wikidata:Q4233718'><img alt='wikidata:Q4233718' src='https://upload.wikimedia.org/wikipedia/commons/thumb/f/ff/Wikidata-logo.svg/20px-Wikidata-logo.svg.png' width='20' height='11' srcset='https://upload.wikimedia.org/wikipedia/commons/thumb/f/ff/Wikidata-logo.svg/30px-Wikidata-logo.svg.png 1.5x, https://upload.wikimedia.org/wikipedia/commons/thumb/f/ff/Wikidata-logo.svg/40px-Wikidata-logo.svg.png 2x' data-file-width='1050' data-file-height='590' /></a>

3.3 Content license

- Creative Commons Attribution-Share Alike 3.0

REFERENCE

TIMELINES OF HISTORY

VOLUME 9

INDUSTRY AND EMPIRE

1800–1900

South Huntington Pub. Lib.
145 Pidgeon Hill Rd.
Huntington Sta., N.Y. 11746

GROLIER
an imprint of
SCHOLASTIC
www.scholastic.com/librarypublishing

Published by Grolier,
an imprint of Scholastic Library Publishing,
Sherman Turnpike
Danbury, Connecticut 06816

© 2005 The Brown Reference Group plc

Set ISBN 0-7172-6002-X
Volume 9 ISBN 0-7172-6011-9

Library of Congress Cataloging-in-Publication Data

Timelines of history.
    p. cm.
  Includes index.
  Contents: v. 1. The early empires, prehistory—500 B.C. — v. 2. The classical age, 500 B.C.—500 A.D. — v. 3. Raiders and conquerors, 500—1000 — v. 4. The feudal era, 1000—1250 — v. 5. The end of the Middle Ages, 1250—1500 — v. 6. A wider world, 1500—1600 — v. 7. Royalty and revolt, 1600—1700 — v. 8. The Age of Reason, 1700—1800 — v. 9. Industry and empire, 1800—1900 — v. 10. The modern world, 1900—2000.
  ISBN 0-7172-6002-X (set : alk. paper) — ISBN 0-7172-6003-8 (v. 1 : alk. paper) — ISBN 0-7172-6004-6 (v. 2 : alk. paper) — ISBN 0-7172-6005-4 (v. 3 : alk. paper) — ISBN 0-7172-6006-2 (v. 4 : alk. paper) — ISBN 0-7172-6007-0 (v. 5 : alk. paper) — ISBN 0-7172-6008-9 (v. 6 : alk. paper) — ISBN 0-7172-6009-7 (v. 7 : alk. paper) — ISBN 0-7172-6010-0 (v. 8 : alk.paper) — ISBN 0-7172-6011-9 (v. 9 : alk. paper) — ISBN 0-7172-6012-7 (v. 10 : alk. paper)
  1. Chronology, Historical

All rights reserved. Except for use in a review, no part of this book may be reproduced, stored in a retrieval system, or transmitted in any form, or by any means, electronic, mechanical photocopying, recording, or otherwise, without prior permission of Grolier.

For information address the publisher:
Grolier, Sherman Turnpike,
Danbury, Connecticut 06816

Printed and bound in Thailand

FOR THE BROWN REFERENCE GROUP PLC

Consultant: Professor Jeremy Black, University of Exeter

Project Editor: Tony Allan
Designer: Frankie Wood
Picture Researcher: Sharon Southren
Cartographic Editor: Tim Williams
Design Manager: Lynne Ross
Production: Alastair Gourlay, Maggie Copeland
Senior Managing Editor: Tim Cooke
Editorial Director: Lindsey Lowe
Writers: Susan Kennedy, Michael Kerrigan, Peter Lewis

PICTURE CREDITS
(t = top, b = bottom, c = center, l = left, r = right)

Cover
Corbis: Christie's Images b.

AKG-images: 20b, Erich Lessing 45b; **The Art Archive:** Eileen Tweedy/School of Oriental & African Studies 24b; **Bridgeman.co.uk:** The British Library, London 29, Paul Freeman/Private Collection 13b, Pro-File Photo Library, Hong Kong 38b; **Corbis:** 21, Paul Almasy 25b, Archivo Iconografico, S.A. 14c, 25t, 38cr, Bettmann 15t, 45t, 46t, Gallo Images/Roger De La Harpe 20cr, Historical Picture Archive 14b, 19, Hulton Deutsch Collection 39, Layne Kennedy 44, Stapleton Collection 13t, 18cl, 27, Werner Forman Archive 9b; **DaimlerChrysler:** 40t; **Getty Images:** 6b, 9t, 24t, 35, 43, Time Life Pictures/Mansell 26cl, 34cl; **Robert Hunt Picture Library:** 17, 34t, 46b; **Mary Evans Picture Library:** 31; **National Archives and Records Administration:** 32c, 33; **Courtesy of Otis Elevator Company:** 26t; **Edgar Fah Smith Collection, University of Pennsylvania Library:** 37; **PhotoDisc:** Larry Brownstein 18t, David Buffington 41t; **Photos12.com:** Pierre Jean Chalençon 11c, Fondation Napoléon 11b, Snark Archives 30; **Photograph by Charles Kerry Studio, Tyrrell Collection. Reproduced courtesy of the Powerhouse Museum, Sydney:** 40b; **Science and Society Picture Library:** 15cl, Science Museum 36, 38t; **TopFoto.co.uk:** 8t, 20tl, 22cl, 26b, 47b, The British Library/HIP 7b, 12, The British Museum/HIP 8b, National Railway Museum, York/HIP 7t, Ann Ronan Picture Library 41c, Ann Ronan Picture Library/James Naysmyth 22cr, Derrick Whitty 6t, Woodmansterne 10.

The Brown Reference Group has made every effort to trace copyright holders ofthe pictures used in this book. Anyone having claims to ownership not identified above is invited to contact The Brown Reference Group.

CONTENTS

How to Use This Book   4

TIMELINE: 1800–1807	6
TIMELINE: 1808–1815	8
NAPOLEON BONAPARTE	10
TIMELINE: 1816–1822	12
TIMELINE: 1823–1830	14
THE LIBERATION OF LATIN AMERICA	16
TIMELINE: 1831–1837	18
TIMELINE: 1838–1845	20
THE INDUSTRIAL REVOLUTION	22
TIMELINE: 1846–1852	24
TIMELINE: 1853–1860	26
COLONIALISM	28
TIMELINE: 1861–1867	30
THE AMERICAN CIVIL WAR	32
TIMELINE: 1868–1873	34
THE AGE OF INVENTION	36
TIMELINE: 1874–1880	38
TIMELINE: 1881–1887	40
THE SCRAMBLE FOR AFRICA	42
TIMELINE: 1888–1893	44
TIMELINE: 1894–1900	46

Facts at a Glance   48
Further Reading   54
Set Index   54

HOW TO USE THIS BOOK

INTRODUCTION

After the epochal events that shook the last decades of the 18th century—the American Revolution and the French Revolution—a casual observer around the year 1820 could have believed that stability had returned to world affairs. Napoleon Bonaparte, who had come to personify France's revolutionary heritage, had been defeated, and France's Bourbon kings had been restored. Everywhere in Europe the old monarchical system was back in control. Across the globe in China and Japan long-established dynasties steadfastly resisted change.

Yet appearances were to prove deceptive. Even if France's revolution had seemingly been reversed, its American counterpart had not; the United States continued to expand a republic that, however imperfect, was still something new in a world of nation-states. To the south the countries of Latin America had taken advantage of the ferment in Europe to break free from the grip of Spain. Meanwhile in first Britain and then in Germany, the United States, and countries around the globe a new force was growing that would eventually transform the world: The Industrial Revolution was literally gathering steam.

For a time in the second half of the century the new force of industrialization would polarize the world. In search of natural resources and new markets for their goods the newly wealthy developed lands expanded their existing mercantile empires into colonial ones. Countries of Asia and Africa that had yet to experience the industrial wave found themselves opened up to its effects willy-nilly under foreign rule. Even the great ancient cultures of Japan and China were not exempt; the pace of change was so rapid that they too were compelled to come to terms, willingly or unwillingly, with new ways.

ABBREVIATIONS	
mi	miles
cm	centimeters
m	meters
km	kilometers
sq. km	square kilometers
mya	million years ago
c.	about (from the Latin word circa)

A NOTE ON DATES
This set follows standard Western practice in dating events from the start of the Christian era, presumed to have begun in the year 0. Those that happened before the year 0 are listed as B.C. (before the Christian era), and those that happened after as A.D. (from the Latin Anno Domini, meaning "in the year of the Lord"). Wherever possible, exact dates are given; where there is uncertainty, the date is prefixed by the abbreviation c. (short for Latin circa, meaning "about") to show that it is approximate.

ABOUT THIS SET

This book is one of a set of ten providing timelines for world history from the beginning of recorded history up to 2000 A.D. Each volume arranges events that happened around the world within a particular period and is made up of three different types of facing two-page spreads: timelines, features, and glossary pages ("Facts at a Glance," at the back of the book). The three should be used in combination to find the information that you need. Timelines list events that occurred between the dates shown on the pages and cover periods ranging from several centuries at the start of Volume 1, dealing with early times, to six or seven years in Volumes 9 and 10, addressing the modern era.

In part, the difference reflects the fact that much more is known about recent times than about distant eras. Yet it also reflects a real acceleration in the number of noteworthy events, related to surging population growth. Demographers estimate that it was only in the early 19th century that world population reached one billion; at the start of the 21st century the figure is over six billion and rising, meaning that more people have lived in the past 200 years than in all the other epochs of history combined.

The subjects covered by the feature pages may be a major individual or a civilization. Some cover epoch-making events, while others address more general themes such as the development of types of technology. In each case the feature provides a clear overview of its subject to supplement its timeline entries, indicating its significance on the broader canvas of world history.

Facts at a Glance lists names and terms that may be unfamiliar or that deserve more explanation than can be provided in the timeline entries. Check these pages for quick reference on individuals, peoples, battles, or cultures, and also for explanations of words that are not clear.

The comprehensive index at the back of each book covers the entire set and will enable you to follow all references to a given subject across the ten volumes.

TIMELINE PAGES

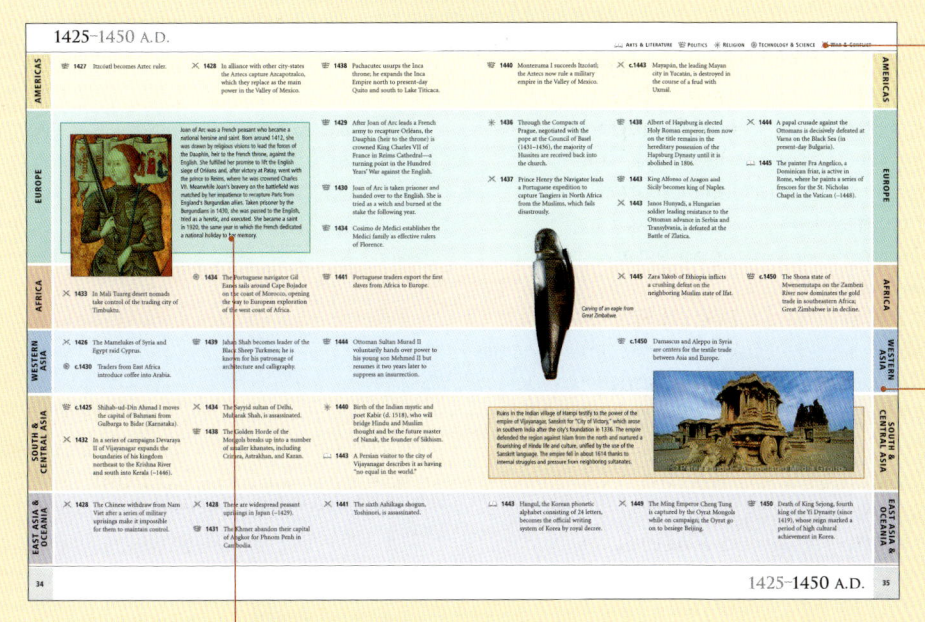

Symbols
Each entry is prefixed by one of five symbols—for example, crossed swords for war, an open book for arts and literature—indicating a particular category of history. A key to the symbols is printed at the top of the right-hand page.

Bands
Each timeline is divided into five or six bands relating to different continents or other major regions of the world. Within each band events are listed in chronological (time) order.

Boxes
Boxes in each timeline present more detailed information about important individuals, places, events, or works.

FEATURE PAGES

Maps
Most features are illustrated with detailed maps that put events into their geographical context.

Text
The features flesh out the bare bones of the timelines by providing essential background information on key topics.

Subject-specific timelines
Each feature has a timeline devoted exclusively to its topic to give an at-a-glance overview of the main developments in its history.

1800–1807 A.D.

AMERICAS

- **1800** The U.S. Library of Congress is founded.
- **1800** John Adams becomes the first U.S. president to live in the Executive Mansion (renamed the White House in 1814).
- **1800** German naturalist Alexander von Humboldt explores the Orinoco and Amazon rivers in South America (–1804).
- **1801** Thomas Jefferson succeeds John Adams as U.S. president after defeating Aaron Burr, who becomes vice president.
- **1803** Through the Louisiana Purchase the United States acquires from France an area including present-day Louisiana, Arkansas, Kansas, Oklahoma, Missouri, the Dakotas, Iowa, Nebraska, and parts of Montana and Wyoming.

A black-headed cacajo monkey, engraved from a sketch by Alexander von Humboldt.

EUROPE

- **1800** Napoleon Bonaparte defeats the Austrian army at the Battle of Marengo in Italy (June) and at Hohenlinden in southern Germany (December).
- **1800** Italian physicist Alessandro Volta invents the voltaic pile, the first chemical battery capable of storing electricity.
- **1801** The Act of Union that makes Ireland part of the United Kingdom of Great Britain and Ireland comes into effect on January 1; it will last until 1922.
- **1801** Paul I, czar of Russia, is murdered by army officers trying to force him to abdicate.
- **1804** The English inventor Richard Trevithick designs the first self-propelling steam engine.
- **1804** Serbian national leader Kara George leads an uprising in Belgrade against Ottoman rule that spreads to the rest of Serbia.

AFRICA

- **1801** French troops withdraw from Egypt following defeat by the British.
- **1801** U.S. ships attack Tripoli and Algiers on the North African coast in an attempt to end piracy in the Mediterranean (–1805).
- **1804** Islamic reformer Usman dan Fodio inspires an Islamic revival and *jihad* (holy war) in the Hausa kingdoms of northern Nigeria.

WESTERN ASIA

- **1800** Captain John Malcolm of the British East India Company visits Tehran in Iran to seek the support of the shah against the Russians.
- **1803** Islamic fundamentalists of the Wahhabi sect occupy the Hejaz in Arabia and seize the holy cities of Mecca and Medina (–1805).
- **1804** Fath Ali Shah, a ruler of Iran's Qajar Dynasty, starts a war with Russia resulting from the Russian annexation of the Kingdom of Georgia.

SOUTH & CENTRAL ASIA

Ranjit Singh won the title of Lion of the Punjab for his victories over Afghans and Pathans, traditional scourges of northern India. The son of a Sikh tribal leader, he took Lahore in 1799 and proclaimed himself maharaja in 1801. Prevented by British power from expanding his kingdom eastward, he turned to the north, waging many victorious campaigns until his death in 1839.

- **c.1800** British traders in India begin to export opium to China.
- **1801** Ranjit Singh, founder of the Sikh Kingdom of the Punjab, declares himself maharaja ("great ruler") at the age of 21.

EAST ASIA & OCEANIA

- **1801** A wave of persecution against Catholics begins in Korea.
- **1801** British naval captain Matthew Flinders circumnavigates the entire continent of Australia and charts its coastline (–1803).
- **1802** Nguyen Anh unifies Vietnam and makes Hué his capital.

| ARTS & LITERATURE | POLITICS | RELIGION | TECHNOLOGY & SCIENCE | WAR & CONFLICT |

AMERICAS

- **1804** Jean-Jacques Dessalines makes himself emperor of Haiti; he is assassinated two years later.
- **1804** Meriwether Lewis and William Clark lead an overland expedition from the Missouri River across the Great Continental Divide to the Pacific Ocean and back (–1806).
- **1806** Congress authorizes the Great National Pike, better known as the Cumberland Road, which will become the first federal highway (although construction will not begin until 1811).
- **1807** Congress passes an act prohibiting the importation of slaves into the United States, effective from January 1, 1808.
- **1807** Robert Fulton starts the first commercial steamboat service in the world on the Hudson River between New York City and Albany.
- **1807** Former Vice President Aaron Burr is indicted for treason but acquitted.

EUROPE

A model of Richard Trevithick's steam engine, the first to run on rails.

- **1805** A British fleet under the command of Admiral Horatio Nelson defeats a combined French and Spanish fleet at the Battle of Trafalgar; Nelson himself is shot and killed.
- **1805** Napoleon wins a decisive victory over the Austrians and Russians at the Battle of Austerlitz.
- **1806** Austrian Emperor Francis II gives up the title of Holy Roman emperor, so bringing the 1,000-year-old Holy Roman Empire to an end.
- **1807** Serfdom is abolished in Prussia.
- **1807** Napoleon marches across Spain (allied with France at the time) to occupy Portugal.

AFRICA

- **1805** Muhammad Ali, an Albanian officer in Ottoman service, proclaims himself viceroy of Egypt.
- **1806** British forces reoccupy Cape Colony on the southern tip of Africa; they had earlier held the territory from 1795 to 1803.
- **1807** Britain ends its participation in the international slave trade.

WESTERN ASIA

- **1805** Janissaries (crack Ottoman troops) take control of Aleppo, Syria.
- **1807** Janissaries opposed to reform lead a revolt against Ottoman Sultan Selim III, who is deposed and replaced by his brother Mustafa IV.

Fath Ali Shah, second ruler of Persia's Qajar Dynasty, who reigned from 1797 to 1834.

SOUTH & CENTRAL ASIA

- **1803** War breaks out between the British and the Maratha rulers of central India (–1805).
- **1803** British forces occupy Delhi.
- **1803** Coastal Ceylon (Sri Lanka) is made a British colony.

EAST ASIA & OCEANIA

- **1803** The first penal colony is established on Van Diemen's Land (now Tasmania).
- **1804** The White Lotus rebellion is brought to an end in China.

1800–1807 A.D.

1808–1815 A.D.

AMERICAS

- **1808** Portugal's prince regent, the future King John VI, sets up a government in exile in Brazil.
- **1810** Father Miguel Hidalgo leads an uprising in Mexico against Spanish rule; he is defeated and executed in 1811.
- **1811** Paraguay declares its independence from Spain.
- **1812** A Russian fur-trading colony is founded at Fort Ross on what will one day be the California coast.
- **1812** Massachussetts governor Elbridge Gerry gives his name to gerrymandering—the practice of manipulating electoral boundaries for political ends.
- **1812** The United States declares war on Britain (the War of 1812), citing as the cause the continued blockading of its ports and attacks on its commerce; U.S. forces invade Canada.
- **1814** British troops burn Washington, D.C., during the War of 1812, which is ended by the Treaty of Ghent, signed in December.

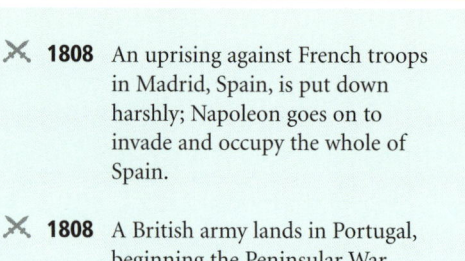

EUROPE

- **1808** An uprising against French troops in Madrid, Spain, is put down harshly; Napoleon goes on to invade and occupy the whole of Spain.
- **1808** A British army lands in Portugal, beginning the Peninsular War against Napoleon (–1814).
- **1809** Andreas Hofer leads an uprising in the Tyrol region of Austria and northern Italy against the French.
- **1809** Sweden cedes Finland to Russia after its defeat in the Finnish War.
- **1809** Death of Joseph Haydn, Austrian composer.

Britain's prince regent, the future King George IV, dressed in ceremonial costume.

AFRICA

- **1808** The British government takes responsibility for Sierra Leone, chosen by opponents of slavery as a colony to resettle freed slaves from North America and Jamaica.
- **1810** Radama I becomes king of the state of Merina in the central highlands of Madagascar; he encourages the spread of mission schools.
- **1814** Said ibn Sultan, ruler of Oman, strengthens Omani control over the Swahili coast of East Africa.

WESTERN ASIA

- **1808** Selim III is assassinated during an uprising intended to restore him as sultan; his cousin Mahmud II takes the Ottoman throne.
- **1811** Mahmud II sends Muhammad Ali Pasha, viceroy of Egypt, with an army to restore order in the Arabian Peninsula.
- **1812** Jabir al-Sabah establishes a sheikhdom in Kuwait.

SOUTH & CENTRAL ASIA

- **1809** Ranjit Singh captures the town of Amritsar; he makes a treaty with the British fixing the eastern boundary of his Sikh kingdom at the Sutlej River.
- **1809** Shoja Shah of Afghanistan signs a treaty with the British.
- **1813** Christian missionaries are allowed for the first time to seek converts in the British-ruled parts of India.

A wooden figure of the Hawaiian war god carved for King Kamehameha I.

EAST ASIA & OCEANIA

- **1810** Kamehameha I conquers rival chiefs to become the first king of the Hawaiian Islands.
- **1811** The Dutch surrender Java to a British invasion force.
- **1814** The Dutch regain control of Sumatra; Java will also be restored to them by treaty two years later.
- **1815** A British expedition explores the ancient Buddhist temple at Borobudur on Java.

ARTS & LITERATURE · **POLITICS** · **RELIGION** · **TECHNOLOGY & SCIENCE** · **WAR & CONFLICT**

AMERICAS

The War of 1812 set the United States against Britain in a struggle linked to Europe's Napoleonic Wars. Much of the inconclusive fighting took place on the Canadian border. The chief U.S. victory took place in January 1815, two weeks after the war had officially ended, when forces under Andrew Jackson repulsed a British attempt to sieze New Orleans (left).

1814 Guyana in South America is transferred from Dutch to British rule and is renamed British Guiana.

1814 José Francia makes himself caudillo (dictator) of Paraguay, which had broken away from Argentina in the previous year.

EUROPE

1810 Spanish artist Francisco de Goya starts work on *The Disasters of War*, a series of 82 prints recording the horrors of the Napoleonic occupation of Spain.

1811 Britain's King George III is declared insane; his son becomes prince regent, marking the start of the Regency period (–1820).

1812 Napoleon's army invades Russia and occupies Moscow, but the severe winter weather forces it to retreat (–1813).

1814 Napoleon abdicates and is exiled to the Mediterranean island of Elba. Louis XVIII, younger son of Louis XVI, is restored as king of France.

1814 The Congress of Vienna meets to decide the political future of Europe in the wake of Napoleon's defeat (–1815).

1815 Escaping from Elba, Napoleon raises a new army in France only to be decisively defeated at the Battle of Waterloo.

AFRICA

1814 Britain takes formal possession of Cape Colony (which it has occupied since 1806) and pays the Netherlands $20 million in compensation.

c.1815 By this date the Mossi kingdoms of Yatenga and Wagadugu in Burkina Faso (central Africa) are in decline.

WESTERN ASIA

1813 The Treaty of Gulistan brings an end to the war between Russia and Persia. Persia loses territory in the Caucasus region.

1813 An Ottoman army retakes Belgrade from Kara George's Serbian nationalist forces.

SOUTH & CENTRAL ASIA

1814 The first Indian museum for arts and natural sciences is established in Calcutta by the Asiatic Society of Bengal.

1815 A border dispute causes British forces in India to go to war with the Gurkhas of Nepal.

EAST ASIA & OCEANIA

1815 Mount Tambora, a volcano in Indonesia, erupts, killing more than 92,000 people; the explosion throws so much ash into the atmosphere that the following year will be known as "the year without a summer."

1815 The first Christian missionaries arrive in New Zealand.

A seated Buddha rests among stupas (circular shrines) at Borobudur on the island of Java (Indonesia).

1808–1815 A.D.

Napoleon Bonaparte

One man dominated world affairs from 1800 to 1815 in an almost unprecedented manner: France's military leader and absolute ruler, Napoleon Bonaparte. Many people in Europe and America saw Napoleon as a hero who used his battlefield successes to spread the ideals of the French Revolution abroad; others detested him for his autocratic ways and the vast number of deaths his expansionist policies left in their wake. What is unchallenged is that he changed France, and the world, forever.

▲ Taking advantage of the career opportunities opened by the French Revolution, Napoleon was a general by the age of 26 and supreme ruler of France four years later. His attempt to reshape Europe on revolutionary lines finally foundered by overstretching the nation's resources.

▶ At the height of his power in 1812 Napoleon dominated a European bloc larger even than Charlemagne's medieval Holy Roman Empire. While Napoleon himself was the driving force behind the entire enterprise, he put individual nations in the hands of trusted subordinates, several of them drawn from his own family.

- **1793** Napoleon wins Toulon from the royalists and is made a brigadier general.
- **1795** Napoleon helps disperse a royalist mob in Paris and is given command of the army of the interior.
- **1796** Napoleon's victories in Italy and Austria win him glory and prestige (–1797).
- **1799** Napoleon becomes first consul.
- **1804** The Napoleonic Code is issued, reforming the laws of France; in the same year Napoleon crowns himself emperor of France in the presence of the pope.
- **1805** Napoleon defeats an Austrian and Russian army at the Battle of Austerlitz.
- **1808** Napoleon crowns his brother Joseph king of Spain.
- **1809** Napoleon defeats the Austrians at the Battle of Wagram.
- **1810** Napoleon divorces his wife Josephine Beauharnais in order to marry Marie-Louise, daughter of Francis I of Austria; a son is born in March 1811.
- **1812** Napoleon invades Russia but is forced to retreat.
- **1814** Napoleon abdicates and is exiled to the Mediterranean island of Elba.

Napoleon Bonaparte was born on the island of Corsica in 1769. His original name was Napoleone Buonaparte, and he spoke Italian until he was 10, when his family sent him to be educated at military schools in France. He graduated as a second lieutenant of artillery in 1785 at the age of 16.

Soon afterward France was plunged into the confusion of the French Revolution. Napoleon proved himself to be a soldier of genius in defense of its goals. He won victories in Italy and Austria that secured the safety of France and led him to see himself as a man of destiny. In 1799 he emerged from the coup that overthrew the ruling Directory as first consul and the most powerful man in France. He immediately set about restoring order to the nation, introducing wide-ranging reforms that established a highly centralized, efficient modern state with himself at its head. In 1804 he proclaimed himself emperor.

Napoleon continued to fight wars abroad, determined to build up France's power in Europe and the rest of the world. In 1805 he defeated the combined armies of Russia and Austria at the Battle of Austerlitz, one of his greatest victories. Unable to overcome the British at sea, he devised the Continental System—economic sanctions designed to exclude Britain from European trade. By 1808 he had made himself master of Europe from Spain to Poland. He redrew the map of the continent, placing members of his own family in positions of power: one brother became king of Spain, another king of Holland, and a third king of Westphalia, while his brother-in-law was made king of Naples.

In 1812 Napoleon sent an army to invade Russia, seeking to compel the czar to uphold the Continental System. The move overstretched his resources and paved the way for his downfall. Defeat in Russia left him greatly weakened, causing the other European powers to ally against him. In 1813 he was defeated at the Battle of Leipzig; in March 1814 the allies entered Paris. Napoleon abdicated and was exiled to the Mediterranean island of Elba, but in less than a year he escaped and returned to France. His attempt to regain power failed when his armies were defeated at Waterloo in June 1815. This time he was exiled to the lonely island of St. Helena in the South Atlantic, from which there was no escape. He died there in 1821, still viewed by many in France as a national hero.

◀ Featuring Napoleon's favorite symbol, the eagle, this imperial coat of arms decorated the back of a throne offered to Bonaparte by the citizens of Strasbourg on the occasion of a state visit. As emperor, Napoleon shocked his radical supporters by creating an imperial nobility to replace the aristocracy of royalist days.

The Campaign of 1812

In June 1812 Napoleon invaded Russia with an army of more than 500,000 men. As they marched toward Moscow, the Russian forces fell back before them, burning the land as they went. Eventually, on September 7 the two armies met in battle at Borodino, just outside the Russian capital. There was terrible loss of life on both sides but no clear victor. A week later Napoleon advanced unopposed into Moscow, which was almost deserted. The defenders who had remained started fires, and soon the whole city was ablaze, leaving the French without food or shelter. Czar Alexander I refused Napoleon's offer of peace, and the emperor had no choice but to retreat. But his army had stayed in Moscow for five weeks, and by now winter was on the way. As the remnants of his forces retraced their route, thousands died of cold and starvation. Others were killed trying to cross the Berezina River. Fewer than 40,000 returned home.

⚔ **1815** Napoleon escapes from Elba and enters Paris in March, having raised a new army on the way. The "100 days" of revived Napoleonic rule end with the emperor's final defeat by British and Prussian forces at the Battle of Waterloo.

👑 **1821** Napoleon dies in exile on St. Helena, a remote island in the Atlantic Ocean.

👑 **1840** Napoleon's remains are returned to France to be reinterred in a marble tomb in Les Invalides, a mausoleum in Paris.

1816–1822 A.D.

AMERICAS

- **1816** Argentina declares its independence from Spain.
- **1816** A slave revolt on the Caribbean island of Barbados is put down.
- **1818** The Stars and Stripes is adopted as the flag of the United States.
- **1818** The 49th Parallel is declared as the border between the United States and Canada.

EUROPE

- **1816** French physician René Laënnec invents the stethoscope, an instrument for listening to the heart and lungs.
- **1818** Mary Shelley publishes her novel *Frankenstein*, telling the story of a scientist who brings a monster to life.
- **1819** Eleven people are killed when cavalry soldiers charge a crowd of protesters in Manchester, England; the event becomes known as the Peterloo Massacre.
- **1820** Danish physicist Hans Christian Ørsted demonstrates that an electric current is able to deflect a magnetized compass needle.
- **1820** The Spanish army leads a revolution against the repressive government of King Ferdinand VII.
- **1821** Greece begins a war to win independence from the Ottoman Empire.

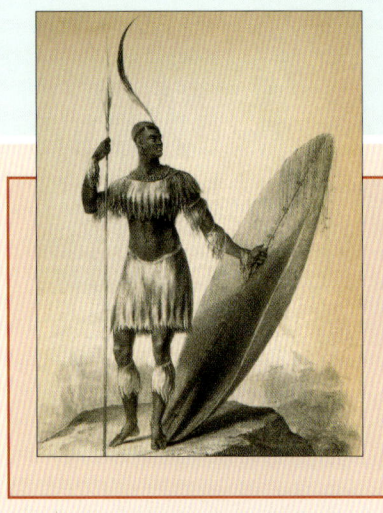

AFRICA

A brilliant but ruthless military leader, Shaka created a Zulu kingdom that took in all the Natal region of present-day South Africa. He created a formidable army of barefoot soldiers armed with long shields and stabbing spears, using it to exterminate neighboring tribes; the remnants were then incorporated into his empire. His triumphs destroyed the tribal structure of the surrounding region, creating widespread devastation and opening up the area to penetration by Boer colonists after his death.

- **1816** The French passenger ship *Medusa* runs aground off the coast of Senegal with great loss of life; the disaster causes a scandal in France and is the subject of a famous painting by French painter Theodore Géricault (1819).

WESTERN ASIA

- **1817** The Ottomans grant the Serbs limited self-government.
- **1819** British warships fire on ports along the Persian Gulf after a series of pirate attacks on British ships in the Indian Ocean.
- **1821** War breaks out again between Persia and the Ottoman Empire. Neither side makes lasting territorial gains (–1823).

SOUTH & CENTRAL ASIA

- **1816** The Gurkhas make peace with the British and agree on the frontier of Nepal, which now comes under British protection.
- **1817** British action against India's *pindari* (wandering bands of warriors) leads to outright war with the Marathas and their final defeat (–1818).
- **1819** Ranjit Singh conquers Kashmir.

EAST ASIA & OCEANIA

- **1816** A British trade mission led by Lord Amherst is expelled from China.
- **1817** Australia is officially named; earlier the island had been known as New Holland.
- **1818** The arrival of European settlers in New Zealand sparks a period of intertribal conflict among the indigenous Maori people known as the Musket Wars (–1835).
- **1819** A British trading station is founded at the southern tip of the Malay Peninsula; it will develop into the modern-day state of Singapore.
- **1820** Minh Manh becomes emperor of Vietnam and revives Confucianism, starting a wave of persecutions against Christians.

| Arts & Literature | Politics | Religion | Technology & Science | War & Conflict |

AMERICAS

- **1818** The *Savannah* is the first steamship to cross the Atlantic.
- **1818** Spain cedes Florida to the United States.
- **1819** Simón Bolívar frees Colombia from Spanish control.
- **1821** Mexico wins independence from Spain.
- **1822** Forces loyal to Jean-Pierre Boyer of Haiti occupy Santo Domingo, uniting the island of Hispaniola under his rule.

EUROPE

The Greek War of Independence was marked by initial Greek successes followed by a successful Ottoman counterattack under Muhammad Ali that culminated in the retaking of Athens in 1827 (left). Foreign intervention saved the Greeks when a joint Russian, French, and British fleet defeated the Turkish navy at the Battle of Navarino soon after. Greek independence was confirmed at the London Conference in 1830.

- **1822** Jean-Francois Champollion uses the Rosetta Stone, discovered by Napoleon's soldiers in Egypt, to decipher ancient Egyptian hieroglyphics (–1824).
- **1822** English mathematician Charles Babbage builds a small prototype model of his "difference engine," or calculating machine, sometimes claimed as the world's first computer.

AFRICA

- **1816** Shaka becomes king of the Zulus and begins to expand Zulu power in southern Africa.
- **1817** Usman dan Fodio establishes the Sokoto Caliphate in the Hausa lands of northern Nigeria and southern Niger.
- **1818** Shehu Ahmad Lobbo establishes an Islamic state in Masina (present-day Mali) with its capital at Hamdallahi, literally "Praise to God" (–1821).
- **1820** British settlers begin to arrive in Cape Colony in great numbers.
- **1820** An Egyptian army led by Ishmail Pasha conquers Sudan on behalf of Muhammad Ali.
- **1822** The first group of freed slaves from the United States arrives to found the city of Monrovia in present-day Liberia, West Africa.

WESTERN ASIA

- **1822** A 30,000-strong Ottoman army invades Greece in an attempt to end the War of Independence.

SOUTH & CENTRAL ASIA

- **1819** The Ajanta Caves in central India are rediscovered: dating from the 2nd century A.D., they contain some of the finest examples of early Buddhist art in India.

EAST ASIA & OCEANIA

- **c.1820** The city of Nan Madol on Pohnpei in the Caroline Islands of Micronesia is abandoned; consisting of a series of artificial stone islets, it was the ceremonial center for the ruling chiefs of the Sandaleur Dynasty.
- **1820** The first Christian missionaries arrive in Hawaii and Tonga.
- **1821** Daoguang becomes emperor of China.

A carved porcelain Chinese brushpot from the reign of Daoguang.

1816–1822 A.D.

1823–1830 A.D.

AMERICAS

1823 U.S. President James Monroe recognizes the newly independent states of Latin America and warns against further European interference in the Americas (the Monroe Doctrine).

1824 The U.S. War Department sets up the Bureau of Indian Affairs, with Ely Parker of the Seneca Nation as its first director.

1824 After a tie in the electoral college the House of Representatives elects John Quincy Adams U.S. president over his rival Andrew Jackson. He will take office in 1825.

1825 The opening of the Erie Canal creates a 363-mile (584-km) waterway connecting the Great Lakes with the Atlantic Ocean.

1827 Joseph Smith, Jr., founder of the Church of Jesus Christ of Latter Day Saints, or Mormons, is given the golden plates of the Book of Mormon by the angel Moroni in a vision.

1827 The Baltimore & Ohio Railroad is chartered as the first commercial railroad to carry both passengers and freight. The first stretch of track will be opened in 1830.

EUROPE

1823 French troops invade Spain in support of Ferdinand VII, bringing the rebellion against his rule to an end.

1824 Charles X succeeds as king of France.

1824 First performance of Beethoven's ninth, and last, symphony; the great composer dies in 1827.

German composer Ludwig von Beethoven, painted by Ludwig Karl Stieler.

1825 The world's first railroad, the Stockton and Darlington Railway, opens in northern England. Regular passenger services begin five years later.

1825 The "Decembrists"—progressive army officers seeking to reform autocratic rule in Russia—stage an unsuccessful uprising.

AFRICA

1823 War breaks out between the British and the Ashanti Kingdom on the Gold Coast of West Africa (–1827).

1823 Muhammad Ali founds the city of Khartoum in Sudan.

1828 The Zulu leader Shaka, who is showing growing signs of insanity, is assassinated.

WESTERN ASIA

1826 Sultan Mahmud II crushes the last mutiny of the Janissaries in Istanbul, thus ending their power.

1827 The Ottoman navy is destroyed by a British, French, and Russian fleet at the Battle of Navarino.

1828 Mahmud II institutes a new western-style dress code, replacing the turban with the fez.

SOUTH & CENTRAL ASIA

1824 The British invade Burma (Myanmar) and capture Rangoon (–1826).

1826 Dost Mohammad becomes ruler of Afghanistan.

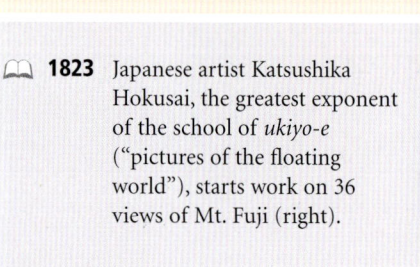

1826 In northern India Sayyid Ahmad of Bareli calls for a jihad (holy war) against the Sikhs.

EAST ASIA & OCEANIA

1823 Japanese artist Katsushika Hokusai, the greatest exponent of the school of *ukiyo-e* ("pictures of the floating world"), starts work on 36 views of Mt. Fuji (right).

1824 An Anglo-Dutch treaty confirms Britain as the dominant colonial power in Malaya and Singapore.

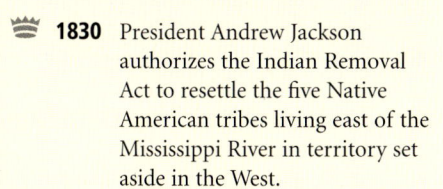

| | ARTS & LITERATURE | POLITICS | RELIGION | TECHNOLOGY & SCIENCE | WAR & CONFLICT |

AMERICAS

- **1829** William Burt patents the first typewriter.
- **1829** Juan Manuel Rosas becomes caudillo (dictator) of Argentina.
- **1830** President Andrew Jackson authorizes the Indian Removal Act to resettle the five Native American tribes living east of the Mississippi River in territory set aside in the West.

As U.S. president from 1817 to 1825, James Monroe negotiated the Canadian boundary dispute with Britain and the takeover of Florida from Spain. He is best remembered now, though, for the Monroe Doctrine, warning the European powers from any further colonization in the Americas while also giving up any U.S. right to intervene in Europe. The doctrine was often invoked in later years, as this 1902 cartoon suggests.

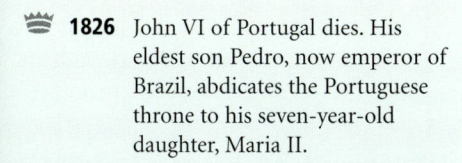

EUROPE

- **1826** John VI of Portugal dies. His eldest son Pedro, now emperor of Brazil, abdicates the Portuguese throne to his seven-year-old daughter, Maria II.
- **1826** French inventor Joseph-Nicéphore Niepce takes the first successful permanent photograph.
- **1829** Turkey recognizes the Greeks' right to rule themselves (although full independence is not granted until 1832).
- **1830** In the July Revolution in France Charles X is forced to abdicate and is succeeded by the populist duke of Orleans, who rules as Louis Philippe.
- **1830** Belgium breaks away from the Netherlands and proclaims its independence.
- **1830** The Poles revolt against Russian rule (–1831).

The first rail locomotive to enter commercial service, kept on display in an English station.

AFRICA

- **1830** A French military force invades Algeria in North Africa, deposes the *dey* (ruler), and occupies the coastal towns.

WESTERN ASIA

- **1828** The Treaty of Turkmanchay ends the second Russo–Persian War, which broke out in 1826.
- **1828** Russia declares war on the Ottoman Empire, already embroiled with Greek rebels.
- **1829** Russia and Turkey make peace at the Treaty of Adrianople; Russia gains land on the Black Sea coast.

SOUTH & CENTRAL ASIA

- **1828** Rammohan Roy, Indian religious reformer, founds the Brahmo Samaj (Society of God) to explore common ground between Hindu and western intellectual thought.
- **1829** The British in India take steps to end the Hindu custom of suttee (the burning of a widow on her husband's funeral pyre).

EAST ASIA & OCEANIA

- **1825** A revolt against Dutch rule on Java is put down with difficulty (–1830).
- **1826** Siam (Thailand) signs a commercial treaty with Great Britain.
- **1827** After Siamese troops devastate the Laotian city of Vientiane, control of northern Laos is divided between Thailand and Vietnam.
- **1828** The Dutch claim possession of the western half of New Guinea.
- **1829** The Swan River Colony is founded for free settlers at Perth in Western Australia.

1823–1830 A.D.

THE LIBERATION OF LATIN AMERICA

IN THE EARLY 19TH CENTURY IT DID NOT TAKE LONG *for Latin America to follow the example of the United States and free itself from colonial rule. The torch of rebellion was lit in 1810, and within 14 years the whole of the Hispanic Empire from Mexico to Argentina had been broken up. In the same period Brazil declared its independence from Portugal.*

▲ A rare combination of thinker and man of action, Simón Bolívar stood not just for the independence of Spain's American colonies but also for cooperation among the Spanish-speaking lands after independence. But his dreams of unity were shattered when Venezuela and Ecuador separated from Colombia in 1830.

Simón Bolívar, the Liberator

Simón Bolívar stands alone in history as the only individual to have had a country, Bolivia, and a currency, the Venezuelan bolivar, named after him. He was born in 1783 to a wealthy family of Spanish descent in Caracas, Venezuela, but spent many years as a young man traveling in Europe, especially Italy and France, where he became an admirer of Napoleon. On his return to South America Bolívar threw his energies into the war against Spain. It took him 11 years to free Venezuela; he then went on to liberate Ecuador and to finally end Spanish resistance in Peru at the Battle of Ayacucho in December 1824. An inspiring leader of men in war, Bolivar dreamed of creating a federation of South American states, but his harsh style of rule once in power alienated many of his former supporters. By the time of his death in 1830 he had ceased to hold any real power, even in Colombia and Venezuela.

By the start of the 19th century the vast Spanish empire in America, stretching from southern California in the north to Chile in the south, was divided into five viceroyalties: New Spain (incorporating Mexico and Central America); New Granada (Venezuela, Colombia, and Ecuador); Peru (Peru and Bolivia); Rio de la Plata (Uruguay, Paraguay, and Argentina); and Chile. The Spanish colonists exported enormous quantities of gold and silver across the Atlantic Ocean from the mines of Mexico and Peru. They created large farming estates known as haciendas and ran them as absentee landlords, living in the coastal towns or returning to Europe for long periods while the Indian peoples were forced to work in the mines or as peons (landless laborers).

In the late 1700s, inspired by the success of the American Revolution and the French Revolution, independence movements began to develop in Latin America. Then, in 1808 Napoleon's army occupied Spain, and Napoleon's brother Joseph Bonaparte was made king, bringing fresh impetus to the demand for

---

1810 There are uprisings against Spanish rule in Mexico, Venezuela, Argentina, and Chile (–1811).

1811 Venezuela declares its independence from Spain (July 5).

1814 Bolívar is driven out of Venezuela by the Spanish and bases himself in Jamaica and Haiti while making repeated raids on the South American mainland.

1816 Argentina wins its independence from Spain.

1817 José de San Martín raises an army in Argentina and crosses the Andes to liberate Chile in partnership with Chilean revolutionary Bernardo O'Higgins.

1817 Bolívar returns to Venezuela, with a base in the Orinoco region.

1819 Bolívar assembles an army of 25,000, including many English and Irish mercenaries, to invade Colombia, where he wins the Battle of Boyacá.

1819 Bolivar proclaims the independent Republic of Colombia (December 17) and makes himself president.

1821 José de San Martín takes possession of Lima, Peru.

1821 Bolivar frees Venezuela from Spanish rule at the Battle of Carabobo (June 24).

1821 Mexico wins its independence from Spain.

1822 Pedro, crown prince of Portugal, declares Brazil's independence from Portugal, with himself as its emperor.

1822 Bolívar and General Antonio José de Sucre liberate Ecuador.

1822 Agustin Iturbide declares himself emperor of Mexico.

1824 Bolívar and de Sucre win the Battle of Ayacucho, defeating the last royalist army in Peru and completing the liberation of South America.

1825 Bolivia—previously part of the Spanish Viceroyalty of Peru—proclaims its independence, taking its name as a tribute to Bolívar.

| Arts & Literature | Politics | Religion | Technology & Science | War & Conflict |

change. Revolution first broke out in Mexico in 1810; but the uprising was quickly put down, and its leader, Miguel Hidalgo, was executed.

In 1811 Paraguay declared its independence, and Simón Bolívar began his fight to liberate Venezuela, his native land. By 1819 he had made himself president of the new Republic of Colombia, and two years later he expelled the Spanish from Venezuela as well. Meanwhile, another revolutionary leader, José de San Martín, first took part in the liberation of Argentina in 1816 and then led an army across the Andes to capture the Peruvian capital of Lima. By 1824, when Bolivar and General Antonio José de Sucre drove the Spanish out of the rest of Peru, all of Spain's empire in the Americas with the exception of the Caribbean islands of Cuba and Puerto Rico had won independence.

Liberation did not extend to everyone in Latin America, however. Power in the new states remained in the hands of people of Spanish descent. Beneath them were the mestizos (individuals of mixed European–Indian descent), and at the very bottom were the native Indians, who had virtually no rights, and the descendants of escaped African slaves. During the following decades there were frequent disagreements and border wars between the new states, many of which fell under the rule of caudillos, dictators who held power through their control of the army.

▶ At the height of his power in 1825 Bolívar governed an empire stretching from Venezuela to the Argentine–Bolivian border. Patagonia was never occupied by the Spanish.

◀ The struggle to liberate the Spanish colonies in America was played out against the background of Spain's involvement in the Napoleonic Wars in Europe. At first Spain allied itself with France, provoking a British attack on Buenos Aires in 1806 (left). Two years later, when French troops occupied Spain, a bitter civil war broke out, leaving the home country in no position to send troops or money to help put down the colonial uprisings.

17

1831–1837 A.D.

AMERICAS

- **1831** Nat Turner leads a slave revolt in Southampton, Virginia, that leaves 55 whites dead.
- **1831** Brazil's first emperor, Pedro I, abdicates and returns to Portugal to help his daughter Maria II regain her throne; he is succeeded by his son Pedro II.

The Alamo, a mission in San Antonio, Texas, played a famous part in the Texan rising against Spanish rule that broke out in 1835. Fewer than 200 defenders held out for 11 days against a Mexican army 3,000 strong; all were eventually killed, but the U.S. cause eventually prevailed.

EUROPE

- **1831** Traveling on the *Beagle*, a British naval vessel, the English naturalist Charles Darwin makes key discoveries that will lead him to formulate his groundbreaking theory of evolution (–1836).
- **1831** Leopold I becomes the first king of Belgium as the newly independent country becomes a constitutional monarchy.
- **1831** The Polish diet (parliament) declares the nation's independence from Russia; Russian forces put down the revolt at the Battle of Ostrolenka.
- **1831** Exiled Italian patriot Giuseppe Mazzini founds the Young Italy independence movement, a model for radical reform groups throughout Europe.
- **1832** The Reform Act in Britain gives the vote to well-to-do men, doubling the electorate from 500,000 to 1 million.
- **1833** After a campaign by antislavery activist William Wilberforce, Britain passes a law abolishing slavery in the empire; it comes into effect on January 1, 1834.

AFRICA

- **1831** The French Foreign Legion is founded in Algeria.
- **1831** Muhammad Ali, viceroy of Egypt, begins a revolt against his Turkish overlords that will see Egypt become an autonomous entity within the Ottoman Empire (his heirs will rule there until 1952).
- **1834** Said ibn Sultan, ruler of Oman, transfers his capital to Zanzibar off the East African coast, making it the center of a commercial empire built on cloves, ivory, and slaves.

WESTERN ASIA

The 1830s marked the start of the Great Trek, which saw thousands of Boers (Dutch settlers in South Africa) moving northward to escape English rule. Known as Voortrekkers, they soon came into conflict with the African peoples of the interior.

- **1832** Muhammad Ali wrests control of Syria from the Ottoman Empire.
- **1833** Austria, Prussia, and Russia agree to uphold the territorial integrity of the Ottoman Empire.

SOUTH & CENTRAL ASIA

- **1834** Sikh forces under the command of Ranjit Singh take the key city of Peshawar on India's Northwest Frontier (now in Pakistan).
- **1835** English is adopted as the language of instruction throughout the areas of India controlled by the British.
- **1835** The ruler of Afghanistan, Dost Mohammad, proclaims himself emir and founds the Barakzai Dynasty.

EAST ASIA & OCEANIA

- **1834** The South Australia Act is passed in the British Parliament, allowing the establishment of a colony there.
- **1834** The British East India Company loses its monopoly on trade with China; the ensuing expansion of trade (especially in opium from British India) will create major friction with China's rulers.
- **1835** The city of Melbourne is founded in the Australian state of Victoria.

| Arts & Literature | Politics | Religion | Technology & Science | War & Conflict |

AMERICAS

- ⚔ **1831** A slave uprising hastens the end of slavery in Jamaica.
- 👑 **1834** The abolition of slavery in the British Empire emancipates almost 700,000 slaves in Britain's Caribbean colonies.
- ⚙ **1835** In the United States Samuel Colt patents his revolving-breech pistol ("revolver").
- ⚔ **1836** Texas wins independence from Mexico in a war that ends at the Battle of San Jacinto; at the Alamo mission 188 defenders hold out against a Mexican army for 11 days before being overwhelmed.
- ⚔ **1836** The federation of Bolivia and Peru is proclaimed; Chile declares war on the new union, which only lasts for three years.
- ⚔ **1837** Two separate revolts, led by Louis Papineau in Lower Canada and William Mackenzie in Upper Canada, break out against British rule in Canada; both are put down.

EUROPE

- 👑 **1834** Under Prussia's leadership the Zollverein (customs union) is founded, embracing most German-speaking territories—an important step toward German unification.
- ⚔ **1834** Civil war erupts in Spain between Carlists (followers of Don Carlos) and the supporters of Isabella II over the disputed succession to the throne (–1839).
- 👑 **1836** In Britain the Chartists (backers of the People's Charter calling for the universal right to vote) found the first national movement representing working people.
- 📖 **1837** British novelist Charles Dickens starts works on *Oliver Twist* (–1839).
- 👑 **1837** Victoria becomes queen of Great Britain, beginning a reign that will last 64 years.

AFRICA

- ⚔ **1834** In the Sixth Xhosa War major clashes take place between Bantu warriors and English settlers in eastern Cape Colony (–1835).
- 👑 **1835** In southern Africa 10,000 Boers (Dutch settlers) protesting the abolition of slavery in Britain's Cape Colony begin the Great Trek north to the Zulu territory of Natal.
- ⚔ **1836** The Dutch Voortrekkers (as the participants in the Great Trek become known) defeat a force of 5,000 Ndebele warriors at the Battle of Vegkop.

WESTERN ASIA

- 👑 **1833** The Ottoman Empire and Russia sign the Treaty of Unkiar Skelessi, which closes access to the Black Sea to all but Russian warships in the event of war.
- 👑 **1833** The Turks recognize the independence of Egypt and relinquish control of Syria (and Aden in southern Arabia) to Muhammad Ali.
- 📖 **1837** Cuneiform script is deciphered by the scholar George Grotefend, leading to a new understanding of the ancient cultures of Mesopotamia (modern Iraq).

SOUTH & CENTRAL ASIA

The Afghan ruler Dost Mohammad and his son, as portrayed by a European artist.

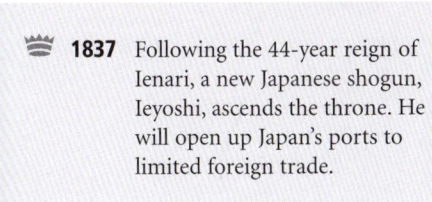

EAST ASIA & OCEANIA

- 👑 **1837** Following the 44-year reign of Ienari, a new Japanese shogun, Ieyoshi, ascends the throne. He will open up Japan's ports to limited foreign trade.
- ⚙ **1837** French explorer Dumont d'Urville starts a three-year Pacific voyage that will lead him to group the Oceanian islands as Melanesia, Micronesia, and Polynesia.

1831–1837 A.D.

1838–1845 A.D.

AMERICAS

- **1838** The confederation of the United Provinces of Central America breaks up as Rafael Carrera leads an Indian uprising in Guatemala, which declares independence the following year.
- **1839** The steamship *Sirius* reaches New York from London after 18 days, becoming the first vessel to cross the Atlantic Ocean solely on steam power.
- **1840** A report prepared by Canada's governor-general Lord Durham recommends the union of Upper and Lower Canada in a single state.

EUROPE

An 1845 photograph by William Henry Fox-Talbot shows the shed where he worked.

- **1838** The first railroad line in Russia links the czar's summer palace to St. Petersburg.
- **1839** In Britain William Henry Fox-Talbot demonstrates his "photogenic drawing" method of photography, while in France Louis Daguerre perfects the daguerrotype.
- **1840** The world's first postage stamp comes into circulation in Britain.
- **1840** Frederick William III of Prussia dies; his son and successor Frederick William IV promises changes but soon crushes liberal hopes for reform of the state.
- **1842** In Britain Parliament passes a law banning women from working below ground in the country's coal mines.

AFRICA

- **1838** As Britain's antislavery law comes into force, thousands of enslaved Africans are freed in Sierra Leone, beginning a southward exodus to their former homelands.
- **1838** British Methodists found a mission to aid Africans on the Gold Coast in West Africa.

Covered wagons and field guns mark the site of the Battle of Blood River.

WESTERN ASIA

- **1839** Ottoman forces invade Syria but are routed by the Egyptians under Ibrahim Pasha at the Battle of Nizip (now in southern Turkey).
- **1839** Ottoman Sultan Mahmud II dies at a critical moment, with the weakened Ottoman Empire under threat of destruction.
- **1839** Under a new sultan, Abdul Mejid, the Ottoman Empire embarks on a program of reform known as the *tanzimat* ("reorganization").

SOUTH & CENTRAL ASIA

- **1838** To forestall Russia's southward expansion, British forces invade Afghanistan, beginning the first of the Afghan Wars; Emir Dost Mohammad is imprisoned.
- **1839** Death of Ranjit Singh, ruler of the Sikh Kingdom of the Punjab.
- **1839** The British install Shah Shuja, an unpopular puppet ruler, in Kabul.
- **1842** An uprising in Kabul forces the British to withdraw their troops.

EAST ASIA & OCEANIA

- **1839** As tensions rise over the import of opium into China, British colonial troops occupy Hong Kong.
- **1840** By the Treaty of Waitangi Britain undertakes to respect the Maoris' right to their own land in New Zealand; the treaty terms are soon violated by unregulated settlers.

Long a standard-bearer of civilization, China reached a low ebb in the 19th century. Foreign powers took advantage of its weakness, notably in two Opium Wars fought by Britain to protect the right of its merchants to import opium into China. Both conflicts ended with China forced to accept humiliating terms.

Arts & Literature Politics Religion Technology & Science War & Conflict

AMERICAS

- **1842** In the United States Crawford Williamson Long performs the first operation using anesthetic (ether).
- **1844** The eastern part of the island of Hispaniola wins independence as Santo Domingo (now the Dominican Republic).
- **1844** The inventor Samuel Morse transmits the first telegraph message, from Washington to Baltimore.
- **1845** The United States annexes Texas.

EUROPE

- **1843** In the wake of the Carlist War 13-year-old Isabella II is finally crowned queen of Spain; her reign is marked by instability.
- **1844** A weavers' uprising in Silesia (southern Poland) is brutally put down by Prussian troops.
- **1845** Potato blight causes a terrible famine in Ireland that will claim the lives of around a million people and drive many more into exile (–1851).

Ireland has suffered many famines, but few as terrible as the one that afflicted it from 1845 on, when potato blight devastated the crop the poor relied on for survival. In all, almost a million people died, and half as many again emigrated, mostly to the United States. Survivors blamed the British government for doing too little to mitigate the famine's effects, leaving a legacy of bitterness to haunt Anglo–Irish relations.

AFRICA

- **1838** At the Battle of Blood River in Natal Boer settlers crush a Zulu army resisting their advance, killing 3,000 warriors.
- **1840** Mzilikazi founds a new Ndebele state in what is now Zimbabwe.
- **1840** Kazembe IV, ruler of the central African territory of Kazembe, dies with his mineral-rich kingdom in the Luapula Valley at its height.
- **1840** The Boer repubic of Natal, founded by the Voortrekkers, is annnexed by the British and made part of Cape Colony (–1844).
- **1843** The British establish the colony of the Gambia in West Africa.

WESTERN ASIA

- **1840** By the Treaty of London Britain, Austria, Russia, and Prussia force Egypt's ruler Muhammad Ali to restore land to the Ottomans.
- **1841** Under the Straits Convention the leading European powers close the Bosporus and Dardanelles to foreign warships in time of peace.
- **1844** South Serbian nationalists led by Ilija Garasanin vow to resist Ottoman rule over the Balkan region.

SOUTH & CENTRAL ASIA

- **1842** The First Afghan War ends in a disastrous defeat for the colonial invaders; only 121 men survive the retreat from Kabul from an original force of over 16,000.
- **1843** The emirs of Sind and the Punjab refuse to cede sovereignty to the British East India Company; Charles Napier's army defeats them at the Battle of Hyderabad.
- **1845** The First Anglo–Sikh War breaks out when Sikh forces invade British territory across the Sutlej River.

EAST ASIA & OCEANIA

- **1840** Britain and China fight the First Opium War after Chinese authorities order the destruction of a large consignment of the drug (–1842).
- **1841** For helping the Sultan of Brunei quell piracy, Sir James Brooke is made raja of Sarawak in Borneo.
- **1842** The Treaty of Nanjing ending the First Opium War secures Britain trading privileges in China and cedes Hong Kong to Britain. It is the first of the so-called "Unequal Treaties," forced on an unwilling China by the western powers.
- **1843** Maoris kill white settlers in New Zealand at the Wairu River, beginning the First Maori War (–1847).
- **1844** China signs a treaty with the United States granting it similar trading rights to those obtained by Britain two years earlier.

1838–1845 A.D.

THE INDUSTRIAL REVOLUTION

FROM AROUND 1750 PROFOUND ECONOMIC and social changes began in western Europe and North America that in time would radically affect people all over the world. Over the next 150 years mechanization and the growth of cities transformed these regions from agricultural commmunities to industrial societies. This period of change came to be known as the Industrial Revolution.

Isambard Kingdom Brunel

Isambard Kingdom Brunel (left) was the greatest engineer of the industrial age. Born into an English engineering family, he was seriously injured in 1828 when a tunnel he and his father were excavating under the Thames River in London collapsed. He made his name in the 1830s, developing England's Great Western Railway. To carry the track, he devised bridges of pioneering design that enhanced his reputation for technical brilliance. Brunel then turned to building iron steamships that revolutionized sea travel, culminating in the massive *Great Eastern*. The ship, which could carry 4,000 passengers, was a technological triumph, but it turned out to be a commercial failure. Exhausted, Brunel died in 1859, just a year after its launch.

- **1733** John Kay invents a mechanical device, the flying shuttle, that speeds up the weaving process.
- **1764** Scottish engineer James Watt improves the steam engine by adding a separate condenser and by devising mechanisms that turn linear into circular motion for powering different machinery (–1774).
- **1776** The Scottish political economist Adam Smith publishes his influential work *The Wealth of Nations*. Smith advocates free trade and modern working practices, including the division of labor.
- **1801** French inventor Joseph Jacquard develops a loom that can produce figured silk fabrics.
- **1815** Scottish engineer John McAdam makes the first paved roads, using crushed stone.
- **1825** The world's first commercial railroad opens to traffic, running between Stockton and Darlington in northern England.
- **1827** France's Benoit Fourneyron develops the water turbine.
- **1833** Britain's Factory Act restricts the use of children in industry.
- **1838** Isambard Kingdom Brunel's iron steamship *Great Western* becomes the first vessel to run regular transatlantic passenger services. The *Great Eastern* will follow 20 years later.
- **1839** American inventor Charles Goodyear discovers how to vulcanize natural rubber, making the material much more durable.
- **1846** The repeal of the protectionist Corn Laws in Britain sees the beginning of the era of free trade between nations.
- **1856** In England Henry Bessemer revolutionizes the manufacture of steel from iron ore, inventing a converter that rids molten pig iron of its impurities and produces cheap, carbon-tempered steel.
- **1862** A machine gun is developed by the U.S. inventor Richard Gatling; 25 years later a much improved version devised by Hiram Maxim will come into widespread service.

22

📖 ARTS & LITERATURE　⛨ POLITICS　☀ RELIGION　⚙ TECHNOLOGY & SCIENCE　⚔ WAR & CONFLICT

▲ The early decades of the Industrial Revolution were marked by low pay and bad working conditions, like those experienced by these children moving coal in a mine. Child labor was finally restricted in Britain in 1833.

◀ James Nasmyth's revolutionary steam hammer was used from 1839 on to press machine parts at the Scottish engineer's foundry in Manchester, England.

The Industrial Revolution began in Britain, where plentiful coal and iron deposits, ready capital, and an empire hungry for exports created ideal conditions. The impetus came first from textiles; the manufacture of cotton and other fabrics, long a cottage industry, was transformed by the invention of mechanical means of spinning and weaving. The new machines were big and expensive, requiring workers to come together in large mills. With this centralizing of production communities changed from making many goods for local consumption to manufacturing a limited range of products for a wider market.

Mechanization also fostered the growth of heavy industry. Early in the 18th century the ironmaster Abraham Darby found a way of producing iron on a large scale, using coke in a blast furnace. Even more important for the huge increase in iron and steel output and in coal extraction later in the century was the supplanting of water power by steam power. The principle of the steam engine had been known since around 1700, and primitive beam engines had been built to pump water from mines; but it was only with James Watt's improvements to the basic design in the 1760s that steam power came of age. Watt and his collaborator, the industrialist Matthew Boulton, produced hundreds of efficient rotary motion engines to drive machinery in factories and mines.

The next step was to apply steam to locomotion. Britain's extensive canal system struggled to carry the ever greater flow of raw materials and goods. The first steam railroad was built to ferry coal from a mine to a waterway in northeastern England in 1825. Within decades the network had expanded enormously, carrying freight and passengers at previously unimagined speeds.

Britain's industrial monopoly was broken early in the 19th century as Belgium and France developed their textile, coal, iron, and arms industries. Even though Germany was still politically fragmented, industrialization began there from the 1840s on. Following unification in 1871, growth accelerated; by 1900 Germany had outstripped Britain in steel production and led the world in chemicals, including synthetic dyes, pharmaceuticals, fertilizers, and explosives. The United States started rather later than the European powers but experienced an extraordinary spurt of growth in the decades following the Civil War that saw it quickly catch up.

The social impact of the Industrial Revolution was also radical. The rural population of most of western Europe fell from 70 to under 10 percent between 1750 and 1914. The new city dwellers experienced overcrowding, poor housing and healthcare, and periodic unemployment. Measures were put in place to curb the worst forms of exploitation, such as child labor and excessive hours. But by the end of the century demands were growing for better political representation for working people, and organized labor in the form of labor unions and socialist parties was beginning to challenge the status quo.

⚙ **1865** Brunel's giant steamship *Great Eastern* lays the first transatlantic telegraph cable.

⚙ **1879** Thomas Alva Edison in the United States and Joseph Swan in England independently develop the electric light; within three years Edison is building power plants to provide electric lighting for homes.

⚙ **1885** German engineers Gottlieb Daimler and Karl Benz devise the internal combustion engine and build vehicles powered by it.

⚙ **1903** Orville and Wilbur Wright undertake the first succesful powered flight of a heavier-than-air machine at Kitty Hawk, North Carolina.

◀ The Industrial Revolution developed in areas with good transport facilities and access to natural resources. Its early heartlands included Britain, Germany, and Belgium.

1846–1852 A.D.

AMERICAS

- **1846** Oregon Territory (Washington, Oregon, and Idaho, with part of British Columbia) is split between the United States and Canada, with the border at the 49th parallel.
- **1846** The U.S. Congress founds the Smithsonian Institution in Washington, D.C.
- **1846** Hostilities break out when the United States and Mexico fail to reach agreement on the purchase of New Mexico; Mexican forces are routed at the battles of Palo Alto and Resaca.

An African–American miner in the California gold rush.

EUROPE

- **1846** A Polish revolt against foreign overlords is suppressed; the Republic of Cracow (in existence since 1815) is dissolved and the territory granted to Austria.
- **1846** In Britain the Corn Laws, which imposed a high import duty on foreign grain, are repealed—a significant victory for free trade.
- **1847** Famine in Ireland drives over 200,000 people to emigrate in a single year, mainly to America.
- **1848** The German political thinkers Karl Marx and Friedrich Engels publish the *Communist Manifesto*, a blueprint for socialist revolution by the working classes.
- **1848** Prodemocracy uprisings take place in many countries across Europe, including Italy, France, Germany, Austria, and Hungary (–1849). In France King Louis Philippe hands over power to the Second Republic.
- **1849** Italian revolutionary Giuseppe Garibaldi helps found the Roman Republic; when French troops restore Pope Pius IX to power, Garibaldi flees to America.
- **1849** Frederick William IV of Prussia spurns the offer of the National Assembly in Frankfurt to be the constitutional monarch of a unified Germany; nascent democracies are crushed throughout Europe.

AFRICA

- **1847** Liberia becomes a free and independent republic.
- **1848** Muhammad Ali's son Ibrahim Pasha dies in Cairo 40 days after taking over as viceroy of Egypt.
- **1848** Now firmly under the colonial control of France, the North African state of Algeria is split into three "departments" (administrative divisions).
- **1849** The French found Libreville in Gabon (equatorial West Africa) as a home for freed slaves.

WESTERN ASIA

- **1848** Nasr al-Din becomes shah of Persia, beginning a 48-year reign in which he will introduce some western ideas to his kingdom.
- **1849** Russian forces occupy the Ottoman Danubian principalities of Walachia and Moldavia, which have risen in revolt.
- **1850** The Bab, an Islamic mystic, is executed for heresy in Persia. His followers are ruthlessly persecuted and eventually expelled (–1864).

SOUTH & CENTRAL ASIA

- **1846** Forces of the British East India Company defeat the Sikhs at Aliwal and Sobraon; the Treaty of Lahore brings the First Anglo–Sikh War to a close.
- **1848** The Second Anglo–Sikh War begins; the British defeat the Sikhs at Chillianwalla and Gujarat, and annex Punjab and Sind by treaty (1849).
- **1851** Rama IV succeeds Rama III as king of Siam (Thailand); the new ruler orders the building of canals and roads, and undertakes administrative reforms.

EAST ASIA & OCEANIA

- **1848** In Australia the explorer Ludwig Leichhardt, who has already probed Queensland and the Northern Territory in 1844–1845, disappears while attempting an east–west crossing of the continent.

Lasting 14 years and costing 20 million lives, the Taiping rebellion devastated China. Led by a visionary who claimed to be Jesus Christ's younger brother, the revolt, which promised egalitarian social reform, only collapsed with the fall of the rebel capital of Nanjing (left) in 1864.

ARTS & LITERATURE | POLITICS | RELIGION | TECHNOLOGY & SCIENCE | WAR & CONFLICT

AMERICAS

- **1848** The Mexican War ends with the United States gaining all lands north of the Rio Grande—California, Arizona, and New Mexico.
- **1848** Thousands of prospectors swarm to the California gold rush.
- **1850** California joins the United States as the 31st state.
- **1850** The Fugitive Slave Act requires all states to return slaves to their former masters, increasing tension between the northern and southern states.
- **1851** U.S. inventor Isaac Singer patents the continuous-stitch sewing machine.
- **1852** Harriet Beecher Stowe publishes her antislavery masterpiece *Uncle Tom's Cabin*.

EUROPE

1848 has gone down in European history as the Year of Revolutions. The first broke out in Paris, and copycat revolts followed in Italy, many German states, and across the Austrian Empire, including Vienna (left). The risings, inspired partly by growing nationalism and partly by middle-class frustration at aristocratic rule, all eventually collapsed in the face of popular alarm at the forces of disorder they unleashed.

- **1851** In London the Great Exhibition showcases the manufactured goods of an industrializing world.
- **1851** Emperor Franz Josef I suspends the Austrian constitution and imposes martial law across the Austro-Hungarian Empire.
- **1851** Louis Napoleon, president of France's Second Republic, stages a coup, creating the Second Empire, with himself as Emperor Napoleon III, in 1852.

AFRICA

- **c.1850** The powerful Zanzibari merchant Tippu Tib leads caravans trading in ivory and slaves into the interior of East Africa, creating a personal empire in the eastern Congo region.
- **1851** British ships lay siege to Lagos in Nigeria in an effort to end the extensive trade in slaves that takes place there.
- **1852** Boer settlers found the republic of Transvaal to the northeast of South Africa; Britain recognizes its sovereignty at the Sand River Convention.

WESTERN ASIA

- **1852** The Bab's successor, taking the name of Baha Ulla ("Splendor of God"), founds the Baha'i faith as a variant form of Babism.

SOUTH & CENTRAL ASIA

- **1852** The Second Anglo-Burmese War breaks out. British forces besiege the capital, Rangoon.

The Aphonphimok Prasat, a disrobing pavilion in the Grand Palace complex in Bangkok, built on the orders of Rama IV.

EAST ASIA & OCEANIA

- **1850** The Taiping Rebellion breaks out in southern China. Lasting 14 years, this insurrection led by Hong Xiuquan is a major challenge to the authority of the ruling Qing (Manchu) Dynasty.
- **1850** The first Chinese immigrants to the United States leave Canton to settle in New York, founding Chinatown; thousands more will follow, mainly to labor on the U.S. transcontinental railroads.
- **1851** In Australia extensive gold deposits are discovered at Bathurst, New South Wales.
- **1852** Britain passes the New Zealand Constitution Act, formalizing the colonial settlement of the country.

1846–1852 A.D.

1853–1860 A.D.

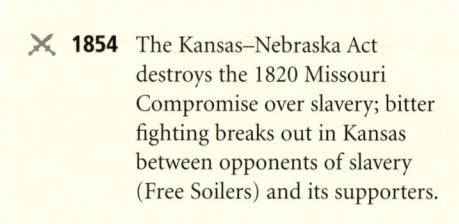

AMERICAS

1854 The Kansas–Nebraska Act destroys the 1820 Missouri Compromise over slavery; bitter fighting breaks out in Kansas between opponents of slavery (Free Soilers) and its supporters.

1854 Through the Gadsden Purchase the U.S. government buys parts of southern Arizona and New Mexico for $10 million in order to facilitate the construction of a southern railroad to the Pacific coast.

Elisha Otis's safety elevator encouraged the development of high-rise buildings.

EUROPE

1856 British inventor Henry Bessemer introduces a process (named after him) for making steel more cheaply and efficiently.

1858 France's Emperor Napoleon III survives an assassination attempt and orders a crackdown on all opponents of his autocratic rule.

1859 The German National Union is founded to lobby for a unified Germany.

AFRICA

1853 Britain grants Cape Colony its own legislative assembly.

1854 In South Africa Britain cedes all territory north of the Orange River to the Boer republics.

1855 Ferdinand de Lesseps is contracted to build the Suez Canal linking the Mediterranean to the Red Sea.

WESTERN ASIA

The Crimean War saw Britain and France make an alliance to prevent further Russian expansion at the expense of the declining Ottoman Empire. The campaign was marked by high loss of life from disease and from futile but heroic actions like the famed Charge of the Light Brigade (left). The war was a setback for Russia, which sued for peace in 1856.

1853 Russia again occupies Walachia and Moldavia; its ships destroy a Turkish Black Sea fleet at Sinope.

1854 The Crimean War breaks out in response to Russian expansion in the Black Sea. Meeting their 1841 treaty obligation, Britain and France invade the Crimean Peninsula of southern Russia.

SOUTH & CENTRAL ASIA

1853 The Second Anglo–Burmese War ends, leaving Britain in control of Pegu (lower Burma). Mindon Min, the new Burmese ruler, develops Mandalay as his new capital.

1853 Britain annexes the Maratha principality of Nagpur in the Deccan region of central India.

1856 Oudh in northern India is annexed by the British.

1856 Persian forces occupy the city of Herat in northwestern Afghanistan, sparking hostilities with Britain.

EAST ASIA & OCEANIA

1853 U.S. Commodore Matthew Perry arrives at Edo Bay, near modern Tokyo, with a fleet of "black ships." By the threat of force he secures an agreement for trade and friendship with imperial Japan.

1854 Taiping rebels overrun Nanjing and make it the center of resistance to Manchu rule.

Commodore Perry as caricatured by a Japanese artist of the time.

1854 Commodore Perry returns to Japan to sign the Treaty of Kanagawa, opening the ports of Hakodate and Shimoda to foreign commerce.

1855 The Miao rebellion against China's Manchu rulers breaks out in the southern province of Guizhou (–1857).

📖 ARTS & LITERATURE   👑 POLITICS   ☀ RELIGION   ⚙ TECHNOLOGY & SCIENCE   ⚔ WAR & CONFLICT

AMERICAS

⚙ **1857** U.S. inventor Elisha Otis installs the first safety elevator in a building in New York City.

👑 **1857** Irish immigrants found the Irish Republican Brotherhood in New York; its supporters ("Fenians") support violence to further Irish independence from Britain (–1858).

👑 **1858** Britain's Queen Victoria selects Ottawa as the capital of Canada.

👑 **1859** Oregon is admitted to the Union as the 33rd state.

⚔ **1859** U.S. abolitionist John Brown raids the armory at Harper's Ferry, Virginia, to arm a slave revolt; he is captured and hanged.

👑 **1860** Abraham Lincoln is elected as 16th president of the United States on a platform opposing the expansion of slavery. His election paves the way for the ensuing secession of the southern slave-owning states from the Union.

EUROPE

👑 **1859** Napoleon III secretly agrees to support Sardinia–Piedmont in its struggle to win Italian independence from Austria.

⚔ **1859** With French backing the Piedmontese army fights the Austrians to a draw at the Battle of Solferino, leaving 30,000 dead.

⚔ **1860** Italian nationalist leader Giuseppe Garibaldi and his "Thousand Redshirts" win control of Sicily and southern Italy.

AFRICA

⚙ **1856** In Egypt a railroad line links Cairo to the Mediterranean port of Alexandria.

👑 **1856** Death of Said ibn Sultan, ruler of Zanazibar and founder of an East African trading empire.

⚔ **1859** Spain conquers Tetuán in Morocco—its first modern colonial venture in Africa.

WESTERN ASIA

⚙ **1855** British nurse Florence Nightingale introduces pioneering standards of sanitation and hygiene into the military hospital at Scutari (Istanbul), saving many lives.

⚔ **1856** After a 322-day siege the key Russian fortress town of Sevastopol in the Crimea falls to British and French forces.

👑 **1856** The Congress of Paris brings the Crimean War to an end. Russia makes concessions in the Balkans, Turkey's independence is guaranteed, and the Black Sea is proclaimed a neutral zone.

Florence Nightingale inspects a ward of her hospital at Scutari in the Crimea.

SOUTH & CENTRAL ASIA

👑 **1857** Shah Nasr al-Din of Persia recognizes the independence of Afghanistan.

⚔ **1857** The Indian Mutiny against British rule erupts, sparked by rumors that new Indian Army rifle cartridges are greased with pork or beef fat, taboo to Muslim and Hindu troops respectively.

👑 **1858** In the wake of the suppression of the Indian Mutiny the Government of India Act transfers sovereignty over the subcontinent from the East India Company to the British crown.

EAST ASIA & OCEANIA

👑 **1856** In Australia the island of Tasmania, formerly a penal colony, is granted self-government.

⚔ **1856** The Second Opium War erupts between Britain and China over the opium trade; British warships besiege Canton and destroy an attacking Chinese fleet (–1857).

👑 **1859** Formerly part of New South Wales, Queensland is made a separate state within Australia.

⚔ **1859** A Franco–Spanish naval force occupies Saigon, marking the start of the French annexation of Cochin China (southern Vietnam) as the nucleus of the future colony of Indochina.

⚔ **1860** An Anglo–French expeditionary force occupies Beijing and destroys the summer palace of the Chinese emperors outside the capital in retaliation for the seizure of envoys under a flag of truce.

1853–1860 A.D.

COLONIALISM

TO SECURE FRESH SOURCES OF *raw materials and to open up new markets for the manufactured goods that began to pour from their factories as the Industrial Revolution gathered pace, European powers sought to expand their existing overseas colonies and win new ones. Having long since established trading empires in Asia and the Americas, they increasingly took on the role of rulers as well as merchants, seeking to impose western standards on distant lands.*

▲ In an archetypal colonial scene Indian villagers report their problems to a visiting district commissioner—the local representative of the British Raj (ruling power).

After the loss of its colonies in North America and the final defeat of Napoleon I in 1815, Britain sought to strengthen its empire and to expand trading opportunities in Asia. In 1819 the colonial administrator Sir Stamford Raffles established the free port of Singapore, which stood at a key point to control trade throughout the region. From 1824 to 1826, following an accord with the Dutch and the founding of the Straits Settlements, Britain consolidated its hold over the Malayan Peninsula. At the same time, British forces from India responding to an invasion of Bengal attacked the neighboring Kingdom of Burma, swiftly overrunning the country's coastal regions. By the mid 1880s the whole country had been annexed to India.

There was soon a booming trade in cotton goods, manufactured in India or increasingly in Britain itself, which were shipped through Singapore to Southeast Asia and China. But a more lucrative trade in another Indian product, opium, caused the outbreak of war between Britain and China in 1840. When China's imperial government ordered the confiscation of the drug, Britain responded with military force. At the end of a one-sided conflict Britain gained the crown colony of Hong Kong, another important East Asian base, which only reverted to Chinese rule in 1997.

In Africa the British colonization of the Cape of Good Hope as Cape Colony began with the founding of a naval base at Simonstown in 1809. In 1835 the original Dutch settlers, protesting a recent British ban

---

1815 At the end of the Napoleonic Wars one-fifth of the world's population is already under the control of the British Empire.

1819 British administrator Sir Stamford Raffles founds the free port of Singapore on the Malaysian Peninsula, which grows into an important trading center.

1824 In the First Anglo–Burmese War the British seize control of the coastal provinces of Arakan and Tenasserim, expanding their empire eastward from Bengal in India (–1826).

1830 The French under King Louis Philippe begin their colonization of Africa by occupying Algeria. The Foreign Legion is founded from international recruits to serve in Africa (–1831).

1835 Dutch settlers in South Africa undertake the Great Trek. After defeating the Zulus at the Battle of Blood River, they found the Republic of Natal (–1838).

1838 The First Afghan War breaks out as British forces invade Afghanistan to prevent the southward spread of the Russian Empire from threatening India (–1842).

1852 Britain annexes the Pegu region of southern Burma during the Second Anglo-Burmese War, leaving Burma a landlocked state (–1853).

1854 France extends and consolidates its hold over Senegal, the center of a growing West African empire.

1857 After quelling the Indian Mutiny, the British transfer control of government of the subcontinent from the East India Company directly to the crown (–1858).

1859 Under their ambitious Emperor Napoleon III the French capture the city of Saigon in Cochin China (Vietnam), beginning their creation of the colony of Indochina.

1859 Spain overruns the Moroccan region of Tetuán, establishing a presence in North Africa that will lead to the establishment of Spanish Morocco in 1912

1863 Napoleon III of France attempts to build an overseas empire in Mexico; the United States pressures French troops to withdraw (–1867).

c.1870 The discovery of valuable minerals (principally gold and diamonds) in southern Africa precipitates the "Scramble for Africa."

28

ARTS & LITERATURE   POLITICS   RELIGION   TECHNOLOGY & SCIENCE   WAR & CONFLICT

The Indian Mutiny

Known in India as the First National War of Independence, the Indian Mutiny broke out in May 1857 among sepoys—Indian troops in British service—stationed in the north of the country. Sparked by rumors that new rifle cartridges from England were smeared with beef or pork fat, respectively taboo to Hindus and Muslims, the uprising was also fueled by nationalist resentment at colonial rule. Quickly gaining support, the rebels captured the capital, Delhi, and besieged outpost garrisons at Lucknow and Kanpur. The revolt was quelled only by the intervention of large-scale reinforcements in mid-1858. India's last Mughal ruler, used by the mutineers as a figurehead, was deposed by the British authorities in the wake of the rebellion. Atrocities hardened attitudes on both sides; Europeans were mercilessly slaughtered in Meerut, while captured mutineers were blown to pieces to discourage native soldiers from further rebellion.

on slave labor, left to travel upcountry on the "Great Trek," in time founding the Boer republics of the Transvaal and Orange Free State. Tension between the two white settler communities was to erupt later in the century in the bitterly fought Anglo–Boer Wars.

France lacked Britain's stability, experiencing revolutions in 1830 and 1848, yet it also embarked on colonization, seizing Algeria, a former Ottoman possession, in 1830. The capital, Algiers, fell after three weeks, but the French were harried by the resistance forces of Abd-el-Kader for a further 15 years. Eager for access to markets in Southeast Asia, France sent an expeditionary force in 1858 to take Saigon. Four years later the emperor of Annam was forced to sign a treaty ceding control of eastern Cochin China (so called to distinguish it from the Cochin region of India) to the foreigners, and over the next two decades the French protectorate was extended to all of Vietnam and neighboring Cambodia.

Yet there were failures too. Emperor Napoleon III overplayed his hand disastrously when he tried to take control of Mexico in 1863. Despite being embroiled in civil war, the United States soon forced the French to abandon the venture, and the unfortunate puppet emperor they had installed, Austria's Archduke Maximilian I, was deposed and executed. Faced with the anticolonial resolve of the Monroe Doctrine, the European powers would make no further attempts to colonize the Americas.

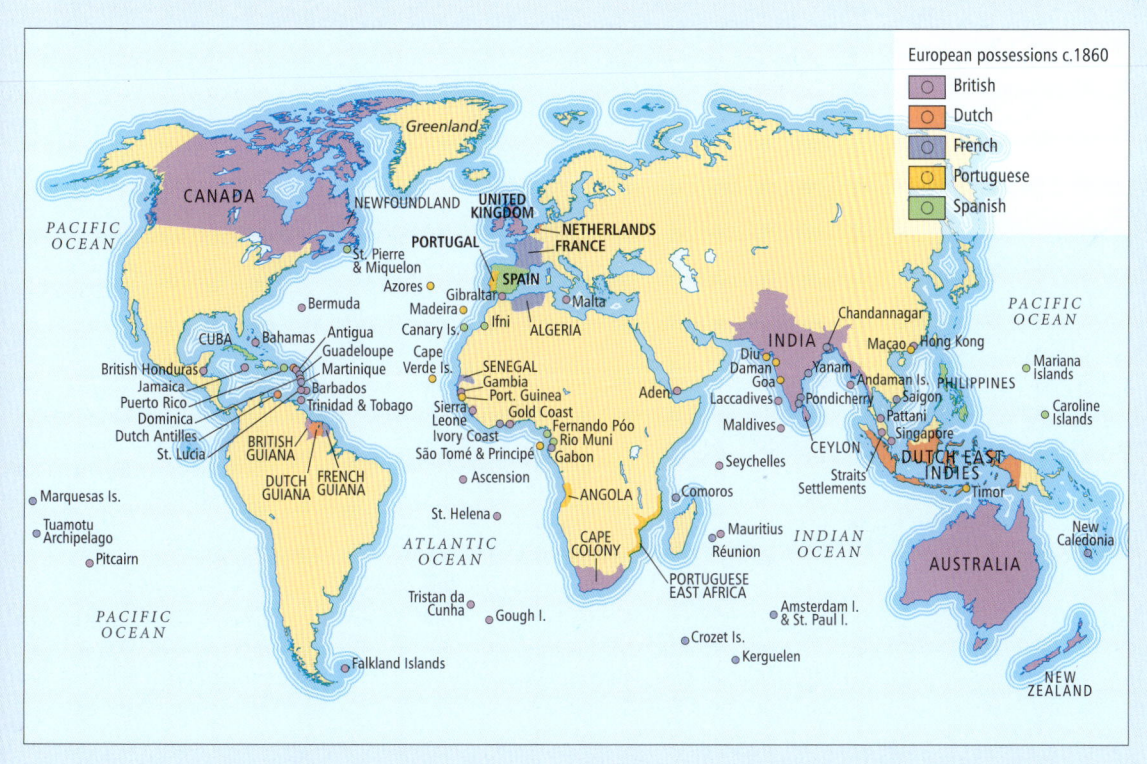

◀ The largest and most widespread colonial empire in the mid-19th century was Britain's, which straddled the world from Canada to Australia. Spain's once-great Latin American empire had been wiped out, leaving the nation with only the Caribbean islands of Cuba and Puerto Rico. The Dutch had retained their East Indian possessions, while the French, who had lost to the British in India and Canada, had expanded into Africa with the occupation of Algeria.

29

1861–1867 A.D.

AMERICAS

- **1861** The American Civil War breaks out when Confederate forces shell Fort Sumter, South Carolina.
- **1863** Abraham Lincoln issues the Emancipation Proclamation, declaring all slaves in rebel states to be free.
- **1863** French forces occupy Mexico City, proclaiming Maximilian of Austria emperor; he is formally inaugurated in 1864.
- **1865** The first transatlantic telegraph cable is successfully laid (–1866).
- **1865** The War of the Triple Alliance sets Paraguay against Argentina, Brazil, and Uruguay. The bloodiest war in Latin American history, it will cost Paraguay 300,000 dead—60 percent of its population at the time (–1870).

EUROPE

- **1861** In the wake of Garibaldi's victories in the south the Kingdom of Italy is proclaimed with Victor Emmanuel, king of Piedmont, as its ruler.
- **1861** Czar Alexander II emancipates Russia's serfs, initiating a series of reforms that includes the setting up of zemstvos (self-governing local councils) three years later.
- **1862** French author Victor Hugo writes *Les Misérables*.
- **1862** Otto von Bismarck becomes premier and foreign minister of Prussia.
- **1863** Polish nationalists stage an unsuccessful insurrection against Russian rule (–1864).
- **1864** Prussia and Austria go to war with Denmark, which is forced to cede the disputed territory of Schleswig–Holstein to Prussia.
- **1864** French scientist Louis Pasteur introduces the pasteurization process, initially for wine.
- **1864** The Red Cross is established by the first Geneva Convention, establishing the principle that battlefield medical facilities are neutral.
- **1865** Austrian monk Gregor Mendel publishes his findings on cross-breeding, initiating the science of genetics (but the significance of his work will not be appreciated for another 35 years).

Laboratory equipment used by Louis Pasteur on display in a French museum.

AFRICA

- **1861** British forces annex the region around Lagos as a British colony.
- **1862** The United States recognizes 15-year-old Liberia as an independent republic.
- **1863** Ismail, the new khedive (ruler) of Egypt, embarks on an ambitious program of modernization.

WESTERN ASIA

- **1861** Abdul Aziz becomes Ottoman sultan on the death of Abdul Mejid. His reign sees the empire opened up to western influences.
- **1866** Abdul Aziz sends troops to Crete to quell an insurrection against Ottoman rule (–1868).
- **1867** Abdul Aziz visits the Great Exhibition in Paris, becoming the first Ottoman sultan to travel to Europe.

SOUTH & CENTRAL ASIA

- **1862** India experiences an economic boom thanks to the increased demand for cotton caused by the American Civil War (–1866).
- **1863** Civil war breaks out in Afghanistan on the death of its ruler, Dost Mohammad (–1870).
- **1865** Russian forces drive into central Asia, conquering Tashkent, which will become the capital of Russian Turkistan two years later.

EAST ASIA & OCEANIA

- **1862** The French establish a protectorate in Cochin China.
- **1863** Muslim rebellions break out in China's Gansu, Qinghai, and Shanxi provinces.
- **1864** The western powers bombard Kagashima and Shimonoseki in Japan in response to attacks on their nationals.
- **1864** Australia starts importing kanaka (native) laborers from the Solomon Islands to work on Queensland sugar plantations.

📖 Arts & Literature 👑 Politics ☀ Religion ⚙ Technology & Science ⚔ War & Conflict

AMERICAS

⚔ **1865** Confederate forces under Robert E. Lee formally surrender at Appomattox Court House; the American Civil War comes to an end soon after.

⚔ **1865** President Lincoln is assassinated.

👑 **1866** Reconstruction gets under way in the southern U.S. states.

⚔ **1867** Maximilian I of Mexico is executed after France withdraws support for his regime.

👑 **1867** Russia sells Alaska to the United States for $7.2 million.

👑 **1867** The British North America Act brings Ontario, Quebec, New Brunswick, and Nova Scotia together in the federal Dominion of Canada.

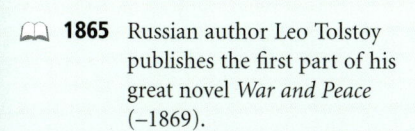

EUROPE

📖 **1865** Russian author Leo Tolstoy publishes the first part of his great novel *War and Peace* (–1869).

⚔ **1866** Prussia defeats its former ally Austria in the Seven Weeks' War.

👑 **1867** Austria becomes Austria-Hungary with the establishment of the Dual Monarchy; already emperor of Austria, Francis Joseph I is now crowned king of Hungary in Budapest.

⚔ **1867** In Italy Garibaldi launches the March on Rome but is defeated and taken prisoner by French and papal troops.

📖 **1867** The German political philosopher Karl Marx publishes the first volume of *Das Kapital* ("Capital").

> No man did more to shape Europe in the late 19th century than Germany's "Iron Chancellor," Otto von Bismarck. As chief minister of Prussia from 1862, he built up the army, then allied with Austria to defeat Denmark, winning Schleswig–Holstein from the Danes. Two years later, in 1866, he went to war with his former Austrian allies, winning a decisive victory in the Seven Weeks' War. His greatest triumph came with the defeat of Napoleon III's France in the Franco–Prussian War of 1870, after which he united most of the German states in a German Second Empire (*Reich*) with William I of Prussia as its emperor.

AFRICA

⚔ **1863** British forces fail to suppress Ashanti raiders attacking the Gold Coast (modern Ghana).

☀ **1866** Scottish explorer–missionary David Livingstone begins his final expedition to Africa.

⚙ **1867** Diamonds are discovered in South Africa.

WESTERN ASIA

SOUTH & CENTRAL ASIA

⚙ **1865** A telegraph service is opened between India and Europe.

Workers lay a section of the Indo–European telegraph cable off Fao in the Persian Gulf.

EAST ASIA & OCEANIA

⚔ **1864** The Taiping Rebellion is finally put down in China with the capture of Nanjing.

👑 **1865** New Zealand's capital moves from Auckland to Wellington.

👑 **1867** The transportation of convicts from Britain to penal settlements in Australia comes to an end.

👑 **1867** Japan's last shogun resigns, bringing almost 700 years of feudal military government to an end.

1861–1867 A.D.

THE AMERICAN CIVIL WAR

IN THE MID-19TH CENTURY THE UNITED STATES TORE ITSELF APART *in a brutal civil war. The principal issue dividing the two sides was slavery, a central part of the economy in the nation's Southern states but deeply unpopular in the North. When Abraham Lincoln won the presidential election of 1860 on an antislavery ticket, 11 Southern states rebelled, joining together to form the Confederate States of America. The conflict that followed lasted four years and cost the nation 162,000 dead.*

▲ A Union soldier leads a charge on Confederate lines in the course of the American Civil War. Advances in rifle technology meant that infantry casualties were regularly high.

▶ Artillerymen from Connecticut pose beside a battery of gigantic mortars employed in the siege of Yorktown, Virginia, in 1862.

- **1854** Violence erupts between pro- and antislavery factions in Kansas, newly opened to settlement.

- **1857** In the Dred Scott case the U.S. Supreme Court decides that descendants of slaves are not entitled to the protection of the U.S. Constitution.

- **1859** Antislavery militants led by John Brown raid a government arsenal at Harper's Ferry (now in West Virginia). Brown is captured and hanged.

- **1860** Abraham Lincoln is elected the 16th president of the United States.

- **1860** South Carolina becomes the first state to secede from the Union. Ten other states will follow its example over the next five months (–1861).

- **1861** The Secessionist states draw up plans to establish the Confederate States of America, with their own government, constitution, and congress.

- **1861** Confederate forces fire the first shots of the civil war by bombarding the Union outpost at Fort Sumter in Charleston Harbor, South Carolina.

- **1861** Confederate forces win an early victory at the encounter known in the South as Manassas and in the North as the First Battle of Bull Run.

- **1862** On the western front Union forces under Ulysses S. Grant win a bloody victory at the Battle of Shiloh.

- **1862** Union forces capture New Orleans, the South's most important port.

- **1862** Confederate forces advancing into Maryland are driven back at the Battle of Antietam (known to Confederates as Sharpsburg).

- **1862** President Lincoln announces his intention to free all slaves in Confederate territories unless the rebel states agree to return to the Union. This Emancipation Proclamation formally comes into force on January 1, 1863.

- **1863** Another Confederate incursion into the north ends in defeat at the Battle of Gettysburg.

- **1863** The Confederate stronghold of Vicksburg on the Mississippi River falls after a short siege.

ARTS & LITERATURE   POLITICS   RELIGION   TECHNOLOGY & SCIENCE   WAR & CONFLICT

Fighting broke out in 1861 and was at first concentrated mainly on two fronts. One centered around the border state of Virginia, where Confederate forces initially gained ground, pressing into Union territory in 1861 and again in 1863. The second front was in the Mississippi Valley, which cut through the Southern heartlands. Here Union General Ulysses S. Grant made deep inroads into Confederate territory, splitting the Southern states in two by 1863.

Although the war was hard fought, the contest was always an unequal one. The North was prosperous and urban, home to well over 20 million people and much of the nation's industrial might. In contrast, the poorer agricultural South had just 9 million inhabitants, 4 million of them slaves. Eventually the North's superior manpower proved decisive, and by early 1865 the Confederate forces were forced to accept surrender.

The great achievement of the Union victory was the abolition of slavery across the United States. Yet the cost was heavy. Nearly one Confederate soldier in four was dead, and much of the South was in ruins. Even the slaves who had nominally won their freedom found in practice that there was little for them to do but go on working for their old masters as sharecroppers, often on terms that were barely better than they had known before. The Civil War left wounds that would take a century or more to heal.

▶ The border states and the South bore the brunt of the fighting in the Civil War. The Confederates' deepest incursion into Union territory was the 1863 campaign that ended at Gettysburg.

Abraham Lincoln

Abraham Lincoln is remembered now as the preserver of the Union, even though at the time of his election as 16th president Southern secessionists accused him of being its destroyer. Born into poverty in a Kentucky log cabin, he was largely self-educated, first rising to prominence in the 1840s as a lawyer in Springfield, Illinois. In his early political career Lincoln was a moderate abolitionist, prepared to accept the continuation of slavery in the Southern states but opposed to its extension to the new lands of the West. Even so, his views were sufficiently marked to bring about immediate confrontation with the South when he took office in 1861. By 1862 he had embraced the policy of emancipation (freedom) for all slaves. His conduct of the war was marked by an unflinching drive to win but also by a lack of rancor toward defeated opponents. His assassination by an embittered Southerner at the war's end caused a national outburst of grief.

✗ **1864** Union General William T. Sherman leads a Union army through Confederate Georgia, capturing Atlanta and spreading devastation in his wake.

✗ **1865** The Confederate capital of Richmond falls to Union forces.

✗ **1865** The Confederate commander Robert E. Lee surrenders to his Union counterpart Ulysses S. Grant at Appomattox Court House, Virginia.

👑 **1865** Five days after Lee's surrender President Lincoln is shot in a Washington, D.C., theater by John Wilkes Booth, a Southern sympathizer; Lincoln dies the following day (April 15).

33

1868–1873 A.D.

AMERICAS

- **1868** U.S. President Andrew Johnson survives impeachment by radicals angered by his obstructive attitude to Reconstruction.
- **1868** A new amendment to the U.S. Constitution (the Fourteenth) grants citizenship to freed slaves.
- **1868** Carlos Manuel de Céspedes leads a rebellion against Spanish rule in Cuba, inaugurating what will become known as the Ten Years' War.

EUROPE

- **1868** A revolution in Spain establishes constitutional monarchy and liberal democratic rule.
- **1870** The Franco–Prussian War breaks out; Prussian forces invade France, defeat the French army at Sedan, and lay siege to Paris. Emperor Napoleon III is taken prisoner, bringing the Second Empire to an end.

The Franco-Prussian War saw France and a newly unified Germany confronting one another for domination of northern Europe. The contest proved onesided when Bismarck's Prussian army defeated Napoleon III's forces at Sedan and went on to besiege Paris. In the ensuing peace settlement France lost the provinces of Alsace and Lorraine, leaving a legacy of bitterness in Franco-German relations that endured well into the 20th century.

AFRICA

- **1868** A British military force frees diplomats held prisoner by Emperor Theodore II of Ethiopia. Theodore commits suicide.
- **1869** The Suez Canal opens.
- **1871** The Fante Confederation of Akan peoples is discouraged by the British, who see it as a threat to their hegemony on Africa's Gold Coast.
- **1871** Henry Morton Stanley of the *New York Herald* tracks down the British missionary and explorer David Livingstone, missing in the East African bush for several years and feared dead.

WESTERN ASIA

A Western caricature of Turkish statesman Midhat Pasha.

- **1869** The Ottoman army is reorganized along Prussian lines.
- **1869** Midhat Pasha becomes the Ottoman governor of Baghdad: his three-year administration will be a time of rapid and radical modernization (–1872).
- **1870** By the Treaty of London the Ottoman Empire is forced to accept Russia's right to build a Black Sea fleet.
- **1870** Sa'ud ibn Faisal deposes his brother Abdallah to rule as emir in Saudi Arabia.

SOUTH & CENTRAL ASIA

- **1868** Two years after being deposed by his half-brothers, Shir Ali Khan reestablishes himself as ruler of Afghanistan.
- **1868** Russia conquers the khanates of Samarkand and Bukhara in central Asia (modern Uzbekistan).
- **1869** Lord Mayo succeeds Lord Lawrence as viceroy of India. His brief term in office will transform the Raj's chaotic finances.

EAST ASIA & OCEANIA

- **1868** In the Meiji Restoration imperial rule is reintroduced in Japan when supporters of the Emperor Mutsuhito overthrow the forces of the Tokugawa Shogunate.
- **1870** Angry crowds in Tianjin, a city near Beijing, kill French diplomats and missionaries amid a rising tide of antiwestern feeling in China.
- **1871** U.S. naval forces strive unsuccessfully to open Korea up to foreign trade.

📖 ARTS & LITERATURE   👑 POLITICS   ☀ RELIGION   ⚙ TECHNOLOGY & SCIENCE   ⚔ WAR & CONFLICT

AMERICAS

⚙ **1869** Teams constructing the Central Pacific and Union Pacific railroads meet at Promontory Point, Utah: the entire North American continent is now crossed by a single railroad.

⚔ **1869** French settlers and French-speaking native tribes in what is now Manitoba rise up against the Canadian Confederation in the Red River Rebellion. (–1870)

👑 **1872** Mexico's reforming President Benito Juárez dies: a succession struggle ensues.

👑 **1873** A financial crash on Wall Street rocks the U.S. economy.

EUROPE

👑 **1870** The annexation of the Papal States means that Italian reunification is almost complete; only the Vatican Palace and its immediate environs remain outside the new nation.

👑 **1871** Germany's Chancellor Otto von Bismarck declares Germany unified under William I, formerly king of Prussia but now emperor of the Second Reich.

⚔ **1871** Paris surrenders to the Prussians. Angry radicals respond by establishing the Commune, a workers' republic suppressed after several weeks of vicious fighting.

👑 **1871** The Treaty of Frankfurt brings the Franco-Prussian War to an end. The French give up the disputed provinces of Alsace and Lorraine to Germany.

👑 **1872** The secret ballot is introduced for elections in Britain.

👑 **1873** William I of Germany, Francis Joseph of Austria, and Alexander II of Russia form the League of the Three Emperors, intended to maintain a common front against Ottoman Turkey.

AFRICA

⚔ **1873** The Second Ashanti War breaks out when British settlers on the coast of Ghana refuse to hand an escaped slave back to the inland Ashanti people; it will end in the burning of Kumasi, the Ashanti capital (–1874).

👑 **1873** Accession of Moulay al-Hassan as sultan of Morocco. His modernizing instincts will bring him into conflict with conservative clerics.

Welsh newsman H.M. Stanley meets David Livingstone at Ujiji in East Africa.

WESTERN ASIA

⚔ **1871** A program of Ottoman expansion in Arabia begins with the conquest of Hasa in the Gulf Coast region. Sheikh Abdallah al-Sabah of neighboring Kuwait also accepts Ottoman overlordship.

👑 **1871** Mirza Husayn, chief minister of Persia, inaugurates a large-scale modernization program but falls foul of conservative factions and is forced out of office (–1873).

⚔ **1872** Ottoman forces conquer Arabia's Red Sea coast, as well as large parts of Yemen to the south.

⚙ **1872** Persia grants the entrepreneur Paul von Reuter a 70-year monopoly to develop modernized transportation, industry, mining, and other facilities in return for regular payments to the state. The concession is later annulled.

SOUTH & CENTRAL ASIA

⚔ **1872** Lord Mayo is assassinated by a convict during a visit to the Andaman Islands prison colony.

👑 **1873** Russia annexes the khanate of Khiva (Uzbekistan).

👑 **1873** The British Raj is reformed to allow more Indian participation at local level.

EAST ASIA & OCEANIA

⚔ **1872** Vientiane, Laos, is sacked by Chinese brigands—mostly deserters from the imperial armies or refugees from civil conflict.

👑 **1872** European settlers finally prevail over New Zealand's indigenous people to end the Maori Wars.

👑 **1873** Siam's young King Chulalongkorn initiates a program of reform.

⚔ **1873** French adventurer François Garnier leads an expedition that takes Hanoi in northern Vietnam.

1868–1873 A.D.

The Age of Invention

The lives of ordinary people in the West *were transformed more radically by technology in the 19th century than they had been in the preceding thousand years. In 1800 most people still lived in the countryside, rising at dawn and going to bed soon after dark by the light of oil lamps and candles. By 1900 railroads crisscrossed the land, the telegraph had been developed, and electricity was harnessed for everyday use in applications ranging from lighting the home to washing clothes.*

▲ Electric power was the force that did most to change people's lives, and by the late 19th century the United States was the world leader in electrical development. It owed its position largely to inventor Thomas Edison, who patented 225 separate devices between 1879 and 1882, including the carbon filament lamp shown above.

The 19th century saw science come out of the laboratories and technology emerge from the mills and mines. Just as steam power revolutionized industry early in the century, so electric power did the same later for everyday life. Electricity was at first little more than a scientific curiosity, its properties demonstrated to wondering gentlefolk at fashionable public lectures. In time, however, its practical applications began to be explored, a process in which British scientist Michael Faraday's discoveries were to prove far-reaching. His work on electromagnetism led to the invention of the electric motor and the transformer, complementary mechanisms from which many later developments would flow.

As the century went on, technological progress developed momentum as fresh inventors built on the work of their predecessors. For example, France's Louis Thimmonier developed the first-ever sewing machine in 1830, but it was left to the American inventor Elias Howe to devise the first practical model for domestic use 15 years later. Samuel Morse conceived the idea of the telegraph in 1832. He and other pioneers then worked on the concept for the next 12 years, producing a series of refinements to improve the system, and by 1866 a telegraph cable had been laid across the Atlantic Ocean. Thomas Edison produced the first practical lightbulb in 1879, although others had produced earlier experimental models. The Scots-born inventor Alexander Graham Bell is credited with the invention of the telephone, although refinements made by Edison were essential to the finished product.

Cumulatively the seperate breakthroughs by individuals of genius made the 19th century the age of invention: By its later decades their discoveries were

Stephenson's *Rocket*

On September 15, 1830, the world's first regular passenger rail service opened in northern England. The inauguration of the Manchester to Liverpool Railway was marked by tragedy when a leading English statesman, William Huskisson, was killed when he fell under a train. Even so, the advantages of the iron way were plain to see, and the day proved a triumph for the *Rocket*, the steam locomotive devised by British engineer George Stephenson that powered the train. Chosen against stiff opposition at the previous year's Rainhill Trials, it raced along, cheered to the skies by festive crowds. Exuberant though they were, they could scarcely guess the importance of what they were witnessing: The railroad would have implications for just about every area of life. Not only would it allow bulk transportation and mass tourism, with all they entailed for economic and cultural life; it would also radically alter people's sense of space and social geography.

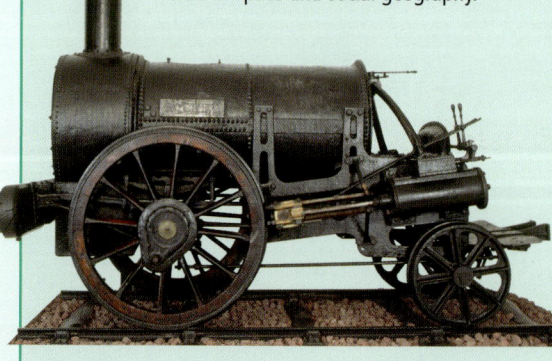

- **1804** Englishman Richard Trevithick invents a working steam locomotive, but the first really successful one will be George Stephenson's *Rocket*, tested in 1829.

- **1821** British scientist Michael Faraday invents the electric motor.

- **1830** France's Louis Thimmonier invents the first known sewing machine.

- **1831** Faraday develops the electric transformer and dynamo.

- **1832** U.S. painter Samuel Morse starts work on the electric telegraph; six years later he perfects his famous code, and 12 years later the first telegraph line is established.

- **1834** An early refrigerator is invented by Jacob Perkins.

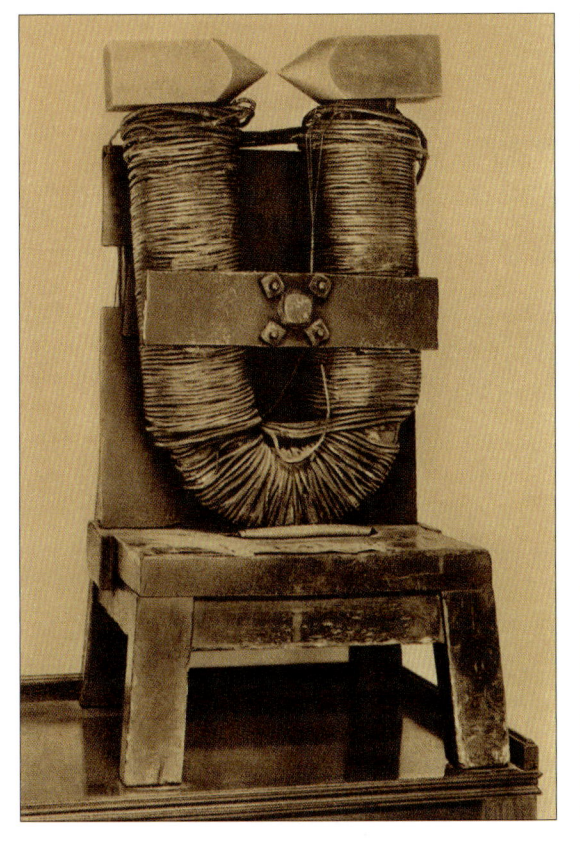

ARTS & LITERATURE   POLITICS   RELIGION   TECHNOLOGY & SCIENCE   WAR & CONFLICT

▲ In 1831 British scientist Michael Faraday helped bring on the electrical era by demonstrating the principle of magnetic induction, using equipment like the electromagnet shown above.

transforming the conditions of daily life. The first, ether-based refrigerator was made by Jacob Perkins in 1834; by the end of the century refrigerated storage and transport were a fact of life. Charles Goodyear's discovery of "vulcanized" rubber (made more resilient by cooking it with sulfur) meant relatively little to the general public in 1839, but it had an effect once John Boyd Dunlop made a practical pneumatic tire in 1889. Dunlop's discovery itself would only come into its own once, by a similarly gradual process of improvement, the modern motor industry was born.

By 1900 railroads had shrunk traveling times dramatically: It took days rather than weeks or months to cross from coast to coast in the United States. Messages could be sent between continents by telegraph, people could speak by telephone from one city to another, sound had been recorded, and electricity was starting to illuminate workplaces and homes. Automobiles were becoming faster and more available, and the Wright Brothers were already contemplating the next great leap forward by thinking about the possibility of powered flight.

▲ The railroad era that got under way with George Stephenson's *Rocket* saw most of Europe crisscrossed with track by 1870. The United States also experienced a railroad boom in the wake of the Civil War; the first transcontinental link was completed in 1869.

✳ **1845** U.S. inventor Elias Howe creates the first successful domestic sewing machine.

✳ **1850** The world's first underwater telegraph cable links Calais, on the coast of France, to Dover, England.

✳ **1858** Hamilton Smith devises the first rotary washing machine.

✳ **1876** Alexander Graham Bell invents the telephone; Thomas Edison's addition of a vibrating-diaphragm microphone the following year will improve its performance dramatically.

✳ **1877** German engineer Niklaus Otto invents what is generally considered to be the prototype for all subsequent internal combustion engines.

✳ **1879** Thomas Edison captures the world's first recorded sound on his phonograph.

✳ **1885** Working independently, German engineers Karl Benz and Gottlieb Daimler develop the first functional automobiles.

✳ **1889** John Boyd Dunlop develops a successful pneumatic tire.

✳ **1898** Rudolf Diesel produces the engine that will be named after him.

1874–1880 A.D.

AMERICAS

A Remington No.1 typewriter of c.1876.

- **1874** The first commercially produced typewriter, the Remington, is introduced.
- **1876** Sitting Bull's Sioux defeat General George Custer's U.S. forces at the Battle of the Little Big Horn.
- **1876** The Molly Maguires workers' movement in the Pennsylvania coalfield is broken by the execution of 10 of its ringleaders.
- **1876** Inventor Alexander Graham Bell patents the telephone.

EUROPE

- **1874** The first Impressionist exhibition is held in France. Claude Monet's painting *Impression: Sunrise* gives the group its name, which is originally intended as a criticism.
- **1875** Rebellion breaks out in Bosnia against Ottoman rule.
- **1876** The Constitution of 1876 restores the Spanish monarchy.

*Claude Monet's painting **Impression: Sunrise**.*

AFRICA

- **1875** Britain buys the Ottoman Empire's share in the Suez Canal, becoming the majority owner.
- **1876** An Anglo–French commission takes financial charge of a bankrupt Egypt.
- **1877** Britain annexes Transvaal, South Africa, held at the time by the Dutch-descended Boers.
- **1879** French forces start an expansionist push across West Africa by moving east from Senegal into the Niger Valley.
- **1879** The Zulu War breaks out in South Africa; British forces suffer a crushing defeat at Isandhlwana.

WESTERN ASIA

- **1874** A financial crisis leaves the Ottoman state bankrupt, leading to confusion and disorder in the empire (–1875).
- **1875** Abdallah ibn Faisal deposes his usurping brother Sa'ud to reclaim the throne of Saudi Arabia.
- **1876** Murad V seizes power as Ottoman sultan in a coup d'état, deposing his autocratic uncle Abdul Aziz.
- **1876** Murad is declared insane following a breakdown. Abdul Hamid II becomes sultan in his place. In deference to western criticism he gives the Ottoman Empire its first written constitution.

SOUTH & CENTRAL ASIA

- **1874** Famine and agrarian unrest bring turmoil to Bengal; the British viceroy Lord Northbrook wins respect for his skillful and humane handling of the situation.
- **1876** Russia seizes Kokand in eastern Uzbekistan. The khan of Kalat (in modern Pakistan) cedes Quetta to the British, who hope to use the city as a bulwark against further Russian expansion.
- **1876** Famine breaks out in India's Deccan region: By 1878, 5 million lives will have been lost.
- **1877** Britain's Queen Victoria assumes the title of empress of India.

EAST ASIA & OCEANIA

- **1874** The Second Treaty of Saigon apparently cements France's hold over Vietnam, but the emperor proves reluctant to honor its terms, and conflict continues.
- **1875** China's Emperor Tongzhi dies without an heir, to be succeeeded by his cousin Dezong, still a small boy. His uncle Prince Gong is his official regent, but real power rests with the dowager (widowed) Empress Cixi.

A Chinese portrait of the dowager Empress Cixi.

| 📖 Arts & Literature | 👑 Politics | ☀ Religion | ⚙ Technology & Science | ⚔ War & Conflict |

AMERICAS

- 👑 **1876** In the revolution of Tuxtepec General Porfirio Díaz seizes power in Mexico in a coup. His hold on power will be endorsed by electors the following year.
- ⚔ **1877** Large-scale labor unrest breaks out in the United States, with railroad strikes and riots.
- ☀ **1877** Thomas Alva Edison develops the phonograph, the first device for playing recorded music.
- ⚔ **1879** The War of the Pacific breaks out as conflict flares between Chile on the one side and Peru and Bolivia on the other; Chile will emerge victorious (–1884).
- ⚔ **1879** In Argentina's War of the Desert General Julio Roca attacks the native peoples of the Pampas, opening land as far as the Río Negro for settlement (–1880).
- 👑 **1880** Ferdinand de Lesseps, builder of the Suez Canal, forms a company to build the Panama Canal.

EUROPE

- ⚔ **1876** A Bulgarian uprising against Ottoman rule is savagely put down.
- 📖 **1876** Composer Richard Wagner produces the complete *Ring* cycle of operas for the first time.
- ⚔ **1877** Russia intervenes in the Balkans in support of local Slavs (Serbs and Montenegrins) rising against Ottoman rule. Britain and Austria ally to oppose Russian expansion in the region.
- 👑 **1878** A show of allied strength compels Russia to back down. The Berlin peace conference confirms the independence of Serbia, Romania, and Montenegro; Austria occupies Bosnia.

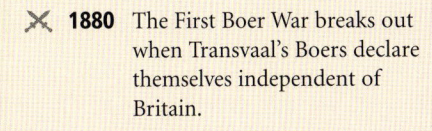

AFRICA

- ⚔ **1880** The First Boer War breaks out when Transvaal's Boers declare themselves independent of Britain.

The Zulu War set British troops and Africans fighting under British colors (left) against Cetshwayo's Zulu nation. After going down to defeat at Isandhlwana, the British forces won the upper hand; Cetshwayo was captured, and his capital was burned.

WESTERN ASIA

- ⚔ **1878** Badly defeated in the Russo–Turkish War, Abdul Hamid II is forced to surrender most of the Ottoman Empire's European possessions under the Treaty of San Stefano. At home he suspends the constitution and takes dictatorial power.
- 👑 **1880** The sheikh of Bahrain surrenders his right to determine foreign policy in return for protection from Britain, starting a trend among the sheikhdoms of the Persian Gulf.
- ⚔ **1880** The Kurds revolt under Shaykh Ubaydallah. The rising is suppressed by joint Ottoman and Persian forces.

SOUTH & CENTRAL ASIA

- ⚔ **1878** Alarmed by Shir Ali Khan's overtures to Russia, Britain starts the Second Afghan War. Shir Ali abdicates in favor of his son Yaqub Khan, but Afghanistan is conquered in 1879.
- 👑 **1880** Britain deposes Yaqub Khan and places Shir Ali's more tractable nephew Abd al-Rahman Khan in power in Afghanistan.
- 👑 **1880** Lord Ripon, a liberal committed to local self-government, is appointed British viceroy of India.

EAST ASIA & OCEANIA

- ⚔ **1875** An uprising in the Malay states against British rule is firmly put down.
- 👑 **1876** New Zealand, formerly six separate provinces, becomes a united dominion of the British Empire.
- 👑 **1876** Japan imposes the Treaty of Kanghwa on Korea, which undertakes to open itself to trade and diplomatic contacts.
- ⚔ **1877** The Satsuma Rebellion breaks out in Japan as a defiant last stand of the samurai class, now marginalized by the introduction of conscription for commoners.
- 👑 **1880** Korea and the United States sign a Treaty of Amity and Commerce.

1874–1880 A.D.

1881–1887 A.D.

AMERICAS

- **1881** James Garfield is assassinated after less than a year as U.S. president.
- **1881** Argentina and Chile resolve a long and bitter border dispute over the division of previously unclaimed Patagonia. Argentina gains the eastern half of Tierra del Fuego, Chile the west.
- **1882** The Chinese Exclusion Act severely restricts Chinese immigration into the United States. Follow-up legislation will effectively end the flow of Asian immigrants.

EUROPE

- **1881** Reforming Russian Czar Alexander II is assassinated by revolutionaries. He is succeeded by his reactionary son Alexander III.
- **1881** The Kingdom of Romania is proclaimed.
- **1882** In the Phoenix Park Murders Britain's chief secretary for Ireland and his undersecretary are assassinated in Dublin by Fenian radicals.

An early Daimler wire-wheel car.

AFRICA

- **1881** French forces occupy Tunisia, nominally still part of the Ottoman Empire but in practice largely independent.
- **1881** In the First Boer War Boer forces win the Battle of Majuba Hill. Under the ensuing Treaty of Pretoria Britain concedes autonomy to Transvaal.
- **1882** British forces occupy Egypt at the request of its Ottoman governor Tawfik Pasha, who has been threatened with a coup by his own officers.
- **1884** Britain's General Charles Gordon and his army are besieged in Khartoum, Sudan, by supporters of Muhammad Ahmad, self-styled Mahdi, or Muslim Messiah.
- **1885** Khartoum falls to the Mahdi's troops, and General Gordon is killed.
- **1885** Leopold II of Belgium is recognized as ruler of the Congo Free State: Millions will die in the brutal colonization process that follows.

WESTERN ASIA

- **1881** Sultan Abdul Hamid issues the Decree of Maharrem, establishing a Public Debt Administration designed to bring Ottoman finances under control.
- **1882** The first wave of Jewish settlement starts in Ottoman Palestine. Some 30,000 people will arrive in the course of the next three decades.
- **1886** Shah Nasr al-Din invites the Islamic visionary Jamal al-Din, known as al-Afghani, to Persia, but he soon becomes a destabilizing presence.

SOUTH & CENTRAL ASIA

- **1882** British viceroy Lord Ripon's Rent Commission recommends a series of reforms to tenancy laws in India, offering greater protection for peasants and their families.
- **1882** The Indian Education Commission is established by Lord Ripon to find ways of extending educational opportunities for Indian children.

A miner seeking his fortune in the Australian gold rush stands by the entrance to a shaft.

EAST ASIA & OCEANIA

- **1884** By the Treaty of Hué France establishes protectorates in Annam and Tonkin (the central and northern parts of modern Vietnam).
- **1885** China and Japan sign the Convention of Tianjin, stipulating that each will remove its forces from Korea.
- **1885** A gold rush begins at Kimberley, Western Australia.

📖 ARTS & LITERATURE 👑 POLITICS ☀ RELIGION ⚙ TECHNOLOGY & SCIENCE ⚔ WAR & CONFLICT

The Statue of Liberty, designed by French sculptor F.A. Bartholdi.

AMERICAS

⚔ **1883** Chile prevails in the War of the Pacific, winning territory from Peru and Bolivia's coastal lands.

⚙ **1885** The Canadian Pacific Railway is completed.

⚙ **1886** New York's Statue of Liberty, a gift from the French people, is dedicated by President Cleveland.

⚔ **1886** Apache Chief Geronimo surrenders to U.S. forces.

EUROPE

👑 **1882** Germany, Austro–Hungary, and Italy join together in the Triple Alliance.

👑 **1884** At the Berlin Conference European powers divide Africa up into spheres of influence.

⚙ **1885** German engineers Gottlieb Daimler and Karl Benz both produce working motor cars.

👑 **1886** William Gladstone's Irish Home Rule Bill fails in the British Parliament, leaving the prime minister's Liberal Party divided.

👑 **1887** The National Union of Women's Suffrage Societies is founded in Britain to advance the cause of votes for women.

AFRICA

⚙ **1886** Gold is discovered in Transvaal and diamonds on Boer territory at Kimberley, confirming Britain's resolve to add these territories to its South African possessions.

👑 **1887** Britain offers to withdraw from Egypt but reserves the right to remain if the peace of the country is under threat.

An early clash between western forces and militant Islam took place in the Sudan in the 1880s. A Nubian named Muhammad Ahmad proclaimed himself the Mahdi, a Muslim Messiah sent to prepare the world for the last days. In 1885 his forces captured Khartoum, killing Britain's General Gordon (right), who had been sent to evacuate Egyptian troops from the area. The Mahdi himself died five months later, probably of typhus, and the rebellion he had inspired was bloodily put down by British forces in the following decade.

WESTERN ASIA

☀ **1887** The Henchak, a revolutionary socialist group, is established by Armenian exiles in Geneva, Switzerland, causing tension to mount in the Ottoman Empire.

SOUTH & CENTRAL ASIA

👑 **1882** Explorer Kishen Singh returns to India, having completed a secret four-year survey of eastern Tibet and the western Gobi Desert on behalf of the British.

👑 **1884** Lord Ripon leaves India after a viceregency that has delighted indigenous Indians but appalled the Anglo-Indian ruling class.

👑 **1885** The Indian National Congress is formed to campaign for independence from Britain.

EAST ASIA & OCEANIA

👑 **1885** Germany and Britain occupy the eastern parts of New Guinea not already under British or Dutch control.

⚔ **1886** The Third Anglo-Burmese War (begun in 1885) concludes in a British victory. Burma is in future to be administered as a part of British India, and its capital is moved from Mandalay to the port of Rangoon.

👑 **1887** China recognizes Portugal's right to administer the trading settlement of Macao.

👑 **1887** The United States acquires the naval base at Pearl Harbor, Hawaii.

1881–1887 A.D.

THE SCRAMBLE FOR AFRICA

BEFORE THE 1870S THE INTERIOR *of Africa had largely escaped the attention of the outside world. Parts of the continent were already well known to foreigners; the coasts had long been exploited by European and Arab merchants, while the North African coastlands had been part of the Mediterranean world since Roman times. In the mid-19th century, however, explorers penetrated to the heart of what Europeans called the "Dark Continent." Their discoveries stirred the interest of the colonial powers, which were soon competing for sovereignty and mineral rights in the newly opened lands.*

▲ A Yoruba craftsman in Nigeria made this carving of Britain's Queen Victoria in the late 19th century. The European colonization of Africa brought about a monumental clash of cultures between peoples with little or no knowledge of each others' ways.

In the 17th and 18th centuries Europe had known West Africa's coasts as a source of slaves and South Africa's Cape of Good Hope as a convenient staging post for ships en route to India. With the 19th century the situation changed radically: For all its incalculable humanitarian benefits, the abolition of the slave trade brought chaos to those African kingdoms that had built power and prosperity around the trade. The leading European nations—Britain and France in particular—offered individual states protection against their local enemies, gaining footholds of trade and political influence for themselves. Farther south British expansion into the Cape hinterland dislodged the region's Dutch-descended Boer farmers, forcing them to make their Great Trek through lands recently destabilized by the expansion of Shaka's Zulu kingdom into the territory of Transvaal.

A series of explorers were meanwhile helping open up Africa to exploitation, even though that was rarely the intention behind their efforts. Early in the century a Scot, Mungo Park, traveled up the Niger River; in its mid years the missionary David Livingstone penetrated to the heart of the continent; while from 1857 on, two Englishmen, Richard Burton and John Hanning Speke, investigated the Great Lakes region, searching for the source of the White Nile.

Whatever the explorers' own motives, the mapping of a region often preceded a colonial claim. By the 1870s opportunistic entrepreneurs in European capitals were studying opportunities for trade and profit in a continent most never even visited. King Leopold II of Belgium took a leading role; as president of the International African Association, he would build up a private kingdom in the Congo Basin

- **1805** Scottish explorer Mungo Park dies while tracing the course of the Niger River.
- **1807** Britain abolishes the slave trade.
- **1835** The Great Trek takes the Boers (settlers of Dutch origin) from Cape Colony on Africa's southern tip overland into the interior of the continent, crossing the Orange and Vaal rivers into the Transvaal.
- **1841** Scottish missionary David Livingstone heads north from the Cape on a decade-long trek across the Kalahari Desert to the Zambezi River, opening a pathway into central Africa.
- **1858** British explorers John Hanning Speke and Richard Burton reach Lake Tanganyika.
- **1862** Speke identifies Lake Victoria as the source of the White Nile.
- **1867** The first major diamond find in Cape Colony is made at Hopetown.
- **1868** French colonists establish a protectorate in Ivory Coast.
- **1876** Leopold II of Belgium establishes the International African Association with a view to undertaking colonial projects.
- **1881** The French occupy Tunisia.
- **1882** British forces occupy Egypt.
- **1884** The Berlin Conference addresses conflicting colonial claims to African territory by European powers.
- **1885** Germany annexes East Africa (now Tanzania). Leopold II of Belgium sets up the Congo Free State.
- **1885** Muslim followers of the Mahdi take Khartoum, Sudan. The killing of General Gordon causes patriotic outrage in Britain.
- **1890** Zanzibar becomes a British protectorate.
- **1895** The territory of the British South Africa Company in what is now Zimbabwe and Zambia is named Rhodesia in Cecil Rhodes's honor.
- **1896** An Italian attempt to seize control of Ethiopia is defeated at the Battle of Adowa.
- **1899** The Second Boer War breaks out between British and Boer settlers in southern Africa.

| Arts & Literature | Politics | Religion | Technology & Science | War & Conflict |

that would in time become notorious for its brutal exploitation of native labor.

By the 1880s the unclaimed lands of Africa had become pawns in a complicated struggle for national prestige played out by most of the major European powers. Britain and France were at first the main players; British dreams of a north–south empire stretching "from the Cape to Cairo" clashed with French ambitions for a band of colonies reaching from the Atlantic to the Indian Ocean. From 1878 on Germany made its voice heard, establishing protectorates in Togo and Cameroon as well as in East and Southwest Africa. Italy laid claim to Somaliland and Eritrea, but its plans to take over Ethiopia also were crushed when its army went down to defeat at Adowa in 1896.

By that time much of the continent, with the exception of Ethiopia and Liberia, had been parceled out among European governments that had little knowledge or understanding of the African populations they presumed to rule. As the name suggests, the Scramble for Africa was largely unplanned and opportunistic; its legacy was a continent whose traditional societies were disrupted in pursuit of interests that were not their own.

▼ The years between 1880 and the outbreak of the First World War in 1914 transformed the map of Africa into a patchwork of European colonies. Only Ethiopia, which drove back an Italian incursion in 1896, and Liberia, originally established with U.S. aid as a home for freed slaves, managed to resist the tide of foreign domination.

European partition of Africa 1880–1913
- Belgian
- British
- French
- German
- Italian
- Portuguese
- Spanish

Cecil Rhodes, Empire-Builder

No individual embraced the colonization of Africa more ambitiously than Britain's Cecil Rhodes, shown in the cartoon above as a colossus bestriding the continent from the Cape of Good Hope to Cairo in Egypt. Rhodes traveled to South Africa as a teenager and stayed to make his fortune; at one time his firm controlled more than 90 percent of the world's production of diamonds. He used his immense wealth to build political influence, buying up newspapers and using them to promote his imperialist views. In 1885 he was instrumental in persuading the British government to establish a protectorate in Bechuanaland, north of Cape Colony; four years later he founded the British South Africa Company, winning for it a charter granting the company the right to exploit the vast tract of land later named Rhodesia in his honor. In 1890 he became prime minister of Cape Colony, devoting much of his energies to his long-held goal of bringing the independent Boer republics of Transvaal and the Orange Free State under British rule in a united, white-ruled South Africa. The Boers took up arms to resist his plans, and the result was the Second Boer War. Although British forces eventually prevailed, Rhodes did not live to see their triumph, dying in 1902, two months before the conflict ended.

43

1888–1893 A.D.

A memorial stone commemorates Sioux dead at Wounded Knee.

AMERICAS

- **1889** Emperor Pedro II of Brazil is forced to abdicate: the country becomes a republic.
- **1889** Ferdinand de Lesseps's Panama Canal scheme collapses.
- **1889** Oklahoma is opened up for settlement.
- **1890** Sioux refugees are massacred at Wounded Knee, South Dakota, by U.S. cavalrymen.

EUROPE

- **1888** Germany's Emperor Frederick III dies and is succeeded by William II.
- **1889** Scottish inventor John Boyd Dunlop develops the pneumatic tyre.
- **1889** Charles Stewart Parnell, leader of the Irish nationalist cause in the British parliament, is brought down by revelations of an adulterous love affair.
- **1889** The Eiffel Tower is built in Paris.
- **1890** William II dismisses Germany's longtime chancellor, Otto von Bismarck.
- **1893** Having been passed by the British House of Commons, Gladstone's Second Irish Home Rule Bill is blocked in Parliament's upper chamber, the House of Lords.
- **1893** Scottish socialist Keir Hardie founds Britain's Independent Labour Party; as the Labour Party, it will become one of the nation's two main political parties (the other being the Conservatives).

AFRICA

- **1889** Ethiopia's new ruler, Menelik II, signs the Treaty of Ucciali with Italy; the Italians will interpret the pact as a license to establish a colonial protectorate.
- **1889** France establishes a protectorate in Ivory Coast; the territory will be made an outright colony four years later.
- **1889** Cecil Rhodes's British South Africa Company is granted a charter to exploit territories to the north of Cape Colony.

WESTERN ASIA

- **1888** The Young Turk movement gets under way in Ottoman Turkey; army officers and intellectuals meet secretly to oppose Sultan Abdul Hamid's despotism.
- **1889** Abdallah ibn Faisal dies; al-Rahman ibn Faisal succeeds him as emir of Saudi Arabia.
- **1889** Abdul Hamid welcomes Emperor William II to Istanbul for a state visit, cementing the growing friendship between the Ottoman Empire and Germany.

SOUTH & CENTRAL ASIA

- **1888** Lord Lansdowne succeeds Lord Dufferin as viceroy of India; his term of office will be a time of relative peace, prosperity, and cautious political reform.
- **1888** The Himalayan Kingdom of Sikkim becomes a British protectorate; its boundary with Tibet is clearly demarcated for the first time.
- **1891** War breaks out after British diplomats visiting Manipur in the Himalayan foothills are killed. The ringleaders are executed, and the small kingdom is absorbed into the province of Assam.

EAST ASIA & OCEANIA

- **1889** Japan's New Constitution establishes a bicameral (two-chamber) diet or parliament but restricts its powers severely. The emperor will be the true ruler of the new Japan.
- **1890** New Zealand holds its first general election based on full male suffrage, electing a Liberal–Labor government that will hold power for more than 20 years.
- **1891** French painter Paul Gauguin settles in Tahiti in search of fresh artistic inspiration.
- **1892** Gold is discovered at Kalgoorlie, Western Australia.
- **1893** France establishes a protectorate in Laos.

Arts & Literature | Politics | Religion | Technology & Science | War & Conflict

AMERICAS

1891 Led by naval officer Captain Jorge Montt, conservative elements in Chile seize power from liberal President José Manuel Balmaceda.

1892 Boll weevils attack the cotton crop in the American South.

1892 Pitched battles break out between striking workers and owners' men at the Homestead Steelworks, Pittsburgh. The eventual outcome is a demoralizing defeat for organized labor.

1892 Ida B. Wells begins her campaign against lynching in the American South.

1893 The failure of a number of major railroad companies causes panic on Wall Street and plunges the U.S. economy into a four-year depression (–1897).

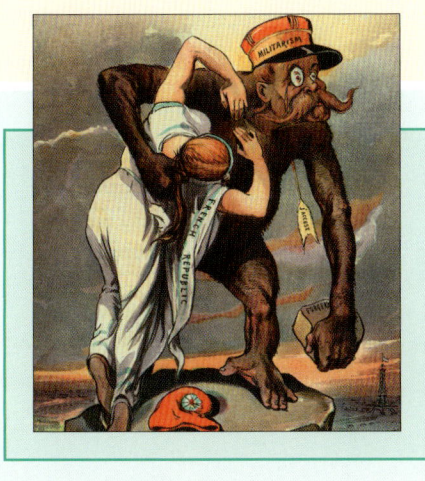

EUROPE

A pro-Dreyfus cartoon shows the French Republic in the grip of brutish militarism. The Dreyfus Affair, in which a Jewish army officer was sent to the Devil's Island prison camp on trumped-up charges for a crime he did not commit, split French public opinion down the middle. Liberals such as the writer Émile Zola charged the anti-Dreyfusards with anti-Semitism and contempt for truth and justice, while opponents of Dreyfus in turn accused the liberals of a lack of patriotism and disrespect for the army.

1893 French army officer Alfred Dreyfus is wrongfully accused of treason in a case that will divide France for over a decade. Convicted by courtmartial in 1894, he will not be finally vindicated until 1906.

AFRICA

1890 Britain takes possession of Zanzibar, giving Germany the Frisian island of Helgoland in exchange.

1890 Cecil Rhodes becomes prime minister of South Africa's Cape Colony.

1891 A British protectorate is established in Nyasaland (now Malawi).

WESTERN ASIA

1891 Jamal al-Din al-Afghani is deported from Iran, the shah having tired of his persistent criticisms of his government.

1891 Muhammad ibn Rashid, ruler of Jabal Shammar, defeats Saudi forces and puts the royal family to flight, bringing to an end the second Saudi state.

SOUTH & CENTRAL ASIA

1892 The Indian Councils Act grants greater powers to local government in British India.

1893 The Durand Line marks the border between India and Afghanistan.

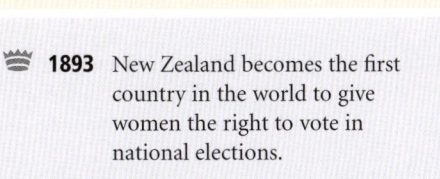

EAST ASIA & OCEANIA

1893 New Zealand becomes the first country in the world to give women the right to vote in national elections.

1893 The Hawaiian monarchy is overthrown in a U.S.-backed coup: The Republic of Hawaii will be proclaimed the next year.

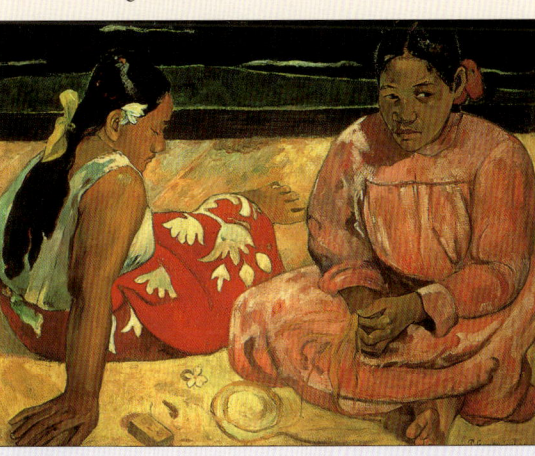

Two Tahitian Women on the Beach, painted by the French expatriate artist Paul Gauguin.

1888–1893 A.D.

1894–1900 A.D.

AMERICAS

- **1894** The U.S. Army imprisons leaders of the Hopi people on Alcatraz Island in San Francisco for seditious conduct.
- **1895** Cuban rebels stage an abortive uprising against Spanish rule.
- **1895** Booker T. Washington's "Atlanta Compromise" speech proposes a cessation of African American political activity in exchange for new educational opportunities.

EUROPE

- **1894** Czar Alexander III dies, to be replaced by his son Nicholas II.
- **1895** France's Lumière brothers present the world's first motion picture show in Paris.
- **1896** The first modern Olympic Games are staged in Athens, Greece.
- **1896** Crete rises against Ottoman rule. The war ends when the European powers impose an international administration (–1898).

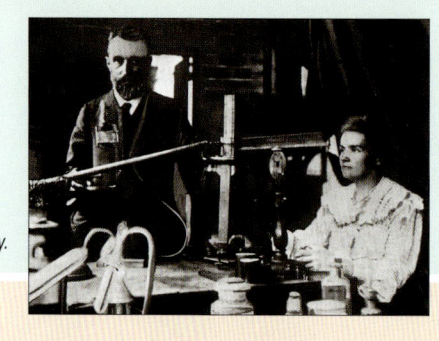

The Curies in their laboratory.

AFRICA

- **1894** The British establish a protectorate in Buganda (Uganda).
- **1895** Territories administered by the British South Africa Company (now Zimbabwe and Zambia) are named Rhodesia in honor of Cecil Rhodes, now the prime minister of Cape Colony.
- **1895** In the Jameson Raid British irregular forces led by L. Starr Jameson attack Transvaal in the hope of provoking an uprising of English-speaking colonists against the Boers. Cecil Rhodes has to resign when the enterprise collapses ignominiously (–1896).
- **1896** Its forces defeated at Adowa, Italy is compelled to recognize Ethiopian independence in the Treaty of Addis Ababa.
- **1896** Ashanti rulers are defeated by Britain in the Fourth (and final) Ashanti War. Britain establishes protectorates in Sierra Leone and East Africa.

WESTERN ASIA

- **1895** Massacres of Armenians begin in Ottoman Turkey; up to 200,000 people will be killed over the next few years.
- **1896** Shah Nasr al-Din of Persia is assassinated by a disciple of the radical Muslim teacher Jamal al-Din al-Afghani.
- **1897** The Young Turks suffer a serious setback when their entire leadership is rounded up and sent into internal exile by the Ottoman government.

SOUTH & CENTRAL ASIA

- **1895** The British rulers of India send an expedition to put down a tribal uprising in Chitral, now in northern Pakistan (–1898).
- **1897** Tribes along British India's Northwest Frontier stage a major revolt.
- **1898** Lord Curzon is appointed viceroy of India.
- **1898** Russia's Transcaspian railroad is extended to Tashkent (Uzbekistan).

EAST ASIA & OCEANIA

Japan embarked on a course of expansion with the Sino-Japanese War of 1894. Its modernized armed forces easily triumphed over China's antiquated army and navy in battles like that of the Yellow Sea (left), and China was compelled to accept humiliating peace terms at Shimonoseki in 1895.

- **1894** Japan invades Korea, triggering the Sino–Japanese War.
- **1894** Sun Yat-sen founds the Revive China Society, a forerunner of the Kuomintang.
- **1895** China acknowledges Korean independence and hands Formosa (Taiwan) over to Japan under the terms of the Treaty of Shimonoseki.

Arts & Literature · Politics · Religion · Technology & Science · War & Conflict

AMERICAS

- **1896** In the *Plessy v. Ferguson* case the U.S. Supreme Court rules that racial segregation is constitutional.
- **1897** The Klondike gold rush begins.
- **1898** The accidental blowing up of the USS *Maine* in Havana harbor gives America the pretext it needs to start the Spanish–American War.
- **1898** By the Treaty of Paris Spain cedes Puerto Rico, Guam, and the Philippines to the United States. Cuba gains its independence.

EUROPE

- **1897** English physicist Joseph Thomson discovers the electron.
- **1898** In France Marie Curie and her husband Pierre discover radium.
- **1898** Russia's Marxist revolutionaries come together to form the Social Democratic Party.
- **1899** At the instigation of Russia's Czar Nicholas II representatives of 26 countries gather for the First International Peace Conference at The Hague in the Netherlands.

AFRICA

- **1898** Herbert Kitchener's two-year campaign to punish the Muslim Mahdists of Sudan culminates in an overwhelming victory for the British at Omdurman. Over 10,000 tribesmen are cut down in the battle.
- **1898** Kitchener pushes south to confront a party of French colonists at Fashoda (Kodok) in southern Sudan, sparking a diplomatic row, the Fashoda Incident.
- **1899** The Second Boer War breaks out between the British and the Boers in South Africa.

Boer fighters take up arms to defend their homeland.

WESTERN ASIA

- **1897** Palestine is chosen as the preferred site for a Jewish national homeland by Theodor Herzl and his Zionist Congress.
- **1898** Emperor Willliam II visits Istanbul, cementing the growing bond between Germany and the Ottoman Empire.
- **1899** Construction of the Istanbul–Baghdad Railroad begins: Germany's involvement upsets rival European powers.

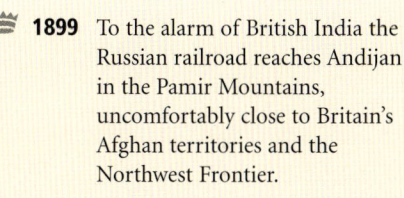

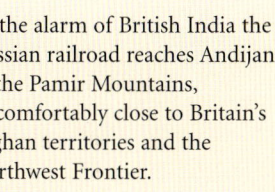

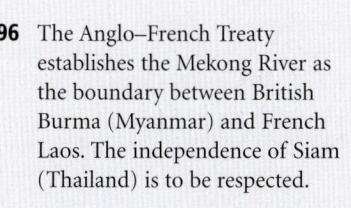

SOUTH & CENTRAL ASIA

- **1899** To the alarm of British India the Russian railroad reaches Andijan in the Pamir Mountains, uncomfortably close to Britain's Afghan territories and the Northwest Frontier.

Britain's newly appointed viceroy in India, Lord Curzon, takes part in an imperial durbar (ceremonial parade) to celebrate his posting.

EAST ASIA & OCEANIA

- **1896** The Anglo–French Treaty establishes the Mekong River as the boundary between British Burma (Myanmar) and French Laos. The independence of Siam (Thailand) is to be respected.
- **1897** German forces seize Kiaochow Bay, China, and establish a trading post there (–1898).
- **1898** Russia leases China's Manchurian port of Lushun, renaming it Port Arthur.
- **1898** Britain secures from China a 99-year lease on Kowloon, the mainland territory across the straits from Hong Kong. Without it the island colony would be unviable.
- **1898** Hawaii is annexed to the United States.
- **1898** The reformist 100 Days Movement agitates for a constitutional monarchy in China, only to be put down on orders of the dowager Empress Cixi.

1894–1900 A.D.

Facts at a Glance

abolitionist
An activist campaigning for the end of slavery.

Afghan Wars
A series of three wars (1838–1842, 1878–1880, and 1919) between Afghan rulers and British forces operating from India to prevent southward Russian expansion. The first campaign brought a major defeat for the British, when its Kabul garrison was forced to retreat to Jalalabad, losing almost all of its 16,000 men on the way.

Akan
A group of peoples linked by language, the Akan originally inhabited the savannah region inland of West Africa's Gold Coast but pushed south into the forest zone in search of gold and slaves. They became key trading partners of the Portuguese.

Anglo–Sikh Wars
Two wars (1845–1846, 1848–1849) fought by Sikhs against British forces in an unsuccessful attempt to prevent the British East India Company from annexing the Punjab. The decisive battle was at Gujarat in the second campaign, where the British defeated 60,000 Sikh warriors.

Apache
Native American people of the southwestern United States, who in the late 19th century fiercely resisted encroachment on their traditional hunting grounds.

Ashanti
After decades of warfare between the various Akan peoples on the Gold Coast, the Ashanti gained the ascendancy, becoming the region's superpower by about 1700 and bartering gold and slaves for the firearms that ensured their dominance.

Ashanti Wars
Series of conflicts between Britain and the Ashanti states of what is now northern Ghana over Ashanti attempts to expand toward the coast.

Bahai faith
Proclaimed in 1863 on the basis of a vision received 11 years earlier, Bahai called for the unification of all creeds. Followers believed that its founder Baha Ulla ("Splendor of God") was not just a prophet but a manifestation of God, along with Zoroaster, the Buddha, Christ, and Muhammad.

Bantus
A group of peoples linked by language, originating in West Africa but dispersed through much of the sub-Saharan region by the early modern period. Kenya's Kikuyu, Zimbabwe's Shona, Namibia's Herero, and South Africa's Xhosa and Zulu are all members of the wider Bantu family.

Boers
From the Dutch for "farmer," the name given to descendants of the original Dutch settlers of South Africa's Cape Colony who spoke their own Dutch-derived language, Afrikaans.

Boer Wars
Wars of 1880 and 1899–1902 in which the Boers of Transvaal and the Orange Free State (combined as the Republic of South Africa) attempted to assert their independence from British rule. Britain finally prevailed, but a lasting legacy of hostility was left.

Buganda
Kingdom west of Lake Victoria in what is now southern Uganda. Established in the 16th century, it came under European dominance and was Christianized in the mid-19th; in 1894 it became a British protectorate.

Carlists
Supporters of Don Carlos (1788–1855), who unsuccessfully claimed the Spanish throne from his three-year-old niece Isabel II in 1833. The Carlists fought three civil wars against Isabel's liberal government (1834–1840, 1846–1849, and 1872–1876).

Canadian Confederation
The union of previously separate British colonies that linked Nova Scotia and New Brunswick with Upper Canada (modern Ontario) and Lower Canada (Quebec) in 1867. Other states subsequently joined the confederation, which was also known as the Dominion of Canada.

Cape Colony
Dutch colony established in 1652 in the region of South Africa's Cape of Good Hope. Britain twice occupied it (from 1795 and 1806) before finally buying it in 1814.

caudillo
A Latin American military strong man claiming to rule in the name of the masses.

Chartists
Members of a radical political movement active in Britain from 1836 to 1848, whose demands for political and social reform, including universal suffrage for men and a secret ballot, were set out in a manifesto called "The People's Charter."

Cochin China
The southern region of Vietnam around the Mekong Delta. In 1862 a French military expedition wrested the area from its indigenous rulers as a colony. It was later allied with the French protectorates of Tonkin, Annam, and Cambodia to form the Union of Indochina.

Commune
The revolutionary regime set up in Paris in 1871 at the end of the Franco–Prussian War while the Prussians were still besieging the city. After two months the French government sent in troops to reassert its control, with heavy loss of life.

communism
A political ideology derived from the writings of Karl Marx (1818–1883) that has as its central tenets the communal ownership of property and the means of production and the creation of an equal society.

Confederate
Supporter of the Confederate States of America—the name taken by the Southern states after their secession from the Union at the time of the American Civil War.

Confucianism
Philosophical system based on the ideas of the celebrated Chinese philosopher Confucius (551–479 B.C.), known in China as Kongfuzi. His teachings, emphasizing learning, respect, and good conduct, became a state religion in China.

Congo Free State
Colonial state created in the valley of the Congo River of central Africa by participants in the Berlin Conference of 1884. It was placed under the personal rule of King Leopold II of Belgium but was open to the trade of all the European powers.

Congress of Vienna
An assembly of European monarchs and statesmen that met in Vienna in 1814–1815 after the defeat of Napoleon to undo the territorial arrangements he had made in Europe and to agree new frontiers.

Conservative Party
In Britain the political party that traditionally upheld the interests of landowners and the church. It was known as the Tory Party until the 1830s, when it adopted the name Conservative.

constitutional monarch
A monarch whose powers are limited by a constitution or laws governing the state.

Continental System
A form of economic warfare waged by Napoleon against Britain by forcing European states to close their ports to British trade.

Corn Laws
Laws used to regulate the import of foreign grain into Britain so as to support home producers. The laws, which became unpopular because they drove up the price of grain, were repealed in 1846.

Cracow, Republic of
A tiny state, consisting of the ancient city of Cracow in southern Poland and surrounding territory, that was created by the Congress of Vienna in 1815 and existed until 1846. It was all that remained at the time of independent Poland.

Crimean War
Fought between 1854 and 1856, this war pitted Russia against a coalition including Britain, France, and the Ottoman Empire intent on restricting Russian naval power in the Black Sea.

cuneiform
A form of writing using wedge-shaped marks (*cuneus* being Latin for "wedge") that was first developed by the Sumerians in about 3000 B.C. Cuneiform characters were impressed in wet clay or wax with the pointed end of a reed.

czar
The title of the ruler of Russia, derived from the Roman imperial title of caesar. It was adopted by Ivan IV (the Terrible) in 1547 and used by his successors until the Russian monarchy was abolished in 1917.

Decembrists
A group of Russian revolutionaries who staged an unsuccessful uprising against Czar Nicholas I in December 1825.

dey
Literally "maternal uncle," the title taken by the rulers of Algeria after 1671, when the country's corsairs rebelled against Ottoman rule. From 1710 to 1830 the dey was to all intents and purposes an independent ruler, owing only nominal allegiance to the Ottoman Empire.

diet
The legislative assembly of certain European countries, especially the German-speaking lands.

Directory
The French revolutionary government set up in 1795, made up of two councils and an executive of five members. Its aim was to prevent power falling again into the hands of one man, as it had under Robespierre during the Reign of Terror.

dominion
Colony accorded self-governing status within the framework of the British Empire.

East India Company (British)
Chartered company established in 1600 that held a trading monopoly on all British commerce with the Indian subcontinent. It traded with the Mughal Empire and engaged in a long struggle for supremacy with its French counterpart. It increasingly became an instrument of colonial administration until its sovereignty over India was formally transferred to the British crown after the Indian Mutiny of 1857.

emancipation
The granting of freedom from slavery.

emir
This Arabic title originally denoted a descendant of Muhammad through his daughter Fatima, but came to be applied to any important commander.

expeditionary force
Military force sent to a distant place, normally to achieve a limited, well-defined objective, such as the lifting of a siege or the quelling of unrest.

Fante Confederation
Alliance of the different states of the Fante people in what is now Ghana against the expansionism of the neighboring (but ethnically distinct) Ashanti peoples. The confederation was organized in 1868, initially with British backing.

Fenians
Members of the Fenian Brotherhood, a clandestine movement organized in Ireland and the United States to achieve Irish independence from Britain, if necessary by violent means.

fez
Named for a city in Morocco, a rimless, cylindrical hat that was adopted by the Ottoman Army in Mahmud II's reforms of the 1820s.

49th Parallel
The line of latitude that in 1818 became the agreed border between the United States and Canada from the Lake of the Woods west to the Rockies. In 1846 the line was extended as far as Vancouver.

Franco-Prussian War
War fought between France and Prussia from 1870 to 1871. Prussia won a rapid victory that caused France's Emperor Napoleon III to abdicate and the the Third Republic to be proclaimed. The peace terms imposed on the French included the loss of Alsace and eastern Lorraine.

free trade
An economic system in which governments do not interfere in the movement of goods between states through the imposition of taxes and tariffs.

Gadsden Purchase
The purchase by the United States from Mexico of a strip of land in what is now southern New Mexico and Arizona, negotiated for the U.S. government by diplomat and railroad entrepreneur James Gadsden in 1853 to facilitate the construction of a southen rail link to the Pacific. The revised treaty was signed in 1854.

Geneva Conventions
International agreement made at Geneva, Switzerland, in 1864 to lay down rules for the treatment of soldiers wounded in war. The provisions were extended at further conventions in 1906, 1929, and 1949 to cover acceptable types of weapons, the treatment of prisoners and the sick, and the protection of civilians in wartime.

Georgia
Country on the eastern shore of the Black Sea. Divided between Persia and the Ottoman Empire for much of the 17th and 18th centuries, it was reunited under Russian rule early in the 19th century.

Gold Coast
A region of coastal West Africa roughly corresponding with modern Ghana, named for its abundant gold reserves. Rich in other minerals too, notably copper and iron, it also became a center for the slave trade.

Great Trek
A series of migrations through the 1830s and 1840s undertaken by South Africa's Boers, angered by British territorial encroachments and the enforced liberation of their slaves. They moved north of the Orange River and set up two republics, Transvaal and the Orange Free State.

Gurkhas
Warriors from the hill tribes of Nepal. After fiercely resisting British encroachment in the early 19th century, they were incorporated from 1860 on into the British Army, where they still form an elite unit.

Hausa
Peoples of what are now northwestern Nigeria and southwest Niger linked by language. From the 14th century a collection of trading states, they were conquered in the 1800s by Fulani warriors and incorporated into the Sokoto Caliphate.

Henchak
Armenian revolutionary organization that took Its name from the Armenian for "bell," implying a call to action. Formed in Geneva in 1887, its aim was a Marxist revolution to free Armenians from Ottoman domination and economic exploitation.

Holy Roman emperor
A title bestowed by the pope on a central European ruler, thought of as the chief secular champion of the Christian cause. The first Holy Roman emperor was the Frankish emperor Charlemagne, crowned in the year 800; the title was abolished by Napoleon in 1806.

Home Rule (Ireland)
The demand that Ireland—united with Britain since the Act of Union (1801)—should have its own parliament to manage its internal affairs. The campaign was a major force in British politics from 1870 on. After 1918 the call for an independent Irish republic replaced that for home rule.

Hopi
Native American people belonging to the Pueblo group who live by farming and are celebrated for their elaborate ceremonial and cultural life.

House of Commons
The elected chamber of the British Parliament.

House of Lords
The upper chamber of the British Parliament, composed in the 19th century of hereditary peers (nobles), bishops, and judges.

House of Representatives
One of the two houses (along with the Senate) of the U.S. Congress. Members are elected for two-year terms and have the power to initiate legislation and to impeach public officials.

impeachment
A judicial procedure in the United States and other countries by which public officials can be put on trial by the legislature for serious offenses committed while in office.

Indian National Congress
Political organization founded in 1885 to promote greater Indian participation in the British raj. In 1920, under the leadership of Mahatma Gandhi, it became a nationwide movement agitating for *swaraj* (self-governance) through a campaign of nonviolent civil disobedience. In 1945–1947 Congress negotiated with Britain for Indian independence.

Irish Republican Brotherhood
The name adopted in later years by members of the Fenian Brotherhood pursuing a policy of armed struggle to win Irish independence from Britain.

Jabal Shammar
Emirate in northern Arabia with its capital at Ha'il. Under Ibn Rashid its forces delivered a crushing setback to Wahhabi expansionism at the Battle of al-Mulaydah (1891).

janissaries
The personal bodyguard of the Ottoman sultan (from the Turkish *yeniçeri*, meaning "new force"), recruited from Christian boys drafted to the sultan's court under the devshirme system.

July Revolution
Revolution that took place on July 27–29, 1830, in France, when the restored Bourbon monarchy of Charles X was overthrown and replaced with the constitutional monarchy of Louis-Philippe, duke of Orléans, known as the Citizen King.

Kalat, Khanate of
Independent state in Baluchistan in northwest India (now Pakistan) under the control of the Mirwari Ahmadzai khans from the 15th century on. It was occupied by the British in 1839.

Kazembe
Kingdom in the Shaba region of what is now the Democratic Republic of Congo, founded by Mwata Kazembe in about 1750. By the mid-19th century it was suffering the encroachments of states centered to the east, in modern Tanzania.

khedive
Derived from a Persian word meaning "lord" or "sovereign," this title was granted by the Ottoman sultan to his viceroy in Egypt in the 1860s and was held by his successors until 1914.

Kokand, Khanate of
Islamic state in the western Ferghana Valley of Central Asia, founded in the early 16th century by the Uzbeks; it developed as a major trade center, with the city of Kokand as its capital from 1740. Kokand was the last major khanate to fall to Russian expansion, in 1876.

Kuomintang
Chinese nationalist movement founded by Sun Yat-sen as the successor to a series of secret societies set up to agitate for the downfall of the Qing Dynasty, the first of which was established in 1894. The Kuomintang became the dominant political force in China following the revolution that overthrew imperial rule in 1911.

Kurds
The once nomadic inhabitants of Kurdistan, a mountainous region now split between southeastern Turkey, Armenia, Syria, Iraq, and Iran. Since the late 19th century Kurds have campaigned for their country to be recognized as a nation-state.

Labour Party
A British socialist political party that was formed to represent trade unions and workers in Parliament. Originally founded as the Independent Labour Party (ILP) in 1893, it became the Labour Representation Committee in 1900 and adopted its present name in 1906.

League of the Three Emperors
An alliance formed in 1873 between the emperors William I of Germany, Francis Joseph of Austria-Hungary, and Alexander II of Russia; the chief architect of the agreement was the German Chancellor Otto von Bismarck.

liberal
Someone embracing the political philosophy of liberalism as developed in 18th- and 19th-century Europe, which stood for limited government and for freedom of the individual, religion, and trade.

Louisiana Purchase
The acquisition in 1803 of French lands west of the Mississippi River by the United States. For the sum of $15 million the U.S. government increased the territory under its control by 140 percent, acquiring not just modern Louisiana but also all or part of 12 other future states.

maharajah
Meaning "great prince" in Sanskrit; the title assumed under the British raj in India by a number of client rulers of princely states who accepted overall British sovereignty while retaining autonomy over the internal affairs of their lands.

Mahdi
The equivalent in Islamic tradition of the Judeo-Christian Messiah, the divine redeemer coming to establish a heaven on earth. The title was claimed by Muhammad Ahmad, who in the 1880s led an uprising in the Sudan.

Manchus
Nomadic people, originally of Tatar stock, from the Liaodong Peninsula in northeastern China. Formerly vassals of the Ming Dynasty, they grew in strength under Nurhachi (1559–1626) and ruled China as the Qing Dynasty from 1644 until 1911.

Maoris
Polynesian people who settled the previously uninhabited islands of New Zealand from the 9th century on.

Marathas
Warrior people of western India who in the 17th and 18th centuries led a Hindu fightback against the expansion of Muslim power. They fought three wars against the British East India Company in the late 18th and early 19th centuries.

martial law
The temporary imposition of military rule in place of civilian government.

Marxists
Followers of the political and economic theories of Karl Marx (1818–1883).

Masina
Islamic state created in the early 19th century in what is now Mali by Fulani holy man Shehu Ahmadu Lobbo: he was inspired by Usman dan Fodio's Sokoto Caliphate, but his state remained separate.

Meiji Restoration
The restoration of imperial rule in Japan, when the last shogun was overthrown by reforming courtiers in 1868.

Merina, Kingdom of
Monarchical state established in the 18th century among the Merina, a people of Malay origin inhabiting the central plateau of Madagascar.

Methodists
Members of the church set up by John Wesley in England in 1729 to renew an Anglican tradition he thought mired in spiritual inertia. The Methodists' reforming zeal inspired many missions to Africa in the mid-19th century.

Mexican War
War fought between the United States and Mexico from 1846 to 1848 in response to the U.S. annexation of Texas in December 1845. It ended in the U.S. occupation of Mexico City and the loss by Mexico of two-fifths of its former territory.

Molly Maguires
Clandestine Irish workers' organization in the Pennsylvania coalfields that organized strikes and attacked police and agents of the mineowners. The movement was eventually broken with the aid of information provided by spies employed by the owners.

Monroe Doctrine
Statement of principle enunciated by U.S. President James Monroe in 1823 to the effect that the United States would in future not tolerate attempts by European powers to plant fresh colonies on the American continent or to interfere in American affairs. In return the U.S. disclaimed any intention of intervening in Europe.

Mormons
Members of the Church of the Latter-Day Saints, established by Joseph Smith on the basis of a mystic revelation whose substance Smith published in 1830 in the *Book of Mormon*.

Mossi
People inhabiting a realm founded by mounted invaders in the 15th century in what is now Burkina Faso, West Africa. They formed two main kingdoms, Wagadugu and Yatenga.

Mughal Empire
The empire established by the Mughals, Islamic successors of Timur the Lame, who conquered northern India in 1526 and subsequently extended their rule over much of the subcontinent.

Napoleonic Code
The body of laws introduced into France by Napoleon Bonaparte as first consul in 1804.

Natal, Republic of
State established by South Africa's Boers in Natal, a region of South Africa's eastern seaboard, after their 1838 defeat of the Zulus, whose heartland it had been. It was seized by the British in 1843 and annexed to Cape Colony in the following year.

Ndebele
Nguni-speaking group who broke away from the Zulus under the leadership of Mzilikazi in the 1820s, eventually establishing a kingdom in central and southern Transvaal. At first they coexisted with the incoming Voortrekkers, but later withstood attacks, making peace in 1852.

Northwest Frontier
Border region between British India and Afghanistan, under British control from the late 1870s. Home to the warlike Pathans, it was difficult to defend and saw frequent uprisings.

Opium Wars
Two wars (1840–1842, 1856–1860) fought between Britain and China over the importation of opium from British India. After trying to halt the trade by seizing shipments, China's Qing Dynasty rulers were defeated and forced to make further trade concessions to foreign powers.

Oregon Territory
An area of North America west of the Rocky Mountains given limited self-government by the U.S. government in 1848 in preparation for statehood. Its extent was substantially reduced by the creation of Washington Territory five years later. The rest became the state of Oregon in 1859.

Ottoman Dynasty
Named for Uthman, a Turkic tribal leader who came to prominence in eastern Asia Minor in 1281, a line of rulers who built a great and enduring empire in western Asia and the eastern Mediterranean from the 14th century on. By the 19th century the empire was in decline, winning the nickname of the "Sick Man of Europe."

Oudh, Kingdom of
Former kingdom now in the northeast Indian state of Uttar Pradesh; Muslim-ruled from the 11th century, it came under British control with the agreement of the Mughals in 1756 and was fully incorporated into British India in 1856.

Panama Canal
Canal across the Isthmus of Panama connecting the Atlantic and Pacific oceans. An attempt to build the canal in the 1880s failed when the company promoting it went bankrupt. The waterway eventually opened in 1914.

Papal States
States in central Italy that were the territorial possessions of the papacy until they became part of the newly unified country of Italy in 1870.

Pathans
Also known as Pushtuns. Pushto-speaking people of the Afghan–Indian border with a reputation as fierce fighters, they remained unsubdued by British camapaigns in the late 19th century, staging major revolts in 1897 and in 1919–1920.

Pegu
Territory in southern Burma ruled from the city of Pegu, founded in 825 A.D. as the capital of the Mon Kingdom and later ruled by the Toungou until the rise of the Konbaung Dynasty in the 1750s.

Peninsular War
The British-led campaign (1808–1814) against French forces occupying the Iberian Peninsula (Spain and Portugal) during the Napoleonic Wars.

protectorate
A state taken under the protection of another state and thereby effectively under that state's control.

Punjab, Kingdom of the
Kingdom established by the Sikh leader Ranjit Singh in 1799 in the Punjab area of northwest India, bordering what is now Pakistan. The kingdom was annexed by the British in 1849 following victory in the Second Anglo–Sikh War.

raj
The Hindi word for "rule"; the term applied to the period of British dominance in India, especially the time of direct rule by the crown from 1858 to 1947. More than 500 princely states kept control over their domestic affairs under British hegemony.

Red Cross
An international humanitarian organization founded by the Swiss philanthropist Henri Dunant (1828–1910) with the purpose of treating the sick and wounded in war.

Redshirts
Volunteers who served under the revolutionary leader Giuseppe Garibaldi (1807–82) in the struggle for Italian unity (the Risorgimento), adopting his distinctive red smock as their uniform.

Regency period
In Britain the period from 1811 to 1820 when George, prince of Wales (the Prince Regent), acted in place of his father King George III.

Roman Republic
Republic established in Rome in the wake of the 1848 revolution by the Italian nationalist leader Giuseppe Mazzini (1805–1872). It lasted for only four months of 1849 before French and Austrian forces restored the authority of Pope Pius IX.

Russo-Persian Wars
Wars fought between Russia and Iran over territories in the Caucasus from 1804 to 1813 and 1826 to 1828. Russia emerged as the victor, taking Georgia, Armenia, and northern Azerbaijan.

samurai
The hereditary class of warriors that dominated Japanese society from the 12th to the 19th century.

Satsuma Rebellion
Uprising led by samurai activists from the southwestern Japanese region of Satsuma, which played a large part in the overthrow of the Tokugawa Shogunate and the Meiji Restoration.

secession
Withdrawal from a group or organization. In U.S. history the term applies to the withdrawal of 11 southern states from the Union at the start of the Civil War.

Second Empire
The period of French history from 1852, when Louis Napoleon (nephew of Napoleon I) took the title of emperor of the French until his abdication in 1870. He called himself Napoleon III, Napoleon II being a son of Napoleon I who had died in 1832 having taken no active role in politics. The First Empire was that of Napoleon I (1804–1815).

Second Reich
Literally "Second Empire," the name given to the period of imperial rule in Germany from unification in 1871 until the founding of the Weimar Republic in 1918 after the nation's defeat in World War I. It had two rulers: William (Wilhelm) I (r.1870–1888) and William II (r.1888–1918). The Holy Roman Empire was regarded as Germany's First Reich; Hitler was to establish the Third Reich in 1933.

Second Republic
The short-lived republic established in France after the overthrow of King Louis-Philippe in February 1848. It survived until 1852, when the Second Empire was proclaimed.

sepoys
Indigenous Indian troops recruited by the British East India Company. The Indian Mutiny of 1857, which began among native soldiers in Meerut, is sometimes known as the Sepoy Rebellion.

serfdom
The status of farm laborers not free to move from the land on which they worked.

shah
Persian for "king." Originally the title of the kings of Persia, it also came to be used by the rulers of other countries in South and Central Asia

shogun
Literally "commander of the imperial guard," the title given from 1192 on to the leader of Japan's ruling warrior family. For almost seven centuries until 1868 the shoguns were the true rulers of Japan, leaving the country's emperors to occupy themselves primarily with ceremonial duties.

Siam, Kingdom of
Successor state in Thailand to the kingdom of Ayutthaya (1351–1767) after the city of Ayutthaya itself was overrun by the Burmese. The capital was subsequently moved to Thon Buri (1767–1782) and then to Bangkok.

Sikhs
Followers of the religion founded in the Punjab area of northwestern India by Guru Nanak (1469–1539). Sikhs believe in a single god who is the immortal creator of the universe and in the equality of all human beings.

Silesia
A region of central Europe belonging to Prussia in the 19th century but now in southwest Poland.

Sind
Now a province of Pakistan occupying the lower Indus Valley, Sind was for many centuries an independent Muslim state until annexed by British forces commanded by Charles Napier in 1843.

Sino-Japanese War
Conflict between China and Japan in 1894–1895 over rival claims to control over Korea. The Chinese were overwhelmed by the modernized Japanese army, agreeing at the Treaty of Shimonoseki to Korean independence and to cede Taiwan and other territories to Japan.

Sioux
Group of seven related Native American tribes of the Great Plains region, later resettled in the Black Hills of Dakota. Resisting incursions following the discovery of gold in the hills, they won a victory over General Custer's troops at the Little Big Horn (1876) but ultimately went down to defeat and massacre at Wounded Knee (1890).

socialism
A political doctrine that aspires to create a more equal society through the redistribution of private property.

Sokoto Caliphate
Islamic state in West Africa established by Usman dan Fodio and his Fulani warriors following their conquest of the Hausa kingdoms in 1804. They went on to create an empire covering much of what is now north and central Nigeria.

Spanish–American War
War between Spain and America fought in 1898 in Spain's Caribbean colonies and in the Philippines. In just four months' fighting the United States established Cuban independence and won Puerto Rico, Guam, and the Philippines, emerging from the war as a substantial colonial power.

Spanish Morocco
Territory taken by Spain around Tetuán, northern Morocco, in 1860. Spanish troops invaded in late 1859 following Moroccan attempts to take back the coastal colonies of Ceuta and Melilla.

Straits Convention
Agreement reached in 1841 between the main European powers (France, Britain, Prussia, Russia, and Austria) that the Dardanelles Straits linking the Black and Mediterranean seas should be closed to all but Ottoman warships in peacetime.

Straits Settlements
Former British colony bordering the strategic Straits of Malacca off the Malay Peninsula, comprising the territories of Malacca, Penang, and Singapore. Founded in 1826, they fell under Japanese control from 1941 to 1945 and were split up in 1946, Singapore becoming a separate colony.

Swan River Colony
Pioneering free colony established at Perth and Fremantle in western Australia by the British naval captain James Stirling in 1829. By 1831 the colony had attracted more than 1,000 settlers.

Taiping Rebellion
A widespread and enduring uprising (1850–1864) in southern China that formed the most serious challenge to Manchu rule. Led by the visionary Hong Xiuquan, it aimed to bring about a "Heavenly Kingdom of Great Peace." The rebels captured Nanjing in 1853, but an attack on Beijing failed. By the time it was put down, the rebellion had cost an estimated 20 million lives.

Ten Years' War
Guerilla struggle waged in Cuba from 1868 to 1878 for independence from Spain. The war ended indecisively with Spanish promises of reform that were not kept.

Tokugawa Shogunate
Japan's third and final shogunate (warrior government), founded by Tokugawa Ieyasu in 1603. Under 15 successive shoguns it brought peace and stability, but at the expense of external isolation. Unable finally to resist foreign incursions, the shogunate ended with the restoration of imperial rule in the Meiji Restoration of 1868.

Transvaal, Republic of
State based in what is now northeastern South Africa, so-called because it lay beyond the Vaal River. First settled by the Afrikaner Voortrekkers in the 1830s, it was long contested between the Boers and the British before finally joining the Union of South Africa in 1910.

Triple Alliance
Secret defensive agreement of 1882 among Germany, Austria–Hungary, and Italy, subsequently renewed at five-year intervals, that pledged the three powers to mutual support in the event of attack by France or Russia.

Unequal Treaties
A series of agreements forced by the western powers on the Chinese that opened up trade with China on punitive conditions. The first, the Treaty of Nanjing, which was signed following China's defeat in the First Opium War, opened up "treaty ports" for British residence and trade. Other nations soon exacted similar concessions.

United Provinces of Central America
Confederation that joined the Central American republics of Costa Rica, Guatemala, Honduras, Nicaragua, and Salvador from 1823 to 1838, shortly after they gained independence from Spain. The union eventually foundered on political rivalries and poor communications.

viceroy
Literally a "deputy king," an individual delegated to stand in for his or her monarch in a colony.

Voortrekkers
Meaning "pioneers'" in Afrikaans, the name given to South African Boers who took part in the Great Trek of the 1830s and 1840s.

Wahhabis
Followers of Muhammad Abd al-Wahhab (1703–1787), a religious leader whose highly conservative interpretation of Islam became closely associated with the rule of the House of Saud in Arabia.

Wall Street
Street at the heart of New York's business district that from the 19th century on has been synonymous with U.S. financial markets.

War of the Desert
Campaign conducted against indigenous peoples in 1879–1880 by General Julio Roca that cleared the southern pampas region of Argentina for agricultural settlement and drove the native inhabitants south of the Rio Negro.

War of 1812
Conflict between the United States and Britain, stirred by British restrictions on trade imposed as part of the war effort against Napoleon. Much of the fighting took place on the Canadian border. The war ended in 1814 with neither side gaining a territorial advantage.

War of the Pacific
War that set Chile against Peru and Bolivia from 1879 to 1884. Chile's forces prevailed, winning Bolivia's only coastal outlet, which became the Chilean province of Antofagasta.

War of the Triple Alliance
Conflict fought between 1865 and 1870 that set Paraguay under its dictator Francisco Solano Lopez against Argentina, Brazil, and Uruguay. The war ended disastrously for Paraguay, which lost over half its population.

Westphalia, Kingdom of
A kingdom created in 1807 by Napoleon for his brother Jerome in Westphalia, a former duchy in what is now northwest Germany; it became a province of Prussia in 1815.

White Lotus Rebellion
The first major rebellion against the Manchu rulers of China, fomented by members of the White Lotus Society. The uprising raged through Shaanxi Province in central China from 1796 to 1804; some pockets of resistance held out until 1813.

Xhosa Wars
A series of wars in the first half of the 19th century sparked by the eastward expansion of Britain's Cape Colony into territories occupied by the Xhosa tribes.

Young Italy
An organization founded by Giuseppe Mazzini in 1831 that sought to develop Italian national feeling among men under 40 years of age. It produced many future leaders of the Italian Risorgimento, including Garibaldi.

Young Turks
Group of young intellectuals and army officers in Ottoman Turkey who called for political reforms, including constitutional rights for citizens and a national parliament.

zemstvos
Regional councils established in Russia in 1864.

Zionists
Supporters of the campaign to establish a homeland for the Jewish people in Palestine, spelled out by Hungarian journalist Theodor Herzl in his 1896 pamphlet *The Jewish State*.

Zollverein
A German customs union, officially constituted in 1834 under Prussian leadership, that was an important stage in the process toward German unification.

Zulus
Warrior people of southern Africa who formed a powerful empire from 1816 under the rule of Shaka, who brought their dispersed, village-based communities together to form a militaristic and aggressively expansionist state.

Zulu War
War between British forces and the Zulu nation fought in 1879. After suffering initial defeat at Isandhlwana, the British forces emerged victorious, capturing the Zulu King Cetshwayo seven months later.

Further reading

Barman, Roderick J. *Brazil: The Forging of a Nation 1798–1852*. Stanford, CA: Stanford University Press, 1994.

Beasley, William G. *The Meiji Restoration*. Stanford, CA: Stanford University Press, 1972.

Beringer, Richard E. *Why the South Lost the Civil War*. Athens, GA: University of Georgia Press, reprint edn., 1991.

Bethell, Leslie, ed. *The Independence of Latin America*. New York, NY: Cambridge University Press, 1987.

Bethell, Leslie, ed. *Spanish America after Independence c.1820–c.1870*. New York, NY: Cambridge University Press, 1987.

Briggs, Asa. *The Age of Improvement 1783–1867*. New York, NY: Longman, 2nd edn., 2000.

Carr, Raymond. *Spain: 1808–1975*. New York, NY: Oxford University Press, reprint edn., 1997.

Carr, William. *The Origins of the Wars of German Unification*. New York, NY: Longman, 1991.

Collins, Bruce. *The Origins of America's Civil War*. New York, NY: Holmes & Meier, 1981.

Crankshaw, Edward. *The Fall of the House of Habsburg*. New York, NY: Penguin, revised edn., 1983.

Englund, Steven. *Napoleon: A Political Life*. New York, NY: Scribner, 2004.

Foner, Eric. *Reconstruction: America's Unfinished Revolution 1863–1877*. New York, NY: Harper & Row, 1998.

Foote, Shelby. *The Civil War: A Narrative*. Alexandria, VA: Time-Life Books, 1998.

Freund, Bill. *The Making of Contemporary Africa: The Development of African Society Since 1800*. Boulder, CO: Rienner, 1998.

Green, Constance. *Eli Whitney and the Birth of American Technology*. Boston, MA: Little, Brown, 1956.

Grosvenor, S., and Morgan Wesson. *Alexander Graham Bell*. New York, NY: Harry N. Abrams, 1997.

Hearder, Harry. *Italy in the Age of the Risorgimento 1790–1870*. New York, NY: Longman, 1983.

Herold, J.C. *The Age of Napoleon*. New York, NY: Mariner Books, reprint edn., 2002.

Hobsbawm, Eric. *Industry and Empire: The Birth of the Industrial Revolution*. New York, NY: New Press, updated edn., 1999.

Hughes, Thomas Parke. *American Genesis: A Century of Invention and Technological Enthusiasm 1870–1970*. Chicago, IL: University of Chicago Press, 2004.

James, Lawrence. *The Rise and Fall of the British Empire*. New York, NY: St. Martin's Press, 1999.

Josephson, Matthew. *Edison: A Biography*. New York, NY: J. Wiley, reprint edn., 1992.

Lynch, John. *The Spanish-American Revolutions 1808–1826*. New York, NY: Norton, 1986.

Macartney, C.A. *The Habsburg Empire 1790–1918*. New York, NY: Macmillan, 1969.

McCord, N. *British History 1815–1906*. New York, NY: Oxford University Press, 1991.

McLynn, Frank. *Napoleon: A Biography*. New York, NY: Arcade Publishing, 2002.

McPherson, J.M. *Battle Cry of Freedom: The Era of the Civil War*. New York, NY: Oxford University Press, 1998.

Mason, Philip. *The Men Who Ruled India*. New York, NY: W.W. Norton & Co., 1985.

Morris, Jan. *Heaven's Command*. New York, NY: Harcourt Brace Jovanovich, 1980.

Morris, Jan. *Pax Brittanica*. New York, NY: Harcourt Brace Jovanovich, 1980.

Painter, Nell Irvin. *Standing at Armageddon: The United States 1877–1919*. New York, NY: W.W. Norton & Co., reissue edn., 1989.

Pakenham, Thomas. *The Scramble for Africa*. New York, NY: Random House, 1991.

Seton-Watson, Hugh. *The Russian Empire 1801–1917*. New York, NY: Oxford University Press, 1990.

Shannon, Richard T. *The Crisis of Imperialism 1865–1915*. London, UK: Hart-Davis MacGibbon, 1974.

Stern, Fritz. *Gold and Iron: Bismarck, Bleichröder, and the German Empire*. New York, NY: Vintage Books, 1979.

Taylor, A.J.P. *The Habsburg Monarchy 1809–1918: A History of the Austrain Empire and Austria-Hungary*. Chicago, IL: University of Chicago Press, 1976.

Taylor, A.J.P. *The Struggle for Mastery in Europe 1848–1918*. New York, NY: Oxford University Press, reissue edn., 1980.

Thompson, J.M. *Napoleon Bonaparte*. New York, NY: Blackwell, 1998.

Thompson, E.P. *The Making of the English Working Class*. Harmondsworth, UK: Penguin, 1968.

Wiebe, Robert H. *The Search for Order 1877–1920*. Westport, CT: Greenwood Press, 1980.

Young, G.M. *Portrait of an Age: Victorian England*. London, UK: Phoenix Press, reprint edn., 2003.

Set Index

Volume numbers are in **bold**. Page numbers in **bold** refer to main articles; those in italics refer to captions.

100 Days Movement **9**:47
1812, War of **9**:8, *9*
Abbas I of Persia **6**:*39*, 43, **7**:6, **8–9**, 15
Abbas II of Persia **7**:23, 31
Abbasid Dynasty **3**:23, *25*, 28, 29, 36, 48 **4**:34, 46
Abd al-Aziz **8**:31
Abd al-Aziz ibn Saud **10**:6, 7
Abdali **8**:10, 46
Abdallah ibn Faisal **9**:38, 43
Abd al-Malik **3**:20, 21, 22
Abd al-Mumin **4**:26, 30
Abd-el-Kader **9**:29
Abdul Aziz **9**:30, 38
Abdul Hamid I **8**:34, 38
Abdul Hamid II **9**:38, 39, 40, 43, **10**:6, 8
Abdul Mejid **9**:20
Abdurrahman III **3**:40
Abelard, Peter **4**:23
Aborigines **1**:10, **8**:*41*, 46
Abu al-Qasim **8**:26

Abubakar II **5**:14, 16, 17
Abu Bakr **3**:16, 19, 22, 23
Abu Hayan **5**:15
Abu'l Hasan **6**:37
Abu Said **5**:15
Abu Zakaria Yahya I **4**:42
Acadia **7**:18, 46, **8**:7, 10, 46
Acamapichtli **5**:26
Aceh **6**:46, **7**:22, 46
Achaean League **2**:46
Achaemenid Dynasty **1**:38, 46
Achille Lauro **10**:40
Achitometl **5**:14
Acolhua **5**:6
Acre **4**:20, 21, **5**:8, 9, 10, 11
Actium, Battle of **2**:46
Adams, John **8**:43, **9**:6
Adams, John Quincy **9**:14
Adams, Will **7**:20–21
Aden **6**:46, **9**:19
Adena Culture **1**:26, *38*, 46, **2**:46, **4**:46
Aditya I **3**:37
Adrianople, Treaty of **9**:15
Aegospotami **2**:9
Aemilianus, Scipio **2**:19
Aeschylus **2**:8, 46

Aetius **2**:45
Afghani, al **9**:41
Afghanistan **3**:44, **8**:23, **9**:8, 28, 30, 34, 39, **10**:30, 39, 44, *46*
Afghan Wars **9**:20, 21, 28, 39, 48
Afonso I of Kongo **6**:23
Afonso Henriques **4**:27
Agadir Incident **10**:8
Agaja **8**:14, 19
Age of Discovery **5**:44–45
Agha Muhammad **8**:43
Aghlabid Dynasty **3**:29, 33, 48
agriculture, development **1**:8–9, 10, 16, *17*, 18
Agrippa **2**:28, 46
Agung **7**:15
Ahab (king of Israel) **1**:31, 46
Ahmad Gran **6**:18, 19, 22, 23, 46
Ahmad ibn Ibrahim al-Yasavi **4**:31
Ahmad Shah Durrani **8**:*22*, 23, 26, 31, 46
Ahmed I **7**:6, 11
Ahmed III **8**:6, *7*, 10, 18
Ahmed al-Mansur **6**:38
Ahmose **1**:19, 24, 25, 46
Ahuitzotl **5**:42
Aidan, St. **3**:17
AIDS **10**:39, 48

Ainu people **3**:29
Aix-la-Chapelle, Treaty of **7**:32, **8**:23, 29
Ajanta **2**:*43*
Ajanta Caves **9**:13
Ajnadyn, Battle of **3**:19
Akbar **6**:27, 30, 31, 34, 35, 36, *37*, 38, 39, 42, **7**:*10*, 38
Akhenaten (Amenhotep IV) **1**:22, 24, *25*, 46
Akkadian Empire **1**:15, 46
Ala al-Din Husayn **4**:30
Ala al-Din Muhammad **4**:35
Alaca Höyük **1**:14, 46
Alamo **9**:*18*, 19
Alaric II **3**:8
Alaska **9**:31
Alauddin **4**:36
Alaunngpaya **8**:26
Albany Congress **8**:27
Albert of Hapsburg **5**:35
Alberti, Leon Battista **5**:38
Albigensian Crusade **4**:42
Albigensians **4**:20, 21, 29, 39, 46
Albuquerque **8**:7
Albuquerque, Afonso de **6**:8, 10, 11
Alcatraz Island **9**:46
Alembert, Jean d' **8**:16, 17

Aleppo 5:35, 9:7
Alexander II of Russia 9:30, 40
Alexander III of Russia 9:40, 46
Alexander the Great 2:10, 11, **12–13**, 32, 46
Alexander Nevsky, St. 4:*43*
Alexandria, Egypt 2:10, 11, *13*, 22, *32*, 33, 34, 46, **3**:19
Alexis I 4:19, 7:27
Alfonso I of Aragon 4:23
Alfonso VI of Castile 4:19
Alfred the Great 3:*37*, 39
Algeria 5:22, 9:15, 18, 24, 28, 29, **10**:27, 28, *29*
Algiers 3:41, 6:11, 15, 34, **8**:30, **9**:6, 29
Ali (Muhammad's son-in-law) 3:20, *22*, 23
Ali Bey 8:34
Allende, Salvador 10:35
Alliance, Treaty of 8:35, 53
All India Muslim League 10:7
Allouez, Claude Jean 7:31
Almeida, Francisco de 6:6, 7, 8
Al Mina 1:46
Almohads 4:22, 26, 27, 30, 35, 38, 39, 46 **5**:6, 46
Almoravids 4:11, 15, 18, 19, 22, 46
Alp Arslan 4:15, 16, 17
alphabets 1:34, 40, **5**:35
Alqas Mirza 6:23
Alsace 9:35, **10**:13
Altan Khan 6:35
Alvardi Khan 8:22
Alvarez, Francisco 6:14
Amangkurat I 7:23
Amasya, Treaty of 6:26, 53
Amazon River 5:43
Amda Siyon 5:14
Amenemhet I 1:24
Amenhotep I 1:19, 46
America
  peopled 1:6–7
  Spanish rule 8:20–21
American Civil War 9:30, 31, **32–33**
American Revolutionary War 8:21, 34, **36–37**, 38, 46
Amin, Idi 10:35, 39
Amina 5:14, 7:10
Amorites 1:18
Amritsar 6:*35*, 9:8, **10**:13, 40
Amsterdam 6:8, 7:36, 37
Anabaptists 6:19, 46
Anasazi Culture 2:26, 46, **3**:16, 32, 48, **4**:22, 26, *32*, *33*, 35, 46, **5**:10, 46
Anatolia 2:12, 46, **3**:40, **5**:33, 39, 46, **6**:26, 46, **7**:46, **8**:46
Anawrahta 4:11, 24, 25
Andagoya, Pascual de 6:15
Andalusia 4:43, 46
anesthetics 9:21
Anga Chan 6:26
Angelico, Fra 5:35
Angkor 3:16, 33, **4**:15, 24, 25, 34, 46 **5**:46, **6**:46,
Angkor Empire 5:11, 14
Angkor Thom 4:34
Angkor Wat 4:23, *24*, 25, 46 **6**:26
Anglo-Burmese Wars 9:25, 26, 28, 41
Anglo-Dutch Wars 7:*26*, 30, 36
Anglo-French Treaty 9:47
Anglo-French War 6:22, 23, 26
Anglo-Saxons 2:42, 46 **3**:*16*, 17, 48, **4**:46
Anglo-Sikh Wars 9:21, 24, 48
Angola 6:13, 38, 43, 7:15, 22, 26, 46, **8**:22, **10**:27, 38
animals, domestication 1:8, *9*, 14, 15
Annam 3:40, 41, 48, **5**:42, **9**:40
Anne of England 8:11
An Qing 2:30
Anselm, St. 4:11

Anson, George 8:23
Antarctica 10:29
Anthony, St. 2:35, 41
Anti-Comintern Pact 10:21, 48
Antioch 4:19, *21*, 31, **5**:8
Antiochos III 2:14, 15, 18, 46
Antiochos IV Epiphanes 2:18, 32
Antoninus 2:29
Antony, Mark 2:23, 25, 50
Antwerp 6:8, 9, 35, 7:37
Anuradhapura 2:7
apartheid 10:38, 48
Aphilas 2:35
Aquino, Benigno 10:40
Aquino, Corazon 10:41
Arab–Israeli wars 10:25
Arab League 10:22, 48
Arabs 3:24, 28, 29
  astronomy 3:33, 37, 44, **4**:6
  conquests 3:16, 17, 19, 20, 21, 22, 25
Arafat, Yasser 10:35, 44, 46, 47
Arameans 1:26, 27, 46
Archaic period, Greek 1:35, 46
Archangel 6:38
Archimedes 2:14, 46
Arcot 8:22, 46
Argentina 9:12, 15, 16, **10**:28
Aristotle 2:8, 11, 46, **7**:46
Arius 2:41, 46
Ark of the Covenant 1:*29*, 46
Armada, Spanish 6:26, *40*, 45, 46
Armenia 2:38, 42, 46 **4**:14, 38
Armenians 9:46, **10**:12
Artaxerxes II 2:7
Artaxerxes III 2:10
artesian wells 4:26
Arthur, *King* 3:9, 32, *33*, 48 **4**:29
Aryabhata 3:9
Aryans 1:18, 19, 22, 26, 46, **2**:46
Asaf Jah 8:14
Ashanti 7:34, 46, **8**:6, 18, 22, 46, **9**:14, 31, 35, 48, **10**:6, 48
Ashanti Wars 9:35, 46, 48
Ashikaga Shogunate 5:19, **6**:15, 31, 46
Ashoka 2:15, 20–*21*, 36, 46
Ashraf 8:18
Ashurbanipal 1:38
Askiya Dynasty 5:42
Assassins 4:*17*, 18, 26, 41, 46
Assurdan II 1:27
Assyrians 1:22, 23, 25, 27, 28, 29, 30, 31, 34, *35*, 38, 46
astrolabes 3:45, **5**:*44*, 46, **7**:*11*, *44*
astronomy, Chinese 2:22, **3**:41, **4**:8
Astyages 1:42, 43
Aswan High Dam 10:28, *29*
Atahualpa 5:37, **6**:17, 18
Atatürk (Mustafa Kemal) 10:*14*, 15, 16, 21
Athabascans 5:10
Athens 1:31, 38, 42, 43, **2**:6, 8–*9*, 22
atoms, splitting 10:18
Attalos III 2:19
Attila 2:45
Augsburg, Peace of 6:25, 27, 51
Augustine, St. 2:43, **3**:13
Augustus (Octavian) 2:23, *28*
Augustus II (the Strong) 8:18
Aum Shinri Kyo cult 10:46
Aurangzeb 6:*37*, 7:11, 26, *27*, 30, 31, 34, 35, 38, 39, **8**:6
Aurelius, Marcus 2:29, 50
Austerlitz, Battle of 9:7, 10
Australia 7:43, **8**:34, **9**:6, 12, 24, 27, 30, 31, **10**:6
  gold 9:25, *40*, 44
  settled by Europeans 8:39, **40–41**, **9**:15, 18
Austria, Duchy of 4:29
Austria-Hungary 9:31

Austrian Succession, War of the 8:22, 23, 25, 29, 53
automobiles 9:37, 41, **10**:10–*11*
Ava, Kingdom of 7:10, 46
Avars 3:12, 13, 21, 48
Avebury 1:14, *15*, 46
Averroës (Ibn Rushd) 4:27
Avicenna 3:44, *45*, **4**:6, 10
Avignon, papacy at 5:15
Avilés, Menéndez de 7:12
Axayacatl 5:38
Axum 2:26, 31, *39*, 46, **3**:12, 17
Ayn Jalut, Battle of 4:41, **5**:7, 8, 9
Ayodhya 45
Ayurveda 2:23, 46
Ayutthaya 4:46, **5**:22, 46, **6**:23, 30, 31, 46, **7**:26, 46, **8**:30, 46
Ayyubid Dynasty 4:30, 43, **5**:6, 7, 46
Azerbaijan 7:11, 46
Azore Islands 5:44
Aztecs 4:39, 42, 46, **5**:11, 14, 22, 26, 34, **36–37**, 38, 42, 46, **6**:7, 46
  account of 6:35
  Cortés and 5:37, **6**:11, 14, *16*, *17*

Bab, the 9:24
Babbage, Charles 9:13, **10**:42
Babur 5:28, **6**:6, 7, 10, 14, 15, 36, 37, 39
Babylon and Babylonians 1:18, 28, 29, 31, *38*, 39, 43, 46, **2**:7, 34
Bach, Johannes Sebastian 8:15
Bacon, Roger 6:44
Bactria 2:*18*, 19, 36, 46
Baghdad 3:23, 28, 45, **4**:14, 41, **5**:27, 31, 38, 7:9, **8**:6, 19
  Mongols and 5:7, 8, 28, *29*
  Ottomans and 6:18, 7:18, **8**:6
Bahadur Shah 8:*10*
Baha'i faith 9:25, **10**:7, 48
Bahama Islands 8:35
Bahmani Sultanate 5:30, *31*, 34, 38, 46
Bahrain 9:39, **10**:17
Bahram 3:13
Bahri Dynasty 5:9, 46
Baird, John Logie 10:18
Bajirao I 8:18
Bakong 4:25
Bakri, al- 4:15
Baku 6:35
Balban 5:10
Balbao, Vasco Nuñez de 6:8, 9, 10
Balearic Islands 1:38, **4**:38
Balfour Declaration 10:13
Bali nightclub bombing 10:47
Balkan Wars 10:9, 48
Balliol, John 5:10, 11
Baltimore 8:15
Banda Bahadur 8:7, 10, 46
Bandaranaike, Sirimavo 10:29
Bangkok 9:25
Bangladesh 10:34, 35, 44
Ban Kao Culture 1:18, 46
Bannockburn, Battle of 5:15
Bantam 7:6, 39, 46
Bantu 3:20, 48, 9:19
Bapheus, Battle of 5:14
Barakzai Dynasty 9:18
Barbados 9:12
Barbarossa 6:*15*, 19, 22, 28, 29, 46
bar Kokba, Simeon 2:33
Barnard, Christiaan 10:33
barometers 7:44
Barquq 5:27, 28
Basil I 3:7, 36
Basil II 3:7, 4:6
Basketmaker Culture 2:*26*, 47
Basra 6:22, 7:31, **8**:35
Bastille, stormed 8:*38*, 39, 45, 46

Batán Grande 3:36
Batavia 7:11, 36, 46, **8**:32, *33*, 46
Batavian Republic 8:43, 46
Baton Rouge, Battle of 8:21
Battani, al- **3**:37
battery, first 9:6
Batu 4:43
Baybars 5:7, 8, 9
Bayeux Tapestry 4:*13*, 17, *28*
Bayezid I 5:27, 29, 30, 33, 42, 43
Bayezid II 6:7, 10
Bayinnaung 6:*26*, 27, 30, 31
Bayon 4:25
Bay of Pigs invasion 10:32, 48
Beaker People 1:10, *11*, 14, 46
Beccaria, Cesare 8:17
Becket, Thomas 4:*30*, 31
Bede 3:25
Beethoven, Ludwig van 9:*14*
Beijing 9:27
Beirut 10:40
Bela III 4:31
Belgrade 8:19
Belisarius 3:6, 9
Benedict, St. 3:*8*, 9
Benedictines 2:41, **3**:48
Bengal 6:46, 7:46, **8**:32, 46, **9**:38, **10**:6
Ben-Gurion, David 10:24
Benin 4:46 **5**:14, 46, **8**:11, *14*, 46
Berbers 3:24, 25, 46, **4**:6, 48, **5**:6, 46
Bering, Vitus 8:15, 22
Berlin Academy of Sciences 8:25
Berlin Wall 10:30, *44*
Bernard of Clairvaux 4:27
Bernard, St. 4:22
Bernoulli, Daniel 8:19
Bhamanid Dynasty 5:19
Bhutan 7:15, 46
Bhutto, Benazir 10:41, 44
Biafra 10:*33*, 34
Bible 2:41, **5**:26, 40, *41*, **6**:24, *25*, 7:10
Bihar 5:43
Bikini Atoll 10:24
Bill of Rights 8:37, 42, 46
Bimbisara 1:43, **2**:6
Biruni, al- 3:44, **4**:11
Bi Sheng 4:8
Bismarck, Otto von 9:30, *31*, 35, 43
Black Death 5:19, **20–21**, 46, **8**:14, 46
Black Monday 10:40
Black September 10:35
Black Sheep Turkmen 5:26, 31, 34, 38
Blainville, Joseph Céloron, sieur de 8:23
Blair, Tony 10:46
blast furnace 8:19
Blenheim, Battle of 8:6, *7*
Blériot, Louis 10:*8*
Blood River, Battle of 9:*20*, 21, 28
Bloody Sunday 10:7
Blue Mosque 7:*7*
Boccaccio, Giovanni 5:21, 22
Bocskay, Istvan 7:7
Boers 6:13, **9**:*18*, 19, 21, 25, 26, 29, 42, *47*, 48
Boer Wars 9:39, 40, 42, 43, 48, **10**:6, *7*, 48
Boethius 2:42, **3**:9
Bolívar, Simón 9:13, *16*, 17
Bolivia 9:19, **10**:20
Bolsheviks 10:6, 12, *13*, 48
bombs
  atom 10:21, *23*, 24, 35
  hydrogen 10:25, 33
Bonampak 3:28, *29*, 35
Boniface, St. 3:25
Boniface VIII, *Pope* 5:11, 14
Book of the Abacus 4:38
Book of Hours 5:*30*
books, earliest printed 3:36

Set Index

Boone, Daniel **8**:*34*, 35
Boris I **3**:36
Borobodur **3**:32, **9**:*9*
Bosnia **9**:38, **10**:45, 46
Boston **7**:12, 18, **8**:34
Boston Tea Party **8**:36
Bosworth Field, Battle of **5**:42
Botticelli, Sandro **5**:42, **6**:20
Boudicca (Boudicea) **2**:27, 47
Bougainville, Louis-Antoine **8**:*31*
Bounty **8**:39
Bourbon Dynasty **6**:39, 46
Bourguiba, Habib **10**:35
Bouvines, Battle of **4**:39
Boxer Rebellion **10**:6, 48
Boyle, Robert **7**:44
Boyne, Battle of the **7**:42
Brahe, Tycho **6**:34
Brahmanas **1**:30, 47
Brahmin priesthood **1**:22, 26, 47
Brahmo Samaj **9**:15
Brazil **6**:26, **8**:*13*, 26, **10**:15
  the Dutch and **7**:15, 18, 26
  the Portuguese and **6**:8, 16, 17, 18, 23, 30, **7**:18, 22, 26, 43
Breda, Treaty of **7**:30
Brennus **2**:10
Brétigny, Peace of **5**:22
Britain
  Iceni tribe **2**:27
  Romans and **2**:23, 25, 26, 42, 44
British Guiana **9**:9
bronze **1**:14, 21, 22, 26, 34, *44*, *45*, **5**:30
Bronze Age **1**:47
Bronzino, Agnolo **6**:19
Brown, John **9**:27, 32
Bruce, James **8**:34
Bruce, Robert **5**:11, 15
Brunel, Isambard Kingdom **9**:*22*, 23
Bruno, Giordano **7**:6
Buddha (Siddhartha Gautama) **1**:42, 43, **2**:6, *20*, 47
Buddhism, growth **2**:20–21, 23, 30, 34, 39, 43, **3**:12, 21, *26*, **4**:6, 24, 46, **6**:47
Buenos Aires **9**:*17*
Bukhara **9**:34
Bulgaria **3**:21, **4**:7, 34, **8**:31, **10**:8
Bulgars **3**:20, 21, 28, 32, 48, **4**:46
Bunker Hill, Battle of **8**:37
Bunyan, John **7**:35
Bureau of Indian Affairs **9**:14
Burji Dynasty **5**:9, 39, 46
Burkina Faso (Upper Volta) **9**:9, **10**:13, 18
Burmans **4**:24
Burr, Aaron **9**:7
Bursa **5**:18
Burton, Richard **9**:42
Burundi **10**:46
Bush, George **10**:41
Bush, George W. **10**:47
Buyids **4**:31, 41, 48, **4**:17, 47
Byzantine Empire **2**:44, 45, **3**:6–7, 12, 20, 32, 40, **4**:6, 13, 31, 34, 47 **5**:14, 27, 46 **6**:47
  and iconoclasm **3**:*24*, 25, 28

cables, transatlantic **9**:23, 30
Cabot, John **5**:43, 44, *45*
Cabot, Sebastian **6**:9
Cabral, Pedro **5**:44, **6**:6, 8, *9*, 16
Cádiz **8**:22
caesarean birth **6**:6
Caesar, Julius **2**:22, 23, *24*, 25, 49
Cahokia **4**:14, 23, 32, *33*, 43, 47, **5**:14
Cairo **3**:19, *37*, 44, **4**:7, 30
caissons **8**:19
calculators **2**:22
Calcutta **7**:42, **8**:18, *33*, **9**:9
  Black Hole of **8**:26

Caleb **3**:8
calendars **1**:10, 11, 15, **2**:23, **3**:18, 34, *35*, **4**:*21*, **6**:38
California **9**:*24*, 25
Caligula **2**:29, 47
Calvinism **6**:*24*
Calvin, John **6**:22, 24, *25*
Cambodia **3**:*36*, 37, **5**:22, 26, **7**:22, 27, **10**:38
Cambrai, League of **6**:7, 50
Cambyses **1**:25, 42, 43
camellias **8**:19
Camoes, Luis de **6**:34
Camp David Accord **10**:38, 39, 49
Canaan **1**:22, 47
Canada **8**:39, **9**:12, 19, 20, 27, 31
Canary Islands **5**:42
Cannae, Battle of **2**:15, 47
cannons **5**:15, **6**:*44*–45
Cano, Sebastian del **6**:8, *9*, 14, 15
Canterbury Tales **5**:26, *27*
Canyon de Chelly **4**:22, 47
Cape Colony **8**:43, 47, **9**:7, 9, 19, 21, 23, 28, 42, 43, 44, 48
Capetian Dynasty **3**:45, 48, **5**:46
Cape Town **7**:27
Caracol **2**:43, **3**:12, 35
caravanseries **4**:22
Cárdenas, Lázaro **10**:20
Carmelites, Discalced **6**:30
Carnatic War **8**:23, 47
Carolina, North and South **7**:47, **8**:15
Carolingian Dynasty **3**:48, **4**:47
Carrera, Rafael **9**:20
Cartagena **8**:20, 22
Carter, Jimmy **10**:38
Carthage **1**:30, 47, **2**:10, 18, 19, 22, 24, 25, 43, 47, **3**:21, 48
Carthaginians **1**:42, **2**:7
Cartier, Jacques **6**:18, *19*
carts, wheeled **1**:13, *21*
Casa Grandes **5**:6
castles, medieval **6**:*45*
Castro, Fidel **10**:28, 29
Catalan Revolt **7**:27, 47
Cateau-Cambrésis, Treaty of **6**:27, 53
Catherine I of Russia **8**:8, 15
Catherine II (the Great) **8**:17, 29, *30*, 43
Catherine de Medici **6**:25, *30*
cathode ray tubes **10**:18
Catholic League **6**:15, 47, **7**:16
cats **1**:15
Ceaucescu, Nicolae **10**:44
Celsius, Anders **8**:22
Celts **1**:27, 31, 39, 40, 47, **2**:14, 15
  La Tène culture **2**:6, 7, 47
ceramics **1**:14
Cervantes, Miguel de **7**:7, 10
Chaco Canyon **3**:40, 49, **4**:26, 30, 32, 47
Chaco War **10**:17, 20, 49
Chaghri-Beg **4**:16, 17
Chalcedon, Council of **2**:41
Chalukya Dynasty **3**:16, 49, **4**:34, 47
Chambord, Chateau of **6**:20, *21*
Champa **2**:31, 43, 47, **3**:16, 49 **4**:25, 34, 47, **5**:38, 47
Champlain, Samuel de **7**:6, *7*, 12
Chan **7**:22, 27
Chancellor, Richard **6**:32
Chan Chan **3**:44, **4**:26, **5**:22, 39
Chandella Dynasty **3**:32, *33*, 49 **4**:26, 31, 34
Chandragupta I **2**:37, 38, 47
Chandragupta II **2**:36–37, 39, 42, 47
Chandragupta Maurya **2**:11, 14, 36, 47
Chang'an **3**:28
Chang Ssu-Hsun **3**:44
Channel Tunnel **10**:45
Chapultepec **5**:11
Charcas **6**:27

Chardin, Jean **7**:34
Charlemagne **3**:29, *30*–31, **4**:44
Charles V, *Holy Roman emp.* **6**:10, *11*, 14, 15, 17, 18, 22, 27
Charles VI, *Holy Roman emp.* **8**:10, 19
Charles I of Great Britain **7**:15, *28*, *29*
Charles II of Great Britain **7**:29, 30, 44
Charles III of France **4**:29
Charles IV of France **5**:18
Charles VII of France **5**:34
Charles IX of France **6**:30
Charles X of France **9**:14, 15
Charles III of Spain **8**:20–21, 27
Charles XII of Sweden **7**:42, *43*, **8**:7
Charles of Anjou **5**:7, 10
Charles the Bold **5**:42
Charles Edward Stuart **8**:23
Charles the Fat **3**:37
Charles Martel **3**:*11*, 25
Charonea, Battle of **2**:11
Charter 77 movement **10**:38, 49
Chartists **9**:19, 48
Chaucer, Geoffrey **5**:26, *27*
Chavin culture **1**:22, *27*, 34, 47 **2**:6, 11, 18, 47
Chávin de Huantar **1**:30
Cheng Tung **5**:35
Chenla **3**:12, 49
Chernobyl **10**:41
chess **3**:9
Chiang Kai-shek **10**:14, *15*, 16, 21, 24
Chiangmai **6**:26, 47
Chiao Wei-Yo **3**:45
Chicago **7**:34
Chichén Itzá **3**:35, 37, 44, 49, **4**:34, 39
Childeric III **3**:28
Chile **9**:16, 19, 41, 45, **10**:8
Chimú **3**:44, 49, **4**:26, *27*, 38, 47, **5**:22, 23, 37, 39, 42,47
China
  Buddhism **2**:20, 21, 30
  Confucius's **1**:10, 44–45
Chinese Exclusion Act **9**:40
Chioggia, Battle of **5**:26
Chittor, fortress **6**:37
chivalry **4**:*20*, 21, 31, 47
chocolate **6**:39, **7**:11
chocolatl **5**:22, 47
Chola Dynasty **3**:37, 44, 49, **4**:7, 10, *11*, 15, 47, **5**:47
Chola State **3**:36
Cholula **3**:15, 25, 49, **4**:18
Choson Dynasty **5**:26, 47
Chrétien de Troyes **4**:29, 31
Christian II of Denmark and Norway **6**:14
Christian IV of Denmark **7**:15, 16
Christianity, spread of **2**:39, 40–41, **3**:13, 21
Christodoulos **4**:10
chronometer **8**:18
Chulalongkorn **9**:35
Churchill, Winston **10**:22, 30
Cicero **2**:47
Cicilia **5**:26, 47
cinema **10**:*18*
circulatory system **7**:15, 44
circumnavigation, first **6**:8, 15
Cistercians **4**:19, 26, 47
Civil Rights Act **10**:32, 33
Cixi **9**:*38*, 47, **10**:8
Clairvaux **4**:22
Claudius **2**:26, 29, 47
Claudius II **2**:44
Clement, VII, *Pope* **6**:7, 24
Cleopatra **1**:25, **2**:22, 23, 25, 47
Clinton, Bill **10**:45, 46
Clive, Robert **8**:26, *27*, 29, 32
clocks **4**:8, 19, *19*, **7**:36
Clontarf, Battle of **4**:6
Clovis **2**:43, **3**:8, *10–11*
Cnut (Canute) **3**:39, **4**:7, *10*, 11

Coatlinchan **5**:6
Cobá **5**:30
Cochin China **9**:27, 28, 29, 30, 48
coelacanths **10**:21
Coercive Acts **8**:36, 47
coffee **5**:34, **8**:14
Cold War **10**:30–31, *40*
Colombia **1**:43, **9**:16, **10**:6
colonialism **6**:47, **9**:28–29
  end **10**:26–27
  see also Scramble for Africa
Colosseum **2**:29, 47
Columba, St. **3**:13
Columbus, Christopher **5**:*42*, 43, 44, *45*, **6**:16
Commodus **2**:31, 47
Commune **9**:35, 48
compasses **2**:27, **4**:11, 18
computer age **9**:13, **10**:*42*–43
Concorde airliner **10**:34, *35*
concrete **2**:18
Confucianism **3**:33, 49, **6**:47, **9**:48
Confucius **1**:*42*, 44, 45, 47, **2**:7, 47
Congo, Democratic Republic of **10**:49
Congo, Republic of **10**:29, 34
Congo Free State **9**:40, 42, 48, **10**:6, 8
conquistadors **5**:37, 47, **6**:9, 11, 14, **16–17**, 22
Conrad II **4**:44
Conrad III **4**:20, 27, 44
Conrad IV **5**:6
Constance, Council of **5**:31
Constance, Peace of **4**:45
Constantine **2**:*38*, 39, 40, *41*, 44, 47
Constantine IV **3**:21
Constantine VI **3**:29
Constantine VII **3**:37
Constantine IX **4**:*15*
Constantine IX Palaeologus **5**:32
Constantinople *see* Istanbul
Constantinople, Treaty of (1479) **5**:42
Constantinople, Treaty of (1784) **8**:38
Constitution, U.S. **8**:*37*, 39
Cook, James **8**:31, *34*, 35, *40*, *41*
Coolidge, Calvin **10**:15
Copán **3**:9, 21, 33
Copernicus, Nicolaus **6**:20, *22*, 23, **7**:44, 47
copper **1**:18, 21
Córdoba **3**:28, 33, **4**:10, 11
Córdoba, Francisco de **6**:11
Corinth **1**:31, **2**:18
corn **1**:10, 26
Corn Laws **9**:22, 48
Cornwallis, Charles **8**:38
Coronado, Francisco **7**:12
Coronado, Vázquez de **6**:22
Corsica **1**:40
Cortenuova, Battle **4**:45
Côrte-Real, Gaspar de **6**:6
Cortés, Hernàn **5**:37, **6**:9, 11, 14, *16*, *17*
Cosmas Indicopleustes **3**:8
Cossacks **7**:22, 27, 34, 40, 41, 47, **8**:47
Costa Rica **4**:10, **5**:*27*
Counter Reformation **6**:23, 24, 25, 47
Coxinga **7**:27, 31, 47
Cranmer, Thomas **6**:27
Crassus **2**:25
Crécy, Battle of **5**:19
Crete **1**:19, **3**:32, **7**:27, 31, **9**:30, 46, **10**:8
  see also Minoans
Crimea **6**:47, **8**:38, 47
Crimean War **9**:*26*, 27, 49
Croatia **10**:45
Croesus **1**:42, 43
Cromwell, Oliver **7**:22, *23*, 28–29
crossbows **2**:*10*
crusader states **4**:22, **5**:9, 11
Crusades **4**:19, **20–21**, 26, 27, 35, 38, 39, 42, *43*, 48, **5**:6, 47
Ctesiphon **2**:31, 34
Cuba **6**:10, 16, **9**:34, 46, 47, **10**:28, 29, 31

Cuban Missile Crisis **10**:30, 31, 49
Cuello **1**:23
Cuicuilco **2**:15, 19
Cultural Revolution **10**:33, 49
Cumberland Road **9**:7
Curie, Pierre and Marie **9**:*46*, 47
Curzon, Lord **9**:*46*, 47, **10**:6
Custer, George **9**:38
Cuzco **5**:37, **6**:17
Cyaxares **1**:38, 47
Cyclades **1**:47
Cyprus **5**:34, **6**:34, **10**:35
Cyrus the Great **1**:29, *43*, 47
Cyrus the Younger **2**:7
Czechoslovakia **10**:45

Dacia **2**:30, 48
Dahomey **8**:23, 47
daimyo **5**:38, 42, 47, **6**:31, 47
Dai Viet **5**:38, **6**:18, 47
Dalai Lamas **5**:*34*, 35, 47, **7**:22, 35, 47, **8**:14, 47, **10**:29, 49
Damad Ibrahim Pasha **8**:11
Damalcherry, Battle of **8**:22
Damascus **3**:16, 17, *22*, 24, **4**:27, **5**:28, 30, 35
Damietta **4**:39, 42, *43*
Damiri, al- **5**:23
Dampier, William **7**:43
Dandanqan, Battle of **4**:10
Danegeld **3**:38, 49, **4**:14, 48
Danes **3**:24, 38, 39
Dante Alighieri **5**:14, 15
Dantidurga **3**:29
Daoguang **9**:*13*
Daoism **4**:*8*
Darby, Abraham **8**:19
Darius **1**:43, **2**:6, 9, 48
Darius III **2**:10, 11, 12, 13, 48
Darwin, Charles **9**:18
David (king of Israel) **1**:26, 28, *29*, 47
David, St. **3**:9
David I **5**:27
Davis, John **6**:38
Dead Sea Scrolls **2**:26, *33*
Decameron **5**:21, 22
Deccani Sultanates **6**:31, 47
Deccan region **2**:31, **4**:34, 48, **5**:47, **7**:47, **8**:6, 47, **9**:38
Decembrists **9**:14, 49
Deerfield **8**:7
Defoe, Daniel **8**:11
Delhi **9**:7
Delhi Sultanate **4**:36, *37*, 38, 42, 48, **5**:7, 11, 15, 22, 26, 27, 30, 47, **6**:15, 47
Demetrius **2**:18
Deng Xiaoping **10**:40
Denkyera, Kingdom of **7**:14, 47
Descartes, René **7**:*19*, 36
Detroit **8**:6
Devaraya II **5**:34
Devolution, War of **7**:32
Dezhnyov, Semyon **7**:23, 41
Dezong **10**:8
Diadochi, Wars of the **2**:48
Diamper, synod of **6**:43
Dias, Bartolomeu **5**:42, 44, *45*
Diaspora, Jewish **1**:29, **2**:32–33, 47, 48, **7**:47
Díaz, Porfirio **9**:39
Dickens, Charles **9**:19
Diderot **8**:16, 17, 23
Dien Bien Phu **10**:26, 27
Din-I Ilahi **6**:38, 48
Diocletian **2**:35, 38, 40, 41, *44*, 45, 48, **3**:49
Diogo I of Kongo **6**:26
Ditch, Battle of the **3**:*18*, 19
Diu **6**:19, 23, 48
Divine Comedy, The **5**:*14*, 15
Diwan **5**:23

Djoser **1**:17, 47
Dmitry, False **7**:7
DNA **10**:*28*
dodo **7**:*38*
Dogen **4**:38
Dolly the sheep **10**:46
Dome of the Rock **3**:*21*, 22
Domesday Book **4**:13, 19, 48
Dominican Republic **9**:21
Dominicans **4**:39, 48, **5**:47
Domitian **2**:41
Donatus **2**:38
Dong Zhou **2**:31, 48
Don Quixote **7**:7, 10
Dorgon **7**:24, 25
Dorset Culture **1**:34, 47, **4**:48, **5**:31, 47
Dost Mohammad **9**:18, *19*, 20, 30
Draco **1**:39, 47
Drake, Francis **6**:35, 41, 42
Dred Scott case **9**:32
Dreyfus Affair **9**:*45*
Druse (Druze) **4**:48, **8**:10, 47, **10**:15, 49
Dunama Dubalemi **4**:39
Dunhuang **2**:39
Dupleix, Joseph **8**:23, 26
Durand Line **9**:45
Dürer, Albrecht **6**:20
Dustbowl **10**:20, 49
Dutch Republic **7**:23, 26, 34, **36–37**
Dutch traders **6**:43, **7**:11, 12, 14, 31, *36*

Easter Island **2**:35, **3**:42, *43*, **8**:14, 47
Eastern Woodlands people **3**:32
Easter Rising **10**:12, 49
East India Company
  British **8**:11, 29, 31, 32, 33, 35, 47, **9**:18, 24, 49
  Danish **8**:15, 47
  Dutch **7**:11, 36, 39, 47, **8**:6, 43, 48
  English **6**:8, **7**:11, 14, 18, 22, 31, 38, 39, 47, **8**:23, *32*
  French **7**:34, 47, **8**:23, 48
  United (VOC) **8**:33
East India trade **8**:32–33
East Timor **10**:27, 39, 47, 49
Ebola virus **10**:46
Ecuador **9**:16
Eddystone Lighthouse **8**:27
Edessa, Treaty of **3**:12
Edington, Battle of **3**:37, 39
Edirne **5**:22, 33
Edison, Thomas Alva **9**:23, *36*, 37, 39, **10**:18
Edo **7**:7, 34, **8**:6, 39
Edward of England **5**:10
Edward I of England **5**:18
Edward II of England **5**:18, 19
Edward IV of England **5**:38
Edward VI of England **6**:40–41
Edward VII of Great Britain **10**:6
Edward the Black Prince **5**:22, 23, 26
Edward the Confessor **4**:12, 13, 14
Egypt **1**:25, 38, 39, **2**:7, 39, **3**:17, 24, 33, **9**:38, **10**:25
  Alexander the Great and **2**:10, 11
  autonomy from Turkey **9**:18
  British occupation **9**:40, 41, 42, **10**:12
  dynasties **1**:10, 11, *14*, 16, 19, 30
  First Intermediate Kingdom **1**:15, 16
  Greek Ptolemies **1**:25, **2**:10, *13*, 18, 32
  Middle Kingdom **1**:50
  New Kingdom **1**:19, 23, **24–25**
  Old Kingdom **1**:*11*, **16–17**
  Second Intermediate Period **1**:52
Eichmann, Adolf **10**:29, 32
Eiffel Tower **9**:43
Einstein, Albert **10**:21
Eisenhower, Dwight D. **10**:28
Elam **1**:22

Elamites **1**:47
El Cid **4**:11, *18*, 19, 48
Eleanor of Aquitaine **4**:27, 28, 29, 30
electricity **9**:36
electrons, discovery **9**:47
elevators **9**:*26*, 27
Elijah **1**:31
Elisha **1**:31
Elizabeth I of England **6**:25, 26, 27, 39, **40–41**, 42
Elizabeth Petrovna **8**:22
Ellora **3**:*28*
El Mirador **2**:7, 15, 18, 23, 27, 31, 48
El Paso **7**:27
emaki **4**:*26*, *27*
Emancipation Proclamation **9**:30
Empire State Building **10**:17
Encyclopedia **8**:16, *17*, 23, 35, 48
encyclopedias, in China **3**:33, 44
Engels, Friedrich **9**:24
engines **7**:43, **9**:6, 23, 37, **10**:10
English civil war **7**:28–29
Enlightenment **8**:**16–17**, *27*, 35, 48
Entente Cordiale **10**:6, 49
Enver Pasha **10**:12
Epic of Gilgamesh **1**:10, 19
Equiano, Olaudah **8**:39
Erasmus **6**:20, *21*
Eratosthenes **2**:15, 48
Erie Canal **9**:14
Erik Bloodaxe **3**:39, 44
Erik the Red **3**:39, 45
Erik "the Saint" **4**:27
Eritrea **10**:25
Esarhaddon **1**:38
Escorial **6**:30, *31*
Esfahan **6**:43, **7**:8, 9, 34, **8**:11, 15, 38, **10**:7
Esmail I of Persia **6**:6, 10, 15, **7**:8
Estates-General **5**:14, 47, **7**:10, 47, **8**:39, 45, 48
Estonia **6**:30, **8**:8, 15
Estrada Cabrera, Manuel **10**:12
Ethiopia **5**:35, 38, **7**:23, *42*, 43, **9**:42, 43, *43*, 46, **10**:12, 15, 20, 39, 40
Etruscans **1**:34, 38, **40–41**, 48, **2**:6, 7, 25, 48
Euclid **2**:14, 48
European Community **10**:41
European Economic Community **10**:*28*, 35
European Union **10**:25, 28, 45, 47, 49
Everest, Mt. **10**:28
Evesham, Battle of **5**:7
exploration
  Age of Discovery **5**:44–45
  Russia's drive to the east **7**:40–41
  in the wake of Columbus **6**:8–9
Exxon Valdez **10**:44

Factory Act **9**:22
Faeroe Islands **3**:29, 39
Fa-hsien **2**:39
Faisal I of Iraq **10**:17
Falklands War **10**:40
"False Messiah" **7**:30, *31*, 48
Family Compact **8**:29, 48
Fa Ngum **5**:22
Fante Confederation **9**:34, 49
Fan Zhongyan **4**:8
Faraday, Michael **9**:36, *37*
Farrukhsiyar **8**:11
Fashoda Incident **9**:47
Fath Ali Shah **8**:43, **9**:6
Fatimids **3**:23, *40*, 41, 44, 49, **4**:14, 18, 19, 48
Fawkes, Guido (Guy) **7**:6
Fehrbellin, Battle of **7**:35
Fenians **9**:27, 49
Ferdinand III, Holy Roman emp. **7**:19
Ferdinand II of Aragon **5**:43, **6**:6
Ferdinand II of Bohemia **7**:16
Ferdinand III of Castile **4**:43

Ferdinand VII of Spain **9**:12, 14
Fermi, Enrico **10**:22
Fernando III **4**:42
feudalism **3**:49, **4**:28–29
Fez **3**:32, 36, **9**:49
Fiji **10**:27, 35, 41
Firdausi **3**:41, **4**:6, 7
Firuz Shah **5**:22, 26
Firuz Shah Bahmani **5**:30, 31
fission, nuclear **10**:21
flagellants **5**:*20*
flight **9**:23, **10**:*8*, 10
Flinders, Matthew **9**:6
Florence **5**:11, 31, 42, **6**:20
Florida **8**:20, 35, **9**:13
flying machines **6**:6
food, genetically modified **10**:45
Forbidden City **5**:31, 48, **7**:48
Ford, Henry, and Ford cars **10**:10–11
Foreign Legion **9**:28
Fort Orange **7**:12
Fort Ross **9**:8
Fourteenth Amendment **9**:34
Fourth of May Movement **10**:13, 49
Fox Talbot, William Henry **9**:*20*
Francis I of France **6**:15, 18, 20, *21*, 23
Francis II Rakoczi **8**:6
Francis of Assisi, St. **4**:*38*, 39, 42
Francis Joseph (Franz Josef) I **9**:25, 31
Franco, Francisco **10**:21, 38
Franco-Prussian War **9**:*34*, 35, 49
Frankfurt, Treaty of **9**:35
Frankish Kingdom **2**:44, **3**:**10–11**, 28, 38, 49
Franklin, Benjamin **8**:*18*, 26, 27, 42
Franz Ferdinand **10**:12
Frederick I Barbarossa **4**:29, 30, 34, 35, 43, 45
Frederick II, Holy Roman emp. **4**:20, 39, 42, 43, **44–45**
Frederick I of Prussia **8**:6, 23, 25
Frederick II (the Great) of Prussia **8**:16, *17*, *24*, *25*, 26, 28, 29, 39
Frederick William of Brandenburg **8**:24, 25
Frederick William I of Prussia **8**:18, 22, 24, 25
Frederick William II of Prussia **8**:25
Frederick William III of Prussia **8**:25, **9**:20
Frederick William IV of Prussia **9**:20, 24
Freedom Riders **10**:32, 49
Free Soilers **9**:26
Fremont Culture **4**:11
French and Indian War **7**:48, **8**:27, *28*, 29, 48
French Revolution **8**:*38*, 42, **44–45**
Frobisher, Martin **6**:35
Froissart, Jean **5**:30
Fuad I of Egypt **10**:14
Fugitive Slave Act **9**:25
Fuji, mt. **8**:7
Fujiwara clan **3**:36, 50, **4**:30, 48
Fujiwara Michinaga **3**:45
Funan **2**:39, 48, **3**:12, 50
Funj **6**:6, 48, **8**:30, 48
Fyodor III of Russia **7**:35, **8**:8

Gadhafi, Muammar al- **10**:34, 40
Gadsden Purchase **9**:26, 49
Gagarin, Yuri **10**:32, *36*
Galatia **2**:14, 15, 48
Galileo Galilei **7**:*11*, 18, 44
Gallipoli **10**:12
Gallipoli Peninsula **5**:33
Gama, Vasco da **5**:43, 44, *45*
Gambia **8**:15, **9**:21
Gandhi, Indira **10**:33, 38, 40
Gandhi, "Mahatma" **10**:12, 14, 16, 17, 20, 21, 23, 25
Gandhi, Rajiv **10**:45
Ganges Valley **1**:30
Gang of Four **10**:39
Gao **4**:30, **5**:16, 18, 26
Gao, *Dowager Empress* **4**:8, 9, 18

Gaozong **4**:9
Gao Zong **4**:26, 27
Garasanin, Ilija **9**:21
Garfield, James **9**:40
Garibaldi, Giuseppe **9**:27, 31
Garnier, François **9**:35
Gaugamela, Battle of **2**:12
Gaugin, Paul **9**:44, *45*
Gaul **2**:25, 44, 48, 2:48
Gaulle, Charles de **10**:22, 32
Gauls **1**:40, **2**:7, 10
Gempei War **4**:34
Genghis Khan **4**:31, 36, 38, 39, *40*, *41*, 42, 48, **5**:12, 13, 48, **8**:48
Geoffrey of Monmouth **4**:29
George I of Great Britain **8**:11
George II of Great Britain **8**:18, 23, 29, 30
George III of Great Britain **8**:29, 30, **9**:9
George V of Great Britain **10**:8, *9*
Georgia (America) **8**:19, 20, 22
Georgia (Caucasus) **4**:34, 38, **5**:48, **7**:11, 48, **9**:49
Gerbert of Aurillac **3**:41, 45
Germany **2**:26, **9**:26, **10**:15
  East and West **10**:24, 44
Geronimo **9**:41
Ghana **10**:28
Ghana, Kingdom of **3**:45, 50, **4**:18, 34, 48, **5**:48
Ghazali, al- **4**:14, 23
Ghazan, Mahmud **5**:11, 15
Ghaznavid Dynasty **3**:44, 50, **4**:10, *16*, 36, 48
Ghazni **4**:30, 31
Ghiasuddin Balban **5**:7
Ghiasuddin Tughluq **5**:15
Ghibellines **4**:*43*, **5**:6, 48
Ghiberti, Lorenzo **5**:30
Ghilzai Afghans **8**:11, 48
Ghuri, Muhammad **4**:31, 34, 36, 37, 38
Ghurid Dynasty **4**:22, 35, 36, 48
Gibraltar **8**:15, 48
Gilbert, Sir Humphrey **6**:38
Gilbert, William **7**:44
Gilgamesh **1**:10, 12, 48
gins, cotton **8**:*43*
Giotto **5**:18
Gladstone, William **9**:41, 43
glassmaking **2**:22
Glenn, John **10**:36
Globe Theater **6**:41
Goa **6**:10, 48, **7**:48, **10**:32
Goband Singh **7**:34
Go-Daigo **5**:*15*, 19
Godunov, Boris **6**:39, *43*
Golden Horde **4**:41, 43, 48, **5**:6, 27, 28, 34, 42, 48, **6**:6, 48
gold rushes **9**:*24*, 25, *40*, 47
Gondar **7**:*42*
Good Friday Agreement **10**:46
Good Hope, Cape of **5**:42, 43, 44
Gorbachev, Mikhail **10**:30, *31*, *40*
Gordon, Charles **9**:40, *41*
Gothic churches **4**:*26*, 48
Goths **2**:34
Government of India Act **8**:33, **9**:27, **10**:20
Goya, Francisco de **9**:9
Gracchus, Tiberius **2**:19, 53
Granada **5**:18, 48
Granada, Treaty of **6**:6, 53
Grand Canal, China **2**:27, **3**:16, **5**:*18*, 19, 31
Granicus, Battle of **2**:12
Great Depression **10**:16, *17*, 50
Great Enclosure **4**:38, *39*
Great Exhibition, London **9**:25
Great Fire of London **7**:30
Great Flood **1**:10, 12
Great Northern War **8**:6, 7, 8, *10*, 15, 48
Great Pharmacopoeia **6**:35

Great Pyramid at Giza **1**:11, 17, 48
Great Schism **5**:26, 31, 48
Great Stupa **2**:23
Great Wall of China **2**:11, *16*, 17, 18, 48, **5**:*39*, 48, **10**:*35*
Great Zimbabwe **4**:34, 49, **5**:30, *35*, 48, **6**:*12–13*, **7**:48
Greco, El **6**:35
Greece **1**:23, 35, **2**:6, 8–9, **4**:23, **9**:12, 13, 15, **10**:24
  city-states **2**:8–9
  Homer's **1**:*32–33*
Greenland, Vikings **3**:39, 45
Gregory VII, *Pope* **4**:15, 17, 19, 44, *45*
Gregory 13, *Pope* **6**:31
Grenada **10**:40
Grosseilliers, Médard Chouart des **7**:27, 31
Guadalupe, Virgin of **7**:23, 53
Guadeloupe **7**:18
Guam **7**:31
Guatemala **1**:31, **6**:15, **9**:20
Guatemala City **8**:34, **10**:12
Guelphs **4**:*43*, **5**:6, 48
Guericke, Otto von **7**:44
Guevara, Che **10**:33
Guido D'Arrezzo **4**:10
Guillaume de Loris **4**:42
guillotines **8**:*45*
Gujarat **4**:26, **6**:48, **7**:48
Gulf War **10**:44, *45*, 50
Gulnabad, Battle of **8**:14
Gulliver's Travels **8**:*15*
Gunbad-i Qabus **4**:*6*
gunpowder **3**:36, **4**:11, 27
Gunpowder Plot **7**:*6*, 7
gunpowder revolution **6**:44–45
Gupta Empire **2**:*37*, 39, 42, 48, **3**:50
Gupta period **3**:*8*
Gurkhas **8**:31, 48, **9**:9, 12, 49
Gustavus I of Sweden **6**:15
Gustavus II Adolphus **7**:10, 14, *16*, 18
Gutenberg, Johannes **5**:38, *40*, 41, 48
Haakon VII of Norway **10**:7
hacienda system **8**:20, 48
Hadrian **2**:29, 30, *31*, 48
Hadrian's Wall **2**:29, 31, 48
Hafiz **5**:23
Haidar Ali **8**:*30*, 31, 34, 35, 38
Haile Selassie I **10**:16, 20, 35
Hairun of Ternate **6**:31
Haiti **8**:13, 42, **9**:7
Halicarnassus, Mausoleum at **2**:10
Halifax, Nova Scotia **8**:23
Hallstatt Culture **1**:27, 31, 48
Hamadi Dynasty **8**:30
Hammadids **4**:6, 49
Hammarskjöld, Dag **10**:32
Hammurabi **1**:*18*, 48
Handel, George Frederick **8**:22
Han Dynasty **2**:19, 26, 31, 48
Hannibal **2**:15, 24, 25, 48
Hanno **2**:7
Hanoi **9**:35
Hanoverian Dynasty **8**:11, 49
Hanseatic League **4**:43, 49, **5**:23, 48
Hanzhou **5**:12
Hapsburg Dynasty **5**:35, 42, 48, **6**:48, **7**:7, 32, 43, 48, **8**:*22*, 49
Hara Castle, massacre at **7**:21
Harald Bluetooth **3**:39
Harappa **1**:14, 18, 20, 48
Hardings, Lord **10**:8
Harding, Warren **10**:14, 15
Harihara II **5**:30
Harington, John **6**:42
Harold II **4**:12–13, 14
harquebuses **6**:*45*, 48
Harrison, John **8**:18
Harshavardhana **3**:16, 17, 20

Hartog, Dirk **8**:40
Harun al-Rashid **3**:23, 29, 32
Harvard University **7**:19
Harvey, William **7**:15, 44
Hasan Pasha **8**:6
Haskalah **8**:16, 49
Hasmonean Dynasty **2**:32, 33
Hassan II of Morocco **10**:38
Hastings, Battle of **4**:12–13, 14
Hastings, Warren **8**:32, 33, 35, 38
Hatshepsut **1**:22, 24, 48
Hattin, Battle of **4**:20, 31, 34
Hausa states **4**:35, 49, **5**:48, **6**:48, **7**:10, **9**:6, 49, **10**:50
Hawaii **9**:13, 45, 47
Hawaiian Islands **2**:42, **3**:42–43
Hawke, Bob **10**:40
Hayam Wuruk **5**:23
Hazen, al- **3**:44, **4**:10
Heidelberg, University of **5**:26
Hein, Piet **7**:15
helicopters **10**:10
Hellenistic Period **2**:32, 48
Hemchandra **4**:26
Henchak **9**:40, 49
Henry III, *Holy Roman emp.* **4**:11
Henry IV, *Holy Roman emp.* **4**:15, 19, 44, 45
Henry I of England **4**:22, 26
Henry II of England, (Henry of Anjou) **4**:28, 29, 30, 31
Henry III of England **5**:6, 7
Henry IV of England **5**:27
Henry V of England **5**:31
Henry VI of England **5**:38
Henry VIII of England **6**:7, 18, 19, 24, 25, 40
Henry II of France **6**:23
Henry III of France **6**:35
Henry IV of France **6**:39, 42, **7**:10
Henry V of Germany **4**:23
Henry the Navigator **5**:31, 35, *44*
Heraclius **3**:7, 16, 17
Herat **5**:39, **9**:26
Herculaneum **2**:27
Hero of Alexandria **2**:27, 48
Herod the Great **2**:22, 23, 32, 48
Herodotus **1**:19, **2**:7, 49
Herschel, William **8**:38
Herzl, Theodor **9**:47, **10**:6
Hesiod **1**:32, 35, 48
Hidalgo, Michael **9**:8
Hidetada **7**:15
Hideyori **7**:10
Hideyoshi **6**:35, *38*, 39, 42, 43, **7**:20
hijra (Hejira) **3**:16, 18, 50
Himiko **2**:34
Hinduism **2**:39, 42, 49, **4**:*23*, **6**:48, **7**:48
Hipparchus **2**:19, 49
Hippo **2**:43
Hippocrates **2**:6, 49
Hiram I **1**:27
Hirohito **10**:15, 44
Hiroshima **10**:23
Hispania **2**:18
Hispaniola **6**:48, **9**:13, 21
Hitler, Adolf **10**:*20*
Hittites **1**:19, 22, *23*, 48
Ho Chi Minh **10**:13
Hofer, Andreas **9**:8
Hohenstaufen family **4**:43, 44, 49, **5**:48
Hohokam Culture **2**:14, 38, 49, **4**:*6*, 26, *32*, *33*, 35, 48, **5**:6, 31
Hojo family **4**:39, 49
Hokusai **9**:*14*
Hollywood **10**:*19*, 25
Holy Land **4**:21, **5**:9
Holy League **6**:10, 48, **7**:39, 48
Holy Roman Empire **3**:*44*, **4**:44–45, **5**:48, **7**:48, **9**:7, 50
Holy Sepulchre Church **4**:7, *21*

Homer **1**:32, 33, 48
hominids **1**:6, 48
Homs, Battle of **5**:8, 10
Hong Kong **9**:20, 21, 28, **10**:*46*, 47
Hongwu **5**:27
Hoover, Herbert **10**:16
Hoover Dam **10**:20, *21*
Hopewell Culture **2**:22, 39, 49, **3**:17, **4**:32, 49
Hormuz **7**:14, 48
Horn, Cape **7**:11
horoscope, earliest **2**:7
horse collars **4**:22
horses **1**:8, *9*, 19, 26
Horthy, Nikolaus **10**:14
Hospitalers **4**:20
Houtman, Cornelis **6**:42, *43*
Huang Di **1**:11, 48
Huan of Qi **1**:44
Huari Empire **2**:43, **3**:12, *13*, 24, 32
Huayna Capac **5**:37, **6**:6
Hubble Space Telescope **10**:37, *45*
Hubertsburg, Peace of **8**:31
Hudson, Henry **7**:7, *10*
Huerta, Victoriano **10**:9
Hugh Capet **3**:45
Hugo, Victor **9**:30
Huguenots **6**:25, 27, 30, 34, 49, **7**:15, 32, 33, 39, 48, **8**:25, 49
Huitziláhuitl **5**:26
Human Genome Project **10**:44, 50
humans, early **1**:6–7
Humayun **6**:*18*, 22, 26, *36*, 37
Humboldt, Alexander von **9**:6
Hundred Years' War **5**:18, 22, 30, 38, 49
Hungary **6**:22, **7**:7, 43, **8**:6, **10**:14, 28
Huns **2**:38, 39, 42, 43, *45*, 49, **3**:50
Hus, Jan **5**:*31*
Husain Baiqara **5**:39
Husain ibn Ali **8**:6
Husainid Dynasty **8**:7, 49
Husayn (grandson of Muhammad) **3**:22, *23*
Husayn, Mirza **9**:35
Husein, Sharif **10**:13
Hussein, Saddam **10**:47
Hussein of Jordan **10**:34, 46
Hussein of Persia **7**:42
Hussites **5**:35, 49
Hussite Wars **6**:44, 49
Huygens, Christiaan **7**:36, 45
Hyderabad **6**:42, **8**:10, 15, 49
Hyderabad, Battle of **9**:21
Hyksos **1**:18, 24–25
Hypatia **2**:42

Ibn Abd al-Hakam **3**:36
Ibn Battuta **5**:15, 16, 18, 22, 26
Ibn Khaldun **5**:19, 23, 27
Ibn Tumert **4**:22, 26
Ibrahim the Mad **7**:*22*, 23
Ibrahim Pasha **9**:24
Iceland **3**:29, 36, 41
Iceni tribe **2**:27
Iconoclast Controversy **3**:50
Idris III Aloma **6**:34, 38
Idrisid Dynasty **3**:29
Ieharu **8**:30, 38
Iemitsu **7**:15, 19, 21, 26
Ienobu **8**:7
Ieyoshi **9**:19
Ifriqiya **4**:42, 49
Igbo Culture **3**:*41*, 50
Igor Svyatoslavich **4**:34
Ilkhan Dynasty **5**:19, 49
Ilkhanids **5**:10, 11, 15
Illuminati, Order of **8**:17, 49
Impressionism **9**:*38*
incanabula **5**:*41*
Incas **4**:27, 38, 49, **5**:34, *36–37*, 39, 42, 49, **6**:6, 16, *17*, 49, **8**:49

Independence, Declaration of **8**:35, 36, 47
Independence, Dutch War of **6**:34
India **1**:23, 30, **9**:30, 46, **10**:12, 16, 20
  arrival of Islam **4**:35, **36–37**
  empires **2**:36–37
  partition **10**:24, *27*
Indian Councils Act **10**:8
Indian Mutiny **8**:33, **9**:27, 28, *29*
Indian National Congress **9**:41, 50
Indian Removal Act **9**:15
Indies, Laws of the **6**:22, 50
Indo-Aryan Culture **1**:23
Indochina **9**:27, 28, **10**:26, 27, 50
Indonesia **10**:16, 24, 26
Indravarman I **3**:37
Industrial Revolution **9**:22–23
Indus Valley civilization **1**:14, 19, **20–21**, 49
Innocent III, *Pope* **4**:20, 21, 35, 39
Innocent, IV, *Pope* **4**:43, **5**:6
Inquisition **4**:43, **5**:49, **6**:49, **7**:18, 48
  Spanish **5**:42, **6**:31
International Peace Conference, First **9**:47
Internet **10**:19
invention, age of **9**:36–37
Investiture Contest **4**:15, 44, *45*, 49
Ionia **1**:31, 32, **2**:6, 8, 49
Ipsos, Battle of **2**:13
Iramavataram **4**:27
Iran **4**:14, **8**:6, 11, **10**:6, 8, 28
Iranian Revolution **10**:39
Iran–Iraq War **10**:39, 50
Iraq **10**:28, 39, 47
Ireland **9**:*21*, 24, 43, **10**:9
  Northern **10**:14, 34, 46
  Vikings **3**:32, 33, 38, **4**:6
Irene, *Empress* **3**:*28*, 29
Irfan **8**:11
iron **1**:18, 23, 26, 31, 32, 38, 39, 44, **2**:6, 7, 10, 15, 31, **4**:8, **8**:19, 26
Iron Age **3**:8, 45
Iron Bridge **8**:*35*
Iroquois **4**:*19*, **5**:23, 49, **7**:49, **8**:49
Irwin Declaration **10**:16
Isabella II of Spain **9**:21
Isabella of Castile **5**:39, 43, **6**:6
Isabella of England **5**:18
Isayu I of Ethiopia **7**:38, 42
Ishmail Pasha **9**:13
Islam **6**:48
  comes to India **4**:35, **36–37**
  Muhammad and **3**:12, 16, **18–19**, 23, **7**:49
  Sunnis and Shiites **3**:22–23
Islam Shah **6**:23
Ismail, Mulay **7**:34
Ismail of Egypt **9**:30
Israel **10**:*24*, 25, 34, 45
Israel, kingdom of **1**:27, **28–29**
Israelites, Exodus **1**:23, 47
Issus River, Battle of the **2**:12, 49
Istanbul (Constantinople) **2**:42, *43*, **3**:6, 9, 20, **4**:39, **5**:7, *32–33*, 38, **6**:7
  mosques **6**:*19*, 27, *29*, **7**:*7*
  Varangians and **3**:*7*, 36, 46–47
Italy **6**:*21*, **10**:24
Iturbide, Agustin **9**:16
Ivan I of Moscow **5**:18
Ivan III of Moscow **5**:39, **6**:6
Ivan the Terrible (Ivan IV) **6**:23, 31, **32–33**, **7**:40
Ivory Coast **9**:42, 43, **10**:18
Izapa **2**:14, 49

Jabir al-Sabab **9**:8
Jabir ibn Aflah **4**:27
Jabir ibn Hayyan **3**:29
Jacobites **8**:11, 49
Jacquard, Joseph **9**:22, **10**:42
Jaffna **5**:10
Jagannath Temple **4**:22, *23*
Jagiellon Dynasty **5**:30, 49

Jahangir **6**:36–37, **7**:6, 7, 11, 15
Jahan Shah **5**:34, 39
Jainism **4**:26, 49, **6**:49
Jalaluddin Rumi **5**:7
Jamaica **7**:27, 34, **8**:43, **9**:19, **10**:*26*, 27
Jamal al-Din al-Afghani **9**:45, 46
James Edward Stuart **8**:11
James I of Aragon **5**:6
James I of England (James VI of Scotland) **6**:41, **7**:6, 15
James II of Great Britain **7**:39, 42
Jameson Raid **9**:46
Jamestown **7**:6, 11, 12, 13, 23, 49
Janissaries **5**:32, *33*, 49, **6**:38, 49, **7**:14, *15*, 27, 49, **8**:18, 49, **9**:*7*, 14, 50
Jansz, Willem **8**:40
Japan **3**:17, **9**:30
  Buddhism **3**:21, *26*, *27*, 33, **4**:39
  closed to foreigners **7**:20–21
  rise of **3**:26–27
Java **3**:32, **5**:11, **7**:15, 23, 36, 39, **8**:32, **9**:8, *9*, 15
Javanese Wars of Succession **8**:6, 11, 49
Jaya Sthiti **5**:26
Jayavarman I **3**:20
Jayavarman II **3**:33, **4**:34
Jayavarman VII **4**:25
Jayavarman VIII **5**:11
Jazz Singer, The **10**:*16*, 18
Jefferson, Thomas **9**:6
Jenkins' Ear, War of **8**:20, 53
Jenné-Jeno **2**:42, **5**:49
Jenner, Edward **8**:43
Jerusalem **1**:26, 29, 35, 42, **2**:27, **3**:16
  crusaders and **4**:19, 20, 29, 31, 42
  taken by Saladin **4**:31, 34
  Temple **1**:27, 28, *29*, 43, **2**:22, 33
Jesuits **6**:22, 23, 39, 49, **7**:31, 49, **8**:11, 20, 27, 30, 31, 34, 49
Jesus Christ **2**:23, 26, 40
Jews **1**:22, **5**:20, 38, **8**:16, **9**:40, 47, **10**:*22*
  Diaspora **1**:29, **2**:32–33
Jezebel **1**:31
Jimmu **1**:38, 49
Jin **2**:6
Jin Dynasty and Empire **4**:*9*, *22*, 23, 26, 38, 39, 40, 43, 49, **5**:12, 49
Jinnah, Muhammad Ali **10**:*21*
Joan of Arc **5**:*34*
John, *king of England* **4**:29, 39
John III Sobieski **7**:35, *38*
John III Vatatzes **4**:38
John IV of Portugal **9**:8, 15
John Paul II, *Pope* **10**:39, 47
Johnson, Andrew **9**:34
Johnson, Lyndon B. **10**:32
Johnson, Samuel **8**:16
John Tzimisces **3**:46
Joinville, Jean de **5**:15
Joliet, Louis **7**:34
Jones, Jim **10**:38
Jordan **10**:24, 25, 45
Joseph I, *Holy Roman emp.* **8**:6
Joseph II, *Holy Roman emp.* **8**:38
Juan Carlos **10**:38
Juan-Juan **2**:42, 49, **3**:12, 50
Juárez, Benito **9**:35
Judah **1**:27, 28, 29, 42, 49
Judea **2**:22, *26*, 33
Jugurtha **2**:19
Julian **2**:39
Julius II, *Pope* **6**:6, 7, 20
July Revolution **9**:15, 50
Jürchen people **4**:22, 23, 49, **5**:49
Justinian I **3**:*6*, 9
Juvenal **2**:31, 49

Kaaba, the **3**:*18*, **6**:*11*, 49
Kabir **5**:34
Kabir, Ali Bey al- **8**:31

Kabul **8**:34, **9**:20
Kabul Khan **4**:40
Kachina Cult **5**:18, 49
Kadesh, Battle of **1**:22, 24, 49
Kahina "the Prophetess" **3**:24
Kaifeng **4**:30, 43, 49
Kairouan **3**:21
Kalka River, Battle of **4**:40
Kamakura Period **4**:34, *35*, 50, **5**:11, 15, 19, 49
Kamchatka Peninsula **7**:40
Kamehameha I **9**:*8*
Kammu **3**:26, 27, 29
Kandahar **6**:42, **7**:14, 15, 18, **8**:7
Kandarya Mahadeva Temple **4**:11
Kandy, Kingdom of **6**:22, 49, **7**:26, 49, **8**:30, 49
Kanem, Kingdom of **3**:32, **4**:39, 50, **6**:49
Kanem-Bornu **4**:19, **6**:34
Kang De **10**:20
Kangxi **7**:*24*, 25, **8**:14
Kanishka **2**:30, 49
Kansas–Nebraska Act **9**:26
Kante Dynasty **4**:34, 50
Kappel, Battle of **6**:18
Kara George **9**:6, 9
Kara-Khitai **4**:40
Karakorum **4**:42
Kara Koyunlu (Black Sheep) **5**:26
Kara Mustafa **7**:*35*, 38
Karanaga people **6**:12, 13
Karbala **3**:20, 22, *23*, **7**:9
Karelia **7**:7, 14
Karim Khan Zand **8**:*35*
Karkar, Battle of **1**:28, 31
Karlowitz, Treaty of **7**:43, **8**:10
Kartarpur **6**:11
Karthoum **9**:40
Kashgaria **8**:27, 49
Kashmir **9**:12, **10**:25, 32
Kashta **1**:34, 49
Kasr al-Kabir **6**:35
Kaunda, Kenneth **10**:44
Kay, John **8**:*18*, **9**:22
Kazembe IV **9**:21, 50
Kemmu Restoration **5**:19, 49
Kennedy, John F. **10**:*32*, 36
Kennedy, Robert **10**:32
Kepler, Johannes **7**:7, 44
Khajuraho, temples **3**:32
Khalil **5**:8, 9, 10
Khalji Dynasty **4**:36, 37, 50, **5**:11
Khalsa Brotherhood **7**:43, 49
Khartoum **9**:14, 41, 42
Khatami, Mohammed **10**:46
Khazan **6**:26
Khazars **3**:16, 44, 50
Khephren **1**:*14*, 49
Khitans **3**:40, 41, 51, **4**:*7*, 9, 50
Khizr Khan **5**:30
Khmer Empire **3**:20, 33, 51, **4**:23, 24, 25, 30, 34, 50, **5**:26, 34
Khmer Rouge **10**:*38*, 39, 50
Khomeini, Ayatollah **10**:32, 38, *39*, 44
Khorasan (Khurasan) **3**:24, **4**:35, 50, **6**:10, 26, 43, 49, **7**:9
Khrushchev, Nikita **10**:28, 33
Khufu **1**:11, 49
Khurram **6**:37
Khusrow I **3**:9, 13
Khusrow II **3**:13, 16
Khwarazm, Kingdom of **4**:40, 41, 50
Khwarazmi **4**:43
Khwarazmian Turks **4**:30, 35, 42
Khwarizmi, Al- **3**:32
Kiev **3**:36, 39, 46, **4**:11, 41, 50
Kilwa **4**:50 **5**:18, **6**:6, 49
King, Martin Luther **10**:32, *33*, 34
King George's War **8**:22, 49
King Philip's War **7**:34, *35*
King Sejong **5**:35

King William's War **7**:38, 42, 43, 49
Kirina, Battle of **5**:16
Kitchener, Herbert **9**:47
Kizimkazi, Friday Mosque **4**:22
knights **4**:*20*
Knights Templar **5**:15, 49
Knossos **1**:*33*, 49
Kobad **2**:43
Kóbé earthquake **10**:46
Koguryo **2**:38, 49, **3**:51
Kojiki **3**:24
Kokand **8**:27, 49, **9**:38, 50
Kokom Dynasty **5**:10
Kolin, Battle of **8**:26, 29
Kongo, Kingdom of **5**:27, 49, **6**:13, 14, 23, 26, 30, 34, 49, **7**:30, 31, 49, **8**:7
Konjaku monogatari **4**:23
Köprülü family **7**:30, 39, 42
Koran **3**:*19*, 20, 40, 51, **4**:27, 50
Korea **1**:15, **2**:*39*, 42, **4**:31, 41, 42, **5**:6, 26, **6**:7, 42, 43, **7**:15, **8**:38, **9**:6, 34, 39, 40, 46, **10**:7, 8
  North and South **10**:24, 47
Korean War **10**:24, 28, 50
Koryo **3**:41, 51, **4**:23, 50
Kosovo **10**:46, 47, 50
Kosovo, Battles of **5**:33
Kotte **6**:10, 22, 26, 50
Kowloon **9**:47
Krak des Chevaliers **4**:*21*
Krakow, University of **5**:22
Kremlin **5**:23
Krishnadevaraya **6**:7
Krishnaraja I **3**:29
Kublai Khan **4**:9, 24, 25, 41, **5**:6, 7, 10, 11, *12*, 13, 49
Kuchuk-Kainarji, Treaty of **8**:35
Kulottunga I of Vengi **4**:15
Kumarapala **4**:26
Kunnersdorf, Battle of **8**:27, 29
Kuomintang **9**:46, 50, **10**:9, 14, 21, 24
Kurds **9**:39, 50, **10**:15, 41, 50
Kush **1**:30, 39, 49
Kushans **2**:26, 27, 30, 34, 35, 36, 37, 49
Kushites **1**:38
Kuwait **10**:32, 44
Kyakhta, Treaty of **8**:14
Kyoto **4**:14, 15, **5**:38

Lalibela **4**:30, 38
Lambart, Thomas **7**:14
lamps (lights), electric **9**:23, 36
Langland, William **5**:22
Lan Na **6**:27
Lannatai **5**:7, 50
Lansdowne, Lord **9**:44
Lan Xang **5**:42, 50, **8**:7, 10, 50
Lao people **5**:22
Laos **6**:50, **7**:49, **8**:6, 10, **9**:15, 35, 44
Laozu **4**:*8*
Lapita Culture **1**:49 **2**:15, 49
Lapita people **1**:23, 26
La Rochelle **5**:23, **7**:15
Lars Porsena **1**:43
La Salle, René-Robert Cavelier, sieuer de **7**:31, 38
las Casa, Bartolomé de **6**:*23*, 26
Las Navas de Tolosa, Battle of **4**:39
La Tène culture **2**:6, 7, 49
Latin America, liberation of **9**:16–17
Latins and Latin kingdoms **4**:22, 23, 50, **5**:9, 50
League of Augsburg, War of the **7**:32, 39, 53
League of Nations **10**:13, 14, 20, 50
Lebanon **10**:14, 22, 38, 40
Lebna Denegel **6**:6, 22
Lechfeld, Battle of **3**:44
Lee, Robert E. **9**:31, 33
Leeuwenhoek, Antoni van **7**:*44*, 45
Legnano, Battle of **4**:34, 43, 45

59

Leif Eriksson 3:*45*
Lenin, Vladimir 10:*13*, 15
Leo III, *Pope* 3:6, 7
Leo X, *Pope* 6:*24*
Leo III, *Emperor* 3:6, 24
Leon Africanus 5:42
Leonardo da Vinci 5:*39*, 43, 6:6, *20*
Leonardo Fibonacci 4:38
Leopold I, *Holy Roman emp.* 8:6, 7, 27
Leopold I of Belgium 9:18
Leopold II of Belgium 9:40, 42–43
Lepanto, Battle of 6:34, *35*
leprosy 4:42
Lesseps, Ferdinand de 9:39
Lessing, Gotthold Ephraim 8:*16*
Lewis and Clark expedition 9:7
Lexington, Battle of 8:34
Liang Dynasty 3:8, 51
Liao 4:23, 50
Liao Dynasty 3:41
Liberia 9:24, 30, *43*
Liberty, Statue of 9:*41*
Library of Congress, U.S. 9:6
Libya 10:27
Liegnitz, Battle of 4:41
Lima 6:17, 19, 22, 8:23
Lincoln, Abraham 9:27, 30, 31, 32, *33*
Lindbergh, Charles 10:10, 16
Linné, Karl (Carolus Linnaeus) 8:16, *19*
Lisbon 4:20, 8:16, 26
Lithuania 5:24–35, 6:31, 10:44
Little Big Horn, Battle of the 9:38
Little Rock high school 10:29
Liu Bang 2:17, 49
Live Aid 10:40, *41*
Livingstone, David 9:31, 34, *35*, 42
Livonia 6:32, 50, 7:14, 49, 8:8, 15
Li Yuanhao 4:10
Llywelyn ap Gruffudd 5:7
Locke, John 7:39, 8:16
Lockerbie 10:41
locomotives 9:*15*, *36*
Lodi Dynasty 5:38, 50
Logstown Treaty 8:26
Lombard League 4:43, 45, 50
Lombards 3:6, *13*, 25, 51, 4:50
London 2:26, 3:41
London, Treaty of 9:21, 34
Longinus 3:13
looms 8:*18*, 9:22
Lorraine 9:35, 10:13
Los Angeles 8:38
lost-wax method 4:14, 51, 5:30, 50
Lothair II 3:11, 4:23, 43
Louangphrabang 8:7
Louis VI (the Fat) 4:22
Louis VII of France 4:20, 27
Louis IX (St. Louis) 4:20, 42, 5:*6*, 7, 8
Louis XII of France 5:43, 6:6
Louis XIII of France 7:10, 14
Louis XIV of France (Sun King) 7:*32*–*33*, 34, 35, 36, 38, 39, 43, 8:7
Louis XV of France 8:*10*, 11, 15, 29
Louis XVI of France 8:35, 39, 42, 45
Louis XVIII of France 9:9
Louisburg 8:22, *29*, 50
Louisiana 8:11, 20
Louisiana Purchase 9:6, 50
Louis Philippe of France 9:*15*, 24, 28
Louis the Pious 3:32, 33
Luba, Kingdom of 7:*6*, 49
Lublin, Union of 6:31, 33, 53
"Lucy" 1:6, 49
Lumière brothers 9:46, 10:18
Luna, Tristán de 6:27
Lunda Empire 7:34, 49
Luther, Martin 6:11, 14, *24*, 25
Lutheranism 6:15, *24*, 50
Lutter, Battle of 7:16

Lützen, Battle of 7:16, 17, 18
Lu Yu 3:29

Maastricht Treaty 10:45
McAdam, John 9:22
Macao 6:8, *27*, 39, 50, 7:*38*, 49, 9:41
Macbeth 4:11
Maccabees, Revolt of the 2:18, 32, 49
Maccabeus, Judas 2:18, *19*, 32, 33
McCarthy, Joseph 10:25
Macchiavelli, Niccolò 6:10
MacDonald, Ramsey 10:15
Macedon 1:39, 49
Macedonian Dynasty 3:7, 36, 51
Machiavelli, Niccolo 6:20
machine guns 9:22
Machu Picchu 5:*36*
McKenzie, Alexander 8:43
McKinley, William 10:6
Madagascar 7:7, 10, 15, 23, 39, 9:8
Madeira Islands 5:44
Madero, Francisco 10:8, 9
Madhav Rao II 8:42
Madras 7:26, 8:23, 32
Madrid, Treaty of 8:20, 26
madrigals 5:19, 50
Magadha 1:50, 2:6, 49
Magdeburg, Siege of 7:17, 18
Magellan, Ferdinand 6:8, *9*, 11, 14
Maghrib 3:32, 51, 4:51, 5:50
Magna Carta 4:29, 39, 51
Magyars 3:36, 40, *44*, 45, 51
Mahabalipuram 3:*24*
Mahabharata 1:27, 50, 6:38, 50
Mahadji Sindhia 8:38
Mahavira 1:42
Mahdi, the 9:41, 42, 50
Mahmud I 8:18, 26
Mahmud II 9:8, 14, 20
Mahmud of Ghazni 3:44, 4:6, 7, 10, 17, 36, *37*, 51
Maine, USS 9:47
Majapahit Dynasty and Kingdom 5:11, *23*, 50, 6:6, 50
Makurra 3:13, 51, 5:23, 50
Malaya 9:14, 10:12, 26
Malaysia (Penang) 8:38
Malaysia, Federation of 10:32
Malcolm Barelegs 4:22
Malcolm, John 9:6
Malcolm X 10:32
Mali, Empire of 4:43, 5:*15*, 16–17, 18, 22
Malik en-Nasir, al- 5:14
Malik Shah 4:15, 17, 18
Malla Dynasty 5:26
Mallet, Paul and Pierre 8:19
Malplaquet, Battle of 8:7
Malta 6:28, 30
Mameluke Dynasty 4:43, 51, 5:6, 7, 8–9, 10, 11, 14, 22, 26, 34, 50, 6:7, 50, 8:10
Mamun, al- 3:32
Manchu (Qing) Dynasty 7:10, 14, 15, 18, *24*–*25*, *35*, 42, 8:11, 14, 27, 9:26, 10:9
Manchuria 4:51, 10:6, 7, 16, 20
Mandela, Nelson 10:*27*, 44, 45
Manipur 9:44
Mansur, al- 3:*23*, 28
Mansuri Maristan 5:10
Manuel I 4:31
Manzikert, Battle of 4:14
Maoris 3:*32*, 50, 5:18, 8:50, 9:12, 20, 21, 35, 50
Mao Zedong 10:16, 21, 24, *25*, 29, 33, 39
Mapungubwe 4:11
Maratha Kingdom 8:22, 26, 30, 34, 38, 42, 50, 9:7, 12
Marathon, Battle of 2:6, 9, 50
March on Rome 9:31, 10:14
Marconi, Guglielmo 10:18
Maria Theresa 8:*22*, 38

Marie Antoinette 8:34
Marie de Medicis 7:10
Marinids 5:6, 11, 19, 22, 50
Marquesas Islands 3:42, 43
Marquette, Jacques 7:34
Marrakesh 4:15, 27
Marseille 1:42
Marshall Plan 10:24, 51
Martinique 7:18
Marwan II 3:25
Marx, Karl 9:24, 31
Mary, Queen of Scots 6:31, 41
Mary I of England 6:24, 25, 26, 27, 41
Masada 2:*27*, 33, 50
Masina 9:13, 51
Massachusetts Bay Colony 7:22
mass media 10:18–19
Matamba, Kingdom of 7:50, 8:22, 50
matchlocks 6:44, *45*, 50
mathematics 3:9, 13, 32
Matsuo Basho 7:*42*
Matthias I Corvinus 5:39
Mau Mau uprising 10:24, 51
Mauretania 2:26, 50
Maurice, *Emperor* 3:13
Mauritius 6:43, 8:14
Mauryan Empire 2:11, 15, 18, 36, 50
Maximilian I of Mexico 9:29, 30
Mayans 1:22, 26, 35, 39, 43, 50, 2:10, 15, 22, 23, 27, 31, 35, 42, 43, 51 3:9, 12, *25*, 28, 34–35, 4:42, 5:50, 6:*34*, 50
decline 3:37, 40, 4:7, 19, 5:30
see also Bonampak; Chichén Itzá; Copán; Mayapán; Palenque; Tikal
Mayapán 4:42, 5:*7*, 10, 35, 38
Mayflower Compact 7:13, 50
Mayo, Lord 9:34, 35
Mazdak 2:43
Mazzini, Giuseppe 9:18
Mecca 3:12, 19, 23, 6:11, 34, 50, 9:6, 10:44
Medes 1:31, 38, 42, 50
Medici family 5:31, 34, 39, 40, 42, 6:19, 20
Medina 3:*18*, 19, 6:34, 9:6
Medusa 9:12
Medway River, Battle of the 7:30
Megalithic Culture 1:26
Mehmed I 5:31
Mehmed II (Mehmet II) 5:*32*–*33*, 34, 38, 42
Mehmed III 6:43
Mehmed IV 7:38
Meji Restoration 9:34
Melfi, Constitutions of 4:45
Menander 2:19, 50
Menelik II of Ethiopia 9:43
Menes 1:10
Mengazi 2:15
Mengel, Gregor 9:30
Mengzi (Mencius) 2:10
Mentuhotep II 1:15, 24, 50
Mercosur 10:46, 51
Meroë 1:42, 2:7, 38, 50
Merovingian Dynasty 3:10, 51
Merv 3:20
Mesa Verde 4:22, *23*, 32, 51
Mesopotamia 1:8, 10, 43, 50, 3:36, 51, 9:9
Messenia 1:35
Metacomet 7:34, 50
Mexican Revolution 10:8, 51
Mexican War 9:25, 51
Mexico 9:13, 28, 29, 35, 39, 10:8, 9, 13
Miao rebellion 9:26
Michael I, *Emperor* 3:31
Michael I of Russia 7:10
Michael VIII Palaeologus 5:6, 7
Michelangelo 6:6, 7, 20
microscopes 7:*44*, 45
Midas 1:34, 50
Midhat Pasha 9:*34*
Milan, Edict of 2:38, 50

Milosevic, Slobodan 10:46
Mimbres pottery 4:*14*, 15, *32*
Minamoto Yoshiie 4:18, 51
Minden, Battle of 8:29
Ming Dynasty 5:13, 23, **24**–**25**, 35, 6:15, 18, 42, 50, 7:15, 18, 27, 50
Minh Manh 9:12
Minoans 1:11, *18*, 22, 32, *33*, 50
Minto, Lord 10:7
miracle plays 5:11, 50
Mir Mahmud 8:11, 14, 15
Mir Wais Hotaki 8:7
Mishnah 2:33, 34
Mississippians 3:33, 51, 4:6, *32*, *33*, 34, 51, 5:14, 50
Mississippi Company 8:14, 50
Mississippi River 7:38
Mithradates I 2:18, 19, 50
Mixtecs 4:15, 51, 5:22
Moche Culture 2:27, 30, *34*, 42, 50, 3:16, 51
Modharites 3:24
Mogollon Culture 4:22, *32*, 34, 51, 5:6, 50
Mohacs, Battle of 6:15
Moldavia 9:24, 26
Molasses Act 8:19
Molly Maguires 9:38, 51
Mombasa 5:38, 6:42, 7:50, 8:15
Mombasa, Sultan of 7:11
Mon 4:25, 6:22, 50
Mona Lisa 6:6, *20*
Monet, Claude 9:38
Mongke 4:41
Mongolia 3:40, 10:9
Mongolian People's Republic 10:15
Mongols 4:38, **40**–**41**, 42, 51, 5:7, 11, 14, 50, 6:50, 7:22, 42, 8:6, 11, 27
and China 4:25, 39, 42, 43, 5:6, **12**–**13**
and India 4:36, 37
and Japan 5:7, 10, 13
Mamelukes and 5:7, 8, 9
see also Genghis Khan; Golden Horde; Timur the Lame
Mon Kingdom 8:22
Monks Mound 4:14, 51
Monongahela, Battle of 8:*28*, 29
Monroe Doctrine 9:14, *15*, 29, 51
Mons Meg 6:44
Montano, Francisco 6:15
Monte Albán 2:*18*, 50, 3:24
Montecorvino, John of 5:14
Montevideo 8:14
Montezuma I 5:35
Montezuma II 5:37, 6:7, 16
Montfort, Simon de 4:29, 5:7
Montgisard, Battle of 4:34
Montgolfier brothers 8:*39*
Montreal 7:22
moon, man on the 10:34, *36*
Moravia 3:32, 40
More, Thomas 6:10, 20
Morgan, Henry 7:34
Moriscos 6:50, 7:7, 10, 50
Mormons 9:14, 51
Morocco 6:26, 27, 38, 7:31, 8:42, 9:27, 28, 35, 10:7, 8, 9
Morse, Samuel 9:21, 36
Moscow 6:34, 9:9
Mossi kingdoms 4:14, 51, 9:9, 51
motors, electric 9:36
Moundsville 4:38, *39*
movies 10:16, *18*, *19*
Mozambique 4:23, 6:7, 8:19, 10:27, 38
Mozart, Wolfgang Amadeus 8:42, *43*
Mu 1:27, 44
Muawiya 3:22
Mubarak Shah 5:34
Mugabe, Robert 10:39, 41

Mughal Empire **5**:28, 51, **6**:*6*, 7, 10, 14, 18, 26, 27, 30, 31, 34, **36–37**, 39, 42, 50, **7**:6, 11, 14, 23, 26, 30, 31, 39, 42, 50, **8**:6, 7, 10, *11*, 15, 19, 31, 50, **9**:51
Muhammad, and Islam **3**:12, 16, **18–19**, 23, **6**:50
Muhammad Ali **9**:7, 8, 13, 14, 18, 19, 21, **10**:8
Muhammad al-Muntazar (Twelfth Imam) **3**:36
Muhammad ibn Saud **8**:31
Muhammad Shah **8**:*11*, 19
Mühlberg, Battle of **6**:23
Mukden **7**:14, 18
mummification **1**:11, *24*
Muqaddimah **5**:23
Murad I **5**:22, 26, 32
Murad II **5**:33, 34, 38
Murad III **6**:34, 35, 38, **8**:6
Murad IV **7**:14, *18*, 19
Murad V **9**:38
Murasaki, Lady **4**:7
Musa **5**:*15*, 16, 17, 19
Musa II **5**:17
Muslim Brotherhood **10**:16
Muslim League **10**:22, 51
Mussolini, Benito **10**:14, 15
Mustafa I **7**:11
Mustafa II **7**:43, **8**:6
Mustafa III **8**:30, 34
Mustafa IV **9**:7
Mutamid, al- **3**:36
Mutasim, Al- **3**:33
Muttawahil, al- **3**:36
Muzaffar ud-Din **10**:7
Mwenemutapa **4**:38, **5**:35, 51, **6**:13, 51, **7**:6, 50
Myanmar (Burma) **4**:24, **6**:19, 22, *26*, **7**:6, 10, 23, **8**:7, 26, 30, **9**:14, 28, **10**:22, 27, 28
Mycenaeans **1**:19, 22, 32, 33, 50
Mysore Wars **8**:31, 42, 43, 46
Mystic **7**:12
Mzilikazi **9**:21

NAACP **10**:*8*
Nabateans **2**:6, 50
Nabopolassar **1**:38, 50
Nadir Kuli (Nadir Shah) **8**:18, *19*, *23*, 50
NAFTA **10**:41, 51
Nagabhak I **3**:25
Nagasaki **6**:8, 34, 39, **7**:19, 20, 22, **10**:23
Najaf **3**:*22*, **7**:9
Nakaya Dynasty **6**:18, 51
Namibia (Southwest Africa) **10**:6, 27
Nam Viet **2**:15, 19, **5**:30, 34
Nanak **5**:38, **6**:11, 19
Nanchao, Kingdom of **4**:25, 51 **5**:6, 12, 51
Nanking **6**:30
Nan Madol **9**:13
Nantes, Edict of **6**:42, **7**:32, 39, 47
Napier, Charles **9**:21
Napoleon III of France **9**:26, 27, 28, 29, 34
Napoleon Bonaparte **8**:42, 43, 45, **9**:6, 7, 8, 9, **10–11**
Narashima Saluva **5**:42
Narmer **1**:*16*
NASA **10**:29, 51
Nasir, al- **4**:34
Nasir Faraj, al- **5**:28
Nasir Muhammad, al- **5**:8, *9*
Nasiruddin Muhammad **5**:30
Nasr al-Din **9**:24, 27, 41, 46
Nasser, Gamel Abdel **10**:28
Natal **9**:21, 28, 51
Natchez Indians **8**:15, 50
Nathan the Wise **8**:17
Nations, Battle of the **8**:25
Native Land Act **10**:9

NATO **10**:25, 28, 30, *31*, 33, 51
Nazca culture **2**:*10*, 27, 0
Nazis **10**:17, 21, 22, 51
Neanderthals **1**:6, *7*, 50
Nebuchadrezzar II **1**:29, 39, 42, 50
Necho II **1**:39, 50
Nectanebo I **2**:10
Nehru, Jawaharlal **10**:24, 32, 33
Nelson, Horatio **9**:7
Nennius **3**:32
Neolithic settlements, Skara Brae **1**:*8*, 11
Nepal **5**:19, 26, **9**:12
Nepos, Julius **2**:42
Nero **2**:26, 27, 29, 40, 50
Nestorians **3**:8, 51
Netherlands **5**:42
Neva River, Battle of the **4**:43
New Delhi **10**:8
New England Confederation **7**:23, 50
New France **7**:12, 50
New Granada **8**:11, 19, 20
New Guinea **1**:19, 22, **6**:15, **9**:15, 41
New Mexico **9**:24
New Plymouth **7**:12
newspapers, English **8**:6, 39
New Sweden **7**:26, 51
Newton, Isaac **7**:45, **8**:16
New York (New Amsterdam) **7**:10, 12, *13*, 15, 30, 34, **8**:13, 22
New Zealand **3**:32, **7**:22, 36, **8**:31, 42, **9**:9, 12, 25, 31, 39, 44, 45
Ngolo Darra **8**:30
Nguyen Anh **9**:6
Niagara Falls **7**:34
Nicaea **4**:19, 38, **5**:18, 51
Nicaea, Council of **2**:50, **3**:28, **4**:51
Nicaragua **10**:9
Nicholas II of Russia **10**:7
Nicomedia (Izmit) **2**:39
Niepce, Joseph-Nicéphore **9**:15
Niger, Pescennius **2**:30
Nigeria **5**:14, **10**:7, 33
Nightingale, Florence **9**:*27*
Nihon Shoki **3**:26
Nijmegen, Treaty of **7**:35
Nile, River **1**:51, **9**:42
Nile, Battle of the **8**:43
Nimrud **1**:30
Nineveh **3**:16
Nixon, Richard M. **10**:30, *35*
Nizam al-Mulk **4**:16, 18
Nizip, Battle of **9**:20
Nkrumah, Kwame **10**:33
Noh theater **5**:23, *27*, 51
Nok culture **2**:*6*, 7, 18, 50
Noriega, Manuel **10**:44
Normans **3**:51, **4**:6, **12–13**, 18, 19, 30, 44
North America
cultures **4**:*32–33*
exploration **6**:19, 22, **7**:6, 7, 10, 27, 31, 34, **8**:43, **9**:7
settling of **6**:38, *39*, **7**:12–13
Vikings **3**:*39*
Northern Wars **7**:27
northwest passage **6**:38, 51, **7**:18, 51, **8**:50
Notre Dame Cathedral **4**:31
Novgorod **3**:36, 46, *47*, **4**:43, 52
Nubia **2**:26, 38, **3**:9, 20, 44, 50
Nubia and Nubians **1**:27, 35, 38, 51, **2**:7, **3**:51
numerals **3**:28, 41, 44
Nur al-Din **4**:27
Nuremberg trials **10**:*25*
Nureyev, Rudolf **10**:32
Nurhachi **7**:10, 14
Nur Jahan **7**:11
nylon **10**:20
Nzinga **7**:14

Oaxaca **1**:23
Obas Akenzua I **8**:11
Oceania, settlement **3**:**42–43**
Oda Nobunaga **6**:31, 34, 35, 38
Odoacer **2**:42, 43, 45
Ogodei **4**:41, 42, 43
Ohio Valley **8**:22
Ojeda, Olonso de **5**:43, **6**:9
Oklahoma **9**:44
Oklahoma City bombing **10**:46
Olaf, *King* **3**:45
Old Believers **7**:30, *31*
Oleg **3**:36, 40, 46–47
Olivares, Count-Duke of **7**:*22*, 51
Olmecs **1**:22, 30, 31, 34, **36–37**, 39, 43, 51, **2**:7, **3**:52
Olympic Games **1**:32, 34, 51, **9**:45, **10**:30, 35
Omai **8**:35
Omar Khayyam **4**:10, 15, 17, 23
Omdurman, Battle of **9**:47
Onin War **5**:38, 42, 51
Opium Wars **9**:*20*, 21, 51
Oregon Territory **9**:24, 51
Orellana, Francisco de **6**:22
Oresme, Nicole **5**:23
Organization of American States **10**:25
Orhan **5**:18, 19
Oriental Entente **10**:21
Orsted, Hans Christian **9**:12
Orthodox Church
Eastern **3**:52, **4**:14, *15*, 52, **6**:51, **7**:51
Russian **7**:30, 31, **8**:8, 52
Osman I (Uthman) **5**:10, 18, 33
Osman II **7**:11, 14
Osman III **8**:*26*
Ostrogoths **2**:39, 43, 45, 50, **3**:12, 52
Otaker I **4**:35
Otto I **3**:*44*
Ottomans **5**:10, 15, **32–33**, 35, 51, **6**:7, 27, 51, **7**:6, 10, 30, 38, 51, **8**:10, 11, 18, 31, 51, **9**:12, 15, 18, 19, 34, 39, 46, 51, **10**:8, 9, 12, 13, 51
battles **5**:14, 27, **6**:10, 15, 34, *35*, **7**:43, **8**:10, 34, **9**:14, 20
conquests **5**:18, **32–33**, 39, 42, **6**:14, 19, 22, 23, 26, 31, 34, 35, **7**:22, 34, **8**:14, 15, **9**:9, 13, 35
and the Safavids **6**:18, 42, **7**:9, **8**:22
see also Janissaries; and names of Ottoman sultans
Oudh **8**:15, 51, **9**:26, 51
Outremer **4**:20, 21, 52
Oyo, Kingdom of **7**:18, 51, **8**:23, 51

Pacal, *King* **3**:17, *34*
Pachacutec **5**:37, **6**:16
Pacific, War of the **9**:41
Pagan **3**:33, **4**:11, *24*, 25, *25*, 52
pagodas **3**:8, *9*, *26*
Pahlavi Dynasty **10**:15, 51
paintings, cave/rock **1**:*6*, *8*, 31
Pakistan **10**:24, 25, 27, 28, 47
Pakubuwono I **8**:6, 11
Pala Dynasty **3**:37, 52, **4**:30, 52
Palenque **3**:*33*, 35
Palestine **2**:33, **4**:18, 19, 22, **9**:40, 47, **10**:6, 13, 14, 16, 25
Palestine Liberation Organization (PLO) **10**:32, 34, 51
Pallava Dynasty **3**:13, *24*, 37, 52
Pan-African Conferences **10**:13, 51
Panama **4**:10, **7**:34, **10**:44
Panama Canal **9**:39, 44, 51, **10**:6, 12, 51
Pandya Dynasty **5**:7, 10, 51
Panipat, Battles of **6**:14, 36, 37
Pankhurst, Emmeline **10**:*6*
Papal States **9**:35, 51
paper **2**:19, 30, **4**:10

papyrus **1**:10, *11*, 51
Paracas Culture **1**:42
Paraguay **9**:8, 9, 17, **10**:20, 44
Parakramabahu I **4**:*30*, 31
Parakramabahu II **4**:43
Parakramabahu III **5**:14
Paramardi **4**:31
Paris Peace Conference **10**:13
Paris, Treaty of
in 1258 **5**:6
in 1763 **8**:30, 31
in 1783 **8**:36, 37, 38
in 1898 **9**:47
Paris University **4**:27
Park, Mungo **8**:42, 51, **9**:42
Parks, Rosa **10**:28
Parnell, Charles Stewart **9**:43
Parsis **3**:24
Parthenon **2**:7, *8*, 9, **7**:39, 51
Parthia and Parthians **2**:14, 22, 30, 34, 44, 50
Pascal, Blaise **7**:*34*
Passarowitz, Peace of **8**:11
Pasteur, Louis **9**:*30*
Patagonia **9**:40
Patrick, St. **2**:41
Paul I of Russia **9**:6
Paul of Tarsus **2**:27, 40, 41
Pavia, Battle of **6**:15
Pazzi family **5**:42
Pearl Harbor **9**:41, **10**:*22*
Peasants' Revolt (England) **5**:21, 26, 51
Peasants' War (Germany) **6**:*14*, 15
Pedro I of Brazil **9**:18
Pedro II of Brazil **9**:44
Pegu **6**:51, **7**:6, 51, **9**:28, 51
Peisistratus **1**:42
Peloponnesian League **1**:42
Peloponnesian Wars **2**:9, 51
Pelusium, Battle of **1**:42
penicillin **10**:15
Peninsular War **9**:8, 51
Penn, William **7**:13, 38, *39*
Pennsylvania **7**:38
Pepi II **1**:15, 16
Pepin of Héristal **3**:11
Pepin the Short **3**:28
Perdiccas **1**:51, **2**:13, 51
Pericles **2**:7, *8*, 51
Perón, Juan **10**:28, 35
Perpetua **2**:34
Perry, Matthew **9**:*26*
Persepolis **2**:*7*, 11, 12, 51
Persia **1**:25, 51, **2**:10, 51, **3**:23, **8**:14, **9**:9, 12, 35
and Greece **2**:6, 8–9, 10
see also Iran
Peru **1**:14, 15, 18, 26, **9**:16, 17, 19
Peter III of Aragon **5**:10
Peter III of Russia **8**:29, 30
Peter the Great **7**:42, **8**:7, **8–9**, 10, 15
Peterloo Massacre **9**:12
Peter Nolasco, St. **4**:39
Petra **2**:6
Petrarch, Francesco **5**:19
pharaohs **1**:17, 24, 51
Pharos of Alexandria **2**:*13*, 14
Philadelphia **8**:42
Philip II of France **4**:39
Philip IV (the Fair) of France **5**:10, 14
Philip VI of France **5**:18
Philip II of Macedon **2**:11, 12, 13, 51
Philip III of Macedon **2**:13
Philip II of Spain **6**:*26*, 27, 30, 31, 38, 39, *40*, 41, 43
Philip III of Spain **7**:7
Philip IV of Spain **7**:16, 27, 30
Philip V of Spain **8**:10
Philip Augustus **4**:20, 29, 34
Philip the Good **6**:44

Philippines 6:30, 34, 7:30, 31, 8:11, 30, 10:6, 7, 8, 23, 24, 27
Phoenicians 1:10, 23, 26, 30, 31, 34, 38, 42, 51, 2:51
phonographs 9:37, 39
photography 9:20
Phrygians 1:26, 51
Picasso, Pablo 10:21
Pilgrims 7:12, 13, 14, 51
Pilgrim's Progress 7:35
pill, birth-control 10:28
Pinatubo, Mt. 10:45
Pinochet, Augusto 10:35, 44
Pires, Thomé 6:15
Pitt, William, the Elder 8:29
Piye 1:25, 34
Pizarro, Francisco 5:37, 6:9, 16, 17, 18, 19, 22
plague 5:19, 7:11, 18, 30
 see also Black Death
Plassey, Battle of 8:27, 29, 32
Plataea, Battle of 2:9, 51
platinum 8:23
Plato 2:8, 10, 51, 6:51
Plessy v. Ferguson 9:47
Plotinus 2:34, 51
Plutarch 2:30, 51
Plymouth Company 7:6, 51
Pocahontas 7:11, 13
Poland 6:31, 7:27, 8:43, 9:15, 18, 24, 30, 10:34
 First Partition 8:25, 34
polio vaccines 10:28
Polo, Marco 5:11, 13
Pol Pot 10:38, 39
Poltava, Battle of 8:7, 8
Polynesia 4:14, 38, 8:42
Polynesians 1:26, 39, 51, 3:52, 4:52
 settling Oceania 3:42–43, 4:35
Pompeii 2:27, 51, 8:23, 51
Pompey the Great 2:22, 25, 51
Ponce de Léon, Juan 6:11
Pondicherry 7:34, 43, 8:28, 32
Pontiac 8:30, 51
Popol Vuh 6:34, 51
porcelain 3:25, 4:42, 5:19, 24, 38, 7:11, 8:26
Portugal 3:22, 10:8, 18
 exploration and trade 6:6, 7, 8, 10, 11, 12, 14, 27
postal services 8:14
potatoes 1:10, 7:14
 sweet 4:14
Potosí, Mt. 6:17, 23
pottery 1:10, 14, 15, 22, 23, 39
Poverty Point Culture 1:19, 51
Powers, Gary 10:30
Powhatan Confederacy 7:12, 15, 51
Prague, Compacts of 5:35
Prague, Defenestration of 7:11, 16, 47
Prague, Peace of 7:17
Prague Spring 10:34, 51
Prajai 6:23
Presbyterians 7:19, 51
Prester John 5:15
printing 3:25, 40, 4:8, 10, 43, 5:40, 40–41, 7:19
Prohibition 10:13, 20, 52
Prose Edda 4:39
Protestantism 6:24, 25, 51, 7:51
Prussia, rise of 8:24–25
Ptolemy, Claudius 2:30, 3:32, 51, 5:51
Ptolemy I Soter 2:10, 11, 13, 51
Ptolemy II Philadelphus 2:14
Pueblo Culture 3:40, 40, 52, 4:52, 5:19, 51
Puerto Rico 6:7
Pugachev, Yemelyan 8:34
Pulakesin II 3:16, 17
pulsars 10:33
Punic Wars 2:15, 18, 24, 25, 51
Pure Land Sect 4:22, 52

Puritans 6:25, 51, 7:52
Puyi 10:8, 9, 20
pyramids 1:11, 14, 16, 17
Pyramid of the Sun 3:15
Pyrenees, Treaty of the 7:27, 32
Pytheas 2:11

Qadisiya, Battle of 3:16, 19
Qaeda, al- 10:47
Qa'itbay 5:39
Qajar Dynasty 8:43, 51, 10:15
Qalat Bani Hammad 4:6
Qalawun 5:8, 9, 10
Qi 1:38, 3:8, 52
Qianlong 8:19, 43
Qin and the first emperor 2:10, 11, 16–17
Qin Zong 4:23
Quakers 7:13, 23, 52, 8:14, 52
Quebec 7:6, 7, 12, 42, 8:28, 42, 10:33
Queen Anne's War 8:7, 10, 52
Quiché 5:30, 52, 6:51
Quiriguá 3:35
Qutbuttin Aibak 4:37, 38
Qutuz 5:7, 8, 9
Quwwat al-Islam mosque 4:36
Qu Yuan 2:15, 51

Rabin, Yitzhak 10:44, 46
radio 10:18
Rahman, Mujibur 10:38
Rahman ibn Faisal 9:44
railroads 9:14, 20, 22, 27, 35, 36, 37, 41, 46, 47
Rainbow Warrior 10:41
Rainulf 4:12
Rajaraja 3:44, 45
Rajaram 7:42
Rajasthan 6:23, 51
Rajendra I 4:6, 7, 10
Rajputs 6:31, 37, 51, 7:52
Raleigh, Walter 6:38, 41, 42, 7:12
Ralambo 7:10
Rama I 8:38
Rama IV 9:24
Ramanuja 4:14
Ramayana 2:14, 51, 4:52
Ramkhamhaeng 5:10
Ramses I 1:24
Ramses II 1:22, 24, 51
Ramses III 1:23, 24, 51
Ranjit Singh 8:43, 9:6, 8, 12, 18, 20
Raphael 6:20
Rashid, Mulay 7:30, 31
Rashtrakuta Dynasty 3:29, 52
Ras Tafari 10:12
Ravenna 2:42
Ravenna, Battle of 6:10
Razi, ar- (Rhazes) 3:40
Raziya 4:42
Reagan, Ronald 10:30, 31, 39, 40
Red Army Faction 10:34
Red Cross 9:30, 51
Red River Rebellion 9:35
Red River Valley 1:18, 22
Red Turbans 5:24, 25, 52
Reform Act 9:18
Reformation 6:24–25, 51
refrigerators 9:36, 37
Rehoboam 1:27, 28, 51
reindeer 2:7
Reis, Piri 6:26
Rembrandt 7:36, 37
Renaissance 5:11, 18, 30, 52, 6:20–21, 51
Restitution, Edict of 7:16, 47
Reuter, Paul von 9:35
revolvers 9:19
Reza Pahlavi 10:28, 38
Rhodes 5:42, 6:28

Rhodes, Cecil 9:43, 43, 44, 46
Rhodesia 9:43, 46
 Southern 10:15, 17, 27
Ribault 6:30
Ricci, Matteo 6:39, 42
rice 1:8, 18, 22, 26, 34, 44, 4:7
Richard I "the Lionheart" 4:20, 31, 35
Richard II 5:26, 27
Richelieu, Cardinal 7:10, 14, 18
Richmond, Virginia 8:19
Rif Republic 10:14
Ripon, Lord 9:40, 41
Roanoke Island 6:38, 39, 42, 7:11
Robert de Hauteville 4:13
Robespierre 8:44, 45
Robinson Crusoe 8:11
Roca, Julio 9:39
Rocket 9:36
Roger II 4:27
Roger de Hauteville 4:19
Rohilkhand, Kingdom of 8:14, 52
Rolf 4:12, 29
Rolfe, John 7:11, 13
Rollo 3:39
Roman Empire 1:51, 2:19, 23, 25, 26, 28–29, 30, 31
Roman Empire (continued)
 divided 2:35, 39, 44
 fall 2:44–45
Romania 9:40, 10:44
Romanov Dynasty 7:10, 52
Romanus 4:17
Rome 1:31, 39, 2:10, 11, 25, 29, 3:33
 rise of 1:34, 43, 2:24–25
 sack of (1527) 6:15
Romulus 2:24, 25, 51
Romulus Augustulus 2:42
Roosevelt, Franklin D. 10:22
Roosevelt, Theodore 10:6, 9
Rose of Lima 7:34
Roses, Wars of the 5:38, 39, 53
Rosetta Stone 2:18, 9:13
Rousseau, Jean-Jacques 8:31
Rowlatt Acts 10:13
Rozvi Dynasty 6:51, 7:26
rubber 9:11, 9:22, 37
Rudolf II Of Hungary 6:35
Rudolf of Hapsburg 5:7
Rum, Sultanate of 4:30, 42, 52
Rurik 3:46
Rus 3:36, 46, 52
Rushdie, Salman 10:44
Russia 10:13, 14
 birth of 3:46–47
 drive to the east 7:19, 23, 40–41
 Kievan 4:7, 11, 14
 Time of Troubles 7:6–7, 10
Russo–Japanese War 10:6, 7, 52
Russo–Persian Wars 9:15, 52
Russo–Turkish Wars 8:31, 35, 38, 52
Ruy Mata 5:22
Rwanda 10:45, 46
Ryswick, Treaty of 7:42

Saadi Dynasty 6:26, 27, 51, 7:52
Saavedra, Alvaro de 6:9
Sable Island 6:43
Sadat, Anwar el- 10:39
Sadi 5:7
Safavids 5:43, 6:6, 15, 18, 22, 39, 42, 43, 52, 7:8, 14, 52, 8:15, 52
Saffarid Dynasty 3:37
Safi I 7:15, 19, 23
Sahagún, Bernadino de 6:15, 35
Sahara Desert 1:16
Said ibn Sultan 9:8, 18, 27
Saigon 9:29
Saikuku 7:39
St. Augustine, Florida 6:30, 7:12

St. Bartholomew's Day Massacre 6:25, 30, 34, 52
St. Basil's Cathedral 6:32, 33
St. Lawrence River 6:18, 19
St. Peter's, Rome 2:41, 6:6
St. Petersburg 8:8, 9, 10:7
Saints, Battle of the 8:38
Sakas 2:31, 36, 51
Saladin 4:20, 30, 31, 34, 35, 52, 5:9
Salado Culture 4:30, 35, 52, 5:52
Salamis, Battle of 2:6, 9, 9, 51
Salazar, António 10:18
Salem 7:42
Salerno 3:40
Salih Ayyub, al- 5:8
Salonika 5:33
Samaria 1:28, 34
Samarqand 5:28, 29, 9:34
Samarra 3:33
Saminids 3:40
Samnites 1:40, 2:11, 14, 52
Samoa 1:26, 8:31
Samudragupta 2:38, 52
samurai 4:18, 52, 9:52
Sanchi 2:37
Sancho of Navarre 4:10
San Diego 8:31
San Francisco 8:20, 10:6, 20
Sanjar 4:31
San Juan Pueblo 6:43
Sankaracharya 3:29
Sankoré, Mosque of 5:43
San Martin, José de 9:16, 17
Sanskrit 1:52, 2:14, 15, 31, 39, 52
Santorini 1:22
Sao Paulo 6:27
Sao Tome 5:39
Sappho 1:39, 52
Saragossa, Treaty of 6:15, 53
Saratoga, Battle of 8:35
Sarawak 9:21
Sardinia 4:14, 8:11
Sargon II 1:34, 35, 52
Sargon the Great 1:13, 14, 52
Sassanians 2:34, 35, 42, 44, 52, 3:8, 9, 12, 13, 16, 17, 52
Satakani (Andhra) Dynasty 2:35
satellites 10:36
Satsuma Rebellion 9:39
Saudi Arabia 9:34, 38, 10:17, 21
Sa'ud ibn Faisal 9:34
Saul 1:28, 52
Savery, Thomas 7:43
Savonarola, Girolamo 5:42
Saxons 3:30, 52
Scandinavia, bronze lurs 1:38
Scheele, Wilhelm 8:34
Schleswig-Holstein 9:30
Schmalkaldic League 6:18, 23, 52
Schouten, Willem 7:11
scientific revolution 7:44–45
Scipio Africanus 2:15, 52
Scramble for Africa 9:28, 42–43
Scythians 1:39, 52, 2:52
Sea Peoples 1:22, 23, 33, 52
Seibal 3:24
Seleucid Kingdom 2:11, 13, 14, 18, 32, 52
Seleucus 2:11, 13, 36, 52
Selim I (the Grim) 6:10, 11, 28
Selim II (the Sot) 6:28, 30, 31
Selim III 8:39, 9:7, 8
Seljuk Turks 3:52, 4:10, 14, 15, 16–17, 19, 30, 31, 17, 52
Sena Dynasty 4:22, 30, 53
Senegal 7:35, 42, 8:27, 35, 38, 9:28
Sennacherib 1:35, 38, 52
Senusret II 1:18, 24, 52
Senusret III 1:18
September 11 attacks 10:47

Serbia 4:34, 5:52, 9:6, 12
Serpent Mound 1:*38*
Settlement, Act of 8:6
Sevastopol 8:38
Seven Weeks' War 9:31
Seven Wonders of the Ancient World 2:10, *13*, 14
Seven Years' War 8:20, *23*, 25, 26, **28–29**, 30
Severus, Septimus 2:*31*, 52
Seville, Treaty of 8:15
Sforza famliy 6:20
Shabako 1:35, 52
Shabbetai Tzevi 7:30, *31*
Shah Alam II 8:32
Shahi family 3:40
Shah Jahan 6:37, 7:*14*, 15, 18, *19*, 26, 30
Shahnama 3:41, 4:*7*, *53*
Shah Rokh 5:30
Shaka 9:*12*, 13, 14
Shakespeare, William 6:*40*, 41, 7:10
Shalmaneser III 1:31, 52
Shang Dynasty 1:19, 22, 23, 44, *45*, 52
Shang Yang 2:10, 16, 52
Shapur II 2:38, 39, 52
Sharpeville massacre 10:28
Shaykh, al- 6:26, 27
Shen Gua 4:19
Shenyang, palace 7:*25*
Sherley, Robert 7:9
Sherman, William T. 9:33
Sher Shah Sur 6:19, 22, 23, 52
Shihuangdi 2:15, *16*, 17, 52
Shirakawa 4:19
Shir Ali Khan 9:34, 39
Shivaji 7:34, 38
Shizu 8:14, *15*, 18
shoguns 4:35, 53, 5:52, 6:52, 7:52, 8:52, 9:31, 52
Shoshenq I 1:25, 26, 28, 52
Shotoku, Prince 3:13, 26, *27*
Shunga Dynasty 2:18, 52
shuttles 8:*18*, 9:22
Siam *see* Thailand
Siberia 7:19, 23, *40*, *41*
Sicán art style 3:36, 52
Sicilian Vespers 5:10, 52
Sicily 1:32, 2:*7*, 9, 3:*33*, 4:*13*, 19, 5:10, 8:11
Sicily, Kingdom of 4:42, 44, *45*, 5:52
Sierra Leone 7:31, 8:11, 38, 52, 9:8, 20, 46
Sigismund II 6:31
Sigismund III Vasa of Poland and Sweden 6:42
Sikander II Lodi 5:43
Sikhs and Sikhism 5:34, 38, 52, 6:52, 7:34, 43, 52, 8:7, 10, 43, 52, 9:14, 18, 21, 24, 52, 10:52
Sikkim 9:44
Silesia 8:52, 9:21, 52
Silesian Wars 8:22
Silk Road 2:19, *22*, 39, 42, 52, 6:6, 52
Silla 3:8, *12*, 13, 21, 28, 32, 37, 52
Sima Guang 4:8, 18
Sima Qian 2:22, 52
Simla Deputation 10:7
Sinagua Culture 5:15
Sinan 6:*19*, 52
Sind 4:35, 9:52
Sind, Ivan 8:30
Singapore 5:19, 9:12, 14, 28
Singhasari Dynasty 5:14
Sino–Japanese War 9:46, 52, 10:52
Sistine Chapel 6:6, *7*, 20, 52
Sivaji 7:26, 30
Six Day War 10:33, 52
Skara Brae 1:*8*, 11, 52
Skopje 5:10
Slave Dynasty 4:36, 37
slavery 7:22, 23, 30, 8:35, 9:27
 end 9:18, 19
 freed slaves 8:38, 9:8, 13, 20, 24, 34

slave trade 6:7, 11, 18, 23, 30, 35, 7:11, 19, 23, 8:**12–13**, 14, 9:25
 banned 8:42, 9:7, 42
Slavs 3:12, 21, 45, 53
Slovakia 3:40
Slovenia 10:45
smallpox, vaccinations 8:43
Smith, Adam 9:22
Smith, John 7:6, 13
Smithsonian Institution 9:24
Socrates 2:9, 10, 52
Sokolov, Kuzma 8:10
Sokoto Caliphate 9:13, 52, 10:52
Solferino, Battle of 9:27
Solidarity union 10:*38*, 39, 52
solmization 4:10
Solomon 1:27, 28, *29*, 52
Solomonid Dynasty 5:7, 52
Solomonids 5:14
Solomon Islands 2:18
Solon 1:42
Somalia 10:29, 39, 45
Somoza, Anastasio 10:39
Sonam Gyatso 6:*34*, 35
Song Dynasty 3:44, 53, 4:7, **8–9**, 15, 18, 19, 22, 23, 30, 43, 53, 5:12, 52
Songhai 5:17, *26*, 38, 42, 52, 6:10, 42, 52, 7:10, 52
Song of Roland 3:28, 4:29
Soninke Dynasty 3:28
Sons of Liberty 8:31
Sophocles 2:8, 52
Soso, Kingdom of 4:34, 38, 42, 53, 5:16, 52
Soto, Hernando de 6:19, 22
South Africa 10:8, 9, 11, 6, 21, 28, 38, 45, 47
Southeast Asian empires 4:**24–25**
Southern Cult 5:19, 52
Southern Song 4:27
South Pacific Forum 10:35
South Sea Bubble 8:14, 52
Soviet Union (USSR) 10:14, 15, 16, 20, 35
space exploration 10:32, **36–37**
space shuttles 10:*37*, 39, 40, *41*
Spain, conquest of 2:28, 3:22, 24, 31
Spanish–American War 9:47, 52
Spanish Civil War 10:21, 52
Spanish Netherlands 6:31, 34, 35, 7:32
Spanish Succession, War of the 7:32, 8:6, 7, 10
Sparta 1:30, 31, 35, 52, 2:6, **8–9**
Spartacus 2:25, 52
Speke, John Hanning 9:42
Spenser, Edmund 6:41
Sphinx, the 1:*14*
Spice Islands (Moluccas) 6:8, 10, 11, 14, 15, 31, 42, 52, 7:14, 30, 31, 50, 8:52
spices and spice trade 6:7, *8*, *9*, *10*, 11, 7:7, 11
spinning wheels 4:10
Spinola, Antonio de 10:35
Sri Lanka (Ceylon) 2:6, 7, 3:33, 45, 5:10, 14, 6:10, 22, 26, 7:26, 8:42, 9:7, 10:25, 27, 28, 35
Srivijaya 3:32, 53, 4:53, 5:52
Stalin, Joseph 10:*16*, 17, 20, 31
Stamford Bridge, Battle of 4:12, 14
Stamp Act 8:31, 36, 52
stamps, postage 9:20
Stanislaw II of Poland 8:31
Stanley, Henry Morton 9:34, *35*
"Star Wars" program 10:30, 37
steamboats and steamships 9:7, 13, 20, 22
steel 8:15, 9:22, 26
Stele of the Vultures 1:14
Stephen Dushan 5:18
Stephenson, George 9:36
Stilicho 2:*39*, 42
Stone Age 1:52
Stonehenge 1:11, 15, 19, 52
Strabo 2:26, 52
Straits Convention 9:21, 52

Stralsund, Peace of 5:23
Stroesser, Alfredo 10:44
stupas 2:*21*, 23, *37*, 3:53
Stuyvesant, Peter 7:26
Suat 7:7
submarines 7:14
Sucre, Antonio José de 9:16, 17
Sudan 6:6, 10:40, 47
Suez Canal 6:7, 9:26, 34, 38, 10:14, 28
Suez Crisis 10:28, 52
suffrage, women's 9:41, 10:6
Sufi, al- 3:44
Sugar Act 8:30
Suger 4:27
Sui Dynasty 3:*13*, 53, 4:53
Sukarno, Ahmed 10:16
sukias 5:*27*
Suleiman II 7:38, *39*, 42
Suleiman, Mansa 5:16, 19, 22
Suleimanye Mosque 6:*19*, 27, *29*
Suleiman the Magnificent 5:33, 6:14, 15, 18, 22, 26, **28–29**, 30
Sulla, Lucius 2:24
Sultaniya 5:28
Sumatra 3:8, 6:11, 7:39, 9:8
Sumerians 1:10, **12–13**, 15, 52
Sunayoshi 7:38, 8:7
Sundiata Keita 4:42, 5:**16–17**
Sunni Ali 5:38
Sunnis and Shiites 3:**22–23**
sunspots 2:23
Sun Tzu 2:6
Sun Yat-sen 9:46, 10:8, 14
Suryavarman I 4:25
Suryavarman II 4:23, 24, 25, 30
Susenyos 8:7
Su Shi 4:10
Suttee 3:8
suttee, custom of 3:53, 9:15
Suu Kyi, Aung San 10:45, 46
Svein Forkbeard 3:39
Sviatoslav, Prince 3:44, 46, 47
Swift, Jonathan 8:*15*
Sydney Harbor Bridge 10:*17*
Synod of Whitby 3:20
Syria 2:22, 3:19, 4:22, 27, 31, 5:14, **28–29**, 35, 8:10, 9:19, 10:14, 15, 24
Syrian Catholic Church 6:43

Tabinshweti 6:19, 23, 26
Tacitus 2:30, 52
Tahmasp I of Persia 6:23, 27, 30, 34
Tahmasp II of Persia 8:19
Taiping Rebellion 9:24, 25, 31, 53
Taiwan (Formosa) 6:11, 7:14, 24, 30, 31, 38, 9:46, 10:24, 41
Taizong 3:17, 4:8
Taizu 3:44, 4:8
Tajikistan 10:16
Taj Mahal 6:37, 7:18, *19*, 53
Takakuni Masamoto 6:15
Takrur 3:32, 53, 5:16, 52
Talas River, Battle of the 3:28
Tale of Genji 3:26, 4:7
Taliban 10:*46*, 52
Talikota, Battle of 6:31
Talmud 2:33, 34, 52
Tamar 4:34
Tambora, Mt. 9:9
Tamil people 3:36, 5:52, 10:53
Tang Dynasty 3:17, *20*, 21, 24, 28, 29, 33, 37, 40, 53
Tangier 7:39
Tanguts 4:8, 11
Tannenberg, Battle of 5:30
Tanzania (Tanganyika) 10:12, 13
Tarascan Kingdom 4:22, 53, 5:26, 52
Tarquin I 1:40, 42, 53
Tarquin II 1:39, 43, 53

Tashkent 9:30
Tasman, Abel 7:22, 36, 8:40
Tasmania 7:36, 8:41, 9:7, 27
Tatars (Tartars) 5:52, 6:6, 34, 52, 7:22, 53
Tawfik Pasha 9:40
Tayasal 7:43
Tbilsi (Tiflis) 8:15, 19, 10:44
Teapot Dome scandal 10:15, 53
Teguder Ahmed 5:10
Tehran, embassy hostage crisis 10:39
telegraph 9:*31*, 36, 37
telephones 9:37, 38
telescopes 6:*42*, 7:*11*, 44
television 10:**18–19**
Telugu language 3:41
Ten Kingdoms 3:40
Tenochtitlán 5:*18*, 37, 38, 6:14, 16, 17
Ten Years' War 9:34, 53
Teotihuacán 2:27, 30, 35, 38, 42, 53, 3:**14–15**, 20, 35
Teresa of Avila, St. 6:30
Teresa of Calcutta, Mother 10:*47*
Terracotta Army 2:15, 16
Tetrarchy 2:44
Teutoburg Forest, Battle of the 2:28
Teutonic Knights 4:20, 21, 38, 42, 43, 52, 5:30, 53, 6:15, 53, 8:53
Texas 8:14, 20, 9:*18*, 19, 21
Texcoco 5:13
Thailand (Siam) 2:14, 4:6, 6:31, 7:31, 8:35, 52, 9:15, 24, 35, 52, 10:17, 21
Thanksgiving Day 7:11
Thatcher, Margaret 10:39, 40, 41, 45
Thebes 2:10, *11*
Theodore II of Ethiopia 9:34
Theodoric 2:43
Theodosius I 2:39
Theophilus 3:33
Thermopylae 2:*7*, 9, 18, 52
Thirty Years' War 7:11, 14, 15, **16–17**, 18, 22
Thomas à Kempis 5:39
Thomas Aquinas 5:7
Thousand Days, War of the 10:6
Three Emperors, League of the 9:35, 50
Three Feudatories 7:34
Three Mile Island 10:38
Thucydides 2:9
Thule culture 4:18, 53
Thutmose I 1:19, 53
Thutmose III 1:22, 53
Tiahuanaco Culture 2:38, 3:8, 16, 53, 4:31
Tiananmen Square 10:*44*
Tiberius 2:29, 53
Tibet 3:29, 5:6, 7:22, *23*, 8:11, 14, 10:6, 9
 Buddhism 3:*16*, 17, 5:15
 invasions by China 8:26, 10:25
Tiglath-Pileser III 1:28, 34, 53
Tikal 2:19, 35, 42, 53, 3:9, *20*, 21, 35
Tilly, Johann 7:16
Timbuktu 5:*17*, 34, 38, 42
Timurid Dynasty 5:28, 30, 53
Timur the Lame 4:36, 37, 5:*22*, 27, **28–29**, 30
Tinchebray, Battle of 4:22
Tingzhou, Battle of 3:29
Tippu Tib 9:25
Tipu Sultan 8:38, *39*, 42, 43, 53
tires, pneumatic 9:37, 43
Titian 6:35
Tizoc 5:42
Tlatilco 1:30
Tlemcen 5:11
Toba 2:53, 4:26
tobacco 7:15
toilets, flush 6:42
Tokugawa Dynasty 7:6, *20*, 26, 53, 8:53, 9:34, 53
Tokugawa Ieshige 8:23
Tokugawa Ieyasu 7:6, 10, 21
Tokusei Decree 5:11

Tolstoy, Leo **9**:31
Toltecs **3**:28, *36*, *41*, 44, 53, **4**:7, 31, 53, **5**:14, 53
Tonga **1**:26, **9**:13, **10**:27, 35
Topiltzin **3**:44
Tordesillas, Treaty of **5**:43, *45*, **6**:16, 53
Toshiro **4**:42
Toussaint, François Dominique **8**:*42*, 43
Toussaint L'Ouverture **8**:13
Tower of London **4**:12, 13
Trafalgar, Battle of **9**:7
trains, bullet **10**:10
Trajan **2**:29, 30, 33, 53
transportation revolution **10**:10–11
Transvaal **9**:25, 39, 40, 41, 42, 46, 53
Trebizond **4**:38, 53
Trent, Council of **6**:23, 25
Trevithick, Richard **9**:6, 36
Triangle Shirtwaist fire **10**:9
Triple Alliance (1600s) **7**:32–33, 34, 53
Triple Alliance (1800s) **9**:41, 53, **10**:8
Triple Entente **10**:8, 53
Tripoli **5**:8, 9, 11, **6**:26, **8**:53, **9**:6, **10**:9, 40
triremes **2**:9
Tristan and Isolde **4**:39
Troy **1**:10, 22, 32, 53
Troyes, Treaty of **5**:31
"True Cross" **3**:16
True Pure Land Sect **4**:39, **5**:43, 53
Truman Doctrine **10**:24, 29, 53
Trundholm **1**:*26*
tsunami **10**:47
Tuareg **5**:17, 34, 53
Tudor Dynasty **5**:42, 53
Tughluq **5**:18
Tughluq Dynasty **5**:*14*, 15, 53
Tughril **4**:35
Tughril-Beg **4**:16, 17
Tughril Khan **5**:7, 10
Tughtigin **4**:22
Tula **3**:*41*, **4**:7, 31
Tulipmania **7**:18, *37*
Tulip Period **8**:11
Tulum **4**:42
Tulunid Dynasty **3**:36, *37*, 53
Tulunids **3**:36
Tuman Bey **6**:10
Tunis **6**:11, 31, 35, **8**:7
Tunisia **9**:40, 42
Tupac Amarú II **8**:*21*, 38
Tupac Yupanqui **5**:37, 39, 42
turbines, water **9**:22
Turkestan **10**:12
Turkey **9**:15, **10**:14, 15, 47
Turner, Nat **9**:18
Tutankhamen **1**:*22*, 24, *25*, 53, **10**:*15*
Tu Yu **3**:33
Twelve Tables, Laws of the **2**:6, 53
Tyler, Wat **5**:26
Tyndale, Matthew **8**:16
Tyndale, William **6**:19, 24, 25
typewriters **9**:15, *38*
Tyre **1**:27, 42, 53, **4**:23, 34
Tyrone, Hugh O'Neill, earl of **6**:42

U2 spy plane incident **10**:30
Ucciali, Treaty of **9**:43
Udayadityavarman II **4**:15
Uganda **9**:46, **10**:35
Ugarit **1**:22, 53
Uighurs **3**:36, 53, **4**:53
Ukbekistan **8**:11
Ukraine **10**:14, 17
Uljaytu, Mahmud **5**:15
Umayyads **3**:17, 20, 22, 23, 25, 53
Uncle Tom's Cabin **9**:25
Union, Act of **8**:7, 46, **9**:6
Union Carbide accident **10**:41
United Arab Republic **10**:29, 53

United Nations **10**:25, 53
United States
 Canadian border **9**:12
 flag **9**:12
 immigrants to **9**:25, 40, **10**:14
Unkiar Skelessi, Treaty of **9**:19
Upanishads **1**:31
Upanishads **1**:53, **2**:6
Uqba ibn Nafi **3**:21
Ur **1**:11, *13*, 27, 53
Urartu **1**:31, 34, 53
Uratu **1**:30
Urban II, *Pope* **1**:20, **4**:19
Ur-Nammu **1**:13, 15
Uruguay **10**:6
Uruk **1**:12, 53
Urukagina of Lagash **1**:15
Urville, Dumont d' **9**:19
Utrecht, Peace (Treaty) of **7**:32, **8**:10, 20
Utrecht, Union of **6**:35, 53
Uzbekistan **9**:34, 35, 38, **10**:12
Uzbeks **6**:53, **7**:15, 18, 53

Valerian **2**:34, 44, 53
Vandals **2**:42, 43, 45, **3**:9, 53
Vanuatu **5**:22
Varangians (Swedish Vikings) **3**:7, 36, 46, *47*, 53
Vargas, Getúlio **10**:15
Vasari, Giorgio **6**:20
Vasudeva **2**:34
Vedas **1**:22, 30, **2**:36, **3**:29, 53
Vedic Age **1**:26
Velazquez, Diego **6**:10, 16
Venezuela **9**:16, 17, **10**:6
Venice **3**:21, **4**:6, **5**:15, 42, **6**:11, 34, **7**:18
Verdun, Treaty of **3**:31, 33, **4**:29
Vermeer, Jan **7**:36
Verrocchio, Andrea del **5**:39
Versailles **7**:*33*, 38, 53, **8**:53
Versailles, First Treaty of (1756) **8**:29
Versailles, Treaty of (1919) **10**:13, 53
Vervins, Treaty of **6**:43
Verwoerd, Hendrik **10**:33
Vesalius, Andreas **6**:23, **7**:44, *45*
Vespucci, Amerigo **5**:43, *45*, **6**:*7*, 8, *9*
Vestini tribe **1**:27
Victor Emmanuel **9**:30
Victoria of Great Britain **9**:19, 38, *42*, **10**:6
Vienna, besieged **6**:15, **7**:38
Vietnam **1**:18, **2**:26, **9**:6, 35, 38, 40, **10**:26, 28, 29, 32
 see also Annam; Champa; Cochin China; Nam Viet
Vietnam War **10**:19, 26, 33, 34, 35, 38, 53
Viiya **2**:6
Vijaya **5**:23
Vijayanagar **5**:19, 23, 30, 31, 34, *35*, 38, 42, 53, **6**:7, 31, 53
Vijayasena **4**:30
Vikings **3**:32, 33, 36, **38–39**, 41, 45, **4**:53, **5**:53
Villa, Pancho **10**:14
Villanova culture **1**:30, 53
Villon, François **5**:39
Vinland **3**:*39*, 45, 53
Virgil **2**:28
Virginia Colony **7**:15, **8**:12
Visigoths **2**:39, 42, 45, 53, **3**:11, 13, 20, 53
Vizcaino, Sebastian **7**:6
Vladimir I **3**:45, *46*, 47, **4**:6
Vlad the Impaler **5**:39, 42
Volstead Act **10**:13
Voltaire **8**:16, *17*, *27*
Von Braun, Werner **10**:36
Voyager (airplane) **10**:40

Wahhabi sect **8**:22, **9**:6, 53
Walachia **9**:24, 26
Waldseemüller, Martin **6**:6, 8

Wales **5**:7, 10
Walesa, Lech **10**:39
Wallace, William **5**:*11*, 15
Wallenstein, Albrecht von **7**:16, *17*, 18
Wall Street Crash **9**:35, **10**:16, 53
Walpole, Robert **8**:*14*, 15
Wang Anshi **4**:8, 15, 18, 22
Wang Mang **2**:26, 53
Wang Wei **3**:21
Wang Yangming **5**:39
Wan-li **6**:34, 38
Warsaw, Battle of **7**:27
Warsaw Pact **10**:28, 30, *31*, 35, 53
washing machines **9**:37
Washington, Booker T. **9**:46
Washington, George **8**:26, 36, *37*, 38, 39
Watergate **10**:35
Waterloo, Battle of **9**:9
Watt, James **9**:22, 23
week, seven-day **4**:6
Wei **2**:35, 39, 42, 53, **3**:53
Wells, Ida B. **9**:45
Wenceslas I **4**:42
West Bank **10**:25, 38, 46
West India Company, Dutch **7**:26, 30, 53
Westminster Abbey **4**:14
Westphalia, Treaty of **7**:*16*, 17, 23, 32, 36
We Zong **4**:23, 26
wheel **1**:12
White Lotus Society **8**:43, 53, **9**:7
White Mountain, Battle of the **7**:14, 16
White Sheep Turkmen **5**:39, 43, **6**:6, 53
Whitney, Eli **8**:*43*
Whittle, Frank **10**:10
Wilberforce, William **9**:18
William I of England **4**:10, 11, 12, 13, 14, 19
William II (William Rufus) of England **4**:13, 22
William II of Germany **9**:44, 47
William III of Orange **7**:34, 36, 37, 42, 53
William of Aquitaine **3**:40
William the Silent **6**:35, 39
Willibrord **3**:25
Wilson, Woodrow **10**:13
Windward Islands **8**:43
witch hunts **5**:42, **7**:*42*
Wolfe, James **8**:27, *28*, 29
Woolens Act **7**:43
World War I **10**:10, *12*, 13, 53
World War II **10**:21–**23**, 53
Worms, Concordat of **4**:23, 44, 45, 47
Worms, Synod of **4**:44
Wounded Knee **9**:*44*
Wright, Orville and Wilber **9**:23, **10**:10, *11*
writing
 cuneiform **1**:*12*, 47, **9**:19, 49
 hieroglyphic **1**:16, 31
Wu Che'eng **6**:42
Wudi **2**:18, 19
Wuh-Teh **3**:44
Wu Sangui **7**:34, *35*
Wu Ti **3**:8
Wu Zetian **3**:21
Wu of Zhou **1**:44
Wycliffe, John **5**:26

Xaltocan **5**:6
Xavier, St. Francis **6**:22, 23, 24, 26, 53, **7**:20
Xenophon **2**:7
Xerxes I **2**:6, 9, 53
Xerxes II **2**:7
Xhosa War, Sixth **9**:19, 53
Xia Dynasty **1**:15, 53
Xuanzang **3**:17

Yakutsk **7**:*41*
Yale University **8**:*6*
Yamato family **3**:24, 26, 53
Yaqub al Mansur **4**:*34*, 35

Yaqubi, Al- **3**:38
Yaqub Khan **9**:39
Yarmuk, Battle of **3**:16
Yaroslav the Wise **4**:7, *11*, 14
Yasodharman **3**:9
Yayoi Culture **1**:*27*, **2**:53
Yazdigird **2**:42
Yazid I **3**:20
Yeager, Chuck **10**:*24*
Yekumo Amlak **5**:*7*
Yeltsin, Boris **10**:44, 45
Yemen **3**:8
Yemenites **3**:24
Yemrahana Krestos **4**:35
Yermak Timofeyevich **7**:*40*
Yi Dynasty **5**:35
Yongle **5**:25
Yoritomo **4**:35
Yoruba people **4**:14, **9**:*42*
Yoshifusa **3**:36
Yoshimune **8**:10, 14, 22, 23, 26
Yoshitane **6**:15
Young Italy **9**:18, 53
Young Turks **9**:43, 46, 53, **10**:8, 9, 53
Yuan Dynasty **5**:*10*, 12, 13, 19, 24
Yuan Shikhai **10**:9, 12, *13*, 53
Yugoslavia **10**:15, 47, 53
Yung-lo **5**:30
Yusuf I **5**:18
Yusuf ibn Tashfin **4**:22

Zab, Battle of the **3**:25
Zagwe Dynasty **4**:26, 27, 30, 53, **5**:53
Zand Dynasty **8**:39, 53
Zangi **4**:26, 27
Zanzibar **4**:22, **7**:27, 43, 53, **9**:18, 42, 43
Zapata, Emiliano **10**:13
Zapotecs **1**:*31*, 43, 53, **2**:6, 53, **3**:24, 53, **5**:22, 53
Zara **4**:38
Zara Yakob **5**:35, 38
Zaria **5**:14, 53
Zedekiah **1**:42
Zeng Gongliang **4**:11
Zenj rebellion **3**:36
Zenobia **2**:34, 35, 53
Zenta, Battle of **7**:43
Zeydis **6**:31, 53
Zhagawa people **3**:17
Zheng-he **5**:30, 31
Zhenzong **4**:8, 9
Zhongdu **5**:12
Zhou Dynasty **1**:44–45, 53 **2**:7, 16, 53, **3**:12
Zhou Enlai **10**:16, 35
Zhu Yuanzhang **5**:23, 24–25
ziggurats **1**:10, *11*, 53
Zimbabwe **3**:45, **4**:38, *39*, **10**:39, 41
Zollverein **9**:19, 53
Zoroaster **1**:53
Zoroastrians **1**:42, 53, **2**:42, 43, 53, **3**:24, 53
Zsitvatörök, Treaty of **7**:6
Zulus **6**:13, **9**:*12*, 13, 14, 21, 53
Zulu War **9**:38, *39*, 53
Zwingli, Ulrich **6**:11, 18